San Francisco: MUNI Metro

W9-CNF-412

Brannan & Embarcadero
2nd St & King (PacBell Park)
Caltrain Station/ (4th St. & King)

Duboce & Church
Duboce Park/ Duboce & Noe
Van Ness
Center

Judah & 9th Ave.
Judah & 19th Ave.
Carl & Cole
UCSF
Church
Castro
16th St.

Judah & Sunset
Church & 18th St.

Ocean Beach
Forest Hill
Church & 24th St.
24th St.

Taraval & Sunset
Taraval & 22nd Ave.
West Portal

San Francisco Zoo
St. Francis Circle
Church & 30th St.
San Jose & Randall

CALTRAIN
BART

Junipero Serra & Ocean
Stonestown
Ocean & Jules
Glen Park

SF State
City College
K
J

Randolph & Arch
Broad & Plymouth
Balboa Park
San Jose & Geneva

Randolph & 19th Ave.

SAN FRANCISCO
SAN MATEO COUNTY
Daly City
BART

0 — 1 mile
0 — 1 kilometer

Legend:
- Ⓝ Judah
- Ⓙ Church
- Ⓛ Taraval
- Ⓜ Oceanview
- Ⓚ Ingleside
- ● Subway station
- ○ Surface station
- ⫢ Subway transfer station
- ⫢ Surface transfer station

San Francisco: BART System

North Concord/Martinez
Pittsburg/ Bay Point
Concord

CONTRA COSTA COUNTY

MARIN COUNTY

Richmond
El Cerrito del Norte
Pleasant Hill

El Cerrito Plaza
Walnut Creek

San Francisco Bay
North Berkeley
Berkeley
Lafayette

Ashby
Orinda

Ft. Cronkhite
Rockridge

MacArthur
19th St./Oakland
Oakland City Center/ 12th St.

Embarcadero
Montgomery St.
Powell St.
Civic Center
West Oakland
Lake Merritt
Fruitvale

16th St./Mission
24th St./Mission
Coliseum/ Oakland Airport

Glen Park
Balboa Park
SAN FRANCISCO
Caltrain

Oakland International Airport
San Leandro
Dublin/ Pleasanton

Daly City
Bay Fair

Colma
Castro Valley
ALAMEDA COUNTY

South San Francisco
San Francisco Bay
Hayward

San Bruno
South Hayward

San Francisco International Airport

SAN MATEO COUNTY
Millbrae

Union City

Fremont

Legend:
- Richmond-Daly City
- Pittsburg/Bay Point-Millbrae
- Fremont-Daly City
- Fremont-Richmond
- Dublin/Pleasanton-SFO
- SFO-Millbrae Shuttle
- CalTrain

0 — 4 miles
0 — 4 kilometers

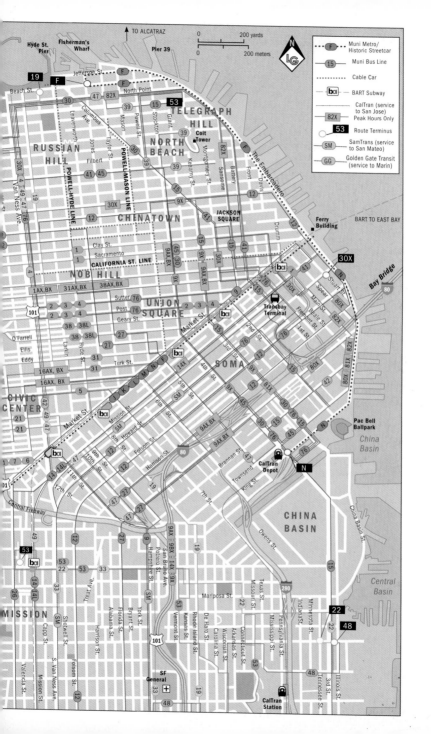

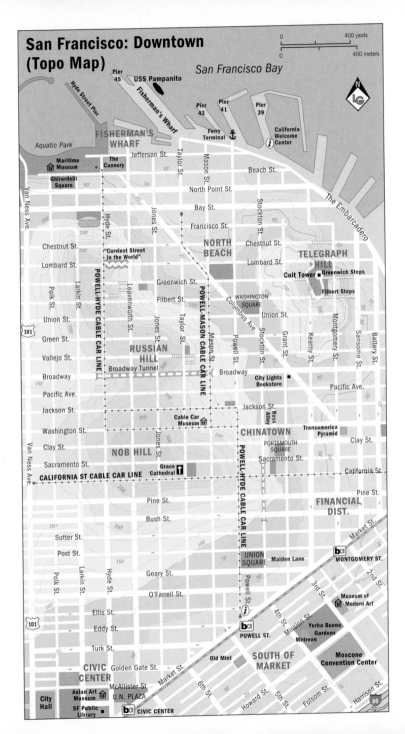

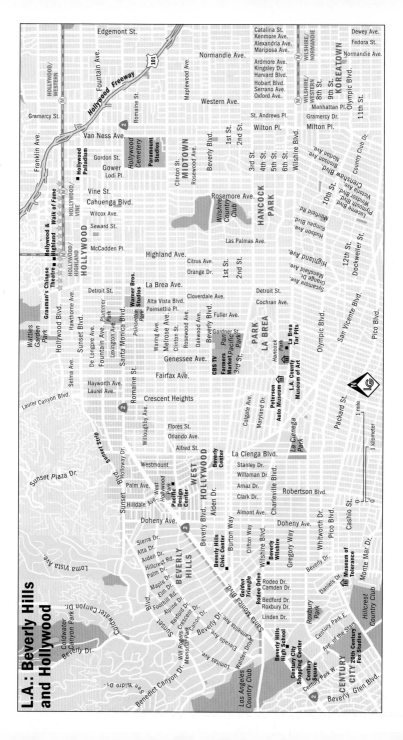

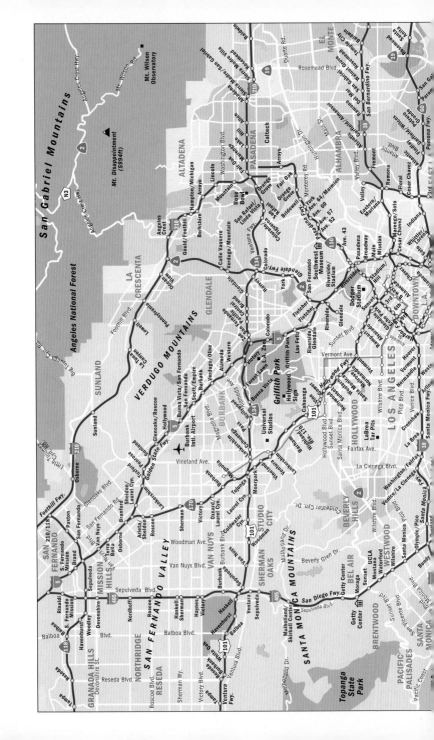

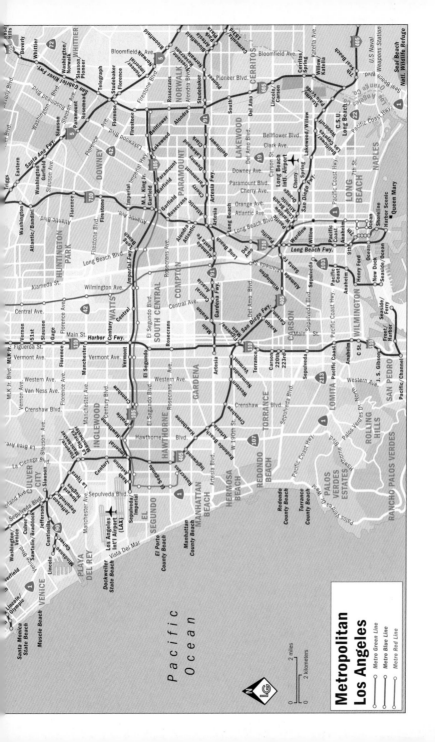

Metropolitan
Los Angeles

Metro Green Line
Metro Blue Line
Metro Red Line

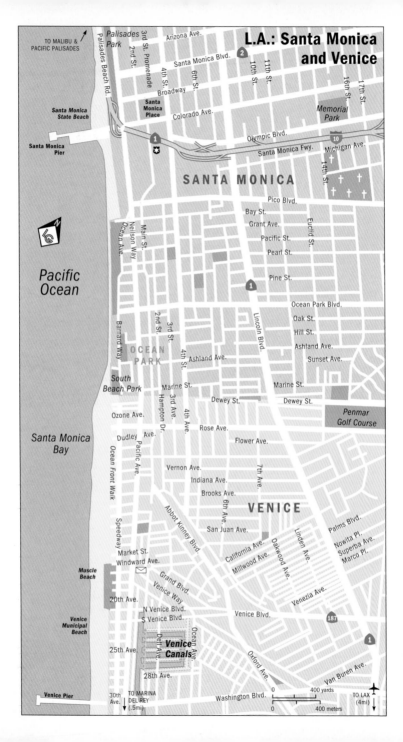

L.A.: Santa Monica and Venice

TO MALIBU & PACIFIC PALISADES

Palisades Park

Palisades Beach Rd.

3rd St.
2nd St.
3rd St. Promenade

Arizona Ave.

Santa Monica Blvd.

4th St.
6th St.
Broadway

10th St.
11th St.

Santa Monica Place

Colorado Ave.

16th St.
17th St.

Memorial Park

Santa Monica State Beach

Santa Monica Pier

Olympic Blvd.

Santa Monica Fwy.

Michigan Ave.

Nielson Way
Ocean Ave.
Main St.

SANTA MONICA

14th St.

Pico Blvd.

Bay St.

Grant Ave.

Pacific St.

Euclid St.

Pearl St.

Pacific Ocean

Pine St.

Ocean Park Blvd.

Barnard Way

2nd St.
3rd St.
4th St.

Lincoln Blvd.

Oak St.

Hill St.

Ashland Ave.

Sunset Ave.

OCEAN PARK

Ashland Ave.

South Beach Park

Marine St.
3rd Ave.
Hampton Dr.
4th Ave.

Dewey St.

Marine St.

Dewey St.

Penmar Golf Course

Ozone Ave.

Ocean Front Walk
Pacific Ave.

Dudley Ave.

Rose Ave.

Flower Ave.

Santa Monica Bay

Vernon Ave.

Indiana Ave.

Brooks Ave.

7th Ave.

6th Ave.

VENICE

Speedway

Abbot Kinney Blvd.

San Juan Ave.

California Ave.

Millwood Ave.

Oakwood Ave.

Linden Ave.

Palms Blvd.

Nowita Pl.

Superba Ave.

Marco Pl.

Market St.

Windward Ave.

Muscle Beach

Grand Blvd.

Venice Way

Venezia Ave.

20th Ave.

Venice Municipal Beach

N Venice Blvd.

S Venice Blvd.

Ocean Ave.

Dell Ave.

Venice Canals

Venice Blvd.

25th Ave.

Oxford Ave.

28th Ave.

30th Ave.

TO MARINA DEL REY (.5mi)

Washington Blvd.

Van Buren Ave.

Venice Pier

0   400 yards

0   400 meters

TO LAX (4mi)

LET'S GO

■ THE RESOURCE FOR THE INDEPENDENT TRAVELER

"The guides are aimed not only at young budget travelers but at the independent traveler; a sort of streetwise cookbook for traveling alone."

—The New York Times

"Unbeatable; good sight-seeing advice; up-to-date info on restaurants, hotels, and inns; a commitment to money-saving travel; and a wry style that brightens nearly every page."

—The Washington Post

"Lighthearted and sophisticated, informative and fun to read. [Let's Go] helps the novice traveler navigate like a knowledgeable old hand."

—Atlanta Journal-Constitution

"A world-wise traveling companion—always ready with friendly advice and helpful hints, all sprinkled with a bit of wit."

—The Philadelphia Inquirer

■ THE BEST TRAVEL BARGAINS IN YOUR PRICE RANGE

"All the dirt, dirt cheap."

—People

"Anything you need to know about budget traveling is detailed in this book."

—The Chicago Sun-Times

"Let's Go follows the creed that you don't have to toss your life's savings to the wind to travel—unless you want to."

—The Salt Lake Tribune

■ REAL ADVICE FOR REAL EXPERIENCES

"The writers seem to have experienced every rooster-packed bus and lunar-surfaced mattress about which they write."

—The New York Times

"Value-packed, unbeatable, accurate, and comprehensive."

—The Los Angeles Times

"[Let's Go's] devoted updaters really walk the walk (and thumb the ride, and trek the trail). Learn how to fish, haggle, find work—anywhere."

—Food & Wine

LET'S GO PUBLICATIONS

TRAVEL GUIDES

Australia 8th Edition
Austria & Switzerland 12th edition
Brazil 1st edition
Britain & Ireland 2005
California 10th edition
Central America 9th edition
Chile 2nd edition
China 5th edition
Costa Rica 2nd edition
Eastern Europe 2005
Ecuador 1st edition **NEW TITLE**
Egypt 2nd edition
Europe 2005
France 2005
Germany 12th Edition
Greece 2005
Hawaii 3rd edition
India & Nepal 8th edition
Ireland 2005
Israel 4th edition
Italy 2005
Japan 1st edition
Mexico 20th edition
Middle East 4th edition
Peru 1st edition **NEW TITLE**
Puerto Rico 1st edition
South Africa 5th edition
Southeast Asia 9th edition
Spain & Portugal 2005
Thailand 2nd edition
Turkey 5th edition
USA 2005
Vietnam 1st edition **NEW TITLE**
Western Europe 2005

ROADTRIP GUIDE

Roadtripping USA **NEW TITLE**

ADVENTURE GUIDES

Alaska 1st edition
New Zealand **NEW TITLE**
Pacific Northwest **NEW TITLE**
Southwest USA 3rd edition

CITY GUIDES

Amsterdam 3rd edition
Barcelona 3rd edition
Boston 4th edition
London 2005
New York City 15th Edition
Paris 13th Edition
Rome 12th edition
San Francisco 4th edition
Washington, D.C. 13th edition

POCKET CITY GUIDES

Amsterdam
Berlin
Boston
Chicago
London
New York City
Paris
San Francisco
Venice
Washington, D.C.

LET'S GO

CALIFORNIA

NAOMI STRAUS EDITOR
JEFFREY J. CLINTON ASSOCIATE EDITOR

RESEARCHER-WRITERS
ANN WHITLOW BROWN
ROHIT CHOPRA
BRIAN EMEOTT
NATHAN ORION SIMMONS
OUSSAMA ZAHR

NICK KEPHART MAP EDITOR
CHARLOTTE DOUGLAS MANAGING EDITOR

ST. MARTIN'S PRESS ✹ NEW YORK

HELPING LET'S GO. If you want to share your discoveries, suggestions, or corrections, please drop us a line. We read every piece of correspondence, whether a postcard, a 10-page email, or a coconut. **Address mail to:**

Let's Go: California
67 Mount Auburn Street
Cambridge, MA 02138
USA

Visit Let's Go at **http://www.letsgo.com,** or send email to:

feedback@letsgo.com
Subject: **"Let's Go: California"**

In addition to the invaluable travel advice our readers share with us, many are kind enough to offer their services as researchers or editors. Unfortunately, our charter enables us to employ only currently enrolled Harvard students.

Maps by David Lindroth copyright © 2005 by St. Martin's Press.

Distributed outside the USA and Canada by Macmillan, an imprint of Pan Macmillan Ltd.
20 New Wharf Road, London N1 9RR
Basingstoke and Oxford
Associated companies throughout the world
www.panmacmillan.com

ISBN: 0-312-33544-X
EAN: 978-0312-33544-1
First edition
10 9 8 7 6 5 4 3 2

Let's Go: California is written by Let's Go Publications, 67 Mount Auburn Street, Cambridge, MA 02138, USA.

Let's Go® and the LG logo are trademarks of Let's Go, Inc.
Printed in the USA.

HOW TO USE THIS BOOK

BOOK ORGANIZATION. Chapter-by-chapter coverage of the Golden State begins in **San Francisco** and the **Bay Area**, moving down Hwy. 1 along the **Central Coast** toward **Los Angeles** and the neighboring towns **Around L.A.** The book then skirts the ocean's edge to **San Diego**, heads south of the border to Mexico's **Baja California**, braves the scorching heat of the **Desert**, cools down in the snowy **Sierra Nevadas**, explores the **Northern Interior** and the **North Coast**, and heads into **Central California**.

COVERAGE. Each chapter begins with the biggest city in the region, and then typically moves north to south through the area, often following major highways.

GETTING ACQUAINTED. The first chapter, **Discover California**, contains highlights of the state, including **Suggested Itineraries** (p. 5) that can help you plan your trip. The **Essentials** (p. 25) section has comprehensive hard information and tips on traveling, including creating a budget, making reservations, renting a car, renewing passports, and more. **Life and Times** (p. 8) has info on California's history, wildlife, and culture that can help you make the most of your visit. **Alternatives to Tourism** (p. 66) describes uniquely Californian opportunities for volunteerism, short-term work, and studying.

GETTING AROUND. Public transportation information is listed for all towns in which it exists. Due to the sheer distances involved in travel within California, not to mention the state's auto-centric culture, most travelers find that a car is extremely helpful for getting around. **Essentials** (p. 25) and the **Practical Information** sections in large cities have information on car rental. The **Desert** chapter (p. 529) has important safety information for driving without getting burnt, stranded, or worse in the Southern California desert.

SCHOLARLY ARTICLES. Our experts assess John Steinbeck's vision of California in *The Grapes of Wrath* (p. 341), survey the history of homosexuality in San Francisco (p. 133), and give the lowdown on interning in the entertainment industry in L.A. (p. 75).

PRICE DIVERSITY. *Let's Go* lists establishments in order of value and quality from best to worst. Our absolute favorites are denoted by the Let's Go thumbs-up (🖎). Since the best value does not always mean the lowest price, we have also incorporated a system of price ranges in the guide. See the Price Diversity chart on p. XX for descriptions of typical establishments within each price range. Price ranges are based on the lowest cost for one person, excluding special discounts. Read listings carefully, as accommodations listed as ❶ may offer higher-priced options, and those listed as ❺ may be much less expensive for those sharing rooms. **All prices are in US dollars**, with the exception of Baja California, where prices are quoted in either US dollars or Mexican pesos.

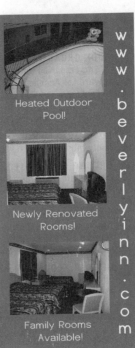

CONTENTS

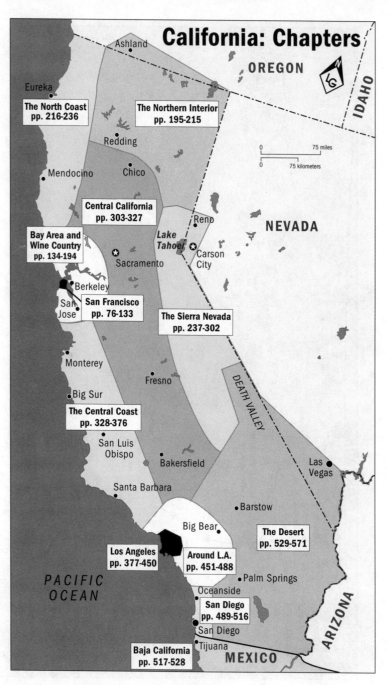

California: Chapters

OREGON

IDAHO

Ashland

Eureka

The North Coast
pp. 216-236

The Northern Interior
pp. 195-215

Redding

0   75 miles

0   75 kilometers

Mendocino   Chico

Central California
pp. 303-327

Reno

NEVADA

Bay Area and Wine Country
pp. 134-194

Lake Tahoe

Carson City

Sacramento

Berkeley

San Jose

San Francisco
pp. 76-133

The Sierra Nevada
pp. 237-302

Monterey

Fresno

DEATH VALLEY

Big Sur

The Central Coast
pp. 328-376

San Luis Obispo

Bakersfield

Las Vegas

Santa Barbara

Barstow

Big Bear

The Desert
pp. 529-571

Los Angeles
pp. 377-450

Around L.A.
pp. 451-488

PACIFIC OCEAN

Palm Springs

Oceanside

San Diego
pp. 489-516

San Diego

ARIZONA

Tijuana

Baja California
pp. 517-528

MEXICO

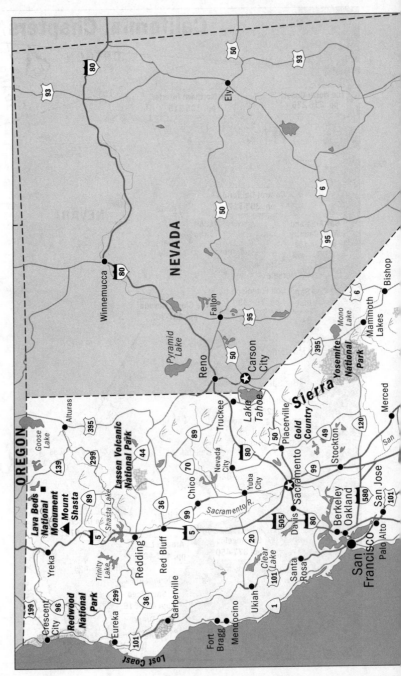

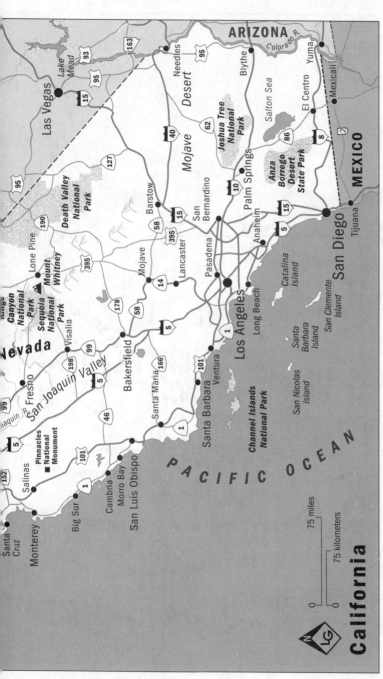

California

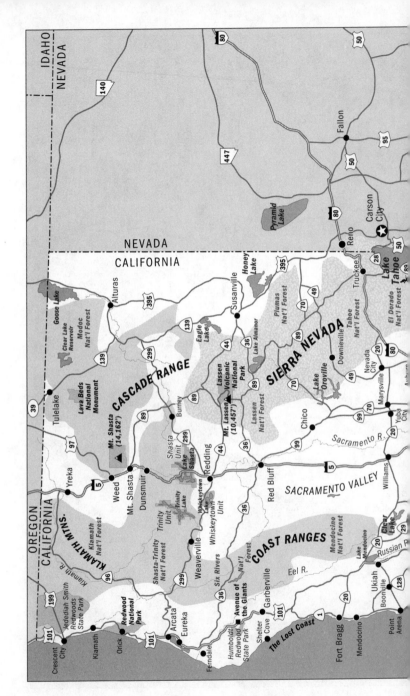

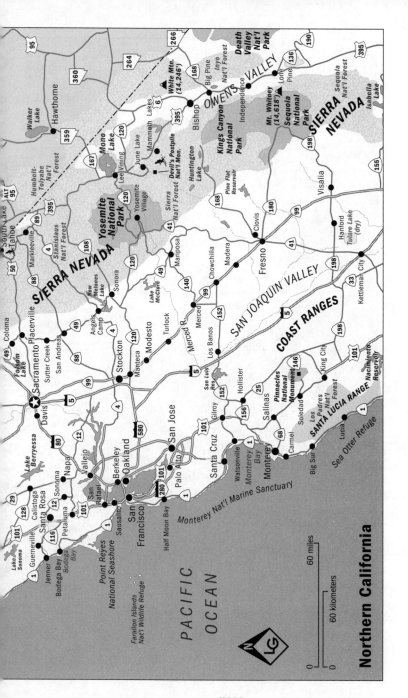

Northern California

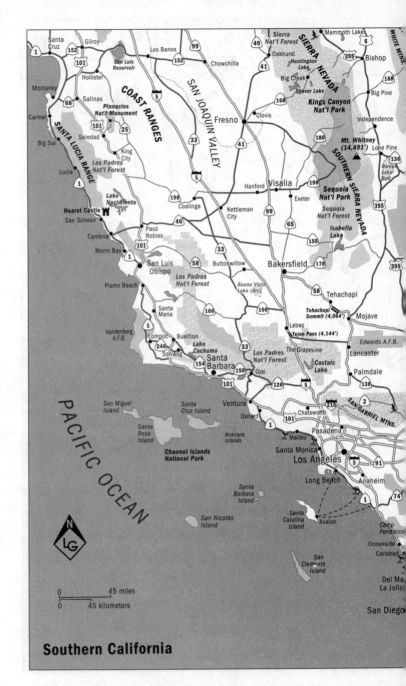

Southern California

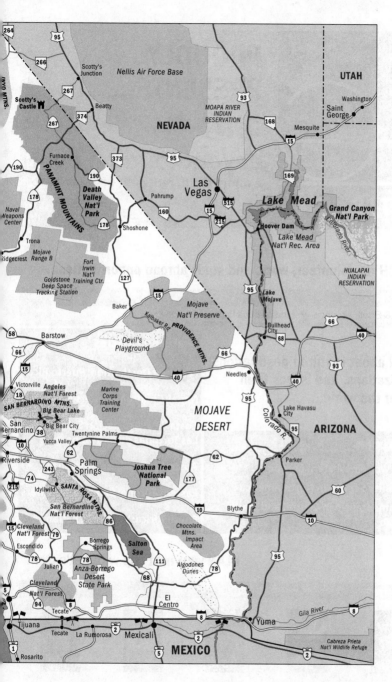

RESEARCHER-WRITERS

Ann Whitlow Brown *Los Angeles, Orange County*

Fresh off her Texas-Oklahoma-Kansas route for *Let's Go USA 2004*, Ann drove into town with her blond locks blowing in the breeze. In no time at all she was navigating L.A. traffic, unearthing new sushi restaurants, and strutting her stuff in L.A.'s hottest clubs like a local. Never fazed by parking nightmares, imperious publicists, or crazy characters, Ann cracked us up during frequent phone calls and sent in consistently thorough research.

Rohit Chopra *San Diego, Baja, The Desert, East of L.A.*

Rohit Chopra put his experience as Harvard College Undergraduate Council President to good use in Las Vegas, negotiating his way into every club and show in town. Always one to get the inside scoop, Rohit tackled 120°F desert in the middle of the summer, fortified only by his car's A/C and the lure of casinos still to come. In Baja, he once again had a run-in with politics before returning to the East Coast to begin work as a consultant.

Brian Emeott *The North Coast, The Central Coast, Marin County South Bay Area, North of L.A.*

As the map editor for *Let's Go California 2004*, Brian got to know the state on paper, and, when given the opportunity to see it in full color, he dove right in. After researching clean-cut Stanford, Brian found himself more at home in the funky town of Arcata, where he stayed as long as we would let him. Despite computer glitches and stolen notebooks, Brian churned out hilarious copy and impeccable maps.

Nathan Orion Simmons *Sierra Nevada, Far North, Central California*

A Berkeley native, Nathan returned to the campgrounds of his youth to give us expert advice on the Sierra Nevadas. A smoothie shop expert, and a bit of a smoothie himself, Nathan braved bears, naked pot-smoking hippies, and insanely windy roads with quiet confidence and impeccable style. Whether discovering new hikes or seeing a familiar sight in a different light, Nathan always captured the spirit of the mountains in his crystal-clear writing.

Oussama Zahr *San Francisco, East Bay, Wine Country*

This literature major took the City by the Bay by storm, lighting up our days with his keenly perceptive research, richly dense prose, and insane stories, and leaving a trail of empty *cafe au lait* mugs and broken hearts in his wake. From taking sartorial inspiration from Rothko paintings to luxuriating in the finest dim sum palaces to ruminating on murals in the Mission, Oussama never ceased to impress us as he emerged a true connoisseur of San Francisco.

CONTRIBUTING WRITERS

Joseph Abel   *Lava Beds National Park, Ashland, OR*

Photographer and mountaineer extraordinaire, Joe sent us insightful coverage of one of the most remote regions of California and some of the best pubs in Southern Oregon.

Katy Bartelma   *Grand Canyon, Lake Mead*

Katy was a desert superstar, chugging through the Southwest to bring us the way low down on hikes in and around the deepest canyon in the US.

Alexandra Hoffer   *Editor, Let's Go: Pacific Northwest Adventure Guide*

Lisa Kennelly   *Associate Editor, Let's Go: Pacific Northwest Adventure Guide*

Chris Schonberger   *Editor, Let's Go: USA*

Julia Bonnheim, Adrienne Taylor Gerken, Michelle Robinson   *Associate Editors, Let's Go: USA*

Susan Gray was a researcher-writer for *Let's Go Greece 1994* and *Let's Go Turkey 1995*. She is now a law student living in San Francisco.

Elizabeth Little was a researcher-writer for *Let's Go China 3rd Ed.* and the editor of *Let's Go China 4th Ed.* She now works for the Trident Media Group.

Susan Shillinglaw is the Director of the Center for Steinbeck Studies and a Professor of English at CSU San Jose.

Stephanie L. Smith has worked as a freelancer for CitySearch Los Angeles and is now working in Hollywood as the features editor/writer for Channel One News online.

ACKNOWLEDGMENTS

TEAM CAL THANKS: Charlotte and her frownies and smileys; Max and Ali—you guys are clutch; Team Road for driving us wild; and our hot, hot RW team and their sweet hot skills.

NAOMI THANKS: Jeff, my hyphenator and partner in crime; Charlotte for Nor Cal pride and format mastery; Nick for making my crazy insets. My crack-team: Max, Mr. Index, for laughing at me all summer; Abigail, the Ultimate Editor; Ali for last-minute boxes; EB for sharing L.A. with me and proofing San Diego. The now-wandering Dane St. Gang, in all its many permutations. Fellow Californians: Leslie, Seth, and Stuart, the opinionated Westside kids; Jon with San Diego beaches; Jim for hardcore O.C.; Gustavo for movies and music; Lane and Jamie, stellar guys who know the best bars and restaurants in L.A.; and my parents, for bringing me into this glorious state.

JEFF THANKS: Naomi for keeping me laughing and for agreeing that nothing prepares you for Alaskan halibut like ahi tartar—intense; Charlotte, who gracefully guided us and supplied Milano cookies—crucial; Nick for masterful mapping; Max, who earns big ups for invaluable help during the homestretch; Jer and Mathias for a crazy summer—we rocked it hard; Mom, Dad, Matt, and Chris for love and support; and Callie, my little buddy.

NICK THANKS: Naomi and Jeff, text-editing machines, for telling me how to fill the blank spaces and for their exquisite job with proofing; Nathan for the copious reference maps; Ann for the billions of L.A. listings; Oussama for solid work in SF; Rohit for a stellar job in Las Vegas; and Brian for his indispensable comments of wisdom and sagacity.

Editor
Naomi Straus
Associate Editors
Jeffrey J. Clinton
Managing Editor
Charlotte Douglas
Map Editor
Nick Kephart
Typesetter
Victoria Esquivel-Korsiak

Publishing Director
Emma Nothmann
Editor-in-Chief
Teresa Elsey
Production Manager
Adam R. Perlman
Cartography Manager
Elizabeth Halbert Peterson
Design Manager
Amelia Aos Showalter
Editorial Managers
Briana Cummings, Charlotte Douglas, Ella M. Steim, Joel August Steinhaus, Lauren Truesdell, Christina Zaroulis
Financial Manager
R. Kirkie Maswoswe
Marketing and Publicity Managers
Stef Levner, Leigh Pascavage
Personnel Manager
Jeremy Todd
Low-Season Manager
Clay H. Kaminsky
Production Associate
Victoria Esquivel-Korsiak
IT Director
Matthew DePetro
Web Manager
Rob Dubbin
Associate Web Manager
Patrick Swieskowski
Web Content Manager
Tor Krever
Research and Development Consultant
Jennifer O'Brien
Office Coordinators
Stephanie Brown, Elizabeth Peterson

Director of Advertising Sales
Elizabeth S. Sabin
Senior Advertising Associates
Jesse R. Loffler, Francisco A. Robles, Zoe M. Savitsky
Advertising Graphic Designer
Christa Lee-Chuvala

President
Ryan M. Geraghty
General Manager
Robert B. Rombauer
Assistant General Manager
Anne E. Chisholm

PRICE RANGES >> CALIFORNIA

Our researchers list establishments in order of value from best to worst; our favorites are denoted by the Let's Go thumbs-up (👍). Since the best value is not always the cheapest price, we have incorporated a system of price ranges for quick reference. Our price ranges are based on a rough expectation of what you will spend. For **accommodations,** we base our price range on the cheapest price for which a single traveler can stay for one night. For **restaurants** and other dining establishments, we estimate the average amount that you will spend in that restaurant. The table below tells you what you will *typically* find in California at the corresponding price range. Keep in mind that a particularly expensive ice cream stand may still only be marked a ❷, depending on what you will spend.

ACCOMMODATIONS	RANGE	WHAT YOU'RE *LIKELY* TO FIND
❶	$1-17	Camping; most dorm rooms, such as HI or other hostels or university dorm rooms. Expect bunk beds and a communal bath; you may have to provide or rent towels and sheets.
❷	$18-34	Upper-end hostels, motels, or small hotels. You may have a private bathroom, or there may be a sink in your room and a shared bathroom.
❸	$35-54	A small room with a private bath. Should have decent amenities, such as phone and TV. Breakfast often included in the price of the room.
❹	$55-79	Similar to 3, but may have more amenities or be in a more touristed area.
❺	$80+	Large hotels, popular B&Bs, or upscale chains. If it's a 5 and it doesn't have the perks you want, you've paid too much.

FOOD	RANGE	WHAT YOU'RE *LIKELY* TO FIND
❶	$1-6	Mostly street-corner stands, pizza places, or fast-food joints. Rarely ever a sit-down meal.
❷	$7-11	Sandwiches, appetizers at a bar, or low-priced entrees. You may have the option of sitting down or getting take-out.
❸	$12-16	Mid-priced entrees, possibly coming with a soup or salad. Tip will bump you up a couple dollars, since you'll probably have a waiter or waitress.
❹	$17-22	A somewhat fancy restaurant or a steakhouse. Either way, you'll have a special knife. Few restaurants in this range have a dress code, but some may look down on t-shirt and jeans.
❺	$23+	Food with foreign names and a decent wine list. Slacks and dress shirts may be expected. Don't order PB&J.

DISCOVER CALIFORNIA

California's iconic Highway 1 epitomizes the abandon and monumentality of this vast state. Crashing waves, sheer coastal bluffs, towering redwoods, and expansive ocean sunsets all converge on this asphalt horizon—exhilaration doesn't begin to describe the way it feels to be poised upon the very western edge of the country, with better times and wilder sights in the cliff-hugging turns ahead, and the past receding in your rearview mirror. This is a state that rejects the time-tested in favor of the unexplored, and discards business suits in favor of shorts and flip-flops; this is where technology, pop culture, and the American dream go to be reborn. Dread-locked hikers head to the sheer granite face of Yosemite's Half Dome, platinum blonde actresses try their luck in Hollywood, speed-demons fly down Lake Tahoe's powdery ski runs, hardcore climbers scramble up gnarled rocks at Joshua Tree, and adventurous diners find their thrills in Berkeley's Gourmet Ghetto and San Francisco's dim sum palaces. Frigid tide pools give way to warm surfing swells, burrito wagons pull up next to farm stands, and San Francisco's colorful Victorians compete with L.A.'s swaying palm trees in the urban beauty contest. Paradoxical, postmodern, and insanely diverse, California's got something new around every bend in the road.

FACTS AND FIGURES

Capital: Sacramento.

State Population: 35,484,453.

State Motto: Eureka! "I have found it!"

Wine Production: 17,000,000 gallons per year.

Length of San Andreas Fault: 754 mi.

WHEN TO GO

Whenever you want! The myth of California as a haven of warmth and sunshine holds true in Southern California, but it fails to incorporate the immense climatic diversity of the state's snowy mountains, cool northern regions, and searing interior desert. Morning and afternoon fog keeps the North and Central Coast at a temperate 50-70°F for most of the year, while coastal Southern California heats up year-round to a comfortable 70-80°F. Along the coast, the summer tourist season runs from Memorial Day to Labor Day. Warm in summer (when campers flood the national parks) and mild in fall, the Sierra Nevada Mountains are smothered in snow from November through March. The Mojave Desert in the state's southern interior scorches in the summer; like the mountain ski resorts of Lake Tahoe, its main tourist season is the cooler period from September to March. For both the coast and the interior, accommodations are cheaper and less crowded in the off season, but some sights may be closed.

THINGS TO DO

Scale a half-mile-high sheer granite cliff face overlooking a glaciated valley or kick back on a sandy beach. Try to revive the "Summer of Love" in the City by the Bay or break into the 'biz in L.A. Crawl past the mirages that emerge from expanses of shimmering sand dunes or frolic in the salty waves with otters, dolphins, and beach bums. Check out the **Highlights** box at the beginning of each chapter for more specific regional attractions; at every turn we'll show you where to start, but in the end it's up to you to define your adventure.

1

DISCOVER

BEST BURRITOS: Taquería Cancún or anywhere else in **the Mission,** San Francisco (p. 99).

BEST "NUDE" BEACHES: Although disrobing on public beaches is illegal, many people celebrate their freedom from the tyranny of clothing at **Red, White, and Blue Beach,** in Santa Cruz (p. 335). **Yuba River** in Nevada City (p. 325) offers sun and seclusion.

BEST SUNSETS: Gnarled plants create striking silhouettes in **Joshua Tree** (p. 531). **Big Sur** (p. 352) has wild cliffs and crashing waves.

BEST SCENIC DRIVE: Roads wind through the misty **Marin Headlands** (p. 158), west of the Golden Gate Bridge.

BEST PLACE FOR VAIN ALCOHOLICS: Beauty Bar, in L.A. (p. 433), serves martinis with a manicure. Beats olives.

BEST REASONS TO LEAVE: Wild and surreal **Las Vegas,** NV (p. 551) sits just over the border. **Oregon Shakespeare Festival,** Ashland, OR (p. 214) presents the Bard and other exceptional theater in a charming small town.

CITIES

San Francisco (p. 76) and Los Angeles (p. 377), California's primary urban centers, are separated by 419 mi. and a great environmental and cultural divide. Most people tend to gravitate toward one city or the other, but love them or hate them, both are too flavorful not to be tried. It's either San Francisco's calf-building hills or L.A.'s 12-lane highways, the land of sunshine or the city of fog, the inheritors of the sexual revolution or the makers of the new mass media.

SAN FRANCISCO. San Francisco evokes images of antique cable cars trundling over hills, of pastel houses and earthy hippies, of the sweeping Golden Gate Bridge and ominous Alcatraz Island. It has inspired its residents to tread off the beaten path, from beatniks in the **Haight** (p. 111) to Ansel Adams and Imogen Cunningham, whose works show at museums in **SoMa** (p. 109). The city's artistic innovation continues with experimental theater, dance, music, and exhibitions at **Fort Mason** (p. 116) and **Yerba Buena Center for the Arts** (p. 109). Even graceful Victorian houses are given a fabulous new life when painted all the colors of the queer rainbow in the **Castro** (p. 111). Vibrant Chicano and Asian-American communities assure an excellent array of food (p. 93) in the **Mission, Richmond,** and **Chinatown** districts. Park land, from the **Presidio** (p. 114) to **Golden Gate Park** (p. 112), blankets the city in green, providing dramatic views and ideal lounging space.

LOS ANGELES. L.A., where every waitress has a headshot and every parking valet has a screenplay, features great weather and a vibrance that comes from knowing that things *happen* here. Host to many a movie premiere, Grauman's Chinese Theater in **Hollywood** (p. 427) often sports celebrities, who strut and pose on the proverbial red carpet outside the theater. The stars still shine in the **Hollywood Walk of Fame** (p. 430), a sidewalk art display of industry greats, past and present. If you insist on knowing where to meet the stars and how to propel yourself into their world, check out our insider's scoop in tidbits such as: **Central Casting** (p. 74) and **The Beverly Hills Celebrity Tour** (p. 418). It ain't much, but it's a start, kiddo.

Once you're through with Hollywood, you can chill in the chic cafes of **Santa Monica** (p. 396) or work on that tan in the thriving beach communities of **Venice** (p. 402) and **Malibu** (p. 401). With its wealth of aspiring rock bands and comedy club kings, **West Hollywood** has some of the most happening, big-time **nightlife** (p. 424) on the planet. And if the traffic jams wipe the smile off your face, get Mickey or Minnie to cheer you up at **Disneyland** (p. 463).

SAN DIEGO. The southernmost of California's major cities, San Diego is a quieter, more conservative alternative to L.A.. It hosts a wide selection of museums in **Balboa Park** (p. 500), and two of the world's best animal habitats in the **San Diego Zoo** (p. 499) and the **San Diego Wild Animal Park** (p. 511). San Diego's laid-back beaches are great for surfing. The city is also a good base for a daytrip to the border town of **Tijuana**, Mexico, a tequila-infused Sodom and Gomorrah (p. 519).

LAS VEGAS. A 5hr. drive from L.A., Las Vegas (p. 551) sits just over the Nevada border, a gloriously overdone sin city filled with grandiose casinos and entertainment spectaculars. Catch the **Cirque du Soleil** in action and gorge on buffets before hitting the Strip for free-booze-fueled **casino hopping** (p. 557). Near Las Vegas, rugged terrain surrounds **Hoover Dam** (p. 561) and the **Grand Canyon** (p. 562).

THE COAST

The home of the Beach Boys and *Baywatch* offers a far wider range of coastal styles than pop culture might suggest. Whether you want to career along the coastal cliffs of the Pacific Coast Highway, bodysurf on powerful waves, explore secluded shorelines, or just lie back with a towel and a novel, California's got a place for you.

HIGHWAY 1. Stretching the length of California, this legendary highway (Hwy. 1, or the Pacific Coast Highway) lays the foundation for a magnificent coastal tour (see **Suggested Itineraries**, p. 5). On the North Coast, Hwy. 1 winds along precarious cliffs between crashing surf and gigantic redwood trees (p. 216). Highlights of the northern route include a meditative stroll to the black sands of **Jones Beach** (p. 233) or a picnic on the ⬛**Mendocino Headlands** (p. 235). In the San Francisco Bay Area, Hwy. 1 passes **Point Reyes National Seashore** (p. 156), where you can stand high on the bluffs over a dramatic drop to the wild, whale-inhabited ocean. Crossing the San Andreas Fault, the highway cuts across the **Golden Gate Bridge** (p. 114) and through San Francisco. Along the Central Coast, the highway skirts laid-back college towns and the precarious cliff-line crawl past forested **Big Sur** (p. 352). A stop at **Pfeiffer Beach** (p. 354) offers unbeatable views. In Southern California, the PCH leads to hot surf spots and legendary beach bum haunts, but yet more shoreline is a ferry ride away at **Catalina Island** (p. 455) and the **Channel Islands** (p. 475).

TOP TEN BEACHES

California's coastline is hundreds of miles long. Highlights include:

1. Mystical Fern Canyon leads to the warm dunes of **Gold Bluffs Beach** (p. 220).

2. The steep trail down to hip, secluded **Black's Beach** (p. 506) makes the warm sand, marine life, and strong surf all the more welcome.

3. Surfers meet Shakespeare at **Stinson Beach** (p. 157), and there's plenty of room for picnics.

4. Fit, beautiful Angelenos play frisbee and lounge on the perfect sands of **Zuma Beach** (p. 402) before hitting the killer waves.

5. **Point Lobos** (p. 351) offers great views of otters, whales, and sea birds.

6. Lively **Cowell Beach** (p. 335) fills with college students playing volleyball and leads to the delightfully kitschy Santa Cruz Beach Boardwalk.

7. **Ocean Beach**, at the far western edge of Golden Gate Park, feels miles away from San Francisco, though it's easily accessible by MUNI.

8. For the classic surfing experience, head to **Huntington Beach** (p. 468).

9. The warm waters of **Pirate's Cove** (p. 364) are particularly merciful to nude bathers.

10. A reef-break at **Del Mar** (p. 512) makes for consistent swells, while newlyweds and families congregate on the palm-shaded sand.

BEACH COMMUNITIES. Beach culture is the sense of lazy, life-long summer vacation that pervades the California coast. The beach communities begin in earnest (and by "earnest" we mean casual lethargy) south of San Francisco and crop up along the coast all the way to the Mexican border.

On the Central Coast, beach communities take the form of college towns that party between the redwood forests and the kelp forests. The waterfront in crunchy, liberal ◪**Santa Cruz** (p. 328) has a crowded beach, sea lions basking beneath the wharf, and the Boardwalk—a whirligig of roller coasters and colorful game booths straight out of the 50s. Farther south, **San Luis Obispo** (p. 360) lies near Pismo Beach, which is a more sedate sand-and-pier locale that can become a raging spring break party spot. Beneath the Spanish Revival architecture that dots its hills, ritzy **Santa Barbara** (p. 366) has stunning sunsets and trendy boutiques.

The Southern California beach scene lacks the wacky students and organic focus of the northern communities, and instead bows to the gods of sun and surf. In L.A., carnivalesque **Venice Beach** (p. 402) features an eye-popping kaleidoscope of street vendors, sand sculptors, and jugglers. Meanwhile, less manic **Santa Monica Beach** (p. 399) crowds with joggers and in-line skaters. Volleyball players spike balls and drinks on **Hermosa Beach** (p. 407), south of L.A. Youthful crowds flock to the noisy bars and grills of San Diego's **Mission Beach** and **Pacific Beach** (p. 498).

SURFING. All along the coast, excellent waves encourage surfers to hang ten. SoCal has the most reliable and warm surf, but the North and Central Coast have some great spots as well. Santa Cruz sensation **Steamer's Lane** (p. 335) and the break next to the pier at **Pismo Beach** (p. 364) rage with wave-riders. North of L.A., **Ventura** (p. 471) sleeps by some of the dreamiest waves on the coast. In Southern California, **Zuma Beach** in Malibu (p. 402) is the best option near L.A. Orange County vets head for the mythical swells of ◪**Huntington Beach** (p. 468), while beginners test the waters at **San Clemente** (p. 471). The San Diego surf scene holds its own, particularly at **Oceanside** (p. 515), **Tourmaline** and **Winandsea Beaches** in La Jolla (p. 506), and beginner-friendly **Ocean Beach** on Point Loma (p. 505).

WILDERNESS

California is an astoundingly diverse landscape of stately mountains, rugged coastlines, fertile valleys, and barren deserts. The vast granite peaks of the **Sierra Nevada** (p. 237) tower over a visually stunning landscape, while austere expanses created by dried lava flows and the snowy splendor of **Mount Shasta** (p. 201) inspire wonder in the **Cascade Range** of the Northern Interior. The North Coast (p. 216) and the Central Coast (p. 328) feature jagged coastlines and giant redwood trees, while the **Desert** (p. 529) is a dry, desolate landscape of rocks and sand dunes.

HIKING. On the hike to Tall Trees Grove in the North Coast's **Redwood National Park** (p. 216), the towering forest canopy blocks off the misty sunlight and the elements, leaving hikers in quiet, cathedral-like spaces. A trek through **Lassen Volcanic National Park** (p. 195) passes the steaming hydrothermal cauldron of Bumpass Hell and the bubbling waters of Cold Boiling Lake. In **Yosemite** (p. 252), the famed jewel of the Sierra, the narrow staircases of the Mist Trail climb through the dispersed sprays and alluvial rainbows of Vernal and Nevada Falls, while the heady bliss of gazing down from Half Dome justifies the harrowing ascent to the top. Not to be outdone by their celebrated neighbor, **Sequoia** and **Kings Canyon National Parks** (p. 269) have stunning and less crowded hikes along Eagle Lake Trail and the easy path through Zumwalt Meadows. Even farther into the Eastern Sierra, the **Whitney Portal Trail** (p. 300) ascends the highest mountain in the continental US, and a trek through the **Ancient Bristlecone Pine Forest** (p. 285) in the White Mountains will bring you face-to-face with the world's oldest living organisms. In the desert, a scramble along Skull Rock Interpretive Walk in **Joshua Tree** (p. 531) is a great way to try out bouldering while learning about flora and fauna in the Mojave.

BIKING. A bike tour of **Wine Country** (p. 150), the hilly region north of San Francisco that produces some of the most celebrated wines in the world, is easy and pleasurable. When the snow melts, **Mammoth Lakes** (p. 286) morphs into a mountain bike park for those who scorn pavement. The most daring ride starts at 11,053 ft. and barrels down the rocky ski trails.

SKIING. The heights of the Sierras boast some of the best powder in North America. **Lake Tahoe** (p. 237) is one of the world's most beautiful places to ski; **Squaw Valley,** host of the 1962 Winter Olympics, and the aptly named **Heavenly** are the top resorts. Many Southern Californians swoosh down **Mammoth Lakes** (p. 286) in the eastern Sierra. **June Mountain** (p. 283), near Mammoth Lakes, is lesser-known but well loved by those who visit. Resorts in **Big Bear** (p. 483) lie within easy daytrip range of L.A., but the skiing conditions are far inferior to those in the Sierra Nevadas. Cross-country skiers find bliss amid the winter scenery of **Yosemite** (p. 264) and **Sequoia and Kings Canyon National Parks** (p. 285).

WATERSPORTS AND FISHING. The waters of **Lake Tahoe** (p. 237) are the ultimate playground for waterskiers, wakeboarders, and sailors. **Kayakers** can tour tranquil, mineral-rich **Mono Lake** (p. 279) or paddle out to the otter-filled kelp forests near **Santa Cruz** (p. 328), **Monterey** (p. 340), or **San Luis Obispo** (p. 360). **Lake Mead** (p. 561), just across the border in Nevada, roars with motor boats and jet skis; the summer sailing at **Big Bear Lake** (p. 483) near L.A. provides a more sedate alternative. **June Lake** (p. 283) is a mountain fishing hot spot, while ocean fishermen harvest the teeming waters off **San Diego** (p. 489) and along the coast.

ROCK CLIMBING. **Joshua Tree** (p. 531) offers footholds for all levels of climbers; its most famed spots are Hidden Valley and Wonderland of Rocks. Experienced climbers tackle the famed granite faces of **Yosemite** (p. 252). Between L.A. and Palm Springs, climbers crank on Tahquitz and Suicide Rocks in rugged **Idyllwild** (p. 451). Popular spots around **Lake Tahoe** (p. 237) include the spectacular climb of Lover's Leap and the 90 ft. wall at Emerald Bay are two of the most popular spots. The River Gorge in **Owens Valley** (p. 292) and the Buttermilks in **Bishop** (p. 292) are lesser-known but thrilling climbs in the Eastern Sierra.

SUGGESTED ITINERARIES

THE BEST OF CALIFORNIA: A 3-WEEK EXPLORATION. Start in **San Francisco** (p. 76) and spend 3 days getting a feel for the Mission, Golden Gate Park, and Alcatraz. Spend a day exploring **Berkeley** (p. 134) or **Wine Country** (p. 160). Then head to **Lake Tahoe** (p. 237) for 2 days on the lake—the hiking, biking, watersports, and skiing there are all sensational. For relief, the breathtaking **Yosemite** (p. 252) is 4hr. away. Spend 3 days traversing its web of trails and bike paths, or admire the scenery from the valley floor. Head back to the coast for 3 days on the Monterey Bay in **Santa Cruz** (p. 328) and **Monterey** (p. 340), strolling on the Beach Boardwalk and exploring the renowned Monterey Bay Aquarium, leaving time for **Carmel's** Point Lobos (p. 351) or a romp across the gorgeous UC Santa Cruz campus. A day of camping in scenic **Big Sur** (p. 352) is a great way to experience the redwood forests. Move on to **Santa Barbara** (p. 366) for breathtaking beaches and an afternoon on State St. Next, wander **L.A.** (p. 377) for 3 days: window-shop in Beverly Hills or actually buy something in Los Feliz, catch a flick at Grauman's Chinese Theater, and take in the view and the gardens at the Getty Museum. Spend a super-happy day at **Disneyland** (see p. 463), then head to **San Diego** (p. 489) to see the famous Zoo and the Wild Animal Park or hang out in Pacific Beach. An excellent daytrip, **Tijuana** (p. 519) provides the ultimate border town experience. Return to the US for a day in **Joshua Tree National Park** (p. 531) to climb boulders or see some of California's most beautiful sunsets. Depending on your travel plans, exit the state and spend a day or two in **Las Vegas** (p. 567), where excess is an art form, or race back up through the middle of the state on I-5, stopping for some Gold Rush flavor in Old Town **Sacramento** (p. 307) and head over to the **North Coast** (p. 216) to gaze at redwoods and get your last glimpse of the Pacific before returning to SF.

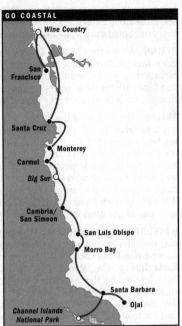
GO COASTAL

THE BEST OF CALIFORNIA

GO COASTAL: A 2-WEEK CRUISE. To savor the best of scenic Hwy. 1, start off in **San Francisco** (p. 76) for 3 days in the foggy City by the Bay, spending time at Golden Gate Park, Haight-Ashbury, and rooting on the Giants in SBC park. Head inland to **Wine Country** (p. 150) for 2 days

of wine-tasting and bicycle rides. Travel south to **Santa Cruz** (p. 328) for 2 days of amusement at the beach Boardwalk, visiting UC Santa Cruz, and learning to surf (p. 335). Jaunt to **Monterey** (p. 340) for a day at the Aquarium and another in nearby **Carmel** (p. 349). A day's drive through **Big Sur** (p. 352) promises big views and bigger redwoods. Don't miss Hearst Castle (p. 358) on your day in **Cambria** and **San Simeon** (p. 355). A day in **San Luis Obispo** (p. 360) allows a stop at Pismo Beach (p. 364) or the Seven Sisters rock formations in **Morro Bay** (p. 366). **Santa Barbara** (p. 366) and its splendid mission are good for 2 days of relaxation. From Santa Barbara, take a daytrip to **Channel Islands National Park** (p. 475) or **Ojai** (p. 375) before driving off into the sunset.

WILD WINTER: 2 WEEKS OF ADVENTURE. Get your extreme-sports fix in the middle of winter—you might even come home with a tan. Start with 3 days of snow at **Lake Tahoe** (p. 237), skiing and snowboarding. For extra kicks, try night skiing at Squaw Valley. Put on the tire chains and head down to **Yosemite** (p. 252), where 2

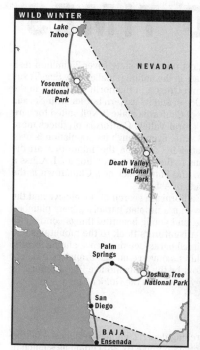

WILD WINTER

Lake Tahoe

NEVADA

Yosemite National Park

Death Valley National Park

Palm Springs

Joshua Tree National Park

San Diego

BAJA
Ensenada

low I-5 up the coast to **Mission San Juan Capistrano** (p. 470), perhaps the most beautiful of the missions, set amongst the rolling hills of Orange County. A 2hr. drive north through L.A. brings you to the **Mission San Fernando Rey de España** (p. 449), an amazing re-creation of the original 1797 structure, which has since burnt down. Farther north, in Ventura, **Mission San Buenaventura** (p. 474) is still used as a parish church. From there, take U.S. 101 north to discover the coastal serenity at **Mission Santa Bárbara** (p. 372), precious Chumash footprints at **Mission Santa Inés** (p. 359), and the colorful Native American frescoes at **Mission San Miguel Archangel** (p. 364). End your trip at the gloriously restored mission in posh **Carmel** (p. 351).

MISSION ACCOMPLISHED

Carmel

San Miguel Archangel

Santa Inés

Santa Bárbara

San Buenaventura

San Fernando Rey de España

San Juan Capistrano

Basílica San Diego de Alcalá

days will give you time to enjoy the park without the summer crowds. Cross-country ski or snowshoe in the South Rim backcountry. Get ready for extreme views, because a day hiking in **Death Valley** (p. 543) is next. Spend 3 days in **Joshua Tree National Park** (p. 531) rock climbing in Hidden Valley and mountain biking alongside the famous gnarled plants. Regain your energy with a day in the spas or casino at **Palm Springs** (p. 537) before heading to **San Diego** (p. 489) to surf at Del Mar and hang glide at Torrey Pines Glider Port. Go south of the border to **Ensenada,** Mexico (p. 526), where you can camp on the beach at Playa el Faro (p. 527), swim in the ocean, play volleyball, and toss back some *cerveza.*

MISSION ACCOMPLISHED: A 1-WEEK TRIP. This drive through history follows **Father Junípero Serra's** 18th-century foot trail, **El Camino Real,** connecting California's missions. Start at **Mission Basílica San Diego de Alcalá** (p. 508) in the historic Old Town district, and then fol-

DISCOVER

LIFE AND TIMES

California commands attention as the most populous state (over 35 million residents) and physically the third-largest state in the nation (smaller only than Texas and Alaska). It stretches over 800 mi. from Oregon in the north to Mexico in the south, and 250 mi. between the Pacific Ocean and its eastern border with Nevada and Arizona. The geography and climate of California make it well suited for agricultural production, especially in the Central Valley: California produces more agricultural products than any other US state, even though its population is over 91% urban and only 15% of its land cultivated. In California, the "minorities" are the majority: one-third of Mexican-Americans in the US live in California, L.A. has a sizable Japanese-American community, and San Francisco's Chinatown is the world's largest Chinese community outside of Asia.

For centuries, settlers have come to California in search of the elusive and the unattainable. Spanish conquistadors saw in it a utopian paradise, 49ers plumbed its depths furiously for the Mother Lode, and young beautiful things continue to strive for stardom on its silver screen. Adventurers flock to the mountains and deserts, and families head off to the national parks, seeking peace among forests, granite cliffs, and lava beds. Flower children converge on San Francisco's Haight Street, while laid-back tan-seekers chill out by the Santa Monica Pier. California's magnetic pull brings millions of people every year to the Golden State.

LAND

Snow-dusted peaks, fertile valleys, scorching deserts, endless beaches—California truly has it all. The Sierra Nevada mountain range (p. 237) dominates much of the eastern third of the state with its jagged granite peaks, the ever-popular Yosemite National Park (p. 252), and the continental US's tallest mountain (Mt. Whitney, p. 301). Parallel to the Sierras is the enormous San Joaquin, or Central, Valley (p. 303), one of the most productive agricultural regions in the world. The formidable Mojave Desert (p. 531) lies southeast of the Valley and the mountains, and those tenacious enough to withstand the heat will be rewarded with otherworldly locales: Death Valley (p. 543), Joshua Tree (p. 531), and, just over the border, Las Vegas (p. 567). And, of course, to the west lies the famed California coast—and several million of the most beautiful sunsets in history.

FLORA AND FAUNA

California's ecosystems vary with the state's geography. Plant life is extremely diverse, ranging from forests on the coast to flowering cacti in the Mojave Desert. California also supports many forms of animal life, including dangerous creatures like rattlesnakes and mountain lions, and the endangered California condor.

PLANTS

SIERRA NEVADA. Giant sequoias, identifiable by their reddish-brown bark and enormous trunks, tower in small groves within the national parks. They are the world's largest single organisms and can live for up to 3500 years; their small cones can cling to the branches for almost 30 years. Few sequoias remain, and battles are constantly being waged between developers and environmentalists over the future of the trees. Also common to the area are **ponderosa** and **lodgepole pines,**

8

which have medium-sized pine cones and golden, scaly bark. Broad-leafed trees such as **pacific dogwood** and **aspen,** with its milky-white bark, make for beautiful fall foliage. During warmer months, wildflowers like the punch-red **Indian paintbrush** and the yellow **monkey flower** flourish in the mountains.

DESERT. Cacti abound in this arid region, among them the brightly flowering cholla, whose "teddy bear" variety looks deceptively soft and inviting. **Joshua trees** are recognizable by their twisted, intertwined branches and upward reaching fronds. Though found throughout the desert, these trees are particularly abundant in Joshua Tree National Park.

PACIFIC COAST. Relatives of the giant sequoias (and just as rare), **redwoods** are the tallest trees in the world. Resilient reddish brown bark protects them and allows them to live for over 2000 years. Grape-sized pine cones and flat needles distinguish the trees. Farther south along the coast, the rushlike **Monterey cypress** and **pine** are found on coastal bluffs alongside the bright orange state flower, the **California poppy.**

DANGEROUS PLANTS. Poison oak is common at elevations below 5000 ft. The plant grows as a shrub or vine, with green, shiny, three-pronged leaves that turn red and drop in the fall. Berries are white or greenish-white. Contact with poison oak will cause an irritating red rash. If exposure is suspected, wash skin immediately with cold water and soap, and launder clothes several times before wearing again. You may want to include itch-relieving ointments in your first-aid kit (p. 32). Never burn poison oak: inhaling its oils can cause serious allergic reactions above and beyond those caused by touching the plant.

ANIMALS

SIERRA NEVADA. Trout swim in high mountain streams. **Deer** are common, and **grizzly** and **black bears** also roam the forest. **Marmots** are found high in the mountains; they are yellow-bellied 5-10 lb. ground squirrels.

DESERT. Most desert animals are nocturnal, although during the day **kangaroo rats** hop across the sand and **roadrunners** (gray birds with fluffy heads and straight tails) race away from wily **coyotes.**

PACIFIC COAST. Sea lions, otters, and seals tend to congregate near Monterey Bay and the Channel Islands, which are National Marine Sanctuaries. From December to March, **gray whales** (or at least their tails and spray) can be seen off the coast as they move between the Arctic Sea and their breeding grounds in Mexico. The **California condor,** with a wingspan of 9 ft. and a life expectancy of up to 40 years, is one of the largest flying birds. Its survival was in question until the success of captive breeding attempts in the 1980s, and now almost 50 condors fly about California, with the total condor population hovering around 200.

DANGEROUS ANIMALS. Rattlesnakes, bears, and sharks can be concerns in parts of California; for info on how to protect yourself, see **Wildlife,** p.56. In addition, cougars, panthers, and coyotes have lost their homes to recent development, and some roam suburban areas at night and in the early morning. Attacks on people are rare, but if walking at night, carry a stick and make noise.

HISTORY

Evidence of California's rich history is readily visible in many parts of the state. The missions throughout the state serve as relics of Spanish colonialism; ghost towns are virtually all that remains of the Gold Rush; and San Francisco's activist enclaves are living remnants of the socially engaged 60s and 70s.

EARLY YEARS AND EXPLORATION

Before California was California, it was Mexico. And before it was Mexico, or even New Spain, it was home to 100 Native American cultures, descendants of the original Paleo-Siberian immigrants, each with their own political system and language. Most tribes were peaceful and survived by hunting, fishing, and gathering.

When Europeans encountered the region, it seemed to them the stuff of dreams. Landing in Baja California in 1535, colonists under the leadership of infamous conquistador **Hernán Cortés** named the region after Queen Califia, the beautiful ruler of a mythical land full of gold and jewels in the Spanish romance *Las Sergas de Esplandian* (1510). In 1542, Spain made its first contact with the tribes of upper California when explorer **Estévan Juan Rodríguez Cabrillo,** a Portuguese conquistador enlisted by the Spanish navy, sailed up the west coast of North America in a poorly provisioned ship manned by conscripts. His mission to find the mythical Strait of Anian failed, but the exploration party reached what is now the Oregon coast.

Many more Spanish ships would follow, establishing a cultural presence that remains strong to this day in everything from language to architecture. After 1769, the Spanish began to settle the area en masse. Coastal cities like San Francisco (founded 1776) and L.A. (founded 1787) cropped up alongside Catholic **missions,** introduced by Father Junípero Serra to convert California's coastal Native Americans and serve as supply outposts for Spanish galleons.

EARLY 19TH CENTURY

At the beginning of the 19th century, Spain's New World colonies rose in revolt against their parent country, and California accompanied them. In Mexico, radical priest **Miguel Hidalgo y Costilla** led the indigenous and mestizo populations in an 1810 uprising that ignited the Mexican Revolution. The revolutionaries persisted even after the capture and execution of Hidalgo, gaining independence for a Mexican state that included California by 1822. With the mission system dissolved by 1833 and regulation from Mexico City ineffective, privileged Mexicans called **rancheros** dominated vast parcels of land, exerting de facto control over California. Staged "revolutionary" battles between ranchero-sponsored factions substituted for governmental checks on power.

BEAR FLAG REPUBLIC

In the following years, a steady trickle of Americans headed west to the mythical land fancifully described as "edenic" in national newspapers. Capitalizing on imminent hostilities between the US and Mexico, which were battling for control of Texas, western settlers joined US Captain John C. Fremont in the **Bear Flag Revolt** of 1846, proclaiming California's independence from Mexico. The Bear Flag Republic proved fleeting, as the US soon went to war with Mexico, acquiring California in the 1848 **Treaty of Guadalupe Hidalgo,** in which Mexico ceded to the US half of its territory, including California for a paltry $15 million.

THE GOLD RUSH

For the US, the timing was golden. Just as the Mexican cession became official, James Marshall discovered **gold** at Sutter's Mill near Sacramento (see **Coloma,** p. 325), and the rush was on. Beginning in 1849, the 49ers, a motley, half-million strong crew of fortune seekers, flooded the region. Thousands of would-be prospectors sailed around South America's stormy Cape Horn, and those in wagon trains encountered savage winters and Native American attacks while crossing the

Rockies and the Sierra Nevadas. The most famous of the doomed settler trains was the **Donner Party,** which was compelled by the fierce winter of 1846-47 to practice cannibalism at a snowbound outpost near what is now Donner Lake in the Sierra Nevadas (see **This Party Bites!,** p.247). By 1859 the new arrivals had mined over 28 million oz. of gold, which would be worth $10 billion at today's prices. In the process, they razed redwood forests, eroded mountains, and annihilated Native American tribes. Five years later, the gold petered out; graveyards and ghost towns have long marked its passing.

The massive influx of prospectors and settlers caused the non-native population to multiply six-fold within four years. Newly independent and economically prosperous, Gold Rush-era Californians quickly wrote their own constitution and inaugurated John C. Fremont as their first governor a full year before receiving the US Congress's 1850 grant of **statehood.** The completion of a transcontinental telegraph system in 1861 linked California with the east and put the ponies out to pasture. Industrialists, including Leland Stanford, Stanford University's founder, invested in the Central Pacific Railroad. Its tracks extended eastward, largely thanks to the very cheap labor of exploited Chinese immigrants. A golden spike linked the Central Pacific and Union Pacific Railroads in 1869 to form the **Transcontinental Railroad,** which made traveling cross-country to California a comparatively easy five-day venture. In the 1870s and 80s, naturalist **John Muir** eloquently advocated wilderness conservation in the Sierra Nevada Mountains, securing the preservation of Yosemite and Sequoia as national parks in 1890.

EARLY 20TH CENTURY

The **great earthquake** of 1906 (7.7 on the Richter scale) destroyed much of San Francisco; city-wide fires from ruptured gas pipes and overturned stoves incinerated the all-wood houses and killed 452 people. In 1904, water bureau superintendent William Mulholland devised a plan to irrigate arid L.A. by constructing an aqueduct from the Owens Valley, 250 mi. northeast of the city. The massive water redirection project fueled the exponential growth of L.A. and enabled the influx of movie studios and entertainers, transforming the once-lush Owens Valley into a desolate expanse in the process. An extensive **streetcar system,** consisting of over 1150 mi. of track and connecting L.A. with four surrounding counties, reached its peak in the 1920s. To capitalize on the oil boom of the 1920s, Standard Oil, Firestone, and General Motors bought out and dismantled the streetcars and subways to make the automobile the only viable mode of transportation.

GREAT DEPRESSION AND WORLD WAR II

California weathered the Great Depression of the 1930s more easily than the rest of the country; its farm income sank to just half of pre-Depression levels. Thousands flocked west to escape the impoverished Dust Bowl of the Southern Plains. These **"Okies"** were perceived as a threat by native Californian workers, and at times local authorities aided farmers in blocking roads against them (as depicted in John Steinbeck's novel *The Grapes of Wrath*). Still, agriculture pressed forward. By 1939, oranges and other produce made California the leading agricultural state in the nation. After the repeal of Prohibition the California grape industry blossomed, and, by 1940, California supplied 90% of the nation's wine, table grapes, and raisins.

Three months after the December 1941 Japanese bombing of Pearl Harbor, President Roosevelt authorized the US military to remove all persons of Japanese ancestry, both American and alien, from the West Coast and relocate them to **internment camps** in the state's interior. Some historians believe that government and public support for Japanese-American internment was based on greed for their land and resources, as many of them owned sizable tracts of farmland in California. Now the internment camps are nothing but a few crumbled building foundations amid the interior wastelands (see **Tule Lake,** p. 213, and **Manzanar,** p. 300).

RADICAL 60S AND PSYCHEDELIC 70S

After the war production boom of the 1940s, construction projects such as the irrigation canals and freeways of Southern California promoted even swifter expansion. In 1964, California redefined the power center of America by overtaking New York as the nation's most populous state. During the early 1960s, the surf culture of Frankie and Annette, Gidget, and the Beach Boys created a carefree, sun-loving, convertible-cruisin' image of California that persists to this day. The beach party ended, however, and waves of political upheaval began to shake the college campuses of California. In Berkeley, clashes between students and police over civil rights spawned the **Free Speech Movement,** a precursor to future student activism and anti-war protests. Beginning in 1965, César Chavez led California grape pickers on a five-year-long strike of California grapes that transformed into a campaign for a nationwide grape boycott. In 1967, San Francisco's Haight-Ashbury district declared a **"Summer of Love,"** and young people voiced their disgust with the Establishment by, in Timothy Leary's words, "turning on, tuning in, and dropping out."

Violence continually marred the flourishing liberal utopianism of the radical 1960s. The 1965 summer riots in **Watts,** L.A., sparked by the arrest of a black man by a white policeman for drunk driving, left four dead and almost 1000 injured. In the midst of mounting antiwar protests based at UC Berkeley, the black empowerment coalition known as the **Black Panthers** challenged white supremacy, **Charles Manson** and his cult grew infamous through a series of ritual murders, and leftist golden child **Bobby Kennedy** was murdered in L.A.'s storied Ambassador Hotel after winning the California primary of the 1968 presidential election. In the same period, conservative Southern California thrust right-wing powerhouse (and former actor) **Ronald Reagan** into the political limelight, electing him governor.

In the 1970s, water and fuel shortages as well as the unbearable L.A. smog forced Californians to alter their ways of life, and attitudes all around lost their earlier sunniness. Governor Jerry "Moonbeam" Brown romanced singer Linda Ronstadt. The Symbionese Liberation Army, the most prominent of a few new revolutionary groups, kidnapped newspaper heiress **Patty Hearst** and temporarily converted her to their cause. The People's Temple of San Francisco gained international notoriety when its leader, **Jim Jones,** poisoned and killed over 1000 members in a mass-suicide service at his religious retreat in Guyana. Meanwhile, **Silicon Valley** (first pioneered by Hewlett-Packard two decades earlier) in the southern Bay Area began its reign as the capital of the computer world.

THE 80S AND 90S

In the 1980s, illegal immigrants streamed across the border from Mexico in increasing numbers. A huge earthquake in 1989 leveled highways in the Bay Area and halted the World Series "Battle of the Bay" between the San Francisco Giants and the Oakland A's. Two years later a massive fire in Oakland burned over 2000 homes. The most severe drought in California history, from 1987 to 1992, tested regional tensions, as Southern Californians continued to tap into depleted Northern California reservoirs.

The 1990s opened with a new wave of racial turmoil and unrest. The 1992 **Los Angeles Riots** were sparked by the acquittal of the four white police officers accused of viciously beating Rodney King (a black man). The passage of **Proposi-**

tion 187, which denied all social services to illegal immigrants, renewed questions of ethnicity and tolerance, though the courts eventually struck down most of the law. Meanwhile, the **O.J. Simpson** trial revealed the gaping divide between black and white perspectives on the objectivity of the American criminal justice system.

After the University of California system prohibited all **affirmative action** programs, the general voting public passed **Proposition 209,** which outlawed affirmative action and quotas in state programs like public education and public employment. Before the proposition (strongly supported by then-governor Pete Wilson) was fully implemented, court injunction brought things to a screeching halt after a coalition of civil rights groups filed a complaint.

The 90s brought about the most comprehensive fight for **marijuana legalization** the state had ever seen. **Proposition 215,** passed by voters in 1996, had allowed individual patients to grow and use marijuana for medicinal purposes only. However, the law was challenged and has since been stripped down considerably.

The **dot-com boom** of the mid- and late 90s was based primarily in Silicon Valley (just outside of San Francisco). During the peak of the dot-com craze, everyone was riding high on the improvements in productivity and information dissemination that could (in theory) result from the Internet and smaller, cheaper computer processors. The NASDAQ stock index kept climbing and money kept appearing magically, and it seemed for a while as though the dot-coms had ushered in a new era of steadily increasing prosperity.

But the dot-com bubble, which seemed indestructible for so long, finally burst when everyone realized that none of these companies was actually making money. Layoffs occurred en masse, and many companies went under altogether. The crazed optimism—in Alan Greenspan's words, the "irrational exuberance"—had faded. That said, the strongest, most innovative high-tech corporations in the world remain in California, and Silicon Valley is still a hotbed of innovation.

TODAY

On October 7, 2003, California hosted the first gubernatorial recall election since 1921. The embattled and widely unpopular Gray Davis was removed from office as 55% of voting Californians supported the recall. Arnold Schwarzenegger, the action movie star and political novice, was ushered into office, winning nearly 50% of the votes cast and defeating 134 other candidates, among them former sitcom star Gary Coleman and pornography magnate Larry Flynt. After several months in office, Schwarzenegger's approval ratings soared as he garnered support across party lines, in part by repealing a controversial car tax increase and by repealing a law that would have allowed illegal immigrants to obtain driver's licenses.

As the political storm surrounding the recall election subsided and Californians warmed to "the governator," more controversy emerged in February 2004 when the mayor of San Francisco, Gavin Newsom, permitted the issuance of marriage licenses to gay and lesbian couples. More than 4000 marriage licenses were handed out before the California Supreme Court issued a temporary stay in March directing officials not to allow additional same-sex marriages. On August 12, 2004, the California Supreme Court ruled that Newsom had exceeded his legal authority and that the same-sex marriages were of no legal effect. The ruling does not resolve the state's same-sex marriage debate; cases directly addressing the constitutionality of the state's marriage laws are working their way through the state's court system and will likely end up before the state Supreme Court.

PEOPLE

With a white non-Hispanic population of only 47%, there is currently no racial majority in California. The Hispanic and Latino population of 32% is projected to rise to 50% by 2040. California's population is 11% Asian, 7% African-American, and 1% Native American. Non-white populations are generally denser in urban areas, while outskirts and suburbs have proportionally more Caucasians—though some small towns have become havens for immigrant communities. In many of California's cities, particularly San Francisco and L.A., distinct ethnic neighborhoods coexist right next to each other, offering an amazing array of food and culture.

CULTURE

FOOD AND DRINK

California's fertile soil and abundant waters have always shaped regional cuisine. Native American tribes feasted on fresh fish, abalone, and acorn mush. When Spanish missionaries arrived, they introduced methods of cultivation that would eventually be adopted throughout the state. During the Gold Rush, prospectors short on yeast perfected the use of bread starters to create **San Francisco sourdough bread,** now hawked to tourists at Fisherman's Wharf. In subsequent years, waves of immigrants adapted the regional cuisines of the South America, Mexico, and many Asian countries to utilize California's unique produce.

In the 1970s Alice Waters revolutionized the gourmet world with her restaurant, Chez Panisse. The **California Cuisine** she still serves there relies on fresh and natural ingredients in fascinating combinations with strong European, Asian, and Latin American influences. While Chez Panisse is out of most budget travelers' price-range, many affordable restaurants abide by the same philosophy. Their emphasis on fresh produce helped spark the explosion of ▩**Farmers Markets,** where you can create your own California Cuisine from whatever excites you as you wander through rows of organic farm-stands.

TIP

AVOCADOS. A staple of the Californian diet, avocados are delicious when eaten ripe. To pick a perfect avocado, gently squeeze the fruit and press it with your thumb. If it's unyielding, it's not ripe enough; if it dents, it's too ripe. Try to find one that yields just a little bit. Then, slice it lengthwise, sprinkle it with a bit of salt, and enjoy!

Apart from California Cuisine, regional food favorites range from hamburgers to alfalfa sprouts. Tiny *taquerías* serve giant **burritos,** and sushi chefs slice inventive cuts of fresh fish. Travelers on the interstates swear by **In-n-Out Burger,** while the health conscious take shots of **wheat grass** juice for a jolt of nutrients. At festivals of strawberries, garlic, and avocados, Californians celebrate the glory of the state's agriculture. Recently, Cypress Grove Chèvre has lead California **cheeses** to critical acclaim with its dreamy Humboldt Fog goat cheese.

The golden hills north of San Francisco host the vineyards of California **wine country.** Since the 1970s, Californian wine has been as famous as its French counterparts, and connoisseurs flock to sample the zinfandels and merlots of Napa and Sonoma counties. In Chico, farther to the northeast of San Francisco, ex-hippies brew Sierra Nevada Pale Ale, one of the most popular craft-beers in the world. And with all the fruit grown in California, cafes all over the state serve fresh and delicious juices and smoothies (a blended mix of fruit, ice, and yogurt).

CUSTOMS AND ETIQUETTE

Laid-back is the word in California (except when looking for parking in L.A.). Don't expect dinner to start exactly when planned, and go with the flow in whatever you do. Dress is generally very relaxed—during the day, shorts and sandals are acceptable for all but the most elite establishments. While you should still mind your pleases and thank-yous, manners and speech are also very casual. In general, Californians are friendly and open, but always trust your instincts when meeting new people.

THE ARTS

California was and is a magnet for innovative artistic talent; its studios and stages are full, and suburbia's garages spawn new bands daily. Digital television, the soaring popularity of DVDs, and worldwide movie premieres allow California to continue to imprint its consciousness on the rest of the planet.

ARCHITECTURE

When he arrived in 1769, **Father Junípero Serra** built Mission San Diego de Alcala out of thick adobe bricks made of mud and straw, covered in white plaster. The rancho adobe style with its arched doorways and red Spanish tile roofs fell out of vogue during the Gold Rush years, but was revived in the late 1900s in the construction of Stanford University and two-story, open-balconied Spanish-style homes. Downtown Santa Barbara remains an impressive example of mission revival architecture. After the 1906 earthquake, San Franciscans rebuilt their city with ornate, brightly colored houses known as "painted ladies." Across the bay, Berkeley filled up with craftsman-style bungalows, and in Pasadena **Charles and Henry Greene** perfected the bungalow style.

In the early 20th century, California embraced an eclectic variety of styles, opening the double-doors for **Julia Morgan's** historicist-romantic palace, Hearst Castle. Opposing this opulence, **Frank Lloyd Wright** abandoned his signature mid-western Prairie style to create Mayan-inspired concrete houses made of pre-fab "textile blocks." The best example of this California Romanza style is Hollyhock house in Hollywood. Following on Wright's heels, **Rudolph Schindler** and **Richard Neutra** brought Modernism to L.A., using reinforced steel and plate glass to coat the Hollywood hills with cascading villas. Modernism lives on in **Richard Meier's** 1998 **Getty Center,** a monumental complex of travertine buildings connected by inventive native landscaping. Beginning in the 1950s, Californian companies began to advertise *with* their buildings, instead of on the side of them. The Capitol Records building at Hollywood and Vine looks like a giant stack of records, and its spire blinks out the message "Hollywood" in Morse code. Cultural critics have identified the kitschy buildings in the shapes of hot dogs or doughnuts that pepper the highways as California's "roadside vernacular."

The current king of California architecture is **Frank Gehry,** who has won critical and popular acclaim for his unique, unorthodox creations. **Walt Disney Concert Hall,** completed in 2003, is slated to rejuvenate downtown L.A. with its gleaming and twisting steel curves.

FINE ARTS

Guy Rose was one of the first Californians to gain international fame as an artist—his impressionist stylings of eucalyptus trees and canyons used French technique to document Californian landscapes. **Dorothea Lange's** 1936 photo *Migrant Mother* became a national symbol of the suffering caused by the Great Depression. During WWII, the federal government hired her to document the relocation of Japanese-Americans, but then censored these photographs for their exposure of the injustices that occurred during the relocation. From 1930 to 1960, **Ansel Adams** showed Yosemite to the rest of the nation. His luminous, iconic photographs of California's landscapes and national parks helped his related efforts in conservation. **Edward Weston** pioneered Modernist photography in California from 1910 to 1940; his sensuous still lifes, portraits, and landscapes are less recognizably "Californian" than Adams's but just as influential. In the mid-20th century, **Richard Diebenkorn** gave rise to the "abstract landscape" with the 1960s *Ocean Park* series of the Santa Monica seashore, found in many California museums. **Robert Crumb's** dementedly insightful comics about the sex, drugs, and rock 'n' roll scene in San Francisco helped fuel the euphoric introspection of late 60s counterculture; his cartoon histories of the blues redefined the comic genre. In the 1980s, British-born **David Hockney** immortalized the suburban pool with his brilliantly-hued, geometric, and pop-arty paintings of Californian residents and residences.

Today, California artists fuse different styles, textures, and mediums, often dabbling in set design, photography, and the more traditional studio arts. Some museums and galleries, like **The Oakland Museum** and **The Pasadena Museum of California Art** exclusively exhibit the work of California residents.

LITERATURE

From the beginning, explorers and settlers heralded California as a paradise in verse and in legend, and with the Gold Rush the literary flow began in earnest. Vestiges of the early California that appeared in the writing of **Bret Harte** and **Mark Twain** can still be seen in the relatively unspoiled hills and ghost towns of Gold Country. Even **Jack London**, Oakland's literary native son, spent time panning for gold while writing pastoral stories on the side. London's 1913 novel *The Valley of the Moon* provides an evocative portrait of the Sonoma and San Joaquin Valleys before they were consumed by wineries and agribusiness. Poet Robinson Jeffers composed his paeans on the Big Sur coast of Monterey County, where novelist Henry Miller also set up camp upon returning from Europe.

California's 20th-century urbanization gave its writers new inspiration. **Raymond Chandler** and **Dashiell Hammett** depicted the wanderings of hard-boiled, world-weary detectives amid the seamy underbellies of L.A. and San Francisco. With *The Day of the Locust* (1939), **Nathanael West** probed the grotesque side of Hollywood, behind the makeup, shams, and illusions, portraying lives warped into empty savagery. **John Steinbeck** won the Nobel Prize in 1962 for his scrutiny of the Depression era. In *The Grapes of Wrath* (1939), he depicted the hard life of Midwesterners displaced to California by drought with heavy-handed symbolism and a sensitivity that earned him the Pulitzer. During the 1950s, **Jack Kerouac** and **Allen Ginsberg** combined candid autobiography with visionary rapture to become the gurus of the Beat Generation. Along with fellow poet and City Lights Bookstore owner **Lawrence Ferlinghetti**, they appropriated San Francisco's North Beach as a spiritual home. After completing the cross-country wanderings fictionalized in his *On The Road* (1957), Kerouac finally settled down and wrote his last novel in and about *Big Sur* (1962). **Thomas Pynchon's** *The Crying of Lot 49* (1966) "went postal" with a paranoid sort of wandering that included potheads and a new slant on stamp collecting. His *Vineland* (1990), an epic mess of pop culture and political conspiracy, romps through California, self-consciously name-dropping every town from Vacaville to Van Nuys. **Armistead Maupin's** *Tales of the City* (1978) captured a wacky assortment of characters living on San Francisco's Barbary Lane, and paved the way for other gay authors. And for the children of this postmodern state, a kinder, gentler author by the name of **Beverly Cleary** penned the delightful *Ramona* series.

Fifth-generation Californian **Joan Didion's** essays examine the less-than-golden sides of the state. Contemporary America owes one of its most pervasive catchphrases to the ennui of Palm Springs's resort culture, which spawned **Douglas Coupland's** *Generation X*. The youthful enthusiasm of the Bay Area, natural or drug-induced, is the subject of **Douglas Rushkoff's** *Ecstasy Club* and **Dave Egger's** *A Heartbreaking Work of Staggering Genius*. **Bruce Wagner's** *I'm Losing You* proves that Hollywood corruption never goes out of style.

MUSIC

With radio stations playing everything from honky-tonk to ranchero to Top 40 hits, California music is as diverse as its population. The California music scene began in earnest in the 1940s and 50s, when **Chet Baker** and others improvised West Coast jazz—known for its laid-back "vo-cools" inspired by California's pace of life and readily available heroin. **Johnny Otis** led the transition from jazz to R&B, which blossomed in 1950s L.A.

The squeaky-clean **Beach Boys** and **Jan and Dean** warbled harmonized odes to sun and fun in the 1960s in L.A. The singer-songwriter movement of the 1970s **(Joni Mitchell, Jackson Browne, James Taylor)** eradicated the last traces of political advocacy from the lone-guitarist idiom it had inherited from American folk music. Bands looking for renewed vigor found it in punk **(X)**, Mexican roots **(Los Lobos)**, or a combination of the two **(The Blasters)**.

From the 1960s to the 1990s, the dissolute sampled several iterations of life in the fast lane. Hollywood produced **The Doors**, the slickly countrified **Eagles,** and the triumphantly sleazy **Guns 'n' Roses**. The guitar gymnastics of Dutch import **Eddie Van Halen** were epoch-making for pop music technique in the early 1980s, while hair-metal **(Mötley Crüe)** and glam-metal **(Poison)** kept the fancy costumes but toned down rock's bluesiness to a limited number of loud, formulaic gestures.

Hippies established a nationally recognized San Francisco sound in the 1960s, as pot and LSD increased audience tolerance for long, indulgent jams grounded in Afro-Caribbean rhythm **(Santana)**, blues **(Big Brother and the Holding Company,** who launched doomed vocalist **Janis Joplin** to stardom), acid **(Jefferson Airplane)**, and folk **(The Grateful Dead)**. Baby boomers mustered great enthusiasm for the Summer of Love in 1967, as copious sex and drugs enhanced the groovy new sound. However, the notorious murder of a Rolling Stones audience member by Hell's Angels in 1969 at Altamont (Woodstock's evil twin) signaled that this "trip" was going bad.

The Bay Area also created several prominent bands that were less dependent on psychedelic motifs. **Sly and the Family Stone's** breathtaking utopian vision of racial integration resonated with the help of slap-bass inventor Larry Graham, and **Credence Clearwater Revival** of El Cerrito credibly impersonated bayou swamp rats. Darby Crash thrust and smashed punk into the California scene in the late 70s as lead singer of **The Germs,** while Penelope Houston and **The Avengers** pioneered punk in San Francisco. And in the midst of 80s suburbia, short-haired skateboarders pounded punk into hardcore **(Dead Kennedys, Black Flag, The Minutemen, Suicidal Tendencies)**.

In the early nineties, the spokesmen of combative gangsta rap **(NWA, Dr. Dre, Eazy E, Ice Cube, Snoop Dogg)** spewed invective straight outta Compton at cops and East Coast rappers. Rap and hard rock were fused into California's diverse milieu of the late 1980s with some leering **(Red Hot Chili Peppers)**, some grooving **(Fishbone)**, and some leftist ranting **(Rage Against the Machine)**. In the mid-90s, L.A. witnessed the emergence of New Swing, a white, middle-class revival of ethnic rhythms first tapped out during the zoot suit-clad Depression era.

To the north, Oakland's rappers **(Digital Underground, Too $hort, Tupac)** built the loping Oaktown sound on Graham's heavy bass foundation. These days, newer artists like **Meat Beat Manifesto** perform electronic music in dance clubs all over the US. Ska music, from Jamaica via the UK, found its way to the Californian suburbs in a ska-revival, or **third wave;** in 1997, radio everywhere blared with Orange County's upbeat **No Doubt,** featuring pop princess Gwen Stefani, and the pseudo-punk "All-Stars" **Smash Mouth.** Despite the death of lead singer Bradley Nowell in 1996, wildly popular **Sublime** continues recording their ska-punk-reggae in remix compilations and tours in the form of the **Long Beach Dub All-Stars.** Meanwhile, the pop punk genre finds its hero in the irreverent **Blink 182,** which crafts references to sodomy, masturbation, and bestiality into pure power chords.

Currently, **Lady Bianca** leads Oakland's rich live blues scene, while local record label **Tigerbeat6** releases glitchy electronica. **Hoobastank** continue the pseudo-alternative California groove. Dublin imports **The Thrills** croon surf-inspired homages to the California coast, and every hip bar hosts indie bands about to make it big.

FILM

SILENT FILM AND PRE-CODE TALKIES. California's film legacy did not begin in Hollywood, but rather at a racetrack in Sacramento, where **Eadweard Muybridge** set up 12 cameras to prove that all four of a running horse's legs are off the ground at once during its stride. Muybridge used the strip of pictures to create a primitive movie machine. When film technique was perfected, the American movie industry began in New York and New Jersey. But within a few years, New York film studios had created a cartel that made making movies nearly impossible for independent film makers. So, lead by **Carl Laemmle** (the founder of Universal Pictures) and lured by the promise of creative freedom and endless sunshine (a boon in the age before adequate artificial lighting), the movie making industry headed to Hollywood.

As the balance of movie power began to shift west, the Hollywood studios created the "star system." For the first time, actors themselves were advertised and used to attract adoring fans to the movies. Laemmle used publicity stunts and an exclusive contract to market **Florence Lawrence** as the first movie star. But it was "America's Sweetheart," **Mary Pickford,** who banked on her golden curls to gain the first million-dollar movie-star contract. **Charlie Chaplin, Buster Keaton, Douglas Fairbanks,** and that lover of lovers, **Rudolph Valentino,** soon joined the girls as rulers of the legendary silver screen.

THE CLASSIC ERA. The 1920s witnessed two major developments: sound and scandal. *The Jazz Singer* (1927), a musical featuring **Al Jolson** in blackface, was the first "talking picture." **Walt Disney** and his animation studio were breaking other ground with colored, talking cartoons beginning with *Steamboat Willie* (1929), which showcased the pervasively lovable Mickey Mouse. Scandals erupted when **Fatty Arbuckle** went on trial for the rape and murder of starlet **Virginia Rappe.** A suspicion that Hollywood was becoming a moral cesspool led to the appointment of Postmaster General **Will Hays** as "movie czar." His vilified Hayes Production Code of 1930 tightly regulated the content and presentation of sex and violence in films, but also prevented the establishment of a federal censorship system that was strongly advocated by the Catholic Church.

American film's golden age took place during the height of the studio era, when Hollywood's four major studios standardized and dominated films. *Gone With the Wind* (1939) was the first large-scale Hollywood extravaganza, blazing the way for other studios to utilize exorbitant budgets, flamboyant costumes, and enormous casts. **Shirley Temple** tap-danced her way into the hearts of Americans, becoming the first child-star, and **Busby Berkeley** created lavish kaleidoscopic dance numbers for the Warner Bros. movie musicals.

In 1941, **Orson Welles** unveiled his intricate masterpiece, *Citizen Kane*, a landmark work that revolutionized the potential of the medium. In the same year, **Humphrey Bogart** smoldered his way through San Francisco in the film noir classic, *The*

Maltese Falcon. Serious directors (including Welles), continued to create these dark detective films throughout the 1940s, while audiences flocked to watch patriotic fluff designed to take their minds off the horrors of WWII.

POST-WAR. Post-war tension with the Soviet Union and conflicts abroad led to widespread communist witch-hunts at home. The film industry, under government pressure, took up the policy of blacklisting any artists with suspected ties to communism. Meanwhile, British import **Alfred Hitchcock** featured Californian landscapes in his iconic thrillers *Psycho* (1960), *Vertigo* (1958), and *The Birds* (1963). The 1950s also saw the emergence of a cult of glamour surrounding the most luminous stars. Cloaked in glitz and scandal, sex symbols **Marilyn Monroe, James Dean, Elizabeth Taylor,** and **Rock Hudson** drew audiences to movies by name recognition alone. These stars, along with actors **Marlon Brando** and **Audrey Hepburn,** brought their own personal mystique to the screen, and added significantly to the art of cinematic performance and tabloid publicity. And in the early 60s, **Sally Field** and **Annette Funicello** boogied their ways through the light-hearted surf-comedy genre in the *Gidget* and *Beach Party* movies.

THE AUTEURS. The late 1960s and early 1970s saw widespread social upheaval and tension between generations. Rethinking their battle plans, many studios enlisted directors influenced by the French New Wave as well as artists from other media to direct features, including **Sidney Lumet, John Frankenheimer,** and **Robert Altman.** Studio head **Robert Evans** made Paramount millions with hit films such as *Rosemary's Baby* (1968), *Love Story* (1970), and *The Godfather* (1972). The introduction of a movie ratings board (MPAA) to replace censorship allowed the work of a number of innovative filmmakers began to enter the mainstream. **Stanley Kubrick** brought a literary importance to filmmaking with *Dr. Strangelove* (1964), *2001: A Space Odyssey* (1968), and *A Clockwork Orange* (1971). **Dennis Hopper's** *Easy Rider* (1969), a film about countercultural youth rebellion and the fruitlessness of the American dream, and the acclaimed documentary *Woodstock* (1970) established film as a viable medium for social critique.

Throughout the 1970s, experimentalism largely gave way to more polished treatment of equally serious issues. Film-schooled directors like **Martin Scorsese** (*Taxi Driver;*1976), **Francis Ford Coppola** (*The Godfather;*1972), and **Michael Cimino** (*The Deer Hunter;*1978) brought technical skill to their exploration of the darker side of humanity. An influx of foreign filmmakers, like **Milos Forman** (*One Flew Over the Cuckoo's Nest;*1975) and Roman Polanski (*Chinatown;*1974), introduced a new perspective to American film.

BACK TO BUSINESS. Driven by the global mass distribution of American cinema and the development of high-tech special effects, the late 1970s and 1980s witnessed the rebirth of the blockbuster. **Steven Spielberg's** *Jaws* (1975) piloted the now tried and true advertising methods of TV previews, movie merchandise, media stunts, and theme song publicity. Following his breakout success with *Jaws,* Spielberg produced the internationally successful *E.T.* (1982) and *Raiders of the Lost Ark* (1981). **George Lucas** followed with his *Star Wars* trilogy. Though such films were criticized for their reliance on special effects and lack of story line, they almost single-handedly returned Hollywood to its former status as king. The revival of the blockbuster continues to this day, particularly during the explosive summer months.

Despite the increasing commercialism of Hollywood, quite a bit of highly imaginative work came out of the 80s, including Rob Reiner's *This is Spinal Tap*, a hilarious send-up of popular music, and David Lynch's *Blue Velvet*, a disturbing exploration of the primal terror beneath the tranquil surface of suburbia. Throughout the 80s and 90s, big studios and independent directors continued to film and set movies in California. For a list of influential "California" movies, see p. 21. Recently, a revolution in digital film technology has spawned such hits as *Shrek* (2001) and *Finding Nemo* (2003), kids' films with intergenerational appeal.

TELEVISION

California has nearly as large an influence on the small-screen as the silver screen. Many of the major studios make their homes in L.A., and even shows that aren't set in California are shot there. In the 1970s, *The Brady Bunch* romped through suburban California and frolicked on an astro-turf lawn. The 1980s saw the Tanner family of *Full House* in the beautiful homes of San Francisco. 1990 was a banner year for L.A.—*Baywatch* splashed onto the Malibu coast and *Beverly Hills 90210* chronicled the lives of wealthy high-school students. The funeral home in HBO's bizarre comedy *Six Feet Under* is in Pasadena, and *The O.C.*, a contemporary, ironizing takeoff of the high-school drama has given Orange County media exposure and an entirely new nickname.

SPORTS

BASEBALL

It's still America's national pastime, and with five teams in the state, baseball excites passions and intrastate rivalries in California. The **San Francisco Giants,** with single-season home run king Barry Bonds, thrive in SBC Park in SoMa, where grand-slams splash into the bay. Across the way, the **Oakland Athletics (A's)** pull off miracles on a minuscule payroll. The popular **L.A. Dodgers** tussle with the hated Giants for second place in the National League West, while the hapless **San Diego Padres** lounge in the cellar. Walt Disney's magic still lives on in the form of the Rally Monkey and the Cinderella 2002 World Champion **Anaheim Angels.**

FOOTBALL

The fall months belong to Major League Baseball's more violent (and thus more popular) competitor, the National Football League (NFL). The resurgent **San Francisco 49ers** are trying to revive the glory days of Montana to Rice and to win back respect in the National Football Conference. In the famed Black Hole are the badboy, blue-collar, precision-passing **Oakland Raiders,** who spent 1982-1995 in the L.A. desert vainly seeking greater profits before maverick owner Al Davis moved them back. L.A. has been devoid of professional football for nearly a decade, ever since the **Rams** fled for St. Louis around the same time that the Raid-uhs up and left for the Bay. The lowly San Diego **Chargers'** odds of having a winning season have improved somewhat under new head coach Marty Schottenheimer.

There are also two big rivalries in college football. The Division-I powerhouse **Stanford Cardinal** (the color, not the bird) annually thrash the UC Berkeley (commonly known as **Cal**) **Golden Bears** to great fanfare and sophomoric pranks the weekend before Thanksgiving in late November. Down south, the **UCLA Bruins** and the **University of Southern California (USC) Trojans** (and their thoroughly inebriated fans) duke it out for supremacy in the City of Angels each year.

BASKETBALL

The **Golden State Warriors,** who play in Oakland, tend to park their backsides on the doormat of the National Basketball Association (NBA). The Western conference powerhouse **Sacramento Kings** are still looking for that first championship ring, despite the best efforts of Chris Webber and his cowbell-clanging fans. Despite a recent string of NBA championships (2000-2002), the L.A. Lakers bowed out miserably in the 2004 NBA Finals against the Detroit Pistons. The poor showing seemed to mark the end of a dynasty; coach Phil Jackson is gone, Shaquille O'Neal was traded to the Miami Heat, and Gary Payton now plays for the Celtics. Despite this recent embarrassment, the Lakers' international brand appeal and coterie of Hollywood stars at every home game tend to make their "rivals," the underachieving **L.A. Clippers,** look pathetic. Star Lisa Leslie and the **L.A. Sparks** have enjoyed success in the Women's National Basketball Association (WNBA).

SOCCER AND HOCKEY

"Ice" and "indoors" are two unfamiliar words to most Californians, but hockey, if it does not thrive, at least survives in the state. The storybook sports year for Anaheim, whose Angels won the World Series for the first time in 2002, ended on a hollow note as the **Mighty Ducks** lost in the National Hockey League's Stanley Cup finals. The Ducks compete with crosstown rivals, the **L.A. Kings.** In the Bay Area, the toothless **San Jose Sharks** skate nightly during the winter. Efforts to popularize soccer (non-American football) are still ongoing. The **San Jose Earthquakes** and **L.A. Galaxy** of Major League Soccer kick it to not-sold-out crowds all summer long.

ADDITIONAL RESOURCES

GENERAL HISTORY

Americans and the California Dream, Kevin Starr. A six-volume series of social, cultural, and political history by the State Librarian of California (Oxford University Press; 1996).

Cadillac Desert: The American West and Its Disappearing Water, Marc Reisner. A look back at how the West was won, one water project at a time (Penguin; 1993).

Bottled Poetry: Napa Winemaking from Prohibition to the Modern Era, James T. Lapsley. A detailed history of the region's growth as a grape-stomping paradise (University of California Press; 1996).

Poet Be Like God: Jack Spicer and the San Francisco Renaissance, Lewis Ellingham and Kevin Killian. An exploration of the literary world in the City by the Bay (Wesleyan University Press; 1998).

TRAVEL BOOKS

A Climber's Guide to the High Sierra, Steve Roper (Random House; 1993).

Nature Writings, John Muir, ed. William Cronon (Library of America; 1997).

Wine Country Bike Rides, Lena Emmery (Chronicle; 1997).

FILM

SAN FRANCISCO/BAY AREA

▨ **The Maltese Falcon** (1941). Hard-boiled San Francisco detective Sam Spade (Humphrey Bogart) mixes with a cast of shady characters in pursuit of a golden, jewel-encrusted falcon statue—"the stuff that dreams are made of." Based on the novel by Dashiell Hammet. A film noir classic.

Vertigo (1958). Alfred Hitchcock's complex tale about an altitude-averse San Francisco detective (Jimmy Stewart) and his encounter with a woman eerily troubled by the past. Features Mission Dolores and Mission San Juan Bautista in fantastic supporting roles.

Dirty Harry (1971). Housewife heartthrob Clint Eastwood plays a dangerous San Francisco cop. In its 1983 sequel *Sudden Impact,* Harry impales his victim on the merry-go-round unicorn at the **Santa Cruz Beach Boardwalk** (p. 333).

The Rock (1996). Alcatraz (p. 118): only one man has ever broken out. Now five million lives depend on two men breaking in. Sean Connery and Nicolas Cage wage battle in California's most famous island prison.

THE COAST

■ **Citizen Kane** (1941). The ultimate classic, loosely based on the life of newspaper giant William Randolph Hearst, who nearly succeeded in purchasing and burning Orson Welles' masterpiece before it was ever shown. Although the film sets the mogul's Xanadu mansion in Florida, its real-world counterpart is **Hearst Castle** (p. 358).

■ **The Graduate** (1967). Young Dustin Hoffman has graduated from college into a meaningless, psycho-erotic void set to the tunes of Simon and Garfunkel's acoustic caterwauling. As he barrels up and down the coast in pursuit of Miss Robinson, catch our hero driving the wrong direction on the Bay Bridge.

The Birds (1963). Birds begin attacking residents of the sleepy seaside town of **Bodega Bay** (p. 236) in this Alfred Hitchcock horror flick.

LOS ANGELES

■ **Chinatown** (1974). Jack Nicholson sleuths through a creepy pastel L.A. Robert Towne's script for this Roman Polanski thriller is one of the most studied screenplays in film schools. Hold your breath for the famous last line.

Pulp Fiction (1993). Quentin Tarantino's ultra-cool, ultra-violent dive into four stories of San Fernando Valley lowlifes, Ezekiel-quoting assassins, washed up boxers, and their French girlfriends. Its hilariously profane dialogue, striking editing, and stylistic flair made it one of the most influential and quotable films of the 90s.

L.A. Story (1991). Steve Martin's love song to the City of Angels. You'll think it's an exaggeration until you go there. He even gets to roller blade in the Los Angeles County Museum of Art (p. 426).

The Big Lebowski (1998). Jeff Bridges is The Dude, L.A.'s most laid-back resident, in this sprawling Coen brothers comedy. With a bowling sequence set to "Hotel California," porn moguls, and German nihilists, it's almost as crazy as the city itself.

Clueless (1995). Alicia Silverstone stars in this meta-fluffy movie about the lives, fashions, and limited but somehow eloquent vocabulary of three high school Beverly Hills girls. The plot's similarities to Jane Austen's *Emma* flick this flick into legitimacy.

Swingers (1996). L.A.'s labyrinthine nightlife serves as backdrop for Mikey's mopey romanticism and Trent's dating escapades. Sadly enough, this comedy has defined the rules of dating and rebound dating for guys everywhere.

Boyz 'N the Hood (1991). A hard-hitting portrayal of life in the poverty-stricken neighborhoods of South Central L.A. Director John Singleton's debut film.

Dogtown and Z-boys (2001). A documentary chronicling the emergence of extreme skateboarding in 1970s L.A., when land-bound surfers began thrashing in empty-pools.

HOLLYWOOD

Sunset Boulevard (1950). Dark, satirical drama about a faded silent movie star in love with a cynical young screenwriter played by William Holden. Gloria Swanson, a former silent film queen herself, embodies a culture of self-absorbed decadence in her portrayal of the aging and vainglorious film star.

Rebel Without a Cause (1955). Teen icon James Dean in this quintessential story of disaffected youth. Shot at Hollywood High and Griffith Observatory.

The Kid Stays in the Picture (2002). Sensational documentary about the rise and fall of Paramount producer Robert Evans, written by and featuring the kid himself.

Swimming with Sharks (1994). A must-see comedy for anyone thinking of entering the industry. Kevin Spacey stars as a cruel studio executive.

THE DESERT

Leaving Las Vegas (1995). A tender romance starring Elisabeth Shue and Nicolas Cage set against a rich backdrop of alcoholism, depression, and prostitution.

Zabriskie Point (1970). Michelangelo Antonioni's counterculture protagonists get down and dirty at Death Valley Monument Zabriskie Point in this bizarre and revolutionary piece. Hang on for the trippy and mind-blowing climax.

THE CENTRAL VALLEY

Psycho (1960). Classic Hitchcock thriller, in which embezzler Janet Leigh has the misfortune to stay in a motel (on a highway between Fresno and Bakersfield) where the caretaker has dangerous, pathological tendencies.

The Grapes of Wrath (1940). John Ford's gripping, naturalistic adaptation of Steinbeck's masterpiece about Depression-era sharecroppers. Many respected critics consider it better than the book. Henry Fonda's final monologue is for the ages.

American Graffiti (1973). Director George Lucas put himself on the Hollywood map with this humorous and lyrical rendering of four Modesto high school graduates' wild adventures one summer night in 1962.

SUGGESTED LISTENING

Al Jolson, "California, Here I Come" (1924).

Beach Boys, "California Girls," *Summer Days (and Summer Nights!)* (1965).

Mamas and the Papas, "California Dreamin'," *California Dreamin'* (1966).

Frank Zappa and the Mothers of Invention, *Freak Out* (1966).

Scott MacKenzie, "San Francisco (Wear Some Flowers in Your Hair)," *San Francisco* (1967).

Marvin Gaye (and the California Raisins), "I Heard it Through the Grapevine," *In the Groove* (1968); originally performed by Gladys Knight and the Pips (1967).

Grateful Dead, *American Beauty* (1970).

The Doors, *L.A. Woman* (1971).

Joni Mitchell, "California," *Blue* (1971).

Led Zeppelin, "Going to California," *Led Zeppelin IV* (1971).

Jackson Browne, *Late for the Sky* (1974).

Eagles, "Hotel California," *Hotel California* (1976).

Bob Seger, "Hollywood Nights," *Stranger in Town* (1978).

Dead Kennedys, "California Über Alles," *Fresh Fruit for Rotting Vegetables* (1980).

Ice Cube, "Once Upon a Time in the Projects," *AmeriKKKa's Most Wanted* (1990).

Sheryl Crow, "All I Wanna Do," *Tuesday Night Music Club* (1993).

Weezer, "Surf Wax America," *Weezer* (1994).

Tupac and Dr. Dre, "California Love," *All Eyez on Me* (1996).

Red Hot Chili Peppers, *Californication* (1999).

Rage Against the Machine, *The Battle for Los Angeles* (1999).

HOLIDAYS AND FESTIVALS

National holidays are accompanied by parades and the closing of businesses and mail service. Festivals are regionally specific focused events celebrating an art form or a piece of cultural history.

DATE IN 2005	HOLIDAY
January 1	New Year's Day
January 17	Martin Luther King, Jr. Day
February 21	Presidents' Day
May 30	Memorial Day
July 4	Independence Day

DATE IN 2005	HOLIDAY
September 5	Labor Day
October 10	Columbus Day
November 11	Veterans' Day
November 24	Thanksgiving Day
December 25	Christmas Day

CALIFORNIA'S FESTIVALS

DATE	NAME AND LOCATION	DESCRIPTION
Jan. 1	▦ **Tournament of Roses Parade and Rose Bowl** (Pasadena)	Floats made entirely of roses parade down Colorado Ave. from 8 to 10am. The football champs of the Pac 10 and Big 10 conferences meet in the afternoon for the Rose Bowl.
late Feb.	**Chinese New Year Celebrations** (SF, L.A.)	Pageants, street fairs, fireworks, and dragons usher in the Chinese New Year in these Chinese-American communities.
May 5	**Cinco de Mayo** (everywhere)	Color, costumes, and *mariachi* bands celebrate Mexican pride throughout the state.
mid-June	**Playboy Jazz Festival** (L.A.)	Two days of entertainment by top-name jazz musicians of all varieties, from traditional to fusion.
mid-July	**National Nude Weekend** (Santa Cruz)	Enjoy bands (playing in the buff) or come paint the posing models (on canvas), at the Lupin Naturalist Club.
July 29-31	**Gilroy Garlic Festival** (Gilroy)	Garlic-laced food, vendors, musicians come together to pay tribute to the stinky rose. Kissing optional.
late July	**North Beach Jazz Festival** (SF)	An assortment of musicians play at this free jazz festival.
late Sept.	**Monterey Jazz Festival**	Big-name blues musicians come to the Bay.
Early Oct.	▦ **World Championship Grape Stomp** (Santa Rosa)	Wine-making on a massive scale in the Sonoma Valley, part of the summer-long Sonoma County Harvest Fair.
Nov. 1	▦ **Dia de los Muertos** (SF)	Follow the drummers and dancing skeletons to the festive Mexican celebration of the dead.

ESSENTIALS

PLANNING YOUR TRIP

> **ENTRANCE REQUIREMENTS**
> **Passport** (p. 26). Required of visitors who are not citizens of the US or Canada.
> **Visa** (p. 28). Generally required of visitors who are not citizens of the US or Canada, but requirement can be waived for residents of certain countries if staying less than 90 days.
> **Work Permit** (p. 28). Required of those planning to work in the US or Canada.
> **Driving Permit** (p. 48). Required of those planning to drive.

EMBASSIES AND CONSULATES

US CONSULAR SERVICES ABROAD

Contact the nearest embassy or consulate to obtain information regarding the visas and permits necessary to travel to the US and Canada. Listings of foreign embassies within the US as well as US embassies abroad can be found at www.embassyworld.com. The **US State Department** (http://foia.state.gov/MMS/KOH/keyoffcity.asp) provides contact info for key officers at US overseas stations.

Australia: Moonah Pl., Yarralumla (Canberra), ACT 2600 (☎61 02 6214 5600; http://usembassy-australia.state.gov). **Consulates:** MLC Centre, Level 59, 19-29 Martin Pl., Sydney, NSW 2000 (☎61 02 9373 9200; fax 9373 9184); 553 St. Kilda Rd., Melbourne, VIC 3004 (☎61 03 9526 5900; fax 9525 0769); 16 St. George's Terr., 13th fl., Perth, WA 6000 (☎61 08 9202 1224; fax 9231 9444).

Canada: 490 Sussex Dr., Ottawa, ON K1N 1G8 (☎1-613-688-5335; www.usembassy-canada.gov). **Consulates:** 615 Macleod Trail SE, Ste. 1000, Calgary, AB T2G 4T8 (☎1-403-266-8962; fax 264-6630); Ste. 904, Purdy's Wharf Tower II, 1969 Upper Water St., Halifax, NS B3J 3R7 (☎1-902-429-2480; fax 423-6861); 1155 St. Alexandre St., Montréal, QC H2Z 1Z2 (mailing address: P.O. Box 65, Station Desjardins, Montréal, QC H5B 1G1. ☎1-514-398-9695; fax 398-0702); 2 Place Terrasse Dufferin, B.P. 939, Québec City, QC G1R 4T9 (☎1-418-692-2095; fax 692-4640); 360 University Ave., Toronto, ON M5G 1S4 (☎1-416-595-1700; fax 595-6501); 1095 W. Pender St., Vancouver, BC V6E 2M6 (☎1-604-685-4311; fax 685-7175).

Ireland: 42 Elgin Rd., Ballsbridge, Dublin 4 (☎353 01 668 8777; www.dublin.usembassy.gov).

New Zealand: 29 Fitzherbert Terr., Thorndon, Wellington (☎644 462 6000; www.usembassy.org.nz). **Consulate:** 23 Customs St., Citibank Building, 3rd fl., Auckland (☎649 303 2724; fax 366 0870).

UK: 24 Grosvenor Sq., London W1A 1AE (☎44 0207 499 9000; www.usembassy.org.uk). **Consulates:** Danesfort House, 223 Stranmillis Rd., Belfast, Northern Ireland BT9 5GR (☎44 0289 038 6100; fax 44 0289 068 1301); 3 Regent Terr., Edinburgh, Scotland EH7 5BW (☎44 0131 556 8315; fax 557 6023).

CONSULAR SERVICES IN CALIFORNIA

Australia: 2049 Century Park East, 19th fl. of the Century Plaza Towers, L.A., 90067 (☎310-229-4800); and 625 Market St., #200, San Francisco, 94105 (☎415-536-1970)

Canada: 550 S. Hope St., 9th fl., L.A., 90071 (☎213-346-2700).

Ireland: 100 Pine St., 33 fl., San Francisco, 94111 (☎415-392-4214)

New Zealand: 12400 Wilshire Blvd., #1150, L.A., 90025 (☎310-207-1605).

South Africa: 6300 Wilshire Blvd., #600, L.A., 90048 (☎323-651-0902).

UK: 11766 Wilshire Blvd., #1200, L.A., 90025 (☎310-481-0031; www.britainusa.com/L.A.); 1 Sansome St., #850, San Francisco, 94104 (☎415-617-1300; www.britainusa.com/SF).

DOCUMENTS AND FORMALITIES

PASSPORTS

REQUIREMENTS
All non-American citizens (except Canadians) need valid passports to enter the US and to re-enter their home countries. Travelers must have a passport valid for at least six months beyond their intended stays. Returning home with an expired passport is usually illegal and may result in a **fine.** Canadians can enter the US (and vice versa) with proof of citizenship along with a photo ID—a driver's license and birth certificate should suffice. Passports, however, are the most convenient and hassle-free method of identification.

NEW PASSPORTS
Citizens of Australia, Canada, Ireland, New Zealand, and the UK can apply for a passport at any passport office and many post offices and courts of law. Any new passport or renewal applications must be filed well in advance of the departure date, though most passport offices offer rush (about 2 weeks) services for a very steep fee, typically $60-200.

PASSPORT MAINTENANCE
Photocopy the page of your passport with your photo, as well as your visas, traveler's check serial numbers, and any other important documents. Carry one set of copies in a safe place, apart from the originals, and leave another set at home. Consulates also recommend that you carry an expired passport or an official copy of your birth certificate in a part of your baggage separate from other documents.

If you lose your passport, immediately notify the local police and the nearest embassy or consulate of your home government. To expedite its replacement, you will need to know all information previously recorded and show ID and proof of citizenship, as well as pay a fee and file a police report. Replacements take approximately 10 days to process, but some consulates offer three-day rush service for an additional fee. A replacement may be valid only for a limited time. Any visas stamped in your old passport will be irretrievably lost. In an emergency, some consulates provide immediate temporary traveling papers that will permit you to re-enter your home country.

VISAS AND WORK PERMITS

VISAS
Citizens of some non-English speaking countries need a visa—a stamp, sticker, or insert in your passport specifying the purpose of your travel and the permitted duration of your stay—in addition to a valid passport to enter the US. Canadian citizens do not need to obtain a visa for admission to the US; citizens of Australia, New Zealand, and most European countries (including the UK and Ireland) can waive US

visas through the **Visa Waiver Program (VWP).** Visitors qualify if they are traveling only for business or pleasure (*not* work or study), are staying for fewer than **90 days,** have proof of intent to leave (e.g., a return ticket), possess an I-94W form (arrival/departure certificate issued upon arrival), are traveling on particular air or sea carriers (most major carriers qualify—contact the carrier for details), and have no visa ineligibilities (e.g., a criminal record). As of October 2004, visitors in the VWP must possess a **machine-readable passport,** though most countries have been issuing such passports for some time. **Children** from these countries who normally travel on a parent's passport will also need to obtain their own machine-readable passports. Additionally, as of June 2004, travelers in the VWP will be able to travel on regular machine-readable passports issued before October 26, 2004, but all passports issued after that date must have **biometric** identifiers to be used as visa waivers. However, most countries in the VWP are not expected to be able to convert to biometric passports by the deadline, so **even VWP travelers to the US with recently issued passports may have to apply for a visa.** Legislation to extend the biometric deadline to 2006 is under consideration by Congress but has not been passed. See http://travel.state.gov/vwp.html or contact your local consulate for a list of countries participating in the VWP as well as the latest information any biometric deadline extensions.

For stays of longer than 90 days in the US, all foreign travelers (except Canadians) must obtain a visa. Visitors to the US under the VWP are allowed to leave and re-enter the US to visit Canada, Mexico, and some neighboring islands, but time spent in those areas counts toward the total 90-day limit. Travelers eligible to waive their visas and who wish to stay for more than 90 days must receive a visa **before** entering the US.

Double-check entrance requirements at the nearest embassy or consulate of the US for up-to-date info before departure (see **Embassies and Consulates Abroad,** p. 25). US citizens can also consult www.pueblo.gsa.gov/cic_text/travel/foreign/foreignentryreqs.html.

WORK PERMITS

Admission as a visitor does not include the right to work, which is authorized only by a work permit. Entering the US to study requires a special visa. Expect slow processing. For more information, see **Alternatives to Tourism,** p. 66.

IDENTIFICATION

When you travel, always carry at least two forms of identification on your person, including a photo ID; a passport and a driver's license or birth certificate is usually adequate. Never carry all of your IDs together; split them up in case of theft or loss, and keep photocopies of all of them in your luggage and at home.

STUDENT, TEACHER, AND YOUTH IDENTIFICATION

The **International Student Identity Card (ISIC),** the most widely accepted form of student ID, provides discounts on some sights, accommodations (20% or more off rooms in many chain hotels), food, and transport (e.g., 5-15% off Alamo Car rentals); access to a 24hr. emergency helpline; and insurance benefits for US cardholders (see **Insurance,** p. 36). Applicants must be full-time secondary or postsecondary school students at least 12 years of age. Because of the proliferation of fake ISICs, some services (particularly airlines) require additional proof of student identity. Particularly in the US, ISICs are less well-recognized than they are abroad, so travelers are advised to have another form of student ID.

The **International Teacher Identity Card (ITIC)** offers teachers the same insurance coverage as the ISIC and similar but limited discounts. For travelers who are 25 years old or under but are not students, the **International Youth Travel Card (IYTC)** also offers many of the same benefits as the ISIC.

Each of these identity cards costs $22. ISIC and ITIC cards are valid through the academic year in which they are issued; IYTC cards are valid for one year from the date of issue. Many student travel agencies (see p. 40) issue the cards; for a list of issuing agencies or more information, see the **International Student Travel Confederation (ISTC)** website (www.istc.org). The **International Student Exchange Card (ISE)** is a similar identification card available to students, faculty, and youth ages 12 to 26. The card provides discounts, medical benefits, access to a 24hr. emergency helpline, and the ability to purchase student airfares. The card costs $25; for more info call ☎ 800-255-8000, or visit www.isecard.com.

CUSTOMS

Upon entering the US, you must declare certain items from abroad and pay a duty on the value of those articles that exceed the allowance established by the US customs service. Note that goods and gifts purchased at **duty-free** shops abroad are not exempt from duty or sales tax; "duty-free" merely means that you need not pay a tax in the country of purchase. Upon returning home, you must likewise declare all articles acquired abroad and pay a duty on the value of articles in excess of your home country's allowance. In order to expedite your return, make a list of any valuables brought from home and register them with customs before traveling abroad, and be sure to keep receipts for all goods acquired abroad. The US does not refund sales tax to foreign visitors.

CURRENCY AND EXCHANGE

The currency chart below is based on August 2004 exchange rates between US dollars (US$), Australian dollars (AUS$), Canadian dollars (CDN$), European Union euros (EUR€), New Zealand dollars (NZ$), and British pounds (UK£). Check the currency converter on websites like www.xe.com or www.bloomberg.com or a large newspaper for the latest exchange rates.

DOLLARS ($)		
AUS$ = US$0.72		US$ = AUS$1.38
CDN$ = US$0.77		US$ = CDN$1.30
EUR€ = US$1.23		US$ = EUR€0.81
NZ$ = US$0.66		US$ = NZ$1.49
UK£ = US$1.81		US$ = UK£0.55

As a general rule, it's cheaper to convert money in the US than at home. While currency exchange will probably be available in your arrival airport, it's wise to bring enough foreign currency to last for the first 24-72hr. of your trip. When changing money, try to go only to banks or other establishments that have at most a 5% margin between their buy and sell prices. Since you lose money with every transaction, **convert large sums, but no more than you'll need.**

If you use traveler's checks or bills, carry some in small denominations (the equivalent of US$50 or less) for times when you are forced to exchange money at disadvantageous rates, but bring a range of denominations since charges may be levied per check cashed. Store your money in a variety of forms; ideally, at any given time you will be carrying some cash, some traveler's checks, and an ATM and/or credit card.

TRAVELER'S CHECKS

Traveler's checks are one of the safest and least troublesome means of carrying funds. American Express and Visa are the most recognized brands. Many banks and agencies sell them for a small commission. Check issuers provide refunds if the checks are lost or stolen, and many provide additional services, such as toll-free refund hotlines abroad, emergency message services, and stolen credit card assistance. They are readily accepted in the US. Ask about toll-free refund hotlines and the location of refund centers when purchasing checks, and always carry emergency cash.

American Express: Checks available with commission at select banks, at all AmEx offices, and online (www.americanexpress.com; US residents only). American Express cardholders can purchase checks by phone (☎800-721-9768). For purchase locations or more info contact AmEx's service centers: in the US and Canada ☎800-221-7282, in Australia 800 68 80 22, in New Zealand 0508 555 358, in the UK 0800 587 6023.

Visa: Checks available (generally with commission) at banks worldwide. For the location of the nearest office, call Visa's service centers: in the US ☎800-227-6811, in the UK 0 800 89 5078; elsewhere, call the UK collect at ☎44 173 331 8949. AAA (see p. 48) offers commission-free checks to its members.

Travelex/Thomas Cook: In the US and Canada ☎800-287-7362, in the UK 0800 62 21 01; elsewhere call the UK collect at ☎44 1733 31 89 50.

CREDIT, DEBIT, AND ATM CARDS

Where they are accepted, credit cards often offer superior exchange rates—up to 5% better than the rate used by banks and other currency exchange establishments. Credit cards may also offer services such as insurance or emergency help, and are sometimes required to reserve hotel rooms or rental cars. **MasterCard** and **Visa** are the most welcomed; **American Express** cards work at some establishments and ATMs and at AmEx offices and major airports.

ATM machines are ubiquitous in the US. Depending on the system that your home bank uses, you can most likely access your personal bank account from the US. ATMs get the same wholesale exchange rate as credit cards, but there is often a limit on the amount of money you can withdraw per day (usually around US$500). There is typically also a surcharge of US$1-5 per withdrawal. The two major international money networks are **Cirrus** (US ☎800-424-7787; www.mastercard.com) and **Visa/PLUS** (US ☎800-843-7587; www.visa.com). Most ATMs charge a transaction fee that is paid to the bank that owns the ATM.

Debit cards are as convenient as credit cards but have a more immediate impact on your funds. A debit card can be used wherever its associated credit card company (usually MasterCard or Visa) is accepted, yet the money is withdrawn directly from the holder's checking account. Debit cards often also function as ATM cards.

GETTING MONEY FROM HOME

If you run out of money while traveling, the easiest and cheapest solution is to have someone back home make a deposit to your bank account. Failing that, consider wiring money or consult the online **International Money Transfer Consumer Guide** (http://international-money-transfer-consumer-guide.info).

It is possible to arrange a **bank money transfer,** which means asking a bank back home to wire money to a bank in California. This is the cheapest way to transfer cash, but it's also the slowest, usually taking several days or more. Note that some banks may only release your funds in local currency, potentially sticking you with a poor exchange rate; inquire about this in advance. Money transfer services like **Western Union** are faster and more convenient than bank transfers—but also much pricier. Western Union has many locations worldwide. To find one, visit www.westernunion.com, or call: in the US ☎800-325-6000, in Australia 800 501 500, in Canada 800-235-0000, in the UK 0800 83 38 33. To wire money within the US using a credit card (Visa, MasterCard, Discover), call ☎800-225-5227. Money transfer services are also available at **American Express** and **Thomas Cook** offices.

COSTS

The cost of your trip will vary considerably depending on where you go, how you travel, and where you stay. The most significant expense will probably be your round-trip (return) **airfare** to California (see **By Plane,** p. 40). Before you go, spend some time calculating a reasonable daily **budget.** Don't forget to factor in emergency reserve funds (at least US$200) when planning how much money you'll need.

STAYING ON A BUDGET

To give you a general idea, a bare-bones day in California (camping or sleeping in hostels/guesthouses, buying food at supermarkets) would cost about US$30; a slightly more comfortable day (sleeping in hostels/guesthouses and the occasional budget motel, eating one meal per day at a restaurant, going out at night) would cost US$50; and for a luxurious day, the sky's the limit.

TIPS FOR SAVING MONEY

Some simpler ways to save money include searching out opportunities for free entertainment, splitting accommodation and food costs with trustworthy fellow travelers, and buying food in supermarkets rather than eating out. Do your **laundry** in the sink (unless you're explicitly prohibited from doing so). That said, don't go overboard. Though staying within your budget is important, don't do so at the expense of your health or a great travel experience.

TIPPING AND BARGAINING

In the US, waitstaff and cab drivers expect tips of 15-20%. Tips are not usually included in restaurant bills, unless you are in a party of six or more. As waitstaff rely almost entirely on tips for their salary, if you tip less than 15% your waiter may chase you out of the restaurant to ask you why you "stiffed" him. At the airport and hotels, porters expect a tip of at least $1 per bag to carry luggage. Except at flea markets, bargaining is generally frowned upon and fruitless in California.

TAXES

Sales tax in California is calculated as a percentage of the price of the good sold. It generally is not included in the listed price of an item. The sales tax rates on normal consumer goods vary by county from 7.25% to 8.75%; there are additional federal taxes on tobacco and alcohol. Most grocery items in California are not taxed. Unless otherwise stated, *Let's Go* does not include taxes in listed prices.

PACKING

Pack lightly: Lay out only what you absolutely need, then take half the clothes and twice the money. The Travelite FAQ (www.travelite.org) is a good resource for tips on traveling light. The online **Universal Packing List** (http://upl.codeq.info) will generate a customized list of suggested items based on your trip length, the expected climate, your planned activities, and other factors. If you plan to do a lot of hiking, also consult **Camping and the Outdoors,** p. 55.

Luggage: If you plan to cover most of your itinerary by foot, a sturdy **frame backpack** is unbeatable. For the basics on buying a pack, see p. 58. Toting a **suitcase** or **trunk** is fine if you plan to live in one or two cities and explore from there. In addition to your main piece of luggage, a **daypack** (a small backpack or courier bag) is useful.

Clothing: For travel in Northern California or the mountains, pack layers of clothing—mornings and evenings tend to be cool year-round and daytime temperatures can vary drastically. A sweater and light jacket may be necessary even in summer. In winter, bring a mid-weight jacket or heavy sweater. No matter when you're traveling, it's a good idea to bring a rain jacket (Gore-Tex® is both waterproof and breathable). Because Southern California is consistently warm and dry, you may not need the rain or cold gear, though restaurants and museums can be heavily air-conditioned, so you might consider carrying a light sweater. If you're hiking in the Sierra Nevadas or Cascades, pack heavy-duty gear. Wherever you go, **sturdy shoes** and **thick socks** can save your feet. **Flip-flops** or waterproof sandals are must-haves for grubby hostel showers, and are worn by Californians everywhere except the nicest restaurants and certain places of worship. You may also want one outfit for going out and a nicer pair of shoes. While Californian fashion tends to be extremely casual, if you plan to visit religious or cultural sites it is respectful to wear something less revealing than the tank tops and cutoff shorts that are acceptable nearly everywhere else.

Converters and Adapters: In the US, electricity is 120 volts AC. **International travelers** using 220/240V electrical appliances should buy an **adapter** (which changes the shape of the plug; around $5) and **converter** (which changes the voltage; $20-30). Don't make the mistake of using only an adapter unless appliance instructions explicitly state otherwise. For more info, visit http://kropla.com/electric.htm.

First-Aid Kit: For a basic first-aid kit, pack bandages, pain relievers, antibiotic cream, a thermometer, a Swiss Army knife, tweezers, moleskin, decongestant, motion-sickness remedy, diarrhea or upset-stomach medication (Pepto Bismol or Imodium), an antihistamine, sunscreen, insect repellent, burn ointment, and a syringe for emergencies (get an explanatory letter from your doctor).

Film: Buying film and developing it in California is fairly affordable and very easy (about $10 for a roll of 24 color exposures at most drug stores). Less serious photographers may want to bring a disposable camera or two. Despite disclaimers, airport security X-rays can fog film, so buy a lead-lined pouch at a camera store or ask security to hand-inspect it. Always pack film in your carry-on luggage, since higher-intensity X-rays are used on checked luggage. A digital camera will allow you to take as many photos as you like without the expense of film or printing.

Other Useful Items: For safety purposes, you should bring a **money belt** and small **padlock.** Basic **outdoors equipment** (plastic water bottle, compass, waterproof matches, pocketknife, sunglasses, sunscreen, hat) may also prove useful. **Quick repairs** of torn garments can be done with a needle and thread; also consider bringing electrical tape for patching tears. To do laundry by hand, bring detergent, a small rubber ball to stop up the sink, and string for a makeshift clothes line. Other things you're liable to forget (but can always purchase once in California) are an **umbrella**; sealable **plastic bags** (for damp clothes, soap, food, shampoo, and other spill-ables); an **alarm clock;** safety pins; rubber bands; a flashlight; earplugs; garbage bags; and a small **calculator.** A **cell phone** can be a lifesaver; see p. 51 for info on acquiring one that will work in California.

Important Documents: Don't forget your passport, traveler's checks, ATM and/or credit cards, adequate ID, and photocopies of all of the aforementioned in case these documents are lost or stolen (see p. 28). Also check that you have any of the following that might apply to you: a hostelling membership card (see p. 52), driver's license (see p. 48), travel insurance forms, ISIC (see p. 28), and/or rail or bus pass (see p. 42).

SAFETY AND HEALTH

GENERAL ADVICE

In any type of crisis situation, the most important thing to do is **stay calm.** Your country's embassy abroad (see p. 25) is usually your best resource when things go wrong; registering with that embassy upon arrival in the US is a good idea. The government offices listed in the **travel advisories** box (see p. 34) can provide information on the services they offer their citizens in case of emergencies abroad.

LOCAL LAWS AND POLICE

California has a strong police presence. Alcohol, drug, and driving laws are strictly enforced. While the police are generally friendly and helpful, the Los Angeles Police Department (LAPD) has become relatively notorious for corruption, though it is in the process of implementing "substantial compliance" with state and federal mandates.

DRUGS AND ALCOHOL

In California, as in the rest of the US, the drinking age is a strictly enforced 21. Never drink and drive—you risk your own life and those of others, and getting caught results in imprisonment and fines. It is illegal to have an open container of alcohol inside a car at any time, even if you are not drinking it. Possession of controlled substances is always illegal. If you carry prescription drugs, it is vital to have a copy of the prescriptions, especially near the Mexican border. Tobacco products may only be purchased by those over the age of 18. Smoking is prohibited on public transportation and in public buildings. Most restaurants and bars have no-smoking policies. Local ordinances vary; check before you light up.

ESSENTIALS

SPECIFIC CONCERNS

NATURAL DISASTERS

While California is famous for its **earthquakes,** they are relatively infrequent and should not discourage visitors. Buildings, bridges, and highways conform to strict safety codes. In the case of an earthquake, open a door to provide an escape route and protect yourself by moving underneath a sturdy doorway, table, or desk.

TERRORISM

In light of the September 11, 2001 terrorist attacks, there is an elevated threat of further terrorist activities in the US. Terrorists often target landmarks popular with tourists; however, the threat of an attack is generally not specific or great enough to warrant avoiding certain places or modes of transportation. Stay current with the daily news and watch for alerts from federal, state, and local law enforcement officials. Allow extra time for airport security and remember that sharp objects in carry-on luggage will be confiscated. For more information on the terror threat to the US, visit www.terrorismanswers.com. The box below lists offices and websites that can provide updated information on your home government's advisories about travel.

> **TRAVEL ADVISORIES.** The following government offices provide travel information and advisories by telephone, by fax, or via the web:
>
> **Australian Department of Foreign Affairs and Trade:** In Australia ☎ 1300 555135; from elsewhere 61 2 6261 1555; www.dfat.gov.au.
>
> **Canadian Department of Foreign Affairs and International Trade (DFAIT):** In the US and Canada ☎ 800-267-8376, elsewhere call 1-613-944-4000; www.dfait-maeci.gc.ca. Call for their free booklet, *Bon Voyage...But.*
>
> **New Zealand Ministry of Foreign Affairs:** ☎ 04 439 8000; www.mft.govt.nz/travel/index.html.
>
> **United Kingdom Foreign and Commonwealth Office:** ☎ 087 0606 0290; www.fco.gov.uk.
>
> **US Department of State:** ☎ 202-647-5225; http://travel.state.gov. For *A Safe Trip Abroad,* call ☎ 202-512-1800.

PERSONAL SAFETY

To avoid unwanted attention, try to blend in as much as possible. Respecting local customs may placate would-be hecklers. Familiarize yourself with your surroundings before setting out, and carry yourself with confidence. Check maps in shops and restaurants rather than on the street. If you are traveling alone, be sure someone at home knows your itinerary, and never admit that you're by yourself. When walking at night, stick to busy, well-lit streets and avoid dark alleyways. If you ever feel uncomfortable, leave the area as quickly and directly as you can.

There is no sure-fire way to avoid all the threatening situations you might encounter while traveling, but a good **self-defense course** will give you concrete ways to react to unwanted advances. **Impact, Prepare, and Model Mugging** can refer you to local self-defense courses in the US (☎ 800-345-5425). Visit the website at www.impactsafety.org for a list of nearby chapters. Workshops (1½-3hr.) start at US$75; full courses (20-25hr.) run US$350-400.

If you are using a **car,** learn local driving signals and wear a seatbelt. Seatbelts in cars and helmets on motorcycles and mopeds are required by California law. Children under 40 lb. should ride only in specially-designed car seats, available for a small fee from most car rental agencies. Study route maps before you hit the road, and if you plan on spending a lot of time driving, consider bringing spare parts. If your car breaks down, wait for the police to assist you. For long drives in desolate areas, invest in a cellular phone and a roadside assistance program (see p. 48). Park your vehicle in a garage or well traveled area, and use a steering wheel locking device in larger cities. **Sleeping in your car** is one of the most dangerous (and often illegal) ways to get your rest. For info on the perils of **hitchhiking,** see p. 49.

POSSESSIONS AND VALUABLES

Never leave your belongings unattended; crime occurs in even the most demure-looking hostel or hotel. Bring your own **padlock** for hostel lockers, and don't ever store valuables in any locker. Be particularly careful on **buses** and **trains;** horror stories abound about determined thieves who wait for travelers to fall asleep. Carry your backpack in front of you where you can see it. When traveling with others, sleep in alternate shifts. When alone, use good judgment in selecting a train compartment: never stay in an empty one, and use a lock to secure your pack to the luggage rack. Try to sleep on top bunks with your luggage stored above you (if not in bed with you), and keep important documents and other valuables on your person.

There are a few steps you can take to minimize the financial risk associated with traveling. First, **bring as little with you as possible.** Second, buy a few combination **padlocks** to secure your belongings either in your pack or in a hostel or train station locker. Third, **carry as little cash as possible.** Keep your traveler's checks and ATM/credit cards in a **money belt**—not a "fanny pack"—along with your passport and ID

ESSENTIALS

cards. Fourth, **keep a small cash reserve separate from your primary stash.** This should be about US$50 sewn into or stored in the depths of your pack, along with your traveler's check numbers and important photocopies.

In large cities **con artists** often work in groups and may involve children. Beware of certain classics: sob stories that require money, rolls of bills "found" on the street, mustard spilled (or saliva spit) onto your shoulder to distract you while they snatch your bag. **Never let your passport and your bags out of your sight.** Beware of **pickpockets** in city crowds, especially on public transportation. Also, be alert in public telephone booths: If you must say your calling card number, do so very quietly; if you punch it in, make sure no one can look over your shoulder.

If you will be traveling with electronic devices, such as a laptop computer or a PDA, check whether your homeowner's insurance covers loss, theft, or damage when you travel. If not, consider purchasing a low-cost separate insurance policy. **Safeware** (☎ 800-800-1492; www.safeware.com) specializes in computers and charges $90 for 90-day comprehensive international travel coverage up to $4000.

PRE-DEPARTURE HEALTH

In your **passport,** write the names of any people you wish to be contacted in case of a medical emergency, along with any allergies or medical conditions. Matching a prescription to a foreign equivalent is not always easy, safe, or possible, so if you take prescription drugs, consider carrying up-to-date, legible prescriptions or a statement from your doctor stating the medication's trade name, manufacturer, chemical name, and dosage. While traveling, be sure to keep all medication with you in your carry-on luggage. For tips on packing a basic **first-aid kit** and other health essentials, see p. 32.

IMMUNIZATIONS AND PRECAUTIONS

Travelers over two years old should make sure that the following vaccines are up to date: MMR (for measles, mumps, and rubella); DTaP or Td (for diphtheria, tetanus, and pertussis); IPV (for polio); Hib (for *haemophilus* influenza B); and HepB (for Hepatitis B). For recommendations on immunizations and prophylaxis, consult the CDC (see p. 37) in the US or the equivalent in your home country, and check with a doctor for guidance.

INSURANCE

Travel insurance covers four basic areas: medical/health problems, property loss, trip cancellation/interruption, and emergency evacuation. Though regular insurance policies may well extend to travel-related accidents, you may consider purchasing separate travel insurance if the cost of potential trip cancellation/interruption or emergency medical evacuation is greater than you can absorb. Prices for travel insurance purchased separately generally run about US$50 per week for full coverage, while trip cancellation/interruption may be purchased separately at a rate of US$3-5 per day depending on length of stay.

Medical insurance (especially university policies) often covers costs incurred abroad; check with your provider. **Canadian** provincial health insurance plans increasingly do not cover foreign travel; check with the provincial Ministry of Health or Health Plan Headquarters for details. **Homeowners' insurance** (or your family's coverage) often covers theft during travel and loss of travel documents (passport, plane ticket, rail pass, etc.) up to US$500.

ISIC and **ITIC** (see p. 28) provide basic insurance benefits to US cardholders, including US$100 per day of in-hospital sickness for up to 60 days and US$5000 of accident-related medical reimbursement (see www.isicus.com for details). **Ameri-**

can Express (US ☎ 800-528-4800) grants most cardholders automatic collision and theft car rental insurance and ground travel accident coverage of US$100,000 on flight purchases made with the card.

INSURANCE PROVIDERS

STA (see p. 40) offers a range of plans that can supplement your basic coverage. Other private insurance providers in the US and Canada include: Access America (☎ 800-284-8300; www.accessamerica.com); Berkely Group (☎ 800-797-4514; www.berkely.com); Globalcare Travel Insurance (☎ 800-821-2488; www.global-care-cocco.com); Travel Assistance International (☎ 800-821-2828; www.europ-assistance.com); and Travel Guard (☎ 800-826-4919; www.travelguard.com). Columbus Direct (☎ 020 7375 0011; www.columbusdirect.co.uk) operates in the UK and AFTA (☎ 02 9264 3299; www.afta.com.au) in Australia.

USEFUL ORGANIZATIONS AND PUBLICATIONS

The US **Centers for Disease Control and Prevention** (**CDC**; ☎ 877-394-7747; www.cdc.gov/travel) maintains an international travelers' hotline and an informative website. The CDC's comprehensive booklet *Health Information for International Travel* (The Yellow Book), an annual rundown of disease, immunization, and general health advice, is free online or US$29-40 via the Public Health Foundation (☎ 877-252-1200; http://bookstore.phf.org). Consult the appropriate government agency of your home country for consular information sheets on health, entry requirements, and other issues for various countries (see **Travel Advisories,** p. 34). For quick information on health and other travel warnings, call the **Overseas Citizens Services** (M-F 8am-8pm ☎ 888-407-4747; after-hours 202-647-4000; from overseas 317-472-2328), or contact a passport agency, embassy, or consulate abroad. For information on medical evacuation services and travel insurance firms, see the US government's website at http://travel.state.gov/medical.html or consult the **British Foreign and Commonwealth Office** (www.fco.gov.uk). For general health info, contact the **American Red Cross** (☎ 800-564-1234; www.redcross.org).

STAYING HEALTHY

Common sense is the simplest prescription for good health while you travel. Drink lots of fluids to prevent dehydration and constipation, and wear sturdy, broken-in shoes and clean socks.

ONCE IN CALIFORNIA

ENVIRONMENTAL HAZARDS

Heat exhaustion and dehydration: Heat exhaustion leads to nausea, excessive thirst, headaches, and dizziness. Avoid it by drinking plenty of fluids, eating salty foods (e.g., crackers), abstaining from dehydrating beverages (e.g., alcohol and caffeinated beverages), and always wearing sunscreen. Continuous heat stress can eventually lead to heatstroke, characterized by a rising temperature, severe headache, delirium, and cessation of sweating. Victims should be cooled off with wet towels and taken to a doctor.

Sunburn: Always wear sunscreen (SPF 30 is good) when spending excessive amounts of time outdoors. If you are planning on spending time near water, in the desert, or in the snow, you are at a higher risk of getting burned, even through clouds. If you get sunburned, drink more fluids than usual and apply an aloe-based lotion. Severe sunburns can lead to sun poisoning, a condition that affects the entire body, causing fever, chills, nausea, and vomiting. Sun poisoning should always be treated by a doctor.

Hypothermia and frostbite: A rapid drop in body temperature is the clearest sign of overexposure to cold. Victims may also shiver, feel exhausted, have poor coordination or slurred speech, hallucinate, or suffer amnesia. *Do not let hypothermia victims fall asleep.* To avoid hypothermia, keep dry, wear layers, and stay out of the wind. When the temperature is below freezing, watch out for frostbite. If skin turns white or blue, waxy, and cold, do not rub the area. Drink warm beverages, stay dry, and slowly warm the area with dry fabric or steady body contact until a doctor can be found.

High Altitude: Allow your body a couple of days to adjust to less oxygen before exerting yourself. Note that alcohol is more potent and UV rays are stronger at high elevations.

INSECT-BORNE DISEASES
Many diseases are transmitted by insects—mainly mosquitoes, fleas, ticks, and lice. Be aware of insects in wet or forested areas, especially while hiking and camping; wear long pants and long sleeves, tuck your pants into your socks, and use a mosquito net. Use insect repellents such as DEET and soak or spray your gear with permethrin (licensed in the US only for use on clothing). **Ticks,** found in rural and forested areas, are responsible for Lyme and other diseases.

Lyme disease: A bacterial infection carried by ticks and marked by a circular bull's-eye rash of 2 in. or more. Later symptoms include fever, headache, fatigue, and aches and pains. Antibiotics are effective if administered early. Left untreated, Lyme can cause problems in joints, the heart, and the nervous system. If you find a tick attached to your skin, grasp the head with tweezers as close to your skin as possible and apply slow, steady traction. Removing a tick within 24 hours greatly reduces the risk of infection. Do not try to remove ticks with petroleum jelly, nail polish remover, or a hot match.

STAYING HEALTHY ■ 39

FOOD- AND WATER-BORNE DISEASES

Prevention is the best cure: be sure that your food is properly cooked and the water you drink is clean. Virtually all tap water in California is chemically treated to be safe for drinking; water from streams and lakes is not safe to drink. If hiking, bring bottled water, or purify your own water by bringing it to a rolling boil or treating it with **iodine tablets.** Note, however, that some parasites such as *giardia* have exteriors that resist iodine treatment, so boiling is more reliable. Always wash your hands before eating or bring a quick-drying liquid hand cleaner.

> **Giardiasis:** Transmitted through parasites (microbes, tapeworms, etc. in contaminated water and food) and acquired by drinking untreated water from streams or lakes. Symptoms include diarrhea, abdominal cramps, bloating, fatigue, weight loss, and nausea. If untreated it can lead to severe dehydration.

OTHER INFECTIOUS DISEASES

AIDS and HIV: For detailed information on Acquired Immune Deficiency Syndrome (AIDS) call the US Centers for Disease Control's 24hr. hotline at ☎800-342-2437, or contact the Joint United Nations Programme on HIV/AIDS (UNAIDS), 20 Ave. Appia, CH-1211 Geneva 27, Switzerland (☎41 22 791 3666; fax 22 791 4187). The INS may reject non-immigrant visa applicants with HIV/AIDS.

Sexually transmitted diseases (STDs): Gonorrhea, chlamydia, genital warts, syphilis, herpes, and other STDs are more common than HIV and can cause serious complications. **Hepatitis B** and **C** can also be transmitted sexually. Though condoms may protect you from some STDs, oral or even tactile contact can lead to transmission. If you think you may have contracted an STD, see a doctor immediately.

OTHER HEALTH CONCERNS

MEDICAL CARE ON THE ROAD

Medical care in the US is world-class and widespread. In more remote regions, however, finding doctors can be difficult and expensive. If you are concerned about obtaining medical assistance while traveling, you may wish to employ special support services. The *MedPass* from **GlobalCare, Inc.,** (☎800-860-1111; www.globalcare.net), provides 24hr. international medical assistance and medical evacuation resources. The **International Association for Medical Assistance to Travelers (IAMAT;** US ☎716-754-4883, Canada 519-836-0102; www.cybermall.co.nz/NZ/IAMAT) has free membership, lists English-speaking doctors worldwide, and offers detailed info on immunization requirements and sanitation. If your regular **insurance** policy does not cover travel abroad, you may wish to purchase additional coverage (see p. 36).

Those with medical conditions (such as diabetes, allergies, epilepsy, or heart conditions) may want to obtain a Medic Alert membership (first year $35, annually thereafter $20), which includes a stainless steel ID tag and a 24hr. collect-call number. Contact the Medic Alert Foundation, 2323 Colorado Ave., Turlock, CA 95382 (☎888-633-4298, outside US 209-668-3333; www.medicalert.org).

WOMEN'S HEALTH

Tampons, pads, and **contraceptive devices** are widely available in California, though your favorite brand may not be stocked—bring extras of anything you can't live without. **Abortion** is legal in the US and Canada; for medical questions or the nearest family planning center, contact Planned Parenthood (☎800-230-7526; www.plannedparenthood.org).

GETTING TO CALIFORNIA

BY PLANE

When it comes to airfare, a little effort can save you a bundle. If your plans are flexible enough to deal with the restrictions, courier fares are the cheapest. Tickets bought from consolidators and standby seating are also good deals, but last-minute specials, airfare wars, and charter flights often beat these fares. The key is to hunt around, to be flexible, and to ask persistently about discounts. Students, seniors, and those under 26 should never pay full price for a ticket.

AIRFARES

Airfares to California peak during the summer; holidays are also expensive. Mid-week (M-Th morning) round-trip flights run US$40-50 cheaper than weekend flights, but they are generally more crowded and less likely to permit frequent-flier upgrades. Not fixing a return date ("open return") or arriving in and departing from different cities ("open-jaw") can be pricier than round-trip flights. Patching one-way flights together is the most expensive way to travel. International flights will be cheapest to San Francisco and L.A.; domestic budget airlines often fly to smaller airports such as Long Beach and Oakland.

If California is only one stop on a more extensive globe-hop, consider a round-the-world (RTW) ticket. Tickets usually include at least five stops and are valid for about a year; prices range US$3400-5000. Try **Northwest Airlines/KLM** (US ☎ 800-447-4747; www.nwa.com) or **Star Alliance**, (US ☎ 800-241-6522; www.staralliance.com) a consortium of 22 airlines including United Airlines .

Fares for round-trip flights to California from the US or Canadian east coast cost $200-700; from the UK, UK£200/UK£400; from Australia AUS$1700/AUS$1900; from New Zealand NZ$2200/NZ$2600.

BUDGET AND STUDENT TRAVEL AGENCIES

While knowledgeable travel agents specializing in flights to California can make your life easy and help you save, they may not spend the time to find you the lowest possible fare—they get paid on commission. Travelers holding **ISIC** and **IYTC cards** (see p. 28) qualify for big discounts from student travel agencies. Most flights from budget agencies are on major airlines, but in peak season some may sell seats on less reliable chartered aircraft.

> **CTS Travel**, 30 Rathbone Pl., London W1T 1GQ, UK (☎0 207 209 0630; www.ctstravel.co.uk). A British student travel agent with offices in 39 countries. In the US, Empire State Building, 350 5th Ave., Ste. 7813, New York, NY 10118 (☎877-287-6665; www.ctstravelusa.com).

> **STA Travel**, 5900 Wilshire Blvd., Ste. 900, L.A., CA 90036, USA (☎800-781-4040; www.sta-travel.com). A student and youth travel organization with over 150 offices worldwide, including US offices in Boston, Chicago, L.A., New York, San Francisco, Seattle, and Washington, D.C. Ticket booking, travel insurance, rail passes, and more. Walk-in offices are located throughout Australia (☎03 9349 4344), New Zealand (☎09 309 9723), and the UK (☎0870 1 600 599).

> **Travel CUTS (Canadian Universities Travel Services Limited)**, 187 College St., Toronto, ON M5T 1P7 (☎416-979-2406; www.travelcuts.com). Offices across Canada and the US including L.A., San Francisco, Seattle, and New York.

> **usit**, 19-21 Aston Quay, Dublin 2 (☎01 602 1777; www.usitworld.com). Ireland's leading student/budget travel agency has 22 offices throughout Northern Ireland and the Republic of Ireland. Offers programs to work in North America.

FLIGHT PLANNING ON THE INTERNET. The Internet may be the budget traveler's dream when it comes to finding and booking bargain fares, but the array of options can be overwhelming. Many airline sites offer special last-minute deals on the Web.

STA (www.sta-travel.com) and **StudentUniverse** (www.studentuniverse.com) provide quotes on student tickets, while **Orbitz** (www.orbitz.com), **Expedia** (www.expedia.com), and **Travelocity** (www.travelocity.com) offer full travel services. **Priceline** (www.priceline.com) lets you specify a price, and obligates you to buy any ticket that meets or beats it; **Hotwire** (www.hotwire.com) offers bargain fares, but won't reveal the airline or flight times until you buy. Other sites that compile deals for you include www.bestfares.com, www.flights.com, www.lowestfare.com, www.onetravel.com, and www.travelzoo.com.

Increasingly, there are online tools available to help sift through multiple offers; **SideStep** (www.sidestep.com; download required) and **Booking Buddy** (www.bookingbuddy.com) let you enter your trip information once and search multiple sites.

An indispensable resource on the Internet is the **Air Traveler's Handbook** (www.faqs.org/faqs/travel/air/handbook), a comprehensive listing of links to everything you need to know before you board a plane.

COMMERCIAL AIRLINES

The commercial airlines' lowest regular offer is the **APEX** (Advance Purchase Excursion) fare, which provides confirmed reservations and allows "open-jaw" tickets. Generally, reservations must be made 7-21 days ahead of departure, with seven- to 14-day minimum-stay and up to 90-day maximum-stay restrictions. These fares carry hefty cancellation and change penalties (fees rise in summer). Book peak-season APEX fares early. Use **Microsoft Expedia** (www.expedia.com) or **Travelocity** (www.travelocity.com) to get an idea of the lowest published fares, then use the resources outlined here to try and beat those fares.

TRAVELING FROM NORTH AMERICA

Standard commercial carriers like American and United will probably offer the most convenient flights, but they may not be the cheapest, unless you manage to grab a special promotion or airfare war ticket. You will probably find flying one of the following "discount" airlines a better deal. **JetBlue** (☎800-538-2583; www.jetblue.com) flies non-stop routes to Long Beach, San Diego, Oakland, Las Vegas, Ontario, San Jose, and Sacramento from various other locations in the US. **Southwest** (☎800-248-4377; www.southwest.com) offers frequent on-line specials to and from eight California cities, Las Vegas, and Reno.

STANDBY FLIGHTS

Traveling standby requires considerable flexibility in arrival and departure dates and cities. Companies dealing in standby flights sell vouchers rather than tickets, along with the promise to get you to your destination (or near your destination) within a certain window of time (typically 1-5 days). You call in before your specific window of time to hear your flight options and the probability that you will be able to board each flight. You can then decide which flights you want to try to make, show up at the appropriate airport at the appropriate time, present your voucher, and board if space is available. Vouchers can usually be bought for both one-way and round-trip travel. You may receive a monetary refund only if every available flight within your date range is full; if you opt not to take an available (but perhaps less convenient) flight, you can only get credit toward future travel. To check on a company's service record in the US, call the Better Business Bureau (☎703-276-0100). Carefully read agreements with any company offering standby flights, as tricky fine print can leave you in the lurch. It is difficult to receive refunds, and clients' vouchers will not be honored when an airline fails to receive payment in time.

TICKET CONSOLIDATORS

Ticket consolidators, or **"bucket shops,"** buy unsold tickets in bulk from commercial airlines and sell them at discounted rates. The best place to look is in the Sunday travel section of any major newspaper (such as the *New York Times*), where many bucket shops place tiny ads. Call quickly, as availability is typically extremely limited. Not all bucket shops are reliable, so insist on a receipt that gives full details of restrictions, refunds, and tickets, and pay by credit card (in spite of the 2-5% fee) so you can stop payment if you never receive your tickets. For more info, see www.travel-library.com/air-travel/consolidators.html.

CHARTER FLIGHTS

Charters are flights a tour operator contracts with an airline to fly extra passengers during peak season. Charter flights fly less frequently than major airlines, make refunds particularly difficult, and are almost always fully booked. Schedules and itineraries may change or be cancelled at the last moment (as late as 48hr. before the trip, and without a full refund), and check-in, boarding, and baggage claim procedures are often much slower. However, the flights can be cheaper. Discount clubs and fare brokers offer members savings on last-minute charter and tour deals. Study contracts closely to avoid an unwanted overnight layover.

GETTING AROUND CALIFORNIA

BY PLANE

It is possible to fly between the Bay Area and Southern California for surprisingly little—in fact, flying is often cheaper than traveling by train or bus. **Southwest Airlines** (☎800-I-FLY-SWA/435-9792; www.southwest.com) frequently offers $39 or $49 one-way deals for travel between Oakland or San Jose and Los Angeles or San Diego. Similarly, **JetBlue** (☎800-JETBLUE/538-2583; www.jetblue.com) frequently offers $49 round-trip tickets for travel between Long Beach and Oakland. **United Airlines** (☎800-241-6522; www.united.com) also has deals for travel between the Bay Area and Southern California.

BY TRAIN

Locomotion is still one of the least expensive ways to tour the US, but discounted air travel may be cheaper, and much faster, than train travel. As with airlines, you can save money by purchasing your tickets as far in advance as possible, so plan ahead and make reservations early. It is essential to travel light on trains; not all stations will check your baggage.

Amtrak (☎800-872-7245; www.amtrak.com) has offices in many cities that directly sell tickets, but tickets must be bought through an agent in some small towns. The web page lists up-to-date schedules, fares, arrival and departure info, and allows you to make reservations. **Discounts** on full rail fares are given to: senior citizens (15% off), Student Advantage cardholders (15% off; visit www.studentadvantage.com to purchase the $20 card), travelers with disabilities (15% off),

ages 2-15 accompanied by a paying adult (50% off), children under two (free with each adult ticket purchased), and current members of the US armed forces, active-duty veterans, and their dependents (15% off; www.veteransadvantage.com). Amtrak's "Rail SALE" online offers provide discounts of up to 90%. Amtrak also offers some special packages—check the website or call for more information.

BY BUS

Buses generally offer the most frequent and complete service between cities and towns in California. A bus is often the only way to reach smaller, more remote towns for those without a car. In rural areas, however, bus lines tend to be sparse. *Russell's Official National Motor Coach Guide* ($16 per issue including postage) is an invaluable tool for constructing an itinerary. Updated each month, *Russell's Guide* has schedules of every bus route (including Greyhound) between any two towns in the US and Canada. *Russell's Guide* also publishes two semiannual supplements—a directory of bus lines and a series of route maps—that are free when ordered with the main issue ($9 each if ordered separately). To order any of the above, write **Russell's Guides, Inc.,** 834 3rd Ave. SE, Cedar Rapids, IA 52403 (☎319-364-6138; fax 362-8808).

GREYHOUND

Greyhound (☎800-231-2222; www.greyhound.com) is the only bus service that operates throughout the entire state. If tickets are purchased with a credit card over the phone at least 10 days in advance, the ticket can be mailed anywhere in the US. In many major cities, tickets purchased online can be picked up at the terminal's designated Will Call ticket line. Ticket purchases can also be made at the terminal up to 1hr. prior to the scheduled departure. Schedule information is available at any Greyhound terminal or agency and on the website.

Advance purchase fares: Reserving space far ahead of time ensures a lower fare, but expect smaller discounts June 5-Sept. 15. Fares are often lower for 14-day, 7-day, or 3-day advance purchases. Greyhound's Super Friendly Fares start at $29 and are capped at $119 with a 7-day advance purchase.

Discounts on full fares: Although the Greyhound Senior Club program has ended, senior citizens with a Greyhound Senior Club Card are still eligible for a 10% discount. Seniors (62+) without the Senior Club Card (5% off); ages 2-11 (40% off); Student Advantage cardholders (up to 15% off); disabled person's attendant ticket 50% off; active and retired US military personnel and National Guard Reserves (10% off with valid ID); Veterans Administration affiliates (25% off with VA form 3068).

Ameripass: Allows unlimited travel through the US. 7-day pass $239; 10-day pass $289; 15-day pass $359; 21-day pass $419; 30-day pass $479; 45-day pass $539; 60-day pass $669. Senior citizen and student discounts available. Children's passes half-price. Before purchasing an Ameripass, total up the separate bus fares between towns to make sure that the pass is more economical or at least worth the flexibility it provides. Call ☎800-454-7277 for more info.

International Ameripass: For travelers from outside North America. 7-day pass $229; 10-day pass $279; 15-day pass $339; 21-day pass $399; 30-day pass $459; 45-day pass $509; 60-day pass $619. Senior citizen and student discounts available. Children's passes half-price. International Ameripasses are not available at the terminal; they can be purchased in foreign countries at Greyhound-affiliated agencies. Passes can also be ordered on the website or by calling ☎800-229-9424 in the US. Call ☎800-454-7277 for info.

BUS TOURS

Green Tortoise, 494 Broadway, San Francisco, CA 94133 (☎800-867-8647; www.greentortoise.com), offers a slow-paced, whimsical alternative to straightforward transportation. Green Tortoise's communal "hostels on wheels"—diesel buses remodeled for living and eating on the road—offer aptly named **Adventure Tours.** All California tours depart from and return to San Francisco; travelers are responsible for getting to San Francisco themselves. Prices include transportation from San Francisco to the destination, sleeping space on the bus, tours of the regions through which you pass, and the cost of food for the communally prepared meals. Green Tortoise offers trips to Yosemite National Park (3 days June-Oct. $185; 2 days Apr.-Sept. $135) and Death Valley National Park (3 days $200), as well as other tours in the continental US. Prepare for an earthy trip; buses have no toilets or showers and little privacy. Reserve one to two months in advance; however, many trips have space available at departure. Reservations can be made by mailing in a completed reservation form (available online) and a $50 deposit.

For those who want someone else to do the itinerary planning for them, **Contiki Travel** (☎ 1-888-CONTIKI/266-8454; www.contiki.com) runs a comprehensive, six-day bus tour called California Highlights ($599). The tour includes accommodations, transportation, and some meals.

BY CAR

RENTING

In a state that glorifies cruisin' the freeway, rental cars can be your ticket to freedom and control over your itinerary. The drawbacks of car rentals include steep prices (a compact car rents for $25-45 per day) and high minimum ages for rentals (usually 25).

COSTS AND INSURANCE

There may be an additional charge for a **Collision Damage Waiver (CDW),** which usually comes to $8-15 per day. Major credit cards (including MasterCard and American Express) will sometimes cover the CDW if you use their card to rent a car; call your credit card company for specifics.

Because it is mandatory for all drivers in the US, confirm with your rental agency that you are covered by **insurance.** Be sure to ask whether the price includes insurance against theft and collision. Some credit cards cover standard insurance. If you rent, lease, or borrow a car, and you are not from the US or Canada, you will need a **green card** or **International Insurance Certificate** to certify that you have liability insurance and that it applies abroad. Green cards can be obtained at car rental agencies, car dealerships, some travel agents, and some border crossings. Remember that if you are driving on an **unpaved road** in a conventional rental car, you are almost never covered by insurance; ask about this before leaving the rental agency.

RENTAL AGENCIES

Car rental agencies fall into two categories: national companies with hundreds of branches, and local agencies that serve only one city or region. National chains often allow one-way rentals, picking up in one city and dropping off in another. There is usually a minimum hire period and sometimes an extra drop-off charge of several hundred dollars.

Most branches rent to customers ages 21 to 24 with an additional fee, but policies and prices vary by location. Small local operations occasionally rent to people under 21, but be sure to ask about the insurance coverage and deductible, and always check the fine print. The rental agencies listed below permit rentals to customers 21-24; however, the surcharges and policies vary—call for details.

Alamo (☎800-GOALAMO/462-5266; www.alamo.com). Compact cars as low as $18 per day. CDW about $9. Under-25 surcharge about $25 per day. Check online for Alamo's "Hot Deals."

Enterprise (☎800-736-8222; www.enterprise.com). Compact cars around $30 per day. Under-25 surcharges around $10-15.

Dollar (☎800-800-4000; www.dollar.com). Compact cars around $30 per day. Under-25 surcharges around $15-20. Check the website for specials.

Thrifty (☎800-847-4389; www.thrifty.com). Compact cars as low as $16 per day. CDW about $9. Under-25 surcharges around $20-25. Check the website for extra savings.

Rent-A-Wreck (☎800-944-7501; www.rent-a-wreck.com). Specializes in supplying vehicles that are past their prime for lower-than-average prices. A bare-bones compact less than 8 years old rents for around $20-25. CDW $15 or less.

AUTO TRANSPORT COMPANIES

These services match drivers with car owners who need cars moved from one city to another. Would-be travelers give the company their desired destination and the company finds a car that needs to go there. Expenses include gas, tolls, and your own living expenses. Some companies insure their cars; with others, your security deposit covers any breakdowns or damage. You must be over 21, have a valid license, and agree to drive about 400 mi. per day on a fairly direct route. Popular transport companies include: **Auto Driveaway Co.,** 310 S. Michigan Ave., Chicago, IL 60604-4298 (☎800-346-2277; www.autodriveaway.com), and **Across America Driveaway,** 936 Hermosa Ave., Hermosa Beach, CA 90254 (☎800-677-6686; www.transportautos/driveaway.htm).

ON THE ROAD

Tune up the car before you leave, make sure the tires are in good condition and are properly inflated, and obtain comprehensive, dependable maps. **Rand McNally's Road Atlas,** covering the US, Canada, and Mexico, is one of the best (available at bookstores and gas stations, $12); for those staying within the state, try **Rand McNally's California state map** ($5). If staying in major California cities for an extended period of time, you may want to invest in a **Thomas Guide** ($20-35, www.thomas.com) for the county or counties in which you are staying. A **compass** and a **car manual** can also be very useful. Always carry a **spare tire** and **jack, jumper cables, extra oil, flares**, a **flashlight**, and **blankets** (in case you break down at night or in winter). If you don't know how to **change a tire,** learn before heading out, especially if you are planning to travel in deserted areas. Blowouts on dirt roads are exceedingly common. If you do have a breakdown, **stay with your car;** if you wander off, there's less likelihood trackers will find you. Those traveling long, isolated stretches of road may want to consider purchasing a **cell phone** (see p. 51) in case of a breakdown.

When traveling in the summer or in the desert, bring lots of **water** (a suggested 5L of water per person per day) for drinking and for the radiator. For essential desert driving tips, see **Desert Survival,** p. 529. The **California Department of Transportation** also has a road conditions hotline at ☎800-427-7623.

When driving, buckle up—seat belts are required by law in California. The speed limit in California varies depending on the road (some rural freeways have speed limits as high as 75mph, while residential areas are generally under 35mph). Heed speed limits at all times; most local police and highway patrolmen make frequent use of radar and airplanes to catch speed demons, for whom fines range from $100-150. Gas in California costs over $2 per gallon, but prices vary widely depending on geographical area and the whims of OPEC. Drivers should take necessary precautions against carjacking, a frequent crime in the state. Carjackers, who are usually armed, approach victims in their vehicles and force them to turn over their cars. **Sleeping in a car or van** parked in the city is both illegal and extremely dangerous. Don't do it.

HOW TO NAVIGATE THE INTERSTATES

A number of major interstates and highways crisscross California. Travelers moving north-south have the choice of three major routes. If you're looking for speed, hop on **Interstate 5,** which runs from Oregon through Sacramento, the San Joaquin Valley, L.A., and San Diego on its way to the Mexican border. I-5 is the fastest and most direct route from L.A. to San Francisco (6-8hr.), but it's also painfully boring, affording at best a numbing view of Central Valley farms, flatlands, and pungent cow pastures. Parallel to I-5, **U.S. 101** winds closer to the coast, through Eureka, Santa Rosa, San Francisco, San Luis Obispo, and Santa Barbara, ending in L.A. With a travel time of 8-10hr. from San Francisco to L.A., it's slower than I-5 but a more scenic drive. A third option is ◪**Highway 1,** which hugs the California coast. Hwy. 1 is very slow, contorted, and often congested, but the scenery is some of the most spectacular in the world, particularly on the breathtaking, cliff-hanging turns of Big Sur (see p. 352). California's east-west routes offer less choice. **I-80** heads east from San Francisco to Sacramento and climbs through the Sierra Nevadas to north Lake Tahoe and Reno. Farther south, **I-10** moves east from L.A. to Palm Springs and Joshua Tree, intersecting near San Bernadino with I-15, which cruises northeast to Las Vegas.

CAR ASSISTANCE

The **American Automobile Association (AAA)** is an exceptional resource for drivers. To join AAA, call ☎800-JOIN-AAA/564-6222 or go to www.aaa.com. AAA offers free trip-planning services, maps, and guidebooks, and 24hr. emergency road service anywhere in the US (☎800-AAA-HELP/222-4357). Also included are free towing and fee-free Visa Travelers Cheques, as well as discounts on Hertz car rental (5-20%), Amtrak tickets (10%), and various motel chains and theme parks. AAA has reciprocal agreements with the auto associations of many other countries, which often provide you with full benefits while in the US. Check with your auto association for details. It costs $64 to join the Southern California branch; it costs extra to add additional adults ($21 each) and dependents ($24 each). Renewals cost $44. Costs at other AAA branches vary slightly.

DRIVING PERMITS AND CAR INSURANCE

INTERNATIONAL DRIVING PERMIT (IDP)

If you do not have a license issued by a US state or Canadian province or territory, you might want an International Driving Permit (IDP). While you may drive in the US with a foreign license for up to a year, the IDP may be helpful if your license is not in English. You must carry your home license with your IDP at all times.

You must be 18 to obtain an IDP, which is valid for one year and must be issued in the country in which your license originates. An application for an IDP usually requires one or two photos, a current local license, an additional form of identification, and a fee. To apply, contact the national or local branch of your home country's automobile association. Be careful when purchasing an IDP online or anywhere other than your home automobile association. Many vendors sell permits of questionable legitimacy for higher prices.

CAR INSURANCE

Collision insurance is required by state law in California. Most credit cards cover standard insurance. If you rent, lease, or borrow a car, you will need a **green card** or **International Insurance Certificate,** to certify that you have liability insurance and that it applies abroad. Green cards can be obtained at car rental agencies, car dealers (for those leasing cars), some travel agents, and some border crossings. Rental agencies may require you to purchase theft insurance in countries that they consider to have a high risk of auto theft.

BY BICYCLE

Safe and secure cycling requires a quality helmet and lock. A good helmet costs about $40—much cheaper than critical head surgery. U-shaped **Kryptonite** locks ($30-60) carry insurance against theft for one or two years. **Bike Nashbar,** 6103 State Rte. 446, Canfield, OH 44406 (☎800-627-4227), will beat any nationally advertised in-stock price and ships anywhere in the US or Canada. Their techline (☎800-888-2710) fields questions about repairs and maintenance. The following books are also useful: *Best Bike Rides in Northern California*, by Kim Grob (Globe Pequot; $13); and *Mountain Bike! Southern California: A Guide to Classic Trails*, by David Story (Menasha Ridge; $16). For more info on bike trips, contact **Adventure Cycling Association,** 150 E. Pine St., P.O. Box 8308, Missoula, MT 59802 (☎800-755-2453; www.adventurecycling.org). It's a national, nonprofit organization that researches and maps long-distance routes and organizes bike tours. Annual membership is $30 and includes access to maps and a subscription to *Adventure Cyclist* magazine.

BY MOTORCYCLE

The wind-in-your-face thrill, burly leather, and muscled roar of a motorcycle has built up quite a cult following, but motorcycling is the most dangerous of road-top activities. Helmets are required by law in California; wear the best one you can find. Those considering a long journey should contact the **American Motorcyclist Association,** 13515 Yarmouth Dr., Pickering, OH 43147 (☎800-262-5646; www.amadirectlink.com), the lynchpin of US biker culture. A full membership

($39 per year) includes a subscription to the extremely informative *American Motorcyclist* magazine, discounts on insurance, rentals, and hotels, and a bad-ass patch for your riding jacket.

 BY THUMB. *Let's Go* strongly urges you to consider the risks before you hitchhike. Hitching means entrusting your life to a randomly selected person. While this may be comparatively safe in some areas of Europe and Australia, it is generally not so in the US or Canada. Find other means of transportation and avoid situations where hitching is the only option.

KEEPING IN TOUCH

BY MAIL

DOMESTIC RATES

First-class letters sent and received within the US take 1-3 days and cost $0.37; **Priority Mail** packages up to 1 lb. generally take two days and cost $3.85, up to 5 lb. $12.15. **All days specified denote business days.** For more details, see www.usps.gov.

SENDING MAIL HOME FROM CALIFORNIA

Airmail is the best way to send mail home from the US. **Aerogrammes,** printed sheets that fold into envelopes and travel via airmail, are available at post offices. Write "airmail" or "par avion," on the front. **Surface mail** is by far the cheapest and slowest

way to send packages. It takes one to two months to cross the Atlantic and one to three to cross the Pacific—good for heavy items you won't need for a while, such as souvenirs or other articles you've acquired along the way that are weighing down your pack. For all the countries below save Canada, postcards and aerogrammes cost $0.70, and letters up to 1 oz. cost $0.80. Airmail should reach any of the following countries in 4-7 days. These are standard rates for mail from the US to:

Australia: Airmail parcel post $14.50.

Canada: Postcards $0.50, aerogrammes $0.70. Airmail parcel post $13.25

Ireland: Airmail parcel post $14.

New Zealand: Airmail parcel post $12.50.

UK: Airmail parcel post $16.

SENDING MAIL TO CALIFORNIA

To ensure timely delivery, mark envelopes "airmail" or "par avion." In addition to the standard postage system whose rates are listed below, **Federal Express** (www.fedex.com; US and Canada ☎ 800-463-3339; Australia 13 26 10; Ireland 1800 535 800; New Zealand 0800 733 339; UK 0800 123 800) handles express mail services from most countries to the US and Canada; for example, they can get a letter from New York to L.A. in two days for $11.55, and from London to L.A. in one to two days for UK£29.50. Sending a postcard within the US costs $0.23, while sending letters (up to 13 oz.) domestically requires $0.37 for the first ounce and $0.23 for each additional ounce.

RECEIVING MAIL IN CALIFORNIA

There are several ways to arrange pick-up of letters sent to you by friends and relatives while you are abroad. Mail can be sent via **General Delivery** to almost any city or town in California with a post office, and is very reliable. Address letters like so:

John SUTTER

General Delivery

Truckee, CA 96161

USA

The mail will go to a special desk in the central post office, unless you specify a post office by street address or postal code. It's best to use the largest post office, since mail may be sent there regardless. It is usually safer and quicker, though more expensive, to send mail express or registered. Bring your passport (or other photo ID) for pick-up. If the clerks insist that there is nothing for you, have them check under your first name as well. *Let's Go* lists post offices in the **Practical Information** section for each city and most towns.

American Express's travel offices throughout the world offer a free **Client Letter Service** (mail held up to 30 days and forwarded upon request) for cardholders who contact them in advance. Some offices will offer these services to non-cardholders (especially AmEx Traveler's Cheque holders), but call ahead to make sure. *Let's Go* lists AmEx office locations for most large cities in **Practical Information** sections; for a complete list, call ☎ 800-528-4800.

BY TELEPHONE

CALLING HOME FROM CALIFORNIA

A **calling card** is probably the cheapest option. Calls are billed collect or to your account. You can frequently call collect without possessing a company's calling card just by calling their access number and following the instructions. **Obtain a calling card** from your national telecommunications service before leaving home. To **call home with a calling card,** contact the operator for your service provider in the US by dialing the appropriate toll-free access number. Before settling on a calling card plan, be sure to research your options in order to pick the one that best fits both your needs and your destination.

You can usually also make **direct international calls** from pay phones. Prepaid phone cards and occasionally major credit cards can be used for direct international calls, but they are generally less cost-efficient. Placing a **collect call** through an international operator is even more expensive, but may be necessary in case of emergency. You can place collect calls through any major service provider even if you don't have one of their phone cards.

 PLACING INTERNATIONAL CALLS. To call the US from home or to call home from the US, dial:

1. The **international dialing prefix.** To call from **Australia,** dial 0011; **Canada** or the **US,** 011; **Ireland, New Zealand,** or the **UK,** 00.
2. The **country code** of the country you want to call. To call **Australia,** dial 61; **Canada** or the **US,** 1; **Ireland,** 353; **New Zealand,** 64; the **UK,** 44.
3. The **area code.** *Let's Go* lists the area codes for cities and towns in California opposite the city or town name, next to a ☎. If the first digit is a zero (e.g., 020 for London), omit the zero when calling from abroad (e.g., dial 20 from Canada to reach London).
4. The **local number.**

CALLING WITHIN THE US

If you are calling locally (within an area code), you do not need to dial the area code. However, if you are calling a different area code in California, you will need to dial 1, the area code, and the seven-digit phone number.

The simplest way to call within the US is to use a coin-operated phone; local calls typically cost $0.35. Prepaid phone cards, which carry a certain amount of phone time depending on the card's denomination, usually save time and money in the long run, although they often require a $0.25 surcharge from pay phones. Another kind of prepaid telephone card comes with a Personal Identification Number (PIN) and a toll-free access number. Instead of inserting the card into the phone, you call the access number and follow the directions on the card. Phone rates typically tend to be highest in the morning, lower in the evening, and lowest on Sunday and late at night.

CELLULAR PHONES

While pay phones can be found in almost every city and town in California, if you already own a cell phone you can avoid much of the hassle of scrounging up change or a phone card. Cell phone reception is clear and reliable in most of the region, although reception can be spotty in remote areas or in the mountains. Your provider may also slap on roaming or extended area fees of up to $1.25 per minute. Call your service provider to check their coverage policies in your destination. The international standard for cell phones is **GSM.** You can make and receive calls in the US with a GSM or GSM-compatible phone. For more info on GSM phones, check out www.telestial.com, www.orange.co.uk, or www.roadpost.com.

TIME DIFFERENCES

California is 8hr. behind Greenwich Mean Time (GMT). The entire state observes Daylight Saving Time, so clocks are set forward 1hr. in the spring and back one hour in the fall.

4 AM	7 AM	NOON	2 PM	7 PM	9 PM
San Francisco	Toronto	London	Istanbul	Beijing	Brisbane
Los Angeles	New York	(GMT)	Jerusalem	Hong Kong	Sydney
Seattle	Philadelphia	Lisbon	Cairo	Manila	Canberra
Vancouver	Boston	Dublin	Riyadh	Singapore	Melbourne

BY EMAIL AND INTERNET

Though in some places it's possible to forge a remote link with your home server, in most cases this is a much slower (and thus more expensive) option than taking advantage of free **web-based email accounts** (e.g., www.hotmail.com and www.yahoo.com). **Internet cafes** and the occasional free Internet terminal at a public library or university are listed in the **Practical Information** sections of major cities. For lists of additional cybercafes in California see www.cypercaptive.com.

Increasingly, travelers find that taking their **laptop computers** on the road with them can be a convenient option for staying connected. Laptop users can call an Internet service provider via a modem using long-distance phone cards specifically intended for such calls. Internet cafes sometimes allow individuals to connect to the wireless network. Newer computers can detect these hotspots automatically; otherwise, websites like www.jiwire.com, www.wi-fihotspot-list.com, and www.locfinder.net can help you find them.

ACCOMMODATIONS

HOSTELS

Many hostels are laid out dorm-style, often with large single-sex rooms and bunk beds, although private rooms that sleep two to four are becoming more common. They often have kitchens and utensils for your use, bike or moped rentals, storage areas, transportation to airports, breakfast and other meals, laundry facilities, and Internet access. There can be drawbacks: some hostels close during certain daytime "lockout" hours, have a curfew, don't accept reservations, impose a maximum stay, or, less frequently, require that you do chores. In California, a dorm bed in a hostel will average around $15-25 per night and a private room around $40.

 A HOSTELER'S BILL OF RIGHTS. There are certain standard features that we do not include in our hostel listings. Unless we state otherwise, you can expect that every hostel has no lockout, no curfew, a kitchen, free hot showers, some system of secure luggage storage, and no key deposit.

HOSTELLING INTERNATIONAL

Joining the youth hostel association in your own country (listed below) automatically grants you membership privileges in **Hostelling International (HI),** a federation of national hostelling associations. Non-HI members may be allowed to stay in some HI hostels, but will have to pay extra to do so. HI's web page (www.hihostels.com), lists the web addresses and phone numbers of all national associations.

Most HI hostels also honor **guest memberships**—a blank card with space for six validation stamps. Each night you'll pay a nonmember supplement (one-sixth the membership fee) and earn one guest stamp; get six stamps, and you're a member. A new membership benefit is the FreeNites program, which allows hostelers to gain points toward free rooms. Most student travel agencies (see p. 40) sell HI cards, as do all of the national hostelling organizations listed below. All prices listed below are valid for **one-year memberships** unless otherwise noted.

Hostelling International-USA, 8401 Colesville Rd., Ste. 600, Silver Spring, MD 20910 (☎301-495-1240; www.hiayh.org). US$28, under 18 free.

Australian Youth Hostels Association (AYHA), 422 Kent St., Sydney, NSW 200 (☎02 9261 1111; www.yha.com.au). AUS$52, under 18 AUS$19.

Hostelling International-Canada (HI-C), 205 Catherine St., #400, Ottawa, ON K2P 1C3 (☎613-237-7884; www.hihostels.ca). CDN$35, under 18 free.

An Óige (Irish Youth Hostel Association), 61 Mountjoy St., Dublin 7 (☎830 4555; www.irelandyha.org). €20, under 18 €10.

Hostelling International Northern Ireland (HINI), 22 Donegal Rd., Belfast BT12 5JN (☎02890 31 54 35; www.hini.org.uk). UK£13, under 18 UK£6.

Youth Hostels Association of New Zealand (YHANZ), Level 1, Moorhouse City, 166 Moorhouse Ave., P.O. Box 436, Christchurch (☎0800 278 299 or 03 379 9970; www.yha.org.nz). NZ$40, under 18 free.

Scottish Youth Hostels Association (SYHA), 7 Glebe Cres., Stirling FK8 2JA (☎01786 89 14 00; www.syha.org.uk). UK£6, under 17 £2.50.

Youth Hostels Association (England and Wales), Trevelyan House, Dimple Rd., Matlock, Derbyshire DE4 3YH (☎0870 770 8868; www.yha.org.uk). UK£14, under 18 UK£7.

BOOKING HOSTELS ONLINE. One of the easiest ways to ensure you've got a bed for the night is by reserving online. Click to the **Hostelworld** booking engine through **www.letsgo.com,** and you'll have access to bargain accommodations from Arcata to San Diego with no added commission.

OTHER ACCOMMODATIONS

HOTELS AND MOTELS

Hotel or motel singles in California cost about US$35-100 per night, doubles US$40-150. Motels are designed for travelers with cars, and will generally include a parking space. Chain motels (such as **Motel 6**) tend to be inexpensive and reliable. Hotels cluster in city centers. Both hotel and motel rooms typically have a private bathroom and shower, although cheaper places may offer shared bath. If you make **reservations** in writing, indicate your night of arrival and the number of nights you plan to stay. The hotel will send you a confirmation and may request payment for the first night. Often it is easiest to make reservations over the phone with a credit card, but great deals can be found on the web—even at the last minute.

BED AND BREAKFASTS (B&BS)

For a cozy alternative to hotel rooms, B&Bs (private homes with rooms available to travelers) range from the cute to the sublime. Rooms in B&Bs generally cost $50-100 for a single and $65-200 for a double in California. Any number of websites provide listings for B&Bs. For more information, check out **The California Association of Bed & Breakfast Inns** (www.cabbi.com), **Bed & Breakfast Inns Online** (www.bbonline.com), **InnFinder** (www.inncrawler.com), **InnSite** (www.innsite.com), **Bedand-Breakfast.com** (www.bedandbreakfast.com), **Pamela Lanier's Bed & Breakfast Guide Online** (www.lanierbb.com), or **BNBFinder.com** (www.bnbfinder.com).

UNIVERSITY DORMS

Many **colleges and universities** open their residence halls to travelers when school is not in session; some do so even during term-time. Getting a room may take a couple of phone calls and require advanced planning, but rates tend to be low, and many offer free local calls and Internet access. **UC Berkeley** (http://www.housing.berkeley.edu/conference/summervis/) offers summer housing.

HOME EXCHANGES AND HOSPITALITY CLUBS

Home exchange offers the traveler various types of homes (houses, apartments, condominiums, etc.), plus the opportunity to live like a native and to cut down on accommodation fees. For more information, contact HomeExchange.Com, P.O. Box 787, Hermosa Beach, CA 90254 (☎800-877-8723; www.homeexchange.com), or Intervac International Home Exchange (☎800-756-4663; www.intervac.com).

Hospitality clubs link their members with individuals or families abroad who are willing to host travelers for free or for a small fee to promote cultural exchange and general good karma. In exchange, members usually must be willing to host travelers in their own homes; a small membership fee may also be required. **Global-Freeloaders.com** (www.globalfreeloaders.com) and **The Hospitality Club** (www.hospitalityclub.org) are good places to start. **Servas** (www.servas.org) is an established, more formal, peace-based organization, and requires a fee and an interview to join. As always, use common sense when planning to stay with or host someone you do not know.

LONG-TERM ACCOMMODATIONS

Travelers planning to stay in California for extended periods of time may find it most cost-effective to rent an **apartment.** A basic one-bedroom (or studio) apartment in San Francisco or L.A. will cost $500-1500 per month. Besides the rent itself, prospective tenants usually are also required to front a security deposit (frequently one month's rent) and the last month's rent. **Craigslist** (www.craigslist.org), a free on-line community message board started in the San Francisco Bay Area and expanded to cover four other California cities, is an incredible resource for short-and-long term rentals.

CAMPING AND THE OUTDOORS

With proper equipment, camping is an inexpensive and relatively safe way to experience California's huge assortment of national parks and other scenic areas. California presents a variety of camping opportunities; few naturally spectacular areas in the world are as accessible to the traveler. The **Great Outdoor Recreation Pages** (www.gorp.com) provides excellent general information for travelers planning on camping or spending time in the outdoors.

 LEAVE NO TRACE. *Let's Go* encourages travelers to embrace the "Leave No Trace" ethic, minimizing their impact on natural environments and protecting them for future generations. Trekkers and wilderness enthusiasts should set up camp on durable surfaces, use cookstoves instead of campfires, bury human waste away from water supplies, bag trash and carry it out with them, and respect wildlife and natural objects. For more detailed information, contact the **Leave No Trace Center for Outdoor Ethics,** P.O. Box 997, Boulder, CO 80306, USA (☎800-332-4100 or 303-442-8222; www.lnt.org).

USEFUL PUBLICATIONS AND RESOURCES

A variety of publishing companies offer hiking guidebooks to meet the educational needs of novice or expert. For information about camping, hiking, and biking, write or call the publishers listed to receive a free catalog.

Family Campers and RVers/National Campers and Hikers Association, Inc., 4804 Transit Rd., Bldg. #2, Depew, NY 14043 (☎716-668-6242; www.fcrv.org). Membership fee (US$25) includes their publication *Camping Today.*

Sierra Club Books, 85 2nd St., 2nd fl., San Francisco, CA 94105 (☎415-977-5500; www.sierraclub.org). Publishes general resource books on hiking and camping, as well as specific guides on California.

The Mountaineers Books, 1001 SW Klickitat Way, Ste. 201, Seattle, WA 98134 (☎206-223-6303; www.mountaineersbooks.org). Over 600 titles on hiking, biking, mountaineering, natural history, and conservation.

Wilderness Press, 1200 5th St., Berkeley, CA 94710 (☎800-443-7227 or 510-558-1666; www.wildernesspress.com). Carries over 100 hiking guides and maps, mostly for the western US.

Woodall Publications Corporation, 2575 Vista Del Mar Dr., Ventura, CA 93001, (☎877-680-6155; www.woodalls.com). Annually updates campground directories.

ESSENTIALS

NATIONAL PARKS

California has eight national parks, which contain some of the most spectacular and varied scenery found in the country. The state's most popular park is **Yosemite** (see p. 252), with extensive trails, jagged peaks, formidable rock faces, and incredible waterfalls. Beyond Yosemite, there are the enormous drive-through trees of **Redwoods** (see p. 216), **Sequoia** and **Kings Canyon** (see p. 269), the rock-climber's paradise of **Joshua Tree** (see p. 531), the scorched desert beauty of **Death Valley** (see p. 543), the marine wildlife on **Channel Islands** (see p. 475), and the volcanic activity of **Lassen** (see p. 195).

The **National Park Service (NPS)**, 1849 C St. NW, Washington, D.C. 20240 (☎888-GO-PARKS/467-2757; www.nps.gov) provides info on the parks. It also sells an annual pass that grants family (or vehicle) admission to all national parks and monuments in the US for $50 per year. Without a pass, most parks charge admission fees upon entering. The passes can be purchased through the NPS or at most park entrance gates.

WILDERNESS SAFETY

THE GREAT OUTDOORS

Staying **warm, dry, and well-hydrated** is key to a happy and safe wilderness experience. For any hike, prepare yourself for an emergency by packing a first-aid kit, a reflector, a whistle, high energy food, extra water, rain gear, a hat, and mittens. For warmth, wear wool or insulating synthetic materials designed for the outdoors. Cotton is a bad choice since it dries painfully slowly.

Check **weather forecasts** often and pay attention to the skies when hiking, as weather patterns can change suddenly. Always let a friend, your hostel, a park ranger, or a local hiking organization know when and where you are hiking. Know your physical limits and do not attempt a hike beyond your ability. For information on outdoor ailments and medical concerns see **Safety and Health,** p. 33.

WILDLIFE

California's wilderness areas teem with wildlife. Most animals are friendly—don't mess with them and they won't mess with you. Below are animals who pose more of a threat, and ways to avoid them.

BEARS. Most California wilderness areas are inhabited by bears; ask local rangers for information on bear behavior before entering any park or wilderness area, and obey posted warnings. No matter how irresistibly cute a bear appears, don't be fooled—they are powerful and unpredictable animals that are not intimidated by humans. If you're close enough for a bear to be observing you, you're too close. California's last grizzly bear was believed to be killed in Sequoia National Park in 1922, so when traveling in California's wilderness, the National Park Service recommends taking precautions against black bears. The most important precaution to take when traveling in bear country is to avoid surprising a bear. Sing or talk loudly on the trail and hike in groups, if possible. If you do encounter a black bear, the National Forest Service recommends trying to scare it off by making noise and throwing sticks and stones in its directions. DO NOT RUN. If the black bear charges or attacks, the National Forest Service recommends that you stand your ground and fight back. Some hikers carry pepper spray for use in such a situation. Please see the National Forest Service bear safety page at www.fs.fed.us/r1/wildlife/igbc/Safety/cwi/menu.htm for more information.

Don't leave food or other scented items (trash, toiletries, the clothes that you cooked in) near your tent. Putting these objects into canisters is now mandatory in some national parks in California, including Yosemite. **Bear-bagging,** hanging edi bles and other scented objects from a tree out of paws' reach, is the best way to keep your toothpaste from becoming a condiment. Bears are also attracted to **perfume**, so cologne, scented soap, deodorant, and hairspray should stay at home.

For more information, consult *How to Stay Alive in the Woods*, by Bradford Angier (Macmillan Press, $8).

SNAKES. Only 18% of snakes in California are venomous. **Rattlesnakes** have broad, triangular heads and a rattle on the end of their tail, and are typically found in dry areas below 6000 ft., but have been known to range as high as 8000 ft. Exercise common sense by watching where you step, sit, reach, and poke. Wear long pants and thick boots when exploring the outdoors. If you encounter a snake, stand still until it slithers away. If the snake is backed into a corner, stay still for a while and then back away slowly, stepping gently. Unless it is surprised and bites reflexively, a rattlesnake will coil defensively and shake its rattle before it strikes. If bitten, get to a medical facility as quickly as possible.

SHARKS. Shark attacks are very rare. Nevertheless, there are generally one or two unprovoked shark attacks per year along the California coast. Sharks hang out near steep drop-offs around sandbars and in prime feeding grounds, identifiable by clusters of birds diving for fish. Sharks are most active at twilight or in darkness; they are attracted to erratic movements and bright colors. To avoid sharks, do not be mistaken for a seal or a fish. Don't wear shiny jewelry, which simulates the sheen of fish scales, and don't enter the water if you're bleeding.

CAMPING AND HIKING EQUIPMENT

WHAT TO BUY
Good camping equipment is both sturdy and light. North American suppliers tend to offer the most competitive prices.

Sleeping Bags: Most sleeping bags are rated by season; "summer" means 30-40°F (around 0°C) at night; "four-season" or "winter" often means below 0°F (-17°C). Bags are made of **down** (warm and light, but expensive, and miserable when wet) or of **synthetic** material (heavy, durable, and warm when wet). Prices range US$50-250 for a summer synthetic to US$200-300 for a good down winter bag. **Sleeping bag pads** include foam pads (US$10-30), air mattresses (US$15-50), and self-inflating mats (US$30-120). Bring a **stuff sack** to store your bag and keep it dry.

Tents: The best tents are free-standing (with their own frames and suspension systems), set up quickly, and only require staking in high winds. Low-profile dome tents are the best all-around. Worthy 2-person tents start at US$100, 4-person at US$160. Make sure your tent has a rain fly and seal its seams with waterproofer. Other useful accessories include a **battery-operated lantern,** a plastic **ground cloth,** and a nylon **tarp.**

Backpacks: Internal-frame packs mold well to your back, keep a lower center of gravity, and flex adequately to allow you to hike difficult trails, while external-frame **packs** are more comfortable for long hikes over even terrain, as they carry weight higher and distribute it more evenly. Make sure your pack has a strong, padded hipbelt to transfer weight to your legs. There are models designed specifically for women. Any serious backpacking requires a pack of at least 4000 in. (16,000cc), plus 500 in. for sleeping bags in internal-frame packs. Sturdy backpacks cost anywhere from $125 to $420—your pack is an area where it doesn't pay to economize. On your hunt for the perfect pack, fill up prospective models with something heavy, strap it on correctly, and walk around the store to get a sense of how the model distributes weight. Either buy a **rain cover** (US$10-20) or store all of your belongings in plastic bags inside your pack.

Boots: Be sure to wear hiking boots with good **ankle support.** They should fit snugly and comfortably over 1-2 pairs of **wool socks** and a pair of thin **liner socks.** Break in boots over several weeks before you go to spare yourself blisters.

Other Necessities: Synthetic layers, like those made of polypropylene or polyester, and a pile jacket will keep you warm even when wet. A **space blanket** (US$5-15) will help you to retain body heat and doubles as a ground cloth. Plastic **water bottles** are vital; look for shatter- and leak-resistant models. Carry **water-purification tablets** for when you can't boil water. Although most campgrounds provide campfire sites, you may want to bring a small **metal grate** or **grill.** For those places that forbid fires or the gathering of firewood, you'll need a **camp stove** (the classic Coleman starts at US$50) and a propane-filled **fuel bottle** to operate it. Also bring a **first-aid kit, pocketknife, insect repellent,** and **waterproof matches** or a **lighter.**

WHERE TO BUY IT

The mail-order/online companies listed below offer lower prices than many retail stores. A visit to a local camping or outdoors store will give you a good sense of the look and weight of certain items.

Campmor, 28 Parkway, P.O. Box 700, Upper Saddle River, NJ 07458, USA (☎888-226-7667; www.campmor.com).

Discount Camping, 880 Main North Rd., Pooraka, South Australia 5095, Australia (☎08 8262 3399; fax 8260 6240; www.discountcamping.com.au).

Eastern Mountain Sports (EMS), 1 Vose Farm Rd., Peterborough, NH 03458, USA (☎888-463-6367; www.ems.com).

L.L. Bean, Freeport, ME 04033 (US and Canada ☎800-441-5713; UK 0800 891 297; www.llbean.com).

Mountain Designs, 51 Bishop St., Kelvin Grove, Queensland 4059, Australia (☎07 3856 2344; www.mountaindesigns.com).

Recreational Equipment, Inc. (REI), Sumner, WA 98352, USA (US and Canada ☎800-426-4840, elsewhere 253-891-2500; www.rei.com).

YHA Adventure Shop, 19 High St., Staines, Middlesex, TW18 4QY, UK (☎1784 458 625; www.yhaadventure.com).

CAMPERS AND RVS

Renting an RV costs more than tenting or hosteling but less than staying in hotels while renting a car (see **Rental Cars**, p. 46). The convenience of bringing along your own bedroom, bathroom, and kitchen makes RVing an attractive option, especially for older travelers and families with children. RV rental rates vary widely by region, season (July and August are the most expensive months), and type of RV. Rental prices for a standard RV are around US$800 per week. **El Monte RVs** (☎800-337-2214; www.elmonterv.com) has 15 locations in California. **Cruise America** (☎800-327-7799 or 480-464-7300; www.cruiseamerica.com), rents and sells RVs in the US and Canada.

ORGANIZED ADVENTURE TRIPS

Organized adventure tours offer another way of exploring the wild. Activities include hiking, biking, skiing, canoeing, kayaking, rafting, climbing, photo safaris, and archaeological digs. Tourism bureaus often can suggest parks, trails, and outfitters. Organizations that specialize in camping and outdoor equipment like REI and EMS (seep. 58) also are good source for info.

Sierra Club, 85 2nd Street, 2nd fl., San Francisco, CA 94105 (☎415-977-5500; www.sierraclub.org). Organizes hikes and other outdoor activities for members (memberships from $25).

Specialty Travel Index, 305 San Anselmo Ave., #309, San Anselmo, CA 94960 (☎888-624-4030 or 415-455-1643; www.specialtytravel.com). Biking, cooking, and other themed tours.

TrekAmerica, P.O. Box 189, Rockaway, NJ 07866 (☎800-221-0596 or 973-983 1144, elsewhere 01295 256 777; www.trekamerica.com). Operates tours in the US, Canada, and Mexico.

Tributary Whitewater Tours, 20480 Woodbury Dr., Grass Valley, CA 95949 (☎800-672-3846; www.whitewatertours.com) Whitewater rafting tours all over California.

SPECIFIC CONCERNS

SUSTAINABLE TRAVEL

As the number of travelers on the road continues to rise, the detrimental effect they can have on natural environments becomes an increasing concern. With this in mind, *Let's Go* promotes the philosophy of **sustainable travel.** Through a sensitivity to issues of ecology and sustainability, today's travelers can be a powerful force in preserving and restoring the places they visit.

Ecotourism, a rising trend in sustainable travel, focuses on the conservation of natural habitats and using them to build up the economy without exploitation or overdevelopment. Travelers can make a difference by doing advance research and by supporting organizations and establishments that pay attention to their impact on their natural surroundings and strive to be environmentally-friendly.

ESSENTIALS

To learn more about the environmental concerns pertinent to California, check *Faultline Magazine* (www.faultline.org), which covers environmental news and information for California. **The California Coastal Conservancy** (www.coastalconservancy.ca.gov) was organized to protect and preserve California's coastal regions. The **California Wild Heritage Campaign** (www.californiawild.org) aims to preserve California's unprotected wilderness and wild rivers. The **California Environmental Health Association** (www.ceha.org) is devoted to enhancing the quality of life by supporting environmental education and protection efforts.

ECOTOURISM RESOURCES. For more information on environmentally responsible tourism, contact one of the organizations below:

The Centre for Environmentally Responsible Tourism (www.c-e-r-t.org).

Earthwatch, 3 Clock Tower Pl., Ste. 100, Box 75, Maynard, MA 01754, USA (☎800-776-0188 or 978-461-0081; www.earthwatch.org).

International Ecotourism Society, 733 15th St. NW, Washington, D.C. 20005, USA (☎202-347-9203; www.ecotourism.org).

TRAVELING ALONE

There are many benefits to traveling alone, including independence and greater interaction with locals. On the other hand, any solo traveler is a more vulnerable target of harassment and street theft. As a lone traveler, try not to stand out as a tourist, look confident, and be especially careful in deserted or very crowded areas. If questioned, never admit that you are traveling alone. Maintain regular contact with someone at home who knows your itinerary. For more tips, pick up *Traveling Solo* by Eleanor Berman (Globe Pequot Press; $18), visit www.travelaloneandloveit.com, or subscribe to **Connecting: Solo Travel Network,** 689 Park Rd., Unit 6, Gibsons, BC V0N 1V7, Canada (☎604-886-9099; www.cstn.org).

WOMEN TRAVELERS

Women exploring on their own inevitably face some additional safety concerns, but it's easy to be adventurous without taking undue risks. If you are concerned, consider staying in hostels that offer single rooms that lock from the inside or in religious organizations with rooms for women only. Stick to centrally located accommodations and avoid solitary late-night treks or metro rides.

Always carry extra money for a phone call, bus, or taxi. **Hitchhiking** is never safe for lone women, or even for two women traveling together. Look as if you know where you're going and approach older women or couples for directions if you're lost or uncomfortable. Generally, the less you look like a tourist, the better off you'll be. Your best answer to verbal harassment is no answer at all; feigning deafness, sitting motionless, and staring straight ahead at nothing in particular are often useful strategies. The extremely persistent can sometimes be dissuaded by a firm, loud, and very public "Go away!". Don't hesitate to seek out a police officer or a passerby if you are being harassed. Memorize emergency numbers, and consider carrying a whistle on your keychain. A self-defense course will both prepare you for a potential attack and raise your level of awareness (see p. 35).

For general information, contact the **National Organization for Women (NOW),** 733 15th St. NW, 2nd fl., Washington, D.C. 20005 (☎202-628-8669; www.now.org), which has branches across the US that can refer women travelers to rape crisis centers and counseling services.

GLBT TRAVELERS

Although California is regarded as a progressive state, prejudice against gay, lesbian, bisexual, and transgendered (GBLT) people is still present. Homophobia may be a problem for the openly gay or lesbian traveler, particularly in rural areas. Many cities, however, have large and active queer communities. San Francisco, of course, is the birthplace of the Gay Pride Parade and the Rainbow Flag, an international icon of GLBT pride, while West Hollywood in L.A. and San Diego's Hillcrest neighborhood are known for their lively gay communities. Even outside the major cities, smaller outposts of gay culture still exist. Palm Springs, known as a resort community for the elderly, increasingly caters to a younger, homosexual clientele. Guerneville, in the Russian River Valley north of San Francisco, is a small town known for its large GLBT population. *Let's Go* includes local gay and lesbian info lines and community centers when available. Listed below are contact organizations, mail-order bookstores, and publishers that offer materials addressing some specific concerns. **Out and About** (www.planetout.com) offers a bi-weekly newsletter addressing travel concerns and a comprehensive site addressing gay travel concerns. The online newspaper **365gay.com** also has a travel section (www.365gay.com/travel/travelchannel.htm).

Giovanni's Room, 1145 Pine St., Philadelphia, PA 19107, USA (☎215-923-2960; www.queerbooks.com). An international lesbian/feminist and gay bookstore with mail-order service (carries many of the publications listed below).

Gay's the Word, 66 Marchmont St., London WC1N 1AB, UK (☎44 20 7278 7654; www.gaystheword.co.uk). The largest gay and lesbian bookshop in the UK, with both fiction and non-fiction titles. Mail-order service available.

International Lesbian and Gay Association (ILGA), 81 rue Marché-au-Charbon, B-1000 Brussels, Belgium (☎+32 2 502 2471; www.ilga.org). Provides political information, such as homosexuality laws of individual countries.

FURTHER READING: GLBT TRAVEL.

Spartacus 2003-2004: International Gay Guide. Bruno Gmunder Verlag ($33).

Damron Men's Travel Guide, Damron Road Atlas, Damron Accommodations Guide, Damron City Guide, and *Damron Women's Traveller.* Damron Travel Guides (US$11-19). For info, call ☎800-462-6654 or visit www.damron.com.

Ferrari Guides' Gay Travel A to Z, Ferrari Guides' Men's Travel in Your Pocket, Ferrari Guides' Women's Travel in Your Pocket, and *Ferrari Guides' Inn Places.* Ferrari Publications (US$16-20).

The Gay Vacation Guide: The Best Trips and How to Plan Them, Mark Chesnut. Kensington Books (US$15).

Gayellow Pages USA/Canada, Frances Green. Gayellow Pages (US$16). They also publish smaller regional editions. Visit Gayellow pages online at www.gayellowpages.com.

TRAVELERS WITH DISABILITIES

Those with disabilities should inform airlines and hotels of their disabilities when making reservations; some time may be needed to prepare special accommodations. Call ahead to restaurants, museums, and other facilities to find out if they are handicapped-accessible. US customs requires a certification of immunization against rabies for **guide dogs** entering the country.

In the US, both Amtrak and major airlines accommodate disabled passengers if notified at least 72hr. in advance. Amtrak offers a 15% discount to physically disabled travelers; call ☎ 800-872-7245 for more info. Greyhound buses will provide a 50% discount for a companion if the ticket is purchased at least three days in advance. If you are without a fellow traveler, call Greyhound (☎ 800-752-4841, TDD 800-345-3109) at least two days before you plan to leave, and they will make arrangements to assist you. For information on transportation availability in individual US cities, contact the local chapter of the **Easter Seal Society** (☎ 800-221-6827; www.easter-seals.org).

If you are planning to visit a national park or attraction in the US run by the National Park Service, obtain a free **Golden Access Passport,** which is available at all park entrances and from federal offices whose functions relate to land, forests, or wildlife. The Passport entitles disabled travelers and their families to free park admission and provides a lifetime 50% discount on all campsite and parking fees.

USEFUL ORGANIZATIONS

Accessible Journeys, 35 W. Sellers Ave., Ridley Park, PA 19078, USA (☎ 800-846-4537; www.disabilitytravel.com). Designs tours for wheelchair users and slow walkers. The site has tips and forums for all travelers.

Directions Unlimited, 123 Green Ln., Bedford Hills, NY 10507, USA (☎ 800-533-5343). Books individual vacations for the physically disabled. Not an info service.

ESSENTIALS

Mobility International USA (MIUSA), P.O. Box 10767, Eugene, OR 97440, USA (☎541-343-1284; www.miusa.org). Provides a variety of books and other publications containing information for travelers with disabilities.

Society for Accessible Travel & Hospitality (SATH), 347 5th Ave., #610, New York, NY 10016, USA (☎212-447-7284; www.sath.org). An advocacy group that publishes free online travel information and the travel magazine *OPEN WORLD* (annual subscription US$13, free for members). Annual membership US$45, students and seniors US$30.

MINORITY TRAVELERS

California is a multicultural state, but not always harmoniously so. Although "minority" groups are now the majority in California, anti-immigrant prejudice persists in many areas, especially toward Mexican immigrants. Racial tensions between blacks and whites have been known to flare up in the inner cities, particularly in historically riot-prone Los Angeles. Racial and ethnic minorities sometimes face both blatant and (more often) subtle discrimination or harassment. Verbal harassment is now less common than unfair pricing, false info on accommodations, or inexcusably slow or unfriendly service at restaurants. Report individual perpetrators to their supervisor or establishments to the **Better Business Bureau** for the region (www.bbb.org); contact the police in extreme situations. *Let's Go* always welcomes reader input regarding discriminating establishments. Be aware that racial tensions do exist even in large, ostensibly progressive areas, and try to avoid confrontations.

In towns along the US-Mexican border, the **Border Patrol** for the US Immigration and Naturalization Service (INS) remains on a constant lookout for Mexican nationals who have crossed the border illegally. In border towns, they may pull over anyone who looks suspicious, search their vehicles for smuggled goods or people, and ask for identification. The INS also runs checkpoints along the interstates south of Los Angeles to catch illegal immigrants. All cars must stop at these points, and the INS workers may search vehicles that arouse suspicion.

DIETARY CONCERNS

Vegetarians should have a food fest in veggie-snacking, soy milk-guzzling California. *Let's Go* often indicates vegetarian options in restaurant listings; other places to look for vegetarian and vegan cuisine are local health food stores, as well as large natural food chains such as ▧**Trader Joe's** and **Wild Oats.** Vegan options are more difficult to find in smaller towns and inland; be prepared to make your own meals. The travel section of the The Vegetarian Resource Group's website, at www.vrg.org/travel, has a comprehensive list of organizations and websites that are geared toward helping traveling vegetarians and vegans. For more information, visit your local bookstore or health food store, and consult *The Vegetarian Traveler: Where to Stay if You're Vegetarian, Vegan, Environmentally Sensitive,* by Jed and Susan Civic (Larson Publications; US$16), or *Vegetarian Restaurants & Natural Food Stores in the US: A Comprehensive Guide to Over 2500 Vegetarian Eateries,* by John Howley (Torchlight Publications; $20). Vegetarians will also find numerous resources on the web; try www.vegdining.com and www.happycow.net, for starters.

Travelers who keep kosher should contact synagogues in larger cities for information on kosher restaurants. Your own synagogue or college Hillel should have access to lists of Jewish institutions across the nation. If you are strict in your

ESSENTIALS

observance, you may have to prepare your own food on the road. A good resource is the *Jewish Travel Guide,* edited by Michael Zaidner (Vallentine Mitchell; US$18). Travelers looking for halal restaurants should check www.zabihah.com.

OTHER RESOURCES

Let's Go tries to cover all aspects of budget travel, but we can't put *everything* in our guides. Listed below are books and websites that can serve as jumping-off points for your own research.

USEFUL PUBLICATIONS

Most of California's big coastal cities offer countless news and entertainment periodicals. In San Francisco, try the *Chronicle, SF Weekly*, and the *Bay Guardian*. The *Bay Area Reporter* covers entertainment and gay culture. In Sacramento, try the *Sacramento Bee* and, for music and activities information, *Alive and Kicking, Inside the City*, and *Sacramento News and Review*. In L.A., pick up copies of the *Times* and *L.A. Weekly*. Industry papers include *Variety* and *The Hollywood Reporter*. For information on gay and lesbian entertainment, try *Fab!, Vibe, Frontiers*, or *Edge*. In San Diego, the *Union-Tribune* provides news and the *Reader* has the nightlife scoop.

WORLD WIDE WEB

Almost every aspect of budget travel is accessible via the web. In 10min. at the keyboard, you can make a hostel reservation, get advice on travel hotspots from other travelers, or buy a bus ticket from L.A. to San Francisco. Listed below are some regional and travel-related sites to start off your surfing; other relevant web sites are listed throughout the book. Because website turnover is high, use search engines (such as www.google.com) to strike out on your own.

 WWW.LETSGO.COM Our freshly redesigned website features extensive content from our guides; community forums where travelers can connect with each other and ask questions or advice—as well as share stories and tips; and expanded resources to help you plan your trip. Visit us soon to browse by destination, find information about ordering our titles, and sign up for our e-newsletter!

THE ART OF BUDGET TRAVEL

BootsnAll.com: www.bootsnall.com. Numerous resources for independent travelers, from planning your trip to reporting on it when you get back.

How to See the World: www.artoftravel.com. A compendium of great travel tips, from cheap flights to self defense to interacting with local culture.

Travel Intelligence: www.travelintelligence.net. A large collection of travel writing by distinguished travel writers.

Travel Library: www.travel-library.com. A fantastic set of links for general information and personal travelogues.

World Hum: www.worldhum.com. An independently produced collection of "travel dispatches from a shrinking planet."

INFORMATION ON CALIFORNIA

GENERAL

California Division of Tourism: www.gocalif.ca.gov. Glossy tourist brochures in e-form, a frightening picture of Arnold and Maria, and useful maps and regional guides.

Maps and Driving Directions: www.mapquest.com. Offers thorough street-level maps of the entire country.

Official California Government Page: www.ca.gov. Lists state government services and contact information.

WorldWeb: www.california.worldweb.com. Information on lodging, tours, attractions, and shopping.

THE OUTDOORS

California State Parks Official Site: www.cal-parks.ca.gov. Maps and reservation info.

California Surf Reports: www.surfrider.org/cal5.htm. A fairly thorough and frequently updated description of surf conditions up and down the California coast.

National Park Service: www.nps.gov. A wealth of information on the US National Park system, including maps and reservation information.

The Ski Report: www.skicentral.com/rpt-california.html. Describes ski conditions at major slopes in California.

ESSENTIALS

ALTERNATIVES TO TOURISM

A PHILOSOPHY FOR TRAVELERS

Let's Go believes that the connection between travelers and their destinations is an important one. We've watched the growth of the "ignorant tourist" stereotype with dismay, knowing that many travelers care passionately about the communities and environments they explore—but also knowing that even conscientious tourists can inadvertently damage natural wonders and harm cultural environments. With this "Alternatives to Tourism" chapter, *Let's Go* hopes to promote a better understanding of California and enhance your experience there.

There are several different options for those who seek to participate in Alternatives to Tourism. Opportunities for **volunteerism** abound, both with local and international organizations. **Studying** can also be instructive, either in the form of direct enrollment in a local university or in an independent research project. **Working** is a way to both immerse yourself in the local culture and finance your travels.

As a **volunteer** in California, you can participate in projects from rehabilitating sick animals to supporting subversive art, either on a short-term basis or as the main component of your trip. Later in this section, we recommend organizations that can help you find the opportunities that best suit your interests, whether you're looking to pitch in for a day or a year.

Studying at a college or language program is another option. California's excellent university system, language institutes, and film schools are three different ways to supplement travel with academics.

Many travelers also structure their trips by the **work** that they can do along the way—either odd jobs as they go, or full-time stints in cities where they plan to stay for some time. From selling concessions at a national park to picking fruit to working as an extra on a movie set, California offers plenty of exciting opportunities for those with a valid work visa.

VOLUNTEERING

Volunteering can be a very fulfilling experience, especially if you combine it with the thrill of traveling in a new place. As the most populous state in the US, California naturally has many problems—and many organizations designed to solve these problems. Migrant workers, inner-city youth, and the homeless all need help. There are organizations designed to preserve California's stunning natural beauty, and others dedicated to fighting for same-sex marriages.

Most people who volunteer in California do so on a short-term basis at organizations that make use of drop-in or once-a-week volunteers. The best way to find opportunities that match up with your interests and schedule may be to check with local or national volunteer centers, either from home or once in California.

More intensive volunteer services may charge you a fee to participate. These costs can be surprisingly hefty (although they frequently cover airfare and most living expenses). Most people choose to go through a parent organization that takes care of logistical details and often provides a group environment and support system. There are two main types of organizations—religious and non-sectarian—although there are rarely restrictions on participation for either.

ART AND CULTURE

High culture, low culture, weird culture—all of it is integral to the vibrancy of life in California. The best and most personal way to become involved is simply to pick up the phone and call your favorite opera, theater, museum, orchestra, arts festival, or venue and ask how you can help. Contacting the **California Arts Council** (www.cac.ca.gov) is another great way to support the arts in a state that thrives on artistic sensitivity.

Heritage Resource Management Department of US Forest Service, P.O. Box 31315, Tucson, AZ 85751-1315 (☎800-281-9176 or 520-722-2716; www.passportintime.com). The Passport in Time program's volunteer opportunities include assisting rock art and historical structure restoration efforts and recording oral histories.

Institute for Unpopular Culture (IFUC), 1592 Union St., Ste. 226, San Francisco, CA 94123 (☎415-986-4382; www.ifuc.org). IFUC supports emerging artists creating subversive attempts to challenge the status quo. The institute sponsors gallery shows, short films, and concerts. Volunteers are needed throughout the year to assist with research and administrative work.

J. Paul Getty Museum, Visitor Services Dept., Volunteer Program, 1200 Getty Center Dr., L.A., CA 90049 (☎310-440-7303; www.getty.edu). Volunteers greet visitors, answer questions, work in offices, and help out with special events. 18+.

Los Angeles Philharmonic Orchestra, 151 S. Grand Ave., L.A., CA 90012 (☎323-850-2165; www.laphil.org). Take part in fundraising, music education, or the support of music in schools. Volunteers can also work with the Hollywood Bowl.

New Conservatory Theatre Center (NCTC), 25 Van Ness Ave., San Francisco, CA 94102 (☎415-861-4914; www.nctcsf.org). Provides entertaining and educational programs for youths, along with a wide array of performances for the entire San Francisco community. The NCTC is always looking for new volunteers, from costume designers to ushers to administrative workers.

ENVIRONMENTAL CONSERVATION

Whether protecting wildlife and endangered species or combating air and water pollution, many Californian institutions devote themselves to ecological conservation. The **California Council for Wildlife Rehabilitators** (www.ccwr.org) lists wildlife rehabilitation centers by region. The **California Coastkeeper Alliance** links to regional branches of its coast protection programs at www.cacoastkeeper.org. The **Trail Center** lists outdoor volunteer opportunities at www.trailcenter.org/links/links-vol.htm. To locate the nearest state park, see the **California State Parks** website (www.parks.ca.gov).

California Wild Heritage Campaign (☎916-442-3155; www.californiawild.org). Aims to preserve California's unprotected wilderness and wild rivers. Volunteers assist with administrative tasks, help local chapters run hikes, and aid public education and outreach personnel. Regional contact information is available on the website.

Ecolutions, 10271 W. Pico Blvd., L.A., CA 90064 (☎310-203-0683; www.ecolutions.org). An environmental education organization; employs creative volunteers in web and graphic design, administration, children's outreach, and one-time events.

Orange County Coastkeeper, 441 Old Newport Blvd., Ste. 103, Newport Beach, CA 92663 (☎949-723-5424; www.coastkeeper.org). Maintains a kelp reforestation program, conducts beach debris surveys, and monitors the harbor. Volunteer opportunities include harbor clean-up efforts and participation in the kelp reforestation program.

Pacific Crest Trail, 5325 Elkhorn Blvd., PMB #256, Sacramento, CA, 95842 (☎916-349-2109; www.pcta.org). Volunteers help maintain and monitor trails, or work as trail cooks. One-time efforts always appreciated. Visit website for the nearest trail crew.

Project Wildlife, Wildlife Care Center, 887½ Sherman St., San Diego, CA 92110 (☎619-449-4145; www.projectwildlife.org). Rescues and rehabilitates sick, injured, and orphaned animals. Volunteers can take part in a number of programs, including transporting and rescuing animals, working at the wildlife care facility, and providing educational presentations. Training is provided.

LITERACY PROGRAMS

Illiteracy negatively affects the lives of thousands of Californians, from recent immigrants to elderly natives to adolescents. Through tutoring and mentoring, volunteers can help these people succeed.

America's Literacy Directory (☎800-228-8813; www.literacydirectory.org/volunteer.asp). A service of the National Institute for Literacy, this online directory allows you to search for volunteer opportunities with more than 5000 literacy programs in the US.

California Literacy, 133 N. Altadena Dr., Ste. 410, Pasadena, CA 91107 (☎626-395-9989; www.caliteracy.org/volunteering.html). Volunteer opportunities include tutoring adult learners in reading and English as a Second Language (ESL).

California Library Literacy Services (www.literacyworks.org). Provides literacy instruction to help adult learners meet their own goals for improvement at public libraries across the state. For information on specific local programs, visit the website.

POLITICAL ACTIVISM

California has a long history of political activism, and on any given day you will find protestors waving signs for their latest cause. Currently, many organizations have sprung up to help in the fight for same-sex marriages and GLBT issues. The organizations listed below are a few of the organizations that spark rallies, demonstrations, and lobbying in California.

Equality California, 2370 Market St., San Francisco, CA 94114 (☎415-581-0005; www.eqca.org). Works on GLBT legislation, as well as GLBT pride. Volunteer tasks might range from the administrative to rallies and outreach.

Marriage Equality California (MECA), P.O. Box 8, Venice, CA 90294 (☎877-356-4125; www.marriageequalityca.org). With chapters throughout California, MECA works to end discrimination toward gay and lesbian marriages. Volunteers always needed for parades, town hall meetings, rallies, and domestic partner registrations.

American Lung Association, 61 Broadway, 6th fl., NYC, NY 10006 (☎800-586-4872/LUNG-USA; www.lungusa.org). Works on anti-smoking campaigns, tobacco prevention in schools, and advocacy in public policies that pertain to lung health.

URBAN ISSUES

In the urban centers of California, as in most cities, some segments of society face serious adverse circumstances, including hunger, domestic abuse, homelessness, and untreated or undiagnosed mental and physical disorders. The high level of immigration to California's cities has prompted the formation of organizations that address language barriers, refugees, and concerns specific to individual ethnic and religious groups. For extensive listings of the volunteer opportunities available in California's three largest cities, check out **The Volunteer Center of San Francisco** (☎415-982-8999; www.thevolunteercenter.net), **Volunteer San Diego** (☎858-636-4131; www.volunteersandiego.org), and **L.A. Works** (☎323-224-6510; www.laworks.com).

Asian Americans for Community Involvement (AACI), 2400 Moonpark Ave., Ste. 300, San Jose, CA 95128 (☎408-975-2730; www.aaci.org/join/volunteers.html). Provides mental health services, domestic violence treatment and prevention programs, and support for refugees and immigrants, among other services. Volunteers can serve as youth counselors and assist at the domestic violence shelter.

Homeless Veteran Program (☎800-827-1000; www.va.gov/homeless). Provides outreach to homeless veterans living on the streets and in shelters. The program offers psychiatric care and information on health care, housing, and employment assistance. The website lists program coordinators by state. AmeriCorps opportunities available.

The Shelter Network, 1450 Chapin Ave., 2nd fl., Burlingame, CA 94010 (☎650-685-5880; www.shelternetwork.org). Offers housing for homeless families and individuals. Volunteers can serve as job search assistants, child care providers, donated clothing and food sorters, and office assistants.

US Department of Housing and Urban Development, 451 7th St. SW, Washington, D.C. 20410 (☎202-708-1112; www.hud.gov). Maintains listings of local homeless assistance programs, shelters, food banks, hospitals, and advocacy groups in every state. **The National Coalition for the Homeless** has a similar directory (www.nationalhomeless.org/local/local.html).

YOUTH AND THE COMMUNITY

Numerous organizations exist to counteract teenage drug and alcohol use, violence, delinquency, and truancy. In California, big sibling programs abound with volunteering opportunities, as do summer camps, day cares, children's museums, tutoring programs, and programs for disadvantaged, disabled, or abused children. Perhaps a less-often recognized population is the elderly, though there are many programs that cater to seniors as well. The **California Department of Aging** (www.aging.state.ca.us) is a helpful place to start.

826 Valencia, 826 Valencia St., San Francisco, 94110 (☎415-642-5905; www.826valencia.org). Literary wunderkind Dave Eggers founded this vibrant center to help children ages 8-18 develop their writing skills. The center runs workshops, mentoring, and publishing with proceeds from an attached pirate store (arrr). Volunteers may help with tutoring, upkeep, or grant writing.

Big Brothers Big Sisters of America, 230 N. 13th St., Philadelphia, PA 19107 (☎215-567-7000; www.bbbsa.org). Provides mentorship, friendship, and support to hundreds of thousands of American kids. Paired "Bigs" and "Littles" work on homework together, visit museums, participate in community service, and just hang out.

Meals on Wheels Association of America, 203 S. Union St., Alexandria, VA 22314 (☎703-548-5558; www.mowaa.org). Visit the website for a list of over 300 communities in California serviced by Meals on Wheels. Buy, prepare, and deliver meals to the elderly and the needy. Public awareness and research projects are also available.

ALTERNATIVES TO TOURISM

STUDYING

Study programs range from basic language and culture courses to college-level classes, often for credit. In order to choose a program that best fits your needs, you will want to research all you can before making your decision—determine costs and duration, as well as what kind of students participate in the program and what sort of accommodations are provided. In programs that have large groups of students, especially ones who speak the same foreign language, the comfort level may be higher, but non-native speakers will not have the same opportunity to better their English by practicing with native Californians, nor will those already proficient in English develop as close ties with the local community. For accommodations, dorm life provides a better opportunity to mingle with fellow students, but there is a lower chance of experiencing the local scene. If you live with a family, there is a potential to build lifelong friendships with locals and to experience day-to-day life in more depth, but conditions can vary greatly from family to family.

VISA INFORMATION

All foreign visitors are required to have a **visa** if they intend to study in the US. In addition, travelers must provide proof of intent to leave, such as a return plane ticket or an I-94 card. Foreign students who wish to study in the US must apply for either an M-1 visa (non-academic or vocational studies) or an F-1 visa (for full-time students enrolled in an academic or language program). See http://educationusa.state.gov for further information on studying in the US. To obtain a visa or study permit, apply at a US embassy or consulate in your home country (see **Embassies and Consulates**, p.25). Most schools require the Test of English as a Foreign Language (TOEFL) for all non-native speakers; it is administered in many countries. The international students office at the institution you will be attending can give you specifics. Contact **TOEFL/TSE Publications**, P.O. Box 6151, Princeton, NJ 08541 (☎877-863-3546, outside the US and Canada 609-771-7100; www.toefl.org). **Visa extensions** are sometimes attainable with a completed I-539 form; call the Bureau of Citizenship and Immigration Service's (BCIS) forms request line (☎800-870-3676) or get it online at www.immigration.gov/graphics/forms-fee/forms/i-539.htm. See http://travel.state.gov/visa_services.html for more information. Recent security measures have made the visa application process more rigorous, and therefore lengthier. **Apply well in advance of your travel date,** especially for visas to the US. The process may seem complex, but it's critical that you go through the proper channels—the alternative is potential deportation.

UNIVERSITIES

Many outstanding American institutions of higher learning are located in California, including Stanford, Caltech, and the superb, three-tiered state university system. The public university system consists of the University of California (www.ucop.edu/pathways), California State University (www.calstate.edu), and the community college system. Community or junior colleges are smaller, do not have graduate schools, and usually serve students who cannot attend school full-time, or who plan to eventually transfer to a four-year school after two years. Unfortunately, public state schools charge non-Californians significantly higher tuition and are extremely popular with residents, who receive priority consideration in admissions. While foreigners may find it difficult to enter the University of California schools, many of the California State Universities have excellent and accessible programs for foreign students.

LANGUAGE SCHOOLS

Language schools can be independently run international or local organizations or divisions of foreign universities. They rarely offer college credit. They are a good alternative to university study if you desire a deeper focus on the language or a slightly less rigorous course load. These programs are also good for younger high-school students who might not feel comfortable with older students in a university program.

Eurocentres, 9500 Gilman Dr., La Jolla, CA 92093 (☎858-964-1050; www.eurocentres.com), or in Europe, Head Office, Seestr. 247, CH-8038 Zurich, Switzerland (☎41 1 485 50 40; fax 481 61 24). Language programs for beginning to advanced students with homestays in California.

Language Studies International, 2015 Center St., Berkeley, CA 94704 (☎510-841-4695; www.lsi.edu) or 1706 5th Ave., San Diego, CA 92101 (☎619-234-2881). Intensive language programs in Berkeley and San Diego for students of all levels. Living options include dorms, homestays, and hotels.

Osako Sangyo University Los Angeles (OSULA) Education Center, 3921 Laurel Canyon Blvd., Studio City, CA 91604 (☎818-509-1484; www.osula.com). Offers intensive and general English classes in a residential college setting in the suburbs of L.A.

Monterey Institute of International Studies, 460 Pierce St., Monterey, CA 93940 (☎831-647-4100; www.miis.edu). The language center runs the 8-week Intensive ESL Program and the more general English for Academic Preparation Program, which offers courses on 3 levels of study. Located in the beautiful coastal city of Monterey.

INTRAX English Institute, 551 Sutter St., San Francisco, CA 94102 (☎415-835-9766; www.intraxinc.com). ESL programs taught in San Francisco and San Diego. Offers courses focused on easing international students into the American college system. INTRAX also operates a Work/Travel service that helps international university students find jobs in the US during their summer vacations, and several Homestay programs in San Francisco, L.A., and San Diego for international youth ages 13-22.

FILM SCHOOLS

Hollywood is the cinematic capital of the universe—there is no better place to gain behind-the-scenes experience than in the studio backlots of Studio City and Burbank. To this end, there are numerous film schools and colleges with high-caliber film programs in the Los Angeles area, many of which run shorter summer and semester programs.

New York Film Academy, 100 E. 17th St., New York, NY 10003 (☎818-733-2600; www.nyfa.com). The L.A. location allows would-be actors, filmmakers, and screenwriters the chance to hone their skills on the Universal Studios backlot. Program lengths vary from one week to one year, with classes in acting, screenwriting, digital imaging, filmmaking, and 3D animation. Programs $1000-25,000.

University of Southern California School of Cinema-Television, Summer Production Workshop, 850 W. 34th St., L.A., CA 90089-2211 (☎213-740-1742; www.usc.edu/schools/cntv/programs/spw). Boasting a luminous alumni list that includes Jedi boy George Lucas, screenwriter John Milius *(Apocalypse Now)*, and producer Laura Ziskin

(Spider-Man), the world-renowned film school offers summer workshops with classes in writing, digital imaging, directing and producing. University housing is available, as are classes for students who have already logged some hours (or years) in the industry.

American Film Institute, 2021 N. Western Ave., L.A., CA 90027 (☎323-856-7600; www.afi.com). Committed to "advancing and preserving the art of the moving image," the L.A. branch of the Institute offers seminars and workshops on topics varying from directing to digital TV editing, notably the "Directing Workshop for Women" which was established in 1974. Some programs are free, but housing and meals are not provided. The annual AFI Fest in the fall lasts for over a week and has numerous screenings and receptions, featuring established and up-and-coming directors.

The Los Angeles Film School, 6363 Sunset Blvd., Ste. 400, L.A., CA 90028 (☎323-860-0789; www.lafilm.com). Located in Hollywood, the L.A. Film School trains students aspiring to careers in many different areas of filmmaking, including directing, screenwriting, production design, and cinematography. 6-week digital camera-based workshops, an 8-month feature development program, and a full-year immersion program are offered. Tuition and equipment costs range from $6500 for a basic 6-week course to $29,000 for international students in the full-year program.

Cinema Make-up School, 3780 Wilshire Blvd., Ste. 300, L.A., CA 90010 (☎213-368-1234; cinemamakeup.com). Numerous courses offered in different styles of make-up from film and television to fashion to beauty and salon. Tuition does not include lab fees or make-up equipment costs. Total costs range from $8250 for Beauty Make-up to $8900 for the Master Make-up course, which is a general introduction to make-up in various mascara-dependent industries.

ALTERNATIVES TO TOURISM

WORKING

As with volunteering, work opportunities tend to fall into two categories. Some travelers want long-term jobs that allow them to get to know another part of the world as a member of the community, while other travelers seek out short-term jobs to finance the next leg of their travels. **Craigslist** (www.craigslist.org) and the classifieds section of any local newspaper will yield dozens of job listings. For those looking for short- or long-term work, temp agencies (try www.adecco.com or www.officeteam.com) can be the ticket to a quick paycheck. Temp agencies require fluent English and a valid work visa (see box below).

VISA INFORMATION

All foreign visitors are required to have a **visa** if they intend to work in the US. In addition, travelers must provide proof of intent to leave, such as a return plane ticket or an I-94 card. A **work permit** (or "green card") is also required. Your employer must obtain this document, usually by demonstrating that you have skills that locals lack. Friends in the US can sometimes help expedite work permits or arrange work-for-accommodations exchanges. To obtain both visas and work permits, contact a US embassy or consulate (see **Embassies and Consulates,** p. 25). Visa extensions are sometimes attainable with a completed I-539 form; call the Bureau of Citizenship and Immigration Service's (BCIS) forms request line (☎800-870-3676) or get it online at www.immigration.gov/graphics/formsfee/forms/i-539.htm. Recent security measures have made the visa application process more rigorous, and therefore lengthier. **Apply well in advance of your travel date.** The process may seem complex, but it's unlikely you'll be hired without the proper permit.

LONG-TERM WORK

If you're planning on spending a substantial amount of time (more than three months) working in California, search for a job well in advance. International placement agencies are often the easiest way to find employment in the US, especially for service jobs. **Internships,** usually for college students, are a good way to segue into working abroad, though they are often unpaid or poorly paid (many say the experience, however, is well worth it). If you want to work in the movie industry, unpaid internships are practically a prerequisite for paid work. Networking (talking to people you know) and the Internet are the best ways to find jobs and internships in Hollywood. To find a job fetching coffee for an industry big-wig, see www.entertainmentcareers.net or www.mandy.com. Be wary of advertisements or companies that claim the ability to get you a job abroad for a fee—often the same listings are available online or in newspapers, or are even out-of-date.

Council Exchanges, 52 Poland St., London W1F 7AB, UK (☎44 020 7478 2000, in the US 617-247-0350; www.councilexchanges.org), charges a US$400-500 fee for arranging short-term work authorizations (generally valid for 3-6 months) and provides extensive information on different job and internship opportunities in California and the US.

Alliances Abroad, 1221 S. Mopac Expressway, Austin, TX 78746, USA (☎888-622-7623; www.alliancesabroad.com) runs a Seasonal Work in the USA program on the H2-B work visa that runs up to 10 months, or a Work & Travel in the USA program on the J-1 visa that arranges employment for students on their summer vacations.

Camp Counselors USA, 570 Eglington Ave. West, Ste. 303, Toronto, ON, M5N 1B7, Canada (☎877-777-7738; www.ccusa.com/HOME), places people aged 18-30 as counselors in summer camps across the US. Also has a work experience placement program.

Association for International Practical Training (AIPT), 10400 Little Patuxent Pkwy. Ste. 250, Columbia, MD 21044-3519, USA (☎410-997-2200; www.aipt.org). The AIPT Experience USA program welcomes students from outside the US during their summer vacations. For up to 4 months, the student will work or train at his or her place of employment while having the freedom to explore the city or country. The organization sponsors a student's J-1 visa application and matches him or her with an American employer. US$50 application fee. Program $800. For internship opportunities in technical fields, **IAESTE** (www.iaeste.org) provides 8- to 12-week programs for college students who have completed 2 years of technical study. US$25 application fee.

AU PAIR WORK

Au pairs are typically women (although sometimes men), aged 18-27, who work as live-in nannies, caring for children and doing light housework in foreign countries in exchange for room, board, and a small spending allowance or stipend. Most former au pairs speak favorably of their experience. One perk of the job is that it allows you to really get to know the country without the high expenses of traveling. Drawbacks, however, often include long hours of constantly being on duty and somewhat mediocre pay. In California, weekly salaries typically fall slightly below $150, with about 45 hours of work expected. Much of the au pair experience depends on the family with whom you're placed. The agencies below are a good starting point for looking for employment as an au pair.

Au Pair in America, River Plaza, 9 W. Broad St., Stamford, CT 06902, USA (☎800-928-7247; www.aupairinamerica.com).

Childcare International, Ltd., Trafalgar House, Grenville Pl., London NW7 3SA, UK (☎44 020 8906-3116; www.childint.co.uk).

InterExchange, 161 Sixth Ave., New York, NY 10013, USA (☎212-924-0446; www.interexchange.org).

SHORT-TERM WORK

Traveling for long periods of time can get expensive; therefore, many travelers try their hand at odd jobs for a few weeks at a time to make some extra cash to carry them through another month or two of touring around. A common way to make some extra cash in California is picking fruit. Those who try agricultural labor should be prepared for a difficult, character-building experience. Go to the local Farm Labor Office for more information. Most agriculture in California is concentrated in the San Joaquin Valley, although regional farms abound up and down the coast as well. The high season for harvest extends from May to October. Another popular option is to work several hours a day at a hostel in exchange for free or discounted room and/or board. Most often, these short-term jobs are found by word of mouth, or simply by talking to the owner of a hostel or restaurant. Due to the high turnover in the tourism industry, many places are always eager for help. Temporary jobs can usually be found in bigger cities like L.A. and San Francisco. For something a bit more glamorous, head to Hollywood, where day-jobs as movie extras abound. *Let's Go* tries to list temporary jobs like these whenever possible; look in the Practical Information sections of larger cities. The organizations listed below offer short-term jobs in popular destinations.

Willing Workers on Organic Farms USA (WWOOF), 309 Cedar St., #5C, Santa Cruz, CA 95060 (☎831-425-3276; www.wwoofusa.org). Room and board at organic farms in California (and other parts of the US) in exchange for a half-day's work. Short or long-term positions available. $20 registration fee.

Concession Services Corporation at Yosemite National Park, P.O. Box 578, Yosemite National Park, CA 95389 (☎209-372-1236; www.yosemitepark.com). Hires part-time and permanent staff to work in the park.

Cenex Central Casting, 220 Flower St., Burbank, CA 91506 (☎818-562-2755; www.entertainmentpartners.com). L.A.'s largest and most reputable casting service places extras on movie sets. Travelers who have a sponsor not eligible to work. Most jobs pay $50-70 for a full day's work. $20 cash for photo fee.

FOR FURTHER READING ON ALTERNATIVES TO TOURISM

Alternatives to the Peace Corps: A Directory of Third World and US Volunteer Opportunities, by Joan Powell. Food First Books, 2000 (US$10).

How to Live Your Dream of Volunteering Overseas, by Collins, DeZerega, and Heckscher. Penguin Books, 2002 (US$17).

International Directory of Voluntary Work, by Whetter and Pybus. Peterson's Guides and Vacation Work, 2000 (US$16).

International Jobs, by Kocher and Segal. Perseus Books, 1999 (US$18).

Overseas Summer Jobs 2003, by Collier and Woodworth. Peterson's Guides and Vacation Work, 2002 (US$18).

Work Abroad: The Complete Guide to Finding a Job Overseas, by Hubbs, Griffith, and Nolting. Transitions Abroad Publishing, 2000 ($16).

Work Your Way Around the World, by Susan Griffith. Worldview Publishing Services, 2001 (US$18).

Invest Yourself: The Catalogue of Volunteer Opportunities, published by the Commission on Voluntary Service and Action (☎718-638-8487).

GOPHER TO THE STARS

One of the few benefits of the egomania that runs rampant in the entertainment industry is an abundance of opportunities for those willing to suffer long hours, low wages, or occasional humiliation. Entertainment types just love their slave labor—as long as it's not associated with their celebrity clothing lines. As a result, there are a ton of openings for interns in and around L.A., perfect if you want to learn more about the entertainment industry or just need a reason to spend a few months in the So Cal sunshine.

I worked one summer as an intern for a screenwriter-turned-director, lured to the area primarily by a strong desire to spend a summer on the beach. I got my wish: our office was small—just me, my boss, and my boss's assistant—and located on a surreal and lovely bit of Malibu coastline. On a typical day, my boss would spend a few hours writing, a few hours talking on the phone, and a few hours negotiating traffic on his way to and from meetings at posh eateries about town. His assistant arranged such outings, all the while deflecting and directing dozens of phone calls a day. When things got slow, the two of them would grab their surfboards and catch a few waves behind the house.

Most of my work consisted of gopher duty. I spent the majority of my time in my car, a cell phone in one hand and a Thomas Map Guide in the other. When my boss needed a present for a colleague or a book from a library in East L.A., I was the go-to girl. I drove up the coast for gourmet coffee beans and to the Pacific Palisades for low-fat organic milk. I kept the kitchen stocked with the basics: Fresca, Kashi, and—perhaps most importantly—Frosty Paws' ice cream for dogs. I spent a lot of time at Kinko's, the post office, and the dry cleaner.

My life in L.A. may not have been the stuff of *A Star Is Born* fantasy, but it did give me the chance to get thoroughly acquainted with the city. Granted, I didn't have to travel much farther than Santa Monica for most of my errands, and the Beverly Center was practically at the edge of my usual territory. But by the end of the summer I managed to visit—and, more often than not, get lost—everywhere from Irvine to the Valley. Not only did I have L.A. traffic patterns down cold, but I had

also managed to discover countless hole-in-the-wall eateries, rare booksellers, and eclectic clothing stores that I might never have known about otherwise.

I also started to get a feel for the ins and outs of industry life. I was able to sit in on brainstorming sessions, make suggestions on script drafts, and attend screenings with technical professionals. All in all, I was involved with three major projects, each in different stages of development. I didn't lend any creative input—nor should any intern expect to, unless they want a sharp reprimand or some time in the hole—but I was expected to pay attention, share my opinions when asked, and occasionally serve as a human thesaurus. It provided an ideal opportunity to learn about the workings of Hollywood in a low-stress, low-risk environment.

And even if the day-to-day aspects of the job were fairly mundane, there were a number of glamorous incidents to keep things interesting. From time to time I would drive onto a studio lot to deliver a package; once my boss arranged for me to visit the set of a big-budget film and meet with the art director and production designer. I fielded the occasional celebrity phone call: I distinctly remember my shock when a barely pubescent voice at the end of the line turned out to be Ron Howard. And my boss was also given to periodic moments of obscene generosity. I was once handed a hundred dollars after returning unscathed from a errand that took me through a nightmarish jam on I-405. Another day my co-worker and I found that our boss had left each of us ten CDs, which he had just picked up while browsing at Amoeba records.

The rewards—both financial and intellectual—of life as a Hollywood gopher are intermittent at best. But if you're interested in the industry and willing to swallow most of your pride, it's a great way to gain some experience. You can also leverage your time as an intern to get a permanent position somewhere in town—particularly if you have access to your office Rolodex. But even for those with less ambitious aspirations, interning allows you to experience L.A., get to know its streets and stores, and hear the latest celebrity gossip.

Elizabeth Little was a researcher-writer for Let's Go China 3rd Ed. *and the editor of* Let's Go China 4th Ed. *She now works in New York City for the Trident Media Group.*

SAN FRANCISCO

If California is a state of mind, San Francisco is euphoria. This city will take you to new highs, leaving your mind spinning, your taste buds tingling, and your calves aching. Though it's smaller than most "big" cities, the City by the Bay more than compensates for its size with personality that simply won't quit. The dazzling views, daunting hills, one-of-a-kind neighborhoods, and laid-back, friendly people have a unique charisma not found anywhere else. The city packs an incredible amount of vitality into its 47 square miles of thriving art communities, bustling shops, and wild nightlife.

San Francisco's history of eccentrics and troublemakers resonates more strongly today in its street culture than in its museums and galleries. The lineage of free spirits and outlaws dates back to the 19th-century smugglers and pirates of the Barbary Coast and the 49ers who flocked here during the madness of the California Gold Rush. As the last stop in America's voracious westward expansion, San Francisco has always attracted artists, dreamers, and outsiders. With the 1950s came the Beats—brilliant young writers who captured the rhythms of be-bop jazz in their freewheeling poetry of discontent. The late 60s ushered in the most famous of San Francisco's rabble-rousers—hippies and flower children, who lounged on the city's lawns making love, not war.

The tradition of subversion persists. Anti-establishment politics have become establishment here as rallies and movements continue to fill the streets and newspapers. The queer community became undeniably visible in the 70s as one of the city's most vocal and powerful groups. In addition, Mexican, Central American, and Asian immigrants have made San Francisco one of the most racially diverse cities in the US. In a wave of mid-90s, computer-crazed prosperity, young techies ditched the bland suburbs of Silicon Valley for the cooler breezes of San Francisco, and upstart Internet companies infiltrated the forgotten spaces of lower-rent neighborhoods. For a while, the SF fight was old-timers and hippies vs. dot-commers, but when the Clinton-era national surplus went the way of the dodo, high-end yuppification collapsed, leaving neighborhoods to reassess their futures. San Francisco is changing with the times but some things stay the same: the Bay will always be foggy, the hills always steep, and the tourists always the only ones wearing shorts. For more extensive coverage, see ▧*Let's Go: San Francisco*.

HIGHLIGHTS OF SAN FRANCISCO

GOLDEN GATE BRIDGE. Yes, it's totally cliché, but it's also beautiful—particularly when viewed from the Presidio (p. 114).

SBC PARK. The bleacher seats at SBC Park come with fabulous views of the game, the city, and the bay. Right-field homers make a splash in the sparkling Bay (p. 126).

MISSION MURALS. This urban art form brilliantly combines technical perfection and community politics. Standouts include Mona Caron's Market St. Mural, Balmy Alley, and a three-building tribute to guitar god Carlos Santana (p. 110).

TWIN PEAKS. The view to end all views; this mountaintop vantage point is perhaps the best way to say hello and goodbye to SF in all its hilly, sunlit glory (p. 111).

 AREA CODE. The area code in San Francisco is **415**.

⚑ INTERCITY TRANSPORTATION

BY PLANE. Busy **San Francisco International Airport** (**SFO**; ☎650-821-8211) is 15 mi. south of downtown by U.S. 101. Plan your transportation from the airport by calling the SFO Travelers Aid (☎650-821-2732; open daily 9am-9pm) or **511** (☎817-1717; www.511.org) the all-purpose Bay Area public transportation, bicycling, and traffic guide or by accessing the ground transport section of www.flysfo.com, which includes links to the web pages of all public transportation services as well as a driving route planner. **Information booths,** located on the arrival levels of all terminals and in the international departures terminal, offer detailed fare and schedule info. **Travelers' Aid Society** booths can be found on the departure levels of all terminals. (Both open daily 9am-9pm.)

The **Bay Area Rapid Transit (BART)** system, which runs throughout the city and connects to other Bay Area destinations, now offers **the most convenient, direct service public transportation** from SFO to downtown ($5). Four BART stops in San Francisco connect to the **San Francisco Municipal Railway (MUNI),** San Francisco's public transportation system. Many **van services** leave from the airport and for $14-17 per person will take you directly to your lodging. For those with heavy luggage, door-to-door commercial **shuttles** are the most convenient way of leaving SFO. Most shuttles circulate at the airport around the lower level central island outside the baggage claim and do not require reservations (reservations recommended for arrivals after 11pm). For a complete list of companies, ask at the SFO Info Booth or check under "ground transport" on www.flysfo.com. **Taxis** to downtown from SFO depart from the lower level central island outside the baggage claim area (about $37). Check free area guides for coupons.

BY FREEWAY. If you are driving into San Francisco **from the south,** approach the city directly on **U.S. 101, I-280,** or **Route 1.** I-280 crosses U.S. 101 in south San Francisco and then continues through eastern Potrero Hill to end just southeast of SoMa. U.S. 101 runs along the border of Potrero Hill and the Mission, then bears left through SoMa and becomes **Van Ness Avenue.** Hwy. 1 turns into **19th Avenue** around San Francisco State University and runs through Sunset, Golden Gate Park, Richmond, and the Presidio.

From the north, U.S. 101 and Hwy. 1 lead over the **Golden Gate Bridge** (southbound-only toll $5). Hwy. 1 eventually turns into **19th Avenue** after running through the Presidio, the Richmond district, and Golden Gate Park, while U.S. 101 turns into **Lombard Street** in the Marina and connects to Van Ness Ave. Going south on Van Ness Ave. takes you to Market St., the main street downtown.

From the east, take **I-5** to **I-580** to **I-80,** which runs across the **Bay Bridge** (westbound-only toll $3) into SoMa and then connects with U.S. 101 just before it runs into Van Ness Ave.

BY REGIONAL PUBLIC TRANSPORTATION. All regional buses operate from the **Transbay Terminal,** 425 Mission St., at 1st St. An information center on the second floor has maps and free phone lines for bus information. (☎495-1569. Open daily 4:30am-12:30am.) **Golden Gate Transit** provides regional fixed-route bus service in San Francisco, Marin, and Sonoma Counties. Limited service is also available between Central Marin and Western Contra Costa Counties. (☎923-2000; www.goldengatetransit.org. Runs M-F 6am-10pm, Sa-Su reduced service; $1.85-6.55 depending on distance; discounts for seniors, disabled, and youth.) **Alameda County (AC) Transit** operates bus service to and in Oakland and Berkeley. (☎800-448-9790; www.actransit.org. $1.25-3.50; discounts for seniors, disabled, and youth.) **San Mateo Transit (SamTrans)** serves the peninsula with hundreds of trips along the Bayshore corridor between Palo Alto and downtown San Francisco. Additional frequent SF service is provided along El Camino Real and Mission St.

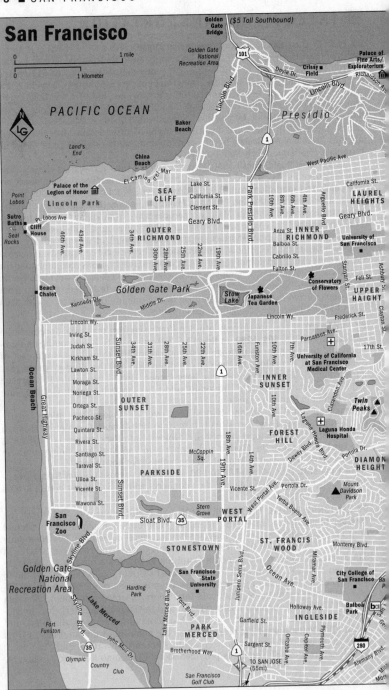

San Francisco

PACIFIC OCEAN

Golden Gate Bridge
($5 Toll Southbound)

Golden Gate National Recreation Area

Crissy Field

Palace of Fine Arts/ Exploratorium

Presidio

Doyle Dr.

Richardson Ave.

Lincoln Blvd.

West Pacific Ave.

Baker Beach

China Beach

Land's End

El Camino del Mar

Lake St.

California St.

California St.

SEA CLIFF

Clement St.

LAUREL HEIGHTS

Geary Blvd.

Geary Blvd.

Palace of the Legion of Honor

Point Lobos

Lincoln Park

Pt. Lobos Ave.

Sutro Baths

Cliff House

Seal Rocks

46th Ave.

43rd Ave.

34th Ave.

OUTER RICHMOND

30th Ave.

28th Ave.

25th Ave.

22nd Ave.

19th Ave.

Anza St.

Balboa St.

INNER RICHMOND

Cabrillo St.

Fulton St.

University of San Francisco

10th Ave.

8th Ave.

6th Ave.

4th Ave.

Arguello Blvd.

Stanyan St.

Fell St.

Asbury St.

Clayton St.

Conservatory of Flowers

UPPER HAIGHT

Beach Chalet

Golden Gate Park

Stow Lake

Japanese Tea Garden

Kennedy Dr.

Middle Dr.

Lincoln Wy.

Frederick St.

Lincoln Wy.

17th St.

Irving St.

Judah St.

Kirkham St.

Lawton St.

Moraga St.

Noriega St.

Ortega St.

Pacheco St.

Quintara St.

Rivera St.

Santiago St.

Taraval St.

Ulloa St.

Vicente St.

Wawona St.

Sunset Blvd.

34th Ave.

31th Ave.

28th Ave.

25th Ave.

22th Ave.

16th Ave.

Funston Ave.

10th Ave.

7th Ave.

Parnassus Ave.

University of California at San Francisco Medical Center

OUTER SUNSET

INNER SUNSET

10th Ave.

Twin Peaks

Laguna Honda Hospital

FOREST HILL

18th Ave.

14th Ave.

Dewey Blvd.

Laguna Honda Blvd.

Portola Dr.

DIAMON HEIGHT

McCoppin Sq.

PARKSIDE

19th Ave.

Vicente St.

West Portal Ave.

Portola Dr.

Mount Davidson Park

Stern Grove

WEST PORTAL

Yerba Buena Ave.

San Francisco Zoo

Skyline Blvd.

Sloat Blvd. 35

STONESTOWN

ST. FRANCIS WOOD

Monterey Blvd.

Golden Gate National Recreation Area

Harding Park

San Francisco State University

Junipero Serra Blvd.

Ocean Ave.

Miramar Ave.

City College of San Francisco

Ba

Lake Merced

Lake Merced Blvd.

Font Blvd.

Holloway Ave.

INGLESIDE

Plymouth Ave.

Capitol Ave.

Balboa Park

ba

Fort Funston

Skyline Blvd.

PARK MERCED

Garfield St.

Ortaza Ave.

280

Olympic Country Club

35

John Muir Dr.

Sargent St.

Brotherhood Way

1

TO SAN JOSE (55mi)

Alemany Ave.

San Francisco Golf Club

Ocean Beach

Great Highway

Ocean Beach

Park Presidio Blvd.

Lincoln Blvd.

0 ___ 1 mile

0 ___ 1 kilometer

N LG

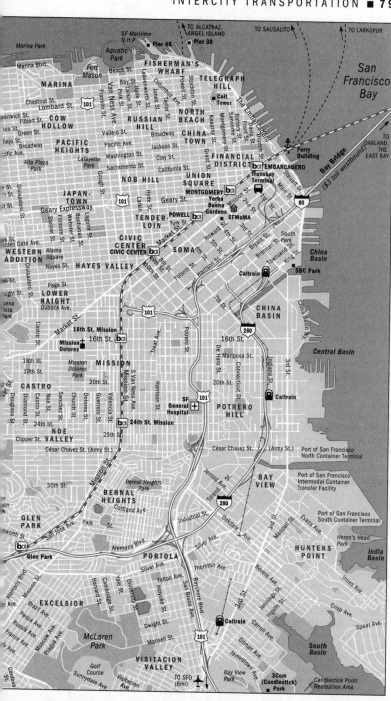

Hundreds of other daily trips serve SFO, Daly City, Hayward, and 20 other cities in the county. (☎800-660-4287 or 650-508-6200; www.samtrans.com. Most routes daily 6am-6pm. $1.25-3.50; discounts for seniors and youth.)

BART is the easiest and speediest way to travel in the Bay Area, with five lines connecting San Francisco with the **East Bay** (see p. 134), including Oakland, Berkeley, Richmond, Concord, and Fremont. All stations provide free maps and schedules and all stops are wheelchair-accessible. (☎989-2278; www.bart.gov. Runs M-F 4am-midnight, Sa 6am-midnight, Su 8am-midnight; times at individual stops may vary. Fare within San Francisco $1.25, to the East Bay up to $5.)

Caltrain (Bay Area ☎800-660-4287, elsewhere 510-817-1717; www.caltrain.com) leaves from the **Caltrain Depot** at 4th and King St. in SoMa and is easily accessible as the terminal of the MUNI N-Judah line (M-F 5am-midnight, Sa 7am-midnight, Su 8am-10pm). Caltrain runs to Palo Alto ($4.25, seniors and under 12 $2) and San Jose ($5.50/$2.75), making many stops along the way. Fares are calculated on the basis of zones and monthly passes are available. Be sure to check ahead as service is somewhat unreliable due to construction.

❉ ORIENTATION

San Francisco is 403 mi. north of L.A. and 390 mi. south of the Oregon border. The city proper lies at the northern tip of the peninsula separating the San Francisco Bay from the Pacific Ocean. (For info on other cities surrounding the bay, see **Bay Area and Wine Country,** p. 134.) San Francisco's diverse neighborhoods are loosely organized along a few central arteries. **Market Street** runs on a diagonal from the Ferry Building through downtown and all the way to the Castro. Most neighborhoods are compact enough to explore comfortably on foot. Check the topographical map in the front of this book and note the steep hills in each district—a two-block detour can sometimes prevent a strenuous climb.

SAN FRANCISCO NEIGHBORHOODS

The following descriptions and the listings of sights and restaurants spiral through the city, beginning in the downtown area. Popular tourist districts, such as North Beach and Chinatown, give way to local favorites SoMa, the Mission, the Castro, and Haight-Ashbury. The waterfront parks, Fisherman's Wharf, and the islands in the bay finish the trip. If you find that neighborhood boundaries get confusing, don't stress—San Francisco, like any living, breathing city, doesn't follow the imaginary lines that books like this must rely on. However, a good map is a must.

UNION SQUARE. Union Square balances big-name retail stores with an unyielding abundance of art galleries; the clothes and the art range from casual to positively swank. As the heart of San Francisco's **theater district,** the area has plenty to offer budget travelers: affordable accommodations, hip cafes, nightlife venues, and—of course—window **shopping.**

CHINATOWN. With over 100,000 residents, Chinatown is not only the most densely populated of San Francisco's neighborhoods, but also the largest Chinese community outside of Asia. Chinese laborers began coming to San Francisco in the mid-19th century as refugees from the Opium Wars and were immediately put to work constructing the railroads. In the 1880s, Californians secured a law against further Chinese immigration to prevent the so-called "Yellow Peril." Stranded in San Francisco, Chinese-Americans banded together to protect themselves in this small section of downtown. To this day, Chinatown remains mostly Chinese, though it has attracted visitors since the 1850s, when sailors staggered down from Barbary Coast saloons looking for women, alcohol, and opium. Today, tourists descend from cable cars looking for porcelain dolls and **dim sum.**

NORTH BEACH. On Columbus Ave. at Broadway, shops shift from selling ginseng and roast duck to selling provolone and biscotti. The legendary **Italian** community of North Beach, also the birthplace of the **Beat movement,** lies north of Chinatown. In the early 1950s, a group of beatnik poets and writers, including Jack Kerouac, Allen Ginsberg, and Lawrence Ferlinghetti, came to North Beach to write, drink, and raise hell. They lashed out at the conformity of postwar America, embraced Eastern religions and be-bop jazz, and lit a fuse that would eventually set off the counterculture explosion of the late 1960s. Today, crowds flock to the dozens of Italian restaurants and cafes around Columbus Ave., named after operas and Italian provinces, before moving on to the cozy Beat-inspired bars and hot live music venues around Broadway and Kearny St.

THE FINANCIAL DISTRICT AND THE EMBARCADERO. Although much of modern-day Bay Area business may be conducted online, the city still has its share of pressed suits and corner offices. Corporate worker bees swarm the Financial District, where towering banks blot out the cheerful sun. A surprising number of parks and architectural standouts add character to the area.

CIVIC CENTER. There's no mistaking the colossal Civic Center, with its mammoth classical buildings arranged around two vast plazas. Home to the opera, symphony, and professional theater, the district is grandest at night, when beautifully lit flags and fountains flank bumper-to-bumper limousine traffic.

THE TENDERLOIN. The indistinctly defined region known as the Tenderloin is economic light years away from its neighbors, Union Square and Civic Center. Sporadic attempts at urban renewal have done a (small) bit to improve the poverty of the quarter and its residents. Nevertheless, **avoid walking here alone,** especially in the rectangle bordered by Ellis St., Van Ness Ave., Leavenworth St., and Golden Gate Ave., and at night.

HAYES VALLEY. To the west of the Civic Center, recently gentrified Hayes Valley is small, glitzy, and increasingly upscale. Currently home to young **artists** and designers, the neighborhood has not always boasted such a swinging scene. Destruction caused by the 1989 earthquake led to a drastic makeover, and the rough-and-tumble district has become San Francisco's latest beauty queen.

NOB HILL AND RUSSIAN HILL. In the late 19th century, Nob Hill attracted the West's great railroad magnates and robber barons. Today, their showy mansions remain, some on **Lombard Street,** the crookedest street in the world. Russian Hill, to the north, is named after Russian sailors who died during an expedition in the early 1800s and were buried on the southeast crest.

PACIFIC HEIGHTS AND COW HOLLOW. Flanked on the east by Nob Hill and Russian Hill and on the west by the Presidio, Pacific Heights and Cow Hollow supplement hoity-toity residential areas with budding commercial areas. Stunning views of both the city and the Bay and elegantly restored **Victorian homes** put Pacific Heights on the map. Just to the north, the neighborhood of Cow Hollow houses herds of San Francisco's elite. Along Fillmore St. and Union St, there are a fair number of vintage shops, boutiques, and worthwhile eateries that make Pacific Heights and Cow Hollow up-and-coming hot spots for the upwardly mobile.

JAPANTOWN (NIHONMACHI). After the neighborhood was destroyed by the 1906 earthquake, Japanese immigrants moved into the area now called Japantown, just south of Pacific Heights and a mile west of downtown. For a time, its closely packed homes and shops constituted one of the largest Japanese enclaves outside Japan. Few returned after the community was broken apart by internment during WWII, but the name stuck.

SOUTH OF MARKET AREA (SOMA). The most visited, culturally vibrant part of SoMa lies north of Folsom St., between 2nd and 4th St. These blocks overwhelm passersby with the concrete and glass expanses of **Yerba Buena Gardens,** Sony Metreon, and the Moscone Convention Center. A joyous Keith Haring sculpture gestures toward the **San Francisco Museum of Modern Art (SFMoMA),** which presides over the cultural milieu. Several blocks south, between **SBC Park** (home of the San Francisco Giants; see p. 126) and the freeway, travelers and locals brave the "cyberspace gulch" of upstart Internet and design companies in search of hidden but worthwhile eateries. The stretch from 7th to 12th St. along Folsom St. as you head toward the Mission is known for hip cafes, inexpensive restaurants, legendary clubs, and several establishments dedicated to the leather scene.

THE MISSION. One of SF's hippest neighborhoods, the Mission houses some of the city's oldest structures and pulses with vibrant Latino and artistic communities. Colorful **murals** celebrate the prominent Latino presence that has long defined the area. West of Mission St., especially along Valencia and Guerrero St., you begin to see evidence of a bohemian subculture that has entrenched itself almost as firmly as the Latino community. Hip new cafes, bars, and shops disappear almost as quickly as they emerge, giving the Mission a sense of both freshness and volatility. Politically, the Mission is the city's most radical pocket, marked by left-wing bookstores, active labor associations, and vegan cafes. Maintaining a cultural precedent that has managed thus far to fend off commercial influx, the Mission richly rewards the traveler who enjoys it on its own terms.

THE CASTRO. Waving in the wind like a flamboyant sentinel, a huge rainbow flag greets locals and tourists to the Castro. Much of San Francisco's **gay** population, along with a smaller number of young lesbians, calls the Castro home. Cruisy bars and cafes are rivaled in quantity only by gyms and fitness centers. Same-sex public displays of affection raise nary an eyebrow, and tank tops and chiseled abs are a dime a dozen. Having recently forfeited some of its fabulous edge to a more mainstream commercialism, the Castro nevertheless remains a sentimental home-we-never-had for the GLBT community.

NOE VALLEY, BERNAL HEIGHTS, AND POTRERO HILL. Although Noe Valley (south of the Castro), Bernal Heights (south of the Mission), and Potrero Hill (south of SoMa) feel like residential versions of their more famous neighbors, each offers some highlights to justify a brief visit on a free afternoon or evening. Noe Valley's worthwhile eateries, Bernal Heights's treasured **lesbian** bars, and Potrero Hill's burgeoning artistic community promise to satisfy jaded city travelers in search of a more laid-back atmosphere. The more bustling areas and thoroughfares include 24th Street in Noe Valley, Cortland Avenue in Bernal Heights, and the area framed by 17th, 20th, Connecticut, and Texas St. in Potrero Hill.

THE HAIGHT. East of Golden Gate Park and smack dab in the center of the city, the Haight has aged with uneven grace since its hippie heyday. Once a haven for conscientious objectors to the Vietnam War, "Hashbury" embraced drug use and Eastern philosophies during anti-war protests and marches. The hippie voyage reached its apogee in 1967's **"Summer of Love,"** when Janis Joplin, the Grateful Dead, and Jefferson Airplane all made music and love here within a few blocks of one another. Today the counterculture hangs out with the over-the-counter tourist culture, especially in Upper Haight. The Lower Haight still clings to the good ol' days despite the recent additions of Internet cafes and smoothie joints.

GOLDEN GATE PARK. Golden Gate Park covers 1017 acres of lush greenery, thoughtfully conceived gardens, and recreational community spaces. Beginning in the 1870s, the city undertook decades of work to transform the desert-like region into a vibrant green expanse of undulating hills and peaceful cloisters. Today, nine lakes, a herd of bison, and two windmills are among the park's many attractions.

THE RICHMOND DISTRICT. Beneath its fog and blank facade of stuccoed buildings, the Richmond district is a riot of immigrant history and student life, home to many Irish-, Russian-, and Chinese-Americans. East of Park Presidio Blvd., the Inner Richmond, teeming with cut-price grocery stores and excellent ethnic cuisine, is known as **"New Chinatown."** The Outer Richmond holds a handful of Russian delis, an abundance of Irish pubs, and an imposing orthodox church.

LINCOLN PARK. Lincoln Park is positioned perfectly for snapping a shot of the Golden Gate Bridge and the bay. Rugged terrain for hiking and biking meets high culture at the **California Palace of the Legion of Honor.** The Sutro Baths offer a Californian version of ancient ruins.

GOLDEN GATE BRIDGE AND THE PRESIDIO. The great span of the Golden Gate Bridge stretches across the San Francisco Bay from Marin County to the Presidio. Originally the northernmost Spanish military garrison in California, the Presidio served first the Mexican and then the American army until the 1990s. Most of the buildings have been converted for civilian use, but the Presidio, covering 1500 acres, can still feel rather deserted. Its miles of paths and hills are wide open to the public and worth a visit. **Crissy Field,** in particular, is a newly restored and beautiful shoreline expanse that serves sunbathers, ballplayers, and nature lovers.

THE MARINA AND FORT MASON. The residential Marina, between Fort Mason to the east and the expansive Presidio to the west, is home to more young, wealthy professionals (and failed dot-commers) than any other part of San Francisco. Fort Mason provides a cultural counterbalance to the area, with theaters and museums. Directly across the lengthy Marina Green near the Presidio stands the breathtaking **Palace of Fine Arts** and the fun-for-kids-of-all-ages **Exploratorium.** On the southern border of the Marina, bustling Chestnut and Lombard St. are packed with motels, eateries, and trendy bars.

FISHERMAN'S WHARF AND THE PIERS. The eastern portion of San Francisco's waterfront is one of its most visited—and most reviled—tourist destinations. Aside from the while-you-wait caricature artists, "olde-fashioned fudge shoppes," penny-flattening machines, and novelty t-shirts, on **Piers 39-45,** the only natives you're likely to find here are the sea lions.

ALCATRAZ AND ANGEL ISLAND. Although the one on Alcatraz is by far the better known, both Alcatraz and Angel Island once housed prisons. Because of its location in the middle of the Bay, Alcatraz was thought to be inescapable and was used to house the nation's hardest criminals. Angel Island was used in the late 19th century as a detention center for Chinese immigrants and then as a WWII POW camp. Today, its shores and trails are surprisingly perfect for picnicking and hiking.

⊑ LOCAL TRANSPORTATION

BY PUBLIC TRANSPORTATION. San Francisco's main public transportation systems are the **MUNI Metro subway** and **bus system,** which operate throughout the city, and **Bay Area Rapid Transit (BART),** which provides wider coverage of the Bay Area and speedy but limited service in San Francisco. Each system is described below and has its own infrastructure, but are all overseen by the **Metropolitan Transportation Commission** (☎ 510-464-7700; www.transitinfo.org), which provides transit information for the nine-county San Francisco Bay Area.

A decent public transit system makes San Francisco something of an anomaly in California; the Bay Area is the easiest place on the West Coast to explore without a car. The system (particularly the Metro system) may be slower and less developed than its counterparts on the East Coast, but the city is so walkable that a combination of foot and MUNI are perfectly adequate for getting around.

Most transportation within the city falls under the authority of the **San Francisco Municipal Railway** (**MUNI;** pronounced MEW-nee; ☎ 673-6864; www.sfmuni.com)—something of a misnomer since the system includes **buses** (electric trolley and diesel), **cable cars** (the only ones in the world still operating), a **subway,** and **streetcars.** The MUNI Metro system, whose cars alternate between subway (below ground) and surface-rail (above ground) transportation at various points in the city, offers more limited but speedier service than the MUNI bus system. Downtown, all six Metro lines (F, J, N, L, M, and K) travel underground along the central artery of **Market Street.** With the exception of the F line, they all run from the **Embarcadero Station** to at least the **Van Ness Station.** As they travel "outbound" (away from the Ferry Terminal and the Embarcadero), they all stop at the **Embarcadero, Montgomery, Powell, Civic Center, and Van Ness stations;** if you're just traveling along this short downtown stretch, it doesn't matter which car you catch. If you're heading west of Van Ness station, however, take care to snag the appropriate car before the lines split. The **J** and **N** emerge from the tunnel at **Church Street** at Duboce St., while the **K, L,** and **M** routes continue underground past **Castro Street** and emerge above ground at the **West Portal Station.** The **F** line runs antique streetcars along Market St., from Castro St. Station to the Embarcadero Station and connects to Fisherman's Wharf via the Northern Waterfront/Embarcadero.

Single-ride fares on MUNI buses, streetcars, and the subway cost $1.25 (seniors and ages 5-17 $0.35, under 5 free); you must take a **free transfer** as **proof of payment** (valid for travel on any MUNI vehicle except cable cars within a 90min. period). Single-ride fares on the cable cars are pricier ($3, seniors and disabled $3, under 6 free; before 7am and after 9pm $1), with no transfers. **MUNI passports,** sold at the Powell St. Visitors Center and at some accommodations, are valid on all MUNI vehicles including cable cars (1-day $9, 3-day $15, 7-day $20). The **Weekly Pass** is cheaper ($12) but must be purchased for a single work week (M-Su) and cable cars cost $1 extra. The **Monthly FastPass** ($45; seniors, disabled, and ages 5-17 $10) includes in-town BART trips (from Embarcadero to Balboa Park) and cable cars.

Cable cars are a classic icon of San Francisco. Declared a national historic landmark in 1964, the colorful trolleys are about image, not practicality. They are noisy, slow (9½ mph), expensive, and usually crammed, making them an unreliable method of getting around. You won't be the first person to think of taking one to Fisherman's Wharf. Still, there is something charming about these relics, and they're worth riding, especially if you have a MUNI passport. To avoid the mobs, get up early and climb the hills with the sunrise, or you can also catch a cable car at one of its stops along the uphill route. All lines run daily from 6am to 1:30am. There are three lines from which to choose: Powell-Mason (PM), California Street (C), and Powell-Hyde (PH). The Powell lines, which board at Powell and Market St., are popular for their views of the Bay.

BY FERRY. Golden Gate Ferry (☎ 923-2000; www.goldengateferry.org) sails across the Bay to Marin County from the **Ferry Building** at the foot of Market St., east of Pier 1. ($6.15, seniors $3.05, ages 6-12 $4.60.) Ferries serve **Larkspur** (M-F 20 per day; first ferry leaves SF 6:30am, last ferry leaves Larkspur 8:50pm; Sa-Su and holidays 5 per day; first ferry leaves SF 12:30am, last ferry leaves Larkspur 5:30pm) and **Sausalito** (M-F 9 per day, first ferry leaves SF 7:40am, last ferry leaves Sausalito 7:20pm; Sa-Su 7 per day; first ferry leaves SF 10:40am, last ferry leaves Sausalito 6:20pm). Both lines are wheelchair accessible. Transfers are free between bus routes and ferries.

The **Blue and Gold Fleet** (☎705-8200, tickets ☎705-5555; www.blueandgold-fleet.com) runs to **Alcatraz** (14 per day; $11.50 round-trip, seniors $9.75, ages 5-11 $8.25; audio tour $4.50, children $2.50.) and **Angel Island** (M-F 4 per day, Sa-Su 3 per day; round-trip $13, ages 6-12 $7.50, under 6 free) and between SF and Tiburon, Vallejo, Alameda, and Oakland. The Blue and Gold also offers an Island Hop to Alcatraz and Angel Island (June-Sept. daily; May 22-30 Sa-Su only; $41.50, seniors $38.75, ages 5-11 $26.75, under 5 free; includes audio tour on Alcatraz and Tram-Tour on Angel Island). The **Harbor Bay Ferry** (☎510-769-5500; www.harborbay-ferry.com) goes between SF and Alameda. The **Red and White Ferry** (☎673-2900; www.redandwhite.com) offers cruise tours of the Bay. The **Baylink Ferry** (☎877-643-3779; www.baylinkferry.com) services SF to Vallejo. All ferries leave the **Ferry Building** near the Embarcadero.

BY BIKE. Though even the hardiest bike couriers have been spotted walking their bikes, San Francisco is a great city to traverse by bike or in-line skates despite the steep, punishing hills. Check out our color topographical map of downtown in the front of this book to plan a flatter route. Most modes of public transportation in the Bay Area accommodate bicycles. When riding on roads also used by cable cars and trains, beware of getting your tires stuck in the grooves.

The Department of Parking and Traffic runs the **SF Bicycle Program** (**SFBP**; ☎585-2453; www.bicycle.sfgov.org), which organizes numbered **bike routes** around the city. Rectangular **signs** showing a silhouetted bike and the Golden Gate Bridge mark the routes. Odd numbers on the signs refer to north-south routes, with the numbers increasing from north to south; even numbers refer to east-west routes, with the numbers increasing from east to west; three-digit numbers refer to loops and spurs. Green signs are local routes, while signs with a Golden Gate Bridge icon indicate crosstown routes. These bike paths may run apart from motor vehicle traffic, alongside traffic in the street in a marked bike lane, or with traffic on a street with a wide-curb lane. The SFBP hotline has info on bike lockers, MUNI racks, and safety resources. The non-profit **SF Bicycle Coalition** (☎431-2453; www.sfbike.org) promotes bike use, advocates for transit improvement, and gets members bike shop discounts.

BY TAXI. Taxis can be hailed on the street in San Francisco, but if you need a cab in a certain place at a certain time, it's often a good idea to call in advance. **San Francisco's Yellow Cab** (☎626-2345), **National Cab Company** (☎648-6444), and **Town Taxi** (☎285-3800) are a few of the local taxi companies.

BY CAR. A car is not necessary for getting around the city and may be more trouble than it's worth, unless you would like the convenience of your own wheels on a daytrip. Contending with the treacherous **hills** is the first task; if you've arrived in a standard (manual) transmission vehicle, you'll need to develop a fast clutch foot, since all hills have stop signs at the crests. If you're renting, get an automatic transmission. Make sure to stop for cable cars because they won't stop for you. **Seat belts** in cars and **helmets** on motorcycles and mopeds are required by law.

Parking in San Francisco is rare and expensive even where legal, and a network of zealous traffic cops doles out tickets despite local protests against the city's rigorous regulations. The many broken parking meters indicate an irate citizenry, but the time limit still applies to such spaces, and you may be ticketed up to three times for a single offense. Whatever you do, don't block a sidewalk disabled-access ramp—the ticket is a whopping $250. You can stow your car all day in the Richmond district or the Sunset, south of Golden Gate Park—just make certain you heed signs indicating weekly street-cleaning times. To park near a popular area, your best bet may be a **parking garage.** Below is a list of car rental agencies.

City, 1748 Folsom St. (☎877-861-1312; www.cityrentacar.com), between Duboce and 14th St. Additional location: 1433 Bush St. (☎866-359-1331), between Van Ness Ave. and Polk St. Compacts from $32-40 per day, $170 per week. 21+. Under-25 surcharge $15 per day. Open M-F 7:30am-6pm, Sa 9am-4pm.

Budget, 321 Mason St. (☎292-8400 or 800-527-0700; www.budget.com), in Union Sq. Compacts from $30 per day. 25+. Open daily 7am-7pm.

Thrifty, 520 Mason St. (☎415-788-8111; www.thrifty.com), at Post St. Compacts around $35 per day. Unlimited mileage. 21+. Under-25 surcharge $25 per day. Open daily 7am-7pm.

 PREVENT RUNAWAYS. The street signs admonishing you to "Prevent Runaways" refer not to wayward youth but to cars parked on hills. When parking facing uphill, turn front wheels away from the curb, and, if driving a standard transmission, leave the car in first gear. If your car starts to roll, it will stop (hopefully) when the tires hit the curb. When facing downhill, turn the wheels toward the curb and leave the car in reverse. *Always* set the emergency brake.

▣ PRACTICAL INFORMATION

TOURIST AND FINANCIAL SERVICES

Visitor Information: Visitor Information Center (☎391-2000, 24hr. info recordings 391-2001; www.sfvisitor.org), in Hallidie Plaza, at Powell St. Open M-F 9am-5pm, Sa-Su 9am-3pm; Nov-June closed Su.

Consulates: Australia, 625 Market St., Ste. 200 (☎536-1970), at New Montgomery St. Open M-F 9am-5pm. **Ireland,** 100 Pine St., 33rd fl. (☎392-4214), at Front St. Open M-F 10am-noon and 2pm-3:30pm. **UK,** 1 Sansome St., #850 (☎617-1300; www.britainusa.com), at Market St. Open M-F 8:30am-5pm.

Currency Exchange: Available at the airport and most banks. **American Express,** 455 Market St. (☎536-2600; www.americanexpress.com), at 1st St. Open M-F 9am-5:30pm, Sa 10am-2pm. **Bank of America Foreign Currency Services,** 1 Powell St. (☎953-5102), at Eddy St., near Market St. Open M-F 9am-6pm, Sa 9am-2pm. **Associated Foreign Exchange,** 221 Sansome St. (☎677-5100), at Pine St. Open M-F 9am-5pm. **Travelex and Thomas Cook Currency Services,** 75 Geary St. (☎362-3452; www.travelex.com). Open M-F 9am-5pm, Sa 10am-4pm.

LOCAL SERVICES

San Francisco Public Library: Main Branch, 100 Larkin St. (☎557-4400; http://sfpl.lib.ca.us), at Grove St. Open M and Sa 10am-6pm, Tu-Th 9am-8pm, F noon-6pm, Su noon-5pm. Other branches: 300 Bartlett St. (☎355-2800), at 24th St. in the **Mission.** 1135 Powell St. (☎335-2888), near Jackson St. in **Chinatown.** 2000 Mason St. (☎274-0270), at Columbus St. in **North Beach.**

Ticket Agencies: Tickets.com (☎478-2277 or 800-225-2277). Open daily 6am-9pm. **TIX Bay Area** (☎433-7827; www.theatrebayarea.org), a kiosk on Powell St. between Geary and Post St. in **Union Square.** Tickets for almost all shows and concerts as well as info about city tours and MUNI passes. Half-price tickets often available on day of show and on Sa-Su for Su-M performances. Open Tu-Th 11am-6pm, F 11am-7pm, Sa 10am-7pm, Su 10am-3pm. Cash or traveler's checks only for half-price tickets.

Road Conditions: CalTrans, ☎800-427-7623 in California, elsewhere 916-445-7623. **511 Travel Guide,** ☎817-1717.

Laundromats: Brain Wash, 1122 Folsom St. (☎255-4866; www.brainwash.com), near 7th St. in **SoMa.** Combo cafe-laundromat (see p. 99). Wash $2.25, dry $0.25 per 6min. Dry cleaning. Open daily 7am-11pm; last wash 9:30pm. **Doo Wash,** 1859 Powell St. (☎885-1222), between Greenwich and Filbert St. in **North Beach.** No self-service. Wash, dry, fold $0.85 per lb. Open M and Th 7am-8pm, Tu-W and F-Su 7am-7pm.

Television: ABC Channel 7; **CBS** Channel 5; **Fox** Channel 2; **NBC** Channel 11; **PBS** Channel 9; **WB** Channel 20.

Radio: National Public Radio KQED 88.5 FM; KALW 91.7 FM.

EMERGENCY AND COMMUNICATIONS

Police: ☎553-0123. **Fire:** ☎558-3200. **Poison:** ☎800-876-4766.

Hotlines: AIDS Hotline, ☎863-2437. **Crisis Line for the Handicapped,** ☎800-426-4263. **Drug Crisis Line,** ☎362-3400. **Rape Crisis Center,** ☎647-7273. **Suicide Prevention,** ☎781-0500.

Medical Services: S.F. General Hospital, 1001 Potrero Ave. (☎206-8000) at 23rd St. in **Potrero Hill.** Emergency room open 24hr. **Haight-Ashbury Free Medical Clinic,** 558 Clayton St. (☎487-5632), at Haight St. Appointments only. Open M-Th 9am-9pm, F 1-5pm. **Lyon-Martin Women's Clinic,** 1748 Market St., #201 (☎565-7667), at Octavia St. Drop-ins Th 1-3pm. Open M-Tu and Th-F 8:30am-5pm, W 8:30am-7:30pm.

Internet Access: Most **public library** locations (see p. 86). A few of the cafes listed in our guide offer **free** wireless or DSL internet for patrons with a laptop, including **Morning Due Cafe** (see p. 100) and **The Butler and the Chef Cafe** (see p. 99). For a thorough list of free venues, check www.cheesebikini.com. Other locations offer desktop computers with internet service for a fee, try **Brain Wash Laundromat and Cafe** in **SoMa** (see p. 99) or **The Horseshoe Cafe** in the **Haight** (see p. 103).

Post Offices: 24hr. automated service, connects to local post offices: ☎800-275-8777. **Bernal Heights Station,** 30 29th St., at Mission St. Open M-F 8:30am-5pm. **Postal Code:** 94110. **Chinatown Station,** 867 Stockton St., at Clay St. Open M-F 9am-5:30pm, Sa 9am-4:30pm. **Postal Code:** 94108. **Civic Center:** Federal Building Station, 450 Golden Gate Ave., at Larkin St. Open M-F 8:30am-5pm. **Postal Code:** 94102. **Geary Station,** 5654 Geary Blvd., at 21st Ave. Open M-F 9am-5:30pm, Sa 9am-4:30pm. **Postal Code:** 94121. **Haight-Ashbury Station,** 554 Clayton St., at Haight St. Open M-F 9am-5:30pm, Sa 9am-4pm. **Postal Code:** 94117.

PUBLICATIONS

The largest Bay Area daily is the *San Francisco Chronicle* ($0.50; www.sfgate.com), run by executive editor Phil Bronstein and owned by the Hearst Corporation. The *San Francisco Examiner* (www.examiner.com), founded by yellow journalist William Randolph Hearst himself, has lunchtime and evening editions. The two papers share a Sunday edition ($1.50). The pink *Datebook* section of the Sunday edition is a worthwhile entertainment resource. Free publications flood San Francisco cafes, visitors centers, and sidewalk boxes, including the progressive *S. Bay Guardian* (www.sfbg.com) and its main competitor, *SF Weekly* (www.sfweekly.com). Harder to find, but worth the effort, are two special-interest rags: *Poetry Flash* (www.poetryflash.org), which has info on literary happenings in the Bay Area and beyond, available at discerning bookstores and the weekly *Bay Area Reporter*, which has articles on gay issues as well as an entertainment section. Various tourist-targeting, coupon-filled free glossies (*Bay City Guide*, *San Francisco Guide*, and *San Francisco Quick Guide*) are in sidewalk boxes at Fisherman's Wharf and Union Square, as well as at visitors centers.

SAN FRANCISCO

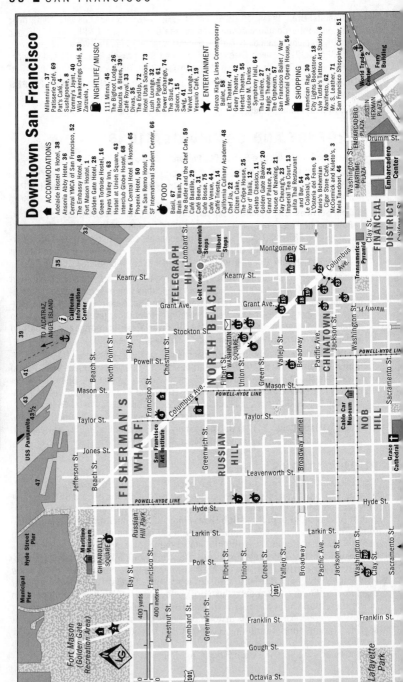

SAN FRANCISCO

⚑ ACCOMMODATIONS

For those who don't mind sharing a room with strangers, many San Francisco **hostels** (see below) are homier and cheaper than most budget **hotels** (see p. 91). Book in advance if at all possible, but since many don't take reservations for summer, you might have to just show up or call early (well before noon) on your day of arrival. Travelers with cars should also consider the **Marin Headlands Hostel,** a beautiful spot just minutes from the city across the Golden Gate Bridge (see p. 155). Some hostels ask for a foreign passport as identification; US citizens are usually welcome but sometimes must prove they are not local residents. None of the hostels listed here impose a curfew or chores. **B&Bs** (see p. 92) are often the most comfortable and friendly, albeit expensive, option.

HOSTELS

▨ **San Francisco International Guesthouse,** 2976 23rd St. (☎641-1411), in the **Mission.** No sign; look for the blue Victorian with yellow trim near the corner of Harrison St. With hardwood floors, wall tapestries, and comfortable common areas, this hostel feels like the well-designed (but totally clean) room of your tree-hugger college roommate. Caters primarily to international visitors; passport with international stamps "required." Free coffee and magazines. TV area, 2 kitchens, guest phones, and free Internet. 5-night min. stay. No reservations, but chronically filled to capacity. All you can do is try calling a few days ahead of time. Dorms $16; doubles $32. ❶

▨ **Adelaide Hostel and Hotel,** 5 Isadora Duncan (☎359-1915 or 877-359-1915; www.adelaidehostel.com), at the end of a little alley off Taylor St. between Geary and Post St. in **Union Square.** The bottom 2 floors, recently renovated with fresh paint and new furniture, entice a congenial international crowd, while the top 2 floors should be avoided until they undergo the same renovations. TV and wash basin in each room. Small, shared hallway bathrooms. Morning shuttle to SFO $8. Free safe deposit. Laundry (wash $1.50, dry $1.50). 4-day max. stay. Check-out 11am. Reserve online or by phone. Dorms $22; singles and doubles from $65. ❷

▨ **Green Tortoise Hostel,** 494 Broadway (☎834-1000; www.greentortoise.com), off Columbus Ave. at Kearny St. in **North Beach.** A ballroom preceded this super-mellow and friendly pad, allowing today's laid-back, fun-seeking young travelers to hang out amid abandoned finery in the spacious common room. Free sauna. Free Internet access. Open mic with free keg Tu. Breakfast and dinner (M,W,F) included. Storage lockers $1 per day; smaller free lockers under every bed. Safety deposit box $10. Laundry (wash $1.25, dry $0.75). Key deposit $20. 10-day max. stay. Reception 24hr. Check-in noon (recommended). Check-out 11am. Reservations recommended, especially for large groups. For walk-in availability, call at noon on your arrival day. 3-, 4-, 5- and 8-bed dorms $19-22; private rooms $48-60. No credit cards. ❷

Fort Mason Hostel (HI-AYH), Bldg. #240 (☎771-7277; sfhostel@norcalhostels.org), in **Fort Mason.** Once you enter the complex at the corner of Bay and Franklin St., the hostel is at the corner of Funston and Pope St. past the administrative buildings. Beautiful surrounding forest and wooden bunks give this 160-bed hostel a campground feel. Not a place for partiers—strictly enforced quiet hours (11pm) and other rules such as no smoking or alcohol. Huge, clean kitchen, and cute cafe with vegetarian dinner. Movies, walking tours, kitchen, dining room, bike storage, lockers, and parking. Laundry (wash $1, dry $1). Check-in 2:30pm. Check-out 11am. Reserve weeks in advance. Dorms $22.50-29, under 13 $15-17. ❷

Interclub Globe Hostel, 10 Hallam Pl. (☎431-0540), off Folsom St. between 7th and 8th St. in **SoMa.** A cool hostel primarily for young international travelers. Happening common room has pool table, TV, microwave, and fridge. No stove. 24hr. Internet access. All rooms have private bath. Passport or out-of-state ID required. Safety deposit box $10. Key deposit $10. Linen $2.50. 14-day max. stay. Check-out noon. 5-bed dorms $18; doubles $45. Weekly dorms $100. No credit cards or personal checks. ❶

Central YMCA of San Francisco, 220 Golden Gate Ave. (☎345-6700; fax 885-5439; www.centralymcasf.org), at Leavenworth St. in the **Tenderloin.** Opened in 1910, the 9-story Tenderloin Y is perfect for travelers seeking exercise facilities such as a gym, pool, and cardio classes. The Y houses 106 simple rooms, some with private baths. TVs available upon request. Continental breakfast included. Cheap parking. Key and remote deposit $20. Dorms $23.50; singles $44; doubles $62, with bath $74; triples $81. Weekly singles $262; doubles $373. ❷

Hostel at Union Square (HI-AYH), 312 Mason St. (☎788-5604; www.norcalhostels.org), between Geary and O'Farrell St. in **Union Square.** A converted hotel, these tidy and unadorned dorm-style triples and quads offer quieter accommodations than the typical hostel. Internet $1 per 10min. $5 deposit for locker, iron, or key. Laundry (wash $1.25, dry $0.75). 21-night max. stay. Reception 24hr. Check-in 2pm. Check-out 11am. Reservations highly recommended. 3-4 bed dorms $22; private rooms $60. Nonmembers $25/$66. Under 13 half-price with parent. ❷

New Central Hotel and Hostel, 1412 Market St. (☎703-9988), between Van Ness Ave. and Polk St., in **Civic Center.** This no-frills hostel is dim and austere, but clean. Lockers, TV room, laundry, and free linens. Passport required. Reception 24hr. Check-out 11am. Dorms $17; private room $40, with private bath $52. Weekly dorms $105. ❶

SF International Student Center, 1188 Folsom St. (☎255-8800; www.sfstudent-center.com), between 7th and 8th St. in **SoMa.** The ownership runs a tight ship (no drinking, no swearing) at this youth hostel, now in its 11th year. Small lounge with couches, microwave, fridge, and toaster. No locals. Reception 8am-11pm. Check-in until 11pm. Check-out 11am. Linen $0.50. Key deposit $5. 3-, 4-, or 5-bed dorms $15. Weekly dorms $100. No credit cards. Prior notice required for personal checks. ❶

HOTELS

▨ **The San Remo Hotel,** 2237 Mason St. (☎776-8688; www.sanremohotel.com), between Chestnut and Francisco St. in **Russian Hill.** Built in 1906, this pension-style hotel features small but elegantly furnished rooms with antique armoires, bedposts, lamps, and complimentary (if random) backscratchers. Sparkling shared bathrooms with brass pull-chain toilets harken back to the end of the 19th century. The hotel's penthouse offers a private garden, bathroom, and windowed rooftop room with an amazing view of the city and Coit Tower. Friendly staff. Free modem connections. Laundry (wash $1.50, dry $1). Check-in 2pm. Check-out 11am. Reservations recommended. Singles and doubles $50-70; triples $70. Penthouse $155; reserve 2-3 months in advance, but cancellations often free up the room. ❸

San Francisco Zen Center, 300 Page St. (☎863-3136; www.sfzc.org), near Laguna St. in the **Lower Haight.** Even if rigorous soul-searching is not for you, the Zen Center offers breezy, unadorned rooms whose courtyard views instill a meditative peace of mind. Breakfast included in daily rates; all meals included in the discounted weekly (10% off) or monthly (25% off) rates. Singles and doubles $66-120. ❹

Phoenix Hotel, 601 Eddy St. (☎776-1380 or 800-248-9466; www.jdvhospitality.com), at Larkin St. in the **Tenderloin.** Delightful cabanas-by-the-pool setup, complete with breezy courtyard and wide-leaved palm trees. Freshly painted rooms and somewhat garish comforters lovingly harken back to the 70s. Parking included. Singles and doubles in high season from $99, in low season from $89. Suites $179-265. ❺

Metro Hotel, 319 Divisadero St. (☎861-5364), between Oak and Page St. in the **Lower Haight.** This conventional retreat, slightly removed from the hubbub, has solid if unremarkable rooms. 14-day max. stay. Reception 7:30am-midnight. Check-out noon. Reserve well in advance. Singles $66; doubles $77; triples $120. ❹

The Embassy Hotel, 610 Polk St. (☎673-1404 or 888-814-6835; www.embassyhotelsf.com), at Turk St. A rare find in **Civic Center**—respectable, affordable, and safe. Rooms are neat, if spartan. Adjoining bar (M-F 11am-1am) and cafe (M-F 6am-4pm), TV, Internet, telephones, and parking included. Continental breakfast (7-9:30am) included. Check-in 3pm. Check-out 11am. Singles $69-109; doubles $79-109. ❹

The Seal Rock Inn, 545 Point Lobos Ave. (☎752-8000; www.sealrockinn.com), at 48th Ave. opposite Sutro Heights Park in the **Richmond.** Surrounded by Golden Gate Park, Sutro Heights Park, and Lincoln Park, the inn's remoteness from the city is its most attractive feature. Solid accommodations with a small pool, patio, and standard hotel furnishings. Some rooms with small kitchen or large living room. Free parking. Check-in 1pm. Check-out 11am. Singles $105-143; doubles $115-153; $10 per additional person, $5 per child. Reduced rates Sept.-May. ❺

Ansonia Abby Hotel, 711 Post St. (☎673-2670 or 800-221-6470; fax 673-9217), between Jones and Leavenworth St. in **Union Square.** Affordable singles and doubles. TV (reception varies) and fridge in every room, and access to DSL-equipped computer lab. Full breakfast included. Dinner included M-Sa. Safe deposit $2.50 per week. Laundry $1.25. Check-out 11am. Singles $56-66; doubles $66, with bath $79. Cheap student weekly rates (from $120 for a double with shared bath and no meals) Sept.-Apr. ❹

BED AND BREAKFASTS

▨ **Hayes Valley Inn,** 417 Gough St. (☎431-9131, reservations 800-930-7999; www.hayesvalleyinn.com), just north of Hayes St. in **Hayes Valley.** European-style B&B with small, clean rooms, shared bath, and lace curtains. Bedrooms range from charming singles with daybeds to extravagant turret rooms with wraparound windows and queen-size beds. All rooms have cable TV, phone, and private sink. Some smoking rooms. Breakfast of cereal, cheeses, and ham. Check-in 3pm. Check-out 11am. Reservations recommended. Singles $47; doubles $53-66; turret rooms $63-71. ❸

▨ **The Red Victorian Bed, Breakfast, and Art,** 1665 Haight St. (☎864-1978; www.redvic.com), west of Belvedere St. in the **Upper Haight.** Inspired by the 1967 "Summer of Love," proprietress Sami Sunchild nurtures guests. Whether you seek the silent meditations of the sparsely adorned Japanese Tea Garden room or the joyous celebrations of the ever-colorful Flower Child room, the unique and specially designed rooms are sure to rejuvenate your spirit. Breakfast included. Reception 8am-9pm. Check-in 2-5pm or by appointment. Check-out 11am. Reservations strongly recommended, especially if you desire a specific room. Rooms $86-200. Discounts for stays longer than 3 days. ❺

▨ **Golden Gate Hotel,** 775 Bush St. (☎392-3702 or ☎800-835-1118; www.goldengatehotel.com), between Mason and Powell St. in **Union Square.** A positively charming B&B, with a staff as kind and solicitous as the rooms are plush and inviting. Wicker chairs, antiques, and big bay windows. German, French, and Spanish spoken. Continental breakfast (8-10:30am) and afternoon tea (4-7pm) included. Garage parking $15 per day. Reservations recommended. Doubles with sink $85, with bath $115. ❺

The Parker House, 520 Church St. (☎621-3222 or 888-520-7275; www.parkerguesthouse.com), near 17th St. in the **Castro.** Extravagant and stylish, the Parker House is regularly voted best LGB B&B in the city. Beautiful parlor, with dark wood paneling, grand piano, and flowers galore. Every room has heavenly down comforters, cable, and modem ports. Spa and steam room downstairs. Breakfast is served in a sunny enclosed porch overlooking rose gardens. Parking $15 per day. 2-night min. stay on weekends; 4-night min. stay some holiday weekends. Check-in 3pm. Check-out noon. Reservations recommended. Rooms from $119, with private bath from $149. ❺

Queen Anne Hotel, 1590 Sutter St. (☎441-2828; www.queenanne.com), at Octavia St. in **Pacific Heights.** Indulge in the extravagance of high Victorian style. The Queen Anne offers posh accommodations painstakingly adorned with antiques. Breakfast, afternoon tea, and sherry served daily. Some rooms with fireplaces and hot tubs. All rooms include TV and private bath. Complimentary evening limo takes you anywhere in the city. Wheelchair accessible. Rooms $140-180; deluxe rooms (fridge, wet bar, DVD player) $160-240; suites (king-size beds, living room) $180-350. ❺

Inn On Castro, 321 Castro St. (☎861-0321; www.innoncastro.com), near Market St. in the **Castro.** An elegant Edwardian exterior, painted in bright and colorful pastels, welcomes guests into this cozy and intimate 8-bedroom inn. Homey design and friendly staff—not to mention a sweeping view of the East Bay. The immaculately clean dining area and comfy common lounge are reminiscent of a compulsive friend's apartment. Full breakfast included. Gay-owned and operated, but straight-friendly. 2-night min. stay on weekends. Reception 7:30am-10:30pm. Singles $85 (shared bath); doubles $145; neighborhood apartments $115-200. ❺

Noe's Nest, 3973 23rd St. (☎821-0751; www.noesnest.com), between Noe and Sanchez St. in **Noe Valley.** The owner of this B&B is in the process of outfitting a more posh 19th-century Grand Victorian B&B. In the meantime, Noe's feels like a home, proudly displaying family memorabilia. The 7 rooms—all with private bath, phone, cable TV, VCR, and modem ports—are designed around individual themes such as the "Oriental Room" with silk fabrics or the romantic "Treehouse" room built behind the main house. Laundry service. 2-night min. stay on weekends. Flexible check-in and check-out. Reservations required. Singles and doubles $109-180. ❺

❏ FOOD

Strolling and sampling the food in each neighborhood is an excellent way to get a taste for the city's diversity. For the most up-to-date listings of restaurants, try the *Examiner* and the *S.F. Bay Guardian.* The glossy *Bay Area Vegetarian* can also suggest places to graze. To make your own meals, try the worker-owned cooperative **Rainbow Grocery,** 1745 Folsom St. (☎863-0620), at 13th St. in **SoMa.** (Open daily 9am-9pm.) **Harvest,** 2285 Market St. (☎626-0805), in the **Castro,** is a "ranch market" with organic food and outdoor benches. (Open daily 8:30am-11pm.) The **Marina Safeway,** 15 Marina Blvd., between Laguna and Buchanan St., is legendary as a spot to pick up more than just groceries. (☎563-4946. Open 24hr.)

UNION SQUARE

While not as ubiquitous as in nearby Chinatown or North Beach, satisfying, inexpensive eateries do exist in the primarily high-end Union Square, provided you move away from the main shopping thoroughfares to the quieter side streets.

▨ **Le Colonial,** 20 Cosmo Pl. (☎931-3600; www.lecolonialsf.com), off Post St. between Taylor and Jones St. Le Colonial presents exquisite French-Vietnamese cuisine in a stunning French-inspired building. The veranda, with its high white adobe walls, ivy-clad lattice, and overhead heating lamps, offers the best opportunity to revel in the architecture and down signature mojitos artfully garnished with lime and kumquat ($8). Veranda and chill lounge perfect for drinks or dessert. Entrees $20-33. F-Sa no athletic wear or torn jeans. Open Su-W 5:30-10pm, Th-Sa 5:30-11pm; lounge open from 4:30pm. ❺

▨ **Millennium,** 580 Geary St. (☎345-3900), in the Savoy Hotel at Jones St. Though the award-winning menu is entirely vegan, Millennium is patchouli free. The dark wood interior, complete with spare detailing and high ceilings, fits the high-class dining. The first restaurant in the US to feature an all-organic wine list. Elaborate entrees, such as Truffled Flageolet Gratin, average $20 and draw upon global influences. Open M-F 5:30-9:30pm, Sa-Su 5:30-10pm. Reservations recommended. ❺

FOOD BY TYPE

AFRICAN
Cafe Ethiopia (100)   MI ❷

AMERICAN AND DINERS
Café Bosse (99)   SM ❶
❖ Home Plate (103)   MA ❷
Marina Submarine (98)   PH ❷
Pat's Café (103)   FW ❶
Orphan Andy's (100)   CA ❶
Tommy's Joynt (98)   TL ❶
❖ Welcome Home (100)   CA ❷

BREAKFAST
❖ Café Bean (95)   US ❶
❖ Home Plate (103)   MA ❶
Kate's Kitchen (102)   HA ❷
Miss Millie's (102)   NP ❸
❖ Pork Store Cafe (102)   HA ❷
Squat and Gobble (102)   HA, CA ❷

CAFES
Brain Wash (99)   SM ❶
❖ The Butler and the Chef Cafe (99)   SM ❶
Caffé Trieste (96)   NB ❶
The Horseshoe Café (103)   HA ❶
Imperial Tea Court (95)   CH ❶
Farley's (102)   NP ❶
Morning Due Cafe (100)   CA ❶
Wild Awakenings Cafe (97)   CC ❶

CALIFORNIA CUISINE
Cafe Venue (97)   FD ❸
❖ California Culinary Academy (97)   TL ❺
Fuzio (102)   CA ❷
❖ Millennium (93)   CC ❺

CHINESE
❖ Chef Jia (95)   CH ❶
❖ Golden Gate Bakery (95)   CH ❶
Grand Palace (95)   CH ❷
❖ House of Nanking (95)   CH ❷
Kay Cheung's Restaurant (95)   CH ❷
❖ Lee Hou Restaurant (103)   RI ❷
Taiwan Restaurant (103)   RI ❷

DESSERT
Bombay Ice Creamery (100)   MI ❶
Citizen Cake (97)   CC ❹
❖ Mitchell's Ice Cream (100)   MI ❶
Gelato Classico (96)   NB ❶
❖ Peasant Pies (102)   NP ❶
Squat and Gobble (102)   HA, CA ❷

FRENCH AND CREPERIES
❖ The Butler and the Chef Cafe (99)   SM ❷
Café Bastille (97)   FD ❹
Citizen Cake (97)   CC ❹
The Crêpe House (98)   RH ❷
Crepevine (100)   MI ❷
❖ La Boulangerie (98)   PH ❶
Patisserie Café (99)   SM ❷
Sophie's Crepes (99)   JT ❶
Squat and Gobble (102)   HA, CA ❷

INDIAN
Bombay Ice Creamery (100)   MI ❶
Mela Tandoori (95)   US ❷

ITALIAN AND PIZZA
Fior d'Italia (96)   NB ❺
Gelato Classico (96)   NB ❶
❖ L'Osteria del Forno (96)   NB ❷
❖ Mario's Bohemian Cigar Café (96)   NB ❷
Marcello's (102)   CA ❶
Pizza Orgasmica (98)   PH ❷

JAPANESE
Sushigroove (98)   NR ❷
Mifune (99)   JT ❷
Isobune (99)   JT ❷

MEDITERRANEAN AND MIDDLE EASTERN
❖ La Méditerranée (98)   CA, PH ❷
Blue Front Café (103)   HA ❷
Zarzuela (98)   NR ❸

MEXICAN
❖ La Canasta (98)   PH ❶
La Taquería (100)   MI ❶
❖ Taquería Cancún (99)   MI ❶

SEAFOOD
McCormick and Kuleto's (104)   FW ❸

SOUTHEAST ASIAN
Basil (99)   SM ❷
❖ Lalitai Thai Restaurant (97)   CC ❸
❖ Le Colonial (93)   US ❺
Le Soleil (103)   RI ❷
❖ Nirvana (100)   CA ❷

VEGETARIAN AND VEGAN
❖ Millennium (93)   US ❺
❖ Peasant Pies (102)   NP ❶

SAN FRANCISCO

CA Castro CC Civic Center CH Chinatown FD Financial District FW Fisherman's Wharf HA The Haight MA Marina MI The Mission NP Noe Valley and Potrero Hill NB North Beach NR Nob Hill and Russian Hill JT Japantown PH Pacific Heights and Cow Hollow RI Richmond SM South of Market TL Tenderloin US Union Square

◪ **Café Bean,** 800 Sutter St. (☎346-9527). A crazy cosmopolitan atmosphere and the restorative powers of Dutch pancakes ($4-7) offer jet-setting diners much-needed respite. Parisian posters, maps of Amsterdam, and German road signs hang above makeshift couches. Creative sandwiches $5-8. Internet $3 per 20min. Open M 6am-8pm, Tu-Sa 6am-7pm, Su 6am-5pm; kitchen closes M-F 2pm, Sa 4pm, Su 3pm. ❶

Mela Tandoori, 417 O'Farrell St. (☎447-4041), between Taylor and Jones St. Offering subtly smoked and sweetly spiced flavor, this Indian and Pakistani restaurant serves inventive entrees ($9-16) and an array of sides (naan $1.50-3). Standard seating or a traditional dining area (shoes blissfully optional) in an elegant interior complete with indoor fountain, ornate metalwork, and authentic clay dishware. Extensive vegetarian options $7. Open M-F 11am-2:30pm and 5:30-10:30pm, Sa 1-11pm, Su 1-9:30pm. ❷

CHINATOWN

San Francisco's Chinese cuisine is widely held to be unsurpassed outside of Asia, but it can be difficult to distinguish the excellent restaurants from the mediocre ones. Chinatown is filled with cheap restaurants whose sheer number and outward similarity can baffle even the savviest of travelers. Finding vegetarian or vegan food is likewise harder than it might seem; many vegetable dishes use oyster sauce or chicken broth, and rice dishes sometimes include egg. The one certainty is Chinatown's universally excellent dim sum. The area is also home to many spectacular bakeries, teahouses, and specialty restaurants.

◪ **Chef Jia,** 925 Kearny St. (☎398-1626), at Pacific St. Insanely cheap and delicious food served in a spacious room with fresh yellow paint and hardwood floors. A local crowd comes for lunch and dinner specials ($4.80) or the celebrated signature dishes, such as rolling lettuce chicken with pine nuts ($9). Entrees $6-10. Open M-F 11:30am-10pm, Sa-Su 5-10pm. No credit cards. ❶

◪ **House of Nanking,** 919 Kearny St. (☎421-1429), near Columbus Ave. Big portions of excellent food compensate for off-putting white tile decor and brusque service in this famous, tourist-laden Chinatown institution. Some regulars trust their server to select their meal. Entrees $8-12. Open M-F 11am-10pm, Sa noon-10pm, Su noon-9:30pm. ❷

Golden Gate Bakery, 1029 Grant Ave. (☎781-2627). This tiny bakery's mooncakes, noodle puffs, and vanilla cream buns (all $0.75-1.50) draw long lines of admirers. Open daily 8am-8pm. No credit cards. ❶

Grand Palace, 950 Grant Ave. (☎982-3705), between Washington and Jackson St. With quick turnover to accommodate the rush of diners, Grand Palace's best dim sum dishes are fried: deep-fried pork dumplings and sesame balls ($1.80-2.50). Even a solitary guest can enjoy the full dim sum experience with an 8-piece sampling plate ($8). Entrees average $8.50. Happy hour 2:30-5:30pm; all beer $2. 2hr. free parking. Open daily 7:30am-10pm. ❷

Kay Cheung's Restaurant, 615 Jackson St. (☎989-6838), at Kearny St. Patrons line up on weekends to sample some of the best dumplings in Chinatown. Seafood entrees, such as the prawns with honey walnut, range $8-13. Dim sum about $2.15 per plate. Open daily 9am-2:30pm (dim sum) and 5pm-9:30pm. ❷

Imperial Tea Court, 1411 Powell St. (☎788-6080 or 800-567-5898; www.imperial-tea.com), at Broadway. This oasis of aromatic serenity affords relief from the bustle of mainstreet Chinatown. Elegantly burnished bird cages and finely painted lanterns hang-

IMME SOME DIM SUM

Dim sum, meaning "little bits of he heart," are the foods tradition-ally eaten at a Cantonese or Southern Chinese *yum cha* ("tea unch"). This heavenly dining experience involves many small dishes eaten in the morning or early afternoon, typically on Sun-days, in mass quantities. Waiters and waitresses push carts laden with all sorts of Chinese "finger oods," from dumplings and buns o chicken feet. When they stop at your table, point to whatever ooks good or use the handy mini-menu below. The waiter will stamp a card to charge you by the dish. Dim sum is sure to steal our heart one piece at a time.

Cha Siu Bao: Steamed barbecue oork buns.

Haar Gao: Steamed shrimp dumplings.

Dan Taat: Tiny tart shells filled vith sweet egg custard.

Siu Mai: Shrimp and pork in a ancy dumpling "basket."

Woltei: The lovingly wrapped pork oot stickers.

iaozi: The classic steamed pork dumplings.

Dou Sha Bao: Steamed buns illed with sweet red bean paste.

Loh Bak Goh: A fried mashed tur-nip patty. Don't knock it until ou've tried it.

Fun Gwor: Chicken and mush-oom dumplings.

uebing: A flaky, frosted pastry vith red bean paste filling.

ing from the ceiling. Tea ceremony includes a brief introduction of the teas ($3-5 per cup). Open M and W-Sa 11am-6:30pm. ❶

NORTH BEACH

In North Beach's tourist-friendly restaurants, California cuisine merges with the bold palate of Italy, inspiring *delicioso* dishes that blend tradition and innovation.

🍴 **L'Osteria del Forno,** 519 Columbus Ave. (☎982-1124), between Green and Union St. This picture-perfect Italian eatery features acclaimed Italian meats. Enthusiastic and devoted staff serves up terrific thin-crust pizzas (slices $2.50-3.75, whole pizzas $10-17) and focaccia sandwiches ($5-7). Salads and antipasti $5-9. Entrees $8-13. Open Su-M and W-Th 11:30am-10pm, F-Sa 11:30am-10:30pm. No credit cards. ❷

🍴 **Mario's Bohemian Cigar Store Café,** 566 Columbus Ave. (☎362-0536), at Union St. on the corner of Washington Sq. The Beats frequented this laid-back cafe, which still serves first-rate grub. The Italian cook at the stove behind the bar deftly prepares hot focaccia sandwiches ($7-8.50; half $4.50) in full view as patrons cup their espressos ($1.50-3.25). Soothing glasses of port $4. Pizza $7-8.50. Open daily 10am-11pm. ❷

Gelato Classico, 576 Union St. (☎391-6667), near Stockton St. Ice cream can't compete with this smooth and extremely creamy gelato. An Italian matron presides over 20 tubs of gelato goodness, swiftly handling the crowd's requests for scoops of sweet spumoni, white chocolate decadenza, or classic tiramisu. Small $2.85, medium $3.65, large $4.25. Open daily winter noon-10pm; summer noon-11pm. No credit cards. ❶

Caffé Trieste, 601 Vallejo St. (☎392-6739), at Grant Ave. in **North Beach.** Although the staff comes across as brusque, Trieste enjoys a rich tradition of serving enthusiastic patrons, including Francis Ford Coppola and Luciano Pavarotti. More fond of opera than Beat literature, the Giotta family (owners since 1956) expresses strong and refreshing regard for the culture of the Italian community. The jukebox still plays Verdi, and, since 1973, there have been live Italian showtune and opera concerts every Sa (1:45-6pm). Espresso drinks $1.60-3.45. Wine from $2.50 per glass. Open Su-Th 6:30am-10:30pm, F-Sa 6:30am-11:30pm. No credit cards. ❶

Fior d'Italia, 601 Union St. (☎986-1886; www.fior.com), near Stockton St. From the decanter of olive oil to the folded paper enclosing the bill, patrons are reminded everywhere that Fior is the oldest continuously operating restaurant in America. What Fior lacks in tasteful subtlety it makes up for in generous portions. Entrees $18-31. Open daily 11:30am-10:30pm. Reservations recommended for inner dining room. ❺

FINANCIAL DISTRICT AND THE EMBARCADERO

In the Financial District, corner cafes vend Mediterranean grub at rock-bottom prices. Pedestrian side streets, nestled between banks, are packed with outdoor bistros. Sit-down restaurants serve haute cuisine with liberal portions of ambience, though you may need an MBA to afford more than an appetizer.

Cafe Venue, 721 Market St. (☎546-1144), between 3rd and 4th St. Cafe Venue's people-watching patio is a perfect place to catch a bite or a bit of gossip. San Franciscans wash down roasted eggplant on sourdough sandwiches ($4.50) with a wheatgrass "shot" ($1). Other menu offerings include pasta ($6) and smoothies ($3.50). Open M-F 7am-7pm, Sa 8am-5:30pm, Su 11am-5:30pm. No credit cards. ❷

Café Bastille, 22 Belden Pl. (☎986-5673), between Kearny and Montgomery St. Enter on Pine or Bush St. In this strip of pricey sidewalk cafes, Bastille stands out for its quality food and playfully chic Parisian decor. The menu is filled with light French offerings such as *boudin noir* (blood sausage; $12.75), chicken and port pâté ($7), and a heavenly chocolate almond dessert crepe ($6). Entrees $17-24. Open daily 11am-11pm. ❹

CIVIC CENTER

Restaurants are surprisingly hard to find in San Francisco's home of opera, musicals, and movies. The Opera Plaza, Van Ness Ave., and McAllister St. have a sprinkling of appetizing eateries hidden among fast-food chains. In this area, worthwhile eateries are often hidden behind nondescript facades. Nearby Hayes Valley has some popular pre-opera offerings as well.

▨ Lalita Thai Restaurant and Bar, 96 McAllister St. (☎552-5744), at Leavenworth St. Mood lighting, a beautifully elaborate water-lily mural, and a touch of plastic foliage complement the daring yet understated flavors of the menu. The deliciously cheap $20 4-course prix-fixe dinner special (available before 9pm) is a favorite of theatre-goers; allow 1½hr. for the entire meal. Most dinner entrees $11 (specialty entrees $15-29), with veggie options. Open M-Sa 11am-10pm. Reservations recommended, especially for weekend nights. ❸

Wild Awakenings Cafe, 142 McAllister St. (☎255-0208), at Hyde and Jones St. Secondhand couches, leather armchairs, a slew of individual tables, 4 DSL-equipped computers ($7 per hr.), and cheap eats (fresh sandwiches $3.75; ice cream $1-4) make this spacious cafe the ideal all-purpose space for the college crowd. A huge selection of Torani Italian sodas, from pomegranate to passion fruit ($1.75), and scrumptious vegan cookies from the Alternative Baking Co. ($2.25). Open summer M-F 7am-10pm, Sa-Su 7am-8pm; in school year from 6am. No credit cards; ATM inside. ❶

Citizen Cake, 399 Grove St. (☎861-2228), at Gough St. With light, fresh California cuisine and to-die-for desserts, this restaurant-*patisserie* is popular with the post-theatre crowd. Patrons are known to make reservations a month in advance during the opera, ballet, and theater seasons. Entrees $18-26. Desserts $8-13. Pastries-to-go $1.25-7. Open Tu-F 8am-10pm, Sa 10am-10pm, Su 10am-5pm and 5:30-9pm. ❹

TENDERLOIN

▨ The California Culinary Academy, 625 Polk St. (☎216-4329), between Turk and Eddy St. Academy students cook behind a window visible from the high-ceilinged Carême dining room. The Tu-W *prix-fixe* 3-course lunch ($16) or dinner ($24) indulges patrons with ambitious and extremely successful culinary combinations. Wine pairings with each course are a steal at $5 total. The Th-F grand buffet lunch ($22) or dinner ($38) draws large crowds; reserve 1 week ahead. Open Tu-F 11:30am-1pm and 6-8pm. ❺

Tommy's Joynt, 1101 Geary St. (☎ 775-4216; www.tommysjoynt.com), at Van Ness Ave. A delicious hybrid saloon, school cafeteria, and beer lovin' sports bar where customers enter the assembly line-style servery for freshly carved sandwiches of barbecue brisket ($5) and sides of hickory baked beans ($1.90). Daily specials $4.85-7. Nearly 100 varieties of beer ($2.50-4.50; pitcher $12.50-16). Open daily 11am-1:45am. ❶

NOB HILL AND RUSSIAN HILL

Zarzuela, 2000 Hyde St. (☎346-0800), at Union St. The Spanish home-style menu features hot and cold tapas ($3.25-9) in a festive, slightly upscale setting. Entrees $8-17. Open Tu-Th 5:30-10pm, F-Sa 5:30-10:30pm. ❸

Sushigroove, 1916 Hyde St. (☎440-1905), between Union and Green St. Without a full kitchen, this chic, inexpensive sushi-*sake* joint (most *nigiri* and *maki* $4) serves up several different rolls (some vegetarian) but nothing that has seen the inside of an oven. Valet parking $10. Open Su-Th 5:30-10pm, F-Sa 5:30-10:30pm. ❷

The Crêpe House, 1755 Polk St. (☎441-2421), at Washington St. Though the crepes here ($5-8) are nothing special, the omelettes ($5-8) garner local praise and the friendly staff makes the place refreshingly mellow. Good selection of salads ($6-9) and sandwiches ($7). High-speed Internet $10 per hr. Open Su-Th 7:30am-9:30pm, F-Sa 7:30am-10:30pm. No credit cards. ❷

PACIFIC HEIGHTS AND COW HOLLOW

La Boulangerie, 2325 Pine St. (☎440-0356; www.baybread.com), at Fillmore St. Homesick Parisians and Francophiles migrate to this French countryside bakery for freshly baked baguettes, loaves, and rounds ($2-7) in brown wicker baskets. Friendly management serves Parisian-style *macarons* ($1.50), richly textured *cannelès* ($1.75), and the most delicious almond croissants ($2.25) this side of the Seine. Small selection of savory tarts and sandwiches ($4.25). Check the website for additional SF locations. Open Tu-Sa 8am-6pm, Su-8am-4pm. ❶

La Méditerranée, 2210 Fillmore St. (☎921-2956; www.cafelamed.com), between Sacramento and Clay St. Additional locations: 288 Noe St. (☎431-7210), at 16th and Market St. in the **Castro;** 2936 College Ave. (☎510-540-7773) in **Berkeley.** Narrow, colorful, and bustling, La Méditerranée harkens back to modest Greek and Lebanese traditions but adds a chic twist. Lunch specials (served until 5pm; $6-8.50) and entrees ($8-10) are light and Mediterranean-inspired. Locals gravitate towards the Middle Eastern platter ($9.75), but the filled filo dough ($9.25) and quiche of the day ($8.25) are also delectable. Open Su-Th 11am-10pm, F-Sa 11am-11pm. ❷

La Canasta, 3006 Buchanan St. (☎474-2627), near Union St. The Mexican food at this local favorite is fresh and cooked in healthy oils. Hard-working cooks in a tiny kitchen whip up tacos, burritos, and salads. Soups made on the spot. Takeout only. Almost everything on the menu under $5. Open daily 11am-10pm. ❶

Marina Submarine, 2299 Union St. (☎921-3990), at Steiner St. Often a long (but worthwhile) wait for excellent subs in several sizes ($4-11.25) and flavorful gelato. Open M-F 10am-6pm, Sa 11am-4:30pm, Su 11am-3:30pm. No credit cards. ❷

Pizza Orgasmica, 3157 Fillmore St. (☎931-5300), at Greenwich St. With pizzas suggestively named "menage à trois" and "doggie style," it's hard not to get excited. Sex sells at a steep price here (pies $15-25) so don't miss the salad, soda, and slice special (M-F 11am-4pm; $5.50) or the all-you-can-eat special (11am-4pm; $7.50). Open Su-W 11am-midnight, Th 11am-2am, F-Sa 11am-2:30am. ❷

JAPANTOWN

Isobune, 1737 Post St. (☎563-1030), in the Kintetsu Bldg. Swipe sushi from little boats as they sail by your moat-side seat in America's first sushi boat restaurant. Isobune patented the idea in 1982. Color-coded plates correspond to prices ($1.80-3.75). *Sake* $3. Open daily 11:30am-10pm. ❷

Mifune, 1737 Post St. (☎922-0337), in the Kintetsu Bldg. Excellent and much-loved noodle restaurant. Choices include *udon* (thick flour noodles) or *soba* (slender buckwheat noodles). Hot noodles from $4.50; cold noodles from $5.25. *Sake* from $2.80. Dinner entrees $10.30-18.50. Open Su-Th 11am-9:30pm, F-Sa 11am-10pm. ❷

Sophie's Crepes, 1581 Webster St. (☎929-7732), on the upper level of the Kinokuniya Bldg. Walk through the **Japan Center** (p. 108) and virtually every group of teens is munching thin and crisp crepes stuffed with fruits, Nutella, or gelato. Savory crepes $2.95-4.95. Sweet crepes $2.45-5.70. Gelato $3-4. Sundaes $4-5. Open Su and Tu-Th 11am-9pm, F-Sa 11am-10pm. No credit cards. ❶

SOUTH OF MARKET AREA (SOMA)

▓ **The Butler and the Chef Cafe,** 155A S. Park Ave. (☎896-2075; www.thebutlerandthechef.com), between Bryant, Brannan, 2nd, and 3rd St. Advertising itself as San Francisco's only authentic French bistro, this stellar reproduction of a Parisian street cafe serves breakfast crepes ($4-10) and baguette sandwiches ($7). The scrumptious *Croque Mademoiselle* ($8) will have you reeling in bliss. Open Tu-Sa 8am-4:30pm. ❷

Patisserie Café, 1155 Folsom St. (☎703-0557; www.patisseriecafe.com), between 7th and 8th St. Enjoy a cheap breakfast (coffee and perfectly buttered croissant $3), a reasonable lunch (gourmet sandwich $7), or a decadent dinner (appetizers around $6; entrees $8-14) while pondering the experimental artistic decor. Open M-F 8am-4pm, dinner Th-F 6:30pm-10pm. ❷

Brain Wash, 1122 Folsom St. (☎255-4866; www.brainwash.com), near 7th St. This combination cafe-laundromat turns a mundane task into a hip way to spend the afternoon. A freewheeling jazz band sometimes entertains in the cafe as customers munch on weekend brunch ($5-7) or inventive sandwiches ($7-8) amid Pop Art-infused decor. Happy hour 4-7pm. $1 off cafe items with laundry. Internet $3 per 20min. Wash $2.25, dry $0.25 per 6min. Dry cleaning. Open daily 7am-11pm. ❶

Cafe Bosse, 1599 Howard St. (☎864-2446), at 12th St. Bright, shiny, and quick, Bosse provides restaurant-quality meals with cafeteria-style decor. Burgers, breakfast omelettes, and lunch specials all $6-7. The Philly cheesesteak is worth the trek. Lots of veggie and salad options. Open M-F 7am-4pm. ❶

Basil, 1175 Folsom St. (☎552-8999; www.basilthai.com), near 8th St. Somberly sophisticated ambience sets the mood for classy Thai food with a dash of spice. Curries and entrees "from the grill" or "from the wok" include "drunken tofu" and piquant "mussels inferno" (all $8-14). F-Sa night $15 min. Open M-F 11:30am-2:45pm, Su-Th 5-10pm, F-Sa 5-10:30pm. ❷

THE MISSION

The dominance of Mexican specialties and gigantic burritos is undeniable in the Mission, but the area also houses a solid contingent of homey diners, quirky vegan-friendly cafes (along **Valencia Street**), and Middle Eastern, Italian, and Thai cuisine.

▓ **Taquería Cancún,** 2288 Mission St. (☎252-9560), at 19th St. Additional locations: 3211 Mission St. (☎550-1414), at Cesar Chavez Ave.; open daily 10am-12:45am. 1003 Market (☎864-6773), at 6th St.; open daily 9am-11:45pm. So good they need three branches to meet customer demand. Delicious burritos ($4; grilled chicken upon request) and scrumptious egg dishes served with chips and salsa, small tortillas, and choice of sausage, ham, or salsa ($5). Open Su-Th 9am-1:45am, F-Sa 9am-3am. ❶

🍴 **Mitchell's Ice Cream,** 688 San Jose Ave (☎648-2300), at 29th St. This take-out parlor gets so busy that you have to take a number at the door. With a list of awards almost as long as the list of flavors (from caramel praline to Thai iced tea), Mitchell's will chocolate dip any scoop. Cone $2.10. Pint $5.10. Open daily 11am-11pm. ❶

La Taquería, 2889 Mission St. (☎285-7117), at 25th St. Despite the dozens of *taquerías* in the Mission, La Taquería's spacious, faux-adobe interior always fills up with customers craving their sizable burritos ($3.25-4.75) and unique all-natural *frescas* made with diced fruit ($2). Open M-Sa 11am-9pm, Su 11am-8pm. ❶

Bombay Ice Creamery, 522 Valencia St. (☎431-1103), between 16th and 17th St. This richly textured ice cream makes for deliciously thick milkshakes. Try a mango *kulfi* ($2.50) with rose water and sweet rice noodles. The *bhel* (a puffed rice dish; $4) and the *dahi puri* ($4) prove that this parlor excels at more than just ice cream. Open Su and Tu-Th 11:30am-9pm, F-Sa 11:30am-9:30pm. ❶

Crepevine, 216 Church St. (☎421-4646), at Market St. Crepevine's vast menu includes Cali-style sweet and savory crêpes ($6-8), all sorts of egg concoctions ($4), french toast ($5), pasta ($7-8), pancakes, sandwiches ($7-8) and salads ($5-7). Kids' menu ($2.95 and under) with breakfast served all day. Open M-Th and Su 7:30am-11pm, F-Sa 7:30am-midnight. No credit cards; ATM inside. ❷

Cafe Ethiopia, 878 Valencia St. (☎285-2728), just north of 20th St. Well-spiced Ethiopian food in a very relaxed environment. Ample vegetarian options. Entrees $6.75-10. Open M and W-Su 11:30am-9:30pm. ❷

THE CASTRO

Campy diners and posh cafes dominate the Castro's culinary offerings, where little is as cheap as in the neighboring Mission district. To find affordable fare, head away from Castro St. along Market St. toward Noe and Sanchez St.

🍴 **Welcome Home,** 464 Castro St. (☎626-3600), near the Castro Theatre. Whether placing a doily under your milkshake ($3.75), giving you the extra shake in a metal cup, or playfully reminding you that shakes and burgers ($8-9) were made for each other, Welcome Home's waitstaff is always, well, welcoming. With a cozy interior and photos of Marilyn Monroe and Judy Garland, this enchanting diner coddles patrons with a familiarity that all but secures their return. Open M-F 8am-9pm, Sa-Su 8am-4pm. No credit cards. ❷

🍴 **Nirvana,** 544 Castro St. (☎861-2226), between 18th and 19th St. Greeted at the door by a metal sculpture of Buddha and a flirty host, patrons come for Burmese cuisine with a twist. Playfully concocted cocktails such as "nirvana colada" and "phat margarita" ($8-9) complement more traditional dishes (from $8) that the gorgeous waitstaff serves up to this young crowd of local scenesters. Open M-Th 4:30-9:30pm, F-Sa noon-10:30pm, Su noon-9:30pm. ❷

Orphan Andy's, 3991 17th St. (☎864-9795), between Castro and Market St. If the desire for diner grub strikes after hours, head to this oh-so campy all hours venue, where you can enjoy a slice of double fudge chocolate cake ($3.85) while disco streams from the jukebox. Open 24hr.; closed Tu 4-6am for maintenance. ❶

Morning Due Cafe, 3698 17th St (☎621-7156), at Church St. A quiet, welcoming place where locals gather to read and type on their laptops while enjoying cheap sandwiches ($4), espresso drinks ($1.25-3), and a wide variety of vegan cookies and pastries (from $1.50). Bookshelves along the wall sell a selection of grrly books on feminism and the like. Wireless Internet. Open daily 7am-9pm. No credit cards. ❶

Marcello's, 420 Castro St. (☎863-3900). No-frills joint serves locally adored pizza with a formidable list of toppings. Slices $2.30-3.50; whole pizzas $10-25. Beer $2. Open Su-Th 11am-1am, F-Sa 11am-2am. No credit cards. ❶

Fuzio, 469 Castro St (☎863-1400; www.fuzio.com), near 18th St. Fuzio's daring menu and full bar make it an obvious choice for those in search of cheap eats before striking out for a night on the town. Barbie-lipstick-red walls complement special martinis and "universal pastas" ($8-9), with international inspiration from Italy to Japan. "2 out of 3" soup, salad, or sandwich lunch special $8. Open Su-Th 11:30am-10pm, F-Sa 11:30am-11pm. ❷

NOE VALLEY, BERNAL HEIGHTS, POTRERO HILL

▨ **Peasant Pies,** 4108 24th St. (☎642-1316; www.peasantpies.com), near Castro St. in **Noe Valley.** These affordable, portable pies, a traditional French staple, are enticingly filled with everything from veggies to seafood and poultry to chocolate and fruit. Handmade fresh every morning, most pies are vegan and low-fat. 2 pies make a meal ($4.25). Single pie $2.50. Open M-Sa 9:30am-7pm, Su 10am-7pm. ❶

Miss Millie's, 4123 24th Street (☎285-5598), near Castro St. in **Noe Valley.** Dishes line the walls on display shelves in what feels like your favorite aunt's rustic country kitchen. Over the weekend hordes of customers wait outside for a chance to taste Millie's famed lemon ricotta pancakes with blueberry syrup ($9.75), the delectably sweet mango bread ($4.50), or any of the elaborate entrees ($9.75-13.75). Insiders know to come for the dinner menu in order to avoid the high-profile brunch rush. Open W-Th 6-9:30pm, F 6-10pm, Sa 9am-2pm and 6-9:30pm, Su 9am-2pm. ❸

Farley's, 1315 18th St. (☎648-1545; www.farleyscoffee.com), between Texas and Missouri St. in **Potrero Hill.** Proudly stocking only 1 cup size and 1 type of milk (whole, of course), Farley's provides a no frills hang-out for everyone from laptop users (no Internet) to motorcycle pups to artists from the local warehouse studios. There's also an arsenal of board games, extensive newsstand, and lots of desserts ($1.25-3.50). Exhibit of local art changes monthly. Open M-F 6:30am-10pm, Sa-Su 8am-10pm. ❶

THE HAIGHT

▨ **Pork Store Cafe,** 1451 Haight St. (☎864-6981), between Masonic Ave. and Ashbury St. in the **Upper Haight.** A breakfast place that charges itself very seriously with the mission to fatten you up—they proudly stock only whole milk. The two delicious healthy options ("Tim's Healthy Thursdays" and "Mike's Low Carb Special"; each $7) pack enough spinach, avocado, and salsa to hold their own against the Piggy Special ($7). Open M-F 7am-3:30pm, Sa-Su 8am-4pm. ❷

Kate's Kitchen, 471 Haight St. (☎626-3984), near Fillmore St. With red and white checkered tablecloths and a no-nonsense menu, Kate's delivers one of the best breakfasts in the neighborhood (served all day). It's often packed (especially weekends), so sign up on a waiting list outside. Items such as the "Farmer's Breakfast" or the "French Toast Orgy" (with fruit, yogurt, granola, and honey; $7.50) fill up rumbly tummies. Open M 9am-2:45pm, Tu-F 8am-2:45pm, Sa-Su 8:30am-3:45pm. No credit cards. ❷

Squat and Gobble, 1428 Haight St. (☎864-8484; www.squatandgobble.com), between Ashbury St. and Masonic Ave. in the **Upper Haight.** Additional locations: 237 Fillmore St. in the **Lower Haight** and 3600 16th St. in the **Castro.** With scores of crepe places to choose from in SF, Squat and Gobble makes its bid with shamelessly indulgent dessert crepes, such as the "very berry nutella" with its discrete bowl of ice cream and dripping berry sauce ($6.75). Equally colossal savory crepes ($6-9) and omelettes ($5-7). Many salads, sandwiches, and vegetarian options. Open daily 8am-10pm. ❷

Blue Front Café, 1430 Haight St. (☎252-5917), between Ashbury St. and Masonic Ave. This genie-marked joint offers a Mediterranean (mostly Middle Eastern) menu in addition to an assortment of basic salads and sandwiches ($6). Smooth hummus and perfectly seasoned chicken shawarma come in a combo plate ($9). Sizeable wraps $7. Open M-Th 7:30am-10pm, F 7:30am-11pm, Sa 8am-11pm, Su 8am-10pm. ❷

The Horseshoe Café, 566 Haight St. (☎626-7297), between Steiner and Fillmore St., in the **Lower Haight.** A combined cafe and high-quality vintage shop, the Horseshoe is a narrow space with lots of seating for munching on cheap cookies ($0.50), croissants, and ice cream ($1 per scoop). The vintage store stocks beautiful lace dresses and plush fur coats ($100) as well as less pricey shirts and skirts ($10-30). Open daily 6am-midnight. No credit cards. ❶

RICHMOND

Some locals claim that Chinese restaurants in the Richmond are better than those in Chinatown, and with good reason. Instead of hastily catering to the daily influx of tourists, Inner Richmond dedicates itself to providing quality grub for the local community. **Clement Street,** between 2nd and 12th Ave., has the widest variety.

▨ **Lee Hou Restaurant,** 332 Clement St. (☎668-8070), at 5th Ave. Some of the best dim sum San Francisco has to offer. The service and decor may seem basic, but Lee Hou is the rare restaurant that indulges patrons with dim sum so fresh that it must be made-to-order. The restaurant helps out non-Chinese speakers with an English menu that lists dim sum dishes ($1.30-3.20). Entrees $3-8. Open Su-Th 8am-1am, F-Sa 8am-2am. ❷

Le Soleil, 133 Clement St. (☎668-4848), between 2nd and 3rd Ave. Vietnamese food in a refreshing and bright setting complete with flowers and a mellow lime-green decor. Huge vegetarian selection (sauteed eggplant with coconut and curry sauce; $7.50) on both the lunch and dinner menus. Lunch $6.50. Dinner entrees average $7-14. Open Su-Th 11am-10pm, F-Sa 11am-10:30pm. ❷

Taiwan Restaurant, 445 Clement St. (☎387-1789), at 6th Ave. Watch cooks fold your dumplings in the window of this cheap, veggie-friendly spot, which serves Northern Chinese dim sum ($1-4.25 per plate) and "Taiwan's version of China's epicurean delights." Lines out the door on weekends. Lunch specials (M-F 11am-4pm) feature select items as low as $3.50. Dinner specials around $10. Open M-Th 11am-9:30pm, F 11am-10:30pm, Sa 10am-10:30pm, Su 10am-9:30pm. ❷

MARINA AND FORT MASON

▨ **Home Plate,** 2274 Lombard St. (☎922-4663), off Pierce St. in the Marina. While diners eagerly await apple buckwheat pancakes ($5.50) or homemade apricot-pistachio granola ($4.25), this inventive breakfast and lunch joint wins them over with complimentary warm scones with homemade mango or mixed fruit jam. Open daily 7am-4pm. ❶

FISHERMAN'S WHARF AND THE PIERS

Pier 39 and Fisherman's Wharf overflow with opportunities to refuel, but because this is tourist central, most eateries charge fairly expensive rates for average food. If you're already down here, you may feel compelled to try some clam chowder and sourdough bread.

Pat's Café, 2330 Taylor St. (☎776-8735), between Chestnut and Francisco St. With playful yellow swirls on the building's facade, Pat's bright decor welcomes diners to a hearty home-cooked meal like mom would make. Burgers, sandwiches, and big breakfasts $5-10). Open M and Th-Su 5:30-9pm, Tu-W 7:30am-3pm. ❶

McCormick and Kuleto's, 900 N. Point St. (☎929-1730), in Ghirardelli Sq. Can't leave the wharf without trying crabcakes or clam chowder, but skeptical about the vendors on the piers? This upscale seafood restaurant offers a comprehensive menu, spectacular view of Aquatic Park, and tasteful maritime decor. Most entrees $10-25. Open Su-Th 11:30am-10pm, F-Sa 11:30am-11pm. ❸

◎ SIGHTS

UNION SQUARE

The three-block radius around Union Square houses prestigious art galleries, the heart of San Francisco's theater district, upscale hotels, several multi-floor shopping centers, and just about every boutique imaginable. Whether you're looking to drop cash at the nine-story **San Francisco Shopping Centre** or merely browse through jaw-droppingly beautiful designer clothes on **Maiden Lane,** the numerous galleries that litter the area allow you to pick up a little culture with your couture. For shopping, see p. 119.

GALLERIES. ◨**Hang** is a sleek urban gallery that fashions an intimate setting in a chrome warehouse. Artists' personal bios explain the individually lit works hanging from exposed ceiling beams. The Hang Annex, located directly across the street, tends to display monthly solo shows, while the original Hang changes its art every few days. Both galleries specialize in the rental of works "by emerging artists for emerging collectors." *(556 Sutter St., between Powell and Mason St. ☎434-4264; www.hangart.com. Open M-Sa 10am-6pm, Su noon-5pm. Annex open Tu-Sa 10-6pm; by request Su-M.)* Architecture enthusiasts will love the artful swirling brick design of **Xanadu Gallery,** the only **Frank Lloyd Wright** building in SF. *(140 Maiden Ln. ☎392-9999; www.xanadugallery.us. Open M-Sa 10am-6pm).* The two-story **Martin Lawrence Gallery** houses America's largest collection of work by painter Marc Chagall, as well as a number of pieces by Keith Haring, Andy Warhol, and Pablo Picasso. This upscale gallery entices passersby with elegant and tasteful street-level exhibits. *(366 Geary St., between Powell and Mason St. ☎956-0345. Open Su-M 10am-6pm, Tu-Th 9am-8pm, F-Sa 9am-9pm.)* If you're more partial to photography, the recently opened **sf black & white gallery** transforms a spare office space into a backdrop for its collection of simple yet classic black and white images of San Francisco. Photographs go for as little as $30. *(619 Post St., at Taylor St. ☎929-9424. Open M-F 9am-9pm; Sa-Su 12pm-9pm.)* **The Academy of Art College** has galleries that showcase student work on a monthly basis. *(410 Bush St., between Kearny St. and Grant Ave. ☎274-8680. Additional locations: 625 Sutter St. and 79 New Montgomery St. Open M-Sa 9am-5pm; if students are milling around, it may be possible to get in later.)*

CHINATOWN

WAVERLY PLACE. This little alley offers off-beat architecture without the garishness of Grant Ave. The fire escapes are painted in pinks and greens and held together by railings made of intricate Chinese patterns. The alley is also home to **Tien Hou Temple,** the oldest Chinese temple in the US. *(Between Sacramento and Washington St. and between Stockton St. and Grant Ave. Tien Hou Temple at 125 Waverly Pl.)*

GRANT AVENUE. The oldest street in San Francisco is today a sea of gaudy Chinese banners, signs, and architecture. During the day, Grant Ave. and nearby streets brim with tourists who stop at every block to buy health balls and chirping boxes while pretending not to notice the Chinese porn mags lining some shop windows. At the intersection of Bush St. and Grant Ave. stands the ornate, dragon-crested **Gateway to Chinatown,** a gift from Taiwan in 1970. "Everything in the world is in just proportion," declare the characters above the gate. Most of the picturesque pagodas punctuating these blocks were designed around or after 1900, not as authentic replicas of Chinese architecture, but as "exotic" temptations for Western tourists. While Grant Ave. is the center of Chinatown, to get a true taste of the neighborhood venture off into the alleys and side streets.

ROSS ALLEY. Ross Alley was once lined with brothels and gambling houses; today, it epitomizes the cramped look of old Chinatown. The narrow street has stood in for the "Orient" in such films as *Big Trouble in Little China, Karate Kid II,* and *Indiana Jones and the Temple of Doom. (Ross Alley is located off Washington St., between Stockton and Grant St.)* Squeeze into a tiny doorway to watch fortune cookies being shaped by hand at the ▇**Golden Gate Cookie Factory.** All cookies that don't come out according to the baker's high standards are put in big tins for free taste-testing. *(56 Ross Alley. ☎ 781-3956. Open daily 9am-8pm. Bag of cookies $3, with "funny," "sexy," or "lucky" fortunes $5.)*

NORTH BEACH

North Beach is worth visiting during both its relaxed daytime and its neon-lit evenings. Over the years, the old Italian community has welcomed beatniks, hippies, and swells of tourists without compromising its Old World feel.

WASHINGTON SQUARE. North Beach's piazza, a pretty, tree-lined lawn, fills every morning with practitioners of *tai chi.* By noon, sunbathers and picnickers take over. This was the site of Joe DiMaggio's wedding to his first wife, Dorothy Arnold (and not, as you may hear, to his second wife, Marilyn Monroe). The **St. Peter and St. Paul Catholic Church** invites tired sightseers to take refuge in its dark, wooden nave. *(666 Filbert St.)* Turn-of-the-century San Francisco philanthropist and party-girl Lillie Hitchcock Coit donated the **Volunteer Firemen Memorial** in the middle of the square after being rescued from a fire as a young girl. *(Washington Sq. is bordered by Union, Filbert, Stockton, and Powell St.)*

TELEGRAPH HILL. Overlooking Washington Park and North Beach, Telegraph Hill was originally the site of a semaphore that signaled the arrival of ships in gold rush days. Today, tourists hike up the hill to visit **Coit Tower** (est. 1933), which stands 210 ft. high and commands a spectacular view of the city and the Bay. During the Depression, the government's Works Progress Administration employed artists to paint the inside of the dome with colorful and surprisingly subversive murals that depict laborers at work. *(MUNI bus #39 goes all the way to Coit tower. By car, follow Lombard St. to the top, where there is free 30min. parking daily 10am-6:30pm. Tower: ☎ 362-0808. Open daily 10am-6:30pm. Free guided tour of the murals Sa 11am. Elevator $3.75, ages 6-12 $1.50, seniors $2.50, under 6 free.)*

THE LOCAL STORY

FORBIDDEN CITY

In the 1930s and 40s, the second floor of 363 Sutter St., below Stockton St., housed Chinatown's Forbidden City, a vaudeville club with a full Asian-American cast performing everything from Sinatra standards to tap, but nothing "traditionally" Chinese. Poised to profit from America's fascination with the "fragile exoticism" of the Far East, proprietor Charlie Low tempted audiences with images of Oriental fantasy but then wowed them with all-American vaudeville acts.

Forbidden City's performers were the victims of open prejudice. They were rarely praised on their own merits, but rather likened to white entertainment icons. The "Chinese Sally Rand" Noel Toy performed as the popular Bubble dancer, but the risqué act shocked her community. Larry Ching was dubbed the "Chinese Frank Sinatra" but was also called "slant eyes" and "chink" by American soldiers during World War II; after the club closed in the 60s, he drove a truck for a local newspaper.

Rather than become a cultural landmark, the venue fell into obscurity after a major fire in the 1980s and a renumbering of the block. Of late, it housed a computer instruction company. Arthur Dong's award-winning documentary, **Forbidden City USA,** supplies the only thorough record of the club's existence by giving its performers the chance to offer their memories to posterity.

SAN FRANCISCO ART INSTITUTE. The oldest art school west of the Mississippi, the San Francisco Art Institute has produced a number of American greats, including Mark Rothko, Ansel Adams, Dorothea Lange, and James Weeks. To the left as you enter is the **Diego Rivera Gallery.** One wall is covered by a huge 1931 Rivera mural entitled *The Making of a Fresco Showing the Building of a City*, which depicts Rivera working on a mural commemorating the working man and his eventual triumph over big business bosses. The gallery hosts weekly student exhibits with receptions *(Tu 5-7pm)*. Farther down the left-hand hallway are the **Walter and McBean Galleries,** which show exhibits by established artists. Outside these galleries and across the airy modern "quadrangle," newly renovated **Pete's Cafe** serves up cheap homemade sandwiches and veggie options, making it a nice picnic spot with fantastic views of the Bay. *(800 Chestnut St., between Leavenworth and Jones St. ☎ 771-7020 or 800-345-7324; www.sfai.edu. 60 free lectures by artists throughout the year; call for additional info. Walter and McBean Galleries open Tu-Su 11am-6pm. Pete's Cafe open in summer 9am-3pm; during the school year 9am-5pm.)*

■ **CITY LIGHTS BOOKSTORE.** Beat writers came to national attention when Lawrence Ferlinghetti's City Lights Bookstore (est. 1953) published Allen Ginsberg's *Howl*, which was banned in 1956 and then subjected to an extended trial at the end of which a judge found the poem "not obscene." A glance around the store confirms the obvious radical leanings of a bookstore rooted in the subversive potential of intellectual countermovements led by daring authors such as Simone de Beauvoir and Pablo Neruda. City Lights has expanded since its Beat days and now stocks wide selection of fiction and poetry, but it remains committed to publishing young poets and writers under its own label. Black and white signs beckon visitors to sit down and read a book. Writers without permanent addresses can have their mail held in the store. See also **Shopping: Books,** p. 120

FINANCIAL DISTRICT AND THE EMBARCADERO

Certain areas of the Financial District's architectural landscape rescue it from the otherwise banal functionalism of the business area. The leading lady of the city's skyline, the **Transamerica Pyramid,** is, according to new-age sources, directly centered on the telluric currents of the Golden Dragon Ley line between Easter Island and Stonehenge. Planned as an architect's joke and co-opted by one of the leading architectural firms in the country, the building has earned disdain from purists and reverence from city planners. Unless you're an employee, tight security means there is no chance of a top-floor view, though the lobby is currently undergoing renovation to modernize a virtual viewing lounge in the Washington St. entrance where you can peer down on the masses from ground-level. *(600 Montgomery St., between Clay and Washington St.)* At the foot of Market St., **Justin Herman Plaza** and its formidable 1971 Vaillancourt Fountain, made of pre-cast aggregate concrete, invite total visitor immersion. Bands and rallyists often rent out the area during lunch. Dubbed "a famous city's most famous landmark" by legendary Pulitzer Prize-winning *SF Chronicle* columnist Herb Caen, the 660 ft. waterfront **Ferry Building,** at the foot of Market St., has regained a bit of its lost grandeur with a 2003 restoration. A. Page Brown designed the elegant port with repeated archways and Corinthian columns to recall Roman aqueducts.

CIVIC CENTER

San Francisco's theater scene dominates the majestic Civic Center. The palatial **San Francisco City Hall,** modeled after Rome's St. Peter's Basilica, is the centerpiece of the largest US gathering of Beaux Arts architecture. *(1 Dr. Carlton B. Goodlett Pl., at Van Ness Ave. ☎ 554-4000. Open M-F 8am-8pm, Sa-Su noon-4pm.)* Overlooking the Civic Center, the **State Building's** grandeur is comparable to City Hall's in both structure and function. Home to the state Supreme Court, it also features a small but interesting art collection in the lobby at the Golden Gate Ave. entrance and an exhibition room near the McAllister St. entrance. (*350 McAllister St., between Polk and Larkin St.*) The **United Nations Plaza** hosts the city's **Farmers Market** and a general assembly of pigeons. (*Farmers Market on Polk St. in summer W and Su 5:30am-5:30pm.*)

The seating in the glass-and-brass **Louise M. Davies Symphony Hall** was designed to give most audience members a close-up view of performers. Visually, the building is a smashing success, as is the **San Francisco Symphony**. (*201 Van Ness Ave.* ☎ *552-8000.*) The highly regarded **San Francisco Opera Company** and the **San Francisco Ballet** perform at the recently renovated **War Memorial Opera House**. (*301 Van Ness Ave., between Grove and McAllister St.*) For performance info, see Entertainment, p. 125.

TENDERLOIN

Do not walk alone here, as the area can be dangerous, especially at night. Witness the scene more safely by day, and also check out the vibrant cultural offerings. The **Luggage Store**, 1007 Market St., near 6th St., and its mother organization, **509 Cultural Center**, at 509 Ellis St., present performing arts events, exhibitions, and arts education initiatives with an emphasis on promoting a rich cultural and artistic tradition to counter the Tenderloin's bad reputation. Started by artists and residents in the late 80s, the group strives to draw on the neighborhood's diversity to gain a sense of community. Activities include comedy open mic (Tu 8pm), an experimental music series (Th 8pm), and the "In The Street" theater festival in early October. (☎ 255-5971; www.luggagestoregallery.org. Gallery open W-Sa noon-5pm; hours vary if there is no show.) The **Art Institute of California**, 1170 Market St., at UN Plaza, near 8th St., hosts occasional student shows in its lobby. The space is great for a brief viewing, but don't expect to find a multitude of works—it cannot hold more than 15 paintings, which rotate quarterly. (☎ 865-0198. Open M-Th 9am-8pm, F-Sa 9am-6pm.)

HAYES VALLEY

A few years ago, artists of all types, from architects to fashion and interior designers, began to open studios on and around Hayes St. As if a natural extension of the artist community, cafes sprung up, providing the essential social and caffeine reprieves. After them came the young trendsetters, and thus a hip neighborhood was born. Success has also brought higher prices—starving artists are few and far between. An established contemporary art stronghold, the **Bucheon Gallery**, 389 Grove St., at Gough St., dazzles the art world with new exhibits of fresh and well-crafted work every five weeks. The gallery, which often donates its space for fundraising events for progressive causes, specializes in displaying the work of emerging and mid-career artists. Receptions are open to the public. (☎ 863-2891; www.bucheon.com. Open Tu-Sa 11am-6pm, occasionally Su. Free.)

NOB HILL AND RUSSIAN HILL

In this expensive, mostly residential area, the main attractions are the views. You'll find more activity as the area merges into Union Sq. and the Tenderloin.

THE CROOKEDEST STREET IN THE WORLD. Captivatingly lush and beautifully manicured flower beds are as stunning as the famously curvy road they flank. The iconically San Franciscan curves of Lombard St. were installed in the 1920s so that horse-drawn carriages could negotiate the extremely steep hill. Tourists standing in the middle of the road to photograph these curves may infuriate drivers trying to navigate them. The top of Lombard St. affords a fantastic view of the city and harbor. The view north along Hyde St. reveals lonely Alcatraz floating in the bay. (*Between Hyde and Leavenworth St., running down Russian Hill.*)

GRACE CATHEDRAL AND HUNTINGTON PARK. The largest Gothic edifice west of the Mississippi, **Grace Cathedral** is Nob Hill's stained glass-studded crown. The main doors that beckon visitors into this concrete version of a cut-stone cathedral are replicas cast from Lorenzo Ghiberti's **Doors of Paradise,** which open on Florence's famed Baptistry. Inside, modern murals mix San Franciscan and national historical events with saintly scenes. The altar of the AIDS Interfaith Memorial Chapel celebrates the church's "inclusive community of love" with a lustrous and intricate Keith Haring triptych. Outside, this all-accepting behemoth of Christian modernity looks onto the turf and trees of **Huntington Park,** equipped with a playground and a reproduction of Rome's "Fountain of the Tortoises." *(1100 California St., between Jones and Taylor St. ☎749-6300; www.gracecathedral.org. Open Su-F 7am-6pm, Sa 8am-6pm. Services: M-F 7:30, 9am, 12:10pm; Sa 9 and 3pm; Su 7:30, 8:15, 11am, 6pm. Additional services Th 5:15pm and mid-Sept. to mid-June Su 3pm. Tours available M-F 1-3pm, Sa 11:30am-1:30pm, and Su 12:30-2pm. Tours may be cancelled due to wedding or funeral services. Suggested donation $3.)*

CABLE CAR POWERHOUSE AND MUSEUM. After the steep journey up Nob Hill, you'll understand the inspiration behind the vehicles celebrated at this museum. More an educational breather than a destination in its own right, the modest building is the working center of San Francisco's cable car system. Look down on 56,300 ft. of cable whizzing by, or view displays to learn more about the cars, some of which date back to 1873. The best place to catch an actual cable car is where Powell or Hyde meet Market St. *(1201 Mason St., at Washington St. ☎474-1887. Open daily Apr.-Sept. 10am-6pm; Oct.-Mar. 10am-5pm. Free.)*

PACIFIC HEIGHTS

Along Union and Sacramento St., Pacific Heights has the greatest number of **Victorian buildings** in the city. The Heights sustained serious damage in the 1989 earthquake—Victorian restoration has become a full-fledged enterprise here. Pierce and Clay St., in particular, have an abundance of grand homes. The Public Library offers free tours of Pacific Heights mansions (www.sfcityguides.com. Tours meet in Alta Plaza atop the stairs at Pierce and Clay St. every Sa and 3rd Tu at 11am.)

You need not be an architecture buff to appreciate **St. Dominic's Cathedral,** 2390 Bush St., at Steiner St., and its towering altar with an elaborate sculpture of Jesus and the 12 apostles or its imposing gray stone and Gothic-style facade. (Open M-Sa 6:30am-5:30pm, Su 7:30am-9pm. Mass M-F 6:30 and 8am, 5:30pm; Sa 8am and 5:30pm; Su 7:30am quiet mass, 9:30am family mass, 11:30am solemn choral, 1:30pm Spanish, 5:30pm contemporary music, 9pm candlelight service.) If you have any breath left after the steep climb up to the **Alta Plaza,** the views will snatch it away. Gaze downhill for a panorama of downtown San Francisco and Twin Peaks, or uphill along Pierce St. to catch a spectacular glimpse of the Bay. Sunbathe on the grassy slopes or swing like a carefree kid in the playground; this is a great place to spend a mellow afternoon or pack a picnic.

JAPANTOWN

Walking all the way through Japantown takes just minutes and is the only way to experience the area. Stores hawk Pokémon paraphernalia and karaoke bars resonate with J-pop along Post St. around the Japan Center. The five-tiered **Peace Pagoda** (on Geary St. between Webster and Laguna St.), a gift to the community from the Japanese government, once sat amid cherry trees and a reflecting pool. It is currently in the midst of a slow restoration process to convert its bleak paved lot into the inviting centerpiece of the Japan Center. A brighter example of Japanese architecture is the **Soto Zen Mission Sokoji Buddhist Temple,** 1691 Laguna St., at

Sutter St., where some meditation services are open to the public. (☎346-7540. Open Su-W and F-Sa 9am-5pm. Public Zazen services Su 8am, Tu 7:30am, W 6:30pm, F 6:30pm.; arrive 15min. early.)

After a draining day of traveling unwind at **Kabuki Springs and Spa,** 1750 Geary Blvd., at Fillmore St., which encourages an environment of respectful silence and meditation. Kabuki treats its patrons—a mix of older professionals, locals, and youngsters—to communal baths, a dry sauna, steam room, cold pool, and hot pool. (☎922-6000; www.kabukisprings.com. Women Su, W, F; Men M, Th, Sa; Coed Tu. Photo ID required. Open daily 10am-9:45pm. $16, after 5pm and on weekends $20. Massages $55-130. Body treatments $50-150. Facials $75-125.)

SOUTH OF MARKET AREA (SOMA)

To the uninitiated, South of Market may appear a bleak stretch of industrial wasteland, but the area is actually home to a good bit of excitement. As a center for modern and experimental art, SoMa has attracted hip youth who in turn bring with them fresh fashion and novel services. The leather and Levi's community has exercised its daring and outlandishness here ever since the 1940s. It's hard to deny the character and complexity of a place where dressing to the nines involves Pop Art-inspired hairstyles for some and chains, restraints, and leashes for others.

■**SAN FRANCISCO MUSEUM OF MODERN ART (SFMOMA).** Fascinating for its architecture as well as its contents, this black and gray marble-trimmed museum houses five spacious floors of art, with an emphasis on design, photography, and audiovisuals. SFMOMA teems with the largest collection of 20th-century art this side of New York, including famous works by Henri Matisse (including the portraits of Michael and Sarah Stein, his SF patrons), Andy Warhol (*National Velvet*), Frieda Kahlo (*Frieda and Diego Rivera*), Jasper Johns, Paul Klee, and Robert Rauschenberg. With new installations and special exhibits, including one that charts the developments in graphic and industrial design, SFMOMA succeeds in showcasing the ever-expanding art world. Daily film screenings in the 2nd floor Koret Center. *(151 3rd St., between Mission and Howard St. ☎357-4000; www.sfmoma.org. Open Sept. 7-May M-Tu and F-Su 11am-5:45pm, Th 11am-8:45pm; June-Sept. 6 M-Tu and F-Su 10am-6pm, Th 10am-9pm. Four free gallery tours per day. $10, students $6, seniors $7, under 13 free. Th 6-9pm half-price. Free 1st Tu of each month. Group discounts.)*

■**CALIFORNIA ACADEMY OF SCIENCES.** The Academy of Sciences, usually in Golden Gate Park, is currently closed for renovations until late 2008. It can be visited at its new location in SoMa near the Yuerba Buena Center for the Arts and the Metreon. The temporary location stills houses most of the original features such as the **National History Museum** and **Steinhart Aquarium,** with the notable exception that the **Morrison Planetarium** is closed to the public. *(875 Howard St. between 4th and 5th St. in SoMa. ☎750-7145; www.calacademy.org. Open daily 10am-5pm. Adults $7; students, seniors, and ages 12-17 $4.50; ages 4-11 $2. Free 1st W of each month.)*

YERBA BUENA CENTER FOR THE ARTS. The center runs an excellent theater and gallery space that emphasizes performance, film, viewer involvement, and local multicultural work—essentially anything that can be considered "adventurous art." It is surrounded by the **Yerba Buena Rooftop Gardens,** an oasis of foliage and gurgling fountains in a predominantly concrete neighborhood. *(701 Mission St., at 3rd St. ☎978-2787; www.yerbabuenaarts.org. Open Su and Tu-W noon-5pm, Th-Sa noon-8pm. Free tours 1st Th of the month 6pm. $6, seniors and students $3. Free 1st Tu of each month, students and seniors free every Th.)*

Within the gardens but a sight unto itself, the **Zeum** is a completely interactive "art and technology center" aimed primarily at children and teens. Beside studios for arts and crafts, claymation, and karaoke, Zeum has a music performance space and an ice skating and bowling center. The best draw is the **carousel,** built in 1906 and

SAN FRANCISCO

TO WED OR NOT TO WED

Ever the leader in raising the quality of life for its gay residents, San Francisco isn't used to riding shotgun in the bandwagon headed for the gay rights horizon. But when the Massachusetts Supreme Judicial Court deemed the gay marriage ban unconstitutional on November 11, 2003, San Francisco suddenly found itself in the backseat.

Refusing to be shown up, SF Mayor Gavin Newsom, in an appeal to the equal protection granted all persons under the state constitution, began issuing marriage licenses on February 12, 2004. After 4037 couples had been married with Newsom's blessing and tearful family, friends, and city officials looking on, California's high court issued a halt on gay marriages on March 11, 2004. Then, on August 12, the California Supreme Court ruled that Newson had overstepped his legal authority and that all of the same-sex marriages were "void and of no legal effect."

Though the ruling came as a blow to gay rights activists, not to mention the thousands of newlyweds, the issue remains far from resolved. Challenges to the constitutionality of California's ban on gay marriage have already been filed. Whatever happens, SF's heady month of marriages will remain an inspiring chapter in the city's history of social activism.

reopened after a 25-year hiatus. *(221 4th St., at Howard St. ☎ 777-2800; www.zeum.org. Open in summer Tu-Su 11am-5pm; in winter W-Su 11am-5pm. $7, students and seniors $6, ages 4-18 $5, under 4 free. Carousel: open daily 11am-6pm. $2 for 2 rides.)*

THE MISSION

The Mission is slowly outgrowing its reputation as one of the most underappreciated neighborhoods in the city. Beyond the fabulous food and kickin' nightlife, the Mission is home to a vibrant community of painters and writers struggling to keep their messages heard in the face of dot-commers and rising rents. **16th Street** is perhaps the most pulsing, pluralistic, personality-filled boulevard in all of San Francisco, where shops cater to various vegetarian diets, political radicals, and literary dissenters.

MISIÓN DE LOS DOLORES (MISSION DOLORES). Located in the old heart of San Francisco, the Mission Dolores is thought to be the city's oldest building. Father Junípero Serra founded the mission in 1776, naming it in honor of St. Francis of Assisi. Later, due to its proximity to the Laguna de Nuestra Señora de los Dolores (Lagoon of Our Lady of Sorrows), the mission became known as Misión de los Dolores. The Basilica (restored after the 1906 earthquake) overwhelms the eyes with a chevron pattern on the ceiling. Bougainvillea, poppies, and birds-of-paradise bloom in the cemetery, which was featured in Alfred Hitchcock's 1958 film *Vertigo. (3321 16th St., at Dolores St. ☎ 621-8203. Open May-Oct. Su-F 9am-4:30pm, Sa 9am-4:30pm; Nov.-Apr. daily 9am-4pm. Mass: in English M-Sa 7:30 in Old Mission, 9am in Basilica, Sa 5pm in Old Mission, Su 8 and 10am, in Spanish Su noon. $3, ages 5-12 $2.)*

MISSION MURALS. The magnificent murals scattered throughout the Mission certainly warrant straying from the main thoroughfare. Continuing a long Mexican tradition made famous by Diego Rivera and José Orozco, the Mission murals have been a source of pride for Chicano artists, schoolchildren, and community members since the 1980s. Standouts include the political murals of **Balmy Alley** off 24th St. between Harrison and Folsom St., a three-building tribute to guitar god Carlos Santana at 22nd St. and Van Ness Ave., the face of **St. Peter's Church** at 24th and Florida St., and the urban living center on 19th St. between Valencia and Guerrero St. The latest addition to the mural scene is Mona Caron's mural at **300 Church St.**, at the corner of 15th St. one block south of Market St. The mural shows the evolution of Market St. since the 1920s. The passage of time flows west to east and charts a history of labor and war protests.

OTHER SIGHTS. The Jack Hanley Gallery specializes in exhibiting fresh talent who use the gallery as a stepping stone to international acclaim. *(395 and 389 Valencia St., at 15th St. ☎522-1623; www.jackhanley.com. Open Tu-Sa 11am-6pm.)* **Osento** is a 25-year-old Japanese-style bathhouse for women, with wet and dry saunas, a hot tub, an outdoor dipping pool, sundecks, and a relaxation room. *(955 Valencia St., between 20th and 21st St. ☎282-6333. Open daily noon-midnight; last admission 11pm. 14+. $10-20, over 70 free, senior discount. 1hr. massage $60-80. No credit cards.)* **Dolores Park** is a prime hang-out for residents of the Mission, the Castro, and Noe Valley. *(18th to 20th St. between Church and Dolores St.)* **La Galería de la Raza** celebrates local Chicano and Latino artists who push the boundaries of standard contemporary art with exhibitions every eight weeks or so. *(2857 24th St., at Bryant St. ☎826-8009; www.galeria-delaraza.org. Open W-Sa noon-6pm. Free.)* Attached to the gallery is **Studio 24,** a space where Chicano, Latino, and Mexican artists sell artwork, crafts, and jewelry. *(Open Sept.-Dec. daily noon-6pm; Jan.-Aug. W-Su noon-6pm.)*

THE CASTRO

Out and proud GLBT folk find comfort and fun on the rainbow flag-lined streets of the Castro. The concept, as well as the reality, of an all-queer neighborhood draws queer tourists and their friends from around the world. Beyond the glitz of shimmering bodies and the gyms where they are sculpted, the Castro harbors a more playful side. A slew of kitschy stores and a contingent of rebellious youth add flair to the picture-perfect streets, where couples make a full-time job out of seeing and being seen. Trevor Hailey, a resident since 1972, is consistently recognized as one of SF's top tour leaders. Her 4hr. **walking tour** covers Castro life and history from the Gold Rush to the present. *(☎550-8110; trvrhailey@aol.com. Tours Tu-Sa 10am. $45; lunch included. Reservations required.)* The steeply sloped areas to the south and west of Castro Village tend to be residential; and the vibrantly painted old **Victorians,** of which Collingwood and Noe St. have their fair share, are worth visiting. For architecture without the walk, head to the **Castro Theatre** at 429 Castro St., an Art Deco appropriation of a Mexican cathedral design.

TWIN PEAKS

Tourist hub by day, lovebird locale by night—the lookout-*cum*-make-out point atop Twin Peaks (not to be confused with the David Lynch TV show) offers what many consider to be the best views of the city. From Alcatraz to the Transamerica Pyramid to a big rainbow flag at the foot of Market St. in the Castro, all major San Francisco landmarks are on display. On rare fogless nights, the views at 922 ft. are particularly sublime; at all times of day, even in summer, the winds are intense and the temperature much chillier than in the valleys below. Local lore maintains that either the peaks were once a married Native American couple parted by the Great Spirit during a vicious squabble or that the mountains are actually the transformed daughters of a Native American chief. The Spanish opted for the more voluptuous interpretation and referred to the peaks as "Los Pechos de la Choca" (the Breasts of the Indian Maiden). Ultimately the name was settled on the far less steamy "Twin Peaks." The peaks are located west of Noe Valley, between Portola Dr., Clarendon Ave., and Upper Market St. From Noe Valley take MUNI bus #48 to Diamond Heights. From elsewhere in the city take MUNI bus K, L, or M to Forest Hills, then MUNI bus #36. For a scenic route by car, bike, or foot, take 17th St. to Clayton St. to Clarendon Ave. and head up Twin Peaks Blvd. to the top.

THE HAIGHT

All around Haight and Ashbury St., vestiges of the 60s exist in semi-harmony with recent upscale recent arrivals such as yuppie cafes and boutiques. Inexpensive bars and ethnic restaurants, action-packed street life, anarchist literature, and shops selling pipes for, um, tobacco come together under the legacy of the free-love era. While the Upper Haight tends to attract a younger tourist crowd, the Lower Haight is the stomping ground for longtime locals.

The former homes of several countercultural legends continue to attract visitors, even though new residents inhabit the often unmarked cribs. From the corner of Haight and Ashbury St., walk up Ashbury St. to #710, just south of Waller St., to check out the house occupied by the **Grateful Dead** when they were still the War-locks. Look across the street for the **Hell's Angels'** house. If you walk back to Haight St., go right three blocks, and make a left on Lyon St. to check out **Janis Joplin's** old abode. (122 Lyon St., between Page and Oak St.) Cross the Panhandle, continue three blocks to Fulton St., turn right, and wander seven blocks toward the park to see where the Manson "family" planned murder and mayhem at the **Charles Manson** mansion. (2400 Fulton St., at Willard St.) The **San Francisco Public Library** sponsors a free walking tour focused on the area's pre-hippie incarnation as a Victorian-era resort. (Tours leave from the Park Branch Library at 1833 Page St., near Cole St. ☎ 557-4266; www.sfcityguides.org. Tours Su 11am.)

Several parks dot the Haight. You may see police lurking in the bushes, as the parks are rumored to be popular places to buy marijuana. **Buena Vista Park,** which runs along Haight St. between Central and Baker St. and continues south, resembles a sprawling jungle complete with a dense canopy. The lush and exotic fauna provides a private/public haven for free spirits. An unofficial crash pad and community center for San Francisco skaters, Buena Vista is supposedly safer than **Alamo Square,** which lies northeast of the Haight at Hayes and Steiner St. Across Alamo Sq.'s gentle grassy slope, a string of beautiful and brightly colored Victorian homes known as the **Painted Ladies** glow against the backdrop of the skyline.

GOLDEN GATE PARK

In-line skaters, neo-flower children, and sunbathers converge in this lush city oasis, which spreads 3½ mi. from the Haight to the ocean, separating the residential Richmond and Sunset districts with half a mile of greenery. It is bounded by Fulton St. to the north, Stanyan St. to the east, Lincoln Way to the south, and Ocean Beach to the west; a strip called the Panhandle juts east between Fell and Oak St. into the Haight. Originally the "carriage entrance," it contains the oldest trees in the park. The busy section of Hwy. 1 running through the park is called Park Presidio By-Pass Dr. going north and Cross-Over Dr. going south.

Inside the park, open green meadows, groves, and myriad little gardens patch together the larger developed areas, namely the museum complex in the eastern third of the park, Stow Lake, the stadium, the golf course, and soccer fields near the western edge. Don't rush through the park—locals bask in it all weekend long. Intriguing museums and cultural events pick up where the lush flora and fauna finally leave off, and athletic opportunities abound. On Sundays, traffic is banned from park roads, and bicycles and in-line skates come out in full force.

CONSERVATORY OF FLOWERS. The impressive conservatory, recently reopened after extensive renovations, presides over Conservatory Valley, whose huge, perfectly manicured flower beds—among the best in the entire park—entice visitors to this marvelous glass greenhouse. (☎ 666-7001; www.conservatoryofflowers.org. Open Tu-Su 9am-4:30pm. $5; ages 12-17, seniors, and students $3; ages 5-11 $1.50; under 5 free. Free 1st Tu of each month.) Across JFK Dr. from the conservatory, just south of **Lily Pond,** the **National AIDS Memorial Grove** rests with a somber, quiet strength among the flowering dogwoods and giant redwoods of **De Laveaga Dell.** (AIDS Memorial: ☎ 750-8340; www.aidsmemorial.org. Call to schedule a 20-min. tour that begins and ends at the Main Portal of the Grove, near the corner of Middle Dr. East and Bowling Green Dr. Free tours available Mar.-Oct. 1st and 3rd Sa of the month 9am-noon; Nov.-Feb. 1st Sa 9am-noon.)

STRYBING ARBORETUM AND BOTANICAL GARDENS. The Strybing Arboretum is home to over 7000 varieties of plants, including collections from Chile, New Zealand, and the tropical, high-altitude New World Cloud Forests. In addition to gardens maintained at Mediterranean and mid-temperate climates, the arboretum offers thematic special collections, such as the **Primitive Plant Garden** near the Friends Gate in the northern part of the Arboretum. On the eastern side, near the **Strybing Store** and **Russell Library of Horticulture,** is the **Garden of Fragrance,** designed especially for the visually impaired—all labels are in Braille, and plants, such as sedge and dwarf honeybush, are chosen specifically for their textures and scents. On the western side is the majestic and spacious **Moon Viewing Garden,** which offers the perfect vantage for basking in lunar rays. *(On Lincoln Way at 9th Ave.* ☎ *661-1316; www.strybing.org. Open M-F 8am-4:30pm, Sa-Su and holidays 10am-5pm. Free guided tours from Strybing Store M-F 1:30pm, Sa-Su 10:30am and 1:30pm; from North Entrance W, F, Su 2pm.)*

OTHER GARDENS. Near the **Music Concourse** off of South Dr., the **Shakespeare Garden,** filled with crab-apples and red brick paths, contains almost every flower and plant ever mentioned by the Bard. Plaques with the relevant quotations are hung on the back wall, and there's a map to help you find your favorite hyacinths and rue. *(Open daily dawn-dusk. Free.)* The **Rhododendron Dell,** between the temporarily closed Academy of Sciences and JFK Dr., honors park designer John McLaren with a splendid profusion of his favorite flower. The 850 varieties of rhododendron bloom the first weeks of spring. Ring-like **Stow Lake** sits in the middle of the park. Cross one of two stone bridges in order to explore the big, green island of **Strawberry Hill.**

OTHER SITES. Brimming **Spreckels Lake,** on JFK Dr. along the northern border of the park, is populated by crowds of turtles that pile onto a big rock to sun themselves. The multi-national collection of gardens and museums in Golden Gate Park would not be complete without something distinctly American...like a herd of **bison.** A dozen shaggy beasts loll about a spacious paddock just southwest of Spreckels Lake. In the northwest corner of the park, the Dutch Windmill has done its last good turn in the cheery **Queen Wilhelmina Tulip Garden,** where 10,000 bulbs burst forth color in March. Rounding out the days of yore is the Children's Playground, in the southeast corner of the park, with its carousel (circa 1912), accompanied by a $50,000 Gebruder band organ. *Let's Go* recommends riding the ▨**lion** or the ▨**green dragon.** *(Open early June-early Sept. daily 10am-4:30pm; early Sept.-early June F-Su 10am-4:30pm. $1.50, ages 6-12 $0.50.)*

BEACH CHALET. The Beach Chalet, a Spanish colonial-style villa built in 1925, sits on the western edge of the park on the Great Hwy., south of Fulton St. During the Great Depression, the WPA enlisted French-born artist Lucien Labaudt to design frescoes for the chalet's walls; the elaborate paintings of 1930s San Francisco were completed just in time for WWII, when the building was used as an army outpost. The restored chalet reopened in 1996, and the building now serves as the official **visitors center** for Golden Gate Park. *(*☎ *751-2766. Open daily 9am-7pm.)*

JAPANESE TEA GARDEN. During the first week of April the **Japanese Cherry Orchard** blooms intoxicatingly, enticing visitors to the elegant **Japanese Tea Garden.** The oldest Japanese garden in the US, created for the 1894 Mid-Winter Exposition, the garden is a serene collection of wooden buildings, carefully pruned trees, and graceful footbridges. *(Lincoln Way and South Dr.* ☎ *752-1171. Open daily in summer 8:30am-6pm; in winter 8:30am-5pm. $3.50, ages 6-12 and seniors $1.25. Free in summer 8:30-9:30am and 5-6pm; in winter 8:30-9:30am and 4-5pm. Half-price Sept.-May 1st W of the month.)*

LINCOLN PARK

At the northwest end of San Francisco, Lincoln Park has spectacular views of the Pacific and the Golden Gate Bridge. The bulky patch of meandering paths and historical sights is ideal for an afternoon hike or summertime picnic.

CALIFORNIA PALACE OF THE LEGION OF HONOR. In the middle of Lincoln Park, between the golf course and the Land's End wilderness, is a magnificent enclave of European proportions. The California Palace of the Legion of Honor was built in 1924 after one of San Francisco's leading ladies, Mrs. Alma Spreckels, fell in love with the temporary "French Pavilion" built in Golden Gate Park for the Panama International Exhibition. The pavilion was a replica of Paris's Palais de la Legion d'Honneur, and Spreckels was determined to build a permanent one of equal stature. A copy of Rodin's *Thinker* beckons visitors into the grand courtyard, where a glass pyramid recalls another Paris treasure, the Louvre. Works from such masters as Rubens, Dalí, and Rodin await inside. Other draws include a pneumatically operated 4500-pipe organ, played in free weekly recitals *(Sa-Su 4pm),* and a gilded ceiling from a 15th-century *palacio* in Toledo, Spain. Free tours given on Saturdays in a different language each week (in order from 1st to 4th Sa: French, Italian, Spanish, Russian). Just outside the Palace, a **Holocaust Memorial** sculpture depicts a mass of emaciated, denuded victims with a single, hopeful survivor in tattered clothing looking out through a barbed-wire fence to the beauty of the Pacific. *(☎863-3330; www.legionofhonor.org. Open Tu-Su 9:30am-5pm. $8, seniors $6, under 17 $5, under 12 free. $7 surcharge for special exhibits. Tu free. $2 discount with MUNI transfer. Wheelchair accessible.)*

CLIFF HOUSE. The precarious Cliff House, built in 1909, is the third to occupy this spot; the previous two burned down. It has slowly deteriorated due to decades of neglect, and the complex is undergoing yet another renovation, scheduled to be completed by September 2004. The **Golden Gate National Recreation Area Visitors Center,** housed within the Cliff House, distributes information on Lincoln Park, Ocean Beach, and the entire GGNRA. Don't feed the coin-operated binoculars that look out over Seal Rocks; instead, head inside for a free look through the GGNRA telescope. *(☎556-8642. Open daily 10am-5pm.)* Overlooking the cliffs and the Pacific, **Camera Obscura** contains a periscope-like mirrored lens on its roof, and, as the lens turns in circles, light from outside is bounced down into the "dark room" and onto a concave viewing plate, displaying the ocean vistas and nearby Seal Rocks, all magnified 700%. *(☎750-0415. Open daily 11am-sunset. $2.)*

SUTRO BATHS AND SUTRO HEIGHTS PARK. Slightly north of Cliff House rest the ruins of Adolph Sutro's 1896 bathhouse, known as the Sutro Baths. Up the hill from the intersection of Point Lobos and 48th Ave., and to the east of the Cliff House and the Baths, is spectacular Sutro Heights Park. Sadly underused, the park offers unparalleled views of the city and surrounding watery expanses. A lion-guarded gate recalls the day when the hill was Adolph's palatial personal garden.

GOLDEN GATE BRIDGE AND THE PRESIDIO

GOLDEN GATE BRIDGE

When Captain John Fremont coined the term "Golden Gate" in 1846, he meant to name the harbor entrance to the San Francisco Bay after the mythical Golden Horn port of Constantinople. In 1937, however, the colorful name became permanently associated with Joseph Strauss's engineering masterpiece—the Golden Gate Bridge. Built for only $35 million, the bridge stretches across 1¼ mi. of ocean, its towers looming 65 stories above the Bay. It can sway up to 27 ft. in each direction during high winds. On sunny days, hundreds of people take the 30min. walk across the bridge. The views from the bridge are amazing, especially from the Vista Point just at the Marin end of the bridge. To see the bridge itself, it's best to get a bit farther away. Fort Point and Fort Baker in the Presidio, Land's End in Lincoln Park, Mt. Livermore on Angel Island, and Hawk Hill off Conzelman Rd. in the Marin Headlands all offer spectacular views of the bridge on clear days. *(MUNI #29 and #28 buses take passengers to the bridge. By car, take Lincoln Blvd.)*

THE PRESIDIO

It is easy to see why the Presidio attracted such attention from Spain, Mexico, and the US. Its expanses are idyllic, secluded, and deeply forested. When Spanish settlers forged their way up the San Francisco peninsula from Baja California in 1769, they established *presidios*, or military outposts, along the way. San Francisco's Presidio, the northernmost point of Spanish territory in North America, was dedicated in 1776. The settlement stayed in Spanish hands for only 45 years before the deed passed to Mexico upon winning its independence from Spain. In 1848, the US took over the Presidio as part of the Treaty of Guadalupe Hidalgo, which ended the Mexican-American War. Gold fever stimulated expansion of the outpost, and a forest barrier was constructed in 1883 to assert military authority and set the post apart from the expanding city. The Presidio assumed greater importance during WWII after the attack on Pearl Harbor. Crissy Field's Intelligence School and the Letterman Army Hospital became leaders in their respective fields during the war. Today, the Presidio is part of the **Golden Gate National Recreation Area (GGNRA),** run by the National Park Service in conjunction with the Presidio Trust, which is raising funds to make the park self-sufficient by 2013 and coordinating the ongoing renovation and modernization of roads, buildings, and trails in the park.

MAIN POST. The once-grand barracks that make up Main Post are now a semi-historic playground for the San Francisco Film Society and any other non-profit agency willing to fork over funds for a lease. Remnants of the original Spanish settlement are on view in the **Officer's Club,** one of the many historic buildings that surround the 1776 Parade Ground. The **William Penn Mott, Jr. Visitors Center** offers free maps, glossy viewbooks, and pocket walking tour guides that explain the park's present and past. *(Temporarily located in the Presidio Officer's club in Building 50, on Moraga Ave.* ☎ *561-4323; www.nps.gov/psrf. Open daily 9am-5pm.)*

SAN FRANCISCO NATIONAL CEMETERY. This 28-acre cemetery, which houses the graves of over 30,000 soldiers and their families, was the first national cemetery on the West Coast. The 450 soldiers of the all-black Buffalo Soldier regiments of the US Army as well as Pauline Cushman Fryer, the Union's most famous female spy, rest here. Maps and registers are available inside the entrance gate. *(Just off Lincoln Blvd. at Sheridan Ave., in the center of the Presidio.* ☎ *650-589-7737.)*

FORT POINT. Fort Point, under the Golden Gate Bridge in the northernmost corner of the park, used to be called "the Gibraltar of the West." During the Civil War, the fort was the West Coast's main defense post against the Confederate Army, housing a garrison of men and nearly 200 guns and cannons. Today, the cavernous fort is open to the public and hosts historical recreations (such as cannon-loading demonstrations), free guided and audio tours, and exhibits. The top tier of the four-story building is windy but the view is worth the climb. *(MUNI buses #28 and 29 stop at the Golden Gate Bridge, where dirt paths and paved roads lead to the fort. By car, take Lincoln Blvd. to Long Ave. to Marine Dr. Limited parking.* ☎ *556-1693; www.nps.gov/fopo. Open F-Su 10am-5pm due to Golden Gate Bridge retrofit. Wheelchair accessible.)*

MARINA

Charming Spanish colonial-style houses with lavish gardens, stunning views of Marin, and a high quotient of young beautiful socialites characterize the residential Marina. You would never know that the area was one of the worst struck by the 1989 earthquake, during which massive fires destroyed several buildings. The main attractions stretch along the waterfront across the northern edge of the city.

⬛ PALACE OF FINE ARTS. The majestic rotunda, curving colonnades, nobly drooping trees, and subtly spraying fountain of the Palace of Fine Arts were reconstructed from remnants of the 1915 Panama-Pacific Exposition, designed to commemorate the opening of the Panama Canal and to exemplify San Francisco's recovery from the 1906 earthquake. To catch the Palace in its most resplendent light, locals come around late afternoon to lounge on its lawn along Baker St. while the setting sun illuminates the rotunda with an ethereal glow. Shakespearean plays are performed here during the summer, and the nighttime lights are glorious. The **Palace of Fine Arts Theater,** located directly behind the rotunda, hosts everything from dance and theater to the Magnetic Fields. *(On Baker St., between Jefferson and Bay St. Open daily 6am-9pm. Free. Theater: ☎563-6504; www.palaceoffinearts.org.)*

■ **EXPLORATORIUM.** *Scientific American* called this "the best science museum in the world," but museum literature describes it as "a vibrant, sprawling landscape of sights, sounds and curiosities" meant to capture the interest of adults and children alike. Displays include interactive tornadoes, computer planet-managing, and giant bubble-makers. Spectators gather for demonstrations such as a cow's eye dissection or changing special exhibitions. Within the Exploratorium dwells the **Tactile Dome,** a pitch-dark maze of tunnels, slides, nooks, and crannies designed to help refine your sense of touch. *(3601 Lyon St. ☎561-0360; www.exploratorium.edu. Open Tu-Su 10am-5pm. Groups of 10 or more required to make reservations. $12; students, seniors, disabled, and ages 9-17 $9.50; ages 4-12 $8; under 3 free. Free 1st W of each month. Tactile Dome: ☎561-0362. $15, includes general admission. Credit card required for reservation; book at least 1 day in advance.)*

WAVE ORGAN. Past the Golden Gate Yacht Club at the end of a long jetty in the west harbor, the Wave Organ is arguably one of San Francisco's most neglected but worthwhile treasures. This acoustic environmental sculpture made of 25 pipes jutting out of the ocean once created musical sounds as waves crashed against it. Conceived by Peter Richards in 1986, sculptor and stone mason George Gonzalez developed the marble and granite design for the seating area, which makes this a perfect solitary getaway. All sorts of carvings can be discerned if you look closely. Regardless of its quiet state of disrepair, the wave organ provides a rare view of the city and Bay unencumbered by tourists, where the only sound you hear is the gentle lapping of the waves in the silence of music's absence.

FORT MASON

Fort Mason Center is home to the original headquarters of the 1906 earthquake relief site. Its initial purpose, quite singular in scope, contrasts now with the diverse cultural museums and resources that inhabit the fort. Nevertheless, with its orderly row of buildings it still seems like a military outpost. From innovative theater to small exhibits of Italian and African-American art, the variety of attractions in Fort Mason remains relatively unknown to both travelers and locals. Fort Mason Center is a quiet waterfront counterpart to the tourist blitz of nearby Fisherman's Wharf. On the first Wednesday of every month, all museums are free and open until 7pm. The grounds are also home to a popular hostel and the headquarters of the **Golden Gate National Recreation Area (GGNRA).** These manicured greens are a swell spot for strolling. (Main Office open M-F 9am-5:30pm, Sa-Su 9am-5pm. ☎441-3400, ext. 3; www.fortmason.org.)

MUSEUM OF CRAFT AND FOLK ART. The tiny but culturally rich MOCFA puts on small but interesting exhibits of crafts and functional art (vessels, clothing, furniture, and jewelry) from past and present, near and far. The museum showcases everything from contemporary Japanese lacquer to wartime commentary made through light bulbs. The 2nd floor is not wheelchair accessible. *(Bldg. A., 1st fl. ☎775-0991; www.mocfa.org. Open Tu-F and Su 11am-5pm, Sa 10am-5pm. $4, seniors $3, under 18 free. Free Sa 10am-noon and 1st W of each month 11am-7pm.)*

AFRICAN-AMERICAN HISTORICAL AND CULTURAL SOCIETY MUSEUM. The museum displays historic artifacts and artwork as well as modern works by African and African-American artists. There is also a permanent collection of works by local artists. *(Bldg. C, #165. ☎441-0640. Open W-Su noon-5pm. $3, seniors and ages 12-17 $1, under 12 free. Free 1st W of each month.)*

MUSEO ITALO AMERICANO. The only museum in the country dedicated solely to Italian and Italian-American art, Museo Italo Americano exhibits a small collection by artists from several centuries and offers a selection of cultural programs, such as language classes and lectures. *(Bldg. C. ☎673-2200; www.museoitaloamericano.org. Open W-Su noon-5pm. $3, students and seniors $2, under 12 free.)*

FISHERMAN'S WHARF AND THE PIERS

Fisherman's Wharf is home to eight blocks of carnivalesque aquatic spectacle. Next to the ubiquitous tourist shops, patrons can catch glimpses of sea lions, Alcatraz, and a rich naval tradition. Unless you harbor a desire to experience a true tourist trap, there's no good reason to come here during the day. Perhaps the best way to appreciate the wharf is to wake up at 4am, put on a warm sweater, and go down to experience the loading and outfitting of small ships, the blanket of morning mist, and the incredible view. The western edge, near Municipal Pier, is quieter than the main Wharf piers.

PIER 39. Dubbing itself "San Francisco's Number One Attraction," Pier 39 is a shamelessly commercial collection of 110 specialty shops, restaurants, vendors, and entertainment. Even the world-famous sea lions—found by the western tip of the pier at platforms J and K—seem to enact a choreographed performance of splashing and snorting. The **California Welcome Center,** located at the top of the Marina Plaza stairs, features an **Internet** cafe ($3 per 25min.), snacks, info, and occasional discounts for attractions in the city and beyond. For some casual entertainment, patrons gather at the end of the pier to unwind with live street performances at **Center Stage** or a jaunt on the **Venetian Carousel** ($2 per ride). The new "V Show" presents an exhilarating variety show twice nightly. *(☎981-7437; www.pier39.com. Shops, attractions, and fast food open Memorial Day-Labor Day Su-Th 10am-9pm, F-Sa 10am-10pm. Restaurants open Su-Th 11:30am-10pm, F-Sa 11:30am-11pm; check website for mid- and peak-season hours. California Welcome Center: ☎956-3493. Open Su-Th 10am-9pm, F-Sa 10am-10pm. V Show: ☎ 888-398-7469; www.vtheshow.com. Daily 6 and 8pm. $44, seniors $39, children $24.)*

PIER 45. Still used by fishermen in the early morning, Pier 45 is also home to the **USS Pampanito** (SS-383). In retirement after sinking six enemy ships during its Pacific patrols, this WWII Balao-class fleet submarine now serves as a National Historic Park museum. *(☎775-1943. Open June-Sept. M-Tu and Th-Su 9am-8pm, W 9am-6pm; Oct.-May M and Th-Su 9am-6pm, F-Sa 9am-8pm. $7, seniors $5, ages 6-12 $4, under 6 free.)* The **Musèe Mèchanique,** recently relocated from its plot near the Cliff House, offers a charming array of coin-operated machines, such as the famously morbid Laughing Sal whose twenty-five cent mechanical cackle has been alternately enchanting and frightening children for 50 years. *(Pier 45 Portwalk. Open daily from 10am. Free.)*

THE CANNERY. Built in 1907 as the del Monte canning factory, once the largest peach cannery in the world, **The Cannery** has recently been converted into a marketplace-style plaza. Three levels of balconies, bridges, and walkways house charming restaurants, shops, and entertainment. Its maze of shady terraces, European-inspired garden courtyards, and brick enclosures offers respite from the wharf's hubbub. *(2801 Leavenworth St., between Jefferson and Beach St. www.thecannery.com. Open June-Labor Day Th-Sa 10am-8:30pm; Labor Day-May M-Sa 10am-6pm, Su 11am-6pm.)*

SAN FRANCISCO

SAN FRANCISCO MARITIME NATIONAL HISTORICAL PARK. This entire sight—including the **Hyde Street Pier** and **Municipal Pier**, a library, museum, a visitors center and the adjacent Victorian Park—is dedicated to the preservation of national maritime artifacts. *(Visitor Center: ☎447-5000; www.nps.gov/safr. Open daily in summer 9am-5pm. Hyde St. Pier: Open daily 9:30am-5:30pm. $5, under 17 free. Guided Pier Walks offered 4 times daily; call for times. Museum: Open daily 10am-5pm. Free admission. Library: Open Tu 1-8pm, W-F 1-5pm, Sa 10am-5pm.)* Along with the curving Municipal Pier, Hyde Street Pier encloses an area of the Bay known as Aquatic Park. Sittin' on the dock of the Bay, you can watch daring locals swim laps in frigid 50°F water. The **South End Rowing Club** and the **Dolphin Club** are open to the public on alternate days for $6.50, and you can thaw out in their saunas. Hyde Street Pier offers guided tours of vessels, schooners, and ferryboats as well as a boat-building class to satisfy your nautical needs. The museum displays maritime artifacts such as a ship's steering wheel, sextant, and ship figureheads. *(Dolphin Club: 502 Jefferson St. ☎441-9329. Open in summer W 11am-6pm; in winter W 10am-5pm. South End Rowing Club: 500 Jefferson St. ☎929-9656. Open in summer Tu, Th, Sa 11am-6pm; in winter Tu, Th, Sa 10am-5pm.)*

GHIRARDELLI SQUARE. Chocolate-lovers' heaven, Ghirardelli Square houses a mall in what used to be a chocolate factory. Everyone's got a golden ticket to the **Ghirardelli Chocolate Manufactory,** with its vast selection of chocolatey goodies, and the **Ghirardelli Chocolate Shop and Caffe,** which sells drinks, frozen yogurt, and a smaller selection of chocolates. Both hand out **free samples** of a delectably smooth milk chocolate square filled with gooey caramel, but on tourist-heavy days, the Caffe is often less crowded. The ever-busy **soda fountain,** an old-fashioned ice-cream parlor, serves huge sundaes ($6.25) smothered with its world-famous hot fudge sauce. *(Mall: 900 N. Point St. ☎775-5500; www.ghirardellisq.com. Stores open in summer M-Sa 10am-9pm, Su 10am-6pm. Ghirardelli Chocolate Manufactory: ☎771-4903. Open Su-Th 9am-11pm, F-Sa 9am-midnight. Soda fountain: Open Su-Th 10am-11pm, F-Sa 10am-midnight. Chocolate Shop and Caffe: ☎474-1414. Open daily May-Dec. 7am-8pm; Jan.-Apr. 7am-7pm.)*

ALCATRAZ

The Blue and Gold Fleet (☎705-8200, tickets 705-5555; www.blueandgoldfleet.com) runs to Alcatraz (14 per day; $11 round-trip, with audio tour $16; over 62 $9.75/$14.25, ages 5-11 $8.25/$10.75). Ticket lines can be painfully long. Often sells out in summer. Reserve at least a day and preferably a week in advance.

Mention Alcatraz and most people think of hardened criminals and daring escapes. In its 29 years as a maximum-security federal penitentiary, Alcatraz did encounter a menacing cast of characters: Al "Scarface" Capone, George "Machine Gun" Kelly, and Robert "The Birdman" Stroud, among others. There were 14 separate escape attempts—some desperate, defiant bolts for freedom, others carefully calculated and innovative. On the Rock, the award-winning cell-house audio tour takes you back to the infamous prison days. Listen to the screaming gulls and booming foghorn and watch the palm trees blowing in the wind outside. From the dining-room window, view the glittering hubbub of San Francisco life and experience some of the isolation that plagued the prison's inmates. But there's more to the history of Alcatraz than gangsters and their antics. A **Park Ranger guided tour** can take you around the island and through its 200 years of occupation: from a hunting and fishing ground for Native Americans, to a Civil War defensive outpost, to a military prison, a federal prison, and finally a birthplace of the movement for Native American civil rights. Now part of the **Golden Gate National Recreation Area,** Alcatraz is home to diverse plants and birdlife. The Agave Trail footpath lets you explore these habitats (open Sept.-Jan.). For general orientation, the dockside theater gives a 13min. video of the Rock's history and resources. Next door is the bookstore, offering videos, audiotapes, books, and gifts to round out the Alcatraz experience. Check the website for occasional book-signings by former prisoners, guards, and residents.

ANGEL ISLAND

The Blue and Gold Fleet (☎ 705-8200, tickets 705-5555; www.blueandgoldfleet.com) runs to Angel Island (20 min.; M-F 2 per day, Sa-Su 3 per day; round-trip $13, ages 6-12 $7.50, under 6 free).

Picturesque **Angel Island State Park** sits in the middle of San Francisco Bay, providing heavenly escape from the bustle of the city, except for those sunny weekends when all of San Francisco shows up. A 20min. ferry ride from San Francisco or Marin brings you to rolling hills, biking and hiking trails, and sprawling picnic grounds. In addition to great views, the island harbors a rich history. For over 2000 years, coastal tribes native to Marin County paddled here to hunt and fish. Spaniard Juan Manuel de Ayala "discovered" the island and gave his name to the sheltered cove he established as a harbor. Mexicans used Angel Island to rear cattle until 1859, when it was taken over by the US Army. The forts left by the Army have housed a Civil War encampment, a Spanish-American War quarantine station (for cholera, typhus, and other diseases), a missile site, and an immigration station. From 1910 to 1940, Angel Island served as a holding site for immigrants, mostly Chinese. During WWII, the station was used as a POW camp. The immigration station is currently undergoing restoration to preserve the Chinese poetry that detainees scrawled on the walls.

Public grills dot the lawn at Ayala Cove. On weekends and summer weekdays, this area fills up with families, but if you came to the island to escape the crowds, serenity is only a hike away. Just behind the picnic grounds, the unstaffed **visitors center** has exhibits and free 20min. orientation videos about the history and activities of the island. Adjacent to the center, the **Park Ranger Station** (☎ 435-5390, reservations 435-3522) offers tours of the Immigration Station, Camp Reynolds, and Fort McDowell. For a leisurely island circuit, the 1hr. **Tram Tour** hits all major historic sites and provides some decent views. (Purchase tickets with your ferry ticket in the dockside cafe, or call ☎ 897-0725. $12.50, seniors $10.50, children $7.50.) **Bikes** can be brought on the ferry or rented near the docks at Ayala Cove ($10 per hr. , $30 per day; helmet included). Bikers are allowed only on the perimeter road and the steeper fire road. The perimeter road balances exhausting uphills with exhilarating downhills. Hikers can choose among several trails to the 788 ft. summit of **Mt. Livermore.** If the exertion leaves you famished, the dockside **Cove Cafe** serves coffee, soft drinks, alcohol, snacks ($3-4), sandwiches, and ice cream. (Cove Cafe, tram tours, and bike rentals operate seasonally; check www.angelisland.com.) Maps at the gift shop are available for $1. If a daytrip isn't enough, you can **camp** at one of the nine eco-friendly 8-person **hike-in sites ❶** ($10) or the larger 20-person **Kayak Camp ❷** ($20). All sites have running water, pit toilets, grills, tables, and food lockers. No wood fires are allowed; bring charcoal or a stove. (☎ 800-444-7275; www.reserveamerica.com. Sites must be reserved; for summer weekends book up to 7 months in advance.)

◻ SHOPPING

For indulgent window-shopping, locals and tourists head to the small enclave known as **Maiden Lane,** between Post and Geary St. in **Union Square.** Also in Union Square, the **San Francisco Shopping Centre,** above Powell Station on Market and 5th St., spirals around six curving escalators (the only ones in the world) that transport shoppers to mid-range retailers such as Guess and Steve Madden. Nordstrom occupies the upper five floors, beginning with an entire level devoted to shoes. (Open M-Sa 9:30am-8pm, Su 11am-6pm. Nordstrom open M-Sa 9:30am-9pm, Su 10am-7pm.) The **Mission** teems with so many countercultural shops that it feels like a true alternative artists' enclave. With vegan clothing boutiques, 'zine bookstores, indie record stores, and the friendliest hipster staffs ever assembled in one district, shopping in the Mission, especially the northern end of **Valencia Street** and along ◙**16th Street**, is a quintessentially San Franciscan delight. Stores in the **Castro** cater to tourists' expectations, with everything from rainbow flags and pride-wear to the latest in GLBT books, dance music, and trinkets of the more unmentionable variety. In the **Haight**, secondhand shops and tie-dye stores hawking 60s-style pipes, clothing, and accessories hold their own against posh boutiques and the much-reviled Gap, at the corner of Haight and Ashbury St. The Haight is the best place to go for hunting down great used clothing or that rare LP that has eluded you for the past five years.

BOOKS

◙ **City Lights Bookstore,** 261 Columbus Ave. (☎362-8193), near Broadway in **North Beach.** This Beat generation landmark, famous for promoting banned books in the 1950s and 60s, has a wide selection of fiction, poetry, art, and, of course, Beat literature. Founder and owner Lawrence Ferlinghetti remains committed to publishing and publicizing the work of new authors. Open daily 10am-midnight. See **Sights,** p. 106.

◙ **Needles and Pens,** 483 14th St. (☎255-1534), near Guerrero St. in the **Mission.** Selling 'zines (pocket-sized magazines endearingly crafted, assembled, and penned by hip but everyday people) of all sorts, Needles and Pens is a unique and high-caliber bookstore. With fashionable handmade clothes ($10-25) and purses (around $30), as well as a backroom gallery exhibiting the edgiest of local punk artwork, this 'zine stop has become a can't-be-missed alternative community space. 'Zines $1-5, compilations $12-25. Open Su and Th-Sa noon-7pm. No credit cards.

A Different Light Bookstore, 489 Castro St. (☎431-0891), near 18th St. in the **Castro.** Though it has shed most of its radical roots in favor of half-naked calendar boys, pornographic DVDs, and self-help books, this bookstore still carries new work by prominent queer authors, who can be heard at free monthly readings. Open daily 10am-11pm.

Green Apple Music and Books, 506 Clement St. (☎382-2272), at 6th Ave. in the **Richmond.** Green Apple's popularity gives it a chaotic marketplace feel—no quiet, comfy-armchair perusing here. The main store covers everything from bestsellers to cooking to transportation; find fiction, music books (from theory to biographies to sheet music), and a cramped yet sprawling DVD and used CD section (mostly alternative and rock) in the **Annex,** 2 doors down at 520 Clement St. Open Su-Th 10am-10:30pm, F-Sa 10am-11:30pm. Annex closes 15min. earlier.

Phoenix Books and Music, 3850 24th St. (☎821-3477; www.dogearedbooks.com), at Vicksburg St. between Church and Sanchez St. in **Noe Valley.** New, remainder, and used books and CDs. Extensive fiction and children's sections, great bargains on hardcovers (most $4-15; art books $20-30), and informative and hilarious left-wing books. Sister stores: **Red Hill Books,** 401 Cortland St. (☎648-5331) and **Dog Eared Books,** 900 Valencia St. (☎282-1901). All open M-Sa 9am-9pm, Su 9am-8pm.

MUSIC

◙ **Aquarius Records,** 1055 Valencia St. (☎647-2272), at 21st St. in the **Mission.** Specializing in obscure music (from kraut rock to 60s psychedelic to experimental electronica), Aquarius works hard so you don't have to. Knowledgeable and friendly employees (a rare find in record stores) affix personally penned reviews to new releases as well as their all-time faves, rewarding customers willing to experiment. New and used. Great vinyl section. Open M-W 10am-9pm, Th-Su 10am-10pm.

Open Mind Music, 342 Divisadero St. (☎621-2244; www.openmindmusic.com), at Page St. in the **Lower Haight.** Insane quantities of new and used vinyl (from house to soul to hip-hop) and collectibles (live bootlegs, rare singles). As the only new and used store in the area that offers listening stations (3 turntables, 1 CD player) to sample before you buy, Open Mind is the best stop for hunting through the backlog you never had. Open M-Sa 11am-9pm, Su noon-8pm.

Amoeba Music, 1855 Haight St. (☎831-1200; www.amoebamusic.com), between Shrader and Stanyan St. in the **Upper Haight.** *Rolling Stone* dubbed this the best record store in the world. Amoeba supplements their staggering collection of rare rock posters, vinyl, and new and used CDs with a large DVD room. The store doubles as a venue for free concerts. Open M-Sa 10:30am-10pm, Su 11am-9pm.

CLOTHES

Manifesto, 514 Octavia St. (☎431-4778), just north of Hayes St. in **Hayes Valley.** Local designers sell 1950s-inspired clothes for men and women in this small but bright and welcoming venue. The retro dresses ($110-150), hip shirts (men's $65-115), and darling blouses ($70-95) are well cut and more flattering than authentic vintage. Open Su noon-5pm, Tu-F 11am-7pm, Sa 11am-6pm.

American Rag, 1305 Van Ness Ave. (☎474-5214), between Sutter and Bush St. north of the **Tenderloin.** A California vintage clothing institution, which nonetheless stocks more new apparel than used. Shopaholics adore the big-name retro styles up front, from 1920s silk dresses ($700) to Christian Dior suits ($300) while bargain-hunters turn to thrifty restored vintage (dresses $10-20). Open M-Sa 9am-10pm, Su noon-7pm.

Buffalo Exchange, 1555 Haight St. (☎431-7737; www.buffaloexchange.com), between Clayton and Ashbury St. in the **Upper Haight.** Additional locations: 1800 Polk St. (☎346-5726) in **Nob Hill** and 2585 Telegraph Ave. (☎510-644-9202) in **Berkeley.** One of those rare thrift stores that actually allows you to be thrifty and fashionable. Almost everything under $20 in this expansive yet utterly organized store. High-quality clothes, shoes, and accessories. Open M-Th 11am-7pm, F-Su 11am-8pm.

TATTOOS AND PIERCINGS

California law states that **you must be 18 years old** to get a tattoo. Generally, minors need an adult present for piercing.

Lyle Tuttle's Tattoo Art Studio, 841 Columbus Ave. (☎775-4991; http://www.lyletuttle-tattooing.com), in North Beach. Lyle Tuttle opened his modern, clean tattoo studio in 1960, and gained street-cred inking Janis Joplin, Joan Baez, and Cher. While the legendary Tuttle, age 73, has since retired from the business, the seasoned yet fresh talent Tanja Nixx, herself covered in tattoos from head to foot, continues the tradition. Tattoos from $80. Open daily noon-9pm. No credit cards.

Mom's Body Shop, 1408 Haight St. (☎864-6667), in the **Upper Haight.** A young, enthusiastic, and incredibly experienced staff tattoo their own fresh designs along with Arabic words, *kanji* (Japanese characters), and custom drawings. Piercings from $10. Tattoos $150 per hr., $60 minimum. Appointments suggested, but walk-ins welcome. Open in summer Su-Th noon-8pm, F-Sa noon-9pm; in winter daily noon-8pm.

EROTICA

Good Vibrations, 603 Valencia St. (☎522-5460; www.goodvibes.com), at 17th St. in the **Mission.** Additional locations: 1620 Polk St. (☎345-0400), at Sacramento St. in **Pacific Heights,** and 2504 San Pablo Ave. (☎510-841-8987) in **Berkeley.** A well-known, woman-run erotica cooperative for enthusiastic do-it-yourselfers (see their "Make Your Own Dildo" kit). A new spacious interior, neatly covered from wall to wall with a huge selection of dildos ($25-88), vibrators ($14-82), and lubes (around $15), is sure to please intrepid shoppers looking for the best way to please themselves or their partners. "Tester" bottles of lube and displays of vibrators and dildos allow you to handle before purchasing. Excellent collection of instructional books $7-25. DVD/VHS rentals $3.50 per night. 18+. Open Su-W 11am-7pm, Th-Sa 11am-8pm.

Mr. S. Leather, 310 7th St. (☎863-7764 or ☎800-746-7677; www.mr-s-leather.com), between Folsom and Harrison St. in **SoMa.** Selections range from $2 cock-rings to mammoth-sized dildos ($50-190) to a $2500 suspended sleep sack/bondage suit. A huge variety of men's leather clothes (jackets $439-595, chaps $275-319) and a helpful staff have made Mr. S. a one-stop shop for the leather community for the last decade. Sister store **Madame S.,** 321 7th St. (☎863-9447; www.madame-s.com), across the street, specializes in leather and latex "hâute fetish couture." Mr. S. open daily 11am-7pm. Madame S. open M and W-Sa noon-7pm, Su 11am-5pm.

MISCELLANEOUS

▨ **Otsu,** 3253 16th St. (☎255-7900), between Valencia and Guerrero St. in the **Mission.** All vegan all the time, this store carries beautiful but sturdy handmade wallets ($16-30), shirts ($14), notebooks (from $30), and purses and messenger bags ($20-80), all made without animal products and according to fair labor practices. "Punk-rock pricing" for animal lovers and the hard-core. Open Tu-Su 11am-7pm.

Under One Roof, 549 Castro St. (☎503-2300; www.underoneroof.org), between 18th and 19th St. in the **Castro.** Perhaps the most service-oriented establishment you're likely to find in the Castro, Under One Roof donates 100% of the sale price of every item—be it an AbFab magnet, scented bath oil, or a Pride holiday ornament—to organizations working to fight AIDS. The all-volunteer staff that has helped raise $10 million to date. Sign-up and orientation are simple for those looking to join, with any degree of commitment. Open M-Sa 10am-8pm, Su 11am-7pm.

Does Your Father Know?, 548 Castro St. (☎241-9865), between 18th and 19th St. in the **Castro.** Dad told you not to waste your money on touristy trinkets. Now you can show him you didn't listen *and* you're queer! DYFK is stocked with the Castro's finest kitsch, from Judy Garland figurines to glow-in-the-dark vibrators and penis-shaped cupcake pans. Open M-Th 9:30am-10pm, F-Sa 9:30am-11pm, Su 10am-9pm.

🎵 ENTERTAINMENT

PERFORMING ARTS

Civic Center gleams with elegant buildings housing concerts, dance, and opera. The San Francisco Symphony, under Music Director Michael Tilson Thomas, reaches world-class status. Downtown, **Mason Street** and **Geary Street** constitute **"Theater Row,"** the city's prime place for theatrical entertainment. **Fort Mason,** near Fisherman's Wharf, is also a popular area. For the latest on shows, check local listings in free mags and the newspaper. TIX Bay Area, in a kiosk in Union Sq. on the corner of Geary and Powell St., offers tickets for almost all shows and concerts and information about city tours and MUNI passes. Assure yourself a seat in advance, or try for cash-only, half-price tickets the day of. (☎433-7827; www.theaterbayarea.org. Open Tu-Th 11am-6pm, F 11am-7pm, Sa 10am-7pm, Su 10am-3pm.)

DANCE

▨ **Alonzo King's Lines Contemporary Ballet,** 26 7th St. (☎863-3040; www.linesballet.org), at Market St. in **Civic Center.** One of San Francisco's premier dance companies, specializing in modern and contemporary ballet. Dancers combine elegant classical moves with athletic flair to the music of great living jazz and world music composers. 2-week fall season and 1-week spring season are performed at the Yerba Buena Center for the Arts. Tickets $20-50.

San Francisco Ballet (☎ 865-2000; www.sfballet.org) shares the Opera House (see below). Season runs Feb.-May. Tickets from $30; available online or by phone M-F noon-4pm. Box office open from noon on performance days only. Discounted standing-room-only tickets at the Opera House 2hr. before performances.

Oberlin Dance Company, 3153 17th St. (☎ 863-9834; www.odctheater.org), between S. Van Ness and Folsom St. in the **Mission.** Dance company with a contemporary world focus. Occasional theater. Attached gallery. Tickets $10-25. Occasional 2-for-1 and "pay what you can" nights. $1 parking across the street. Box office open W-Sa 2-5pm.

MUSIC

Louise M. Davies Symphony Hall, 201 Van Ness Ave. (☎ 864-6000; www.sfsymphony.org), near the **Civic Center,** houses the **San Francisco Symphony** in an impressive Modernist structure. The cheapest seats are on the center terrace, directly above the orchestra; the acoustics are slightly off, but you get an excellent (and rare) head-on view of the conductor (and the rest of the audience). Box office open M-F 9am-5pm.

War Memorial Opera House, 301 Van Ness Ave. **San Francisco Opera** (☎ 864-3330; www.sfopera.com). Season runs Sept.-early Dec., June-early July. Tickets from $25. Standing-room-only tickets ($10, cash only) available from 10am on day of performance and student rush ($15 for orchestra seats, cash only) at 11am on day of performance. Open in-season M-Sa 10am-6pm, Su matinees 10am-1st intermission; off-season M-F 10am-6pm.

Herbst Theatre, 401 Van Ness Ave. (☎ 392-4400), near the **Civic Center** in the War Memorial Veterans Bldg. A plush setting for year-round schedule of classical soloists, quartets, and smaller symphonies, plus occasional lectures by renowned authors, artists, and other intellectuals. Box office at 180 Redwood St., Ste. 100, off Van Ness Ave., between McAllister and Golden Gate St. Box office open M-F 9:30am-5:30pm for walk-ups, Sa 10am-4pm by phone only.

THEATER

🎭 **Theatre Rhinoceros,** 2926 16th St. (☎ 861-5079; www.therhino.org), at S. Van Ness Ave. in the **Mission.** From the drag queen starlet to the audacious onstage lesbian lovers, the mural in the foyer says it

THE HIDDEN DEAL

A NIGHT AT THE OPERA

Opera has a bad rap as an aristocratic art form that turned into a bourgeois privilege. The diva glides across the stage with a girth to match her voluminous voice. The tenors are loud and pompous. The music is inaccessible and archaic, and the foreign language libretto doesn't help. What's worse, operas are *way* too long.

But the SF Opera offers a very cheap opportunity to dispel all these myths. **Student rush tickets** (available after 11am on the day of the performance) are $15 (cash only) regardless of the original purchase price, which means you can snag a $215 orchestra seat. Popular operas and singers can attract a line that forms by 10am or earlier, particularly on peak-season weekends.

The SF Opera enjoys a seat in the upper echelons of quality American opera. The 2004-2005 season already promises sweet returns, with West Coast appearances from last year's Met season. More daring productions come off with intellectual aplomb. In short, a trip to the SF Opera pays off in dividends.

301 Van Ness Ave., in the ***War Memorial Opera House.*** *☎ 864-3330; www.sfopera.com. Season runs Sept.-early Dec. and June-early July. Open M-Sa 10am-6pm, Su matinees 10am-1st intermission; in off season M-F 10am-6pm.*

all: queer, fabulous, diverse. The oldest queer theater in the world. Call in advance for wheelchair access. $15-30. $5 off for students, seniors, and groups of 10+. Box office open W-Su 1-6pm.

Magic Theatre, Bldg. D, 3rd fl. (☎441-8822; www.magictheatre.org), in **Fort Mason.** Use Fort Mason Center entrance. Sam Shepard was playwright-in-residence here from 1975 to 1985. Today, under the guidance of artistic director Chris Smith, this daring theater stages both international and American premieres. Tickets Tu-Th $24-37; F-Su $29-41; previews $20-29. Senior and student rush tickets available 30min. before the show ($10). Shows at 8 or 8:30pm. Box office open Tu-Sa noon-5pm.

Geary Theater, 405 Geary St. (☎749-2228; www.act-sfbay.org), at Mason St., in **Union Square.** Home to the renowned American Conservatory Theater, the jewel in SF's theatrical crown. The elegant theater is a show-stealer in its own right. Tickets $11-73 (cheaper for previews and on weekdays). Half-price student, teacher, and senior tickets available 2hr. before showtime. Box office open Su-M noon-6pm, Tu-Sa noon-8pm.

The Orpheum, 1192 Market St. (☎512-7770; www.bestofbroadway-sf.com), at Hyde St. near the **Civic Center.** This famous San Francisco landmark hosts the big Broadway shows. The Orpheum box office also serves the two sister theaters in the area: **Golden Gate Theatre,** 1 Taylor St., at Market St.; and **Curran Theatre,** 445 Geary St. Individual show times and prices vary. Box office open M 10am-6pm, Tu-Sa 10am-8:30pm; also Su 11am-7pm on performance days.

848 Community Space, 848 Divisadero St. (☎922-2385; www.848.com), between Fulton and McAllister St., near the **Upper Haight.** Basically a glorified living room, the 848 tries to do a little of everything. Comedy troupes, one-act plays, and music dominate the calendar but everything from night-long tribal rituals to live erotica readings have taken place here. Check the website for listings. Tu night contact improv classes ($8) and jams ($5). Shows free-$20, sliding scale. No credit cards.

Exit Theater, 156 Eddy St. (☎931-1094, reservations 673-3847; www.theexit.org), between Mason and Taylor St. in the **Tenderloin.** Also at 277 Taylor St., between Eddy and Ellis St. 2 locations and 4 stages produce independent and experimental theater for a youthful, urban audience. Special events include the sassy DIVAfest, 2 weeks in May devoted to "theater of a female persuasion," and the big daddy of national indie theater, the SF Fringe Festival, showcasing 250 performances over 12 days in Sept. Tickets $12-20; $8 and under for San Fran Fringe. Reservations held until 15min. before the performance. Cash only at the box office.

LIVE MUSIC

The live music scene in San Francisco is a vibrant mix of class and brass, funk and punk, hippies and hip-hop, and everything in between. Wailing guitars and scratchy voices still fill the halls of San Francisco's most famous rock clubs, where several stars in the classic rock pantheon got their start. If you're in a mellow mood, low-profile, funked-up soul seems to draw today's pimped-out booty shakers. The distinction between bars, clubs, and live music venues is hazy. Most bars occasionally have bands, and small venues have rock and hip-hop shows. Start looking for the latest live music listings in *SF Weekly* and *The Guardian*. *The List* is an online calendar of rock gigs all over Northern California (http://jon.luini.com/thelist.txt).

JAZZ AND BLUES

Boom Boom Room, 1601 Fillmore St. (☎673-8000, bar 673-8040; www.boomboomblues.com), at Geary St., near **Japantown.** Once owned by John Lee Hooker, Boom Boom is known as the city's home to "blues and boogie, funk and bumpin' jazz" and features live music, often big-name acts, daily at 9pm. This place is leading the revival of the 50s Fillmore Jazz scene with style. Happy hour 4-7:30pm. Beer $2.50, mixed drinks $4. Cover $4-10. Open M-F 4pm-2am, Sa-Su 3pm-2am.

Biscuits & Blues, 401 Mason St. (☎292-2583; www.biscuitsandbluessf.com), at Geary St., in **Union Square.** "Dedicated to the preservation of hot biscuits and cool blues," this basement joint serves up Southern fare such as a spicy jambalaya, but it's the nightly live blues acts that really make things simmer. Entrees $11-16. Drinks $3-7. Happy hour until 7:30pm; $2 draught, $4 specialty drinks. All ages. Tickets $5-20. Dinner served M-Sa 6pm, Su 5pm. Open M-Sa 6pm-1am, Su 5-10pm.

Saloon, 1232 Grant Ave. (☎989-7666), between Columbus Ave. and Vallejo St., in **North Beach.** The oldest bar in San Francisco (est. 1861) hardly looks like a saloon. A largely working-class crowd congregates here to relax after a hard day's work. Live bands M-Th 9:30pm-2am, F-Su 4-8pm and 9:30pm-2am. Cover F-Sa $5; 1-drink min. other nights. Open daily noon-2am. No credit cards.

ROCK AND HIP-HOP

🎸 **Bottom of the Hill,** 1233 17th St. (☎626-4455, 24hr. info 621-4455; www.bottomofthehill.com), between Missouri and Texas St., in **Potrero Hill.** Intimate rock club with tiny stage is the best place to see up-and-comers before some of them nab major label contracts; The White Stripes, Incubus, and Kid Rock all passed through here. Most Su afternoons feature local bands and all-you-can-eat barbecue for $5-10 (from 4pm, music from 5pm). Usually 21+, with occasional all-ages shows. Cover $6-25. Shows typically start around 8:30pm or 9pm.

🎸 **The Independent,** 628 Divisadero St. (☎771-1421), at Hayes St. in the **Lower Haight.** Formerly under another name and known for live hip-hop, this live venue has expanded to include everything from indie rock and punk to funk, jazz, and reggae. With a fully raised stage and some ambitious light designs, shows feel more like concerts here than at other SF venues. Cover $10-25. Box office open M-F 11am-6pm and 1hr. before the show. Check website for listings.

Café du Nord, 2170 Market St. (☎861-5016), between Church and Sanchez St. in the **Castro.** This red velvet club with a speakeasy ambience caters to a mixed gay/straight crowd. Excellent live music nightly—from noise pop and 1940s swing to alternative country. Local favorites include vintage jazz, blues, and R&B. Happy hour daily until 7:30pm with swank $2.50 martinis, Manhattans, and cosmos. Upstairs, the **Swedish-American Hall** accommodates larger, nationally touring acts. Frequently sells out; buy tickets online at www.ticketweb.com. Cover $7-25 after 8:30pm. 21+. Open M-Th 7pm-2am, F 5pm-2am, Sa-Su 6pm-2pm.

Amoeba Music, 1855 Haight St. (☎831-1200; www.amoebamusic.com), just east of Stanyan St., in **Upper Haight.** Occasional free concerts in the store—while you stand in the aisles. Some fairly well-known acts. Weekly DJ series. Open M-Sa 10:30am-10pm, Su 11am-9pm. See shopping, p. 121.

MOVIES

For a complete listing of features and locations, check the weekly papers or call **MovieFone** (☎777-3456).

🎬 **Castro Theatre,** 429 Castro St. (☎621-6350, automated 621-6120; www.thecastrotheatre.com), near Market St. in the **Castro.** This landmark 1922 movie palace has live organ music before evening showings. Specializes in revivals, festivals (the most famous is January's film noir), and double features. Bawdy crowds turn many a movie, or even documentary, into *The Rocky Horror Picture Show.* In addition to premiering sought-after first-run films, the theater also screens the occasional lighthearted musical

CLEANING OUT THE BATHHOUSE

When you mention SF sex clubs to unknowing visitors, they might ask, "Don't you mean bathhouses?" But, indeed there is a difference. The City's Department of Public Health shut down bathhouses in 1984, finding them partially responsible for the spread of HIV during the 1980s. Since bathhouses would rent private rooms to patrons, it was impossible for employees to enforce the safe-sex practices. As a response to this crackdown, sex clubs, which have no private rooms, blossomed.

Clubs enforce strict rules to ensure safety and hygiene. Onlookers must maintain a certain distance from a couple or group, and must respect refusals of sex. Patrons who break the rules are kicked out immediately. No alcohol is served, and anyone drunk is denied entry. Employees break up couples that aren't using condoms (free condoms and lube are available all around the club).

The **Power Exchange** is one of SF's most famous sex clubs. The bottom two floors (with a basement "dungeon") are mixed straight, trans, and gay, while the top two floors are men only and have a kinky wrestling ring. Courtship usually amounts to darting glances, a quick introduction, and a hunt for space. Privacy is a limited to a dark corner or tent with patches of transparent mesh.

Power Exchange, 74 Otis St. (☎ 487-9944), in **SoMa.**

sing-along. Adults $8.50, seniors and under 12 $5.50. Matinees W and Sa-Su $5.50. Box office opens 1hr. before 1st show. No credit cards.

🎬 **Roxie,** 3117 16th St. (☎863-1087; www.roxie.com), off Valencia St. in the **Mission.** Specializing in film festivals, this trendy movie house shows sharp indie films and fashionably foolish retro classics. The "Little Roxie," which recently opened next door, screens edgier films and political documentaries. Walk with a companion at night. Candy, popcorn, and soda starting at $1.25. $8, seniors and under 13 $4. 1st show W and Sa-Su $5, seniors and under 13 free. Discount pass (good for 5 shows) $22. No credit cards.

Midnight Mass, 3010 Geary Blvd. (☎267-4893; www.peacheschrist.com), at the Bridge Theatre in the **Haight,** presents a series of summer midnight Sa screenings of campy classic films. $10.

The Lumière, 1572 California St. (☎885-3201, showtimes 267-4893; www.landmarktheatres.com), between Larkin and Polk St. in **Nob Hill.** This famous theater hosts an array of indie, foreign, and art films as well as documentaries. Films $9.50; seniors, children, and 1st show of the day $7.25 (before 6pm).

SPECTATOR SPORTS

The **San Francisco Giants** (☎ 800-734-4268, tickets 510-762-2277; www.sfgiants.com) play baseball at the newly opened **SBC Park** (formerly Pac Bell Park) in SoMa, near the water off Townsend St. The Giants' season is April through October. Most games sell out before the season even starts, except for 500 seats reserved for day-of-game sale. (Tickets $10-42. Tours of the park $10.) The five-time Super Bowl champion **49ers** (☎468-2249; www.49ers.com) still play at San Francisco's old-time field—the notoriously windy **Candlestick Park** (☎467-1994). Now officially called **3COM Park,** the stadium is 8 mi. south of the city with its own exit off U.S. 101. MUNI offers express roundtrip service to the park via the 9x, 28x, and 47x buses. (www.sfmuni.com. $6; seniors, disabled, youth $4; with a MUNI pass $3; under 5 free.) Football pre-season starts in early August. The main season runs from September through January.

▧ NIGHTLIFE

Nightlife in San Francisco is as varied as the city's personal ads. Everyone from "shy first-timer" to "bearded strap daddy" to "pre-op transsexual top" can find a place to go on a Saturday (or Tuesday) night. The spots listed below are divided into coffeehouses, bars, and clubs, but these lines get pretty blurred after dark. Every other bar calls itself a cafe, every second cafe is a club, and half the clubs in town declare themselves lounges. Don't fret—there are hundreds of night spots in the city, and you're sure to find something that suits your fancy. If the spots listed below don't inspire you, check out the nightlife listings in *SF Weekly*, the *Guardian*, and *Metropolitan*. **Unless otherwise noted, all clubs are 21+ only.** San Francisco is not a particularly friendly city to underagers.

BARS AND LOUNGES

■ **Noc Noc,** 5574 Haight St. (☎861-5811), between Steiner and Fillmore St. in the **Lower Haight.** This lounge, creatively outfitted as a modern cavern complete with faux industrial piping, seems like the only happening place before 10pm—neo-hippies and other inheritors of the Haight aesthetic mingle at high-backed bar stools, relax cross-legged on the padded floor cushions, or otherwise ensconce themselves in dimly lit nooks and crannies. Happy hour daily 5-7pm; pints $2.50. Open daily 5pm-2am.

■ **111 Minna St.,** (☎974-1719; www.111minnagallery.com), at 2nd St. in **SoMa.** A funky gallery by day, hipster groove-spot by night. The bar turns club W 5-10pm for a crowded night of progressive house music. Check for openings and receptions. Cocktails and beer $4. Cover $5-15 for bands and progressive house DJs. Gallery open M-F noon-5pm. Bar open Tu 5pm-9pm, W 5pm-11pm, Th-F 5pm-2am, Sa 10pm-2am.

■ **Lush Lounge,** 1092 Post St. (☎771-2022; www.thelushlounge.com), at Polk St. in **Nob Hill.** Oh-so-lush, with ample vegetation, sassy classic Hollywood throwback decor, and frozen margaritas ($3). Either way, you'll be happy to kick back as the best in 80s nostalgia, from ABBA to Madonna, streams through the speakers. Open daily 4pm-2am; in summer M-Tu from 5pm. No credit cards.

Swig, 561 Geary St. (☎931-7292; www.swig-bar.com), between Taylor and Jones St., in **Union Square.** Outfitted with an artful, intimate back room and an upstairs smoking lounge—not to mention the walnut bar and Brazilian cherry wood floor—this hip new bar has already entertained Eminem, D12, and the Wallflowers. Caters to a fashionable semi-professional crowd. 21+. No cover. Open daily 5pm-2am.

Place Pigalle, 520 Hayes St. (☎552-2671; www.place-pigalle.com), between Octavia and Laguna St. in **Hayes Valley.** After a long day at work, the designers, boutique owners, and artists of Hayes St. relax on vintage velvet sofas at this dark, spacious bar. On weekend nights the wine flows freely, the music blares, and crowds of young bohemians pack the place. Occasional DJs and a rotating art exhibit liven up the back room. Happy hour daily 4-7pm; beer and house wines $2.75. Open daily 4pm-midnight.

Comet Club, 3111 Fillmore St. (☎567-5589) at Filbert St. in the **Marina.** Seductively illuminated with candles in red vases, this lounge attracts mobs of late-night scenesters. DJs get the dance floor packed with classic 70s and 80s funk, house, and groove F-Sa. Happy hour 6pm-9pm; $3 select premium beer and Miller Lite. Cover F-Sa $3. "Smart attire" after 9pm. Open Tu-W and Su 7pm-2am, Th-Sa 6pm-2am.

Matrix Fillmore, 3138 Fillmore (☎563-4180), between Filbert and Greenwich St. in **Cow Hollow.** The freestanding Art Deco fireplace, huge specialty cocktail selection ($7-10) and hoity-toity appetizers from brie to seared ahi tuna ($4-12) make this a favorite nighttime hot spot for chill young professionals. DJs spin "deep SF lounge" music M and W-Su. Flat-screen TVs play movies everywhere, even the bathroom. Open daily 5:30pm-2am.

Hi-Fi Lounge, 2125 Lombard St. (☎345-8663), at Fillmore St. in the **Marina.** This bar draws a young crowd F-Sa nights with old-school, underground, and Top 40 hip-hop. Housing one of the few dance floors in the Marina, Hi-Fi is absolutely packed over the weekend, with people crowded against the blue vinyl bar or squeezed into the diner-style white booths. Well drinks $5, beer $4. Cover F-Sa $5.

Lingba Lounge, 1469 18th St. (☎355-0001), at Connecticut St. in **Potrero Hill.** With a name that means "crazy monkey," the bar's motif manifests itself everywhere, from the jungle/tiki/rainforest decor and lush vegetation to the flaming Bowl of Monkeys (a scorpion bowl variation; $21). DJs spin hip-hop, house, jazz, and new lounge every night except Tu (live Brazilian bossa nova). Appetizers $7-9, platters $22-30. Open Su-W 5pm-1am, Th-Sa 5pm-2am.

Vesuvio Café, 255 Columbus Ave. (☎362-3370), at Jack Kerouac Alley, in **North Beach.** More accurately described as a bar with a literary edge, Vesuvio Café is decorated with everything from portraits of James Joyce to paintings by local artists. The wooden, tiled, and stained-glass bar with an upstairs balcony was Kerouac's favorite watering hole and remains a great place to drink. Draught beers $4.50, pitchers $9-12. Happy hour M-Th 3-7pm; draught $1 off, pitchers and bottles of wine $3 off. Open daily 6am-2am. No credit cards.

Hush Hush, 496 14th St. (☎241-9944), at Guerrero St. in the **Mission.** You'll feel oh-so-hip when you find Hush Hush, since this hot spot is too cool for a sign; look for the blue awning with 496 in white. Large leather booths, pool, and local DJs spinning almost every night have everyone whispering about this place. Tu $1 PBR, $2 vodka drinks. F "Divination" DJ Soulsalaam spins funked-up world music. Cover $3-5 after 9-10pm. Open Su-M 9pm-2am, Tu and Sa 7pm-2am, W-F 6pm-2am. No credit cards; ATM inside.

Café Royale, 800 Post St. (☎441-4099) at Leavenworth St. in **Nob Hill.** This bar/lounge actually offers a menu to justify the cafe in its name. Deep burgundy velvet couches complement the mellow jazz and soft lighting, whether you're enjoying a *croque monsieur* (fresh sandwiches $7.50) or a Soju *sake* creamsicle cocktail ($6). W live music 8-10:30pm. 3rd Th of each month wine and cheese tastings 6:30-8:30pm ($10). 1st Th of each month art opening reception 8pm-midnight. Happy hour M-F until 7pm; draught beers $3, Soju cocktails $4. Open Su-Th 4pm-midnight, F-Sa 4pm-2am.

The Dubliner, 3838 24th St. (☎826-2279) between Sanchez and Church St. in **Noe Valley.** A grand pub and sports bar that devotes its 11 TVs to broadcasting every NFL game playing on a given day. With less comprehensive coverage of hockey, baseball, and basketball, the bar fills up with a good-natured crowd of working-class locals and dot-commers. Domestic beer $3.50, imported $4. Toasted sandwiches $4. Open M-Th 2pm-2am, F 1pm-2am, Sa noon-2am, Su 9:30am-2am (NFL season) and noon-2am (off-season); opens earlier during college football season.

The Bigfoot Lodge, 1750 Polk St. (☎440-2355), between Clay and Washington St. in **Nob Hill.** A gigantic Big Foot and Girl Scout bartenders up the camp-factor at this log cabin retreat. Easygoing crowd. Beer $3.50-5.50. Cocktails $5.50-8.50. Happy hour M-F 3pm-7pm; well drinks $3, $1 off other drinks. Open M-F 3pm-2am, Sa-Su noon-2am.

Hotel Utah Saloon, 500 4th St. (☎546-6300; www.thehotelutahsaloon.com), at Bryant St., in **SoMa.** Excellent and unpretentious saloon with a handcrafted bar from Belgium and one of the friendliest crowds around. Above average bar food includes build-your-own burgers ($8) and homemade fare. A balcony overlooks the intimate stage space, which hosts live rock or country music nightly and one of the best open mics in the city on some M (shows begin 8:30-9pm; sign up by 7:30pm). Beer $4. 21+. Cover around $6. Open M-F 11:30am-2am, Sa-Su 6pm-2am.

CLUBS

🌀 **El Rio,** 3158 Mission St. (☎282-3325), between César Chavez and Valencia St. in the **Mission.** This club sprawls in all directions, from the chill lounge with pool table to the large boisterous outdoor patio to the dance floor. Each area has its own bar, but the patio—with its picnic tables, tiered sections, and movies projected on the wall—is center stage for the young, occasionally punk, but always stylin' urbanites who play cards and smoke cigars. Diverse queer and straight crowd. M $1 drinks. Tu $2 margaritas, free pool. W and Sa live Bay area bands. Th "Arabian Nights." F world music. Su live salsa (mainly GLBT) 3-8pm; salsa lessons 3-4pm. Cover M $2, Th after 10pm $5, Su $7. Open M 5pm-1am, Tu-Sa 5pm-2am, Su 3pm-midnight. No credit cards.

Pink, 2925 16th St. (☎431-8889), at South Van Ness Ave. in the **Mission.** With a new set of French owners, this venue plays it chic. Pink satin and gossamer draperies lend a lounge feel during the week but expect clubbers F-Sa. DJs spin a mix of world music, soulful house, Cuban jazz, and Afro beats. 21+. Cover $5, F-Sa $10. Open Su and Tu-Th 9:30pm-2am, F-Sa 9:30pm-3am.

Velvet Lounge, 443 Broadway (☎788-0228; www.thevelvetlounge.com), between Kearny and Montgomery St., in **North Beach.** Decked-out twenty- and thirty-somethings pack this posh club and thump along to house, hip-hop, and funk on F and a 70s, 80s, 90s mix on Sa. No hats F-Sa. No sneakers, athletic wear, or torn or faded jeans. 21+. Special events Su-W. Cover usually $10. Open Th-Sa 9pm-2am.

The Top, 424 Haight St. (☎864-7386), between Webster and Fillmore St., in the **Lower Haight.** Host to some of the finest house DJs in SF. A definite must for turntable loyalists. Biggest nights are Tu "Phuturo" drum and bass and F "S.W.A.T." house. Su and W-Th house. M hip-hop. Sa broken beat. Happy hour daily until 10pm; $3 well drinks. Cover $5 after 10pm. Open daily 9pm-2am. No credit cards.

GLBT NIGHTLIFE

■ **Divas,** 1081 Post St. (☎928-6006; www.divassf.com), at Polk St. in the **Tenderloin.** With a posh starlet collecting covers at the door and a savvy pin-striped madam working the bar, this full-time transgender nightclub is simply fabulous. 1st level bar, 2nd level dance floor, 3rd level TV lounge. Tu Talent (singing, comedy, lip synching); $50 prize. W-Th pole dancers. F-Sa midnight drag show. Happy hour M-F 5-7pm; $2.75 well drinks, wine, domestic beer. Cover W-Th $7, F-Sa $10. Open daily 6am-2am. No credit cards.

■ **The Bar on Castro,** 456 Castro St. (☎626-7220), between Market and 18th St. An urbane **Castro** staple with padded walls and dark plush couches perfect for eyeing the stylish young crowd, scoping the techno-raging dance floor, or watching *Queer as Folk* on Su. Happy hour M-F 3-8pm; beer $2.25. Su beer $1.75. Open M-F 4pm-2am, Sa-Su noon-2am. No credit cards.

■ **SF Badlands,** 4121 18th St. (☎626-0138), near Castro St. in the **Castro.** Strutting past the sea of boys at the bar, the Castro's prettiest faces and bodies cruise an enclosed circular dance floor where the latest Top 40 divas shake their thangs in enthralling tele-projection. Cover F-Sa $2. Open daily 2pm-2am. No credit cards.

■ **Wild Side West,** 424 Cortland Ave. (☎647-3099), at Wool St., in **Bernal Heights.** The oldest lesbian bar in SF is a friendly neighborhood favorite for women and men alike. There's pool, a cool jukebox, cheap beer (domestic $2), and a playful blend of classical art and Hollywood stills on the walls. The hidden highlight is a backyard jungle with benches, fountains, and scrap-art statues contributed by patrons, not to mention shady overhanging vegetation and stunning fuchsias. Open daily 1pm-2am. No credit cards.

The EndUp, 401 6th St. (☎646-0999; www.theendup.com), at Harrison St. in **SoMa.** Beautiful people inevitably end up here for euphoric after-hours fun. DJs spin progressive house for mostly straight Th KitKat, F pretty-boy Fag, and a blissful hetero-homo mix during popular all-day Sa-Su parties. Sa morning "Otherwhirled" party 6am. Infamous Su "T" Dance (27 years strong) 6am-8pm. Cover $10-15. Open Th 10:30pm-4am, F 10pm-6am, Sa 6am-noon and 10pm-4am, Su 6am-8pm. No credit cards.

The Stud, 399 9th St. (☎863-6623), at Harrison St. in **SoMa.** This legendary bar and club (a 38-year-old stallion) recreates itself every night of the week. Cruisy gay crowd. Go Tu for the wild and wacky midnight drag and transgender shows known as "Trannyshack," Th for Page Hodel's legendary hip-hop/R&B mix, F for electro-80s/pop, and Sa for "Sugar." Cover $5-9. Open M, W, Su 5pm-2am, Tu and F 5pm-3am, Th and Sa 5pm-4am. No credit cards; ATM inside.

The Lexington Club, 3464 19th St. (☎863-2052), at Lexington St., in the **Mission.** The only bar in SF that is all lesbian, all the time. Jukebox plays all the grrly hip-hop and alternative favorites. Campy portraits of nurses and ballerinas decorate the spare interior. Not much room for dancing, but still an enjoyable night with the ladies. M blue-collar night; $1 PBR, $2 Jim Beam drinks. F secret DJ. 2nd Sa "Sprung" party scene. Happy hour M-F 3-7pm; $2 well drinks. Open daily 3pm-2am. No credit cards.

Esta Noche, 3079 16th St. (☎861-5757), at Valencia St. in the **Mission.** The Mission meets the Castro in this boy-happy Latino bar. Regular drag shows. The bar is quite popular and space is tight on weekends. Happy hour daily 4-9pm; domestic bottles $2.25, margaritas $3. Cover F-Su $7. Open M-Th 1pm-2am, F-Su noon-3am. No credit cards.

Detour, 2348 Market St. (☎861-6053) at Castro St. in the **Castro.** The tamer, younger sister bar of SF Badlands (see above). Tom of Finland drawings and a chain-link fence add to the decor. Happy hour daily until 8pm; 2-for-1 well or call drinks. Dancing W-Su. Open M-Sa 4pm-2am, Su 2pm-2am.

The Café, 2367 Market St. (☎861-3846), between 17th and 18th St., in the **Castro.** Chill in the afternoon, with patrons strolling leisurely about the handsomely designed multi-tiered interior and faux adobe patio. Come evening, the club's maze-like nooks and corners fill to capacity with young bodies thumping to the latest house and pop remixes, with the dance floor, balcony, and patio crowds rotating in a constant game of see-and-be-seen. Cover F-Sa $2. Open M-F 3pm-2am, Sa-Su 2pm-2am. No credit cards.

▓ FESTIVALS

An astounding array of seasonal events take place in San Francisco no matter what time of year you visit. The summer is especially full, and events like Pride, which can draw crowds of more than 700,000 (as big as the population of the city!), make finding a hotel room or parking space difficult. Events below are listed chronologically. The visitors center (☎391-2001) has a recording of current events.

SPRING

San Francisco International Film Festival (☎561-5000; www.sffs.org). Apr. 1st-May 5th, Kabuki and Castro Theaters. The oldest film festival in North America, showing nearly 200 international films of all genres over 2 weeks, range $8-12.

Cinco de Mayo, the weekend nearest May 5. The Mission explodes with colorful costumes and mariachi bands to celebrate the day that a small, untrained Mexican army defeated Napoleon III's army, an event that led to Mexico's definitive freedom from the French five years later.

Bay to Breakers (☎359-2800; www.baytobreakers.com). 3rd Su in May starting at the Embarcadero at 8am. The largest foot race in the US, with up to 100,000 participants, covers 7½ mi. in inimitable San Francisco style. Runners win not only on their times but on their costumes as well. Special centipede category.

Carnaval (☎920-0125; www.carnavalSF.com). Memorial Day weekend. San Francisco's take on Mardi Gras, featuring Latino, jazz, and samba Caribbean music and more.

SUMMER

▓ **Pride Day** (☎864-3733; www.sfpride.org). The last Su in June. The High Holy Day of the queer calendar. Officially it's called Lesbian, Gay, Bisexual, Transgender Pride Day, with a **parade** and events downtown starting at 10:30am. Pink Saturday, the night before, brings a sea of bodies to the Castro for a huge block party. **San Francisco International Gay and Lesbian Film Festival** (☎703-8650; www.frameline.org). 11 days leading up to Pride Day, at the Roxie (at 16th and Valencia St.) and Castro Theatre (at Castro and Market St.). California's 2nd-largest film festival and the world's largest lesbian and gay media event. Tickets go fast. $6-15.

North Beach Jazz Festival (☎971-7577; www.nbjazzfest.com). The last week of July or beginning of Aug. at venues from Washington Sq. Park to Telegraph Hill. Free-$20.

Nihonmachi Street Fair (☎771-9861; www.nihonmachistreetfair.org). Early Aug. in Japantown. Lion dancers, taiko drummers, and karaoke wars.

FALL

San Francisco Fringe Festival (☎931-1094; www.sffringe.org). Starts the 1st Th after Labor Day, at several theaters downtown. Experimental theater at its finest, with over 60 international companies presenting short shows, all less than $8.

Ghirardelli Square Chocolate Festival (☎775-5500; www.ghirardellisq.com). Early Sept. in Ghirardelli Sq. Welcome to chocolate heaven. All kinds of chocolate goodies to be sampled, with proceeds going to Project Open Hand.

Día de los Muertos (Day of the Dead; ☎821-1155) Nov. 2. in the Mission. Follow the drummers and dancing skeletons to the festive Mexican celebration of the dead. The party starts in the evening at the Mission Cultural Center, 2868 Mission St. at 25th St.

Vivas Las Americas! (☎705-5500; www.pier39.com). Mid-Sept. at Pier 39. Music and dance performances celebrating Hispanic heritage.

Folsom Street Fair (☎861-3247; www.folsomstreetfair.com). Last Su in Sept. (Sept. 25 in 2005), on Folsom St. between 7th and 11th St. Pride Day's raunchier, rowdier brother. The Hole in the Wall gang lets it all hang out in leather and chains.

WINTER

Chinese New Year Celebration (☎982-3000) and **Parade** (☎391-9680; www.chineseparade.com). All Feb. in Chinatown. North America's largest Chinese community celebrates the new year in San Francisco's largest festival. Includes a Flower Fair, Miss Chinatown USA Pageant, and a Community Street Fair. Watch the Parade (Feb. 19th 2005 at 5:30pm) from Market and 2nd St. to Columbus Ave. The Chinese New Year Treasure Hunt is a crowd favorite (www.sftreasurehunt.com). Free.

OVER THE RAINBOW

Though SF Pride is possibly the gayest day of the year, with an ebullient block party in the Castro on Pink Saturday and a wild parade and street fair in Civic Center on Sunday, inevitably somebody had to do a lot of work so that everyone else could play.

On June 27, 1970, a handful of activists marched towards City Hall. In solidarity with the patrons of New York's Stonewall Bar who, a year earlier, had struck back at the policemen who harassed them, these activists demanded basic rights. At a time when same-sex couples couldn't hold hands and a known homosexual couldn't be served a drink, such a demonstration was radical and risky.

While there have certainly been swells in this political wave, today SF Gay Pride is primarily about celebration. At the street fair, you thread through dozens of buff shirtless men, fabulous drag queens, excited twinks, and bike dykes. Some tables educate and hand out condoms, others sell anything rainbowed, and those near City Hall pass out pins and launch letter campaigns. Stages feature the hottest queer music acts and famous headliners.

Amid all this celebration, you might wonder if people remember Stonewall. But traces of those political victories resound quietly with every couple holding hands and every hand that accepts a complimentary condom.

San Francisco Independent Film Festival (☎ 820-3907; www.sfindie.com). In Jan. or Feb. The best of Bay Area indie films at various locations.

Dr. Martin Luther King Jr.'s Birthday Celebration (☎ 510-268-3777; www.norcalmlk.org). Jan. 19-21 in Yerba Buena Gardens. Includes a candlelight vigil and "Making the Dream Real" march and rally on Jan. 21 to honor the great civil rights leader.

When confronted with the exuberant face of San Francisco's gay population, one might easily imagine a prospector striking gold...gold lamé, that is. Although it ould have been difficult to pan for gold platrm go-go boots, the Gold Rush of 1849 indeed lped lay the foundation for SF's image as a bean of tolerance.

By late 1849, "Gold Fever" had attracted wards of 40,000 fortune-seekers. Due to this ady influx of miners, the population of San ancisco was roughly 90% male throughout the 50s and remained disproportionately high for ars. Mine work meant laboring in a remote cation with long absences from women, and ch conditions helped foster a homosexual sublture. Tales of all-male barn dances, where the rtner dancing the woman's steps wore a red ndana on his arm, circulate in gay folklore as a ssible source of the contemporary "hanky de." San Francisco's new arrivals mingled with ilors, transients, and travelers. They patronized e saloons and brothels of the infamous Barbary ast, a subversive action for the time, earning e city one of its earliest nicknames, "Sodom By ie Sea." By the late 19th century, some estabhments catered exclusively to a gay clientele; e city's earliest gay bar, The Dash, was located 574 Pacific Street. The saloon, with a dance ll that featured female impersonators, was shut wn by city officials in 1908.

The onset of World War II contributed to the y's reputation as a haven for "outlaws" of tradinal society. The Bay was a point of departure d reentry for over 1.5 million servicemen in the ir, thousands of whom were discharged by the litary for homosexuality. Rather than return me, many opted to remain in San Francisco. e number of gay bars and restaurants in the y multiplied during the war years. Military pernnel seeking out such establishments got inadrtent assistance from the armed services emselves—lists of off-limits bars were rouely posted on military bases.

In the 1950s, right-wing politicians like Joseph cCarthy and Californian Richard Nixon prooted a discourse in which homosexuality was par with communism as an "anti-American" reat. At the same time, the Beat movement ined momentum, which influenced and was luenced by the attitudes and social scene of e emerging gay culture. Jack Kerouac immorized one of SF's best-known gay bars, the ack Cat Café, as the bohemian bar in On The ad. Establishments that catered to a gay and lesbian clientele in the 40s and featured drag shows throughout the 50s bore the brunt of officially sanctioned anti-gay activity. Because homosexuality was illegal, the state Alcoholic Beverage Commission would police gay bars and close them for serving drinks to self-identified homosexuals. In response to such harassment, owners of primarily gay establishments formed the Tavern Guild in 1962. The Guild became the first overtly gay business association in the country and offered an organizational backbone for the gay community.

San Francisco's gay population found further political empowerment during the mayoral election of 1960. Incumbent conservative George Christopher was accused by his opponent of allowing the city to become a safe harbor for homosexuals. The smear tactic failed and Christopher was reelected, but in the course of the debate both candidates' homophobia alienated voters. In 1964, *Life Magazine* ran a full-photo feature naming San Francisco the country's "Gay Capital." During the 60s, gays found the counterculture and anti-war movements sympathetic to their own struggle. New York's watershed Stonewall Riot in 1969 led to explosive progress in gay consciousness and activism. The growing identity of the gay community manifested itself publicly in 1970 with the first Gay Pride Parade. In 1978, local artist Gilbert Baker designed a visual symbol for the community by creating the Rainbow Flag, which is now recognized by the International Congress of Flag Makers.

The best-known figure of SF's gay social and political scene was Harvey Milk, who in 1977 became the first openly gay member of the city's Board of Supervisors. Milk, along with Mayor George Moscone, worked to successfully defeat the Briggs Initiative (a proposal barring the employment of gay people as teachers), but on November 27, 1978, Milk and Moscone were murdered by ex-Supervisor and anti-gay spokesperson Dan White. White escaped first-degree murder charges and received a lighter manslaughter sentence after his attorney presented a "Twinkie Defense," arguing that his client could not be held accountable for his actions due to a sugar high from eating cupcakes and drinking Coke. When the sentence was announced, enraged citizens staged one of the biggest riots in San Francisco history, known as White Night.

For further reading try *Gay by the Bay: A History of Queer Culture in the San Francisco Bay Area* (1996) by Susan Stryker, et al.

Susan Gray was a researcher-writer for Let's Go Greece 1994 *and* Let's Go Turkey 1995. *She is now a law student living in San Francisco.*

BAY AREA AND WINE COUNTRY

Surrounding the San Francisco peninsula are a number of dynamic counterparts to the City by the Bay: Berkeley's cafes, Oakland's blues, the Wine Country's vineyards, and Silicon Valley's tech industry. The blustery cliffs, winding roads, and foggy beaches in Marin and San Mateo County are beautiful and easy escapes from the city. In general, the Bay Area has better weather and more trees than San Francisco proper, and Wine Country delights visitors with nearly year-round sunshine and plenty of tasting opportunities.

HIGHLIGHTS OF THE BAY AREA AND WINE COUNTRY

TELEGRAPH AVENUE. The bookstores and cafes of this Berkeley street still pulse with vigorous political ferment (p. 142).

PANORAMIC HIGHWAY. North of San Francisco, this curvy road winds next to Mt. Tamalpais and Muir Woods, offering breathtaking views (p. 158).

GUERNEVILLE. With hot nightlife, a cool river, and quiet vineyards, Guerneville (p. 175) offers a youthful alternative to touristy Napa and Sonoma Valleys.

EAST BAY

Longer and older than its Golden Gate counterpart, the **Bay Bridge** carries San Francisco traffic east to **Oakland,** where freeways fan out in all directions. Oakland's urbanized port sprawls north into **Berkeley,** an assertively post-hippie college town. The two towns have long shared an interest in activism, reflected in wonderfully progressive and effective city government and policies. Berkeley, bookish and bizarre as ever, offers outstanding boutiques and cafes. Oakland is harder to navigate, but reverberates with progressive blues and jazz.

BERKELEY ☎ 510

Berkeley implanted itself in the nation's consciousness as a progressive leader and haven for iconoclasts in 1964, when activist Mario Savio led the UC Berkeley student body in a series of highly visible protests. While the town remains staunchly liberal, true radicals may chuckle at the irony of today's yuppified Berkeley, where polished storefronts sell organic goods to a niche market of Marxists with bourgeois incomes. Hirsute hippies stalk down Telegraph Ave., which teems with stylishly dressed down students, while the posh boutiques and pricey eateries of Shattuck Ave. and 4th St. avoid such ambiguity with an unapologetic embrace of upscale living. Berkeley's craftsman bungalows are surrounded by stunning flowerbeds, its restaurants range from high California cuisine to family-run Asian takeout, and its bookstores provide the perfect intellectual material for an afternoon spent sunning in the park, making the city an ideal day- or weekend trip from San Francisco.

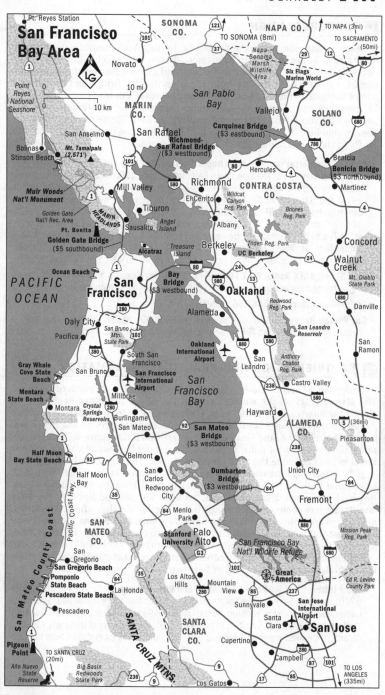

San Francisco Bay Area

▐▌ TRANSPORTATION

Freeway congestion can make driving in the Bay Area frustrating, especially during rush hours. As in San Francisco, drivers in Berkeley face numerous one-way streets, vexing concrete planters, and a sometimes lengthy quest for a parking spot. If you're driving from SF, cross the Bay Bridge on **I-80** and take one of the four Berkeley exits. The **University Avenue exit** leads most directly to UC Berkeley and downtown. Reasonably priced public lots (most are $10-15 per day) let you ditch your car and explore on foot. Those headed for downtown would be better off taking the BART, while those in search of parks and far-flung sights can manage more easily with a car.

Public Transportation: Bay Area Rapid Transit (BART; ☎465-2278; www.bart.gov) has 3 Berkeley stops. The Downtown Berkeley station, 2160 Shattuck Ave., at Center St., is close to the western edge of campus, while the North Berkeley station, at Delaware and Sacramento St., lies 4 blocks north of University Ave. To get to Southern Berkeley, take the BART to the Ashby stop at the corner of Ashby and Adeline St. (20-30min. from downtown SF, $3.05). **Alameda County (AC) Transit** city buses #15, 40, 43, and 51 run from the Berkeley BART station to downtown Oakland on Martin Luther King, Jr. Way, Telegraph Ave., Shattuck Ave., and College Ave., respectively ($1.50; seniors, disabled, and ages 5-12 $0.75; under 5 free; 1hr. transfers $0.25).

Ride Share: KALX Radio, 90.7 FM (☎642-5259), broadcasts a daily list of those needing or giving rides at 10am and 10pm. Call to put your request on the air for free.

Taxi: Yellow Express (☎548-2561). Runs 24hr.

Car Rental: Budget, 600 Gilman St. (☎800-763-2999), at 2nd St. Prices vary; call for current prices. 25+. Open M-F 7am-6pm, Sa 7am-4pm, Su 9am-4pm.

▐▌ ▐▌ ORIENTATION AND PRACTICAL INFORMATION

Berkeley is just across the Bay Bridge from San Francisco, north of Oakland. The **Marina** rests on the western side of the city while **Tilden Regional Park** climbs the sharp grades to the east. Undergraduates from **UC Berkeley** tend to gather on the campus's south side. **Downtown Berkeley,** around the BART station at Shattuck Ave. and Center St., is where you'll find more upscale restaurants, shops, a slew of pubs, some banks, and public libraries, while **Addison Street** is fast becoming the area's theater district. The signature Berkeley thoroughfare, **Telegraph Avenue** runs south from the Martin Luther King Jr. Student Union and is lined with bookstores, cafes, palm readers, and panhandlers. North of campus on **Shattuck Avenue,** between Virginia and Rose St., the **Gourmet Ghetto** has some of California's finest dining. Farther afield, **4th Street,** near the waterfront (take AC bus #51 bus west), and **Solano Avenue** to the northwest (take AC bus #43 north) are home to excellent eateries and shops. The intersection at **College** and **Ashby Avenue** (take AC bus #51 south) also offers delectable dining. Quality cafes, music stores, and specialty shops grace the **Rockridge** district on the border between Berkeley and Oakland.

Visitor Information: Berkeley Convention and Visitor Bureau, 2015 Center St. (☎549-8710), at Milvia St. Helpful maps, friendly service, up-to-date practical info, accommodation resources, and tons of brochures. Open M-F 9am-1pm and 2-5pm. **UC Berkeley Visitors Center,** 101 University Hall (☎642-5215), at the corner of University Ave. and Oxford St. Detailed maps and campus info. Guided campus tours depart from the center M-F 10am; from Sather Tower Sa 10am, Su 1pm. Open M-F 8:30am-4:30pm. **UC Berkeley Switchboard** (☎642-6000) can direct you to info on everything from community events to drug counseling. Open M-F 8am-5pm.

GLBT Organizations: UC Berkeley Queer Council/Queer Resource Center, 305 Eshleman Hall (☎643-8429; http://queer.berkeley.edu), at Bancroft Way and Telegraph Ave. Open Sept.-May M-F 10am-9pm, but usually staffed until 5pm only; June-Aug. by appointment only. **Pacific Center,** 2712 Telegraph Ave. (☎548-8283; www.pacific-center.org), at Derby St. Counseling and info on events, housing, and clubs. Open M-F 10am-10pm, Sa noon-3pm, Su 6-9pm.

Police: Berkeley Police, 2100 Martin Luther King Jr. Way (☎981-5900). **Campus Police,** in the basement of Sproul Hall (☎642-6760). Open 24hr.

Medical Services: Berkeley Free Clinic, 2339 Durant Ave. (☎800-625-4642 or 548-2570; www.berkeleyfreeclinic.org), between Ellsworth and Dana St. 2 blocks west of Telegraph Ave. Call for hours of service; the best times to talk to a real person are M-F 3pm-9pm, Sa 9am-2pm and 6-9pm, Su 4-7pm. Provides the following services: **STD Clinic and HIV/AIDS Testing:** Gay Men's Health Collective (☎644-0425). Service provided regardless of orientation. Drop-ins accepted Su 5-7pm. **City of Berkeley Public Health Clinic,** 830 University Ave. (☎981-5350), at 6th St. Medical help on a sliding payment scale. Open M-W and F 8am-5pm, Th 10am-7pm; closed daily noon-1pm.

Library and Internet Access: Berkeley Public Library, 2090 Kittredge St. (☎981-6100). Open M-Tu noon-8pm, W-Sa 10am-6pm. **Berkeley Espresso,** 1900 Shattuck Ave. (☎848-9576). Free wireless Internet access with purchase (bring your own laptop). Open daily 6am-11pm. No credit cards. For a list of cafes with free wireless connections consult www.cheesebikini.com.

Post Office: 2000 Allston Way (☎649-3155), at Milvia St. Open M-F 9am-5pm, Sa 9am-3pm. **Postal Code:** 94704.

ACCOMMODATIONS

There are surprisingly few cheap accommodations in Berkeley. The **Berkeley-Oakland Bed and Breakfast Network** (☎547-6380; www.bbonline.com/ca/berkeley-oakland) coordinates some great East Bay B&Bs with a range of rates ($85-175). Many travelers stay in SF and make daytrips to Berkeley (for San Francisco accommodations, see p. 90). No-frills motels line **University Avenue** between Shattuck and Sacramento streets, while ritzier joints are downtown.

UC Berkeley Summer Visitor Housing, 2700 Hearst Ave. (☎642-1676; www.housing.berkeley.edu), in Stern Hall, at Highland St. College dorm rooms in a great location. Shared baths. Free Internet in computer room, local phone calls, games, and TV room. Cafeteria-style meals and photocopying available. Laundry (wash $1.35). Check-out noon. Reservations online or by phone. Open June to mid-Aug. Availability limited by season due to construction. Singles $54; doubles $68; 7th night free. ❸

YMCA, 2001 Allston Way (☎848-6800), at Milvia St. Barely adequate rooms in the coed hotel portion of this YMCA make it functional if not pleasant. Shared bath. Free use of pool and fitness facilities. Communal kitchen, computer room, and TV lounge. Some rooms wired for DSL connection. 18+. 10-night max. stay. Reception daily 7am-9:30pm. Singles $39; doubles $50; triples $65. ❸

Capri Motel, 1512 University Ave. (☎845-7090), at Sacramento St. Unremarkable rooms with cable TV, A/C, and fridge. Jacuzzi bath in some rooms. 18+. Check-in 1pm. Check-out 11am. Singles from $65; doubles from $85. ❹

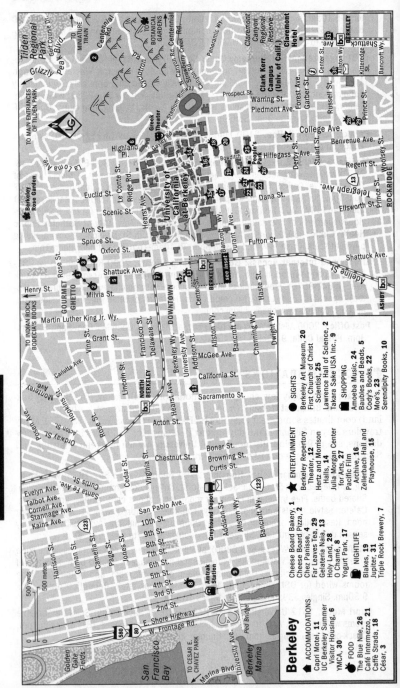

Berkeley

▲ ACCOMMODATIONS
Capri Motel, **11**
UC Berkeley Summer
Visitor Housing, **6**
YMCA, **30**

🍴 FOOD
The Blue Nile, **26**
Café Intermezzo, **21**
Caffè Strada, **18**
César, **3**
Cheese Board Bakery, **2**
Cheese Board Pizza, **4**
Chez Panisse, **1**
Far Leaves Tea, **29**
Gelateria Naia, **13**
Holy Land, **14**
O Chamé, **8**
Yogurt Park, **17**

★ ENTERTAINMENT
Berkeley Repertory
Theater, **12**
Hertz and Morrison
Halls, **14**
Julia Morgan Center
for Arts, **27**
Pacific Film
Archive, **16**
Zellerbach Hall and
Playhouse, **15**

🎵 NIGHTLIFE
Blakes, **19**
Jupiter, **31**
Triple Rock Brewery, **7**

● SIGHTS
Berkeley Art Museum, **20**
First Church of Christ
Scientist, **25**
Lawrence Hall of Science, **9**
Takara Sake USA Inc., **2**

🛍 SHOPPING
Amoeba Music, **24**
Baubles and Beads, **5**
Cody's Books, **22**
Moe's, **23**
Serendipity Books, **10**

FOOD

Berkeley's **Gourmet Ghetto,** at Shattuck Ave. and Cedar St., was the birthplace of California Cuisine and still houses restaurants serving fresh food in all price ranges. Since Berkeley has to feed thousands of starving students, the town is also home to pizza joints and hamburger stands. The north end of **Telegraph Avenue** caters to trendy liberal student appetites and wallets with late-night offerings along **Durant Avenue,** including an enclave of **Asian cuisine** (just east of Telegraph Ave.) with storefronts encircling a small courtyard. If you'd rather talk to a cow than eat one, you're in luck because Berkeley does greens like nowhere else. **Solano Avenue,** to the north, is great for Asian fare, while **4th Street** is home to trendy upscale eats. A **Farmers Market,** run by the Ecology Center (☎548-3333), sprouts up Saturdays at Center St. and Martin Luther King, Jr. Way (10am-3pm) and Tuesdays at Derby St. and MLK Way (2-7pm). Both markets are open rain or shine.

Chez Panisse, 1517 Shattuck Ave. (☎548-5525, cafe 548-5049; www.chezpanisse.com). The birthplace of California Cuisine, opened by chef Alice Waters in 1971. Alice still prepares the nightly fixed menu (4 courses; $50-75) in the downstairs restaurant. Upstairs, the more casual cafe serves similar, but less expensive fare. Starters $7-13. Entrees $15-20.) Reservations for restaurant or cafe strongly recommended; available up to 1 month in advance. Cafe open M-Th 11:30am-3pm and 5-10:30pm, F-Sa 11:30am-3:30pm and 5-11:30pm. Restaurant open for dinner M-Sa; seatings at 6-6:30pm and 8:30-9:30pm. ❺

Cheese Board Pizza, 1512 Shattuck Ave. (☎549-3055), between Cedar and Vine St. Though it only prepares one type of pizza per day (always vegetarian), customers line up halfway down the block to walk away with a slice. Live jazz music while you wait. Whole pizza $18, half $9, slice $2.25. Open Tu-F 11:30am-2pm and 4:30-7pm, Sa noon-3pm and 4:30-7pm. The neighboring worker-owned and operated **Cheese Board Bakery** (☎549-3183) offers a selection of over 300 international cheeses, most around $5-10 per lb. but some as much as $30 per lb. Open M-F 7am-6pm, Sa 10am-5pm. ❶

César, 1515 Shattuck Ave. (☎883-0222; www.barcesar.com), south of Vine St. A swank bar self-consciously dressed up as a breezy Mediterranean haunt, César offers savory tapas ($3.75-13), *bocadillos* (a small sandwich on French bread; $7), desserts (about $5), and an impressive list of spirits. Open daily noon-midnight. Kitchen open Su-Th noon-3pm and 4-11pm, F-Sa noon-3pm and 4-11:30pm. ❹

Gelateria Naia (☎883-1568; www.gelaterianaia.com), between Center and Addison St. 3 types of gelato with that Berkeley charm—patrons can opt out of the creamier, traditional variety for either a sorbetto (nondairy in-season fruit ice) or soy gelato (nondairy, no refined sugars). Cones or cups $3.25-5.25. Open Su-Th noon-11pm, F-Sa noon-midnight. ❶

Yogurt Park, 2433 Durant Ave. (☎549-2198, for daily yogurt flavors 549-0570), just west of Telegraph Ave. A Berkeley icon. Frozen yogurt $1.85-2.30; additional toppings $0.65. Huge portions. Open daily 11am-midnight. No credit cards. ❶

Holy Land, 2965 College Ave. (☎665-1672), just south of Ashby Ave. This family-owned kosher-style Middle Eastern restaurant invites patrons to spend a quiet evening in its cozy interior. Falafel $5. Shawarma $5-6. Pitas $5-6. Lunches $8. Dinner after 4pm $15-20. Open M-F and Su 11am-9:30pm. ❸

O Chamé, 1830 4th St. (☎841-8783), between Virginia and Hearst St. Innovative Japanese fusion cooking, with dishes such as Kona crab with mustard greens and bean sprouts ($12.50). Patrons enjoy a bowl of *soba* or *udon* noodles while getting tipsy on *sake* ($7-9) in a peaceful rustic setting. Appetizers $6-10. Entrees around $16. Open M-Th 11:30am-3pm and 5:30-9pm, F-Sa 11:30am-3pm and 5:30-9:30pm. ❸

BAY AREA AND WINE COUNTRY

The Blue Nile, 2525 Telegraph Ave. (☎540-6777), between Blake and Dwight St. With low ceilings, dim lighting, and bamboo shoot curtains separating the tables, this venue is impressively removed from the hubbub of the street. Waitresses in traditional gowns serve huge portions of traditional Ethiopian food. Variety of vegetarian dishes (lentils abound; $11-13). Open Tu-Su 5-10pm. Reservations recommended. ❸

CAFES

▧ **Café Intermezzo,** 2442 Telegraph Ave. (☎849-4592), at Haste St. A favorite staple of the Cal crowd, this veggie-lover's paradise serves heaping salads ($3.50-7) with home-made dressing, huge sandwiches on freshly baked bread, and hot soups. Salad and sandwich combo $5.50. Sandwiches $5. Open daily 10am-10pm. No credit cards. ❶

Caffè Strada, 2300 College Ave. (☎843-5282), at Bancroft Way. The glittering jewel of the caffeine-fueled intellectual scene. Go to be seen, discuss philosophy, or just enjoy the beautiful terrace. All espresso drinks under $2.50. The Strada Bianca (white hot chocolate; $1.90) is a decadent pleasure. Open daily 6:30am-midnight; in summer until 11 or 11:30pm. No credit cards. ❶

Far Leaves Tea, 2979 College Ave. (☎665-9409; www.farleaves.com), just south of Ashby Ave. Meditative tea shop offering a vast selection of teas ($3-6), with an emphasis on traditional Chinese and Taiwanese green and oolong blends. Brew your own while you sit on floor pillows and sip with a book, a friend, or your own reflections. Chinese tea tasting 1st and 3rd Su of each month, 3-4pm. Open daily 11am-9pm. ❶

◉ SIGHTS

UC BERKELEY

The campus is bound on the south by Bancroft Way, on the west by Oxford St., on the north by Hearst Ave., and on the east by Tilden Park. Maps of campus are posted everywhere; the visitors center (see p. 136) hands out campus maps ($0.10) and offers free tours.

In 1868, the private College of California and the public Agricultural, Mining, and Mechanical Arts College united as the **University of California.** The stunning 178-acre university was the first of the nine University of California campuses, so by seniority it has sole right to the nickname "Cal." With over 30,000 students and 1350 full professors, the university is particularly active when classes are in session, from late August to mid-May. If you'd like to sit in on some classes, track down a course catalog and schedule at the campus bookstore or online (www.berkeley.edu). Remodeling often occurs during academic downtime, so watch for closings.

▧ **BERKELEY ART MUSEUM.** With its 11 galleries, BAM is most respected for its collection of 20th-century American and Asian art, in particular the Hofmann Collection. Rotating exhibits showcase experimental work. BAM is also associated with **The Pacific Film Archive.** *(2626 Bancroft Way, at College Ave. ☎642-0808; www.bampfa.berkeley.edu. Open W and F-Su 11am-5pm, Th 11am-7pm. $8; students, seniors, disabled, and ages 12-17 $5. 1st Th of each month free.)*

SPROUL PLAZA. In October 1964, students protested the arrest of one of their own who had been distributing civil rights pamphlets, galvanizing a series of confrontations that lasted several years. Mario Savio, a student and member of the widely influential Free Speech Movement, addressed a crowd from the steps of the plaza, arguing for students' rights to free expression and assembly. Savio was eventually jailed and expelled, but in 1997 the plaza steps were named in his honor. It's still a popular social (and activist) hangout during the school year.

SATHER TOWER. Better known as the **Campanile** (roughly Italian for "bell tower"), this 1914 monument to Berkeley benefactor Jane Krom Sather, is the third-tallest freestanding clock tower in the world (at 307 ft.). For a great view, take the elevator to its observation level at 200 ft. *(Open M-F 10am-4pm. $2. Very top is not wheelchair accessible).* A 61-bell **carillon** plays during the school year on weekdays at 7:50am, noon, and 6pm, with a longer concert on Sundays at 2pm.

LAWRENCE HALL OF SCIENCE. High atop the eucalyptus-covered hills east of the main campus is one of the finest science museums in the Bay Area. Ever-changing exhibits stress hands-on activities, which cater to children but are fun for all ages. The plaza offers a life-size model whale, a stunning view of the bay, and free stargazing workshops on clear Saturday evenings. Visit the Planetarium for its "Constellations Tonight" show and be sure to check out the outdoor "Forces That Shape The Bay" exhibit. *(On Centennial Dr. Bus #65 runs directly from the Berkeley BART station to LHS. Get a transfer ($0.25) for $2 off admission. Alternatively, catch UC's week-day Local Shuttle (☎643-5708; $0.50) at Center St. and Shattuck Ave. then transfer to the Hill Service Shuttle at the Hearst Mining Circle on campus or brace yourself for a long, steep walk. ☎642-5132; www.lawrencehallofscience.org. Open daily 10am-5pm. Stargazing workshops 1st and 3rd Sa of each month. $8.50; students, seniors, and ages 5-18 $6.50; ages 3-4 $4.50.)*

OTHER UC BERKELEY SIGHTS. In the northeastern part of the main campus, the impressive marble **Hearst Greek Theatre,** built in 1903, is modeled after a classical amphitheater in Epidaurus, Greece. Used for university ceremonies and concerts, the Grateful Dead used to play here annually. *(☎642-4864.)* Though the bulk of its impressive collection is rarely, if ever, on display, the **Phoebe Hearst Museum of Anthropology** is a pleasant, quick stop for exhibits of objects from California, ancient Egypt, and pre-Colombian Peru. *(103 Kroeber Hall, at the corner of Bancroft Way and College Ave. ☎643-7648; http://hearstmuseum.berkeley.edu. Open W-Sa 10am-4:30pm, Su noon-4pm. $4, seniors $3, students with ID $1, under 13 free. Free Th.)* Though primarily a research facility, the **UC Museum of Paleontology** has exhibits open the public, including a complete Tyrannosaurus rex skeleton. *(1101 Valley Life Sciences Bldg. ☎642-1821; www.ucmp.berkeley.edu. Open M-Th 8am-10pm, F 8am-5pm, Sa 10am-5pm, Su 1-10pm; summer hours vary. Free.)* The **Botanical Gardens** contain approximately 12,000 species of plant life from around the world, including a huge number of rare and endangered plants. Agatha Christie supposedly came here to examine a rare poisonous plant whose deadly powers she later put to use in a mystery novel. The **Stephen Mather Redwood Grove** across the street is also worth a visit. *(200 Centennial Dr., in Strawberry Canyon, between UC Stadium and Lawrence Hall of Science. ☎643-2755; http://botanicalgarden.berkeley.edu. Open daily 9am-5pm; Memorial Day-Labor Day W-Su until 8pm; closed 1st Tu of each month. $3, seniors $2, ages 3-18 $1; Th free.)*

OFF CAMPUS

TELEGRAPH AVENUE. You haven't really visited Berkeley until you've strolled the first five or so blocks of **Telegraph Avenue,** which runs south from Sproul Plaza as far as downtown Oakland. Close to the university, Telegraph Ave. is lined with a motley assortment of cafes, bookstores, and used clothing and record stores. Businesses come and go at the whim of the marketplace, but the scene—a rowdy jumble of 60s and contemporary counterculture—persists. Vendors push tie-dye, Tarot readings, and jewelry; the disenfranchised hustle for change; students add an indefatigable energy; and characters looking like Old Testament prophets carry on hyperdimensional conversations, transmitting knowledge and meditations accrued from years of Berkeley experience.

FIRST CHURCH OF CHRIST SCIENTIST. Built in 1910, architect Bernard Maybeck's masterpiece is a conglomeration of Gothic, Renaissance, Classical, Japanese, Mediterranean, and industrial styles. *(2619 Dwight St., at Bowditch St. ☎ 845-7199. Open during services W 8pm, Su 11am, and 1hr. before and after each service. Tours at 12:15pm on the 1st Su of each month.)*

TAKARA SAKE USA INC. Learn the history and science of making *sake* through a museum and video, and sample 15 different types. The knowledgeable hosts won't laugh in your face when you wobble out the door, another victim of Japan's merciless firewater. *(708 Addison St., just west of 4th St. Take bus #51 to 4th St. and walk down to Addison St. ☎ 540-8250; www.takarasake.com. Open daily noon-6pm. Free.)*

TILDEN REGIONAL PARK. In the pine and eucalyptus forests east of the city lies the beautiful anchor of the East Bay park system, **Tilden Regional Park.** Hiking, biking, running, and riding trails crisscross the park and provide impressive views of the Bay Area. The **ridgeline trail** makes for an especially spectacular bike ride. *(By car or bicycle, take Spruce St. to Grizzly Peak Blvd. to Canon Dr. AC Transit bus #67 runs from the Berkeley BART station to the entrances at Canon Dr. and Shasta Rd. on weekdays; over the weekend the #67 bus enters at Canon Dr., continues throughout various sights in the park, and exits on Shasta Rd. ☎ 843-2137. Open daily dawn-dusk.)* For those looking to frolic without getting sweaty, the 1906 **carousel** inside the park is a fun option. *(Open daily 11am-5pm; after Labor Day open only Sa-Su. $1.)* Also inside the park, the small, sunny beach at **Lake Anza** is a popular swimming spot during the hottest summer days, though not the place to go for a quiet, romantic dip, as the lake tends to become crowded with families. *(Open in summer 11am-10pm. No lifeguard 6-10pm. $3.50, seniors and children $2.50.)* The **Environmental Education Center** offers exhibits and naturalist-led programs. *(At the north end of the park. ☎ 525-2233. Open Tu-Su 10am-5pm. Free.)* **Grizzly Peak** and **Inspiration Point** provide breathtaking panoramas of the entire Bay Area. **Wildcat Canyon** is a less developed park than Tilden, with gorgeous hiking through grassy meadows and wooded canyons. *(Adjacent to Tilden Park. Open daily dawn-dusk.)*

OTHER PARKS. Berkeley's parks provide respite from the craziness of campus life. North of campus, the ◪**Berkeley Rose Garden,** built by the Works Projects Administration in the Depression era, spills from one terrace to another in a vast semicircular amphitheater. The roses are pruned in January in preparation for Mother's Day, when the garden is at its glorious peak. *(Open May-Sept. daily dawn-dusk.)* Berkeley's biggest confrontation between the People and the Man was not fought over freedom of speech or the war in Vietnam, but over a muddy vacant lot between Dwight and Haste St. In April 1969, students, hippies, and radicals christened the patch of university-owned land **People's Park,** tearing up pavement and laying down sod to establish, in the words of the *Berkeley Barb,* "a cultural, political freak out and rap center for the Western world." When the university moved to evict squatters and build a parking garage on the site, resistance stiffened. Governor Ronald Reagan sent in 2000 troops, and the conflict ended with helicopters dropping tear gas on students in Sproul Plaza, one bystander shot dead by police, and a 17-day National Guard occupation. The park's grassy existence represents a small victory over the establishment. The basalt face of **Indian Rock** challenges thrill-junkies with short but demanding climbs. For the vertically challenged, side steps lead to an impressive view of the Headlands. *(At the north end of Shattuck Ave. Open daily dawn-dusk.)*

BAY AREA AND WINE COUNTRY

⬛ SHOPPING

Telegraph Avenue is an excellent source for books, music, and secondhand clothing, along with homemade tie-dye, jewelry, and pipes. If you are willing to walk or drive a few miles off Telegraph, you will be rewarded with some of Berkeley's best bookstores and sex shops. Chain stores seem misplaced in this happy land of independent, locally supported stores. The dabbler in beads, bracelets, and necklaces will be in heaven at **Baubles and Beads,** 167 Shattuck Ave., between Lincoln and Virginia St., which has devoted two full-sized storefronts to the art of ad hoc jewelry. (☎644-2323. Open M-W 10:30am-6:30pm, Th 10:30am-8pm, F-Sa 10:30am-6:30pm, Su 11am-5pm). Though less massive and comprehensive than its San Francisco incarnation, the original ■**Amoeba Music,** 2455 Telegraph Ave., near Haste St., still offers CDs by local artists, a plenitude of used CDs and vinyl, and an experimental section that draws customers from around the Bay Area. (☎549-1125; www.amoebamusic.com. Open M-Sa 10:30am-10pm, Su 11am-9pm.) If you're looking for a gargantuan, warehouse-sized store with more thorough selection (especially for goth and punk), then the SF location (see p. 121) will better suit your buy-sell-trade fancies.

Berkeley's book trade is truly astounding. Leave yourself more time to browse than you think you'll need. Telegraph Ave. is home to some good book nooks, including ■**Moe's,** 2476 Telegraph Ave., between Dwight and Haste St., which was featured in *The Graduate* (see p. 22) and has four well-arranged floors' worth of secondhand books as well as new books at a 10% discount. "More Moe's" has art and antiquarian books on the fourth floor. (☎849-2087; http://moesbooks.com. Open daily 10am-11pm.) The independently owned **Cody's Books,** 2454 Telegraph Ave., prevails against corporate rivalry with two expansive floors of new books as well as bestselling hardcovers and paperbacks. Local authors, small press publications, special orders, strong academic sections, and two to three author readings per week make supporting the little guy more than worthwhile. (☎559-9500; www.codysbooks.com. Open daily 10am-10pm.) An inspiring prose paradise beckons on University and Shattuck Ave. The dusty collection at ■**Serendipity Books,** 1201 University Ave., at Curtis St., has earned Bay Area-wide respect as the place to go for rare books, first editions, manuscripts, archives, and fine printing of 20th-century fiction and poetry. (☎841-7455. Open M-Sa 9am-5pm.)

♫ ENTERTAINMENT

Berkeley's innumerable publications, which can be found in corner boxes and at cafes, are invaluable for an up-to-date list of happenings around town, including the latest goings-on in San Francisco. Look in bookstores and bins for the free weekly *East Bay Express* (www.eastbayexpress.com), filled with theater, film, and concert listings. If you can find a recent edition of *Resource*, the guide given to new Berkeley students, grab it (try the visitors center at 101 University Hall). The *Daily Californian* (www.dailycal.org), which publishes twice a week in the summer and daily during the academic year, carries university news and features.

ON CAMPUS

CAL Performances (☎642-9988; www.calpers.berkeley.edu), in Zellerbach Hall. Info and tickets for concerts, plays, and movies. Open Tu-F 10am-5:30pm, Sa-Su 1-5pm, and 1 hr. before performances.

Zellerbach Playhouse, near the corner of Bancroft Way and Dana St. Shared by professional dance and theater companies and student ensembles, Zellerbach is a community favorite. Summertime shows are usually musicals and romantic comedies. Tickets during the academic year $6-12; in summer $5-10, students and seniors $3-6.

Hertz and Morrison Halls (☎642-2678), between Bowditch St. and College Ave. The Cal music department hosts concerts (W noon) during the academic year with a mostly classical line-up, from early music to contemporary. Past student ensembles include the African Music Ensemble, the Berkeley Contemporary Chamber Players, the Javanese Gamelan, and the 1991 Grammy-nominated University Chamber Chorus.

OFF CAMPUS

▨ **Pacific Film Archive,** 2575 Bancroft Way (☎642-0808; www.bampfa.berkeley.edu), near Bowditch St. With a new facility and a huge collection of archived foreign and independent films, the PFA is a great place to catch any number of underground, experimental, and hard-to-find flicks. Generally evening shows, sometimes a Sa or Su matinee. Tickets $8; non-UCB students, seniors, disabled, under 12 $5. For double bills, additional feature $2. Ticket office open M-Th 1-5pm.

▨ **Berkeley Repertory Theater,** 2025 Addison St. (☎647-2949; www.berkeleyrep.org). The best-known and arguably the finest theater in the area, with an eclectic repertoire of classics and unknowns. Tickets $43-55; previews $40. Half-price tickets may be available Tu-F on the day of the show—line up at the box office at noon. Half-price student and seniors tickets available 30min. before the show. $20 advance tickets available to those under 30 except for Sa night. Box office open Tu-Su noon-7pm.

Julia Morgan Center for Arts, 2640 College Ave. (☎845-8542, tickets 925-798-1300; www.juliamorgan.org), at Derby St. Regular performances by the **Berkeley Opera** as well as traveling performing artists. The theater shares space with a preschool and yoga center in a beautiful building, Morgan's first public commission. Originally a church, it still retains all the original fixtures, including the pews (though the windows have been boarded up to keep light from interrupting the performances). Center open M-F 9:30am-5:30pm. Ticket lines open M-Sa 10am-6pm, Su noon-5pm.

▣ NIGHTLIFE

Since Berkeley is so close to SF proper, when hard-core clubbers need to bump and grind, they just take BART into the city. What Berkeley does offer is an unrivaled array of casual brewpubs and brainy cafes. Crowded at almost any hour of the night or day, they serve as surrogate libraries, living rooms, and lecture theaters; espresso drinks and microbrews loosen the tongues of an already talkative city. Many bars have some great live music offerings as well.

▨ **Jupiter,** 2181 Shattuck Ave. (☎843-8277), near the BART station. The church pews and elaborate Gothic paneling are only noticeable if the place is empty—but it won't be. Patrons seat themselves but may wait up to an hour on busy nights before tasting the terrific wood-fired pizza (9 in. pie $7-8). Live jazz music in the spacious beer garden Tu-Sa. Th Night "Beat Down" features a DJ spinning trance and hip-hop. "Americana Unplugged" bluegrass Su 5-8pm. No cover. Open M-Th 11:30am-1am, F 11:30am-2am, Sa noon-2am, Su noon-midnight.

Blakes, 2367 Telegraph Ave. (☎848-0886), near Durant Ave. A jam-packed and unabashed meat market. The pint-sized upstairs gets loud, while the middle floor is mellow with more seating. In the basement (18+), kick it to the loud beats of local bands (W-Sa). Cocktails $5-6.75. Appetizers $2.60-7. Popular meals include fish 'n' chips ($7.20), burgers (up to $8), and ribs ($6-8). Happy hour M-F 4-7pm; $0.75 off pints and cocktails. Drink specials 9pm-midnight; W $1 PBR, Th $2.75 well drinks. Cover $2-12. Open M-Sa 11:30am-2am, Su noon-1am.

Triple Rock Brewery, 1920 Shattuck Ave. (☎843-2739; www.triplerock.com), between Hearst Ave. and Berkeley Way. Frequented by local beer aficionados, the Rock was the first of Berkeley's many brewpubs. Long and ever-changing menu of ales, stouts, and porters (made 3-4 times a week in a hands-on 7-barrel process). Award-winning Red Rock Ale $3.75. Open Su-W 11:30am-midnight, Th-Sa 11:30am-1am or later. Rooftop garden closes 10pm. Kitchen closes Su-W 10pm, Th-Sa 11:30pm.

OAKLAND ☎510

Newcomers to the Bay Area too easily forget that Oakland, with 400,000 people, 81 languages, and considerable land mass, is a thriving city in its own right. Despite economic limitations, Oakland has maintained a commercial center and some beautiful residential neighborhoods. These regions sometimes run into one another, giving the city an indefinite character—it's neither bustling nor quiet, not quite action-packed but never entirely boring. An afternoon in downtown museums, a gourmet dinner in Rockridge, and a legendary live music scene are just a short car or BART ride away from San Francisco.

▢ TRANSPORTATION

Drivers take **I-80** from San Francisco across the Bay Bridge to **I-580** and connect with Oakland **I-980 South,** which has downtown exits at 12th St. and 19th St. For traffic updates, call ☎817-1717.

Buses: Greyhound, 2103 San Pablo Ave. (☎834-3213, schedules and reservations 800-231-2222). Be careful around the station at night. F-Su rates slightly higher. Buses depart daily to: **L.A.** (7-8hr., $48); **Sacramento** (1½hr., $14.50); **Santa Cruz** (2½hr., $11.50). F-Su rates slightly higher. Seniors and child discount; call for rates.

Public Transportation: Bay Area Rapid Transit (BART; ☎465-2278; www.bart.gov) is the most convenient way to travel to and within Oakland. BART runs from downtown **San Francisco** to Oakland's stations at **Lake Merritt** (Dublin/Pleasanton or Fremont trains), **Oakland City Center/12th Street** (Richmond or Pittsburg/Bay Point trains), **19th Street** (Richmond or Pittsburg/Bay Point trains), **Rockridge** (Pittsburg/Bay Point trains), and **Coliseum** (Dublin/Pleasanton or Fremont trains). **Alameda County (AC) Transit** (☎817-1717; www.actransit.org). $1.50; seniors, disabled, and ages 5-12 $0.75; under 5 free. 1½hr. bus-to-bus transfers $0.25. 1½ BART-to-bus transfers $1.25, seniors, disabled, and children $0.55. **Transbay** routes to San Francisco ($3/ $1.50). All AC buses are wheelchair accessible and equipped with bike racks.

Ferries: Alameda/Oakland Ferry (☎522-3300; www.eastbayferry.com). Purchase tickets on board. Ferries run between Oakland, Alameda, the SF Ferry Building, and Pier 41/Fisherman's Wharf. $5.25, seniors and disabled $3, ages 5-12 $2.50, under 5 free. Free AC and MUNI transfers; MUNI transfers must be validated on ferry.

Taxi: Oakland Yellow Cab (☎251-0130). Runs 24hr.

◼◼ ◪ ORIENTATION AND PRACTICAL INFORMATION

The scarcity of noteworthy sights and cheap and safe accommodations make Oakland a better daytrip than vacation destination. Oakland's major artery is **Broadway,** which runs northeast under the Nimitz Fwy. (I-880) at 5th St., and separates **Old Oakland** (to the west) from **Chinatown** (to the east). The city center is at 13th St. and Broadway, but the greater downtown area occupies all of **Lake Merritt,** including Lakeside Park on the north side and the Lake Merritt Channel on the south side. North-south addresses are numbered to match the east-west cross streets; for example, 1355 Broadway is between 13th and 14th St. To get to **Jack London Square** and the waterfront from the 12th St. BART stop, just head down Broadway away from the hills. North of downtown, past some of Oakland's poorest areas, are a few Berkeley-esque neighborhoods with boutiques, grocers, and restaurants. **Rockridge** (take Broadway north off I-580), with its well-kept lawns, lies toward Berkeley and is accessible from downtown Oakland by BART or AC Transit bus #51.

Visitor Information: Oakland Visitors Information Bureau, 463 11th St. (☎839-9000), at Broadway in the Marriott building. Free maps of the city and brochures. Open M-F 8:30am-5pm. **Port of Oakland Information Booths** (24hr. info ☎866-295-9853; www.jacklondonsquare.com), on Broadway in Jack London Sq. under the Barnes & Noble bookstore. Info focuses on waterfront sights. Also at Oakland International Airport. Hours vary.

Police: 455 7th St. (nonemergency ☎777-3333).

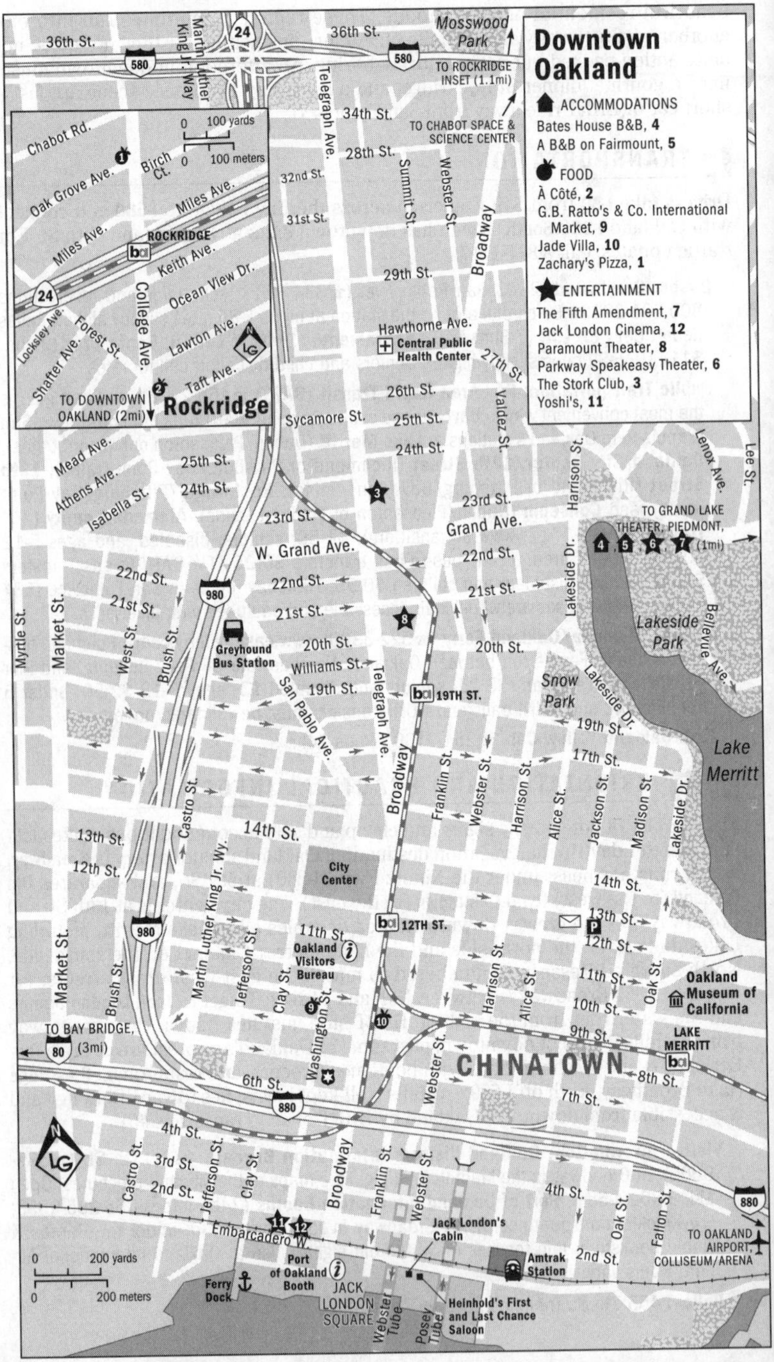
Downtown Oakland
ACCOMMODATIONS
Bates House B&B, 4
A B&B on Fairmount, 5
FOOD
À Côté, 2
G.B. Ratto's & Co. International Market, 9
Jade Villa, 10
Zachary's Pizza, 1
ENTERTAINMENT
The Fifth Amendment, 7
Jack London Cinema, 12
Paramount Theater, 8
Parkway Speakeasy Theater, 6
The Stork Club, 3
Yoshi's, 11
Rockridge
Chabot Rd.
Oak Grove Ave.
Birch Ct.
Miles Ave.
ROCKRIDGE
Keith Ave.
Ocean View Dr.
College Ave.
Locksley Ave.
Forest St.
Shafter Ave.
Lawton Ave.
Taft Ave.
TO DOWNTOWN OAKLAND (2mi)
0 100 yards
0 100 meters
Mosswood Park
TO ROCKRIDGE INSET (1.1mi)
TO CHABOT SPACE & SCIENCE CENTER
36th St.
34th St.
28th St.
32nd St.
31st St.
29th St.
Martin Luther King Jr. Way
Telegraph Ave.
Summit St.
Webster St.
Broadway
Hawthorne Ave.
Central Public Health Center
27th St.
26th St.
25th St.
24th St.
Sycamore St.
Valdez St.
Mead Ave.
Athens Ave.
Isabella St.
23rd St.
Grand Ave.
W. Grand Ave.
22nd St.
21st St.
20th St.
Harrison St.
Lenox Ave.
Lee St.
TO GRAND LAKE THEATER, PIEDMONT, (1mi)
Lakeside Dr.
Lakeside Park
Bellevue Ave.
Snow Park
Lake Merritt
Myrtle St.
Market St.
West St.
Brush St.
Greyhound Bus Station
Williams St.
19th St.
San Pablo Ave.
19TH ST.
17th St.
Franklin St.
Alice St.
Jackson St.
Madison St.
Castro St.
14th St.
13th St.
12th St.
City Center
11th St.
Oakland Visitors Bureau
12TH ST.
Jefferson St.
Clay St.
Washington St.
Oak St.
10th St.
9th St.
Oakland Museum of California
LAKE MERRITT
TO BAY BRIDGE, (3mi)
CHINATOWN
8th St.
7th St.
6th St.
4th St.
3rd St.
2nd St.
Embarcadero W.
Fallon St.
TO OAKLAND AIRPORT, COLLISEUM/ARENA
Jack London's Cabin
Amtrak Station
Port of Oakland Booth
Ferry Dock
JACK LONDON SQUARE
Webster Tube
Posey Tube
Heinhold's First and Last Chance Saloon
0 200 yards
0 200 meters
580
24
980
80
880

Medical Services: Highland Hospital, 1411 E. 31st St. (☎437-4800), at 14th Ave. 24hr. emergency care.

Pharmacy: Leo's Day and Night Pharmacy, 1776 Broadway (☎839-7900), at 19th St. Open M-F 9am-6pm.

Post Office: 1675 7th St. (☎251-3373), west of Peralta St. Open M-F 8:30am-midnight. **Postal Code:** 94615

ACCOMMODATIONS

Although Oakland is full of motels, few downtown are as safe, clean, or economical as those in San Francisco and Berkeley. Motels clustered along **West MacArthur Boulevard** near the MacArthur BART station are around $45 per night for a room with private bath. Ask to see the room before checking in. Commercial inns and hotels (cleaner and safer, but bland) are also clustered around **Broadway** at Jack London Sq. Try one of the beautiful and affordable B&Bs sprouting up in the northern part of the city. For more information, contact the **Berkeley-Oakland Bed and Breakfast Network** (www.bbonline.com/ca/berkeley-oakland).

Bates House B&B, 399 Bellevue St. (☎893-3881), at Van Buren Ave. 1 block north of Grand Ave. A lavish, yet entirely homey B&B surrounded by rose beds. The 4 rooms are painstakingly adorned with captivating antique, oriental, and contemporary furnishings. Three are suites with expansive, fully furnished sitting rooms (TV, sofas, chairs). Outdoor patio. Check-in 2pm. Check-out noon. 10% off stays of 7+ days. Doubles $95-175. ❺

A B&B on Fairmount, 600-block Fairmount Ave. (☎653-7726; www.bbonline.com/ca/fairmount), in Oakland near Piedmont. Beautiful Craftsman home-stay B&B with 3 airy rooms, all with private bath. Living room with views of Mt. Tamalpais and the hills. Healthy breakfasts, made with ingredients from vegetable garden in back, are served in the sunny kitchen. No smoking. 29 stairs to front door; rooms on 2nd floor. 2-night min. stay. 2-week max. stay. Check-in to be arranged after 3pm. Check-out 11am. Exact address revealed with reservations. Singles from $85; doubles from $95. Every consecutive 7th night is free. No credit cards. ❺

FOOD

All-American staples like burger joints, breakfast diners, and barbecue shacks dominate in Oakland. More gourmet cafes, mostly open for breakfast and lunch, have sprung up on **Washington** and **Clay Streets** between 7th and 12th St. Oakland's **Chinatown,** west of Broadway around 9th St., features a cluster of dim sum restaurants, Vietnamese and Cambodian cuisine, and Asian markets. Every Friday the **Oakland Village Farmers Market** takes over 9th St. between Broadway and Clay St., offering fresh fruits, vegetables, and some of the best baked goods in the Golden State. (☎745-7100. F 8am-2pm.) A similar **market** takes over a corner of Jack London Sq. on Broadway, near the waterfront. (☎800-949-3276. Su 10am-2pm.)

▨**Zachary's Pizza,** 5801 College Ave. (☎655-6385), at Oak Grove Ave. Named "Best Pizza" by *East Bay Express* for almost 2 decades straight, Zachary's attracts a large crowd that spills over the counters and out the door waiting for a taste of the signature stuffed pizza. Slices ($3) not served after 4pm. Pies $8.15-26.50. Open Su-Th 11am-10pm, F-Sa 11am-10:30pm. No credit cards. ❶

Jade Villa, 800 Broadway (☎839-1688), at 8th St. Widely acknowledged as the best dim sum in Oakland. High-quality dim sum ($1.90-5.50) includes such specialties as spinach shrimp dumplings and walnut prawns. Dim sum dinner special $9. Beef, poultry, and seafood entrees $7-38. Open M-F 9:30am-9:30pm, Sa-Su 9am-9:30pm. ❷

À Côté, 5478 College Ave. (☎ 655-6469), at Taft Ave. Critics rave about the French-inspired tapas menu, and customers savor artistically arranged cheese plates ($7) and succulent dinner dishes such as pancetta wrapped chicken breast ($12). Tapas dishes $5-12 (expect to order 2 dishes per person). Open Su-Tu 5:30-10pm, W-Th 5:30-11pm, F-Sa 5:30pm-midnight. ❹

G.B. Ratto's & Co. International Market, 821 Washington St. (☎ 832-6503), between 8th and 9th St. While the deli counter prepares their no-frills sandwiches ($3.50-6.75), locals shop for Italian preserves, French honey, and self-serve spices in this century-old cosmopolitan grocery store. Open M-F 9am-6pm, Sa 9:30am-5pm. ❶

🔵 SIGHTS

Haunted by Gertrude Stein's withering observation that "there is no there there," Oakland's tourist literature combats the cynicism of its former resident by assuring visitors that **City Square** is "always here for you" and "there is shopping there." Free walking tours of the city (☎ 238-3234; www.oaklandnet.com) highlight the *thereness* of downtown's best sights, including Roslyn Mazzilli's City Square sculpture, defiantly entitled "There!" For a slightly militant view of the city, take the **Black Panther Legacy Tour.** Former chief-of-staff David Hillard guides visitors through a first-hand account of the events, locations, and personalities that defined the Party. (☎ 986-0660; www.blackpanthertours.com. Reservations required. Tours last Sa of each month. $25.)

OAKLAND MUSEUM OF CALIFORNIA. The three garden-topped levels of Bauhaus-inspired poured concrete at the Oakland Museum of California showcase the collections of three established area museums, brought together in 1969 to reflect the collective artistic, historical, and environmental legacy of Oakland and California. The **Cowell Hall of History** documents the cultural and political forces that shaped centuries of Californians. **The Natural Sciences Gallery** on the first floor re-creates the state's eight biotic zones, allowing you to "Walk Across California" from the shore to the mountains while observing flora and fauna. The **Gallery of California Art** includes the state's largest collection of Dorothea Lange photography, photography by Ansel Adams, paintings by Richard Diebenkorn, and myriad modern masterpieces. The "What's Goin' On?" exhibit (open through Feb. 27, 2005) uses oral histories, film, music, and over 500 historical artifacts to chronicle the impact of the Vietnam War on America and California. (*1000 Oak St., on the southwestern side of the lake. From the Lake Merritt BART station, walk 1 block north on Oak St. toward the hills. ☎ 238-2200 or 888-625-6873; www.museumca.org. Open Su noon-5pm, W-Sa 10am-5pm, 1st F of each month until 9pm. $8; seniors, students, and ages 6-18 $5; under 6 free. 2nd Su of each month free.*)

LAKE MERRITT. Lake Merritt was dammed off from the San Francisco Bay in 1869 and now provides a site for sailing, biking, and jogging—not to mention political protest. Activity revolves around **Lakeside Park,** which has the nation's oldest urban bird sanctuary. The **Lake Merritt Boating Center** rents boats and leads lake tours. (*Park: ☎ 238-7275. Parking $2. Lake: ☎ 238-2196. Boating Center: 568 Bellevue Ave. ☎ 238-2196; www.oaklandnet.com/parks/programs/boating.asp. Boats $6-12 per hr. Deposit $10 deposit. 50% off for seniors and disabled. Open June-Aug. M-F 9am-6pm, Sa-Su 10am-6pm; Sept.-Oct. daily 10:30am-5pm; Nov.-Feb. M-F 10:30am-3:30pm, Sa-Su 10:30am-4pm; Mar.-May M-F 10:30am-4pm, Sa-Su 10:30am-5pm.*)

JACK LONDON SQUARE. This eight-block commercial district is named for Oakland's native son, author of *White Fang* and *The Call of the Wild.* **Jack London's Cabin,** near Webster St., is a reproduction made from the original wood of the author's home during his prospecting days in the Yukon in the 1890's. (*Along the waterfront. Take Broadway south.*) Next to the cabin, the small wooden **Heinold's First and Last Chance Saloon** has barely changed since London's days, except, presumably, for the addition of the London-themed mural. The same gaslight still burns, the sunken floor and bar from 1906 still slant, and 120-odd years of knick-knacks continue to pile up on the walls. *(48 Webster St. ☎839-6761; www.heinoldsfirstandlastchance.com. Open M-Th noon-11pm, F-Sa noon-2am, Su 11am-11pm. No credit cards.)*

CHABOT SPACE AND SCIENCE CENTER. This incredible four-year-old complex offers stargazing both indoors at the **Planetarium** and outdoors with high-powered telescopes, daily screenings in the **Tien MegaDome Theater,** and interactive exhibits in various science and computer labs. *(10000 Skyline Blvd, in Joaquin Miller Park in the Oakland Hills. ☎336-7300; www.chabotspace.org. Open Sept.-June F-Sa 10am-10pm, Su noon-5pm; July-Aug. Tu-Th 10am-5pm, F-Sa 10am-10pm, Su 11am-5pm. $13; students, seniors, and ages 4-12 $9; under 3 free. Planetarium and Tien MegaDome Theater open same hours as Science Center plus April-Oct. F-Sa dusk-11pm; Nov.-Mar. 7-10pm. $6; students, seniors, and ages 4-12 $5; under 3 free.)*

🎵 🎭 ENTERTAINMENT AND NIGHTLIFE

LIVE MUSIC

The **live music scene** is one of the best reasons to make the trip to Oakland. Whether it's West Coast blues, Oaktown hip-hop, or progressive jazz, Oakland's music venues are unsurpassed. Because many artists lack institutional representation, check posters and local papers for shows. The daily *Oakland Tribune* (www.oaklandtribune.com; $0.50, Su $1.25) is a good resource available in newsstands throughout the city. The **Paramount Theater,** 2025 Broadway, at 21st St., has hosted national music acts such as Nina Simone and George Benson. *(☎465-6400; www.paramounttheater.com. Box office open June-Aug. Tu-F noon-6pm; Sept.-May Tu-F noon-6pm, Sa noon-5pm; and 2hr. before performances. Guided tours begin at Box Office entrance on 21st St. ☎893-2300. 2hr. 1st and 3rd Sa of each month 10am. $1. Films $6.)*

🎵 **Yoshi's,** 510 Embarcadero W. *(☎238-9200; www.yoshis.com),* in Jack London Sq. Every major jazz musician over the past 30 years has passed through Yoshi's sushi dinner-jazz concert venue. Big names command higher prices; tickets sometimes sell out but are often available at the door. Cover $10-30. 1-drink min. Local musician nights (usually M) $8-15. Su family matinee: parent $15, child $5. Shows M-Sa 8 and 10pm; Su 2 and 8pm. Box office open daily 10am-11pm.

The Fifth Amendment, 3255 Lakeshore Ave. *(☎832-3242),* at Lake Park Ave. Not the most famous, but one of the best. Local jazz, soul, and blues musicians take the stage in this downtown club frequented by a mature crowd that's serious about music. Cover F-Sa $5. 2-drink min. 21+. Shows Th-Su usually at 8pm or 9pm, F 5:30pm. Open M and W-Su 4pm-2am.

The Stork Club, 2330 Telegraph Ave. *(☎444-6174; www.storkcluboakland.com).* Laid-back country-western bar by day, rock party by night. Kitschy Christmas and Barbies decor year-round. The only Oakland live music venue open 6 days a week. Indie rock, punk (at least twice a week), and underground Tu-Sa around 9pm. Don't walk alone late at night. Cover usually $5. Open Tu-Su 4pm-2am. No credit cards.

CINEMA AND FINE ARTS

The **Paramount Theater,** 2025 Broadway *(☎465-6400),* at 21st St., is an exquisite Art Deco movie palace that screens classic Hollywood films on Fridays ($6). The Paramount shares its stage with the **Oakland East Bay Symphony** and the **Oakland Ballet.** The Symphony performs five Friday concerts yearly, with open rehearsals the preceding Thursday afternoon. The ballet performs several programs, including "Revolutionary Nutcracker Sweetie." (Symphony ☎444-0801; www.oebs.org. Ballet ☎286-8914; www.oaklandballet.org. Symphony tickets $15-65. Ballet tickets $8-45. Box office open June-Aug. Tu-F noon-6pm; Sept.-May Tu-F noon-6pm, Sa noon-5pm; and 2hr. before performance.) Another groovy place to see a movie is the **Parkway Speakeasy Theater,** 1834 Park Blvd., a theater with lounge seating where you can order pizza ($3 per slice), pasta, sandwiches, and wine or beer by the pitcher ($12) or pint ($4.50) right at your seat. Keep an eye open for special Thrillville features. (Movie hotline ☎814-2400, office 848-1994; www.picturepubpizza.com. Tickets $5. 21+ after 4pm. Rocky Horror Picture Show F midnight; $6. 17+. Sa matinees $3, all ages. 2nd floor not wheelchair accessible.) The classic **Grand Lake Theater** features Wurlitzer organ music before Friday and Saturday evening shows and all the latest, hottest movies. (☎452-3556; www.rrfilms.com. Tickets $9; children, seniors, and matinee $6.) Also, there's the more mainstream **Jack London Cinema,** on Washington St. at Embarcadero. (Showtimes ☎433-1320; theater 433-1325. Tickets $9.25, seniors and matinees $6.75.)

SPORTS AND FESTIVALS

Baseball's **Oakland Athletics (A's)** and football's **Oakland Raiders** both play in the **Oakland Coliseum,** 7000 Coliseum Way (☎569-2121), at the intersection of the I-880 (Nimitz Fwy.) and Hegenberger Rd. The Coliseum has its own BART station. The NBA's **Golden State Warriors** play basketball in the **Coliseum Arena,** adjacent to the Oakland Coliseum. (Box office open M-F 10am-6pm, Sa 10am-4pm.) **California Canoe & Kayak,** 409 Water St., in Jack London Sq., rents paddling equipment, offers classes, and plans adventure trips. (☎893-7833, reservations 800-366-9804; www.calkayak.com. Boats due back 1hr. after last rental. $15-25 per hr., $25-60 per day. Open M-Th 10am-7pm, F-Sa 10am-8pm, Su 10am-6pm. Boat rentals M-Th 11am-5pm, F-Sa 11am-6pm, Su 11am-4pm.)

A calendar of events is available at www.oaklandcvb.com. **Art & Soul,** during Labor Day weekend, is Oakland's premier art and music festival, celebrating the arts with impressive music line-ups and gallery exhibits (☎444-2489; www.artandsouloakland.com. Tickets $5, under 12 free.) In the middle of June, **Juneteenth** commemorates the anniversary of the Emancipation Proclamation and black history and culture with parades, soul food, blues, and R&B. In summer, there's free **Shakespeare** in the park. (☎415-422-2222 or 800-978-7529; www.sfshakes.org.)

NORTH BAY AND WINE COUNTRY

MARIN COUNTY ☎415

Just across the Golden Gate Bridge, the jacuzzi of the bay—Marin (muh-RIN) County—bubbles over with enthusiastic residents who casually blend the chic and the radical. Marin is strikingly beautiful, politically liberal, and visibly wealthy. On the eastern side of the county in the upscale towns dotting U.S. 101, locals might initially seem a bit stand-offish, but protective scowls give way to pleasant smiles when visitors appreciate the land and care for it as their own. On the county's west side, the cathedral stillness of ancient redwoods, sweet smell of eucalyptus (though not a native species), brilliant wildflowers, high bluffs, and crashing surf along Hwy. 1 are ample justification for civic pride and earnest preservation concerns. Best of all, this unspoiled natural wonder is just minutes from San Francisco, making it entirely possible to hike all day and party all night.

▐ TRANSPORTATION

The Marin peninsula lies at the northern end of the San Francisco Bay and is connected to the city by **U.S. 101** via the **Golden Gate Bridge.** U.S. 101 extends north inland to Santa Rosa and Sonoma County, while **Highway 1** winds north along the Pacific coast. The **Richmond-San Rafael Bridge** connects Marin to the East Bay via **I-580. Gas** is scarce and expensive in West Marin, so fill up in town before you head out for the coast. If you start running low in West Marin, head toward Point Reyes Station, where you'll find one of few gas stations in the area. Drivers should exercise caution in West Marin, where roads are narrow, sinuous, and perched on cliff-edges.

Public Transportation: Golden Gate Transit (☎455-2000, in SF 923-2000; www.gold-engate.org; phones operated M-F 7am-7pm, Sa-Su 8am-6pm). Provides bus service between San Francisco and Marin County via the Golden Gate Bridge, as well as local service in Marin. Within Marin County, bus #63 runs on the weekends from Marin City through Mount Tamalpais State Park and Stinson Beach. $2, seniors and disabled $1, under 6 free. Rates and service subject to change; check website or call first. **West Marin Stagecoach** (☎526-3239; www.marin-stagecoach.org) now provides **weekday service** connecting West Marin communities to the rest of the county. Stops include: Muir Beach, Pt. Reyes Station, Samuel P. Taylor Park, and Stinson Beach. Anyone can flag the bus to pull over or drop off between scheduled stops. Free Golden Gate Transit transfers. Call or check the website for specific schedules and more detailed routes. $1.50; seniors, disabled, and under 18 $0.75.

Taxi: Belaire Cab Co. (☎388-1234). 24hr.

Bike Rental: Cycle Analysis (☎663-9164; www.cyclepointreyes.com), a trailer in the empty, grassy lot at 4th and Main St. off Hwy. 1 in **Point Reyes Station.** Rents unsuspended bikes ($10 per hr., $32 per day), front-suspension mountain bikes ($12/$35), and child trailers ($30 per day). Helmets included. Emergency repairs and advice for self-guided tours. Open M-Th by appointment, F-Su 10am-5pm.

◼◢◪ ORIENTATION AND PRACTICAL INFORMATION

National seashore and parkland constitutes most of West Marin. The **Marin Headlands** sit 10 mi. from downtown San Francisco, just across the Golden Gate Bridge. Beaches and coastal wonders line **Highway 1** (also called **Shoreline Highway**), which splits from U.S. 101 north of Sausalito and runs up the Pacific coast through Muir Beach, Stinson Beach, Olema, and Pt. Reyes Station. About 4 mi. north of the split, the **Panoramic Highway** branches off Hwy. 1 and winds up to **Mount Tamalpais,** reconnecting with Hwy. 1 near Stinson Beach. Access Muir Woods from **Muir Woods Road,** which splits from both the Panoramic Hwy. winding toward Mt. Tamalpais and from Hwy. 1 about 1½ mi. later. Slightly inland, Mt. Tamalpais is about 15 mi. northwest of San Francisco; the state park encompasses a large area just inside the coast from Muir Beach to around Stinson Beach. The **Point Reyes National Seashore,** a near-island surrounded by almost 100 mi. of isolated coastline, is a wilderness of pine forests, chaparral ridges, and grassy flatlands, about 15 mi. northwest of San Francisco. **Point Reyes Station** sits about 2 mi. north of Olema and about 20 mi. northwest of San Francisco.

Visitor Information: Marin County Visitors Bureau, 1013 Larkspur Landing Cr. (☎925-2060; www.marincvb.org), near the Sir Francis Drake Blvd. exit off U.S. 101, by the ferry terminal. Open M-F 9am-5pm.

Park Visitor Information:

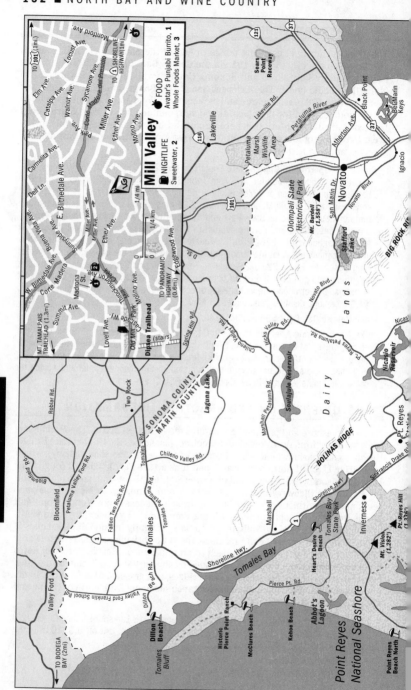

Mill Valley

● FOOD
Avatar's Punjabi Burrito, **1**
Whole Foods Market, **3**

● NIGHTLIFE
Sweetwater, **2**

Marin County

ACCOMMODATIONS
Green Gulch Farm Zen Center, 4
Marin Headlands Hostel, 5
Point Reyes Hostel, 1
West Point Inn, 3

CAMPSITE
Kirby Cove, 6
Samuel P. Taylor State Park, 2

Trailhead
Ferry Route
Federal Parkland
State Parkland
Other Parkland
Trail

Sausalito

FOOD
Real Food Company, 2
Sushi Ran, 3
Venice Gourmet Delicatessen, 5

NIGHTLIFE
No Name Bar, 4
Smitty's Bar, 1

PACIFIC OCEAN

San Pablo Bay

San Francisco Bay

San Francisco

Drakes Bay

Pt. Reyes Lighthouse

Point Reyes Beach South

Sir Francis Drake Blvd

Drake's Beach

Drakes Estero

Limantour Beach

Sculptured Beach

Arch Rock

Mt. Wittenburg (1,407')

1906 Earthquake Epicenter

Coast Camp

Limantour Rd. Bear Valley Visitor Center

Coast Nisqik Indian Village

Olema

Samuel P. Taylor State Park

Five Brooks Trailhead

Glen Camp

Wildcat Camp

Alamere Falls

Phillip Burton Wilderness

Coastal Trail

Palomarin Trailhead

Bass Lake

Bolinas Lagoon

Bolinas

Mesa Rd.

Horseshoe Hill Rd.

Audubon Canyon Ranch

Stinson Beach

Muir Beach

Marin Headlands Visitor Center

Pt. Bonita Lighthouse

MARIN HEADLANDS AREA

Conzelman Rd.

Bunker Rd.

Kirby Cove

Golden Gate Bridge

Battery Spencer

The Presidio

Belvedere

Tiburon

Angel Island State Park

Richardson Bay

Sausalito

see Sausalito inset

Marin City

Golden Gate National Rec. Area

Muir Woods Nat'l Mon.

Mt. Tamalpais (2,571')

Mt. Tamalpais State Park

Pan Toll Ranger Station

Panoramic Hwy.

W. Ridgecrest Blvd.

Pine Mtn. (1,762')

Alpine Lake

Kent Lake

Marin Municipal Water Dist.

Lake Lagunitas

Phoenix Lake

Bon Tempe Lake

Tempe Oaks

Larkspur

Ross

Corte Madera

Mill Valley

see Mill Valley inset

Ring Mtn.

Paradise Dr.

Corte Madera

Kentfield

San Anselmo

Fairfax

Woodacre

San Geronimo

Lagunitas

Forest Knolls

Sir Francis Drake Blvd.

Fairfax Bolinas Rd.

Butterfield Dr.

Sleepy Hollow

Terra Linda

Marinwood

San Rafael

Point San Pedro Rd.

San Pedro Rd.

China Camp State Park

McNears Beach

Richmond-San Rafael Bridge

TO SAN FRANCISCO

Red Hill Ave.

Magnolia Ave.

Valley Rd.

Lucas Valley Rd.

Golden Gate Nat'l Rec. Area

580

101

131

1

0   2 miles
0   2 kilometers

Sausalito inset

TO SF BAY MODEL, MILL VALLEY

Sausalito Point

Sausalito Yacht Harbor

Gabrielson Park

Municipal Fishing Pier

Tiffany Beach

Swedes Beach

Bridgeway Blvd.

Buckley Ave.

Art that Makes You Laugh

PLAZA VINA DEL MAR

Richardson St.

Main St.

Valley St.

Second St.

Third St.

North St.

San Carlos Ave.

Harrison Ave.

Bridgeway Blvd.

Santa Rosa Ave.

Locust St.

Johnson St.

Pine St.

Litho St.

Caledonia St.

Cazneau Ave.

Crescent Ave.

Filbert Ave.

Spencer Ave.

Glen Dr.

Prospect

Alexander Ave.

Edwards Ave.

Golden Gate National Recreation Area

TO GOLDEN GATE BRIDGE, HEADLANDS

TO SAN FRANCISCO (2.5mi.)

Rainbow Tunnel

101

0   1/2 mi
0   1/2 km

A WILD RIDE. Travel on Hwy. 1 is not always life in the fast lane. A mere 10 mi. may be entirely composed of 15 mph curves and stunning ocean views. Take your time, enjoy the view, and if there are more than three cars behind you, pull over to let them pass. Hopefully the ancient RV sputtering in front of you will return the favor.

Point Reyes National Seashore Headquarters (also referred to as Bear Valley Visitor Center; ☎464-5100; www.nps.gov/pore), on Bear Valley Rd., ½ mi. west of Olema. Rangers lead guided hikes and distribute camping permits, maps, and sage advice on trails, tides, and weather conditions. Excellent exhibits on the cultural and natural history of Pt. Reyes. Open M-F 9am-5pm, Sa-Su and holidays 8am-5pm.

Pan Toll Ranger's Station, 801 Panoramic Hwy. (☎388-2070), in Mt. Tamalpais State Park, about 2½ mi. inland from Stinson Beach. Bus #63 stops on the weekends (about 5 per day). Operates Mt. Tam's campgrounds and trails. Rangers offer suggestions and explain restrictions on the trails. Open daily June-Aug. 9am-6pm; Sept.-May intermittently.

Muir Woods National Monument Visitors Center (☎388-2596; www.nps.gov/muwo), near the entrance to Muir Woods. Muir Woods trail map $2 (free download on website). Great selection of hiking, biking, and driving maps of Marin and Mt. Tam. Open daily Sept.-May 9am-6pm; June-Aug. 8am-8pm.

Marin Headlands Visitors Center, Bldg. 948, Fort Barry (☎331-1540), at Bunker and Field Rd. Talk to the helpful staff about hiking and biking in the park and pick up maps, trail advice, and permits for free campsites. The center is also a museum and a store with artifacts. Wheelchair accessible. Open daily 9:30am-4:30pm.

Police: Marin County Sheriff: ☎479-2311, 24 hr. In Sausalito ☎289-4170, in Point Reyes 663-1151, in San Anselmo 258-4610.

Medical Services: Marin General Hospital and Community Clinic, 250 Bon Air Rd. (☎925-7000, clinic 488-1500), in **Greenbrae,** off the U.S. 101 San Anselmo exit. 24hr. emergency care. Clinic open by appointment only M-Th 8am-8pm, F 8am-5pm.

Library and Internet Access: Stinson Beach Library, 3521 Shoreline Hwy. (☎868-0252). Free Internet. Open M 10am-1pm, Tu 1-5pm and 6-9pm, F 10am-1pm and 2-6pm, Sa 10am-1pm.

Post Office: Sausalito, 150 Harbor Dr., off Bridgeway. Open M-Th 8:30am-5pm, F 8:30am-5:30pm. **Postal Code:** 94965. **Stinson Beach,** 15 Calle Del Mar, at Shoreline Hwy. Open M-F 8:30am-5pm. **Postal Code:** 94970.

ACCOMMODATIONS

Marin has a few well-run hostels in amazing natural surroundings. A number of pricey, upscale inns are available in Sausalito, Mill Valley, and Stinson Beach.

West Point Inn (info ☎388-9955, reservations 646-0702), on Mt. Tamalpais, 2 mi. up Stage Rd. Park at the Pan Toll Ranger Station ($6, seniors $5) and hike or bike up. Not the lap of luxury, but one hell of an experience. Built in 1904 and hasn't changed much since. Propane-generated heat, light, and refrigeration; no other electricity. Bring your own linens, sleeping bags, food, and flashlight, but not your pets. Pancake breakfast ($7), even for non guests, May-Oct. on the 2nd Su of the month 9am-1pm. 7 private rooms, 5 private cabins, and a well-equipped shared kitchen. Reservations required. Sa vacancies are rare. Closed Su-M nights. $35, under 18 $17.50, under 5 free. ❷

Point Reyes Hostel (HI-AYH; ☎663-8811; norcalhostels.org), just off Limatour Rd. 2 mi. from Limatour beach in the Point Reyes National Seashore. Miles from civilization, this excellent hostel provides shelter and solace for a stay in the wilderness.

Linen $1; sleeping bags encouraged. Towels $1. Check-in 4:30-9:30pm. Check-out 10am. Lockout 10am-4:30pm. Dorms $16, under 17 $10. One private room reserved for families with children under 5. ❶

Green Gulch Farm Zen Center, 1601 Shoreline Hwy. (☎383-3134; www.sfzc.org). Tranquil silence, serene nature, and a yurt. If a guest stay isn't enlightened enough, Green Gulch's guest student program allows serious students of Zen to meditate, work, and study at the center for $15 per night (5-day min. stay, 6-week max. stay). Singles M-Th $75-90, F-Su $90-105; doubles M-Th $125-140, F-Su $140-155. ❹

Marin Headlands Hostel (HI-AYH), Bldg. 941 on Rosenstock (☎331-2777 or 800-909-4776, ext. 168; http://headlandshostel.homestead.com), up the hill from the visitors center and next to the Headlands Center for the Arts. 2 spacious and immaculate Victorian houses, with 100 beds, a game room, kitchens, and common rooms. Internet $0.10 per min. Linen $1. towels $0.50. Laundry $1.50. Key deposit $20. 15-day max. stay per year. Check-in 3:30-10:30pm. Check-out 11am. No lockout. Reservations recommended 2 months in advance for private rooms and weekends. Dorms $18, under 18 $9. Private rooms for 2 adults and 2 kids $54. ❷

▚ CAMPING

The Headlands (☎331-1540; www.nps.gov/goga/camping/index.htm) offers 3 small walk-in campgrounds with 11 primitive campsites for individual backpackers and small groups. No water. No fires or pets allowed. Showers and kitchen ($2 each) at Headlands Hostel (see p. 155). Free cold showers at Rodeo Beach. 3-day max. stay per site; 9-day max. stay per year. Reserve up to 90 days in advance. All individual sites free with a permit from the Marin Headlands Visitors Center (see p. 154). ❶

Kirby Cove (☎ 800-365-2267), off Conzelman Rd. west of the Golden Gate Bridge, in the Marin Headlands. 4 car-accessible sites in a grove of cypress and eucalyptus trees on the shore. Designed for larger groups. Fire rings and pit toilets. No water. No pets. 3-day max. stay. 1 weekend reservation per group per year. Open Apr.-Nov. Sites $25. ❷

Point Reyes National Seashore (☎663-8054; www.nps.gov/pore; open for reservations M-F 9am-2pm, walk-in 9am-5pm). Walk-in sites. 2 camps are coastal (Coast and Wildcat) and 2 are inland (Sky and Glen). Some have exquisite ocean views. Charcoal grills, running water (non-potable at Wildcat Camp), picnic tables, food storage lockers, and pit toilets. 4-night max. stay. Reservations recommended up to 3 months in advance. Sites for 1-6 people $12-15. Boat-in camping at Tomales Bay north of the state park; call or check web for info. Pick up permits at Point Reyes Headquarters (see p. 154). ❶

Samuel P. Taylor State Park, P.O. Box 251 (☎488-9897, reservations through Reserve America, 800-444-7275; www.parks.ca.gov), on Sir Francis Drake Blvd., 15 mi. west of San Rafael in Lagunitas. The park contains 6 family campgrounds along Sir Francis Drake Blvd. in a lush setting beneath stately, second-growth redwoods. Often crowded on weekends. Sites are shady, though not always quiet. Running water, flush toilets, and hot coin showers. Day-use parking $6. 7-night max. stay. Check-out noon. Reservations recommended. Sites $20, seniors $18. Hike/bike sites $3 per person, 2-night max. stay, and no reservations. ❶

◗ FOOD

Marinites take their fruit juices, tofu, and nonfat double-shot soy cappuccinos very seriously, and pay dearly for them. Stock up for the ferry ride home in Sausalito with the organic produce from **Real Food Company,** 200 Caledonia St. (☎332-9640. Open daily 9am-9pm.) In Mill Valley on the outskirts of town, **Whole Foods,** 414 Miller Ave., specializes in organic groceries. (☎381-1200. Open daily 8am-8pm.)

▨ **Venice Gourmet Delicatessen,** 625 Bridgeway (☎332-3544; www.venicegourment.com), in **Sausalito**. Serves a wide variety of sandwiches ($3.75-6.50) and side dishes ($1.50-5) in a Mediterranean-style marketplace. Waterside seating with a stunning view of the San Francisco skyline across the Bay. Open daily 9am-6pm; summer weekends until 7pm. ❷

▨ **Avatar's Punjabi Burrito,** 15 Madrona St. (☎381-8293), in **Mill Valley**. Take chickpeas, rice, chutney, yogurt, and spice; add tofu and meats; and wrap in yummy Indian flatbread, for an inspired and filling meal. Burritos $5.50-8.50. Rice plates, salads, and mango lassi also available. Open M-Sa 11am-8pm. ❷

Bubba's Diner, 566 San Anselmo Ave. (☎459-6862), in **San Anselmo**. A local favorite that serves all the essentials. All-day breakfast menu, including "chocoholic" pancakes ($8). Open M and W-F 9am-9pm, Sa-Su 8am-9pm. ❸

Sushi Ran, 107 Caledonia St. (☎332-3620; www.sushiran.com), in **Sausalito**. A local favorite. Upscale Japanese fare, including *sake* and vegetarian *maki*. Sushi $4-15. Open M-F 11:45am-2:30pm and 5:30-11pm, Sa 5:30-11pm, Su 5:30-10:30pm. ❺

Comforts, 335 San Anselmo Ave (☎454-9840), in **San Anselmo**. Gourmet deli counter goods, like pasta, chili, and salads $3.25-4.25 per ½ lb. Made-to-order sandwiches ($6.50-7) until 3pm. Open M-F 6:30am-7pm, Sa 7:30am-7pm, Su 8:30am-3pm. ❷

👁 ⚠ SIGHTS AND OUTDOOR ACTIVITIES

Marin's proximity to San Francisco makes it a popular daytrip destination. Virtually everything worth seeing or doing in Marin is outdoors. An efficient visitor can hop from park to park and enjoy several short hikes along the coast and through the redwood forests in the same day, topping it off with a pleasant dinner in one of the small cities. Those without cars, however, may find it easier to use one of the two well-situated hostels as a base for hiking or biking explorations.

POINT REYES

POINT REYES NATIONAL SEASHORE. Surrounded by nearly 100 mi. of isolated coastline, the Point Reyes National Seashore is a wilderness of pine forests, chaparral ridges, and grassy flatlands. Five million years ago, this near-island outcropping was a suburb of L.A., but it hitched a ride on the submerged Pacific Plate and has been creeping northward along the San Andreas Fault ever since. In summer, colorful **wildflowers** attract crowds of gawking tourists, but with hundreds of miles of amazing trails, it's quite possible to stroll alone. *(Hwy. 1 provides direct access to the park from the north or south; Sir Francis Drake Blvd. comes west from U.S. 101 at San Rafael.)* The park headquarters are at the **Point Reyes National Seashore Headquarters,** just west of Olema. Rangers distribute camping permits and can suggest trails, drives, beaches, and picnic areas. *(☎464-5100; www.nps.gov/pore. Open M-F 9am-5pm, Sa-Su 8am-5pm.)* The **Earthquake Trail** is a half-mile walk along the infamous San Andreas Fault Line that runs right through Bear Valley. Lovely **Limantour Beach** sits at the end of Limantour Rd., 8 mi. west of the visitors center. A keen eye will see that the dramatic landscape around the hostel is still scarred with a few charred reminders of a major forest fire that torched the region in 1995, although lush regrowth has covered most traces of the inferno. Both Limantour and Point Reyes Beaches have high, grassy dunes and long stretches of sand, but strong ocean currents along the point make swimming very dangerous. Swimming is safest at **Heart's Desire Beach,** in separate Tomales Bay State Park north of the visitors center on sheltered **Tomales Bay.** To reach the dramatic **Point Reyes Lighthouse** at the very tip of the point, follow Sir Francis Drake Blvd. to its end (20 mi. from the visitors center). From December to February, migrating gray whales can be spotted from the overlook. *(Lighthouse Visitors Center ☎669-1534. Open M and Th-Su 10am-4:30pm.)*

MARIN COAST

Highway 1 reaches the Pacific at Muir Beach and then twists its way up the rugged coast. It's all beautiful, but the stretch between Muir and Stinson Beaches is the most breathtaking, especially when driving south on the sheer-drop-to-the-ocean side of the highway. If you're riding a bike, don't expect the white-knuckled drivers of passing cars to allow you much elbow room.

BEACHES. Sheltered **Muir Beach** is scenic and popular with families. The crowds thin out significantly after a 5min. climb on the shore rocks to the left. *(Open dawn-9pm.)* Six miles to the north, **⬛Stinson Beach** attracts a younger, rowdier, better-looking surfer crowd, although cold and windy conditions often leave them languishing on dry land. *(Bus #63 runs from Sausalito to Stinson Beach on weekends and holidays. Open 9am-1hr. after sunset.)* The Bard visits Stinson Beach from July to October during **Shakespeare at Stinson**. *(☎868-1115; www.shakespeareatstinson.org.)* Between Muir and Stinson Beaches lies **Red Rocks Beach**, a secluded spot reached by a steep hike down from a parking area 1 mi. south of Stinson Beach. where many beachgoers do without their swimsuits.

ZEN CENTER. Just inland from Muir Beach is the **Green Gulch Farm Zen Center**, a Buddhist community, retreat, and organic farm. Visitors are free to explore the tranquil grounds and gardens. On Sunday mornings the public is welcome at meditation instruction (8:15am) and meditation (9:25am) followed by a lecture on Zen Buddhism (10:15am), tea, and lunch. Would-be Zen masters are asked to wear dark, loose-fitting clothing for *zazen* meditation. *(1601 Shoreline Hwy. ☎383-3134; www.sfzc.org. Lunch $8. Su parking $5; free when 3+ people carpool.)*

BOLINAS. Continuing a few miles northwest from Stinson Beach along Hwy. 1, you'll find the **Audubon Canyon Ranch.** Dedicated to preserving the surrounding lands as well as other areas in Marin and Sonoma counties, the ranch provides educational programs and conducts several research projects. Come watch great blue herons and great egrets nest, or go for a hike on the 8 mi. of hiking trails. *(Across from the Bolinas Lagoon. ☎868-9244; www.egret.org. Open mid-Mar. to mid-July Sa-Su 10am-4pm, Tu-F by appointment.)* Immediately past the lagoon is the unmarked turn-off for the village of Bolinas—a tiny colony of hippies, artists, and writers. Many of the art galleries and eateries that dot the town have no set hours, and watching three generations of bohemians walk side-by-side down the street emphasizes the village's strong atemporal vibe. Eccentric Bolinas residents have included authors Richard Brautigan *(Trout Fishing in America)* and Jim Carroll *(The Basketball Diaries)*. Try Northern California cuisine at **Coast Cafe ❹**, but don't tell them we sent you. *(46 Wharf Rd. ☎868-2298. Average dinner entree $16.50. Open for breakfast and lunch M-Th 7:30am-2pm, F-Su 7:30am-3pm; dinner Su-Tu 5-8:30pm, W-Sa 5-9pm.)* For years, locals have hoped to discourage tourist traffic by tearing down any and all signs marking the Bolinas-Olema road. Press coverage of the "sign war" won the people of Bolinas exactly the publicity they wanted to avoid, but for now, at least, the town remains unspoiled in ways that Sausalito is not—and they intend to keep it that way, so don't expect to feel welcomed. *(Driving north from Stinson Beach, the Bolinas-Olema road is the first left after coming around the lagoon; turn and follow the road to the end. From Olema, take Hwy. 1, and hang a right after Horseshoe Hill Rd. before the lagoon.)*

MOUNT TAMALPAIS AND MUIR WOODS

MOUNT TAMALPAIS STATE PARK. Between the upscale towns of eastern Marin and the rocky bluffs of western Marin rests beautiful **Mount Tamalpais State Park** (tam-ull-PIE-us). The park has miles of hilly, challenging trails on and around Mount Tamalpais (2571 ft.). The bubbling waterfall on **Cataract Trail** (off Hwy. 1, follow signs) and the **Gardner Lookout** on Mount Tam's east peak are worthy destinations. *(☎388-2070. Free. Parking $6, $5 seniors.)* Visit the **Pan Toll Ranger Station,**

BAY AREA AND WINE COUNTRY

BURNING GREASE

People have been riding bikes "off-road" for as long as they have been riding bikes, but mountain biking (the extreme, knee-shattering sport) was born in Marin County in the early 70s, when a group of hotshot road racers headed out to Mt. Tamalpais's rocky fire roads.

Gary Fisher, Charlie Kelly, Joe Breeze, and others rode 1930s-era bikes with fat balloon tires and coaster brakes that handled the rough terrain better than their fancy road bikes. Eventually, someone made the fateful claim, "I'm fastest," and in October 1976, the first **Repack race** was held on northern Mt. Tamalpais, down a steep, winding 2 mi. course with a 1300 ft. drop. By the course's end, all the grease in the bike's coasters had vaporized, and the racers finished trailing a plume of smoke. After each race, the brakes needed to be re-packed with grease (hence the race's name).

Enthusiasts came together early at Repack, trading ideas to improve the sport and their equipment. Fisher added derailleur gears and Breeze built the first modern frame. In 1979, Fisher, Kelly, and Tom Ritchey collaborated to create MountainBikes, the first exclusively off-road bike company. Today, Mt. Tamapais is still a prime mountain-biking spot.

on Panoramic Hwy., for trail suggestions and biking restrictions. Although this is the birthplace of the mountain bike, cyclists that go off designated trails and fire roads risk incurring the wrath of eco-happy Marin hikers. On weekends and holidays, bus #63 stops at the ranger station between the Golden Gate Bridge and Stinson Beach. At the center of the state park is **Muir Woods National Monument,** a 560-acre grove of old coastal redwoods. Spared from logging by the steep sides of Redwood Canyon, these massive, centuries-old redwoods are shrouded in silence. The level, paved trails along the canyon floor are lined with wooden fences, but a hike up the canyon's sides will soon take you away from the tourists and put you face-to-face with wildlife. *(5 mi. west of U.S. 101 on Hwy. 1. ☎388-2595. Open 8am-sunset. $3 charge 9am-6pm, under 17 free.)*

MARIN HEADLANDS
The fog-shrouded hills just west of the Golden Gate Bridge constitute the Marin Headlands. These windswept ridges, precipitous cliffs, and hidden sandy beaches offer superb hiking and biking minutes from downtown. For instant gratification, drive up to any of the lookouts and pose for your own postcard-perfect shot of the Golden Gate Bridge and the city skyline, or take a short walk out to Point Bonita. If you intend to do more serious hiking or biking, choose one of the coastal trails that provide easy access to dark sand beaches and dramatic cliffs of basalt greenstone. The visitors center, at Bunker and Field Rd., offers helpful maps (free or $1.50). Either way, bring a jacket in case of sudden wind, rain, or fog.

POINT BONITA. One of the best short hikes leads to the lighthouse at Point Bonita, a prime spot for seeing sunbathing California sea lions in summer and migrating gray whales in the cooler months. The little lighthouse at the end of the point really doesn't seem up to the job of guarding the whole San Francisco Bay, but has done so valiantly since 1855; in fact, its original glass lens is still in operation. At the end of a narrow, knife-like ridge lined with purple wildflowers, a short tunnel through the rock and a miniature suspension bridge lead to the lighthouse. The trail is gated off at the tunnel when the lighthouse is closed, but the short walk provides gorgeous views on sunny days. *(Lighthouse: 1 mi. from visitors center, ½ mi. from nearest parking. Open M and Sa-Su 12:30-3:30pm. Guided walks M and Sa-Su 12:30pm. Free. No dogs or bikes through the tunnel.)*

MILITARY GUNS. Formerly a military installation charged with defending the San Francisco harbor, the Headlands are dotted with machine-gun nests, missile sites, and soldiers' quarters dating from the Spanish-American War to the 1950s. ▓**Battery Spencer,** on Conzelman Rd. immediately west of U.S. 101, offers superb views of the city skyline, and the Golden Gate Bridge seems close enough to touch. It's a perfect photo-op, especially around sunset on the (rare) clear day. Farther into the park is the **NIKE Missile Site** on Field Rd., where disarmed Cold War missles sit hauntingly. (*Battery Spencer on Conzelman Rd. just west of U.S. 101. NIKE Missile Site on Field Rd., at Fort Berry and Fort Cronkite.* ☎ *331-1453. Open W-F and 1st Su of the month 12:30-3:30pm. Tours every hour.*)

OTHER ACTIVITIES. The 1 mi. walk from the visitors center down to sheltered **Rodeo Beach,** a favorite of cormorants and pelicans, is easy and pleasant. The **Wolf Ridge** and **Tennessee Valley** trails are perennial favorites; ask rangers for other suggestions and camping info. The **Marine Mammal Center** is a working hospital for sick sea creatures and provides some information about the animals and their rehabilitation. (*Off Bunker Rd.* ☎ *289-7325; www.marinemammalcenter.org. Open daily 10am-4pm.*)

SAUSALITO

The city at Marin's extreme southeastern tip was originally a fishing center of bars, bordellos, and houseboats populated by outlaws, radicals, and outlaw radicals (such as wanted members of the violent 60s political group the Weather Underground). Today, its saltiness has given way to retail boutiques and overpriced seafood restaurants. The palm trees and 14 ft. elephant statues of **Plaza de Viña del Mar Park** look out over a wonderful view of San Francisco Bay, making for a sunny, self-consciously Mediterranean-esque excursion. The sheer number and variety of quality art galleries in the small town make it worth checking out, regardless of the touristy feel. Half a mile north of the town center is the **Bay Model and Marinship Museum,** 2100 Bridgeway, a massive working model of San Francisco Bay covering 3 acres. Built in the 1950s to test proposals to dam the bay, the water-filled model recreates tides and currents in great detail. (☎ 332-1851. Open Tu-F 9am-4pm, Sa 10am-5pm. Free.)

SAN RAFAEL

San Rafael (San Ra-fell) is the largest city in Marin County, but it holds little of interest to the budget traveler. If you do stop here on your way to or from San Francisco, the main strip for eating and shopping lies along **4th Street.** Visitors with a car have the option of picnicking at **China Camp State Park,** an expanse of grassy meadows east of the city. Named for the ramshackle remains of a Chinese fishing village that once housed thousands of laborers who were forced from the city. (☎ 456-0766. Open daily 8am-sunset. Visitors center open daily 10am-5pm. Parking $5.) Six miles north of San Rafael is an exit for Lucas Valley Rd., where Jedi master George Lucas toils away at **Skywalker Ranch,** (www.george.lucas.net), crafting the next installment of the Star Wars saga. Don't try stopping for a sneak preview—the ranch is fiercely guarded by Imperial Stormtroopers.

BAY AREA AND WINE COUNTRY

▓ NIGHTLIFE

If you really wanted to party, you'd head back to the city, but Marin County does offer a number of low-key live music venues and easygoing watering holes. San Rafael probably has the most action, with many more bars than are listed here.

Sweetwater, 153 Throckmorton (☎ 388-2820), in **Mill Valley.** Popular spot to booze during happy "hour" (all day every day until 7pm; pints $3.50, well drinks $2.25) before listening to live blues, folk, bluegrass, or rock music by locals (like Bonnie Raitt, for example) and visiting celebs alike. Music Su-Th from 8:30 or 9pm, F-Sa from 9:30pm. Cover $6-15; around $25 for a more famous artist. Open daily 12:30pm until the music stops (between 12:30-2am).

No Name Bar, 757 Bridgeway (☎332-1392), in **Sausalito**. Once a haunt of the Beats, the bar with no name now serves a mixed crowd of tourists and locals. Cozy heated garden patio out back. Live blues or jazz most nights. The biggest draw is Dixieland jazz every Su afternoon. Sandwich menu noon-4pm. Open 10am-2am.

Smitty's Bar, 214 Caledonia St. (☎332-2637), in **Sausalito**. This bar resisted upward mobility to remain a rough-around-the-edges favorite of Sausalito's "boat people." Shuffleboard, pool, 3 TVs, and a wall of billiards trophies to admire. Domestic pints $3.50-4.50, schooners (32 oz.) $0.75-6.25, pitchers $10-12. Open daily 10am-2am.

Fourth Street Tavern, 711 4th St. (☎454-4044), between Lincoln and Tamalpais Ave. in **San Rafael**. A small-town pub, this local favorite features an eclectic line-up that runs the gamut from bluegrass and junkabilly to hip-hop and funk from 9:30pm daily. Happy hour Tu-F 5-7pm; drink specials $3. Open M 7pm-2am, Tu-Su 3pm-2am.

NAPA VALLEY   ☎707

Napa catapulted American wine into the big leagues in 1976, when a bottle of red from the area's Stag's Leap Vineyards beat a bottle of critically acclaimed (and unfailingly French) Château Lafitte-Rothschild in a blind taste test in Paris. While not the oldest, and not necessarily the best, Napa Valley is certainly the best-known of America's wine-growing regions. Its golden hills, natural hot springs, and consistently gorgeous weather inspired Gold Rush millionaires to build luxury spas here in the 1850s. From the well-to-do urbanite staying in a high-priced B&B to the group of tourists cruising in a rental limousine, Napa attracts the most diverse crowd of visitors in Wine Country, and you can always expect insufferable traffic congestion, especially at the south end of Napa where all the major highways meet. Regardless of tourist traffic, Napa's dense collection of vineyards rewards the budget traveler who splurges on a single day's car rental, promising winery after winery of intoxicating pleasure and vistas that are equally disarming.

▐ TRANSPORTATION

If you're planning a weekend trip from San Francisco, avoid Saturday mornings and Sunday afternoons; the roads are packed with like-minded people. From San Francisco, take U.S. 101 over the Golden Gate Bridge, then follow Rte. 37 east to catch Rte. 29, which runs north to Napa.

Public Transportation: Napa City Bus, or **Valley Intercity Neighborhood Express (VINE),** 1151 Pearl St. (☎800-696-6443 or 255-7631, TDD 226-9722), has a few bus services that cover the entire stretch of Napa Valley from Vallejo to Calistoga M-F 5:20am-9:20pm, Sa 6am-8:10pm, Su 8:15am-6pm. $1-2.50, students $0.75-1.80, seniors $0.50-1.25. Ask for a free transfer as you board the bus. The nearest **Greyhound** station is in Vallejo at 1500 Lemon St. (☎643-7661 or 800-231-2222).

Airport Service: Evans Airport Transport, 4075 Solano Ave. (☎255-1559), in Napa, runs daily shuttle buses from the **San Francisco** and **Oakland** airports via Vallejo to northern Napa. To **Napa** ($29, children 12 and under $14.50, $5 local resident discount; cash only) and **Vallejo** ($24; cash only.).

✱ ▐ ORIENTATION AND PRACTICAL INFORMATION

Scenic **Route 29 (Saint Helena Highway)** runs north from **Napa** through Napa Valley and the well-groomed villages of **Yountville** and **Saint Helena** (where it's called Main St.) to **Calistoga's** soothing spas. The relatively short distances between wineries

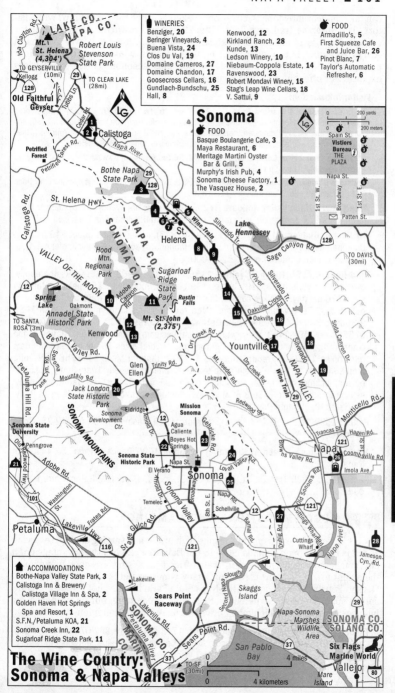

WINERIES
Benziger, **20**
Beringer Vineyards, **4**
Buena Vista, **24**
Clos Du Val, **19**
Domaine Carneros, **27**
Domaine Chandon, **17**
Goosecross Cellars, **16**
Gundlach-Bundschu, **25**
Hall, **8**

Kenwood, **12**
Kirkland Ranch, **28**
Kunde, **13**
Ledson Winery, **10**
Niebaum-Coppola Estate, **14**
Ravenswood, **23**
Robert Mondavi Winery, **15**
Stag's Leap Wine Cellars, **18**
V. Sattui, **9**

FOOD
Armadillo's, **5**
First Squeeze Cafe
and Juice Bar, **26**
Pinot Blanc, **7**
Taylor's Automatic
Refresher, **6**

Sonoma

FOOD
Basque Boulangerie Cafe, **3**
Maya Restaurant, **6**
Meritage Martini Oyster
Bar & Grill, **5**
Murphy's Irish Pub, **4**
Sonoma Cheese Factory, **1**
The Vasquez House, **2**

Vistiors Bureau
THE PLAZA

ACCOMMODATIONS
Bothe-Napa Valley State Park, **3**
Calistoga Inn & Brewery/
Calistoga Village Inn & Spa, **2**
Golden Haven Hot Springs
Spa and Resort, **1**
S.F.N./Petaluma KOA, **21**
Sonoma Creek Inn, **22**
Sugarloaf Ridge State Park, **11**

The Wine Country:
Sonoma & Napa Valleys

BAY AREA AND WINE COUNTRY

can take unpleasantly long to cover on weekends, when the roads crawl with visitors. The **Silverado Trail,** parallel to Rte. 29, is less crowded, but watch out for cyclists. Napa is 14 mi. east of Sonoma on **Route 12.** Although harvest season in early September is the most exciting time to visit, winter weekdays are less packed and allow for more personal attention. Most accommodations are also less expensive or offer specials in the winter.

Visitor Information:

Napa Conference & Visitors Bureau, 1310 Town Ctr. (☎226-7459; www.napavalley.com/ nvcvb.html). Very friendly staff. Provides free maps and info. The *Napa Valley Guidebook* ($6) has more comprehensive listings and fold-out maps. Ask about any specials during your visit (they come in daily) and pick up coupons from local businesses. Open daily 9am-5pm.

St. Helena Chamber of Commerce, 1010A Main St. (☎963-4456; www.sthelena.com). Eager to help. Open M-F 10am-5pm, Sa 11am-3pm.

Calistoga Chamber of Commerce, 1458 Lincoln Ave. (☎942-6333; www.calistogafun.com). Open M-F 10am-5pm, Sa 10am-4pm, Su 11am-3pm.

Winery Tours: Napa Valley Holidays (☎255-1050; www.napavalleyholidays.com). Afternoon tours $75 per person, with round-trip transportation from San Francisco $85 .

Car Rental: Budget, 407 Soscol Ave. (☎224-7846), in Napa. Cars about $40 per day. Unlimited mileage. 25+ with credit card. Promotional specials often available; call Budget Reservation Center at ☎800-527-7000.

Bike Rental: ◪St. Helena Cyclery, 1156 Main St. (☎963-7736; www.sthelenacyclery.com). Hybrid bikes $10 per hr., $30 per day; road bikes $50 per day; tandem bikes $70 per day. All bikes come with maps, helmet, and lock; hybrid and tandem with picnic bag. Reservations recommended for road and tandem bikes. Open M-Sa 9:30am-5:30pm, Su 10am-5pm. **Getaway Adventures,** 1522 Lincoln Ave. (☎942-0332 or 800-499-2453; www.getawayadventures.com), behind the gas station at the corner of Rte. 29 and Lincoln Ave., in Calistoga. Hybrid bikes $6 per hr., $24 per day; road bikes $12/$28; mountain bikes $9/$30; tandem bikes $14/$56. 2hr. min. rental. Also leads "Sip 'n' Cycle" bike tour to 5 wineries (usually 10am-3pm) $115 per person; includes bike rental and lunch. Open Su-F 9am-5:30pm, Sa 9am-6pm; in low season usually M and W-Su 8:30am-5pm. Additional location: 2228 North Point Pkwy. ☎568-3040, in Santa Rosa.

Police: 1539 1st St. (☎253-4451), in Napa; 1235 Washington St. (☎942-2810), in Calistoga.

Medical Services: Queen of the Valley Hospital, 1000 Trancas St. (☎252-4411), in Napa.

Post Office: 1625 Trancas St. (☎255-0190), in Napa. Open M-F 9am-5pm. **Postal Code:** 94558.

♠♣ ACCOMMODATIONS AND CAMPING

Rooms in Napa Valley go quickly despite high prices and varying quality; reserving ahead is best. Though Napa is close to the Bay Area and has the advantages of a city, smaller towns will prove more wallet-friendly. Calistoga is a good first choice; the quaint town is a short drive from many wineries and is close to Old Faithful Geyser, Petrified Forest, and Bothe-Napa State Park. It is also home to natural hot-spring spas. The least expensive alternative is camping, but be prepared for intense summer heat, which might drive you back into air-conditioned civilization.

◪ **Golden Haven Hot Springs Spa and Resort,** 1713 Lake St. (☎942-6793; www.goldenhaven.com), a few blocks from Lincoln Ave. in Calistoga. Well-sized and tastefully decorated rooms, especially when compared to other options in this price range. TV and private bath in all rooms. Rooms with king-size beds, kitchenettes, hot tubs, vaulted ceilings, and saunas also available. Mineral swimming pool and hot tub access. No children under 16 F-Sa. 2-night min. stay on weekends. Room with queen-size bed $89, with private sauna $149; king-size bed $99, with kitchenette $139, with private hot tub $189. Nov.-Mar. M-Th $10-40 less. ❹

▨ **Calistoga Inn and Brewery,** 1250 Lincoln Ave. (☎942-4101; www.calistogainn.com), at the corner of Rte. 29 in Calistoga. 18 clean, simple, country inn rooms that barely accommodate a queen-size bed. Shared bathrooms. Microbrewery and restaurant downstairs; open M-Th 11:30am-9:30pm, F 11:30am-10pm, Sa-Su 10am-10pm. Rooms Su-Th $75, F $110, Sa $125. ❹

The Calistoga Village Inn & Spa, 1880 Lincoln Ave. (☎942-0991), has small clean, basic rooms with unremarkable decor, cable TV, phones, and private bath. Rooms with hot tub available. Heated mineral pools and hot tub. On-site spa; 10% off spa treatments for guests. Rooms with full-size bed $89; queen-size bed $99, with sitting area $119, with kitchenette and hot tub $169; king-size bed with sitting area and Roman tub $149; 2 bedrooms $129. Su-Th rooms $10 less; 2-bedroom unit $20 less. Nov.-Mar. Su-Th 15% off. Ask about special packages for lodging, spa, and meals. ❺

Bothe-Napa Valley State Park, 3801 Rte. 29 (☎942-4575, reservations 800-444-7275; www.napanet.net/~bothe), north of St. Helena. The 50 quiet sites near Ritchey Creek Canyon often fill to the max; reserve up to 7 months in advance for summer weekends. Fairly rustic, though there are toilets, fire pits, and picnic tables at each site. Pool $3, under 17 $1. Hot showers $0.25 per 3min. Check-in 2pm. Park open daily 8am-dusk. Sites for up to 8 people and 1 vehicle $20. Picnic area day use $4. ❷

◖ FOOD

Extremely cheap eats aren't an option in Wine Country, but you can find great meals at a moderate price. Picnics are an inexpensive and romantic alternative—numerous delis and grocery stores in the area sell supplies. Most wineries have shaded picnic grounds, often with excellent views, but most require patronage. The **Napa Farmers Market,** 500 1st St., at Soscol Ave., offers a sampling of the valley's produce. (☎252-7142. Open Tu and Sa 7:30am-noon.)

Taylor's Automatic Refresher, 933 Main St. (☎963-3486), on Rte. 29 across from the Merryvale Winery, in St. Helena. A 50s-style roadside stand dishing up big burgers ($5.50-10) and popular super-thick milkshakes ($4.60). Ample outdoor seating around the stand. Beer and wine available. Open daily 11am-9pm. ❷

First Squeeze Cafe and Juice Bar, 1126 First St. (☎224-6762), in Napa. A friendly staff serves up healthy favorites such as the Vanessa (grilled tofu with avocado on health nut bread), *huevos rancheros* ($8), or fresh fruit smoothies ($4). Beer and wine $2.50-3.50. Breakfast served until 2pm. Open M-F 7am-3pm, Sa-Su 8am-3pm. ❷

Pinot Blanc, 641 Main St. (☎963-6191), on Rte. 29 in St. Helena. All the charm of a French country inn, though most diners take lunch on the lush patio. Dinner entrees such as duck leg confit, average $17. Lunch $9-20. W "Local night" 3-course dinner $28. Free corkage. Open M-Th 5:30-9pm, F-Sa noon-5pm and 5:30-9:30pm, Su noon-3pm and 5:30-9pm. Reservations recommended W and F-Sa. ❹

Armadillo's, 1304 Main St. (☎963-8082), in St. Helena. Cali-Mexican dishes in a kitschy pueblo-style interior with delightfully painted chairs and tables. Enchiladas $7.75-14. Strawberry margarita $4. Beer and wine available. Open Su-Th 11am-9pm, F-Sa 11am-10pm. ❷

⚡ WINERIES

There are more than 250 wineries in Napa County, nearly two-thirds of which line **Route 29** and the **Silverado Trail** in Napa Valley, home of Wine Country's heavyweights. Nationally recognized vineyards include Inglenook, Fetzer, and Mondavi. Some wineries have free tastings and some have free tours; all have large selections of bottled wine available for purchase at prices slightly cheaper than those in stores and less than half the price of those in restaurants. Many wineries offer reduced rates to visitors who purchase a tasting or become a club member. Style and atmosphere, from architecture to visitor hospitality, vary from estate to estate; experiencing both the larger touristy operations and the smaller-name vineyards adds to the fun. No matter their marketing approach, the wineries listed below (from south to north) have two things in common: each claims to make the best Cabernet (a.k.a "Cab") in the Valley and each cards for underage drinkers; **you must be 21+ to taste or purchase alcohol.**

A good way to begin your Napa Valley experience is with a tour such as the ones offered at **Domaine Carneros** or **Beringer**, or a free tastings class, like the one on Saturday mornings at **Goosecross Cellars**, 1119 State Ln., in Yountville. (☎944-1986; www.goosecrosscellars.com. Open by appointment daily 11am-4pm. Classes Sa 11am-12:30pm.)

NAPA AREA

Kirkland Ranch, 1 Kirkland Ranch Rd. (☎254-9100; www.kirklandranchwinery.com), south of Napa off Rte. 29. Reminiscent of an upscale ranch, this family-operated winery has windows overlooking the production facilities. True to its country-western style, the winery's walls are adorned with family pictures of cattle-herding cowboys. Tours by appointment. Tastings $5. Open daily 10am-4pm.

Domaine Carneros, 1240 Duhig Rd. (☎257-0101), off Rte. 121 between Napa and Sonoma. Picturesque estate peacefully removed from the main drag, with an elegant terrace modeled after a French château; "Be prepared to feel like royalty" is their slogan. Owned by Champagne Taittinger and known for its sparkling wines, Carneros also makes a great Pinot Noir. The free tour and film (daily 10:15am and every hr. 11am-4pm) is a great way to kick off a day of wine tasting. No tastings, but wines by the glass $5-10 with complimentary hors d'oeuvres. Open daily 10am-6pm.

YOUNTVILLE AREA

🕯 Clos Du Val Wine Company, Ltd., 5330 Silverado Trail (☎259-2225; www.closduval.com), north of Oak Knoll Rd., in Yountville. Stakes its claim with wines that age with balance and subtlety. Small, elegant grounds and plenty of name recognition attract lots of tourists. Delightful *petanque* court in the back where visitors play the French version of bocce ball. Tastings $5; price applicable toward wine purchase. Free tours by appointment. Open daily 10am-5pm.

Domaine Chandon, 1 California Dr. (☎944-2280 or 800-934-3975; www.chandon.com), in Yountville. Owned by Moët Chandon (the French makers of Dom Perignon), the winery sells over 300,000 cases of sparkling wine annually. Sprawling grounds with manicured gardens, tree canopy, and spraying fountains make the sleek visitors center feel like a decadent cloister. French restaurant on site. 3 tastes for $9-14, by the glass $5-13. Open daily 10am-6pm.

Stag's Leap Wine Cellars, 5766 Silverado Trail (☎944-2020; www.cask23.com). "The tiny vineyard that beat Europe's best," reads the souvenir glass that comes with the portfolio ($10) or flights ($30) tasting at this small but formidable winery. Call in advance to arrange a 1hr. tour ($20; includes a tasting). Open daily 10am-4:30pm.

OAKVILLE

Robert Mondavi Winery, 7801 Rte. 29 (☎963-9611 or 888-766-6328; www.robert-mondaviwinery.com), 8 mi. north of Napa. Massive and touristy, with a beautiful mission-style visitors complex, 3 tasting rooms selling by the glass ($4-15), and the atmosphere of a luxury summer resort. Offers a variety of tours. Vineyard and Winery tour daily every hr. 10am-4pm $15; includes 3 tastes and hors d'oeuvres. Reserve 1hr. in advance. The other 5 tours (some seasonal) are each given one day per week between 10am and 11am, and cost $25-95 per person. Open daily 9am-5pm.

Niebaum-Coppola Estate Winery, 1991 St. Helena Hwy. (☎968-1100, tours 968-1161). Famed director Francis Ford Coppola and his wife bought the historic 1880 Inglenook Chateau and Niebaum vineyards in 1975. Restoring the estate to production capacity, Coppola also added a free family history museum upstairs that contains film memorabilia, including the desk from *The Godfather* and his Oscar and Golden Globe statues. 4 tastes and commemorative glass for $12-30. Vineyard tours ($25) daily 11am; rubicon tours ($50) by reservation Th and Sa-Su 1pm. Open daily 10am-6pm.

ST. HELENA

◪ V. Sattui, 1111 White Ln. (☎963-7774 or 800-799-2337; www.vsattui.com), at Rte. 29, in St. Helena. Named "Best Winery in California" at the 2004 California State Fair, V. Sattui is one of the few wineries in the valley that only sells at its winery. Cutting out the middle man means good prices for visitors. The family-owned operation has a gourmet cheese counter, meat shop, and bakery. Picnic area for customers. Very popular and crowded free tastings. Open daily Mar.-Oct. 9am-6pm; Nov.-Feb. 9am-5pm.

Hall, 401 St. Helena Hwy. (☎967-2626), in St. Helena. Don't let the lack of cars and crowds outside deter you; the attentive staff within this small lodge takes its hospitality very seriously. Garden patio perfect for savoring wine as you enjoy modern sculpture from Texan owners' private collection. 5-7 tastes for $10. Open daily 10am-5:30pm.

Beringer Vineyards, 2000 Main St. (☎963-4812; www.beringer.com), off Rte. 29, in St. Helena. This sprawling estate is mobbed with tourists. Historic district tours of the stunning Queen Anne Victorian mansion and grounds daily at 10:30am ($18; 21+); tour includes a tasting of 3 exclusive wines. Introductory tour, including tasting, every hr. 10am-5pm ($5, under 21 free). Tastings $5-16 for 3 wines. Open daily 10am-6pm.

🅖 🅜 SIGHTS AND OUTDOOR ACTIVITIES

Napa's gentle terrain makes for an excellent bike tour. The area is fairly flat, although small bike lanes, speeding cars, and blistering heat can make routes more challenging, especially after a few samples of wine. The 26 mi. **Silverado Trail** has a wider bike path than Rte. 29. **◪St. Helena Cyclery** (see p. 162.) rents bikes.

CALISTOGA. Calistoga is known as the "Hot Springs of the West." Sam Brannan, who first developed the area, meant to make the hot springs the "Saratoga of California," but he misspoke and promised instead to make them "The Calistoga of Sarafornia." The **Sharpsteen Museum** adjoins one of his restored resort cottages and traces the town's development in exhibits designed by a Disney animator. *(1311 Washington St. ☎942-5911; www.sharpsteen-museum.org. Open daily 11am-4pm; in winter noon-4pm. Suggested donation $3.)* Calistoga's luxuriant mud baths, massages, and mineral showers will feel even more welcome after a hard day of wine-tasting. Be sure to hydrate beforehand; alcohol-thinned blood and intense heat do not mix. A basic package consisting of a mud bath, mineral bath, eucalyptus steam, and blanket wrap costs around $50. Salt scrubs and facials are each about $50. **The Calistoga Village Inn and Spa** gives friendly service. (☎942-0991. *Mud bath $50. 50min. massage $75. 25min. facial $49. Body wrap $80.)* **Golden Haven** also offers full spa services. *(☎942-6793. Mud bath $64. 30min. massage $48. 30min. facial $48. Less in winter.)*

OLD FAITHFUL GEYSER OF CALIFORNIA. This steamy wonder should not be confused with its more famous namesake in Wyoming. The geyser regularly jets boiling water 60 ft. into the air. Though it "erupts" about every 40min., weather conditions affect its cycle; winter eruptions can occur as often as every 5-15min., though at half the usual height. The ticket vendor will tell you the estimated time of the next spurt. *(1299 Tubbs Ln., off Hwy. 128, 2 mi. outside Calistoga. ☎942-6463. Open daily 9am-7pm; in winter 9am-6pm. $8, seniors $7, ages 6-12 $3, disabled free.)*

MARINE WORLD. This 160-acre Vallejo theme park specializes in animal shows and special attractions including a butterfly walk, and the Shark Experience. The park was recently purchased by Six Flags, eclipsing zoo and oceanarium exhibits with an array of roller coasters. *(Off Rte. 37, 10 mi. south of Napa. Vallejo is accessible from San Francisco by BART. ☎643-6722. Open Mar.-Aug. Su-F-10am-8pm, Sa 10am-9pm; Sept. Sa-Su 10am-8pm; Oct. F 4-10pm, Sa 10am-10pm, Su 10am-9pm. $46, seniors $36, under 48 in. $25. Parking $10.)*

OTHER SIGHTS. The Petrified Forest, 4100 Petrified Forest Rd., west of Calistoga proper, was formed over three million years ago when molten lava from a volcano eruption 7 mi. northeast of Mt. St. Helena covered a forested valley and preserved the trees. The half-mile trail is wheelchair accessible. *(☎942-6667. Open daily 9am-7pm; in winter 9am-6pm. $6, seniors and ages 12-17 $5, ages 6-11 $3, under 3 free.)* Experience an authentic Venetian gondola ride on Napa River with **Gondola Servizio Napa,** inside Hatt Market. *(540 Main St. ☎257-8495, reservations and live operator 866-737-8494. Open May-Oct. Th-Su. 30min. private ride $55 per couple, 1hr. $100, 1hr. plus wine and collectible glass $135; $10 per additional person, $15 per additional person for the wine package.)* **Napa Valley Wine Train** travels from Napa to St. Helena and back and offers gourmet meals and full cocktail service on board in the style of the early 1900s. *(1275 McKinstry St. ☎253-2111 or 800-427-4124; www.winetrain.com. Reservations recommended. Dining excursions about 3hr. Available for lunch, brunch, and dinner. Ticket and meal plans $40-140. Advanced payment required.)* Swimming, sailing, and sunbathing in the cool waters of **Lake Berryessa** are a popular family activity. *(20 mi. north of Napa off Hwy. 128. ☎966-2111.)*

❊ FESTIVALS

The annual **Napa Valley Wine Festival,** in which around 50 vintners raise money for public education through dinners, tours, and rare vintage auctions, takes place in early November. From January through April the **Mustard Festival** (☎259-9020; www.mustardfestival.org) lines up different musical or theatrical presentations as well as art exhibits. The annual **Napa County Fair** (☎942-5111; www.napacountyfairgrounds.com) hosts a July 4th weekend celebration with concerts, fireworks, and a rodeo. In the summer, there are free afternoon concerts at **Music-in-the-Park,** downtown at the riverfront. Contact Napa Parks and Recreation Office (☎257-9529) for more info.

SONOMA VALLEY   ☎707

Sprawling Sonoma Valley is a quieter alternative to Napa, but home to bigger wineries than the Russian River Valley. Many wineries are on winding side roads rather than a freeway strip, creating a more intimate wine-tasting experience.

Sonoma Plaza is surrounded by art galleries, novelty shops, clothing stores, and Italian restaurants. Petaluma, west of the Sonoma Valley, has more budget-friendly lodgings than the expensive wine country.

▐ TRANSPORTATION

From San Francisco, take **U.S. 101 North** over the Golden Gate Bridge; then follow Rte. 37 E to Rte. 116 N, which turns into Rte. 121 N and crosses Rte. 12 N to Sonoma. Alternatively, follow U.S. 101 N to Petaluma and cross over to Sonoma by Rte. 116. Driving time from San Francisco is about 1-1½hr. For road conditions, call ☎817-1717.

Buses: Sonoma County Transit (☎576-7433 or 800-345-7433; www.sctransit.com) serves the entire county. Bus #30 runs from **Sonoma** to **Santa Rosa** (daily every 1-1½hr. 6am-7pm; $2.25, students $1.90, seniors and disabled $1.05, under 6 free); #44 and 48 go from **Santa Rosa** to **Petaluma** (daily; $1.90, students $1.60, seniors and disabled $0.90). Within Sonoma, county buses must be flagged down at bus stops (daily 8am-4:25pm; $1, students $0.80, seniors and disabled $0.50). **Golden Gate Transit** (from Sonoma County ☎541-2000, from SF 415-923-2000) runs buses frequently between **San Francisco** and **Santa Rosa. Volunteer Wheels** (☎800-992-1006) offers door-to-door service for people with disabilities. Open daily 8am-5pm.

Bike Rental: Sonoma Valley Cyclery, 20093 Broadway (☎935-3377), in Sonoma. Mountain bikes $6 per hr., $20 per day; includes helmet, lock, bags. Open M-Sa 10am-6pm, Su 10am-4pm.

▐▐ ORIENTATION AND PRACTICAL INFORMATION

Route 12 traverses the length of Sonoma Valley, from **Sonoma** through **Glen Ellen** to **Kenwood** in the north. The center of downtown Sonoma is **Sonoma Plaza,** which contains City Hall and the visitors center. **Broadway** dead-ends at Napa St. in front of City Hall. Numbered streets run north-south. **Petaluma** lies to the west and is connected to Sonoma by **Route 116,** which becomes **Lakeville Street** in Petaluma.

Visitor Information: Sonoma Valley Visitors Bureau, 453 1st St. East (☎996-1090; www.sonomavalley.com), in Sonoma Plaza. Maps $2. Open daily 9am-5pm. **Petaluma Visitors Program,** 800 Baywood Dr. (☎762-2785), at Lakeville St. The free visitor's guide has listings of restaurants and activities. Open daily 9am-5pm.

Police: In Petaluma ☎778-4372, in Sonoma ☎996-3602.

Medical Services: Petaluma Valley Hospital, 400 N. McDowell Blvd. (☎778-1111).

Post Office: Sonoma, 617 Broadway (☎996-9311), at Patten St. Open M-F 8:30am-5pm. **Postal Code:** 95476 **Petaluma,** 120 4th St. (☎769-5352). Open M-F 8:30am-5pm, Sa 10am-2pm. **Postal Code:** 94952.

▐▐ ACCOMMODATIONS AND CAMPING

Pickings are pretty slim for lodging; rooms are scarce even on weekdays and generally start at $85. Less expensive motels cluster along **U.S. 101** in Santa Rosa and Petaluma. Campers with cars should try the **Russian River Valley** (see p. 175).

▩ **Sonoma Creek Inn,** 239 Boyes Blvd. (☎939-9463 or 888-712-1289), west off Hwy. 12, in Sonoma. Just 10min. from the Sonoma Plaza. Bold and colorful rooms exude a character utterly lost in most Wine Country inns in this price range. All rooms with fridge, cable TV, phone, and full bath. Rooms Su-Th $79, with patio $89, F-Sa $149/$159. ❹

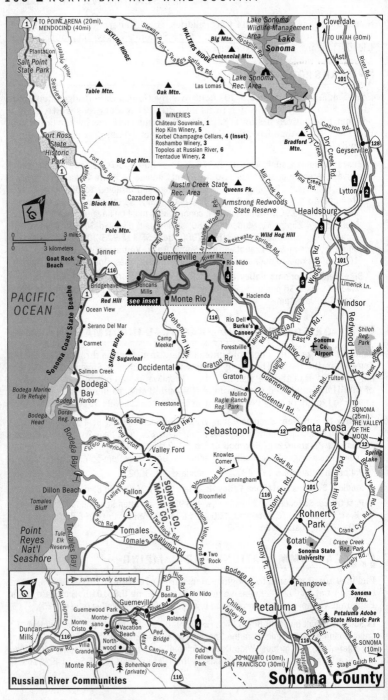

WINERIES

Château Souverain, **1**
Hop Kiln Winery, **5**
Korbel Champagne Cellars, **4 (inset)**
Roshambo Winery, **3**
Topolos at Russian River, **6**
Trentadue Winery, **2**

see inset

PACIFIC OCEAN

BAY AREA AND WINE COUNTRY

TO POINT ARENA (20mi), MENDOCINO (40mi)

TO UKIAH (30mi)

Lake Sonoma Wildlife Management Area

Cloverdale

Lake Sonoma

Salt Point State Park

Plantation

Big Mtn.

Rockpile Rd.

Centennial Mtn.

Asti

Stewart Point–Skaggs Springs Rd.

SKYLINE RIDGE

WALTERS RIDGE

Lake Sonoma Rec. Area

101

Table Mtn.

Oak Mtn.

Las Lomas

Canyon Rd.

Fort Ross State Historic Park

Big Oat Mtn.

Bradford Mtn.

W. Dry Creek Rd.

Geyserville

128

Dry Creek Rd.

Wine Creek Rd.

1

2

Lytton

Austin Creek State Rec. Area

Queens Pk.

Armstrong Redwoods State Reserve

Healdsburg

Cazadero

Black Mtn.

Pole Mtn.

Old Cazadero Hwy.

Cazadero Hwy.

Armstrong Woods Rd.

Wild Hog Hill

3

101

West Side Rd.

Mill Creek Rd.

Sweetwater Springs Rd.

Limerick Ln.

Jenner

Goat Rock Beach

116

Guerneville

River Rd.

Rio Nido

4

5

Windsor

Bridgehaven

Duncans Mills

Monte Rio

Hacienda

Redwood Hwy.

Shiloh Reg. Park

Red Hill

Ocean View

116

Rio Dell

Burke's Canoes

Russian River

Sonoma Co. Airport

East Side Rd.

Serano Del Mar

Carmet

Camp Meeker

Forestville

6

Sonoma Rd.

Bohemian Hwy.

Mirabel Rd.

Sugarloaf

SHEEP RIDGE

Salmon Creek

Occidental

Graton Rd.

Graton

Guerneville Rd.

Fulton Rd.

Fulton

Mark West Springs Rd.

Santa Rosa

Bodega Marine Life Refuge

Bodega Bay

Bodega Harbor

Freestone

Molino

Ragle Ranch Reg. Park

Occidental Rd.

TO SONOMA (25mi), THE VALLEY OF THE MOON

Bodega Head

Doran Reg. Park

Bodega

Bodega Hwy.

Sebastopol

12

12

Spring Lake

Bodega Bay

Valley Ford Cutoff

Estero Americano

Valley Ford

Knowles Corner

Todd Rd.

101

Petaluma Hill Rd.

Bennett Valley Rd.

Dillon Beach

Fallon

Bloomfield Rd.

Cunningham

Bloomfield

116

Stony Pt. Rd.

Rohnert Park

Tomales Bluff

SONOMA CO. MARIN CO.

Dillon Beach Rd.

Fallon–Two Rock Rd.

Petaluma Valley Ford Rd.

Crane Cyn.

Crane Creek Reg. Park

Pressly Rd.

Point Reyes Nat'l Seashore

Tule Elk Reserve

Tomales

Two Rock

Tomales–Petaluma Rd.

Cotati

Sonoma State University

Penngrove

Sonoma Mtn.

Petaluma Adobe State Historic Park

Bodega Rd.

Chileno Valley Rd.

Petaluma

Adobe Rd.

TO NOVATO (10mi), SAN FRANCISCO (30mi)

116

Lakeville Hwy.

Petaluma River

Stage Gulch Rd.

Frates Rd.

TO SONOMA (10mi)

D. St.

Russian River Communities

summer-only crossing

Duncan Mills

116

Moscow Rd.

Villa Grande

Monte Rio

Monte Cristo

Montesano

Guernewood Park

Northwood

Vacation Beach

Bohemian Grove (private)

Guerneville

River Rd.

El Bonita

Rio Nido

Rolands

Ped. Bridge

Hulbert's Canyon Rd.

Odd Fellows Park

4

116

Sonoma County

Redwood Inn, 1670 Santa Rosa Ave. (☎545-0474), in Santa Rosa. At least 30min. drive from Sonoma. Comfortable motel-style rooms with cable TV, phone, and bath. Some with kitchenette. Rooms with 1 bed $55-75, 2 beds $65-85. $5 less in winter. ❹

Sugarloaf Ridge State Park, 2605 Adobe Canyon Rd. (☎833-5712), off Rte. 12, north of Kenwood in the Mayacamas mountains. 49 sites with tables and fire rings. Arranged around a central meadow with flush toilets and running water (but no showers). In summer and fall, take advantage of Ferguson Observatory inside the park; see www.rfo.org for details. Reserve sites through ReserveAmerica (☎800-444-7275; www.reserveamerica.com). Sites $12-19. ❶

San Francisco North/Petaluma KOA, 20 Rainsville Rd. (☎763-1492, reservations 800-992-2267; www.petalumakoa.com), in Petaluma off the Penngrove exit. Suburban camp with 300 sites plus a recreation hall with activities, petting zoo, heated pool, store, laundry facilities, and hot tub. Many families. Hot showers. Check-in 1pm. Check-out 11am. 1-week max. tent stay. Reservations recommended. 2-person sites $29-36; $6 per additional adult, $4 per child. RVs $38-50. Cabins (sleep 4; no linens or kitchenware) $56-61; $70 over holiday weekends. ❸

FOOD

Seasonal produce is available directly from area farms or at roadside stands and farmer's markets. *Farm Trails* maps are free at the Sonoma Valley Visitors Bureau. Those in the area toward the end of the summer should ask about the ambrosial **crane melon,** a tasty hybrid of fruits grown only on the Crane Farm north of Petaluma. The **Sonoma Market,** 520 W. Napa St., in the Sonoma Valley Center, is an old-fashioned grocery store with deli sandwiches ($5-7) and produce. (☎996-0563. Open daily 6am-9pm.) The **Fruit Basket,** 18474 Sonoma Hwy., sells inexpensive fruit. (☎996-7433. Open daily 7am-7pm.) Groceries can be found at **Safeway,** 477 W. Napa St. (☎996-0633. Open 24hr.)

Maya, 101 E. Napa St. (☎935-3500; www.mayarestaurant.com), at the corner of 1st St. East in Sonoma's Historic Town Sq. The festive decor, mouthwatering Yucatan food, and extensive wine and tequila menu are truly impressive. Margaritas $5. Entrees $10-23. Occasional live music in summer. Open M-Th 11:45am-9:30pm, F-Sa 11:45am-10:30pm, Su 4pm-9pm. ❸

Murphy's Irish Pub, 464 1st. St. East (☎935-0660; www.sonomapub.com), tucked in an alleyway off Sonoma Plaza. A delightful local pub. Good-natured Irish staff welcomes newcomers with a big smile and a perfectly pulled pint. Local favorites include fish 'n' chips ($12) and anything from the thoughtful selection of beers and ales. Very popular open mic night on the 2nd and 4th M of each month at 8pm. Live music Th-Su 8pm. Open Su-Th 11am-11pm, F-Sa 11am-midnight. ❷

Meritage Martini Oyster Bar and Grill, 165 W. Napa St. (☎938-9430; www.sonomameritage.com), in Sonoma. With a new location and more upscale design, including handblown glass lights, this bistro serves equally well as an indulgent breakfast joint (orange brandy french toast with mascarpone ($7), decadent gelato getaway (3 scoops for $5), or trendy lounge. Lunch specials $7-10. The oyster bar is a favorite ($1.75-2.50 per piece; 2-person sampling platter $15). Pastas and entrees $9-20. Brunch served Sa-Su until 3pm. Open M-Th 11am-9pm, F 11am-10pm, Sa-Su 10am-10pm. ❹

The Vasquez House, 414 1st. St. East (☎938-0510), in El Paseo de Sonoma. Inconspicuously tucked behind touristy shops, this historic house hides a library and a miniscule tea room serving coffee, tea, and lemonade ($0.75), along with freshly baked "indulgences" ($1). Open Th-Sa 2-4:30pm. No credit cards. ❶

Basque Boulangerie Cafe, 460 1st. St. East (☎935-7687), in Sonoma Plaza. Though not on par with the exquisite French cafes and bakeries in SF, this little cafe is always packed. Below the wall of freshly baked French breads is a counter filled with tarts, mini-gateaus, and pastries ($2-20). Lunch sandwiches $3.50-8. With 24hr. notice they'll arrange a box lunch ($11) for vineyard picnicking. Open daily 7am-6pm. ❸

Sonoma Cheese Factory, 2 Spain St. West (☎996-1931 or 800-535-2855; www.sono-majack.com), in Sonoma. No-frills deli lets you sample familiar cheeses while waiting for a sandwich (from $5.50). Open Su-Th 8:30am-6pm, F-Sa 8:30am-7:30pm. ❶

⚡ WINERIES

Sonoma Valley's wineries, near Sonoma and Kenwood, are less touristy but just as elegant as Napa's. As an added bonus, there are more complimentary tastings of current vintages. Take a close look at the *Let's Go* map or bring an extra one along (they're all over the place and free), as there are few winery signs to guide you.

SONOMA AREA

🏛 **Gundlach-Bundschu,** 2000 Denmark St. (☎938-5277; www.gunbun.com), off 8th St. E. Established in 1858, this is the 2nd-oldest winery in Sonoma and the oldest family-owned and run winery in the country. Delightfully fragrant wines (e.g., Tempranillo Rosé), German offerings (e.g, Gewürztraminer), and Zinfandels draw people from across the country and set this winery apart from its peers. Ensconced among rolling hills against a backdrop of mountains, the winery hosts outdoor events such as a Mozart series. Free wine storage cave tours Sa-Su every 30min. noon-3:30pm. Tastings $5 for 4-6 samples with the extremely personable staff. Open daily 11am-4:30pm.

Buena Vista, 18000 Old Winery Rd. (☎938-1266; www.buenavistawinery.com). Take E. Napa St. from Sonoma Plaza and turn left on Old Winery Rd. The oldest premium winery in the valley. Famous stone buildings are preserved just as Mr. Haraszthy built them in 1857 when he founded the California wine industry. Theater shows July-Sept. Historical presentation and guided tour daily at 11am and 2pm ($15). All other tours are self-guided. Tastings $5; includes glass. Open daily 10am-5pm.

Ravenswood, 18701 Gehricke Rd. (☎933-2332 or 888-669-4679; www.ravenswood-wine.com), north of Sonoma. If you make the faux pas of asking for a white Zinfandel, you'll hear the Ravenswood mantra about "no wimpy wines." An otherwise congenial staff lend this Zinfandel house a pleasant and bustling air. Price of tastings ($5 or $10) applicable to wine purchase (up to $5 only). Tours by appointment daily at 10:30am. Open daily 10am-4:30pm.

GLEN ELLEN

🏛 **Benziger,** 1883 London Ranch Rd. (☎888-490-2739 or 935-4014; www.benziger.com). One of the few wineries in the US certified as biodynamic, this winery brings a great deal of care to the winemaking process in order to preserve the natural character of the property and its grapes. Tourists flock here for the acclaimed 45min. tram ride tour ($10, under 21 $5) through the vineyards, which runs in the summer (daily every 30min. 11am-3:30pm) and includes reserve tasting and 20% off purchases. Self-guided tours lead from the parking lot through the vineyards and peacock aviary. Tastings of current vintage $5, estate and reserves $10. Open daily 10am-5pm.

KENWOOD

🏛 **Ledson Winery and Vineyards,** 7335 Sonoma Hwy. (☎833-2330; www.ledson.com). A relatively new Merlot estate that does not market its wines. The stunning French-Normandy "castle" houses a lavish parlor and an equally impressive gourmet marketplace featuring fine cheeses, chocolate wine sauces, and exclusive fruit spreads. Monthly events themed around holidays. Tastings $5-10. Open daily 10am-5pm.

Kunde, 10155 Sonoma Hwy. (☎833-5501; www.kunde.com), near Kenwood. The cave tours at Kunde offer respite from the sun, and you may catch a glimpse of the impressive 125-year-old Zinfandel vines. Known for its Chardonnays. Free cave tours every hr. Su and F-Sa 11am-3pm. Tastings estate $5 (redeemable toward purchase), reserves $10 (includes glass but not redeemable). Open daily 10:30am-4:30pm.

Kenwood, 9592 Sonoma Hwy. (☎833-5891; www.kenwoodvineyards.com). Known for its Jack London Wolfe wine (they buy the grapes from the author's estate). Current vintage tastings free, private reserves $5. Open daily 10am-4:30pm.

👁 🌸 SIGHTS AND FESTIVALS

SONOMA STATE HISTORIC PARK. Within the park, an adobe church stands on the site of the **Mission San Francisco-Solano,** the northernmost and last of the 21 Franciscan missions. Marking the end of El Camino Real, or the "Royal Road." Built in 1826 by Padre Jose Altimira, the mission contains a fragment of the original California Republic flag, the rest of which was burned in the 1906 San Francisco earthquake fires. In 1841, the present chapel replaced its more unstable predecessor, which had been damaged by a rain storm. *(E. Spain and 1st St., in the northeast corner of Sonoma. ☎938-1519. Open daily 10am-5pm. $2, children under 17 free. Includes admission to Vallejo's Home, Sonoma Barracks, and Petaluma Adobe.)*

GENERAL VALLEJO'S HOME. This site is often referred to by its Latin name, *Lachryma Montis,* meaning "Tears of the Mountain." The "Yankee" home of the famed Mexican leader, who also was mayor of Sonoma and a California senator, is open for tours of the museum, pond, pavilions, and gardens. The grounds are graced with a serene picnic area designed in part by Vallejo and his wife. *(Located on W. Spain St. at 3rd St. ☎938-1519. Open daily 10am-5pm. $2, under 17 free.)*

JACK LONDON STATE PARK. Around the turn of the 20th century, hard-drinking and hard-living Jack London, author of *The Call of the Wild* and *White Fang,* bought 1400 acres here, determined to create his dream home. London's hopes were frustrated when the estate's main building, the **Wolf House,** was destroyed by fire in 1913. Arson had been the widely accepted explanation until a recent forensic study revealed that the fire started when a pile of rags damp with linseed oil spontaneously ignited one hot August night. London died three years after the fire and is buried in the park, his grave marked by a volcanic boulder originally intended for the construction of the home. The nearby **House of Happy Walls,** built by London's widow in fond remembrance of him, is now a two-story museum devoted to the writer. The park's scenic half-mile **Beauty Ranch Trail** passes the lake, winery ruins, and quaint cottages. There are many longer, more challenging trails. Take **Lake Trail** (1 mi.) from the parking lot to the lake. There, follow **Mountain Trail** (½ mi.) to a lovely vista point. Continue on Mountain Trail all the way to the Park Summit (2½ mi.) or circle around Woodcutter's Meadow on the **Fallen Bridge Trail** (1¼ mi.) to return. *(Take Hwy. 12 4 mi. north from Sonoma to Arnold Ln. and follow signs. ☎938-5216. Park open daily 10am-5pm during standard time; 10am-7pm during daylight savings time. Museum open daily 10am-5pm.)* **Sonoma Cattle and Napa Valley Trail Rides** also amble through the fragrant forests. *(☎255-2900; www.napasonomatrailrides.com. 2hr. ride $55.)*

FESTIVALS. Sonoma Plaza hosts festivals and fairs nearly every summer weekend; check www.sonomavalley.com for a calendar of events. Kenwood heats up July 4 for the **Kenwood Footrace,** a tough 7½ mi. course through hills and vineyards. A chili

BAY AREA AND WINE COUNTRY

TASTING 101

While European wines are often known by their region of origin, California wines are generally known by the type of grape from which they are made. California white wines include Chardonnay, Riesling, and Sauvignon Blanc; reds include Pinot Noir, Merlot, Cabernet Sauvignon, and Zinfandel, which is indigenous to California. Blush or rosé wines come from red grapes that have their skins removed during fermentation, leaving just a kiss of pink. Dessert wines, such as Muscat, are made with grapes that have acquired the "noble rot" (botrytis) at the end of picking season, giving them an extra sweet flavor. When tasting, be sure to follow the proper procedure. Always start with a white, moving from dry to sweet. Proceed through the reds, which range from lighter to more full-bodied, depending on tannin content. Ideally, you should cleanse your palate between wines with a biscuit, some *fromage* cheese, or fruit.

Tasting proceeds thus: stare, sniff, swirl, swallow. You will probably encounter tasters who slurp their wine and make concerned faces. These are serious tasters who are aerating the wine into their mouths to better bring out the flavor. Key words to help you seem more astute during tasting sessions are: dry, sweet, buttery, light, crisp, fruity, balanced, rounded, subtle, rich, woody, and complex.

cook-off and the **World Pillow Fighting Championships** continue the party. At the championships, eager contenders hover over a mud pit and beat each other with wet pillows. (See opposite.)

SANTA ROSA ☎ 707

Famed horticulturist Luther Burbank once said of Santa Rosa (pop. 140,000), "I firmly believe, from what I have seen, that this is the chosen spot of all the earth, as far as nature is concerned." But whatever natural beauty Luther admired yielded long ago to the concerns of developers, who cast tract housing here and shopping malls there, effectively surrendering Santa Rosa's ecological superiority to Sonoma County to suburban torpor. Now most people stop in Santa Rosa just for a quick bite on their way between the Bay Area and Wine Country.

TRANSPORTATION. Greyhound, 435 Santa Rosa Ave. (☎545-6495 or 800-231-2222), 4 blocks from 2nd St., runs **buses** to San Francisco (2 per day, $16). **Golden Gate Transit** (☎541-2000; www.goldengatetransit.org) bus #80 runs throughout the day to Civic Center in San Francisco; catch it at Piner Rd. and Industrial Dr. or at the Santa Rosa Transit Mall at 2nd and B St. ($7.25, 2½ hr.). **City Bus** (☎543-3333) covers the main streets of Santa Rosa ($1, seniors and disabled $0.50, students K-12 $0.25, under 5 free). Carry exact change and get a schedule at the visitors bureau. **Rincon Cyclery,** 4927 Sonoma Hwy., at Rte. 12, rents mountain and road bikes, hybrids, and tandems. (☎538-0868 or 800-965-2453; www.rinconcyclery.com. Free maps. Mountain and road bikes $7 per hr., $25 per day. Tandem or full-suspension mountain bikes $10/$40. 2hr. min. rental. Open M-F 10am-6pm, Sa 9am-6pm, Su 10am-5pm.)

ORIENTATION AND PRACTICAL INFORMATION. Santa Rosa is at the intersection of **U.S. 101** and **Route 12,** 57 mi. north of downtown San Francisco. **Cleveland Avenue** marks the city's western edge. The town center is occupied by a mall that interrupts A, 2nd, 3rd, 4th, and 5th St. **Mendocino Avenue** and **4th Street** define the bustling yet spotless downtown area. **Railroad Square,** bounded by 4th, 5th, and Wilson St., houses Santa Rosa's trendiest shops and most charming cafes. The neighborhoods surrounding the heart of the city are not the safest; **exercise caution after dark.**

The **Greater Santa Rosa Convention and Visitor Bureau,** 9 4th St., at Wilson St., in the old North-Western Pacific train depot, sells maps and brochures. (☎577-8674 or 800-404-7673; www.visitsantarosa.com. Open M-Th and Sa 9am-5pm, F 9am-6pm, Su 10am-5pm.) The **Sonoma County Wineries Association,** 5000 Roberts Lake Rd., east of U.S. 101 in Rohnert Park, sells maps of area wineries and a tasting directory. (☎586-3795; www.sonomawine.com. Open M-F 9am-5pm.) Other local services include: the **police** (☎543-3600); **Santa Rosa Memorial Hospital,** 1165 Montgomery Dr. (☎546-3210); and the **post office,** 730 2nd St., between D and E St. (☎528-8783; open M-F 8am-6pm, Sa 10am-2pm). **Postal Code:** 95402.

⌂ ACCOMMODATIONS. Santa Rosa has a number of basic roadside motels in addition to a few swanky downtown lodgings. **The Redwood Inn ❹,** 1670 Santa Rosa Ave., offers limited local calls and cable TV in slightly cramped rooms. All rooms have breakfast snacks and coffee, some have kitchenettes. (☎545-0474. Rooms with 1 bed $50-75; 2 beds $60-85. 10% senior discount Su-Th.) **The Country Inn ❹,** 2363 Santa Rosa Ave., has tidy, darkly painted rooms with cable TV, phone, refrigerator, and coffeemaker. There is also an outdoor pool. (☎546-4711. Rooms with 1 bed $59-79, 2 beds $69-89. Winter $10 less. 10% discount for seniors.) The historic **Hotel La Rose ❺,** 308 Wilson St., across from the visitors center, is located in Railroad Sq., which adds to its charm and price. Lavish rooms come with A/C, cable TV, phones, a continental breakfast, and access to a rooftop hot tub. (☎579-3200 or 800-527-6738; www.hotellarose.com. Check-in after 3pm. Check-out noon. Rooms $129-250. 10% AAA and AARP discount.)

⬛ FOOD. Fresh produce can be found at the weekly **Farmers Market** along 4th St. between B and D St. (www.srdowntownmarket.com. Open Memorial Day-Labor Day W 5-8:30pm.) **Organic Groceries,** 2481 Guerneville Rd., near Fulton St., has all the organic food you'll need. (☎528-3663. Open M-W 10am-7pm, Th 10am-6:30pm, F-Su 10am-4:30pm.) **The Rose Pub & Restaurant ❸,** 2074 Armory Dr., serves classic Irish dishes like Kerry Pie ($10) and seafood options like black tiger shrimp ($11). The puffed pastry filled with potatoes, carrots, mushrooms, and peas in a curry sauce ($9) will delight vegetarians. (☎546-7673; www.therosepubandrestaurant.biz. Open Tu-Th 3pm-midnight, F-Sa 3pm-2am. Kitchen open Tu-Th 4-9pm, F-Sa 4-10pm.) **Mixx ❹,** 135 4th St., has modern American dishes as well as an extensive award-winning wine list at great prices. (☎573-1344; www.mixxrestaurant.com. Lunch $7-16. Dinner $17-29. Happy hour M-F 3pm-6:30pm; well drinks $3.50. Open M-F 11:30am-2pm and 5:30-9pm, Sa 11am-2pm and 5:30-9pm.)

PILLOWFIGHT!

From opposite sides of a creek, two competitors slide along an aluminum pole to the center of a mud pit. A referee, waist-deep in mud, hands a wet pillow to each contender. Two more refs seated in lawn chairs at each end of the pole squirt water from their hoses into the pit to dilute the thick mud. Both contenders straddle the pole...

The fights at the annual July 4th **Kenwood World Pillow Fighting Championships** are an odd union of jousting and mud-wrestling. The rules are simple—the first contender to knock his opponent off the pole twice moves on to the next round—but the competition is fierce. A local radio station provides amusing commentary for cheering spectators, who sun themselves, down foamy beer, and gnaw on giant turkey drumsticks.

The festivities also include body painting, rock climbing, ring tossing, and a cushy kiddie ring for future champions. The church across the street starts the day with a pancake breakfast, and the finals end at 4:30pm. Though only locals can enter, watching is just as entertaining.

On Warm Springs Rd. off Hwy 12 in Sonoma, close to Sonoma Plaza. Tickets $5. Free parking along the street. Contact Sonoma Valley Visitor's Bureau (☎707-996-1090; see p. 171) for more info.

⑥ 🏞 SIGHTS AND OUTDOOR ACTIVITIES. The **Luther Burbank Home and Gardens**, at Santa Rosa and Sonoma Ave., is a great place to stop and smell the chamomile. At the age of 26, the horticulturist Burbank fled to California from Massachusetts to carry out his extensive plant-breeding experiments, with the aim of improving the quality of plants and increasing the world's food supply. Though he created over 800 new varieties of plants, only some are exhibited due to the difficulty in tracking them down. Regardless, the gardens still grow the most beautiful and fragrant roses you're likely to find in the Bay Area. (☎524-5445. Gardens open daily Apr.-Oct. 8am-7pm; Nov.-Mar. 8am-5pm. House open Apr.-Oct. Tu-Su 10am-4pm. Free. Tours $4, seniors and ages 12-18 $3, under 12 free.)

Four attractions pay tribute to Peanuts comic strip artist **Charles M. Schulz**, who lived in Santa Rosa from 1958 until his death in 2000. The **Redwood Empire Ice Arena**, 1667 W. Steele Ln., is decorated with original stained glass artwork inspired by characters from the Peanuts comic strip. (☎546-7147. $7, under 11 $5.50; skate rental $2.) The adjoining **Warm Puppy Cafe ❷** serves burgers (from $6.50), sandwiches, and popular root beer floats. (Open M-Th 7am-8:30pm, F-Sa 7am-9pm, Su 7am-7pm). Next door, **Snoopy's Gallery** continues the ice rink's artistic theme. Good grief! They sell every souvenir imaginable! (Open daily 10am-6pm.) The **Charles M. Schulz Museum**, 2301 Hardies Ln., celebrates the legacy of Mr. Schulz and the Peanuts gang with an approach more akin to a fine art museum than a Disney theme park. The museum theater screens a series of seven cartoons and documentaries each day. (Take the Guerneville Rd./Steele Ln. exit off U.S. 101 N. ☎579-4452; www.schulzmuseum.org. Open M and W-F noon-5pm, Sa-Su 10am-5pm. $8; seniors, students, and ages 4-18 $5; under 4 free. Theater included in admission.)

If you are biking or driving, Sonoma County's back roads offer scenery that surpasses even that on Rte. 12. **Bennett Valley Road,** between Kenwood and Santa Rosa, **Petaluma Hill Road,** between Petaluma and Santa Rosa Ave., and **Grange/Crane Canyon Road,** connecting the two, provide beautiful views of the countryside. If you are biking, be alert; the surroundings can distract you from the blind turns, hills, and drivers. Conversely, drivers along these routes should watch for bikers.

🎭 🎪 ENTERTAINMENT AND FESTIVALS. **Luther Burbank Center for the Arts,** 50 Mark West Springs Rd., is the new state-of-the-art venue for big-name concerts as well as lesser-known talent. The 2004 summer season hosted artists such as Smokey Robinson, Natalie Merchant, Melissa Etheridge, and Seal. (☎546-3600; www.lbc.net. Box office open Tu-Sa noon-6pm.)

Annual events include the **Wine Country Vintage Jazz Festival** (☎539-3494; www.sonomacountydixiejazz.org), with nonstop music and dancing in late August or early September. **The Green Music Festival** (☎664-3147; http://festival.sonoma.edu.) at California State University Sonoma, 1801 E. Cotati Ave., in Rohnert Park, is a celebration of music, art, and ideas. Events are scheduled throughout July. The **Sonoma County Fair** (☎545-4200; www.sonomacountyfair.com) is a two-week extravaganza from late July to early August. In the first weekend of October, Santa Rosa celebrates local food, wine, and artists at the **October Harvest Fair.** Events include the ▪**World Championship Grape Stomp Contest,** pumpkin carvings, a jazz stage, and hay rides. There are over 500 wines represented. (☎545-4203; www.harvestfair.org. Admission $7. Tasting tickets additional.) Both fairs take place at the fairgrounds on Bennett Valley Rd. at Brookwood Ave. in Sonoma.

RUSSIAN RIVER VALLEY ☎707

The Russian River Valley is a well-kept secret. Though many of its wineries have been operating nearly as long as their counterparts to the southeast, they are neither as well known nor as crowded. Beyond its small, intimate vineyards, the area is home to beautiful coastline, second-growth redwoods, and a scenic river. In quiet Sebastopol, hippies and farmers coexist peacefully. Unpretentious Guerneville is a small, gay-friendly community that caters to those hoping to experience both the great outdoors and hot nightlife. Farther northeast, Healdsburg is a wealthy and beautiful town, and makes a good base for winery exploration.

🚌 TRANSPORTATION

To reach Sebastopol, travel west on **Route 12** from Santa Rosa.

Buses: Sonoma County Transit (☎576-7433 or 800-345-7433; www.sctransit.com). County-wide bus #20 to the Russian River area. Leaves from 2nd and B St. in **Santa Rosa.** (15 per day 5am-8pm; to Sebastopol $1.55, to Guerneville $2.25.)

Bike Rental: Bicycle Factory, 195 N. Main St. (☎829-1880), in Sebastopol. Mountain bikes $8 per hr., $24 per day; includes helmet, lock, and water bottle. Open M-F 10am-6:30pm, Sa 10am-5pm, Su 10am-4pm.

☀🛈 ORIENTATION AND PRACTICAL INFORMATION

The **Russian River** winds through western Sonoma County before reaching the Pacific Ocean at Jenner. The river flows south, roughly following **U.S. 101** until **Healdsburg,** where it veers west. A number of small towns line this western stretch of river, including **Guerneville, Monte Rio,** and **Forestville.** This area is quite compact by California standards; none of the towns are more than a 40min. drive apart. **Sebastopol,** not a river town itself, claims a kind of kinship to those towns because of its location on **Route 116,** "the crossroads to the Russian River and Sonoma County."

Visitor Information: Sebastopol Area Chamber of Commerce, 265 S. Main St. (☎823-3032; www.sebastopol.org). Open M-F 10am-noon and 1:30-4pm. **Healdsburg Chamber of Commerce,** 217 Healdsburg Ave. (☎433-6935; www.healdsburg.org). Open M-F 9am-5pm, Sa 9am-3pm, Su 10am-2pm. **Guerneville Chamber of Commerce and Visitors Bureau,** 16209 1st St. (☎869-9000). Open M and F-Sa 10am-6pm, Tu-Th and Su 10am-5pm.

Post Office: Sebastopol, 290 S. Main St. (☎823-2729). Open M-F 8:30am-5pm. **Postal Code:** 95472. **Healdsburg,** 404 Center St. (☎433-8142). Open M-F 8:30am-5pm. **Postal Code:** 95448.

🏠🏕 ACCOMMODATIONS AND CAMPING

The Russian River Valley's least expensive option is camping, for the tourist industry on the Russian River caters to a well-heeled, elegant, B&B-patronizing crowd. Nonetheless, there are a couple of indoor options that won't break the bank.

▨ **Inn At The Willows,** 15905 River Rd. (☎869-2824 or 800-953-2828), in Guerneville, directly on the Russian River. Staying here is more like pitching a tent in someone's backyard than camping in the woods, especially since the price includes free use of canoes and kayaks, outdoor hot tub, and a semi-outdoor kitchen. Campers can escape their dockside abode for the comforts of the cozy and intimate living room complete with fireplace and piano. The inclusive atmosphere caters to a diverse crowd and welcomes all. The inn's lodgings feel like home, with limited rooms available for children and pets. Inquire about event weekends. Full wellness spa. Rooms $79-159; sites $25, $10-25 per additional person. ❹

Johnson's Beach Resort (☎869-2022), on 1st St. in the center of Guerneville. This family-run, family-oriented resort is a throwback to younger, more innocent days; burgers, hot dogs, and beers are all $1.50, and the speakers play Sinatra. Boat rentals (canoes and kayaks $8 per hr., $25 per day; paddle boats $8 per hr.; inner tubes $4 per day) are the cheapest on the river. The campground looks like a parking lot. Free river access. Recreation and laundry room. No pets. The **Russian River Jazz Festival** (Sept.) and **Blues Festival** (June) are held here. Reservations available for cabin rentals of 1 week or more. Open mid-May to mid-Oct. Cabins with fridge and TV $45-50; sites $10, $2 per additional person, RVs $20-25. Weekly cabins $225-250. No credit cards. ❶

River Village Resort & Spa, 14880 River Rd. (☎869-8139 or 888-342-2624; www.rivervillageresort.com), in Guerneville, across the street from the Russian River. Pool and spa treatment. Cabins have pleasing layouts, especially the suites, but the decor tends to be quaint. Pets allowed in some cottages. Reservations advised for weekends and holidays; minimum stay may be required. Rooms $90-175. ❺

🍴 FOOD

Health-conscious Russian River Valley sprouts good and good-for-you restaurants. Most venues pride themselves on using local ingredients and organic produce.

▨ **Sparks,** 16248 Main St. (☎869-8206), in Guerneville. Serves organic vegetarian and vegan fare in an extremely pleasant, laid-back atmosphere. Unique plates such as barbecue Seitan Pizza ($9.25) and seasonal beverages like the hibiscus and mint cooler ($2) make for an exquisite dining experience. Menu changes often. Inquire about cooking classes. Open M-Tu and Th 11am-2pm, W 5:30-9pm, F 11am-2pm and 5:30-9pm, Sa-Su 10am-3pm and 5:30-9pm. ❸

▨ **Screamin' Mimi's,** 6902 Sebastopol Ave. (☎823-5902), in Sebastopol. The best ice cream and sorbet around ($0.60 per oz., scoops $2.50-5.75). This colorful shop offers rich homemade delights with quality you can taste. Popular flavors include the signature Mimi's Mud (espresso, fudge, and Oreo), though flavors change with the availability of the best ingredients. They also have a full line of coffees and teas. Open June-Sept. daily 11am-11pm; Oct.-May Su-Th 11am-9:30pm, F-Sa 11am-11pm. ❶

▨ **Willow Wood Cafe Market,** 9020 Graton Rd. (☎823-0233), off Rte. 116 in Graton. This out-of-the-way cafe and country market is worth the detour. Food so fresh you'd think they harvest each order individually. Menu items range from a roast pork tenderloin sandwich ($9.75) to polenta with goat cheese ($9.75). Chai and double lattes ($2.75) come in big ceramic bowls. Open M-Sa 8am-9pm, Su 9am-3pm. ❷

Raymond's Bakery, 5400 Cazadero Hwy. (☎632-5335; www.raymonds-bakery.com), in Guerneville. Take Rte. 116 west and turn right onto Cazadero Hwy. Owned by a friendly young couple, this French country-style *boulangerie* is quickly becoming a local favorite. Tucked 12 mi. back in the redwoods, the bakery's freshly baked breads ($2-5.25 loaf), homemade cookies ($0.95), and pastries ($1.75-3.50) make it well worth the trip. Customers enjoy the onion rolls and fresh focaccia sandwiches ($5) while taking advantage of ample seating. Open M and Th-Sa 8am-6pm, Su 8am-3pm. ❶

East-West Cafe, 128 N. Main St. (☎829-2822), in Sebastopol. Mediterranean platters, along with some Mexican, Indian, and Californian dishes, make this the best local vegetarian-friendly restaurant. The Hi Protein Wrap ($7) is a popular weekday breakfast special. Free-range chicken or tofu fajitas $9.50. Beverages include Thai iced tea, ginger honey lemonade, organic wine, and beer. Open daily 8am-9pm. ❷

◉ ⚠ SIGHTS AND OUTDOOR ACTIVITIES

Russian River Valley **wineries** are typically smaller, more remote, and less crowded than those in Napa and Sonoma. The *Wine Country Map of the Russian River Wine Road*, free at every visitors center in Wine Country, has an excellent map and lists every winery in the area, complete with hours, services, and products. Some *Let's Go* favorites follow. Traveling a few miles northwest along Rte. 116 from Sebastopol brings visitors to **Forestville,** the site of **Topolos at Russian River Vineyards,** 5700 Rte. 116 (Gravenstein Hwy.), known best for their Zinfandels and efforts toward an all-organic vineyard. (☎887-3344 or 800-867-6567. Restaurant open W-Su 11:30am-2:30pm and 5:30-9:30pm; Su brunch from 10:30am. Tasting room open daily 11am-5:30pm.) Just outside Guerneville, the **Korbel Champagne Cellars,** 13250 River Rd., conduct free tours, covering the cellars, brewery, rose gardens, and tasting room. Korbel is also home to the biggest bottle of champagne in the world (350 lb.) and a **deli ❶** that offers gourmet sandwiches for $6. (☎824-7000. Open daily 9am-5pm; in winter 9am-4:30pm. Tours every hr. M-F 10am-3pm.) The unpretentious **Hop Kiln Winery,** 6050 Westside Rd., in Healdsburg, is a historic landmark where hop flowers were once dried for the flavoring of beer. Visitors are welcome to complimentary wine (limit 4), as well as weekend tastings of olive oil and chutney. (☎433-6491; www.hopkilnwinery.com. Open daily 10am-5pm for tasting. Grounds close 5:15pm.) Those with an interest in art will appreciate **Roshambo Winery,** 3000 Westside Rd., 3 mi. south of Healdsburg. Its modern and contemporary art gallery is a rarity in Wine Country and overlooks miles of vines framed by rolling, gold-green mountains. They emphasize their wines' accessibility by refusing to label their bottles with longwinded, flowery descriptions. Special events include the August drag brunch and a roshambo ("rock, paper, scissors") tournament. (☎888-525-9463. Open daily 10:30am-4:30pm.) Fountains abound at the more intimate **Trentadue Winery,** 19170 Geyserville Ave., 1 mi. south of Geyserville, one of the few wineries that also specializes in port. The decadent chocolate and port pairing ($10 for 4 pairings) is a must-try. Two arbors outside make for a perfect picnic under a canopy of grape leaves, clematis, and potato lions. (☎433-3104 or 888-332-3032. Open daily 10am-5pm.) Across the way from Trentadue, the award-winning **Château Souverain,** 400 Souverain Rd. (turn left at the Independence Ln. exit off U.S. 101), offers luxury wines at sensible prices. An elegant **cafe ❹** looks out on the winery and its magnificent expanse of vineyards. (☎433-8281. Tastings daily 10am-5pm. Cafe open M-Th 11:30am-2:30pm, F-Sa 11:30am-2:30pm and 5:30-8:30pm, Su 11am-2:30pm and 5:30-8:30pm.)

Burke's Canoe Trips rents canoes for the 10 mi. river trip to Guerneville. The fee includes a ride back; shuttle buses run every 30min. (☎887-1222; www.burkescanoetrips.com. Canoes $50 per day. Call ahead for return service to your car. Open May-Oct. M-F 9:30am-6pm, Sa-Su 9am-6pm. No credit cards.) Just 10min. north of Guerneville, enjoy the shaded beauty of the redwoods in the **Armstrong Woods State Park** (☎869-2015). Hiking, biking, and horseback riding opportunities abound. **Horseback Adventures** (☎887-2939; www.redwoodhorses.com) leads riding tours of the park. Packages range from $60 for 2½ hr. rides to $250 for an overnight tour. The 1 mi. **Pioneer Trail** starts at the visitors center parking lot and skirts Fife Creek. For a challenging trek, take the **East Ridge Trail** (5½ mi.), which climbs 300 ft.

🄴 🎇 NIGHTLIFE AND FESTIVALS

Guerneville is *the* nightspot in the Russian River Valley. Despite the predominantly gay scene, no one is made to feel unwelcome. 🄺**Stumptown Brewery,** 15045 River Rd., 1 mi. east of Guerneville, is a popular venue with unique in-house brews ($4-

7), smokehouse eats (rack of ribs $17), and live bluegrass and country (Su 4-8pm). An outdoor patio looks out over the Russian River. Their flagship ale, the Rat Bastard Pale Ale, took home the blue ribbon at the 2004 California State Fair. (☎ 869-0705. Open daily noon-2am. Kitchen closes 9pm. Cash only; ATM inside.) The **Rainbow Cattle Co.**, 16220 Main St., with its posters of men in thongs and stickers stating "Hate Stops Here," proudly welcomes everyone. (☎ 869-0206. Happy hour daily until 8pm. Open daily 6am-2am.)

Sebastopol's **Apple Blossom Festival,** in late April, has entertainment, crafts, and food; the **Sebastopol Music Festival** (☎ 800-648-9922) occurs concurrently. The annual **Festival of Art and Wine** (☎ 824-8717), in Duncans Mills, occurs in late June. The **Russian River Valley Winegrowers Grape to Glass Weekend** (☎ 521-2534; Aug. 19-21 in 2005), is the big event of the season, when over 30 wineries offer free tours and tastings. **The Russian River Jazz Festival** is a major event at Johnson's Beach Resort, blasting trombone, trumpet, and piano melodies down the river the weekend after Labor Day. (☎ 510-655-9471; www.jazzontheriver.com. Tickets from $42.)

SOUTH BAY

The San Francisco peninsula extends southward into what was once a valley of fruit orchards and is now the breeding ground of America's electronics industry. From Stanford University to San Jose, the entire area known as Silicon Valley is as sterile as its dot-com offices.

SAN JOSE   ☎ 408

Founded in 1777 in a bucolic valley of fruit and walnut orchards, California's first civilian settlement is now its third most populous city (pop. 896,000). The area's primary business was agriculture until the technology sector began to develop in the middle of the 20th century. In 1939, the first computer company, Hewlett-Packard, began modestly in Dave Packard's garage. By the early 1970s, many of San Jose's orchards had been replaced by offices, and the moniker "Silicon Valley" had stuck. For several decades, the self-proclaimed "Capital of Silicon Valley" has been the country's foremost center of technological innovation, with its residents raking in the second-highest average disposable incomes of any US city. Shifting economic conditions in recent years have caused San Jose to broaden its focus to include other industries. Museums, restaurants, hotels, and vineyards have all sprouted up around the city as part of San Jose's expansion beyond the world of microchips and barefoot techies.

▐ TRANSPORTATION

Airport: San Jose International, 1661 Airport Blvd. (☎ 277-5366). Take Guadalupe Pkwy. off U.S. 101. Also accessible by **Valley Transit Authority (VTA)** light-rail. Free shuttles connect the terminals.

Trains: Amtrak, 65 Cahill St. (☎ 287-7462 or 800-USA-RAIL/872-7245; www.amtrak.com), at W. San Fernando St. To **L.A.** (11hr., $45-108). **CalTrain,** 65 Cahill St. (☎ 291-5651 or 800-660-4287), to **San Francisco** (2hr.; every hr. M-F 5am-10pm, Sa 6am-10:30pm, Su 7am-9pm; $5.50), with stops at peninsula cities.

Buses: Greyhound, 70 S. Almaden Blvd. (☎ 295-4151 or 800-231-2222; www.greyhound.com), at Post St. Open M-F 5:15am-11:30pm, Sa-Su 5:15am-12:45am. Good security. Luggage lockers for ticketed passengers ($2 per 6hr., $4 for 1 day, $5 per day after 1st day). To **L.A.** (7hr., $48) and **San Francisco** (1¼hr., $5.50).

Downtown San Jose

▲ ACCOMMODATIONS
Sanborn Park Hostel (HI-AYH), **9**
Super 8, **1**

◆ FOOD
Bella Mia, **2**
House of Siam, **3**

✦ ENTERTAINMENT
Camera 12, **4**
City Lights, **8**
Student Union, **5**

♦ NIGHTLIFE
Agenda, **6**
South First Billiards, **7**

Public Transportation: Santa Clara Valley Transportation Agency (VTA), 2 N. 1st St. (☎321-2300; www.vta.org), offers modern buses and a light-rail system. ($1.50, day pass $4.50; ages 5-17 $1.25/$3.75; seniors and disabled $0.75/$1.75. Exact change required.) **Bay Area Rapid Transit (BART;** ☎510-441-2278). Bus #180 serves the Fremont station from 1st and Santa Clara St. in downtown San Jose (40min., $1.50-3). To **San Francisco** (45-55min., $4.70).

■ ORIENTATION

San Jose lies at the southern end of the San Francisco Bay, about 45 mi. from San Francisco (via U.S. 101 or I-280) and 45 mi. from Oakland (via I-880). I-280 is renowned for its roadside scenery along the stretch called Junípero Serra Fwy. and is often less congested than U.S. 101. (For info on reaching San Jose from San Francisco using public transit, see **CalTrain,** p. 184.)

The city centers on the convention-hosting malls and plazas near the intersection of east-west **San Carlos Street** and north-south **Market Street.** Bars, restaurants, and clubs crowd around 1st St. in the so-called **SoFA District.** The **Transit Mall,** the center of San Jose's bus and trolley system, runs along 1st and 2nd St. in the downtown area. The grassy grounds of **San Jose State University (SJSU)** span several blocks between S. 4th and S. 10th St. Founded in 1857, SJSU is the oldest public college in California.

▪ PRACTICAL INFORMATION

Visitor Information: Visitor Information and Business Center, 150 W. San Carlos St. (☎726-5673 or 888-SAN-JOSE/726-5673, events line 295-2265; www.sanjose.org), at Market St. in the San Jose McEnery Convention Center. Free maps. Open M-F 9am-5pm, Sa 11am-5pm.

Police: 201 W. Mission St. (☎277-8900, info 277-2211).

Hotlines: Rape Crisis, ☎287-3000. **Suicide Prevention/Crisis Intervention,** ☎279-3312.

Medical Services: San Jose Medical Center, 675 E. Santa Clara St. (☎998-3212, emergency 977-4444), at 14th St. Open 24hr.

Library and Internet Access: Martin Luther King, Jr. Public Library (☎808-2000; www.sjlibrary.org), at the intersection of E. San Fernando and 4th St. Internet free with library card (obtained by providing picture ID and proof of address). Open M-W 8am-8pm, Th-Sa 9am-6pm, Su 1-5pm.

Post Office: 105 N. 1st St. (☎292-0487). Open M-F 8:30am-5pm, Sa 7am-noon. **Postal Code:** 95113.

▐▐ ACCOMMODATIONS AND CAMPING

Chain motels and county park campgrounds surround the city. Enjoy peace and quiet at the **Sanborn Park Hostel (HI-AYH) ❶,** 15808 Sanborn Rd., in Sanborn-Skyline County Park, 20 mi. west of downtown San Jose. This rustic log cabin hideaway feels like home. (☎741-0166. Linen $0.50, towels $0.25. Reception 5-10pm. Checkout 9am. Curfew 11pm. Dorms $14, nonmembers $16-$17, under 18 $7.) Convenient and comfortable, albeit rather expensive, **Super 8 ❹,** 1860 The Alameda, is close to many attractions and 2 mi. from the San Jose airport. It has a pool, cable TV, free parking, continental breakfast, and restaurant. (☎293-9361. Singles $79; doubles $89. Seniors and AAA 10% off.) **Mount Madonna County Park ❶,** on Pole Line Rd. off Hecker Pass Hwy., has 117 sites in a beautiful setting. (☎842-2341 or 842-6761, reservations 355-2201; www.parkhere.org. Toilets and coin-operated showers. Entrance fee $4 per vehicle. Sites $15; RVs $25.) The area around **Saratoga ❶**, on Rte. 85, 14 mi. southwest of San Jose, has a number of campsites, as well as miles of horse and hiking trails in **Sanborn-Skyline County Park.** From Rte. 17 S, take Rte. 9 to Big Basin Way and turn left onto Sanborn Rd. (☎867-9959, reservations 355-2201; www.parkhere.org. Walk-in camping closed mid-Oct. to late Mar. Sites $8; RVs $25.)

◖ FOOD

Familiar fast-food franchises and pizzerias surround SJSU. Diverse independent cheap eats lie along **South 1st Street** or near **San Pedro Square,** at St. John and San Pedro St. A **farmers market** takes place at San Pedro Sq. (May-Dec. F 10am-2pm.) **House of Siam ❸**, 55 S. Market St., boasts of their award-winning Thai entrees and vegetarian options ($8-14). Beware the spice level! (☎279-5668. Open M-F 11am-2:30pm and 5-9:30pm, Sa-Su noon-10pm. A larger branch at 151 S. 2nd St.; ☎295-3397; open M-F 11am-3pm and 5-10pm, Sa-Su noon-10pm.) **Bella Mia ❹**, 58 S. 1st St., serves regional Italian-American cuisine in a classy and upscale (but still inviting) atmosphere. The lasagna ($15) and chicken foresta ($16) are especially popular. Also holds special dinner nights (F 8 and 10pm, Sa 7 and 9pm), such as Murder Mystery or Comedy Cocktail; ask the host for tickets. (☎280-1993. Open M-Th 11:30am-9pm, F 11:30am-10pm, Sa 4:30-10pm, Su 4:30-9:30pm.)

◉ SIGHTS

San Jose lives in the shadow of its cosmopolitan neighbor to the north. Despite its reputation as the capital of Silicon Valley, many of the corporate headquarters and high-tech giants (like Intel and Hewlett-Packard) are actually farther up north on the peninsula in Mountain View and Sunnyvale. Still, drawing vitality from SJSU, San Jose has plenty to offer the traveler, including well-funded and interesting museums.

TECH MUSEUM OF INNOVATION. Curious kids and their parents love the hands-on, cutting-edge science exhibits and IMAX theater at this tourist-savvy attraction. The museum is underwritten by high-tech firms and housed in a sleek geometric building. *(201 S. Market St. ☎795-6224; www.thetech.org. Open daily 10am-5pm; Oct.-Mar. closed M. $9, seniors $8, ages 3-12 $7. Exhibits and IMAX film $16/$15/$13.)*

WINCHESTER MYSTERY HOUSE. This odd Victorian house is little more than that, but will amuse those with a penchant for the unusual. Sarah Winchester was the eccentric heir to the Winchester rifle fortune. After the death of her daughter and husband, she was convinced by an occultist that the spirits of all the men ever killed by her family's guns would seek revenge if construction on her home ever ceased. Work on the mansion continued 24hr. a day for over 38 years. A 160-room maze of doors, windows, and stairs elaborately designed to "confuse the spirits" is the end result. *(525 S. Winchester Blvd. Near the intersection of I-880 and I-280, west of town. ☎247-2101. Open mid-Oct. to Aug. daily 9am-7pm; Sept. to mid-Oct. Su-Th 9am-5pm, F-Sa 9am-7pm. $20, ages 6-12 $14, over 65 $17, under 6 free.)*

ROSICRUCIAN EGYPTIAN MUSEUM AND PLANETARIUM. Rising out of the suburbs like the work of a mad high priestess, this grand structure houses the largest exhibit of Egyptian artifacts in the western US, with over 4000 ancient Egyptian artifacts, including a walk-in tomb and spooky animal mummies. This collection belongs to the ancient and mystical Rosicrucian Order, whose past members include Amenhotep IV, Pythagoras, Sir Francis Bacon, Rene Descartes, Benjamin Franklin, and Isaac Newton. Join a tour lead by the friendly, knowledgeable staff, roam the surrounding ornate gardens, or catch a planetarium show. *(1660 Park Ave., at Naglee Ave. ☎ 947-3635; www.egyptianmuseum.org. Open Tu-F 10am-5pm, Sa-Su 11am-6pm. Planetarium shows Tu-F 2pm, Sa-Su 3:30pm. $9, students and seniors $7, ages 5-10 $5, under 5 free.)*

THE SAN JOSE MUSEUM OF ART. Neighbor to the Tech, this modern museum not only features contemporary art but is itself progressive in design and mission. Admission is free to encourage public awareness of 20th- and 21st-century art, and the museum offers a wide range of exhibits, lectures, programs, and hands-on events for adults and children. *(110 S. Market St. ☎ 294-2787; www.sjma.com. Open Tu-Su 11am-5pm. Free.)*

OTHER MUSEUMS. The Children's Discovery Museum is filled with hands-on, science-based toys for young children. *(180 Woz Way, across from the light-rail station. ☎ 298-5437; www.cdm.org. Open M-Sa 10am-5pm, Su noon-5pm, closed M during school year. $7, seniors $6.)* The **San Jose Institute of Contemporary Art** *(451 S. 1st St. ☎ 283-8155; www.sjica.org. Open Tu-W 10am-5pm, Th 10am-8pm, F 10am-5pm, Sa noon-5pm)* holds innovative new works. **Movimiento de Arte y Cultura Latino Americana** is an alternative Latino art center. *(510 S. 1st St. ☎ 998-2783; www.maclaarte.org. Open W-Th noon-7pm, F-Sa noon-5pm.)*

MISSION SANTA CLARA AND SANTA CLARA UNIVERSITY. The first California mission to honor a woman—Clare of Assisi—as its patron saint, Mission Santa Clara was established on the Guadalupe River in 1777, moving to its present site in 1825. Summer masses are held in the mission's beautiful church, complete with a functional organ. *(Mass M-F noon, Su 10am.)* **Santa Clara University,** built around the mission, was established in 1851, making it California's oldest institution of higher learning. Subsequent restorations have refitted the structures to match the beauty and bliss of the surrounding rose gardens and 180-year-old olive trees. Get a free parking pass from the university security guard as you drive in. *(500 El Camino Real, 5 mi. northwest of downtown San Jose off The Alameda. ☎ 554-4000; www.scu.edu.)*

AMUSEMENT PARKS. Paramount's Great America theme park is a jungle of roller coasters, log rides, and other fiendish contraptions designed to spin you, flip you, soak you, drop you, and generally separate you from your stomach. *(☎ 988-1776; www.pgathrills.com. Off U.S. 101 at Great America Pkwy. in Santa Clara, 8 mi. northwest of downtown San Jose. Open June-Aug. Su-F 10am-9pm, Sa 10am-10pm; Sept.-Oct. and Mar.-May Sa 10am-10pm, Su 10am-9pm. $48, seniors and disabled $40, ages 3-6 or under 48 in. $34, under 3 free. Parking $10.)* The area's best collection of waterslides, Paramount's **Raging Waters,** is great on a hot day, but don't expect to be the only one seeking a soaking. *(☎ 654-5450; www.rwsplash.com. Off U.S. 101 at the Tully Rd. exit, about 5 mi. east of downtown San Jose. Open June-Aug. daily 10am-6pm; May and Sept. Sa-Su 10am-6pm. $26, under 48 in. $20, seniors $16. After 3pm $19, under 48 in. $14.)*

🎵 🎎 ENTERTAINMENT AND FESTIVALS

For information on entertainment and events, look for the weekly *Metro*, available for free on downtown street corners, or check www.artsopolis.com and www.sjdowntown.com. **City Lights,** 529 S. 2nd St. *(☎ 295-4200; www.cltc.org),* at William St., offers unique, cutting-edge theater in an intimate and flexible seating space. Local actors put on a variety of performances—classics, adaptations, and some original work. The brand-new **Camera 12 Cinema,** 201 S. 2nd St., shows art-house, independent and Hollywood first-run films. *(☎ 998-3300; www.cameracinemas.com.)* The **Student Union and Concert Hall,** 1 Washington

Sq. (☎924-1120), at SJSU, hosts concerts and other performances. Concert hall performances are free on Thursdays during the school year.

San Jose is home to many beloved annual events, like the **Blues Festival** (☎924-6262) in May and the **Miller Music in the Park** and **Music in the Other Park** summer concert series, where alternative, R&B, reggae, rock, and jazz acts perform weekly in the Plaza de Caesar Chavez and St. James Park. (www.sjdowntown.com. Th 5:30-9pm. Free.) On a weekend in early fall, the **San Pedro Square Brew-Ha-Ha** fills the downtown area with microbrew sampling, stand-up comedy, and fun for all. (☎279-1775; www.sjdowntown.com.) From the week before Thanksgiving to Martin Luther King, Jr. Day, downtown converts into a winter wonderland with **Downtown Ice,** the South Bay's largest outdoor ice skating rink. (☎279-1775; www.sjdowntown.com.)

The NHL **San Jose Sharks** (☎287-7070; www.sjsharks.com) play at the HP Pavilion, while the Major League Soccer **San Jose Earthquakes** (☎260-6300; www.sjearthquakes.com) let loose at Spartan Stadium, on 7th St. off I-280.

■ NIGHTLIFE

The flashiest nightspots are in the **SoFA District,** a strip of downtown along 1st St. **Agenda,** 399 S. 1st St., serves New American cuisine ($10-19) on its outdoor patio, where you can hear the hottest acid jazz in town. It gets crowded, so plan on eating early to get great tables. Upstairs lounge serves 15 microbrews and all three floors bust out dance music at night. (☎287-3991. Live music from 7:30pm. Cover $10 for non-diners; free with meal. Restaurant open Tu-Sa 5:30-9pm. Nightclub open W-Sa 9pm-2am, Su 9pm-1:30am.) If a pool party is more your scene, try one of 26 tables at **South First Billiards,** 430 S. 1st St., a stylish bar and billiard combo that serves beer (pints from $2), standard bar fare (pizza $6, burger $8), and unique drinks ($7.50), such as the frozen Lava Lamp. (☎294-7800. Happy hour M-F 4-7pm; half off selected appetizers, $2.50 well drinks, pool $6 per hr. Live music on the 2nd Su of each month. Pool $6-15 per hr. depending on day and time. Open daily 4pm-2am. Kitchen closes at 12:30am.)

PALO ALTO   ☎ 650

Dominated by the beautiful 8000-acre Stanford University campus, Palo Alto looks like "Collegeland" at a Disney theme park. Stanford's perfectly groomed grounds, sparkling lake, and Spanish mission-style buildings have a manufactured quality that suits the

THE LOCAL STORY

CARDINAL RITUALS

Though 20 years younger than its rival school, UC Berkeley, Stanford makes up for its youth with a plethora of odd traditions.

The sun in Palo Alto is nearly as bright as the students, so for years, Stanford undergrads have beaten the heat in a strange ritual they call fountain hopping. The beach is 30 mi. west, so students find the next best thing in the eight large fountains on campus. Stripped to bikinis or roughing it in clothes (and occasionally accompanied by inner tubes), Stanfordites cool off in the school's fountains.

In the mood for some school spirit? At the start of every quarter at 11pm, the inventive Stanford Band dons costumes and head dresses in preparation for the band run. The musicians march through dorms trumpeting fight songs to draw students out of their rooms. After collecting a critical mass of the campus, the student body and their beloved band run to the main quad for more band sound, school spirit, and booty shakin'.

During the rivalry-ridden week leading up to the "Big Game" between Cal and Stanford, zealous Stanford fans have been known to construct a bear (the Cal mascot) from papier-mâché and fill it with spaghetti-Os. When thrown on a sharp sculpture called the "claw," the poor state school bear bleeds and oozes pasta guts.

university's speedy rise to international acclaim. The city that Stanford calls home is equally manicured, with a tidy downtown strip of restaurants, bookstores, and boutiques. Its nightlife caters to students and suburbanites, while weekday happy hours help singles wind down.

■ TRANSPORTATION

Palo Alto is 35 mi. southeast of San Francisco, near the southern shore of the bay. Take **U.S. 101** to the University Ave. exit, or take the Embarcadero Rd. exit directly to the Stanford campus. Alternatively, motorists from San Francisco can split off onto **I-280 (Junípero Serra Highway)** for a longer but more scenic route. From I-280, exit at Sand Hill Rd. and follow it to the northwest corner of Stanford University.

The **Palo Alto Transit Center,** 95 University Ave., at Alma St., serves local and regional buses and trains. (☎323-6105. Open M-F 5am-12:30am.) A train-only depot lies on California Ave., 1¼ mi. south of the transit center. (☎326-3392. Open M-F 5:30am-12:30am.) The transit center connects to points north via **San Mateo County buses** (SamTrans) and to Stanford via the free **Marguerite Shuttle.**

Trains: CalTrain, 95 University Ave. (☎800-660-4287). Street-side stop at Stanford Stadium on Embarcadero Rd. To **San Francisco** ($4.25; seniors, disabled, and youth under 18 $2) and **San Jose** ($3/$1.50). Operates M-F 5am-11pm, departing approximately 10min. and 40min. past the hour. Operates Sa 6:30am-11pm and Su 7:30am-9:30pm, departing 30min. past the hour.

Buses: SamTrans (☎800-660-4287). To downtown **San Francisco** ($3, under 17 $1.25) and **San Francisco International Airport** ($1.10). To reach Palo Alto from SF, take SamTrans express bus KX from the Transbay Terminal in San Francisco to the Stanford Shopping Center. Operates daily 6am-10pm, departing every 30min.

Public Transportation: Santa Clara Valley Transportation Authority (**VTA**; ☎408-321-2300 or 800-894-9908). Local and county-wide transit. $1.25, ages 5-17 $0.70, seniors and disabled $0.40. Day pass $3/$1.75/$1. Express buses $2. The **Marguerite Shuttle** (☎723-9362) provides free service around Stanford University, stopping at red-and-white shuttle stop signs and the Caltrain station. Operates M-F 6am-8pm, with extended hours during the academic year. The city of Palo Alto provides a free **crosstown shuttle**, operating M-F 7am-6pm, and an **Embarcadero shuttle** (☎329-2520; www.cityofpaloalto.org/transportation/shuttle), operating M-F 7-9:30am, 11:45am-1:45pm, 3:05pm-6:30pm.

Taxi: Yellow Cab (☎321-1234 or 888-512-1234). 24hr. Base fare $2, $2.50 per mi.

Car Rental: Budget, 4230 El Camino Real (☎424-0684, reservations 800-527-0700; www.budget.com). From $40 per day. Unlimited mileage. 21+ with credit card. Under-25 surcharge $20 per day. Open M-Sa 7am-6pm, Su 9am-5pm.

Bike Rental: Campus Bike Shop, 551 Salvatierra Ln. (☎723-9300), across from Stanford Law School. $15 per day. Helmets $5, under 18 free. Lock, basket, light, and repairs included. Major credit card, $150-300 cash deposit, or check deposit. Open M-F 9am-5pm, Sa 9am-3pm.

■ ■ ORIENTATION AND PRACTICAL INFORMATION

The pristine lawns of residential Palo Alto are not easily distinguished from Stanford's campus. Despite its name, **University Avenue,** the main thoroughfare off US 101, is more town than gown. Cars coming off US 101 onto University Ave. pass very briefly through **East Palo Alto,** which once had one of the highest vio-

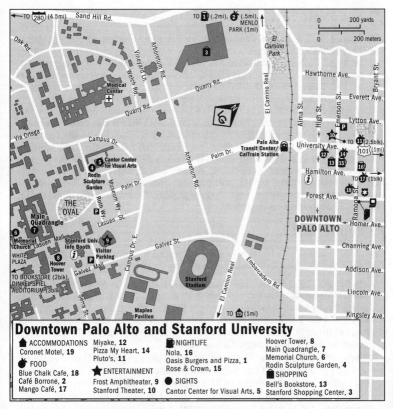

Downtown Palo Alto and Stanford University

🏠 ACCOMMODATIONS
Coronet Motel, **19**

🍴 FOOD
Blue Chalk Cafe, **18**
Café Borrone, **2**
Mango Café, **17**

Miyake, **12**
Pizza My Heart, **14**
Pluto's, **11**

★ ENTERTAINMENT
Frost Amphitheater, **9**
Stanford Theater, **10**

🎵 NIGHTLIFE
Nola, **16**
Oasis Burgers and Pizza, **1**
Rose & Crown, **15**

● SIGHTS
Cantor Center for Visual Arts, **5**

Hoover Tower, **8**
Main Quadrangle, **7**
Memorial Church, **6**
Rodin Sculpture Garden, **4**

🛍 SHOPPING
Bell's Bookstore, **13**
Stanford Shopping Center, **3**

lent crime rates in the nation. The town has cleaned up its act and grown safer in recent years, but the contrast with immaculate Palo Alto is still striking. **Stanford University** spreads out from the west end of University Ave. Abutting University Ave. and running northwest-southeast through town is **El Camino Real** (part of Rte. 82). From there, University Ave. turns into Palm Dr., which accesses the **Main Quad** of Stanford's campus.

Visitor Information: Palo Alto Chamber of Commerce, 122 Hamilton Ave. (☎324-3121), between Alma and High St. Open M-F 9am-5pm. **Stanford University Information Booth** (☎723-2560), across from Hoover Tower in Memorial Auditorium. Supplies parking passes ($12 per day), maps, and information about the university. Free student-led 1hr. **tours** depart daily 11am and 3:15pm. Open daily 8am-5pm.

Police: 275 Forest Ave. (☎329-2406, after hours 329-2413).

Library and Internet Access: Palo Alto Main Library, 1213 Newell Rd. (☎329-2436), off Embarcadero Rd. Free Internet. Open M-W 10am-9pm, Th noon-9pm, F-Sa 10am-6pm, Su 1-5pm. **Downtown Branch,** 270 Forest Ave. (☎329-2641). Free Internet. Open Tu-F 11am-6pm.

Post Office: Main Office, 2085 E. Bayshore Rd. (☎321-1423). Open M-F 8:30am-5pm. **Postal Code:** 94303. **Hamilton Station,** 380 Hamilton Ave. (☎323-2650). Open M-F 8:30am-5:30pm, Sa 9am-1pm. **Postal Code:** 94301.

BAY AREA AND WINE COUNTRY

♠ ACCOMMODATIONS

Motels are plentiful along **El Camino Real,** but rates can be steep. Generally, rooms are cheaper farther away from Stanford. More reasonably priced accommodations may be found farther north toward Redwood City. Many Palo Alto motels cater to business travelers and are actually busier on weekdays than on weekends. Close to Stanford, **Coronet Motel ④**, 2455 El Camino Real, at California St., has reasonably priced and rather generic rooms with big windows, cable TV, pool, telephone, private baths, and kitchenettes. (☎326-1081. Check-out 11am. Singles $55; doubles $60. $5 per additional person. Weekly rates available.) **Hidden Villa Ranch Hostel (HI-AYH) ①**, 26870 Moody Rd., about 10 mi. southwest of Palo Alto in the Los Altos Hills was the first hostel on the Pacific Coast (est. 1937). It functions as a working ranch and farm in a wilderness preserve. Recent renovations have completely rebuilt dorms and extended the living, kitchen, and dining rooms. Heated cabins house 35 beds in dorm, family, and private rooms. (☎949-8648. Reservations required for weekends and groups. Open Sept.-May. Dorms $15, nonmembers $18, children $7.50; private cabins $30-42.)

◖ FOOD

The posh restaurants of University and California Ave. form the core of Palo Alto dining. Those watching their wallets should stay on University Ave.

Café Borrone, 1010 El Camino Real (☎327-0830), at Santa Cruz Ave., next to Kepler's Books in Menlo Park. Bustling, brasserie-style cafe spills out onto a large patio. Borrone serves freshly baked bread, sinful desserts ($2-5), coffee drinks, Italian sodas, and wine ($6-9 per glass). Check the chalkboard for daily specials or choose from a wide range of delicious salads ($4-10) and sandwiches ($6-10). Open M-Th 7am-11pm, F 7am-midnight, Sa 8am-midnight, Su 8am-5pm. ②

Pluto's, 482 University Ave. (☎853-1556). Out-of-this-world cafeteria-style restaurant with hefty portions. Design your own salad from heaps of fresh fixings ($5-6) or choose from grilled meats and veggies to fill a sandwich ($5.15-5.75). Open M-Th 11am-10pm, F 11am-11pm, Sa 11:30am-11pm, Su 11:30am-10pm. ①

Mango Café, 435 Hamilton Ave. (☎325-3229), 1 block east of University Ave. Reggae music and Caribbean cuisine. Seriously spicy Jamaican "jerked joints" ($7.25) and tropical smoothies ($3.50). Veggie options. Entrees range from $8-13, lunch specials from $5-11. Delicious bread pudding $3. Open M-F 11:30am-2:30pm and 6-10pm, Sa 6-10pm, Su 6-9pm. ②

Pizza My Heart, 220 University Ave. (☎327-9400), in the heart of downtown. Catering to the late-night crowd, this surf-themed pizzeria serves beer by the pint ($3) and pitcher ($9), not to mention a mean slice ($2.50-3.50). Students, bar hoppers, and local teens come at all hours for the great food and deals—like salad, slice, and soda for $5.75. Open Su-Th 11am-midnight, F-Sa 11am-2am. ①

Miyake, 140 University Ave. (☎323-9449). Silicon-chic rules the palate at this sushi joint. Taste the IBM roll ($7.50), then email your critique using the free wireless Internet. Music starts thumping at 6pm to signify the beginning of the wild sake bombing. Favorites include the chicken teriyaki ($5) and the ebi tempura roll ($5). Open Su-Th 11:30am-10pm, F-Sa 11:30am-11pm. ③

Blue Chalk Cafe, 630 Ramona St. (☎326-1020). What began as a Stanford Business School project became an instant hit with both students and tech professionals. Southern inspired lunches ($8-10) and dinners ($18-22) include a variety of salads ($5-12). Happy hour M-Sa 4-7pm. The kitchen closes at 9:30pm, just before the fun-loving bar crowd arrives around 10pm. Open M-Sa 11am-1:30am. ④

SIGHTS

STANFORD UNIVERSITY

Undoubtedly Palo Alto's main tourist attraction, the secular, co-educational **Stanford University** was founded in 1885 by Jane and Leland Stanford to honor their son who died of typhoid. The Stanfords loved Spanish colonial mission architecture and collaborated with **Frederick Law Olmsted,** designer of New York City's Central Park, to create a Spanish-tiled sandstone campus of uncompromising beauty. Often called "a hotbed of social rest," the school has produced such eminent conservatives as Chief Justice William Rehnquist.

MAIN QUADRANGLE. The oldest part of campus is the site of most undergraduate classes. The walkways are dotted with diamond-shaped, gold-numbered stone tiles that mark the locations of time capsules put together by each year's graduating class. *(Serra St., between Lasuen and Lomita Mall. Free tours daily at 11am and 3:15pm depart from Information Booth in Memorial Auditorium.)*

MEMORIAL CHURCH. Memorial Church is a nondenominational gold shrine with stained glass windows, glittering mosaic walls, and a 7,777-pipe organ. *(Just south of the Main Quad, at Escondido Mall and Duena. ☎ 723-3469; http://religiouslife.stanford.edu/memorial_church. Open M-F 8am-5pm. Free tours F 2pm.)*

HOOVER TOWER. The tower's observation deck has views of campus, the East Bay, and San Francisco. *(East of the Main Quad, near Serra St. ☎ 723-2053. Open daily 10am-4:30pm. Closed during finals and academic breaks. Adults $2, seniors and under 13 $1.)*

IRIS AND B. GERALD CANTOR CENTER FOR VISUAL ARTS. This visual arts center displays its eclectic collection of painting and sculpture for free. Highlights include a copy of Rodin's *The Thinker* and a plaster death mask of Leland Stanford, Jr. *(328 Lomita Dr., at Museum Way off Palm Dr. ☎ 723-4177; www.stanford.edu/sept/ccva. Open W and F-Su 11am-5pm, Th 11am-8pm. Free tours W noon, Sa-Su 1pm.)*

RODIN SCULPTURE GARDEN. This extensive garden contains a stunning bronze cast of *Gates of Hell,* among other large figures. It's an ideal spot to enjoy a picnic lunch. *(At Museum Way and Lomita Dr. ☎ 723-4177. Free tours first Su of the month 2pm; meet at the Main Quad.)*

⌐ SHOPPING

Bell's Bookstore, 536 Emerson St. (☎ 323-7822). Family-run since 1935, Bell's is a favorite among locals and Stanfordites. Packed floor to ceiling with used, new, and rare books arranged by subject. Selection includes a large range of hardback and out-of-print texts. Open M-Th 9:30am-5:30pm, F 9:30am-9pm, Sa 9:30am-5pm.

Stanford Shopping Center (☎ 617-8585 or 800-772-9332; www.stanfordshop.com), at the corner of Sand Hill Rd. and El Camino Real. Designer clothes, department stores, specialty food shops, and restaurants line tree-shaded avenues. Patio cafes perfect for people-watching. Open M-F 10am-9pm, Sa 10am-7pm, Su 11am-6pm.

Stanford Bookstore, 519 Lasuen Mall (☎ 329-1217 or 800-533-2670; www.stanfordbookstore.com), on campus. An array of books split shelf space with ridiculous amounts of Stanford-emblazoned clothing and knick-knacks. Open M-Th 8am-8pm, F 8am-7pm, Sa 9am-6pm, Su 11am-6pm.

BAY AREA AND WINE COUNTRY

♫ ENTERTAINMENT

The Stanford-run *Palo Alto Daily* and local *Palo Alto Weekly* both contain listings of what's going on all over town. The free *Metro* and *Palo Alto Daily News*, available in downtown sidewalk boxes, also publish the local lowdown.

Dinkelspiel Auditorium, 471 Lagunita Dr., adjacent to Tresidder Union. Called "the Dink" by locals, the auditorium hosts classical concerts and other events sold through the Tressider Union ticket office (☎725-2787). Open M-F 10am-5pm, Sa noon-4pm.

Stanford Theater, 221 University Ave. (☎324-3700). Dedicated to Hollywood's "Golden Age." Devotes exhibition seasons to directors and stars, such as Billy Wilder and Cary Grant. The Wurlitzer organ plays before and after the 7:30pm show and accompanies silent films every W. Double features $6, seniors $4, under 18 $3.

The Lively Arts at Stanford (☎723-2551; http://livelyarts.stanford.edu) brings semi-big-name concerts to Frost Amphitheater and Memorial Auditorium at discount prices ($20-50). The Memorial hosts movies on Su during term-time. Films $3, students $2.

◙ NIGHTLIFE

Though Palo Alto can't compete with San Francisco's wild nightlife, it still has a couple of hot spots and bars perfect for sitting back and having a few beers. The upscale aspirations of Palo Alto force drinkers to throw out a few extra bucks, but visitors mix easily with Stanford students and Silicon Valley geeks.

Nola, 535 Ramona St. (☎328-2722). There is a fiesta everyday in this vibrant, super-popular bar. Colorful strings of lights and patio windows open onto a cool courtyard dining area. The late-night New Orleans-themed menu offers Cajun quesadillas ($8-9), Creole prawns ($17), and gumbo ($7) to accompany cocktails ($6.50-9.50). Open M-F 11:30am-2am, Sa-Sun 5:30pm-2am. Kitchen closes M-Th 10pm, F-Sa 11pm, Su 9pm.

Oasis Burgers and Pizza, 241 El Camino Real (☎326-8896; www.theoasisbeergarden.com). Locals and students loosen up at this watering hole and late-night dive, affectionately known as "The O." Beer flows by the pint ($2.40-4) or the pitcher ($6.50-10) in semi-private booths and on the outdoor patio. Burgers ($5.25) and pizza ($18-23) served amidst tables and walls crudely carved by patrons past. Open daily 11am-2am. Kitchen closes 1:30am.

Rose & Crown, 547 Emerson St. (☎327-7673). This low-key pub with an Ace jukebox is good for throwing darts or quietly nursing a Guinness. British bar menu includes fish and chips ($6.50-10.50), bangers and mash ($9.25), and ploughman's lunch ($7). Happy hour M-F 4-6pm. Jazz night Su 7:30pm. Comedy showcase M 9pm, Quiz Night Tu 8:30pm. Open M-F 11:30am-1:30am, Sa noon-1:30am, Su 1pm-1:30am.

SAN MATEO COUNTY ☎650

The bluffs of the San Mateo County coast obscure the hectic urban pace of the city to the north. Most of the energy here is generated by the coastal winds and waves. Hwy. 1 maneuvers along the rocky shoreline past colorful beach vistas, generations-old ranches, and the small communities of Pacifica, Half Moon Bay, and Pescadero. The forests of La Honda and the suburban sprawl of Burlingame rest inland.

▣ TRANSPORTATION

On this stretch of the Pacific coast, it's good to have a car. Stunning ocean views off **Highway 1** compete with the road for drivers' attention. If traveling by public transportation you'll have a tougher time. SamTrans services the area only somewhat successfully (see below). Bus route maps are available at some CalTrain and BART stations, but calling customer information is the most reliable way to get updated info on the buses. The shore from Pacifica to Half Moon Bay is serviced by buses #17 and 294.

Public Transportation: San Mateo County Transit (SamTrans), 290 and 1100 California Dr. (☎508-6455 or 800-660-4287; www.samtrans.com), in Burlingame. Buses #17 and 294 service Half Moon Bay on a limited basis. #17 runs along the coast between Moss Beach and Half Moon Bay M-F 6:18am-5:30pm, Sa 6:32am-6:32pm. #294 runs from Hillsdale in San Mateo to Linda Mar Park-and-Ride M-F 5:40am-7:35pm; Sa-Su only from Linda Mar to Half Moon Bay (Sa 6:32am-6:32pm; Su northbound 8:45, 11:45am, 2:45pm; southbound 10:42am, 1:42, 4:42pm). Bus route maps are available at some CalTrain and BART stations; call for specific schedules. Adults $1.25, seniors and disabled $0.60, ages 5-17 $0.75, under 5 free. Monthly pass $40, seniors and disabled $18, ages 5-17 $22.

Bike Rental: The Bike Works, 20 Stone Pine Ctr. (☎726-6708), off Main St. Friendly staff will set you up with a mountain bike ($7 per hr., $35 per day; helmet included). Open M-F 10am-6pm, Sa 10am-5pm, Su 11am-4pm.

✳🔢 ORIENTATION AND PRACTICAL INFORMATION

Hwy. 1 winds along the San Mateo County coast from San Francisco to **Big Basin Redwoods State Park.** This expanse of shore is scattered with isolated, sandy beaches, most of which are too cold for swimming. Keep your eyes peeled for the stunning, unmarked, crowdless beaches.

Visitor Information: Half Moon Bay Coastside Chamber of Commerce and Visitors Bureau, 520 Kelly Ave. (☎726-8380; www.hmbchamber.com), in a Victorian house just east of Hwy. 1. Amiable staff, numerous brochures, and local bus service maps. Open M-F 9am-4pm. **San Mateo County Convention and Visitors Bureau,** Seabreeze Plaza, 111 Anza Blvd., #410 (☎800-288-4748). From the Broadway exit of Rte. 101, follow signs to Airport Blvd., take a left, and follow road to Anza Blvd. Turn left; it's the mirrored building on your right, across the street from the Embassy Hotel. Near SFO, this sleek office offers info on the Central Coast and San Francisco area, including brochures and helpful maps. Open M-Th 8:30am-5pm, F 8:30am-4pm.

Police: Half Moon Bay, 537 Kelly Ave. (☎726-8288). **San Mateo Police General Information,** ☎522-7710.

Library and Internet Access: Half Moon Bay Library, 620 Correas St. (☎726-2316), off Main St. Free Internet and wireless connection. Open M-W 10am-8pm, Th 1-8pm, F 10am-6pm, Sa 10am-5pm, Su 1-5pm.

Post Office: Half Moon Bay, 500 Stone Pine Rd. (☎726-4015). Open M-F 8:30am-5pm, Sa 8:30am-noon. **Postal Code:** 94402 **San Mateo,** 1630 S. Delaware St. (☎358-8490). Open M-F 8:30am-5pm, Sa 8:30am-12:30pm. **Postal Code:** 94019.

🔳🔳 ACCOMMODATIONS AND CAMPING

🔲 **HI-AYH Pigeon Point Lighthouse Hostel,** on Hwy. 1 (☎879-0633), 6 mi. south of Pescadero. 4 houses, each with a homey common room and well-equipped kitchen. Ocean views from bedrooms and a hot tub just feet from the surf spray. 53 beds. Small chores required. Check-in 4:30pm. Check-out 10am. Lockout 10am-4:30pm. Curfew 11pm. Reservations recommended. Wheelchair accessible. Dorms $18, nonmembers $21; doubles $51, nonmembers $57. ❶

BAY AREA
WINE COUNTRY

San Benito House, 356 Main St. (☎726-3425). 12 airy, pristine rooms, each impeccably decorated with antique furnishings. Most rooms have private baths with claw-footed bathtubs. Communal access to gleaming hall showers and sauna. Bar open M-F 3pm-around midnight, Sa-Su 4pm-around midnight. Continental breakfast included. Check-in after 3pm. Check-out 11am. Reservations recommended. Rooms M-Th $75, F-Su $90; with private bath $90/$100, with living room suite $125/$160. ❹

Costanoa, 2001 Rossi Rd. (☎879-1100 or 877-262-7848; www.costanoa.com), on the east side of Rte. 1, 25 mi. south of Half Moon Bay between Pigeon Pt. and Año Nuevo. The Ritz Carlton of roughing it. All accommodations include access to dry sauna and showers with heated floors. Activities include horseback riding, bike rentals, naturalist-led hikes, and Native American storytelling. Canvas cabins (includes heated mattress) $95-185; lodges $165-350; tent and RV sites $40-55. ❸

Francis Beach Campground, 95 Kelly Ave. (☎726-8820), on Francis Beach. 52 sites with fire pits and picnic tables. Clean bathrooms. June-Sept. 7-night max. stay; low-season 15-night max. stay. 1-night max. stay for hike/bike. Check-out noon. Wheelchair accessible. Hot showers $0.25 per 2min. Sites $20, seniors $18; Hike/bike sites $3 per person. Day-use of beach $6, seniors $5. ❶

HI-AYH Point Montara Lighthouse Hostel (☎728-7177), on Lighthouse Point, at Hwy. 1 and 16th St., 25 mi. south of San Francisco and 8 mi. north of Half Moon Bay. SamTrans #294 stops 1 block north, though bus drivers will often drop you off at the lighthouse if you ask. Revel in this isolated 45-bed facility with 2 kitchens and serene surroundings. Ask for a room with a view of the coast. Laundry $2. Check-in 4:30-10pm. Lockout 10am-4:30pm. Curfew 11pm. Make reservations well in advance for weekends, groups, and private rooms. Wheelchair accessible. Dorms $18, nonmembers $21, under 18 with parent $12; $15 extra for private rooms. ❶

🔲 FOOD

Despite the area's remote feel, a surprising number of restaurants cater to hungry travelers. Those looking for late-night snacks or planning to picnic can find a 24hr. **Safeway,** 70 N. Cabrillo Hwy. (☎726-1143), at the junction of Hwy. 1 and 92.

🔳 **The Flying Fish Grill** (☎712-1125), at Main St. and Rte. 92, by Tom and Pete's Market. Small roadside cafe serves cheap local seafood. Famous fish tacos $2.95-4.15. Other oceanic offerings $8.45-12.95. Takeout available. Open Tu-Su 11:30am-8:30pm. ❷

Half Moon Bay Brewing Co., 390 Capistrano Rd. (☎728-2739; www.hmbbrewingco.com), at the edge of Pillar Point Harbor in Princeton. One of Half Moon Bay's singles hot spots. Ocean-view seating and patio with fire pit. Fresh seafood $15-21.50. Pub grub $9.50-15. Micro-brewed beers $4.25 per pint. Live music and dancing Su 4-8pm. Open daily 11:30am-10pm. Kitchen closes 9pm. ❷

Taqueria La Cumbre, 28 N. B St. (☎344-8989), at Baldwin St. in San Mateo. Take the 3rd Ave. W exit off U.S. 101 and turn right on Delaware St., left on 1st Ave., and right onto B St. This restaurant and its San Francisco branch have won the "best burrito" award in every major Bay Area magazine. Filling and piquant Mexican meals for $8.50-10. Long lines at lunchtime. Open Su-Th 11am-9pm, F-Sa 11am-10pm. ❷

3-Zero Cafe, 8850 Hwy. 1 (☎728-1411; www.3-zero.com), at the Half Moon Bay Airport. Watch planes take off while you stay grounded with your huge and hearty home-style breakfast ($4-11). Menu and owner come equipped with wit and charm. Also serves "launch" (lunch $5-12). Visit website for discounts. Open daily 7am-3pm. ❷

Jeffrey's, 42 S. B St. (☎348-8698), at 1st Ave. in San Mateo. Take the 3rd Ave. W exit off U.S. 101, turn right on Delaware St., and then left on 1st Ave. Somewhere between a dive and a nice family restaurant comes this hearty independent hamburger joint. Try an avocado burger ($5.80) or choose from another pleasantly cheap menu item ($4.60-10). Open Su-Th 11am-9pm, F-Sa 11am-10pm. ❶

Moon Juice, Stone Pine Ctr. (☎712-1635), off Main St. in Half Moon Bay. Head south on Main St.; Stone Pine Ctr. is on your left. When terrestrial simply won't do, head to this little juice and smoothie store, which serves up out-of-this-world concoctions, like the Beetaholic. Deli sandwiches ($5-6) and stuffed hot pretzels ($3) make this a great place for a light meal or snack. Juices $4.25-5.75. Smoothies $3.75-4.75. Open M-Tu and Th-Su 10am-8pm. ❷

👁 🏔 SIGHTS AND OUTDOOR ACTIVITIES

Time in San Mateo County is best spent enjoying the myriad outdoor opportunities, but there are plenty of quirky sights for those foggy days. The following sights and outdoor activities are listed in roughly north-south order.

COYOTE POINT RECREATION AREA AND MUSEUM.
The recreation area features a kid-oriented nature museum and a small but impressive array of live animals in natural habitats, including an aviary and small fish tank. The park also offers great waterside views of the planes flying into SFO. *(1651 Coyote Point Dr. From San Francisco, take U.S. 101 to the Poplar Ave. exit just south of the airport and follow the signs. Recreation Area: ☎573-2592. Open daily Apr.-Sept. 8am-8pm; Oct.-Mar. 8am-5pm. Park entrance fee $5 per car. Museum: ☎342-7755. Open Tu-Sa 10am-5pm, Su noon-5pm. $6, seniors and ages 13-17 $4, ages 3-12 $2, under 3 free. 1st W of each month free.)*

BURLINGAME MUSEUM OF PEZ MEMORABILIA.
The largest public display of Pez Candy dispensers in the world fits into two small rooms and dispenses loads of childhood nostalgia one sweet pellet at a time. Enjoy the bite-sized things in life at this once-in-a-lifetime stop. *(214 California Dr., between Burlingame and Howard Ave. Exit U.S. 101 at Broadway Ave., head west, and turn left on California Dr. Also accessible by CalTrain; get off at the Burlingame Station. ☎347-2301; www.burlingamepezmuseum.com. Open Tu-Sa 10am-6pm. $3, ages 4-12 and over 65 $1, under 4 free.)*

FILOLI ESTATE.
If "old money" is your bag, check out this rare example of an early 1900s country estate, including a pristine Gregorian Revival House and a magnificent 16-acre garden. *(On Canada Rd. From San Francisco, take I-280 S. to Edgewood Rd. W. and turn right on Canada Rd. ☎364-8300; www.filoli.org. House and Garden tours Mar.-Oct. Tu-Sa 10am-2:30pm. $10, students $5, children 7-12 $1, under 7 free.)*

THE LOCAL STORY

LSD: FROM THE MAN TO THE PEOPLE

In 1938, in Basel, Switzerland Albert Hoffman synthesized a compound called lysergic acid diethylamide (LSD). The new wonder drug was said to cure psychosis and alcoholism. In the early 50s, the CIA adopted LSD fo **Operation MK-ULTRA,** a series o Cold War mind-control experiments. By the late 60s, the drug had been tested on 1500 military personnel in a series of ethically shady operations. Writers Ken Kesey, Allen Ginsberg, and the Grateful Dead's Robert Hunter were first exposed to acid as subjects in government experiments.

The CIA soon abandoned the unpredictable hallucinogen, but Kesey, a Stanford graduate student at the time, had already made it his mission to share i with the world. The proto-hippies in the Haight were among the first of its adherents. Amateur chemists began producing the compound, and intellectuals like Timothy Leary and Aldous Huxley advocated its use as a means o expanding consciousness. In October 1966, the drug was made illegal in California, and Kesey's Merry Pranksters hosted their first public **Acid Test,** immortalized in Tom Wolfe's journalistic novel *The Electric Kool-Aid Acid Test.* Acid became an ingredient in much of the youth culture of the time, juicing up anti-war rallies and love-ins across the Bay and the country.

DOWNTOWN HALF MOON BAY. Independent shops and a small-town atmosphere characterize **Main Street,** which splits off from the town's main thoroughfare, **Highway 1.** A couple of historical relics are on Johnston St., which runs parallel to Main St. one block east. The **Community United Methodist Church,** built in 1872, stands as a well-kept example of the city's registered landmarks. *(529 Johnston St., at Miramontes Ave. ☎726-4621.)* The **Half Moon Bay Jail,** just two houses north of the church, was built in 1911 and used as an incarceration facility for the entire county. Today, the austere building houses artifacts from Half Moon Bay's Spanishtown. *(505 Johnston St. ☎726-7084. Open Sa-Su 1-4pm.)* **Johnston House,** built in 1853 by 49er James Johnston, is the earliest American home still standing along the San Mateo County coastline, as well as one of the few examples of "New England" salt box architecture on the West Coast. *(Drive to south end of Main St. and make a left on Higgins Purissima Rd. ☎726-0329; www.johnstonhousehmb.org. Open Jan.-Sept. 11am-3pm on the 3rd Sa of the month. Call ahead for tours.)*

HILLER AVIATION MUSEUM. This impressively packed museum features flying machines from past and present, as well as imaginative renditions of future models. *(601 Skyway Rd., at the San Carlos Airport. From San Francisco, take U.S. 101 S to the Holly St./Redwood Shores Pkwy. exit. Head east onto Redwood Shores Pkwy., right onto Airport Rd., and right onto Skyway Rd. ☎654-0200; www.hiller.org. Open daily 10am-5pm. $8, seniors and ages 8-17 $5, under 8 free.)*

LA HONDA. A winding cross-peninsular trip down **Route 84** will bring you to the little logging town in the redwoods where author Ken Kesey lived with his merry pranksters in the 1960s, before it got too small and they took off across the US in a psychedelic bus. The shady, scenic drive makes this detour worthwhile, even if you aren't familiar with Kesey's gang, but *Let's Go* recommends reading a copy of Tom Wolfe's ▨*The Electric Kool-Aid Acid Test* before making the journey.

PARKS AND TRAILS. Memorial County Park offers 65 mi. of redwood trails, stretching through three parks open to hiking, horseback riding, and bicycling. *(On Pescadero Rd. Go east from Hwy. 1 to Cloverdale Rd. ☎879-0212. Visitor Center open daily May-Sept. 10am-4pm.)* The **Heritage Grove** spans 12 sq. mi. and has the oldest and largest redwood trees in the Santa Cruz mountains. *(On Pescadero Rd. to Alpine, and make a right. Butano: 5 mi. south of Pescadero. From the north, take Pescadero Rd. east from Hwy. 1 to Cloverdale Rd. From the south, take Gazos Creek from Hwy. 1 to Cloverdale. ☎879-2040.)* Among the many redwood parks, **Butano State Park** stands out for its sweeping views of the Pacific Ocean. Its 3200 acres offer 20 mi. of hiking and mountain biking trails. *(Off Pescadero Rd., 7 mi. east of Hwy. 1 from the north, 3 mi. east from the south.)* For those who prefer concrete but still want scenic settings, the **Sawyer Camp Trail** is popular among the local bicyclist, in-line skater, jogger, and hiker set. It stretches 10 mi. along the Crystal Springs reservoir. *(1801 Crystal Springs Rd. ☎589-4294. Open M-F.)*

AÑO NUEVO STATE RESERVE. This wildlife reserve has several hiking trails that offer views of **Año Nuevo Island,** the site of an abandoned lighthouse now overrun with birds, seals, and sea lions. The visitors center features real-time videos displaying the animal adventures on the island as well as a fascinating informational video about the seals and Point Año Nuevo. From mid-December to late March, the reserve is the mating place of the 15 ft., 4500 lb. **elephant seal.** Thousands of fat seals crowd the shore and, like frat boys looking to score, the males fight each other for dominance over a herd of females. Before mid-August, you can still see the last of the "molters" shedding their fur and the young who have yet to find their sea legs. Don't get too close—if they don't get you, the cops might; law requires staying 25 ft. away at all times. Allow about 2hr. total to make the 3 mi. round-trip hike to the seal viewpoints. *(50 mi. south of San Francisco, 25 mi. south of Half Moon Bay, and 20 mi. north of Santa Cruz. Park information ☎ 879-0225. No pets. Open daily 8am-sunset. Visitors center open daily 10am-3:30pm; although hours sometimes vary. Free hiking permits available at the ranger station at the visitors center. Seal-viewing permits are only issued until 3:30pm. Parking $6, seniors $5.)*

◪ BEACHES

Wide, sandy, and fairly deserted **state beaches** dot the coast along Hwy. 1 (Cabrillo Hwy.) in San Mateo County. Unless otherwise noted, each state beach charges $6, a fare that covers admission to all state parks for the entire day. All beaches have parking lots and restrooms and are open daily from 8am-sunset. Keep your eyes peeled for unmarked beaches along the coast; they're often breathtaking, crowdless spots with free parking. The water is too chilly for most swimmers, and surfers always wear full-body wetsuits. Rip currents and undertows are frequent, so be careful if you choose to brave the cold. The creeks near these beaches are often contaminated—signs will be posted at entrances to warn you, but simply staying out of them is generally a good idea. Dogs are not allowed on the state beaches.

GRAY WHALE COVE BEACH. This stunning beach, shielded by high bluffs from the highway above, used to be one of the more popular private nude beaches in the Bay Area. Now legendary as the first "clothing-optional" state beach, Gray Whale Cove offers some of the most gorgeous and not so gorgeous views on the coast. *(12 mi. south of San Francisco, in Devil's Slide—the curvy, cliffy stretch of Hwy. 1—a few mi. south of Pacifica. You'll know it by the large parking lot on your left. Free.)*

HALF MOON BAY STATE BEACH. Lining the coast next to town, Half Moon Bay State Beach is actually composed of several smaller beaches. The **Coastal Trail,** a paved path perfect for joggers, bikers, and dog walkers, runs 3 mi. along all four beaches and then continues north. At the end of Kelly Ave., **Francis Beach** lies closest to town and is the southernmost of the four. Although it's the least scenic of the bunch, it is the only one with a campsite (see p. 190), a guard station that operates year-round, and wheelchair accessibility. *(☎ 726-8820.)* To the north of Francis, the wider and prettier **Venice Beach** is down a flight of stairs at the end of a dirt road leading from Venice Blvd. off Hwy. 1. **Dunes Beach** and **Roosevelt Beach** are at the end of a short, steep trail at the end of Young Ave. off Hwy. 1. Strong tides and undertows make swimming dangerous, but they also create great waves and winds for board- and windsurfing. Windsurfers have to go a ways out to sea to catch the strong gusts, as the half-moon shape of the bay protects the shores, making for wonderful picnicking and sunbathing options. *(On the coast right next to the town of Half Moon Bay.)*

SAN GREGORIO AND POMPONIO STATE BEACHES. These two beaches are dramatically set below one of **the most scenic stretches of Hwy. 1.** Of all the beaches in the area, they are arguably the most picturesque—and often the most deserted. Walk to the northern end of San Gregorio or the southern end of Pomponio to find little caves in the shore rocks. Between San Gregorio and Pomponio State Beaches, there allegedly rests a gorgeous, less frequented beach at the unmarked turnout at Marker 27.35 along Hwy. 1. It's difficult to find without aid; keep an eye out for cars mysteriously parked along the highway. *(San Gregorio: 11 mi. south of Half Moon Bay. Pomponio: 13 mi. south of Half Moon Bay. $6.)*

PEBBLE BEACH AND PIGEON POINT. Though threatening signs discourage them from doing so, kids tend to pocket handfuls of tiny, smooth pebbles from **Pebble Beach.** Law-abiding parents have been known to mail the stolen stones back to the Half Moon Bay Visitors Center. A paved and level trail leads south from the parking lot along the bluffs; reaching the tide pools below for exploration requires a bit of a climb down. (*19 mi. south of Half Moon Bay, 2 mi. south of Pescadero Rd. $6.*) **Pigeon Point,** 4 mi. south of Pebble Beach, takes its name from a hapless schooner that crashed into the rocky shore on its inaugural voyage in 1853. The point turns heads with its tide pools, 30 ft. plumes of surf, and 115 ft. operating lighthouse (the tallest on the West Coast), which houses a four-ton lens. (*23 mi. south of Half Moon Bay, 6 mi. south of Pescadero Rd. Lighthouse and Point info ☎ 879-2120.*)

NORTHERN INTERIOR

North from Redding to the Oregon border and east into the tall, densely forested Cascade Mountains, California's vast, oft-forgotten Northern Interior offers rugged and isolated beauty. This region offers plenty of activities for the small-town enthusiast, the nature-lover, and the outdoor adventurer. Vast golden plains, rock-strewn hills, and swift rivers reign in the relatively unpopulated Northern Interior. The Cascade Mountains interrupt the expanse of farmland to the southeast with quiet peaks, lush wilderness, and the two enormous glaciated mountains of Mt. Shasta and Mt. Lassen. Past and present volcanic activity has left behind a surreal landscape of lava beds, cratered mountains, lakes, waterfalls, caves, and recovering forest areas. Tremendous opportunities for recreation, hiking, and adventure await those who make the trek north.

HIGHLIGHTS OF THE NORTHERN INTERIOR

MOUNT SHASTA. The stunning, sacred Mount Shasta (p. 201) inspires bikers, hikers, climbers, and odd mystical legends.

LAVA BEDS NATIONAL MONUMENT. Under dry grasses, sagebrush, and rock formations, this otherworldly landscape (p. 214) is riddled with fascinating caves.

OREGON SHAKESPEARE FESTIVAL. The Bard's greatest hits reign again in Ashland, Oregon at this renowned annual theater festival (p. 214).

LASSEN VOLCANIC NATIONAL PARK ☎ 530

Lassen Volcanic National Park—the most geothermally active area in the Cascade Range—is one link in a chain of seismic and volcanic sites around the Pacific Rim intimidatingly dubbed the "Ring of Fire." Mt. Lassen's most recent large-scale volcanic activity occurred in 1914, when tremors, lava streams, black dust, and a series of enormous eruptions ravaged the area. The geological ruckus climaxed a year later when Mt. Lassen spewed a cloud of smoke and ash 7 mi. into the sky. Shortly thereafter, in 1916, the area was established as a national park. Even now, remnants of the eruption are discernible in Lassen's unearthly pools of boiling water, barren lava rock, occasional sulphur stench, and young, revitalized forests.

AT A GLANCE: LASSEN VOLCANIC NATIONAL PARK

AREA: 106,372 acres.

CLIMATE: Crisp in the summer (sometimes with near-freezing temperatures at night), during the winter Lassen gets snowed in.

FEATURES: Cold Boiling Lake, Mt. Lassen, the Devastated Area.

HIGHLIGHTS: Hiking Mt. Lassen, braving Bumpass Hell, showshoeing by Emerald Lake.

GATEWAYS: Redding (p. 201), Chico (p. 312) Red Bluff.

CAMPING: Camping 7- to 14-day max. stay, backcountry 14-day max. stay. Free wilderness permit is required for backcountry camping.

FEES AND RESERVATIONS: Entrance fee $10 per vehicle, $5 per pedestrian or cyclist. Valid for 7 days. $25 annual fee.

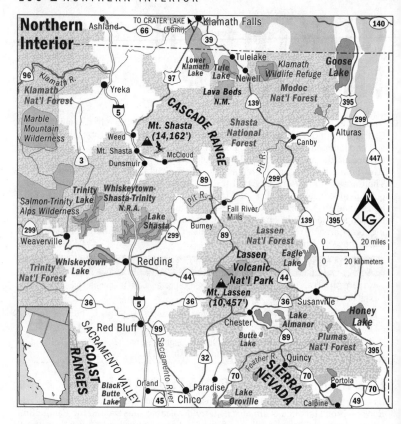

ORIENTATION AND PRACTICAL INFORMATION

Lassen National Park is located squarely in the middle of Lassen National Forest, 48 mi. east of Redding (via Rte. 44) and Red Bluff (via Rte. 36). **Route 89** passes through the park and connects to Rte. 44 at the northern entrance and Rte. 36 at the southern entrance. From **Chester** (71 mi. east of Red Bluff on Rte. 36), two dirt roads enter the park from the southeast, one leading north to Juniper Lake and the other northwest to Warner Valley. Rte. 89 winds through the major attractions on the west side of the park and can be followed all the way through the park once the snow melts (usually by late June). The park's eastern side is less developed. The **Pacific Crest Trail** (see **From Crest to Crest: The Trail of the West**, p. 237) winds through the center of the park, crossing Warner Valley in the south.

There are two information stations in Lassen that provide wilderness permits, publications, and information about the entire park: **Park Headquarters,** in Mineral (☎595-4444; open daily 8am-4:30pm), and the **Loomis Museum,** at Manzanita Lake, near the north entrance (☎595-4444, ext. 5180; open daily June 27-Sept. 1 9am-5pm; closed Sept. 21-May 30; open the rest of the year Su and F-Sa 9am-5pm). A **park entrance fee** of $10 per vehicle ($5 per bike or pedestrian) is valid for seven days. Annual passes cost $25. Backcountry camping requires a free permit.

> **WHEN TO GO.** Lassen is one of the least visited national parks and is fairly quiet until July, when the summer hikers show up. The park is open year-round; rangers ski to work when the roads close. Those visiting Lassen in the winter should have outdoors experience.

ACCOMMODATIONS AND CAMPING

INSIDE THE PARK

Due to the danger of rock slides and lava flows, few permanent structures exist in the park. The only indoor lodging in Lassen is the upscale and charming **Drakesbad Guest Ranch ❺**, in Warner Valley in the park's southern end. This 110-year-old guest ranch isn't cheap, but it comes with three meals a day and scenic, secluded surroundings. Take Rte. 36 to Chester, turn right at the firehouse, and follow the signs. (☎529-1512, ext. 120; www.drakesbad.com. Open early June-Oct. Reservations necessary. Singles and doubles from $121 per person; bungalows from $139 per person.) Fortunately, **camping** in the park is beautiful and abundant. Unfortunately, temperatures approach near-freezing at night, even in August, and snow often keeps campgrounds closed well into June; check the weather and snow reports before leaving. **Backcountry camping ❶** is limited to 14 days per year with a free wilderness permit. Fires are prohibited, as is the use of all soaps (even biodegradable ones) in the lakes. Portable propane or gas stoves are allowed. Stop by Park Headquarters, in Mineral, for info on safety, ecological rules, and a list of restricted areas. Geothermally active sites such as Bumpass Hell and Devil's Kitchen are closed to backcountry camping.

▧ **Summit Lake North,** 6700 ft., 17½ mi. south of the Manzanita Lake entrance. Summit Lake's deep blue water glitters through the pine trees surrounding 46 popular sites. Summit Lake North and its cousin on the south side are usually the first to fill up. Drinking water and flush toilets. 7-day max. stay. Open July-Sept. Sites $16. ❶

▧ **Summit Lake South,** 6700 ft., just around the lake from the Summit North campground. All 48 sites have the same views as North Summit. Many trails begin here. Drinking water. No showers or flush toilets. 7-day max. stay. Open July-Sept. Sites $14. ❶

Manzanita Lake, 5900 ft., just inside the park border, near the northwest entrance. Because most of the 179 sites lack privacy, this campground may be more suitable for families than for those seeking solitude. Pay phone, concession services, motorless boating, drinking water, flush toilets, laundry, showers, dump station, and gas. 14-day max. stay. Open early June-late Oct. Sites $16; late Sept.-late Oct. $10. ❶

Butte Lake, 6100 ft., 6 mi. south on a dirt road from Rte. 44, 17 mi. east of Old Station. Less crowded than the Manzanita and Summit Lake campsites. Bathtub Lake promises the warmest water in the park for swimming. Once the snow melts in late summer, the number of available sites increases from 46 to 101. Flush toilets and piped water. Boating and fishing access. Open late May-late Sept. Sites $14. ❶

OUTSIDE THE PARK

The indoor accommodations closest to the northern entrance of the park are 14 mi. north, in Old Station. There are also a handful of motels in Mineral near the southern entrance. Less costly motels are in Redding, 48 mi. west on Rte. 44 (p. 201); Red Bluff, 50 mi. west on Rte. 36; and Chester, southeast on Rte. 36. Lassen National Forest, which surrounds the park, has several developed campgrounds. Six of them line Rte. 89 for the first 10 mi. north of the park. Campgrounds are generally open May through October. **Big Pine ❶**, 4500 ft., is the closest. (19 sites. Piped water, vault toilets. Sites $10.) **Bridge ❶**, 4000 ft., and **Cave ❶**, 4300 ft., both

NORTHERN INTERIOR

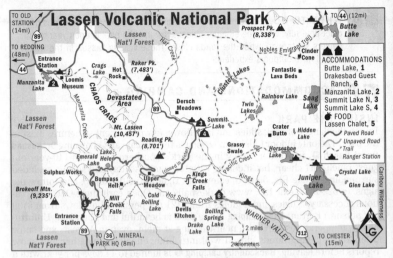

Lassen Volcanic National Park

TO OLD STATION (14mi) 89
TO REDDING (48mi) 44

Entrance Station
Manzanita Lake
Crags Lake
Loomis Museum
Hot Rock
Raker Pk. (7,483')
Devastated Area
Dersch Meadows
Summit Lake
Mt. Lassen (10,457')
Reading Pk. (8,701')
Lake Helen
Emerald Lake
Sulphur Works
Bumpass Hell
Brokeoff Mtn. (9,235')
Upper Meadow
Mill Creek Falls
Cold Boiling Lake
Kings Creek Falls
Entrance Station
Devils Kitchen
Drake Lake
Boiling Springs Lake
Grassy Swale
Horseshoe Lake
Hot Springs Creek
Kings Creek

Prospect Pk. (8,338')
Butte Lake
Nobles Emigrant Trail
Cinder Cone
Fantastic Lava Beds
Rainbow Lake
Twin Lakes
Crater Butte
Hidden Lake
Snag Lake
Juniper Lake
Crystal Lake
Glen Lake
Caribou Wilderness
WARNER VALLEY

Lassen Nat'l Forest
Hat Creek
Cluster Lakes
Chaos Crags
Manzanita Creek
Pacific Crest Tr.

TO 44 (12mi)

ACCOMMODATIONS
Butte Lake, **1**
Drakesbad Guest Ranch, **6**
Manzanita Lake, **2**
Summit Lake N, **3**
Summit Lake S, **4**
◆ **FOOD**
Lassen Chalet, **5**
▱ Paved Road
▱ Unpaved Road
--- Trail
▲ Ranger Station

Lassen Nat'l Forest
89 TO 36, MINERAL, PARK HQ (8mi)
0   2 miles
0   2 kilometers
312 TO CHESTER (15mi)

have drinking water and trailer-only sites for $11, though tents may be used if you don't mind bumpy ground. Several campgrounds also lie east of Mineral on Rte. 36, in the Almanor Ranger District (☎258-2141). A number of campgrounds sit on the southwestern shore of **Eagle Lake,** in the eastern part of Lassen National Forest. **Christie, Merrill,** and **Aspen Grove** have piped water and are in the Eagle Lake Ranger District. (☎257-4188. Sites $13-15.) Once an active fire lookout, **McCarthy Point ❹** has since been converted into a guest cabin, which has a kitchen and a bedroom that accommodates up to six. (☎258-2141. Reserve at least 2 weeks ahead. Sites Su-Th $40, F-Sa $60. Security deposit $200.)

🍴 FOOD

Meals in Lassen can be hard to come by: restaurants are few and far between, and groceries tend to be limited and overpriced. Those opting to prepare their own food should consider purchasing supplies before entering the park. For prepared meals, try the **Lassen Chalet ❶,** a cafeteria-style restaurant and gift shop just inside the southwest entrance. Their large burgers ($4-6) are filling but only available until 5pm. (☎595-3376. Open daily 9am-6pm; late May-late June and Sept. to mid-Oct. 9am-4pm.) For a wider selection, try the **Mineral Lodge Cafe ❶,** 1 mi. east of Park Headquarters on Rte. 36, which serves huge breakfasts, burgers, and sandwiches for around $6. (☎595-4422. Open M-Th 8am-3pm and 5-8pm, F-Su 8am-8pm.) Across the street is a small grocery store, the **Gas Mart and Deli.** (☎595-3222. Open M-Sa 8am-6:30pm, Su 8am-5pm.) At the park's north end, the **Manzanita Camper Service Store,** at the Manzanita Lake campground, has a small selection of pricey groceries, a snack bar, fishing licenses, gasoline, guides, and maps. It also launches lakeworthy boats. (☎335-7557. Open daily summer 8am-8pm; late May-late June and Sept. to mid-Oct. 9am-5pm. Snack bar closes 1hr. before store.)

👁 🏔 SIGHTS AND OUTDOOR ACTIVITIES

Lassen is very car-friendly; roadside sights are clearly numbered, and most are accessible from Rte. 89, depending on snow conditions. Check with Park Headquarters before heading out at all times of the year. At any park entrance ranger station, drivers can pick up the *Lassen Road Guide* ($6), which expounds upon the numbered roadside sights. A comfortable drive through the park (including a few stops) should take 2hr., but allow a full day to accommodate short hikes.

MOUNT LASSEN. Lassen is the world's largest plug-dome volcano—a volcano with lava flow so viscous and slow that it solidifies as it emerges and plugs the volcano vent. A steep, 2½ mi., 4-5hr. trek leads to the 10,457 ft. summit. Even if it's sunny and warm, take along extra clothes (especially a windbreaker) for the gusty peak. Solid shoes are also important; 18 in. of snow can clog the upper 2 mi. of trail even in summer. Those opting out of the hike can still get excellent views of Reading Peak, Mt. Harkness, and Lake Almanor at ▧**Panorama Point,** a pull-off 1 mi. from the Mt. Lassen trailhead.*(Mt. Lassen parking area is little over 1 mi. from Bumpass Hell on Rte. 89. Guidebooks $0.50 at the trailhead.)*

HIKES FROM THE LOOMIS MUSEUM VISITORS CENTER. There are a few easy, relaxing walks in the area surrounding the Loomis Museum Visitors Center at Rte. 89's north entry into the park. The hike to **Crags Lake** starts 500 yd. from the Visitors Center and runs 1¾ mi. one way, climbing 700 ft. (2-4hr. round-trip). The walk winds through dense forest, emerging above a huge rocky basin and the warm lake. For two shorter, easier hikes, head across the street from the visitors center. One hike curls around Lily Pond (1 mi.), with informative placards along the way. The second path goes around Reflection Lake (¾ mi.). For an especially relaxing stroll, consider the 1½ mi. trail around Manzanita Lake.

ALONG ROUTE 89. Many of the park's most popular sights are conveniently located just off Rte. 89 and are accessible by car or foot. Snow can keep some of these sights closed well into the summer, so check at Park Headquarters before venturing off. Coming from the south, the first sight (or smell) is **Sulphur Works,** where a short boardwalk runs above some of Lassen's active sulphur vents. Although the guard rails may prevent you from getting burned, changes in wind direction are apt to provide you with a face full of rotten-egg mist. The boardwalk is wheelchair accessible. About 4½ mi. farther along Rte. 89 is **Emerald Lake.** When partially thawed by the sun, it shimmers bright green with icy cold, 300 ft. deep waters around a snowy center. Swimming is fine for fish but too cold (40°F) for the warm-blooded. No fishing is allowed.

The 1½ mi. hike to **Bumpass Hell,** the largest group of hot springs west of Yellowstone, wanders through the park's largest hydrothermal area. Volcanic heat 6 mi. below makes its presence known by boiling the surface of this huge cauldron of water and mud. The man who discovered Bumpass Hell lost his leg to the stew, but a clearly marked trail and boardwalk makes such a fate unlikely for present-day hikers. Snowbound **Cold Boiling Lake** is 1¾ mi. farther on the same trail. The lake water always appears to boil or simmer due to its placement above a flatulent fissure.

About 5 mi. from Mt. Lassen is the **King's Creek Picnic Area,** near a wildflower meadow. From here, trails depart for Cold Boiling Lake (¾ mi.), Bumpass Hell (4 mi.), Crumbaugh Lake (1¼ mi.), and Southwest Campground (5¼ mi.). A little farther north on Rte. 89, at mile marker 32, is the trailhead to King's Creek Falls, Summit Lakes, and Drakesbad. The trail to **King's Creek Falls** follows the idyllic, cascading King's Creek 1½ mi. to the rushing falls. **Summit Lake** can be reached on foot from King's Creek or from Rte. 89, 5 mi. farther on, if the road's open. **Dersch Meadow,** north of Summit Lake, is a good place to spot grazing deer and circling birds of prey.

A little over 3 mi. from Summit Lake, a short trail leads to what is left of **Devastated Area,** the forested zone that was annihilated by debris spewed out of Mt. Lassen in 1915. Conifers have reclaimed the land here, and as the forest nears maturity, it becomes difficult to see any traces of the destruction from many years ago. In a decade or so, the forest will look virtually as it did before the eruption. A paved trail with informative signs highlighting various remnants of the eruption traverses the region. **Hot Rock** sits 2 mi. farther along Rte. 89. The 300-ton boulder was once a part of Mt. Lassen, but it was swept down to its current location by a massive lava flow. Though it never melted from the lava, the rock got so hot that it boiled the mud around it for months.

Chaos Crags and Jumbles, 6 mi. from Hot Rock, is a broken, messy field of rock that avalanched down several volcanic domes and now looks like the landscape of another planet. The final stop, at the northernmost end of Rte. 89, is the **Loomis Museum** (p. 199), which showcases an extensive collection of photographs of the volcanic activity of the 1910s.

OVERNIGHT HIKES. A network of trails explores much of the wilder eastern portion of the park, rising and dipping through coniferous forests, hidden lakes, and the occasional lava bed. Of the 150 mi. of trails (including a stretch of the Pacific Crest Trail), the **Manzanita Creek Trail,** near Manzanita Lake campground (see p. 197), and the **Horseshoe Lake** area, east of Summit Lake, are the driest throughout the summer. Both trails make enjoyable overnight trips. Manzanita Creek Trail parallels a creek through rolling woodlands that bear little resemblance to the boiling cauldrons to the south. To the east, the Horseshoe Lake area is rich in ice-cold lakes and deer-filled pine forests. A number of scenic loops also start from the Summit Lake North campground. The 10 mi. loop to Lower Twin Lake and the Cluster Lakes features, unsurprisingly, many beautiful lakes. The 11½ mi. loop around Grassy Swale that heads to Lower Twin Lake is greener and less crowded. Wilderness permits are required for backcountry camping.

By mid-summer, the shallow waters of Manzanita Lake and Summit Lake can warm up enough to make swimming possible. Bathtub Lake in the northeast corner of the park is traditionally the warmest of all. Several lakes in the park have native rainbow trout, and Hat Creek is stocked. A state license is required to go fishing, and some areas have additional rules. (Manzanita, for example, has "catch and release" and barbless hook policies.)

OTHER SIGHTS. Lassen is near three less-traveled and less-developed wilderness areas. If you're not driving a 4WD vehicle, ask about the road conditions at Park Headquarters. Pick up a free wilderness permit from the US Forest Service. A topographic map of the area ($4), available at ranger stations, is invaluable for finding trails and determining what sights are nearby. All wilderness areas have a no-trace policy: everything packed in must be packed out.

Caribou Wilderness, a gently graded plateau, borders the park to the east. For the easiest access, take Rte. 44 or 36 to Hwy. A-21 for 14 mi., then take Silver Lake Rd. to the **Caribou Lake Trailhead.** Its numerous quiet, clean lakes support water lilies and wildflowers in early summer and treat hikers to solitude. The more desolate **Cone Lake Trailhead** can be reached by taking Forest Service Road (F.S.) 10, off Rte. 44 north of Hwy. A-21. For the ultimate in isolated beauty, make the trek to the **Hay Meadows Trailhead.** Head north on F.S. 10 from Rte. 36 (near Chester), then turn left after 14 mi. F.S. 10 can be rough; a 4WD vehicle is necessary.

Thousand Lakes Wilderness can be accessed from F.S. 16, 4 mi. north of the park's northern entrance, off Rte. 89. Seven miles from Rte. 89 on F.S. 16, the road forks; F.S. 16 continues to the right toward **Magee Trailhead.** The strenuous trail leads to Magee Peak, 8594 ft., and deserted Magee Lake, where insect repellent is a must. The left fork continues to **Tamarack Trailhead.** The trail there is more manageable and goes to Lake Eiler via Eiler Butte. Going north, take F.S. 33 N25 and turn left just after Wilcox Rd. When the road forks, turn left onto F.S. 33 N23Y. This 7 mi.

stretch of road requires 4WD. **Subway Cave** is part of the Thousand Lakes Wilderness is easily accessible by car—it's off Rte. 89, just past the Rte. 44 split near the north entrance station. The 1300 ft. long lava tubes were created when lava flowing in a trench began to harden on top. The lava below kept flowing through the trench, leaving large hollow tunnels. The cave is pitch-black and cool with uneven footing, so bring a friend, a sweater, sturdy shoes, and a lantern or strong flashlight with extra batteries.

The spectacular **Ishi Wilderness,** named for the last survivor of a Yahi Yana tribe, is at a comparatively low altitude for such rugged terrain, making it ideal for off-season exploration. Take Rte. 36 from Red Bluff 20 mi. to Payne's Creek Rd. Then take a right on Plum Creek Rd., and another right on Ponderosa Way. This rough road skirts the eastern edge of the wilderness, where most trailheads lie. Ishi is a series of river canyons with dense islands of Ponderosa pine and sparse, sun-scorched grasslands in the south; it swelters in the summer. **Mill Creek Trail** runs along the 1000 ft. canyon, where gentle waters await swimmers. Keep an eye out for red-tailed hawks and golden eagles. The Tehana Deer Herd, the largest migratory herd in California, spends its winters in Ishi. The **Deer Creek Trail** is another scenic hike, with a trailhead at the southern end of the Ishi Wilderness on Ponderosa Way.

MOUNT SHASTA   ☎ 530

Rising dramatically out of completely flat plains to a frosted, 14,162 ft. peak, Mount Shasta attracts nature buffs, mineral-bath pilgrims, and extreme sports enthusiasts, all entranced by the striking vista. In 1873, one Shasta worshipper described the mountain as "lonely as God, white as a winter moon." Local Native American tribes believed that a great spirit dwelled within the volcano, and modern-day spiritualists are drawn to the mountain by its mystical energy. Thousands of believers gathered in 1987 to witness the great new-age clerical event of Harmonic Convergence, which climaxed when a resident turned on her TV and saw an angel displayed on the screen. Spiritual significance aside, climbers come to tackle the slopes and Bay Area yuppies flock to relax in the fragrant mountain air. The town of Mount Shasta is moderately touristy and quite crunchy: it has vegetarian restaurants, spiritual bookstores, outdoor equipment shops, and a friendly, pervasive serenity.

▐ TRANSPORTATION

Trains: Amtrak's closest station is in Dunsmuir (9 mi. south on I-5), 5750 Sacramento Ave. (☎800-872-7245). Unattended. Prices range greatly depending on demand, so call ahead. To: **Redding** (2hr., 1 per day, $9-18); **San Francisco** (8½hr., 1 per day, $29-62); **Portland, OR** (10½hr., 1 per day, $38-82).

Buses: Greyhound (☎800-231-2222) has a flag stop in the parking lot at 4th St. and Mt. Shasta Blvd. To **San Francisco** ($52-56) and **Redding** ($15). Cash only.

Public Transportation: Siskiyou Stage (☎800-247-8243) offers minibus transit between Weed, Mt. Shasta (next to the Black Bear Diner in the Mt. Shasta Shopping Center), and Dunsmuir. Operates M-F; call for times. $2-5.

▟▐ ORIENTATION AND PRACTICAL INFORMATION

The town of Mt. Shasta is 60 mi. north of Redding on **Interstate 5,** 50 mi. west of Lassen Volcanic National Park, and 275 mi. north of San Francisco. The town can be used as a base for daytrips to Lava Beds, Lassen, Burney Falls, and the Shasta Recreation Area. Everitt Memorial Hwy. leads to the Mt. Shasta trailheads.

Visitor Information: Mount Shasta Visitors Center, 300 Pine St. (☎800-397-1519). Open M-Th 9am-5:30pm, F-Sa 9am-6pm, Su 9am-4pm. **Shasta-Trinity National Forest Service,** 204 W. Alma St. (☎926-4511), across the tracks from the intersection of Alma St. and Mt. Shasta Blvd., has loads of info on outdoor activities in and around Mt. Shasta. Find out which campgrounds and trails are open, and grab maps, brochures, or fire and wilderness permits. Mountain climbers and hikers must sign the trail register outside. Open M-Sa 8am-4:30pm, Su 9am-3pm.

ATM: Bank of America, 100 Chestnut St. (☎926-8950 or 800-521-2632). Open M-Th 10am-4pm, F 10am-5pm.

Equipment Rental:

House of Ski and Board, 316 Chestnut St. (☎926-2359; www.hosab.com), 1 block behind Mt. Shasta Blvd. Rents, sells, and services skiing, climbing, and snowboarding equipment at reasonable rates. Boots, bindings, and skis $10 per day, $18 for 3 days. Snowboard and boots $17/$32. Snowshoes $8 per day. Open M-F 9am-6pm, Sa 8am-6pm, Su 10am-5pm. A **cycle shop** is in the same building and rents mountain bikes. $22 per half-day, $26 per day, $75 per week.

5th Season, 300 N. Mt. Shasta Blvd. (☎926-3606), rents camping gear, outdoor equipment, skis, and bikes. Sleeping bag with pad $6 per day. 2-person tent $40 for 3 days. Skis $40 for 3 days. Bikes $36-48 per day. Also offers mountain-climbing and alpine touring equipment. Open spring-fall M-F 9am-6pm, Sa 8am-6pm, Su 10am-5pm; winter daily 8am-6pm.

Weather, Climbing, and Skiing Conditions: 24hr. Weather, ☎842-4438. **Climbing Conditions,** ☎926-9613. **Ski Report,** ☎926-8686.

Library and Internet Access: Mount Shasta Library, 515 E. Alma St. (☎926-2031). 1hr. free Internet. Open M and W 1-6pm, Tu noon-6pm, Th and Sa 1-5pm.

Laundromat: Launderland, in Mt. Shasta Shopping Center off Lake St. Wash $1.50, dry $0.25 per 8 min. Open M-Sa 7am-9pm, Su 8am-9pm.

Police: 303 N. Mt. Shasta Blvd. (☎926-7540), at Lake St. Notify the sheriff (☎841-2900 or 800-404-2911) of missing climbers.

Hospital: Mercy Medical Center, 914 Pine St. (☎926-6111).

Post Office: 301 S. Mt. Shasta Blvd. (☎926-1343). Open M-F 8:30am-5pm. **Postal Code:** 96067.

■ ACCOMMODATIONS AND CAMPING

South Mount Shasta Boulevard, south of McCloud Ave., is lined with chain motels that promise convenience. There are also a few independent accommodations that provide a more personal experience. The US Forest Service (☎926-4511) runs area campgrounds. The campgrounds closest to town, however, are primarily commercial. Pick up a campground map from the visitors center. No-fee campgrounds require a campfire permit, available at the Forest Service station.

Alpenrose Cottage Guest House, 204 E. Hinckley St. (☎926-6724; www.hostels.com/alpenrose), Roses, wind chimes, pets, and a sundeck view of Mt. Shasta. Joyful owner Betty Brown is friendly and helpful. Wood-burning stove, open kitchen, TV room, and library. Hummingbird viewing in summer. Free laundry. With only 4 beds available, reserve in advance. Rooms $30-35 per person. No credit cards. ❸

Finlandia Motel, 1612 S. Mt. Shasta Blvd. (☎926-5596). A clean, 2-level motel with a dilapidated exterior. More personality than other options in the area. Deluxe rooms have vaulted ceilings and bathtubs, while economy rooms are more like standard motel rooms. Some rooms with mountain views. All have access to a spa and sauna. Economy singles from $60, with kitchen $65; doubles from $75; deluxe rooms from $67. Low-season about $10 less. ❹

Lake Siskiyou Campground (☎926-2618 or 888-926-2618; www.lakesis.com), 3 mi. southwest of town. Exit I-5 via Lake St., follow Hatchery Ln. ¼ mi., then go south on Old Stage Rd. and W.A. Barr Rd. This family-oriented site provides a not-quite-roughing-it experience, complete with paved roads and video arcade. Beach access with a phenomenal view of Mt. Shasta and rental paddleboats, motorboats, and canoes. Coin-operated laundry, flush toilets, hot showers. Reserve in advance. Sites $19; RV sites with hookup and TV $25. ❷

Panther Meadow, 7500 ft., sits on Mt. Shasta 8 mi. down the road from McBride Springs. Astounding views. High elevation means it is cold at night, even during the summer. Call the Forest Service to make sure it's not snowed in. 10 walk-in sites with pit toilets; no water. 3-night max. stay. Free. ❶

McBride Springs Campground, 5000 ft., 5 mi. east of Mt. Shasta off Everitt Memorial Hwy. This compact and secluded campground has 9 drive-up sites with nice views, and hiking access. Water and well-maintained outhouses. 7-night max. stay. Sites $10. ❶

🍴 FOOD

Mt. Shasta has many grocery stores, the largest of which is **Ray's Food Place,** 160 Commercial Way, in the Mt. Shasta Shopping Center off Lake St. near I-5. (☎926-3390. Open daily 7am-11pm.) In the summer, **produce stands** across the street provide cheaper, fresher fruits and veggies. **Berryvale Natural Foods,** 305 S. Mt. Shasta Blvd., caters to the health-conscious with organic produce, soy products, great microbrews, and enough tie-dye to make you dizzy. (☎926-1576. Open M-Sa 8:30am-7:30pm, Su 10am-6pm.)

▧ Laurie's Mountain View Cafe, 401 N. Shasta Blvd. (☎926-4998). Looks more like a hippie's kitchen than a cafe, and its employees treat you more like a good friend than a customer. Try their original sandwich creations (salmon, pesto, and cheese $7), and fresh fruit smoothies ($3.50). Sa barbecue. Occasional live music in summer. Open June-Oct. Su-Th 7am-4pm, F-Sa 7am-8pm; Nov.-May daily 7am-4pm. ❷

Lily's, 1013 S. Mt. Shasta Blvd. (☎926-3372). Don't let the white picket fence or delicate white table cloths fool you; hiding in this little house is perhaps the most extensive and creative menu in town. For breakfast, both vegetarian eggs benedict ($8) and non-veggie Benedict Arnold ($9) are enticing. Dinner entrees $15-22. Drink specials change with the seasons. Open daily summer 7am-10pm; winter 8am-9pm. ❹

THE LOCAL STORY

LEGEND OF THE LEMURIANS

While most people are familiar with the mythical city of Atlantis at the bottom of the Atlantic Ocean, its Pacific Ocean counterpart, Lemuria, is lesser-known. According to legend, the tall and beautiful Lemurians became refugees when their continent sunk into the depths of the Pacific. After Lemuria sank, the Lemurians supposedly relocated to a golden city in the middle of Mt. Shasta, emerging only to trade gold nuggets for supplies in Mt. Shasta city. A scientist who studied Mt. Shasta alleged that, while aiming his telescope at the base of the mountain, several golden domes appeared. As the sun set to a moonless night, the same area was illuminated bright white.

Another story involves a prospector who accidentally found a tunnel that had been carved into solid rock near the mountain. He entered the tunnel, followed it for a while, and found a cavern, lined with sheets of copper and containing various artifacts, such as giant bones and drawings. Worried that his employer would seize his discovery, the man waited 30 years until he retired, told his story, and assembled a group to help him search, only to disappear the night before the search.

The lack of recent Lemurian sightings has led some to theorize that they may have relocated to a less conspicuous location, such as the Himalayas, but there's always a chance they'll reemerge.

Serge's Restaurant, 531 Chestnut St. (☎926-1276). This small French restaurant prepares simple, traditional fare for an upscale crowd. Sit outside on the sun deck for an amazing view of Mt. Shasta. The menu varies, but a typical dinner goes for $15-20. Open Su and W-Th 5pm-9pm; F-Sa 5pm-9:30pm. ❹

Black Bear Diner, 401 W. Lake St. (☎926-4669; www.blackbeardiner.com). Busy, small chain draws folksy locals and hikers hungering for the huge portions, friendly service, and Black Bear merchandise. Historic photographs of Mt. Shasta, newspaper menus, and a juke box complemented by old-time hospitality. Hungry Bear's Breakfast ($8) is truly huge. Dinners ($8-11) are heaping plates of comfort food. Vegetarian options. Open daily 5:30am-11:30pm. ❷

👁 🛆 SIGHTS AND OUTDOOR ACTIVITIES

MOUNT SHASTA

At 14,162 ft., Mt. Shasta is not an easy climb, and requires mountaineering skills even on its easiest route. Weather conditions are notoriously unpredictable. 17 routes lead to the Shasta summit, each with its own challenges and rewards.

All climbers must stop at the US Forest Service (see p. 202) for weather updates, maps, climbing conditions, safety registration, a free wilderness permit, a summit pass for climbs over 10,000 ft. ($15), and the mandatory human waste pack-out system. Mt. Shasta rangers are particularly knowledgeable, friendly, and helpful, whether you're going for a jump in a lake, an afternoon hike, or an all-out trip to the summit. Parking is free at trailheads.

AVALANCHE GULCH SUMMIT. The most popular and accessible route to the summit starts at Bunny Flat on the mountain's southwest side, off Everitt Memorial Hwy. A short, steep trail leads to Horse Camp, where hikers will find the historic **Sierra Club Cabin ❶**, which is occupied in the summer by a caretaker. This is a good place to set up base camp for the necessary early morning ascent. *(No accommodations in the cabin itself. $5 fee to camp near the cabin; $3 for a bivy sack.)* **First-night camping ❶** is also permitted on the Bunny Flat parking lot or anywhere in the surrounding area, as long as you have a wilderness permit (see p. 202). While the **Avalanch Gulch** climb can be done in one day, most first-time climbers choose to spend the night at **Helen Lake** (10,443 ft.). Though Avalanche Gulch is not a technical climb, it does require crampons, a helmet, and an ice axe, even in summer.

 Since Mt. Shasta City sits below the mountain at only 3500 ft., take a few mini-climbs in order to acclimate to Mt. Shasta's extreme elevations before attempting to summit.

DAY HIKES AND SCENIC ROADS. Mount Shasta attracts experienced climbers and casual hikers, but those without the will or the time to lace-up their hiking boots can enjoy it from the comfort of their cars. The **Everitt Memorial Highway** provides excellent views of the mountain as it winds 14 mi. from the town of Mt. Shasta to the Ski Bowl trailhead. Parking is available at Bunny Flat and at the end of the road. Before the snow melts (usually around mid-July), Everitt Memorial Hwy. is closed above Bunny Flat; when it finally gets warm enough, Panther Meadow campground (see p. 203), the highest car accessible point, opens. A number of **day hikes** begin in this area, including the steep 2mi. hike to Grey Butte and another two mile hike through Red Butte to Squaw Meadows from the Old Ski Bowl (three-quarters of a mile from Panther Meadow). The **Horse Camp Trail,** at Horse Camp, is an especially scenic 2mi. hike that begins at Bunny Flat

Mount Shasta Area

and affords great views of Avalanche Gulch. Because these "trails" are often unlabeled and ill-defined, it's a good idea to plan your route with a map from the Ranger Station before setting out.

MOUNT SHASTA SKI PARK. Downhill skiers and snowboarders tackle the intermediate-level ski trails of **Mount Shasta Ski Park,** while cross-country skiers use the ski park's **Nordic Center** or go for challenging backcountry skiing; pick up maps and info from the ranger service. In summer, **mountain bikers** rage down the snow-free ski trails. Logging roads in the national forests make excellent backcountry biking trails. **Climbers** of all skill levels love the park's outdoor wall. *(10 mi. east of I-5 on Hwy. 89. ☎926-8600 or 800-754-7427; www.skipark.com. Hours vary by season. Opens for the summer on June 26th; opening date in winter depends on snow. Lift tickets $35, ages 8-12 and over 64 $19, under 8 $5. Tu adults $26. Night skiing W-Sa 4-10pm $20/$13/$3. Ski rental packages from $23. Nordic Center: trail pass and rental $22/$18/$9. Biking $12/$4/$8. Bikes $20 per half-day. Climbing: 2 climbs $5, 3hr. $12.)*

BEYOND MT. SHASTA

MCCLOUD RIVER AREA. Somewhat out of the way, but well worth the drive, the McCloud area features 13 mi. of rivers and storybook waterfalls, all easily accessible by foot. Many places are perfect for swimming, boating, hiking, and camping. The area is growing in popularity, but many trails and facilities are still unmarked. Lower, Middle, and Upper Falls, each a short drive or hike off Hwy. 89, are distinctly beautiful and striking. Maps are posted in the parking lot at Lower Falls. **Fowlers Camp,** 3600 ft., is the only overnight campground in the area and has toilets, picnic units, water, and handicap facilities. *(10 mi. east of the town of Mt. Shasta on Hwy. 89. First come, first camp. Sites $12.)*

SQUAW VALLEY CREEK TRAIL. Unique vegetation and a thick carpet of moss line Squaw Valley Creek, which connects pristine waterfalls and pools suitable for fishing and swimming. The gentle 5mi. trail is ideal for catching glimpses of black tailed deer and black bears. *(Trailhead 9 mi. south of McCloud; follow the signs to Squaw Valley Creek Rd.)*

CASTLE CRAGS STATE PARK. The dramatic spires of Castle Crag resemble medieval fortifications; but in fact, the crags are easily accessible and provide stunning views. Twenty-eight miles of well-maintained hiking trails span the area. To see Mt. Shasta in its glory, try the strenuous 2.7 mi. **Castle Crags Trail,** accessible from the Vista Point parking area. The first three quarters of the hike are steep in parts but walkable; however, bouldering and trailblazing is required to reach Castle Dome, 2250 ft. higher than the parking lot. Water supplies can be replenished at Indian Spring, 1.6 mi. from the trailhead. Buy a topographical map ($1) from the ranger station at the park's entrance. The **Pacific Crest Trail** (see **From Crest to Crest: The Trail of the West,** p. 237) runs for 19 mi. through the wilderness, curving around serene alpine lakes. Access the trail at the south fork of Sacramento Rd. Maps and permits are available at the Forest Service. Be cautious: much of the stone here is dangerous and unstable. Nearby **Cantara Loop** has good rock faces for beginners. **Pluto's Cave,** a tube formed by a 190,000 year old basaltic lava flow, is gated due to vandalism, but still provides a stunning glimpse of volcanic action. For more climbing info, call 5th Season (see p. 202) or the US Forest Service (see p. 202). Camping is free in the area of the Shasta-Trinity National Forest surrounding Castle Crags, and the state park runs a full service campground. Abutting the wilderness area is **Castle Lake,** which offers beautiful hiking trails as well as fishing, swimming, and camping, though camping is restricted within 200 ft. of the lake. *(Off I-5, 15 mi. south of Shasta. ☎ 235-2684.)*

STEWART MINERAL SPRINGS. Brought to these springs on the brink of death, Mr. Stewart attributed his subsequent recovery to the healing qualities of the mineral water and the beauty of the surrounding environment. Spiritual properties aside, the secluded saunas and hot tubs make for a relaxing soak. *(4617 Stewart Springs Rd., in Weed. ☎ 938-2222; www.stewartmineralsprings.com. Open May-Sep. Su-W 10am-6pm, Th-Sa 10am-10pm; Oct.-Apr. daily 10am-6pm. Mineral baths $20. Tent and RV sites $15. Motel rooms $45, with kitchen $49-79; cabins $59-89.)*

MOUNT SHASTA STATE FISH HATCHERY. The oldest operating hatchery west of the Mississippi monitors the production of nearly 10 million baby trout every year. The dense masses of swimming trout in the hatchery troughs are truly a spectacle. Visitors can toss in fish food to incite total pandemonium. Guided tours and easy-to-use maps are provided. *(3 Old State Rd. ☎ 926-5508. West of the Lake St. exit off I-5. Open Mar.-Dec. daily 7am-dusk. Free.)*

AREA LAKES

The alpine lakes around Mt. Shasta—including Deadfall Lake, Castle Lake, Toad Lake, and Heart Lake—are ideal for secluded swimming and fishing. Of the lakes, **Lake Siskiyou** is the most popular and accessible, though it tends to be crowded. Stop by the Shasta-Trinity National Forest Service station in Mt. Shasta for detailed info on these spots. At all lakes, beach use is $1.

SHASTA LAKE. Shasta Lake is the largest reservoir in California. Campgrounds and picnic areas pepper the lake's 450 mi. of coast, most of which is beachless. While the lake is popular with watersports enthusiasts, it may also be enjoyed simply by jumping into the sapphire blue water. *(Shasta Lake sits on I-5 30min. south of Mt. Shasta and 15min. north of Redding.)* Completed in 1945, the **Shasta Dam,** off I-5 at the

Shasta Dam Blvd. exit, is three times taller than Niagara Falls, and, after the Grand Coulee in Washington, is the second-largest dam in the US. The views from the dam are amazing. *(Dam Visitor Center in Dam Park. ☎275-4463. Open daily M-F 8am-4:30pm, Sa-Su 8:30am-5pm.)* **Bailey Cove,** has five RV sites (no hookups) and seven tent sites on Lake Shasta. Drinking water and flush toilets are among the few amenities available. *(Just off I-5. ☎275-1857. Open Mar.-Nov. Sites $15.)*

WHISKEYTOWN UNIT. Eight miles west of Redding are the popular beaches, marinas, campsites, and hiking trails of **Whiskeytown Lake and Recreation Center,** which is easily accessible from Rte. 299. In the peak summer season, boat traffic is heavy and the large number of visitors makes for crowded conditions. Nevertheless, the lake is a scenic escape from the endless pavement of nearby Redding. The recreation area has many well-maintained **campgrounds ❶**—though some RV sites are really just crowded parking lots with little shade. *(Park entrance fee $5 per vehicle per day, $10 per week.)* The **Whiskeytown Unit Visitors Center,** at Rte. 299 and Kennedy Memorial Dr., south of the lake, sells day-use permits for $5. Reserve campsites through Biospherics *(☎800-365-2267; http://reservations.nps.gov).* The **Oak Bottom Campground,** off Rte. 299, has 22 RV sites (no hookups) and 100 developed tent sites near a beach, picnic area, snack bar, and marina, as well as drinking water and flush toilets. *(Sites May 15-Sept. 15 $16, lakeside $18; Sept. 16-May 14 $8.)* Nearby **Oak Bottom Marina** rents ski boats, sailboats, patio boats, and canoes. *(☎359-2269. Canoes $21 for 3hr.; sailboats $42 for 3hr. Open M-Th 7am-8pm, F-Su 7am-9pm.)* To escape the crowds, you can pick up backcountry camping and hiking permits at **Park Headquarters,** which provides info on a number of primitive **campsites ❶.** *(☎246-1225. 14-day max. stay. Open daily spring-fall 9am-6pm; in winter 10am-4pm. Sites $10 per night; in winter $5.)*

ASHLAND
☎541

Just over the California border, Ashland (pop. 20,000) mixes hip youth and stunning outdoors to set an unlikely but intriguing stage for the world-famous Oregon Shakespeare Festival. Though stores cater to school groups descending for their yearly dose of the Bard, Ashland's food, nightlife, and culture are astounding for a town of this size. When the setting sun hits the mountain ranges on either side of this charming hamlet, the hills light up in sonnet-inspiring glory.

▐ TRANSPORTATION. Coming from California, take I-5 north and get off at the Ashland/Klamath Falls exit. Merge onto Siskiyou Blvd. and follow it into town. **Greyhound** (☎482-8803) runs from Mr. C's Market, where I-5 meets Rte. 99 north of town. Three buses per day go to: Portland (6¾hr., $50-54); Sacramento (6¼hr., $50-54); and San Francisco (10½hr., $60-64). **Rogue Valley Transportation District (RVTD;** ☎779-2877; www.rvtd.org), runs the #10 bus between the transfer station at 200 S. Front St. in Medford and the plaza in Ashland (35min.) before making several stops on a loop through downtown. In-town rides are free. Bus #10 runs through Ashland every 30min. from 5am-7pm.

▟▐ ORIENTATION AND PRACTICAL INFORMATION. Ashland sits in the foothills of the Siskiyou and Cascade Ranges, 15 mi. north of the California border and 285 mi. south of Portland, near the junction of **I-5** and **Route 66.** Rte. 99 cuts through the middle of town on a northwest-southeast axis. It becomes **North Main Street** as it enters town from the west, and then splits briefly into **East Main Street** and **Lithia Way** as it runs through the highly walkable downtown. Farther south, Main St. changes name again to **Siskiyou Boulevard,** where Southern Oregon University (SOU) is flanked by affordable motels.The Ashland **Chamber of Com-**

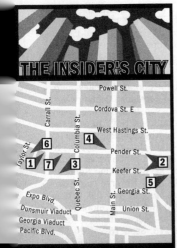

Powell St.

Carrall St.

Columbia St.

Cordova St. E

West Hastings St.

Taylor St.

6

4

Pender St.

1 **7** **3**

2

Keefer St.

Quebec St.

5

Georgia St.

Expo Blvd.

Main St.

Union St.

Dunsmuir Viaduct

Georgia Viaduct

Pacific Blvd.

DRINK DEEP ERE YOU DEPART

Ashland's nightlife scene is denser than a dark microbrewed stout—you could easily enjoy a week of partying in the clubs and bars in the town square. All pubs are 21+ unless otherwise noted.

1 Mellow out on the huge outdoor deck at the **Ashland Creek Bar & Grill**, 92 N. Main St. (☎482-4131). W DJ, F-Sa blues, ska, and reggae. Cover $1-3. Open daily 11am-2am.

2 Head next to the **Siskiyou Brew Pub**, 31 Water St. (☎482-7718), the most laid-back bar in town. Occasional live music 21+ after 9pm. Cover $5-10. Open M-Th from 4pm, F-Su from 3pm.

3 If you shoot pool, the place to be is **Q's Bar & Grill**, 140 Lithia Way (☎488-4880). W live music, Th college night (well drinks $1-3), Sa shot night. Open Su-W 11am-1am, Th-Sa 11am-2:30am.

merce, 110 E. Main St., has tons of brochures on the area. (☎482-3486; www.ashlandchamber.com Open M-F 9am-5pm.) The **police station** (☎488-2211) is at 20 E. Main St. The newly expanded **Ashland Library,** 410 Siskiyou Blvd., at Gresham St., offers 18min. of free **Internet access** on three computers and free wireless. (☎482-1151; www.jcls.org. Open M-Tu noon-7pm, W-Th 10am-6pm, F-Sa noon-5pm.) **Evo's Java House** (see below) also provides free access on one computer or via their wireless network. The **post office** is at 120 N. 1st St., at Lithia Way. (☎800-275-8777. Open M-F 9am-5pm.) **Postal Code:** 97520.

✝ ACCOMMODATIONS. In the winter, Ashland is a budget traveler's paradise of motel vacancies and low rates; in summer, every room in town fills in the blink of an eye and rates rise sky-high. Only rogues and peasant slaves arrive without reservations. The Victorian parlor and sturdy bunks of the ✪**Ashland Hostel ❷,** 150 N. Main St., play host to theater-goers, Pacific Coast Trail hikers, and other Ashland visitors. It's conveniently located near the theaters and town square. (☎482-9217; www.ashlandhostel.com. No A/C. Linen $2. Check-in 5-10pm. Lockout 10am-5pm. Dorms $21; private rooms $50. Cash only.) **Columbia Hotel ❸,** 262½ E. Main St. oozes charm. Each room is decorated with antique-style furniture. A reading alcove and morning tea round out this historic home-turned-Euro-style hotel. Even better, its only two blocks from the theaters and has free wireless Internet. (☎482-3726 or 800-718-2530; www.columbiahotel.com. Doubles June-Oct. $69, with bath from $105; Mar.-June $49-89. 10% HI discount in low season.) Save money by camping at **Mt. Ashland Campground ❶,** 20min. south of Ashland off I-5 at Exit 6. Follow signs for Mt. Ashland Ski Area through the parking lot. Nine sites in the forest overlook the valley and Mt. Shasta, and can be snowy into June. (No drinking water. Free.)

▢ FOOD. The plaza at N. and E. Main St. has restaurants whose quality matches that of the theater festival. **The Ashland Food Cooperative,** 237 N. 1st St., stocks cheap and organic groceries in bulk. (☎482-2237; www.asfs.org. Open M-Sa 8am-9pm, Su 9am-9pm.) Cheaper groceries are available at **Safeway,** 585 Siskiyou Blvd. (☎482-4495. Open daily 6am-midnight.) Whether it's breakfast on the rose-entwined wooden porticos or lunch by the fireplace, ✪**Morning Glory ❷,** 1149 Siskiyou Blvd. charms diners with its decor and its organic coffee. Incredible scrambles, and waffles, and sandwiches are all around $9. (☎488-8636. Open daily 7am-2pm.) If you're hungry and sick of the Man keeping you down, fight back at

Evo's Java House and Revolutionary Cafe ❶, 376 E. Main St. , where the politics are as radical as the vegetarian burritos and sandwiches ($3.50-5) are tasty. Once or twice a week you can listen to live folk, punk, or metal. (☎774-6980. Free wireless Internet. Occasional cover for music. Open M-Sa 7am-5pm, Su 7am-2pm.) Load up on delicious Indian food at **Three Rivers ❷**, 1640 Ashland St. (☎482-0776. All-you-can-eat lunch buffet $8, dinner buffet $9. Open M-Su 11:30am-2:30pm and 5-9pm.)

📷🎶 **SIGHTS AND ENTERTAINMENT.** At the 📷**Oregon Shakespeare Festival** (☎482-4331; www.osfashland.org), professional actors perform 11 plays in repertory, only three or four of which are by Shakespeare. Performances run on the three Ashland stages from mid-February through October. The 1200-seat **Elizabethan Stage,** an outdoor theater modeled after a 17th-century London design, is open from mid-June to mid-October and hosts three plays per season (usually by Shakespeare). The **Angus Bowmer Theater** is a 600-hundred seat indoor stage that shows a variety of comedies and dramas. The **New Theater,** still awaiting a $7 million donor for a name, seats 250-350, shows experimental work, and serves as a modern replacement for the aging Black Swan Theater, which is now used for festival lectures and rehearsals. The 2005 schedule includes *Twelfth Night, Richard III, Love's Labours Lost*, and several contemporary plays.

To ensure seats, purchase tickets up to six months in advance. The **Box Office,** 15 S. Pioneer St., is next to the Elizabethan and Bowmer Theaters, across the street from the New Theater. Last-minute theatergoers should not abandon hope. At 9:30am, the box office releases **unsold tickets** for the day's performances. Arrive at least 1hr. early; local patrons have been known to leave their shoes in line to hold their places. When no tickets are available, limited priority numbers are given out. These entitle their holders to a designated place in line when the precious few returned tickets are released (noon for matinees, 6pm for evening shows). For those truly desperate for their Shakespeare fix, the Box Office also sells 20 clearview **standing room tickets** for sold-out shows on the Elizabethan Stage ($13; available on the day of the show). Half-price **rush tickets** are occasionally available 1hr. before performances not already sold out. All three theaters hold full-performance **previews** in the spring at considerable discounts. Unofficial ticket transactions take place all the time just outside the Box Office, but those "buying on the bricks" should check the date and time on

4 Let the dancing begin at **Tabú,** 79 N. Pioneer St. (☎482-3900). Good acoustics and a great bar area give this place a classy feel. Th and Sa salsa, F DJ. Cover $3. Afterwards, relax downstairs at the gay-friendly bar **Abajo.** W ladies night, F-Sa martini bar. Restaurant open W-Su 11:30am-3pm, daily 5-10pm. Club open Th-Sa 10pm-2:30am. Lounge open W-Th 7:30pm-1am, F-Sa 5am-1am.

5 Regain your saucy edge with an ale from **Black Sheep,** 51 N. Main St. (☎482-6414), one of the only authentic English pubs in Oregon. In the afternoon, they make great scones. 18+ after 11pm. Open daily 11:30am-1:30am.

6 If drinking ballads aren't your thing, go techno at **Kat Wok,** 62 E. Main St. (☎482-0787). By day it's a restaurant/sushi bar, by night a club with laser lights and a glow-in-the-dark pool table. Th hip-hop and R&B, F alternative, Sa dance mix. Cover $3-5. Open daily from 5pm.

7 Finally, to sample a slice of student life, visit **Louie's,** 41 N. Main St. (☎482-9701), a sports bar with cheap beer that is packed with SOU students during the school year. Bar open Th-Sa until 1:30am.

the ticket carefully and pay no more than face value. (Box Office: ☎482-4331; www.osfashland.org. Open Tu-Su 9:30am-performance, M and non-performance days 9:30am-5pm. No children under 6. Mail-order and phone ticket sales begin Jan. Tickets $29-55; spring previews and fall shows $23-44. $5 fee per order by phone, fax, or mail. Ages 6-18 25% off in summer, 50% off in spring and fall. For complete ticket info, visit the website.)

Backstage tours provide a wonderful glimpse of the festival from behind the curtain. Tour guides (usually actors or technicians) divulge all kinds of anecdotes—from the story of bird songs during an outdoor staging of *Hamlet* to the time a door on the set used for almost every stage entrance and exit locked itself midway through the show, provoking over 30min. of hilarious improvisation before it was fixed during intermission. (Tickets available at the Box Office. 2hr. tours leave from the Black Swan Tu-Su at 10am. $11, ages 6-17 $8.25; no children under 6.) In mid-June, the **Feast of Will** celebrates the annual opening of the Elizabethan Theater with dinner and merry madness in Lithia Park. (Call the Box Office for details. Tickets $12.) **Festival Noons,** a mix of lectures and concerts held in the courtyard just outside the Elizabethan Theatre, occur almost every day at noon beginning in mid-June. Most are free, but some require tickets ($7-9).

Before it imported Shakespeare, Ashland was naturally blessed with **lithia water,** which contains dissolved lithium salts reputed to have miraculous healing powers. It is said that only one other spring in the world has a higher lithium concentration. To try the water, hold your nose and head for the circle of **fountains** in the plaza center. Besides these aquatic phenomena, **Lithia Park** features free concerts, readings, nature walks around hiking trails, a Japanese garden, and swan ponds. An artisans' market sets up in the park on summer weekends.

LAVA BEDS NATIONAL MONUMENT ☎530

At first glance, Lava Beds National Monument appears a stark sea of arid grasses, sagebrush, and craggy rocks. But beneath this 73 sq. mi. expanse lies a complex web of more than 500 lava-formed caves and otherworldly tunnels. Cool, quiet, and often eerie tubes range from claustrophobic 12 in. crawl spaces to 80 ft. cathedrals. The product of lava flows from the Mammoth Crater around 30,000 years ago, these tubes were formed when the outer layer of a flow contacted the colder ground or air around it and hardened to create a sheet that insulated the molten lava inside. The hot, fluid lava continued to flow away, leaving hollow conduits under the earth after the lava flow ceased. In spring and fall, nearby Tule Lake Refuge provides a stopover for migratory birds, some of which come from as far away as Siberia. The fall migration is particularly spectacular, when a million ducks and half a million geese literally darken the sky. In winter, this is the best place in the contiguous US to see a bald eagle. For people, however, Lava Beds and the Tule Lake Refuge present a more challenging destination, due mostly to their remoteness and harsh climate; expect blistering heat and little water in the monument. Local accommodations are sparse, and those seeking less desolate motels should plan on making the drive to Mt. Shasta (see p. 201).

✦ ⊓ ORIENTATION AND PRACTICAL INFORMATION

Although cold weather can pervade the high desert climate at any time of the year, summer weather tends to be arid, with hot days (75-80°F and not an inch of shade) and cool nights (50°F). It takes a full day to really appreciate the park, and you'll need a car not only to access the park but also to explore its northern reaches. The nearest spot to catch a bus, rent a car, or find a hospital is across the Oregon border in **Klamath Falls,** 50 mi. north of Lava Beds.

Lava Beds is southwest of the tiny town of **Tulelake** (pop. 1000) and northeast of **Mt. Shasta.** The **southeast entrance** (25 mi. south of Tulelake) is closest to the visitors center and follows a seriously potholed road. The two northern entrances are closer to Klamath Basin Wildlife Refuge and the Oregon border. The **north entrance** is on Hill Rd., which can be reached from State Rd. 161 (State Line Rd.). County Rd. 111 splits from Rte. 139 about 8 mi. southeast of Tulelake and leads to the **northeast entrance** before winding through the wilder northern areas of the monument for 25 mi. to the visitors center. Visitors coming from the south on I-5 should take a circuitous route, following U.S. 97 North, then Rte. 161 East to S. Hill Rd. For cheap gas, hop over the Oregon border on Rte. 139 N to Merrill.

Lava Beds Visitors Center, in the park's southeast corner, has exhibits on Modoc culture and the battles that took place around the monument. The well-informed staff lends flashlights to explorers (free; return them by 5:30pm, in winter by 4:30pm) and sells souvenir hardhats for $3.90. (☎667-2282; www.nps.gov/labe. Open daily May 26-Aug. 8am-6pm; Sept.-May 25 8am-5pm. One guided cave tour leaves the visitors center daily at 2pm. The Tulelake **police** station (☎800-404-2911 or 667-5284) is located at the corner of 24th St. and C St. **Bring plenty of water and food**—there are no concessions at the monument.

🏠🍴 ACCOMMODATIONS AND FOOD

There are a few roadside motels in Tulelake. Each is fairly isolated, set between agricultural fields and Rte. 139. The best of the bunch is the **Ellis Motel ❸**, 2238 Rte. 139, 1 mi. north of Tulelake, which sits behind a manicured lawn with only a row of large shady trees separating it from the highway. There are 11 small, simple rooms, some with kitchens. (☎667-5242. Singles from $35; doubles from $45.) The only developed campground in Lava Beds is **Indian Well ❶**, opposite the visitors center, featuring 43 well-spaced sites with picnic tables, fire pits, and a fantastic view of the stars. Fortunately, you can now bypass the hellish walk across the jagged volcanic rocks to this long-used Indian camp by driving right up to the sites. Drinking water and flush toilets. No reservations. Sites $10.) The monument has two wilderness areas separated by the main north-south road for **backcountry camping ❶**. A wilderness permit is not required. Cooking is limited to stoves, and camps must be at least 1 mi. from trailheads, roads, and parking areas, and 150 ft. from cave entrances. **Modoc National Forest** borders the monument and offers free **camping ❶**. Fifteen miles south of the monument, **Medicine Lake** and **Hemlock** campgrounds ❶ have water and flush toilets, as well as opportunities to fish, swim and boat. (Sites $7.) More info is available at the **Modoc Doublehead Ranger Station,** 1 mi. south of Tulelake on Rte. 139, near a set of metal silos. (☎667-2246. Open M-F 8am-4:30pm.) If you're looking for a little more of a wilderness experience, ask park rangers about the **Bulls Eye Lake** campgrounds.

Jock's, at the corner of Modoc and Main St., in Tulelake, is a decently sized grocery store. (☎667-2612. Open M-Sa 7am-8pm, Su 9am-6pm.) **Captain Jack's Stronghold Restaurant ❷**, 5 mi. south of Tulelake, and 1 mi. south of the turn-off to Lava Beds, serves homemade soups and breads and has a sizable salad bar. The diverse menu, prime location, pleasant outdoor porch, and welcoming floral decorations attract locals and tourists. (☎664-5566. Breakfast and lunch $6-8. Dinner $8-13. Open Feb.-Nov. Tu-W 7am-8pm, Th-Sa 7am-9pm, Su 9am-8pm.)

👁 🚶 SIGHTS

SPELUNKING

The lava beds, mostly linear lava tubes, offer novice cavers relatively easy expeditions into the underground. But "easy" is not to say that the caves aren't pitch black, perfectly silent, and generally spooky. Though never more than a few hundred feet below the surface, the caves can inspire a sense of isolation that few other experiences provide. Hardhats, on sale at the visitors center for $3.90, or other helmets are essential unless you're under 12 in. tall; the unusually sharp ceilings have an uncanny affinity for human heads. Another necessary cave-going accessory is a sweatshirt or jacket; the sun-swept desert can be scorching, but the caves below are cool and damp. Perhaps the most essential piece of equipment is a flashlight or two, which you can pick up for free at the visitors center. Cave tours, leaving from the visitors center for a different cave each day, explain the fascinating phenomena associated with the caves. (Tours mid-June-Aug. daily 2pm.) Solo exploring is not recommended but is allowed; bring at least two flashlights.

Of the hundreds of caves in the park, nearly three dozen can be explored by the public. All caves are technically public, but under the Cave Protection Act, only a few can have their location disclosed. The most worthwhile caves are among the disclosed caves; it is generally not worth looking for the unmarked caves. The **Mushpot Cave**, 500 ft. down the hill from the visitors center parking lot, has a short, well-lit trail to acquaint visitors with cave formations. **Valentine Cave**, south of the visitors center, is perhaps the best and most surreal of the area's caves, with unnaturally smooth walls due to its more recent formation. The **Skull Cave**, 3½ mi. north of the visitors center, is the widest in the park, with 80 ft. high ceilings. It gets its name from the two human skeletons found chilling alongside wagonloads of bighorn sheep skulls. The sheep were lured in by the moisture emanating from the cave (there is year-round ice at the bottom), but now serve as a testament to the importance of a helmet and flashlight. The human skeletons are still a complete mystery. The 2¼ mi. **Cave Loop Road**, which starts and finishes at the visitors center, passes by 20 caves, but gives little guidance beyond the entrance stairways. Parking is available at each entrance. **Sentinel Cave**, one of the last on the loop, has crisscrossing tunnels, skylights, and two entrances. **Golden Dome** is structurally unremarkable, save for some impressive lavacicles, but the hydrophobic bacteria-encrusted ceiling has an incredible golden hue. The most complex of the public tunnels is the **Catacombs Cave**, where the ceiling dips as low as 1 ft. Visitors crawl a good deal of the over 1 mi. of interconnected passageways. Ask for a photocopy of the technical map at the visitors center or buy the book with technical maps of the whole park ($4.50), and allow 4-6hr.

HIKING

Trails of varying difficulty wander through the park. Hikers should keep in mind that the area is essentially a desert, with little shade and extreme heat. The **Whitney Butte Trail** leads through rocky brush to the black Callahan Lava Flow, a 3½ mi. (one way) route from the trailhead at Merrill Cave. The **Mammoth Crater** is more a sight than hike, offering all the excitement of a huge volcanic crater with none of the annoying molten rock and exploding cinder. For an overnight hike, the **Lyons Trail** traverses 10 mi. from Skull Cave to Hospital Rock over the rocky, hot moonscape in the park's eastern reaches. It's a great hike for those who enjoy hiking on sharp, unstable rocks in intense heat. Consult a ranger before you go.

Four miles north of the visitors center is **Schonchin Butte.** The steep, three-quarter mile ascent takes about 30min. and leads to a fire lookout that provides a broad view of the landscape rising up to the massive white face of Mt. Shasta. Close to Lava Bed's northern entrance is **Captain Jack's Stronghold,** a natural lava fortress where Modoc warriors and US troops battled during the Modoc War. Be sure to stop at the visitors center before you go to pick up the interpretive guide. **Petroglyph Point,** just outside the northern entrance, is the cliff wall of a former island (the lake surrounding the island was drained), covered with a large collection of native rock carvings. Native Americans had to paddle across a lake to the cliff, where they engraved mountain- and human-like images. A few carvings from before 1950, such as Japanese characters engraved by prisoners of the internment camps, are also historic. The ugly barbed wire fence guarding the walls prevents further efforts to leave inscrutable messages for posterity.

BEYOND LAVA BEDS   ☎ 530

Tule Lake and **Lower Klamath National Wildlife Refuge** are most easily accessed via Lava Beds. The first wildlife refuge in the US set aside specifically for waterfowl, the Lower Klamath National Wildlife Refuge absolutely teems with them. The drive from Tulelake to Lava Beds runs through the Tule Lake Refuge. Over a million birds migrate through the refuge each year, including bald eagles and pelicans; the best time to see the eagles is winter. **Lower Klamath and Tule Lake Wildlife Refuge Visitors Center and Headquarters,** on Hill Rd., 4 mi. south of Rte. 161 and 18 mi. north of Lava Beds Visitors Center, has a small **museum** with a high-quality slide show and many a stuffed bird and beast. A canoe route is open from July through September, and has 2 mi. of marked "trails" for quiet and up-close observation. Ask at the visitors center for directions. (☎ 667-2231; www.klamathbasinrefuges.fws.gov. Open M-F 8am-4:30pm, Sa-Su 10am-4pm.) Car tours are available in the Tule Lake and Lower Klamath Refuges. The "Tule Lake tour" is best.

The **Tule Lake internment camp** is a relic of a dark side of American history. More than 18,000 Japanese-Americans were held here by the US government during WWII. The camp is in Newell, 4 mi. north of Petroglyph Point. Not much remains except a plaque, a couple of ruined buildings, and old fence-lines.

YREKA   ☎ 530

Yreka (why-REE-ka; pop. 7500) is a good ol' American town—strip malls, motels, and gas stations. Founded as a Gold Rush town in 1852 and named after a nearby mountain range, today Yreka is the trade center for Siskiyou County. Among the town's few attractions are the largest gold display south of Alaska and numerous historic buildings. Yreka makes a good stop on the way to the wealth of outdoor activities in the area, but is hardly a destination in and of itself.

◪ ⁊ ORIENTATION AND PRACTICAL INFORMATION. Yreka is conveniently stationed on I-5, 22 mi. south of the Oregon border, 40 mi. north of Mt. Shasta, and 260 mi. north of Sacramento. **Greyhound,** 115 E. Miner St. (☎ 842-3145; open daily 8am-5pm) runs to: Mt. Shasta (50min., 1 per day, $10-11); Redding (2hr., 3 per day, $25-27); San Francisco (9-10hr., 3 per day, $57-61); Portland, OR (8-9hr., 2 per day, $61-66). The **Chamber of Commerce,** 117 W. Miner St., is the most reliable source for visitor information. (☎ 842-1649; www.yrekachamber.com. Open M-Sa 9am-5pm, Su 10am-4pm; winter M-F 9am-5pm.) Other services include: **Klamath National Forest Headquarters** and **Clouds National Forest Ranger,** 1312 Fairlane Rd. (☎ 842-6131; open M-F 8am-4:30pm); the **hospital,** 444 Bruce

CLOSE, BUT NO SECESSION

Imagine a state with no taxes and the slogan, "Our roads are not passable, hardly jackassable." Such a state was nearly established during the 1941 secession of the "State of Jefferson." Due to the lack of sufficient roads and bridges to Northern California and Southern Oregon, the region's abundant supply of minerals and timber was inaccessible, and for nearly 100 years, Sacramento and Salem had refused to recognize the isolated area.

In November of 1941, representatives from the mountain border counties of Lassen, Modoc, Siskiyou, Del Norte, and Curry met in Yreka to form an alliance to obtain federal aid for the construction and repair of bridges and roads. The Siskiyou Daily News offered a $2 prize to name the 49th state—"Jefferson" won. Later, Yreka was designated state capital, and members of the rebellion stopped traffic on Hwy. 99 to pass out their Proclamation of Independence. A governor was elected and the streets closed in celebration. Newsreels recorded the festivities, which were scheduled to air nationally on Dec. 8. But when Pearl Harbor was bombed on Dec. 7, focus shifted, and the rebellion movement ended. Today, a lone barn roof on the side of I-5 emblazoned with "The State of Jefferson" is the only reminder of the proud little state that almost was.

St. (☎842-4121); and the **post office,** 401 S. Broadway at Center St. (☎842-9372; open M-F 8:30am-5pm). **Postal Code:** 96097.

⚐❒ ACCOMMODATIONS AND FOOD. The southern end of Main St. is the most promising for high-value accommodations. **The Klamath Motor Lodge ❸,** 1111 S. Main St., is a friendly spot with large, immaculate rooms, phones, microwaves, popcorn, cable TV, A/C, and a grassy picnic area with a grill and pool. (☎842-2751 or 800-551-7255. Singles from $52, doubles $64; in winter singles $48, doubles $59.) **The Miner's Inn ❹,** 122 E. Miner St., off I-5, is a step above the standard motor lodge. Spacious, spotless rooms have cable TV, phone, and coffee, while suites are two-bedroom apartments with kitchens. The grounds include two heated pools. (☎842-4355. Singles and doubles $74-84; suites $105. In winter $3-5 less.)

Yreka fare ranges from truck-stop convenience to organic nutrients to tourist taverns. **Nature's Kitchen ❷,** 412 S. Main St., is decorated with faux vines, fresh flowers, candles, and a mishmash of Christian and Hindu iconography, but it's all charming. Try a Monterey Jack and avocado sandwich with a sesame-and-garlic seasoned salad or a bowl of soup for only $6. An organic bakery and espresso bar are attached. (☎842-1136. Open M-Sa 8am-3pm.) Another local favorite, **Poor George's Family Restaurant ❶,** 108 W. Oberlin Rd., just west of Main St., is what Denny's wishes it could be. Seniors and skaters munch on burgers (around $6), sandwiches ($4-6), salads ($3-6), and steak and eggs ($8) amid a juke box, paintings of bald eagles, and other Americana. Breakfast ($4-9) is served all day. (☎842-4664. Open M-F 6am-7:45pm, Sa-Su 7am-1:45pm.)

REDDING   ☎530

At first glance, Redding may seem little more than urban planning gone awry. The city is virtually unwalkable, riven with freeways, and dispersed without a central downtown. Despite its lack of charm, Redding is a convenient, if not essential, supply stop when headed to Shasta Lake, Lassen Volcanic National Park, or the Trinity Wilderness; the city is strategically located at the crossroads of I-5 and Rtes. 44 and 299, and has a large number of hotels and gas stations. Recent construction of a "sundial" footbridge designed by world-famous Spanish architect Santiago Caltraveras has brought national attention and increased beauty to this gateway to the mountains.

TRANSPORTATION. There is an unstaffed **Amtrak** train station at 1620 Yuba St. (☎800-USA-RAIL/872-7245). Buy a ticket on the train or directly through Amtrak. Trains depart to: Sacramento (4hr., 1 per day, $26); San Francisco (6hr., 1 per day, $40); and Portland, OR (12-13hr., 1 per day, $77). **Greyhound buses,** 1321 Butte St. (☎241-2531 or 800-231-2222), at Pine St., depart from the 24hr. station to: Sacramento (4hr., 6 per day, $23); San Francisco (5-8hr., 6 per day, $35); and Portland, OR(8-10hr., 5 per day, $54).

ORIENTATION AND PRACTICAL INFORMATION. Redding is on I-5, 160 mi. north of Sacramento and 100 mi. south of Yreka. Shasta Lake is 16 mi. north of Redding on I-5, and Mt. Shasta is 60 mi. north. Get informed at the **Visitors Bureau,** 777 Auditorium Dr., off Rte. 299 at the Convention Center exit. (☎225-4100 or 800-874-7562; www.visitredding.com. Open M-F 8am-6pm, Sa-Su 10am-5pm.) Call the **Shasta Lake Ranger District,** 14225 Holiday Rd., for local conditions or camping info. (☎275-1589. Open M-Sa 8:30am-5pm, Su 8am-4:30pm.) Other services include: **police,** 1313 California St. (☎225-4200); **Redding Medical Center,** 1100 Butte St. (☎244-5400), at East St.; and the **post office,** 2323 Churn Creek Rd. (☎223-7523; open M-F 8:30am-5:30pm, Sa 9am-3pm). **Postal Code:** 96049.

ACCOMMODATIONS AND FOOD. The Visitors Bureau has free vacation planners with a variety of coupons for area and state accommodations. Standard, inexpensive rooms can be found at the **Hilltop Lodge ❸,** 2240 Hilltop Dr. The rooms are a little scuffed but clean and comfortable, and all have phone, cable TV, A/C, and access to an outdoor pool. (☎221-5432. Singles and doubles M-F $39, Sa-Su $49.) **Best Western Ponderosa Inn,** 2220 Pine St., is a step above most motels in Redding. Its 69 rooms are spacious and have cable TV, A/C, and pool access. (☎241-6300. Continental breakfast included. Singles $59-64; doubles $59-70.) Campers can choose from the numerous options at Whiskeytown Lake and Shasta Lake (p. 206). For those who want to do their own cooking, **Safeway,** 2275 East St., has an extensive selection of groceries, fresh produce, a deli, and a coffee shop. (☎243-2985. Open daily 7am-midnight.) ❖**Buz's Crab ❷,** 2159 East St., next to Safeway, offers a huge selection of the best seafood in the area at fantastic prices. Order from the gigantic menu as you enter, then sit down below the hanging anchors and fishnets to wait for your meal. Fish (or oysters or calamari) and chips ($3-8), hot crab sandwiches ($6.25), and crabcake burgers ($7.50) are all delicious. (☎243-2120; www.buzscrab.com. Open daily 11am-9pm.)

NORTHERN INTERIOR

THE NORTH COAST

Windswept and larger than life, the North Coast winds from the San Francisco Bay Area to the Oregon border. Redwoods tower over undiscovered black-sand beaches, and otters frolic next to jutting rock formations—the North Coast's untouched wilderness is simply stunning. From the Marin Headlands, Hwy. 1 snakes along craggy cliffs between pounding surf and monolithic redwoods. The quaint coastal hamlets spaced along the highway offer opportunities to recover from the heart-stopping journey. Be prepared, however, for slow trailers on the road and sky-high prices. The least expensive and most rewarding options are out-doors—camping, hiking, and picnicking. The coast is also home to some of the loveliest inns and B&Bs around, which may persuade travelers to splurge after a week in the wilderness. An hour north of Fort Bragg, Hwy. 1 turns sharply inland and travels away from the coast, merging with U.S. 101 for the journey north. The highway skips a stretch of coastline known as the Lost Coast, which contains some of the most rugged scenery in the state. Lost Coast marijuana farmers are (in)famous for cultivating what smokers consider to be some of the strongest bud in the world. U.S. 101 brings travelers to the Avenue of the Giants, home of the red-woods that make the region famous. North of the lively liberal towns of Eureka and Arcata, U.S. 101 winds back to the coast where more redwoods tower peace-fully, protected within the long strips of Redwood National and State Parks.

HIGHLIGHTS OF THE NORTH COAST

SAMOA COOKHOUSE. The only operational lumberjack-style cookhouse in the country serves meals huge enough to fuel hikes through the redwoods (p. 227).

KINETIC SCULPTURE RACE. Eccentric Humboldt County outdoes itself in this annual race of bizarre, artistic vehicles (p. 225).

MENDOCINO HEADLANDS. Blustery cliffs overlooking the Pacific make for solitary hiking or romantic, windswept picnicking (p. 235).

REDWOOD NATIONAL AND STATE PARKS ☎ 707

With ferns as tall as humans and redwood trees the size of skyscrapers, Redwood National and State Parks celebrate nature's awe-inspiring extremes. The red-woods are the last remaining stretch of the old-growth forest that used to blanket two million acres of Northern California and Oregon. Within the parks, wildlife runs free; black bears and mountain lions roam the backwoods and Roosevelt elk graze the meadows. While a short tour of the big sights and the drive-through trees certainly allows ample photo opportunities, a more intimate experience of the red-woods requires heading down a trail into the quiet of the forest, where you can see trees as they have stood for thousands of years.

⊞ ORIENTATION

Redwood National and State Parks is an umbrella term for four contiguous red-wood parks. The parks span 40 mi. of coast and two counties, with information centers and unique attractions throughout. **Redwood National Park** is the southern-most of the four; the others, from south to north, are **Prairie Creek Redwoods State Park, Del Norte Coast Redwoods State Park,** and **Jedediah Smith Redwoods State Park. U.S. 101** traverses most of the parks. The slower but more scenic **Newton Drury Parkway** runs parallel to U.S. 101 for about 9 mi. from Klamath to Prairie Creek

AT A GLANCE: REDWOOD NATIONAL PARK

AREA: 105,516 acres.

CLIMATE: Cool and foggy.

FEATURES: Tall Trees Grove, Fern Canyon, Battery Point Lighthouse.

HIGHLIGHTS: Whale-watching at Patrick's Point, hiking to the Boyscout Tree, exploring tide pools in Crescent City.

GATEWAYS: Orick, Klamath.

CAMPING: Developed and undeveloped sites. Many accept reservations. Backcountry camping permitted

FEES AND RESERVATIONS: Entrance to the National Park is free. $4 entrance fee at Jedediah Smith, Del Norte Coast, and Prairie Creek Redwoods State Parks.

(watch for bikers). **Crescent City,** with park headquarters, grocery stores, and plenty of fast food, is at the far northern end of the park region. The **Klamath** area to the south consists of a thin stretch of parkland connecting Prairie Creek with Del Norte State Park. The town itself consists of a few stores stretched over 4 mi.; the main attraction here is the spectacular coastline. **Orick** (pop. 650) is a somewhat desolate town overrun with souvenir stores selling burl sculptures (expensive hand-crafted wood carvings) and cows (which outnumber the people). However, it also has a post office and a market for campfire groceries. Just south of town is an extremely helpful ranger station.

▐ TRANSPORTATION

Greyhound, 500 E. Harding St. (☎ 464-2807), in Crescent City, runs one or two buses daily, one in the morning and one in the evening, to San Francisco ($61-71) and Portland, OR ($61-71). The station is only open for bus arrivals. Call for exact rates and departure times. **Redwood Coast Transit (RCT),** 421 U.S. 101 (☎ 464-9314), off Cooper St., runs buses from Crescent City to Klamath along U.S. 101, with various stops on the way ($1, under 6 free. M-Sa 6:30am-7:30pm). RCT also provides **dial-a-ride** M-F 7am-7pm and Sa 9am-5pm. Rides after 6pm must be prearranged a day in advance. $2.50, seniors and disabled $1, under 4 free.

▓ PRACTICAL INFORMATION

Entrance Fees: Charges vary by park and are different for camping, parking, and hiking. While there is usually there is no charge to enter, a day-use fee ($4 per car) for parking and picnic areas is typical.

Auto Repairs: AAA Emergency Road Service (☎ 800-222-4357). 24hr.

Visitor Information:

Jedediah Smith State Park Information Center (☎ 464-6101, ext. 5113), on US 199 across from the Hiouchi Ranger Station in the campground. Open June-Sept. daily 10am-4pm; Oct-May Su and W-Sa 10am-2pm.

Hiouchi Ranger Station (☎ 464-6101, ext. 5067), on U.S. 199 across from Jedediah Smith Redwoods Park. Open June-Sept. daily 9am-5pm.

Redwood National Park Headquarters and Information Center, 1111 2nd St. (☎ 464-6101, ext. 5826), in Crescent City. Headquarters of the entire national park, though ranger stations are just as well informed. Open daily 9am-5pm. Nov.-Mar. closed Su.

Crescent City-Del Norte County Chamber of Commerce, 1001 Front St. (☎ 464-3174 or 800-343-8300; www.northerncalifornia.net), in Crescent City. Free coffee, brochures, and coupons. Knowledgeable and friendly staff. Open June-Aug. daily 9am-5pm, Sept-May M-F 10am-4pm.

Prairie Creek Information Center (☎ 464-6101, ext. 5301), on the Newton Drury Scenic Pkwy. in Prairie Creek Redwood State Park. Open June-Aug. M-Th 9am-5pm, F-Su 9am-6pm, though hours may vary; Sept.-May daily 10am-5pm.

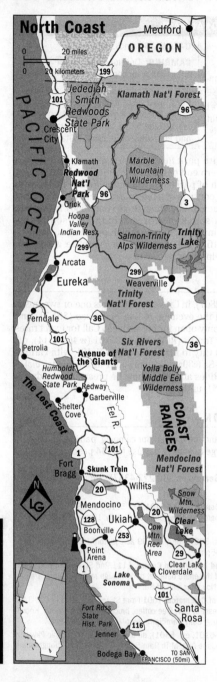

North Coast

OREGON

Medford ●

PACIFIC OCEAN

Jedediah
Smith
Redwoods
State Park

Crescent
City

Klamath

Redwood
Nat'l
Park

Orick

Hoopa
Valley
Indian Res.

Arcata

Eureka

Ferndale

Petrolia

Avenue of
the Giants

Humboldt
Redwood
State Park   Redway

The Lost Coast

Shelter
Cove   Garberville

Eel R.

Fort
Bragg   Skunk Train

Willits

Mendocino

Ukiah
Boonville

Point
Arena

Lake
Sonoma

Fort Ross
State
Hist. Park

Jenner

Bodega Bay

Klamath Nat'l Forest

Marble
Mountain
Wilderness

Salmon-Trinity
Alps Wilderness

Trinity
Lake

Weaverville

Trinity
Nat'l Forest

Six Rivers
Nat'l Forest

Yolla Bolly
Middle Eel
Wilderness

COAST RANGES

Mendocino
Nat'l Forest

Snow
Mtn.
Wilderness

Cow
Mtn.
Rec.
Area

Clear
Lake

Clear Lake

Cloverdale

Santa
Rosa

TO SAN
FRANCISCO (50mi)

N
LG

Six Rivers National Forest Station (☎457-3131), on U.S. 199 in Gasquet, has info about recreation opportunities in the Smith River National Recreation area and nearby campgrounds Panther Flat, Grassy Flat, and Big Flat. Open Jun.-Aug. M-Sa 8am-noon, 12:30-4:30pm; Sept.-May M-F 8am-noon, 12:30-4:30pm.

Thomas H. Kuchel Visitors Center (☎464-6101, ext. 5265), on U.S. 101, 1 mi. south of Orick. Shows an informative video on redwoods. Several maps available. Info on trails and campsites doled out by enthusiastic and helpful rangers. Open daily 9am-5pm.

ATMs: Bank of America, 240 H St., at 2nd St., in Crescent City. **Klamath Market,** 166 Klamath Blvd. (☎482-0211), in Klamath. Open M-Sa 8am-9pm, Su 9am-5pm. **Orick Market,** 121175 U.S. 101 (☎488-3225), in Orick. Open M-Sa 8am-7pm, Su 9am-6pm.

Laundromat: 101 Laundromat and Dry Cleaners, 503 L. St. (☎464-9230), in Crescent City. Wash $1.75, dry $0.25 per 8min. **Laundromat,** 110 Klamath Circle, in Klamath. Open daily 6am-8pm. Wash $1.50, dry $0.25 per 10min.

Hotlines: Rape Crisis Line, ☎465-2851. 24hr. **Road Conditions,** ☎800-427-7623.

Medical Services: Sutter Coast Hospital, 800 E. Washington Blvd. (☎464-8511), in Crescent City.

Library and Internet Access: Del Norte County Library, 190 Price Mall (☎464-9793), at the corner of K St. and Front St., in Crescent City. $1 per 30min. Open M and W-Th 10am-6pm, Tu 10am-8pm. **Orick School Library,** 120918 U.S. 101 (☎488-2821), in Orick. Free Internet June-Aug. W 11am-3pm; Sept.-May W 3-6pm.

Post Office: Crescent City, 751 2nd St. (☎464-2151) at H St. Open M-F 8:30am-5pm, Sa noon-2pm. **Postal Code:** 95531. **Orick,** 121147 U.S. 101 (☎488-3611). Open M-F 8:30am-noon and 1-4pm. **Postal Code:** 95555. **Klamath,** 141 Klamath Blvd. (☎482-2381). Open M-F 8am-1pm and 1:30-4:30pm. **Postal Code:** 95548.

ACCOMMODATIONS

Redwood Youth Hostel (HI-AYH), 14480 U.S. 101 (☎482-8265; www.redwoodhostel.com), at Wilson Creek Rd., 7 mi. north of downtown **Klamath.** The young family that runs this hostel welcomes travelers of all ages. Breathtaking sunsets from 2 ocean-view sundecks—the beach is just across the street. Simple chores and rules (no shoes inside) keep the house immaculate. Free parking. Check-in 5-10pm. Check-out 10am. Lockout 10am-5pm; day-use available for a fee. Curfew 10pm. Reservations recommended in summer. Dorms $18-19; under 18 half-price; doubles $45. ❷

Patrick Creek Lodge & Historical Inn, 13950 Hwy. 199 (☎457-3323; www.patrickcreeklodge.com), in **Gasquet,** northeast of Hiouchi. A sunny home away from home since 1926. Fish along the Smith River, swim in the pool, and enjoy the toasty fire and "creative cuisine" at night (dinner entrees $16-22). Extensive champagne brunch Su 10am-2pm ($19). Credit card required for reservations and check-in. Singles $47.50; doubles $80-90; cabins $130 for 2 people, each additional person up to 6 $20. ❸

Historic Requa Inn, 451 Requa Rd. (☎482-1425 or 866-800-8777), west off U.S. 101, about 1mi. from the **Klamath** overlook. Lace-curtained windows look out over the picturesque Klamath River. Breakfast (included) served in the Victorian parlor. Elegant evening dining M-Sa (entrees $12-22). Reservations recommended June-Sept. Rooms May-Sept. $85-135, Oct.-Apr. $79-120. ❺

Ravenwood Motel, 151 Klamath Blvd. (☎482-5911), off U.S. 101 in **Klamath.** A cute dog and his friendly owner run this motel conveniently located next to a market, cafe, and laundromat. Doubles $58; family units with full kitchen $105. ❸

Redwood National Park

▲ ACCOMMODATIONS
Camp Marigold, 9
Historic Requa Inn, 10
Patrick Creek Lodge & Historical Inn, 2
Penny Saver Inn, 4
Ravenwood Motel, 12
Redwood Youth Hostel (HI-AYH), 8

▲ FEE CAMPING
Big Flat, 7
Big Lagoon County Park, 15
Elk Prairie, 14
Gold Bluffs Beach, 13
Jedediah Smith Redwoods S.P., 3
Mill Creek, 6
Panther Flat, 1
Patrick's Point S.P., 16

△ FREE CAMPING
Flint Ridge, 11
Nickel Creek, 5

▲ Groves
ʎ Trailheads
Trail

THE LOCAL STORY

ELK MACHISMO

Easy to spot thanks to their massive size and signature cream-colored rumps, Roosevelt elk have rebounded from near extinction to populate the prairies of Sinkyone Wilderness State Park and Redwood National and State Parks. While the elk are normally no danger unless threatened, travelers should be extremely cautious around these potentially deadly animals, especially in the late summer and early fall. In mating season, male elks (bulls) form rivalries over control of an entire group of females, known as a "harem." A challenger bull approaches an already spoken-for harem and bugles, urinates, and kicks up turf in a show of desire. If the bull-in-residence answers the challenge, some poor cream-rump could end up losing an antler. However, one of the bulls usually backs down before things escalate to an antler clash, as should visitors who make the mistake of getting too close.

During calving season in early June, female elk are particularly protective of their young, making any human contact a dangerous situation. Should you meet an elk in the wild, keep your distance, stay still, and don't draw attention to yourself. Backing away slowly is a good idea, since running might entice the animal to chase you. It is particularly important to keep dogs away from elk, as dogs are known to chase elk down and elk will often stomp dogs to death in return.

Camp Marigold, 16101 U.S. 101 (☎482-3585 or 800-621-8513), 3 mi. north of **Klamath Bridge.** High-tech meets rustic in log cabins with cable TV. Tent sites and RV hookups available. 1-bed studios $48; 6-person lodge with kitchen $210; sites $10. ❸

Penny Saver Inn, 665 L St. (☎464-3142 or 888-717-3669; www.pennysaverinn.com), in **Crescent City.** A penny saved is a penny earned at this downtown motel, convenient to amenities you just can't find in the woods. Indoor heated pool. Singles and doubles $55. Reduced rates in winter. ❹

🏕 CAMPING

Redwood National Park offers several backcountry campsites; all are free and accessible only by hiking from roads or parking lots. **Nickel Creek Campground,** at the end of Enderts Beach Rd., outside Crescent City, has ocean access and toilets, but no showers or water. **Flint Ridge** is off the end of Redwood National and State Parks Coastal Dr., and has neither water nor showers, but toilets are available. There are also **State Park campsites ❶,** which are easily accessible and have most of the amenities except electricity. Contact ReserveAmerica (☎800-444-7275; www.reserveamerica.com) for reservations, which are necessary in summer. (Sites usually $17-20.) North of Crescent City on U.S. 199 is **Jedediah Smith Redwoods State Park ❶.** Amenities include picnic tables, grills, water, restrooms, and showers. Free campfire programs (M-Sa 8:30pm) and nature walks (M-F, times vary) also offered during the summer. (Sites $20; day-use $5; hike/bike $2.)

The Del Norte Coast Redwoods State Park offers magnificent ocean views and inland camping at **Mill Creek Campground ❶,** right off U.S. 101. Camping in Prairie Creek Redwoods State Park is possible at **Elk Prairie ❶,** where elk munch away and ignore tourists as long as the cameras stay at a distance. The sound of the crashing waves lulls campers to sleep at ▨**Gold Bluffs Beach.** Smith River National Recreation Area at **Six Rivers National Forest** (☎457-3131) has several campgrounds. **Big Flat Campground ❶,** ideal for those seeking serious isolation, is 14 mi. down South Fork Rd. off U.S. 199 (No hookups. Sites $8). Situated directly on the Smith River, **Panther Flat ❶,** on U.S. 199, 2½mi. east of the Six Rivers National Forest Station in Gasquet, has water, showers, and a day-use picnic area. (Sites $16).

▨**Patrick's Point State Park ❶,** 15 mi. south of Orick along U.S. 101, is an excellent spot for **watching whales** and seals. The 70 sites offer terrific ocean views, lush vegetation, and teeming tide pools.

(☎677-3570, reservations 800-444-7275; www.reserveamerica.com. Showers and flush toilets. No dumpsite. No hookups. Reservations strongly recommended. Sites June-Aug. $20 per car; Sept.-May $15. Day-use $6 per car.) **Big Lagoon County Park ❶**, 35 mi. north of Eureka on U.S. 101, is a favorite. The park has 25 sites with flush toilets, coin showers, drinking water, and a big lagoon for swimming, canoeing, and kayaking. (☎445-7652. No hookups. No reservations; arrive early. Sites $15 per vehicle. Day-use $2.)

FOOD

There are more picnic tables than restaurants in the area, so the best option for food is probably the supermarket. In Crescent City, head to the 24hr. **Safeway,** 475 M St. (☎465-3353), on U.S. 101 between 2nd and 5th St. The **Klamath Market,** 166 Klamath Blvd., also has an ATM. (☎482-0211. Open M-Sa 8am-9pm, Su 9am-5pm.) **Orick Market** has reasonably priced groceries. (☎488-3225. Open M-Sa 8am-7pm, Su 9am-6pm.) Crescent City is a fast food lover's dream, but is also home to a number of slower joints. **Glen's Bakery and Restaurant ❶**, at 3rd and G St. in Crescent City, opened in 1947 and has always been a family affair. The multitude of loyal regulars love the huge pancakes ($4) and sandwiches ($5-6.50). It serves breakfast all day. (☎464-2914. Open Tu-Sa 5am-6:30pm.) The mom-and-pop **Palm Cafe ❷**, on U.S. 101, is one of the few places to eat in Orick. Locals and visiting hikers and bikers savor the homemade pies ($2.25); fruit, coconut, and chocolate are the favorites. (☎488-3381. Open daily 5am-8pm.)

SIGHTS AND OUTDOOR ACTIVITIES

The best way to experience the redwoods is to get out of the car. The National Park Service and the California Department of Parks and Recreation conduct many ranger-led activities for all ages in the summer. (See **Visitor Information,** p. 217, or call the Redwood Information Center at ☎464-6101). Hikers should take particular care to wear protective clothing—**ticks** and **poison oak** thrive in these dark places. **Roosevelt elk** roam the woods and are interesting to watch but dangerous to approach, as encroachers on their territory are promptly circled and trampled. Also look out for the **black bears** and **mountain lions** that inhabit the park. Before setting out, get advice and trail maps at the visitors center. All plants and animals in the park are protected—even feathers dropped by birds of prey are off-limits. California **fishing licenses** (1 day $10) are required for fresh and saltwater fishing off any natural formation, but fishing is free from any man-made structure (check out Battery Point in Crescent City). There are minimum-weight and maximum-catch requirements specific to both fresh and saltwater fishing. Call the **Fish and Game Department** (☎445-6493; www.dfg.ca.gov) for more information on how to obtain a permit.

HIOUCHI AREA

This inland region, known for its rugged beauty, sits in the northern part of the park region along U.S. 199 and contains some excellent hiking trails, most of which are in **Jedediah Smith Redwoods State Park.** Several trails lie off Howland Hill Rd., a dirt road that winds through scenic **Stout Grove,** which compares favorably to the Avenue of the Giants. Take the wheelchair-accessible **Stout Grove Trail** (½ mi.) to get close to the ancient redwoods. The trailhead is near the eastern end of Howland Hill Rd. The **Mill Creek Trail** is a moderate 4 mi. hike with excellent swimming, accessible from the Mill Creek Bridge on Howland Hill Rd., and from the footbridge in the Jedediah Smith campground during summer. The more strenuous **Boy Scout Trail** off Howland Hill Rd. has an unmarked, easy to miss split after 3 mi.; the right-hand path goes to the monstrous **Boy Scout Tree,** and the left ends at **Fern Falls.** From U.S. 199, turn onto South Fork Rd. in Hiouchi and right onto Douglas Park Rd., which then becomes Howland Hill Rd. From Crescent City, go south on U.S. 101, turn left onto Elk Valley Rd., and right onto Howland Hill Rd.

Two miles west of Jedediah State Park on U.S. 199 lies the **Simpson-Reed Grove,** a circular trail through an old stand of redwoods. The untapped beauty of **Six Rivers National Forest** (☎ 457-3131) is directly east of Hiouchi. The Smith River, the state's last major undammed river, rushes through rocky gorges on its way from the mountains to the coast. This area offers the best salmon, trout, and steelhead fishing around, and excellent camping awaits on the riverbanks. There are also numerous hiking trails throughout the forest.

CRESCENT CITY AREA

An outstanding base from which to explore the parks, Crescent City calls itself the city "where the redwoods meet the sea." Perched on a causeway jutting out from Front St., the **Battery Point Lighthouse** houses a museum open only during low tide. Turn left onto A St. at the top of Front St. (☎ 464-3089. Open Apr.-Sept. W-Su 10am-4pm, tide permitting; Nov.-Mar. F-Sa low tide. $3, children $1.) From June through August, the national park offers **tidepool walks,** which leave from the Enderts Beach parking lot. (At the turn-off 4 mi. south of Crescent City; call ☎ 464-6101, ext. 5064, for schedules.) The trail to the tidepools begins at the **Crescent Beach Overlook** on Enderts Beach Rd., just off U.S. 101. A scenic drive from Crescent City along **Pebble Beach Drive** to **Point Saint George** snakes past coastline that resembles the rocky surf of New England; craggy cliffs, soft meadows, and an old lighthouse add to the atmosphere.

KLAMATH AREA

The **Klamath Overlook,** where Requa Rd. meets the steep **Coastal Trail** (8 mi.), is an excellent **whale-watching** site (especially Nov.-Dec. and Mar.-May). The view is fantastic provided fog doesn't obscure it, though the overlook can be crowded by North Coast standards. The mouth of the **Klamath River** is a popular commercial fishing spot in fall and spring, when salmon spawn, and in winter, when steelhead trout do the same. Contact the Redwood National Park Headquarters (☎ 464-6101, ext. 5064.) to obtain a permit. In spring and summer, sea lions and harbor seals congregate along Coastal Dr., which passes by the remains of the **Douglas Memorial Bridge** and continues along the ocean for 8 mi. of incredible views. A 200 ft. tall Paul Bunyan (who talks and waves to youngsters who climb on his boots) and his blue ox Babe mark the entrance to **Trees of Mystery,** 15500 U.S. 101, just north of Klamath. The tourist trap's **Sky Trail,** a multi-million-dollar gondola, shoots up the hill, offering an exclusive bird's-eye view of the towering trees. A three-quarter-mile walk through a maze of curiously shaped trees and elaborate chainsaw sculptures is mysteriously accompanied by audio stories. Along the way, a small Native American **museum** displays ornate costumes, baskets, and tapestries. (☎ 482-2251 or 800-638-3389. Trail open daily 8am-5:30pm. Gift shop open 8am-7pm. Museum open 8am-6:30pm. $12, seniors $10, ages 4-10 $5.) Those looking for a great reward for minimal exertion can trek the easy half-mile to **Hidden Beach.** The unspoiled beach is inaccessible by car and swarms with bright purple and orange starfish (and other sea life) at low tide. The trailhead is across U.S. 101 from Trees of Mystery, on the northern edge of Trees Motel.

PRAIRIE CREEK AREA

Accessible off the Newton B. Drury Scenic Pkwy., the Prairie Creek Area is equipped with a ranger station, visitors center, and state park campgrounds. The area is perfect for hikers, who can explore over 70 mi. of trails across the park's

14,000 acres. Be sure to pick up a trail map ($1) at the ranger station before heading out; the loops of crisscrossing trails can be confusing. Starting at the Prairie Creek Visitors Center, the **James Irvine Trail** (4½ mi. one way) snakes through a prehistoric garden of towering old-growth redwoods. Winding past small waterfalls that trickle down 30 ft. fern-covered walls, the trail ends at enchanting **Fern Canyon** on **Gold Bluffs Beach.** Beautiful blossoms line **Rhododendron Trail** (7¾ mi. one way); if you get tired, take **South Fork Trail,** a convenient short-cut. To see large fauna and flora, elk-watch on the meadow in front of the ranger station or cruise part of the **Foothill Trail** (¾ mi.) to the 1500-year-old, 306 ft. high **Big Tree** (also accessible just off the Scenic Pkwy. by car). This behemoth is a satisfying alternative for those who don't want to trek to **Tall Trees Grove** (see **Orick Area,** below). The **Elk Prairie Trail** (1½ mi.) skirts the meadow and loops around to join the nature trail. The **Revelation Trail** is occasionally frequented by elk and is wheelchair accessible.

ORICK AREA

The Orick Area covers the southernmost section of Redwood National and State Parks. A popular sight is the **Tall Trees Grove,** a trail accessible by car to those with permits (free from the Orick Visitors Center) when the road is open. Allow at least 3-4hr. to hike the trail. From the trailhead at the end of Tall Trees Access Rd., off Bald Hills Rd. from U.S. 101 north of Orick, it's a 1¼ mi. hike down (about 30min.) to some of the tallest trees in the world. The return hike up is steep—allow 1hr. Hardy souls can hike the 11 mi. round-trip from **Dolason Prairie Trail** to **Emerald Ridge Trail,** which connects with **Tall Trees Trail.**

South of Orick, **Patrick's Point State Park** offers one of the most spectacular views along the coast, and merits a day or two from hikers and nature enthusiasts heading north to the redwoods. During **whale-watching** season (Nov.-Dec. and Mar.-May), observe migrating gray whales from the towering cliffs of the point.

FESTIVALS

Annual highlights in Crescent City include the **World Championship Crab Races,** featuring races and crab feasts on the third Sunday in February. Enjoy a deck party, live music, market fair, parade, and the largest fireworks show north of San Francisco on the 3rd and **4th of July.** The **Sea Cruise,** a parade of over 500 classic cars, happens over three days on the first or second weekend in October. Call the Crescent City/Del Norte County Chamber of Commerce (☎800-343-8300) or check www.northerncalifornia.net for information regarding any of these events. On the second weekend in July meet the Rodeo King and Queen and taste deep-pit beef barbecue at the **Orick Rodeo.**

ARCATA   ☎707

Arcata (ar-KAY-ta; pop. 16,900) is like a slice of Berkeley transplanted to the remote northern corner of California. At the intersection of U.S. 101 and Rte. 299, the town typifies the laid-back North Coast lifestyle, with many murals, Victorian homes, and dread-locked characters living alternative lifestyles. Arcata's neighbor, California State University, focuses on forestry and marine biology (Earth First! was founded here). All over Humboldt County, students get baked in the sun—and on the county's number one cash crop.

▶ PRACTICAL INFORMATION. Arcata Chamber of Commerce/California Welcome Center, 1635 Heindon Rd., off U.S. 101 at the Giuntoli Ln. exit, has visitor information. (☎822-3619. Open daily 9am-5pm.) An **ATM** is at US Bank, 953 G St. **Humboldt County Library, Arcata Branch,** 500 7th St., has free **Internet access.** (☎822-5954. Open

IN RECENT NEWS

A NATURALLY CONTENTIOUS ISSUE

Amidst the ongoing battle to save the redwoods, Northern Californians find themselves on the cutting edge of another earth-friendly debate. Many of the residents of Humboldt County are passionate about organic foods and are looking for a way to ban the growing of genetically modified (GMO) plants and animals in the county. In June of 2004, a petition of 5950 signatures qualified an initiative for the November ballot, which, if passed, will ban the growing of GMO crops in Humboldt County. Mendocino County, farther south, has already approved such a ban, and similar measures are on the ballots of four other California counties.

The future of the ban is unclear, but a trip to the North Coast Co-op in downtown Arcata makes passage seem likely. Nearly all of the store's produce is local and organic, as are many of the products lining its shelves. A survey of the 10,000 members of the co-op (in a town of just under 17,000) shows that over 98% support the anti-GMO initiative.

Organic-friendly residents should not yet celebrate an easy victory, however. Biotech companies spent upward of $700,000 in opposition of a similar initiative in Mendocino County, and will likely spend nearly as much to protect their Northern California assets.

Tu 2-5pm, W 1-8pm, Th-Sa 10am-5pm.) For a downtown **laundromat** try **Emerald City Laundry,** at the corner of 12th and G St. (825-6802. Open M and Th-F 7:30am-11pm, Tu 7:30am-midnight, Sa-Su 8am-11pm; last wash 1½hr. before closing.) **Adventure's Edge,** 650 10th St., rents outdoor equipment. (☎822-4673. Tents $23 for the first 3 days, $4 per additional day. Sleeping bags $16/$3. Cross-country ski packages $20/$4. Sea kayaks $25 same-day return, $35 per 24hr. Open M-Sa 9am-6pm, Su 11am-5pm.) Other services include **Mad River Hospital,** 3800 Janes Rd. (☎822-3621), and the **post office,** 799 H St. (☎822-3370; open M-F 8:30am-5pm). **Postal Code:** 95521.

♨♨ ACCOMMODATIONS AND CAMPING. Many budget motels cluster off U.S. 101 at the Giuntoli Ln. exit. The least expensive is **Motel 6 ❸,** 4755 Valley West Blvd. It offers cable TV, a pool, and A/C. (☎822-7061. Singles Su-Th $40, F-Sa $58; 2nd adult $6 extra, additional adults $3 extra; under 17 free. AARP discount.) Find classier, pricier digs at the historic **Hotel Arcata ❹,** 708 9th St., at G St., in downtown. (☎826-0217 or 800-344-1221; www.hotelarcata.com. Singles Su-Th $79, F-Sa $84; doubles $8/$93.)

Popular **Clam Beach County Park ❶,** on U.S. 101, 7½ mi. north of Arcata, has dunes and a huge beach with seasonal clam digging; call ahead. (☎445-7651. Water and pit toilets. No reservations. Sites $10. Hike/bike $3.)

◨◧ FOOD AND NIGHTLIFE. The **North Coast Co-op,** on 8th St. at I St., is a standard supermarket except for the unusual amounts of organic products, tofu, ginseng cola, and soy milk lining its shelves. (☎822-5947. Open daily 6am-10pm.) A **Farmers Market** offering tie-dyed dresses, candles, and the usual fresh produce, livens up the Arcata Plaza on Saturdays. Several local bands playing at full volume make the affair a weekly party. (Apr.-Nov. Sa 9am-1pm.) **Golden Harvest Cafe ❷,** 1062 G St., a popular breakfast venue, has extensive options for vegetarians and vegans. (☎822-8962. All dishes $4-10. Open M-F 6:30am-3pm, Sa-Su 7:30am-3pm.) Set in a beautifully restored Victorian home, **Crosswinds ❸,** 860 10th St. at I St., offers a number of breakfast and lunch variations in large portions ($5-13). Vegan substitutes are available for all meat used in the Mexican, Italian, and Californian specialties. (☎826-2133. Open W-Su 7:30am-2pm.) **Los Bagels ❶,** 1061 I St., bakes specialty breads and tops bagels ($2-3.50) with cream cheese, guacamole, hummus, or smoked tofu. (822-3150. Open M and W-F 7am-6pm, Sa 7am-5pm, Su 8am-3pm.) **Folie Douce ❹,** 1551 G St., is a chic, tucked-away venue for dinner and drinks with a seasonal

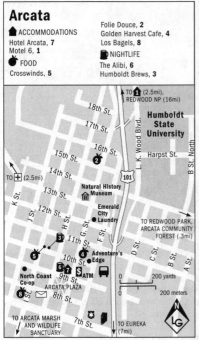

Arcata

▲ ACCOMMODATIONS
Hotel Arcata, **7**
Motel 6, **1**

● FOOD
Crosswinds, **5**

Folie Douce, **2**
Golden Harvest Cafe, **4**
Los Bagels, **8**

◗ NIGHTLIFE
The Alibi, **6**
Humboldt Brews, **3**

menu. (☎822-1042. Appetizers $8-9.50. Wood-fired pizzas $10-14. Entrees $18-30. Open Tu-Th 5:30-9pm, F-Sa 5:30-10pm.)

As a college town, Arcata maintains its share of bars, most of which are on 9th St. in the town square. **The Alibi ❶**, 744 9th St., serves charbroiled burgers ($4.75-6.55) and stiff drinks ($3.50-6.75). Choose from 69 different martinis and nine Bloody Marys. (☎822-3731. Open daily 8am-2am. Kitchen closes 11pm.) **Humboldt Brews ❷**, 856 10th St. at I St., is a popular local microbrewery with burgers ($6.25), salads ($5-8.75), and wings by the pound ($8). Unusual beers like the Red Nectar Ale go well with a game of pool. (☎826-2739. Occasional live DJ. Open M-Tu 4pm-midnight, W-Sa noon-midnight.)

◩ ▓ SIGHTS AND FESTIVALS. Experience Arcata by taking a short stroll around the **Arcata Plaza,** in the center of town near the intersection of 8th and H St. The plaza hosts folk music on the weekends and an annual **Summer Solstice Festival** on the weekend nearest the summer solstice. The **Natural History Museum,** at 13th and G St., is a brief walk from the plaza and home to a modest collection of prehistoric fossils. (Open Tu-Sa 10am-5pm. Suggested donation $2.) Nearby **Redwood Park,** at 14th and Union St., contains lots of nooks for picnicking among giant trees. Behind the park lies **Arcata Community Forest,** which has picnic spaces, meadows, redwoods, and hiking trails. A former "sanitary" landfill, the 75-acre **Arcata Marsh and Wildlife Sanctuary** lies at the foot of I St., across from Samoa Blvd. Visitors can take a tour to see how this saltwater marsh/converted sewer system works with treated waste, or wander the trails around the lake. The 4½ mi. of trails along marsh, ponds, and the Humboldt Bay make for great bird-watching opportunities. (☎826-2359. Tours Sa 8:30am, meet at the foot of I St., and at 2pm, meet at the info center on S. G St. Open daily 9am-5pm.)

The 36-year-old **Kinetic Sculpture Race,** held annually over Memorial Day weekend, is Humboldt County's oddest festival. A few dozen insane and artsy adventurers attempt to pilot unwieldy homemade vehicles (like the squash-shaped "Gourd of the Rings") on a grueling three-day, 42 mi. trek from Arcata to Ferndale over road, sand, and water. Vehicles from previous competitions are on display at a museum in Ferndale (see p. 228).

EUREKA
☎707

Eureka (pop. 27,218) was born out of the demands of incoming 49ers who wanted a more convenient alternative to the tedious overland route from Sacramento. The Humboldt Bay provided a landing spot, and Eureka was founded as its port. The decline of the region's gold mining and lumber businesses has led Eureka to shift

THE NORTH COAST

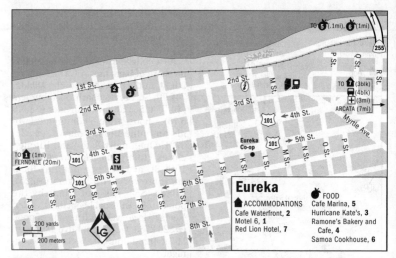

Eureka

▲ ACCOMMODATIONS
Cafe Waterfront, **2**
Motel 6, **1**
Red Lion Hotel, **7**

● FOOD
Cafe Marina, **5**
Hurricane Kate's, **3**
Ramone's Bakery and
Cafe, **4**
Samoa Cookhouse, **6**

from a reliance on natural resources to fishing and tourism. While the town is less attractive than its northern neighbors, Old Town Eureka offers some historical appeal. Victorian buildings clustered next to the harbor contain a series of shops, restaurants, and art galleries. Don't judge Eureka solely on the basis of a drive through town on U.S. 101. The city's perimeter may appear a bit gritty, but the center of Eureka retains a pleasant, old-town charm.

◪ **TRANSPORTATION. Greyhound buses** depart twice a day for San Francisco ($34.50-38) and once or twice a day for Crescent City ($20-22) from 1603 4th St. at Q St. (☎442-0370 or 800-231-2222. Open M-F 9am-1pm and 8-10pm; Sa 9am-noon and 8-10pm.) The **Humboldt Transit Authority,** 133 V St., runs regional buses between Scotia and Trinidad ($1.40-2) via Arcata. Most buses pick up passengers along 5th St. or Broadway. (☎443-0826; www.hta.org. Open M-F 8am-noon and 1-4:30pm.)

◪◪ **ORIENTATION AND PRACTICAL INFORMATION.** Eureka straddles **U.S. 101,** less than 7 mi. south of Arcata and 280 mi. north of San Francisco. To the south, U.S. 101 is referred to as Broadway. In town, U.S. 101 is called 4th St. (heading south) and 5th St. (heading north). The **Eureka/Humboldt Visitors Bureau,** 1034 2nd St., will answer specific questions. (☎443-5097 or 800-346-3482. Open M-F 9am-5pm.) Eureka's **Chamber of Commerce,** 2112 Broadway, has information and brochures. (☎442-3738. Open M-F 8:30am-5pm; extended summer hours.) **Bank of America,** near the corner of E and 4th St., and at the **Eureka Co-op** on 5th St. at L. St., has **ATMs.** Clean up at **Summer Street Laundromat,** 111 Summer St. (☎443-7463. Wash $2.55-4.50, dry $0.25 per 7min. Open daily 7am-9pm.) **Internet access** is free at the **Humbolt County Library,** 1313 3rd St. (☎269-1900; www.humlib.org. Open Tu, Th, Sa noon-5pm, W noon-8pm, F 10am-5pm.) Services include: the **police** (☎441-4000); **Eureka General Hospital,** 2200 Harrison Ave. (☎445-5111, ext. 4699); the **post office,** 337 W. Clark St., near Broadway (☎442-1768; open M-F 8:30am-5pm and Sa noon-3pm). **Postal Code:** 95501.

◪◪ **ACCOMMODATIONS AND CAMPING.** Travelers will find many budget motels off U.S. 101, but most are unappealing; be selective. Walking around alone at night, especially along Broadway, is not recommended. For an indulgent night, head to ▦**Cafe Waterfront** ❺, in Old Town at 1st and F St. The restaurant owns two plush Victorian bedrooms with a kitchen and breakfast nook to share. It feels like a private harbor-view apartment. (☎444-1301. Breakfast included. Rooms in summer $150-175; in winter $125-150.) **Motel 6** ❸, 1934 Broadway, south of town off U.S. 101, is a sure bet and offers satellite TV. (☎445-9631. Singles Su-Th $48, F-Sa $56; doubles $54/$62. $3 per additional person.) Pricey but dependable, the **Red Lion Hotel** ❺, on U.S. 101 at the northern edge of town, has immaculate rooms. (☎445-0844. Singles $104-119; doubles $114-125. Prices vary widely throughout the year. $10-15 AAA discount.)

⊓ FOOD. Old Town Eureka is suitable for evening dinners and strolls. **Eureka Co-op,** 1036 5th St., at L St., sells organic produce, deli foods, and typical groceries. (☎443-6027. Open M-Sa 7am-9pm, Su 8am-9pm.) There are also two **Farmers Markets** that run in the summer and fall. (Old Town Gazebo June-Sept. Tu 10am-2pm; Henderson Center July-Sept. Th 10am-2pm.) Family-style servings of traditional meat-and-potatoes fare are big enough for Paul Bunyan at the ▦**Samoa Cookhouse** ❸, 79 Cookhouse Ln., in Samoa. Take Hwy. 255 off U.S. 101 over the Samoa bridge, the first left onto Samoa Blvd., and then the first left onto Cookhouse Ln. The only operational lumber camp-style cookhouse in North America serves huge and delicious breakfasts in a room that seats up to 300 burly men. (☎442-1659; www.humboldtdining.com/cookhouse. Breakfast $9. Lunch $10. Dinner $14. Reduced rates for children under 12 and seniors. Open M-Sa 11am-3:30pm and 5-9pm, Su 7am-9pm.) At **Hurricane Kate's** ❸, 511 2nd St., the menu of tapas-style small plates and traditional entrees changes frequently, as does the genre of the live music that occasionally accompanies dinner. Fusion cuisine like Caribbean tacos ($11) and crab and sweet corn cheesecake ($12), and home-infused vodkas (kumquat-ginger or lavender-honey-hazelnut $5.50) spice up lunch or dinner. (☎444-1405. Open Tu-Sa 11:30am-2pm and 5-9pm.) **Cafe Marina** ❸, 601 Startare Dr., is off U.S. 101 at the Samoa Bridge exit (Hwy. 255); from there, take the Woodley Island exit north of town. Outdoor dining on the marina is the perfect way to enjoy fresh seafood, like the spicy blackened snapper ($16). Come evening, local fishermen crowd around the polished bar. (☎443-2233. Sandwiches $7-14. Entrees $10-17. Open daily June-Aug. 7am-10pm; Sept.-May 7am-9pm.) **Ramone's Bakery and Cafe** ❶, 209 E St., between 2nd and 3rd St., specializes in homemade truffles, fresh-baked pies, and the ever-popular "Chocolate Sin," a chocolate and liqueur torte ($3.50). Sandwiches ($4.25-4.50), soups ($3), and salads ($4) are also available. (☎445-2923. Open M-Sa 7am-6pm, Su 7am-4pm.)

⊙ ⚑ SIGHTS AND OUTDOOR ACTIVITIES. Eureka prides itself on its colorful **Victorian homes.** Free self-guided tour maps are available at the Chamber of Commerce. Some of the more handsome houses are now expensive B&Bs. If you drive by, don't miss the much-photographed, dramatically stark **Carson Mansion,** on M St. at 2nd St., which belonged to a prominent logger in the 1850s. **Art galleries** are downtown Eureka's other attraction. **First Street Gallery,** 422 1st St. (☎443-6363), **The Ink People Gallery,** 411 12th St. (☎442-8413), and the **Morris Graves Museum of Art,** 636 F St. (☎442-0278) display eclectic art and frequently changing exhibits. Ask the Chamber of Commerce about current exhibits.

The **Dunes recreation area,** in Samoa off Rte. 255 (past the Samoa Cookhouse and left at Samoa Bridge, on the north end by the jetty), was once a thriving dune ecosystem. Now, the peninsula offers beach access and dune hiking. The **M.V. Madaket** sets sail from the foot of C St. for 75min. narrated **cruises of the Humboldt Bay.** (☎445-1910. Cruises M-Tu 1pm; W-Sa 1, 2:30, and 4pm; Su 1 and 2:30pm. $12.50, seniors and ages 13-17 $10.50, ages 5-12 $6.50, under 5 free. 1hr. non-narrated cocktail cruise W-Sa 5:30pm.)

FERNDALE ☎ 707

Ferndale (pop. 1320) exemplifies small-town perfection, and is a convenient gateway to either the Lost Coast or the Avenue of the Giants. The amphitheater-like **cemetery** near **Russ Park** on Ocean Ave. gives a sense of the town's history and provides a breathtaking view of the Victorian town and its grazing dairy cattle. One of Ferndale's oddest traditions, the annual Arcata Kinetic Sculpture Race (see p. 225), ends at the studio of the event's founder, **Hobart Galleries,** 393 Main St., at Brown St. See kooky contraptions from past races in the form of a raccoon, dragon, bumblebee, flying saucer, and purple crayon at the **Ferndale Kinetic Sculpture Museum,** inside the **Arts and Cultural Center,** 580 Main St., at Shaw Ave.

Accommodations here are mainly exorbitant B&Bs, but if you have been saving for a splurge, this is the place. Founded in 1854, the Carpenter Gothic Revival-style (Victorian, in laymen's terms) **Shaw House ❺,** 703 Main St., has eight rooms, a sit-down hot breakfast, afternoon tea, and wireless Internet. (☎786-9958; www.shawhouse.com. Check-in 4-6pm. Check-out 11am. Doubles $100-245.) Frozen in time, **Candystick Fountain and Grill ❶,** 361 Main St., scoops ice cream into homemade waffle cones ($2.50-3.50), splits a mean banana ($5.50), and dishes up burgers ($4.50-6) and hot dogs ($1.75-3.25) amidst Ferndale High sports memorabilia dating from 1914. (☎786-9373. Open M-Th and Sa 11am-6pm, F 11am-7pm, Su 11am-5pm.)

AVENUE OF THE GIANTS ☎ 707

About 10 mi. north of Garberville on U.S. 101 in the Humboldt Redwoods State Park, the Avenue of the Giants (the actual name of the road) splits off the highway and winds its way through 31 mi. of redwoods, the world's largest living organisms above ground level. Hiking, swimming, fishing, biking, and rafting opportunities abound in this rugged area. Garberville is the main town along the Avenue and is connected to its smaller neighbor, Redway, by Redwood Dr., the main street in both towns. Moving north up the Avenue, drivers encounter the tiny towns of Phillipsville, Miranda, Myers Flat, Weott, Redcrest, and Pepperwood.

◪◪ TRANSPORTATION AND PRACTICAL INFORMATION. Greyhound (☎800-231-2222) runs buses out of Garberville to Arcata (W-Su 2 per day, $22.75), San Francisco (2 per day, $48.50), and Portland, OR (2 per day, $96). Meet the bus in front of Waterwheel Restaurant, 942 Edwood Dr. The **Humboldt Redwoods State Park Visitors Center,** just south of Weott on the Avenue, has very knowledgeable staff who can describe the Avenue's groves, facilities, trails, and bike routes and provide safety tips for camping. The center also has videos and displays about local wildlife and history, some of which are hands-on and kid-friendly. (☎946-2263. Open daily Apr.-Oct. 9am-5pm; Oct.-Apr. 10am-4pm.) The **Garberville-Redway Chamber of Commerce,** 782 Redway Dr., in the Redwood Drive Center, downtown Garberville, offers info on local events and attractions. (☎800-923-2613. Call for hours.) **Treats,** 764 Redwood Dr., in Garberville, has **Internet access.** (☎923-3554. $0.10 per min. Open M-F 8:30am-6pm, Sa 9am-6pm, Su 10am-6pm.) The Garberville **post office** is at 368 Sprowl Creek Rd., just off Redwood Dr. (☎923-2652. Open M-F 8:30am-5pm.) **Postal Code:** 95542.

◪ ACCOMMODATIONS. Foggy weather may make staying indoors an attractive, if expensive, option. **Myers Inn ❺,** in Myers Flat, is a former stagecoach stop and the Avenue's only B&B. It has ten homey bedrooms and offers boating and fishing tours. (☎943-3259 or 800-500-6464; www.myersinn.com. Expansive continental breakfast. Rooms $125-175. AAA discount.) The **Brass Rail Inn ❹,** 3188 Redwood Dr., in Redway, has retired its former roles of brothel, dinner house, and teahouse, and is now a perfectly respectable motel rumored to be home to a friendly ghost named George. (☎923-3931; Singles $55-60.50; doubles $66.) For city convenience, stay in the **Sherwood Forest Motel ❹**, 814 Redwood Dr., in downtown Garberville. (☎923-2721, www.sherwoodforestmotel.com. Fridge, microwave, and coffeepot in every room. Check-in by 10pm. Singles $66; doubles $77.) At cozy **Madrona Inn ❹**, 2907 Ave. of the Giants, in Phillipsville, guests sleep in pink cottages, some with kitchens and two bedrooms. Friendly owners allow pets for a $5 fee. (☎943-1708. Cottages $60-100; $6 per additional person.)

⚑ CAMPING. Camping options are plentiful in **Humboldt Redwood State Park ❶**. Each developed campsite offers coin showers, flush toilets, and fire rings. (☎946-1811, reservations 800-444-7275; www.reserveamerica.com. Sites May 16-Sept. 15 $20; Sept. 16-May 15 $15. Day-use $6. Hike/bike $3.) The most remote site, wildlife-filled **Albee Creek,** on Mattole Rd., 5 mi. west of U.S. 101 near Rockefeller Forest, has access to biking and hiking trails and is open from Memorial Day to Labor Day. **Hidden Springs,** near Myers Flat, has 154 semi-secluded sites with hot showers situated on a hillside in a mixed forest. Few hiking trails start directly at the campsite, but the South Fork of Eel River is a short hike away. (Open Memorial Day-Labor Day.) Conveniently located next to the visitors center, **Burlington** offers fully developed campsites, but is near the drone of the nearby freeway.

   Richardson Grove State Park ❶, off U.S. 101, 8 mi. south of Garberville, has sites with toilets and showers. (☎247-3318. Sites May 16-Sept. 15 $20; Sept. 16-May 15 $15.) **Grasshopper Trail Camp ❶** is near the summit of Grasshopper Peak. (Primitive sites with pit toilets. No fires or pets. Register and get information in advance at headquarters. $3 per person.)

▯ FOOD. Garberville offers a number of civilized eating options. **Sentry Market,** on Redwood Dr., is the largest supermarket for miles. (☎923-2279. Open daily 7am-10pm.) Locals highly recommend **Calico's Cafe ❷,** on Redwood Dr. next to Sherwood Forest Motel, for its homemade pastas, salads, and burgers. Try the garlicky fettuccine gorgonzola ($9) made from scratch. (☎923-2253. Open daily Jun.-Aug. 11am-10pm; Sept.-May 11am-9pm.) **Nacho Mama's ❷,** at Redwood Dr. and Sprowl Creek Rd., is an organic Mexican food stand with burritos, dolphin-free albacore tacos, and vegan, wheat-free chocolate chip cookies. (☎923-4060. Entrees $3-9. Open M-Sa 11am-7pm.) For a burger made with 100% grass-fed local beef ($5-8), stop by the **Chimney Tree Coffee Shop ❷,** 1111 Ave. of the Giants, just south of Phillipsville. There is also a hokey "hobbit" trail ($5, ages 5-11 $3) and a free burnt-out, hollow "Chimney" redwood. (☎923-2265. Open daily 10:30am-7pm.)

⚠ ❀ OUTDOOR ACTIVITIES AND FESTIVALS. Scattered throughout the area are several tourist traps, such the **Drive-Thru Tree** ($1.50) in Myers Flat, and plenty of Bigfoot merchandise. Indispensable maps for longer trails are available at the visitors center ($1) or at any of the campsites. There are a number of short day hikes near the Avenue. The very worthwhile half-mile loop at **Founder's Grove** features the 1300- to 1500-year-old **Founder's Tree,** and the former tallest tree in Humboldt Redwoods State Park, the fallen 362 ft. **Dyerville Giant,** whose massive, three-story root-ball looks like a mythic entanglement of evil. Half a mile north of Miranda, the **Stephens Grove Trail** is an easy three-quarter-mile walk that passes the remnants of a campsite wiped out by a flood in 1964. South of the visitors center, the half-mile **Kent-Mather** loop trail begins at the **Garden Club of America Grove** and wanders through redwood sorrel and lady ferns; look for ospreys near the river.

THE NORTH COAST

Uncrowded trails wind through **Rockefeller Forest** in the park's northern section, which contains the largest grove of continuous old-growth redwoods in the world. The **Grasshopper Peak Trail**, a strenuous 14 mi. round-trip hike, starts at the Big Tree parking lot, 4 mi. west of the Avenue on Mattole Rd. This is a hilly, all-day backcountry hike and will take you 3379 ft. high to a gorgeous view of the Giants.

With its sizable population of artists, Garberville's **art festivals** run all summer. **Summer Arts Fair** begins in late June, followed by the popular **Shakespeare at Benbow Lake** in late July. Early August brings a marathon of jam sessions on the banks of the Eel River with **Reggae on the River,** a wild three-day festival. For more info on these annual events, call the Chamber of Commerce (☎800-923-2613).

LOST COAST

The Lost Coast can elude even the most observant visitor. When Hwy. 1 was built, the rugged coastline between Usal and Ferndale had to be bypassed and the highway moved inland, leaving jagged mountains, rocky shores, and black sand beaches undeveloped. To explore the area, bring a map and a 4WD vehicle, as many roads are unpaved, steep, and poorly marked; it's easy to get, well, lost.

> **:TIP:** **THESE DOGS HAVE THE MUNCHIES.** Due to its remote location, the Lost Coast is home to many illegal marijuana farms. If you drive up a dirt road and are greeted by large guard dogs, you've probably stumbled upon someone's stash and are not welcome. Turn around immediately!

KING RANGE NATIONAL CONSERVATION AREA
☎707

Stretching 24 mi. along the coast between Shelter Cove and Petrolia, the King Range National Conservation Area provides some of the best primitive camping in California, with clean creeks, beaches, and an abandoned lighthouse. It also contains one of North America's most unstable mountain ranges, which sits on a fault line between three different tectonic plates. Intense earthquakes push the ocean floor upward an average of 10 ft. every 1000 years. In 1992, a single earthquake raised King Range almost 4 ft. in a matter of minutes. 4WD vehicles are necessary to traverse many of the roads.

■ **ORIENTATION.** **King Peak Road** travels through dense forest in the central part of the conservation area and leads to **Lightning, Saddle Mountain,** and **Horse Mountain Creek** trailheads and the **Horse Mountain** and **Tolkan** campsites. No motor homes or trailers are permitted north of Horse Mountain Campground. **Chemise Mountain Road** meanders through Douglas fir and leads to Roosevelt elk at the **Hidden Valley** trailhead (where the southern **Lost Coast Trail** begins), the **Nadelos** and **Wailaki campsites,** and **Sinkyone Wilderness State Park.** Use low gears on downgrades, watch for oncoming traffic, and allow faster cars behind you to pass.

■ **CAMPING.** Before setting out into King Range National Conservation Area, all organized groups accessing the backcountry must acquire a permit. Fire permits are required for everyone and can be obtained for free at the **King Range Bureau of Land Management (BLM)** office, on Shelter Cove Rd., 9 mi. from Shelter Cove. (☎986-5400; www.ca.blm.gov/arcata. Open M-Sa 8am-4:30pm.) Of all the sites, **Wailaki Campground ❶** is slightly closer to civilization and more developed. (Toilets, fire pits, drinking water, and picnic tables. Sites $8.) **Tolkan ❶** is windy,

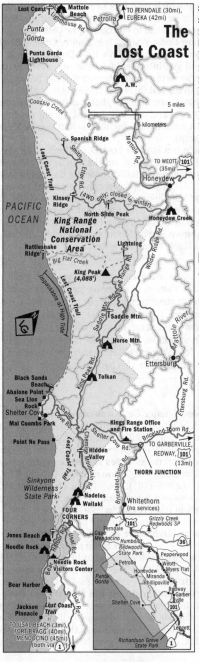

The Lost Coast

secluded, and on a steep ridge. (13 sites, picnic tables, pit toilets, fire rings. No water. No RVs. Sites $8.) **Horse Mountain Camp ❶**, which is not located by the trailhead, is the most remote developed campground. Its nine sites are windy and cool, but lack water. (Sites $8.) **A.W. Campground ❶**, between Honeydew and Mattole on Mattole Rd., is managed by Humboldt County and sits on the Mattole River. (Flush toilets, showers. Sites May 16-Sept. 15 $20, Sept. 16-May 15 $15.) **Mattole Beach Campground ❶**, at the northern part of King Range, is at the end of Lighthouse Rd., 45min. north of Honeydew off Mattole Rd. (Pit toilets. Water must be filtered before drinking. Sites $5. Day use $1.)

◐▲ SIGHTS AND OUTDOOR ACTIVITIES. The windy, flat beach in King Range is framed by steep grass-covered mountains and rolling dunes. Here visitors can enjoy the **Mattole River Estuary**, a nursery for young salmon and a home to egrets and brown pelicans, or take off on the challenging three-day **Lost Coast Trail** (25 mi. one way to Shelter Cove). Although it is possible to hike the trail one way and then backtrack to your vehicle, some campers use the privately run **Lost Coast Trail Transport Service.** (☎986-9909; www.lostcoast-trail.com. Call ahead of time for rates and availablity.) Others bring two cars. The trek is long but rewarding with ever-changing vistas of mountains and coastline, and occasional encounters with sea lions, shore birds, and black-tailed deer. The trail has several springs along the way, but this water must be purified before drinking; it is a good idea to come prepared with some bottled water. You may also see a black bear, especially if your camp is not clean. **Bear canisters** are required on all King Range land and can be rented at the BLM office ($5; credit card deposit $75). Always be on the lookout for poison oak, ticks, and rattlesnakes. A portion of the trail is impassable during high tide; it is necessary to check **tide tables.** Do this at the King Range BLM, or buy them in Garberville or Petrolia. It's a good idea to stop by the BLM office or call ahead to let them know your plans.

The northern 25 mi. portion of the Lost Coast Trail ends in Shelter Cove at **Black Sands Beach,** which is open to beachcombing only at low tide. Do not attempt a swim here; dangerous **riptides** will pull you into the deep blue sea. From Black Sands Beach, those who want to experience the seaside beauty without hiking the entire Lost Coast Trail can hike north to **Big Flat** (8½ mi.). This stretch is all beach hiking and portions of it are impassable during high tide, but it remains a favorite with hard-core surfers seeking killer waves and camping enthusiasts enjoying the large coastal terrace. From Big Flat, a great inland day hike is **Rattlesnake Ridge Trail** (4 mi. one way to Bear Hollow Camp).

Hikes abound in King Range. Three miles into the Lost Coast Trail, from Mattole, lies the **Punta Gorda Lighthouse.** First lit in 1917, it was known as the Alcatraz of lighthouses due to its remote location and reputation for being the assignment with which to punish deviant keepers. Allow half a day for the journey there and back, as most of the trail is slow-going sand hiking. **King Peak Trail** climbs 4087 ft. to reach a panoramic view of endless forested peaks and more than 100 mi. of Pacific coastline. The hike is a rigorous uphill climb from Lightning trailhead (2½ mi. one way) or a very gradual ascent from Saddle Mountain trailhead (5 mi. one way). There is a spring near the top at Maple Camp for water.

> **▌!** **SLEEPER WAVES.** Sleeper waves are overpowering waves that crash ashore and then forcefully pull back whatever or whomever they happen upon. Many beaches have posted warnings about such dangerous currents, and it is safest to simply stay out of treacherous waters. However, if a sleeper wave yanks you into the surf, do not swim toward shore. Doing so will only tire you out in a futile battle against the current. Instead, swim parallel to the beach until you're out of the wave's clutches. To avoid these waves, heed ranger advice that may save your life: stay watchful and never turn your back on the ocean.

SHELTER COVE ☎ 707

The tamest part of the wild Lost Coast, Shelter Cove was once a trading post. Native Americans bartered with each other on Point Delgada and settlers built a shipping port for fishing and wood products. Still home to a tiny community of fishermen, Shelter Cove now welcomes vacationers as well. Tourists can view adorable sea lions perched on coastal rocks at **Sea Lion Rock,** along lower Pacific Dr., or inspect tide pools and an historic lighthouse at **Mal Coombs Park,** next to **Mario's Marina,** 533 Machi Rd. (☎986-1401), the site for chartering and launching boats. The complex also houses a restaurant overlooking the cove and a motel with two queen-size beds in each room. (☎986-7595; www.mariosofsheltercove.com. Restaurant open M-F 8am-noon and 5pm-9pm. $93.50.) The pricier but plush ▧**Oceanfront Inn and Lighthouse ❺,** 10 Seal Ct., has seaside rooms and homey suites, all with private beach access and a private deck overlooking the ocean. (☎986-7002. Suites with kitchen available. Rooms with 1 king-size bed $125; private lighthouse suite $175.) The **Cove Restaurant ❸** is on the inn's first floor. (☎986-1197. Lunch $7-13. Dinner $8-19. Open Th-Su 11:30am-4pm and 5-9pm.) Pick up news and advice at the **Shelter Cove Campground and Deli ❷,** 492 Machi Rd., the only place in town where you can get fish 'n' chips ($7), Shelter Cove souvenirs, a tide table, and aspirin all at once. The closest thing in town to an information booth, the deli is also the headquarters for over 100 campsites near the marina. (☎986-7474. Open daily 7am-7pm. Tent sites $20; full hookup $30.) The rooms at the **Shelter Cove Beachcomber Inn ❹**, 412 Machi Rd., are the best deals on this stretch of coast. Some have kitchens and fireplaces. (☎986-7551 or 800-718-4789. Singles and doubles $55-95.)

SINKYONE WILDERNESS STATE PARK   ☎707

To get to Sinkyone take U.S. 101 to Redway and follow the signs to **Shelter Cove** along Briceland-Thorn Rd. At the Thorn Junction, turn left. Ten miles down is the Four Corners intersection. To the left is Usal Rd., which eventually leads south to Usal Beach along a drive that makes Hwy. 1 seem like child's play (4WD required). Sinkholes and weather conditions make Usal Rd. impassable for more than nine months of the year and even 4WD vehicles get stuck year-round. Rangers warn that travelers should use this road only to reach Usal Beach from the south and should **avoid using Usal Rd. north of the beach.** To the right is Chemise Mountain Rd., which leads back to Shelter Cove, offering vistas of the rugged Lost Coast. Allow 2hr. to travel the winding, wooded route.

On the west side of the Four Corners intersection, Briceland-Thorn Rd. becomes **Bear Harbor Rd.**—a gravel road so narrow it only fits one car at a time. As you pull around the numerous blind hairpin turns, don't be bashful about announcing your presence with a firm honk. The mountain road passes by **Jones Beach, Needle Rock,** and the **Needle Rock Visitors Center,** which sells camping permits and firewood. (Visitors center opening hours vary, but always closes 5pm. Pit toilets; no water. 14-night max. stay. No reservations. Fills in summer. Sites $20.) The road eventually leads to **Bear Harbor,** growing increasingly difficult toward the end (in fact, the stretch beyond Needle Rock is closed during the winter). The dedicated, however, will find their reward in the rustic beauty of the three neighboring campgrounds: **Orchard, Railroad,** and **Bear Harbor.** Surrounded by lush ferns, black sand, and transplanted eucalyptus trees, the sites are a half a mile's hike from the road. Be prepared to share your space with the **Roosevelt elk**. The blocked-off road to **Jones Beach** is just 2 mi. down Bear Harbor Rd.

One of the more popular Lost Coast beaches, **Usal Beach ❶** has a self-registration kiosk and camping areas (unmarked sites $10-12, trail camps $2-3. Open July 1-Sept 15). About 300 ft. farther up the dirt road is a short bridge and turn-off leading to a parking area and some windy beachside sites (no drinking water). The southern trailhead of the difficult **Lost Coast Trail** begins at Usal and leads 52 mi. up the coast to **Mattole River.** However, most people hike the Lost Coast north to south so that the wind is with them. Many also only travel from the **Mattole Campground** to **Black Sands Beach,** near Shelter Cove, because that 25 mi. stretch hugs the coast.

MENDOCINO   ☎707

Teetering on bluffs over the ocean, isolated Mendocino (pop. 1107) is a charming coastal community of art galleries, craft shops, bakeries, and B&Bs. The town's weathered shingles, white picket fences, and clustered homes seem out of place on the West Coast; Mendocino was able to masquerade for years as the fictional Maine village of Cabot Cove in the TV series *Murder, She Wrote*.

▐ TRANSPORTATION. The nearest **Greyhound bus** station (☎800-231-2222) is two hours away in Ukiah. **Mendocino Transit Authority,** 241 Plant Rd., in Ukiah, makes one round-trip daily between Mendocino and Santa Rosa ($16), stopping at Willits ($2.75) and Ukiah ($4.25) on the way. Catch the bus in Mendocino at the Cookie Company at the corner of Lansing and Ukiah St. (☎800-696-4682. Over 61 and disabled half-price.) Although driving is the easiest way to reach Mendocino, once there, the tiny town is best explored on foot. **Catch a Canoe and Bicycles, Too!,** at Hwy. 1 and Comptche-Ukiah Rd., less than half a mile south of downtown Mendocino, specializes in handcrafted redwood canoes but also rents quality bikes and kayaks. Call ahead for tide info. (☎937-0273. Canoes $20 per hr., $60 per day; bikes $12/$36; kayaks $12/$36. Open daily 9am-5pm.)

⚡📧 ORIENTATION AND PRACTICAL INFORMATION. Mendocino sits on **Highway 1,** right on the Pacific Coast, 30 mi. west of U.S. 101 and 12 mi. south of Fort Bragg. In Fort Bragg, Hwy. 1 is known as North and South **Main St.** Mendocino, like all northern coast areas, can be very chilly, even in summer. Travelers should prepare for 40-70°F temperatures. For visitor information, head to the **Fort Bragg-Mendocino Coast Chamber of Commerce,** 332 N. Main St., in Fort Bragg. (☎961-6300 or 800-726-2780. Open M-F 9am-noon and 12:30-5pm, Sa 9am-3pm.) For park-related general information, call ☎937-5804 or go to the **MacKerricher State Park Visitors Center,** 2½ mi. north of Fort Bragg. (☎964-8898. Open in summer Su-M, W, F-Sa 10:30am-4:30pm; limited hours in winter.) **Lost Coast Kayaking** gives fantastic 2hr. guided tours of Van Damme State Park. (☎937-2434; www.lostcoastkayaking.com. Daily 9, 11:30am, and occasionally 2pm. $50. Reservations are necessary but walk-ins may get lucky. Open May-Oct.) For clean clothes, head to **Colombi Laundromat,** 647 Oak St., five blocks east of Main St., in Fort Bragg. (☎964-5773. Wash $1.75, dry $0.25 per 8½min. Open daily 6am-10pm.) **Internet access** is available at the **Fort Bragg Library,** 499 Laurel St., at the corner of N. Whipple and Laurel St., four blocks east of Main St. in Fort Bragg. (Open Tu and Th 10am-6pm, W noon-8pm, F-Sa 10am-5pm.) Emergency services include the **police** (☎964-0200), with a station in Fort Bragg, and a **rape crisis line** (☎964-4357). **Mendocino Coast District Hospital** is located at 700 River Dr. (☎961-1234), in Ft. Bragg, and the Mendocino **post office** is at 10500 Ford St., two blocks west of Main St. (☎937-5282; open M-F 7:30am-4:30pm). **Postal Code:** 95460.

📧 ACCOMMODATIONS. Jug Handle Creek Nature Center ❶, about 3 mi. north of Mendocino off Hwy. 1, across the street from the Jug Handle State Reserve, is a beautiful 134-year-old house sitting on 39 acres of gardens, campsites, and small rustic cabins. Trails from the property lead to coastal access. (☎964-4630. Reservations recommended in summer; walk-ins welcome. Rooms $27, students $21; cabins $35 per person; sites $11; $5 off for 1hr. of chores.) **Abigail's Bed & Breakfast Inn ❷,** 951 Ukiah St., is in the heart of town, right next to great restaurants and a little over a block from the ocean. (☎937-0934 or 800-962-0934. Phones, TV, and breakfast are available in the Hospitality Living Room. 2-night min. stay on weekends, 3-night min. stay on holidays. All reservations must be paid in half in advance. Rooms $99-299.) Less expensive and less eye-pleasing options can be found in Fort Bragg. The most budget-friendly option is **Colombi Motel ❸,** 647 Oak St., five blocks east of Main St. It has clean single and double units with cable TV, phones, and private bath; some have a full kitchen. (☎964-5773. Motel office inside market. Check-out 11am. In summer singles M-F $45, Sa-Su $50; doubles M-F $55, Sa-Su $60. In winter singles M-F $40, Sa-Su $45; doubles M-F $50, Sa-Su $55.)

There are also scores of campsites nearby; contact ReserveAmerica (☎800-444-7275) to make reservations, which are strongly advised in summer. **MacKerricher State Park campground ❷,** 2½ mi. north of Fort Bragg, has excellent views of tide pool life, passing seals, sea lions, and migratory whales, as well as 9 mi. of beaches and a murky lake for trout fishing. Around this lake is **Lake Cleone trail** (1 mi.), a short, easy hike that features thick cypress trees and a pretty marsh. Access the trail from Cleone Camp or Surfwood Camp. (☎937-5804. Showers, bathrooms, and drinkable water. Sites $20.) Woods and fog shelter 30 sites at **Russian Gulch State Park campground ❷,** 8 mi. south of Fort Bragg on Hwy. 1. Campers have access to a beach, redwoods, hiking trails, and a 35 ft. waterfall. The **Falls Loop trail** (6¼ mi.)

leads from the campground to a smattering of second-growth redwoods and rock-pounding falls. (☎937-5804. Coin showers and flush toilets. No hookups. Open Apr.-Oct. Sites $20. Senior discount. Hike/bike $3. Day use $6.)

◻ **FOOD.** Mendocino's breads are freshly baked, its vegetables locally grown, and its wheat unmilled—and the prices are accordingly high. Picnicking on the Mendocino Headlands is the cheapest option and should be preceded by a trip to **Mendosa's Market,** 10501 Lansing St., the closest thing in Mendocino to a real supermarket. It's pricey, but most items are fresh and delicious. (☎937-5879. Open daily 8am-9pm.) For a more typical supermarket experience, head to **Safeway,** 660 Main St., in Fort Bragg. Restaurants in Mendocino often close unusually early. **Lu's Kitchen ❷,** 45013 Ukiah St., west of Lansing St., is a local favorite. It serves leafy vegetarian cuisine in an informal, outdoor atmosphere. (☎937-4939. Entrees $5-9. Open daily Apr.-Sept. and Dec.-Jan. 11:30am-5pm.) At **Lipinski's Mendo Juice Joint ❶,** Ukiah St., just east of Lansing St., grab a sandwich, bagel, or salad to go with your Buddah Boost ($2.70) smoothie, Blemish Blaster ($3) organic blended veggie juice, or Wet Lawn ($2) wheat grass shot. (☎937-4033. Free Internet. Open M-Th 6:30am-7pm, F-Sa 6:30am-11pm, Su 6:30am-9pm.) **Bay View Cafe ❸,** 45040 Main St., serves affordable meals with a sweeping view of the ocean. Popular hot crab sandwiches are $14. (☎937-4197. Entrees $7-16. Open daily 8am-8pm.) **Cafe Beaujolais ❺,** 961 Ukiah St., at the corner of Evergreen, has a welcoming garden. To enjoy the fresh goods (loaves $2.95-4.25) from their on-site, brick-oven bakery, wake up early—they run out quickly. Dinners are likewise superb. (☎937-5614. Entrees $23-34. Bakery open daily 11am-4:30pm. Dinner served daily 5:45-9pm.) **Albion Inn ❻,** 3790 N. Hwy. 1, south of Mendocino, has a spectacular ocean view and award-winning food. The menu changes periodically, but you can always count on roasted garlic caesar salad ($8), lime and ginger grilled prawns ($24), and grilled Pacific king salmon ($23) to satisfy your taste buds. (☎937-1919 or 800-479-7944. Open M-F 5:30-9pm, Sa-Su 5-9:30pm. Reservations recommended.)

◫◪ **SIGHTS AND ENTERTAINMENT.** Mendocino's greatest natural feature lies 900 ft. to its west, where the earth comes to a halt and falls off into the Pacific, forming the impressive coastline of the ▧**Mendocino Headlands.** The windy quarter-mile stretch of land that separates the town from the rocky shore remains an undeveloped meadow of tall grass and wildflowers.

In **Fort Bragg,** the California Western Railroad, also called the **Skunk Train,** at Hwy. 1 and Laurel St., makes for a jolly, child-friendly diversion as it chugs along its scenic Redwood Route. A steam engine, diesel locomotive, and vintage motorcar take turns running between Fort Bragg and Northspur. (☎964-6371 or 866-457-5865; www.skunktrain.com. 3½hr. round-trip. Call or check website for details. Diesel and motorcar $35, children 3-11 $20, under 3 free; steam engine $45/$20/free. Reservations recommended.)

Poor drainage, thin acidic soil, and ocean winds have created unusually stunted vegetation 3 mi. south of town at the **Pygmy Forest** in **Van Damme State Park ❷** (sites $20; day use $6). The forest, off Hwy. 1 past the park (after turning onto Little River Airport Rd., drive 3 mi. to a parking lot and look for a sign) allows free hiking. The **ecological staircase** at **Jug Handle State Park** is a terrace of five different ecosystems formed by a combination of erosion and tectonic uplift, with each ecosystem roughly 100,000 years older than the one below it. Hike the **Ecological Staircase Nature Trail** (a 5 mi. loop) to see another Pygmy Forest.

Farther south on Hwy. 1 in Mendocino County, the fog-shrouded **lighthouse** and **museum** of **Point Arena** deserve a stop. The 115 ft. lighthouse is vintage 1906, built after the San Francisco earthquake demolished the 1870 original. (Open daily May-

THE NORTH COAST

Sept. 10am-4:30pm; Oct.-Apr. 11am-3:30pm. Free guided tours. $5, under 13 $1.) Nearby **Manchester State Beach ❶** has 46 tent sites and hike/bike sites. (☎707-937-5804. Toilets. Sites $15, seniors $13; hike/bike $3; day use free.)

From July 18th to July 30th, enjoy the **Mendocino Music Festival,** a two-week melee of classical music, opera, and cultural dance. Tickets for some events go quickly. (☎937-2044; www.mendocinomusic.com. Tickets $18-45, youth $15.)

JENNER
☎**707**

Jenner sits on Hwy 1. at the mouth of the Russian River. The town's **Goat Rock Beach,** with its astounding waves and coast, is the site of a famous harbor seal rookery. Twelve miles north of Jenner is **Fort Ross State Historic Park,** a lonely walled fort clinging to the ocean bluffs that marks the eastern limit of former imperial Russia. Russians migrated here from Alaskan outposts to hunt otters and find farmland, but left in 1841 after decimating the otter population and losing vast sums of money. John Sutter, of mill and creek fame, bought the fort for a song, primarily to get the redwood threshing table inside. The fort now houses a small museum and bookstore, and features the only reconstructed Russian buildings in the continental US. (☎707-847-3437. Visitors center open 10am-4:30. Museum open daily 10am-4:30pm. Entrance fee $6 per car, seniors $5.)

Reef Campground and Day Use Area ❶, 2 mi. south of the fort, offers 21 primitive campsites with fire rings, toilets, and picnic tables. (Open Apr.-Nov. Sites $15. Day use $6.) **Salt Point State Park ❶,** north of Fort Ross, 20 mi. from Jenner, comprises 6000 acres, including 6 mi. of rugged coast. **Gerstle Cove** and **Woodside** campgrounds provide a total of 109 sites with fire pits and picnic tables. (☎707-847-3221, reservations 800-444-7275. No showers. Dogs allowed. Drinking water and toilets. Drive-in sites $20, seniors $18; walk-ins $18. Day-use $6, hike/bike $3.)

BODEGA BAY
☎**707**

Just north of Point Reyes, Bodega Bay is the sleepy fishing village featured in Alfred Hitchcock's 1963 film *The Birds* (see p. 22). The visitors center has pictures from the filming. The small town displays its seafaring roots in the incredibly fresh salmon and crab at ocean-side restaurants. On the Sonoma coast west of Bodega Bay, the **Bodega Head Loop** (1½ mi.) is a short coastal hike with pristine beach and ocean views. To reach the trail, turn left on E. Shore Rd., turn west on Bay Flat Rd., and continue around the bay past Spud Point Marina to Bedge Head parking, the trailhead's location. The **visitors center,** 850 Hwy. 1, has info on the North Coast. (☎707-875-3866. Open M-Th 10am-6pm, F-Sa 10am-8pm, Su 10am-7pm.) **Sonoma Coast State Beach** begins just north of Bodega Bay off Hwy. 1. The 5000 acres of land offer 16 mi. of beach, spectacular views, and places to picnic, hike, and camp. However, unpredictable currents make swimming dangerous.

The most popular coastal campgrounds are **Bodega Dunes ❶** (hot showers; sites $20, seniors $18. Day-use $6/$4; hike/bike $3) and **Wright's Beach ❷** (sites $30). Call ReserveAmerica for reservations at ☎800-444-7275. If the campgrounds are full, the antique-decorated rooms at **Bodega Harbor Inn ❹,** off Hwy. 1 in Bodega Bay, are your cheapest bet. (☎875-3594; www.bodegaharborinn.com. Rooms $65-90.)

THE SIERRA NEVADA

The Sierra Nevada Mountain Range is known as California's backbone. It runs 450 mi. along the line where two gigantic tectonic plates, the Pacific and North American, collided 400 million years ago. Stretching from stifling Death Valley to just below the Oregon border, the range is a living record of the tireless work of the elements—a product of Mt. Lassen's volcanic activity hundreds of millions of years ago and granite-smoothing glaciation a mere few thousand years ago. It also nurtures some of the most breathtaking scenery in the country, including Lake Tahoe's crystalline waters, Mono Lake's giant tufa formations, Sequoia National Park's towering redwoods, and Yosemite's incredible waterfalls. The entire range is worthy of homage and exploration.

Temperatures in the Sierra Nevada are as diverse as the terrain. Even during the generally warm summer, overnight lows can dip below 30°F (check local weather reports). Normally, only U.S. 50 and I-80 are open during the snow season. Exact dates of road closures vary from year to year; check with a ranger station for road conditions, even through June. In summer, protection from exposure to ultraviolet rays at high elevations is necessary; always bring sunscreen and a hat. For additional outdoors advice, see **Camping and the Outdoors,** p. 55.

HIGHLIGHTS OF THE SIERRA NEVADA

GENERAL SHERMAN. The largest living thing in the world, this massive sequoia tree in Sequoia National Park towers over its nearly-as-tall neighbors in Giant's Grove (p. 275).

ANCIENT BRISTLECONE PINE FOREST. The oldest living organisms on Earth put things in perspective—these trees have been alive for almost 5000 years (p. 294).

MT. WHITNEY. The tallest mountain in the contiguous US makes for brag-worthy hiking and stunning vistas (p. 300).

FROM CREST TO CREST: THE TRAIL OF THE WEST. The longest hiking route in North America, the **Pacific Crest Trail (PCT)** snakes, scales, and scrambles up 2650 mountainous miles from Mexico to Canada, passing through some of the most pristine wilderness on the West Coast and many different climates along the way, from deserts to subarctic regions. True to its name, the PCT always keeps to the crest; the trail maintains an average elevation of over 5000 ft., topping out at the summit of **Mount Whitney** (14,494 ft.), the highest peak in the contiguous US. Although work on the PCT began in 1968, the trailblazing task was so immense that it was not officially completed until 1993. No matter how much of the trail you choose to tackle, proper supplies and conditioning are vital. The **Pacific Crest Trail Association** (☎916-349-2109 or 888-728-7245; www.pcta.org) gives tips on how to prepare.

LAKE TAHOE   ☎530/775

Beautiful Lake Tahoe and its surrounding towns and mountains became a popular destination for wealthy San Franciscans after the 49ers cut roads to the area. Today, posh resorts and massive casinos still attract moneyed vacationers, but the area's abundant outdoor activities make Tahoe's wonders accessible to all. Shimmering blue water, pristine beaches, immense mountains, and an unobtrusive but

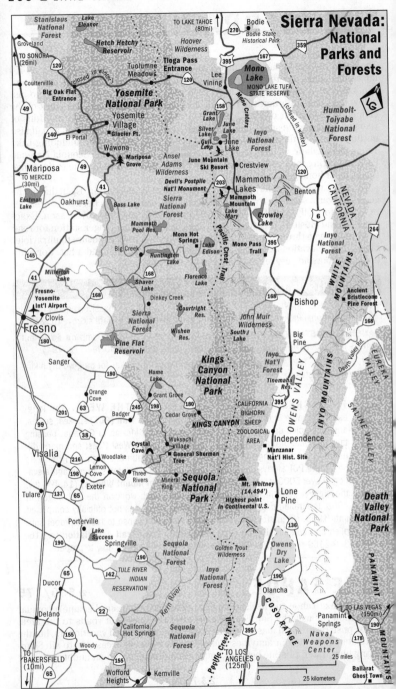

ubiquitous commercial presence make Tahoe an ideal destination for boating, fishing, sunning, skiing, hiking, and spending money. Each season brings wonders of its own to Tahoe; accordingly, tourist season is yearlong.

 The area code for Lake Tahoe is **530** unless otherwise specified. The Nevada side is **775.**

SIERRA NEVADA

⌨ TRANSPORTATION

Trains: Amtrak (☎800-USA-RAIL/872-7245). Trains running between Chicago and San Francisco stop at the Truckee Depot in downtown Truckee. 1 west-bound train daily to **Sacramento** (4½hr., $22-40) and **Oakland/San Francisco** (6½hr., $45-93), and 1 east-bound train to **Reno** (1hr., $10-21).

Buses: Greyhound (☎800-231-2222), at the Truckee Depot. To: **Sacramento** (3hr., 4 per day, $21-24); **San Francisco** (5½hr., 4 per day, $31-35); **Reno, NV** (1hr., 3 per day, $10.50-12.50).

Public Transit:

Tahoe Casino Express (☎775-785-2424 or 800-446-6128). Provides shuttle service between the Reno airport and South Shore Tahoe casinos. (Daily 6:15am-12:30am; $20, under 12 free.)

Tahoe Area Regional Transport TART (☎550-1212 or 800-736-6365; www.laketahoetransit.com). Connects the western and northern shores from Incline Village through Tahoe City to Meeks Bay, where it joins with South Lake Tahoe (STAGE) buses in the summer at a transfer station. Stops daily every 30min.-1hr., depending on the route. Buses also run from Tahoe City to Truckee and Squaw Valley and back (5 per day 7:30am-4:45pm). $1.25, day pass $3. Exact fare required.

South Tahoe Area Ground Express STAGE (☎541-7149). Operates in both NV and CA on the South Shore. It runs several routes between the Stateline, NV casinos and the Hwy. 89/50 intersection. Runs 6:40am-12:40pm. $1.25, day pass $2, 10-ride pass $10.

Bus Plus (☎541-7149) runs door-to-door service within city limits (24hr., $3) and within El Dorado County (7am-7pm, $5).

Car Rental: Many agencies have branches in Nevada casinos. **Avis** (☎775-588-3361), in Caesars Tahoe, Stateline, NV. **Enterprise** (☎775-586-1077), in the Horizon lobby, Stateline, NV. **Hertz** (☎775-586-0041), in Harvey's, Stateline, NV.

⛰ ORIENTATION

Located in the northern Sierra Nevadas on the California-Nevada border, Lake Tahoe is a 3hr. drive from San Francisco. The lake rests about 100 mi. northeast of Sacramento (via **Highway 50**) and 35 mi. southwest of Reno (via **Highway 395** and **431**). Coming from the south, **Highway 395** runs 20 mi. east of the lake. Lake Tahoe is divided into two main regions, **North Shore** and **South Shore.** The North Shore includes **Tahoe City** in California and **Incline Village** in Nevada, while the South Shore includes **South Lake Tahoe** in California and **Stateline** in Nevada. "The Most Beautiful Drive in America," Hwy. 50 combines with Hwy. 28 and 89 to form a 75 mi. asphalt ring around the lake; the entire winding loop takes nearly 3hr. to complete by car.

Tahoe City centers around the intersection of **Highways 89** and **28.** Hwy. 89 is called **West Lake Boulevard** and heads south to the beaches and parks of the west shore, and Hwy. 28, a large commercial street, is known as **North Lake Boulevard** in central Tahoe City. **Highway 50 (Lake Tahoe Boulevard)** is the main drag of South Lake Tahoe and Stateline, NV. At the western end of South Lake, Hwy. 89 heads up the lake's shore. The major cross streets in South Lake are **Ski Run Boulevard, Wildwood Avenue,** and **Park Avenue.**

SIERRA NEVADA

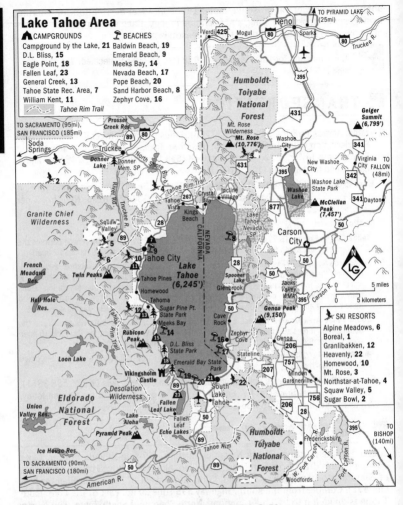

Lake Tahoe Area

⛺ CAMPGROUNDS
Campground by the Lake, **21**
D.L. Bliss, **15**
Eagle Point, **18**
Fallen Leaf, **23**
General Creek, **13**
Tahoe State Rec. Area, **7**
William Kent, **11**

🏖 BEACHES
Baldwin Beach, **19**
Emerald Beach, **9**
Meeks Bay, **14**
Nevada Beach, **17**
Pope Beach, **20**
Sand Harbor Beach, **8**
Zephyr Cove, **16**

~~~ Tahoe Rim Trail

🎿 SKI RESORTS
Alpine Meadows, **6**
Boreal, **1**
Granlibakken, **12**
Heavenly, **22**
Homewood, **10**
Mt. Rose, **3**
Northstar-at-Tahoe, **4**
Squaw Valley, **5**
Sugar Bowl, **2**

🛈 PRACTICAL INFORMATION

Visitor Information:

North Lake Tahoe North Visitors Bureau, 380 North Lake Blvd. (☎ 583-3494; www.mytahoevaca-tion.com), in Tahoe City. Tons of info on the area. Open M-F 9am-5pm, Sa-Su 9am-4pm.

Lake Tahoe Visitors Authority, 1156 Ski Run Blvd. (☎ 544-5050 or 800-288-2463; www.virtualta-hoe.com), in South Lake. An information clearinghouse for the entire lake with an emphasis on the South Shore. Open M-F 8:30am-5pm.

Tahoe-Douglas Chamber of Commerce and Visitors Center, 195 Hwy. 50 (☎ 775-588-4591; www.tahoechamber.org), in Stateline, NV. Open daily May-Oct. 9am-6pm; Nov.-Apr. 9am-5pm.

Taylor Creek Visitors Center (USFS), (☎ 543-2674; www.fs.fed.us/r5/ltbmu), 3 mi. north of South Lake Tahoe on Hwy. 89. A good resource for planning outdoor excursions, with detailed maps of the area. Issues permits for camping in the Desolation Wilderness. Camping fee $5 per person per night, $10 per person for 2 or more nights, annual pass $20; under 12 free. Reservations (☎644-6048, $5) available for overnight permits mid-June through Labor Day. Open daily Memorial Day weekend to mid-June and Oct. 8am-4pm; mid-June to Sept. 8am-5:30pm.

Bank: US Bank, 705 North Lake Blvd. (☎583-2346), in Tahoe City. Open M-Th 9am-5pm, F 9am-6pm. **Bank of the West,** 2161 Lake Tahoe Blvd. (☎531-3390), in South Lake. Open M-Th 9am-5pm, F 9am-6pm, Sa 9am-1pm. Both banks have **24hr. ATM.**

Library: Tahoe City Library, 740 North Lake Blvd. (☎583-3382). Free Internet. Open Tu and Th-F 10am-5pm, W noon-7pm, Sa noon-4pm. **El Dorado County Library: South Lake Tahoe Branch,** 1000 Rufus Allen Blvd. (☎573-3185). Free Internet. Open Tu-W 10am-8pm, Th-Sa 10am-5pm.

Laundromats: Big Tree Cleaners, 531 North Lake Blvd. (☎583-2802), in Tahoe City. Wash $1.50, dry $0.25 per 10min. Open daily 7am-10pm. **Uncle Bob's Laundromat,** 2180 Lake Tahoe Blvd. (☎542-1910), in South Lake. Wash $1.25, dry $0.25 per 8min. Open daily 7am-10pm.

Road Conditions: California ☎800-427-7623; Nevada 877-687-6237 or 775-793-1313; elsewhere 800-546-5253, ext. 43.

24hr. Road Service: ☎587-6000 or 800-937-4757.

Police: Placer County Sheriff, 2501 North Lake Blvd. (☎581-6330), east of Tahoe City on Hwy. 28. **South Lake Police,** 1352 Johnson Blvd. (☎542-6100), off Al Tahoe Blvd.

Crisis Hotlines: General, ☎800-992-5757. **Gamblers Anonymous,** ☎573-2423. **Tahoe Women's Services,** ☎546-3241.

Medical Services: Incline Village Community Hospital, 880 Alder Ave. (☎775-833-4100), off Hwy. 28 in Incline Village. **Barton Memorial Hospital,** 2170 South Ave. (☎541-3420), at 3rd St. and South Ave. off Lake Tahoe Blvd. in South Lake.

Post Office: Tahoe City, 950 North Lake Blvd. (☎800-275-8777). In the Lighthouse Shopping Center. Open M-F 8:30am-5pm. **Postal Code:** 96145. **South Lake Tahoe,** 1046 Al Tahoe Blvd. (☎800-275-8777). Open M-F 8:30am-5pm, Sa noon-2pm. **Postal Code:** 96151.

⌐ ACCOMMODATIONS

The South Shore hosts many of the cheapest motels in the region and a few high-priced casino-hotels. With few exceptions, motels in the South offer nothing more than basic amenities. Accommodations in the North Shore, while fewer in number, are generally more polished and refined. Accordingly, rates in the North are relatively high. In Tahoe City and Incline Village, the priciest lodgings tend to be booked solid for weekends and holidays; reserve well in advance. Fall and spring are the most economical times of the year to visit Tahoe. Look for discount coupons in free publications at the visitors centers. Whatever your budget, the area's campgrounds are great options in warmer months.

■ **Tahoe Valley Lodge,** 2214 Lake Tahoe Blvd. (☎800-669-7544 or 541-0353; www.tahoevalleylodge.com), in **South Lake.** Decorative detail and exquisite comfort (and comforters) in spacious rooms with a simple log-cabin theme. All rooms have queen-size beds, cable TV, and coffeemakers; many have microwaves, refrigerators, and in-room spas. Reception 24hr. Singles $95; doubles $125. ❺

■ **Firelite Lodge,** 7035 North Lake Blvd. (☎800-934-7222 or 546-7222), in Tahoe Vista 8 mi. east of **Tahoe City.** Right across from a sandy beach, this hotel has understated, relaxing rooms with microwaves, refrigerators, coffeemakers, and cable TV. Some rooms with balconies overlooking the pool. Laundry service available. Reception 8am-11pm. Singles and doubles summer and winter from $59; spring and fall from $49. ❸

Royal Inn, 3520 Lake Tahoe Blvd. (☎544-1177), in **South Lake.** Generic, well-maintained rooms with cable TV. Heated pool and laundry facilities. Singles Su-Th $28-35; doubles $39-49. Rates inflate greatly on weekends and holidays. Mention *Let's Go* for a possible discount. ❷

Tahoe City Inn, 790 North Lake Blvd. (☎581-3333 or 800-800-8246; www.tahoecity-inn.com), in downtown **Tahoe City.** Standard rooms include queen-size beds, coffee-makers, mini-fridges, and cable TV. Deluxe rooms come with kitchenettes, hot tubs, and access to an extensive video library. Rooms late Apr. to mid-June and late Sept.-late Nov. $85-160; mid-June to late Sept. and late Sept.-late Apr. $59-140. ❹

Doug's Mellow Mountain Retreat, 3787 Forest Ave. (☎544-8065). From the north, turn left from Hwy. 50 onto Wildwood Rd. west of downtown **Stateline,** then left on Forest Ave. A woodsy house in a residential neighborhood. Along with well-sized, basic rooms, Doug supplies a modern kitchen, BBQ, and fireplace. Internet $5 per hr. Dorms $15; private rooms $25. Discounts for stays over a week. ❶

Tamarack Lodge, 2311 North Lake Blvd. (☎583-3350 or 888-824-6323), 3 mi. north of **Tahoe City,** across from Lake Forest Beach. Clean, friendly lodge in the woods. Outdoor BBQ and fireplace, phones, and cable TV. Some rooms come with kitchenettes and some cabins with full kitchens. Rooms from $54; low season from $44. Cabins (sleep 4) $125; low season $105. ❸

⚑ CAMPING

The Taylor Creek Visitors Center (see p. 240) provides up-to-date information on camping. Campgrounds ring the entire lake, but **Route 89** is inundated with sites between Tahoe City and South Lake Tahoe. Sites can be booked on weekends in July and August, and it pays to reserve in advance; call the **California State Parks Reservation Center** (☎800-444-7275) or the **National Recreation Reservation System** (☎877-444-6777; www.reserveamerica.com) for California Land Management. Backcountry camping is allowed in designated wilderness areas with a permit from the Forest Service (see p. 240). The listings below run from north to south.

Tahoe State Recreation Area (☎583-3074), on the eastern edge of **Tahoe City** off Hwy. 28. In these 39 compact sites within walking distance of downtown Tahoe City (and adjacent to a shopping center), you may not feel like you're camping. Both sunny and shady sites. Water, flush toilets, and showers ($0.50). Open May-Nov. Sites $15; $4 per additional vehicle. ❶

William Kent (☎583-3642), on Hwy. 89, 2 mi. south of **Tahoe City.** One of the most popular campgrounds on the west shore, with 95 shady sites, beach access, clean flush toilets, and water. Open June-Sept. 6. Sites $16; $5 per additional vehicle. ❶

General Creek (☎525-7982), in Sugar Pine Point State Park, 1 mi. south of **Tahoma** off Hwy. 89. This popular, family-friendly campground has 175 sites, tennis courts, bike and cross-country ski trails, as well as a nature center, historic mansion, and lakeside dock. Water, barbecue pits, and flush toilets. Showers $0.50. Sites $15; $4 per additional vehicle. ❶

D.L. Bliss (☎525-7277), 11 mi. south of **Homewood** off Hwy. 89. One of the most scenic campgrounds on the lake. Access to Lester Beach and the trailheads for Rubicon and Lighthouse Trails. 168 sites with grills, water, flush toilets, and showers. Open late May-Sept. Sites $15-19; $5 per additional vehicle. ❶

Eagle Point (☎541-3030), in Emerald Bay State Park 12 mi. north of **South Lake Tahoe** off Hwy. 89. 100 sites with breathtaking views of Emerald Bay. Grills, water, flush toilets, and showers. Open late May-Sept. Sites $15; $5 per additional vehicle. ❶

Fallen Leaf (☎544-0426), 2 mi. north of **South Lake Tahoe** off Hwy. 89. 206 shady sites beside Fallen Leaf Lake with access to Baldwin and Pope Beaches. A good option for those looking to mix the gambling action of South Lake Tahoe with the call of the wild. Water, flush toilets, but no showers. Open late May-Sept. Sites $18. ❷

Campground by the Lake (☎542-6096), at Hwy. 50 and Rufus Allen Blvd. in **South Lake Tahoe.** 170 bare-bones sites across from a beach and picnic areas. Free casino shuttle, showers, and flush toilets. Open Apr-Oct. Sites $21; RV hookups $29. ❷

◪ FOOD

In the south, casinos offer low-priced buffets, but grilles and burger joints around the lake promise superior food at reasonable prices. The Tahoe City **Farmers Market,** at Dollar Hill off Hwy. 28, opens every summer. (☎823-6183; www.foothillfarmersmarket.com. Open June-Oct. Th 8am-1pm.) For year-round foraging, try **Safeway,** 850 North Lake Blvd. (☎583-2772; open daily Sept.-June 6am-10pm; July-Aug. 6am-1am), or 1020 Johnson Blvd., at Lake Tahoe Blvd. in South Lake (☎542-7740; open 24hr.).

Jakes on the Lake, 780 N. Lake Blvd. (☎583-0188), in Boatworks Shopping Mall in **Tahoe City.** A taste of the South Seas in a relaxed wood-paneled dining room. Hawaiian-inspired creations alongside options like the New Rack of Lamb ($22). Open M-F 11:30am-2:30pm and 5:30-9:30pm, Sa-Su 11:30am-2:30pm and 5-9:30pm. ❹

Sprouts Natural Foods Cafe, 3123 Harrison Ave. (☎541-6969), at the intersection of Lake Tahoe Blvd. and Alameda Ave. in **South Lake.** Young, hip waiters dish out creative natural foods to an intelligent and healthy crowd. Try a breakfast burrito with avocados ($5), a smoothie ($3-3.75), or a shot of wheat grass ($2). Open daily 8am-10pm. ❶

The Red Hut Cafe, 2723 Lake Tahoe Blvd. (☎541-9024), in **South Lake,** and another location at 22 Kingsbury Grade (☎588-7488). A Tahoe original since 1959. Friendly staff serves homestyle cooking. Waffles piled with fruit and whipped cream $5.75, avocado burgers $6.50. Open daily 6am-2pm. No credit cards. ❶

Syd's, 550 North Lake Blvd. (☎583-2666), in **Tahoe City.** Cheap smoothies ($3.75) and humorously named sandwiches, such as Hummus Humongous ($4.50) and The Gobbler ($5). Open Sept.-June daily 6:30am-5pm; July-Aug. 6am-7pm. ❶

Sancho's, 7019 North Lake Blvd. (☎546-7744), in Tahoe Vista, 8 mi. east of **Tahoe City.** This *taqueria* with a view serves huge portions of tacos ($1.50), burritos ($4.50), and tostadas ($3.75) filled with carne asada, carnitas, or chorizo. Try the terrific tostada ceviche with shrimp and mahi-mahi ($4.50). Open daily 11am-9pm. ❶

Lakeside Beach Grill, 4081 Lakeshore Blvd. (☎544-4050), on the water between Park and Stateline Ave., near **South Lake.** Lake-front location draws hordes of beach-goers. Unique and satisfying entrees ($7-11) such as the calamari burger go well with any of their numerous domestic beers ($3). Open June-Sept. daily 11am-7pm. ❷

◪ OUTDOOR ACTIVITIES

SUMMER ACTIVITIES

BEACHES

Lake Tahoe's many beaches provide the perfect setting for a day of sunning and people-watching. Parking generally costs $3-7; bargain hunters should leave cars in turnouts on the main road and walk to the beaches.

NORTH SHORE. Sand Harbor Beach, 2 mi. south of Incline Village on Hwy. 28, has gorgeous granite boulders and clear waters that attract crowds of swimmers, sunners, snorkelers, and boaters to its marina. The parking lot ($5) often fills by late morning. **Tahoe City Commons Beach,** in the heart of Tahoe City off North Lake Blvd., has a playground, sandy beach, and pristine lake waters great for swimming.

SOUTH SHORE. Baldwin Beach and neighboring **Pope Beach,** near the southernmost point of the lake off Hwy. 89, are popular, shaded expanses of shoreline. Quiet spots can be found on the edges of both beaches. **Nevada Beach,** on the east shore, 3 mi. north of South Lake Tahoe off Hwy. 50, is close to the casinos but offers a sandy sanctuary away from the jangling slot machines. Recently renovated **Zephyr Cove Beach,** 5 mi. north of South Lake Tahoe, hosts a youthful crowd keen on beer and bikinis.

WEST SHORE. Meeks Bay, 10 mi. south of Tahoe City, is a family-oriented beach with picnic tables, volleyball courts, BBQ pits, campsites, and a store. The minimal **D.L. Bliss State Park,** 17 mi. south of Tahoe City on Hwy. 89, is home to **Lester** and **Calawee Cove Beaches** on striking Rubicon Bay. It's also the trailhead for the Rubicon Trail, which leads to the Vikingsholm mansion. Parking ($5) is limited; check the visitors center at the entrance or park on the road and walk in.

HIKING

Hiking is an excellent way to explore the Tahoe Basin. Visitors centers and ranger stations provide detailed info and maps for all types of hikes. Backcountry hikers must obtain a wilderness permit (see p. 249) for any hike into Desolation Wilderness; 700 hikers are allowed in this area on any given day. Due to erratic weather conditions in the Sierra, hikers should always bring a jacket as well as drinking water. Ask where the snow has melted—it's not usually all gone until July. **Alpenglow Sports,** 415 North Lake Blvd., in Tahoe City, offers a wide array of outdoor gear. (☎ 583-6917. Open M-F 10am-6pm, Sa-Su 9am-6pm.)

After decades of work, the 165 mi. **Tahoe Rim Trail** has finally been completed. The route encircles the lake, following the ridge tops of the Tahoe Basin. The trail welcomes hikers, equestrians, and, in most areas, **mountain bikers.** Camping is allowed on most parts of the trail, but backcountry permits are required in Desolation Wilderness. Hiking is moderate to difficult. On the western shore, the route is part of the Pacific Crest Trail. There are eight trailheads around the lake; consult a ranger station for a trail suited to your interests. Popular trailheads include **Spooner Summit,** at the junction of Hwy. 50 and 28, and **Tahoe City,** on Fairway Dr. off Hwy. 89.

NORTH SHORE. At 10,776 ft., **Mount Rose** is one of the tallest mountains in the region as well as one of the best climbs. The panoramic view from the summit includes the lake, Reno, and the surrounding Sierra Nevadas. The 12 mi. round-trip trek begins as an easy dirt road but ascends switchbacks for the last few miles. Take Hwy. 431 north from Incline Village to the trailhead. The rugged trails and mountain streams of **Granite Chief Wilderness,** west of Squaw Valley, wind through forests in 5000 ft. valleys up to the summits of 9000 ft. peaks. The **Alpine Meadows Trailhead,** at the end of Alpine Meadows Rd. off Hwy. 89 between Truckee and Tahoe City, and the **Pacific Crest Trailhead,** at the end of Barker Pass Rd. (Blackwood Canyon Rd.), provide easy access to secluded wilderness.

SOUTH SHORE. The southern region of the basin includes many moderate to strenuous hiking trails. The picturesque **Emerald Bay,** on Hwy. 89 between South Lake Tahoe and Tahoe City, is best explored on foot. Waterfalls cascade down the mountains above this partially enclosed bay, which contains Lake

Tahoe's only island, Fannette. ⬛Emerald Bay State Park, which abuts Desolation Wilderness, offers hiking and biking trails of varying difficulty, as well as camping. One of the best hikes in Tahoe is Rubicon Trail, which wraps 6 mi. around the beach and granite cliffs of Emerald Bay. There are trailheads at D.L. Bliss State Park and Vikingsholm. The challenging Eagle Falls Trail ascends into the barren Desolation Wilderness and provides spectacular views of the High Sierra. The trail starts from the Eagle Lake parking lot. Permits, available at the Taylor Creek Visitors Center (see p. 240), are required for this hike. The nature trails around the Taylor Creek Visitors Center, 3 mi. north of South Lake Tahoe on Hwy. 89, are more leisurely. The Lake of the Sky Trail (½ mi. round-trip) includes several informative signs. The centerpiece of the visitors center is the River Profile Chamber, which displays a cross-section of a Tahoe creek ecocosm. The chamber is accessible via Rainbow Trail (½ mi. round-trip). Lower and Upper Echo Lakes, off Hwy. 50 south of South Lake Tahoe, are much smaller, wilder versions of Tahoe; granite tablets and pine trees tower over the lakes, and extend for miles into the backcountry. Echo Chalet, 2 mi. west of Hwy. 50 on the near shore of Lower Echo, operates boat service across the lake. (☎659-7207. Runs in high season M-Th 8am-6pm, F-Su 8am-7pm. $7 one-way; pets $3.) Once across, a well-maintained stretch of the Pacific Crest Trail leads you past the Upper Echo boat landing and into Desolation Wilderness. Day hiking wilderness permits are available at the chalet; mandatory overnight permits are issued at the Taylor Creek Visitors Center (see p. 240). Another 2 mi. along Hwy. 50, just before Twin Bridges, is the Horsetail Falls trailhead. These stunning falls are accessed by a short (1¼ mi.) but challenging hike through the slippery canyon. Inexperienced hikers should exercise caution—each year, Forest Service helicopters rescue a few sight-seekers.

ROCK CLIMBING

Alpenglow Sports, 415 North Lake Blvd., in Tahoe City, provides rock and ice climbing literature and know-how. (☎583-6917. Shoe rental $8 per day. Open M-F 10am-6pm, Sa-Su 9am-6pm.) Pleasant climbs abound in Lake Tahoe, but safety precautions and equipment are a must. The inexperienced can try bouldering in D.L. Bliss State Park. The South Shore has many popular climbing spots, including the celebrated Ninety-Foot Wall at Emerald Bay, Twin Crags at Tahoe City, and Big Chief near Squaw Valley. Lover's Leap, in South Lake Tahoe, is an incredible, albeit crowded, route spanning two giant cliffs. East of South Lake Tahoe off Hwy. 50, Phantom Spires has amazing views, while Pie Shop is a more difficult climb.

WINTER ACTIVITIES

DOWNHILL SKIING

With world-class alpine slopes, 15 ski resorts, knee-deep powder, and California sun, Tahoe is the stuff of skiers' dreams. Visitors centers provide info, maps, and free publications like *Ski Tahoe* and *Sunny Day*. Daily ski info updates are online at www.visitortips.com/tig/skitahoe. Skiing conditions range from winter storms to t-shirt weather, and snow (artificial or otherwise) covers the slopes into early summer. Low-season skiing may not compete with winter powder, but it's cheaper. Rates listed below are for peak season. All the major resorts offer lessons and rent equipment. Look for multi-day packages that offer significant discounts over single-day rates. Lifts at most resorts operate daily 9am-4pm; arrive early for the best skiing and shortest lines. Prices do not include ski rental, which generally costs $20-30 per day. Numerous smaller ski resorts offer cheaper tickets and shorter lines. Granlibakken

(☎583-4242 or 800-543-3221) is the oldest ski resort at Lake Tahoe and sells the cheapest lift tickets ($18); **Homewood Mountain Resort** (☎525-2992) has top-notch tree skiing, great views of the lake, and 1260 acres.

Squaw Valley (☎583-6985 or 888-766-9321; www.squaw.com), 5 mi. north of Tahoe City off Hwy. 89. The site of the 1960 Olympic Winter Games, and it still shows; the groomed bowls make for some of the West's best skiing. 4000 acres of terrain across 6 Sierra peaks. 33 ski lifts, including the 110-passenger cable car and high-speed gondola, access high-elevation runs for all levels. Open late Nov.-May. Full day $59; half-day $43, ages 13-15 and 65-75 $29, under 12 $5, 76 and over free. Night skiing mid-Dec. to mid-Apr. daily 4-9pm; $20.

Heavenly (☎775-586-7000), on Ski Run Blvd. off South Lake Tahoe Blvd. The largest and most popular resort in the area, with over 4800 acres, 29 lifts, and 84 trails. Its vertical drop is 3500 ft., Tahoe's most extreme. Few shoots or ridges. Lifts and slopes straddle the California-Nevada border and offer dizzying views of both states. Full day $57, ages 13-18 $47, seniors and ages 6-12 $29.

Northstar-at-Tahoe (☎562-1010; www.skinorthstar.com), on Hwy. 267, 13 mi. north of Tahoe City. Family-oriented ski area emphasizes beginning and intermediate trails. 200 new acres on Lookout Mountain cater to advanced skiers, and its 2420 total acres are the most on the North Shore. Full day $57, ages 13-22 $44, under 13 $19.

Alpine Meadows (☎583-4232 or 800-441-4423), on Hwy. 89, 3 mi. north of Tahoe City. Family vacation spot and local hangout. Over 2000 skiable acres. Friendlier than the bigger resorts, with long expert bowls and good powder skiing. Full day $39, ages 7-12 $10, over 70 $10, under 6 free.

Mt. Rose (☎800-754-7673 or 775-849-0704), 11 mi. from Incline Village on Rte. 431. A local favorite. Long season, short lines, and advanced-level focus. Full-day $48, ages 13-17 $38, seniors $28, ages 6-12 $12, over 70 (mid-week) and under 6 free; half-day $38, ages 13-17 $33. Tu 2-for-1, W students $19, Th women $19.

Sugar Bowl (☎426-9000), off I-80 at the Soda Springs/Norden exit, then 3 mi. east on Donner Pass Rd. From Tahoe city, take Hwy. 89 to I-80 west. Home to the first chairlift in California and the first gondola in the country, Sugar Bowl has 1500 acres with trails for all experience levels. Full day $35 midweek, $54 weekend; half-day $35, kids $13.

Boreal (☎426-3663), off I-80, 10 mi. west of Truckee. From Tahoe City, take Hwy. 89 to I-80 west. With mostly beginner and intermediate runs, and a crowded snowboard park, Boreal is a popular choice for Bay Area travelers who don't want to drive all the way to Lake Tahoe. 9 lifts, 41 trails, and night skiing. Full-day $34, ages 5-12 $10, over 60 $18, over 70 and under 5 free.

CROSS-COUNTRY SKIING AND SNOWSHOEING

One of the best ways to enjoy the solitude of Tahoe's pristine snow-covered forests is to **cross-country ski** along the thick braid of trails around the lake. **Porters,** 501 North Lake Blvd., in Tahoe City, rents cross-country skis for $10-15. (☎583-2314. Open daily Oct.-Apr. 8am-6pm; May-Sept. 9am-6pm.) **Royal Gorge,** off I-80 at the Soda Springs/Norden exit, is the nation's premiere cross-country ski resort. Its 90 trails cover over 200 mi. of beginner and expert terrain. (☎800-500-3871 or 426-3871. Midweek $21.50, weekend $26; children $12/$14.) **Spooner Lake,** at the junction of Hwy. 50 and 28, offers 57 mi. of machine-groomed trails and incredible views. (☎775-749-5349. $19, children $3.) **Tahoe X-C,** off Hwy. 28, 2 mi. northeast of downtown Tahoe City on Dollar Hill, maintains 40 mi. of trails for all abilities that wind through North Shore forests. (☎583-5475. $18; mid-week $13; children $6.) **Snowshoeing** is easier to pick up. Follow hiking or cross-country trails, or trudge off into the woods. Equipment rentals are available at sporting goods stores for about $15 per day. Check local ranger stations for ranger-guided winter snowshoe hikes.

⚑ NIGHTLIFE

In Tahoe City, the nightlife centers around the pub scene. Pick up a copy of *Action* newspaper, available in the Lighthouse Shopping Center in Tahoe City, for happenings around town. In South Lake Tahoe, casinos dominate the nightlife, and gambling is an all-hours pursuit. To get into bars or casinos, you must be 21 and have a government-issued form of picture ID.

Pierce Street Annex, 850 North Lake Blvd. (☎583-5800), in the Lighthouse Shopping Center in **Tahoe City.** The most popular bar in town; crowded nightly. All sustenance comes in liquid form. Free pool on Su, DJ W-Sa, locals night Th. Open daily 2pm-2am.

Caesar's Palace, 55 Hwy. 50 (☎888-829-7630 or 775-588-3515). A Roman theme pervades the casino/restaurant/club complex. The popular **Club Nero** (☎775-586-2000) heats up for dancing and drinking. $1 drinks M. Latino night Tu. Wet t-shirt contests and free admission for ladies W. Ladies night with free admission and well drinks until midnight Th-Sa. $1 drafts Su. Cover $5-25. Open daily from 9pm on.

The Brewery, 3542 Lake Tahoe Blvd. (☎544-2739). Stop in and try one of the 7 microbrews on tap. The sassy Bad Ass Ale packs a fruity punch, and pizzas (from $10) come crammed with as many toppings as you want. Laid-back atmosphere makes this spot a favorite for locals. Open Su-Th 11am-10pm, F-Sa 11am-2am.

⚑ DAYTRIP FROM LAKE TAHOE

DONNER MEMORIAL STATE PARK. A short drive from Lake Tahoe, Donner Memorial State Park features hiking and biking trails, picnic areas, and the serene Donner Lake. Several hikes depart from the Donner Summit Trailhead, 8 mi. west of Donner Lake on I-80 near the Castle Peak Area/Boreal Ridge Rd. exit. The **Summit Lake Trail** follows the PCT through thick forest before branching off toward tranquil, trout-filled Summit Lake. The **Pacific Crest Trail** (12 mi. round-trip) climbs from the Donner Summit Trailhead to the summit of Mt. Judah, passing by huge granite boulders. **Climbing** at Donner Summit is world-renowned. Over 400 climbs along Old Hwy., off I-80, range from beginner to advanced.

THE LOCAL STORY

THIS PARTY BITES!

Today, memorials honoring the Donner Party are ubiquitous in Truckee. Their tragic story began in April 1846, when a group of Midwesterners (led by George Donner) set off for the Edenic lands of California. Unfortunately, the ill-fated party took a "shortcut" in Wyoming advocated by explorer Lansford Hastings, who had never actually seen the route. They hacked through the wilderness, losing cattle and abandoning wagons along the way. When they rejoined the main trail, they were three weeks behind.

By late October they arrived at Truckee Meadows (present-day Reno) but were exhausted, demoralized, harassed by Paiute Indians, and out of food. When they reached Truckee (now Donner) Lake around November 4, snow was already on the ground. The party made three unsuccessful attempts to cross the pass over the Sierras and was finally forced to settle around the lake. The thaw they hoped for never came, and, trapped by 22 ft. of snow, many resorted to cannibalism before they were finally rescued in April 1847. Only 47 of the initial 89 people survived. After national news of the horrific incidents emerged, migration to California fell off for several years until the torrent of the Gold Rush washed away all memories of that winter. Today, an Annual Donner Party Hike (☎587-2757) reenacts the fateful journey every October (meal not included).

School Rock (beginner) and Snow Shed (advanced) are some of the most popular ascents. *(From Tahoe City, take Hwy. 89 to I-80 west and exit at Donner Lake Rd.)*

THE BIG SPLURGE

FROM THE HEAVENS

Walk through the main floor of any casino in Reno and you're sure to witness some gamblers at the highest of highs, and others at the lowest of lows. But what to do when your bottom begins to sore, your right arm tire, and your pocket book swell from hours of success on the slots? Head outside, look up, and you just may see your answer. The Ultimate Rush stands high above the Reno skyline, equal parts hang gliding, bungee jumping, and sky diving.

The perfect way to let loose from the pressures of gambling or the regrets of a quick hitch, the Ultimate Rush is a fall from a 185 ft. tower (attached to an elastic wire). The view from the top is utterly spectacular and terrifying at the same time. You're sitting on top of the world, hanging above the biggest little city in the world. You can even take 2 of your friends with you on the Ultimate Rush to share the thrill. The plan is simple: stop by the casino, win yourself $25, and then visit the Reno Hilton and experience the Ultimate Rush—sure beats going all in on a single poker hand and having to hitch a ride home.

The Ultimate Rush is at the Reno Hilton, 2500 E. 2nd St. ☎ 800-427-7247. Open daily noon-10pm.

RENO   ☎775

With decadent casinos only a die's throw away from the snowcapped Sierras, Reno embodies both the opportunist frenzy and the natural splendor of the West. Catering to those interested in making a fast buck or saying a quick vow, the city has become known for its crazed gamblers and its equally delirious lovers. Reno continues to be the Sierra's answer to Las Vegas, attracting risk-takers who crave the rush of hitting it big without the theme-park distractions.

▐ TRANSPORTATION

Flights: Reno-Tahoe International Airport, 2001 E. Plumb Ln. (☎328-6499 or 888-766-4685), off Hwy. 395 at Terminal Way, 3 mi. southeast of downtown. Most major hotels have free shuttles for guests; otherwise, take Citifare bus #13 (daily 6:15am-1:30am). Taxi from downtown to airport $10-12.

Trains: Amtrak, 135 E. Commercial Row (☎329-8638 or 800-872-7245). Ticket office open daily 8:30am-5pm. Purchase tickets at least 30min. in advance. 1 train per day heads to **Sacramento** (5hr., $65), continuing to **San Francisco** (via Emeryville; 7½hr., $71).

Buses: Greyhound, 155 Stevenson St. (☎322-2970 or 800-231-2222), between W. 1st and W. 2nd St. Open 24hr. To: **San Francisco** (12 per day, 5-6hr., $30-32) and **Las Vegas, NV** (1 per day, 10hr., $72).

Public Transportation: Reno Citifare (☎348-7433) serves the Reno-Sparks area. Main terminal between Plaza St. and E. 4th on Center St. Major routes operate 24hr. $1.50, ages 6-18 $1.25, seniors and disabled $0.75. **Sierra Spirit** (☎348-RIDE/7433) circles downtown Reno, hitting stops along Sierra and Center St. between 9th and Liberty St. every 10min. Runs Su-W 10am-8pm, Th-Sa 10am-midnight. $0.50.

Taxi: Whittlesea Checker Taxi, ☎322-2222. **Reno-Sparks Cab,** ☎333-3333.

Car Rental: Alamo (☎323-7940 or 888-426-3296), **Avis** (☎785-2727 or 800-831-2847), and **Budget** (☎800-527-7000 or 800-527-0700) are all in the airport. Outside the airport are **Enterprise,** 809 W. 4th St. (☎328-1671 or 800-736-8222), and **Rent-A-Wreck,** 295 Gentry Way (☎322-7787 or 877-880-5603).

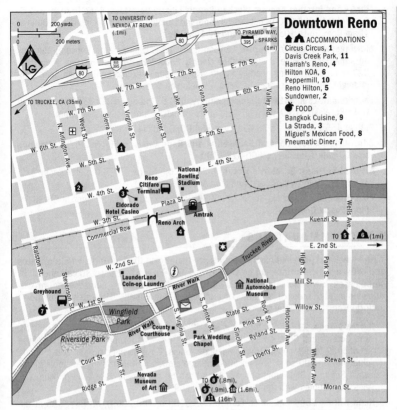

Downtown Reno

♠♠ ACCOMMODATIONS
Circus Circus, **1**
Davis Creek Park, **11**
Harrah's Reno, **4**
Hilton KOA, **6**
Peppermill, **10**
Reno Hilton, **5**
Sundowner, **2**

● FOOD
Bangkok Cuisine, **9**
La Strada, **3**
Miguel's Mexican Food, **8**
Pneumatic Diner, **7**

✦ ORIENTATION

Fifteen miles from the California border and 445 mi. north of Las Vegas, Reno sits at the intersection of **I-80,** which stretches between Chicago and San Francisco, and **Highway 395,** which traces the eastern slope of the Sierra Nevadas from Southern California to Washington.

Many of the major casinos are in the **downtown** area between West and Center St., and 2nd and 6th St. The neon-lit streets of downtown Reno are heavily patrolled, but **avoid straying too far east of the city center at night.** Relatively cheap accommodations, outlying casinos, and numerous strip malls can be found south of the Truckee River along **Virginia Street,** indisputably Reno's main drag. The #1 bus services Virginia St. from downtown Reno to Meadowood Mall. The *Reno/ Tahoe Visitor Planner,* available at information kiosks throughout the city, contains a local map and is a helpful city guide. **The drinking and gambling age is 21.**

✦ PRACTICAL INFORMATION

Visitor Information: Reno-Sparks Convention and Visitors Authority, 1 E. 1st St. (☎ 800-367-7366; www.renolaketahoe.com), on the 2nd fl. of the Cal-Neva Building. Open M-F 8am-5pm.

Library and Internet Access: Washoe County Library Downtown Reno Branch, 301 S. Center St. (☎327-8300), between Ryland and Liberty St. Free Internet access. Open M 10am-8pm, Tu-Th 10am-6pm, F and Su 10am-5pm.

Marriage: Men and women over 18 (and those 16-17 with parental consent) can pick up a marriage license at the **Washoe County Recorder's Office,** 75 Court St. (☎328-3275), for \$55. All you need is a partner of the other sex and an ID. Open daily 8am-midnight. Numerous chapels in Reno will help you tie the knot.

Laundromat: LaunderLand Coin-op Laundry, 680 E. 2nd St. (☎329-3733), at 2nd and Wells St. Wash \$1.75, dry free. Open daily 7am-10:30pm; last wash 9:30pm.

Police: 455 E. 2nd St. (☎334-2121 or 334-COPS/2677).

24hr. Crisis Lines: General Counseling and Rape Crisis, ☎800-992-5757. **Compulsive Gamblers Hotline,** ☎800-522-4700.

Medical Services: St. Mary's Hospital, 235 W. 6th St. (☎770-3000, emergency 770-3188), between West St. and Arlington Ave. Open 24hr.

Post Office: 50 S. Virginia St. (☎786-5936), at the corner of Mill St. Open M-F 8:30am-5pm. **Postal Code:** 89501.

ACCOMMODATIONS

While weekend prices at casino resorts are usually on the high side, weekday rates and off-season discounts can be very affordable. Prices fluctuate, so call ahead. In some cases, low rates may reflect a lack of wholesomeness—heterosexual prostitution is legal in most of Nevada (though not in Reno itself). The rates below don't include Reno's **12% hotel tax.**

Harrah's Reno, 219 N. Center St. (☎800-427-7247 or 786-5700), between E. 2nd St. and Commercial Row. A Reno staple, Harrah's provides luxurious rooms in a central location. 2 towers house 964 immaculate rooms, 7 restaurants, a pool, and a health club. The 65,000 sq. ft. casino attracts large crowds with Reno's highest table limits, while Sammy's Showroom and the Plaza host top performers. Free valet parking. Singles and doubles M-Th from \$49, F-Su from \$89. ❸

Reno Hilton, 2500 E. 2nd St. (☎800 648-5080 or 789-2000), off Hwy. 395 at the Glendale exit. With more than 2000 elegant rooms, a 9000-seat outdoor amphitheater, a driving range, a 50-lane bowling center, a health club and spa, and a shopping mall, this is Reno's biggest, most extravagant hotel-casino. Press your luck in the 115,000 sq. ft. casino, or, for something even more stomach-churning (depending on how you wager), check out the Ultimate Rush reverse bungee. Rooms \$35-149. ❸

Circus Circus, 500 N. Sierra St. (☎329-0711), at 6th St. Over 1500 rooms fill the 2 towers of this fun-loving hotel-casino. The exterior looks a bit dated compared to other downtown hotels, but the spotless rooms and free circus acts make Circus Circus feel young. Rooms \$35-189. ❸

Sundowner, 450 N. Arlington Ave. (☎800-648-5490 or 786-7050), between W. 4th and W. 5th St. This working man's casino represents the meat and potatoes of Reno's gambling industry. Standard, no frills rooms. Pool, hot tub, and jacuzzi on the premises. Rates are among the lowest. Rooms Su-Th from \$26, F \$50, Sa \$70. ❷

Peppermill, 2707 S. Virginia St. (☎800-648-6992 or 826-2121), between Carano Ln. and Brinkby Ave. Just south of downtown, the Peppermill grew, in a quarter of a century, from a small coffee shop to a sprawling hotel and renowned casino. Each of the 1100 rooms is adorned with mirrors and marble. Work on your tan at the grandiose Waterfall Pool and Spa. Home to 7 restaurants and 12 themed bars. Rooms Su-Th \$59 (as low as \$39 in off season), F-Sa \$119. ❸

CAMPING

To escape the jangling slot machines, drive to the woodland campsites of **Davis Creek Park ❶,** 18 mi. south of Reno on Hwy. 429, off Hwy. 395. Volleyball courts and trout-packed Ophir Creek Lake offer pleasant diversion. (☎ 721-4901. Showers and toilets on site. Sites $15, each additional car $5; pets $1.) Adventurous campers hike the challenging Ophir Trail (6 mi. one way), which ascends over 4000 ft. to meet the Tahoe Rim Trail. Closer to the action is the **Hilton KOA ❷,** 2500 E. 2nd St. (☎ 888-562-5698 or 789-2147), next to the Reno Hilton. There's no grass in sight, but campers have access to the Hilton's pool, tennis courts, and fitness center. (RV hookups $27-38.)

FOOD

Casinos offer a wide range of all-you-can-eat buffets and next-to-free breakfasts, but you can escape the clutches of these giants to find inexpensive eateries.

Pneumatic Diner, 501 W. 1st St. (☎ 786-8888 ext. 106), at the corner of Ralston and W. 1st St., in the Truckee River Lodge. This funky, cramped diner creates Italian, Mexican, French, and Middle Eastern food from all-natural ingredients. Spend some time reading the lengthy, confusing menu, which includes definitions, and, as you exit, take a peak at the various Spam products located on a shelf above the door. Beverage concoctions (try the Snoopy; $1.50-4), breakfast ($1.50-6.50), sandwiches (ratatouille baguette $5.50), domestic beers ($3.75), and other delights ($4-7.50). Open M-F 11am-11pm, Sa 9am-11pm, Su 8am-11pm. ❷

Miguel's Mexican Food, 1415 S. Virginia St. (☎ 322-2722). Miguel's is a Reno classic. Substantial lunch menu ($6-9) offers delicious fare in generous servings. Don't miss the outstanding guacamole ($7) and *sopapillas* (free with your meal). Dinner entrees $5-14. Open Su noon-8pm, Tu-Th 11am-9pm, F-Sa 11am-10pm. ❷

Bangkok Cuisine, 55 Mt. Rose St. (☎ 322-0299), at S. Virginia St. The savory Thai food and an elegant setting create a welcome haven from Reno's ubiquitous steaks and burritos. All sorts of soups ($4-7), noodles ($8-12), fried rices ($8-12), curries ($8-10), and specialties (stuffed Thai omelette; $8). Open M-Sa 11am-10pm. ❷

La Strada, 345 N. Virginia St. (☎ 348-9297), in the Eldorado Hotel. Serves award-winning Italian cuisine in the heart of the Eldorado. Pastas made fresh daily $10-20. Beef and fish entrees $13-24. Open daily 5pm-10pm. ❸

SIGHTS AND ENTERTAINMENT

The newly reopened **Nevada Museum of Art,** 160 W. Liberty St., is housed in a postmodern building with sharp angles and huge, misshapen panes of glass inspired by Black Rock Desert. The museum has galleries and a sculpture plaza; it also hosts visiting shows by the likes of Diego Rivera, Edward Hopper, and Dennis Oppenheim. (☎ 329-3333. Open Tu-W and F-Su 11am-6pm, Th 11am-8pm. $7, students and seniors $5, ages 6-12 $1, under 6 free.)

Reno is like a giant adult amusement park, with casinos the main attractions. Prudently, casinos offer free gaming lessons. The most popular games and minimum bets vary by establishment, but slots are ubiquitous. Drinks are usually free if you're gambling; beware alcohol's inhibition-lowering effects.

Almost all casinos offer live nighttime entertainment, but most shows are not worth the steep admission prices. **Harrah's,** 219 N. Center St. (☎ 786-3232), offers a particularly good deal with its **Night on the Town** packages, which cost slightly more than the price of a show ticket, but allow you to dine in one of Harrah's award-winning restaurants and then take in a show in Sammy's Showroom. At **Circus Circus,** 500 N. Sierra St., a small circus on the midway above the casino floor performs "big top" shows approximately every 30min. (☎329-0711. Shows M-Th 11:30am-11:30pm, F-Su 11:15am-11:45pm). For more entertainment listings and info on casino happenings, check out the free *This Week* or *Best Bets* magazines. *The Reno News & Review*, published every Thursday, provides an alternative look at weekly happenings and events off the beaten casino path.

❊ FESTIVALS

Cultural events heat up in the summer. The popular **Artown** festival (☎322-1538; www.renoisartown.com) is held every July for the entire month. The event features dance, jazz, painting, and theater, and almost everything is free. August roars in with the chrome-covered, hot-rod splendor of **Hot August Nights** (☎356-1956; www.hotaugustnights.com), a celebration of classic cars and rock 'n' roll.

For the more athletically inclined, the annual **Reno Rodeo** (☎329-3877; www.renorodeo.com), one of the best in the West, takes place over eight days in late June. In September, the **Great Reno Balloon Race** (☎826-1181), in Rancho San Rafael Park, and the **National Championship Air Races** (☎972-6663; www.air-race.org), at Reno/Stead Airport, draw an international group of contestants who take to the sky as spectators look on. If you prefer more exotic modes of transportation, nearby Virginia City hosts **Camel Races** (☎847-0311) during the weekend after Labor Day, in which both camels and ostriches scoot about town.

NATIONAL PARKS AND FORESTS

Far from the urban centers and the industry of coastal California, the central Sierra Nevadas are wilderness in all its unbridled majesty. Clear streams flow through endless forest below untouched high Sierra peaks. This rugged wilderness is the legacy of a long-standing conservation movement pioneered by John Muir in the late 19th century. The two main park areas in the Sierra Nevadas are Yosemite National Park (near Stanislaus National Forest and Mono Lake) and Sequoia and Kings Canyon National Parks (framed by Sierra National Forest to the north and Sequoia National Forest to the south). National parks attract hordes of sightseers, each with a camera and endless rolls of film, as well as some who retreat to the remote backcountry. National Forests are larger, their attractions more spread out, and visitors fewer and farther between. Both offer tremendous beauty and countless outdoor activities.

YOSEMITE NATIONAL PARK   ☎209

Yosemite became a national park over 100 years ago, but geologic work on the park began eons before that. About 50 million years ago, the flat floor and granite walls of Yosemite Valley, the park's most spectacular and popular area, were no more than a slow-moving river and rolling hills. Then the Sierra Nevadas rose, the Merced River deepened the terrain 3000 ft., and glaciers carved out the valley's trademark "U" shape. Today, the valley is home to some of the most amazing and well-known natural wonders in the world. Yosemite Falls, the tallest waterfall in North America, spills gently over one of the walls. The massive El Capitan, claimed to be the largest single monolith of granite in the world, stands on guard at the valley's entrance. Half Dome looms seemingly out of reach, but, as the park's most distinctive monument, it dominates most valley views. While tourists make crowding in Yosemite Valley inevitable, the park has no shortage of secluded areas, from the high country and Tuol-

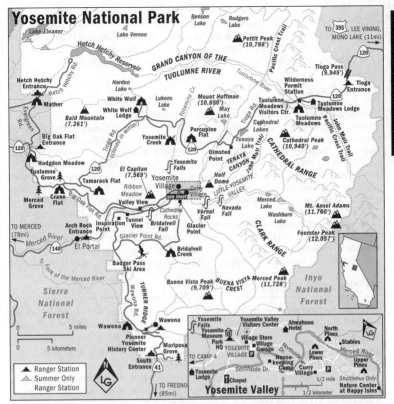

umne Meadows to Wawona and the Mariposa Grove of Giant Sequoias. Yosemite is the most famous of the national parks and for good reason; world-class sightseeing, outdoor activities, and an unimaginable geologic history are just a few of Yosemite's offerings. Yosemite Valley, at the bustling, awe-inspiring heart of the park, still lives up to its old name: "The Incomparable Valley."

AT A GLANCE: YOSEMITE NATIONAL PARK

AREA: 1189 sq. mi.

CLIMATE: Temperate forest.

FEATURES: Tuolumne (tah-WALL-um-ee) Meadows, Half Dome, Hetch Hetchy Reservoir, Yosemite Valley.

HIGHLIGHTS: Swimming in Tenya Lake, climbing El Capitan, getting sprayed at Bridalveil Falls.

GATEWAYS: Fresno (p. 316), Merced (p. 315), Manteca, and Lee Vining (p. 279).

CAMPING: Reservations necessary. 7-night max. stay in the valley and Wawona; 14-night max. stay elsewhere. Free wilderness permit is required for backcountry camping in the high country; backcountry camping is not permitted in Yosemite Valley.

FEES AND RESERVATIONS: Entrance fee $20 per car, $10 per pedestrian, cyclist, or bus passenger. Valid for 7 days. Good for one week. Annual pass $40.

WHEN TO GO. Yosemite's moderate climate makes it a comfortable destination year-round. Less snow means more tourists, however, and Yosemite Valley is generally overrun from June to Sept. Those seeking a quiet visit to this national wonder should consider going during the colder winter months.

ORIENTATION

Yosemite covers 1170 sq. mi. of mountainous terrain, 95% of which is officially designated as wilderness. The center of activity in the park, **Yosemite Valley** contains the area's most enduring and photographed monuments, including **El Capitan, Half Dome,** and **Yosemite Falls.** The immense valley and all its granite monoliths were carved out by glaciers over thousands of years. **Yosemite Village,** the valley's service, shopping, and information center, is perhaps the least natural part of the park. Facing the sheer southern wall of the valley and offering incomparable views, **Glacier Point** brims with summertime tourists. **Tuolumne Meadows,** in the park's northeastern corner, is a beautiful rock-strewn alpine meadow surrounded by snow-capped peaks and swift streams. **Mariposa Grove** is a forest of giant sequoia trees at the park's southern end. Wawona, just north of Mariposa Grove, is a historic, upscale development that includes museums, the luxurious Wawona hotel, and a golf course. The vast majority of the park, however, is wild.

TRANSPORTATION

Yosemite lies 200 mi. east of San Francisco (a 4hr. drive) and 320 mi. northeast of L.A. (a 6-9hr. drive, depending on the season). It can be reached via Rte. 140 from Merced, Rte. 41 from Fresno, or Rte. 120 from Manteca or from Lee Vining.

BY PLANE. Fresno/Yosemite International Airport, 4995 E. Clinton Way (☎559-621-4500), is 2½hr. from Yosemite via South Entrance, and is the closest airport to the park. Most flights are from western US cities like L.A., San Francisco, and Las Vegas. Five national rental car agencies serve the airport and VIA runs buses from the terminal to the park.

BY BUS OR TRAIN. Yosemite runs public **buses** that connect the park with Fresno, Merced, and Mariposa. **Yosemite VIA** runs buses from the Merced bus station, at 16th and N St. (☎384-1315 or 800-842-5463. 4 trips per day. $10.) Buses also make stops in Cathy's Valley, Mariposa, Midpines, and El Portal. VIA meets Amtrak trains from San Francisco arriving at the Merced train station. Tickets can be purchased from the driver. (☎384-1315. Buses run M-F 8am-5pm. Fares include Yosemite entry.) **Yosemite Gray Line (YGL)** runs buses to and from **Fresno Yosemite International Airport (FYI),** Fresno hotels, and Yosemite Valley ($20). Yosemite Area Regional Transportation System, or **YARTS,** provides four daily trips to Yosemite from Merced, making stops similar to those of VIA along the way, and sends one bus a day along Rte. 120 and Rte. 395, hitting Mammoth and June Lakes, Lee Vining, and Tuolumne Meadows. (☎877-989-2787 or 388-9589. Buses depart Merced bus station 7, 8:45, 10:30am, 5:25pm. $20 round-trip from Merced, Mammoth and June Lakes, Lee Vining, Tuolumne Meadows; other fares less. Fares include Yosemite entry.) **Amtrak** runs a bus from Merced to Yosemite (4 per day, $22) and trains (☎800-USA-RAIL/872-7245) to Merced from San Francisco (3½hr., 5 per day, $22-29) and L.A. (5½hr., 4 per day, $28-51). The trains connect with the YGL bus.

The best bargain in Yosemite is the **free shuttle bus,** which runs in Yosemite Valley, and, in summer, between Wawona and Mariposa Grove and Tioga Pass and Tenaya Lake (every 10-20min. 7am-10pm). Comfortable but often crowded, the buses have knowledgeable drivers and wide viewing windows. **Hikers' buses** run daily to Glacier Point and to Tuolumne Meadows/Lee Vining. (☎372-1240; www.yosemiteparktours.com. Late June to Sept. 6. Round-trip $20.50.) To get to the shuttle, drive into the valley and park near Curry and Yosemite Villages.

BY CAR. Driving is the most convenient way to enter the park, though traffic and parking hassles can rival those of rush-hour L.A. on summer weekends. Be sure to fill the tank before heading out, as there is no gas in Yosemite Valley except for **emergency gas** at the Village Garage ($15 for 5 gallons). There are overpriced 24hr. gas stations at Crane Flat, Tuolumne Meadows, and Wawona. Within the valley, there is really no reason to drive since the shuttle system is free and very convenient. Those intending to visit the high country in spring and fall should arm cars with snow tires (sometimes required even in summer). Of the five major approaches to the park, **Route 120** to the Big Oak Flat entrance is the curviest. A less nauseating alternative is **Route 41** from Fresno into the valley, featuring the famous **Inspiration Point** from which explorers reputedly first beheld the valley. The eastern entrance, **Tioga Pass**, is closed during snow season, with snow often lasting until July, but makes for a spectacular summer drive. (For info on winter driving, see **Wintertime in Yosemite,** p. 264.) For auto repairs, head to **Village Garage** (☎372-8320), in the center of the village. The garage has emergency gasoline and 24hr. towing. (Open daily 8am-noon and 1-5pm. AAA and National Auto Club accepted.)

BY BICYCLE. Cycling into the park is permitted from any of the entry points and will land you half-off admission price. Cycling is a great way to see Yosemite Valley; many sights are within 2 mi. of the valley center and easily viewed from the area's 12 mi. of paved, flat bike paths. One popular bike route follows the wide, paved road from the valley campgrounds to Mirror Lake (6 mi. round-trip), which is closed to motorized vehicles. Yosemite's bike paths are ideal for leisurely rides and circumventing automobile traffic; serious cyclists should not expect a workout. Off-road mountain biking is not permitted in the park, but all paved roads are open to cyclists. (See **Outdoor Activities,** p. 260, for more information on bike trails.) Both **Yosemite Lodge** (☎372-1208) and **Curry Village** (☎372-8319) rent bikes ($5.50 per hr., $21 per day). A driver's license or credit card is required as a security deposit. (Both open daily 8:30am-7pm, weather permitting; open on a limited basis after Sept. 6.)

THE LOCAL STORY

BUFFALO SOLDIERS

When Yosemite first gained National Park status, the National Park Service did not exist, but the Department of the Interior needed some way to protect the park's cherished natural wonders.

In 1903, when the Army was charged with protecting the National Parks, the soldiers of the 24th Mounted Infantry and the 9th Cavalry, both African-American regiments, were among a group of black soldiers assigned to the area who became known as the Buffalo Soldiers. Roughly 400 of these men made the trip from San Francisco to Yosemite on horseback, becoming, in essence, the park's first rangers. Their task was unforgiving: the park's tremendous acreage and varied terrain was nearly impossible to navigate, and sheepherders had already begun to devastate Yosemite's land by using it for grazing. But the Buffalo Soldiers completed their mission, standing guard over staggering granite peaks, roaring rivers, graceful waterfalls, and lush meadows.

When the National Park Service was created over a decade later, Yosemite's flawless beauty had been preserved. And today, a little over a century since these proud troops were deployed, the millions who visit the park are unwittingly appreciating the work of the Buffalo Soldiers, for without them, Yosemite would not be the park we know today.

SIERRA NEVADA

⊅ PRACTICAL INFORMATION

Visitor Information: (☎372-0200; general info www.nps.gov/yose, visitor info www.yosemite.org). Info on weather, accommodations, and activities. Free maps and copies of *Yosemite Guide* and *Yosemite Today* are distributed at park entrances and all visitors centers. **All hours listed are valid late May-Sept. unless otherwise noted.**

Camp Reservations: ☎800-436-7275, outside the U.S. or Canada 301-722-1257; www.reservations.nps.gov.

Yosemite Valley Visitors Center (☎372-0299), in Yosemite Village at shuttle bus stops #5 and 9. Sign language interpreter in summer. Books, maps, exhibits, and the *Spirit of Yosemite* orientation film every 30min. Open daily 8am-6pm; winter 9am-5pm.

Wilderness Center, P.O. Box 545, Yosemite National Park 95389 (☎372-0745; www.nps.gov/yose/wilderness), in Yosemite Village. Wilderness permit reservations up to 24 weeks in advance (☎372-0740; $5 per person per reservation; M-F 8:30am-4:30pm), or first come, first served (free). 40% of backcountry quota is held for first come, first camp. The center's staff cannot plan your trips but has tons of info. Bear canisters, maps, and guidebooks for sale. Open daily 7:30am-6pm; closed in late fall and winter.

Tuolumne Meadows Visitors Center (☎372-0263), on Tioga Pass Rd., 55 mi. east of Yosemite Village. The high-country headquarters, with visitor services. Open in summer 9am-7pm.

Wilderness Permit Station, off Tioga Rd. on the road to Tuolumne Lodge. Issues permits. Open daily 8am-5pm.

Big Oak Flat Info Station (☎379-1899), on Rte. 120 W, just inside the Big Oak Flat entrance station. Knowledgeable National Park Service rangers, Yosemite Association staff, books, maps, and wilderness permits (until 4:30pm). Open daily 8am-5pm.

Wawona Info Station (☎375-9531), on Rte. 41, 6 mi. from the southern entrance near Mariposa Grove, on the Wawona Hotel grounds. Wilderness permits issued. Large selection of books. Open daily 8am-4:30pm.

LOCAL SERVICES

Wheelchair Access: Wheelchairs available at Yosemite Lodge (☎372-1208) and Curry Village (☎372-8319) for $5 per hr., $20 per day.

Equipment Rental: Yosemite Mountaineering School (YMS; ☎372-8344), in Curry Village; 2nd location on Rte. 120 at Tuolumne Meadows. Sleeping bags $10.50 per day; backpacks $8.50 per day. 3rd day half-price. Climbing shoes rented to YMS students only. Driver's license or credit card required for deposit. Rock climbing classes daily. Open daily 8:30am-noon and 1-5pm. For info on ski and snowshoe rental, see **Wintertime in Yosemite,** p. 264.

24hr. ATM: Bank of America, in Yosemite Village. The bank also has a check-cashing service. Open daily 8am-4pm. There are also ATMs in Village Store, Yosemite Lodge, Curry Village market, Wawona store, and El Portal.

Laundromat: Laundry facilities open at **Housekeeping Camp.** Wash $1.25, dry $0.25 per 10min. Open daily 8am-10pm. In winter, laundry facilities available at **Camp 6,** across the street from the Village Store. Open daily 7am-10pm.

Swimming Pools: At Yosemite Lodge, Wawona Hotel, Awahnee Hotel, and Curry Village. $2 per day; free for guests of Ahwahnee Hotel, Wawona Hotel, Yosemite Lodge, and Curry Village. All open daily 10am-5pm.

Showers: Housekeeping Camp ($2, children $1.50). Includes towel and soap. Open daily 8am-10pm. **Curry Village** (free for guests). Open 24hr. Also at **Tuolumne Meadows** and **White Wolf Lodges** ($2). Open daily noon-3:30pm.

Weather and Road Conditions: ☎372-0200. 24hr.

EMERGENCY AND COMMUNICATIONS

Medical Services: Yosemite Medical Clinic (☎372-4637), 2 blocks from the eastern end of Yosemite Village. 24hr. emergency room. Open M-Sa 8am-5pm. **Dental services** (☎372-4200 or 372-4637) available next door.

Internet Access: Yosemite Bug Hostel (☎966-6666), on Rte. 140, 30 mi. west of Yosemite in Midpines (see p. 259). $1 per 10min.

Post Office: Yosemite Village, next to the visitors center. Open M-F 8:30am-5pm, Sa 10am-noon. **Curry Village,** near the registration office. Open June-Sept. 6 M-F 2:30-4pm. **Yosemite Lodge** open M-Th 11:30am-2:45pm, F 11:30am-4:30pm. **Wawona** open M-F 9am-5pm, Sa 9am-1pm. **Tuolumne Meadows** open M-F 9am-5pm, Sa 9am-1pm. **Postal Code:** 95389.

CAMPING

One of the first views of Yosemite a visitor gets during the summer may be of the endless "tent cities" in the valley. Don't expect to get a spot without reservations, which have to be made well in advance for summer visits. (☎800-436-7275, TDD 888-530-9796, outside the US 301-722-1257; http://reservations.nps.gov. Reservations available by phone or website daily 7am-7pm, Pacific time, or mail NPRS, P.O. Box 1600, Cumberland, MD 21502. Reservations become available on the 15th of the month, 5 months in advance. Spots in the valley usually fill up within a few days of becoming available.) Cancellation lotteries are held at the campground reservations office in Curry Village (daily 8am and 3pm) but the odds are low. Camp 4, in the valley, does not accept reservations, but people line up for spots in the mornings. Camping is plentiful and usually easily available in the surrounding national forests; these are good alternatives if you can't get a spot in Yosemite. During the summer, there is a seven-night maximum stay for those in the valley or at Wawona and a 14-night maximum stay for campers outside the valley. All drive-in campsites provide picnic tables, fire pits or grills, a cleared tent space, parking, and a food storage area. Natural stream water (serving Tamarack Flat, Yosemite Creek, and Porcupine Flat) must be boiled, filtered, or treated to prevent giardia (an intestinal disease; see **Food- and Water-borne diseases,** p. 39). Iodine water treatments can be bought at any supply store. Backcountry camping is prohibited in the valley but encouraged outside of it (see **Backcountry,** p. 264). Toilet facilities are everywhere, but Tamarack Flat, Yosemite Creek, and Porcupine Flat only have vault toilets. RVs are prohibited in Tamarack, Yosemite Creek, and walk-in sites. Dump stations are available in the valley (year-round) and in Wawona and Tuolumne Meadows (summer only). Only the Upper Pines and Camp 4, in the valley, Wawona, and Hodgdon Meadow campgrounds are open year-round; the rest are open in summer, usually from June to Sept.

IN YOSEMITE VALLEY

All drive-in campsites require reservations, which should be made as far in advance as possible on the 15th of the month, up to five months prior to camping. **All valley campgrounds fill completely every summer night.**

Camp 4, 4000 ft., at the western end of the valley, past Yosemite Lodge. 150 yd. from the parking lot. 35 walk-in sites fill up before 9am most mornings. Caters to seasoned climbers swapping stories of exploits on vertical rock faces. Be prepared to meet new friends, since every site is filled with 6 randomly assembled people. Water, flush toilets, and tables. No reservations. Limited parking. Sites $5 per person. ❶

Lower Pines, 4000 ft., in Yosemite Valley's busy eastern end. Commercial, crowded, and plagued by car traffic. Next to the comparable **North Pines** campground (4000 ft.; open Apr.-Sept.; 81 sites) and **Upper Pines** campground (4000 ft.; 238 sites). Water, toilets, tables, and showers. Reservations required. Sites $18. ❷

BEYOND YOSEMITE VALLEY

Outside the valley, campsite quality vastly improves. Reservations should be made in advance.

Tuolumne Meadows, 8600 ft., on Rte. 120, 55 mi. east of the valley. Across from the gorgeous meadow of the same name, this campground lies next to the relaxing Tuolumne River and near Lembert Dome. Large drive-in sites offer some privacy, while the 25 sites in the backpackers camp are truly secluded. Nightly ranger programs, complete with a campfire and giddy kids. Pets allowed in western section only. 152 sites require advance reservations, 152 saved for same-day reservations. Open July-Sept., depending on snow. Drive-in sites $18; backpacker sites $3 per person. ❶

Crane Flat, 6200 ft., centrally located on Big Oak Flat Rd. near the Tioga Rd. turn-off. Convenient for access to the valley, Crane Flat's 166 spacious sites are well shaded; many include small boulders or views of a peaceful meadow. Reservations required. Open June-Sept. Sites $18. ❷

Bridalveil Creek, 7200 ft., 25 mi. south of the valley on Glacier Point Rd. Peaceful, beautiful grounds convenient for serious backpackers aiming for Glacier, Dewey, and Taft Points. Popular among mosquitoes in early summer. A 2 mi. walk to McGurk Meadow. 110 sites. No reservations. Open July-early Sept. Sites $12. ❶

White Wolf, 8000 ft., off Rte. 120 E, 31 mi. from the valley. Near Tuolumne Meadows and the rest of the High Sierra, these 74 sites are ideal for those trying to avoid crowds. Open July-early Sept., depending on snow. Sites $12. ❶

Hodgdon Meadow, 4900 ft., on Rte. 120 near Big Oak Flat Entrance, 25 mi. from the valley. Warm enough for winter camping. 105 compact sites with little privacy increase the likelihood of making new friends (or enemies). Water, toilets, and tables. May-Sept. sites $18 and reservations required; Oct.-Apr. $12 and first come, first camp. ❷

Porcupine Flat, 8100 ft., 15 mi. from Tuolumne Meadows off Tioga Rd. RV sites in the front section. 52 first come, first camp sites. Open late July-Sept. Sites $8. ❶

Wawona, 4000 ft., off Rte. 41, 1 mi. outside Wawona, 27 mi. from Yosemite Valley. 93 open, unshaded sites near the South Fork of the Merced River. Water, flush toilets, and tables. Pets allowed. May-Sept. sites $18, reservations required; Oct.-Apr. sites $12. ❷

Tamarack Flat, 6300 ft., 23 mi. northeast of the valley. Take Rte. 120 east on Tioga Rd. and follow the rough road for 3 mi. (only if your car can take it; not recommended for RVs and trailers). 52 rustic drive-in sites. Fewer amenities, but campers can enjoy peace and quiet. First come, first camp. Open June-Sept. Sites $8. ❶

⚑ ACCOMMODATIONS

INSIDE THE PARK

When American Transcendentalist Ralph Waldo Emerson visited Yosemite in 1884, the park's accommodations were so simple that he was awakened in the morning by the clucking of a hen climbing over his bed. These days, Yosemite's lodgings have become much more comfortable, but at times rooms are scarce. Spring, summer, and weekend rates are high (suites at the luxurious Ahwahnee Hotel start at $357) and space is tight. Reservations are necessary and can be made up to one year in advance by calling ☎559-252-4848 or going online at www.yosemitepark.com. The rates given below are for summer weekends. Check-in is usually around 11am. **All park lodgings provide access to dining and laundry facilities, showers, and supplies.**

▩ **Curry Village** (☎252-4848), 2 mi. southeast of Yosemite Village. Originally created as an economical alternative to camping, Curry Village is in the shadow of Glacier Point above, making it the shadiest and coolest valley lodging in the summer. 18 hotel rooms, 103 cabins with private bath, and 80 cabins and 427 canvas tents with shared bath. Pool, store, outdoor amphitheater, and ice rink (Nov.-Feb.). Standard motel room $112; cabins $77, with bath $92; canvas tent cabins $60. ❹

Housekeeping Camp (☎372-8338), ¼ mi. west of Curry Village. This army barracks-style camp feels less hotel-like than other lodgings. Canvas-capped concrete "camping shelters" hold up to 4 people (6 with cots) and include 2 bunk beds, a double bed, a picnic table, a fire pit with grill, and lights. Camping equipment rental. Shelters $64. ❶

Tuolumne Meadows Lodge (☎372-8413), on Tioga Rd., in the park's northeastern corner. In the high country, these rustic cabins are across from Tuolumne Meadows and just steps from the Tuolumne River. Popular among day hikers and those on their way to High Sierra Camps; convenient for non-campers who want to enjoy this beautiful area. Canvas-sided cabins, wood stoves, no electricity. Cabins $67; $9 per additional adult, $4 per additional child. ❹

White Wolf Lodge (☎372-8416), on Tioga Rd. in the park's western area. A good base for several day hikes, this high-country lodge has 4 cabins with baths and 24 canvas cabins with shared baths. Open late June to early Sept. Cabins with bath $84; canvas cabins $63. $9 per additional person. ❹

Yosemite Lodge (☎372-1274), west of Yosemite Village and directly across from Yosemite Falls. Located on the site of Fort Yosemite, the park headquarters of the U.S. Army Cavalry, the lodge contains 245 spacious hotel rooms. Pool, cocktail lounge, bike rental, outdoor amphitheater. Lodge rooms $146; standard rooms $110. $11 per additional person. ❺

OUTSIDE THE PARK

Lodging in the park may be convenient, but it's also expensive and hard to get. For the same price as a canvas cabin in the valley, you can find high-quality hotel accommodations in scenic and, surprisingly, more pristine areas. For more info on gateway towns and accommodations, access the **Yosemite Area Traveler Information (YATI)** website (www.yosemite.com). YATI has computer terminals at the Yosemite Valley Visitors Center (see p. 256), the Greater Merced Chamber of Commerce (see p. 315), and the Tuolumne County Visitors Bureau (see p. 256).

Yosemite Bug Hostel (☎966-6666; www.yosemitebug.com), on Rte. 140, in Midpines, 25 mi. west of Yosemite. Look carefully for the sign. A woodsy, spirited resort spot. International backpacking crowd lounges in hammocks. Beer on tap, full guest kitchen, library with games, cafe with exceptional food, and a swimming hole with a waterfall. Occasional live music outdoors. Discounts on public transportation to park ($10 round-trip; 3-day pass $20). Internet $1 per 10min. Dorms $16; private rooms $40-70, with bath $55-115; tent sites $17. ❷

Evergreen Lodge, 33160 Evergreen Rd. (☎379-2606; www.evergreenlodge.com), 7 mi. off Rte. 120, 1 mi. before Big Oak Flat Entrance. Over 80 years old and advertised almost exclusively through word-of-mouth, this lodge near the quieter Hetch Hetchy region is secluded and cozy. The spacious cabins have porches, outdoor patios, and grills. On-site restaurant, bar, deli, and market. Standard cabins $79; family cabins $99-$104. $10 more during summer. ❹

Yosemite View Lodge (☎379-2681 or 800-321-5261; www.yosemite-motels.com), on Rte. 140, 2 mi. east of El Portal, just outside the park. Descend from the mountains and kick back in luxury. Huge hotel on the banks of the Merced River. 3 pools, 6 hot tubs (2 right on the banks of the Merced), and vaulted wood ceilings. Kitchenettes in every elegant room. Rooms $139-209. $50 less in off season. ❺

🍴 FOOD

The **Village Store** is your best bet for groceries, with a huge selection and only moderately inflated prices. (Open daily June-Sept. 8am-10pm; Oct.-May 8am-9pm.) Smaller, pricier stores are in the Yosemite Lodge (open daily June-Sept. 8am-

10pm; Oct.-May 8am-9pm), at Wawona (open daily 8am-8pm), Crane Flat (open daily 8am-8pm), El Portal (open daily 8am-8pm), and Tuolumne Meadows (open daily June-Sept. 8am-8pm). Consider buying all of your cooking supplies, marshmallows, and batteries in Merced or Fresno before entering the park.

IN YOSEMITE VALLEY

Yosemite's center of commerce is crammed at lunchtime. Make like a forest animal and carry your meal away to eat in seclusion.

Mountain Room Restaurant (☎372-9033), in Yosemite Lodge. Outstanding views of Yosemite Falls from nearly every seat in the restaurant make this ideal for a post-hike meal. Filling portions of hearty American fare $17-28. Open daily 5:30-9pm. ❺

Ahwahnee Dining Room (☎372-1489). Linen tablecloths, 34 ft. high ceilings, chandeliers, and strict dress codes in this stately National Historic Landmark. Elegant and expensive American cuisine $30-50. Open M-F 7-10:30am, 11:30am-3pm, 5:30-9:15pm; Su brunch 7am-3pm. Bar open 11am-11pm. Reservations recommended. ❺

Degnan's Delicatessen (☎372-8454), in Yosemite Village. Inside a convenience store and adjacent to an ice-cream parlor and pizza place. Huge sandwiches and small veggie sandwiches $5.75. Open daily 7am-7pm. ❷

BEYOND YOSEMITE VALLEY

Other restaurants in the park are generally in hotels. Check Yosemite's publications for lunchtime bargains. The moderately upscale Tuolumne Meadows and White Wolf Lodges both offer American-style dishes. Tuolumne Meadows also has a small grill with reasonably priced, filling food. Wawona has an expensive restaurant in its hotel and a snack shop in the golf store. Glacier Point also has a snack shop. Call ☎372-1000 for current dining information. Cheaper, often better dining opportunities can be found just outside of the park. The **Yosemite View Restaurant** ❸, on Rte. 140 at the Yosemite View Lodge in El Portal, offers fine dining in a gleaming building with a high wooden ceiling, stone fireplace, and lots of tourists. It's a better deal than the Ahwahnee but the atmosphere can't compare. Fuel up at its breakfast buffet for $10. (☎379-9307. Entrees $13-24. Open daily 7-11am and 6-10pm.) Seven miles down the road, the **Cedar Lodge Restaurant** ❸, on Rte. 140 in El Portal, serves somewhat overpriced food until late at night. (☎379-2316. Entrees $9-19. Open daily 7am-10pm. Lounge open until 1:30 am.)

◪ OUTDOOR ACTIVITIES

SCENIC DRIVES

Although the view is better if you get out of the car, you can see a large portion of Yosemite from the bucket seat, and if you only have one day in the park, exploring it by car is the only way to see all the sights. The **Yosemite Road Guide** ($3.50 at every visitors center) is keyed to roadside markers and outlines a superb tour of the park; it's like having a ranger riding shotgun. Spectacular panoramas and beautiful glades are omnipresent along **Route 120 (Tioga Road)** from Crane Flat to Tuolumne Meadows. This stretch of road is the highest highway strip in the country; as it winds down from Tioga Pass through the park's eastern exit, it plunges a mile down to reach the lunar landscape of Mono Lake. The drive west from the pass brings you past **Tuolumne Meadows,** with its colorful grasses and rippling creeks, to shimmering Tenaya Lake. No less incredible are the views afforded by the southern approach to Yosemite, **Route 41.** Most recognizable is the Wawona Tunnel turnout (also known as **Inspiration Point**), which affords views many visitors will recognize from many Ansel Adams photographs. From here, **Yosemite Valley** unfurls its famed, humbling beauty. **El Capitan,** a gigantic granite monolith (7569 ft.), looms over awestruck crowds. If you stop and look closely (with binoculars if possible), you will see what appear to be specks of dust moving on the mountain face. They are actually world-class climbers inching toward fame, and at night their flashlights shine from impromptu hammocks hung from the granite. Opposite El Capitan, **Bridalveil Falls** drops 620 ft. A drive into the heart of the valley leads to the staggering **Yosemite Falls** (the highest waterfall in North America at 2425 ft.). Incredible views of the falls are available at numerous parking lots and turnouts, making it possible to avoid areas with shoulder-to-shoulder tourists photographing the sight. In the valley's eastern end stands **Half Dome,** a monolithic rock formation. Half Dome can be seen from virtually everywhere in the valley, but the closer you get, the more impressive it appears.

Glacier Point Rd., off Rte. 41 in the southern part of the park, meanders past lush meadows and rounded domes to the southeast. At its end, **Glacier Point** gives a bird's-eye view of the valley floor, which is considered one of the most spectacular views on Earth. Half Dome arcs majestically from the valley's east side and water seems to tumble down Nevada Falls in slow motion. When the moon is full, this is an extraordinary (and very popular) place to visit. Arrive at sunset and watch the fiery colors fade over the valley as the stars and moon appear.

HIKING IN YOSEMITE VALLEY

With two or more days in Yosemite, it's worthwhile to explore some of its trails. World-class hiking abounds for anyone willing to lace up a pair of boots, though sneakers will suffice for a few trails. Daytrip trails are well populated—at nearly any point in the day, you may find yourself stuck behind groups of other tourists. Hiking just after sunrise is the best and sometimes the only way to beat the crowds, but even then, trails like Half Dome are already busy. A colorful trail map of short day hikes from the valley with difficulty ratings and average hiking times is available at the visitors center ($0.50). The popular Mist Trail (6 mi.) starts at Happy Isles trailhead (shuttle bus stop #16) at the valley's eastern end. The trail runs parallel to the Merced River to the base of Vernal Falls. From there, steep and slippery steps carved out of the granite put you next to the falls, which sprays hikers with its mist. The trail ends at the top of the fall.

The strenuous hike to the top of **Half Dome** is a popular option. This hike, which starts at the Happy Isles trailhead, affords the thrill of conquering Yosemite's most recognizable monument. (The demanding hike has inspired an "I made it to the top" t-shirt.) The 16 mi. hike is recommended for those in good condition and comfortable with heights. Half Dome attracts lightning, and midsummer thunderstorms make early morning departures advisable. Or, spread the trek over two days by camping in Little Yosemite Valley for a night (wilderness permit required). Rising 4800 vertical ft., this climb makes comrades out of complete strangers who make the ascent.

The **Mirror Lake Loop** is a level 3 mi. walk past Mirror Lake (½ mi.), up Tenaya Creek, and back. The **Lower Yosemite Falls Trail** is a favorite of all ages and starts just opposite the Yosemite Lodge. On moonlit nights, mysterious moonbows (a nighttime rainbow) can sometimes be spotted off the water. Both the Lower Yosemite and Bridalveil Falls trails are wheelchair accessible. **Upper Yosemite Falls Trail,** a backbreaking 3½ mi. trek to the windy summit, climbs 2700 ft. but rewards the intrepid hiker with an overview of the vertiginous 2425 ft. drop. Those with energy to spare can trudge on to **Yosemite Point** or **Eagle Peak,** where views of the valley below rival those from Glacier Point. The trail begins with an extremely steep, unshaded ascent. Leaving the marked trail is not a wise idea—a sign warns, "If you go over the waterfall, you will die." An easy quarter-mile stroll from the

Bridalveil Falls parking lot, or its shuttle bus stop, leads to the base of Bridalveil Falls. You probably won't work up a sweat, but if you do, the cool mist of the waterfall's water should refresh you.

From **Glacier Point,** the steep **Four Mile Trail** (actually 4½ mi. long) is a switch-backed descent to the valley floor. Walk through forests of white firs and sugar pines with sporadic valley views as you gain a sense of the valley's 3000 ft. depth. The wildflower-laden **Pohono Trail** also starts from Glacier Point, crosses Sentinel Creek (spectacular **Sentinel Falls,** the park's second-largest cascade, lies to the north), and parallels the south rim of the valley on its way to **Taft Point, Dewey Point,** and other secluded lookouts.

HIKING OUTSIDE THE VALLEY

Tioga Rd. slices through the park, making its way into windswept high country other-wise inaccessible to day hikers. From the west, the lush and relatively flat **White Wolf** trails depart from the campground and head to fishing and swimming at **Harden** (3 mi. northwest) and **Lukens Lakes** (1 mi. east, uphill). The 5 mi. hike down to **North Dome,** which provides great views of Yosemite Valley and Half Dome, isn't too difficult, but the hike back up is more strenuous. The trailhead is 5 mi. past where Tioga Rd. crosses Yosemite Creek. At a turn-off about 8 mi. from the creek crossing, the hike to **Mt. Hoff-mann** (10,850 ft.) is a moderate 3 mi. to the top of the geographic center of the park. Along the way, you'll pass gorgeous **May Lake.** Halfway between the turn-off for Mt. Hoffmann and Tenaya Lake is the turnout for **Olmsted Point,** a must-see vista of Tenaya Canyon, stretching out to Yosemite Valley with views of the backside of Half Dome. Two miles farther east is **Tenaya Lake,** a large, clear alpine lake popular with swimmers.

Tuolumne Meadows (8600 ft.), a park village in the high country at the eastern end of Tioga Rd., is the second most popular area in the park after Yosemite Val-ley. A huge number of greatly rewarding day hikes weave through the region. The 3½ mi., 1000 ft. ascent to **Cathedral Lakes** is moderately difficult and leads to a swimming spot with an incredible view of the unmistakable Cathedral Peak, the jagged high-country mountain. It's an easier 2 mi. haul to **Elizabeth Lake,** another outstanding glacier-carved mountain lake situated at the base of Uni-corn Peak. The visitors center has info on the many hiking opportunities in the region. Nearly every hike in Yosemite gives hikers jaw-dropping views and quiet moments of serenity. For a taste of "real" rock climbing without the requisite equipment and training, Yosemite day hikers and climbers clamber up **Lembert Dome** above Tuolumne Meadows. This gentle (by rock climbing standards), solid granite incline is riddled with foot- and handholds. The 1½ mi. hike to the dome begins 200 yd. east of the Dog Lake parking area.

For views rivaling those of the valley without the hordes of tourists, head to the much less visited **Hetch Hetchy Reservoir.** John Muir spent many of his later years in an ultimately futile fight to prevent Hetch Hetchy Valley (which was acknowl-edged to be as stunning as Yosemite Valley) from being turned into a big water trough for San Francisco. Take Rte. 120 west to the Big Oak Flat Entrance, turn right (1 mi.) on Evergreen Rd., and continue for 16 mi. Park by the O'Shaughnessy Dam. The area has several idyllic day hikes, but backcountry access can be even more stunning. Permits are available one day before or on the day of the hike at the Hetch Hetchy Entrance, or make advance reservations for $5 per person (☎372-0740). The **Wapama Falls** trail (2½ mi.) is a fairly easy hike with spectacular views at every turn. The trail continues to **Rancheria** (an additional 4 mi.), a popu-lar place to camp. **Bring bear canisters—the bears here are particularly aggressive.**

OTHER SUMMER ACTIVITIES

The world's best **climbers** come to Yosemite to test themselves at angles beyond vertical. Join the stellar rock climbers by taking a lesson with the hard-core **Yosemite Mountaineering School** (see p. 256). Classes range from basic techniques to alpine ascents and lead climbing; most are 7hr. long. Reservations are useful and require advance payment, though drop-ins are accepted. (☎372-8344. In Curry Village open daily 8:30am-noon and 1-5pm; in Tuolumne Meadows daily 9am-5pm. Classes in Curry Village begin at 8:30am. 3-6 people $70; individual courses $170. Intermediate lessons on weekends and alternating weekdays $80-90.) The energetic guides of **Incredible Adventures,** 350 Townsend St., in San Francisco, lead excellent hiking and sightseeing trips to great Yosemite spots, catering to young, spirited backpackers. (☎415-642-7378 or 800-777-8464; www.incadventures.com. 3-day/3-night trips depart from San Francisco June-Oct. W and Su; $190 including meals, entrance fee, equipment, transportation, and tax. 2-day trips $150. Daytrips run throughout the year; $95, with free hotel or hostel pickup.) **Green Tortoise** sends its "hostels on wheels" from San Francisco on two-day (Apr.-Sept.) and three-day (June-Oct.) tours of Yosemite. For details, see p. 44.

Guided **horseback rides** start at $51 for a 2hr. ride. All-day rides are $94. There are stables at: Yosemite Valley (☎372-8348; open Apr.-Sept. daily 7:30am-5pm); Wawona (☎375-6502; open early summer daily 7:30am-5pm); and Tuolumne Meadows (☎372-8427; open June-Sept. daily 7:30am-5pm).

Fishing is allowed from April through November in any of Yosemite's lakes, streams, or rivers, but prospects are notoriously bad. Anglers undaunted by the dismal odds may obtain a fishing license from grocery or sporting goods stores in Yosemite Valley, Wawona, Tuolumne, or White Wolf. (Nonresident 10-day license $30, under 16 free. There are also 2 free fishing days per season. Consult the *Fishing in Yosemite National Park* handout for specific guidelines.) Tackle is available at the **Village Sport Shop.** (☎372-1286. Open daily 8:30am-6pm.) Those frustrated with Yosemite's so-called fishing can **bird-watch** instead; the visitors center gives out field checklists.

Rafting is permitted on the Merced River (10am-4pm) in June and July or when deemed safe, but no motorized crafts are allowed. Rafts can be rented at the Curry Village Recreation Center. For organized rafting trips, **All Outdoors,** 1250 Pine St. (☎925-932-8993 or 800-247-2387), in Walnut Creek, leads trips on the north fork of Stanislaus River (leave from Calaveras Big Trees State Park), the Merced River (Mt. View Store, Midpines), the Kaweah River (Kaweah General Store), and Goodwin Canyon (Stanislaus River Park, Sonora). Most full-day trips cost $119 during the week and $144 on weekends. **Swimming** is allowed throughout the park except where signs to the contrary are posted. Those who prefer their water chlorinated can swim in the public pools at Curry Village, Yosemite Lodge, and Wawona. (Open daily 10am-6pm. $2 for nonguests.)

ORGANIZED ACTIVITIES

Open-air tram tours (☎372-1240) leave from Curry Village, Ahwahnee Hotel, Yosemite Lodge, and the Village Store. Tickets are available at lodging facilities and the Village Store tour desk. The basic 2hr. **Valley Floor Tour** points out Half Dome, El Capitan, Bridalveil Falls, and Happy Isles. (Departs daily 10am-3pm on the hr. and at 6pm. $20.50, seniors $18.50, ages 5-12 $15.50.) The 4hr. **Glacier Point Tour** climbs 3200 ft. to the point for a view of the valley 7300 ft. below. (Departs daily June-Oct. 8:30, 10am, and 1:30pm from Yosemite Lodge. $29.50, ages 5-12 $16.50). The 2hr. **Moonlight Tour,** on nights with a full (or nearly full) moon, offers unique nighttime views of the valley ($20.50).

Park rangers lead a variety of informative hikes and other activities for visitors of all ages. Daily **junior ranger** (ages 7-10) and **senior ranger** (ages 11-13) activities allow children to hike, raft, and explore aquatic and terrestrial life. (Free with the purchase of a coloring handbook. Reservations required in advance through the Yosemite Valley Visitors Center; see p. 256.) Rangers also guide a number of free walks. **Discover Yosemite Family Programs** address a variety of historical and geological topics. (3hr. Daily 9am. Most wheelchair accessible.) Rangers also lead strenuous 4-8hr. **Destination Hikes** into the high country from Tuolumne Meadows. Other free, park-sponsored adventures include 2hr. **photographic walks,** which are lessons/adventures led by professional photographers. (Hikes leave Tu, Th, Sa-Su at 9am. Sign up and meet at the Ansel Adams Gallery; see p.265.) Free **Sunrise photo walks** leave most mornings from the Yosemite Lodge tour desk at 6:30am. The **Glacier Point Sunset Photo Shoot** is offered Saturday nights from June to September. Bring lots of film; this is an incredible spot, especially at sunset. Late in the day, the valley's dusky hues become a photographer's dream. The workshop with a professional photographer is free, but the scenic tram ride up to the point is not (departs 1hr. before the meeting time and returns 4hr. later, $20.50). However, you can always drive and meet the group at the Glacier Point Amphitheater.

WINTER ACTIVITIES

Winter is Yosemite's least busy season, but the park still has a lot to offer and the visitor's experience is guaranteed to be more personal and serene. The valley, which, at 4000 ft., has relatively mild temperatures, undergoes a face lift; waterfalls freeze, meadows frost over, and granite peaks get sprinkled with white. Morning and evening bring a romantic quality, as the angle of the sun fills the walls of the valley with light. While the valley remains accessible year-round, other parts of the park close with the arrival of snow. **Route 140** from Merced, a designated all-weather entrance, is usually open and clear. Although Tioga Pass and Glacier Point Rd. invariably close at the first sign of snowfall, **Route 41** from the south and **Route 120** from the west typically remain traversable. Verify road conditions before traveling (☎372-0200) and carry chains. Camping is generally permitted in Lower Pines, Camp 4, Hodgdon Meadow, and Wawona; most indoor accommodations offer big off-season reductions (with the notable exception of the Ahwahnee). Park tours move "indoors" to heated buses; even the Merced and Fresno buses (see **Transportation,** p. 254) operate, road conditions permitting.

Several well-marked trails for **cross-country skiing** and **snowshoeing** cut into the backcountry of the valley's South Rim at Badger Pass and Crane Flat. Rangers host snowshoe walks from mid-December through March, but the hushed winter forests are perhaps best explored without guidance. Snowshoes and cross-country skis can be rented from the **Yosemite Mountaineering School** (see p. 256). **Badger Pass Rental Shop** (see below) also rents winter equipment and downhill skis. Backcountry skiers can stay at Ostrander Ski Hut, 9 mi. south of Badger Pass, or Glacier Point Hut, at the end of Glacier Point Rd. Both provide heated accommodations and meals and require reservations. Guided cross-country skiing trips (☎327-8444) with meals and accommodations at the huts are also available.

The state's oldest ski resort, **Badger Pass Ski Area,** on Glacier Point Rd. south of Yosemite Valley, is the only downhill ski area in the park. The resort's powder may not rival Lake Tahoe's, but its family-fun atmosphere is good for beginners. Various lessons and package deals are available. Free shuttles connect Badger Pass with Yosemite Valley. (☎372-8430. Lifts open 9am-4:30pm. Group ski lessons $22 per 2hr., private lessons from $44. Rental packages $18 per day, under 12 $13. Lift pass M-F $22, under 12 $13; Sa-Su $28/$13.)

Ice skating at Curry Village is a beautiful (if cold) experience, with Half Dome towering above a groomed outdoor rink encircled by snow-covered pines. (☎372-8319. Open in winter M-F noon-9:30pm, Sa-Su 8:30am-9:30pm. $5; skate rental $2.) **Sledding** and **tobogganing** are permitted at Crane Flat, off Rte. 120.

BEYOND YOSEMITE VALLEY: THE BACKCOUNTRY

Most folks moseying through Yosemite never leave the valley, but a wilder, more isolated Yosemite awaits those who do. The Wilderness Center in Yosemite Valley offers maps and personalized assistance for such adventurers. (For advice on keeping yourself and the wilderness intact, see **Wilderness Safety,** p. 56.) Topographical maps (most around $8) and hiking guides are especially helpful in navigating Yosemite's nether regions. Equipment can be rented or purchased at the Mountaineering School at Tuolumne Meadows (see p. 256) or at the Mountain Shop at Curry Village, but backpacking stores in major cities are less expensive.

Backcountry camping is prohibited in the valley (those caught face a $60 fine and park eviction), but is generally permitted along the high-country trails with a free wilderness permit (see p. 256); each trailhead has a limited number of permits. The five wildly popular **High Sierra Camps** (situated between 5¾ and 10 mi. from each other) allow multi-day hikers to take a break from backcountry camping and sleep on mattresses, eat real food, and take showers. Request a lottery application by calling ☎559-252-4848, but do so far in advance. There is a 40% quota held on 24hr. notice at the Yosemite Valley Visitors Center, the Wawona Ranger Station, and Big Oak Flat Station (see **Visitor Information,** p. 256). Popular trails like Little Yosemite Valley, Clouds Rest, and Half Dome fill quickly. (Permits free; reservations $5. Call ☎372-0740 or write Wilderness Permits, P.O. Box 545, Yosemite National Park 95389.) In the high country, many hikers stay at undeveloped mountain campgrounds, which offer a few bear lockers. Hikers can also store food in hanging bear bags (see **Bears,** p. 56) or in rented plastic canisters from the Yosemite Valley Sports Shop ($5 per day). **Bear canisters** are highly recommended and mandatory in some areas—bear-bagging is considered more of a delay tactic than a safety precaution.

With over 800 mi. of trails, backcountry hiking opportunities are virtually limitless. Many of the most popular trails start from Happy Isles Nature Center in the valley and Tuolumne Meadows. The extraordinary 211 mi. **John Muir Trail** connects with the **Pacific Crest Trail** at Tuolumne Meadows and then heads south to Kings Canyon and Sequoia National Park and the highest peak in the lower 48 states, Mt. Whitney (elev. 14,494 ft.). Making a go at any portion of this trail, including the 27 mi. journey to Tuolumne Meadows from the valley, makes for an unforgettable experience. Traversing the entire trail takes anywhere from three weeks to a few months.

🔘 🎵 SIGHTS AND ENTERTAINMENT

Rangers lead different, usually free, activities, from nature walks to historical presentations to star-gazing, every day at nearly every park village. Check *Yosemite Today* or local bulletin boards and ranger stations for schedules and information.

The **Ansel Adams Gallery,** next to the visitors center, is a gift shop and activity center featuring work by famous wilderness photographers and artists including, of course, the man himself. Sign up for a fine-print viewing to see the precious stuff—you'll most likely be shown around with a group of people, but occasionally the staff will give private showings. The gallery offers free camera walks three times a week at 9am from the village. (☎372-4413; www.anseladams.com. Open daily 9am-6pm; in winter 9am-5pm.) The **Art Activity Center,** in Yosemite Village next to the store, takes pride in its artist-in-residence program and offers an art instruction class. (☎372-1442. Open daily 9:30am-4:30pm. Class offered daily 10am-2pm. Advance sign-up recommended. Supplies for sale but not included.)

Just behind the gallery, Native American cultural events take place in the **Miwok-Paiute Village,** a collection of Native American sweatlodges, roundhouses, *umachas* (homes), placards describing indigenous fauna, and an interactive diorama. The large *Hangie* (roundhouse) is a humbling piece of construction still serving as a cultural center for local Miwok and Paiute Indians (village open dusk to dawn).

Additional information can be garnered at the **Yosemite Village Museum,** next to the visitors center. Inside is a reconstruction of Ahwahnee village life, Native American craft demonstrations, and a display of the park's enormous art collection, including watertight woven baskets and amazing headdresses. (Open daily 9am-4:30pm.) Pick up the guide at the visitors center and tour the resting places of Native Americans and others who played important roles in the park's formation at the **Yosemite Cemetery,** across from the museum.

In 1903, John Muir gave President Theodore Roosevelt a now-famous tour of Yosemite. Thespian Lee Stetson has assumed Muir's role, leading free 1hr. hikes along the same route. Stetson also presents one-man shows such as **The Spirit of John Muir, Conversation with a Tramp,** and **Wild Stories with John Muir.** Stetson has recently begun a new show reenacting the encounter between Muir and Roosevelt entitled **The Tramp and the Roughrider.** There are six different theatrical presentations, changing from year to year. (Shows play 3 times per week at 8pm; usually M, W, F. $7.50, children $3.25.)

STANISLAUS NATIONAL FOREST ☎209

One of the oldest National Forests, Stanislaus takes its name from the rushing Stanislaus River. Occupied first by the Miwok Indians and then overrun with gold prospectors over a century ago, Stanislaus has since quieted down and become overshadowed by its celebrity neighbor to the southeast, Yosemite. The park's varied landscape, from golden hills and raging rapids to crystalline alpine lakes and dense forests, remains relatively pristine. The 900,000 acres of central Sierra forest, including nearly 200,000 acres of untrammeled wilderness, teems with trails and recreational opportunities. The over 800 miles of river and streams make for endless fishing and boating. The park is organized into four ranger districts: Calaveras, Groveland, Miwok, and Summit. It also encompasses parts of the Carson-Iceberg, Emigrant, and Mokelumne federal wilderness areas.

Maps, brochures, permits, and advice can be found at **Park Headquarters,** 19777 Greenly Rd., across from the county library in Sonora. (☎532-3671. Open M-F 8am-4:30pm.) Permits are required for overnight trips into the wilderness areas and for building campfires outside of developed campsites. Dispersed camping (camping outside of developed campgrounds) is permitted throughout most of Stanislaus and requires no permit or fee. Exceptions include recreation areas like Pinecrest and Alpine Lake and wilderness areas, all of which require permits. One or two campsites in each district accept reservations.

SUMMIT DISTRICT. Encompassing large sections of the Emigrant Wilderness, the family-friendly Pinecrest Recreation Area, a number of glacial lakes, and subalpine meadows, the Summit Ranger District serves as both an entry point into the backcountry and a venue for less remote fishing, camping, biking, and nordic skiing. The **ranger station,** 1 Pinecrest Lake Rd., off Rte. 108 at Pinecrest Lake, has info on all the camping and recreational activities in the area. (☎965-3434. Open daily 8am-5pm; in winter M-Sa 8am-4:30pm.) The district hosts 25 campgrounds, most at 6000-7000 ft. Campsites abound to the east along Rte. 108 (free-$17). **Cascade Creek ❶,** 6000 ft., 11 mi. from Pinecrest, and **Niagara Creek ❶,** 6600 ft., 17 mi. from Pinecrest on Eagle Meadow Rd., both have beautiful, forested sites (12 and 10 sites respectively, $6) with fire rings and vault toilets, but no running water. **Pinecrest ❷,** the largest campsite in the district, is right next to the Pinecrest Recreation Area, and offers swimming, fishing, boating, and hiking. The 200 campsites have piped water and flush toilets and require a reservation. (Reservations ☎877-444-6777, TDD 877-833-6777; www.reserveamerica.com. Open May-Oct. Sites $19.) The only free campground is **Beardsley ❶,** 3400 ft., on the Beardsley Reservoir, 7 mi. off Rte. 108 on Beardsley Rd., with 10 RV sites (no hookups) and 16 tent sites. **Herring Creek ❶,** 7350 ft., with seven sites, and **Herring Reservoir ❷,** 7350 ft., with 42 sites, both on Herring Creek Rd. off Rte. 108, only request a donation. All sites are open May-Oct. ▓**Pinecrest Lake,** about 30 mi. east of Sonora on Rte. 108, is popular with families. The perfect alpine lake, set amid granite mountains and pine trees, serves as a small resort area, offering a swimming area, fishing pier (and rainbow trout stocking), picnic sites, and a 4 mi. hiking trail around the lake. **Boat rentals** are available at the marina. (☎ 965-3333. Kayaks $7 per hr.; paddleboats $10 per hr.; motorboats $30 per 2hr.; party boats $175 per half-day.) Every June, the lake hosts a **fishing celebration** (☎ 532-3671) that includes a fishing and casting contest and a free lunch.

Route 108 is a 60 mi. drive northeast through the forest, starting in Sonora and ending at the Sonora Pass on the border of the Toiyabe National Forest. The scenic drive is rich with history. Pick up an audio cassette tour at the Pinecrest Lake ranger station to play in your car as you make the trip. There are also many day hikes off Rte. 108, all between 1 and 4 mi. long and ranging in difficulty from quite easy to moderate. A few of them, such as the **Trail of the Gargoyles** (3 mi.), which is lined with twisted geological formations, and the **Trail of the Ancient Dwarfs** (2½ mi.), which follows a line of natural bonsai trees, can be supplemented with guides from the ranger station that point out items of geological and botanical interest. Many backcountry hikes into the Emigrant and Carson-Iceberg Wildernesses start along Rte. 108; obtain a wilderness permit, topographical maps, and more information at the ranger station. For stunning views of the **Stanislaus River** and its dammed reservoir, take Rte. 108 18 mi. east of Pinecrest to **Donnell Vista.** The popular and excellent **Gooseberry-Crabtree Trail** is a 15 mi. gravel and dirt road **mountain biking** loop that makes a difficult 2000 ft. ascent but rewards the tenacious biker with awesome vistas.

CARSON-ICEBERG WILDERNESS. Occupying the northeast corner of the park and bordered to the north by Rte. 108, to the south by Rte. 4, and to the east by Rte. 395, Carson-Iceberg is 160,000 acres of volcanic peaks, granite canyons, sinuous creeks, and pure solitude. While the high elevations, steep terrain, and scarcity of lakes eliminate this region from most itineraries, adventurous travelers are rewarded with unspoiled wilderness terrain all to themselves. What lakes the area does have are heavily visited, especially Sword Lake and Lost Lake. Major trailheads are at Wheat's Meadow and County Line.-Stanislaus Peak and Sonora Peak are accessible from the Pacific Crest Trail (for more info, see **From Crest to Crest: The Trail of the West,** p. 237), and give persevering climbers a humbling panorama of the Sierra. The Pacific Coast Trail includes a 5 mi. round-trip cross-country scramble from **Saint Mary's Pass,** 1 mi. before **Sonora Pass** on Rte. 108. It has a great view of the Central Valley, but the 3000 ft. climb is tiring. All mechanized vehicles (including bicycles) are prohibited in the wilderness.

CALAVERAS DISTRICT. In the northwest corner of the forest, the Calaveras Ranger District is blessed with quiet lakes, high-elevation hikes, the best rock climbing around, and the raging North Fork Stanislaus River. The **ranger station,** 5341 Rte. 4, at Hathaway Pines, exhibits the Dardanelles, a series of volcanic byproducts. (☎ 795-1381. Open M-F 8am-5pm, Sa 8:30am-2pm; in winter M-F 8am-4:30pm, Sa 9am-1pm.) **Wa Ku Luu Hep Yoo Campground ❶,** on Boardscrossing-Sourgrass Rd. off Rte. 4 in Dorrington, is shady and cool and has water, flush toilets, and hot showers at its 49 sites, as well as commercial rafting opportunities. The camp is on the site of an ancient Miwok village and features a number of preserved artifacts. (Open June-Oct. Sites $13.) Daredevil **rock climbing** and more bouldering opportunities abound here. Box Canyon offers 70-100 ft. technical climbs (rated moderately at 5.5-5.9). Park in the parking lot half a mile east of the Bear Valley junction with Rte. 4. More challenging climbs can be found at Spicer Road Crags and Spicer Terraces, both along Spicer Reservoir Rd. Guided expeditions are available through **Mountain Adventure Seminars** (☎ 753-6556 or 800-362-5462).

GROVELAND DISTRICT. Covering the area south of Sonora and west of Yosemite, Groveland District is best known for its lakeside recreation and its run of the Tuolumne Wild and Scenic River. The **Ranger Station,** 24545 Rte. 120, is 9 mi. west of Groveland. (☎962-7825. Open daily 8am-5:30pm; in winter 8am-4:30pm; Apr.-May Su-F 8am-5:30pm.) **The Pines ❶,** 3200 ft., 9 mi. west of Groveland on Rte. 120, is the closest campground to the entrance. The 12 sites have piped water and vault toilets. (Open year-round. Sites $10.) **Cherry Lake Campground ❶,** 4700 ft., 20 mi. down Cherry Lake Rd. off Rte. 4, has 46 sites, water, and access to boating and fishing on Cherry Lake. (Open Apr.-Oct. Sites $12.) **Cherry Valley,** a bit scarred from a fire, is half a mile north of Cherry Lake, just west of Yosemite. The stark glacier-carved canyon has space for hikers. A bridge crossing the South Fork Tuolumne on Rte. 120 marks the site of the popular swimming hole **Rainbow Pool,** where young children cavort in nature. Short hikes crisscross the area but the only extended hikes are in the mountainous Emigrant Wilderness, an area marked by alpine meadows and rocky hills. A trailhead at **Eagle Meadow** leads down to Coopers Meadow and **Three Chimneys,** a brick-red volcanic formation.

SIERRA NATIONAL FOREST   ☎559

Extending from the foothills of the San Joaquin Valley to the sheer walls of the High Sierras, the 1.3 million acres of the Sierra National Forest are characterized by steep gorges, glacial lakes, and endless conifers. Nearly half of the forest is federally designated wilderness of sweet solitude, while the region's crowded rivers and lakes serve as recreational centers, primarily for fishing.

Information on popular activities and the forest's 60 campgrounds can be obtained at the **Sierra National Forest Supervisor's Office,** 1600 Tollhouse Rd., off Rte. 168 in the gateway town of Clovis. (☎297-0706. Open M-F 8am-4:30pm.) A **backcountry permit** ($5 per person) is required for overnight stays in all of the designated wilderness areas (Ansel Adams, Dinkey Lakes, John Muir, Kaiser, and Monarch), which constitute 46% of the forest. Obtain permits for the Ansel Wilderness by writing the Mariposa/Minarets Ranger District and for the John Muir and Kaiser Wilderness areas by writing the Pineridge/Kings River District (for addresses, see below). Trailhead quotas are in effect from May through October. Forty percent of the permits are offered daily on a first-come, first-served basis, but these quotas fill quickly. It is also possible to write away for an advance reservation. Mail requests should be sent 20 days in advance.

NORTHWESTERN MARIPOSA DISTRICT. In summer, parched San Joaquin Valley residents crowd **Bass Lake,** where the marinas bustle with activity. The lake is well stocked with salmon, catfish, trout, crappie, bluegill, and bass. To join the water fun, rent equipment from **Miller's Landing,** 37976 Rd. 222. (☎642-3633; www.millerslanding.com. Canoes $5 per hr. Jet skis $85 per hr. Patio boats $180 for 5hr.) **Lupine** and **Cedar Bluff Campgrounds ❷** are right on the lake and stay open year-round for strong-willed ice fishers or wintertime Yosemite patrons. Between the two, there are 113 sites, all with flush toilets and water. (Sites $16.) Some of the best **hikes** in the Sierra are also nearby. Off Sky Ranch Rd. from Rte. 41, **Nelder Grove** is a large tract of pine trees, fir trees, incense cedars, and 106 seldom-visited giant sequoias. The grove also contains a campground used for thousands of years by the Southern Sierra Miwok Indians. Another trail winds to the **Bull Buck Tree,** a 246 ft. giant that is even more impressive without the crowds of gaping tourists common in other parts of the Sierra. The more challenging **Willow Creek Trail** passes both Angel Falls and the aptly named **Devil's Slide Waterfall** en route to McLeod Flat Rd.; the meandering **Mono Trail** is another option. Take Rte. 41 to the Bass Lake turn-off and follow Rd. 222 about 4 mi. to the parking lot at the trailhead. Information on the northwestern Mariposa District can be obtained by calling or writing the **Mariposa/Minarets Ranger District Office,** 57003 Rd. 225, P.O. Box 10, North Fork, CA 93643. (☎877-2218. Open M-F 8am-4:30pm.)

KINGS RIVER DISTRICT. The far reaches of the Kings River District rise to 13,000 ft. at the Sierra Crest. Most of the region's activity centers on the Dinkey Creek area and the Pine Flat Reservoir. The **Kings River Trail,** beginning at the end of Garnet Dike Rd. on the north side of Kings River, is the most popular in the area, winding through the tranquil wilderness. The 269 ft. **Boole Tree,** at the end of Converse Basin Rd., 5 mi. past Grant Grove off Rte. 180, is the largest giant sequoia outside of the national parks system. Four free **camping** sites, located along Kings River, are open during the summer. **White-water rafting** on the Kings River is a popular pastime, especially in spring when melting snow raises the water levels. **Kings River Expeditions** offers a variety of guided trips; get a group together to reduce costs. (☎233-4889. Open M-F 8am-5pm.) Trail bikes and 4WD vehicles raise dust on five off-highway routes that provide access to camping and fishing.

PINERIDGE DISTRICT. Easily accessible from Rte. 168, the Pineridge District is the forest's most popular region due to its wealth of swimming, boating, biking, rafting, fishing, hiking, and camping opportunities. **Camp Edison ❷** is a centrally located private campground with its own marina, convenience store, trout farm, and lake access. (☎841-3134. 252 well-spaced sites with electric hookup, flush toilets, showers, tables, and fire pits. Sites from $22.) The **Pineridge/Kings River Ranger District Office,** 29688 Auberry Rd., in Prather, is one of the forest's busiest centers. The office offers weekly ranger talks and guided hikes followed by marshmallow roasts—call for details. (☎855-5360. Open daily 8am-4:30pm.)

HUNTINGTON LAKE. Just one reservoir in the Big Creek hydroelectric system developed by Southern California Edison, Huntington Lake, 21 mi. farther east along Rte. 168, is known for its excellent boating and summertime regattas, windsurfing, waterskiing, and fishing. The lake's two marinas turn blue and white with sailboats in the summer. The best hiking from the lake ventures into the Kaiser and Dinkey Lakes Wilderness Areas. Seven **campgrounds ❶** cluster around the lake; register at the **Eastwood Visitor Center** at the junction of Rte. 168 and Kaiser Pass Rd. (Sites $16.) Past Kaiser Pass, the road narrows—honk your horn on the sharp turns to announce your presence. The terrain at the end of this road is definitively High Sierra—alpine lakes, green crowds of conifers, craggy summits, and crisp mountain air. **Mountain bikers** can speed down dozens of trails from the leisurely Tamarack Trail to the 66 mi. Dusy/Ershin Rd.

SEQUOIA AND KINGS CANYON NATIONAL PARKS

☎559

Protected from deforestation nearly as soon as it was discovered by European Americans, Sequoia National Park, which was expanded in the 1940s to include Kings Canyon to the north, is the nation's second-oldest national park, after Yellowstone. Though they cover only a small portion of the parks, the most popular attractions are the groves of giant sequoia, the earth's most massive living things. The largest specimen, the General Sherman Tree, in Giant Forest, weighs over 2.7 million pounds and has a base circumference of over 100 ft. In that same small grove stand four of the world's five largest trees, each about as old as Western civilization. The parks themselves stretch north-south along the middle elevations of the Sierra Nevadas, through an abundance of meadows and braided creeks. In addition to the sequoias, the parks contain the 6000 ft. Kern Canyon and Kings Canyon, the deepest in North America, carved out by the deep blue rapids and falls of Kings River. Most of these sights can be reached by car or by short walking expeditions, but the majority of the parks' lands are completely undeveloped, their gorges and wild rivers attracting serious hikers and backpackers to their 800 miles of backcountry trails.

AT A GLANCE: SEQUOIA AND KINGS CANYON NATIONAL PARKS

AREA: 864,411 acres.

CLIMATE: Temperate redwood forests.

FEATURES: Giant Forest, Cedar Grove, Moro Rock.

HIGHLIGHTS: Stretching your neck to see the General Sherman Tree, spelunking in the Crystal Cave, hiking the Congress Trail.

GATEWAYS: Fresno (p. 316), Visalia, Three Rivers.

CAMPING: Some campgrounds accept reservations. Free wilderness permit is required for backcountry camping.

FEES AND RESERVATIONS: Entrance fee $10 per car; $5 per pedestrian, cyclist, or motorcyclist. Valid for 7 days. Annual pass $20.

WHEN TO GO. Just like other areas of the Sierra Nevada, the parks are overrun with tourists in the summer. Nonetheless, this is the best time for hikes and water activities, since winter and spring weather is unreliable and can be quite frigid. The roads are often smothered with more than 15 ft. of snow in the winter, making tire chains a necessity.

⊏ TRANSPORTATION

By car, the two parks can only be accessed from the west. From **Fresno**, Rte. 180 runs east 60 mi. to Kings Canyon's **Big Stump** entrance, passes **Grant Grove**, and ends 30 mi. later in **Cedar Grove** at the mouth of King's Canyon. The drive into the Canyon is steep and curvy, making extra caution, and possibly downshifting, necessary. The Canyon is generally off-limits from late October to late April, as Rte. 180 closes just past the Hume Lake turn-off due to the threat of winter storms and falling rocks. From **Visalia**, Rte. 198 winds its way past Lake Kaweah to Sequoia's Ash Mountain entrance, where it becomes the **Generals Highway,** named for its route between the General Grant and General Sherman trees. A serpentine and sometimes unpredictable speedway, Rte. 198 climbs through 2000 vertical feet of hairpin turns. Drivers should exercise caution; switching into a low gear on downhill grades is recommended. The drive from Ash Mountain through Sequoia's Giant Forest to Grant Grove takes about 2hr. The road is usually open from mid-May to October. During the winter, entry points to Grant Grove and Giant Forest, and the Generals Highway connecting the two, are kept open when weather permits. The **Mineral King** turn-off branches from Rte. 198 just before Sequoia's Ash Mountain entrance. This drive is accented by high-country panoramas, but marred by five unpaved miles and endless switchbacks. **No gas is officially sold in the park,** so be sure to fill up before entering. In a pinch, Hume Lake and Kings Canyon Lodge, in Sequoia National Forest (see p. 269) off Rte. 180 between Grant and Cedar Groves, sell gas at a premium. Stony Creek Village, on the Generals Highway between Giant Forest and Grant Grove, also has gas and offers 24hr. credit card access. The only park access from the east is by trail; enter either park from the **John Muir Wilderness** and **Inyo National Forest,** both accessible from spur roads off U.S. 395. One of the most popular trails begins in Onion Valley and enters the park over Kearsarge Pass. Hikers from the east should secure backcountry permits in advance.

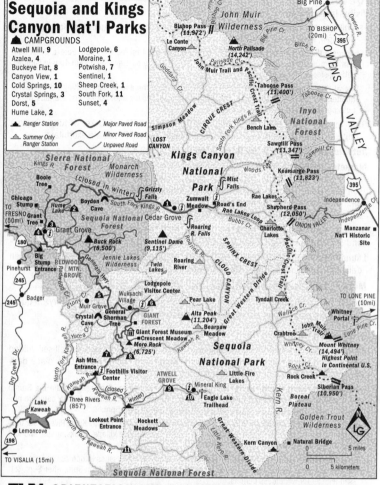

Sequoia and Kings Canyon Nat'l Parks

▲ CAMPGROUNDS

Atwell Mill, **9**	Lodgepole, **6**
Azalea, **4**	Moraine, **1**
Buckeye Flat, **8**	Potwisha, **7**
Canyon View, **1**	Sentinel, **1**
Cold Springs, **10**	Sheep Creek, **1**
Crystal Springs, **3**	South Fork, **11**
Dorst, **5**	Sunset, **4**
Hume Lake, **2**	

▲ Ranger Station
▲ Summer Only
Ranger Station

Major Paved Road
Minor Paved Road
Unpaved Road

SIERRA NEVADA

ORIENTATION AND PRACTICAL INFORMATION

The parks' most popular sights are concentrated in three areas: **Giant Forest** in Sequoia, and **Grant Grove** and **Cedar Grove** in Kings Canyon. Pristine backcountry comprises the eastern two-thirds of Sequoia and the southern two-thirds of Kings Canyon. Seasonal changes are dramatic in this part of the Sierra. Anything beyond the frontcountry of Generals Hwy. is accessible only during the summer, as snow lasts throughout the year on some peaks. Dogwood, aspen, and oak trees display brilliant colors in the fall. Snow season is from November to March, and, although trails are open year-round, they may have snow as late as mid-June. Spring here is unpredictable, bringing late storms, low fog, runoff flooding, and falling rock. Camping supplies, amenities, gas, and groceries in the parks are no-frills but expensive. The **Central Valley** (see p. 303), **Three Rivers** (8 mi. southwest on Rte. 198), and **Visalia** (25 mi. southwest on Rte. 198) offer a better selection of supplies.

SIERRA NEVADA

SEQUOIA

Visitor Information:

Foothills Visitor Center (☎565-3341), just inside the Ash Mountain entrance station. Open daily 8am-5pm; in winter 8am-4:30pm.

Lodgepole Visitor Center (☎565-4436), on Generals Hwy. 4 mi. east of Giant Forest. Open daily 8am-5pm, with reduced hours after Sept. 6. Wilderness permits available 7am-4pm in summer; self-register in winter.

Mineral King Ranger Station (☎565-3764), 1 mi. before the end of Mineral King Rd. The headquarters for the remote Mineral King region offers maps, hiking info, books, first aid, and wilderness permits. Open daily 8am-4:30pm.

Gas: The nearest reasonable option is in Three Rivers, Hume Lake, or Kings Canyon Lodge, a 15min. drive from Grant Grove in Kings Canyon. Prices are exorbitant.

Auto Repair: AAA Emergency Road Service ☎800-400-4222.

Markets: Lodgepole Market, near Lodgepole Visitor Center, is well stocked with food and outdoor supplies at reasonable prices. Open daily in summer 8am-8pm; in low season 9am-6pm. Two stores in Three Rivers, **Village Market** (open M-Sa 8am-8pm, Su 9am-6pm) and **Three Rivers Market** (open daily 7:30am-8pm), offer better selections on food and gear. **Silver City Resort** (☎561-3223), in Mineral King, sells supplies.

Showers: Opposite the Lodgepole Visitors Center. $2. Open daily May-Sept. 8am-1pm and 3-7:45pm; Oct.-Apr. 9am-1pm and 3-5:45pm.

Laundromat: In the Lodgepole Market Center. Wash $1.25, dry $0.50 per 10min. Open daily Oct.-Apr. 9am-4:30pm; May 9am-6pm; June-Sept. 8am-8pm.

Medical Services: Kaweah Delta Hospital (☎624-2000), off Rte. 198, in Visalia.

Post Office: At Lodgepole. 24hr. stamp machine in lobby. General Delivery: Sequoia National Park, CA. Open M-F 8am-1pm and 2-4pm. **Postal Code:** 93262.

KINGS CANYON

Visitor Center: In addition to providing info, the following visitors centers sell self-guided tour maps. Walks, talks, and slide shows at Grant and Cedar Groves take place daily during the summer and on winter weekends.

Grant Grove Visitor Center (☎565-4307), in Grant Grove Village, 2 mi. east of the Big Stump entrance by Rte. 180. Books, maps, local wilderness permits, and exhibits. Nightly campfire programs and daily hikes. Open daily 8am-6pm; in low season 8am-5pm.

Cedar Grove Visitor Center (☎565-3793), 30 mi. farther down Rte. 180 by Kings River. Near trailheads into Kings Canyon high country, ½mi. south of Cedar Grove Village. Books, maps, and first aid. Open daily mid-June to Sept. 6 9am-5pm.

Road's End Kiosk (☎565-3791), 6 mi. east of Cedar Grove Village. Issues wilderness permits, sells maps, and rents bear canisters. Open daily mid-June to Sept. 21 7:30am-3pm; after Sept. 21, self-register for wilderness permits.

Gas: There are 2 options along Rte. 180: **Hume Lake Christian Camp** (☎335-2000), 11 mi. north of Grant Grove, and **Kings Canyon Lodge** (☎335-2405), 17 mi. north of Grant Grove. More reasonable prices can be found at Three Rivers, south of the park on Rte. 198. Only emergency gas is available at Grant Grove Market.

Auto Repair: Attendants at Grant Grove (☎335-5500) can handle minor repairs and lockouts. For major repairs or service outside the Grant Grove area, call **Michael's** (☎638-4101), in Reedley. **AAA Emergency Road Service,** ☎800-400-4222.

ATM: At Grant Grove Market and Cedar Grove Market. $2 surcharge.

Markets: Grant Grove Market, Cedar Grove Market, and the **Hume Lake General Store** carry a limited selection of camping basics and groceries. Grant Grove Market open daily 8am-9pm. Cedar Grove Market open daily 7am-9pm. Hume Lake General Store open Su-F 8am-7pm, Sa 8am-10pm.

Showers: Cedar Grove Village. $3; towel $1. Open daily 8am-7pm. **Grant Grove Village.** $3; towel $1. Open daily 11am-4pm.

Laundromat: Cedar Grove Village. Wash $1, dry $0.25 per 15min. Open daily 8am-7pm.

Medical Services: Fresno Community Hospital (☎459-6000), at Fresno and R St., in Fresno.

Post Office: Grant Grove Village (☎335-2499), near the visitors center. Hours vary widely, but generally M-F 9am-3:30pm, Sa 9am-12:30pm. A stamp machine and mailbox are next to the visitors center. General Delivery: Kings Canyon National Park, CA. **Postal Code: 93633. Hume Lake,** at the Hume Lake Christian Camp. Open June-Oct. M-F 9am-4:30pm, Sa 9:30am-2pm. **Postal Code: 93628.**

ACCOMMODATIONS

For those who just want a roof over their heads, motels with all the creature comforts can be found in outlying towns. Within the parks, lodges are the cheapest option. When traveling in a group, look for hotels with suites or cabins, which usually work out to be significantly less per person than doubles. The **Kings Canyon Park Service,** P.O. Box 909, Kings Canyon National Park, CA 93633 (☎335-5500) is in charge of accommodations and reservations in the park. **Grant Grove Lodge and John Muir Lodge ❸** (☎335-5500, reservations 866-522-6966; www.sequoia-kingscanyon.com), in Grant Grove Village, have wooden structures with canvas tops, no electricity, and communal baths (from $45); rustic wooden cabins with or without electricity ($55 or $60); and cabins with private bath and electricity (from $100). The cheapest indoor accommodations hover at higher rates at the **Cedar Grove Lodge ❺** in Cedar Grove Village. (☎565-0100; www.sequoia-kingscanyon.com. Rooms $99, with kitchenette and patio $110.) Outside the park, small spots can be a better value but are still pricey. Motels and lodges abound in **Three Rivers,** 6 mi. west of the park on Rte. 198. **Visalia,** 30 mi. southwest of the park on Rte. 198, is home to standard motels and a few finds.

The Sierra Lodge, 43175 Sierra Dr./Rte. 198 (☎561-3681), in Three Rivers. This funky pastel motel sits just outside Sequoia's Ash Mountain entrance. Spacious rooms have valley and river views, coffeemakers, and balconies. 5 suites feel like condos, with kitchen and fireplace. Large pool. Rooms from $49; in winter $39. Suites $100-160. ❸

The Sequoia Motel, 43000 Sierra Dr./Rte. 198 (☎561-4453; www.sequoiamotel.com), in Three Rivers. This recently remodeled motel has 11 rooms and 4 fairly standard cabins with fireplaces. Pool, picnic area, and extensive garden. Even the smallest room has a patio and private bath. Rooms from $66; 6-person cabins $110-165. ❹

Ben Maddox House, 610 N. Encinia St. (☎800-401-9800), in Visalia. This stately 4-room ground-level B&B built from sequoia trees in 1876 sits on a well-groomed lot with palm trees. Amenities include 14ft. ceilings, a pool, patio, spa, full breakfast, and in-room Internet connections. Singles $85-95; doubles $90-110. ❺

CAMPING

Although campgrounds fill quickly, a few spots should still be available on most weekends. **Dorst** is the campground in Sequoia that accepts reservations. (☎800-365-2267; http://reservations.nps.gov.) Most campgrounds are open from mid-May to October, with a 14-night maximum stay during the summer and one month total per year. There are no RV hookups in the parks, but dump stations are available at Potwisha, Lodgepole, Dorst, and Princess. Contact a ranger station for more info. **Backcountry camping** permits are free (see **Practical Information,** p. 272).

SIERRA NEVADA

 BEARS WILL EAT YOU...OR YOUR FOOD. Black bears are common in both parks. Though bears seldom attack humans, all odorous items, edible or not, should be locked away in bear boxes provided at developed campsites. Backcountry campers can rent a bear canister at visitors centers.

SEQUOIA

■ **Buckeye Flat,** 2800 ft., past park headquarters, a few miles from the Ash Mountain entrance on Rte. 198. All 28 sites are spacious and lie in a grove of low, shady buckeye trees and stark rock outcroppings. Great views of the mountains above; refreshing swimming in the sparkling water below. Closed to RVs. Flush toilets, drinking water. Open May 21-Oct. 12. Sites $18. ❷

Potwisha, 2100 ft., near Buckeye Flat. A full-service campground with 42 well-spaced sites where RVs are welcome. No RV hookups, but dump stations available. Good swimming across the street. Flush toilets, drinking water. Sites $18. ❷

Atwell Mill, 6650 ft., and **Cold Springs,** 7500 ft., 20 mi. along Mineral King Rd. in the Mineral King area. 2 secluded campgrounds a mile apart. Pit toilets, piped water, and picnic tables for the 61 tent sites overlooking a stream. Steep, winding roads and a ban on trailers keep the RVs away. On-site pay phones. Store, restaurant, and showers are 2-3 mi. away in Silver City. Open June-Oct. Sites $12. ❶

South Fork, 3600 ft., on South Fork Rd., 13 mi. from Rte. 198. 10 sites near the ranger station, a river, and some backcountry roads. Vault toilets, no drinking water. Not recommended for trailers or RVs. Sites $12. ❶

Dorst (☎800-365-2267), 6800 ft., 12 mi. north of Giant Forest and 8 mi. north of Lodgepole. Huge campground with 204 sites convenient to Sequoia attractions. The wide paved road and wood-chip paths wind through gentle hills, a small stream, and enormous pines. Dump station and pay phone. Open late May-Sept. Sites $20. ❷

KINGS CANYON

■ **Sunset, Azalea,** and **Crystal Springs,** 6500 ft., are within a stone's throw of Grant Grove Village (and all its services) but remain quiet. Sunset (200 sites) features gentle wooded hills and brilliant views of the San Joaquin Valley but is often closed unless other sites start to overflow. Azalea (113 sites), open year-round (free in winter), is well forested and often calm but packed with RVs during busy weekends. Crystal Springs (62 sites) is the smallest and most remote. Like Sunset, it is also frequently closed. All offer flush toilets, water, and privacy. Azalea has a dump station. Sites $18. ❶

Sheep Creek, Sentinel, Canyon View, and **Moraine,** 4600 ft., on Rte. 180 at Kings River near Cedar Grove, 32 mi. east of Grant Grove. Within a few miles of Road's End and Kings Canyon trailheads. All are well forested and near Kings Creek. Sheep Creek (111 sites) has more secluded tent sites in the back of the campground. Sentinel's 82 sites are flatter and near the Cedar Grove Amphitheater. Moraine, with its canyon vistas, serves primarily as overflow and opens only on the busiest weekends. All have flush toilets, water, and dump stations. Canyon View accepts group reservations. Usually closed Oct.-May. Sites $18. ❶

 MARMOTS WILL CHEW ON YOUR CAR. These sneaky rodents have been known to chew on hoses and wiring on parked cars. Be sure to check with a ranger to make sure it is safe to park in Mineral King.

◗ FOOD

If you have a small camp stove and some barbecue briquettes (available at park markets), or don't mind a cold meal, you can stock up on provisions at a park market (see p. 256) or in Three Rivers. **Village Market** in Three Rivers may help you produce an affordable meal. (☎561-4441. Open M-Sa 8am-8pm, Su 9am-6pm.)

Grant Grove Restaurant (☎335-5500), in Grant Grove Village, across from the visitors center. A restaurant that feels more like a cafeteria. Good portions of standard American fare. Breakfast $4-8. Lunch $6-8. Dinner $10-18. Pizza availablenoon-2pm and 5-10pm. Open in summer daily 7am-9pm; in low season M-F 7:30am-2pm and 4:30-7pm, Sa 7am-8pm, Su 7am-7pm. ❸

Serrano's Mexican Restaurant, 40869 Sierra Dr. (☎561-7283), in Three Rivers. This colorful, painted *cocina* serves up delicious and authentic Mexican food in healthy portions. Free chips and *salsa fresca* warm up the taste buds for large dinner plates ($8-10). Great lunch special (2 items for $5). Open daily 9am-10pm. ❷

Anne Lang's Emporium, 41651 Sierra Dr. (☎561-4937), in Three Rivers. Lingering scents of potpourri and coffee permeate the air in this friendly deli that overflows with potted plants. Terraces overlook the Kaweah River. Large sandwiches ($5) come with potato salad and fruit. Salads $3-6. Open M-F 9:30am-5:30pm, Sa-Su 10am-5pm. ❶

◙ ⚠ SIGHTS AND OUTDOOR ACTIVITIES

SEQUOIA
Giant Forest contains the largest of the giant sequoia trees, including the most massive of them all, **General Sherman.** John Muir named the grove during his extensive explorations of the area and recounted his epiphanous experiences to the American public in his plea for conservation, *My First Summer in the Sierra.* Branching off eastward from the Giant Forest Museum on Generals Hwy., the Moro Rock-Crescent Meadow Rd. is a 3 mi. dead-end road that leads to Moro Rock, Crescent Meadow, and **Tunnel Log** (2¾ mi. from the village). This giant sequoia fell in 1937 and was hollowed out so cars could drive through it.

GENERAL SHERMAN TREE. The tallest of the park's marvels, this towering pine was discovered in 1879 and named by a Civil War veteran after William Tecumseh Sherman. Standing 275 ft. tall, measuring 102 ft. around its base, weighing over 1385 tons, and estimated to be around 2500 years old, the **world's largest living thing** looms regally over the forest. It also generates a line of children and adults waiting to get their picture taken in front of the massive tree and the marker that identifies it. Many sequoias in the forest are over 3000 years old; their extensive root systems, fire-resistant bark, and insect-repelling juices make them the ultimate survivors. The 2 mi. **Congress Trail,** the park's most popular trail, leaves from the General Sherman Tree parking lot, boomerangs around General Sherman and other trees named for US political big shots, and passes through the heart of the grove. **Big Trees Trail** (¾mi.) is a short, wheelchair-accessible loop lined with informative panels. It starts at the Giant Forest Museum, which is easy to find with the trail guides available at all park visitors centers.

MORO ROCK. The granite monoliths and meadows of the Giant Forest area are perhaps more impressive than the trees that made it famous. If you've ever wanted to feel like a daredevil rock climber without the peril, the 400-step granite staircase leading up Moro Rock will oblige, and if the arduous climb up the stairs doesn't leave you breathless, the stunning 360° view of the southern Sierra will.

The Great Western Divide lies to the east, while foothills recline into the San Joaquin Valley to the south and the west. The bare face of the dome is prone to lightning strikes; never take this hike in a storm.

CRESCENT MEADOW. At the end of the Moro Rock-Crescent Meadow Rd., beyond the parking lot, rests this fabulous bed of flowers, which Muir called "the gem of the Sierra." The Park Service requests that you stay on marked trails, but to avoid crowds, take the short hike to **Tharp's Log,** a hollowed-out sequoia that housed the first Anglo settler in the area. For ultimate serenity, venture out from the meadow along the High Sierra trail to Mt. Whitney, 71 mi. to the east.

CRYSTAL CAVE TOURS. Crystal Cave Rd. branches off Rte. 198 a few miles south of the Giant Forest Museum and winds 6 mi. to Crystal Cave. Discovered by two trail construction workers fishing on their day off in 1918, this is one of the few caves on the park's western side that are open to the public. Half a mile from the road, the cave is lined with smooth limestone stalagmites and stalactites, moistened by a dark underground stream, and inhabited by hordes of Mexican freetailed bats. Tours last 45min. and proceed along lighted walkways, stopping often to note interesting features. **Marble Hall,** the cave's largest chamber, is 141 ft. long and over 40 ft. high. The temperature inside is a constant 50°F, so wear warm clothing. (☎ 565-3159. Tickets must be purchased 1½hr. in advance at the Lodgepole or Foothills Visitors Centers. Tours given May 31-Sept. 6 daily every 30min. 11am-4pm; less frequently the rest of the year. $10, ages 6-12 $5, 62 and older $8, under 6 free.)

OTHER ACTIVITIES. For those craving the underground scene, **Boyden Cavern** lies on Rte. 180, 10 mi. west of Cedar Grove, in Kings Canyon itself. (☎ 866-762-2837. 45min. tours Apr.-Nov. every hr. 11am-4pm; June-Sept. 10am and 5pm. $9, ages 3-13 $4.50, under 3 free. National park entrance fee required. No reservations necessary.) Whitewater rafters can ride the bucking rivers with **Kaweah White Water Adventures,** on Rte. 198 in Three Rivers. May and June are the best months for high water. (☎ 561-1000 or 800-229-8658. Class III rapids, half-day $80 per person; Classes IV and V, full-day $130 per person.) Visitors interested in renting horses can contact the stables at Grant Grove, Cedar Grove, or Horse Corral. All offer guided rides. (Grant Grove ☎ 335-9292, Cedar Grove 565-3464, Horse Corral 565-3404. Open mid-May to mid-June daily 8am-6pm. $25 per hr., $100 per day.) Bicycles, off-road vehicles, and snowmobiles are not permitted on hiking trails or in the backcountry.

KINGS CANYON

GRANT GROVE. The most developed portion of Kings Canyon is Grant Grove, named for its commanding attraction, the General Grant Tree. The 3500-year-old general, the third-largest sequoia in the world, is famed for its archetypal shape. It has been designated the "Nation's Christmas Tree" and serves as the only living shrine to the American war dead. The **Grant Tree Trail,** just past the Sunset Campground, is a paved loop (½ mi.) that passes the mammoth sequoia. At the trailhead, a $1 trail guide with information on significant trees along the trail is available. The huge **Fallen Monarch** (a felled sequoia) once housed a saloon and a stable, and has been lying on the forest ground undecayed for an unimaginably long time. The 24 ft. wide **Centennial Stump** stubbornly resisted nine days of hacking. When it arrived at the 1876 Centennial Exposition in Philadelphia, Easterners refused to display it, dismissing it as "another California hoax."

CEDAR GROVE. The most incredible sights in Kings Canyon lie in the canyon itself, 30 mi. east of Grant Grove on Rte. 180. Over countless millenia, glacier movement and the powerful Kings River cleaved a groove here deeper than even the Grand Canyon. Sheer rock walls and fertile hills rise up around the turbulent blue-green river that tumbles down below. Once within the grove, you can explore the banks of Kings River and marvel at the depth of the canyon (8200 ft. in some spots). Roaring River Falls and Mist Falls are at their best in late spring and early summer, when the streams that feed them are swift and swollen. The **Roaring River Falls** plunge into a large rocky basin before flowing out to the river and are easily reached by a 5min. walk from Rte. 180, 3 mi. east of Cedar Grove Village. Look for signs just beyond the village. **Mist Falls,** a 9 mi. hike from the trailhead at Road's End, 5½ mi. east of Cedar Grove Village, takes about 4hr. The breathtaking **Grizzly Falls,** located 7 mi. west of Cedar Grove in Sequoia National Forest, is a leisurely 50 yd. walk from the highway.

OTHER SIGHTS AND HIKES. For an easily accessible view, head to **Panoramic Point,** at the end of a steep 2¼ mi. road that leaves from behind the Grant Grove Visitor Center. If the road is closed, use the 2 mi. North Boundary Trail, 1 mi. west of Grant Grove Village. **Buena Vista Peak,** a 1 mi. hike from Generals Hwy., 7 mi. south of Grant Grove, and **Big Baldy,** a moderately difficult 2 mi. hike from the trailhead 8 mi. south of Grant Grove afford tremendous views. **Park Ridge Trail** is one of the most scenic and well-marked treks in the park. The 1½ mi. round-trip hike along the **Dead Giant Loop** borders national park and national forest lands, and provides information on the differences between the two. Just north of the park entrance on Rte. 180 lies the **Big Stump Basin Trail,** a 1 mi. self-guided walk through an 1890s-era logging camp that laid the area's sequoias to waste.

◈ BACKCOUNTRY HIKING

In the backcountry, visitors should be wary of bears, which are adorable, fuzzy, and fond of human food (see **Bears,** p. 56). **Group tours** led by the park's pack stations (☎ 563-3445) provide safety in numbers. *Backcountry Basics,* a guide to backcountry safety, is available at the visitors center ($10).

Near Giant Forest, **Little Baldy Trail** starts at Little Baldy Saddle, 9 mi. north of General Sherman on the Generals Hwy., and climbs 1¾ mi. with a 700 ft. vertical ascent to the rocky summit. The more challenging **Garfield Trail** climbs 4½ mi. to the Garfield sequoia grove from South Fork Campground. **Moro Rock Trail** leads 4½ mi. from Moro Rock, a short drive behind the Giant Forest Museum, to Roosevelt Tree and Triple Tree (three trees grown together).

Redwood Mountain Grove, the world's largest grove of redwood trees, lies near Quail Flat, 6 mi. south of Grant Grove and 4 mi. north of Giant Forest Village. A 10 mi. trail makes two shorter loops through the grove along **Redwood Creek,** a tributary of the Kaweah River's North Fork, where azaleas bloom in May and June. The route passes small waterfalls, young sequoias, and Tunnel Tree. **Mist Falls Trail** heads out from Road's End on 5 mi. of relatively flat ground to a grand waterfall. The trail continues another 3 mi. to Paradise Valley. The long and strenuous **Don Cecil** and **Hotel Creek Trails,** which begin within walking distance of the village, head toward Cedar Grove and the awesome canyon, making for full-day hikes.

The extensive system of backwoods trails presents even more spectacular views. The **Marble Falls Trail** (7 mi. round-trip) begins by the Potwisha Campground and twists through hills to a 2000 ft. peak at the foot of **Marble Falls.** For those who want the easy payoff, the top of Marble Falls can also be accessed from a much shorter trail off Cave Rd. Ask for directions to **Admiration Point** at a ranger station. The moderately strenuous hike from the Lodgepole Visitors Center to the glistening **Twin Lakes** (13½ mi. round-trip) reminds visitors that some of the beauty of the park can be found in little things as well; flowers, brooks, and chipmunks abound in picturesque Cahoon Meadow. A few trails lead deep into the park, connecting with the Pacific Crest Trail and crossing into Inyo National Forest. Ask a ranger about the High Sierra Trail and the Woods Creek Trail.

The **Mineral King** area was acquired by the park system in 1978 after lawsuits prevented the Walt Disney Corporation from building a ski resort on the site. Some of the best scenery in the park awaits those willing to brave the winding drive with blind corners and steep drop-offs. The valley is 7500 ft. deep with steep trails leading up to mountain lakes and meadows. A booming mining area in the 1800s, the region now offers magnificent backcountry hiking and climbing. The walk to **Aspen Flat** from Mineral King Pack Station is an easy, rewarding day hike, flanked by soda springs and wildflowers. The moderately difficult **Eagle Lake Trail** (6¾ mi. round-trip) starts 1 mi. down the road from the ranger station. Look for the sinkhole where Eagle Creek disappears underground—no one knows where the water ends up. Furry marmots and pikas along the trail will whistle if you startle them.

Road's End is a naturally U-shaped glacial valley at the eastern end of Rte. 180. The most popular backcountry foray from Road's End is **Rae Lakes Loop,** which traverses an all-star list of the Sierra's best: glaciated canyons, gentle meadows, violent rapids, and inspiring lakes. Along the five-day trail are two backcountry ranger stations, open only during the summer, and campgrounds at 7 mi. intervals. Trails into the High Sierra (including the **Pacific Crest Trail**) also depart from here. Obtain permits at the **Road's End Kiosk** (see p. 272).

SEQUOIA NATIONAL FOREST   ☎ 559

Sequoia National Forest is on the southern end of the majestic Sierra Nevada range, which peters out in the Mojave Desert 60 mi. south of the park. The forest is best known for its 38 groves of towering giant sequoia trees and the Hume Lake Dam, the first multiple arch concrete dam built in the US. It is bound on the north by the Kings River, on the west by the San Joaquin Valley, on the east by the Owens Valley, and on the south by Telephone Ridge. The Kern River slices through its southeast region.

■🔌 **ORIENTATION AND PRACTICAL INFORMATION.** The **Forest Headquarters,** 900 W. Grand Ave., on Rte. 65 in Porterville, has detailed maps of the forest ($7.50) highlighting its six designated wilderness areas. (☎784-1500. Open M-F 8am-4:30pm.) Backcountry excursions to the **Golden Trout Wilderness** require wilderness permits, available at any district ranger's office. The **Hume Lake Ranger District Office,** 35860 E. Kings Canyon Rd., on Rte. 180 in Dunlap, 32 mi. east of Fresno near the forest entrance, provides camping info. (☎338-2251. Open June-Sept. 6 M-Sa 8am-4:30pm; Sept. 7-May M-F 8am-4:30pm.) There is a $10 fee to enter the park from the north, due in part to the fact that this entrance also serves Sequoia and Kings Canyon National Parks.

🔭 **CAMPING. Camping** in the forest is abundant, quiet, and mostly free. While numerous campgrounds are available, camping outside designated campgrounds is allowed unless otherwise posted. You must be at least 100 ft. away from any water's edge and obtain a campfire permit. In the Hume Lake District, **Big Meadow** ❶ (7600 ft.), on Big Meadow Rd. 13 mi. southeast of Grant Grove from Generals Hwy., has 25 sites for tents and trailers at no charge, though there's no water available. More popular sites in the area include **Stony Creek** ❶ and **Upper Stony Creek** ❶ (6400 ft.), both 14 mi. southeast of Grant Grove on Generals Hwy. Some sites at each may be reserved in advance. (☎877-444-6777. Stony Creek sites $16; Upper Stony Creek sites $12.) As the name implies, **Quaking Aspen** ❶ (7000 ft.), in the Tule River/Hot Springs District, is surrounded by beautiful quaking aspen. It lies next to a small meadow, and some sites are very secluded. (Water, toilets. Sites $14.)

◙ ⚠ SIGHTS AND OUTDOOR ACTIVITIES. The **Giant Sequoia National Monument** extends from Kings River in the north to Telephone Ridge in the south. With 38 groves of giant sequoia, the monument is the focal point of the forest. A strenuous 40 mi. stretch of the **Pacific Crest National Scenic Trail** passes through the forest on its 2600 mi. journey between Canada and Mexico (see **From Crest to Crest: The Trail of the West,** p. 237). The **Trail of 100 Giants,** in Giant Sequoia National Monument, is a more relaxing, interpretive 35min. walk in the southern section of the forest. From Springville, take U.S. 190 until it turns into Western Divide Hwy. and continue for 13 mi. until you see signs for the trailhead. One of the most popular trails in the National Monument, it has signs emphasizing the ecology of giant sequoias and information about the grove. **Needles Trail** is a moderate 2½ mi. hike from Forest Service Rd. 21 SO5. From Springville, take U.S. 190 24 mi. until it turns into Western Divide Hwy., then, after 1 mi., take Forest Service Road 21 SO5. The hike, which begins at the end of a dirt road, ascends to the top of the Needles Fire Lookout, providing stunning views of the Kern River, Mt. Whitney, and Dome Rock. The moderately strenuous 2 mi. **Sherman Pass Trail** starts from the Sherman Pass parking lot on Sherman Pass Rd. and climbs to the mountain's peak for a view of the surrounding forest, recently devastated by fire. These trails are open to off-road vehicles and horses. One hundred fifty miles of **backcountry hiking** can be found in the **Golden Trout Wilderness,** accessible on Rte. 190 and Rte. 395, and **Monarch Wilderness,** accessible on Rte. 180. These areas are remote and unforgiving; expeditions require serious preparation. **Outdoor Adventures** (☎ 800-323-4234; www.kernrafting.com) runs two-day **whitewater rafting trips** on the Lower Kern for about $300 per person, day and half-day trips on the Upper Kern for $100-150, and serious three-day trips on the Class V rapids of the North Fork Kern for $750-800. **Whitewater Voyages** provides kayaking instruction and also has Kern, Kings River, and Tuolumne River rafting trips. (☎ 800-488-7238; www.whitewatervoyages.com. 2- to 4-day kayaking courses $250-500. Rafting $100-200 per day.)

The forest also includes several historic sights. The **Boole Tree** is the largest giant sequoia in the National Forest system, the eighth-largest in the world, and was spared from logging due to its size. The tree is in Converse Grove, 6 mi. north of Kings Canyon National Park's Grant Grove on Hwy. 180. **Stump Meadow** is part of Converse Grove and is filled with sequoia stumps resulting from 19th century logging. **Hume Lake Dam,** at Hume Lake, off Hwy. 180, is the first reinforced concrete multiple-arch dam ever built in the US. Designated a National Historic Landmark, it holds Hume Lake, which allows boating, fishing, picnicking, and swimming.

EASTERN SIERRA

Unlike the western side of the Sierra Nevada, which descends leisurely into the Central Valley foothills, the eastern side's jagged heights drop off precipitously, drawing a dramatic silhouette against the skies. This striking topography resulted from lifting and faulting that shaped the Sierra Nevada ridge 10 million years ago. Die-hard fishermen are drawn to the June Lake area, downhill enthusiasts flock to the incomparable snow and mountain biking trails of Mammoth Lakes, and outdoorsmen in search of the Wild West wander the high-elevation trails of Lone Pine.

LEE VINING AND MONO LAKE   ☎ 760

As the snow thaws in June, Rte. 120 over the stunning Tioga Pass opens to motorists, transforming the town of Lee Vining (pop. 315) into a great eastern gateway to Yosemite or a quiet getaway destination itself. The town's focus is the vigilant preservation of nearby natural marvel Mono Lake. Sitting at the western flank of the Great Basin desert and home to similarly saline lakes like Pyramid and The Great Salt Lake, Mono Lake is sustained by freshwater inflows from surrounding mountains. Without any natural outlet, evaporation is the sole equilibrating force in the lake, but because salts and minerals are left behind as the lake dries, salinity has built up to two to three times that of ocean levels. This process of drainage by evaporation has been going on for nearly a million years, making Mono Lake one of the oldest in the Western Hemisphere. The lake's mythological appearance is marked by tufa, spires of calcium carbonate that form when calcium-rich springs well up in the carbonate-filled salt water. In some places, these spires reach nearly 15 ft. above the water.

Today, Mono supports not only its own delicate and unique ecosystem, but also the water needs of greater metropolitan L.A. Although Mono Lake's water has always been too salty to use, its freshwater inflows are extremely pure. L.A.'s rapid growth, lack of freshwater supplies, and political might resulted in these inflows being completely diverted in 1941. By 1982, the lake's levels had dropped 50 ft., its volume had halved, and its salinity had doubled. Various parts of the ecological fabric in the area quickly began to fray. Delicate tufa were exposed, riparian forests withered, local trout populations were depleted, and the Californian shore's gulls and brine shrimp faced tough prospects for survival. In the past 20 years, however, locals and lake-lovers have rejoiced to see the lake rise 15 ft. as the combined efforts of Congress, the US Forest Service, the Audobon Society, and the Mono Lake Committee succeeded in reducing the flow south by half.

The small town of Lee Vining happily serves as host to Yosemite adventurers and Mono Lake visitors. Although quite small (the town only stretches about 4 city blocks), its visitors center has a wealth of information about outdoor activities in the area, and its restaurants and accommodations take care of the basics, sometimes with admirable success.

■ 🛈 ORIENTATION AND PRACTICAL INFORMATION

Lee Vining provides stunning access to Yosemite via **Inyo National Forest** and is the best access point to Mono Lake and Bodie. The town is 70 mi. north of Bishop on U.S. 395 and 10 mi. west of the Tioga Pass entrance to Yosemite. Bodie is 28 mi. northwest of Lee Vining off U.S. 395. Addresses in Lee Vining consist only of P.O. Box numbers, so general directions or cross-streets are provided here instead.

Visitor Information:

■ **Mono Lake Committee and Lee Vining Chamber of Commerce** (☎647-6595; www.mono-lake.org or www.leevining.com), in the orange and blue clay building at Main and 3rd St., in Lee Vining. Like a friendly eco-gift shop, with exhibits, posters, books, and extensive lake and preservation info. Walking and canoe tours (see **Sights and Outdoor Activities,** p. 282). Internet $2 per 15min. Open daily late June-Sept. 6 9am-10pm; Sept. 7-late June 9am-5pm.

Mono Basin National Forest Scenic Area Visitors Center (☎873-2408; www.fs.fed.us/r5/inyo), in Inyo National Forest, off U.S. 395 ½ mi. north of Lee Vining. This new angular structure resembles a modern-day cathedral or *Architectural Digest* centerfold. Interpretive tours, an informative film, patio talks, and info on Mono County's wilderness areas. Topographical maps ($6-20) and free wilderness permits. Open M-F 9am-5:30pm; in winter F-Su 9am-4pm. Summer tours of the tufa towers daily at 10am, 1, 6pm ($3, under 18 free).

ATMs: In the Mobile station on the southern end of town, in the Chevron station on the northern end of town, and in the Lee Vining Market near Main and 4th St.

Kayak Rental: Caldera Kayaks (☎935-4942; www.calderakayak.com), at Crowly Lake Marina, in Mammoth Lakes. Single kayaks $25 per half-day, $35 per day; tandem $5 more. Natural history kayak tour of Mono Lake $65 per day.

Laundromat: Mono Vista RV Park (☎647-6401), at the north end of the town. Wash $1.25, dry $0.50. Showers $2 per 5min. Open 9am-6pm.

Weather Conditions: ☎935-7663.

Post Office: (☎647-6371), in the big brown building on 4th St., in Lee Vining. Open M-F 9am-2pm and 3-5pm. **Postal Code:** 93541.

ACCOMMODATIONS

When Tioga Pass is open (early June-Sept.), Lee Vining is an ideal stop on the way from Reno or Death Valley to Yosemite, making hotel vacancies scarce on Friday afternoons and holidays. Lodgings are easier to arrange for weekdays, but camping and picnics are always cheaper alternatives to motels and restaurants. Many hotels and campgrounds are closed in winter; call ahead. Most cheap options are on **Main Street** or 10 mi. south of town on the 14 mi. **June Lake Loop** (see p. 283).

El Mono Motel (☎647-6310), at Main and 3rd St. Popular among young, outdoorsy types. The has rooms that are small but cozy; their plush furnishings and framed Mono Lake photos make them feel luxurious. Cable TV, shared bath, no phone. Pets allowed. Open Apr.-Oct. Singles and doubles with shared bath $49; quads $82. ❸

Tioga Lodge (☎647-6423 or 888-647-6423), 2 mi. north of Lee Vining on the western shore of Mono Lake. Each cabin-like room in this complex of blonde wood is beautifully decorated with a turn-of-the-century Sierra theme. Excellent views of the lake. Idyllic small meadow has a swing, gazebo, and creek. Singles $97; doubles $107. Rooms from $58 before Tioga Pass opens. ❺

CAMPING

None of the area's campgrounds take reservations but sites are ubiquitous; a pre-noon arrival time will all but guarantee a spot. Most sites are clustered west of Lee Vining toward Yosemite along Rte. 120. There are many **Inyo National Forest Campgrounds ❶** on Rte. 120 heading into town. **Lundy** and **Lower Lee Vining** are the best locations for travelers headed for Mono Lake. (No water. Open May-Oct. Sites $7.) The **June Lake Loop ❶** area, south on U.S. 395, has six sites (see **Camping**, p. 284). Most sites are $15, but **Bloody Canyon Trailhead** is free. **Ellery Lake ❶**, 9500 ft., on Tioga Pass Rd. at Rte. 120, across from Tioga Pass Resort, has 12 sites near a brook with fishing and swimming in the nearby lake. (Running water, chemical toilets. Sites $13.)

FOOD

Due to its size, Lee Vining is host to a limited number of dining options, though the quality of food in town is high. **Lee Vining Market,** on U.S. 395 at the southern end of town, is the closest thing to a grocery store. (Open daily 7am-10pm.) **Tioga Gas Mart,** at the intersection of Rte. 120 and Rte. 395, is not your average gas station. It offers fancy coffees, chai, pizza, deli, grilled food, groceries, a gourmet food selection, and 93-octane gas. The grassy picnic area overlooks Mono Lake. (☎647-1088. Open daily 7am-10pm. Gas 24hr.)

Nicely's (☎647-6477), on Rte. 395, 3 stores north of the visitors center. A local favorite. Hot sandwiches ($5-7) like "The Gobbler" with turkey, Swiss cheese, and chilis on sourdough bread. Other typical diner offerings. The large maroon interior is often packed. Open daily 6am-9pm; in winter M-Tu and Th-Su 6am-9pm. ❷

Mono Cone (☎647-6606), on Rte. 395, at the northern end of town. This hamburger stand is a local institution; its opening signals the beginning of summer. The guacamole burger ($4), milk shakes ($2.95), and soft-serve ice cream ($1.50) are all filling and satisfying. Open daily 11am-9pm. ❶

👁 🔟 SIGHTS AND OUTDOOR ACTIVITIES

MONO LAKE

When John Muir first came to the Sierra Nevada, he described what is today **Mono Basin National Forest Scenic Area** as "a country of wonderful contrasts, hot deserts bordered by snow-laden mountains, cinders and ashes scattered on glacier-polished pavement, frost and fire working in the making of beauty." To reach the scenic area, take U.S. 395 S to Rte. 120, then go 4 mi. east and take the Mono Lake South Tufa turn-off 1 mi. south to Tufa Grove. The **South Tufa Formations** features the greatest concentration of these dramatic calcium carbonate spires, which cluster on the shore and pierce the smooth, icy blue surface of this inland sea. Free summer tours led by knowledgeable naturalists depart from the South Tufa parking lot daily at 10am, 1, and 6pm. (Entrance $3, under 19 free. Golden Eagle, Golden Age, and Golden Access passes accepted.) Five miles north of Lee Vining on US 395 and 1 mi. east on Cemetery Rd. is **Mono Lake County Park,** a public playground with a wheelchair-accessible boardwalk trail to a smaller tufa grove, as well as bathrooms, picnic tables, and swings. Rangers lead a number of free hikes throughout the summer, including bird-watching excursions, a hike to Panum Volcano, and stargazing trips. Inquire at the visitors center about schedules.

The Mono Lake Committee offers **canoe tours** of the lake that include a crash course in conservation and Mono's natural history. (☎647-6595. 1hr. tours depart from South Tufa at Mono Lake mid-June to early Sept. Sa-Su 8, 9:30, 11am. Bird-watching is better on earlier tours. Arrive 30min. early for life jacket fitting and photo-taking. Tours $17, ages 4-12 $7. Reservations required.) Caldera Kayaks offers full-day **kayak tours and rentals** (see p. 280).

In this arid basin, the summer temperatures at high noon inspire tourists to seek shade. The 20min. slide show presentation at the Mono Lake Committee is beautifully done, informative, rabble-rousing, and free. **The US Forest Service Scenic Area Visitors Center** shows a film. ($3; includes 20min. film, exhibits, and access to South Tufa area.) The **Mono Basin Historical Society Museum,** in Guss Hess Park, in Lee Vining, is a great way to get informed about the Basin's rich past. Housed in the old Mono Lake schoolhouse, this museum has the standard balance of Gold Rush trinkets and Native American artifacts. (☎647-6461. $1.)

BODIE

Considered to be the best and most well-preserved historic ghost town in the country, Bodie was named after Waterman S. Body, who discovered gold here in 1859. During its heyday in the 1870s, Bodie was home to 10,000 people, three breweries, dozens of saloons, and, in its most treacherous times, up to one homicide per day. "Good-bye, God, I'm going to Bodie!" wrote one little girl in her diary, coining a phrase that captured the town's rough-and-tumble character. The toughest town in the West survived until 1932, when the infamous Bodie Bill, a 2½-year-old child, incinerated 90% of the town with one match. The remaining 10%, however, is now ghost town—absolutely genuine and brimming with a haunting romantic appeal. Bodie is off U.S. 395 32 mi. north of Lee Vining, then 13 mi. east on Hwy. 270. (Open daily June-Sept. 6 8am-7pm; Sept. 7-May 8am-4pm. Entrance $3. Self-guided tour booklet $1.) The small **Bodie Museum** displays some Wild West stories and artifacts. (Open daily in summer 8am-7pm; in winter 8am-4pm.) For more info, contact the Bodie State Historic Park at ☎647-6445 or P.O. Box 515, Bridgeport, CA 93517.

HIKING

The unique terrain of this geological gallery—from the flat, alien landscape around Mono Lake to the mountainous forests along Rte. 120—makes it a great place for hikers of all levels. Easier trails include a quarter-mile boardwalk to tufa and the lake, **Old Marina Area Trail,** 1 mi. north of Lee Vining on Rte. 395; the 1 mi. **Lee Vining Creek Trail,** which begins behind the Mono Basin Visitors Center; and the **Panum Crater Trail,** 5 mi. south on U.S. 395 near the South Tufa turn-off, which leads to a volcanic dome. Those undaunted by the prospect of a punishing trek should head 10 mi. east of U.S. 395 on Rte. 120, where an exceptionally steep trail leads 1 mi. to the glistening **Gardisky Lake.** Another peaceful but tough hike starts at **Lundy Lake,** off U.S. 395, 7 mi. north of Lee Vining, and leads to **Crystal Lake** and the remains of an old mining town. The well-maintained hike gains 2000 ft. in its 3 mi. ascent and offers little shade. Bring plenty of sunscreen and bug spray. Other moderate-to-difficult trails also depart from Lundy Lake, including the 5½ mi. trail through **Lundy Canyon** to 20 Lakes Basin and the 3½ mi. trail out of Lundy Canyon to **Lakes Canyon.**

JUNE LAKE LOOP ☎ 760

The townsfolk of this glacier-carved valley off Rte. 395 resolutely ignore the dramatic wilderness around June Lake in their focus on fishing and skiing at the smaller lakes and mountains forming the June Lake Loop. From the last Saturday in April to the end of October, the four beautiful lakes traced by the loop become hot spots for the cult of fishing. Locals and thousands of visitors flock to the town's marinas on quests for the elusive monster trout, trophies to mount back home, or just something for the frying pan. In the winter, the family-friendly June Mountain and the slopes around the loop make for excellent skiing and snowsports, with smaller crowds and lower fees than at Mammoth.

▐▀ TRANSPORTATION

Buses: CREST (☎ 800-922-1930) runs buses from **Carson City, Nevada** to June Lake firehouse (Tu and Th-F, $13). Reserve tickets in advance. **Greyhound** (☎ 800-24-9424) makes stops in Carson City from around the country.

Boat Rental: June Lake Marina (☎ 648-7726) has 6-horsepower (half-day $39, full-day $44) and 15-horsepower ($49/$54) motorboats. Open daily 6am-7pm. **Gull Lake Marina** (☎ 648-7539) has motorboats (half-day $37, full-day $48), large pontoon boats ($90/$150), and paddleboats ($10 per hr.). Open daily 6am-7pm.

▐◆▌▐⁊ ORIENTATION AND PRACTICAL INFORMATION

Just off U.S. 395, 7 mi. south of Lee Vining, the 14 mi. **June Lake Loop** winds by Grant, Silver, Gull, and June lakes before rejoining U.S. 395. In June Lake Town, Boulder Dr. is also referred to as Main St. before it becomes Loop Rd. There are no addresses on the June Lake Loop; go by general directions or cross streets instead.

Visitor Information: June Lake Chamber of Commerce (☎ 648-7584; www.junelake-chamber.com) offers tourist info. Open M-F 8am-5pm. Another info kiosk at the south entrance of the lake. **June Lake Properties** (☎ 648-7705) makes reservations.

Laundromat: Carson Peak Laundromat, across from the Fern Creek Lodge. Wash $2, dry $0.25 per 8min. Open 8am-9pm.

Weather: 24hr. snow report (☎ 873-3213 or 888-586-3686).

Emergency: 24hr. Sheriff, ☎ 932-7549. **Forest Service,** ☎ 647-6525.

Post Office: On Boulder Dr. (☎ 648-7483), across from Trout Town Joe Cafe. Open M-F 9am-2pm and 3-5pm. **Postal Code:** 93529.

SIERRA NEVADA

ACCOMMODATIONS

True to its resort town character, there are numerous pleasant, yet pricey accommodations. Still, rates are significantly lower than in Mammoth Lakes, and the many cabins, condos, and suites available provide cheap and comfortable lodging for larger groups. **A 12% tax applies to all indoor accommodations in Mono County.**

Fern Creek Lodge (☎ 648-7722 or 800-621-9146; www.ferncreeklodge.com), on Rte. 158, 13 mi. from Lee Vining, 2 mi. past June Lake Town. Accommodations range from small, rustic cabins to nearly full-sized houses. All have well-equipped kitchens and cable TV. 2-person cabins $60-65; 14-person cabins from $230. ❹

Reverse Creek Lodge (☎ 648-7535 or 800-762-6440; www.reversecreeklodge.com), on Loop Rd. Chalets, big log cabins, and small cabins all come with private bath, kitchen, cable TV, and a patio with a grill. A-frame chalets (for up to 6 people) are larger, include 2 full baths, gas fireplaces, and grills, and look out on nearby Carson Peak. Small cabins $65; 2-bedroom cabins $85-120; chalets $125-140. ❹

June Lake Motel, (☎ 648-7547, reservations 800-648-6835; www.junelakemotel.com), on Boulder Dr. A fisherman's dream; in addition to a hot tub, sauna, barbecues, and cable TV, the motel has fish-cleaning stations, fish-freezers, fish rags, and free ice. Motel rooms from $62; 4-person rooms with kitchen from $92; cabins $92-135; condos with lake view from $145. ❹

June Lake Villager Inn (☎ 648-7712 or 800-655-6545; www.junelakevillager.com), on Boulder Dr. Though lacking great views, these motel rooms, suites, and cabins are charming. All rooms have phone, cable TV, VCRs, and coffee. Fish-cleaning station and patio with grill on site. For winter there's an indoor hot tub and firewood for rooms with fireplaces. Singles $50-75, with kitchen $60-105; cabins $125-195. ❸

CAMPING

There are six Inyo National Forest campgrounds, as well as a few private sites. Most are open only during fishing season (last Saturday in April to October).

Grant Lake Resort (☎ 648-7964), 7600 ft., off Rte. 158 toward Lee Vining, in the most remote part of the June Lake Loop. Tackle shop, marina, and boat rental (half-day $30, full day $40). Each site has water, hookup, and fire pit. Most sites offer shade and many overlook the big and somewhat less crowded Grant Lake, which has good fishing. Reservations recommended in the summer. Send a check for camping fee to P.O. Box 627, June Lake, CA 93529. Open late Apr.-Oct. Sites $15, seniors $12. ❶

Oh! Ridge Pine Cliff Resort (☎ 648-7558), 7600 ft., by the June Lake shore. Private RV site and campground. General store, gas, propane, laundry (8am-8pm), basketball court, and showers. Fish-cleaning station and licenses available. Open mid-Apr. to Oct. Tent sites $12; water and electric hookup $17; full RV hookup $22. Trailer rentals $185-460 per week. ❶

Oh! Ridge Campground, 7600 ft. This National Forest Service Campground has access to a swimming beach and flush toilets. The campground is rarely filled, RVs are few, and sites are large. Quiet and spacious sites. Open Apr.-Nov. Sites $15. ❶

June Lake Campground, 7600 ft., next to the marina. On a busy lake near shops and a restaurant, this densely vegetated campground feels like it's set aside from the main rush of campers and RVs, despite being near Main St. 28 sites, 6 for walk-in tent campers only. Water and flush toilets. Showers at marina. Sites $15. ❶

Silver Lake Campground, 7200 ft. A National Forest site. Right on the lake, considerably far from June Lake Town, near a number of trailheads. The grassy campsites have little shade but plenty of elbow room. 63 sites with flush toilets and water. Good fishing access. Open late Apr. to Oct. Sites $15. ❶

◖ FOOD

The **June Lake General Store** is a supermarket, hardware store, liquor store, and deli in one. (Open daily 8am-7pm.) Options outside of the June Lake Loop include the smaller market at **Fern Creek Lodge** (☎648-7722; open daily 8am-9pm; slightly reduced winter hours) and the **Silver Lake Resort Store** (open daily 7am-9pm).

Tiger Bar (☎648-7551; www.thetigerbarcafe.com), at Knoll Ave. and Rte. 158. A small section of the menu features surprisingly good Mexican food, while the rest is standard American fare. Pool table, TV, and pinball machine. Huge Tostada Grande $8.25. Burgers with french fries or chips $7-8. Full breakfasts $4-7. American-style dinners $9-15. Open daily 8am-close. Kitchen open until 10pm. ❷

Trout Town Joe, 2750 Boulder Dr. (☎648-1155), across from the post office. A stylish and comfy coffeehouse popular with locals, TTJ is the perfect place for a creative salad or sandwich ($4-7), or a cup of coffee ($1.25-3). Open daily 7am-3pm. ❷

Eagle's Landing Restaurant, (☎648-7897), at the Double Eagle Resort, 2 mi. outside of June Lake, is *the* place to go to treat yourself. This beautiful new lodge has gorgeous mountain views from every table. Grab a drink at the **Eagle's Nest Saloon** and watch a game on their 42 in. plasma screen TV. The house specialty is rotisserie chicken basted in lemon-herb garlic and barbecue sauce ($16). Logger-type breakfasts $6-11. Burgers $7. Entrees $14-26. Open daily 7am-8:30pm. ❸

◉ ⚐ SIGHTS AND OUTDOOR ACTIVITIES

In the summer months, all minds in June Lake are on **fishing.** The June Lake Loop (Rte. 158) traces the outer edge of four bountiful lakes: **June Lake** (☎648-7726), closest to the South June Lake junction with Rte. 395; **Gull Lake** (☎648-7539); **Silver Lake** (☎648-7525); and the expansive **Grant Lake** (☎648-7964) to the north. There are also a number of fishable streams in the Loop, such as Rush and Alger Creeks, as well as lakes accessible only by foot or horse. Each of the four main lakes sells California fishing licenses (required for anyone over 16) and has its own tackle shop and a marina that rents motorboats ($40-50 per day). The lakes are stocked twice a month with rainbow, brook, and German brown trout. Although all the lakes yield big fish every day, many serious anglers prefer Gull and Grant Lakes. June Lake is a popular spot for sunbathing, swimming, and recreational boating. Quieter **Walker Lake** and **Parker Lake** are accessible by short day hikes from trailheads just north of Grant Lake. **Rush Creek, Agnew Lake,** and **Gem Lake** can all be accessed from the **Rush Creek Trail,** which starts across from the Silver Lake campground (2¼ mi. to Agnew Lake; 3 mi. to Gem Lake).

There are a few moderate **day hikes,** most leading to trout-filled lakes, and some excellent backcountry trails into the Ansel Adams Wilderness, which connects to the John Muir Trail. Across from the June Lake firehouse, the trail to **Yost Lake** is a moderate 5 mi. hike through the aspen and fir forest of the June Mountain Ski Area. The separate **Yost Creek Trail,** departing about 1 mi. south of Silver Lake, leads to two beautiful and quiet lakes. About a mile into the hike, the trail forks near a waterfall; the right branch leads a steep 1½ mi. to Fern Lake, while the left trail is a moderate 2½ mi. to Yost Lake. Much of the backcountry can be explored on **horseback. Frontier Pack Train** (☎648-7701) offers guided horseback trips including overnight packing trips. ($25 per hr., $55 per half-day, $85 per day.)

Increasingly popular but still much less crowded than Mammoth Mountain, **June Mountain Ski Resort** caters to the snowboarding crowd, dedicating nearly half the mountain to "enhanced terrain" parks with half-pipes, rails, and jumps perfect for catching huge air. Excellent powder, tremendous views, and short lines (if any) make this an attractive alternative to the larger resort to the south. It's also less expensive to ski here. (☎648-7733; www.junemountain.com. Lift-ticket $50, ages 19-23 $45, ages 13-18 $38, seniors and under 13 $25.)

MAMMOTH LAKES ☎760

Home to one of the most popular ski resorts in the US, the town of Mammoth Lakes (pop. 7093) has evolved into a giant year-round playground. With an average annual snowfall of over 350 in. and 3500 acres of skiable terrain, it's prime skiing ground. High altitudes mean that snow lasts as late as July some years, cutting the low season down to four months. As soon as the snow melts, mountain bikers invade the town by thousands to take on Mammoth Mountain, skateboarders come to test their skills in some of the stiffest competitions in the country, and fisherfolk come to the magma-warmed creeks to catch some hot fish. Beyond all the hair-raising adventure, Mammoth Lakes also supports a significant cultural scene with concerts, festivals, and a small but very lively nightlife. With plenty of restaurants, hotels, and activities, Mammoth is more developed than most Sierra towns and happily caters to tourists.

▐ TRANSPORTATION

Airport: Reno-Tahoe International (☎775-328-6400). Served daily by major carriers. Mammoth Shuttle provides bus connections to town (see below).

Bus: CREST (☎800-922-1930) runs buses Tu and Th-F at 1:45pm from **Carson City**, arriving in **Mammoth Lakes** around 4:40pm. $15.

Public Transit:

Inyo-Mono Dial-A-Ride (☎872-1901; www.countyofinyo.org) leaves from McDonald's in Mammoth Lakes and K-Mart in Bishop, with service to **Bishop, Bridgeport, Lee Vining, June Lake,** and **Crowley Lake.** (M, W, Sa; fare depends upon location.)

Mammoth Shuttle Service (☎934-3030) On-call service for intercity travel M-Th 8am-midnight, F-Sa 8am-2am.

Mammoth Area Shuttle (MAS; ☎934-3030) offers a red line shuttle to town and the main ski lodge. During ski season, shuttles connect to chairlifts every 15min. daily 7am-midnight. Free. In summer, a shuttle daily runs every 20min. from main lodge to Reds Meadow, Devils Post Pile, and 8 other stops in the forest. Runs daily 7:30pm-5:30pm. Shuttle required in these areas 7am-7pm. Last run out of Reds Meadow 8pm. Day pass ($7) good for duration of trip if camping.

Sierra Express (☎924-8294) Door-to-door shuttle service runs 7am-2am. Rates fluctuate.

Car Rental: U-SAVE, 49 Laurel Mt. Rd., (☎934-4999 or 800-207-2681). 4WD vehicles from $56 per day, $372 per week. Compacts $42/$252. Single-day rates 10% higher. Rentals are also available at the **Chevron** (☎934-8111) next to the post office. Cars $40-90 per day.

Auto Repairs: AAA Emergency Road Service (☎800-400-4222.)

✈ ▐ ORIENTATION AND PRACTICAL INFORMATION

Mammoth Lakes is off U.S. 395, 160 mi. south of Reno, 325 mi. north of L.A., and 40 mi. southeast of the eastern entrance to Yosemite. Rte. 203 runs through the town as **Main Street** and then becomes Lake Mary Rd. as it heads to the area's lakes. In winter, the normally desolate U.S. 395, which runs directly below the brooding heights of the Eastern Sierra, is packed with weekend skiers from L.A. making the 6hr. journey up to the slopes.

Visitor Information: Inyo National Forest Visitors Center and Chamber of Commerce (☎924-5500; www.visitmammoth.com), on Rte. 203 west of U.S. 395, north of town. Offers area info, discounts on accommodations and food, *Mammoth Times* ($0.50), free video, exhibits, and walks. Accommodation reservations. Open daily 8am-5pm.

Equipment Rental: Footloose Sports Shop, 3043 Main St. (☎934-2400; www.footloos-esports.com), rents skis, snowboards, and mountain bikes. Ski tuning, boot fitting, and trail info. Ski packages $20-28 per half-day, $25-35 per day; snowboard packages $20/$25. Mountain bikes $6-15 per hr., $20-45 per half-day, $24-60 per day. Open in summer daily 8am-8pm; in winter Su-W 7am-8pm, Th-Sa 7am-9pm.

Rick's Sport Center, 3241 Main St. (☎934-3416). Fishing rods $10 per day. 10-day nonresident fishing license $30; annual pass $83. Package fishing deal (waders, boo-ties, fins, and float tube) $30 per day. Fly-fishing lessons available for $110 per half-day. Open daily 6am-8pm; in low season 7am-7pm.

Bank: Bank of America, 3069 Main St. (☎934-6830). Open M-Th 9am-5pm, F 9am-6pm, Sa 9am-1pm. **24hr. ATM.**

Laundromat: Mammoth Lakes Laundromat, 24 Laurel Mountain Rd. (☎934-8207), off Main St. Wash $1.50, dry $0.25 per 7½min. Friendly staff. Open daily 8:30am-6:30pm; last wash 1½hr. before closing.

Weather Conditions: ☎934-7669.

Ski Conditions: Mammoth Mountain Snow Conditions ☎934-6166. **Mammoth Mountain Ski Area** ☎934-2571.

Medical Services: Mammoth Hospital, 85 Sierra Park Rd. (☎934-3311). 24hr.

Post Office: 3330 Main St. Open M-F 8:30am-5pm. **Postal Code:** 93546.

▓ ACCOMMODATIONS

As in most ski resort towns, lodging in Mammoth Lakes is much more expensive in the winter. Condo rentals are a comfortable choice for groups of three or more and start at $100 per night. **Mammoth Reservation Bureau** can make rental arrangements. (☎800-462-5571; www.mammothvacations.com. Open M-Th 8am-6pm, F 8am-7pm, Sa-Su 8am-5pm.) For lone travelers, dorm-style motels are the cheapest option. Reservations are highly recommended for winter stays. **A 12% tax applies to all indoor accommodations in Mono County.**

▓ **Davison St. Guest House,** 19 Davison Rd. (☎924-2188, reservations 619-544-9107; www.mammoth-guest.com), at Lake Mary Rd. A living room with 5 comfy couches and a fireplace, a sundeck with barbecue, cushy dorm rooms, and 2700 sq. ft. capable of accommodating groups of up to 26 make this homey lodge the best value in town. Dorms $21-25; private rooms $45-60, with bath $62-75; entire lodge $450-650. ❷

Holiday Haus, 3905 Main St. (☎934-2414; www.holidayhausmammoth.com). Spacious and pleasant rooms and cabins, some with views, fireplaces, and kitchens. Spa on site. Owned by friendly locals. All rooms have phone and cable TV. Doubles in winter from $50; in summer from $45. Suite for up to 6 with kitchen from $70. ❸

Swiss Chalet, 3776 Viewpoint Rd. (☎934-2403 or 800-937-9477; www.mammoth-swisschalet.com), just off Main St. 21 hilltop motel rooms with vaulted wood ceilings and stunning mountain views. Cable TV, refrigerator, ski rack, and coffee in each immaculate room. Sundeck, hot tub, and sauna make for easy relaxation after a day on the slopes. Rooms in winter $65-120; in summer $60-95. ❹

BLACK BEAR FRIGHT

Throughout my years of camping, 've seen the photos of cars mangled by bears—doors ripped off, trunks no more, drivers missing. These images seemed particularly frightening, however, as I set off as a solo camper. My dad had reminded me not to eat in the car, training me to check every square inch of the station wagon's interior for even the slightest crumb. Unfortunately, I had ignored his advice, and my first night alone, I lay in my tent, scared to death. After five minutes, I emerged, flashlight in hand, to check the car once more. It was clear and I returned to my tent. But not for long. As I reached to wipe my nose, a strong food smell came from my fingers. Paranoia filled my mind. Would a bear's powerful nostril pick up this odor? Would a sharp claw in search of food soon be ripping through my tent's taut fabric? The odor now seemed to fill my dark, cold sleeping place. I ran to the bathroom and scrubbed my hands, and returned to my tent to wait out the night. I lay tense through the long hours of the night, waiting for the bear to come. In the morning, the chirping of birds indicated I had survived, but had my car? I opened the driver-side door, and there, in plain view, sat a half-eaten sandwich. In my anguish to secure the car, I had forgotten to check the most obvious place. Luckily for me, the bear hadn't checked either.

— *Nathan Orion Simmons*

⚑ CAMPING

There are nearly 20 Inyo Forest public **campgrounds** ❶ (sites $13-16) in the area, sprinkled around Mammoth Lakes, Mammoth Village, Convict Lake, Red's Meadow, Agnew Meadow, and June Lake. All sites have piped water and most are near fishing and hiking. Contact the **Mammoth Ranger District** (☎924-5500) for info. Reservations can be made at nearby Sherwin Creek for New and Old Shady Rest (☎877-444-6777; www.reserveusa.com).

▓ **Twin Lakes,** 8600 ft., ½ mi. off Lake Mary Rd., about 2 mi. outside town. In a pine forest, the 95 lush sites are a 1min. walk from fishing and swimming at Twin Lakes. Perfect view of Twin Falls rushing into the southern end of Upper Twin Lake. General store nearby with essentials and showers. Piped water and flush toilets. 7-night max. stay. Open late May-late Oct. Sites $16. Showers $2. ❶

Lake Mary, 8900 ft., on Lake Mary Loop Rd. The most crowded campground in the area, and for good reason; its 48 sites are right on the beaches of Lake Mary. Close to great boating, fishing, and hiking. General store nearby. 14-night max. stay. Open mid-June to mid-Sept. Sites $14. ❶

New Shady Rest, 7800 ft., on Rte. 203 across from McDonald's. A great option for convenient camping, within walking distance of stores and restaurants. The 165 sites are in a pine forest but traffic noise is omnipresent. 14-night max. stay. Sites $15. ❶

◖ ◗ FOOD AND NIGHTLIFE

Mammoth Lakes is packed with delis, cafes, and pizza joints to feed the high-adrenaline, low-funds crowd, but adventurous palates need not despair. The town is often called the culinary capital of the Sierra, with plenty of restaurants offering creative menus, which often charge prices as high as the neighboring peaks.

▓ **Paul Schat's Bakery and Cafe,** 3305 Main St. (☎934-6055, Vermeer Deli 934-4203). At 8000 ft., the highest bakery in Northern America is also the best in town. Over 30 varieties of bread (around $3), wonderful cookies and biscotti (from $1), and cappuccino ($2.75). Inside the bakery, the **Vermeer Deli** ❷ encourages picnicking with famously fresh sandwiches like the albacore tuna with sun-dried tomatoes ($7.50). Bakery open daily 5:30am-6pm. Deli open daily 10am-2pm. ❶

Whiskey Creek (☎934-2555), at Lake Mary Rd. and Minaret St. This modern, upscale restaurant with an ever-changing menu serves meaty and experimental American cuisine (entrees $18-23) in a sophisticated, dimly-lit atmosphere. The large bar area is a nightlife hub with a DJ W and live music F-Sa. Microbrews $3. Happy hour M-F 5-7pm; $1 drafts. Open daily 5pm-1:30am. Kitchen open 5:30-10pm. ❹

Nick-n-Willies Pizza & Subs, 76 Old Mammoth Rd. (☎934-2012). The best pizza in the Sierra Nevadas; try the Sierra (pesto, sausage, mushrooms, feta, and mozzarella; $15-27). Slices from $3. Small pizzas $11-15. Hot subs $6-9. Open daily 11:30am-9pm. ❶

Base Camp Cafe (☎934-3900), on Main St., across from the post office. Excellent and inexpensive joint plastered with skate company stickers. Breakfast for as little as $2. Sandwiches ($4-6) include mouthwatering turkey breast with cranberries on a French loaf. Brown bag lunches available as early as 7:30am ($8; call ahead). Open M-W 7:30am-3pm, Th-F and Su 7:30am-8pm, Sa 7:30am-9pm. ❷

⊙ SIGHTS

There's plenty to see in Mammoth Lakes, much of which is accessible by the **MAS shuttle service** (see p. 286). This mandatory shuttle was introduced to keep the area from being completely trampled and runs from the Mammoth Mountain Gondola Building to the Devil's Postpile Monument, Agnew Meadows, and numerous trailheads and **campgrounds ❶** (sites $12-14). Park your car in the massive lot at the gondola building and relax on the shuttle ride. The shuttle system makes the Gondola Building the hub for many outdoor activities in the area. Day passes and camping passes are $7.

DEVIL'S POSTPILE NATIONAL MONUMENT AND RAINBOW FALLS. One of the world's finest examples of columnar basalt, **Devil's Postpile** is a stunning 60 ft. wall made of eerily uniform hexagonal rock columns that formed less than 100,000 years ago. After the basalt lava that oozed through Mammoth Pass cooled and contracted, a glacier plowed through the area, carving away a chunk of the solidified basalt and exposing this cross-sectional view. The middle fork of the San Joaquin River drops 101 ft. into a glistening green canyon pool at **Rainbow Falls,** a pleasant 2 mi. walk from the Devil's Postpile Monument. A shorter hike with more shade departs from the Rainbow Falls trailhead MAS stop. On sunny afternoons, look for the rainbow that forms at the base of the falls. Although Postpile and Rainbow Falls are the most popular attractions, the park has more to offer; take a stroll around Sotcher Lake, steep yourself in Fisher Creek Hot Springs, or hike part of the John Muir Trail to fully appreciate the marvels on display. To really get to know Postpile, camp at one of the six area **campgrounds,** all of which have piped water. *(From U.S. 395, the Devil's Postpile/Rainbow Falls trailhead can be reached by parking at the Mammoth Mountain Gondola Building and boarding the MAS shuttle on Rte. 203. Driving in is prohibited. For campers, shuttle passes valid for the duration of the trip; mention this when purchasing. Guided ranger walks daily 11am. Campgrounds 7600-8400 ft.; sites $14.)*

VOLCANOES. Created about 500 years ago, the **Inyo Craters** are open pits 600 ft. across with blue-green water at the bottom. Formed when underground magma caused a giant steam explosion (the magma never reached the surface), they provide eerie examples of the area's volcanic history. *(The ¼ mi. jaunt to the craters can be reached from Mammoth Scenic Loop Rd., north of town off U.S. 395.)* **Obsidian Dome** is an odd mass of different colored blocks of solid volcanic matter resulting from the quick chilling of lava 1000 years ago. *(14 mi. north of Mammoth Junction and 1 mi. west of U.S. 395 on Obsidian Dome Rd. Follow the signs on the dirt road.)*

SIERRA NEVADA

MAMMOTH SKI MUSEUM. This recently opened museum houses one of the largest single collections of skiing art, literature, and heritage in the world. With work dating from the 1500s, the museum's **Beekley Library** contains over 2500 books in 11 different languages. A state-of-the-art theater, seasonal exhibits, and educational programs are among the highlights. *(100 College Pkwy. From Rte. 203, turn left on Meridian Blvd. and then left on College Pkwy. ☎ 934-6592; www.mammothskimuseum.org. Open Tu-Su noon-5pm. $3, ages 5-18 $2, college students free.)*

◢ OUTDOOR ACTIVITIES

Mammoth is like a sports-drink commercial come to life—extreme activities abound, from climbing to dogsledding. **Mammoth Mountain High Adventure's** climbing wall stands like a shrine to extreme sports, beckoning both the inexperienced and the professional. (☎ 924-5683. Open daily 10am-6pm. $6 per climb, $13 per hr., $22 per day; discount for groups of 3 or more.) Their Map and Compass Course simulates an escape from the jungle. ($15 for 2hr. course; includes compass rental, map, and intro lesson.) Swing, tightrope walk, and rappel in the High Ropes Course. (4hr.; Th-Sa 1pm, Su 10am. $43, group rate $40 per person.)

The **Mammoth Mountain Gondola** affords a mile-high view. (☎ 934-2571. Open daily 9am-4:30pm. Round-trip $16, children $8. Day pass for gondola and trail use $25. Chair-lift $10 round-trip, children $5.) A mountain biking extravaganza with more than 80 mi. of twisted trails in **Mammoth Mountain Bike Park** is at the top of the mountain. The ride starts at 11,053 ft. and heads straight down on rocky ski trails. (☎ 934-0706. Helmets required. Open 9am-6pm. Day pass $29, children $15. Unlimited day pass and bike rental $62/$31.)

HIKING

Day hikes in the area cluster around the Mammoth Lakes Basin and Reds Meadow. A quick half-mile hike from the Twin Lakes turn-off on Lake Mary Rd. culminates in spectacular views of Owens Valley and Crowley Lake from the **Panorama Dome.** Lake Mamie has a picturesque picnic area and many short hikes leading out to **Lake George,** where exposed granite sheets attract climbers. For short but stunning hikes through wildflowers and amazing scenery, trek the **Crystal Lake Trail** (2½ mi.) or the **Barrett Lake Trail,** both of which leave from the Lake George entrance parking lot. **Horseshoe Lake** is a popular swimming spot and also the trailhead for the impressive **Mammoth Pass Trail.** The fork in the trail leads to **McLeod Lake** on the left or **Reds Meadow** on the right. In Agnew Meadows (take the MAS shuttle), moderate trails lead from the campground to tranquil **Shadow Lake** (3½ mi.) and **Ediza Lake** (6½ mi.). Also departing from Agnew Meadows is a very challenging day hike or a less strained overnighter—the trail to **Thousand Island Lake** (10 mi.). **Mammoth Sporting Goods** (☎ 934-3239) and **Sandy's Ski & Sport** (☎ 934-7518) can equip more experienced hikers with gear and info on more challenging climbs.

FISHING

Not one of the over 100 lakes near town (60 are within a 5 mi. radius) actually goes by the name of Mammoth Lake. The area's largest, most pristine lake, the 1 mi. long **Lake Mary,** is popular for boating, sailing, and fishing. Anglers converge on the Mammoth area each summer to test their skills on some of the best **trout lakes** in the country. Permits are required for anyone over 16 (the visitors center has info on other regulations) and can be expensive for nonresidents. Fanatics will find the frequent fishing derbies well worth the price of entry, but less competitive types might prefer to try their luck at the area's serene and well-stocked backcountry waters. Man-made reservoir **Crowley Lake** in Owens Valley, 12 mi. south of town, is a fishing mother lode, yielding over 80 tons of rainbow trout each summer and attracting a city's worth of people on opening day. The lake has **campsites ❷** with full hookup. (☎935-4301. Parking $6 per day. Motorboat rental $55 per day; parking included. Sites $25.) Just south of town on Rte. 395, **Convict Lake** teems with monster trout, but its deep water and windy surroundings can make catching one a challenge. **Campsites ❶** are $13. (☎934-3800. Fishing boats $15 per hr., $65 per day.) **Owens River** is a great spot for fly-fishing; head south on Rte. 395 to Benton Crossing Rd. and then 3 mi. to a bridge and a dirt road that follows the river.

The **Hot Creek Geothermal Area,** 5 mi. south of town off U.S. 395 at Hot Creek Rd., also allows catch-and-release fishing. The waters here are warmed by the liquid magma sending up steam from miles below the creek bed following a toasty volcanic blast. Hungry trout bathe in these warm waters year-round. Several trails lead to the springs, but be careful—the steam can cause severe burns. Tours of the hot springs and trout hatchery are given daily from 8am to 4pm.

WINTER RECREATION

With 3500 acres, 3100 vertical ft., 385 in. of snow, and 300 days of sunshine, Mammoth is one of the country's premier winter resorts. California's highest ski elevation also has the longest season—Mammoth's runs are open from November to June; in a good year, downhill skiing can last through July. Avoiding weekends and major holidays keeps costs lower. Rent skis in town (see **Equipment Rental,** p. 287); resort shops usually charge 10-20% more. Mammoth Mountain lift tickets can be purchased at the Main Lodge at the base of the mountain on Minaret Rd. Group ski lessons are available for all levels ($54, beginners $35) every day. A special first-timers package includes rentals, day pass, and a lesson for $78. (☎934-2571. Open daily 7:30am-3pm. Full-day lift tickets $57, weekend $62; afternoon $46/50.) A free shuttle bus (MAS) transports skiers between lifts, town, and the Main Lodge (see p. 286). The US Forest Service provides info on the area's cross-country trails.

Mammoth has miles of trails and open areas for **snowmobiles.** The **Mammoth Lake Snowmobile Association** maps out open and restricted areas. Visitors over 16 years old with a driver's license can rent snowmobiles at **Center Street Polaris DJ Snowmobile.** (☎934-4020. Open M-Sa 8am-4:30pm. One-seater $85 for 2hr., $167 for 4hr.; two-seater $115/$245.) Mammoth has lately pioneered **bobsledding;** although runs are slow enough for non-Olympians, they can be exhilarating, especially at night. **Bobsledz,** on Minaret Rd. halfway to the lodge, can help fulfill your pipe dreams. (☎934-7533. Open daily 10am-4pm; in summer 4:30-7:30pm.)

FESTIVALS

Almost every weekend in every season Mammoth is host to some wild festival, from triathlons to skateboarding contests, from dogsledding to canoe races. At the **Mammoth Festival of Beers and Bluesapalooza,** in early August, chug truckloads of over 40 microbrews and piles of barbecue dishes to the sounds of some of the country's best blues. (☎934-0606. Unlimited beer and 4 food coupons $36; music only $28.) The **Mammoth Lakes Jazz Jubilee,** in mid-July, is a local favorite, with thousands of spectators and dozens of bands packed into handful of venues. (☎934-2478; www.mammothjazz.org. Day entry $35, 3-day pass $70.) The **Mammoth Motorcross Race** (☎934-0642), in late June, is one of the area's most popular athletic competitions, and the **National Mountain Biking Championships** (☎934-0651), in early September, attracts nearly 50,000 people.

Winter festivities include cross-country ski races, a **Snowshow Play Day** (☎934-7566) in February, a **Winterfestival** (☎934-6643) in March, and a **marathon** (☎934-2442) in late March.

BISHOP AND OWENS VALLEY ☎760

Situated in the northern end of Owens Valley minutes from world-class hiking, climbing, horseback riding, and fishing, Bishop is the place for visitors to stop and recharge en route to the surrounding rivers, mountains, and desert valleys. The largest city in the Eastern Sierras, this resort town has many amenities missing from the rest of the region, such as international cuisine, bookstores, and coffeehouses, as well as some things that are better off missed, like casinos and strip malls. Opportunities to fish in the clear lakes of Bishop Creek Canyon, boulder in the Buttermilks, or enjoy the seasonal festivals make the town worth visiting. Owens Valley is wedged between the Sierras and the towering White Mountains, making it "the deepest valley on Earth." In the early 20th century, the valley's freshwater streams provided water for the budding city of L.A., leading to the water scandal that the movie *Chinatown* (see p. 22) fictionalized.

▐ TRANSPORTATION

Bus: CREST (☎800-922-1930) runs from **Carson City** Tu and Th-F at 2pm, arriving in Bishop at 6:30pm. One-way $20.

Public Transportation: Dial-A-Ride (☎872-1901 or 800-922-1930) runs fixed routes around town ($0.50) and will travel up to 1 mi. off-route for an additional $0.75. Call ahead for flexible stops M-Th 8am-5pm, F-Sa 8am-midnight (last call 11:30pm). Door-to-door buses also serve the area. Shuttles run twice daily (7am and 5:30pm) to **Mammoth** ($5.50) and **Crowley Lake** ($3).

Auto Repairs: AAA Emergency Road Service, ☎872-8241 or 800-400-4222.

Road Conditions, Caltrans ☎800-427-7623.

▐▌ ORIENTATION AND PRACTICAL INFORMATION

Bishop is located on Rte. 395 in the northern end of Owens Valley. Lone Pine, at the base of Mt. Whitney, is 60 mi. south. The town is 140 mi. from Yosemite via the Tioga Pass. Death Valley is 165 mi. to the southeast, L.A. is 270 mi. south, and Reno is 205 mi. north via Rte. 395.

Visitor Information:

Bishop Area Chamber of Commerce and Visitors Bureau, 690 N. Main St. (☎888-395-3952 or 873-8405; www.bishopvisitor.com), at City Park. Area maps and info. Get a free copy of *Bishop, California Vacation Planner* for up-to-date listings of special events. Open mid-Apr. to mid-Oct. M-F 9am-5pm, Sa-Su 10am-4pm; mid-Oct. to mid-Apr. M-F 9am-4:30pm, Sa-Su 10am-4pm.

White Mountain Ranger Station, 798 N. Main St. (☎873-2500; www.fs.fed.us/r5/inyo). Campground and trail info for all of Inyo National Forest. Weather report and message board. Reserve wilderness permits up to 6 months ahead. Walk-in permits for all trails. Open mid-May to mid-Sept. daily 8am-5pm; mid-Sept. to mid-May M-F 8am-4:30pm.

Bank: Washington Mutual, 400 N. Main St. (☎873-5031). **24hr. ATM.** Open M-F 9am-6pm, Sa 9am-1pm.

Laundromat: Sierra Suds, 163 Academy St. (☎873-8338). Wash $1.25, dry $0.25 per 10min. Open daily 7am-9pm; last wash 8pm.

Fishing Licenses: Culver's Sporting Goods, 156 S. Main St. (☎872-8361). For nonresidents, 10-day license $30.70, annual $82.45. Open Apr.-Oct. M-Th 6am-8pm, F-Sa 8am-9pm; Nov.-Feb. daily 7am-5pm; Mar. daily 7am-6pm.

Police: Bishop Police Department, 207 W. Line St. (☎873-5866).

Hospital: Northern Inyo Hospital, 150 Pioneer Ln. (☎873-5811), off W. Line St. 24hr. emergency care.

Library and Internet Access: Inyo County Free Library, 210 Academy St. (☎873-5115). 30min. free Internet. Open M-Th 10am-8pm, F 10am-6pm, Sa 10am-1pm.

Post Office: 595 W. Line St. (☎873-3526 or 800-275-8777). Open M-F 7:30am-4pm, Sa 9am-1pm. **Postal Code:** 93514.

ACCOMMODATIONS

Accommodations in Bishop are plentiful but expensive. Thrifty travelers are better off camping. Those traveling in groups, especially those looking to fish, may find a cabin the best option. Try the **Cardinal Village Resort ❺**, at the North Fork of Bishop Creek Canyon (☎873-4789; www.cardinalvillageresort.com), or **Bishop Creek Lodge ❺**, 2100 S. Lake Rd., at the south fork of Bishop Creek Canyon. (☎873-4484; www.bishopcreekresorts.com. 2- to 3-night min. stay, $90-275.)

El Rancho Motel, 274 Lagoon St. (☎872-9251 or 888-872-9251), 2 blocks west of Main St. A quintessential motel; drive right up to your door. 16 rooms with TV, A/C, coffeemaker, and refrigerator. Kitchen $8 extra. Singles $38-55; doubles $45-70. $5 per additional person. ❸

Bardini House, 515 Sierra St. (☎873-8036, 872-4413, or 872-1348). A house in a residential neighborhood with small but comfortable rooms. Kitchen, grill, and back patio for guest use. 10-night max stay. Reservations required. Dorms $10. ❶

Chalfant House, 213 Academy St. (☎800 641-2996 or 872-1790). A homey B&B is with hardwood floors, patchwork quilts, and wood stove in the parlor. Breakfast and refreshments included. Check-in 3-7pm. Singles and doubles $80-105. ❺

Bishop Village Motel, 286 W. Elm St. (☎872-8155 or 888-668-5546). Caters to fishermen with a grilling area and fish-freezing facilities. Quiet, comfortable rooms 1 block from Main St. Heated pool. Rooms have refrigerator, microwave, and cable TV; some with kitchen. Rooms $39-49; suites $69-89. ❸

CAMPING

Most campgrounds around Bishop are well kept and easily accessible. Sites host a consistent flow of campers throughout the summer but are especially crowded during the Mule Days celebration over Memorial Day weekend and the Tri-County Fair over Labor Day weekend (book a year in advance).

There are over 30 **Inyo National Forest** campgrounds in the Bishop Ranger District (most open May-Oct.). The closest campgrounds to town are private, however, and can be found on or near Rte. 395 close to Bishop. **Millpond ❶**, 4500 ft., 6 mi. north of Bishop on Saw Mill Rd., has 70 cool, shady spots near Millpond County Park and McGee Creek. (☎873-5342. Open Mar.-Oct. Sites from $16.) Southwest of town on Rte. 168 are many Forest Service campgrounds. The wheelchair- accessible **Four Jeffrey ❶**, 8100 ft., boasts 100 open sites on a hillside above the south fork of Bishop Creek. (Open late Apr. to Oct. Sites $14, extra vehicle $5.) For wilder camping, **North Lake ❶**, 9500 ft., and **Sabrina Lake ❶**, 9000 ft., both have stunning scenery, trail access to the John Muir Wilderness, and fishing, of course. The chilly sites have vault toilets and water. (7-day max. stay. North open mid-June to Sept.; Sabrina mid-May to Sept. Sites $14, extra vehicle $5.) **Pleasant Valley ❶**, 4100 ft., 6½ mi. north of town off Hwy. 395, is home to 200 sites for year-round camping near the Happy and Sad Boulders and Owens River Gorge. (Water and toilets. 14-day max. stay. Sites $10.) **Free** camping can be found 5 mi. west of Hwy. 395 on Round Valley Rd. (off Saw Mill Rd.) at **Horton Creek,** 5000 ft. Fifty-three unshaded sites have vault toilets, but no drinking water. (14-day max. stay. Open May-Oct.)

Some of the best camping can be found north of town, between Bishop and Mammoth Lakes, on Rte. 395. **Rock Creek ❶,** 7000-10,000 ft., has 10 campgrounds with over 300 sites scattered about the canyon, nearly all of which are secluded and shady. Excellent fishing, mountain biking, climbing, and hiking abound. Most sites have piped water and flush toilets. (Open May-Oct. Sites $15-16.)

◖ FOOD

Stock up on groceries at **Manor Market,** 3100 W. Line St., which offers natural foods (☎873-4296; open M-Sa 6am-9pm, Su 6am-8pm), or **Vons,** 1190 N. Main St. (☎872-9811; open 24hr.). Saturdays in summer bring the **Bishop-Eastern Sierra Farmers Market** to Sierra St. at U.S. 395. (☎873-1038. Open July to Oct. Sa 9am-noon.)

Taqueria Las Palmas, 136 E. Line St. (☎873-4337). This authentic *taqueria* is popular with locals and climbing bums. The friendly waitstaff dishes out specialty *flautas,* buffalo burritos ($9), and a full range of Mexican beers. Open daily 11am-9pm. ❷

Western Kitchen, 930 N. Main St. (☎872-3246). Despite the name, this Western kitchen also serves Eastern dishes. Try an omelette ($5-7) or steak ($7-9), or choose from an extensive list of Thai specials ($7.50-9.50). Open daily 6am-9pm. ❷

Erik Schat's Bakery, 763 N. Main St. (☎873-7156). Breads and pastries ($3-5) are baked daily and served with coffee. Hearty salads, soups, and sandwiches ($3.50-7) such as the "Mule Kick," are particularly rejuvenating after a day in the hills. Try the sheepherder's bread. Open May-Oct. M-Th and Sa 6am-6:30pm, F 6am-10pm, Su 6am-8pm; Nov.-Apr. M-Th and Sa 6:30am-6:30pm, F 6am-10pm, Su 6:30am-7pm. ❶

Kava Coffeehouse, 206 N. Main St. (☎872-1010). Serves healthy eats like Kava Quiche ($5). Coffee and fresh smoothies ($4). Local artists' wares grace the cabinets. Free wireless Internet access. Chess night Tu 5-8pm. Open M-F 6:30am-8:30pm, Sa 7am-8:30pm, Su 7am-3:30pm. ❶

◤ OUTDOOR ACTIVITIES

EAST OF BISHOP

To escape the crowds gallivanting on the western slopes of the valley, head east; you'll see more cows than people. The mountains forming the Owens Valley are a backpacker's Eden. In the eastern half of Inyo National Forest, which is split by Hwy. 395, the yellow sands of the **White Mountains** rise to heights that rival the Sierra Nevadas. If it's elevation you want, tackle the tough 7½ mi. slog to the top of **White Mountain Peak** (14,246 ft.), the third-tallest mountain in California. The hike gains 2500 ft. on the way to the summit from the locked Bancroft Gate at the White Mountain Research Station. Park your car at the station on White Mountain Rd., 26 mi. from Hwy. 168 and 38 mi. from Big Pine.

Scattered across the face of the White Mountains are California's **bristlecone pines,** the oldest living organisms on the planet. Gnarled, twisted, and warped into fantastic shapes, the trees may grow only one inch taller every 100 years. The preservative qualities of the cold, dry altitudes (the trees grow at extreme elevations of up to 12,000 ft.) have allowed the "Methuselah" specimen in the

Schulman Group to survive for 4700 years (to prevent vandalism, visitors are not told which one it is). Known as the trees that rewrote history, the bristle-cones were used to calibrate the radiocarbon dating process, allowing scientists to pinpoint the dates of early civilizations. To reach the **Ancient Bristlecone Pine Forest** (☎873-2500 or 873-2573), follow Hwy. 168 off Hwy. 395 at Big Pine for 12 mi. and turn left at the sign. The 11 mi. paved road climbs to **Schulman Grove,** at nearly 10,000 ft. Before the grove, 8 mi. down the road, you'll come to **Sierra View Overlook.** The Sierra Nevadas stand opposite this viewpoint, stretching like a massive wall for miles in either direction, legitimizing their reputation as California's backbone. Two short **hikes** head out from Schulman Grove. The moderately strenuous 4½ mi. **Methuselah Trail** takes you deep into the grove and past the oldest tree in the world. The easy 1 mi. **Discovery Trail** leads through the hills and past the first tree dated at over 4000 years. The drive to the even-higher **Patriarch Grove,** home of some of the most astonishing trees, is a beautiful but unpaved 12 mi. from Schulman.

A number of valleys are tucked beneath eastern slopes of the White and Inyos, including Fish Lake Valley, Deep Springs Valley (home of **Deep Springs College**), part of Death Valley, and the uninhabited ▧**Eureka Valley,** directly northwest of Death Valley. Eureka's magnificent and haunting sand dunes (the tallest in California) create one of the region's most surreal landscapes. If the sand is cool, flip off your shoes, climb to the top of the dunes, and roll down. The friction between the sand you disturb and the grains beneath it produces a deep resonation that sounds like a bizarre hum. Native Americans called it "the singing of the sands." Death Valley Rd., off Hwy. 168 east of Big Pine, passes through Eureka Valley on its way to Scotty's Castle. The paved and gravel road runs 37 mi. southwest from the intersection with Hwy. 168 before turning off near Eureka Valley Rd., a 10 mi. gravel and dirt track that cuts across the valley floor to the dunes. 4WD is preferable, especially if there's snow or if the road is washed out; see **Desert Survival,** p. 529.

WEST OF BISHOP

Outdoor fun abounds near Bishop in Big Pine and Bishop Creek Canyons, to the south and west, and in Buttermilk Country and Rock Creek, to the west and northwest. Wilderness permits are required year-round for overnight trips in the **John Muir Wilderness,** which includes most of the Eastern Sierra from Mt. Whitney to Mammoth. All trailheads within the wilderness have usage quotas, but 40% of permits are available on a walk-in basis. To reserve a permit, call ☎873-2483. ($5 fee.) Head south on Hwy. 395 to Big Pine, then west on Crocker St. for 10 mi. to reach the mouth of **Big Pine Canyon,** which was cut into the thick groves of Jeffery Pines by Big Pine Creek. This area is home to the southernmost glaciers in the US, remnants from the last Ice Age. The largest of these glaciers is **Palisade Glacier,** 2 mi. in length and several hundred feet thick. The **North Fork Trail** (or **Big Pine Lakes Trail**) is a popular route for hikers, as well as rock and ice climbers looking to access the glacier or Palisades, the rock pinnacles above it. The 18 mi. round-trip trail passes First, Second, and Third Lakes as well as the stone cabin of Hollywood legend Lon Chaney before reaching the foot of Palisade Glacier, with a 4500 ft. total elevation gain. Hikers in good condition can navigate the North Fork Trail to the base of Palisade Glacier, but **only those with ice-climbing experience should continue up the glacier.** The summit of North Palisade (14,242 ft.), one of the tallest peaks in the Sierras, is another 2000 ft. higher. For great **fishing,** take Big Pine's obscure **South Fork Trail,** which leads to lakes full of trout. The route becomes extremely steep above Willow Lake (4 mi. from trailhead).

Six miles north of Big Pine and 7 mi. south of Bishop on Hwy. 395 are **Keough's Hot Springs.** The natural springs are now a full-fledged business, complete with a pool, lifeguards, and snack bar. (☎872-6911. $7.) At night, however, the water that was diverted into the pool continues down the hill and makes for terrific free hot-tubbing in the creek. To reach these healing waters, turn onto Keough Hot Springs Rd. from U.S. 395 and make a right turn down to the creek after half a mile.

Follow Line St. (Hwy. 168) west of Bishop to the lakes and campgrounds of **Bishop Creek Canyon.** Within the canyon walls, 15 mi. down the highway, the road splits. Turning left at the fork will take you to **South Lake** (9700 ft.; 9 mi.), while continuing straight will take you to **Lake Sabrina** (9125 ft.; 5 mi.). Both stunning mountain reservoirs teem with fish and offer trailhead access into the Sierras. The official angling season lasts from late April to late October. Contact the Chamber of Commerce (☎873-8405) for general fishing and tournament info. From South Lake, hikers can pick up the **Bishop Pass Trail,** which connects with trails leading to Green, Treasure, and Chocolate Lakes, as well as mountain meadows that fill with wildflowers in the spring. More adventurous hikers can forge deeper into the wilderness along the trail and tackle some of the nearby 13,000 ft. peaks, including **Mount Goode** (13,085 ft.). From the fork, Hwy. 168 continues 4 mi. west to **Sabrina Basin,** which offers secluded hiking and fishing opportunities. On the southern side of the road **Cardinal Pinnacle** features a number of multi-pitch routes on superb granite. Lake Sabrina is the trailhead for routes up to pristine alpine lakes including Blue, Hungry Packer, and Midnight Lakes. **North Lake** can be accessed by a single-lane dirt road heading north just before Lake Sabrina. From the campground at North Lake, the **Paiute Pass Trail** follows the north fork of Bishop Creek up to Paiute Pass (11,423 ft.), where it joins the **John Muir Trail.**

Nearly 8 mi. up Hwy. 168 from U.S. 395, the Buttermilk Rd. turn-off leads to some world-famous boulders in **Buttermilk Country.** Named for the dairy farms that once refreshed stagecoach travelers, the area is characterized by giant granite boulders great for climbing and mountain biking. About 4 mi. down the road, you'll come to the **Peabody Boulders,** the most celebrated of the outcroppings.

The forests and mountains along **Rock Creek Canyon** are frequented year-round. Hair-raising precipices, plunging canyons, and alpine wildflowers mesmerize photographers and casual onlookers alike. Take Hwy. 395 24 mi. north of Bishop, head west on Rock Creek Rd., and continue up Rock Creek Canyon as far as you can go: in the summer, Mosquito Flat (10 mi.), and in the winter, the locked gate. **Little Lakes Valley,** at the canyon's west end, cradles a necklace of trout-filled lakes in the shadow of 13,000 ft. peaks. The **Little Lakes Trail** sets out from Mosquito Flat and climbs gradually to explore the upper valley's lakes and meadows. **Mono Pass Trail,** which branches off from the Little Lakes Trail about a quarter of a mile from the trailhead, traverses the canyon's northern wall, affording spectacular views of the valley and lakes below and leading to beautiful **Ruby Lake** and its staggering sheer granite walls. It continues to Mono Pass (12,040 ft.) and connects with the John Muir Trail. Rock Creek also boasts some great mountain biking on the **Lower Rock Creek Trail,** which starts at Tom's Place. There is day parking at each of the three trailheads. In winter, the evergreen forests and lake basins of this "range of light" (as Muir described the Eastern Sierra) make for spectacular **cross-country skiing.**

🎵 🎆 ENTERTAINMENT AND FESTIVALS

There might not be a hopping bar scene in Bishop, but hog-riders and other wild spirits manage to find excitement at the few watering holes that line **Main Street** (Hwy. 395). **Rusty's,** 112 N. Main St is among the most popular—and darkest. (☎873-9066. Open daily 8am-2am.) Although activity and excitement seem to permeate everyday life in Bishop, several annual events add more spice to the metropolis. Haul your ass to town during Memorial Day weekend for the largest mule event in the world; **Mule Days** (☎872-4263; www.mule-days.org) features 110 mule sporting events, 30,000 mule-obsessed fans, 700 mules, and the famous Mule Days Parade, which is long enough to be listed in the Guinness Book of World Records. The **Hotrods, Hippies & Polyester 50s-70s Dance** (☎873-3588) grooves every February, and the **Air Show** usually flies by on Fourth of July weekend. The City Park (behind the visitors center) has hosted **evening concerts** in the gazebo for 40 consecutive summers. (Shows June-Aug. M 8-9pm. Free.) Food, games, and fun characterize the massive **Tri-County Fair** (☎873-3588) over Labor Day weekend, with rodeos, homemade salsa, beer and wine contests, and a demolition derby.

LONE PINE   ☎760

Flanked to the west by the unrivaled Mt. Whitney and to the east by Death Valley, it's no wonder that Lone Pine (pop. 2404) has attracted the attention of Hollywood's location scouts. *Roy Rogers, The Lone Ranger, Gladiator,* and *Gone in 60 Seconds* are a only few of the over 3400 commercials, TV shows, and films shot in this striking landscape. Still, Lone Pine remains unspoiled by its celebrity associations; the town is still more focused on Mt. Whitney than on the movies. Hikers, mountaineers, anglers, mountain bikers, rock climbers, and artists all flock to this legendary American wilderness for a serious outdoor experience.

▐ TRANSPORTATION

Airport: Inyokern Airport (IYK; ☎377-5844), in Inyokern, 70 mi. south on Rte. 395. United Airlines (☎377-5000; www.ual.com) flies daily to L.A. (round-trip $200-300).

Buses: Getting to Lone Pine by bus is rather difficult. You can take Greyhound or Amtrak to Carson City, where **CREST** (☎800-922-1930) departs on Rte. 395 Tu and Th-F at 1:45pm and arrives in **Bishop,** 60 mi. north of Lone Pine, at 6:30pm. A separate, non-connecting bus passes through Bishop on its way to Lone Pine (M, W, F).

Car Rental: Lindsey Automotive, 361 S. Washington St. (☎876-4789). From $60 per day, with 150 mi. included. 21+ with credit card. Open M-F 8am-5pm. After-hours service available for a charge. **Avis** (☎446-5556) has an office at the Inyokern Airport.

Auto Repairs: Don's Garage, 1506 S. Main St. (☎876-4600). Open M-F 8am-5pm, Sa 9am-3pm. **AAA Emergency Road Service:** ☎872-8241.

▚ ▞ ORIENTATION AND PRACTICAL INFORMATION

Straddling U.S. 395, Lone Pine is the first Sierra town northeast on Rte. 136 from Death Valley. Independence, the Inyo county seat, is 15 mi. north, while Bishop is 60 mi. north. L.A. is a 4hr. drive away, 212 mi. south along U.S. 395, and southwest along Rte. 14. Yosemite is 210 mi. north on U.S. 395, a 5-6hr. drive. Upon reaching Lone Pine, U.S. 395 becomes **Main Street; Washington Street** is one block west. **Whitney Portal Road** intersects Main St. at the town's only traffic light and extends west to the base of Mt. Whitney.

Visitor Information:

Interagency Visitors Center (☎876-6222), at U.S. 395 and Rte. 136, 1½ mi. south of town. Joint venture between a number of agencies, including the Forest Service and University of California. Excellent maps and guidebooks, plus small exhibits. Informative handouts on hiking in the area. Open daily 8am-4:50pm.

Lone Pine Chamber of Commerce, 120 S. Main St. (☎876-4444 or 877-253-8981; www.lonepinechamber.com), in Lone Pine. Same services as the visitors center. Open M-F 7:30am-4:30pm.

Mount Whitney/Inyo National Forest Ranger Station, 640 S. Main St. (☎876-6200; www.fs.fed.us/r5/inyo), in Lone Pine. Brochures on regional wildlife and history. Topographical and trail maps for backcountry camping. Gives out free **wilderness permits,** which are required for overnight backcountry trips. All trails within the Ansel Adams, John Muir, Hoover, and Golden Trout Wildernesses have overnight usage quotas May-Oct. (usually 10-30 people). Reserve permits ($5 fee) up to 6 months in advance for the quota season; self-register in the winter. 40% of trail quotas are saved for walk-ins during the quota season. Each day, Mt. Whitney has 60 overnight and 130 day-use **Mt. Whitney permits,** all of which must be reserved in advance. All permit applications must be submitted in Feb. (the earlier in the month, the better). Contact the ranger station or visit the website for an application, which must be mailed or faxed in. Some spots are usually left over, and can be reserved beginning in May. Non-Mt. Whitney **Wilderness Reservations** can be phoned in daily 10am-4pm at ☎760-873-2483. Station open daily 8am-6pm.

Laundromat: Coin-Op Laundromat, 105 W. Post St., just off Main St. Wash $1.25, dry $0.25 per 12min. Open daily 7am-9pm.

Showers: Kirk's Barber Shop, 114 N. Main St. (☎876-5700). Showers $4. **Whitney Portal Store,** on the mountain. $3.

Police: Inyo County Sheriff, Lone Pine Substation, 210 N. Washington St. (☎876-5606). County Headquarters (☎878-0383).

Medical Services: Southern Inyo Hospital, 501 E. Locust St. (☎876-5501).

Library and Internet Access: Lone Pine Public Library (☎876-5031), on S. Washington St. 30min. max. Open M-Tu and Th-F 9am-noon and 1-5pm, W 6-9pm, Sa 10am-1pm.

Post Office: 121 Bush St. (☎876-5681), between Jackson and Main St. Open M-F 9am-5pm. **Postal Code:** 93545.

▚ ACCOMMODATIONS

Many clean but high-priced motels are available in Lone Pine. Weekdays are cheapest, but rates fluctuate widely depending on demand; make reservations or arrive early. During the Badwater Ultramarathon and the Lone Pine Film Festival, reservations should be made well in advance.

Historical Dow Hotel, 310 S. Main St. (☎876-5521, reservations 800-824-9317; www.dowvillamotel.com). Built during Lone Pine's Hollywood heyday to house pouty movie stars, the welcoming lobby of this old hotel has a TV, tea and coffee, and a fireplace. Pool and hot tub open 24hr. Doubles from $40, with bath from $50. ❸ Next door is the more upscale **Dow Villa Motel,** which has newer rooms, more amenities, and great mountain views. Rooms (some sleeping up to 6 people) $75-115. ❹

Comfort Inn, 1920 S. Main St. (☎876-8700; www.comfortinn.com), 1 mi. south of Lone Pine. This chain motel is removed from Lone Pine's minimal bustle. Above-average rooms with fridge, microwave, and cable TV. Heated pool. Singles Apr.-Oct. from $59; Nov.-Feb. $49. $10 extra for double, patio, or balcony. 10% AAA discount. ❹

De La Cour Ranch (☎876-0022), 2½ mi. past Lubken Canyon Rd. on Horseshow Meadow Rd., off Whitney Portal Rd. outside of Lone Pine. Secluded, spacious cabin in the foothills, with a bedroom and living room, full kitchen, and bathroom. Feels like home. Futon and loft sleep 4 inside; 2 tent bungalows sleep another 4. Reserve in advance. Cabin $150, weekly $750. ❺

▚ CAMPING

Camping is cheap, scenic, and conveniently located. As with motels in the area, make reservations or arrive early.

▨ **Whitney Portal Campground** (Mt. Whitney ranger ☎876-6200, reservations 877-444-6777; www.reserveamerica.com), 8000 ft., on Whitney Portal Rd., 13 mi. west of town. Surrounding evergreens, a rushing stream, and phenomenal views. Served by the **Whitney Portal Store,** which carries light food, guidebooks, and outerwear. Store open May-Oct. daily dawn-dusk. Pay phone and a small restaurant. 7-night max. stay. Some sites accept reservations. Open June-Oct. Sites $14; group sites $30. ❶

Lone Pine Campground (☎877-444-6777), 6000 ft. Take Whitney Portal Rd. from Lone Pine for about 7 mi. 43 immaculate sites in close proximity to numerous trailheads, stellar views of soaring granite faces, and soft gravel for tent pitching. Water and vault toilets. 14-night max. stay. Open mid-April to Nov. Sites $12, seniors $6. ❶

Diaz Lake Campground (☎876-5656), 3700 ft., on U.S. 395, 3 mi. south of Lone Pine. Formed when the massive earthquake of 1872 dropped the valley floor 20 ft., Diaz Lake is home to 200 secluded sites, tremendous fishing, and various watersports. Grills, flush toilets, and showers. 15-day max. stay. Sites $10. ❶

Portagee Joe, 3800 ft., ½ mi. from Lone Pine on Whitney Portal Rd., within walking distance of town. Tree-lined camping by a small stream. 15 sites. Water and vault toilets. 14-day max. stay. Sites $10; walk-in sites $6. ❶

◨ FOOD

Lone Pine has a smattering of diners, cafes, and a few fancier restaurants. Grab groceries in town at **Joseph's Bi-Rite Market,** 119 S. Main St., which also has a hearty hot deli. (☎876-4378. Open daily 8am-9pm.) This may not be the place for international cuisine, but reasonably priced homey meals are abound.

High Sierra Cafe, 446 Main St. (☎876-5796). Down-to-earth food and prices. The barbecue beef sandwich ($5.50) is a great post-climb treat. A local favorite. Open 24hr, and the entire menu is available at all hours. ❷

Mt. Whitney Restaurant, 227 S. Main St. (☎876-5751). Decorated with memorabilia and photos from Westerns shot in the Alabama Hills, this diner serves classic American grub for $6-14 and claims to have the best burger in town. The large breakfasts (around $6) provide good fuel for a day's hike. Open 6:30am-9:30pm. ❷

Seasons Restaurant (☎876-8927), at the corner of Rte. 395 and Whitney Portal Rd. The most upscale restaurant in town, serving Continental cuisine ($10-25) including some excellent seafood entrees. There are precious few vegetarian options but a great selection of wines, and microbrews. Open daily 5-10pm; in winter M-Sa 5-10pm. ❹

◉ SIGHTS

Lone Pine is surrounded by strange, beautiful scenery, from the deserts in the east to the rolling foothills and striking mountains in the west. All of the Sierra's tallest peaks are here, including the famous **Mount Whitney** (elevation 14,494 ft.). Nearly 3 mi. from Main St., off Whitney Portal Rd., is **Movie Road,** which winds 12 mi. through the famous **Alabama Hills.** A bouldered dreamscape of golden-brown granite formations, the hills provided the backdrop for fictionalized Hollywood cowboy 'n' Indian tales like the 1920s *How the West Was Won,* television shoot-'em-ups like *Bonanza* and *Rawhide,* and countless SUV commercials. Recent flicks include *Maverick, Star Trek: Generations,* and *Gladiator.* In all, over 400 commercials, feature films, and shows were shot here. The Chamber of Commerce dispenses a **movie location map** with a

1hr. self-guided driving tour. The annual **Lone Pine Film Festival** every Columbus Day weekend, screens films shot in the region. (☎876-9103; $25 for all screenings and a tour of the hills)

The **Eastern California Museum,** 155 N. Grant St., off Market St. in Independence, exhibits local Paiute and Shoshone handicrafts, preserved equipment used by locals to construct the Los Angeles aqueduct, and a display on the Manzanar internment camp. Just behind the museum is a re-creation of a small 1880s pioneer village, Little Pine. (☎878-0258. Open Su-M and W-Sa 10am-4pm. Donation appreciated.) On U.S. 395, between Lone Pine and Independence, lies the **Manzanar National Historic Site,** a symbol and relic of one of the most shameful chapters in American history. Previously known as a "relocation" camp, it was the first of 10 internment centers that the US established after Japan's 1941 attack on Pearl Harbor to contain Japanese Americans, whom the government saw as potential enemy sympathizers. From 1942 to 1945, 11,400 people were brought here to the dusty, bare Owens Valley floor with whatever they could manage to carry in two suitcases. Conspicuously ignored by the government and America's collective memory, the camp is reduced to a few building foundations and some barbed wire. A new visitors center and park headquarters provide information and exhibits about the site. On the last Saturday of every April, an annual pilgrimage of former internees, their descendants, and the public, is held at the camp's cemetery.

Owens Dry Lake, 5 mi. south of town on Rte. 395, was once a 30 ft. deep lake used to transport bullion and supplies for the mines at Cerro Gordo before the city of Los Angeles diverted the fresh-water streams that fed the lake in order to fill the L.A. aqueduct. Today, the lake is dry, though its bed is rich with colorful minerals. The pretty green and pinkish hues are the results of algae and bacteria. The dry salts exposed when the water disappeared have caused a serious dust problem in the area; in fact, the Environmental Protection Agency has deemed the area around Owens Lake the dustiest in the US.

One of the best-preserved ghost towns in the state, **Cerro Gordo** (☎876-1860), or "Fat Hill," once produced nearly 10,000 lb. of silver a day, where it accounted for one-third of all business transactions in the L.A. port. After the silver was exhausted, zinc briefly revived the mines in the early 1900s. Today, the town's remains are private property. Call ahead to visit the deserted old-time hotels, offices, a brothel, mining structures, and a museum. Cerro Gordo is 8 mi. down a dirt road from Keeler, off Rte. 270 south of Lone Pine.

⚑ HIKING

MOUNT WHITNEY

Climbing Mount Whitney requires significant preparation, physically and logistically. Unlike other Inyo trails, the main Mt. Whitney trail requires a permit for both overnight trips and day hikes. During the low season there is no limit to the number of permits issued, but between May 15 and November 1 there are daily quotas. Throughout the month of February, lottery applications (☎873-2483; www.fs.fed.us/r5/inyo) are accepted for both day and overnight permits for the quota season. In this lottery, overnight hikers have about a 60% chance of getting a spot, while day hikers have about a 90% chance, though these odds depend on date and group size. A small number of permits for the quota season go unissued every year and can be reserved beginning in May.

As one of the most popular trails in the nation, the **Mount Whitney Trail** to the **highest point in the lower 48 states** is popular with both experienced and amateur adventurers looking for bragging rights. The **trailhead** for Mount Whitney, at the end of Whitney Portal Rd., is at 8365 ft.; the trail ascends over 6000 ft. to the 14,491 ft. summit. Hikers should be wary of the effects of altitude, hiking slowly and allotting extra time in their itinerary. Spend some time hiking at higher altitudes to avoid altitude sickness; many campers spend a few days in the area before attempting higher climbs. Also remember that this is bear country. Ingenious bears rip apart backpacks and BMWs alike to get at anything odorous (see **Bears,** p. 57). Rent a bear-proof food container at one of the ranger stations ($5 per trip). The 11 mi. trek to the top of Mt. Whitney usually takes two to three days, though the very fit and acclimated can summit and return in one long day. While more of a strenuous hike than a mountain climb, this nontechnical route is feasible only in late spring and summer when there is no ice. Temperatures can dip below freezing on the mountain at any time of year, so only attempt the journey with proper equipment and outerwear. For rock climbers, Mt. Whitney's **East Face** is a year-round technical challenge. A backcountry route to the Mt. Whitney summit, the **Cottonwood Lakes Trail** (10,000 ft. at the trailhead) continues over 40 mi. between the forests that abut the John Muir Wilderness and Sequoia National Park, passing some of the most incredible nature spots in the country along the way. Follow Whitney Portal Rd. for 4 mi. from Lone Pine and take Horseshoe Meadow Rd. 20 mi. to the trailhead. The trail is on the quota system from June to September 15.

OTHER HIKES

Many moderate **day hikes** explore the Eastern Sierra out of the Whitney Portal, at the end of Whitney Portal Rd. The 1hr. hike along **Horseshoe Meadow Trail** to **Golden Trout Wilderness** passes several dozen high mountain lakes that reflect the Inyo Mountains. **Horseshoe Meadow** has walk-in **camping ❶** (sites $6) and equestrian facilities ($12 per horse). The **Meysan Lake Trail** is a tough 4¾ mi. haul from Whitney Portal to an exquisite high-altitude lake and a number of rock climbing opportunities. Consider buying a topographical map, as the trail can be difficult to follow at times. The **Whitney Portal Trail** offers a more challenging 6hr. hike from the Lone Pine Campground to Whitney Portal Campground. The trail follows Lone Pine Creek and offers incredible views of Mt. Whitney and the Owens Valley.

If you've got bulletproof muscles and high-octane willpower, you may want to line up for some of the toughest footraces in the world. On the first Saturday in May, Lone Pine stages the high-elevation **Wild Wild West Marathon,** considered

BADASS

In 1977, Al Arnold inaugurated one of the world's most painful endurance races when he ran from Badwater, in Death Valley the lowest point in the Western Hemisphere, to the top of Mt Whitney, the highest peak in the contiguous US. It took him 84hr and he shed 17 lb. during the journey. Now this brutal run is the Annual Badwater Ultramarathon.

Each year, in Death Valley's blazing July heat, 70-80 runners embark on this grueling 135 mi. run halfway up Mt. Whitney. There's no prize money; there's no relief. But there are scorching temperatures that reach 130°F, 13,000 ft. in cumulative elevation change, and 4700 ft of joint-rattling descents. IVs are prohibited and there are no official aid stations. Members of runners' support crews have passed out from the heat as they sat in their cars. To the AP, two-time finisher Greg Minter reported hallucinating: "I saw a dinosaur around mile 108." Runners get a belt buckle if they finish.

Pam Reed, a 42-year-old mother from Arizona, has won twice, finishing in just under 28hr. She never ate or slept, sustaining herself on an all-liquid diet, including eight Red Bull energy drinks. Her four-person support crew raced to spray her down with water every quarter-mile.

Al Arnold, now 75, addresses the runners every year. When he's done, he shouts "BANG!" at 6am sharp, and they're off.

the seventh most difficult marathon in North America. Interested athletes can enter by contacting the Chamber of Commerce. For the truly masochistic, there is the 135 mi. **Badwater Ultramarathon** (☎510-528-3263; www.badwaterultra.com; see p. 301) in sweltering late July. Traveling from Death Valley's Badwater, the lowest point in the Western Hemisphere, to Mt. Whitney, this is the ultimate test of endurance. This invitation-only odyssey usually takes two to three days for the world's top endurance athletes to complete. The unimaginably tough winners tend to finish in just over a full day of pain, sucking down a liquid diet of Red Bull and lactic acid, though they're never far from the stocked and well-marked cars that accompany them. You're unlikely to find a more intense athletic event anywhere in the world.

CENTRAL CALIFORNIA

Sandwiched between the Coastal Range and the Sierra Nevadas, Central California doesn't conform to the California stereotype, though it's really the most golden part of the Golden State. During the Gold Rush, steamboats chugged out of Sacramento to bring prospectors and provisions to towns in the foothills of the Sierra Nevadas. Today, Gold Country is little more than a historical relic, but the Central Valley still has pay dirt—its fertile soil nurtures the agriculture that fuels much of California's economy. With golden hills, summer heat, and a rural, laid-back feel, Central California presents an older, gentler version of crazy California.

HIGHLIGHTS OF CENTRAL CALIFORNIA

INTERSTATE 5. This long, straight highway may be dull, but it's the fastest way to traverse the state, and there are plenty of cows to keep you company.

A SACRAMENTO KINGS HOME GAME. With the noisiest fans in the NBA, a Kings game at Arco Arena is one of the best ways to catch the Sac Town spirit (p. 309).

YUBA RIVER. The cool waters of this river rush through Gold Country, offering prime opportunities for whitewater rafting or swimming-hole skinny-dipping (p. 326).

THE CENTRAL VALLEY

California's Central Valley minds its own agribusiness. Lifestyles here revolve around agriculture and college life. One of the most productive regions in the world, the San Joaquin Valley stretches from the Tehachapi Range south of Bakersfield to just north of Stockton, where it becomes known as the Sacramento Valley. From there, the Valley continues north past Chico, before it is engulfed by the Cascades. The land is flat, the air is oven-hot, and endless rice fields, almond orchards, and cow pastures dominate the landscape along the razor-straight slashes of I-5 and Rte. 99.

SACRAMENTO ☎ 916

California's more glamorous cities often overshadow the state capital. Best known for its political and agricultural activity, Sacramento (area pop. 1.9 million) is also the nation's most diverse city, not to mention the home of a vibrant arts scene and excellent cuisine. In 1848, Swiss emigré John Sutter, fleeing debtor's prison back home, purchased 48,000 dusty acres from the Miwok tribe for a few trinkets. His trading fort became the central pavilion for the influx of gold miners to the Valley in the 1850s. Over the next century, mansions and suburban bungalows gradually transformed the landscape, paving the way for future residents Ronald Reagan and Arnold Schwarzenegger. Today, Sacramento is one of the fastest growing regions in the US, though its pace balances the bustle of San Francisco to the west and the tranquility of the Sierra Nevadas to the east. An impressive fleet of law enforcement officials patrols the city, especially the area surrounding the capitol building, but **exercise caution at night downtown.**

CENTRAL
CALIFORNIA

The Central Valley

TRANSPORTATION

Airport: Sacramento International (☎929-5411; http://airports.co.sacramento.ca.us), 12 mi. north of the city on I-5. 2 terminals host 12 airlines serving hundreds of destinations worldwide. Cabs are expensive ($22-25 to downtown) but vans are cheaper ($9-10); call **SuperShuttle** (☎800-258-3826) for pick-up. **Yolo Bus** (☎530-666-2877) runs public buses downtown (every hr. 5am-10pm, $1.25).

Trains: Amtrak, 401 I St. (☎800-USA-RAIL/872-7245), at 5th St. Open daily 5am-midnight. To: **L.A.** (8-14hr., 4 per day, $42); **San Francisco** (2hr., 5 per day, $19); **Reno, NV** (3hr., 7 per day, $20). **Be careful around the station at night.**

Buses: Greyhound, 715 L St. (☎444-6858 or 800-229-9424), between 7th and 8th St. Lockers available. Open 24hr. To: **L.A.** (7-9hr., 10 per day, $44-51); **Reno** (3hr., 10 per day, $21-23); **San Francisco** (2-3hr., 20 per day, $14.50-16); **Seattle** (16-20hr., 6 per day, $73.50-78.50). **Be careful around the station at night.**

Public Transit: Sacramento Regional Transit Bus and Light Rail, 1400 29th St. (☎321-2877; www.sacrt.com). Bus operates 5am-10pm, light rail 4am-midnight. $0.50-$1.50, day pass $3.50.

Taxi: Yellow Cab (☎444-2222 or 800-464-0777). 24hr.

Car Rental: Enterprise, 2700 Arden Way (☎486-9900). Cars from $34 per day, and as low as $20 per day on weekends. 21+ with major credit card. Open M-F 7:30am-6pm, Sa 9am-1pm.

Bike Rental: American River Bike Shop, 9203 Folsom Blvd. (☎363-2671). Other locations at 256 Florin Rd. and 2645 Macaroni Ave. Grab a friend for a tandem ride ($6 per hr., $30 per day) around the American River. Bikes $4 per hr., $20 per day. Open M-F 9am-7pm, Sa 9am-6pm, Su 10am-5pm.

Sacramento

🏠 ACCOMMODATIONS
Courtyard by Marriott, **13**
Sacramento Hostel
(HI-AYH), **2**
Vagabond Inn Midtown, **9**

🍴 FOOD
33rd St. Bistro, **6**
Cafe Bernardo, **8**
Ernesto's, **12**

The Fox and Goose, **10**
Maalouf's Taste of Lebanon, **1**
Zelda's Pizza, **7**

🍷 NIGHTLIFE
Faces, **4**
Old Ironsides, **11**
Torch Club, **3**
True Love Coffeehouse, **5**

〰 Sacramento Light Rail

✦ 🛈 ORIENTATION AND PRACTICAL INFORMATION

Sacramento is at the center of the **Sacramento Valley**. Five major highways converge on the capital: **I-5** and **Route 99** run north-south, with I-5 to the west, **I-80** runs east-west between San Francisco and Reno, and **U.S. 50** and **Route 16** bring traffic westward from Gold Country. Numbered streets run north-south and lettered streets run east-west in a grid. The street number on a lettered street corresponds to the number of the cross street (2000 K St. is near the corner of 20th St.). The capitol building, parks, and endless cafes and restaurants occupy the **downtown area** around 10th St. and Capitol Ave. Old Sacramento is located just west of downtown, on the Sacramento River.

Visitor Information: Sacramento Convention and Visitor Bureau, 1303 J St., #600 (☎264-4740; www.sacramentocvb.org). Open M-Sa 8am-5pm.

Police: 5770 Freeport Blvd. (☎264-5471; www.sacpd.org), at I St.

Medical Services: UC Davis Medical Center, 2315 Stockton Blvd. (☎734-2011), at Broadway.

Hotlines: Suicide Prevention and Crisis Response (☎368-3111). Open 24hr.

Library and Internet Access: Sacramento Public Library, 828 I St. (☎264-2700), between 8th and 9th St. 1hr. free Internet. Open M and F 10am-6pm, Tu-Th 10am-9pm, Sa 10am-5pm, Su noon-5pm.

Post Office: 801 I St. (☎556-3415). Open M-F 8am-5pm. **Postal Code:** 95814.

ACCOMMODATIONS AND CAMPING

Sacramento has many hotels, motels, and B&Bs, but lawyers, businesspeople, and politicians often flood accommodations, making it hard to find a room. Advance reservations are always a good idea. **West Capitol Avenue** has many cheap hotels, but they might be on the seedy side, so investigate before making plans. Within Sacramento proper, **16th Street** is home to many hotels and motels. Rates fluctuate seasonally, but standard chain hotel and motel rooms usually go for $50-150 per night. **Camping** is most popular with RVers, but tent sites are usually available, even in the metropolitan area.

■ **Sacramento Hostel (HI-AYH),** 900 H St. (☎443-1691; reservations 800-909-4776, ext. 40), at 10th St. Built in 1885, this pastel Victorian mansion looks more like an elegant B&B than a hostel with its high sloping ceilings, grand mahogany staircase, and stained-glass atrium. Huge modern kitchen, 3 large living rooms, library, laundry facilities, TV/VCR, and an extensive selection of video rentals ($1). Dorm-style rooms are spacious and immaculate. Family, couple, and single rooms available. Parking $5 per night. Check-in 7:30-9:30am and 5-10pm. Check-out 9:30am. Lock out 10am-5pm. 11pm curfew, speak to the receptionist before going out. Dorms $21-23, nonmembers $24-26. Group rates available. ❷

Courtyard by Marriott, 4422 Y St. (☎455-6800), at the UC Davis Medical Center. A full-fledged hotel at a relatively low price. Grounds include an exercise room, pool, whirlpool, restaurant, cocktail lounge, and coffee shop. Rooms have cable TV, irons, hairdryers, and high-speed Internet connections. Doubles from $74. ❺

Vagabond Inn Midtown, 1319 30th St. (☎454-4400; www.vagabondinn.com), between M and N St. Low rates, well-kept rooms, and above average amenities. Rooms have cable TV, phone, Internet, and free newspapers. Continental breakfast included. Doubles from $50; online rates from $48. ❸

KOA Sacramento (☎371-6771, reservations 800-562-2747). Take I-80 west of downtown and exit at W. Capitol Ave. Centrally located. Site $27; RV with hookup $37; cabins $46.) ❷

FOOD

Food in Sacramento is plentiful and good, thanks to a hip midtown, varied immigrant populations, and a dose of Californian culinary inventiveness. Many eateries are concentrated on **J Street** or **Capitol Avenue** between 19th and 29th St. The stretch of **Fair Oaks Boulevard** between Howe and Fulton St. is also home to great restaurants of all price ranges. Old Sacramento is filled with gimmicky restaurants that tend to be on the more expensive side. The **Downtown Certified Farmers Market** is held three times a week and is a great place to sample fresh produce from local farmers. (☎442-8575; www.downtownsac.org. Open Tu 10am-2pm at 10th and P St., W 10am-2pm at 10th and J St., and Th 10am-2pm at 4th and K St.)

■ **Zelda's Pizza,** 1415 21st St. (☎447-1400), at N St. A local favorite. Posters of Italy, year-round Christmas lights, and a varied clientele enliven this windowless pizza joint. Simple yet satisfying salads ($6) fill the 30min. wait for superb Chicago-style pizza ($8-18) served fresh from the oven. Open M-Th 11:30am-2pm and 5-10pm, F 11:30am-2pm and 5-11:30pm, Sa 5-11:30pm, Su 5-10pm. ❷

Ernesto's, 1901 16th St. (☎441-5850; www.ernestosmexicanfood.com), at the corner of S St. Often awarded best Mexican food in Sacramento, this spacious restaurant dishes out upscale Mexican food at reasonable prices. The extensive vegetarian menu includes whole bean soup ($7) and fajitas with marinated zucchini, mushrooms, onions, and bell peppers ($9). Huge burritos ($7-9), quesadillas ($7), and salads ($6-8). Open Su-W 11am-10pm, Th 11am-11pm, F-Sa 9am-midnight. ❷

Cafe Bernardo, 2726 Capitol Ave. (☎443-1189; www.cafebernardo.com), at 28th St. Inspired by European cafes but infused with earth tones and stainless steel, Cafe Bernardo prepares delectable sandwiches ($6-8), salads ($2-7), and soups ($2-4). Order at the counter at this bright cafe and wait for one of the energetic waiters to serve your meal. Outdoor seating. Open Su-Th 7am-10pm, F-Sa 7am-11pm. ❷

The Fox and Goose, 1001 R St. (☎443-8825), at 10th St. Situated in a huge brick factory with colored windows built in 1913 and renovated in the 1970s, the Fox and Goose blends authentic English public house atmosphere and American alternative culture. Primarily a brunch spot, though filling meals served 3 times a day. Serves everything from a proper pot of tea to European beer ($3), bangers ($5), pasties ($6), and fish and chips ($6). Open mic nights and live music Th-Sa. Open M-F 7am-2pm and 5:30pm-midnight, Sa-Su 8am-2am. ❶

33rd St. Bistro, 3301 Folsom Blvd. (☎455-2233), at the corner of 33rd. St. Opened by 2 classically trained chef brothers who weren't afraid to experiment, this bistro mixes flavors of the Pacific Northwest, American South, Mediterranean, and Caribbean seamlessly and successfully. Exquisite desserts include seasonal fresh fruit cobblers ($6). Outdoor seating. Entrees $9-19. Salads $5-15. Open Su-Th 8am-10pm, F-Sa 8am-11pm. ❸

Maalouf's Taste of Lebanon, 1433 Fulton Ave. (☎972-8768), east of downtown. Bold and flavorful kebab and schwarma sandwiches ($3-5) and appetizer favorites like kibbe and falafel ($2-4) combine Middle Eastern and Mediterranean influences. Frequented by the local Lebanese community. Open M-Sa 11am-9:30pm. ❶

◗ SIGHTS

Since the Gold Rush, Sacramento has been more of a pit stop on the way to the lakes and mountains in the east than a destination in itself, but the city's numerous historical sights and museums have been growing in popularity.

GOVERNMENT BUILDINGS. Debates about the budget and water shortages, as well as a considerable amount of Arnold-spotting, occur daily in the elegant **State Capitol.** *(10th St. and Capitol Ave. ☎324-0333. 1hr. tours depart daily every hr. 9am-4pm. Free tickets distributed in Room B27 on a first come, first served basis.)* Colonnades of towering palm trees and grassy lawns transform Capitol Park into a shaded oasis in the middle of downtown's busy bureaucracy. The **State Historic Park Governor's Mansion** was built in 1877, and its faded, weathered exterior makes it look not a year younger. The mansion served as the residence of California's governor and his family until then-governor Ronald Reagan opted to rent his own pad. *(At the corner of 16th and H St. ☎324-0539. Open daily 10am-4pm. Tours every hr. $2, under 16 free.)*

OLD SACRAMENTO. This 28-acre town of historic buildings constructed in the early 1800s attracts nearly five million visitors annually and has been refurbished to resemble its late 19th-century appearance. Today, tourists trod on the wooden planked sidewalks, browsing gift shops or eating at one of the many restaurants. Attractions include a restored riverboat, California's first theater, and a military museum. The world-renowned 100,000 sq. ft. ◪**California State Railroad Museum** exhibits 23 historic locomotives, half of which you can walk through, and is widely regarded as the finest railroad museum in North America. (125 I St., at 2nd St. ☎ 445-6645. Open daily 10am-5pm. 1hr. train rides from the Train Depot in Old Sacramento Apr.-Sept. weekends; $6, ages 6-12 $3, under 6 free. Museum $4, under 17 free.)

CALIFORNIA HISTORY. Sutter's Fort was the only remaining property of John Sutter after the rest were overrun by gold-seekers. These days, busloads of tourists and local school children come to see the restored fort and its educational exhibits. (2701 L St., between 26th and 28th St. ☎ 445-4422. Open daily 10am-5pm. $4, ages 6-16 $1, under 5 free.) The **California State History Museum** relates the story of California with artifacts and documents from the state archives. Multimedia exhibits include a virtual trip on a 1936 bus with a video of immigrant narratives and a glimpse of the state constitution. (1020 O St., at 10th St. ☎ 653-0563; www.ss.ca.gov/museum/intro.htm. Open Tu-Sa 10am-5pm, Su noon-5pm. $5, ages 6-13 $3, seniors $4, under 6 free.)

CROCKER ART MUSEUM. This relatively small museum packs in excellent art with permanent works by Brueghel, Rembrandt, and Jacques-Louis David, as well as large rotating exhibits downstairs. What makes the Crocker stand apart, however, is its superb collection of contemporary Californian art, including pieces by local burnout artist Robert Arneson. (216 O St., between 2nd and 3rd St. ☎ 264-5423; www.crockerartmuseum.org. Open Tu-W and F-Su 10am-5pm, Th 10am-9pm. Tours available; book a week in advance. $6, seniors $4, ages 7-17 $3, under 7 free.)

LAND PARK. Chimps, hippos, giraffes, lions, white tigers, and an albino alligator are among the nearly 400 critters at the **Sacramento Zoo**. It sits in a beautiful eucalyptus-filled park and emphasizes protection of endangered species and the careful recreation of natural habitats. (On William Land Park Dr. off I-5 at the Sutterville exit. ☎ 264-5885; www.saczoo.com. Open daily Nov.-Jan. 10am-4pm; Feb.-Oct. 9am-4pm. $6.75, ages 3-12 $4.50, under 3 free.) Across the street, **Fairytale Town** is a children's park dedicated to promoting the imagination, creativity, and education of children. Since 1959, kids have enjoyed the town's amusement rides, live reproductions of fairy tales, and seven resident animals. (On William Land Park Dr. ☎ 264-5233; www.fairytaletown.org. Open daily Mar.-Aug. 9am-4pm; Sept.-Oct. 10am-4pm; Nov.-Dec. W-Su 10am-4pm. $3.50, Sa-Su $3.75; ages 3-12 $3.25/$3.50; under 3 free.)

◪ OUTDOOR ACTIVITIES

The American River is within a short drive of Sacramento, and its rushing waters make **river rafting** an opportunity for adventure seekers. Rent rafts at **American River Raft Rentals**, 11257 S. Bridge St., in Rancho Cordova, 14 mi. east of downtown on U.S. 50. Exit on Sunrise Blvd. and take it north 1½ mi. to the American River. (☎ 635-6400. 4-person rafts $38; kayaks $27. $2 launch fee. Return shuttle $3.50 per person. Open daily 9am-6pm; rentals available until 1pm.) The **American River Recreation Trail and Parkway**, spanning over 30 mi. from Discovery Park to Folsom Lake, is a nature preserve with a view of the downtown skyline. Five million people a year visit to cycle, jog, swim, fish, hike, and ride horses. You can enter the trail in Old Sacramento or at designated entrance points along the river. **Folsom Lake State Recreation Area**, 25 mi. east of town on I-80 (take Douglas Blvd.), hosts a giant 11,000 acre reservoir perfect for swimming, boating, fishing, and wake-boarding. Over 100 mi. of trails wind through the surrounding hills. (☎ 988-0205. Open daily 6am-10pm. $2-6 per vehicle.)

◪ ENTERTAINMENT

In summer Sacramento bustles with free afternoon concerts and cheap food. The Friday edition of the *Sacramento Bee* contains a supplement called *Ticket*, which gives a rundown of events, restaurants, and nightlife. For weekend performances and activities, check the free weeklies, such as *Sacramento News and Review* and *Inside the City*. The free *Alive and Kicking* has schedules and information about music and arts throughout the city. **Bass tickets,** 1409 28th St., Ste. 206 (☎453-2730; www.tickets.com), is the largest ticket vendor in the area; call them for event times, locations, and prices.

Aside from the ubiquitous multiplexes, Sacramento has a good number of art film theaters. The unique **Crest Theater,** at 10th and K St., was built in 1913 as a vaudevillian stage and now screens an impressive parade of independent films. Inside are three cinemas with palatial stairways, gilded ceilings, crystal chandeliers, and decadent paisley carpet. It is also a popular local venue for live indie rock and other big-name performances; contact Bass for tickets. (☎442-5189. Films $5-8.) Since 1942, the **Sacramento Theatre Company,** 1419 H St., has been staging classic and contemporary plays. Seven productions, often lesser-known critical hits, go up each year from September to May. (☎443-6722. Tickets $18-36.)

If you're visiting Sacramento in the spring, catch a **Sacramento Kings** basketball game and scream alongside the Kings fans, reputed to be the loudest in the NBA. The Kings play at the Arco Arena, 1 Sports Pkwy. To order single-game tickets by phone, call ☎649-8497, 530-528-8497, or 209-485-8497. Baseball fans can feed off the youthful spirit of minor league baseball at a **Sacramento Rivercats** game. From early April to September, games are played at Raley Field, 400 Ballpark Dr., in West Sacramento. Pick up a schedule at the Visitors Bureau. For tickets, call ☎800-225-2277 or visit www.rivercats.com.

Second Saturday Art Walk (www.sacramento-second-saturday.org). On the 2nd Sa of each month, art galleries in Sacramento stay open late, allowing art lovers to wander about and check out the local art scene. Some galleries serve refreshments. Pick up a copy of the *Sacramento News and Review* for a list of participating galleries. Free.

Friday Night Concert Series (☎442-2500), in Cesar Chávez Park, at 10th and I St. Live bands (rock, blues, jazz, folk, and pop), food stands, and beer gardens. In summer F 5-9pm. Free.

Dixieland Jazz Jubilee (☎372-5277; www.sacjazz.com). Over 100 bands play every Memorial Day weekend in Old Sac, attracting more than 100,000 listeners.

International Street Fair, on 11th St. between J and L St. A celebration of Sacramento's diversity. Food, vendors, kids' activities, and performances. Mid-July 5-9pm.

Shakespeare Lite (☎442-8575), in St. Rose of Lima Park, at 7th and K St. Comedic abridged versions of the Bard's work. Pack a picnic. June to mid-July Th noon-1pm.

California State Fair (☎263-3000; www.bigfun.org). This classic agricultural fair doesn't skimp on spinning rides, fairway food, pig races, or bungee jumping. Mid-Aug. to early Sept. Tickets $7, seniors $5, children $4.50.

◙ NIGHTLIFE

Capital-dwellers slink about in their natural habitat of brass- and mahogany-lined bars and coffeehouses. Sacramento's midtown entertainment parlors, on the other hand, afford a view of city residents who have more body-piercings per capita than their representatives in the government. The **Fox and Goose** (see p. 307) is a splendid nightlife option. Nightclubs are scattered around Sacramento's periphery.

◙ **True Love Coffeehouse,** 2406 J St. (☎492-9002; www.truelovesacto.com), at 24th St. A cozy, quirky hangout thriving on the pulse of Sacramento's alternative culture. Small stage is given over to all sorts of unusual and compelling entertainment, from movie screenings to waffle night to documentary films and, of course, live music. Check out the large, shaded patio out back. Usually no cover, but some performances $6-7. Open Su-Th 5pm-midnight, F-Sa 5pm-2am.

Old Ironsides, 1901 10th St. (☎443-9751; www.theoldironsides.com), at 10th and S St. The 1st bar in Sacramento to get its liquor license after Prohibition, Old Ironsides is split into 2 rooms, one for grooving and one for boozing. Both are filled with laid-back and interesting locals. Lipstick DJ Tu. Open-mic W. Live music Th-Sa; $5-10 cover. Open M-F 11am-1:30am, Sa-Su 6pm-1:30am.

Torch Club, 904 15th St. (☎443-2797; www.thetorchclub.com), at I St. The ultimate blues and bluegrass venue in town with an atmosphere to prove it. Blues legends rambling through town and the local upstarts attract hardcore soul music enthusiasts. Deep wailing and foot-stomping exuberance gives these tunes a redemptive, releasing vitality. Live bands play every night. Cover varies, often free. 21+. Open daily 10am-2am.

Faces, 2000 K St. (☎448-7798; www.faces.net), at 20th St. *The* mid-town gay club scene, also voted Sacramento's best dance club. 5 bars, 2 dance floors, an outdoor patio, and a variety of music including country, karaoke, disco, and salsa. Su barbecue 5:30pm. Occasional amateur stripteases Th night. 21+. Open daily 4pm-1:45am.

DAVIS   ☎530

Fourteen miles west of Sacramento on I-80, Davis (pop. 60,300) prides itself on higher education, agriculture, and two-wheeled transportation. Davis's residents own more bicycles per capita than any other US city, and several intersections even feature bike-specific traffic lights. The diverse student body of University of California at Davis (UCD) shapes the unique character of the town, and activity centers around the campus and adjacent downtown.

🚺 PRACTICAL INFORMATION. Amtrak, 840 2nd St. (☎800-872-7245), provides **train** service to Sacramento (16 per day, $5.50) and San Francisco (11 per day, $17). **Unitrans** (☎752-2877) connects downtown and the UCD campus ($0.75). **Yolo Bus** (☎666-5842) serves Davis and Sacramento ($1.25, seniors, disabled, and ages 5-12 $0.50). Get info at the **Visitors Bureau,** 105 E St. (☎297-1900; www.davisvisitor.com; open M-F 8:30am-4:30pm) or the **UC Davis Information Center,** in the Memorial Union on campus (☎752-2222, campus events 752-2813; open M-F May-Aug. 10am-4pm; Sept.-Apr. 8am-7pm). Other services include: **Bank of America,** 325 E St. (☎757-5046) with 24hr. **ATM; Rite Aid Pharmacy,** 655 Russell Blvd. (☎759-7804); **Yolo County Library, Davis Branch,** 315 14th St. (☎757-5591; 1hr. of free **Internet access;** open M 1-9pm, Tu-Th 10am-9pm, F-Sa 10am-5:30pm, Su 1-5pm); **post office,** 2020 5th St. (☎800-275-8777; open M-F 7am-5:30pm, Sa 9am-4pm). **Postal Code:** 95616.

🏠🍴 ACCOMMODATIONS AND FOOD. Motels in Davis do not come cheap, and rooms are scarce during university events. **University Park Inn ❹,** 1111 Richards Blvd., off I-80 at the Richards Blvd. exit, is six blocks from campus and four from downtown. It has 45 spotless rooms with cable TV, refrigerators, A/C, and a pool. (☎756-0910. Continental breakfast included. Doubles $75-85 $85. AAA discount.) The **University Inn Bed and Breakfast ❹,** 340 A St., near Central Park, has the feel of a country home in the middle of town. The innkeeper serves breakfast, and amenities include private bathrooms and cable TV. (☎756-8648. Doubles $65, with breakfast $78.)

Wednesday nights in the summer bring locals to Central Park (at 3rd and C St.) for the renowned **Farmers Market.** Among the market's attractions are fresh organic produce, booths housed by local restaurants, and live music. (☎756-1695; www.davisfarmersmarket.org. Sa 8am-1pm; Oct.-Mar. W 2-6pm; Apr.-Oct. W 4:30-8:30pm.) A true college town, Davis abounds with ethnic restaurants and quirky cafes. The downtown area between E and G St. south of 3rd St. is always a sure bet for a slice of pizza, a vegetarian smorgasbord, or a cup of joe. The

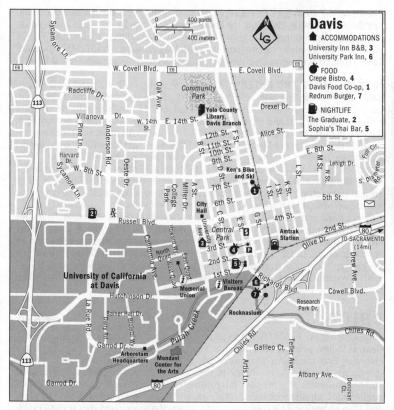

Davis Food Co-op, 620 G St., has a colossal selection of organic produce, fresh deli foods, international wines, and offers 15min. of free Internet access. (☎758-2667. Open daily 8am-10pm.) Practically a Davis legend, the **Crepe Bistro ❷**, 234 E St., is right in the middle of downtown and is staffed by longtime, heavily tattooed Davis residents who happily share their opinions. The bistro serves substantial crepes ($3-7) and a mean breakfast omelette ($4-8) in a delightful outdoor seating area. (☎753-2575. Open M-F 10:30am-10pm, Sa-Su 9:30am-10pm.) **Redrum Burger ❷**, 720 Olive Dr., is a 50s style diner with a bizarre history and attracts a diverse clientele. True carnivores come for the full 1 lb. burgers ($9). Ostrich burgers ($5.50) add an exotic twist, and super-thick milkshakes ($3.70) complement patties of any kind. (☎756-2142. Open daily 10am-10pm.)

◪ OUTDOOR ACTIVITIES. Of the UC schools, the **University of California at Davis** is the largest in square miles and also tops the list in agriculture and viticulture (vine cultivation). Step into nature at the **UCD Arboretum** on Putah Creek, which features trees and plants of Mediterranean climate from around the world, a soothing break from the summer heat. (☎752-4880. Open 24hr.)

Davis is marked by more than 40 mi. of bike trails and rocks. For trail maps and ratings, stop by the Visitors Bureau or a bike shop in town. **Ken's Bike and Ski**, 650 G St., rents bikes. (☎758-3223. Street bikes $10 per day, $6 per half-day; mountain bikes $28/

$14. Open M-F 10am-8pm, Sa 9am-7pm, Su noon-5pm.) For some practice before hitting the rocks outside, check out the **Rocknasium,** 720 Olive Dr., Ste. Z, in a warehouse just past Redrum Burger (see above), which offers climbing for all levels. The 70 routes include a bouldering cave and extensive lead climbing. (☎757-2902. Open M-F 11am-11pm, Sa 10am-9pm, Su 10am-6pm. $12, students $10. Equipment rental $8/$6.)

☜ ♫ NIGHTLIFE AND ENTERTAINMENT. At night, students party on the huge dance floor of **The Graduate,** 805 Russell Blvd., in the University Mall. Friday evenings bring drink specials and swarms of students. The walls usually reverberate with mainstream pop and hip-hop, but the music can be hit-or-miss; beware line-dancing nights. (☎758-4723. Open daily 10:30am-2am.) An older and more sophisticated crowd gathers at **Sophia's Thai Bar,** 129 E St., a tiny bar with tropical decor, aquariums, outdoor seating, and occasional live music. (☎758-4333. Open M-Sa 5pm-2am, Su 5-10pm.) South of 3rd St., **G Street** also houses many bars that get rowdy during the school year and early summer. For information on happenings around town, stop by the visitors bureau and pick up a copy of the *Davis Downtown Business Association News and Info* newspaper.

For cultural entertainment, check out the schedule at the new **Mondavi Center for the Arts,** on Mrak Hall Dr. at Old Davis Rd. Built for UCD by wine tycoon Robert Mondavi, this striking sandstone performance center draws heavyweights such as Joshua Redman, Ladysmith Black Mambazo, and Salman Rushdie, and is easily at the center of cultural enrichment in Davis. (Box Office at 1 Shields Ave. ☎754-2787; www.mondaviarts.org. Open M-F 10am-6pm, Sa noon-6pm, and 1hr. before performances. Tickets $20-50.)

CHICO   ☎530

Little Chico (pop. 66,676) fights a valiant war against the heat and boredom of the Central Valley, offering cool streams, shady streets, and plentiful beer to hikers emerging from the Sierra Nevadas or drivers desperate for an end to the freeway's monotony. A college town, home to the nation's second-largest municipal park and headquarters of a premier micro-brewery, Chico is a strange collection of intellectuals, hippies, rednecks, frat-boys, and hipsters. Founded in 1860 by General John Bidwell and his teetotalist wife, Annie, the town began as a genteel ranch with an Italianate mansion and a school for the improvement of Native Americans. By the 1980s the ranch had become a town, and the school had become California State University Chico, which Playboy Magazine named the number one party-school in America. Since the beer-sodden riots of 1989, Chico has more or less cleaned up its act, and the town bustles with a thriving independent arts scene and an incredible park that winds through and above the town.

▛ TRANSPORTATION. Chico is 90 mi. north of Sacramento on Rte. 99. The **Amtrak** train station (☎872-7245) is just a platform on Orange St., at W. 5th St. One train daily to: L.A. (15hr., $81); Oakland (4½hr., $30); Sacramento (2hr., $20). **Greyhound,** 450 Orange St. (☎343-8266), at the Amtrak station, sends three buses per day to: Red Bluff (45min., $13-14.50); Sacramento (2½hr., $15.50-17.50); and San Francisco (5½hr., $30.50-33). There is public **parking** at the lot at 2nd and Wall St., in the garage on Salem St. between 2nd and 3rd St., and at street meters.

▛ ▟ ORIENTATION AND PRACTICAL INFORMATION. A stroll through Chico's **downtown,** the area on Main St. and Broadway between 1st and 5th St., reveals a bustling scene of cafes, restaurants, shops, and bars, and the laid-back townies that frequent them. Downtown, numbered streets run northeast-southwest. Don't confuse the downtown numbered streets with the numbered **avenues**

Chico

🏠 ACCOMMODATIONS
Town House Motel, 1
Vagabond Inn, 5

🍎 FOOD
Sierra Nevada
  Brewing Co., 6
Tacos de Acapulco, 4
Upper Crust Bakery
  and Cafe, 3

🌙 NIGHTLIFE
Madison Bear Garden, 2

that start north of Big Chico Creek and intersect the **Esplanade** (es-plan-AID), which runs northwest through town, splitting to become Main St. and Broadway in downtown. The **Chamber of Commerce**, 300 Salem St., at 3rd St., has wall-to-wall tourist brochures. (☎891-5556 or 800-852-8570; www.chicochamber.com. Open M-F 9am-5pm, Sa 10am-3pm.) The **library,** 1108 Sherman Ave. (☎891-2761), at 1st Ave., offers 30min. free **Internet** access. (Open M-Th 9am-8pm, F-Sa 9am-5pm.) Other services: the **police,** 1460 Humboldt Rd. (☎895-4981); **Enloe Hospital,** 1531 W. 5th Ave. (☎332-7300), at the Esplanade; and the **post office,** 550 Vallombrosa Ave. (☎343-2068. Open M-F 8:30am-5:30pm, Sa 9:30am-12:30pm.) **Postal Code:** 95926.

🏠🏕 **ACCOMMODATIONS AND CAMPING.** Chico has plenty of inexpensive motel rooms, many for as low as $40 per night. **Town House Motel ❸,** 2231 the Esplanade, is a quiet, remodeled motel close to downtown. Standard rooms have cable TV and A/C. (☎343-1621. Singles from $39; doubles from $42.) **The Vagabond Inn ❹,** 630 Main St., on the edge of downtown, centers on a swimming pool. All rooms have HBO, and some have kitchens. (☎895-1323; www.vagabondinns.com. Continental breakfast included. Singles $59-69; doubles $69-70, with kitchen $77-89.)

To avoid the valley heat, Chicoan campers head to the Lassen National Forest, a short distance east of Chico. Lassen (see p. 195) has many campgrounds on Rte. 32, about 35 mi. north of Chico, near Lake Almanor. The camping closest to Chico is at the **Woodsen Bridge State Park Campground ❷.** Take Rte. 99 N for 12 mi., turn left on South Ave., and drive about 3 mi. There are over 35 shady sites with water and toilets. (☎800-444-7275. Self-register. Sites $18.) Numerous campgrounds also lie a little farther afield at **Lake Oroville,** 30 mi. from Chico on Rte. 99 S (9 mi. from Oroville Dam exit), which offers fishing, swimming, boating, and a 35 mi. bike trail. **Bidwell Canyon ❷** is very close to the water and used mostly by RVs. (☎534-2409. Full hookup $20.) **Loafer Creek ❶** is more forested and less crowded than Bidwell, with a beach and swimming area. (☎538-2219. Sites $14.)

📖 **FOOD.** It's not hard to find great-tasting, ridiculously inexpensive food and drink in Chico, given the unrelenting demand of the college population. A lavish **Farmers Market** fills the parking lot at 2nd and Wall St. (☎893-3276. Sa 7:30am-1pm.) Produce takes a back seat to live music and craft stalls when the entire town turns out for the **Thursday Night Market,** on Broadway between 2nd and 5th St. (Apr.-Oct. Th 6-9pm). ◪**Tacos de Acapulco** ❶, 429 Ivy St., at 5th St., is the stuff of drunken legend. Mexican pop plays through the night as revelers from the party hub of "5 and I" stumble in for gigantic and delicious burritos ($4). During the day it's more sedate, but the *carnitas* are always fresh and filling. (☎892-8176. Open daily 8am-3am.) Beer flows at the **Sierra Nevada Brewing Co.** ❸, 1075 E. 20th St., home to the brewery and an elegant taproom restaurant. Its California cuisine is overshadowed by Sierra Nevada on tap for a mere $2.50 per pint. Ask for the $8.50 tasting plate of all 15 seasonal beers. (☎345-2739. Lunch $6-10. Dinner $8-21. Open Su and Tu-Th 11am-9pm, F-Sa 11am-10pm.) Locals head to the **Upper Crust Bakery and Cafe** ❶, 130 Main St., for homemade baked goods and soups. A great place to read, it's conveniently located next to **The Bookstore,** which has a vast selection of used books. (Upper Crust: ☎895-3866. Open M-Sa 6:30am-9pm, Su 7:30am-4pm. The Bookstore: ☎345-7441. Open M-W 10am-9pm, Th-F 10am-8pm, Sa 11am-9pm, Su 11am-8pm.)

🔲🔃 **SIGHTS AND OUTDOOR ACTIVITIES.** Everyone agrees that the best things to do in Chico are to frolic in the awesome park and to indulge in the youthful revelry of this party-school town. With over 3600 acres, ◪**Bidwell Park** (☎895-4972) is one of the nation's largest municipal parks and undoubtedly Chico's most cherished attraction. Though throngs flock to its trails, parks, golf course, and swimming holes on hot summer days, it never feels overcrowded. The park has entrances along Vallombrosa Ave., Manzanita Ave., and 4th St., and is divided into two sections: Upper Park and Lower Park. Upper Park is largely undisturbed canyonland (save for a beautiful golf course), while Lower Park is more shady and developed for jogging, biking, playing baseball, and sunbathing. In Upper Park, **North Rim Trail,** on Wildwood Ave. upon entering the park, cuts through the hardy, rugged terrain. **Bear Hole,** the first of many swimming holes here, is often overrun with college kids. Farther north, the trails get rougher but the swimming holes get better (and more secluded). **One-Mile,** in Lower Park, near downtown by 4th St., is a well-groomed spot for picnicking, playing frisbee, or swimming in the amazing public swimming pool built into the river. The **Chico Creek Nature Center,** 1968 E. 8th St., is dedicated to exploring and preserving the park's wildlife. (☎891-4671. Open Tu-Su 11am-4pm. Free talks, exhibits, and nature walks.)

Besides Bidwell Park, Chico offers a number of worthwhile sights and cultural experiences. Pay homage to the malt and barley wizards at **Sierra Nevada Brewing Co.,** 1075 E. 20th St., with a tour of the impressive brass-and-mahogany brewery or equally expansive gift shop. (☎896-2198. Gift shop open daily 10am-6pm. Tours Tu-F 2:30pm, Sa noon-3pm.) The Chamber of Commerce has a walking tour pamphlet of charming downtown Chico. Highlights of the tour include: a stroll around the leafy campus of **California State University Chico,** at W. 2nd St. and Normal Ave. (☎898-6118 for guided tours); a visit to the **National Yo-Yo Museum,** home of the world's largest yo-yo (256 lb.), inside Bird in Hand gift shop at Broadway and W. 3rd St. (☎893-1414; open M-Sa 10am-6pm, Su noon-5pm); and a tour through historic **Bidwell Mansion,** 525 the Esplanade, the Pepto Bismol-pink home of Chico founders John and Annie Bidwell (☎895-6144; 45min. tours on the hour M-F noon-4pm, Sa-Su 10am-4pm; $2, under 16 free).

🔲🔃 **ENTERTAINMENT AND NIGHTLIFE.** On any given night, Chico overflows with cultural events and insanely cheap drink specials. Pick up the free *Chico News & Review* (www.newsreview.com/chico) for weekly entertainment listings. Escape the summer heat at the **Pageant Theatre,** 351 E. 6th St., an indie movie theater with sofas in the front row, brewers' yeast for the popcorn, and a mural of Godzilla on the wall. (☎ 343-0663; www.pageantchico.com. Tickets $5.75, under 12 and seniors $4.25. Cheap Skate M $2.50; get there early.) The **Blue Room,** 139 W. 1st St., shows bold, often unconventional plays to an appreciative audience and occasionally hosts traveling productions. (☎ 895-3749. Tickets $12, students with ID $10; Th $6. Box office open W-Sa noon-5pm.) The summer **Concert in the Park Series** hosts free musical and theatrical performances in Downtown Park Plaza, at 5th and Main St. (☎ 345-6500. May-Sept. F 7-8pm.) In the summer, local thespians take over Cedar Grove in Lower Park for **Shakespeare in the Park.** (☎ 891-1382. Call for schedule.) To truly experience the Chico party scene, head to the intersection of 5th and Ivy St. **(5 and I),** where college students stumble to bars or perform keg stands on the large front lawns of dilapidated frat houses. Among the many student bars in town, the **Madison Bear Garden,** 316 2nd St., at Salem St., is a classic, with its goofy decor and cheap beer. An enormous outdoor patio, dance floors, pool tables, and frequent specials ($1 pints Sa 9pm-1am) make this a hot spot for hundreds of rowdy revelers. Look for the horse and buggy hung from the ceiling. (☎ 891-1639. Burgers, salads, and sandwiches $5-7. Open daily 11am-2am.)

MERCED ☎ 209

The wide streets of downtown Merced (pop. 63,893) project an order and openness shared by the entire town. A good-natured atmosphere makes Merced one of the best places to stop before heading for Yosemite's northern entrance.

⌷ TRANSPORTATION. Self-titled the "Gateway to Yosemite," Merced has excellent public transportation into the park. The regional **YARTS** provides bus trips directly to Yosemite. Call ahead to ask about the varying schedules. (☎ 877-989-2787; www.yarts.com. Round-trip $20, seniors and under 16 $14, under 16 free with purchase of adult ticket. Fare includes park admission.) **Greyhound,** 710 W. 16th St. (☎ 722-2121 or 800-231-2222), runs buses to L.A. (9 per day, $35) and San Francisco (6 per day, $29-33). **Amtrak,** 324 W. 24th St., runs to L.A. and Reno, among other destinations. (☎ 800-USA-RAIL/872-7245. Open daily 7:15am-8:45pm.) Public transportation within Merced, simply called **The Bus,** may be flagged down at any street corner along designated routes. (☎ 384-3111 or 800-345-3111. Runs M-F 7am-6pm, Sa 9am-5pm. $1; day pass $3-4.)

▟▞ ORIENTATION AND PRACTICAL INFORMATION. Situated on Rte. 99 at the midpoint between Sacramento and Fresno, Merced maintains a small-town image along its quaint Main St. The area north of Bear Creek hosts standard suburban mall and restaurant chains. The **Merced Chamber of Commerce** and the **California Welcome Center,** 690 W. 16th St., have information on activities and Yosemite road conditions, as well as maps and brochures detailing local restaurants, accommodations, and transportation options. (Chamber of Commerce: ☎ 384-7092. Open M-F 8:30am-5pm. Welcome Center: ☎ 384-2791. Open daily 8am-5pm.) Other services include: the **police,** 611 W. 22nd St. (☎ 385-6912); **Mercy Hospital and Health Services,** 2740 M St. (☎ 384-6444; open 24hr.); and the **post office,** 2334 M St. (☎ 723-3741; open M-F 8am-5:30pm). **Postal Code:** 95340.

▛▟ ACCOMMODATIONS AND FOOD. The friendly hosts of the six-bed **Merced Home Hostel (HI) ❷** pick up guests from the bus and train stations between 5 and 9pm. Visitors must call in advance; without reservations, the address is not disclosed. (☎ 725-0407. Dorms $15, nonmembers $18; private rooms $34/$39.) Over half a dozen budget-friendly motels lie along the appropriately named **Motel Drive,**

two exits south of downtown Merced on Rte. 99, where there are plenty of chain motels like the refurbished **Days Inn ❹** (☎722-2726; singles $59-79; doubles $59-108) and the **Sierra Lodge ❸**, 951 Motel Dr. (☎722-3926; singles $45; doubles $55).

While fast-food joints are abundant, especially along Olive Ave., cheap home-grown eats can also be found. **Mandarin Shogun ❷**, 1204 W. Olive Ave., has an all-you-can-eat buffet (lunch $6; dinner $8) with a variety of entree and dessert choices. (☎722-6313, delivery 722-1881. 10% senior discount. Open Su-Th 11am-2:30pm and 5-9:30pm, F-Sa 11am-2:30pm and 5-10pm.) In the heart of downtown, **The Cinema Cafe ❸**, 661 W. Main St., alternates traditional diner breakfasts with more elaborate dinner cuisine ($10-15) that includes fresh fish and lamb. (☎722-2811. Breakfast and lunch around $6. Open M-F 6am-2pm, Sa-Su 6am-1pm; in summer also F-Sa 5-9pm.) All over Merced small, hole-in-the-wall Mexican joints serve tasty Mexican dishes and margaritas. Try **La Nita's ❷**, 1327 W. 18th St. (☎723-2291. Entrees $6-10. Open Tu-Sa 9am-9:30pm, Su 8am-9:30pm.)

◨ **SIGHTS.** Though most visitors see Merced as only a portal to Yosemite's wilderness, the area houses three small attractions. The old **Courthouse,** at 21st and N St., is the oldest building in Merced and houses a museum. Volunteers lead free tours, sometimes adding colorful, personal anecdotes. (☎722-6291. Open W-Su 1-4pm.) **Applegate Park** and its **Zoo,** 1045 W 25th St., provide 23 shady acres in which to escape the valley heat. The zoo houses rescued animals native to California, including mountain lions, bobcats, foxes, the occasional one-eyed animal, and an American black bear named Sissy. (☎385-6840. Open daily 10am-5pm; in winter 10am-4pm. $1.25, ages 3-10 $0.75, over 60 $0.50, under 3 free.) To the northwest of Merced is the **Castle Airport** and **Air Museum,** 5050 Santa Fe Dr., in Atwater. Aviation buffs and history enthusiasts can wander among the restored aircraft and a small collection of Air Force memorabilia. (☎723-2178. Open Dec.-Oct. M and W-Su 9am-5pm, Tu 10am-5pm. $7, seniors and children $5, under 7 free.)

FRESNO ☎559

Fresno (pop. 448,500) struggles to reconcile its agricultural past with an ever-growing urban population. Truly an asphalt jungle, the city is dusty, hot, and in many places crime-ridden. However, some interesting attractions, decent digs, and cheap eats are available for travelers headed for the mountains.

◨◪ **TRANSPORTATION AND PRACTICAL INFORMATION. Greyhound,** 1033 Broadway Ave. (☎268-1829), runs buses to L.A. (14 per day, $24) and San Francisco (7 per day, $26-$31). **Amtrak,** 2650 E. Tulare St., Bldg. B, sends trains to San Francisco and L.A., with more expensive tickets. (☎800-872-7245/USA-RAIL. Open daily 7:15am-8:45pm.) Local transportation is provided by **Fresno Area Express (FAX),** 2223 G St. (☎498-1122). For schedules and routes, visit the transportation offices at the Manchester Shopping Center, at Shields and Blackstone Ave. The **Fresno Chamber of Commerce,** 2331 Fresno St. (☎495-4800; www.fresnochamber.com; open M 9am-5pm, Tu-Th 8am-5pm, F 8am-4:30pm), and the **Convention and Visitor Bureau,** 848 M St., in the Water Tower (☎233-0836; open M-F 8am-5pm), have info on accommodations, food, and attractions. The main **post office** is located at 1900 E St. (☎497-7566. Open M-F 8:30am-5:30pm.) **Postal Code:** 93721.

◪◪ **ACCOMMODATIONS AND FOOD.** Chain motels line the highways that run through Fresno. The most inexpensive accommodations can be found off Rte. 99, with rooms averaging $40, but the area around Motel Dr. requires **extra caution.** Accommodations near **Shaw Avenue,** the major east-west thoroughfare, may be a safer (though more expensive) alternative. The **Red Roof Inn ❸**, 5021 N. Barcus

Ave., is a good choice with large, clean rooms. (☎276-1910 or 800-733-7663. Pool, cable TV, A/C. Pets allowed. Singles with queen-size bed from $49.) **Piccadilly Inn** ❺, 2305 W. Shaw Ave., is a high-end place where you get what you pay for: quiet, spacious, well-maintained rooms. A pool, spa, cable TV, A/C, and restaurant all add to the luxury. (☎226-3850. Singles from at $85.)

The trendy **Tower District,** on E. Olive Ave. between N. Palm Ave. and N. Blackstone Ave., is Fresno's best bet for good eats, as well as the gathering place of the young, the trendy, and the artsy. The **Daily Planet** ❸, 1121 N. Wishon Ave., masters contemporary American flavor in a dining room with Art Deco flair. Though the diners are often a mature crowd, the bar attracts a wider range of ages. (☎266-4259; www.thedailyplanet.us. *Prix fixe* dinners $10-17.) **Cafe Revue** ❶, 620 E. Olive Ave., is the place to see and be seen. A friendly staff serves up coffeehouse favorites in a chic cafe and patio area, and poetry books grace the tables. (☎449-1844. Drinks and pastries $1-4. Open M-Th 7am-11pm, F 7am-midnight, Sa 8am-midnight, Su 8am-11pm.) At **Livingstone's Bar** ❸, 831 Fern St., an eclectic cast of characters enjoys good eats. (☎485-5198. Dinner $10-20. Late-night happy hour W 10pm-midnight; drinks $2. Su brunch 10am. Open daily 11am-2am.)

⑥ SIGHTS. If you have time for only one thing in Fresno, stop by the ▨**Baldasare Forestiere Underground Gardens,** on Shaw Ave., one block east of Rte. 99. Forestiere migrated to Fresno from Sicily around the turn of the century to farm. But when he found hardpan instead of fertile topsoil, he moved underground, gardens and all, to escape the heat. His descendants now lead tours through the tunnels of his 40-room, dirt-walled house. (☎271-0734. Tours in summer W-Su at 10am, noon, and 2pm; in low season Sa-Su at noon and 2pm. $8, seniors $7, under 18 $6.) The **Fresno Metropolitan Museum,** 1515 Van Ness Ave., displays Ansel Adams photography, an educational science exhibit, and the largest institutional collection of puzzles in the US. (☎441-1444. Open Tu-W and F-Su 11am-5pm, Th 11am-8pm. $7, students and seniors $4, ages 3-12 $3. Th nights $1.) **Roeding Park** and **Chaffee Zoological Gardens,** 894 W. Belmont St., one block east of Rte. 99, are great for picnics. The 700-animal zoo is fairly standard, but offers camel rides when weather permits. (☎498-2671; www.chaffeezoo.org. Park entrance $1. Zoo open daily Mar.-Oct. 9am-5pm; Nov.-Feb. 10am-4pm. Zoo entrance $6, seniors and ages 2-12 $4.) Baseball enthusiasts and families enjoy the recently completed, $46 million Grizzlies Stadium, 1800 Tulare St., where the **Fresno Grizzlies** (☎442-1994, tickets 442-1047; www.fresno-grizzlies.com) play AAA-baseball.

BAKERSFIELD ☎661

Virtually every West Coast chain store has a home (or two, or three) in Bakersfield (pop. 230,771). The second-fastest growing city in the nation, Bakersfield is home to the world's largest ice-cream plant and the country's largest marketing cooperative and second-largest snack food. Convenient for the scores of long-haul truckers looking for a place to rest on the road to Fresno, Bakersfield is more of a pit stop than a tourist destination.

◨▨ TRANSPORTATION AND PRACTICAL INFORMATION. Greyhound, 1820 18th St. (☎327-5617), runs frequent buses to Fresno ($13), L.A. ($17), and San Francisco ($38). Bakersfield is serviced by **Golden Empire Transit (GET),** a reliable public transportation system. (☎869-2438; www.getbus.org. $0.75; day pass $1.75; monthly pass $25.) **The Greater Bakersfield Chamber of Commerce,** 1725 Eye St., is located at the intersection of 18th St. (☎327-4421. Open M 9am-5pm, Tu-F 8am-5pm.) Other services include: the **police,** 1601 Truxtun Ave. (☎326-7111); **Bakersfield Memorial Hospital,** 420 34th St. (☎327-1792; open 24hr.), at Union Ave.; and the **post office,** 1730 18th St. (☎861-4346). **Postal Code:** 93302.

CENTRAL CALIFORNIA

⌐◻ ACCOMMODATIONS AND FOOD. Bakersfield's reputation as a good overnight stop is well earned, as it teems with motels. Clean, safe chain motels cluster at the Olive St. exit off Hwy. 99 N and price wars keep things cheap. For a non-chain option, try the **California Inn ❸**, 3400 Chester Ln., behind Carl's Jr. at Real Rd., which offers a pool, spa, and sauna, as well as mini-fridges, microwaves, TV, laundry, and free wireless Internet access in every room. (☎328-1100. Singles $45-49; doubles $49-59.) **E-Z 8 Motels ❸**, 5200 Olive Tree Ct., offers a pool, spa, laundry, and rooms with TV and mini-fridge. (☎392-115. Singles $34; doubles $47.)

For a departure from typical freeway fare, head to **Wool Growers Restaurant ❹**, 620 E. 19th St., for French Basque food. Try the lamb chops ($18) or garlic chicken ($14), served in heaping portions. (☎327-9584. Open M-Sa 11:30am-2pm and 6-9:30pm.) **Jake's Tex-Mex Cafe ❷**, 1710 Oak St., is a local favorite for its Texas-style barbecue. The tri-tip beef ($8) and Jake's famous chocolate cake ($2) are unbeatable. (☎322-6380. Open M-Sa 11am-8:30pm.) For a sweet taste of Bakersfield tradition, hit up **Dewar's ❶**, 1120 Eye St. The candy shop and old-fashioned soda fountain have been in operation since 1909, and all their treats are perfected art. (☎322-0933. Ice cream and floats $1-5. Open Su-Th 10am-9pm, F-Sa 10am-10pm.)

◪ SIGHTS. Do-si-do over to **Buck Owens' Crystal Palace**, 2800 Buck Owens Blvd., a sort of Hard Rock Cafe for country music, with a restaurant, theater, and museum. Live music and dancing Wednesday through Saturday nights is popular with locals and tourists. (☎328-7560. Entrees $7-27. Cover $6-10. Open daily 11am-midnight.) The 16-acre **Kern County Museum** complex, 3801 Chester Ave., has over 50 structures dedicated to Kern County's history and culture. Buildings focus on local themes, including agriculture, community development, and native cultures. The new interactive petroleum exhibit traces the history of oil and its influence on Bakersfield. (☎852-5000; www.kcmuseum.org. Open M-Sa 10am-5pm, Su noon-5pm. Ticket office closes 3pm. $6, seniors and students $5, children $4.)

GOLD COUNTRY

In 1848, California was a rural backwater of only 15,000 people. That year, sawmill operator James Marshall wrote in his diary: "This day some kind of mettle…found in the tailrace…looks like gold." Rumors began spreading of untold riches buried in the hills, but media skepticism muted the excitement until President James K. Polk declared the rumors to be true in December 1848. By the end of the next year, some 90,000 miners from around the world had set off for California and its Mother Lode, a 120 mi. expanse of gold-rich seams. "Gold fever" prompted a stampede of over half a million prospectors over the next decade. Many of the first prospectors found the rumors to be accurate and made fortunes mining easily accessed surface gold. These stores were rapidly depleted, however, and few subsequent prospectors struck it rich. Miners, sustained by dreams of instant wealth, worked long and hard, but most could barely squeeze sustenance out of their fiercely guarded claims. Many died of malnutrition; Mark Twain described the miner diet as "beans and dishwater for breakfast, dishwater and beans for dinner. And both articles warmed over for supper." In Coloma, during one miner's funeral, a mourner spotted "color" (gold) in the open grave. In the ensuing frenzy, the coffin was removed, and everyone in attendance, including the preacher, took to the ground with shovels. Five years after the big discovery, the panning gold was gone, and miners could survive only by digging deeper and deeper into the rock or by using the highly erosive techniques of dredging and sluicing. By the 1870s, all but a few mines—and most of the towns around them—had been abandoned.

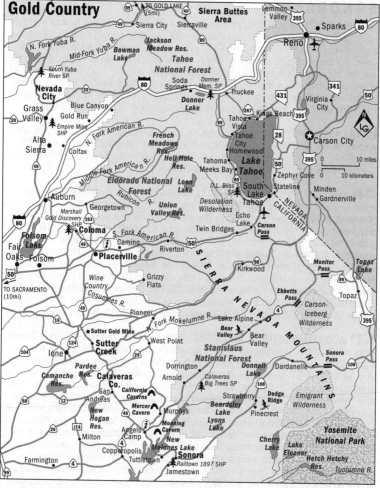

These days, you may only find a few old-timers panning for gold in local rivers or aimlessly guiding a metal detector, but remnants of the Gold Rush still attract a light, steady flow of tourists that makes up the bulk of the area's economy. The wealth once associated with the area hasn't carried over to the tourist industry, however, and residents of Gold Country seem aloof to the endless stream of cars entering their towns. Still, there is no shortage of historical landmarks or restored towns. Strung along the appropriately named Rte. 49, which winds through the tawny Sierra foothills, "Gold Rush Towns" are relaxed and dotted with the relics of the Gold Rush era. Traffic from the coast connects with Rte. 49 via I-80 through Sacramento, which serves as an apt starting point for a Gold Country tour. For those who tire of Gold Country lore, vineyard touring, river rafting, and spelunking are popular in the area. Most of Gold Country is about 2hr. from Sacramento and 3hr. from San Francisco.

SONORA
☎ 209

A band of roaming prospectors from Sonora, Mexico, were the first to stumble upon gold in the canyons around this area. The settlers named their small mining encampment after their homeland and created a famously wild Mexican frontier town. As news of gold spread, however, 49ers converged on the town and drove out the Mexican settlers with a steep foreigner mining tax. Today, only the most naïve come to Sonora in search of gold, though the city's tourist industry continues to benefit from its golden past. Situated close to the Sierra Nevadas, this quiet town attracts history buffs and curious hikers emerging from the mountains.

☐ TRANSPORTATION. Sonora is about a 2½hr. drive from Sacramento (100 mi.). **Amtrak** (☎ 800-USA-RAIL) has an unstaffed bus station outside the Sonora Days Inn. Buses depart to Sacramento (3hr., 3 per day, $29-31), San Francisco (4hr., 1 per day, $39), and Reno (9½ hr., 2 per day, $46-80).

◨◪ ORIENTATION AND PRACTICAL INFORMATION. Sonora's layout is complicated by the fact that two highways enter the town from three directions. **Washington Street** runs north-south through town and becomes Rte. 49 N at the north end. At the south end, it branches, and the east fork becomes Rte. 108. In the middle of town, Washington St. intersects with **Stockton Street,** which becomes Rte. 49 S. The **Visitors Bureau,** 542 W. Stockton Rd., gives out local info pamphlets and free maps of the county. (☎ 533-4420 or 800-446-1333; www.thegreatunfenced.com. Open M-F 9am-7pm, Sa 10am-6pm, Su 10am-5pm.) Other services include: the **police,** 100 S. Green St. (☎ 532-8143); **Tuolumne General Hospital,** 101 Hospital Rd. (☎ 533-7100; 24hr. emergency care); and the **post office,** 781 S. Washington St. (☎ 536-2728; open M-F 8:30am-5pm, Sa 10am-2pm). **Postal Code:** 95370.

◨◪ ACCOMMODATIONS AND FOOD. Built in 1896, the Spanish-style **Sonora Days Inn ❹,** 160 S. Washington St., stands out from most chain motels with its age and authenticity. The spacious rooms all have floral wallpaper, colonial furniture, A/C, and cable TV; most have fridges and microwaves. The hotel also houses a rooftop pool, steakhouse, and saloon. (☎ 532-2400 or 800-329-9466. Doubles from $70. Less in winter.) Cheaper accommodations that are only slightly less convenient lie on Rte. 108 east of Sonora. **Camping** is abundant in the Stanislaus National Forest (see p. 266), 15 mi. east of Sonora on Rte. 108. The Miwok Ranger District is closest to town, but has few developed campgrounds. **Dispersed camping** is free and does not require a permit in most of the forest, though campfire permits are often required and restrictions posted on roadside signs are strictly enforced.

Local farmers gather once a week in the summer for the Sonora **Farmers Market,** at Theall and Stewart St. (☎ 532-7725. Open May-Oct. Sa 8am-noon.) **Nanna's Cafe ❷,** 362 S. Stewart St., has a charming outdoor arbor perfect for a casual meal. This popular, subtly elegant cafe/deli serves up wood-fired pizzas and delicious sandwiches for $7-13. The large tri-tip sandwich is perfectly seasoned with caramelized onions and hot mustard. (☎ 533-3289. Open M-Th 7am-8pm, F 7am-9pm, Sa 8am-9pm, Su 11am-5pm.) **Banny's Cafe ❸,** 83 S. Stewart St., a block east of Washington St., has eclectic lunches ($6-11) and dinners ($11-15) that fuse Mediterranean, Southwestern, and Asian flavors. Entrees such as the grilled eggplant ($8) and the andouille sausage sandwich ($7) are welcome variants to standard miner fare. (☎ 533-4709. Open M-Sa 11am-9pm, Su 11am-8pm.)

◧◩ SIGHTS AND ACTIVITIES. Columbia State Historic Park is considered the best preserved Gold Rush town in all of Gold Country. Settlers first came to Columbia in 1850, and the town is virtually stuck in time, with proprietors in 19th-century dress, a 100-year-old stagecoach, and an active gold mine. The only transportation option in the park is horse and buggy for around $5. Take Rte. 49 N from Sonora to Parrot's Ferry Rd. and look for signs to the park. An office at 11255 Jackson St. has tourist info. (☎ 532-0150; www.parks.ca.gov. Open daily 8am-4:30pm. Free.) Just 10min. south of Sonora in Jamestown, **Railtown 1897 State Historic Park** is home to one of America's last authentic, operating railroad roundhouses. The park's locomotives and cars have appeared in over 200 films and television shows, causing Railtown to be nicknamed "The Movie Railroad." Tours and weekend train rides are offered. From Sonora, take Rte. 49 S. to 5th St. (☎ 984-4936. Open daily Apr.-Oct. every hr. 9:30am-4:30pm; Nov.-Mar. 10am-3pm. Train rides Apr.-Oct. 11am-3pm. $6, under 12 $3.) Just north of Sonora on Rte. 49 is **Tuttletown,** Mark Twain's one-time home, though there is now little more to see than a historic marker. The Stanislaus National Forest (see p. 266) offers fine hiking, fishing, mountain biking, and rafting opportunities. Gear up at the **Sierra Nevada Adventure Co.,** 173 S. Washington St. (☎ 532-5621. Kayaks and canoes from $45 per day.)

CALAVERAS COUNTY ☎ 209

Unsuspecting Calaveras County turned out to be literally sitting on a gold mine—the most bountiful, southernmost part of the "Mother Lode"—when the big rush hit. Over 550,000 lb. of gold were extracted from the county's earth during its heyday. A journalist from Missouri named Samuel Clemens, a hapless miner but a gifted spinner of yarns later known as **Mark Twain,** allegedly based "The Celebrated Jumping Frog of Calaveras County" on a tale he heard in Angels Camp Tavern. This short story single-handedly put both the county and the writer on the map, and Calaveras has capitalized on it since 1928 by holding the annual **Calaveras County Fair and Jumping Frog Jubilee** in the third week of May. The town gets hopping with over 35,000 spectators and upwards of 2000 frog competitors for the four-day event. (☎ 736-2561; www.frogtown.org. Tickets $11-13 per day.)

A drive along scenic **Route 49** is a great way to glimpse Calaveras County. Pint-sized **San Andreas,** at the junction of Rte. 26 and 49, is the county's hub and most densely populated area. The **Calaveras County Information Center,** in downtown Angels Camp, is a great historical resource and the place to go for frog-related apparel. (☎ 736-0049 or 800-225-3764; www.visitcalaveras.org. Open M-F 9am-6pm, Sa 11am-6pm, Su 11am-4pm.)

🌄 🏞 **SIGHTS AND OUTDOOR ACTIVITIES.** Calaveras County encompasses dramatically varied landscape, from rolling Sierra foothills in the west to 8000 ft. peaks in Stanislaus National Forest (see p. 266) in the east. Opportunities for outdoor recreation abound in the forest and in **Calaveras Big Trees State Park,** just inside Stanislaus National Forest on Rte. 4, about 35min. from Angels Camp. (☎ 795-3840, reservations 795-2334. Day-use $4.) Augustus T. Dowd discovered the first Sierra redwoods, **the world's oldest and largest living organisms,** in Calaveras's North Grove in 1852. Preservation of the North Grove was the objective when the area became a State Park in 1931. Today, two timeless groves, as well as numerous streams and lakes, comprise the park's 6500 acres. There are three primary trails. **North Grove Trail** (1 mi.), which begins at the visitors center parking lot, is a leisurely walk and has numbered markers highlighting historically significant redwoods. Pick up *A Guide to the Calaveras North Grove Trail* ($0.50 donation) for descriptions that correspond to the markers. The slightly more difficult, half-mile long **Grove Overlook Trail** looks down on the North Grove from the surrounding hills, providing impressive views of the treetops. About ten times as many trees (over 1000) can be found at the end of the more challenging—and hence quieter—3½ mi. **South Grove Trail.** Just after Beaver Creek Bridge along South Grove Trail is the trailhead to **Bradley Grove** (2½ mi.), which offers a chance to see young (about 30-year-old) sequoias. **Fishing** is permitted in the Stanislaus River and the stocked Beaver Creek with a license (available at local gas stations and sporting goods stores; late Apr. to mid-fall; 5 fish per day limit). **Camp** at **North Grove ❶**, right inside the park entrance, or **Oak Hollow ❶**, 4 mi. inside the park, both with piped water, flush toilets, and showers. (Sites $15, seniors $13.) In winter, family-friendly skiing at **Bear Valley** is the main activity. The mountain features 1900 vertical feet and 67 runs, including a half-pipe and terrain park. (☎ 753-2301; www.bearvalley.com. Day passes $43, ages 13-23 $36, ages 8-12 $15, ages 65-74 $10, under 7 and over 74 free.)

CAVERNS. Traditionally, those who flocked to Calaveras County were most interested in pay dirt underground. Today, many still head underground, but they're generally not looking for gold. A labyrinthine limestone cave network snakes below ground, offering tourists an exciting chance to view the Calaveras underworld. Three caverns have been developed for visitors. Descend the 100 ft. staircase into ▩ **Moaning Cavern,** 5350 Moaning Cave Rd., which holds the largest public vertical chamber in the state. Deep enough to hold the Statue of Liberty, the cavern is also the site where some of the oldest human remains in America were found. The Family Tour guides visitors down the 234 steps, while the more adventurous (over 18 or over 12 with parental consent) can rappel their way down. Reservation-only 3hr. adventure trips begin with the rappel and end with a guided journey through the depths of the undeveloped chambers and passages. (☎ 736-2708. Open daily in summer 9am-5pm; in winter 10am-4pm. Family Tour $12, ages 3-13 $6. Rappel $45. Adventure trip $99.) **Mercer Cavern,** off Rte. 4 on Sheep Rd. in Murphys, is a three-million-year-old living limestone cave. Royalty and a President have visited the cavern to see Mercer's brilliant multi-colored crystalline formations. All tours are 45min. and descend by walkway into six ten-million-year-old chambers. (☎ 728-2101; www.mercercaverns.com. Open Su-Th 9am-5pm, F-Sa 9am-6pm; in winter daily 10am-4:30pm. Tours $10, ages 5-12 $6.) During the Gold Rush, **California Caverns,** at Cave City, 9 mi. from San Andreas off Mountain Ranch Rd., served as a naturally air-conditioned bar and dance floor, and a shot of whiskey could be purchased for a pinch of gold dust. The caverns sobered up on Sundays for church services, and one stalagmite served as an altar. Now the caverns are host to 1hr. walking tours and various rugged spelunking trips that explore cramped tunnels, waist-high mud, and underground lakes. (☎ 736-2708. Open daily 10am-5pm. 1hr. walking tour $11, ages 3-13 $5.50. 2hr. spelunking expeditions $99, ages 8-16 $65.)

WINERIES. Calaveras County winemaking is as old as gold prospecting. Most of the area's nine flourishing vineyards are located on Rte. 49, just north of San Andreas, and on Rte. 4, near Murphys. The largest vineyard in the county, **Stevenot Winery,** 2690 San Domingo Rd., 3 mi. north of Main St. in Murphys, was established in 1973 by fifth-generation Calaveras resident Barden Stevenot and has won hundreds of awards for its bold creations. (☎ 728-0638; www.stevenotwinery.com. Main tasting room open daily 10am-5pm. 2nd tasting room at 451 Main St., in Murphys, open daily 10:30am-5:30pm.) **Ironstone Vineyards,** on Six Mile Rd., 1½ mi. south of Main St., produces 250,000 cases a year. Ironstone's wine-aging caverns were blasted out of the limestone using dynamite in 1989 and also served as the first tasting room. Today, spacious new visitor facilities include a museum, tasting room, demonstration kitchen, gallery, and deli. (☎ 728-1251; www.ironstonevineyards.com. Open daily 11am-5pm. Free 45min. tours daily 11:30am, 1:30, 3:30pm. Sa additional tour 2:30pm.)

SUTTER CREEK ☎ 209

With a more refined tourist set than its Gold Country neighbors, and its jettisoning of Gold Rush sentimentality in favor of a more contemporary approach, Sutter Creek is not your average Gold Rush town. This former mining encampment, named after the pioneering prospector John Sutter, was one of the Gold Rush's few success stories. Its bounty made fortunes for mine owners like Leland Stanford, who used his earnings to start a railroad business, become governor, and establish a university. Today, Rte. 49 turns into a short and quaint Main Street lined with shops and beautiful Victorian houses.

◼◪ TRANSPORTATION AND PRACTICAL INFORMATION. Sutter Creek is 67 mi. east of Sacramento via Rte. 50 to Rte. 49, and 90 mi. west of South Lake Tahoe. In town, Rte. 49 becomes Main St., which hosts the majority of historical sights and commercial activity. **Amador Regional Transit System** (☎223-2877; www.amadortransit.com) sends two buses per day to and from Sacramento to Rancho Murieta, where another bus goes to Sutter Creek for $1. Visitor information can be found at the **Sutter Creek Visitors Center,** at the end of Eureka St. in Knight's Foundry. (☎267-1344. Open M-F 9:30am-4pm, Sa 10am-3pm.) Other services in Sutter Creek include the **police** (☎267-5646) and the **post office,** 3 Gopher Flat Rd., near Main St. (☎267-0128; open M-F 8:30am-5pm). **Postal Code:** 95685.

◪◻ ACCOMMODATIONS AND FOOD. There are well over a dozen B&Bs within walking distance of town, including charming **Grey Gables ❺,** 161 Hanford St. (☎267-1039; www.greygables.com), and elegant **The Foxes ❺,** 77 Main St. (☎267-5882). Both have typical B&B decor and amenities for around $120-250 per night. The **Sutter Creek Inn ❺,** 75 Main St., a well-decorated Greek Revival house on a relaxing yard, claims to be California's first B&B. (☎267-5606; www.suttercreekinn.com. Doubles with bath from $82.)

Food in town is not cheap, with a number of restaurants specializing in fine dining and expensive wines. For those who prefer a home-cooked meal, check out the Sutter Creek **Farmers Market,** on Eureka St. at Rte. 49. (☎296-5504. Open Jun.-Oct. Sa 8-11am.) **The Back Roads Coffeehouse ❶,** 74 Main St., serves light lunch fare, freshly baked pastries and bagels, and caffeinated beverages. (☎267-0440. Open Tu-F 7am-3pm, Sa-Su 7am-4pm). The **Sutter Diner ❷,** 291 Hanford St., specializes in home cooking and hickory-smoked barbecue. Ask the friendly owners about daily barbecue offerings—they aren't on the menu. Most dishes cost $7-10. (☎267-1551. Open M-Tu 7am-2pm, W-Sa 7am-8pm, Su 7am-7pm.)

◙ SIGHTS. Most sights in town are on Main St. **Knight's Foundry,** at the end of Eureka St., built and serviced hard-rock mining equipment and is still in operation. The huge, outdated contraption operates on water power, just as it did in 1873. (☎267-0201. Call for a tour.) **Sutter Gold Mine,** 1 mi. north of town on Rte. 49, takes you into an abandoned hard rock gold mine. The family tour transports visitors on an underground shuttle, while the more strenuous 3½hr. deep mine exploration showcases a modern gold mine in action. (☎866 762-2837. Open daily 8am-6pm; in winter 9am-5pm. 1hr. family tours $10. Deep mine exploration $99 by reservation only.) Before Napa and Sonoma became California's wine country, the Sierra foothills were the state's biggest producer. Prohibition hit the region hard, however, and the area's 40 **vineyards** have only recently begun to prosper again. **Sutter Ridge Vineyards,** 14110 Ridge Rd., 1 mi. south on Rte. 49 and 2½ mi. east on Ridge Rd., is a 170-acre vineyard run by a fourth-generation wine-making family. (☎267-1316. Open F-Su 11am-4pm.) **Argonaut Winery,** 13825 Willow Creek Rd., 11 mi. from town, northwest via Rte. 49 and south via Willow Creek Rd., is a small vineyard with weekend tastings. (☎245-5567. Open Sa-Su 10am-5:30pm.)

PLACERVILLE   ☎530

In its Gold Rush prime, Placerville (pop. 9300) was the third-largest town in California. Today, restaurants and shops fill its restored, historic downtown. Beyond downtown, however, chain stores dominate and Placerville's Gold Rush charm is nowhere to be found. Relative to other Gold Country towns, Placerville seems less concerned with history and more comfortable as a contemporary small town.

⚹🔊 TRANSPORTATION AND PRACTICAL INFORMATION. About one-third of the way from Sacramento to Lake Tahoe on U.S. 50, Placerville is strategically positioned to ensnare campers, boaters, and skiers. Most streets, like **Main Street**, run parallel to U.S. 50 to the north. **Route 49** also bisects the town, running north to Auburn (10 mi.), and south toward Calaveras County. **Greyhound** (☎800-231-2222) makes drop-offs and pick-ups at 222 Main St. at Pacific St., going to Sacramento (1½hr., 2 per day, $12) and Reno (6hr., 1 per day, $20). The **Chamber of Commerce**, 542 Main St., has maps and info. (☎621-5885. Open M-F 9am-5pm.) Other services include the **police,** 730 Main St. (☎642-5210; www.hangtowncops.org) and the **post office,** 3045 Sacramento St., south of U.S. 50. (☎642-5280; open M-F 8:30am-5pm, Sa 8:30am-noon). **Postal Code:** 95667.

⚹📭 ACCOMMODATIONS AND FOOD. One of the best deals in this consistently overpriced town is the **National 9 Inn ❹**, 1500 Broadway, which has spotless new rooms, cable TV, A/C, and comfortable king-size beds. (☎622-3884. Singles $49; doubles $55-75.) **Camping** is plentiful in the Eldorado National Forest, east of town. **Sand Flat ❶**, 3800 ft., has 29 sites on U.S. 50, 28 mi. east of town. (Vault toilets, water. Sites $12.) **Dispersed camping** is free and does not require a permit, though campfire permits are required for fires and stoves.

For a *Dukes of Hazzard* experience, saunter into ⬛**Poor Red's ❸**, on El Dorado's Main St., 5 mi. south of Placerville on Rte. 49. The split-level bar and small dining room of this barbecue joint are always packed. Their famous two-glass "Golden Cadillac" (responsible for 3% of American consumption of galliano) is only $6. (☎622-2901. Sandwiches around $6. Entrees $9-17. Open M-Sa 5-11pm, Su 2-11pm.) The historic **Cozmic Cafe and Bar ❶**, 594 Main St., dates from 1859. It may initially look unexceptional, but in the back there is seating in a 150 ft. walk-in mine shaft. (☎642-8481. Sandwiches $5-6. Smoothies $3.50-5. Espresso $1.50-2.50. Th movie night. F open mic. Sa live band. Shows start around 7pm. Open M-W 7am-3pm, Th 7am-8pm, F-Sa 7am-11pm, Su 8am-3pm.) **Sweetie Pies ❷**, 577 Main St., is known for its huge cinnamon buns, full espresso bar, light lunches (sandwiches $6), and popular breakfast menu ($4-7). Homemade pie by the slice ($3.25) is delicious. Eat on the charming front patio. (☎642-0128. Open M-W 6:30am-4pm, Th-Su 7am-9pm.) Alternatively, forage for fresh food at the **Farmers Market** in the Ivy House parking lot. (Open Th 5-8pm, Sa 8am-noon.)

⚹🔊 SIGHTS AND OUTDOOR ACTIVITIES. Placerville was once known as "Hangtown, USA" due to its reputation for handing out speedy justice at the end of a rope. Now the **Historic Hangman's Tree,** 305 Main St., is a friendly neighborhood bar with a life-size replica of a hanged man (George) outside, and a ghost (Willy) inside. The old-fashioned bar keeps old-fashioned hours. (☎622-3878. Open M-Sa 6am-10pm, Su 6am-5pm.) The hills around Placerville are filled with fruit. By bike and car, travelers can tour the apple orchards and wineries off U.S. 50 in the area known as **Apple Hill.** The fall is particularly busy with public events, concerts, and plenty of apple-picking. **Larsen Apple Barn** (☎644-1415) has 12 varieties of apples and a large picnic area in which to enjoy them. A complete listing and map of orchards is available from the Chamber of Commerce (see p. 324) and at many orchards. Locals claim that **Denver Dan's,** 4354 Bumblebee Ln. (☎644-6881), has the best apple prices, while **Kid's,** 3245 N. Canyon Rd. (☎622-0184), bakes the best apple pie in the area. Most orchards are open only September through December, but **Boa Vista Orchards,** 2952 Carson Rd. (☎622-5522), stays open year-round, selling fresh pears, cherries, and other fruits from a huge open barn. For a free wine tasting, try **Lava Cap Winery,** 2221 Fruitridge Rd. (☎621-0175. Open daily 11am-5pm.) Also visit **Madroña Vineyards,** 2560 High Hill Rd. (☎644-5948), or the sophisticated **Boeger Winery,** 1709 Carson Rd. (☎622-8094; open daily 10am-5pm). Those visiting in June should not miss **Brewfest,** when hordes of middle-aged locals pony up $20 for a small tasting glass and wander to over 30 downtown businesses for free beer. (☎672-3436. Usually in late June.)

COLOMA

☎530

The 1848 Gold Rush began in Coloma at John Sutter's water-powered lumber mill, operated by James Marshall. Today the tiny town (pop. 175) is overshadowed by its Gold Rush history and the adjacent American River. The town revolves around the **James Marshall Gold Discovery State Historic Park.** A replica of the original mill sits near the site where Marshall first struck gold. (☎622-3470. Open daily 8am-dusk. Park entrance fee $4 per car, seniors $3; pedestrians $2, under 16 free.) Picnic grounds across the street surround the **Gold Discovery Museum,** 310 Back St., which presents the events of the Gold Rush through dioramas, artifacts, and film. (☎622-3470. Open daily 10am-4:30pm.) The real reason to come to Coloma is its wild natural beauty. The **American River's** class III currents, among the most accessible rapids in the West, attract thousands of rafters and kayakers each weekend. Farther north along Rte. 49, the river flows into **Folsom Lake** (see p. 308) and a deep gorge perfect for hiking and swimming. Many of the **rafting** outfitters in the county offer tours. Contact **Zephyr Whitewater** (☎800-359-9790), **Motherlode River Trips** (☎800-427-2387), **Oars Inc.** (☎800-346-6277), or **Whitewater Connection** (☎800-336-7238) to arrange an expedition. (Half-day trips $69-79, full-day $89-109.)

Camping can be found 2 mi. downstream at **Camp Lotus ❷,** 700 ft., on Basie Rd. off Lotus Rd. The sites are large and shady, and sit on the banks of the American River. (☎622-8672. Water, flush toilets, free hot showers, nearby store, and sand volleyball courts. Check-in from 2pm; check-out noon. Sites Su-Th $18, F-Sa $24.)

NEVADA CITY

☎530

Nevada City's Main St. is similar to that of many Gold Country towns, with restored buildings and an old-time feel. The historic facade, however, can't mask a vaguely new-age interior. The city's downtown caters to its health-conscious, sophisticated residents; organic produce, herbal tea, and a good read are never far away. A small town with a community feel, Nevada City is less touristed than other Gold Country towns.

⌂⌂ ACCOMMODATIONS AND FOOD. The ▧**Outside Inn ❹,** 575 E. Broad St., is a redesigned 40s-era motel, frequented by and supportive of outdoors lovers. The themed rooms range from the Celestial Room, with glowing stars, to the River Room, with photos of the Yuba River. For the cheapest rates, ask for the Autumn Room. (☎265-2233. Library with maps and recreational info, patio, grill, swimming pool, A/C, and Internet in every room. Rooms from $65, with kitchenette from $85.) The US Forest Service and California Parks Department operate **campgrounds** east of town on Rte. 20. **Scotts Flat Lake Recreation Area ❶,** 9 mi. east of town at Scotts Flat Rd., has 185 wooded RV and tent sites near Scotts Flat Reservoir. (☎265-5302. Water, flush toilets, hot showers. Sites $14-23.) To get a little farther from the crowds, free sites are available at **Bowman Lake,** 16 mi. north of Rte. 20 on Bowman Lake Rd. (4WD recommended.)

Nevada City's pesticide-reviling eaters congregate at **Earth Song ❸,** 135 Argall St., a natural foods market and cafe where vegetarians stock up on soy burgers, Welsh and Cornish cuisine, and organic produce. Delicious, largely organic entrees run $7-18. (☎265-9392. Market open daily 8am-9pm. Cafe open daily 11am-3pm and 5-8pm.) Another popular hangout is **Cafe Mekka ❷,** 237 Commercial St. The interior looks like a set designer's studio. Browse children's books, modern art, and chaises over an artichoke heart, pesto, and brie sandwich ($7), or sip coffee with the evening crowd. (☎478-1517. Open M 8am-7pm, Tu-Th 8am-10pm, F-Sa 8am-12am, Su 8am-11pm.)

◉ ⚠ **SIGHTS AND OUTDOOR ACTIVITIES.** Many buildings in town are of historical interest, including the dozens of **Victorian homes,** the **National Hotel** (claiming to be the nation's oldest in continual operation), and the historic 1860 **Firehouse.** A museum in the firehouse features exhibits on pioneer life, mining, the Nisenan and Maidu Indians, and the once-large Chinese population. (Open daily 11am-4pm; in winter M-Tu and Th-Su 10am-3pm. Free.) A walking tour map is available from the **Chamber of Commerce** at the end of Commercial St., near the Shell station and bank. (☎265-2692 or 800-655-6569. Open M-F 9am-5pm, Sa 11am-4pm.) Most historic buildings in Nevada City have been transformed into cappuccino bars, liberal bookstores, and vegetarian eateries.

History lives dankly on at the **Empire Mine State Historic Park,** at the Empire St. exit off Rte. 20 west of town. Peering down the cool, dark mine shaft, you may wonder if you'd risk a 12,400 ft. drop for big money—5.8 million ounces of gold were extracted from the mine during its 106 years of operation. The surrounding estate and woods make for peaceful hikes. Tours are offered on summer weekends. (☎273-8522; www.empiremine.org. Open daily May-Aug. 9am-6pm; Sept.-Apr. 10am-5pm. $2, under 17 free.)

The Nevada City area has trails for hikers of every ability. The **Nevada City Ranger Station,** 631 Coyote St., of the Tahoe National Forest, provides information on recreation and camping. (☎265-4531. Open M-F 8am-5pm, Sa 8am-4:30pm.) Take the **Loch Leven Trail** (3½ mi.) to the Loch Leven chain of granite-bed glacial lakes. The trailhead is just east of the Big Bend Visitors Center, at the Big Bend exit off I-80 east of Nevada City. **South Yuba State Park,** in Penn Valley off Rte. 20, features a number of hikes including an easy 1¼ mi. jaunt over the largest covered bridge in the West and around the river canyon. The **South Yuba River,** immortalized in countless miner and hippie songs, flows into idyllic swimming holes, many of which sit just under or around the covered bridge. More remote holes perfect for skinny dipping can be accessed by hiking the **Independence Trail.** Whitewater rafting and kayaking are great ways to experience the rugged beauty of the area. **Wolf Creek Wilderness,** 595 E. Main St. (☎477-2722), in Grass Valley, rents kayaks year-round and runs multiple kayaking trips and clinics. In the winter, they rent snowshoes and cross-country skis and hold snowshoe tours and avalanche clinics.

SIERRA BUTTES AREA   ☎530

A craggy ridge of volcanic peaks north of Donner Pass, the **Sierra Buttes** are the highlight of the **Lakes Basin Recreation Area,** a stretch of wilderness spanning Plumas and Tahoe National Forests. The snow-capped Sierra Buttes themselves rise dramatically farther up Gold Lake Rd., amid the surrounding small alpine lakes and densely forested hills. For trail access, take the Sardine Lake turn-off from Gold Lake Hwy., 1 mi. north of Rte. 49, bear right past Sardine Lake, and continue 1½ mi. past Packer Lake. (4WD recommended.) The mountains and over 40 glacial lakes in the area are among the least-traveled outdoor destinations in the state. Hiking trails lead through the small but beautiful range, while the lakes are ideal for fishing and boating. The area is 6 mi. north of Sierra City. Five miles east of Sierra City, on the corner of Rte. 49 and Gold Lake Hwy., lies **Bassetts Station,** an all-purpose establishment that has offered **lodging ❹,** dining, gas, and supplies for over 125 years. Stop in for info. (☎862-1297. Open daily 7am-9pm. Rooms $70-75.)

The Gold Lake Hwy. leads to **Sardine Lake,** 1 mi. from Rte. 49 past Bassetts Station. A number of self-register campsites sit on this small, shallow lake. Five miles farther on Gold Lake Hwy. is **Gold Lake** itself. The adjacent **Gold Lake Pack Station** offers guided horseback rides around the area, usually from 9am to 4pm; call for schedules. (☎283-2014. $28-98 per person, depending on the length of the ride.) The turn-off for **Frasier Falls** is 6 mi. north of Bassetts Station off Gold Lake Hwy., across from the first Gold Lake turn-off. The roads can be rough. Follow signs for 4 mi. to the Frasier Falls parking lot. The falls are then a 30min. walk. There are six **campgrounds ❶** along the route from the Bassetts turn-off to Frasier Falls. Most have toilets but no water or showers. (Sites range from free to $16.)

THE CENTRAL COAST

The 400 mi. stretch of coastline between L.A. and San Francisco embodies all that is purely Californian—rolling surf, a seaside highway built for cruising, dramatic bluffs topped by weathered pines, self-actualizing new-age adherents, and always a hint of the offbeat. This is the solitary magnificence that inspired John Steinbeck's novels and Jack Kerouac's musings. Clear skies, sweeping shorelines, dense forests, inland farming communities, and old seafaring towns beckon enticingly. The landmarks along the way—Hearst Castle, the Monterey Bay Aquarium, the historic missions—are well worth visiting, but the real highlight of the Central Coast is the journey itself.

HIGHLIGHTS OF THE CENTRAL COAST

SANTA CRUZ. Santa Cruz unites hippies, surfers, and students with fog-drenched forests, a bustling downtown, and a carnivalesque beachside milieu (p. 328).

MONTEREY BAY AQUARIUM. Elaborate displays at the immense aquarium create habitats for delicate sunfish, luxuriant kelp forests, and critters of the deep (p. 347).

BIG SUR. The quiet forests and roaring coastline of Big Sur continue to inspire eccentric mystics and solace seekers (p. 352).

HEARST CASTLE. Media mogul William Randolph Hearst's hilltop mansion fabulously commemorates its namesake's wealth and international travels (p. 358).

HIGHWAY 1

The apotheosis of Californian roads, **Highway 1** stretches along much of the state's coastline. Begun in 1920, the highway required $10 million and 17 years to complete. From San Francisco, the highway runs along the craggy shorelines of San Mateo County to loopy Santa Cruz and sedate Monterey. South of Monterey, the highway follows the 90 mi. strip of thinly inhabited coast known as **Big Sur** (see p. 352). Snaking through Big Sur's mountains, Hwy. 1 inches to the edge of jutting cliffs that hang precipitously over the surf. William Randolph Hearst's **San Simeon** (see p. 358) anchors the southern end of Big Sur. Between **San Luis Obispo** (see p. 360) and genteel **Santa Barbara** (see p. 366), the route winds past vineyards, fields of wildflowers, and miles of beaches. From Santa Barbara to lazy, surf-crazed Ventura, the highway curves and finally skirts the coastal communities of L.A. The **Bay Area** (see p. 134), **North Coast** (see p. 216), and **Los Angeles** (see p. 377) chapters cover other parts of the highway.

SANTA CRUZ   ☎ 831

One of the few places where the 1960s catchphrase "do your own thing" still applies, Santa Cruz (pop. 56,000) embraces sculpted surfers, aging hippies, free-thinking students, and same-sex couples. The atmosphere here is fun-loving but

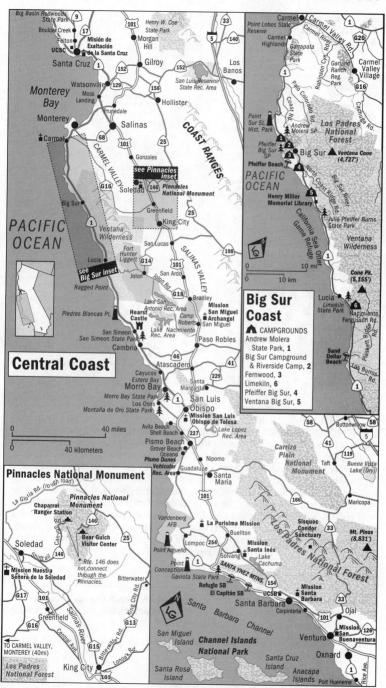

THE CENTRAL COAST

Central Coast

Big Sur Coast

▲ CAMPGROUNDS
Andrew Molera
State Park, **1**
Big Sur Campground
& Riverside Camp, **2**
Fernwood, **3**
Limekiln, **6**
Pfeiffer Big Sur, **4**
Ventana Big Sur, **5**

Pinnacles National Monument

TO CARMEL VALLEY,
MONTEREY (40mi)

THE CENTRAL COAST

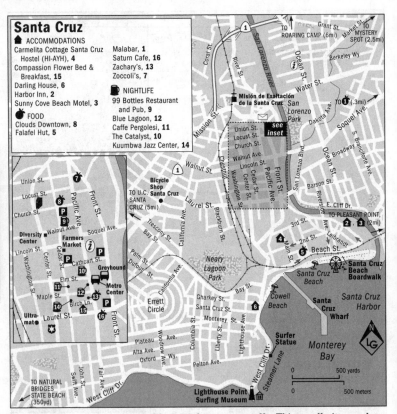

Santa Cruz

ACCOMMODATIONS
Carmelita Cottage Santa Cruz
  Hostel (HI-AYH), **4**
Compassion Flower Bed &
  Breakfast, **15**
Darling House, **6**
Harbor Inn, **2**
Sunny Cove Beach Motel, **3**

FOOD
Clouds Downtown, **8**
Falafel Hut, **5**

Malabar, **1**
Saturn Cafe, **16**
Zachary's, **13**
Zoccoli's, **7**

NIGHTLIFE
99 Bottles Restaurant
  and Pub, **9**
Blue Lagoon, **12**
Caffe Pergolesi, **11**
The Catalyst, **10**
Kuumbwa Jazz Center, **14**

far from hedonistic, intellectual but nowhere near stuffy. This small city exudes both Northern California cool and Southern California fun, whether you find it gobbling cotton candy on the Boardwalk or sipping wheatgrass at poetry readings.

Along the beach, tourism and surf culture reign supreme. Nearby Pacific Ave. teems with independent bookstores, cool bars, trendy cafes, and pricey boutiques. On the inland side of Mission St., the University of California at Santa Cruz (UCSC) sprawls luxuriously across miles of rolling forests and grasslands filled with prime biking routes and wild students. Restaurants offer avocado sandwiches and industrial coffee, while merchants hawk UCSC paraphernalia alongside flyers for courses. Be careful about visiting on Saturday or Sunday, since the town's population virtually doubles on summer weekends, clogging area highways as daytrippers make their way to and from the Bay Area.

TRANSPORTATION

Resident-traffic-only zones, one-way streets, and dead-ends can make Santa Cruz frustrating to navigate by car. It's cheapest to park at a motel or in free 3hr. public lots bordering Cedar St. and Front St. downtown.

Trains: Amtrak (☎ 800-872-7245). The closest train station is in **San Jose,** which can be reached by Greyhound bus.

Buses: Greyhound, 425 Front St. (☎423-1800 or 800-231-2222). Open daily 8:30-11:30am and 1-6:45pm. To: **L.A.** (6 per day; $44); **San Francisco** (M-Sa 4 per day, Su 5 per day; $11.50); **San Jose** (M-Th 4 per day, Su 5 per day; $6).

Public Transportation: Santa Cruz Metropolitan Transit District (SCMTD), 920 Pacific Ave. (☎425-8600, TDD 425-8993; www.scmtd.com), in the Metro Center. Open M-F 8am-4pm. The free *Headways* has route info. Buses run daily 6am-11pm. $1.50, seniors and disabled $0.75, under 46 in. free; day pass $4.50/$2.25/free. The bus to **San Jose** departs M-F 4:50am-9:25pm approximately every hr., Sa-Su 5:50am-9:05pm less frequently. $4, seniors and disabled $2. A **free beach shuttle** runs June-Aug. daily every 15min. 11am-7pm between the downtown Metro Center and beach boardwalk.

Taxi: Yellow Cab (☎423-1234). Base $3, $2.25 per additional mi. 24hr.

Bike Rental: The Bicycle Shop Santa Cruz, 1325 Mission St. (☎454-0909). Mountain or round-the-town bikes $10 per hr., $40 per day. 2hr. min. rental. Open M-Sa 10am-6pm, Su 11am-5pm. **Family Cycling Center,** 914 41st Ave. (☎475-3883). Kid trailers $15 per day; beach cruisers $25 per day; mountain bikes $30 per day. Open M-Sa 10am-6pm, Su 10am-5pm.

◪ 🛈 ORIENTATION AND PRACTICAL INFORMATION

Santa Cruz is on the northern tip of Monterey Bay, 65 mi. south of San Francisco. Through western Santa Cruz, Hwy. 1 becomes **Mission Street.** The **University of California at Santa Cruz (UCSC)** blankets the hills inland from Mission St. Southeast of Mission St. lie the waterfront and the downtown. Down by the ocean, **Beach Street** runs roughly east-west. The narrow **San Lorenzo River** runs north-south, dividing the boardwalk scene from quiet, affluent residences. **Pacific Avenue** is the main drag downtown. Along with **Cedar Street,** Pacific Ave. carves out a nightlife niche accessible from the beachside motels. It's about a 15min. walk between the beach and downtown.

Visitor Information:

    Santa Cruz County Conference and Visitor Council, 1211 Ocean St. (☎425-1234 or 800-833-3494; www.santacruz.org). Extremely helpful staff. Publishes the free *Santa Cruz County Traveler's Guide,* which has tourist info and discounts. Cyclists should pick up the extensive "bike adventure kit." Open M-Sa 9am-5pm, Su 10am-4pm.

    Downtown Info Center, 1126 Pacific Ave. (☎459-9486). Open daily noon-6pm. An information **kiosk** (☎421-9552) sits to the left of the Santa Cruz Wharf. Open June-Aug. daily 10am-5pm.

    California Parks and Recreation Department (☎429-2850). Info on camping and beach facilities in Santa Cruz; for reservations. Open M-F 8am-5pm.

GLBT Organizations: Diversity Center, 177 Walnut Ave. (☎425-5422; www.diversity-center.org). Distributes *Manifesto* ("the ultimate gay guide to Monterey Bay") and the *Lavender Reader,* a quarterly. Helpful staff. Info about events. Open daily; hours vary.

Laundry: Ultramat, 501 Laurel St. (☎426-9274), at Washington St. Wash $2, dry $0.25 per 7min. Morning wash special M-Th 7-11am ($1.25). Open daily 7am-midnight; last wash 10:30pm.

Police: 155 Center St. (☎471-1131). Open 24hr.

Hotlines: Weather Conditions, ☎656-1725. 24hr. **Women's Crisis Line,** ☎685-3737. 24hr. **Suicide Prevention Service,** ☎458-5300. 24hr.

Medical Services: Santa Cruz Dominican Hospital, 1555 Soquel Dr. (☎462-7700). Take bus #71 on Soquel Dr. from the Metro Center. Open 24hr.

Library and Internet Access: 224 Church St. (☎420-5730). Internet available in 1hr. sessions, but expect a wait. Internet is free with library card (current California library card and proof of address in that library's jurisdiction required) or $5 per hr. Open M-Th 10am-8pm, F 10am-5pm, Sa 10am-5pm, Su 1-5pm.

Post Office: 850 Front St. (☎426-8184). Open M-F 9am-5pm. **Postal Code:** 95060.

⌐ ACCOMMODATIONS

Santa Cruz gets jam-packed during the summer, when room rates skyrocket and availability plummets. Surprisingly, the nicer motels tend to have reasonable summer weekend rates but more expensive rates at other times. Reservations are always recommended. Shop around—price fluctuation can be outrageous. Camping may be the best budget option.

Carmelita Cottage Santa Cruz Hostel (HI-AYH), 321 Main St. (☎423-8304), 4 blocks from the Greyhound stop and 2 blocks from the beach. Centrally located but in a quiet neighborhood, this 40-bed Victorian hostel is run by a young staff. Chores requested. Storage lockers available. Linens included. Towels $0.50. Overnight parking free; day permits $1.25. July-Aug. 3-night max. stay. Reception 8-10am and 5-10pm. Lockout 10am-5pm. Strict curfew 11pm. Call for reservations. Dorms $18, nonmembers $21, ages 12-17 $14, ages 4-11 $10, under 3 free. ❷

Harbor Inn, 645 7th Ave. (☎479-9731). Take Murray St. west from downtown until it turns into Eaton St; the inn is a few blocks north of Eaton St. A beautiful 19-room inn well off the main drag. In late June, you can pick plums from the trees out back. Rooms have queen-size bed, cable TV, microwave, coffeemaker, and fridge. Some rooms with shared bath. Check-in 2-7pm; call to arrange late check-in. Check-out 11am. Reservations recommended. High-season singles Su-Th $70-115, F-Sa $105-125; doubles Su-Th $90-115, F-Sa $125-135. Low-season singles Su-Th $50-70, F-Sa $70-85; doubles Su-Th $70-85, F-Sa $85-95. ❺

Compassion Flower Bed & Breakfast, 216 Laurel St. (☎466-0420). Beautifully restored Victorian home in downtown. Gourmet breakfast, garden patio, and hot tub. Run by two women and their children, who take extra care to be environmentally friendly. Will cater to vegan, vegetarian, and special diets. 2-night min. stay may be required on weekends. Singles and doubles Su-Th $115-155, F-Sa $125-175. ❺

Darling House, 314 West Cliff Dr. (☎458-1958; www.darlinghouse.com). A 1910 oceanfront mansion B&B on lovely gardens. Shared bathrooms, but each room has a sink. Continental breakfast included. Usually 2-night min. on weekends. Singles and doubles $95-260, depending on view. Check with visitors center for discounts. ❺

Sunny Cove Beach Motel, 2-1610 E. Cliff Dr. (☎475-1741), near Schwan Lagoon. Far from downtown, but the pleasant, well-kept suites have kitchens and cable TV. Outdoor pool. Market and beach 1 block away. Pets $5 per day. Rooms $50-90; in summer $80-150. Weekly rates available. ❸

⌐ CAMPING

Reservations for state campgrounds can be made through ReserveAmerica (☎800-444-7275) and should be made early. Sites below are listed from north to south. Big Basin Redwoods State Park is accessible by public transportation. As with any other kind of lodging in Santa Cruz, campgrounds fill up quick and early.

▨ Big Basin Redwoods State Park, 21600 Big Basin Way (☎338-8860; www.bigbasin.org), in Boulder Creek, 23 mi. northwest of Santa Cruz. Go north on Rte. 9 to Rte. 236 through Boulder Creek. Removed from the city, Big Basin offers the best camping in the region. 80 mi. of cool, breezy trails, including the most picturesque 17 mi. of the 2-day, 30 mi. **Skyline-to-the-Sea Trail** (trailhead parking $6). To reserve one of the 145 campsites with coin showers, call ReserveAmerica (☎800-444-7275); for tent cabins, call ☎800-874-8368. Registration for backpacking mandatory ($5 fee). Sites $20. Day use $6 per car, backcountry camping (including parking) $10. ❶

Sunset State Beach, 201 Sunset Beach Rd. (☎763-7063), in Watsonville, on Hwy. 1, 16 mi. south of Santa Cruz. Exit on San Andreas Rd., follow San Andreas Rd. for about 6 mi., and turn right onto Sunset Beach Rd. Wind through eucalyptus-lined roads and end up by a stunning beach. Food lockers, picnic tables, and coin showers. 90 sites with fire rings. Reservations highly recommended in summer. Sites $20. Day use $6, seniors $5; hike/bike $3. ❶

Manresa Uplands State Beach Park, 205 Manresa Rd. (☎761-1795), in La Selva Beach, 13 mi. south of Santa Cruz. Exit Hwy. 1 at San Andreas Rd., follow San Andreas Rd. for about 3.5 mi., and turn right on Sand Dollar Dr. 64 walk-in tent sites. Sites $20; day use $6 per car, seniors $5, disabled $3. ❶

▌ FOOD

Santa Cruz offers an astounding number of budget eateries. The healthful restaurant community goes out of its way to embrace vegans—tofu can be substituted for just about anything. Fresh local produce sells at the **Farmers Market** at Lincoln and Cedar St. downtown. (W 2:30-6:30pm.)

▨ Zoccoli's, 1534 Pacific Ave. (☎423-1711). This phenomenal Italian deli makes hot and cold sandwiches for $4.50-5.25. Daily pasta specials (small $4-5, large $6-7) come with salad and garlic bread. Only the freshest ingredients. Open daily 9am-6pm; in summer M-Sa 9am-7pm, Su 10am-6pm. ❷

▨ Malabar, 1116 Soquel Ave. (☎423-7906), between Cayuga St. and Seabright Ave. Healthy, vegetarian Sri Lankan cuisine. Incredible flatbread served by candlelight with *ghee* and garlic ($3). Hefty entrees are reasonably priced ($8.50-9.50). Open M-Th 11am-2:30pm and 5:30-9pm, F 11am-2:30pm and 5:30-9:30pm, Sa 5:30-9:30pm. ❷

▨ Saturn Cafe, 145 Laurel St. (☎429-8505), at Pacific Ave. A 50s diner with a funky modern attitude, Saturn Cafe orbits in its own unique world with deals like "Tu-Tu Tuesday" ($2 fry baskets; $2 pints; 2 PBRs for $2) and "Wednesday Wigout" (all patrons wearing wigs get 20% off their meal). Interesting display-box tables make great conversation starters as you gulp and grub until the wee hours of the morning. Open daily 11:30am-3am. Kitchen closes 1:45am. ❷

Zachary's, 819 Pacific Ave. (☎427-0646). With savory potatoes, freshly baked bread, and enormous omelettes, laid-back Zachary's will give you reason to laze about on the beach for the rest of the day. Breakfast (2 eggs, oatmeal-molasses toast, and hash browns) for under $5. Eat at the counter to avoid the wait. Open Tu-Su 7am-2:30pm. ❶

Falafel Hut, 309 Beach St. (☎423-0567), across the street from the Boardwalk. A good place for a quick late-night snack, serving a variety of Middle Eastern and American dishes. The Lebanese owners pride themselves on their falafel sandwiches ($4.25), but the chicken ($5) is hard to beat. Open daily 11am-11pm. ❶

Clouds Downtown, 110 Church St. (☎429-2000). Fresh American cuisine with a Pacific Rim influence in a modern and friendly atmosphere. Attracts a more mature, affluent crowd. Salads $5-12. Lunch $9-10. Dinner $9-16. Open M-Th 10am-11pm, F-Sa 11am-11pm, Su 11am-10pm. Bar open F-Sa until 2am. ❹

◔ SIGHTS

SANTA CRUZ BEACH BOARDWALK. Santa Cruz has a great beach but the water is frigid. Many casual beachgoers catch their thrills on the Boardwalk, a three-block strip of over 25 amusement park rides, guess-your-weight booths, shooting galleries, and corn-dog vendors. It's a gloriously tacky throwback to 50s-era beach culture, providing a loud, lively diversion that seems to attract every

SURF'S UP!

As a proud Michigander, I am always quick to assert that the Great Lakes *do* have beaches, but after surfing on the Pacific coast I must admit Lake Michigan's ripples simply don't count as waves.

I was a little intimidated as I approached my first surfing lesson and my instructor, Corey. It didn't help that he was a sculpted, bronze Adonis and I was a pasty, pudgy Casper. Nevertheless, I signed my life away on a release form and grabbed a 7 ft. board marked with the nicks and dents of novice surfers and, for all I knew, shark bites.

With the rush that comes only from jumping full-force into 55°F water, I paddled out into the oncoming waves. After a number of failed attempts, I was ready to conquer what would be the last wave of the day. I was shooting fast on a wall of water, clutching my board for dear life, until it dawned on me to attempt standing up and maybe even some kind of neat backflip that would make the girls swoon. I was crouched and ready to join the ranks of surfing legends. I was nearly standing. I was exhilarated. I was...quickly head over heels in the swirl of the ocean.

I emerged (eventually) from the arms of the sea, exhausted and physically drained, but filled with a respect for surfers and a desire to hit the waves again—if only to win back my self-respect.

—Brian J. Emeott

sun-drenched family, couple, and roving pack of teenagers in California. Highly recommended is the ◨**Giant Dipper,** a 1924 wooden roller coaster, where Dirty Harry met his enemy in 1983's *Sudden Impact*. If stomach-turning rides don't sound appealing, there's always Buccaneer Bay Miniature Golf or arcade games, both inside Neptune's Kingdom. While the Boardwalk is relatively safe, be cautious of the surrounding area at night. *(Boardwalk open daily June-Sept. 6, plus many low-season weekends and holidays. Some height restrictions. $30 per 60 tickets, with most rides 4 or 5 tickets; Day pass $26. Miniature golf $5.)*

UNIVERSITY OF CALIFORNIA AT SANTA CRUZ (UCSC).

Five miles northwest of downtown sprawls this 2000-acre campus, accessible by bus (#10, 12, 15, 16, 19, 20, or 22), car, or bicycle (for those who brave the uphill climb). In the 1960s, governor Ronald Reagan's plan to make UCSC a "riot-proof campus" (free of a central point where radicals could inflame a crowd) had a beneficial side effect: the university's decentralized and forested layout. Although the campus appears tranquil, spread out over spectacular rolling hills and redwood groves, Santa Cruz is famous (or infamous) for its leftist politics and conspicuous drug culture. Once the "safety school" of the UC system, UCSC now turns away scores of aspiring Banana Slugs (the school's mascot). Student-led tours of the campus are available by reservation only. *(Parking permit required M-F; available at the kiosk inside the main campus entrance, the police station, or the parking office; $4.)* Trails behind the campus are perfect for day hikes. The UCSC **Arboretum,** one of the finest in the state, grows some of the world's rarest flowers. *(Open daily 9am-5pm; July-Aug. F until 7pm. Free)* Also impressive is the UCSC **Farm and Garden,** where students of the Center for Agroecology and Sustainable Food Systems are hard at work growing acres of vegetables, plants, and flowers. The **Seymour Marine Discovery Center,** at Long Marine Laboratory, is another fascinating spot for nature lovers. Located on the bluffs overlooking Monterey Bay, the center exhibits current scientific research for the public to observe and touch. *(100 Shaffer Rd. ☎ 459-3799. $5; students, ages 6-16 and over 60 $3; under 5 free. 1st Tu of every month free.)*

SURFER STATUE AND SANTA CRUZ SURFING MUSEUM.

The bronze Surfer Statue, just northeast of the lighthouse on W. Cliff Dr., is a monument "dedicated to all surfers, past, present, and future." This inspirational figure, erected in 1991, is often graced with a *lei*. Inside the lighthouse is a small surfing museum, which opened in 1986. The main room displays vintage artifacts, photos, and videos, concentrating on the personal stories of local surfers from the 1920s to the present. *(At Pelton Ave. near Steamer's Ln. ☎ 420-6289. Open M and Th-Su 10am-5pm. Free.)*

SANTA CRUZ WHARF. Jutting off Beach St. is the longest car-accessible pier on the West Coast. Seafood restaurants and souvenir shops will try to distract you from the expansive views of ocean, beach, and Boardwalk. Munch on homemade saltwater taffy or fudge in a variety of flavors from local favorite **Marini's Munchies** while watching sea lions hang out on rafters beneath the end of the pier. *(Parking $2 per hr., under 30min. free. Disabled patrons get 90 min. free parking. Marini's Munchies: ☎ 423-7258. Taffy $2.50 per lb. Fudge $3.50 per lb.)*

OTHER SIGHTS. The peaceful adobe church and fragrant garden at **Misión de Exaltación de la Santa Cruz** offer contemplative quiet. *(130 Emmet St. Head north on Emmet St. off Mission St. ☎ 426-5686. Open Tu-Sa 10am-4pm, Su 10am-2pm. Donation requested.)* The **Mystery Spot** is a cult-favorite tourist trap of supposedly unexplainable optical illusions. *(465 Mystery Spot Rd., off Market St. northeast of downtown. ☎ 423-8897; www.mysteryspot.com. Open daily 9am-7pm. Tours last 30-45min. $5, under 4 free.)*

BEACHES AND OUTDOOR ACTIVITIES

The **Santa Cruz Beach** (Cowell Beach) is broad, reasonably clean, and packed with volleyball players. If you're seeking solitude, you'll have to venture farther afield. Away from the main drag, beach access points line Hwy. 1. Railroad tracks, farmlands, and dune vegetation make several of these points somewhat difficult to reach, but the beaches are correspondingly less crowded. Beach maps are listed in the *Santa Cruz Traveler's Guide*, available at the visitors center on Ocean St. (see p. 331). Many of the sites listed under **Camping** (see p. 332) open onto pristine and unfrequented beaches. Those who want to **bare everything** are known to head north on Hwy. 1 to the **Red, White, and Blue Beach,** down Scaroni Rd. A piece of wood and mailbox painted in patriotic colors that marks the elusive turn-off to the beach. Sunbathers must be 18 or accompanied by a parent. (Beach open daily Feb.-Oct. 10am-6pm. $10, after 3pm $15.) For a free all-over tan and party atmosphere, others try the **Bonny Doon Beach,** off Hwy. 1 at Bonny Doon Rd., 6 mi. north of Santa Cruz. Magnificent cliffs and rocks surround this windy and deserted spot.

The best vantage points for watching **surfers** are along W. Cliff Dr. To learn more about the activity, stop in at **Steamer's Lane,** an area of deep water off the point where surfers have flocked since Hawaiian "Duke" Kahanamoku kick-started California's surf culture here nearly 70 years ago. Surfers also gather at the more remote "Hook" along **Pleasure Point,** south of Santa Cruz in Live Oak. For surfing lessons, contact the **Richard Schmidt Surf School.** Schmidt is locally respected for his ability to get anyone surfing. (☎ 423-0928; www.richardschmidt.com. 1hr. private lesson $80; 2hr. group lesson $80. Equipment included.)

Around the point at the end of W. Cliff Dr. is **Natural Bridges State Beach.** Only one natural bridge remains standing, but the park offers a pristine beach, awe-inspiring tide pools, and tours during **monarch butterfly** season (Oct.-Mar.). In November and December, thousands of the stunning butterflies swarm along the beach and cover the nearby groves with their orange hues. (☎ 423-4609. Open daily 8am-dusk. Parking $6, seniors $5, disabled $3.) During whale-watching season (Dec.-Mar.), boats depart from the Santa Cruz Municipal Wharf. Trip costs vary, but hover around $30. Some tours guarantee sightings. For more info, contact the Santa Cruz Visitors Info Center (☎ 425-1234).

THE CENTRAL COAST

THE CENTRAL COAST

Watersports enthusiasts will find ample activities in Santa Cruz. Parasailing and other pricey pastimes are popular on the wharf. **Kayak Connection,** 413 Lake Ave., offers 3 hr. tours of the Elkhorn Slough (9:30am or 1:30pm; $45) and the Monterey Bay ($40), and rents ocean-going **kayaks** at decent rates. Take Murray St. east. Murray St. becomes Eaton St. Kayak Connection is one block south of Eaton St. on Lake Ave. (Slough tours ☎724-5692, bay tours 479-1121. Open-deck single kayak $30 per day, closed-deck single kayak $33. Paddle, life jacket, brief instruction, and wetsuit included with rentals. Open M-F 10am-5pm, Sa-Su 9am-6pm.) Beware of cheaper rental agencies that don't include instruction sessions; closed-deck ocean kayaking can be dangerous. You must provide American Canoe Association certification for a closed-deck kayak unless you go to **Elkhorn Slough,** a beautiful estuary where it is relatively safe for inexperienced kayakers to use a closed-deck kayak. This incredible spot has an amazing array of wildlife.

Get a grip **rock climbing** on 13,000 sq. ft. of artificial terrain at **Pacific Edge,** 104 Bronson St., #12. The gym also includes a weight room, cardio equipment, a sauna, and showers. Take Murray St. east, turn left on Seabright Ave., and an immediate right onto Watson St.; Pacific Edge is in view where Watson St. meets Bronson St. (☎454-9254. Day pass for experienced climbers $14, ages 11 and under $7. Basic safety classes for beginners over 12 years old offered Th 7-9pm, Sa-Su 10:30am-12:30pm and 3:30-5:30pm. $31.50. Open M 4-10pm, Tu and Th 8am-10pm, W and F 11am-10pm, Sa 10am-9pm, Su 10am-7pm.)

🎵🎭 ENTERTAINMENT AND NIGHTLIFE

Underage kids and those asking for spare change gather downtown, especially along Pacific Ave. Nevertheless, this strip is also home to a host of buzzing coffee shops and a few laid-back bars. There are comprehensive weekly events listings in the free local publications *Good Times* and *Metro Santa Cruz*, and also in *Spotlight* in Friday's *Sentinel* (all available at cafes and bookstores). The Boardwalk bandstand hosts free summertime concerts, usually by oldies bands, on Friday around 6:30 and 8:30pm. The Santa Cruz Parks and Recreation Department (see p. 331) publishes info in the free *Summer Activity Guide.*

📷 **99 Bottles Restaurant and Pub,** 110 Walnut Ave. (☎459-9999). Try one of 99 beers (pints $4) to complement standard bar fare (burgers $6.80-8.30) or if you have a lot of time to kill and superhuman tolerance, try all 99 to join the wall of fame. This modest but lively bar in the heart of downtown is more than a beer lover's dream, with M karaoke and W quiz night. Happy hour M and F 4-6pm, Tu and Th 4-6pm and 10pm-1:30am; beers $3, pitchers $8.75. 21+ and appetizers only after 10pm. Open M-Th 11:30am-1:30am, F-Sa 11:30am-2am, Su 11:30am-midnight.

Blue Lagoon, 923 Pacific Ave. (☎423-7117). Mega-popular gay-straight club has won lots of local press awards, from "best bartender" to "best place you can't take your parents." 3 pool tables and dancing people everywhere. Happy hour daily 4-9pm; $2.75 drinks. Stronger-than-the-bouncer drinks $3-4. Cover $1-3. Open daily 4pm-1:30am.

The Catalyst, 1011 Pacific Ave. (☎423-1338). The town's primary music and dance venue draws national, college, and local bands. Pool, darts, and bar upstairs, Mexican food ($8-10) and bar downstairs. Shows W-Sa. Fat Tuesday 18+ dance party 9pm. W dollar night (show, drinks, and pizza $1 each; 21+). Th-Sa dance party 21+. Open daily 9am-2am. Kitchen closes 1am.

Caffe Pergolesi, 418A Cedar St. (☎426-1775). Chill coffeehouse/bar with small rooms and a roomy patio for reading, writing, or socializing. Four types of hot chocolate. Homemade cookies and pie ($1.75-3.50) and other coffee shop snacks. Live music ranging from acoustic to punk on F or Sa night from around 8pm; check ahead for details. $3 pints daily 5-7pm. Cheap coffee M-F 1-2pm. Open M-Th 6:30am-11:30pm, F-Sa 7:30am-midnight, Su 7:30am-11:30pm.

Kuumbwa Jazz Center, 320 Cedar St. (☎427-2227; www.kuumbwajazz.org). Known throughout the region for great jazz and innovative off-night programs. Even those under 21 are welcome in this small and low-key setting. Coffees, sodas, beer, and wine. The big names play here on M at 7 and 9pm; locals have their turn Th 7pm. Tickets ($12-23) sold through **Logos Books and Music,** 1117 Pacific Ave. (☎427-5100) Su-Th 10am-10pm, F-Sa 10am-11pm, as well as at www.ticketweb.com.

✺ FESTIVALS

Migration Festival (☎423-4609), at the Natural Bridges State Park. In early Feb. Celebrate the journeys of the migrating elephant seals, salmon, shorebirds, whales, and monarch butterflies that pass through the Central Coast. Music, crafts, and booths.

Santa Cruz Blues Festival (☎479-9814; www.santacruzbluesfestival.com). 2 days in late May. Big-name blues musicians. Tickets $30, children under 12 $20.

Lesbian, Gay, Bisexual, Transgender, Intersex, and Questioning Pride Day (☎761-9652; www.santacruzpride.org). 1st Su in June. Parade, speakers, and music.

Surf City Classic: Woodies on the Wharf (☎420-5273; www.santacruzwharf.com). Late June. More than 150 classic surf vehicles roll into the beautiful Santa Cruz Municipal Wharf. These so-called "woodies" generate a fine fuss. 50s and 60s music and food.

Musical Saw Festival (☎335-4484), at Roaring Camp Railroads, in Felton. Late June. Musicians and listeners are invited to workshops for jam and open mic sessions featuring musical saws and folk instruments from around the world. Parking $6.

Shakespeare Santa Cruz (☎459-2159; www.shakespearesantacruz.org), at UCSC Mid-July to Sept. Nationally acclaimed, innovative outdoor festival. Tickets $29-36; seniors, students with ID, and children under 18 (Su-F) $26. All-show passes available.

Cabrillo Festival (☎426-6966). 1st 2 weeks in Aug. Held downtown in the Civic Auditorium, the festival brings contemporary classical music to the Central Coast. Purchase tickets in advance for good seats. Tickets $20-40.

SALINAS AND SALINAS VALLEY ☎831

The heart of John Steinbeck Country beats in Salinas, an agricultural town 90 mi. south of San Francisco and 25 mi. inland from Monterey. Steinbeck, the first of two American authors to win both the Pulitzer and Nobel Prizes, lived here until he was 17, and his ashes are buried here today. Salinas is where Steinbeck set *East of Eden* and *The Red Pony*, and appears to a lesser extent in many of his other works. Aside from real-life echoes of Steinbeck's writing and a highly acclaimed rodeo, Salinas also offers travelers pieces of Great Depression and WWII culture. For most, though, the town is simply a brief diversion while driving along U.S. 101 or Rte. 68 to Monterey.

South of Salinas, U.S. 101 heads for faraway San Luis Obispo, running through the wide, green Salinas Valley, where the towns of Gonzales, Soledad, Greenfield, and King City (all 10-15 miles apart) serve mainly as farming communities and truck stops. Framed by the rolling hills, acre upon acre of lettuce, artichokes, broccoli, cauliflower, carrots, grapes, and chili peppers thrive in the self-proclaimed "salad bowl of the world." Driving down U.S. 101, beware of the speed trap around King City, where wily highway patrolmen dwell. For a more intimate, scenic route, take smaller roads like Rte. 146.

THE CENTRAL COAST

⌐ TRANSPORTATION

Trains: Amtrak, 30 Railroad Ave. (☎422-7458 or 800-872-7245), off Station Pl. in Salinas. Offers bus/train combo and train-only service. Waiting room open daily 10:30am-2:30pm and 4-8pm. To: L.A. (bus/train and train-only $45-69) and **San Francisco** (bus/train $20-25).

Buses: Greyhound, 19 W. Gabilan St. (☎424-4418 or 800-231-2222), in Salinas, 1 block from the MST Center. Open daily 5am-midnight. Several buses per day to: **L.A.** ($41-45.50); **San Francisco** ($18.50-20.50); **Santa Cruz** ($13-15).

Public Transportation: Monterey-Salinas Transit (MST), 110 Salinas St. (☎424-7695), at Central Ave. in Salinas. Fare per zone $1.75; seniors, ages 5-18, and handicapped $0.85. 1-zone day pass $3.50/$1.75; Multiple-zone day pass $7/$3.50. Same-zone 2hr. transfers free. Bus #20 or 21 goes to **Monterey.**

⁊ PRACTICAL INFORMATION

Visitor Information: Salinas Valley Chamber of Commerce, 119 E. Alisal St. (☎424-7611), at Soledad St. in Salinas. City maps ($2) and plenty of info on the Salinas Valley and Monterey Peninsula. Open M 9:30am-5pm, Tu-F 8:30am-5pm. **King City Chamber of Commerce and Agriculture,** 203 Broadway (☎385-3814). Staff members are available to answer questions but are short on brochures (maybe because the region is short on tourist activities). Open M-F 10am-1pm and 2-4pm.

Police: 222 Lincoln Ave. (☎758-7321), in Salinas; 415 Bassett St. (☎385-8311), in King City.

Medical Services: Salinas Valley Memorial Hospital, 450 E. Romie Ln. (☎757-4333), in Salinas.

Post Office: Salinas, 100 W. Alisal St. Open M-F 8:30am-5pm. **Postal Code:** 93901 **King City,** 123 S. 3rd St., at Bassett St. Open M-F 8:30am-4:30pm. **Postal Code:** 93930.

⌐ ACCOMMODATIONS

Generally, the farther south from Salinas accommodations are, the lower the cost. Salinas has some expensive hotels, but standard chain motels cluster off U.S. 101 exits, such as the E. Market St. exit and along N. Main St. near the California Rodeo Salinas stadium. **Traveler's Hotel ❸,** 16½ E. Gabilan St., is the best moderately priced option in Salinas. Rooms include cable TV, mini-fridge, coffeemaker, and private bath. (☎758-1198. Coin-operated laundry. No off-street parking. Singles $45-66; doubles $55-77. 10% discounts for AARP and AAA members, seniors, and military.) **El Dorado Motel ❹,** 1351 N. Main St., is flanked by fast-food joints, but offers pleasant rooms including cable TV. (☎449-2442 or 800-523-6506. Laundry. Apr.-Sept. singles $45-65; doubles $77-85. Oct.-Mar. singles $45; doubles $55.)

⌂ FOOD

Though the freeway is clogged with fast-food chains, there's no reason to settle for grease. Those visiting Old Salinas by the Steinbeck Center can stop by the popular **First Awakenings ❷,** 171 Main St., for apple cinnamon pancakes ($6.50) or one of many egg dishes—crepes, omelettes, frittatas, or the "your way" eggs Benedict for $5.25-7.75. (☎784-1125. Open daily 7am-2pm.) The more upscale **Monterey Coast Restaurant and Brewery ❸,** 165 Main St., serves typical brewpub fare with a few sophisticated entrees like pork chops with red wine, apples, and potatoes ($15) and artichoke, sun-dried tomato, and goat cheese pizza ($12). They also make their own brews and host a wide variety of live music on Sa from 9pm. (☎758-2337. Open M-F 11am-10pm, Sa 11:30am-midnight, Su 11:30am-10pm.) **Hullaballoo ❹**, 228 S. Main St., is more expensive ($9-25) but has more "bold American cooking" options and very large portions. They also have a cafe in the Steinbeck Center. (☎757-3663. Open M-Th 11:30am-9pm, F 11:30am-10pm, Sa 4:30-10pm, Su 4:30-9pm.) **Mi Tierra ❶**, 18 E. Gabilan St., at Monterey St., is a simple Mexican joint serving *combinaciones* with rice, beans, and salad ($4.50-8) and other Mexican favorites accompanied by chips and salsa. (☎422-4631. Open daily 8am-8:30pm.)

🔘 🌾 SIGHTS AND FESTIVALS

The town of Salinas salivates over Nobel and Pulitzer Prize winner and hometown author, John Steinbeck. The modern 40,000 sq. ft., **National Steinbeck Center,** 1 Main St., uses movies, games, and stories to evoke Steinbeck's inspiration: the Salinas Valley. Even without having read any of his works it is easy to appreciate this interactive and provocative journey into Steinbeck's world of small-town culture. The center often teems with schoolchildren who love the hands-on multimedia approach. A more relaxing atmosphere pervades the art gallery, whose works depict the Salinas area. The new 6500 sq. ft. exhibit called "Valley of the World" celebrates Salinas's other claim to fame: its agricultural riches. (☎775-4721; www.steinbeck.org. Open daily 10am-5pm. $11; students $9; teachers, military, and ages 13-17 $8; ages 6-12 and over 62 $6; under 6 free.) The nearby **gravesite**, at 758 Abbot St. and Romie Ln., and **Steinbeck House,** 132 Central Ave., are less dazzling but more intimate ways to enter Steinbeck's world. The house is now a **restaurant ❷.** (☎424-2735. Open Tu-Sa 11:30am-2pm.)

The **Mission Nuestra Señora de la Soledad (Our Lady of Solitude),** 36641 Fort Romie Rd., in Soledad off Arroyo Seco, was built in 1791. Though floods destroyed the building, it was restored in 1955 and now has a small museum. An annual fiesta is held the first Sunday in October, and a barbecue takes place on the last Sunday in June. (☎678-2586. Open daily 10am-4pm.) Visitors can see how movie-star animals are housed, nurtured, and trained for film and television at **Wild Things,** 400 River Rd., 4 mi. off Hwy. 68, between Salinas and Monterey. (☎455-1901; www.wildthingsinc.com. Tours daily 1pm; Jun.-Aug. also at 3pm. $10, under 15 $8. Private tours $15/$10; 4-person min.) Salinas's biggest non-literary tourist pull is the **California Rodeo Salinas,** 1034 N. Main St., at Bernal Dr. The rodeo is the fourth-largest in the world, attracting bull wrestlers and riders from across the West in the third week of July. Though the rodeo lasts only four days, related events like cowboy poetry readings take place from May to July. (☎800-549-4989; www.carodeo.com. $12-19, discounts for children, seniors, and disabled. Season tickets $64-76.)

PINNACLES NATIONAL MONUMENT   ☎831

Towering dramatically over the dense, dry brushwood east of Soledad, Pinnacles National Monument consists of the spectacular remnants of an ancient volcano. Set aside as a national monument in 1908, it preserves the erratic, unique spires and crags that millions of years of weathering carved from prehistoric lava flows. Thirty miles of hiking trails wind through the park's low chaparral, boulder-strewn caves, and pinnacles of rock, many of which challenge even experienced climbers. The monument also offers opportunities for caving; flashlights are required on cave trails. **Bench Trail** is an easy 2 mi. path with access to park facilities from Pinnacles Campground, Inc., along Chalone Creek. At the end of Bench Trail are links to Bear Gulch and Old Pinnacles. **Bear Gulch** (1 mi.) is a moderate, shaded walk at the bottom of a valley connecting to the Bear Gulch Visitors Center and Chalone Creek. **Old Pinnacles** traverses the shady canyon bottom but is slightly easier and longer (2¼ mi.). Both trails will lead toward cave-exploring options: **Bear Gulch Cave Trail** and **Balconies Cave Trail**, respectively. The **High Peaks Trail** runs a strenuous 5½ mi. across the park between the east and west entrances, offering amazing views of the surrounding rock formations. A magnificent array of wildflowers blooms in the spring, and the park offers excellent bird-watching year-round. The area is home to has a wide range of **wildlife,** including mountain lions, bobcats, coyotes, rattlesnakes, golden eagles, California condors, and peregrine falcons. Since Pinnacles is far from city lights and has very few clouds, the night sky over the monument puts on quite a show. Taking Rte. 25 to Rte. 146, the **Park Headquarters** are at the eastern entrance, but maps, water, and restrooms are also available at a station on the west side off Rte. 146 from U.S. 101. (☎389-4485. Open daily in summer 7:30am-9pm; in low season until 6 or 7pm, call ahead. Park entrance $5.)

There is no camping at the monument, but east of the monument is **Pinnacles Campground, Inc. ❶,** a privately owned campground with 100 tent sites (6-person max.), 12 group sites, 36 RV sites, a pool, flush toilets, and hot showers. Reservations available. (☎389-4462. 4-night max. stay. Sites $7, with hookup $11.) There are five other campgrounds on the east side of Pinnacles: **Bolado Park ❶,** 27 mi. north of the park (☎628-3421; $7.50 per vehicle, $12 per RV); **Hollister Hills State Vehicular Recreation Area ❶,** 35 mi. north (☎637-3874; $10 per vehicle); **Mission Farm RV Park ❷,** 40 mi. north (☎623-4456; RVs $28-31); **McAlpine Lake and Park ❷,** 50 mi. north (☎623-4263; sites $25, hookup $33); **Fremont Peak State Park ❶,** 52 mi. north (☎623-4255; sites June-Aug. $15, Sept.-May $11). There is no road access from the east side of the park to the west side (the drive is 70 mi. around to the other side), although it is possible to hike through. Campgrounds to the west are: **Salinas Valley Fairgrounds ❶,** in King City (☎385-3243; trailers and RVs only; hookups $15 ; **San Lorenzo Regional Park ❶,** in King City (sites $16; RVs $19; hookups $21); and **Cuidad del Rey Motel and Trailer Park ❷,** 2 mi. south of King City (☎385-4828; hookups $25).

MONTEREY ☎831

Monterey (pop. 33,000) makes good on its claim to have preserved more of its heritage than any other Californian city. Although luxury hotels and tourist shops abound and the Cannery Row of Steinbeck fame has all but vanished, a number of important sites testify to the city's colorful past. The "Path of History," marked by little yellow medallions embedded in the sidewalks, passes by such landmarks as Colton Hall, the site of the California Constitutional Convention in 1849, and the Robert Louis Stevenson House, where the author took refuge in 1879. Most of this history owes its preservation to Monterey's other distinguishing feature: abundant wealth. Multi-million-dollar homes and golf courses line the rocky shoreline, and droves of luxury cars cruise the pristine city streets, cutting a sharp contrast with Monterey's gritty industrial past. While Monterey used to pack marine life into sardine cans, today the peninsula's oceanic riches flourish in the surrounding waters of the Monterey Bay National Marine Sanctuary and the impressive Aquarium.

▐ TRANSPORTATION

Motorists approach Monterey from **U.S. 101** via **Route 68** west through Salinas or from coastal **Highway 1.** Frustrated visitors can park for free in the Del Monte Shopping Center and explore by foot and shuttle instead. Free 1-2hr. parking lines downtown streets; parking lots and garages are reasonably priced ($0.50-0.75 per 30min.) and conveniently located near the aquarium, Cannery Row, Fisherman's Wharf,

THE CENTRAL COAST

The Grapes of Wrath is, for many, Steinbeck's quintessential California novel, the book that brings together his compassion for social outcasts, his vision of place, and his awareness of the unrealized possibilities inherent in westward migration. It is a book that owes as much to its journalistic roots as to its mythic underpinning—an exiled people in flight to the promised land. "You know he was a missionary," said Toby Street, a Stanford friend of Steinbeck's. "He was trying to expose, not from the standpoint of interfering with lives of people, but more from the standpoint of exposition. He was always trying to show you what a bad time we were having."

In the summer of 1936, George West, editorial page editor of the liberal San Francisco News, asked Steinbeck to cover the migrant situation in California. As reporter and witness, Steinbeck traveled first to Hoovervilles—makeshift roadside settlements—in Kern County and then toured Arvin Camp, a new migrant camp near Bakersfield that was depicted in John Ford's classic 1940 film adaptation of the novel and that still houses migrant workers today. Arvin Camp was the second of a projected 15 federally funded camps to be established in California to alleviate housing problems for Southwest migrants pouring in from the Dust Bowl regions. While at Arvin, Steinbeck gathered material by reading manager Tom Collins's detailed reports of the migrants' woes and by speaking to destitute Oklahomans. In October 1936, the News published his series of six articles, titled "The Harvest Gypsies." Each article was accompanied by Dorothea Lange's photos of the migrants' desperate lives. Both the photos and Steinbeck's lucid exposés compelled readers to participate in the actuality of migrant poverty; his prose nudged readers on a visual tour of dilapidated shacks and leaking tents. By December 1936, Steinbeck knew that his next "big book" would be the migrants' story.

The Grapes of Wrath touched a national (and international) chord. Over 45,900 copies were sent to bookstores before it was even published on April 14, 1939, and it sold 83,361 copies in its first month, a record for Viking Press. California writer Frank Taylor wrote in Forum in November 1939, "Californians are wrathy over The Grapes of Wrath....Though the book is fiction, many readers accept it as fact." Accepting the book purely as an historical document was the initial reaction of many readers, both in California and in Oklahoma. In Steinbeck's home state, impassioned charges were leveled against many of the novel's implications. The book treated California's Associated Farmers—one of the most virulent organizations in American history—with well-deserved contempt, implying that landowners lured thousands of migrants to the state in order to keep wages low with overabundant cheap labor. It suggested that police were in league with the powerful elite in hounding the migrants. And it depicted an unthinkable level of human poverty, misery, and hunger.

Those initial objections suggest much about the California quality of The Grapes of Wrath. The book is concerned with contours of power and how those who wield control—whether banks, tractors, landowners, or angry mobs—strip freedom from those they control. In California, the powerless have long been migrants: Chinese, Japanese, Filipino, Mexican, and "Okie." The Grapes of Wrath also presents a probing assessment of what it means to have ownership of land and water rights in the state. California has a long history of rapacious dealings in land—and this book is very much about the use and misuse of California's vast resources: land, water, produce. The Californian dream and its dark underside are evident; Steinbeck balances prosperity and plenty against failure, waste, and shame, deconstructing the mythic Western sagas of gunslingers, horse thieves, and the likes of Billy the Kid. The rugged loner is exchanged for the embrace of the family, and the real story of western expansion is told.

It was and is a definitive American book—a book about movement, the dream of a new home and land, and the resilience of realigned families. Steinbeck's most famous and controversial novel is a text so thoroughly engrained in the American social conscience that even now it speaks eloquently of poverty, exile, and self-determination. Steinbeck reported in a 1938 interview, "These people have that same vitality that the original Americans who came here had; and they know just what they want." These Okies were, for Steinbeck, the state's newest pioneers.

Susan Shillinglaw, Ph.D., is the Director of the Center for Steinbeck Studies and a Professor of English at CSU San Jose. She is the editor of the journal Steinbeck Studies (University of Idaho Press) and co-editor of American and Americans and Selected Nonfiction, and has also written many introductions to Steinbeck's classics.

downtown, and Monterey State Beach.
Monterey's primary attractions are all
within striking distance of **Alvarado
Street.** Another great way to see the
peninsula is by **bicycle,** but exercise
caution on the narrow, twisting road.

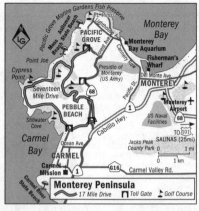

Monterey Peninsula
🚩 17 Mile Drive   ⬛ Toll Gate   ⚑ Golf Course

Airport: Monterey Airport (☎648-
7000; www.montereyairport.com).
From Hwy. 1, take Rte. 68 1½ mi. east;
exit onto Olmsted Rd. Intrastate and
national service.

Buses: Greyhound, 1042 Del Monte
Ave. (☎373-4735 or 800-231-2222),
at the gas station on the corner. To:
San Francisco (4-9hr., 5 per day,
$18.50-20.50); **Santa Barbara** (6-
7hr., 3 per day, $35.50-39); **Santa
Cruz** (1hr., 3 per day, $13-15).

Public Transportation: Monterey-Salinas Transit (MST; ☎899-2555, TDD 393-8111;
MST phone lines open M-F 7:45am-5:15pm, Sa 10am-2:30pm). The free *Rider's
Guide,* available on buses, at motels, and at the visitors center, contains route info.
MST serves the region from Watsonville in the north (where it connects to SCMTD; see
Santa Cruz, p. 328) to Carmel in the south, as well as inland to Salinas. Many buses
stop at the **Transit Plaza** downtown, where Munras, Tyler, Pearl, Alvarado, and Polk St.
converge. MST has 4 zones, each encompassing 1 or 2 towns. Fare per zone $1.75;
seniors, ages 5-18, and disabled $0.85. Same-zone transfers free up to 2hr. Exact change
required. MST offers the following 3 extra services: The free **Waterfront Area Visitors
Express (WAVE)** goes to Monterey sights from the Del Monte Shopping Center. The free
MST Trolley runs 2 routes: 1 goes between the Transit Plaza and the aquarium, stopping at Fisherman's Wharf and Cannery Row on the way (Memorial Day-Labor Day daily
every 10-12min. 10am-7pm), another runs a loop including downtown Pacific Grove,
the Natural History Museum, and the aquarium (early July-Labor Day Tu-Sa every 10-
12min. 10am-6pm). **Bus #22** runs twice daily May-Oct. between Monterey and Big Sur
($3.50; seniors, ages 5-18, and disabled $1.75).

Taxi: Yellow Cab (☎646-1234). $2.50 base; $2 per mi. 24hr.

Bike Rental: Bay Bikes, 585 Cannery Row (☎646-9090), at Hoffman Ave. Recreation
Trail. There is also a smaller, usually less crowded location on the bike path near **Fisherman's Wharf.** Bikes $5.50 per hr., $17 per 4 hr., $25 per day; Includes lock and hel-
met. Will deliver and retrieve bikes for day rentals. Open daily 9am-7pm. Fisherman's
Wharf location open daily 10am-5pm.

✴ 🔢 ORIENTATION AND PRACTICAL INFORMATION

The Monterey Peninsula, 116 mi. south of San Francisco, consists of **Monterey,** the
residential **Pacific Grove,** and the exclusive golfing community of **Pebble Beach.
Alvarado Street** runs north-south through Old Monterey and hosts most local nightlife. **Pacific Street,** a main thoroughfare, runs parallel to Alvarado St. At its northern
end stand luxury hotels and the giant Monterey Conference Center; beyond the
plaza lies a parking lot, the marina, and Fisherman's Wharf. Perpendicular to Alvarado St., **Del Monte Avenue** runs northeast to the coast; on the other side, **Lighthouse
Avenue** leads northwest through Pacific Grove, where it turns into **Central Avenue**
and changes back to Lighthouse Ave., ending at Point Piños Lighthouse.

Visitor Information: Monterey Peninsula Visitor and Convention Bureau, 150 Olivier St. (☎657-6400, 649-1770, or 888-221-1010; www.montereyinfo.org). Free pamphlets and *Walkabout Map*. The free 168-page *Visitor's Guide* is chock-full of info. Open M-F 7am-5pm. There is also a smaller **visitors center,** 401 Camino El Estero (☎649-1770). Open May-Sept. M-F 10am-6pm, Sa-Su 10am-5pm; Oct.-Apr. daily 10am-5pm.

Laundromat: Wash n' Dry, 615 Lighthouse Ave. Wash $1.50, dry $0.25 per 10min. Soap $0.50. Change machine. Open 24hr.

Police: 351 Madison St. (☎646-3830), at Pacific St.

Hotlines: Rape Crisis, ☎375-4357. 24hr. **Road Conditions,** ☎800-427-7623. **Suicide Prevention,** ☎649-8008. 24hr.

Library and Internet Access: Monterey Public Library, 625 Pacific St. (☎646-3930; www.monterey.org/library), diagonally across from City Hall. Free Internet. Pleasant courtyard. 2hr. free parking. Open M 1-9pm, Tu-W 10am-9pm, Th-F 10am-6pm, Sa 10am-5pm, Su 1-5pm.

Post Office: 565 Hartnell St. (☎372-3021). Open M-F 8:30am-5pm, Sa 10am-2pm. **Postal Code:** 93940.

⌂⌂ ACCOMMODATIONS AND CAMPING

Inexpensive hotels line the 2000 block of **Fremont Street** in Monterey (bus #9 or 10). Others cluster along **Munras Avenue** between downtown Monterey and Hwy. 1. The cheapest hotels in the area are in the less appealing towns of Seaside and Marina, just north of Monterey. Prices fluctuate widely depending on the season, day of the week, and local events. In Monterey, camping is an excellent option for the budget traveler. Call **Monterey Parks** (☎755-4895 or 888-588-2267) for camping info and ReserveAmerica (☎800-444-7275) for reservations.

Monterey Carpenter's Hall Hostel (HI-AYH), 778 Hawthorne St. (☎649-0375), 1 block west of Lighthouse Ave. This 45-bed hostel is fairly new and perfectly located. Modern facilities and a large, comfy living room with a piano, library, and games. Make-your-own pancake breakfast with tea, hot chocolate, and coffee every morning (small donation appreciated). Parking included. Limited shower time: visitors get 2 tokens per day, each good for 3min. of hot water. Towels $0.50. No sleeping bags; linens provided. Lockout 10:30am-5pm. Curfew 11pm. Reservations essential June-Sept. Dorms $22, nonmembers $25, ages 7-17 with adult $17; private rooms for 2-5 people $60-74. ❷

Del Monte Beach Inn, 1110 Del Monte Blvd. (☎649-4410), near downtown, across from the beach. Cute, Victorian-style inn with pleasant rooms. Near a fairly loud road. One room has kitchenette. Continental breakfast and tea in sunny main room. Check-in 2-8pm. Reservations recommended. Rooms $55-88; with bath $88-99. ❹

Butterfly Grove Inn, 1073 Lighthouse Ave. (☎373-4921) in Pacific Grove. 28 rooms with TV, phone, microwave, refrigerator, coffeemaker, and private bath. Continental breakfast and pool. Full kitchens, fireplaces, and hot tub available. Rooms in summer $99-179; in winter from $69. ❺

Sunset Inn, 133 Asilomar Blvd. (☎375-3936), in Pacific Grove. In a quiet neighborhood less than 1 mi. from the ocean. Cottage-like rooms have cable TV, phone, coffeemaker, and private bath. Some have a fireplace and hot tub. Continental breakfast included. Prices can vary widely; reserve ahead. Rooms Apr.-Sept. Su-Th from $119, F-Sa from $149; Oct.-Mar. Su-Th$59, F-Sa $79. Walk-ins may snag lower prices. ❻

THE CENTRAL COAST

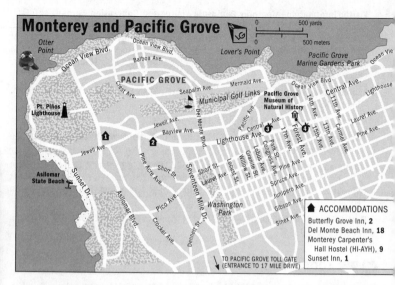

Monterey and Pacific Grove

ACCOMMODATIONS
Butterfly Grove Inn, **2**
Del Monte Beach Inn, **18**
Monterey Carpenter's
 Hall Hostel (HI-AYH), **9**
Sunset Inn, **1**

Veterans Memorial Park Campground (☎646-3865), in Monterey. 1½ mi. from downtown. Take bus #3. From Rte. 68, turn left onto Skyline Dr. From downtown, go south on Pacific St., turn right on Jefferson St., and follow the signs. Located on a hill with a view of the bay. Playground, barbecue pits, and hot showers. 40 sites. 3-night max. stay. No reservations; arrive before 3pm in summer and on weekends. Sites $20. ❷

Laguna Seca Recreational Area (☎758-3604 or 888-588-2267), on Hwy. 68 near the racetrack, 10 mi. east of Monterey. This hilly, oak-strewn camp overlooks valleys and the Laguna Seca Raceway. Of the 175 sites, 99 have hookups. If nobody is on duty, pitch your tent and rangers will come by and collect. Gun range, restrooms, barbecue pits, tables, and free hot showers. Reservations accepted. Sites $22; hookups $30. ❷

🍴 FOOD

Once a hot spot for the canned sardine industry (hence the name Cannery Row), Monterey Bay now yields crab, red snapper, and salmon. Seafood is bountiful but often expensive; look for free chowder samples or early-bird specials (usually 4-6pm). Monterey's culinary wealth extends beyond the sea; artichokes and strawberries also abound. Nibble on free samples of fruit, cheese, and seafood at the **Old Monterey Market Place,** on Alvarado St. between Pearl St. and Del Monte Ave. (☎655-2607. Open Tu 4-7pm; in summer 4-8pm.) **Whole Foods,** 800 Del Monte Ctr. (☎333-1600), off Munras Ave., is a healthy grocery store conveniently located at the Del Monte Shopping Center.

CANNERY ROW AND DOWNTOWN

Kalisa's, 851 Cannery Row, across from the Monterey Bay Aquarium. This simple yellow structure was the inspiration for La Ida Cafe in Steinbeck's *Cannery Row.* Hearty, healthy, inexpensive sandwiches and salads from $5. Lappert's ice cream from Hawaii ($2.50-4.50) and fresh coconuts drilled for drinking ($3) add a tropical flair. F night belly dancing show from 9pm (cover $5). Sa "Bohemian Night" from 8pm (cover $5-10). Open Su-Th 9am-6:30pm, F-Sa 9am-2am; in summer also Su-Th 6:30-9pm. ❷

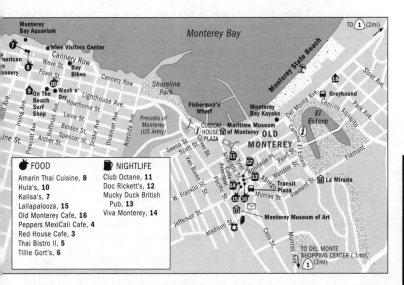

FOOD

Amarin Thai Cuisine, **8**
Hula's, **10**
Kalisa's, **7**
Lallapalooza, **15**
Old Monterey Cafe, **16**
Peppers MexiCali Cafe, **4**
Red House Cafe, **3**
Thai Bistro II, **5**
Tillie Gort's, **6**

NIGHTLIFE

Club Octane, **11**
Doc Rickett's, **12**
Mucky Duck British
Pub, **13**
Viva Monterey, **14**

Old Monterey Cafe, 489 Alvarado St. (☎646-1021), serves locally acclaimed breakfasts ($4-10.95), from Old Monterey banana pancakes ($5.50) to cinnamon raisin swirl french toast ($6). Burgers and sandwiches $6-9.50. Athenian Greek salad $9.50. Open daily 7am-2:30pm. ❷

Amarin Thai Cuisine, 807 Cannery Row (☎373-8811), near the aquarium in a complex of touristy shops. Fresh and unique California-style Thai food. Many vegetarian dishes such as tofu with vegetables and chili pepper sauce ($13). Lunch $7-11. Dinner $9-17. Open M and W-Sa 11:30am-3:30pm and 5:30-9:30pm, Su noon-3:30pm. ❸

Lallapalooza, 474 Alvarado St. (☎645-9036). This American steak house and martini bar serves immense portions of meat and other dishes ($9-30). Excellent service, high ceilings, and vivid paintings create a classy atmosphere for your meal or nightcap (or two). 32 specialty martinis $6-8. Open M-Th 4-11:45pm, F-Sa 4pm-12:45am, Su 4-11pm. Kitchen closes M-Th 11pm, F-Sa midnight. ❹

LIGHTHOUSE AVENUE AREA

🍴 **Thai Bistro II,** 159 Central Ave. (☎372-8700), in Pacific Grove. Graced with a flower-encircled patio, this bistro offers top-quality Thai cuisine in a comfortable atmosphere. Mixed vegetable curry and tofu $8. Lunch combos ($7-9) come with soup, salad, egg roll, and rice. Extensive vegetarian menu. Open daily 11:30am-3pm and 5-9:30pm. ❷

🍴 **Tillie Gort's,** 111 Central Ave. (☎373-0335), in Pacific Grove. This vegetarian restaurant has been in the business for over 30 years. Large portions of fresh dishes like Mexican fiesta salad ($8.25), eggplant francese ($8.50), or spinach ravioli ($10.50), and sweet treats like berry cheesecake or chocolate vegan cake ($4.50) will please even the most devout carnivore. Beer and wine. Open June-Oct. M-F 10am-10pm, Sa-Su 8am-10pm; Nov.-May M-F 11am-10pm. ❷

Red House Cafe, 662 Lighthouse Ave. (☎643-1060). Simple American favorites with a gourmet sensibility. Only the freshest ingredients from local growers are used. Daily specials often include fresh local fish, especially in summer. Long lines at lunchtime. Lunch $8.50-13. Small dinner plates $9-11. Dinner entrees $14-22. Open Tu-F 11am-8:30pm, Sa-Su 8am-8:30pm. ❹

Peppers MexiCali Cafe, 170 Forest Ave. (☎373-6892), between Lighthouse and Central Ave. Serves fresh-Mex fare like Yucatan snapper ($12.50) in a fun, lively setting with chile pepper decorations. Beer, wine, and margaritas available. Open M-Sa 11:30am-10pm, Su 4-10pm. Reservations strongly recommended in evenings. ❸

Hula's, 622 Lighthouse Ave. (☎655-4852). Try Hawaii-inspired dishes like macadamia encrusted ono ($18) and Duke Luau's pork plate ($12.50), or have a wrap or rice bowl ($10.50-13). Similar menu with slightly lower prices for lunch. Beer, wine, and sake available. Open Tu-Sa 11:30am-2:30pm and 5:30-10pm. ❸

🅖 SIGHTS

▨MONTEREY BAY AQUARIUM. The largest of Monterey's attractions, this extraordinary aquarium benefits from the area's superb marine ecology. Gaze through the **world's largest window** at an enormous marine habitat containing green sea turtles, giant ocean sunfish, large sharks, and yellow- and blue-fin tuna in one million gallons of water. Don't miss the provocative exhibit connecting the shape, movement, and beauty of jellyfish to various art forms, or the new exhibit exploring the myth and mystery of sharks. Kids and adults love watching the **sea otters** during feeding time, walking through the **shorebird aviary,** perusing the living kelp forest housed in a two-story glass aquarium, and checking out the petting pool of damp bay creatures (stingrays included). Be patient; the lines for tickets, admission, viewing, and food can be unbelievably long. Save 20-40min. by picking up tickets the day before. *(886 Cannery Row. ☎648-4888 or 800-756-3737; www.monterey-bayaquarium.org. Open daily June-early Sept. and holidays 9:30am-6pm; early Sept.-late May 10am-6pm. $20, over 65 $18; students and ages 13-17 $16; disabled and ages 3-12 $9.)*

CANNERY ROW. Lying along the waterfront east of the aquarium, Cannery Row was once a dilapidated street crammed with languishing sardine-packing plants. The three-quarter-mile row has since been converted into a different commercial venture of tourist-packed mini-malls, bars, and a pint-sized carnival complex. All that remains of the earthiness and gruff camaraderie celebrated by John Steinbeck in *Cannery Row* and *Sweet Thursday* are a few building facades: 835 Cannery Row was the Wing Chong Market, the bright yellow building next door is where *Sweet Thursday* took place, and Doc Rickett's lab, 800 Cannery Row, is now closed to the public. Take a peek at the **Great Cannery Row Mural;** local artists have covered 400 ft. of a construction-site barrier on the 700 block with depictions of 1930s Monterey and what "The Row" was like in its heyday. The "Taste of Monterey" **Wine Visitors Center** on the second floor of the 700 building offers a sampling of the county's booming wine industry with well-priced bottles and winery maps. The wide variety of wine, plus the knowledgeable staff and inspiring view of the bay, makes it a good starting place for tasting tours. *(700 Cannery Row. ☎888-646-5446. Open daily 11am-6pm. 6 tastings $5; fee can go toward wine purchases.)*

SUNSET DRIVE. West of Monterey in Pacific Grove, Sunset Dr. provides a free, 6 mi. scenic alternative to 17 Mile Drive (see below). Appropriately, Sunset Dr. is the best place in the area to watch the sun go down. People arrive a full 2hr. before sunset in order to secure front-row seats along the road, also known as Ocean Blvd. At the western tip of the peninsula stands **Point Piños Lighthouse,** the oldest continuously running Pacific Coast lighthouse, which houses exhibits on Coast Guard history. *(☎648-3116. Open Th-Su 1-4pm. Free.)*

PACIFIC GROVE. Pacific Grove took root as a Methodist enclave over 100 years ago, and many of the Victorian houses are still in excellent condition. This unpretentious town (which falls eerily quiet at night) has a beautiful coastline, numerous lunch counters, and lots of antique and artsy home furnishing stores. Browse second-hand clothing, book, and music stores along Lighthouse Ave., or outlet-shop-'til-you-drop at the **American Tin Cannery,** on Ocean View Blvd. near New Monterey. Thousands of **monarch butterflies** winter in Pacific Grove from October to March. Look, but don't touch; bothering the butterflies is a $1000 offense. The **Pacific Grove Museum of Natural History,** at Forest and Central Ave. one block north of Lighthouse Ave., has traveling exhibits as well as on monarchs and other local wildlife. The stuffed birds are top-notch. (☎648-5716. Open Tu-Sa 10am-5pm. Free.)

17 MILE DRIVE. The famous 17 Mile Drive meanders along the coast from Pacific Grove through **Pebble Beach** and the forests around Carmel. Once owned by Del Monte Foods, Pebble Beach has become the playground of the fabulously well-to-do. Its enormous, manicured golf courses creep up almost to the shore's edge in bizarre contrast to the dramatically jagged cliffs and turbulent surf. The drive is rolling, looping, and often spectacular, though plagued by slow-driving tourists and a hefty $7.50 entrance fee. To drive in and out as you please in one day, present your receipt to the guard and have him record your license plate number. Save money by biking it (bicyclists and pedestrians are allowed in for free) or drive along Sunset Dr. instead (see above). Along 17 Mile Drive, make sure to stop at **Fanshell Overlook** to where massive harbor seals and their pups rest up on the shore, and at the **Lone Cypress,** an old, gnarled tree growing on a rock promontory, valiantly resisting the onslaught of determined, jostling photographers. An image of this tree is now the official logo of the Pebble Beach community.

MARITIME MUSEUM OF MONTEREY. This haven for sea buffs illustrates the maritime history of Monterey with ship models, photos, navigation tools, logs, and a free 14 min. film. The museum's centerpiece is the original Fresnel lens of Point Sur Lighthouse. The entire lens is a two-story structure of gear-works and cut glass that was later replaced by the electric lighthouse. (5 Custom House Plaza, across from Fisherman's Wharf in downtown Monterey. ☎374-2608. Open daily 10am-5pm. $8; ages 13-17 $3; over 60, military, and disabled $6; under 12 free.)

PATH OF HISTORY WALKING TOUR. Monterey's early days spawned a unique architectural trend that combined flourishes from the South, like wraparound porches, with Mexican adobe features, like 3 ft. thick walls and exterior staircases. The Path of History, marked by yellow sidewalk medallions, snakes through Monterey State Historic Park in downtown, passing numerous historic buildings including the **Royal Presidio Chapel,** built in 1794, and the **Larkin House,** home to the US consul to Mexico during the 1840s. Use the visitors center brochure to walk the path unguided, or join a free tour led by state park guides. (☎649-7118. Houses open daily 10am-5pm; in winter 10am-4pm. Tour times and starting locations vary; call for details.)

OTHER SIGHTS. Catch a glimpse of otters in the wild from **Otter Point** or from any of the several other areas nearby. Touching an otter is illegal, and "harassing" one in Monterey Bay carries a $10,000 fine. (In Pacific Grove, 2½ mi. south from the Coast Guard Pier.) The **Monterey Museum of Art** has two locations. The Civic Center branch holds changing shows, mostly of California artists. (559 Pacific St. ☎372-5477. Open W-Sa 11am-5pm, Su 1-4pm. $5, students and military $2.50, under 12 free.) **La Mirada,** off Fremont across from Lake El Estero, has exhibits on California's history and collections of Asian and Pacific Rim art. (720 Via Mirada. ☎372-3689. Open W-Sa 11am-5pm, Su 1-4pm. $5, students and military $2.50, under 12 free.)

◼◼ BEACHES AND OUTDOOR ACTIVITIES

Monterey's neighbors to the west and north have more dramatic coastlines and more impressive surf than those in town. Around the northern end of the peninsula, the beach runs uninterrupted for nearly 4 mi., first as **Pacific Grove Municipal Beach,** then as **Asilomar State Beach.** Bus #2 stops within four blocks of the ocean in Pacific Grove. The numerous tide pools along the rocky shore encourage exploration. Several companies on Fisherman's Wharf offer critter-spotting boat trips around Monterey Bay. The best time to go is during **gray whale migration season** (Nov.-Mar.), but the trips are hit-or-miss year-round. The lucky spot dolphins frolicking in the current; the unlucky see millions of gallons of water. **Chris's Fishing Trips,** 48 Fisherman's Wharf, offers daily whale-watching tours and fishing boat charters. (☎375-5951. 2-3hr. whale-watching tours May-Nov. 11am and 1pm. $25, under 13 $18. 2hr. gray whale migration tours Dec.-Apr. $18, under 13 $12. Open daily 4am-5pm.)

The local swells provide a good (and cold) testing ground for enthusiastic water-goers. **On The Beach Surf Shop,** 693 Lighthouse Ave., rents surfboards, boogie boards, and wet suits. (☎646-9283. Surfboard rentals $10 per half-day, $20 per day; boogie boards $5/$10. Wet suits $6/$12. Open M-Th 10am-7pm, F-Sa 9am-8pm, Su 10am-6pm; June-Aug. closes 1hr. later.) Sea kayakers on Monterey Bay float above kelp forests and among otters. **Monterey Bay Kayaks,** 693 Del Monte Ave., provides rentals and tours. (☎373-5357 or 800-649-5357. $30 per person per day; includes gear, wet suit, and instruction. 3hr. guided kayak tours of the bay. Open in summer Su-Th 9am-6pm, F-Sa 9am-8pm; in winter daily 9am-6pm.)

There are several designated bike paths in the area. The best is the **Monterey Peninsula Recreation Trail,** which follows the coast for approximately 20 mi. from Castroville to Asilomar St. in Pacific Grove beside spectacular views of pristine coastline, cyprus trees, and marine life. Bikers can then continue through Pacific Grove to Pebble Beach along famous 17 Mile Drive (see p. 349). The Recreation Trail shares the road with cars after **Lover's Point,** 2½ mi. from Fisherman's Wharf.

🎵 🎭 ENTERTAINMENT AND FESTIVALS

Laguna Seca Raceway (☎800-327-7322; www.laguna-seca.com), on Hwy. 68 east of Monterey. Late May-early Oct. Motorcycle racing (July), Historic Automobile Races (mid-Aug.), the Monterey Grand Prix Indy Car World Series (early Sept.), and the Sportscar Championship: Lemans Series (mid-Oct.). Office open M-F 8am-5pm.

AT&T National Pro-Am Golf Tournament (☎649-1533 or 800-541-9091; www.attpb-golf.com), at Pebble Beach. Feb. 7-13, 2005. Celebrity and PGA tour matchups.

Monterey Bay Blues Festival (☎394-2652; www.montereyblues.com). Brings big-name blues musicians to the bay for 3 days in late June.

Monterey Bay's Theatrefest (☎622-0700; www.pacrep.org), at the Custom House Plaza. Late June. Free afternoon theater Sa-Su 11am-5pm. Tickets $15, students and seniors $8.

Annual Winemaker's Celebration (☎375-9400; www.montereywines.org). Over 25 Monterey County wineries release new vintages and special wines in late Aug. Also features educational exhibits on topics like grapevine pruning and cork display, live music, and a silent auction.

Monterey County Fair (☎372-5863; www.montereycountyfair.com), at Monterey County Fairgrounds, in mid-Aug. Livestock exhibitions, live music, midway, and food.

Monterey Jazz Festival (☎373-3366; www.montereyjazzfestival.org), at the Monterey Fairgrounds. Sept. 16-18, 2005. The longest-running jazz festival in the world. Miles Davis and Dizzy Gillespie played here.

🎷 NIGHTLIFE

Monterey knows how to cut loose at night, but some areas of the peninsula quiet down early. The main action is downtown along **Alvarado Street;** there are also a few **Lighthouse Avenue** bars. Those under 21 have few options.

■ **Mucky Duck British Pub,** 479 Alvarado St. (☎655-3031). Parking lot in back. Empty front window booths might fool you—many patrons are in the back beer garden, listening to music, having a smoke, or staying warm around a coal-burning fire. Monterey locals have voted the pub's beer the city's best for 7 years in a row. Come early to avoid waits. Live music, karaoke, or DJ from around 9pm; some live music during the day. Salads, sandwiches, and appetizers $4.25-10.25. Open daily 11:30am-2am.

■ **Club Octane,** 321-D Alvarado St. (☎646-9244; www.cluboctane.com), on the 2nd floor at Del Monte Ave. Parking structure adjacent. Strobe lights and heavy smoke machines throb like teenage hormones. 3 bars and 4 dance floors with different DJs. Pool tables and a smoking deck. Male and female burlesque M 9:45pm. Live music W. No hats, tennis shoes, or beach flip-flops. Cover M $7; Tu, Th, Su free; W $5-25; F $5; Sa $10-15. Open daily 9pm-1:45am.

Viva Monterey, 414 Alvarado St. (☎646-1415). A less polished crowd lives it up amid papier-mache table-tops and bottle-cap wall art at Monterey's oldest bar. 2 pool tables. Only Monterey nightspot with daily live music. Open Su-M and W-Sa 7:30pm-2am, Tu 3:30pm-2am. Shows M-Su 9:30pm.

Doc Rickett's, 180 East Franklin St. (☎649-4241). Named after Ed Ricketts, the marine biologist who inspired Steinbeck's doctor characters. Tu country night with cash prize karaoke. W live DJ with house music. F-Sa comedy and dancing. Clubbing dress code enforced. Open M-Sa 5pm-2am.

CARMEL ☎831

Moneyed Californians migrate to Carmel (officially Carmel-by-the-Sea; pop. 4400) to live out their fantasies of small-town life. Carmel has beautiful beaches, a main street lined with boutiques and art galleries, and a carefully manufactured aura of quaintness. Local ordinances forbid address numbers, parking meters (though police chalk tires to keep track of how long cars have been parked), live music in bars, billboards, and, at one time, eating ice-cream cones outside—all considered undesirable symbols of urbanization. Though the waters off the coast are too cold for swimming, the white-sand beaches of Carmel are beautiful, the mission is extraordinary, and your heart may race to see resident and former mayor Clint Eastwood. Still, the town proper may simply be too snooty for some.

▐ TRANSPORTATION

Carmel lies at the southern end of the Monterey Peninsula off **Highway 1,** 126 mi. south of San Francisco. The town's main street, **Ocean Avenue,** cuts west from

THE LOCAL STORY

HANGING 10 AND OTHER SURFER FAUX PAS

Brian, a 19-year-old surfer dude from San Jose, was spotted with his longboard and wet suit at Carmel City Beach.

LG: How long have you been surfing?

A: 'Bout 12 years.

LG: And exactly how long did it take you to actually stand up on the board and "catch a wave"—is that the proper terminology nowadays?

A: No that's fine, some people still say that....And it took me a good year until I could ride a wave.

LG: But how long did it take you to even stand up on the board? [It took our researcher 2hr.]

A: I think just about anyone could do it in a day with some instruction.

LG: [Feeling validated—he said *day*] What are the big rules of surfing?

A: The biggest one is that up-wave surfers have the right of way. So, like, if someone is on a wave before you then it is his and you can't get in his way.

LG: Now getting back to the issue of jargon or slang, you said that some people will say "catch a wave." What are some other examples of contemporary surfing parlance?

A: Um, like, what do you mean?

LG: I mean, what words would you use to describe a fantastic surfing expedition? "Gnarly," "rad," "wicked"? And does anyone say "hang ten"?

A: [Pensive] I guess I say "killer" a lot and call going out to surf a "sesh" [short for session]. "Hang ten" is not something I hear.

the freeway to (surprise) the ocean. All other east-west avenues are numbered; numbers ascend toward the south. **Junípero Avenue** crosses Ocean Ave. downtown and leads south to the mission at **Rio Road.** Free town maps are available at most hotels and the visitors center. A public lot on the corner of Junípero Ave. and 3rd St. has **free all-day parking.**

Public Transportation: Monterey-Salinas Transit (MST; ☎899-2555, TDD 393-8111). Buses #4, 5, and 24 go through Carmel. Bus #22 runs to Big Sur (2 per day, $3.50). Schedules available at the Monterey info and transit centers. Fare per zone $1.75; seniors, disabled, and ages 5-18 $0.85; same-zone transfers free up to 2hr.

Bike Rental: Bay Bikes (☎646-9090), based in Monterey, delivers to Carmel with 24hr. notice for a $5 fee. Bikes $25 per day; includes helmet and lock. Open daily 9am-7pm.

Visitor Information: Carmel-by-the-Sea Chamber of Commerce and Visitor Information Center (☎624-2522 or 800-550-4333; www.carmelcalifornia.org), on the 2nd fl. of the Eastwood Bldg. on San Carlos St. between 5th and 6th St. Free city maps. Open M-F 9am-5pm, Sa 11am-5pm.

Internet Access: Mail Mart (☎624-4900), at Dolores Ave. and 5th St. $3 per 15 min. Open M-F 8:30am-5:30pm, Sa 9am-3pm.

Post Office: (☎624-3630) 5th Ave. between San Carlos St. and Dolores Ave. Open M-F 9am-4:30pm, Sa 10am-2pm. **Postal Code:** 93921.

ACCOMMODATIONS

The inns and lodges in Carmel usually offer only double-occupancy rooms (which fall below $90 only midweek or in winter) and usually include full breakfasts. A 15min. bus ride to Monterey will yield lower rates at places with less charm. Camping is illegal within city limits, and no state parks are nearby. There is, however, a private campground 4½ mi. east at **Saddle Mountain Ranch ❷,** 27625 Schulte Rd. The 50 sites have showers and pool access. (☎624-1617. Reserve ahead. $25.)

Carmel Sands Lodge (☎624-1255 or 800-252-1255), on San Carlos St. between 4th and 5th Ave. This upscale motel is one of the least expensive options in downtown Carmel. All rooms have cable TV, phone, and private bath. Some have fireplace, wet bar, or lanai balcony. Free off-street parking and pool. Rooms in high season $85-189; in low season $68-145. AAA and AARP discounts. ❹

Wayfarer Inn (☎624-2711 or 800-533-2711), at 4th Ave. and Mission St. Immaculate, simple English country-style rooms with TV, VCR, phone, refrigerator, and private bath. Most have fireplaces, some have kitchenettes. Welcoming staff. Buffet breakfast in the morning, snacks in the afternoon. Rooms June 16-Sept. 20 Su-Th $129-189, F-Sa $159-229; Sept. 21-June 15 Su-Th $89-139, F-Sa $119-159. ❺

The Green Lantern Inn (☎624-4392 or 888-414-4392), at 7th Ave. and Casanova St. Each room is modeled after a country cottage and includes TV, phone, refrigerator, private bath, and private entrance. Breakfast buffet and afternoon refreshments. No pets or smoking. Street parking. Rooms $129-229; in winter $89-189. ❺

Coachman's Inn (☎624-6421 or 800-336-6421), on San Carlos at 7th Ave. Motel style gone deluxe. All rooms with fridge, coffeemaker, microwave, VCR, phone, and cable TV. Many rooms have fireplaces. Outdoor patio, hot tub, sauna, light continental breakfast basket, and afternoon sherry and cookies available. English country rooms $115-350. Check visitors center for midweek deals. 10% AAA, AARP, and senior discounts. ❺

FOOD

Food, like everything else in Carmel, is overpriced. It is, however, occasionally good enough to justify the expense.

Em Le's (☎625-6780), on Dolores Ave between 5th and 6th Ave. This cafe is known for its fabulous breakfasts. Offering omelettes with potatoes or cottage cheese and toast ($8-12); unique French toast $9. Many lunch options $6-11. Dinner entrees $14-20, but early birds (4:30-7pm) can get an entree with soup or salad for $9.95. Soda fountain. Open daily 7am-3pm and 4:30-10pm. ❸

The Forge in the Forest (☎624-2233), at the southwest corner of 5th Ave. and Junipero St. Voted best outdoor dining in Monterey County for the last 13 years, this popular restaurant serves pasta, seafood, and grill items ($15-28), and gourmet pizza (roasted duck and caramelized onion $13) on a gorgeous garden patio complete with open-fire forge. Su brunch until 2:30pm. Open Su-Th 11:30am-9pm, F-Sa 11:30am-10pm. ❹

The Tuck Box (☎624-6365), on Dolores Ave. between Ocean and 7th Ave. Built in 1927, this historic building is now home to the Tuck Box English Tea Room, famous for scones ($4.25), preserves, and a fairy tale-esque facade. Salads $4.50-10. Omelettes $8-10. Open daily 7:30am-2:50pm. ❷

Jack London's (☎624-2336), on Dolores Ave. between 5th and 6th Ave. British pub with salads ($5.25-11), fish or fowl ($10.25-15), burgers (from $9.25), and sandwiches (from $9.50). Sit in the courtyard or near the action-packed bar. The only night-owl eatery in town. Open daily 11:30am-12:30am. ❸

🔵🔵 SIGHTS AND BEACHES

🔲 **POINT LOBOS RESERVE.** This extraordinary 550-acre, state-run wildlife sanctuary is popular with skin divers and day hikers. Bring binoculars to view otters, sea lions, seals, brown pelicans, gulls, or migrating whales from the paths along the cliffs. At the water, Point Lobos offers tide pools and scuba access. No dogs are allowed. *(On Hwy. 1, 3 mi. south of Carmel. Park on Hwy. 1 before the tollbooth and walk or bike in for free. Accessible by MST bus #22. ☎624-4909. Open daily Apr.-Oct. 9am-7pm; Nov.-Mar. 9am-5pm. Free daily nature tours; call for times. $8 per car, seniors $4. Map $1. Day-use free for campers registered with one of the state parks. Divers must call ☎624-8413 or email ptlobos@mbay.net for reservations. Dive fee $7.)*

MISSION BASILICA SAN CARLOS BORROMEO DEL RÍO CARMELO (CARMEL MISSION). Established at its present site in 1771 by Father Junípero Serra, "the great conquistador of the cross," this mission converted 4000 Native Americans before it was abandoned in 1836. Fastidiously restored in 1931, the mission's marvels continue to astound. Complete with a stone courtyard, bell tower, lavish gardens, and a daily mass, the mission is one of the most extensive in California. Buried here are Father Serra and over 2300 Native Americans. The three museums display the original silver altar furnishings, handsome vestments, and a library. *(3080 Rio Rd. and Lasuen Dr., off Hwy. 1. ☎624-1271. Open M-Sa 9:30am-4:30pm, Su 10:30am-4:30pm. $4, ages 6-17 $1, under 6 free.)*

CENTER FOR PHOTOGRAPHIC ART. The Sunset Cultural Center, which once housed Ansel Adams and Edward Weston's Friends Photography, is now home to the Center for Photographic Art. The Center exhibits top-notch work by local and international artists. Recently shows included Dennis Hopper, Linda McCartney, and Rodney Smith. *(San Carlos St. between 8th and 9th Ave. ☎625-5181; www.photography.org. Open Su and Tu-Sa 1-5pm. Free.)*

BEACHES. The northern Big Sur coast begins at the end of Ocean Ave., at **Carmel City Beach,** a white, sandy crescent framing a cove of chilly waters. The beach ends abruptly at the base of red cliffs, which make a fine grandstand for sunsets. **Carmel River State Beach,** just south of City Beach, is windier and colder than Carmel City

Beach, but it is blessed with better surf and parking and smaller crowds. Bring a jacket or sweater, even in summer. *(To get to Carmel River State Beach, walk about 1 mi. along Scenic Rd., or drive to the end of Carmelo St. off Santa Lucía. Parking lot closes at dusk.)*

BIG SUR ☎ 831

Big Sur's enormous appeal shines from its outdoor offerings—redwood forests with freshwater rivers and rocky shores with surf crashing on golden beaches. More of a region than a precise destination, a fair amount of driving is required to get around and no signs tell you that you are actually in the town of Big Sur, which hosts a handful of pricey restaurants and campsites booked up months in advance.

✈ ORIENTATION

Monterey's Spanish settlers called the entire region below their town *El Sur Grande*—the Big South. Today, Big Sur is a more explicitly defined coastal region, bordered on the south by San Simeon and on the north by Carmel. There is a town called Big Sur, but to the traveler it is nothing more than a slight concentration of buildings along Hwy 1. The coast is thinly inhabited, dotted with a few gas stations and exorbitant "getaway" hotels. Almost everything—fuel, food, toiletries, beer—costs more in Big Sur. Last-chance stops for the thrifty are at **The Crossroads,** the supermarket complex on Rio Rd. in Carmel, and the market in Morro Bay.

Despite its isolation, Big Sur can be reached by public transit in the summer (see p. 353), though once you arrive, you'll want a car. The stretch of Hwy. 1 from Carmel to Big Sur is simply amazing but curvy and crowded, so go slowly and find a time (early mornings are recommended) when traffic won't impede your enjoyment of the seaside splendor. Spring is the optimal time to visit Big Sur, when delicate wildflowers are in bloom. No matter what the season, layered clothing is essential—mornings are typically foggy, afternoons sunny, and evenings chilly.

As places in Big Sur do not have street addresses, general directions are provided. All of Big Sur's attractions lie along Hwy. 1; accordingly, listings are ordered from north to south. Most stops along Hwy. 1 are well marked and obvious, as they are the only interruptions amid miles of coast and forest.

☎ TRANSPORTATION AND PRACTICAL INFORMATION

In general, it's best to plan a trip to Big Sur ahead of time and bring all necessary supplies along. In town, there is a Shell **gas station** and an **ATM** (near the post office), but visitors are better off taking care of such matters in Carmel to the north or Cambria to the south before going to Big Sur.

Public Transportation: Monterey-Salinas Transit (MST; ☎ 899-2555). Bus #22 through Big Sur leaves from the Monterey Conference Center and runs as far as Nepenthe, 29 mi. south of Carmel, stopping at various points en route (May-Sept. 2 per day). Limited space for bikes; call ahead. Fare per zone $1.75, seniors and under 18 $0.85. From Monterey or Carmel to Big Sur $3.50/$1.75.

Visitor Information: Big Sur Chamber of Commerce (☎ 667-2100; www.bigsurcalifornia.org). Leave a message any time to have a Big Sur travel brochure sent to you. Open M, W, F 9am-1pm. **Big Sur Station (**☎ 667-2315), ½ mi. south of Pfeiffer Big Sur entrance on Hwy. 1, about 22 mi. south of Carmel. Multiagency station includes the State Park Office, the US Forest Service (USFS) Office, and the CalTrans Office. Permits, maps, and info on hikes. Open daily June-Sept. 8am-6pm; Oct.-May 8am-4:30pm.

Hotlines: Road Conditions, ☎ 800-427-7623. **Highway Patrol,** ☎ 805-549-3261. **Emergency: Ranger Dispatch,** ☎ 649-2810.

Post Office: 47500 Hwy. 1 (☎667-2305), next to the Center Deli in Big Sur Center. Open M-F 8:30am-4pm. **Postal Code:** 93920.

CAMPING

Camping in Big Sur is heavenly, but neglecting to bring equipment is a big mistake; what little equipment is available is expensive. Low site availability reflects the high demand for camping in the area, so reserve well in advance by calling ReserveAmerica (☎800-444-7275; $7.50 fee). If all sites below are booked, check with the **US Forest Service.** Camping is free in the **Ventana Wilderness,** a backpack-only site at the northern end of Los Padres National Forest (permits at Big Sur Station). Detailed trail maps are necessary for this kind of backcountry camping; ask Big Sur rangers for essential information on current conditions.

Andrew Molera State Park (☎667-2315), on Hwy. 1, about 15 mi. south of Carmel next to a horseback riding facility. A level ½ mi. trail leads to hike-in, tent-only campgrounds near the beach. 24 sites. Ornithology center, picnic tables, fire rings, drinking water, and flush toilets. No showers. 7-night max. stay. Sites $9. Day use $8. No pets. ❶

Big Sur Campground and Cabins (☎667-2322), on Hwy. 1, about 18 mi. south of Carmel on the Big Sur River. Hot showers and laundry. Reservations recommended. Sites for 2 people $27, $4 per additional person. 5-person max. Hookup $4. Tent cabins for 2 people $57, 3rd person or dogs $12. Cabins $121-258. Low-season day use $10. ❷

Riverside Camp (☎667-2414), next to the Big Sur Campground. Slightly dustier sites. Reservations $4. 2 people and 1 vehicle $28; $4 per additional person (over 5), $3 per dog. Additional untowed vehicle $6. Electricity and water hookup $4. 2 cabins ($130) and 5 rooms ($75-130) are also available. No pets allowed in rooms. ❷

Fernwood Resort and Campground (☎667-2422), on Hwy. 1, about 19 mi. south of Carmel, downhill behind the Fernwood Bar and Grill (see p. 354). 60 small but well-situated campsites and 2 swimming holes in a redwood forest on the Big Sur River. Several state park trails start from the campground. Hot showers. Reservations recommended. Sites for up to 6 people $27; 2 people and 1 vehicle with hookup $29. $5 per additional person. Vehicles $5. Dogs $3. ❷

Pfeiffer Big Sur State Park (☎667-2315), on Hwy. 1, about 22 mi. south of Carmel, just south of Fernwood Resort and Campground. The diverse wildlife and terrain, the beautiful Big Sur River, and several hiking trails ensure that all 218 bustling campsites are always filled. Fire pits, picnic tables, softball field, flush toilets, and hot showers. As one ranger put it, "Your grandma can camp here." Trail maps available ($1). Park open sunrise-sunset. Sites Feb.-Oct. $25-35, seniors $23-33; Nov.-Jan. $20-30/$18-28. Disabled half off. Hike or bike-in $3. Day use $8. Second vehicle $8. ❶

Ventana Big Sur (☎667-2712; www.ventanawildernesscampground.com), on Hwy. 1, about 24 mi. south of Carmel. 80 shady sites in a gorgeous redwood canyon with picnic tables, fire rings, flush toilets and water faucets. Hot showers. Sites for 2 people and 2 vehicles Su-Th $27, F-Sa $35. $5 per additional person; 5-person max. Pets $5. ❷

Limekiln State Park (☎667-2403), on Hwy 1, about 50 mi. south of Carmel and 4 mi. south of Lucia. Many of the 33 sites sit along a bubbling creek or have ocean views. Fire rings, picnic tables, hot showers. Sites $15, seniors $13. Day use $6. ❶

FOOD

Grocery stores are at Big Sur Lodge (in Pfeiffer Big Sur State Park), Pacific Valley, and Gorda, and some packaged food is sold in Lucia and at Ragged Point, but it's better to arrive prepared because prices in Big Sur are generally high. Restaurants are listed from north to south along Hwy. 1.

THE CENTRAL COAST

■ **The Roadhouse** (☎667-2264), off Hwy. 1, about 19 mi. south of Carmel, just south of Riverside Camp. A relatively new dining venue with a lively, intimate atmosphere and flavorful food, like sweet corn risotto with grilled vegetable salad ($15). Small, selective menu changes frequently. Patio seating available. Soups and salads $7-15. Entrees $12-22. Desserts $3-6.50. Beer and wine. Open M and W-Su 5:30-9pm. ❸

Redwood Grill at Fernwood (☎667-2129), on Hwy. 1 in the Fernwood complex, about 19 mi. south of Carmel. Highly popular outdoor patio under a redwood canopy. Chicken breasts, veggie burritos, and hamburgers from $6.50. Sandwiches and salads $1-10. Daily fish, grill, or barbecue specials $11-13. Live music weekly in the summer. Connected to a separately run full bar and adjacent to a small grocery store. Open daily in summer noon-9pm; reduced low-season hours. Bar open Su-Th noon-midnight, F-Sa noon-1am. Grocery store open daily 8am-10pm. ❷

Center Deli and General Store, 47520 Hwy. 1 (☎667-2225), beside the post office in Big Sur Center, about 23 mi. south of Carmel, 1 mi. south of Big Sur Station. The most reasonably priced goods in the area. Sandwiches ($4-5.50) include veggie options like avocado and egg salad. Pasta salads $5 per lb. Open daily 7:30am-8pm. ❶

■ **Big Sur Restaurant and Bakery** (☎667-0520, bakery 667-0524; www.bigsurbakery.com), just south of the post office by the Shell gas station and the Garden Gallery. Enjoy 12 in. wood-fired pizzas ($11-17) and entrees using free-range meats and fresh local vegetables ($19-23) in a garden setting. The bakery specializes in organic breads and pastries. Beer and wine available. Open Tu-Su 11:30am-3pm and 5:30-9:30pm. Bakery open Tu-Su 8am-9:30pm. Closed Tu in winter. ❸

Ceilo (☎667-4240), off Hwy. 1, about 24 mi. south of Carmel, just south of Big Sur Station in the same complex as the Ventana Big Sur campground. One of the most chic and pricey restaurants in the area, but unlike many other establishments, Ceilo offers more for your money than just a great al fresco ocean view; the food and atmosphere are first-rate as well. If dinner entrees ($25-38) are too steep, try a smaller plate ($8-19). Lunches feature salads ($7-16), sandwiches ($13-14), and main courses like chardonnay braised beef short ribs ($17). Open daily noon-5:30pm and 6-9pm. ❺

Coast Gallery Cafe (☎667-2301), on Hwy. 1, about 28 mi. south of Carmel, 2 mi. south of the Henry Miller Memorial Library. From its elevated location above a free art gallery displaying Henry Miller watercolor paintings, this roadside cafe has a sweeping ocean view for minimal cost. Sandwiches, salads, burgers, wraps, and quiche ($4.25-9). Beer and wine. Open Mar.-Oct. daily 9am-5pm.

👁 🏃 SIGHTS AND OUTDOOR ACTIVITIES

Big Sur's state parks and **Los Padres National Forest** beckon to outdoor enthusiasts of all types. Their **hiking** trails penetrate redwood forests and cross low chaparral, offering even grander views of Big Sur than those available from Hwy. 1. The northern end of Los Padres National Forest, accessible from the Big Sur Station, has been designated the **Ventana Wilderness** and contains the popular **Pine Ridge Trail,** which runs 10 mi. through primitive sites to the Sikes Hot Springs. Big Sur Station, about 22 mi. south of Carmel and half a mile south of Pfeiffer Big Sur State Park, supplies maps and permits for the wilderness area (see p. 352). Directions to sights are given in relation to Big Sur Station, the main hub for outdoor info.

Within **Pfeiffer Big Sur State Park** are seven trails of varying lengths ($1 map available at park entrance). **Pfeiffer Falls** (1½ mi. round-trip) and **Valley View** (2 mi. round-trip) are short, easy to moderate hikes. The easier of the two, Pfeiffer Falls, is a scenic hike through redwoods along Pfeiffer Big Sur Creek to a 60 ft. waterfall. The slightly more difficult Valley View Trail offers views of Point Sur and Big Sur Valley. **Oak Grove Trail** is a bit more challenging, a 3 mi. round-trip from the Big Sur

Lodge, and intersects with the Pfeiffer Falls trail. It features redwood groves, oak woodlands, and dry chaparral. The strenuous **Mt. Manuel Trail** (8 mi. round-trip) begins at the Oak Grove Trail and is a steep, dry, minimally maintained, and often overgrown climb to the 3379 ft. Manuel Peak. **Buzzard's Roost Trail** is a rugged 2hr. hike up very rigorous switchbacks, but at its peak, hikers are rewarded with panoramic views of the Santa Lucia Mountains, Big Sur Valley, and the Pacific Ocean.

Big Sur's most fiercely guarded treasure is the USFS-operated **Pfeiffer Beach** ($5). Travel 1 mi. south of Pfeiffer Big Sur State Park on Hwy. 1, at the stop sign just past the bridge by Loma Vista. Follow the road 2 mi. to the parking area, where a path leads to the beach. An offshore rock formation protects sea caves and seagulls from the pounding ocean waves. Other beaches can be found at **Andrew Molera State Park** (7 mi. north of Big Sur Station; $8), **Sand Dollar Beach** (33 mi. south of the Big Sur Station near Kirk and Plasket Creek campsites; $5), and **Jade Cove** (36 mi. south of Big Sur Station; free). Roughly at the midpoint of the Big Sur coast, about 10 mi. south of Big Sur Station, lies **Julia Pfeiffer Burns State Park,** where picnickers find refuge in the redwood forest and sea otters in **McWay Cove.** At the point where McWay Creek flows into the ocean is a spectacular 80 ft. waterfall, visible from a semi-paved path a quarter-mile from the park entrance. This absolutely majestic view overlooking McWay Cove epitomizes the raw beauty that draws visitors to the Big Sur coast. **Ewoldsen Trail** (4½ mi. round-trip) starts among redwoods at McWay Creek, follows McWay Canyon, and climbs upwards, sometimes steeply, to reveal coastal views. **Tan Bark Trail** starts east of Hwy. 1 at Partington Cove. The 5½ mi. round-trip hike traverses oaks and redwoods to the Tin House and has excellent coastal views. To shorten the trip, take the road at the end of the trail. It leads back to Hwy. 1, 1 mi. south of the trailhead.

Many state park trails are usually crowded, but solitude seekers can avoid the crowds by following highway turn-offs that lead to secluded inlets with terrific rock formations and crashing waves. One can also spend some time learning about one of the area's most celebrated former residents—Henry Miller. The **Henry Miller Memorial Library,** just south of Nepenthe and Cafe Kevah and 26 mi. south of Carmel, displays books and artwork by the famous author of *Tropic of Cancer*, a novel banned in the US for 27 years after its 1934 publication in Paris. Miller's late works introduced his readers to Big Sur, and many readers of his more explicit works came to Big Sur seeking a nonexistent sex cult that he purportedly led. While the sex cult is no longer a tourism draw, the cult of authorship suffices nicely. (☎ 667-2574; www.henrymiller.org. Open June-Oct. M and W-Su 11am-6pm; Nov.-May Th-Su 11am-6pm and by special arrangement.) The library sells books and hosts concerts like the **Big Sur Experimental Music Festival** (last weekend in May) and readings such as the **West Coast Championship Poetry Slam** (3rd weekend in July). There is also a unique sculpture garden featuring a computer-and-wire crucifix and mammoth cocoon.

CAMBRIA AND SAN SIMEON ☎ 805

The original Anglo-Saxon settlers of the southern end of Big Sur were awe-struck by the stunning pastoral views and rugged shoreline, reminiscent of the eastern coast of England. In homage to the natural beauty of their homeland, they gave this equally impressive New World territory the name Cambria, after the ancient Roman name for Wales. Today, Cambria is a small country town offering travelers a pleasant place to enjoy food, shopping, and timeless views. Ten miles north of Cambria, neighboring New San Simeon is a strip town along Hwy. 1 with few roads and many motels near spectacular beaches. It's the last stop for travelers heading north to Big Sur or those making the pilgrimage to Hearst Castle. Old San Simeon is north of New San Simeon and consists only of the 150-year-old Sebastian Store, and the homes of Hearst Corporation ranchers. Newspaper tycoon William Randolph Hearst built Hearst Castle, an extravagant hilltop villa that puts Disney to shame, over the course of 28 years (1919-1947) inviting the rich and famous (and his mistress, Marion Davies) to visit him there.

▐ TRANSPORTATION

Regional Transit Authority (RTA; ☎541-2228) formerly known as Central Coast Area Transit (CCAT), runs a bus (#12) from San Luis Obispo to Morro Bay ($1-1.50), Cambria ($1.50), and San Simeon ($2.25); you may have to flag buses down. Carry exact change. Buses run Monday through Saturday. **Cambria Village Transit** (☎927-0468) is a free trolley service through Cambria (M and F-Su every 30min. 9am-6pm). There is no public transportation to Hearst Castle.

▐ PRACTICAL INFORMATION

Visitor Information: Cambria Chamber of Commerce, 767 Main St. (☎927-3624), provides maps of the area. Open M-F 9am-5pm. **San Simeon Chamber of Commerce,** 250 San Simeon Ave. (☎927-3500), on the west side of Hwy. 1; look for tourist info signs. Open Apr.-Oct. M-Sa 9am-noon and 1-4pm; Nov.-Mar. M-F reduced hours.

24hr. ATM: Bank of America, 2258 Main St., in Cambria.

Police: Sheriff, ☎800-834-3346.

Library and Internet Access: Cambria Branch Library, 900 Main St. (☎927-4336), in Cambria. Open Tu-F 11am-5pm, Sa noon-4pm.

Post Offices: Cambria, 4100 Bridge St. (☎927-8610). Open M-F 9am-5pm. **Postal Code:** 93428. **San Simeon** (☎927-4156), on Hwy. 1, in the back of Sebastian's General Store. Take the road opposite the entrance to Hearst Castle. Open M-F 8:30am-noon and 1-5pm. **Postal Code:** 93452.

▐▌ ACCOMMODATIONS AND CAMPING

Cambria has lovely but pricey B&Bs; budget travelers will have better luck in San Simeon. The arrival of the national chain Motel 6 set off a pricing war that has led to wildly fluctuating rates, so it is always a good idea to call ahead. Beware of skyrocketing prices in summer, when tourists storm the castle.

▨ **San Simeon State Beach Campground** (☎927-2020, reservations 800-444-7275), just north of Cambria on Hwy. 1. San Simeon Creek has showers at its 134 developed sites near the beach. Neighboring Washburn sits on a breezy hill overlooking the ocean and has primitive camping, pit toilets, and cold running water. San Simeon Creek sites $20, seniors $18. Washburn sites $15/$13. Hike/bike $2. ❶

▨ **Bridge Street Inn,** 4314 Bridge St. (☎927-7653), in Cambria. Originally built in the 1890s for the preacher of the church next door. The sunny and sparkling rooms in this recently renovated house have sturdy bunk-beds. Individual bed curtains provide some nighttime privacy. White picket fence encloses a yard for volleyball and croquet. Pleasant living room with fireplace. Continental breakfast and linen included. Reception 5-9pm. Dorms $20; private rooms $40-70. ❷

Creekside Inn, 2618 Main St. (☎927-4021 or 800-269-5212), in Cambria. Look for a yellow cottage-like building. Some rooms have balconies overlooking the creek, and all have TVs and VCRs. Rooms with queen-size bed Su-Th $89, F-Sa $125-145; king-size bed with balcony Su-Th $99, F-Sa $129; double beds with balcony $109, F-Sa $139. $40 less in winter. Prices fluctuate with room availability. ❺

Sands by the Sea, 9355 Hearst Dr. (☎927-3243 or 800-444-0779), in San Simeon, west of Hwy. 1 near the beach. All rooms have king-size bed, cable TV, and coffee makers. Some have VCRs. Coffee, muffins, and juice served in the morning. Indoor heated pool. Rooms July-Aug. Su-Th $65-95, F-Sa $125-145; May-Jun. and Sept.-Oct. $65-80; Nov.-Apr. $35-65. $5 per additional person. ❹

Motel 6, 9070 Castillo Dr. (☎927-8691), in San Simeon off Hwy. 1. The benefits of chain consistency and economies of scale are manifest in these big, clean, and comfy rooms with cable TV. May-Sept. singles Su-Th $63, F-Sa $83; doubles Su-Th $69, F-Sa $89. Oct.-Apr. singles from $40; doubles from $46. $3 per additional person. ❸

◗ FOOD

Food is more plentiful in Cambria than in San Simeon. Though most places have pre-established opening and closing times, they may close early if business is slow, so plan ahead, especially if you want to dine after 8:30pm. Groceries are available at **Soto's Market,** 2244 Main St., in Cambria. (☎927-4411. Open M-Th 7am-8pm, F-Sa 7am-9pm, Su 8am-6pm.) Buy fresh local produce at the Cambria **Farmers Market** every on Main St. next to the Veteran's Hall. (F 2:30-5:30pm). All the establishments below are located in or close to Cambria.

▨ **Robin's,** 4095 Burton Dr. (☎927-5007). Many San Luis Obispo residents consider this the only reason to drive the 30 mi. to Cambria. Eclectic international cuisine in a Craftsman-style bungalow with outdoor gardens. Lunch sandwiches $7.50-12.50. Veggie options like Thai curry tofu $13. Entrees $12-18. Extensive wine list. Open daily 11am-9pm or later. Reservations recommended for evenings. ❸

Bistro Sole, 1980 Main St. (☎927-0887). This bistro cultivates an intimate, welcoming dining atmosphere and specializes in creative dishes (polenta napoleon $15), all made from scratch and changing seasonally. Su brunch features live music. Lunch entrees $7.50-13. Dinner entrees $16-24. Open M-Th 11:30am-2:30pm and 5-9pm, F-Sa 11:30am-2:30pm and 5-9:30pm, Su 11am-2:30pm and 5-9pm. ❹

Creekside Gardens Cafe, 2114 Main St. (☎927-8646), at the Redwood Shopping Center. Locals frequent this petite eatery for hearty "California country cookin'." Indoor or patio dining. Pancakes $4.50-6. In the evening, "Creekside de Noche" serves Mexican food such as combination plates with beans and rice ($8.25). Desserts ($2-3) made fresh daily. Open M-Sa 7am-2pm and 5-9pm, Su 7am-1pm. No credit cards. ❶

Main St. Grill, 603 Main St. (☎927-3194). Extremely popular eatery serves fast, cheap, high-quality grill food in a spacious, sports-themed restaurant. The patio seating is pleasant on a sunny day. Burgers $3.70. Baby-back ribs $10. Salads $7-8.50. Open daily 11am-8:30 or later. Cash only; ATM inside. ❷

The Hamlet at Moonstone Gardens (☎927-3535), off Hwy. 1, approximately 2 mi. north of Cambria at Moonstone Gardens. Don't judge from the driftwood exterior; the hamlet has a spectacular ocean view and lovely outdoor seating for lunch. Soft, live music often plays for a more mature dinner crowd on F-Sa. "Sunset Jazz" series on alternate Su at 4pm (cover $15) and 7:15pm (cover $12). Lunch specials (11am-4pm), like quiche lorraine ($8.50) or calamari and chips ($10). Bowls of chowder $6. Entrees $12-30. Open daily 11:30am-8:30pm. Bar usually open until 10pm. ❹

French Corner Cafe and Bakery, 2214 Main St. (☎927-8227). A cute little corner cafe and bakery modeled after Parisian cafes and *boulangeries*. Indoor and outdoor seating. Seeded baguette $3. Cream puffs $2. Fresh berry tarts $2.50. Open daily 7am-6pm. ❶

THE CENTRAL COAST

👁 🏖 SIGHTS AND BEACHES

🏛 HEARST CASTLE

On Hwy. 1, 3 mi. north of San Simeon and 9 mi. north of Cambria. Info ☎ 927-2010, reservations 800-444-4445, wheelchair accessible reservations 927-2070 or toll free 866-712-2286. Visitors center open 8am-6pm. **Tours:** *Call in advance, as tours often sell out. Each tour involves climbing 150-370 staircase steps. 4 different types of daytime tours leave frequently. Tours 1, 2, 3, and 4 last approximately 1¾hr. $24, ages 6-12 $12, under 6 free. Tour 5, available on most weekend evenings during the spring and fall, features costumed docents acting out the castle's legendary Hollywood history (2hr.; $30, ages 6-12 $15, under 6 free). During the low season (Sept. 16-May 14) tours 1-4 cost $20, ages 6-12 $10. National Geographic Theater:* ☎ *927-6811. 40min. IMAX films daily every 45 min. 8:15am-5:15pm. Tickets $8, ages 6-17 $6, under 6 free. A film ticket is included with the purchase of a Tour 1 pass. $2 discount on movie admission with tours 2, 3, and 4.*

Newspaper magnate and multi-millionaire owner William Randolph Hearst casually referred to it as "the ranch," or, in his more romantic moments, "La Cuesta Encantada" (Spanish for "the Enchanted Hill"). Today, officially referred to as the Hearst San Simeon State Historic Monument, and popularly known as Hearst Castle, the estate does indeed stand as a monument to Hearst's unfathomable wealth and Julia Morgan's architectural genius. An indescribably decadent dreamland of limestone castle, shaded cottages, exquisite pools, fragrant gardens, and Mediterranean *esprit*, the complex rests high on grassy hills sloping down to the Pacific. Architectural planning began in 1919 and construction lasted 28 years until 1947.

While traveling in Europe with his mother at age 10, young Hearst caught a bad case of art-collecting fever. He spent the rest of his life gathering Renaissance sculpture, tapestries, and ceilings, and telling his architect to incorporate them into his castle's design. Julia Morgan, the first woman to receive a certificate in architecture from the prestigious Ecole des Beaux-Arts in Paris, orchestrated this artistic chaos into a coherent triumph of the Mediterranean Revival style, blending elements of ancient Greece, Spanish cathedrals, and red-tiled villas. Scores of celebrities and luminaries such as Greta Garbo, Charlie Chaplin, Charles Lindbergh, and Winston Churchill visited the castle to bask in Hearst's legendary hospitality. While countless memorable cast parties were held on these grounds, the only things ever filmed here were 30 seconds of *Spartacus* and the end of a Kodak Funsaver commercial. Hearst Castle is also famous for what was not filmed here—Orson Welles's masterpiece, *Citizen Kane* (see p. 22), which bears more than a passing resemblance to Hearst's life (Hearst reportedly tried to prevent the film from ever seeing the light of a film projector).

Before going to see the castle, your experience will be enhanced by stopping by the **visitors center** at the base of the hill, which features a surprisingly frank portrait of Hearst's failed days at Harvard University, his central role in yellow journalism, and the scandals of his life. At one point, Hearst's mistress, Marion Davies, had to sell her jewels so that construction of her indebted lover's mansion could continue without interruption. Five different tours are run by witty and knowledgeable guides from the State Parks Department. Tour 1 includes well-rounded exposure to both the interior and exterior of the monument as well as a viewing of a National Geographic IMAX documentary on the architectural wonder.

BEACHES

Big Sur's dramatic coastline comes to a stunning end in San Simeon. Sea otters, once near extinction, now live in the kelp beds of **Moonstone Beach,** on Moonstone Dr. off Hwy. 1, just south of San Simeon at the northern end of Cambria. Along this stretch of coast, surfers are occasionally nudged off their boards by playful seals (and, far more rarely, by not-so-playful great white sharks, who thrive in these waters; see **Sharks,** p. 57). Scenic **Leffingwell's Landing** offers the best spot for **whale-watching.** In addition to providing the best swimming for miles, **San Simeon** and **Hearst State Beaches,** just across from Hearst Castle, are ideal for beachcombing .

SANTA YNEZ VALLEY ☎ 805

To the northwest of Santa Barbara along Rte. 154 lies the lovely **Santa Ynez Valley,** home to thousands of acres of vineyards, hundreds of ostriches, and Michael Jackson's **Neverland Ranch,** named after J. M. Barrie's fantasy world. The free *Santa Barbara County Wineries Touring Map*, available at the Santa Barbara Visitors Center, provides comprehensive listings. One of the prettiest vineyards is **Gainey Vineyard,** 3950 E. Rte. 246, at Rte. 154. (☎ 688-0558. Open daily 10am-5pm. Tours daily 11am, 1, 2, 3pm. Tastings $5; includes 9 tastes and logo glass.)

At the intersection of Rte. 246 and U.S. 101 is the town of **Buellton,** home of **Pea Soup Andersen's ❶,** where the split pea soup ($4) has been served thick, hot, and fresh since 1924. For $8, patrons feast on all-you-can-eat soup, pumpernickel, and Danish cheese bread plus a soda or thick milkshake. (☎ 688-5581. Open daily 7am-10pm.) Four miles east on Rte. 246, thatched roofs cluster in **Solvang Village,** a supremely quaint Danish haven. Crammed with northern European gift shops, restaurants, and *conditoris* (bakeries), this overpriced, Disney-esque town is a tribute to its Danish ancestors and a peculiar tourist attraction. The **Solvang Bakery,** 460 Alisal Rd., bakes fresh bread ($4), assembles deli sandwiches ($5) and claims to be "Solvang's favorite coffeehouse." (☎ 688-4939. Open daily 7am-6pm; in summer F-Sa until 8pm.) Behind the bakery is the graceful **Mission Santa Inés,** 1760 Mission Dr. Look for the footprint of a Chumash child in the Chapel of the Madonnas and the graves of 1700 Chumash people. (☎ 688-4815. Open daily Feb.-Nov. 9am-7pm; Dec.-Jan. 9am-5:30pm. $3, under 16 free.)

Farther northwest, at the juncture of Hwy. 1 and Rte. 246, is the city of **Lompoc,** home to the nation's largest producer of flower seed. The acres upon acres of blooms, which peak near the end of June, are both a visual and olfactory explosion. Lompoc holds a **flower festival** (☎ 735-8511) at the season's peak, usually the last weekend in June. **La Purisma Mission State Park,** 2295 Purisma Rd., has the most fully restored of Father Serra's missions and 12 mi. of trails. Follow Rte. 246; the entrance is off Mission Gate Rd. (☎ 733-7781. Open daily 9am-5pm. Parking $4.)

THE LOCAL STORY

HAP-PEA DAYS

When Danish immigrants Anton and Juliette Andersen opened a small restaurant named "Andersen's Electric Cafe" (after their new electric stove), they probably had no idea that they had flipped the switch on a craze that would bring their establishment fame for over 80 years. Just three years after they served their first bowl of split pea soup, the Andersen needed to order one ton of peas to fill their customers' rapidly growing hunger for the concoction. Lacking adequate storage space, Anton put the peas in the restaurant window and proclaimed the cafe "The Home of Split Pea Soup"—and the rest is history.

Today, Pea Soup Andersen's still dishes out hot, fresh bowls of its namesake specialty in the magnitude of thousands of servings a day. The recipe for the soup is no secret. In fact, Andersen's even sells bags of split peas along with instructions for creating your own home version of the murky magic. Still, many customers claim that their soup can't match the unique flavor of Andersen's own. The restaurant suggests that "perhaps it's the magical touch that Juliette lent to the cauldrons and ladles so many years ago."

Whatever it is, it continues to make repeat customers out of the hundreds of hungry travelers who count this a favorite rest stop. On a daily basis, the line to be seated is as thick as, well, pea soup.

SAN LUIS OBISPO ☎805

Amid sprawling green hills close to the rocky coast, (San Luis Obispo ; san-LEW-is oh-BIS-boh; frequently condensed to SLO; pronounced "slow") is a town that lives up to its nickname but by no means stands still. While the mission has reigned as the center of local life since 1772, this area only became a full-fledged town after the Southern Pacific Railroad laid tracks here in 1894. Ranchers and oil refinery employees comprise a large percentage of today's population (44,359), and California Polytechnic State University (Cal Poly) students add a young, energetic component to the mix. Along the main roads in downtown, hip students mingle with laid-back locals in outdoor eateries, trendy shops, and music-filled bars.

⌐ TRANSPORTATION

Trains: Amtrak, 1011 Railroad Ave. (☎541-0505 or 800-USA-RAIL/872-7245), at the foot of Santa Rosa St., 7 blocks south of Higuera St. Open daily 5:45am-8:30pm. To: **L.A.** ($30); **San Francisco** ($36); **Santa Barbara** ($18-20). It's cheapest to reserve at least a week in advance.

Buses: Greyhound, 150 South St. (☎543-2121 or 800-231-2222), ½ mi. from downtown. Open daily 7:30am-6pm; in summer also open 8:30-9pm. To **L.A.** (4½-5hr., 5 per day, $27.50-29.50) and **San Francisco** (6-7hr., 5 per day, $45-48). To get to downtown from the station, walk west on South St., then north on Higuera St.

Public Transportation: The **Regional Transit Authority** (**RTA;** ☎541-2228; www.slorta.com) formerly known as Central Coast Area Transit (CCAT) links SLO to: **Los Osos** (#11, 12; $0.75-1); **Morro Bay** (#12, $1.50); **Paso Robles** (#9, $1.75); **Pismo Beach** (#10, $1). Day pass $3. Buses depart from City Hall at Osos and Palm St. On Sa, only buses #9 (north to San Miguel), #10 (south to Santa Maria) and #12 (north to San Simeon) operate. **SLO Transit** (☎541-2877; www.rideshare.org) runs buses throughout the city; they're faster than the acronym would suggest. Buses run M-F 6:45am-8:30pm, Sa-Su 8am-6:20pm. Sa only buses #2-6 operate; Su only buses #2-5 operate. $1, seniors and disabled $0.50; free transfers. SLO Transit's **downtown trolley** runs Th 3:30-9pm, F-Sa 12:30-9pm, Su 10am-3:30pm. Additional service to hotels along Monterey St. $0.25. **Ride-On** (☎541-8747) offers safe rides ($2 per person) and other shuttle services. **Safe rides** (☎235-SAFE/7233) runs Th-Sa 9pm-2:30am.

◢ ② ORIENTATION AND PRACTICAL INFORMATION

San Luis Obispo is at the heart of the Central Coast. It sits inland on **U.S. 101,** burrowed among ranch-laden mountains. This small town serves as a hub between the smaller towns of Morro Bay, 12 mi. north on Hwy. 1, and Avila Beach, Shell Beach, and Pismo Beach, all about 12 mi. south on Hwy. 1.

Downtown, **Monterey** and **Higuera Streets** (north-south) and **Broad** and **Garden Streets** (east-west), are the main drags. Walking here is easy and there is plenty of cheap parking. One-hour **free parking** is available on streets and in parking structures downtown at the Palm St. (at Morro St.) and Marsh St. (at Chorro St.) lots.

Visitor Information: Visitors Center for the Chamber of Commerce, 1039 Chorro St. (☎781-2777; www.visitslo.com). Watch for signs on U.S. 101. Staff and brochures. Open M 10am-5pm, Tu-W 8am-5pm, Th 8am-8pm, F 8am-7pm, Sa 10am-7pm, Su 11am-5pm.

Laundromat: California Coin Laundry, 552 California Blvd. (☎544-8266). Wash $2, dry $0.25 per 8-10min. Open 24hr.

Police: 1042 Walnut St. (☎781-7317).

Hotlines: Counseling and referrals, ☎800-549-8989. 24hr. **Weather Conditions,** ☎541-6666, ext. 580.

Medical Services: French Hospital Medical Center, 1911 Johnson Ave. (☎543-5353).

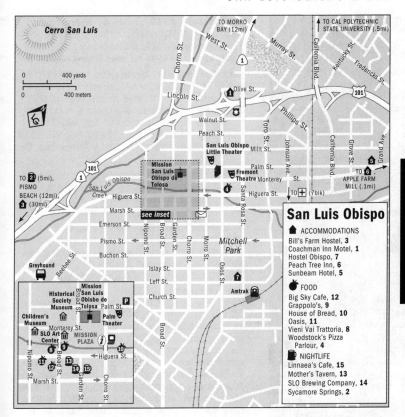

Library and Internet Access: San Luis Obispo Branch Library, 995 Palm St. (☎781-5989), on the 2nd fl. Open M-W 10am-8pm, Th-Sa 10am-5pm. **SLO Perk,** 1028 Chorro St. (☎541-4616). $1.50 per 15min., $5 per hr. Open daily 7am-6pm.

Post Office: 893 Marsh St. (☎541-9138). Open M-F 8:30am-5:30pm, Sa 10am-5pm. **Postal Code:** 93406.

ACCOMMODATIONS

Hotel rates in San Luis Obispo fluctuate daily, depending on the weather, the season, the number of travelers that day, and even the position of the moon. In nearby **Pismo Beach** and **Morro Bay** the prices are more stable. It is often cheapest to stay in hotels downtown during the week and in hostels during the weekends. Make a reservation well in advance during summer weekends and events; Cal Poly commencement is in mid-June.

Hostel Obispo (HI-AYH), 1617 Santa Rosa St. (☎544-4678; www.hostelobispo.com). Convenient location just 1 block from the Amtrak station (exit to your right) and 6 blocks from downtown. Tight-knit atmosphere. The relaxing common room is great for conversations with fellow travelers. Homemade sourdough pancakes included. Linen

COME ON, VOGUE

The **Madonna Inn**, in south SLO, is probably the only hotel in the world that sells postcards of each room. Alex S. Madonna, the contractor behind the construction of much of U.S. 101 and I-5, decided in 1958 to build a Queen Anne-style hotel of 12 rooms fit for the most discerning material girl. He put his wife, Phyllis, in charge of the design.

By 1962, the vision had grown into a hot-pink behemoth of 101 rooms on 2200 acres of land. The men's room is truly a work of art, featuring a giant laser-operated waterfall that doubles as a urinal.

Each room has its own theme. Take a holiday in the Caveman Room, or express yourself in the Daisy Mae Room. One room even has a working waterwheel serving as a headboard.

Nonguests can cherish coffee and a bun from the Madonna's oven or dine on steak in bubble-gum pink booths surrounding a giant gold-cast tree, illuminated by flower-shaped electric bulbs. You can also check out the photo album of the rooms in the reception area. At night, there's swing music from 7 to 11pm in the lounge to keep things hoppin'.

100 Madonna Rd., off U.S. 101; take the Madonna Rd. exit. ☎ *543-3000. Rooms $127-320.*

included. Towel $0.50. Laundry $1. Reception 7:30-10am and 4:30-10pm. Lockout 10am-4:30pm. Dorms $18, nonmembers $20; private family room for 2-4 people $50-85, children half-price. No credit cards. ❷

Peach Tree Inn, 2001 Monterey St. (☎543-3170 or 800-227-6396). Cozy, creek-side country-style inn with motel appearance, located on the edge of town. Rooms with TV, coffeemaker, and telephone. Continental breakfast included. Rooms Apr.-Oct. Su-Th $59-99, F-Sa $79-130; Nov.-Mar. Su-Th $59-89, F-Sa $79-120. 10% discount for seniors, AAA, and AARP members. ❹

Sunbeam Hotel, 1656 Monterey St. (☎543-8141). Looks like an apartment complex. Spartan rooms have cable TV, A/C, fridges, phones, and coffeemakers. Pastry breakfast included. Rooms May-Sept. M-Th $36-59, F-Sa $69-99; Oct.-Apr. $36-59. ❸

Coachman Inn Motel, 1001 Olive St. (☎544-0400), a few blocks from downtown, near the Hwy. 101 S exit. Sizable, immaculate rooms come with cable TV and fridges. Pets $10. May-Sept. singles and 3doubles M-Th $37-89, F-Su $89-198. Oct.-Apr. singles $30-40; doubles $35-49. ❸

Bill's Farm Hostel, 1040 Cielo Ln. (☎929-3647), in Nipomo, 30 mi. south of SLO. Exit U.S. 101 S. on Tefft St., turn right on Tefft St., left on Orchard St., and right on Primavera St.; Cielo Ln. is on the left. Not for the prissy or picky traveler, Bill's cluttered retreat offers a real secluded farm feel and a unique experience. Those without cars need to arrange a ride with Bill into town for public transport. Linen $1. Check-in by 9pm. Lights out 10pm. Wake-up call (with bugle) 8am. Donation of $14 can be replaced with 2½hr. of farm work, like milking the goats. Required chore, musical performance, or $4. ❶

🏕 CAMPING

All state park sites can be reserved through **ReserveAmerica** (☎800-444-7275) up to seven months in advance. In summer, you need reservations at beach parks; particularly crowded parks require reservations year-round.

Montaña de Oro State Park (☎528-0513), on Pecho Rd., 7 mi. south of Los Osos, 12 mi. from SLO via Los Osos Valley Rd. 50 primitive sites in a gorgeous, secluded park. Outhouses and cold running water (but bring your own drinking water). Reserve weeks in advance for sites June-Sept. 6. Sites $15; in low season $11. ❶

Morro Strand State Beach (☎772-2560), off Hwy. 1, at the northern edge of Morro Bay. 76 contiguous sites along a beautiful stretch of sandy beach. Toilets and water but no hot showers. 24 ft. vehicle length limit. Your receipt allows you to use the showers at Morro Bay State Park without paying another entrance fee. Sites $20, seniors $18; in low season $15/$13. ❷

Pismo Beach State Park (☎ 489-1869), on Hwy. 1, just south of scenic Pismo Beach. A huge campground split into 2 areas. **North Beach** has 103 tent sites with water, coin showers, and restrooms. Sanitary disposal. **Oceano** has 40 tent sites and 42 RV hook-ups. Water, flush toilets, and showers. North Beach sites are larger and closer to the beach. Call for reservations. Sites $20, seniors $18; RVs $29; hike/bike $2. ❶

⬛ FOOD

Higuera Street and its cross streets are lined with restaurants and cafes that serve greasy-spoon fare alongside many healthy, organic choices. The area south of the mission along the creek is popular with lunchtime crowds. A weekly **Farmers Market** (Th 6-9pm) takes over Higuera St. between Nipomo and Osos St.

▨ **Big Sky Cafe,** 1121 Broad St. (☎ 545-5401). Voted "Best Restaurant in SLO" in a recent magazine poll and winner of many local awards, Big Sky delivers vegetarian-friendly food under the stars on the outdoor patio or under the tiled ceiling. Lunch sandwiches $7-11. Dinner entrees $7.75-20. Local wines $4-6 per glass. Margaritas $3.50. Open M 7am-9pm, Tu-Sa 7am-10pm, Su 8am-9pm. ❷

▨ **Oasis,** 675 Higuera St. (☎ 543-1155). Lavish surroundings and belly dancers enhance the Mediterranean and Moroccan cuisine. The Oasis feast (appetizer, soup or salad, entree, baklava or cup of mint tea; $24) satisfies even the most weary desert traveler. Lunch entrees $7-15. Dinner entrees $13-16. Belly dancing F-Sa 7-9pm. Open daily 11am-10pm. Reservations highly recommended. ❸

Woodstock's Pizza Parlour, 1000 Higuera St. (☎ 541-4420). This hangout invariably sweeps annual best pizza awards. Young crowds keep it lively into the night. Lunch specials like all-you-can-eat pizza and bottomless soda $7. Single slice $1.90, whole pies $5.50-20. Toppings $0.60-2.20. Happy hour M-W 8-11pm; pitchers $4-8, slices $1.50. Open Su-W 11am-midnight, Th-Sa 11am-1am; slightly reduced winter hours. ❷

House of Bread, 858 Higuera St. (☎ 542-0255). Enticing smells will lure you into this warm bakery, which uses chemical-free Montana wheat in its delicious bread products. Free samples. Raspberry pinwheel or huge cinnamon roll $2. Open M-W and F 7am-7pm, Th 7am-9pm, Sa 7am-6:30pm, Su 8am-5pm. ❶

Grappolo's, 1040 Broad St. (☎ 788-0260). This Italian restaurant and bar overlooks San Luis Obispo Creek. Dishes range $10-24 and the wine list is one of the most extensive in town. After dinner, head downstairs to the intimate, dimly lit basement bar. Kitchen open Su-Th 11:30am-9pm, F-Sa 11:30am-11pm. Bar open daily until 1am. ❸

Vieni Vai Trattoria, 690 Higuera St. (☎ 544-5282). Homemade organic pasta and ravioli with lots of vegetarian sauces ($8-13). Half-order portions are plenty for mid-sized appetites. Seafood, chicken, and veal $13-17. Pizza $9-12. Similar lunch menu $7-12. Full bar. Open Su-Th 11am-10pm, F-Sa 11am-11pm. Bar open F-Sa until 1am. ❸

◉ 🔼 SIGHTS AND OUTDOOR ACTIVITIES

MISSION SAN LUIS OBISPO DE TOLOSA. San Luis Obispo grew around the Mission San Luis Obispo de Tolosa, and the city continues to hold celebrations and general lunchtime socializing near its front steps. Founded in 1772, the mission was once covered in white clapboards and crowned with a steeple in the New England style. In the late 1800s, however, the town began reviving the mission's Spanish origins; by the 1930s it was fully restored. The mission still serves as one of the Catholic parish churches for SLO. It also houses a small museum, which displays objects from the early days of the mission and a small collection of Chumash artifacts. (☎ 543-6850; www.missionsanluisobispo.org. Open daily early Apr.-late Oct. 9am-5pm; late Oct.-early Apr. 9am-4pm. Suggested donation $2.) The mission faces beautiful Mission Plaza, where Father Serra held the area's first mass. At the edge of the plaza sits the **SLO Art Center,** which features lectures, art classes, poetry readings, exhibits by regional artists, and the Pleinair Painting Festival in early October. *(1010 Broad St. ☎543-8562. Open Su-M and W-Sa 11am-5pm. Open July 4-Labor Day Tu 11am-5pm. Free, but donations are appreciated.)*

OTHER SIGHTS. The nearby **Jack House** is a restored Victorian residence with original 19th-century furnishings and a gazebo and garden outside. *(536 Marsh St. ☎781-7308, tour info 781-7300. Open Su 1-4pm. 45min. tours $2.)* Kids enjoy dabbling at the **SLO Children's Museum,** where craft time is included in the price of admission. *(1010 Nipomo St. ☎544-5437. Open Tu-Sa 11am-5pm, Su noon-4pm. Craft time Tu 11:20am-1pm, Th 2-3:30pm, Sa noon-2pm. $5, under 2 free.)* The old public library now houses the **SLO Historical Society Museum.** Changing exhibits depict eras of San Luis Obispo's history. *(696 Monterey St. ☎543-0638. Open W-Su 10am-4pm. Free.)*

MONTANA DE ORO STATE PARK. Gray whales, seals, otters, dolphins, and the occasional orca frequent **Montana de Oro State Park,** whose 8000 acres and 7 mi. of shoreline remain relatively secluded. **Spooner's Cove,** across from the campground three-quarters of a mile north of Coralina Cove, has tide pools and whale-watching spots at Bluff's Trailhead. Get info about hikes at the Ranger's Office in the old ranch house. *(30min. west of SLO on Los Osos Valley Rd. ☎528-0513. Ranger's Office ☎772-7434. Open in summer daily 8:30am-9:30pm; in winter M-Th 8:30am-3:30pm, F-Su noon-4pm.)*

WINERIES. The wineries near SLO are well respected. **Paso Robles** is vintner central. The SLO Chamber of Commerce and the Paso Robles **Chamber of Commerce** have a list of wineries, including visiting hours, tours, and tastings. *(1225 Park St., 25 mi. north of SLO on U.S. 101. ☎238-0506. Open M-F 8:30am-5pm, Sa 10am-4pm.)* Wild Horse, Justin Winery, and Steven Ross are some renowned labels. To taste in San Luis Obispo proper, try **Central Coast Wineries.** *(712 Higuera St. ☎544-8761. Open Su-W 11am-6pm, Th 11am-9pm, F-Sa 11am-8am. Local winemakers host tastings Th 6-9pm for $4.)*

MISSION SAN MIGUEL ARCHANGEL. Rocked by the 2003 San Simeon earthquake, much of the mission is closed until the estimated $16 million in restoration is complete. For now the gift shop remains open and offers a two-room self-guided tour. *(43 mi. north of San Luis Obispo in San Miguel, just off U.S. 101; take the San Miguel exit. ☎467-3256. Open daily 9:30am-4:30pm. Suggested donation $1.)*

BEACHES. Two unmarked beaches just southwest of San Luis Obispo are frequented by distinctly different crowds. Some wear their swimsuits, and others don't at **Pirate's Cove,** which has unusually warm water, kind to nude bathers' pleasure and pride. *(Take U.S. 101 S from San Luis Obispo to the Avila Rd. exit. Follow signs for Avila Beach, but turn left on Cave Landing Rd. Park in the dirt lot and take a 500 yd. path to the cove.)* The rocky shore of **Shell Beach** is the launching point for many kayaks. *(1 mi. down U.S. 101 south of Avila Beach and Pirate's Cove. Take the Shell Beach exit from U.S. 101 S and turn left on Shell Beach Rd. A right on Cliff Ave. will lead to Ocean Blvd. Park at the gazebo.)* Avila and Pismo Beaches are both more developed and crowded than Shell Beach. **Avila Beach** is smaller and known for its gaggle of fishermen. The adjoining city streets seem determined to mimic the boardwalk atmosphere of Pismo. *(Off U.S. 101 at the Avila Beach Dr. exit.)* **Pismo Beach** is the most developed and congested beach in the area; the lines for the public restrooms are practically social events. **Beach Cycle Rentals** rents all kinds of beach equipment just south of the pier. *(519 Cypress St. ☎773-9400. Open daily 9am-6pm.)* When the sun sets behind the hills that jut into the sea, Pismo Beach lights up with a gorgeous sand-on-fire effect. *(Off U.S. 101 1½ mi. south of Shell Beach. Accessible by Regional Transit Authority and Greyhound.)*

PISMO DUNES. Head to this State Vehicular Recreation Area to take your car or all-terrain vehicle (ATV) down onto the dunes. *(South of Pismo Beach on Grover Beach. There are 2 entrances to the dunes: Grover Beach on Grand Ave. off Hwy. 1 and Pier Ave. in*

Oceano, 1 mi. south off Hwy. 1. ☎ *473-7223. Day-use $5, seniors $4.)* Rent ATV equipment from **Steve's ATV.** *(1206 W. Grand Ave. in Grover Beach.* ☎ *474-6431; www.stevesatv.com. 1 hr. ATV rental including helmet $25-75. Hummer beach tours $35, under 12 $15. Open daily 8am-6pm.)* Those surpassing the speed limit of 15 mph risk paying a very hefty fine and their lives, as careless, fast driving on the dunes can be deadly. At the south end of the park is **Oso Flaco Lake ❶,** accessible by hiking. Camping here is an option only for the most serious budget traveler; on weekends, prepare for revving engines and squealing tires. *(*☎ *473-7223. Sites $10, seniors $8.)*

🎵 🎭 ENTERTAINMENT AND NIGHTLIFE

Half of SLO's population is under the age of 24, so the town can't help but party. It gets particularly wild along **Higuera Street** between Nipomo and Osos St. after the Thursday night **Farmers Market,** which often resembles a raging block party more than a produce bazaar. **San Luis Obispo Little Theater,** 888 Morro St., has performances by local thespians. (☎ 786-2440. Shows F and Su 8pm, Sa 2 and 8pm. $17, students and seniors $15.) The **Palm Theater,** 817 Palm St., screens artsy and revival films at odd times; call for a schedule. (☎ 541-5161. Films $7, seniors and children $4; matinees $4; M night $4.) Standard Hollywood flicks often run at the grand **Art Deco Freemont Theatre,** 1035 Monterey St., designed in 1942 by the preeminent Southern Californian architect Charles Lee. The main theater maintains the original murals. (Films $7.50, seniors and children $5.50; matinees before 5:30pm $5.50.) Weekdays in SLO slow down a bit as the students attempt to salvage their grades. Consult the free weekly *New Times* available at restaurants and motels regarding other local happenings; nightlife options range from disco dancing and live big bands to pool clubs and gallery openings.

🏆 **Mother's Tavern,** 725 Higuera St. (☎ 541-8733). This Yukon-inspired bar and restaurant with mounted animal heads draws mostly Cal Poly students who pile in for the DJ Tu-F. Tu 80s night. Free karaoke Su-M. Happy hour M-F 3-6pm; half-price pitchers, $1 off pints and call drinks. Live music Sa 9:30pm-1:30am and Su 3-6pm (usually draws more mature crowds). 21+ after 9pm. Cover $1-5. Open daily 11:30am-1:30am. Kitchen closes 9pm.

SLO Brewing Company, 1119 Garden St. (☎ 543-1843). Winner of the World Beer Cup 2000 for its India Pale Ale, the Brewing Co. also features amazingly good porter ("Cole Porter"; pints $4). Happy hour M-F 4-5:30pm; half-price pitchers. Live funk, reggae, and rock downstairs Th-Sa at 9:30pm (cover varies). 7 billiard tables upstairs ($4-8 per hr.). Strict dress code (no gang paraphernalia). Downstairs open M-W 11:30am-10pm, Th-Sa 11:30am-1:30am, Su 11:30am-9pm. Upstairs open daily 11:30am-midnight, as late as 2am depending on the crowd.

Linnaea's Cafe, 1112 Garden St. (☎ 541-5888; www.linnaeas.com). Evening hangout for the artsy set. Displays local artists' works on the walls and features eclectic live music from classical to hard rock (F-Sa 8:30-10:30pm). No cover, but a hat is passed around after each performance. Open M-W 6:30am-11pm, Th-Sa 6:30am-midnight, Su 6:30am-2pm and 6-11pm. No credit cards.

Sycamore Springs, 1215 Avila Beach Dr. (☎ 595-7302), about 5 mi. south of SLO. Take Avila Beach Dr. exit from U.S. 101 S and follow Avila Beach Dr. about 1 mi. toward Avila Beach. Private outdoor redwood hot tubs with sulfurous mineral water provide nearly around-the-clock relaxation. Tubs hold up to 8 people. Each tub $20 per hr. for first person; $10 per hr. per additional person. Reservations recommended 8pm-2am, especially on weekends. Open daily 7am-2am.

✿ FESTIVALS

Free **Concerts in the Plaza** bring live music to downtown's Mission Plaza on Friday evenings in summer. (☎541-0286; www.downtownslo.com. Live music June-Aug. F 5:30-7:30pm.) The **Mozart Festival** in August is also a favorite. Concerts are held at the Cal Poly theater, the Cohan Center, the mission, local wineries, and local churches. (For info, call ☎781-3009 or write 1160 Marsh St., #310, San Luis Obispo, CA 93401. For tickets call ☎756-2787 or 888-233-2787. Tickets $17-47.) The acclaimed **Central Coast Shakespeare Festival** runs two Shakespeare plays for six weeks. (☎546-4224; www.ccshakes.org. Starting the 1st or 2nd week in July. Performances Th-Su. $17. No credit cards.) The four-day **International Film Festival** features independent films, documentaries, and seminars. (☎546-3456; www.slofilmfest.org. Late Oct. or early Nov.)

MORRO BAY   ☎805

The Seven Sisters, a chain of small ex-volcanoes, are remnants of a time when SLO County was highly volcanically active. The lava that once flowed here formed the dramatic shorelines along Hwy. 1 from Morro Rock to SLO. The northernmost sister, Morro Rock, and three large smokestacks from an electric company shadow the tiny burg of Morro Bay, just north of its namesake park. **Morro Bay State Park** is home to coastal cypresses that are visited by Monarch butterflies from November to early February. The park's modern, hands-on **Museum of Natural History** flexes its curatorial might on the aquatic environment and wildlife of the coastal headlands. A bulletin board near the entrance lists free nature walks led by park docents. (☎772-2694. Open daily 10am-5pm. $2, under 17 free.) South Bay Blvd., which links the town and the park, winds through the new **Morro Bay National Estuary,** a sanctuary for great blue herons, egrets, and sea otters. Take the trail or rent a kayak or canoe to explore the estuary. Pack a basket and paddle out to the sand dunes for a picnic lunch. Check for tides to avoid (or take advantage of) numerous sandbars. **Kayak Horizons,** 551 Embarcadero, rents kayaks and offers instruction. (☎772-6444; www.kayakhorizons.com. Kayaks $8-16 per hr. Open daily 9am-5pm.)

Along the beach, the **Embarcadero** is the locus of Morro Bay activity and fish 'n' chips bargains. The modest **Morro Bay Aquarium,** 595 Embarcadero, is a rehabilitation center for distressed marine animals and has over 100 ocean critters. The seal-feeding station is a rare opportunity to see these animals only feet away. (☎772-7647. Open daily 9am-6:30pm; in winter 9:30am-5:30pm. $2, ages 5-11 $1, under 5 free.) Morro Bay's pride and joy is the **Giant Chessboard,** 800 Embarcadero, in Centennial Park across from Southern Port Traders. The board is 256 sq. ft., with 18-20 lb. carved redwood pieces. (Call the Morro Bay Recreation office at ☎772-6278 to set up a game or watch for free M-F 8am-5pm. $38 per game.)

RTA bus #12 serves Morro Bay from SLO. (Info ☎541-2228. Runs M-F. $1.50.) Motels here are often cheaper here than in SLO. **Morro Bay Chamber of Commerce,** 880 Main St., has maps and listings. (☎772-4467 or 800-231-0592. Open M-F 8:30am-5pm, Sa 10am-3pm.)

SANTA BARBARA   ☎805

Santa Barbara (pop. 92,500) epitomizes worry-free living. The town is an enclave of wealth and privilege, but in a significantly less aggressive or flashy way than its SoCal counterparts. Spanish Revival architecture predominates on State St., a lively pedestrian-only, palm-lined promenade of cafes, thrift stores, boutiques, and galleries. The city's golden beaches, museums, historic missions, and scenic drives make it a frequent weekend escape for the rich and famous, and an attractive destination for surfers, artists, and backpackers.

⌐ TRANSPORTATION

Driving in Santa Barbara can be bewildering, as dead-ends, one-way streets, and congested traffic abound. Beware of intersections on State St. that surprise motorists with quick-changing traffic lights. Many downtown lots and streets offer 1¼hr. of **free parking,** including two underground lots at Pasco Nuevo, accessible on the 700 block of Chapala St. All parking is free on Sundays. **Biking** is a nice alternative; most streets have special lanes. The **Cabrillo Bikeway** runs east-west along the beach from the Bird Refuge to the City College campus.

Flights: Santa Barbara Municipal Airport (☎683-4011; www.flysba.com), in Goleta. Offers intrastate and limited national service.

Trains: Amtrak, 209 State St. (☎963-1015 or 800-USA-RAIL/872-7245). Be careful around the station after dark. Reserve in advance. Open daily 5:45am-9pm. To **L.A.** (5-6hr., 4-5 per day, $20-25) and **San Francisco** (7hr., 3 per day, $48-68).

Buses: Greyhound, 34 W. Carrillo St. (☎965-7551), at Chapala St. Open M-F 5:30am-8pm, Sa-Su 7am-8pm. To **L.A.** (2-3hr., 9 per day, $12) and **San Francisco** (9-10hr., 5 per day, $34). **Santa Barbara Metropolitan Transit District (MTD),** 1020 Chapala St. (☎683-3702), at Cabrillo Blvd. behind the Greyhound station, is a transit and visitors center that provides bus schedules and serves as the transfer point for most routes. Open M-F 6am-7pm, Sa 8am-6pm, Su 9am-6pm. The MTD runs a purple electric **crosstown shuttle** from Franklin Center on Montecito St. to Mountain and Valerio, running through the transit center on Chapala St. $1.25, seniors and disabled $0.60, under 45 in. free; transfers free. Runs M-F 7am-6pm. The **downtown-waterfront shuttle** along State St. and Cabrillo Blvd. runs every 15min. Su-Th 10am-6pm, F-Sa 10am-10pm. Stops designated by circular blue signs. $0.25.

Taxi: Yellow Cab Company (☎965-5111). 24hr.

Car Rental: U-Save, 510 Anacapa St. (☎963-3499). Cars from $20 per day with 150 free mi., $134 per week with 1050 free mi.; each additional mi. $0.20. 21+ with major credit or ATM card. Open M-F 8am-6pm, Sa 8am-4pm.

Bike Rental: Wheel Fun Rentals, 22 State St. (☎966-2282). Surreys, choppers, slingshots, regular mountain bikes, and beach cruisers ($14-44 per hr.), as well as boogie boards, scooters, and in-line skates ($7-15 per hr.). Safety gear included. Open daily 8am-8pm; in summer until 9pm.

✦ 🄻 ORIENTATION AND PRACTICAL INFORMATION

Santa Barbara is 92 mi. northwest of L.A. and 27 mi. from Ventura on **U.S. 101.** Since the town is built along an east-west stretch of shoreline, its street grid is slightly skewed. The beach lies at the south end of the city, and **State Street,** the main drag, runs northwest from the waterfront. All streets are designated east and west from State St. The major east-west arteries are **Cabrillo Boulevard** and **U.S. 101,** which runs east-west between Castillo St. and Hot Springs Rd.

Visitor Information: Tourist Office, 1 Garden St. (☎965-3021 or 800-676-1266), at Cabrillo Blvd. across from the beach. Parking $1.50 per hr. (first 15min. free in summer and Sa-Su). Hordes of folks clamor for maps and brochures. Open July-Aug. M-Sa 9am-

THE CENTRAL COAST

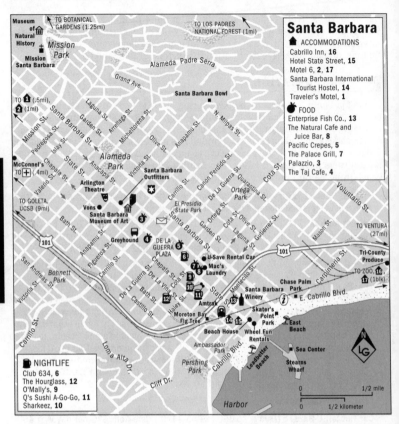

Santa Barbara

▲ ACCOMMODATIONS
Cabrillo Inn, **16**
Hotel State Street, **15**
Motel 6, **2, 17**
Santa Barbara International
  Tourist Hostel, **14**
Traveler's Motel, **1**

● FOOD
Enterprise Fish Co., **13**
The Natural Cafe and
  Juice Bar, **8**
Pacific Crepes, **5**
The Palace Grill, **7**
Palazzio, **3**
The Taj Cafe, **4**

■ NIGHTLIFE
Club 634, **6**
The Hourglass, **12**
O'Mally's, **9**
Q's Sushi A-Go-Go, **11**
Sharkeez, **10**

6pm; Su 10am-5pm; Sept.-Nov. and Feb.-June M-Sa 9am-5pm, Su 10am-5pm; Dec.-Jan. M-Sa 9am-4pm, Su 10am-4pm. Outdoor 24hr. computer kiosk with information on services, dining, shopping, hotels, and entertainment. **Hotspots,** 36 State St. (☎564-1637 or 800-793-7666), is an espresso bar with free tourist info, a hotel reservation service, and an **ATM.** Cafe open 24hr. Tourist info M-Sa 9am-8pm.

GLBT Organization: The Pride Foundation's Gay and Lesbian Resource Center, 126 E. Haley St., #A-11 (☎963-3636). Counseling for alcohol and drug abuse. AIDS hotline, testing, and social services. Open M-F 9am-5pm. For info on events, news, and gay-friendly establishments, consult www.gaysantabarbara.org.

Laundromat: Mac's Laundry, 35 Haley St. (☎966-6760). Wash $1.50, dry $0.25 per 12min. Open M-F 9am-10pm, Sa-Su 6am-10pm; last wash 9:30pm.

Police: 215 E. Figueroa St. (☎897-2300).

Hospital: Cottage Hospital, Pueblo St. (☎682-7111), at Bath St.

Library and Internet Access: Santa Barbara Public Library, 40 E. Anapamu St. (☎962-7653). Open M-Th 10am-9pm, F-Sa 10am-5:30pm, Su 1-5pm.

Post Office: 836 Anacapa St. (☎564-2226), 1 block east of State St. Open M-F 8am-6pm, Sa 9am-5pm. **Postal Code:** 93102.

 ACCOMMODATIONS

A 10min. drive north or south on U.S. 101 will reward you with lodging cheaper than that in Santa Barbara proper. All Santa Barbara accommodations are more expensive on the weekends (peaking in July and August and on holidays).

■ **Hotel State Street,** 121 State St. (☎966-6586), next to the train station, 1 block from the beach and next to the train station. Welcoming, comfortable, and meticulously clean, this European-style inn offers a relatively cheap night's sleep. Common bathrooms are pristine. Rooms have sinks and cable TV; a few have skylights. Reservations recommended. Rooms Sept.-June $50-70; July-Aug. $60-80. ❸

Santa Barbara International Tourist Hostel, 134 Chapala St. (☎963-0154; sbres@bananabungalow.com). Great location near the train station, the beach, and bustling State St. draws a young staff and clientele. A converted day care, this hostel has a more functional feel than others on the coast. Bike, boogie board, and in-like skate rentals ($6/$5/$4 per hr.). Internet $1 per 10min. Laundry (wash $1.50, dry $0.75). Key deposit $5. 6- to 8- person dorms $21-23. Doubles Oct.-Apr. $49-55; May-June and Sept. $55-59; Jul-Aug $59-65. ❷

Motel 6, 443 Corona Del Mar Dr. (☎564-1392). Affordable, standard room near the beach. Singles Su-Th $86, F-Sa $100; doubles Su-Th $92, F-Sa $106. Low-season singles Su-Th from $60, F-Sa from $80; doubles Su-Th from $66, F-Sa $86. Additional location: 3505 State St. (☎687-5400). Singles Su-Th $70, F-Sa $86; doubles Su-Th $76, F-Sa $91. Low-season singles Su-Th from $50, F-Sa from $60; doubles Su-Th from $56, F-Sa from $66. ❸

Traveler's Motel, 3222 State St. (☎687-6009). Take bus #6 or 11 from downtown. Although it's a bit far from the downtown spread, this motel is clean and spacious. Cable TV, A/C, direct-dial phone, microwave, and fridge. Complimentary fruit and coffee 8am-noon. Singles June-Sept. Su-Th $55-70, F-Sa $129-149; Oct.-May Su-Th $40, F-Sa $69-99. Palatial rooms with kitchenette $10-15 more; $5 per additional person. ❹

Cabrillo Inn, 931 E. Cabrillo Blvd. (☎966-1641 or 800-648-6708). 1 mi. east of Stearns Wharf at State St. Directly across from East Beach. This is the best oceanfront value in town. 2 swimming pools. Breakfast lounge with ocean view. Continental breakfast included. 2-night min. stay on weekends. Rooms May-Sept. Su-Th from $109, F-Sa from $139; Oct.-Apr. Su-Th from $89, F-Sa from $109. $30 extra for full ocean view. Ask about vacation home rentals by the week and month. ❺

■ CAMPING

State campsites can be reserved through ReserveAmerica (☎800-444-7275) up to seven months in advance. To reach **Carpinteria Beach State Park ❶**, 12 mi. south of Santa Barbara, follow the signs from U.S. 101 (entrance is at the end of Palm Ave.) or take bus #20 express to Carpinteria. It has 261 developed sites with coin-operated hot showers. (☎684-2811. Sites $21, hookup $30. Day-use $8.) There are three other state beaches within 30 mi. of Santa Barbara, but these are not served by buses. All three are scrunched between the railroad tracks and U.S. 101. **El Capitán ❶**, north of Santa Barbara off U.S. 101, has 142 well-kept sites, some with views of the Channel Islands. It usually fills up months in advance. (☎968-1033. Sites $21; low season $16.) **Refugio ❶** has 84 crowded, wheelchair-accessible sites just steps from the beach. (☎968-1033. Sites $21; low season $16.) **Gaviota ❶**, 10 Rugio Beach Rd., about 30 mi. northwest of Santa Barbara off U.S. 101, has 43 sites. Though it's in a parking lot environment, it's near the beach and has a marsh. (☎968-1033. No reservations. Sites $21; low season $16. Cash only.)

◘ FOOD

Santa Barbara may well have more restaurants per capita than anywhere else in America, so finding a place to eat is not exactly a problem. State and Milpas St. are especially diner-friendly; **State Street** is hipper while **Milpas Street** is cheaper. Ice cream lovers flock to award-winning **McConnel's ❶**, 201 W. Mission St. (☎569-2323. Scoops $2.90. Open Su-Th 11am-10:30pm, F-Sa 11am-11pm.) There's an open-air **Farmers Market** packed with bargains on the 500 and 600 blocks of State St. (Tu in summer 4-7:30pm; in winter 4-6:30pm) and another on Santa Barbara St. at Cota St. (Sa 8:30am-12:30pm). **Tri-County Produce,** 335 S. Milpas St., sells both fresh produce and groceries. (☎965-4558. Open M-Sa 9am-7:30pm, Su 9am-6pm.) Those looking for a downtown grocery store can head to **Vons,** 34 W. Victoria St. (☎963-2420), at the corner of Victoria and Chapala St.

▧ **Palazzio,** 1026 State St. (☎564-1985). The reproduction of the Sistine Chapel ceiling is nearly as impressive as the enormous pasta dishes ($17-20, half-portion $12-15), amazing garlic rolls, and serve-yourself wine. Lunch pasta dishes $7.75-10. Open Su-Th 11:30am-3pm and 5:30-11pm, F-Sa 11:30am-3pm and 5:30pm-midnight. ❸

The Palace Grill, 8 E. Cota St. (☎963-5000). Bourbon Street spice meets Santa Barbara class at this vibrant Cajun-Creole-Caribbean restaurant. Vegetarian dishes are available, but it may prove difficult to resist fish and grill selections ($13.95-26) like the house specialty, filet mignon stuffed with crawfish tails and Creole spices ($26). Magician (F) and live zydeco music (Sa) entertain from around 6pm. Open Su-Th 11:30am-3pm and 5:30-10pm, F-Sa 11:30am-3pm and 5:30-11pm. ❹

Enterprise Fish Co., 225 State St. (☎962-3313). If you've come to Santa Barbara looking for seafood, follow the locals here for daily $25 specials: M-Tu 2 lb. live Maine lobster, W-Th 1 lb. Alaskan king crab legs. Dinner $10-50. Happy hour M-F 4-7pm and 9pm-close. Open daily 11:15am-11pm. Bar open F-Sa until midnight. ❺

The Taj Cafe, 905 State St. (☎564-8280). Traditional village-style Indian cooking made with all-natural ingredients. Dishes include tandoori chicken in a sweet, tangy mango sauce ($11). Lunch buffet 11:30am-2:40pm ($9). Vegetarian entrees $6.50-8.50. Open M-Th 11:30am-3pm and 5-10pm, F-Sa 11:30am-3pm and 5-11pm. ❷

Pacific Crepes, 705 Anacapa St. (☎882-1123). This comfortable cafe is not only filled with the delicious smells of crepes; it's also *authentique*—owned and run by a French couple who only speak French. Luckily, there's an English menu. Appetizer, meal crepe, and dessert crepe $15. Open Tu-Sa 10am-3pm, 5:30-9pm, Su 9am-3pm. ❷

The Natural Cafe and Juice Bar, 508 State St. (☎962-9494). Casual dining with a healthy appeal. A variety of fresh salads, sandwiches, and hot entrees ($3.75-8.25). Smoothies with supplements like protein powder or bee pollen (from $3) will keep you charged all day. Open daily 11am-9pm or later depending on the crowd. ❷

◉ ◪ SIGHTS AND OUTDOOR ACTIVITIES

Santa Barbara is best explored in three sections—the beach and coast, commercial State St., and the mountains. The free *Independent* lists local events and is published every Thursday. Pick up *Santa Barbara's Red Tile Tour*, a walking tour guide (free at the visitors center; $0.25 inside the courthouse).

COASTAL SANTA BARBARA

Santa Barbara's supreme coastal views are along **Cabrillo Boulevard,** the first leg of the city's "Scenic Drive." Follow the green signs as they lead you on a loop into the mountains and around the city, winding through the hillside bordering the town along Alameda Padre Serra. This part of town is known as the American Riviera for its elegance and high concentration of wealthy residents.

SANTA BARBARA ZOO. This delightfully leafy habitat has such an open feel that the animals seem kept in captivity only by sheer lethargy. A mini-train provides a tour of the exhibits, including a miniaturized African plain where giraffes stroll lazily, silhouetted against the Pacific. *(500 Niños Dr., off Cabrillo Blvd. from U.S. 101. Take bus #14 or the downtown-waterfront shuttle. ☎ 962-5339. Open daily 10am-5pm. $9, seniors and ages 2-12 $7, under 2 free. Train $1.50, children $1. Parking $3.)*

STEARNS WHARF. The oldest working pier on the West Coast, Stearns Wharf houses the newly renovated **Sea Center** along with restaurants and shops. The center, slated to reopen in December 2004, is a working lab with hands-on exhibits for visitors. *(At State St. and Cabrillo Blvd. ☎ 962-0885. Sea Center open daily 10am-5pm. Touch tank open daily noon-5pm. $4, seniors and ages 13-17 $3, ages 3-12 $2. Parking $2 per hr. First 1½hr. parking free when stamped by a wharf merchant.)*

BEACHES AND ACTIVITIES. Santa Barbara's beaches are breathtaking, lined on one side by swaying palm trees and on the other by countless sailboats. **East** and **Leadbetter Beaches** flank the wharf on either side. **Skater's Point Park,** along the waterfront on Cabrillo Blvd., east of Stearns Wharf, is a free park for skateboarders and can be an entertaining place to watch thrills and spills. Helmets and gear are required, although the rule does not seem to be strictly enforced. **Wheel Fun Rentals** will rent beachgoers a **retro surrey**—a covered, Flintstone-esque bicycle. You and up to eight friends can cruise the beach paths in this stylish buggy. (See p. 367.) **Beach House,** rents surfboards and body boards plus all the necessary equipment. *(10 State St. ☎ 963-1281. Surfboards $7 per hr., $35 per day; body boards $4/$16; wet suits $3/$16. Credit card required.)* **Paddle Sports** offers kayak rentals and lessons. *(177B Harbor Way. ☎ 899-4925. $20-40 per 2hr., $40-60 per day. Open in summer daily 10am-7pm; in winter Su and Sa 10am-5pm, Tu-F noon-6pm.)* Across the street from the visitors center is idyllic **Chase Palm Park,** a beautiful public park complete with shipwreck playground and a vintage 1916 carousel. *(Carousel operates Sept.-June M 10am-6pm, Tu-Su 10am-7pm; July-Aug. daily 9am-9pm. $2.)*

FOUR SEASONS. For the best ocean view around, have a drink at the bar at the Four Seasons Biltmore Hotel. Appetizers run up to $145 (for caviar). This five-star lodging is prohibitively expensive for most travelers, but the view of the Pacific is priceless. Free live music often plays in the evening. *(1260 Channel Dr., in Montecito. Take U.S. 101 S to Olive Mill Rd. exit. Park across the street; valet parking runs $50. ☎ 969-2261. Dress for the bar is casual, but no beach attire is allowed.)*

STATE STREET
State St., Santa Barbara's monument to city planning, is a straight, tree-lined 2 mi. path through the center of the city. Cultural and historical landmarks are scattered among countless shops and restaurants. Everything that doesn't move—malls, mailboxes, telephones, and restrooms—has been slathered in Spanish tile.

SANTA BARBARA COUNTY COURTHOUSE. To take in the city's architecture and a killer view of the ocean, go up the elevator in the courthouse to the observation deck. The courthouse is distinguished from the more prosaic Mission Revival buildings found elsewhere with a sculpted fountain, sunken gardens, historic murals, wrought-iron chandeliers, and a hand-painted vaulted Gothic ceiling. *(1100 Anacapa St. ☎ 962-6464. Open M-F 8am-5pm, Sa-Su 10am-4:45pm. Tours M-Tu and F 10:30am and 2pm, W-Th and Sa 2pm. Free.)*

SANTA BARBARA MUSEUM OF ART. The impressive collection of classical Greek, Asian, and European artwork spans 3000 years. The 20th-century and Hindu collections are especially worthwhile. Over 90% of the permanent collection consists of gifts from Santa Barbara residents. *(1130 State St. ☎ 963-4364. Open Tu-Su 11am-5pm. $7, seniors $5, students and ages 6-17 $4, under 6 free. Su free.)*

THE CENTRAL COAST

ARLINGTON THEATRE. This live-performance venue and movie theater comfortably seats over 2000 people. The murals over the entrance of the Spanish-Moorish building depict scenes from California's Hispano-Mexican era. Its tower is one of the few structures in this low stucco town that rival the palm trees in height. The actual theater space resembles a Mexican village. Call the box office for info on upcoming events. *(1317 State St. ☎ 963-4408. Films $8, seniors and ages 2-12 $5.50; 1pm matinee and twilight show before 6pm $5.50.)*

OTHER SIGHTS. Brought from Australia by a sailor in 1876, the gnarled branches of the **Moreton Bay Fig Tree** now span 176 ft.; it can provide shade for more than 1000 people at once. *(At the corner of Montecito Ave. and Chapala St.)* If you'd rather drink than stand in the shade with 999 other people, sample award-winning wine at the **Santa Barbara Winery.** *(202 Anacapa St. ☎ 963-3633. Open daily 10am-5pm. Tastings $5 for 6 wines.)*

MOUNTAINS

Up in the northern part of town, things are considerably more pastoral. The awe-inspiring, rugged mountain terrain is artfully balanced by the well-manicured lawns and carefully trimmed hedgerows of the area's multi-million-dollar homes.

MISSION SANTA BARBARA. Praised as the "Queen of Missions" when built in 1786, this mission was restored after the 1812 earthquake and assumed its present incarnation in 1820. Towers with splayed Moorish windows stand around a Greco-Roman temple and facade, while a Moorish fountain bubbles outside. The museum contains items from the mission archives. The main chapel is colorful and solemn; visitors are welcome to attend mass. Today the Mission is not only a museum and parish, but also an infirmary and Franciscan friary. *(At the end of Las Olivas St. Take bus #22. ☎ 682-4149. Open daily 9am-5pm. Self-guided museum tour starts at the gift shop. Mass M-F 7:30am, Sa 4pm, Su 7:30, 9, 10:30am, noon. $4, under 12 free.)*

SANTA BARBARA MUSEUM OF NATURAL HISTORY. Unlike a typical indoor museum, the only way to get from one exhibit to the next in the Museum of Natural History is by going outside. The founder's proposal to establish a museum of comparative oology (no, not zoology) was vetoed by a Board of Trustees who thought that devoting the space to the study of eggs was silly. Intead they hatched the current exhibitions, which include the largest collection of Chumash artifacts in the West, a natural history gallery, and a planetarium. *(2559 Puesta del Sol Rd. Follow signs to the parking lot or take bus #22. ☎ 682-4711. Open daily 10am-5pm. Planetarium shows in summer daily 1:15, 2, 3pm; in winter W 3pm; Sa-Su 1, 2, 3pm. $7, seniors and ages 13-17 $6, under 12 $4, under 2 free. Planetarium $3 extra.)*

SANTA BARBARA BOTANICAL GARDEN. Far from town but close to Mission Santa Barbara and the Museum of Natural History, the Botanical Garden offers an amazing array of native vegetation along easy, meandering paths. Over 5 mi. of hiking trails wind through 65 acres of native Californian trees, wildflowers, and cacti. The garden's water system was built by the Chumash and is now one of the last vestiges of the region's native heritage. *(1212 Mission Canyon Rd. ☎ 682-4726. Open Mar.-Oct. M-F 9am-5pm, Sa-Su 9am-6pm; Nov.-Feb. M-F 9am-4pm, Sa-Su 9am-5pm. Garden tour on the 1st Sa of every month at 2pm. $6, seniors $4, students and ages 13-19 $3, ages 5-12 $1, under 5 free. Dogs allowed.)*

HIKING. Very popular **Inspiration Point** is a 3½ mi. round-trip hike that climbs 800 ft. Half of the hike is an easy walk on a paved road; the other half consists of a series of mountainside switchbacks. The reward on a clear day is an extensive view of the city, the ocean, and the Channel Islands. Following the creek upstream will lead to **Seven Falls.** *(From Mission Santa Barbara, drive toward the mountains and turn right onto Foothill Rd. Turn left onto Mission Canyon Rd. and continue 1 mi. Bear left onto Tunnel Rd. and drive 1¼ mi. to its end.)* **Rattlesnake Canyon Trail** is a moderate 3½ mi. round-trip hike to the Tunnel Trail junction with a 1000 ft. gain. It passes many waterfalls, pools, and secluded spots, but is highly popular—expect company. *(From Mission Santa Barbara, drive toward the mountains and turn right onto Foothill Rd. Turn left onto Mission Canyon Rd. and continue for ½ mi. Make a sharp right onto Las Conas Rd. and travel 1¼ mi. Look for a large sign on the left side of the road.)* Hiking the **San Ysidro Trail** will bring you by a popular swimming hole and then to a beautiful view at E. Camino Cielo Rd. The moderate hike is 3¾ mi. round-trip with a 1200 ft. gain. Allow 2-3hr. *(Take U.S. 101 S to the San Ysidro exit. Turn left and go to the light at East Valley Rd. Turn right and then drive to Park Ln. Take a left, and when you reach the fork, veer left, the trailhead will be on your right.)* The strenuous trek from the **Cold Springs Trail** to **Montecito Peak** is 7¼ mi. round-trip and gains 2462 ft.; even longer, at 9 mi. round trip and a 2675 ft. elevation gain **Camino Cielo** rewards hikers with great views. *(From U.S. 101 S, take the Hot Springs Rd. exit and turn left. Travel 2½ mi. to Mountain Dr., turn left, drive 1¼ mi., and stop by the creek crossing.)* For a more extensive listing of trails, try the **Santa Barbara Outfitters** store or the visitors center in town. Santa Barbara Outfitters has a selection of local hiking books and maps as well as a friendly staff with hiking experience. *(1200 State St. ☎564-1007. Books $12-15. Maps $8.)* Another option is to join the local **Sierra Club** on their group hikes. *(For more information, call ☎564-6694. Social hike at Mission Santa Barbara 6:15pm. Strenuous hike departs from Hope Ave. by the Bank of America Sa-Su 9am. Led by expert hikers. Free.)*

UNIVERSITY OF CALIFORNIA AT SANTA BARBARA (UCSB). This beautiful outpost of the UC system is stuck in Goleta, a shapeless mass of suburbs and coffee shops, but the beachside dorms and gorgeous student body more than make up for the lackluster town. The excellent **art museum** houses the Sedgwick Collection of 15th- to 17th-century European paintings. *(From Santa Barbara, take U.S. 101 N to Ward Memorial Hwy., or take bus #11. ☎893-7564. Open W-Su noon-5pm. Free.)*

OTHER SIGHTS. The beach at **Summerland** is southeast of Montecito. Its biggest food attraction is **The Big Yellow House,** a Victorian-estate-turned-restaurant reported to be inhabited by two ghosts; Hector haunts the wine cellars, while his mistress dwells in the women's bathroom upstairs. Ask to eat in the bedroom with the secret door. *(108 Pierpoint Ave. Take Bus #20. ☎969-4140. Open Su-Th 7am-9pm, F-Sa 8am-10pm.)* **Rincon Beach,** 3 mi. southeast of Carpinteria, has some of the county's best surfing. **Gaviota State Park,** about 30 mi. northwest of Santa Barbara, also has good surf. **Whale-watching** season runs from late November to early April, when the Pacific gray whales migrate past Santa Barbara.

▣ SHOPPING

State Street features 2 mi. of mildly trendy shops and the upscale **Paseo Nuevo Mall,** between Cañon Perdido and Ortega St. Local craftspeople line Cabrillo Blvd. for the **Arts and Crafts Show,** where they sell their handcrafted wares every fair-weathered Sunday from 10am to dusk.

▣ ▣ ENTERTAINMENT AND NIGHTLIFE

Every night of the week, the clubs on **State Street,** mostly between Haley and Cañon Perdido St., are packed. Consult the *Independent* to see who's playing on any given night. Beer on State St. is usually $4; search for specials.

✍ **Sharkeez,** 416 State St. (☎963-9680; www.sharkeez.net). UCSB's *Daily Nexus* voted this wild college hangout 2004's best place to dance, best cheap bar, and best sports bar. If that doesn't impress you, maybe the live mermaids swimming in the tank behind the bar will (Th-Sa 11pm). Affordable eats during the day give way to nightly drink deals like Tu 2-for-1 margaritas or mai tais and 4 Coronas for $8. F $2 martinis. Sa 2-for-1 beers, shots, cocktails, and pitchers (9:30-11pm). M international night. Come early to beat the line, especially on Th during the school year when UCSB party animals take this surf hut over. Open M-F 11am-2am, Sa-Su 10am-2am. Kitchen closes 10pm.

Q's Sushi A-Go-Go, 409 State St. (☎966-9177). A 3-level bar, 8 pool tables, and dancing. Sushi $3-13.50; accompanied by *sake* for $3-5. Happy hour M-Sa 4-7pm; 20% off sushi rolls, 50% off drinks and selected appetizers. M Brazilian night. Tu 80s night (10pm-close). W karaoke. Th college night; $1 hot dogs. All-you-can-eat sushi M-Sa 7-9:30pm ($16). Cover Sa $5 after 9pm. Open M-Sa 4pm-2am.

The Hourglass, 213 W. Cota St. (☎963-1436; www.hourglassspas.com). Soak in an intimate indoor bath or watch the stars from a private outdoor tub; there are 9 spas to choose from. No alcohol. Towels $1. 2 people $28 per hr.; each additional person $8. $2 student discount per tub with ID; under 13 free with parent. Sauna available in winter. Reservations recommended. Open June-Sept. Th and Su 6-11pm, F-Sa 6pm-midnight; Oct.-May W-Th and Su 5-11pm, F-Sa 5pm-midnight.

Club 634, 634 State St. (☎564-1069). Cocktails, dancing, and large back patio. Live bands (Th-Sa) and DJs. Su-M, and W karaoke. Th Red Bull and vodka $3. F select beers $1.50 (5-8pm). Open M-F 2pm-2am, Sa-Su noon-2am.

O'Mally's, 525 State St. (☎564-8904). An Irish pub and sports bar. DJs and dancing Th-Su. Plush upstairs cigar lounge with pool table. Cover charged only 5 times a year during major local events. Open daily 1pm-1:30am. Lounge open Th-Sa from 8pm.

🎊 FESTIVALS

One of the most special events in Santa Barbara is not organized by human hand. Starting in October, and assembling most densely from November to February, hordes of **monarch butterflies** cling to the eucalyptus trees in Ellwood Grove, just west of UCSB, and at the end of Coronado St., off Hollister Ave.; take the Glen Annie/Storke Rd. exit off U.S. 101. Other events include:

Hang Gliding and Paragliding Festival (☎965-3733; www.flyaboveall.com), at Mesa Flight Park. Jan. 1, 2005. Participate in or watch the colorful spectacle as flyers from all over the state take to the skies.

Santa Barbara International Film Festival (☎963-0023; www.sbfilmfestival.org). Jan. 28-Feb. 6, 2005. Sponsored by the Arlington Theatre, among others (see p. 372). Premieres foreign and US independent films and boasts celebrity patronage.

Gay Pride Festival (☎962-1403; www.gaysantabarbara.org). Late Sept. 2 days of speakers, music, dancing, and food on the steps of city hall in De La Guerra Plaza. Free.

I Madonnari Italian Street Painting Festival (☎569-3873; www.imadonnarifestival.com). Memorial Day weekend. Professional and amateur chalk paintings decorate the Old Mission Courtyard, continuing a tradition begun in Italy during the 16th century.

Summer Solstice Festival (☎965-3396). June 25, 2005. A colorful parade of color, music, and dance proceeds down State St. at noon. No words (on posters), no motorized vehicles, no signs, no religious faith symbols, and no animals allowed.

Old Spanish Days Fiesta (☎962-8101; www.oldspanishdays-fiesta.org). Early Aug. Spirited *fiesta*, celebrated for the last 80 years, with rodeos, carnivals, parades, dancing, live flamenco guitar everywhere, and plenty of margaritas and sangria.

Music Academy of the West, 1070 Fairway Rd. (☎969-4726; www.musicacademy.org), holds a series of inexpensive concerts throughout the summer. Stop by for a brochure.

Santa Barbara Festival of Art and Jazz, (☎ 695-8686 or 800-538-1881; www.santabarbarafestival.com), in the sunken gardens of the Santa Barbara Courthouse and Anapamu St. Columbus Day weekend. Festive cuisine, works by over 200 artists, and performances by local, regional, and national jazz bands. Tickets $5.

LOS PADRES NATIONAL FOREST   ☎805

Once the land of the Chumash Indians and California condors, the vast **Los Padres National Forest** (district office ☎968-6640) stretches north of Santa Barbara into San Luis Obispo County and beyond.

Los Padres is a leader in wildlife recovery programs, reintroducing a number of endangered plant and bird species—including the bald eagle—into the wild. In the forest, the **San Rafael Wilderness** contains 125 mi. of trails and a sanctuary for the nearly extinct California condor. The **Adventure Pass,** needed in all recreation areas in the forest, is available at the **Santa Barbara Ranger Office,** 3505 Paradise Rd. Take Rte. 154 for 10 mi. and turn right on Paradise Rd.; the office is 5 mi. down. (☎967-3481. Open M-Sa 8am-4:30pm. Pass $5 per day, $30 per year.) The **Los Padres Ojai Ranger Office,** 1190 E. Ojai Ave. also sells Adventure Passes. (☎646-4348. Open M-F 8am-4:30pm.) Ask Rangers about trails to the **Punchbowl,** a canyon turn where river water swirls. At nighttime, look for "moon bowls" (small pools of water near local waterfalls) and "moon rocks" (gleaming sandstone boulders).

A nearby, separate county park, **Cachuma Lake,** 15 mi. from U.S. 101 on Rte. 154, is a gorgeous, dark emerald-colored water source for the area, as well as a **campsite ❶** and recreational area. (☎805-686-5055. Sites $18. Day-use $6.) Ask for trail information at the entrance. The nearby **Chumash painted cave** is 20min. north of Santa Barbara. The impressive red ochre handiwork of native shamans dates to 1677. Take U.S. 101 to Rte. 154 to Painted Cave Rd., go past the village and down into the oak glen; the cave is up on the right, parking is scarce.

OJAI   ☎805

Lying only 80 mi. north of L.A., Ojai (OH-hi) is a pleasant retreat from the city. Its wooded valleys and mountain vistas have long been known to make mystics out of passersby. The town has capitalized on age-old traditions and made them New Age; Ojai is now home to chichi health spas, organic farms, and spiritual centers.

🖪🔁 TRANSPORTATION AND PRACTICAL INFORMATION. The Ojai valley sits 15 mi. north of Ventura, just east of the Santa Ynez Mountains and south of Los Padres National Forest. To reach Ojai from L.A., take U.S. 101 N toward Santa Barbara, heading north off the Rte. 33 exit. Fifteen miles of tree-lined roads lead to Ojai, where Rte. 33 becomes **Ojai Avenue,** the town's east-west spine. The city of Ojai runs a **trolley.** Stops are indicated by green and red wooden posts, which have the trolley schedule listed on them. Schedules are also available in the Chamber of Commerce. (Runs M-Sa 7:30am-5:30pm, Su 7:30am-4:30pm. $0.25.) Free parking is available along Ojai Ave. The **Ojai Valley Chamber of Commerce,** 150 W. Ojai Ave., provides maps and info on Ojai's galleries, campgrounds, and spa services. (☎626-8126; www.ojaichamber.org. Open M and W-F 9:30am-4:30pm, Sa-Su 10am-4pm.)

🦷 ACCOMMODATIONS. Nestled in a beautiful valley, the secluded **⧆Ojai Farm Hostel ❶** epitomizes the town's earthy aura—any fruit in the organic orchard is yours for the pickin'. The owner is extremely knowledgeable about the area and is often willing to help out with transportation. Free pickup from the Ventura Greyhound bus station (with prior reservation) is offered, along with two TV rooms and a video library, and free bike use. There are two small lodges with a total of 12 beds; one is for couples and women, the other for men. (☎646-0311; www.hostel-handbook.com/farmhostel. Proof of international travel, such as a recent plane ticket, required. Free Internet. Reservations are required; the hostel location will not be disclosed to anyone not staying at the hostel. $15 per person.) The **Capri Motel ❺**, 1180 E. Ojai Ave., is situated in a perfect locale. Tall palms frame the pool and hot tub. (☎877-589-5860. Rooms with cable TV, A/C, fridge, microwave, and balconies. Standard rooms $80-110, with balcony $100-125. Weekly discounts available.) The **Rose Garden Inn ❺**, 615 W. Ojai Ave., has spacious and well-furnished wood-paneled rooms surrounding a heated pool, hot tub, sauna, and well-kept rose garden with hammocks. (☎646-1434 or 800-799-1881; www.rosegardeninnofojai.com. Singles $80-110; doubles $90-120. AAA discount.)

◫ 🏔 SIGHTS AND OUTDOOR ACTIVITIES. Ojai was once the playpen of the Hollywood elite, who came to romp in the area's spas and natural hot springs. But when Eastern philosophy luminary Jiddu Krishnamurti had a spiritual awakening under an Ojai tree, the town added a glow of enlightenment to the sheen of glamour. Today, many visitors forego body wraps, masks, and scrubs ($55-200) at Ojai spas and come to free their minds for free. The **Krotona Institute of Theosophy,** 2 Krotona Hill, operates a quiet library, bookstore, and school of theosophy. From downtown Ojai, drive west on Rte. 33 and turn right on Krotona Rd. (☎646-2653; www.theosophical.org/centers/krotona. Open Tu-F 10am-5pm, Su-Sa 1-5pm.) Other spiritual centers are the **Krishnamurti Library,** 1070 McAndrew Rd. (☎646-4948; open W-Su 1-5pm) and the **Meditation Mount,** at the end of Reeves Rd. The Mount has a meditation room, a garden, and amazing views that soothe the soul. (☎646-5508. Open daily 10am-dusk. Weekly meditation classes open to the public. Donations appreciated.)

Trace the history of the area, from Chumash to New Age, at the **Ojai Valley Museum,** 130 W. Ojai Ave. (☎640-1390. Open Th-F 1-4pm, Sa-Su noon-4pm. $3, ages 12-17 $1, under 12 free.) The **Ojai Center for the Arts,** 113 S. Montgomery St., hosts poetry readings, workshops, and theater. (☎646-0117. Galleries open Tu-Su noon-4pm.) **Bart's Books,** on the corner of Canada and Matilija St., could only exist in Ojai. This open-air fortress of books has bookshelves outside the gates on the street where after-hour browsers can pay for their selections by dropping coins into a box. The books are cheap and plentiful, but the selection is better inside. (☎646-3755; www.bartsbooksofojai.com. Open daily 10am-5:30pm.) A 10min. drive south of town on Rte. 33 leads to the **Old Creek Ranch Winery,** 10024 Old Creek Rd. Built in 1981 on the site of an 1880s historic winery—the oldest in Ventura County—this winery offers handmade premium wines. Buy a bottle and enjoy the quiet of the valley. (☎649-4132. Tastings Sa-Su 11am-5pm.) Ojai is also the southernmost gateway to **Los Padres National Forest** (see p. 375).

LOS ANGELES

Despite what you may have heard, there's a reason 17 million people choose to live in the the the spawling collection of neighborhoods and freeways they call the City of Angels. Yes, the traffic is terrible, the smog is worse, the socio-economic divisions are tense, and the plastic surgery rate is high. However, L.A. also has the nicest beaches, freshest clubs, hottest artists, best ethnic food, and balmiest weather of any city in the world. Flowers bloom year-round, and you're never more than half an hour from the beach or the mountains. Movie premieres, surfing competitions, and opera openings fill social calendars, and for every overpriced bar there's a free beach or hilltop museum. At the turn of the 20th century, L.A. was a quiet agricultural region of orange groves and streetcars, but the arrival of the freeway and the movie studios transformed it into the vibrant, messy metropolis it is today. In many ways, L.A. is still a "company town"— everyone either works in the entertainment industry or is related to someone who does, and Angelenos take their movie-going seriously. If you decide to join them at the theater, buy your tickets early and expect the audience to sit through the end of the credits; that kid next to you just may be the third gaffer. But L.A. has also become incredibly diverse, liberal, and self-aware; pollution levels today are lower than they were in the 1970s, and there is no racial majority in the city.

The metropolitan area known as Los Angeles covers L.A., Orange, San Bernardino, Riverside, and Ventura Counties, encompassing a desert basin center, two mountain ranges, and 81 mi. of dazzling coastline. But despite its scale, L.A. divides into smaller neighborhoods conducive to exploration, and with the right timing, driving L.A.'s freeways is a thrilling and speedy way to soar through the city. As a visitor, it can be difficult to get a grasp on L.A.'s rapidly evolving scene; bars come and go, a club with lines out the door on Monday may be dead by Thursday, and the best *tamale* shop may up and move to another strip mall without warning. While the beaches and the Hollywood sign stay pretty much in one place, if you're looking to dig deeper find a local willing to show you around; otherwise, keep your eyes, ears, and Thomas Map Guide wide open.

HIGHLIGHTS OF LOS ANGELES

THE GETTY CENTER. This stunning travertine complex sits in the Brentwood hills. While its art collection is impressive, the beautiful gardens and panoramic view of the L.A. Basin are the best reasons to spend an afternoon here. Plus, it's free (p. 413).

ZUMA BEACH. Right off the Pacific Coast Hwy. in Malibu, Zuma Beach (p. 402) has the best surfing and softest sand in the area. Dolphins frolic in the waves just off the coast, encouraging their human friends to come and play.

THE MOVIES. Hollywood (p. 427) packs in the famous silver-screen sights, while the new movies are made in the Valley (p. 448). Mann's Village Theater in Westwood (p. 391) is a great place to take in a blockbuster or stalk celebrities at a premiere.

THE SUNSET STRIP. Rockers, celebrities, and all-night party people converge on the Sunset Strip (p. 422), a super-saturated stretch of clubs along Sunset Blvd.

◪ INTERCITY TRANSPORTATION

BY PLANE. Los Angeles International Airport (LAX) is in **Westchester,** about 15 mi. southwest of downtown and 10 mi. south of Santa Monica. LAX can be a confusing airport, but there are electronic information kiosks everywhere in English, Chinese, French, German, Japanese, Korean, and Spanish. **LAX information** (☎310-646-

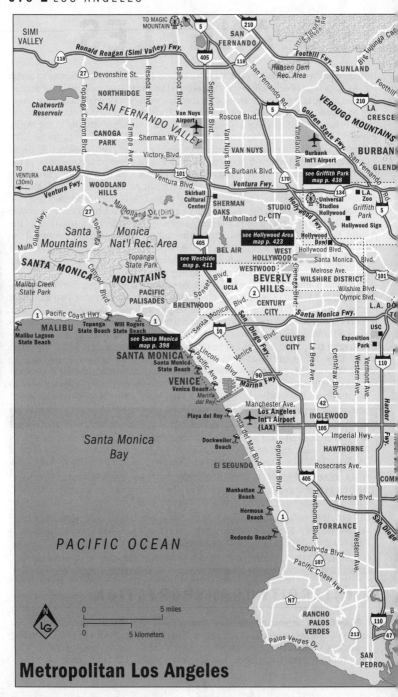

Metropolitan Los Angeles

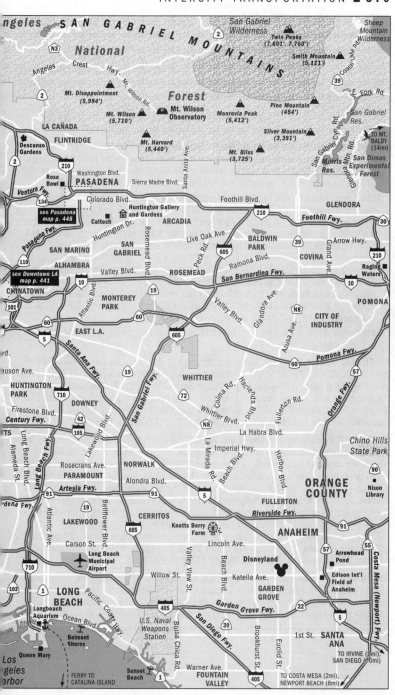

5252) aids Spanish and English speakers. **Airport police** (☎310-646-7911) patrol 24hr. **Traveler's Aid,** a service for airport info, transportation and accommodation suggestions, and major transit emergencies, is in all terminals. (☎310-646-2270. Open M-F 9am-5pm.) There is also a **First Aid Station.** (☎310-215-6000. Open daily 10am-10pm.) Currency exchange is available at **International Currency Exchange (ICE) Currency Services** in all terminals; however, local American Express offices generally offer more attractive exchange rates (see p. 386).

Besides renting a car, there are several other **transit** options from the airport. Check with your place of lodging before hopping into any of the vehicles below; many accommodations offer deals on transportation from the airport.

Metro Rail Subway: Metropolitan Transit Authority (MTA; ☎800-COMMUTE/266-6883; www.mta.net) oversees subway and bus transportation, including the local DASH buses. The **Green Line Metro Rail shuttle** leaves every 10-15min. from any terminal to the Green Line Metro Rail Aviation station. Runs daily 4:30am-11:30pm.

MTA Buses: Orange signs highlight the traffic island where airport shuttle "C" transports bus-bound passengers to the transfer terminal at Vicksburg Ave. and 96th St. To go to: **downtown,** take #42 (M-Sa 5am-7pm, Sa 5am-7pm, Su 7am-7pm; after hours, bus #40 picks up this route and runs all night) or the #439 express (every 40min.; M-F 5am-10pm, Sa-Su 6am-10pm); **Hollywood,** from West Hollywood, #217 along Hollywood Blvd. (every 10-20min.; daily), #2 or #3 along Sunset Blvd. (every 10-30min.; M-F 5am-2am, Sa 6am-2am, Su 6:30am-2am), or #4 along Santa Monica Blvd. (every 15-20min.; daily); **Long Beach,** #232 (M-F 5:15am-11pm, Sa-Su 6am-11pm); **West Hollywood** and **Beverly Hills,** #220 (every hr.; M-F 6:30am-7:30pm, Sa-Su 7:30am-7:30pm); **Westwood/UCLA,** Culver City Bus #6 eastbound (every 15min.; M-Th 5:39am-10:52pm, Sa-Su 6am-10pm).

Taxi: Follow yellow signs. Fare from airport to Hollywood $40; to Santa Monica $25. See p. 383 for taxi companies.

BY TRAIN. Amtrak rolls into **Union Station,** 800 N. Alameda St. (☎213-683-6729 or 800-USA-RAIL/872-7245), at the northeastern edge of downtown. When it opened in 1939, Union Station brought together the Santa Fe, Union Pacific, and Southern Pacific railroads. It was later featured in many films, including *Bugsy* and *The Way We Were.* From the station, take MTA bus #33 (1½hr., every 15min., $1.35) or Santa Monica Big Blue Bus #10 (every 30min., $1.75) to **Santa Monica.**

BY BUS. If coming by **Greyhound bus** (☎800-231-2222 or 213-629-8401), consider bypassing its downtown station, 1716 E. 7th St. (☎213-629-8536), at Alameda St., which is in an extremely rough neighborhood. If you must get off in downtown, be very careful near 7th and Alameda St., one block southwest of the station, where you can catch MTA bus #60 traveling north to the Gateway Transit Plaza at **Union Station.** The new terminal in **Hollywood,** 1715 N. Cahuenga Blvd. (☎323-466-1249), is at a great location close to many hotels, restaurants, and sights. There are several other Greyhound terminals in L.A. Route maps cost $3.

From Union Station, 800 N. Alameda St., buses run to: **Las Vegas** (19 per day, $38); **Santa Barbara** (9 per day, $12); **San Diego** (every hr., $15); **San Francisco** (15 per day, $48, round-trip $90); and **Tijuana** (4-5 per day, $20).

BY CAR. Three major freeways connect L.A. to the rest of the state. **I-5,** which travels the length of California, bisects L.A. on a north-south axis; it continues north to Sacramento and south to San Diego. **U.S. 101** links L.A. to other coastal cities, heading west from Pasadena before turning north toward San Francisco and running parallel to I-5. **I-10** comes in from the east, providing access to Las Vegas and Arizona.

✦ ORIENTATION

Los Angeles, 420 mi. south of San Francisco and 130 mi. north of San Diego, presides over the flatland basin between the coast of Southern California (SoCal) and the inland San Gabriel Mountains. You can still consider yourself "in" L.A. even if you're 50 mi. from downtown; in fact, the metropolis includes a vast conglomeration of over 80 cities and suburbs, including those in Orange, Riverside, San Bernardino, and Ventura Counties.

A busy web of crisscrossing interstate and state highways ensnares nearly 10 million vehicles in the L.A. basin every day. Unless you have inside knowledge of local surface streets in the city, plan to spend intimate, quality time with your car while in the city. The dozen major freeways, along with their offshoots and extensions, can seriously confuse even the savviest map readers. Stick to the main six freeways (commonly referred to by names rather than numbers) and it's smooth sailing. **I-5 (Golden State Freeway), I-405 (San Diego Freeway), I-110 (Harbor Freeway), U.S. 101 (Hollywood Freeway),** and **Pacific Coast Highway (PCH or Highway 1)** all run north-south. **I-10 (Santa Monica Freeway)** runs east-west, connecting Santa Monica to downtown and beyond. I-5 intersects I-10 just east of downtown and serves as one of the two major north-south thruways. I-405, which stretches from Orange County in the south all the way through L.A., parallels I-5 on a route closer to the coast, separating Santa Monica and Malibu from the inland Westside. The best way to orient yourself is by learning a couple of important freeways and remaining aware of L.A.'s natural landmarks; the ocean is west and the mountains are east.

Santa Monica (see p. 396) reigns over the coast with its superior shopping and well-kept houses. Its wealthier neighbor to the north, **Malibu** (see p. 401), is purely focused on the beach, and its seaside cliffs are home to many incognito celebrities. **Venice** and **Marina del Rey** (see p. 402) extend south along Santa Monica's ocean beach path and into crazier territory. Drum circles and in-line skaters characterize Venice, while Marina del Rey caters to the yachting set. Even farther down the coast, the **South Bay** (see p. 405) beaches are relaxed and fun.

East of I-405, the **Westside** sits comfortably along **Santa Monica Boulevard.** This is the cleanest, most happening part of the city. UCLA brings students to **Westwood** and **West L.A.** (see p. 408), while the neighboring hills of **Bel Air, Brentwood,** and **Pacific Palisades** (see p. 413) accommodate stellar homes and the impressive Getty Center. **Beverly Hills** (see p. 415) is, as always, the land of luxury shopping and gaudy mansions. Still on the Westside, but inching toward eastern messiness, predominantly gay **West Hollywood** (see p. 419) is the center of much of the city's best nightlife and shopping. South and east of West Hollywood, the **Wilshire District** and **Fairfax** (see p. 425) house museums and Jewish food, respectively.

Hollywood (see p. 427), in all its faded glamour and neon excitement, lies just up Sunset Blvd. from West Hollywood. It's a good place for late-night eats and celebrity stalking, and holds many of the city's most famous landmarks. Lodging here is among the cheapest available. East of Hollywood are the bohemian neighborhoods and greenery of **Los Feliz, Silver Lake,** and **Griffith Park** (see p. 434). Southeast, **downtown L.A.** (see p. 438) *does* exist and is undergoing a minor rejuvenation with the recent construction of Frank Gehry's Walt Disney Concert Hall. Farther east, at the foot of the San Gabriel Mountains, **Pasadena** (see p. 444) has old-time charm and hosts the Rose Bowl. Movies are made and theme parks reign in the **San Fernando Valley** (see p. 448), north of downtown on I-5.

▣ LOCAL TRANSPORTATION

Whether they're driving pimped-out low-riders or sparkling luxury sedans, Angelenos love their cars with a fervor that comes from constant contact with the road. The city boasts the greatest density of Mercedes-Benzes outside Europe, and there's no shortage of vehicles sporting BMW, Audi, and Lexus logos either. L.A.'s roadways are often jammed. New freeway construction projects, including those that may eventually alleviate the infamous congestion, are vociferously protested by L.A. residents who fear relocation and are tired of construction.

As a result of this obsession with driving, public transportation systems are limited and inconvenient. Though renting a car is expensive, especially if you are under 25, your own set of wheels is by far the best way to navigate the sprawling city. If you must forego the rental, use the subway and the bus to get around. See the **Transportation** sections for **Hollywood,** p. 427, and **Santa Monica,** p. 396, for info on navigating those areas of the city.

PUBLIC TRANSPORTATION

In the 1930s and 40s, General Motors (GM), Firestone, and Standard Oil bought up L.A. streetcar companies and intentionally ran them out of business. After the rails were torn up by these companies, the city grew increasingly reliant on buses and later on cars. In 1949, GM was convicted in federal court of criminal conspiracy—but by then the trolleys were becoming obsolete.

Six **Metropolitan Transit Authority (MTA) Metro Customer Centers** are available to point mass transit users in the right direction. They have MTA schedules and route maps, as well as a friendly staff to help plan your trip. **Downtown:** Arco Plaza, 515 S. Flower St., Level "C" (open M-F 7:30am-3:30pm); Gateway Transit Center, Union Station E. Portal (open M-F 6am-6:30pm). **East L.A.:** 4501-B Whittier Blvd. (open Tu-Sa 10am-6pm). **San Fernando Valley:** 14435 Sherman Way, Van Nuys (open M-F 10am-6pm). Centers are also located in Baldwin Hills and Wilshire.

For travelers who know where they want to go, MTA provides informative telephone and online assistance. (☎800-COMMUTE/266-6883; www.mta.net. Open M-F 6am-8:30pm, Sa-Su 8am-6pm.) MTA's hotline covers the metro rail subway and bus routes, as well as DASH connections. L.A. County's commuter rail, **Metrolink,** is under separate management (see below).

BY DASH. The local **DASH shuttle** ($0.25), designed for short distance neighborhood hops, serves major tourist destinations in many communities, including downtown, Hollywood (along Sunset Blvd.), Fairfax, Midtown, Crenshaw, and Van Nuys/Studio City, and, in the summer, Venice. (☎213-808-2273; www.ladottransit.com. Information open M-F 6:30am-7pm.)

BY MTA BUS. L.A.'s buses are slow but not altogether useless. The MTA used to be known as the RTD (Rapid Transit District), and some of its older buses may still be labeled as such. The name change was apt—most L.A. buses are not rapid in any sense of the word. Given the over 200 routes and several independent municipal transit systems that connect to the MTA, it's no easy task to study the timetables. Ninety percent of MTA routes have wheelchair-accessible buses. Appropriate bus stops are marked with the international symbol for disabled access.

Using the MTA to sightsee in L.A. can be frustrating, as attractions tend to be spread out. If you don't have a car, base yourself in Hollywood (where there are plenty of sights and bus connections) or in a beach community. Santa Monica (see p. 396) has an excellent bus system. Bus service is dismal in the outer reaches of the city. Transfers often involve waits of an hour or more, and traffic congestion hinders everyone.

MTA's basic fare is $1.25 (transfers $0.25), for seniors and disabled $0.45 (transfer $0.10); exact change is required. Weekly passes ($14) are available at customer service centers and local grocery stores. Transfers can be made between MTA lines or to other transit authorities. **Unless otherwise noted, all route numbers are MTA**; BBBus stands for **Big Blue Bus** and indicates Santa Monica buses (see p. 396).

BY SUBWAY. L.A.'s system of light-rail connections continues to expand, although it is still far from complete. Where rails do exist, they can often save commuters time otherwise wasted in traffic snarls. Several stations have park-and-ride lots available. The **Blue Line** runs from downtown to the southern L.A. communities and Long Beach. The **Green Line** goes along I-105 from Norwalk to Redondo Beach, with shuttle service to LAX at Aviation/I-105. The **Red Line** runs from downtown through Hollywood to the San Fernando Valley. The new **Beige Line** (Pasadena line) runs from Union Station to Sierra Madre Villa in Pasadena. Other lines go west to Wilshire and east to Union Station. A one-way trip costs $1.25, with transfers to bus and rail $1.60; seniors and disabled are $0.45, with transfers $0.55. All lines run daily 5am-12:30am.

BY METROLINK TRAIN. Metrolink trains run out of the city from Union Station to Ventura and Orange Counties (M-F), and to Riverside via San Bernardino, Santa Clarita, and Antelope Valley (M-Sa). One-way fares are $4.50-11.25, depending on the destination. You can only buy them from machines in the station within 3hr. of your departure time. Discounts are available if traveling Saturday or during off-peak hours (8:30am-3:30pm and after 7pm). Beware—trains come and go up to 5min. ahead of schedule. For more info, call ☎800-371-5465.

BY TAXI. If you need a cab, it's best to call **Independent** (☎213-385-8294 or 800-521-8294), **LA Taxi/Yellow Cab Co.** (☎800-711-8294 or 800-200-1085), or **Bell Cab** (☎888-235-5222). Be prepared to wait at least 15min. Fare is about $2 per mi. anywhere in the city and approximately $30-35 from the airport to downtown.

NON-PUBLIC TRANSPORTATION

▨**BY CAR.** L.A. may be the most difficult city in the US to navigate without a car. Luckily, parking is seldom a problem. There are many lots in L.A. (about $8 per day) and most accommodations offer free parking. Metered parking is on every major street, but authorized hours vary, so be sure to read all the signs. A quarter buys you anywhere from 7½-30min. With many offices in greater L.A., the **Automobile Club of Southern California**, 2601 S. Figueroa St., at Adams Blvd., has additional driving info and maps. Club privileges are free for AAA members and cost $2-3 for nonmembers. Their *Westways* magazine is a good source for daytrip or vacation planning. (☎213-741-3686, emergency assistance 800-400-4222. Open M-F 9am-5pm.) If you're staying in the city for more than a few days, a **Thomas Guide** ($20), a comprehensive book of detailed street maps of the city, is indispensable. The guides are sold in most gas stations and bookstores.

It is extremely difficult for young travelers to **rent** a car. Most places will not rent to people under 21, and the ones that do will likely impose a costly surcharge. Drivers between 21 and 25 incur a lower surcharge. National rental agencies usually have more dependable cars, but the high demand for rental cars assures that even small local companies can survive, and many offer much lower rates. Though these are worth looking into, car rental is not the best thing to skimp on. National agencies will replace a broken-down car hassle-free; if you want to use a local place, make sure they will do the same. Local rental companies might quote a very low daily rate and then add extra fees when you return the car. The prices quoted below are intended to give a very rough idea of what to expect; ask about airline-related and other discounts. National companies also offer free transportation services to and from LAX.

Alamo (☎310-649-2242 or 800-327-9633; www.alamo.com), at LAX. Cars $27-35 per day, $110-155 per week. Unlimited mileage. Collision Damage Waiver (CDW) $9 per day. Under-25 surcharge $25 per day. Open 24hr.

Avis, 11901 Santa Monica Blvd. (☎310-914-7700; www.avis.com), between Barrington Ave. and Bundy St. Pickup available. Cars from $34 per day, $149 per week. Unlimited mileage. CDW $9 per day. 25+. Open M-F 8am-6pm, Sa 8am-2pm, Su 9am-2pm.

Avon, 7080 Santa Monica Blvd. (☎323-850-0826; www.avonrents.com), at La Brea Ave. Cars $29 per day with 150 mi. free, $179 per week with 750 mi. free, $550-600 per month with 3325 mi. free. CDW $9 per day. No under-25 surcharge. Open M-F 6am-7pm, Sa-Su 7am-5pm.

Enterprise (☎310-649-5400 or 800-RENT-A-CAR; www.enterprise.com), at LAX. Economy cars $23-40 per day, $175 per week. Unlimited mileage. CDW $9 per day. Under-25 surcharge $10 per day. Open daily 5am-10pm.

Lucky, 8620 Airport Blvd. (☎310-641-2323 or 800-400-4736). Economy cars $20-30 per day with 150 mi. free, $109-169 per week with 1050 mi. free. CDW $9 per day. Under-25 surcharge $5-15 per day. Open M-Sa 8am-6pm, Su 8am-1pm.

Thrifty (☎310-645-1880 or 800-367-2277; www.thrifty.com), at LAX. As low as $25 per day. Unlimited mileage in CA, NV, and AZ. CDW $9 per day. Under-25 surcharge $25 per day. Open daily 6am-midnight.

Universal Rent A Car, 920 S. La Brea Ave. (☎323-954-1186). Cars from $20 per day with 150 mi. free, $140 per week with 1050 mi. free. No under-25 surcharge. Open M-F 8am-6pm, Sa-Su 9am-5pm.

FREEWAYS. Comprising over 527 mi. of concrete, L.A.'s freeways are an enduring image of the city. No matter what may separate Angelenos—race, creed, or class—the one thing that unites them all is a maze of 10- and 12-lane roadways. In planning your route, note that heavy traffic moves toward downtown from 7 to 10am on weekdays and streams outbound from 4 to 7pm. However, since L.A. has a huge population that doesn't work 9-to-5, traffic can occasionally be as bad at 1pm as it is at 6pm. No matter how crowded the freeway is, though, it's almost always quicker and safer than taking surface streets to your destination, unless traveling under the guidance of a seasoned local.

Uncongested freeways offer the ultimate in speed and convenience; the trip from downtown to Santa Monica on a wide-open I-10 can take as little as 15min. A nighttime cruise on I-110 (Harbor Fwy.) beneath the tangle of interchanges and iconic L.A. skyscrapers can be quite exhilarating. For freeway info, call **CalTrans** (☎213-897-3693), listen religiously to the frequent traffic reports on KFWB (980 AM), and refer to the **L.A. Overview map** (see p. 378).

BY BICYCLE. Except for recreational purposes, bicycles are fairly useless in L.A. Air quality is poor, distances are long, and drivers are very overprotective of their road space. Always wear a helmet; it's illegal and unsafe to bike on the road without one. For those who really want to explore on two wheels, **L.A. Bike Tours,** 6731 Hollywood Blvd., offers great advice as well as tours of Hollywood, Beverly Hills, and Venice Beach that range from 3hr. to an entire day. They offer a daily bike tour to the Hollywood sign at 2pm; just show up. Advanced rides to the Hollywood Sign, the Getty, and a two-day coastal adventure to Santa Barbara are all available by request. (☎323-466-5890 or 888-775-2453; www.labiketours.com. Bikes $25 per day, $80 per week. Tours $50-94; includes bike rental and snack.)

If you are not in a group, it's best to rent a bike and stick to one of many designated bike paths. The most popular route for the casual rider is the **South Bay Bicycle Path,** which runs from Santa Monica to Torrance (19 mi.), winding over the sandy beaches of the South Bay past sunbathers and spandex-clad in-line skaters. The path continues to San Diego. The new **L.A. River Bike Path** runs from Long Beach to Dodger Stadium. The **Nichols Canyon** to **Mulholland Drive Path** attracts many local riders. It also gives a mini-tour of celebrities' homes. Other bike paths include: **San Gabriel River Trail,** a 37 mi. pedal along the river, with views of the San Gabriel Valley; **Upper Rio Hondo** (9 mi.) and **Lario Trails** (22 mi.), which are free of traffic; and **Kenneth Newell Bikeway,** a 10 mi. glide through residential Pasadena. For the more serious rider, the **Donut Ride** in Palos Verdes, South Bay, provides hill after hill after hill.

BY FOOT. L.A. pedestrians are a hapless breed. Unless you're training for the L.A. Marathon, moving from one part of the city to another on foot is a ludicrous idea—distances are just too vast. Nevertheless, some colorful areas, such as Melrose, Westwood, Hollywood, Third St. Promenade in Santa Monica, and Old Town Pasadena, are pedestrian-friendly and best explored by foot. Just remember that outside these sanctuaries, Californians will stare (and possibly run) you down, and cops may ticket you for setting foot in a crosswalk without a "Walk" signal. For coastal culture lovers, Venice Beach is one of the most enjoyable (and popular) places to walk, with nearby sights and shopping areas. *LA Now,* the official tourist publication, has an excellent list of walking tours (see **Publications,** p. 387). Since some of the best tour companies are one-person operations, schedules and prices are not written in stone. Look for themed tours (e.g., Graveyard) of celebrity homes geared toward your obsessions. The **Los Angeles Conservancy** offers 2½hr. tours of the downtown area every Saturday at 10am. (☎213-623-2489; www.laconservancy.org. Tours $8. Advance reservations required. No strollers or young children.) Call **Tree People** (☎818-753-4600) for info about the Full Moon Sunday walking tours in Coldwater Canyon Park, which occur once a month on the Sunday closest to the full moon.

Once the sun sets, those on **foot,** especially outside the Westside and off well-lit main drags, should exercise caution, particularly when alone. Plan your pedestrian routes very carefully—it is worth a detour to avoid passing through heavily crime-ridden areas.

HITCHHIKING. If you hitchhike in L.A., you will probably die. Hitchhiking is exceptionally dangerous, not to mention illegal. There are many other options. Don't even consider it.

⁊ PRACTICAL INFORMATION

TOURIST AND FINANCIAL SERVICES

Visitor Information:

L.A. Convention and Visitor Bureau, 685 S. Figueroa St. (☎213-689-8822; www.visitlanow.com), between Wilshire Blvd. and 7th St. in the Financial District. Staff speaks English, French, German, and Japanese. Detailed bus map of L.A. available. California road map $3. Distributes *LA Now,* a free booklet with tourist and lodging info. Open M-F 8:30am-5pm.

National Park Service, 401 W. Hillcrest Dr. (☎818-597-9192), in Thousand Oaks, in the Conejo Valley. Info on the Santa Monica Mountains (including outdoor activities and special events) in *Outdoors,* a quarterly events calendar. Open daily 9am-5pm.

Sierra Club, 3435 Wilshire Blvd. #320 (☎213-387-4287; www.angeleschapter.org), between Normandy and Vermont St. Stores throughout L.A.; call for locations. Hiking, biking, skiing, and backpacking info. 4-month event schedules $10. Open M-F 10am-6pm.

Budget Travel: STA Travel, 7280 Melrose Ave. (☎323-934-8722, 24hr. booking 800-777-0112). Open M-Sa 10am-6pm, Su 10am-5pm. **Los Angeles/Santa Monica HI-AYH,** 1434 2nd St. (☎310-393-3413), in Santa Monica next door to the hostel. Info and supplies for travelers. Guidebooks, backpacks, money belts, rail passes, and ISICs. Open M-F 9:30am-5pm, Sa 9am-5pm.

Consulates: **Australia,** 2049 Century Park East, 19th fl. (☎310-229-4800). Open M-F 9am-5pm. Visa desk open M-F 9am-1pm. **UK,** 11766 Wilshire Blvd., #1200 (☎310-481-0031). Open M-F 8:30am-5pm. Visa desk open 8:30-11:30am. Consular services open 8:30am-12:30pm and 2-4pm.

Currency Exchange: At most airport terminals, but rates are exorbitant. **American Express** offices have better rates, but charge a $5 fee to change currency and a 1% fee on traveler's checks if you are not a cardholder. **AmEx Beverly Hills,** 327 N. Beverly Hills Dr. (☎310-274-8277). Open M-F 10am-6pm, Sa 10am-3pm. **AmEx Pasadena,** 269 S. Lake Ave. (☎626-449-2281). Open M-F 9am-6pm, Sa 10am-2pm. Other locations in **Torrance** and **Costa Mesa. Banknotes Exchange,** 520 S. Grand Ave., Ste. L-100 (☎213-627-5404), has no fee for changing currency, but charges a 3% fee for traveler's checks. Open M-F 9am-5pm, Sa 9am-1pm.

LOCAL SERVICES

Library: **Central Public Library,** 630 W. 5th St. (☎213-228-7000; www.lapl.org), between Grand Ave. and Flower St. in downtown. Validated parking available at 524 S. Flower St. with L.A. library card. Present ID with current local address to get a library card. Reading room open to all cardholders. Foreign-language books, weekly exhibits, and activities including readings, films, and workshops. Tours M-F 12:30pm, Sa 11am and 2pm, Su 2pm. Open M-Th 10am-8pm, F-Sa 10am-6pm, Su 1-5pm.

Ticket Agency: **Ticketmaster** (☎213-480-3232) charges high per-ticket fees. A better bet is to contact the box office directly.

Surf Conditions: ☎310-457-9701. Recorded info on Malibu, Santa Monica, and South Bay. Most FM radio stations have a surf report at noon.

Weather Conditions: ☎213-554-1212. Detailed region-by-region report.

Highway Conditions: ☎800-427-7623 for recorded info. KFWB 980 AM and KNX 1070 AM give reports every 10min.

LOCAL MEDIA

Television Stations: **ABC** Channel 7; **CBS** Channel 2; **Fox** Channel 11; **KTLA/WB** (Channel 5; **NBC** Channel 4; **UPN** Channel 13.

Radio Stations: **Classical** KKGO 10.51 FM; **Country** KZLA 93.9 FM; **Hip Hop** "Power 106" 105.9 FM; **National Public Radio** 91.5 FM; **Oldies** KRTH 101.1 FM; **Old School/R&B** "Hot" 92.3 FM; **Pop/Rock/Top 40** "Star" 98.7 FM; **Pop/Top 40** KIIS 102.7 FM; **Rock** KROQ 106.7 FM; **Smooth Jazz** "The Wave" 94.7 FM; **Spanish** "El Sol" 96.3 FM.

EMERGENCY AND COMMUNICATIONS

Hotline: **Rape Crisis,** ☎310-392-8381.

24hr. Pharmacy: **Sav-On,** 3010 S. Sepulveda Blvd. (☎310-478-9821), in West L.A. For other 24hr. locations, call ☎800-627-2866.

Hospitals: **Cedars-Sinai Medical Center,** 8700 Beverly Blvd. (☎310-423-3277, emergency 423-8605). **Good Samaritan Hospital,** 616 S. Witmer St. (☎213-977-2121, emergency 977-2420). **UCLA Medical Center,** 10833 Le Conte Ave. (☎310-825-9111, emergency 825-2111).

Medical Assistance: **Planned Parenthood** (☎323-223-4462) has various locations in the city; call for the nearest one. Birth control, prenatal care, STD treatment, abortions, pregnancy testing, HIV testing, and counseling. Call 1 week in advance for appointments. Hours and fees vary. **Hollywood-Sunset Free Clinic,** 2815 Sunset Blvd. (☎213-989-1981). Provides general medicine, family planning, and psychiatric care for people without an insurance policy or HMO. No mandatory fees. Appointments only; call M, W, F 10am-noon. **Valley Free Clinic,** 6801 Coldwater Canyon (☎818-763-8836), in North Hollywood. Women's health, birth control, medical counseling, drug addiction services, and free HIV testing. Appointments only; call weeks in advance M-F 10am-4pm.

Post Office: Central branch at 7001 S. Central Ave. (☎800-275-8777). Open M-F 7am-7pm, Sa 7am-3pm. **Postal Code:** 90052.

> **AREA CODES.** L.A. is big. Really big. There are many area codes:
> **213** Downtown.
> **323** Hollywood, Vernon, Huntington Park, Montebello, and West Hollywood.
> **310** Santa Monica, Malibu, and the Westside.
> **562** Long Beach and southern L.A. County.
> **626** San Gabriel Valley and Pasadena.
> **818** Burbank, Glendale, and the San Fernando Valley.
> **909** San Bernardino and Riverside.

PUBLICATIONS

The *Los Angeles Times* (newsstand $0.50, Su $1.50) defeats all rival papers west of the Rockies. The *Times* "Calendar" section has the scoop on the current L.A. scene. The free *LA Weekly*, which comes out on Thursdays, is the definitive source of entertainment listings. L.A. has a number of "industry" (i.e. movie) papers; the best known are *Variety* and *The Hollywood Reporter*. The *Los Angeles Sentinel* is L.A.'s largest **African-American** paper. UCLA's **student** paper, *The Daily Bruin*, comes out during the school year. Four of the most popular **gay and lesbian** entertainment magazines are *fab!*, *Vibe*, *The Frontiers*, and *Edge*. L.A. also has numerous foreign-language publications. The **Spanish** *La Opinión* is the largest, but two **Korean** papers (*The Korean Central Daily* and *The Korea Times*) each have circulations approaching 75,000. The *International Daily News* and the *Chinese Daily News* serve the **Chinese**-speaking community. **World Wide,** 1101 Westwood Blvd., at Kinross Ave., is a fine example of L.A.'s massive newsstands. (Open daily 7am-midnight.)

◪ ACCOMMODATIONS

ACCOMMODATIONS BY PRICE

$1-17 (❶)

◪ Hollywood Bungalows International Youth Hostel (427)	HW
Hollywood Hotel and Hostel (428)	HW
Hostel California (403)	VN
◪ Venice Beach Cotel (403)	VN

$18-34 (❷)

Cadillac Hotel (403)	VN
Hollywood International Hostel (428)	HW
◪ Los Angeles/Santa Monica (HI) (397)	SM
Los Angeles South Bay (HI) (406)	SB
◪ Los Angeles Surf City Hostel (406)	SB
Orange Drive Manor (428)	HW
Orbit Hotel and Hostel (419)	WH
Student Inn International Hostel (428)	HW
◪ USAHostels Hollywood (427)	HW
Venice Beach Hostel (403)	VN

$35-54 (❸)

Hotel Claremont (409)	WW
Jolly Roger Hotel (403)	VN
The Little Inn (409)	WW

$55-79 (❹)

Bevonshire Lodge Motel (419)	WH
◪ Days Inn Metro Plaza Hotel (438)	DT
Hotel del Flores (415)	BH
Hotel Stillwell (438)	DT
Liberty Hotel (428)	HW
Milner Hotel (439)	DT
Moon Lite Inn (406)	SB
Seaview Motel (397)	SM
The Beverly Hills Reeves Hotel (415)	BH

OVER $80 (❺)

Hotel California (397)	SM

BH Beverly Hills **DT** Downtown **HW** Hollywood **SB** South Bay **SM** Santa Monica **VN** Venice **WH** West Hollywood **WW** Westwood

Cheap accommodations in L.A. are often unsafe. It can be difficult to gauge quality from the exterior, so ask to see a room before committing. For those willing to share a room and a bathroom, hostels are a saving grace, though Americans should be aware that some only accept **international travelers.** These hostels require an international passport, but well-traveled Americans with proof of travel (passports, out-of-state identification, or plane tickets often do the trick) may be permitted to stay. It never hurts to ask for low-season or student discounts, and occasionally managers will lower prices to snare a hesitant customer.

In choosing where to stay, the first consideration should be location. If you don't have wheels, decide which element of L.A. appeals to you the most. Those visiting for beach culture should choose lodgings in Venice or Santa Monica. Avid sightseers will be better off in Hollywood or the more expensive (but cleaner and nicer) Westside. Downtown L.A. has public transportation connections, but is unsafe after dark. Even those with cars should choose lodgings close to their interests to keep car-bound time to a minimum. **Listed prices do not include L.A.'s 14% hotel tax.**

⚑ CAMPING

L.A. has no campgrounds convenient to public transportation. Even drivers face at least a 45min. commute from downtown. One nearby L.A. County campground, **Leo Carrillo State Beach ❶**, lies on Hwy. 1 (PCH), 20 mi. north of Malibu. It has 135 developed sites with flush toilets and showers. (☎805-488-5223. Sites $13.) Nearby **Point Mugu** has 57 sites at **Sycamore Canyon ❶** with flush toilets and showers ($13) and 75 primitive sites in the **Thornhill Broome ❶** area with chemical toilets and cold showers ($13). **Malibu Creek State Park ❶**, off Las Virgenes Rd., 6 mi. north of Hwy. 1, has over 50 sites with flush toilets and showers. (☎818-880-0367. Sites $15.)

◖ FOOD

From celebrity eateries to taco wagons, there's never a shortage of great food in L.A. This expansive range of culinary options is a direct result of the city's ethnic diversity. Jewish and Eastern European food is most prevalent in Fairfax; Mexican in East L.A.; Japanese, Chinese, Korean, Vietnamese, and Thai around Little Tokyo, Chinatown, Koreatown, and Monterey Park in downtown; and seafood along the coast. Listings of **late-night** restaurants and cafes are on p. 422. If you're looking to cook, ◙**Trader Joe's** specializes in budget gourmet food. They save by doing their own packaging, and, as a result, amazing deals like $3 bottles of good Napa wines abound. There are 74 locations in SoCal; call ☎800-SHOP-TJS/746-7857 to find the nearest one. (Most open daily 9am-9pm.

MARKETS. L.A. boasts enormous public markets that supply a variety of local foodstuffs and crafts. ◙**Farmers Market,** 6333 W. 3rd St., at Fairfax Ave., attracts about 3 million people every year and has over 160 produce stalls, as well as international food booths, handicraft shops, souvenir stores, and a phenomenal juice bar. There's delectable produce, but bargains are becoming increasingly rare. You can also take lunch upstairs to the **Beverly Hills Art League Gallery** and munch among paintings by local amateur artists. (☎323-933-9211; www.farmersmarketla.com. Open M-F 9am-9pm, Sa 9am-8pm, Su 10am-7pm.) A less touristy and less expensive source of produce is the **Grand Central Public Market,** 317 S. Broadway, a large building between 3rd and 4th St. downtown. Entrances are on both Broadway and Hill St. Grand Central has more than 50 stands selling produce, clothing, housewares, costume jewelry, vitamins, and fast food. If you are around during Thanksgiving, be sure to vie for a frozen gobbler in the turkey giveaway. (☎213-624-2378. Open daily 9am-6pm.) Santa Monica (see p. 397), also has an excellent market.

FOOD BY TYPE

AFRICAN
Nyala Ethiopian Cuisine (425) FX ❷

AMERICAN
🔊 The Apple Pan (409) WLA ❷
🔊 Aunt Kizzy's Back Porch (404) MR ❸
Cow's End (404) VN ❷
Big Daddy's (404) VN ❶
Big Dean's "Muscle-In" Cafe (399) SM ❶
Bob's Big Boy (449) VA ❷
Duke's Coffee Shop (420) WH ❷
🔊 Fair Oaks Pharmacy (444) PA ❷
Hennessy's Tavern (406) SB ❸
Lawry's (416) BH ❺
Malibu Chicken (401) MA ❷
🔊 The Pantry (439) DT ❷
Pie 'n Burger (444) PA ❷
Pink's Hot Dog Stand (429) HW ❶
Roscoe's Chicken and Waffles (428) HW ❷
Sidewalk Cafe (404) VN ❷
The Zuma Cafe (402) MA ❶

BREAKFAST
🔊 A la Tarte (413) PP ❷
Blueberry Country Kitchen (399) SM ❷
Bread & Porridge (399) SM ❷
Duke's Coffee Shop (420) WH ❷
Fred 62 (434) LF ❷
Millie's (434) SL ❷
Roscoe's Chicken and Waffles (428) HW ❷
🔊 The Griddle Cafe (420) WH ❷
🔊 The Pantry (439) DT ❷

CAFES
17th St. Cafe (399) SM ❸
Cafe Dolcini (439) DT ❶
Casbah Cafe (435) SL ❶
Lilly's (404) VN ❹
🔊 Rose Cafe and Market (403) VN ❷

CALIFORNIA CUISINE
17th St. Cafe (399) SM ❸
Holly Street Bar & Grill (444) PA ❹
🔊 The Bungalow Club (428) HW ❹

CHINESE
Chin Chin (420) WH ❷
Xi'an (416) BH ❸

DELIS AND SANDWICHES
Cafe Dolcini (439) DT ❶
🔊 Canter's (425) FX ❷

Martha's Corner (406) SB ❷
Nate 'n Al Delicatessen (416) BH ❷
🔊 Phillipe, The Original (439) DT ❶
🔊 Rose Cafe and Market (403) VN ❷

DESSERT
🔊 Al Gelato (416) BH ❸
🔊 Diddie Riese Cookies (409) WW ❶
🔊 Fair Oaks Pharmacy (444) PA ❷
Pie 'n Burger (444) PA ❷

ITALIAN AND PIZZA
Bossa Nova (420) WH ❹
🔊 Fritto Misto (399) SM ❷
Miceli's (449) VA ❸
Mulberry Street Pizzeria (416) BH ❶
Zucca Ristorante (439) DT ❹

JAPANESE
🔊 Asahi Ramen (409) WLA ❶
Sushi Mac (448) VA ❸
Tenmasa Sushi Bar (420) WH ❸
Yu & Mi Sushi (416) BH ❹

MEDITERRANEAN AND MIDDLE EASTERN
Cobras and Matadors (420) WH ❹
Pita! Pita! (444) PA ❷
Zankou Chicken (430) HW ❶

MEXICAN
Jose Bernstein's (410) WW ❶
La Luz del Día (439) DT ❷
🔊 Malo (434) SL ❸
Mariasol (399) SM ❸
Wahoo's Fish Tacos (406) SB ❶

SEAFOOD
Chez Jay (399) SM ❹
Duke's Malibu (401) MA ❸
Gladstones 4 Fish (413) PP ❺
Neptune's Net Seafood (402) MA ❷
Tony P's Dockside Grill (404) VN ❹
Wahoo's Fish Tacos (406) SB ❶

LATIN AMERICAN
Bossa Nova (420) WH ❹
Carlitos Gardel (429) HW ❹
Versailles (425) FX ❸

VEGETARIAN
Native Foods (410) WW ❷
The Spot (406) SB ❷

LOS ANGELES

BH Beverly Hills **DT** Downtown **FX** Fairfax **HW** Hollywood **LF** Los Feliz **MA** Malibu **PA** Pasadena **PP** Pacific Palisades **SB** South Bay **SL** Silver Lake **SM** Santa Monica **VA** Valley **VN** Venice **WH** West Hollywood **WLA** West L.A. **WW** Westwood

⊙ SIGHTS

The majority of L.A.'s tourist sights are in **Hollywood** (see p. 427), where remnants of the golden age of film coexist with sex shops and currency exchanges. The **Wilshire District** (see p. 425) is home to the Miracle Mile, a cluster of museums and parks. **Downtown** (see p. 438) also has a fair number of sights and museums, including the L.A. MoCa and the new Walt Disney Concert Hall. Other excellent art museums are in **Pasadena** (see p. 444) and **Bel Air** (see p. 413). To see where the stars live and shop, head to the Westside and take our **driving tours of celebrity homes** (see p. 414 and p. 418). Movies are made in the San Fernando Valley, and you might catch a bit of live filming at **Universal Studios** (see p. 449). Of course, you can't come to L.A. without heading to the beach. Soak up the sun in **Malibu** (see p. 402), **Santa Monica** (see p. 399), **Venice** (see p. 404), and **South Bay** (p. 405).

⬚ SHOPPING

In L.A., shopping isn't just a practical necessity; it's a way of life. The ornate buildings on the Golden Triangle in **Beverly Hills** (see p. 415) hold the greatest concentration of designer stores. Popular shopping areas like Santa Monica's **Third St. Promenade** (see p. 396), Pasadena's **Old Town** (see p. 444), the **Century City Shopping Complex** (see p. 412), and the **Beverly Center** (see p. 417) are lined with chain boutiques and the latest cookie-cutter fashion of the moment. Nevertheless, a number of cool specialty shops with more one-of-a-kind items are tucked away from the shuffle. **West Hollywood** (see p. 419), **Los Feliz and Silver Lake** (see p. 437), 3rd St. and Robertson Blvd. in **Beverly Hills** (see p. 417), and Montana Ave. in **Santa Monica** (see p. 400) have local designers' boutiques and vintage shops.

⬚ ENTERTAINMENT

FILM AND TELEVISION STUDIOS

A visit to the world's entertainment capital isn't complete without some exposure to the actual business of making a movie or TV show. Fortunately, most production companies oblige. **Paramount** (☎323-956-5000), **NBC** (☎818-840-3537), and **Warner Bros.** (☎818-954-1744) offer 2hr. guided tours that take you onto sets and through backlots. The best way to get a feel for the industry is to land yourself tickets to a taping. Tickets are free, but studios tend to overbook, so holding a ticket does not always guarantee you'll get in; show up early. **NBC,** 3000 W. Alameda Ave., at W. Olive Ave. in Burbank, is your best bet. Arrive at the ticket office on a weekday at 8am for passes to Jay Leno's **Tonight Show,** filmed at 5pm the same evening (2 tickets per person, must be 16+). Studio tours run on the hour. (☎818-840-3537. Tours M-F 9am-3pm. $7.50, ages 5-12 $4.) Many of NBC's "Must-See TV" shows are taped at **Warner Bros.,** 4000 Warner Blvd. (☎818-954-6000), in Burbank. Sitcoms such as the *Drew Carey Show* and *Everybody Loves Raymond* are taped from August to May—call the studio at least five business days in advance to secure tickets.

A **CBS box office,** 7800 Beverly Blvd., next to the Farmers Market (see p. 388) in West Hollywood, hands out free tickets to Bob Barker's game-show masterpiece *The Price is Right* (taped M-Th) up to one week in advance. Audience members must be over 18. (☎323-575-2458. Open M-F 9am-5pm.) You can request up to ten tickets on a specific date by sending a self-addressed, stamped envelope to *The Price is Right* Tickets, 7800 Beverly Blvd., Los Angeles, CA 90036, about four to six weeks in advance. If all else fails, **Audi-**

ences Unlimited, Inc., 100 Universal City Plaza, Building 4250, Universal City, CA 91608 (☎818-506-0067; www.tvtickets.com), is a great resource. To find out which shows are available during your visit, send in a self-addressed, stamped envelope or check the website.

MOVIES

L.A.'s movie palaces show films the way they were meant to be seen—on a big screen, in plush seats, and with top-quality sound and air-conditioning. It would be a cinematic crime not to partake of the city's incredible moviegoing experiences. The gargantuan theaters at **Universal City,** as well as those in **Westwood Village** near UCLA, are incredibly popular, especially on weekends; expect long lines. In **Santa Monica,** there are 22 screens within the three blocks between Santa Monica Pl. and Wilshire Blvd. along Third St. Promenade.

To ogle the stars as they walk the red carpet into the theater for a **premiere,** check the four main premiere venues: **Grauman's Chinese** (about 2 per month), **El Capitán** (Disney films only), and **Mann's Village** and **Bruin,** in Westwood. For info on what's playing, call ☎323-777-3456 or read the daily Calendar section of the *LA Times.*

Devotees of second-run, foreign-language, and experimental films are rewarded by the Santa Monica theaters away from the Promenade. Foreign films play consistently at the eight **Laemmle Theaters** in Beverly Hills (☎310-274-6869), West Hollywood (☎323-848-3500), Santa Monica (☎310-394-9741), Pasadena (☎626-844-6500), and downtown (☎213-617-0268).

L.A.'s giant movie industry does not, surprisingly, include world-class film festivals like Cannes or Sundance. On the other hand, the city hosts a number of smaller, less expensive, and more accessible film showings, including **Outfest,** (☎213-480-7065; www.outfest.org; films $7-12), a GLBT film festival in July, and the **Asian Pacific Film and Video Festival** (☎213-680-4462, ext. 68; films $8, seniors and students $5), in May. The largest film festival is the pricey **AFI L.A. International Film Festival,** held from late October to early November, which shows 150 shorts, documentaries, and features from around the world. (☎866-AFI-FEST/234-3378; www.afifest.com. Week matinee pass $50, $250 for the entire festival.)

MOVIE THEATERS

▧ **Grauman's Chinese Theatre,** 6925 Hollywood Blvd. (☎323-464-8111), between Highland and La Brea Ave., in **Hollywood.** Hype to the hilt. For details, see **Hollywood Sights,** p. 430. Tickets $10, ages 3-12 and over 65 $7; 1st show of the day $7.50.

▧ **Archlight Hollywood Cinerama Dome,** 6360 Sunset Blvd. (☎323-466-3401), near Vine St., in **Hollywood.** The ultimate cineplex for the serious moviegoer. 14 movie screens surround a gigantic dome that seats 820 people and displays a screen that expands from 80 to 180 ft. A spectacular, rumbling sound system. First-run movies only. Don't be late—doors close 7min. after movies begin. Tickets $7.75-14.

▧ **Loews Cineplex** (☎818-508-0588), atop the hill at Universal City Walk, in the **San Fernando Valley.** Opened in 1987 as the world's largest cinema complex, its 18 wide-screen theaters and Parisienne-style cafe put all competition to absolute shame. Tickets $9, seniors and under 13 $6; before 4pm $6.75. $2 parking rebate with purchase of 2 or more movie tickets.

El Capitán, 6838 Hollywood Blvd. (☎323-467-7674 or 800-347-6396; www.elcapitantickets.com), across from Grauman's, in **Hollywood.** A spectacle straight out of *Fantasia.* Disney movies and live Disney stage shows and exhibitions. Tickets $11, seniors and ages 3-11 $8; live stage show $13-24/$11-20.

Mann's Village Theatre, 961 Broxton Ave. (☎310-208-0018), in **Westwood.** Vibrant neons illuminate the Art Deco facade. One huge auditorium, one big screen, and one great THX sound system. Watch the balcony for late-arriving celebrities. Frequent premieres. Tickets $10, students $7.50, seniors $7, under 12 $6.50; M-F before 6pm $7.

Vine Theatre, 6321 Hollywood Blvd. (☎323-463-6819), just west of Vine St., in **West Hollywood.** Selection is limited, but you can't beat the price. 1 theater plays 2 recent movies back-to-back starting around 2pm. Tickets $7, 2nd movie free.

REVIVAL THEATERS

☒ **Nuart Theatre,** 11272 Santa Monica Blvd. (☎310-478-6379), just west of I-405 at Sawtelle Ave., in **West L.A.** Perhaps the best-known revival house. The playbill changes nightly. Classics, documentaries, animation festivals, and foreign and modern films. *The Rocky Horror Picture Show* screens Sa night at midnight with a stellar live cast. Tickets $9.50, seniors and under 12 $7.25pm. Discount card (5 tickets for $35).

LACMA's Bing Theater, 5905 Wilshire Blvd. (☎323-857-6010; www.lacma.org), at the L.A. County Museum of Art, in the **Wilshire District.** Classic films on the big screen, sometimes for less than a video rental. Shows Tu 1pm and F-Sa 7:30pm only. Tickets F-Sa $8, students and seniors $6; Tu $2/$1

Egyptian Theatre, 6712 Hollywood Blvd. (☎466-3456; www.egyptiantheatre.com), 1 block west of Las Palmas St., in **Hollywood.** For each old or new film it shows, the theater brings in the main actor, director, or producer to talk with the audience about the filming process. Films change regularly. Tickets $9, seniors and students $8.

LIVE THEATER

L.A.'s live theater scene does not hold the weight of New York's Broadway, but its 115 "equity waiver theaters" (under 100 seats) offer dizzying, eclectic choices for theatergoers, who can also view small productions in art galleries, universities, parks, and even garages. Browse listings in the *LA Weekly* to find out what's hot.

Geffen Playhouse, 10886 LeConte Ave. (☎310-208-5454), in **Westwood.** Currently undergoing a $17 million renovation. Home to Off-Broadway and Tony award-winning shows. Tickets $34-46; $10 student rush tickets available 1hr. before each.

Pasadena Playhouse, 39 S. El Molino Ave. (☎626-356-7529 or 800-233-3123; www.pasadenaplayhouse.org), in **Pasadena.** California's premier theater and historical landmark has spawned Broadway careers and productions. Tickets $35-60. Call for rush tickets. Shows Tu-F 8pm, Sa 5 and 9pm, Su 2 and 7pm.

Pantages, 6231 Hollywood Blvd. (☎213-365-3500), across from the Metro Red Line's Hollywood/Vine station in **Hollywood.** Hosted the premieres of *Cleopatra* and *Spartacus.* Broadway national tour performances and cabaret acts. Tickets from $30.

LIVE MUSIC

L.A.'s music venues range from small clubs to massive amphitheaters. The **Wiltern** (☎213-380-5005) shows alterna-rock/folk acts. The **Hollywood Palladium** (☎323-962-7600) is of comparable size with 3500 seats. Midsized acts head for the **Universal Amphitheater** (☎818-622-4440). Huge indoor sports arenas, such as the **Great Western Forum** (☎310-330-7300) and the newer **Staples Center** (☎213-742-7100), double as concert halls for big acts. Few dare to play at the 100,000-seat **Los Angeles Memorial Coliseum and Sports Arena;** only U2, Depeche Mode, Guns 'n' Roses, and the Warped Tour have filled the stands in recent years. Call Ticketmaster (☎213-480-3232) to purchase tickets for any of these venues.

☒ **Hollywood Bowl,** 2301 N. Highland Ave. (☎323-850-2000), in **Hollywood.** The premier outdoor music venue in L.A., the Bowl hosts a summer music festival from early July to mid-Sept. Although sitting in the back of this outdoor, 18,000-seat amphitheater makes the L.A. Philharmonic sound like it's on a transistor radio, bargain tickets and a panoramic view of the Hollywood Hills make it worthwhile. Free open house rehearsals by the Philharmonic and visiting performers usually Tu and Th at 10:30am, but the schedule is sometimes irregular. Parking at the Bowl is limited and pricey ($11-12). This is also stacked parking, which means lengthy leaving time; it's better to park at one of the lots away from the Bowl and take a shuttle (parking $5, shuttle $2.50; departs every 10-20min. starting 1½hr. before showtime). There are also lots at 10601 and 10801 Ventura Blvd., near Universal City; at the Kodak Theatre at 6801 Hollywood Blvd.; and at the L.A. Zoo, 5333 Zoo Dr. in Griffith Park. MTA bus #163 runs from Burbank and Hollywood and bus #156 goes west from downtown or east from the Valley. Call Ticketmaster (☎213-480-3232) to purchase tickets.

Music Center, 135 N. Grand Ave. (☎213-972-7211), at the corner of 1st St. **downtown.** Includes the Mark Taper Forum, the Dorothy Chandler Pavilion, the Ahmanson Theatre, and the spanking new Gehry-designed Walt Disney Concert Hall. Performance spaces host the L.A. Opera, Broadway and experimental theater, and dance. Parking $7 after 6pm, but you pay less at the many lots nearby.

The Greek Theatre, 2700 N. Vermont Ave. (☎665-5857; www.greektheatrela.com), nestled in the hills of **Griffith Park.** From I-10 or U.S. 101, take the Vermont Ave. exit north. Winner of the Best Small Outdoor Venue of the Year award for the last 3 years, this theater is a 6000-seat venue that has played host to some of the biggest names in music entertainment. A constant line-up of pop, classical, reggae, rock, and more; call ahead or check the website to find out the schedule. Parking $10.

SPORTS

Exposition Park and the often dangerous city of **Inglewood,** southwest of the park, are home to many sports teams. The **USC Trojans** play football at the **L.A. Memorial Coliseum,** 3911 S. Figueroa St. (☎213-740-4672), which seats over 100,000 spectators. It is the only stadium in the world to have had the honor of hosting the Olympic Games twice. The torch that held the Olympic flame still towers atop the Coliseum's roof. Basketball's doormat, the **L.A. Clippers** (☎213-742-7500), and the dazzling, star-studded 2002 NBA Champion **L.A. Lakers** (☎310-426-6000) play at the new **Staples Center,** 1111 S. Figueroa St. (☎213-742-7100, box office 213-742-7340), along with the **L.A. Kings** hockey team (☎888-546-4752) and the city's women's basketball team, the **L.A. Sparks** (☎310-330-3939). Lakers tickets start at $23, Kings at $24.50, and Sparks at $7.50. Call Ticketmaster (☎213-480-3232) for tickets.

About 3 mi. northeast of downtown, **Elysian Park** curves around the northern portion of Chavez Ravine, home of **Dodger Stadium** and the popular **L.A. Dodgers** baseball team. Single-game tickets ($6-21) are a hot commodity during the April-October season, especially if the Dodgers are playing well. Call ☎323-224-1448 for info and advance tickets.

If you crave the rush of adrenaline that only comes from athletic participation, hop in your car and drive east to **Perris Valley Skydiving,** 2091 Goetz Rd., in Perris Valley, near Riverside (2hr.). Not the most budget-savvy activity, but this is the place to fulfill that urge to leap from 12,500 ft. Dives accommodate both experienced jumpers and first-timers, who jump with an instructor strapped tightly to their backs. After a 1min. freefall, enjoy a 7min. canopy descent. (☎909-657-1664 or 800-832-8818. Dives $199 cash, $209 with credit card; extra charge for people over 200 lbs. Group discounts and lessons available.)

Both surfers and beach bums should check out the annual **surfing competitions** held in late July on Huntington Beach in Orange County (see p. 468), just south of L.A. The multi-day festival features surfing and extreme sports such as skateboarding and BMX, as well as drunken revelry and suntanned bodies. For more information, call ☎310-473-0411 or visit www.fusion.philips.com.

▓ NIGHTLIFE

L.A.'s nightlife scene is constantly shifting. Pick up a copy of *L.A. Weekly* or the *L.A. Times*'s Calendar section (see p. 387) for the latest entertainment news. Given the extremely short shelf life and unpredictability of the L.A. club scene, **late-night restaurants** have become the reliable fallback option of L.A. nightlife, popular with underage club kids and celebs in rehab. Most are in the Hollywood area (see p. 432), though many are chains with outposts in other neighborhoods. Many **coffeehouses** stay open late and have open-mic nights or live music. Bring a book to hide behind as you scope out the scene, or a laptop for working on your new screenplay. L.A.'s **comedy clubs** are among the best in the world. Although prices are steep, it's worth the setback to catch the newest and wackiest comedians or watch skilled veterans hone new material.

Though it's hard to barhop when the best places are a 30min. drive away from each other (*Let's Go* does not recommend drinking and driving) L.A.'s **bars** run the gamut from casual beach hangouts to swanky hotel lounges. Unless otherwise specified, **bars in California are 21+**. With the highest number of bands per capita in the world and more streaming in every day, L.A. is famous for its club scene. The **Sunset Strip** (see p. 432) holds many of the city's best clubs. Most clubs are able to book top-notch acts and pack 'em in every night. The distinction between music and dance clubs is murky in L.A.—most music clubs have DJs a few times a week, and many dance clubs have occasional live music. Club events designed by promoters for specific venues are prevalent and popular. When promoters move their events to different clubs, they're often followed by die-hard fans. Consequently, club venues may host completely different crowds on different nights.

L.A. clubs are often expensive, but many are still feasible on a limited budget. Coupons in *L.A. Weekly* and those handed out inside clubs can save you a bundle. To enter the club scene, it's best to be at least 21 (although it also helps to be a beautiful woman). Nevertheless, if you're over 18, you can still find a space to dance, though it may mean a hefty cover charge in a less desirable venue. **All clubs are 21+ unless otherwise noted.**

▼ GLBT NIGHTLIFE

The slice of **Santa Monica Boulevard** in **West Hollywood** (see p. 424) is the Sunset Strip of GLBT nightlife. Still, many "straight" clubs have gay nights; check *LA Weekly* or contact the Gay and Lesbian Community Services Center. Free weekly magazine *fab!* lists happenings in the gay and lesbian community. **All clubs are 21+ unless otherwise noted.**

❊ FESTIVALS

▓ **Tournament of Roses Parade and Rose Bowl** (☎626-449-7673; www.tournamentofroses.com), in Pasadena. New Year's Day is always a perfect day in Southern California. Some of the wildest New Year's Eve parties happen along Colorado Blvd., the parade route. If you miss the parade, which runs from 8-10am, you can still see the floats (made entirely from fresh flowers) on display that afternoon and on Jan. 2 on Sierra Madre Blvd. between Washington Blvd. and Sierra Madre Villa Ave. ($6). The champs of the Pac 10 and Big 10 conferences meet on the afternoon of Jan. 1 for the Rose Bowl, and every 4 years, the championship game of the NCAA Football's **Bowl Championship Series (BCS)** is held here. Only a few end-zone tickets are available to the public; call ☎626-449-4100 after Nov. 1.

Chinese New Year Parade (☎213-680-0243; www.chinatownla.com), in Chinatown, along Broadway Ave. Fireworks and dragons usher in this Chinese celebration in Feb.

UCLA Mardi Gras (☎310-825-6564), at the athletic field. Billed as the world's largest collegiate activity. Festivities 7pm-2am on Fat Tuesday in Feb. Proceeds to charity.

Playboy Jazz Festival (☎310-449-4070), at the Hollywood Bowl. A weekend of entertainment by top-name jazz musicians of all varieties, from traditional to fusion. Sorry, no bunnies. Call Ticketmaster (☎213-381-2000) for prices.

NIGHTLIFE BY TYPE

BARS

▨ 3 of Clubs (433)	HW
Acapulco (413)	WW
Beauty Bar (433)	HW
Cafe Boogaloo (408)	SB
Daddy's (433)	HW
El Carmen (424)	WH
Formosa Cafe (436)	HW
The Gallery Bar (436)	DT
The Lava Lounge (434)	HW
Lucky Strike (434)	HW
Maloney's (412)	WW
▨ Miyagi's (424)	WH
Musso & Frank Grill (436)	HW
North (424)	WH
The Polo Lounge (436 and p. 416)	BH
The Room (433)	HW
The Roost (438)	LF
Rusty's Surf Ranch (401)	SM
▨ Standard Lounge (433)	HW
▨ Temple Bar (401)	SM
Trader Vic's (436)	BH
Westwood Brewing Company (413)	WW
Ye Coach and Horses (434)	HW
Zen Sushi (438)	SL

CLUBS

7969 Peanuts (424)	WH
The Derby (438)	LF
The Ice House (447)	PA
The Larchmont (434)	HW
Key Club (424)	WH
▨ Largo (424)	WH
Lighthouse Cafe (408)	SB
Q's Billiard Club (448)	PA
Roxy (424)	WH

The Shelter (424)	WH
Twin Palms (448)	PA
Whisky A Go-Go (424)	WH

COFFEEHOUSES

Anastasia's Asylum	SM
Bourgeois Pig (433)	HW
Catalina Coffee Company (408)	SB
▨ Elixer (422)	WH
G.A.L.A.X.Y. Gallery (433)	HW
Gypsy Cafe (413)	WW
▨ Highland Grounds (433)	HW
Stir Crazy (433)	HW
UnUrban Coffeehouse (401)	SM

COMEDY CLUBS

The Comedy and Magic Club (408)	SB
Comedy Store (422)	WH
Groundling Theater (433)	HW
The Laugh Factory (422)	WH

GLBT NIGHTLIFE

▨ Abbey Cafe (424)	WH
Arena (425)	WH
Here (425)	WH
Micky's (424)	WH
The Palms (425)	WH
Rage (425)	WH
Trunks (425)	WH

LATE-NIGHT RESTAURANTS

Barney's Beanery (433)	HW
Jerry's Famous Deli (422)	WH
▨ The Kettle (408)	SB
Mel's Drive In (422)	WH
The Rainbow Bar and Grill (422)	WH

BH Beverly Hills **DT** Downtown **HW** Hollywood **LF** Los Feliz **PA** Pasadena **SB** South Bay **SL** Silver Lake **SM** Santa Monica **WH** West Hollywood **WW** Westwood

LOS ANGELES

Gay Pride Celebration (☎ 323-969-8302), funded by the Christopher Street West Association. The last or second-to-last weekend in June. L.A.'s GLBT communities celebrate in West Hollywood. Art, politics, dances, and a huge parade. Tickets $12.

Shakespeare Festival/L.A. (☎ 213-481-2273; www.shakespearefestivalla.org), in downtown and Palos Verdes. June-July. This theater company aims to make Shakespeare more accessible. Youth program performs Shakespeare adaptations in early Aug. downtown shows begin at 8pm in Pershing Sq. between 5th and 6th St. and Hill and Olive Ave. Canned food donation accepted in lieu of admission at downtown performances. Palos Verdes admission $15.

Día de los Muertos, along Olvera St., downtown. Nov. 1. Rousing Mexican cultural celebration for the spirits of dead ancestors revisiting the world of the living. Food, vendors, costumes, and Halloween accoutrements.

Las Posadas (☎213-485-9777), along Olvera St., downtown. In Dec. This celebration includes a candlelit procession and the whacking of a piñata.

SANTA MONICA ☎310

Santa Monica's charming bungalows and Art Deco apartment buildings are deceptively modest; though the city (pop. 87,000) basks in laid-back charm, it's actually one of L.A.'s priciest places to live. Lush residential areas, populated by screen superstars and comfortable yuppies, sit blocks away from shopping districts and beaches. The Third St. Promenade is the city's most popular spot to shop by day and schmooze by night, but locals head to Montana Ave. or Fred Segal for more unique and pricey items. In spite of (or perhaps due to) its prime beachfront location and excellent weather, liberal Santa Monica struggles to reconcile itself with rampant homelessness.

▐ TRANSPORTATION

From downtown L.A., it takes about 30min. driving on I-10 (Santa Monica Fwy.) with no traffic to reach Santa Monica. **MTA #33/333** connect L.A. and Santa Monica. Santa Monica's Big Blue Bus (BBBus) system connects to MTA routes.

Public Transit: Santa Monica Municipal Bus Lines (☎451-5444; www.bigblue-bus.com). With over 1000 stops in Santa Monica, L.A., and Culver City, the "Big Blue Bus" **(BBBus)** is faster and cheaper than the MTA. Route **#1** connects Santa Monica to West L.A. via Santa Monica Blvd., **#2** runs along Wilshire Blvd.; **#3** goes to LAX; **#10** provides express service from downtown Santa Monica (at 7th St. and Grand Ave.) to downtown L.A. Most routes $0.75; transfer tickets for MTA buses $0.25; transfers to other BBBuses free. The **Tide Shuttle** runs from Broadway south along Ocean Ave. to Marine St. and north along Main St. back to Broadway ($0.25). Signs with route info litter downtown Santa Monica. Runs every 15min. Su-Th noon-8pm, F-Sa noon-10pm.

✦▐ ORIENTATION AND PRACTICAL INFORMATION

The **Santa Monica Freeway (I-10)** runs west from L.A. to the PCH (Hwy. 1.). Just north of the freeway, traffic crawls east-west on **Santa Monica Boulevard.** The car-free **Third Street Promenade** stretches north from Broadway to Wilshire Blvd. Boutique shopping and restaurants make for a slightly less generic environment on **Montana Avenue. Pico Boulevard,** to the south of I-10, has edgier coffee shops and art galleries. Palm tree-lined **Ocean Avenue** runs up the coast before heading into the hills of Pacific Palisades. Much of Santa Monica and Venice is best seen by foot or bike, so plan on parking in one of the main lots near Third St. Promenade.

Visitor Information: Santa Monica Visitors Center, 395 Santa Monica Pl. (☎393-7593), on the 2nd floor of the Third St. Promenade mall. Open daily 10am-6pm. **Information kiosk** at 1400 Ocean Ave. Open daily 10am-5pm.

Equipment Rentals:

Perry's Beach Rentals (☎458-3975; www.actionsportsrentals.com), in the blue buildings north and south of the pier and just before Venice Beach. 4 locations: 2400 and 2600 Ocean Front Walk, 930 and 1200 Hwy. 1. In-line skates and bikes $7 per hr., $20 per day; tandem bikes $12/$35. Boogie boards $6/$18. Group discounts. Open daily 9am-dark.

Skate City, 111 Broadway (☎319-9272). In-line skates $5 per hr., $10 per day. Open M-F 10am-7pm, Sa-Su 10am-8pm.

Blazing Saddles Bike Rentals, 320 Santa Monica Pier (☎393-9778). Bikes $6-11 per hr., $18-30 per day. Tandems and baby seats also available. Helmets, locks, and racks included. Open M-F 9:30am-7:30pm, Sa-Su 8:30am-7:30pm.

Parking: 6 lots flank Third St. Promenade. 3 are accessible from 4th St., and 3 from 2nd St. First 2hr. free, $1 each additional 30min. Santa Monica Place Mall has free parking for up to 3hr. ($3 flat fee after 5pm). Metered spots $0.50 per hr. Downtown streets have meters as well ($0.50 per hr.). All-day beachside parking $6-10.

Currency Exchange: Western Union, 1454 4th St. (☎394-7211), at Broadway. Open M-F 9am-6pm, Sa 10am-2pm.

Library: L.A. Public Library, Santa Monica Branch, 1324 4th St. (☎458-8600), at Santa Monica Blvd. Temporary location while the main branch undergoes construction through 2005. Open M-Th 10am-9pm, F-Sa 10am-5:30pm, Su 1-5pm.

Medical Services: Santa Monica/UCLA Medical Center, 1250 16th St. (☎319-4765). Emergency room open 24hr.

Police: 333 Olympic Dr. (☎395-9931).

Post Office: 1248 5th St. (☎576-6786), at Arizona Ave. Open M-F 9am-6pm, Sa 9am-3pm. **Postal Code:** 90401.

ACCOMMODATIONS

Accommodations in Santa Monica range from cheap oceanfront hostels to expensive oceanfront hotels. In general, the closer you stay to the beach, the more you dish out. Depending on the establishment, the tax on your room may be 8.5% or 14%. Everything fills quickly in summer; book early. Drivers should look for accommodations that include parking or consider staying farther from the beach, since overnight parking near the beach is very limited.

Los Angeles/Santa Monica (HI-AYH), 1436 2nd St. (☎393-9913; www.hilosangeles.org), 1 block from the promenade and 2 blocks from the beach. From Santa Monica Blvd., turn south onto 2nd St. Or take MTA #33 or BBBus #10 from Union Station to 2nd St. and Broadway, or BBBus #3 from LAX to 4th St. and Broadway. Next door to the associated SaMo Travelers Center. Welcoming travelers of all backgrounds and ages, this popular hostel surrounds a courtyard and fountain with small but well-attended rooms and common spaces. Frequent discounted tours, outings, comedy shows, open mic, and movie nights. Dining room, newly renovated kitchen, game room, TV room, pool table, Internet access, and library. Swipe keys enhance security. No-alcohol policy, and strict 10pm-8am quiet hours. Breakfast $1-5. Laundry $1.75. 10-day max. stay. In summer, reserve by phone or online. 4- to 10-bed dorms $28, nonmembers $31; doubles $70/$72. Group packages available for 8 or more. ❷

Seaview Motel, 1760 Ocean Ave. (☎393-6711). Tastefully decorated rooms, a patio ideal for sunbathing, and a path straight to the beach. Prime location at a reasonable price. Singles to quads $65-80. ❹

Hotel California, 1670 Ocean Ave. (☎393-2363 or 866-571-0000; www.hotelca.com), between Pico and Colorado Blvd. Well worth the price for its private beachfront location and well-furnished rooms. Satellite TV, mini-fridge, and wireless Internet in every room. Suites with kitchenette, dining table, pullout bed, stereo, and balcony available. Rooms (sleep up to 4) $129-279. 20% off for stays over a week. ❺

FOOD

Al fresco dining is *de rigueur* under the giant, colorful table umbrellas sprouting from sidewalk patios along **Third Street Promenade** and **Ocean Avenue. Montana Avenue** hosts innovative upscale restaurants, and most menus cater to deep-pocketed health buffs with organic and vegetarian options.

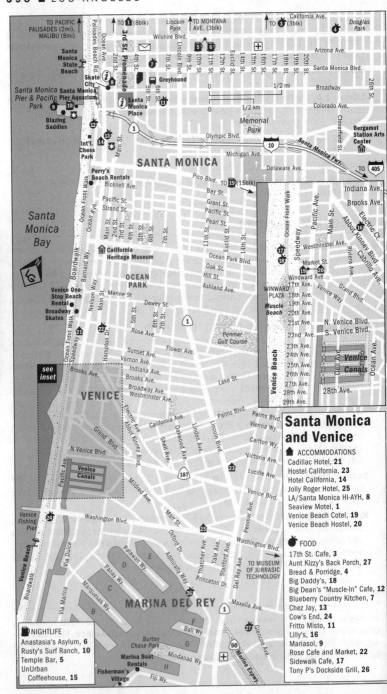

TO PACIFIC PALISADES (2mi), MALIBU (8mi)

TO **1** (8blk)

Lincoln Park

TO MONTANA AVE. (3blk)

California Ave.

TO **3** (3blk)

Douglas Park

Wilshire Blvd.

Arizona Ave.

Santa Monica Blvd.

Broadway

Colorado Ave.

Santa Monica State Beach

Palisades Beach Rd.

Ocean Ave.

3rd St. Promenade

2nd St.

4th St.

5th St.

6th St.

7th St.

Lincoln Blvd.

9th St.

11th St.

12th St.

14th St.

15th St.

16th St.

17th St.

18th St.

19th St.

20th St.

26th St.

Euclid St.

5 **6**

7

Greyhound

Skate City

8

Santa Monica Pier & Pacific Park

Santa Monica Pier Aquarium

Santa Monica Place

9 **10**

Blazing Saddles

11

12

Int'l. Chess Park

13

14

Main St.

Santa Monica Bay

SANTA MONICA

Memorial Park

Olympic Blvd.

Michigan Ave.

Delaware Ave.

Santa Monica Fwy.

Santa Monica St.

Cloverfield St.

10

Bergamot Station Arts Center

TO **405**

Perry's Beach Rentals

Bicknell Ave.

Pacific St.

Strand St.

Ocean Front Walk

Ocean Ave.

Main St.

2nd St.

3rd St.

4th St.

5th St.

6th St.

7th St.

Pico Blvd.

TO **15** (15blk)

Bay St.

Grant St.

Pacific St.

Pearl St.

Ocean Park Blvd.

Oak St.

Hill St.

Ashland Ave.

11th St.

14th St.

Euclid St.

Indiana Ave.

Brooks Ave.

Ocean Front Walk

Speedway

Pacific Ave.

Main St.

Abbot Kinney Blvd.

Electric Ct.

Westminster Ave.

16

17

18

Market St.

Riviera Ave.

Cabrillo Ave.

19

20

Windward Ave.

WINWARD PLAZA

Muscle Beach

7th Ave.

18th Ave.

19th Ave.

20th Ave.

21st Ave.

22nd Ave.

23rd Ave.

24th Ave.

25th Ave.

26th Ave.

27th Ave.

28th Ave.

29th Ave.

Venice Way

Grand Blvd.

N. Venice Blvd.

S. Venice Blvd.

Venice Canals

Dell Ave.

Ocean Ave.

28th Ave.

Venice Beach

California Heritage Museum

OCEAN PARK

Barnard Way

Neilson Way

Main St.

Marine St.

Dewey St.

Rose Ave.

Venice One-Stop Beach Rental

Broadway Skates

Ocean Front Walk

Speedway

Hampton Dr.

5th St.

6th St.

7th St.

Sunset Ave.

Vernon Ave.

Indiana Ave.

Brooks Ave.

Broadway Ave.

Westminster Ave.

21

22

Flower Ave.

Penmar Golf Course

see inset

VENICE

Venice Canals

Electric Ave.

Abbot Kinney Blvd.

Pacific Ave.

Grand Blvd.

N Venice Blvd.

Brooks Ave.

California Ave.

Oakwood Ave.

Shell Ave.

Milldred Ave.

Linden Ave.

Lincoln Blvd.

Lake St.

Palms Blvd.

Palms Blvd.

Vienna Way

Carlton Wy.

Victoria Ave.

Lucille Ave.

Venice Blvd.

Penmar Ave.

23

187

Venice Fishing Pier

24

Venice Beach Boardwalk

Via Marina

Via Dulce

Washington Blvd.

Marr St.

Oxford Dr.

Admiralty Way

Thatcher Ave.

Yale Ave.

Stanford Ave.

Princeton Dr.

Del Rey Ave.

Washington Blvd.

25

TO MUSEUM OF JURRASIC TECHNOLOGY

1

Maxella Ave.

26

27

Glencoe Ave.

Marquesas Wy.

Panay Wy.

Palawan Wy.

F

E

D

C

B

MARINA DEL REY

Marina Boat Rentals

Fisherman's Village

Burton Chase Park

Ball Wy.

Mindanao Wy.

Fiji Wy.

G

H

90

Marina Expwy.

Santa Monica and Venice

▲ ACCOMMODATIONS

Cadillac Hotel, **21**
Hostel California, **23**
Hotel California, **14**
Jolly Roger Hotel, **25**
LA/Santa Monica HI-AYH, **8**
Seaview Motel, **1**
Venice Beach Cotel, **19**
Venice Beach Hostel, **20**

🍎 FOOD

17th St. Cafe, **3**
Aunt Kizzy's Back Porch, **27**
Bread & Porridge, **4**
Big Daddy's, **18**
Big Dean's "Muscle-In" Cafe, **12**
Blueberry Country Kitchen, **7**
Chez Jay, **13**
Cow's End, **24**
Fritto Misto, **11**
Lilly's, **16**
Mariasol, **9**
Rose Cafe and Market, **22**
Sidewalk Cafe, **17**
Tony P's Dockside Grill, **26**

🎵 NIGHTLIFE

Anastasia's Asylum, **6**
Rusty's Surf Ranch, **10**
Temple Bar, **5**
UnUrban Coffeehouse, **15**

0   1/2 mi

0   1/2 km

Santa Monica Bay

Boardwalk

▓ **Fritto Misto**, 601 Colorado Ave. (☎458-2829), at 6th St. "Neighborhood Italian Cafe" with cheery waitstaff lets you create your own pasta (from $6). Vegetarian entrees $8-12. Daily pasta specials $8. Weekend lunch special of all-you-can-eat calamari and salad $12. Omelettes Su 11:30am-4pm ($7-8). Open M-Th 11:30am-10pm, F-Sa 11:30am-10:30pm, Su 11:30am-9:30pm. ❷

Big Dean's "Muscle-In" Cafe, 1615 Ocean Front Walk (☎393-2666). When on the beach, you don't need to venture far for the "burger that made Santa Monica famous" ($7). Veggie burgers $5. Happy hour M-F 4-8pm; $2 domestic beers. Open M-F 10am-dark, Sa-Su 10:30am-dark, or until the regulars clear out. ❶

Mariasol, 401 Santa Monica Pier (☎917-5050). Prime sunset views accompany your meal in the glass-enclosed dining room, or, weather permitting, on the oceanfront patio. Regardless of location, you are always within earshot of the friendly *mariachi* band. Locals recommend the *campechana* ($12), a combination of shrimp, octopus calamari, and ceviche. Appetizers $6-14. Entrees $9-15. Open Su-Th 10am-10pm, F-Sa 10am-11pm. Reservations recommended for 2nd floor dining room. ❸

Bread & Porridge, 2315 Wilshire Blvd. (☎453-4941). Yuppie mummies and daddies push strollers to this trendy breakfast and lunch spot. Prides itself on exceptional service and an egalitarian division of labor—dishwashers, busboys, servers, cashiers, and cooks all rotate jobs and share in the daily tips. Excellent pancakes $6-8. Omelettes $10. Sandwiches and entrees $8-13. Open M-F 7am-2pm, Sa-Su 7am-3pm. ❷

Chez Jay, 1657 Ocean Ave. (☎395-1741). This 43-year-old "celebrity hideaway" serves classic and pricey dishes. Owners Jay and Michael mug for the camera on old-school movie posters. Steak and seafood $17-21. Open M-F noon-2am, Sa-Su 9am-1:30am. Reservations recommended. ❹

Blueberry Country Kitchen, 510 Santa Monica Blvd. (☎394-7766), near 5th St. Blueberries are the muse here, though there are plenty of options for those not fond of the fruit. The sweet staff suggest the signature "Blue Cakes" ($7 short stack, $8.50 for 3). Lunch options include a BLT with a Santa Monica twist ($9). Don't miss the blueberry lemonade ($2). Open M-F 8am-3pm, Sa-Su 6am-3pm. ❷

17th St. Cafe, 1610 Montana Ave. (☎453-2367). Weary Montana Ave. shoppers refresh in this airy cafe. Popular for unique salads such as the Oak Smoked Salmon Salad with feta cheese ($11). Steeper dinner prices, though most pasta dishes are $10-13. Open Su-Th 8am-9:30pm, F-Sa 8am-10pm. ❸

◉ ◗ **SIGHTS AND BEACHES**

Given the cleaner waters and better waves at beaches to the north and south, Santa Monica is known more for its lively shoreside scene than for its surf. Filled with hawkers, the area on and around the carnival pier is the hub of local tourist activity. The fun spills over onto the pedestrian-only Third St. Promenade (see p. 400), where street performers and a Farmers Market add a bit of spice to the outdoor mall-ish ambience. Farther inland, along Main St. and beyond, a smattering of galleries, design shops, and museums testify to the city's love for art and culture.

SANTA MONICA PIER AND PACIFIC PARK. The famed pier is the heart of Santa Monica Beach and home to the carnivalesque Pacific Park. Adrenaline fanatics over 4 ft. tall can twist and turn on the five-story West Coaster or soar 100 ft. above the ocean in the first solar-powered Ferris wheel. Along the pier, amidst pizza joints and souvenir shops, look for free TV show tickets (usually variety and late-night shows) near the north entrance. Achieve temporary hipness at booths along the strip in the form of a painless henna tattoo for $5-20, or pose for a portrait by one of the many artists for $20. (*Off Hwy. 1 on the way to Venice Beach from Santa Monica Beach.* ☎458-8900; http://santamonicapier.org. *Pier open 24hr. Park open in summer Su-Th*

11am-11pm, F-Sa 11am-12:30am; winter hours vary. Ticket window closes 30min. before the park closes. Free Twilight Dance Series June-Sept. Th 7:30pm. Tickets $2 each; most rides 2-3 tickets. Day pass $20, children under 42 in. $11.) Under the Santa Monica Pier lies the **Santa Monica Pier Aquarium,** a high-tech interactive aquarium where kids can watch ocean movies and get their fingers fishy in the "touch tank." *(☎ 393-6149. Open July 1-early Sept. M-F 2-6pm, Sa-Su 12:30-6:30pm, but hours subject to change; reduced winter hours; call ahead. Suggested donation $5, under 12 $3.)*

BEACH SIGHTS. The paved **Ocean Beach Path** is a mini-freeway of cyclists, skaters, and runners; stretching 20¼ mi. along the beach between Santa Monica and Torrance. Immediately south of the pier on Ocean Front Walk, skilled players match wits at the public chess tables at the **International Chess Park.** Opposite the chess masters is the original location of **Muscle Beach** (now in Venice Beach), where bodybuilders and athletes used to show off chiseled physical perfection in the 1930s, 40s, and 50s.

BERGAMOT STATION ARTS CENTER. Once a train depot, these converted warehouses are now helping to promote contemporary L.A. area artists. While the art is pricey, viewing it is free and entertaining. The **Gallery of Functional Art,** in building E3, sells inspired object art, such as bowls made from fresh fruit and vegetables that have been dried, pressed, and aged. The **Santa Monica Museum of Art,** in building G-1, showcases the work of emerging artists. Featured art rotates regularly. Bergamot Station also houses a reasonably priced **Gallery Cafe ❶,** as well as a **Colleagues Gallery** (in building A4) with more affordable works. *(2525 Michigan Ave., near the intersection of Olympic and Cloverfield Blvd. ☎ 586-6467. Gallery of Functional Art open M 9am-4pm, Tu-F 9am-5pm, Sa 10am-5pm. Free. Santa Monica Museum of Art open Tu-Sa 11am-6pm; call ahead because it often closes for installation changes. Suggested donation $3, students and seniors $2. Colleagues Gallery open M noon-2pm and Th 10am-4pm. Free.)*

▐ SHOPPING

Angelenos always claim that nobody walks in L.A., but the rules change on the **Third Street Promenade,** between Broadway and Wilshire Blvd., an ultra-popular three-block stretch of mosaic art tiles, chain clothing stores, movie theaters, and patio restaurants. Cars are prohibited so that everyone can shop, people-watch, and dine in peace. The Promenade truly heats up when the sun sets: street artists strum guitars, break-dance, and sketch caricatures, while families and couples window-shop and eat ice cream. The trendy shopping runs from overpriced bikini shops to some of L.A.'s best bookstores, left over from the Promenade's artier days. On Wednesday and Saturday mornings, the area transforms into a popular **Farmers Market** selling fresh California-grown flowers and produce, with Saturdays featuring exclusively organic products. On the first Saturday of the month, local chefs give cooking demonstrations. To reach the Promenade, take the 4th St. exit off I-10. One block east of the Promenade, **Fred Segal,** 420 Broadway, hides a grotto of high-end clothing and beauty products behind a 60s-style red, white, and blue storefront. *(☎ 458-9940. Open M-Sa 10am-7pm, Su noon-6pm.)*

Beginning at Colorado Ave. and heading south to Venice, **Main Street** mixes old-fashioned charm with designer knick-knack shops. It's much artsier and more urbane than the Third St. Promenade, with numerous art galleries, open-air coffee shops, and restaurants. The historic Victorian-style Roy Jones House, which holds the **California Heritage Museum,** 2612 Main St., half a mile south of Pico Blvd., contrasts with other Main St. architecture. The museum has restored rooms and hosts temporary exhibits. *(☎392-8537. Open W-Su 11am-4pm. $5, students and seniors $3, under 12 free.)*

Just south of an exclusive residential district, **Montana Avenue's** art galleries, vintage stores, high-end boutiques, delicious bakeries, and dozens of restaurants make for a delightful strolling area. A local favorite is the **Culture Shop Gallery,** 1511A Montana Ave., between 15th and 16th St., which sells funky furniture and jewelry. (☎310-656-2656. Open M-F 11am-6pm, Sa 10am-6pm, Su noon-5pm.)

NIGHTLIFE

Temple Bar, 1026 Wilshire Blvd. (☎393-6611). Dark "eastern" decor and cool live music give Temple Bar a smooth vibe. Food and drink complete the eclectic mix with house favorites such as jerk chicken enchiladas with plantains ($8.50) and mojitos ($10). Live music nightly. Open daily 8pm-2am.

Anastasia's Asylum, 1028 Wilshire Blvd. (☎394-7113). Gourmet coffee in huge mugs and rumors of a ghost draw locals to Anastasia's. The menu features ample vegetarian selection and inventive sandwiches, such as Anastasia's Aubergene ($7.50). Frequent live music upstairs. Open Su-Th 6:30am-1am, F-Sa 6:30am-2am.

UnUrban Coffeehouse, 3303 Pico Blvd. (☎315-0056). 3 separate rooms of funky old furniture, campy voodoo candles, Mexican wrestling masks, musty books, and leopard-print couches. Iced mocha blends $3.50. Italian sodas $2. Open mic poetry W 8pm. Open mic comedy Th 7:30pm. Open mic songwriters F 8pm. Music showcase Sa 7pm. Sign up for open mic 30min. before the show. No cover. Open M-Th 7am-midnight, F 7am-1am, Sa 8am-1am, Su 8am-7pm.

Rusty's Surf Ranch, 256 Santa Monica Pier (☎393-7437). Locals love Rusty's impressive surfboard collection and old-school feel. M night pool tournaments and karaoke. Live music F-Sa. Open daily June-Aug. noon-midnight; Sept.-May 4pm-midnight.

MALIBU ☎310

Malibu makes its southern neighbors look like a carnival; it has no amusement parks and no boardwalk—just sand, mountains, and surf. Although Tom Cruise, Bob Dylan, Martin Sheen, Diana Ross, Sting, and Cher are just a few of Malibu's better-known residents, it is not a see-and-be-seen type of town. The quiet shores and the 27 mi. of beautiful beaches that trace the Pacific Coast Highway will soothe the traffic-weary.

TRANSPORTATION

From inland L.A., take I-10 all the way to **Highway 1** (PCH), and head north. Malibu's beaches and restaurants are all directly on the PCH. **Bus #434** runs from downtown to Malibu via Santa Monica.

FOOD

Cheap eats are hard to come by at Malibu's shoreside restaurants, which charge as much for their view as for their food. Celebrity residents sip lattes at the "Star"bucks in the Cross Creek Rd. shopping center.

Malibu Chicken, 22935 Hwy. 1 (☎456-0365), downstairs from Malibu Ocean Sports (see p. 402). Celebrate sun, surf, and fun with sandwiches named after old beach-movie idols, like "Gidget" (grilled chicken breast; $8) and "Big Kahuna" (chicken breast, eggplant, and feta; $8). The "Dora" (2 roast chickens, 4 large sides, salad, and bread; $30) feeds a whole family. Open daily 11:30am-9pm. ❷

Duke's Malibu, 21150 Hwy. 1 (☎317-0777), at Las Flores Canyon Rd. Sit with your feet in the sand at the "Barefoot Bar" and watch the Pacific pound the rocks. Surfing history covers the wall, and you can't go wrong with the parmesan- and herb-crusted fish ($12). Happy hour M-F 4-7pm; entrees half-price. Entrees $8-20. Open M-Th 11:30am-9:30pm, F-Sa 11:30am-10:30pm, Su 10am-9:30pm. ❸

Neptune's Net Seafood, 42505 Hwy. 1 (☎457-3095). It's worth the drive north for this friendly, lively restaurant known for some of the best (and most affordable) seafood in Malibu ($8-10). It's Hell's Angels' heaven on Sundays. Open M-Th 10:30am-8pm, F 10:30am-9pm, Sa-Su 10am-8:30pm. ❷

The Zuma Cafe, 30066 Hwy. 1 (☎457-3143). This classic beachfront stand refuels surfers and swimmers with breakfast ($2.50-6), burgers, and hot dogs. Most items $2-6. Open daily 8am-6pm. ❶

🔵🔲 SIGHTS AND BEACHES

North of Santa Monica along the PCH, the cityscape gives way to appealing stretches of sandy, sewage-free shoreline. Stop along the coast and you may see dolphin pods swimming close to shore, or at least surfers trying to catch a wave. Malibu's beaches are clean and relatively uncrowded—easily the best in L.A. County for surfers, sunbathers, and swimmers. Surfers jet through the wave tubes at **Surfrider Beach,** a section of Malibu Lagoon State Beach north of the pier at 23000 PCH. Walk there via the Zonker Harris Access Way (named after the beach-obsessed Doonesbury character), located at 22700 PCH. **Malibu Ocean Sports,** 22935½ PCH, across from the pier, rents gear, offers surfing lessons, and leads kayak tours of the Pacific coastline. (☎456-6302. Surfboards $10 per hr., $25 per day. Kayaks single $15/$35; tandem $20/$50. Boogie boards $12 per day. Wet suits $10 per day. Surfing lessons $100 for 2hr., includes full-day gear rental. Open M-F 10am-6pm, Sa-Su 9am-6pm.)

🔲**Zuma Beach,** L.A. County's northernmost, largest, happiest sandbox, stretches along the 3000 block of PCH. A convenient location makes sections #5-7 a big draw for swarms of local kids, while a long walk from the only entrance means sections #9-11 are less crowded. Swimmers should stay as close as possible to lifeguard stations; due to the strong **riptide,** rescue counts are high. A trailer directly in front of the Zuma Cafe (see above) rents boogie boards ($10 per hr., $25 per day), kayaks ($15/$35), and bikes ($10/$25). Free parking along PCH is coveted, so expect to use the beach lot ($6, after 6pm $2). Although it's disguised as a deli, **Malibu Ranch Market,** 29575 PCH, in the Zuma Beach Plaza at Busch Rd., also rents boogie boards and sells deli sandwiches, snacks, and alcohol. (☎457-0171. Boogie boards $8-10 per day. Open daily 9am-10pm. Deposit $40.)

Corral State Beach, a tiny windsurfing and swimming haven off the side of the road, lies on the 26000 block of PCH. The larger and generally uncrowded **Point Dume State Beach** (main entrance near 29000 PCH; look for signs) is just north of Corral State Beach, offering better currents for scuba diving. To see one of the country's prettiest university locations, stop by the 830-acre campus of **Pepperdine University,** 24255 PCH, at the intersection of Las Virgenes and PCH. Wide lawns and sand-colored buildings stretch out on a Malibu hillside over the Pacific. Contact admissions (☎506-4000; www.pepperdine.edu) for tours.

VENICE AND MARINA DEL REY ☎310

Venice is a carnivalesque beach town where guitar-toting, wild-eyed, tie-dyed residents sculpt masterpieces in sand or compose them in graffiti, all before hitting the waves. Grab a corn dog and head to Ocean Front Walk; a stroll through in-line skating, bikini-flaunting, tattooed Venice is truly memorable. Inland restaurants and shops cater to a more conservative crowd, with dainty cafes and designer-laden boutiques. Marina del Rey, Venice's neighbor to the immediate south, is older, more expensive, and considerably more sedate. While it does have a swimming beach, residents spurn sunbathing in favor of boating. Once a duck-hunting ground, the area was used as an oil field in the late 1930s and was reincarnated in 1965 as a yacht harbor. Marina del Rey is now the largest man-made marina in the world, with 6000 pleasure boats and 3000 boats in dry storage.

TRANSPORTATION

To reach Venice or Marina del Rey from downtown L.A., take **Bus #33/333**; during rush hour take **#436**. From Santa Monica, take Santa Monica **BBBus #1** or **2**. Avoid meters by **parking** in the lot at Pacific Ave. and Venice Blvd ($5 per day).

ACCOMMODATIONS

Venice Beach Cotel, 25 Windward Ave. (☎399-7649; www.venicebeachcotel.com). From LAX, take BBBus #3, transfer to #2 at California Ave., get off #2 at the post office, and walk 1 block toward shore. Easily identifiable with its international flag display. International staff and guests enliven the cramped quarters. Aqua Lounge features big-screen TV and a BYOB bar where guests chill at night (open 7pm-midnight). Free tea and coffee. Tennis rackets, table tennis, and boogie boards ($20 deposit). **Passport required.** Key deposit $5. Reservations always recommended. 3-, 4-, and 6-bed dorms with ocean view and bath $15-19; doubles $36-52; triples with bath and view $66. ●

Venice Beach Hostel, 1515 Pacific Ave. (☎452-3052; www.caprica.com/venice-beach-hostel), just north of Windward Ave. Central location, friendly staff, and lively atmosphere make this a popular hostel for backpackers. 2 enormous lounges, and 10 super-comfy couches encourage mingling. Lockers, storage rooms, and linen included. Free Internet in every room. Laundry (wash $1, dry $1). Security deposit $25-100. 4- to 10-bed dorms $21-23; private rooms for 1-2 people $58. Weekly discounts available. ❷

Cadillac Hotel, 8 Dudley Ave. (☎399-8876; www.thecadillachotel.com), off Ocean Front Walk. Sauna, rooftop deck with great views, and well-equipped gym. Rooms have TVs, lockers, and private baths. Lounge with cable TV, jukebox, and Internet. **Passport required.** Airport shuttle $10 ($5 per extra person). Discounted car rental. Free pickup and parking. Laundry (wash $0.75, dry $0.50). Reserve ahead. 4-person dorms $25; private rooms $89; family rooms $99. ❷

Hostel California, 2221 Lincoln Blvd. (☎305-0250; kschmahle@aol.com). Park free in the lot off Lucille Ave., 1 block north of Venice Blvd. 1mi. from the beach. Spacious lounge with couches, pool table, and big-screen TV. **Passport** with proof of travel or **out-of-state driver's license required.** Coed and single-sex dorms. Bikes $10. Lockers, linen, laundry included. Key deposit $5. Check-in until midnight. Military-style, 30-bunk barracks $14-16; small, dark, 6-bed dorms $18-19; doubles $40-44. 1 day free for week-long stay. ●

Jolly Roger Hotel, 2904 Washington Blvd. (☎822-2904 or 800-822-2904; www.jollyrgr.com), near Abbot Kinney Blvd., in Marina del Rey. Hotel and motel in the same complex. Though located on a busy street, the hotel is a great mid-range option, especially for stays over a week. Pleasant rooms with A/C, satellite TV, and wireless Internet. Outdoor hot tub and pool, continental breakfast, and free parking. Rooms from $80. Weekly rooms from $350. ❸

FOOD

Venetian cuisine runs the gamut from greasy to ultra-healthy, as befits its beach bum and hippie crowd. The boardwalk has cheap snacks in the fast-food vein; hit up its cafes and restaurants during happy hour for specials on food and drink.

Rose Cafe and Market, 220 Rose Ave. (☎399-0711), at Main St. A rose-lined entrance leads to a bright, floral-themed facade. The cafe's interior features local art, industrial architecture, and healthy deli specials, including sandwiches ($6-8) and salads ($6-8) available from 11:30am. Limited menu after 3pm. Open M-F 7am-5:30pm, Sa 8am-6pm, Su 8am-5pm. ❷

■ **Aunt Kizzy's Back Porch,** 4325 Glencoe Ave. (☎578-1005), in a huge strip mall at Glencoe Ave. and Mindanao Way in Marina Del Rey. A little slice of Southern heaven, offering down-home cooking like sweet potato pie ($3). Dinner $12-$15. All-you-can-eat brunch buffet Su 11am-3pm ($15). Open Su-Th 11am-9pm, F-Sa 11am-11pm. ❸

Sidewalk Cafe, 1401 Ocean Front Walk (☎399-5547), just north of Windward St. A large capacity and prominent boardwalk location attract crowds. Sandwiches include the Hemingway, a 6 oz. steak on a bun, served with fries, and soup or salad ($12). Big social bar. Happy hour daily 4-8pm; pints $2, pitchers $7; appetizers $3-4. Open Su-Th 8am-midnight, F-Sa 8am-1am. ❷

Lilly's, 1031 Abbot Kinney Blvd. (☎314-0004). French cafe and bar with beautiful outdoor garden. Pollock-esque local art adorns the walls. $10 lunch and Su brunch specials. Have *creme brulee* for dessert ($6). Entrees $16-22. Open M-Th noon-2pm and 6-10pm, F-Sa noon-2pm and 6-10:30pm, Su 11:30am-2pm. ❹

Big Daddy's, 1425 Ocean Front Walk (☎396-4146), across Market Ave. Surfboard tables and Beach Boys tunes make this the ultimate beach food shack. The grill masters serve up everything the heart desires but knows it shouldn't. Hot dog combo includes a small hot dog, fries, and drink for $3. Vegetarian pizza $2.75. Churros from an authentic Mexican machine with chocolate, strawberry, or caramel sauce center $4. Open M-F 11am-dark, Sa-Su 9am-dark. ❶

Cow's End, 34 Washington Blvd. (☎574-1080), in Venice. With its asymmetrical whole-pane windows, uneven brick floor, 2 floors, pool table, and scantily clad beach patrons, the Cow's End is riotously popular. Sandwiches from $6.25. Smoothies from $3.75. Open daily 6am-midnight. ❷

Tony P's Dockside Grill, 4445 Admiralty Way (☎823-4534), in Marina del Rey. Pleasant marina views enhance the steak and seafood fare. Tavern walls are covered with framed and signed sports paraphernalia, TVs tuned to the day's sport games, and over 400 beer taps. Lunch entrees $8-10. Dinner entrees $10-22. Martinis shaken at your table $7. Kitchen open M-Th 11:30am-10pm, F 11:30am-11pm, Sa 9am-11pm, Su 9am-10pm. Bar stays open 1hr. longer. ❹

◉ ◤ SIGHTS AND BEACHES

VENICE

At the turn of the 20th century, legendary real-estate developer Abbot Kinney envisioned a re-creation of the famed Italian city on the California coast—a touch of Old World charm, with mustachioed gondoliers plying the canals and the social elite strolling on an elegant ocean-side promenade. Instead, Kinney ended up with a massive dose of New World neuroses. **Ocean Front Walk,** Venice's main beachfront drag, is a seaside three-ring circus of fringe culture. Street people converge on shaded clusters of benches, evangelists drown out off-color comedians, and bodybuilders of both sexes pump iron in skimpy spandex outfits at **Muscle Beach,** 1800 Ocean Front Walk, closest to 18th St. and Pacific Ave. Fire-juggling cyclists, master sand sculptors, bards in Birkenstocks, and **"skateboard grandmas"** define the bohemian spirit of this playground population. Meanwhile, vendors of jewelry, henna body art, snacks, and beach paraphernalia overwhelm the boardwalk.

The best way to experience Venice Beach is to join in the fray. **Boardwalk Skates,** 201½ Ocean Front Walk, rents bikes and skates. (☎450-6634. Bikes $5 per hr., $15 per day; tandem bikes $7/$20. In-line skates $5/$12. Open M-F 10am-7pm, Sa-Su 9am-7pm.) Or cross the bike path to **Venice One-Stop Beach Rental,** located in the bright yellow boxcar, and receive a free map. (Bikes or skates $6 per hr., $10 per 2hr., $17 per day.) Those who got game can ball it up at the popular **basketball court** at 18th St. and Ocean Front Walk, which was featured in the movie *White Men Can't Jump*, but be warned: the competition is fierce and the trash-talking even fiercer.

Toward Culver City is the **Museum of Jurassic Technology**, 9341 Venice Blvd., four blocks west of Robertson Blvd. The museum walks a fine line between an elaborate practical joke and a profound statement on the ultimate inaccessibility of history. It is the only museum of its kind, with an unapologetic and unexplained juxtaposition of exhibits as incongruous as mole rat skeletons, fake gems, and trailer park art. Despite the professional displays, intoned audio narration, and deadpan introductory slide show, you might wonder if it's all designed to make fun of you and/or itself. The museum is not easily accessible by foot from the beach. By car, take I-10 to Robertson Blvd. S and turn right onto Venice Blvd. (☎ 836-6131; www.mjt.org. Open Th 2-8pm, F-Su noon-6pm. Suggested donation $5, students and seniors $3.)

MARINA DEL REY

For a low-key slice of seaside life in L.A., take a walk along the marina or drive down to **Fisherman's Village** (at the eastern end of Fiji Way off Lincoln Blvd.). The small but pleasant wharf-meets-strip-mall is home to a handful of restaurants, gift shops, and boating stores. The village does not warrant a full day, but a relaxing weekend afternoon can be spent in a boat rented from **Marina Boat Rentals**, 13719 Fiji Way. (☎ 574-2822. 4-person powerboats and sailboats $35-90 per hr.; 8-person electric boats $65 per hr.; kayaks $15-25 per hr.; 2-person pedal boats $15 per hr.) No experience is necessary for most rentals, but reservations are recommended. For more rental information visit www.boats4rent.com. Relax afterward on the central patio, where locals gather to hear live music on weekends.

SOUTH BAY   ☎ 562

Head to L.A. County's more casual southern communities for the most precious of SoCal souvenirs: a tan. Manhattan Beach is one of the best-maintained L.A. beaches, filled with yuppie married couples and uncommitted singles enjoying the good life. Immediately to the south lies Hermosa Beach, whose sweet waves, popular boardwalk, and swimsuit competitions attract high concentrations of surfers, volleyball players, and partiers. Redondo Beach is smaller and more commercial, known more for its marina and pier than its beach. Ritzy Rancho Palos Verdes is a different breed of coastal town, but down below the haughty cliffs are sandboxes overrun by gaggles of eager skaters, volleyball players, surfers, and sunbathers. The drive on PCH along the splendid cliffs of Palos Verdes will coax out your romantic side. San Pedro is home to Worldport L.A., the nation's busiest harbor, which somehow supports huge ships and marine life at the same time.

▐▀ TRANSPORTATION

From downtown L.A., take I-10 to **Highway 1** (PCH) and head south. **Bus #439** runs from downtown through Manhattan, Hermosa, and Redondo Beaches. From Redondo Beach, take **Bus #225** to Rancho Palos Verdes and San Pedro.

▐▖ ACCOMMODATIONS

South Bay's hostels represent two extremes in beach living: the contemplative roost at San Pedro and the party-going pad at Hermosa Beach. Budget motels pepper the Pacific Coast Highway.

LOS ANGELES

▓ **Los Angeles Surf City Hostel,** 26 Pier Ave. (☎798-2323), in Pier Plaza in **Hermosa Beach.** Right in the center of the local scene. Free airport pickup 8am-8pm; $10 drop-off. Or take bus #439 to 11th and Hermosa St., walk 2 blocks north, and make a left on Pier Ave. A relaxed atmosphere with a young, mostly international clientele enjoying the nightlife. On the bottom floor of the building is a popular bar and night-club. Discount car rentals, showers, and Internet access. Boogie boards, breakfast, and linen included. **Passport or driver's license required.** Key deposit $10. 28-night max. stay; 3-day max. stay for US citizens. Reservations recommended. 4- to 6-bunk dorms $19; private rooms $48. ❷

Los Angeles South Bay (HI-AYH), 3601 S. Gaffey St., Bldg. #613 (☎831-8109), in Angels Gate Park (entrance across from 36th St.) in **San Pedro.** Free parking. The 180° view from the hilltop location is unbeatable, but the quarters are simple—the hostel was once an army barracks. TV room and basketball court. International or out-of-state residents preferred. Linen $2. 7-night max. stay. Parking included. Reservations in advance with credit card. 5-bed dorms for men, 16-bed dorms for women $19; semi-private rooms with 2-3 beds $22; private rooms $42. Nonmembers $3 more. ❷

Moon Lite Inn, 625 S. Pacific Coast Hwy. (☎540-4058), 2 blocks from the ocean, in **Redondo Beach.** Numerous amenities include: cable TV, A/C, fridge, microwave, phone, and parking. Rooms with 2 beds $65-85; king-size bed with beautiful marble hot tubs $90. Show your *Let's Go* book for a 1-bed rate of $50-65. ❹

⛏ FOOD

Each South Bay community offers more quality restaurants than you will have time to taste-test. Restaurants on the water may offer good views of both beach and beachgoers, but many popular food joints also lie a block or two inland.

Wahoo's Fish Tacos, 1129 Manhattan Ave. (☎796-1044), in **Manhattan Beach.** Opened in 1988 by 2 Hawaiian surfers, the Wahoo family now operates 32-store empire stretching all the way to Colorado. Each funky shack pays homage to surfing with a nonstop surfing video, decal stickers, and surfing posters plastered over its counters and plywood walls. Famous for cheap, flavorful Mexican-inspired grub such as beer-battered Maui onion rings. Try the signature Wahoo bowl (flame-broiled, blackened, or teriyaki Polynesian shrimp on rice with either black or white beans and salsa; $4.25). Mug of Ono Ale $2. Open daily 10:30am-9:30pm. ❶

Hennessy's Tavern, 8 Pier Ave. (☎372-5759), in **Hermosa Beach.** This restaurant and bar offers the best sunset views in South Bay, especially from the 2nd floor deck. 3 full bars open all day. Sandwiches $7-10. Entrees $11-20. Specials include 2-for-1 breakfast and burgers Tu and Luck of the Irish W (after 5pm, flip an Irish coin; if you call it correctly, any dinner entree is free). Free martini with dinner Sa after 5pm. Happy hour F 4-7pm. Open daily 7am-2am. Kitchen closes 12:30am. ❸

The Spot, 110 2nd St. (☎376-2355; www.worldfamousspot.com), in **Hermosa Beach.** Opened in 1977, this is one of the oldest vegetarian restaurants in the L.A. area and is still a favorite with the resident hippie population. Fat-free, non-dairy-based fare in the outdoor garden. Tempeh, tofu, and tahini entrees hit the spot. Homemade bread and desserts $3.50. Trademarked "Inflation buster" combos such as the "Dear George" include veggies served on pasta or rice with tofu ($5-7). Open daily 11am-10pm. ❷

Martha's Corner, 25 22nd Street (☎379-0070), in **Hermosa Beach.** A popular spot for the young and clean-cut. Fresh sandwiches, salads, and soups $3-7. Grilled panini with your choice of 3 ingredients $6. Open M-F 7am-3:30pm, Sa-Su 7am-4pm; extended summer hours. ❷

👁 🌊 SIGHTS AND BEACHES

MANHATTAN BEACH. Manhattan Beach's main drag, **Manhattan Avenue,** is lined with popular cafes and shops and slopes down to the Manhattan Beach Pier. The small **Roundhouse Marine Studies Lab and Aquarium** displays Santa Monica Bay marine life and includes a shark aquarium. *(At the end of the pier. ☎ 379-8117. Open M-F 3pm-dusk, Sa-Su 10am-dusk. Suggested donation $2.)* Casual players can bump volley-balls on the courts by the pier; the games are often more skilled and competitive farther north, at the corner of Marin and Highland Ave.

HERMOSA BEACH. The core of Hermosa Beach's scene is **Pier Plaza,** at the end of Pier Ave. between Hermosa Ave. and the beach. South Bay's best bars, cafes, and surf boutiques sit in this small, pedestrian-only promenade. **The Strand** bike path runs along Manhattan Ave. from Hermosa Beach to Marina del Rey until it hits the bike/skate path along Ocean Front Walk, which stretches north to Santa Monica. **Surfing lessons** are offered at **Pier Surf.** *(25 Pier Ave. ☎ 372-2012. $100 per 1½hr.; includes board.)* **Gallery C** is the largest art gallery in the South Bay dedicated to contemporary painting, sculpture, and installation by California artists. *(1225 Hermosa Ave. ☎ 798-0102. Open Su noon-5pm, Tu-W and F-Sa 11am-6pm, Th 11am-8pm.)*

REDONDO BEACH. Redondo Beach is slightly less upscale than the other beach communities. Its main attractions are the pier, boardwalk, and marina complex. Beginning in July, the city sponsors free concerts on the pier every Tuesday and Friday night that range from rock to jazz to Latin to country. Adjacent **King Harbor** shelters thousands of pleasure boats and hosts some excellent sport fishing. The **Monstad Pier** supports many restaurants, bars, and the local fishing community.

RANCHO PALOS VERDES. Spanish haciendas and ranch houses cover the stunning cliffs and tawny hills of this lovely wealthy peninsula. For prolific Southern Californian plant life, head to **South Coast Botanic Gardens.** This former landfill has been redeemed by an 87-acre garden, where over three quarters of the plants are drought-resistant. *(26300 Crenshaw Blvd., off Hwy. 1. ☎ 544-6815. Open daily 9am-5pm. $6, students and seniors $4, ages 5-12 $1.50. Free 3rd Tu of each month.)* The all-glass **Wayfarer's Chapel** sits on the south side of the hills. Known as the "glass church," the chapel was designed by Frank Lloyd Wright's son, **Lloyd Wright.** Like his father, Wright incorporates his architecture into its surroundings. *(5755 S. Palos Verdes Dr. ☎ 377-1650. Open daily 7am-5pm. Chapel closes for weddings and services; call ahead. Free.)*

SAN PEDRO. Farther southeast, still water, tidepools, and a nearby harbor draw families to **Cabrillo Beach.** *(At the end of Rte. 213. Beach parking $7; free parking in surrounding neighborhood.)* The **Cabrillo Marine Aquarium** presents touch tanks, marine history exhibits, and pickled squid and whale skeletons. *(3720 Stephen White Dr. From Rte. 110, exit at Harbor Blvd. in San Pedro. Take a right onto Harbor Blvd., turn right onto 22nd St., and take a left onto Pacific Ave. Take a left onto 36th St. and Stephen White Dr. ☎ 548-7562. Open Tu-F noon-5pm, Sa-Su 10am-5pm. Suggested donation $5, children and seniors $1. Parking $7.)* Cafes and antique shops line **6th Street.** The **Fort MacArthur Military Museum,** inside the 64-acre **Angel's Gate Park,** is a nearly intact coastal fortification. *(3601 Gaffey St. ☎ 548-2631. Open Tu, Th, Sa-Su noon-5pm. Free.)* Right down the hill from the museum is the **Korean Friendship Bell,** a popular daytime recreation spot with amazing views of the ocean. The bell was featured in *The Usual Suspects.* *(Open daily 10am-6pm.)*

🔎 NIGHTLIFE

▧ **The Kettle,** 1138 N. Highland Ave. (☎545-8511), at the corner of Manhattan Beach Blvd. in **Manhattan Beach.** The Kettle steams with heaping platefuls of home-style cooking. Come nightfall, surfers take over the carved-wood tables. The menu is only a guide—creativity is encouraged. Salads and sandwiches $7-9. "Hangover" omelette with green chiles and jack cheese $7. Beer and wine served until midnight. Open 24hr.

Catalina Coffee Company, 126 N. Catalina Ave. (☎318-2499; www.catalinacoffee.com), in **Redondo Beach.** Not your average bohemian coffeehouse, Catalina Coffee Company provides plush couches, antique chess sets, a working fireplace, Internet access, a mystery library, and smooth jazz. Coffee made from beans roasted on site $1.50-4. Teas $2.25. Gourmet sandwiches $6-7. Baked goods $2-4. Open M-F 6:30am-10pm, Sa-Su 7am-10pm.

The Comedy and Magic Club, 1018 Hermosa Ave. (☎372-1193; www.comedyclubandmagicclub.com), just south of the Pier in **Hermosa Beach.** This premier comedy club usually features 3 comedians, 1 magician, and 1 experimental performance (like juggling) nightly. Recent performances by Jerry Seinfeld, Jay Leno, and Howie Mandel. Tickets $12-30, but big names can cost up to $50. 2-drink min. Shows Tu-F 8pm, Sa 7 and 9:15pm, Su 7pm.

Cafe Boogaloo, 1238 Hermosa Ave. (☎318-2324), in **Hermosa Beach.** Top-notch blues, beautiful people, killer shrimp appetizers, and addictive cocktails ($7) with a dash of Louisiana soul. Full bar with 27 microbrews on tap ($4.50). Smokers put a coaster over their glass to indicate they're coming back to finish drinking. Dinner from $10. Shows nightly from 9pm. Happy hour M-F 5-7pm. Cover F-Sa $10-15. Open M-Th 5pm-midnight, F 5pm-2am, Sa 3pm-2am, Su 1pm-midnight.

Lighthouse Cafe, 30 Pier Ave. (☎372-6911; www.thelighthousecafe.net), in the Pier Plaza in **Hermosa Beach.** Frequented by bronzed volleyball players, this cool dance club plays music ranging from reggae to 80s. The Pacific Rim Party Platter serves 2 or more with Thai wings, fried dumplings, egg rolls, and fresh pineapple ($10). Jazz brunch Su 11am-3pm. Cover Th-Sa $5. Open M-Th 6pm-2am, F 4pm-2am, Sa-Su 11am-2am.

🎇 FESTIVALS

Dubbed the Wimbledon of beach volleyball, the **Manhattan Beach Open** (☎426-8000; www.avp.com) draws crowds to the pier in high summer to watch some of the best pro players in the world bump, set, and spike from morning to night. **Manhattan Beach Concerts in the Park,** 1601 Manhattan Beach Blvd., is a summer-long series of free concerts in Polliwog Park. (☎802-5417; www.citymb.info. Late June-early Sept. 5-7pm.) The **International Surf and Health Festival** is one of the more established annual festivals of the beach cities. Each year at the end of July or beginning of August, hundreds participate in two days of competitions, food, music, dance, drink, and tans. Competitions include bodysurfing, beach volleyball, surfing, swimming, sand-castle building, fishing, and running. Registration is open to all but must be done at least a month in advance. Contact the Manhattan Beach Chamber of Commerce or print out registration forms at www.surffestival.org. The **Hermosa Beach Open,** on the same pro tour as the Manhattan Beach Open, awards more prize money than any other beach volleyball tournament. Call the Hermosa Beach Community Center (☎318-0280) for info.

WESTWOOD AND WEST L.A.　☎310

Wedged between the exclusive neighborhoods of Brentwood and Beverly Hills, Westwood hosts the large student population of University of California at Los Angeles (UCLA) and its many thousands of students. Movie theaters, boutiques, outdoor cafes, and coffeehouses clutter in Westwood Village; most cater to college kids, though some are rather upscale. The nebulous district of West L.A. south of Westwood is largely residential, but hides the occasional quirky store or perfect ethnic hole-in-the-wall restaurant.

TRANSPORTATION

Westwood Village, the triangular area just south of the University of California at Los Angeles (UCLA) and bordered by Weyburn, Glendon, and Broxton Ave., caters to the tens of thousands of students who live in the area. **Santa Monica Boulevard** runs through West L.A., which ends just west of I-405. Take the Wilshire/Westwood Village or Santa Monica Blvd. exits to reach the neighborhoods. **Bus #20** runs from downtown along Wilshire Blvd. through Westwood; **#4** runs along Santa Monica Blvd., connecting West L.A. with West Hollywood and Santa Monica. **BBBus** also runs to UCLA, Westwood Village, and West L.A.

ACCOMMODATIONS

The youthful vibe and compact nature of Westwood village make it a very attractive place to stay. Reserve far in advance if you're coming in June, when parents flock to UCLA's graduation.

Hotel Claremont, 1044 Tiverton Ave. (☎208-5957 or 800-266-5957), near UCLA in Westwood Village. A house-like hotel in a beautiful area, still owned by the same family that built it 60 years ago. All rooms with ceiling fans and private baths. Fridge and microwave next to a Victorian-style TV lounge. Reservations recommended. Singles $56; doubles $62; 2 beds (sleep up to 4) $71. ❸

The Little Inn, 10604 Little Santa Monica Blvd. (☎475-4422). A classic motel that looks like a collection of cottages from the outside. Inside, the furniture is mismatched, but all rooms have A/C, cable TV, and fridge. Parking included. Check-out 11am. 1 bed (for up to 2) $50-65; 2 beds $55-70. $5 per extra person. During high season, expect prices to rise $15. Ask for weekly discounts. *Let's Go* readers get $5 off Sept. 20-June (excluding major holidays). ❸

FOOD

Westwood overflows with cheap food and beer. In West L.A., inexpensive family-owned restaurants pop up on **Santa Monica Boulevard.** Japanese restaurants and stores abound on **Sawtelle Boulevard** south of Santa Monica Blvd. between Missouri St. and W. Olympic Blvd.

Asahi Ramen, 2027 Sawtelle Blvd. (☎479-2231). A tiny, simple Japanese restaurant that serves huge bowls of ramen soup ($5) and the freshest *gyoza* ($3.50) ever. Well worth the frequent wait. Open M-W and F-Su 11:30pm-9pm. Cash only. ❶

The Apple Pan, 10801 W. Pico Blvd. (☎310-475-3585), 1 block east of Westwood Blvd. across from the Westside Pavilion. Suburban legend has it that *Beverly Hills 90210*'s Peach Pit was modeled after The Apple Pan, so lean on the white counter and make like it's 1992. Famous original apple pies $4. Hickory-smoked burgers $6. Fries $2. Open Su and Tu-Th 11am-midnight, F-Sa 11am-1am. No credit cards. ❷

Diddie Riese Cookies, 926 Broxton Ave. (☎208-0448). Cookies baked from scratch every day. Lines stretch down the block (but move fairly quickly) for a $1 ice cream and cookie sandwich (any two cookies with your choice of ice cream). $1 also buys you 2 cookies and milk, juice, or coffee. Popular late-night spot. Open M-Th 10am-midnight, F 10am-1am, Sa noon-1am, Su noon-midnight. ❶

Jose Bernstein's, 935 Broxton Ave. (☎208-4992). Bargain burritos and other Mexican fare. Try the "Tacominator Special"—2 tacos, beans, rice, and a medium drink for only $4. Vegetarian burrito $4. Open M-Th 7am-1am, F 7am-2am, Sa 8am-2am, Su 9am-1am; reduced hours during summer and winter break holidays. ❶

Native Foods, 1110½ Gayley Ave. (☎310-209-1055; www.nativefoods.com). Order at the counter and fight for a seat at this completely vegan eatery. Locals love the "jerk burger with guacamole" ($7) and the "moby dick," a fried tempeh sandwich served on a whole wheat bun ($7). Open daily 11am-10pm. ❷

◉ SIGHTS

UNIVERSITY OF CALIFORNIA AT LOS ANGELES (UCLA)

Directly north of Westwood Village and west of Beverly Hills. By car, take I-405 (San Diego Fwy.) to the Wilshire Blvd./Westwood exit and head east into Westwood. Take Westwood Blvd. north off Wilshire Blvd. and go through Westwood Village directly into the campus. By bus, take MTA #2 along Sunset Blvd., #21 along Wilshire Blvd., #720 from Santa Monica, #761 from the San Fernando Valley, or Santa Monica BBBus #1, 2, 3, 8, or 12. Parking pass ($6) is valid all day at 14 different parking structures. Maps free.

A prototypical California university, UCLA sports an abundance of grassy open spaces, dazzling sunshine, massive brick buildings, and deeply tanned bodies on 400-acres in the foothills of the Santa Monica Mountains. Once voted the #1 jock school in the country by *Sports Illustrated*, UCLA also boasts an illustrious film school whose graduates include James Dean, Jim Morrison, Oliver Stone, Francis Ford Coppola, and Tim Robbins.

UCLA and Westwood are navigable on foot, so pay for a parking pass from campus information stands at any entrance, then park and walk. UCLA parking cops live to ticket unsuspecting visitors. **Tours** are offered by the Alumni Center, which is directly north of Westwood Plaza and parking structures #6 and 8. (☎825-8764; www.admissions.ucla.edu/tours. Tours M-F 10:15am and 2:15pm.) Outdoor highlights include the **Murphy Sculpture Garden,** in the northeast corner of campus, which contains over 70 pieces by major artists such as Auguste Rodin and Henri Matisse, and the UCLA **Botanical Gardens,** in the eastern part of campus, at the intersection of Le Conte and Hilgard Ave, where approximately 5000 plant species from all over the world flourish.

The **UCLA Central Ticket Office** (☎825-2101; www.tickets.ucla.edu) sells tickets for on-campus arts events (including concerts and dance recitals), UCLA sporting events, and discounted tickets to local movie theaters and water parks (discounts not limited to UCLA affiliates). It also has a Ticketmaster outlet. The renowned School of Film and Television Archive sponsors various film festivals, often with foreign films and profiles on groundbreaking filmmakers. (☎206-3456; www.cinema.ucla.edu. Double features $7, students $5; select films free.)

UCLA HAMMER MUSEUM OF ART. The UCLA Hammer Museum houses the world's largest collection of works by 19th-century French satirist Honoré Daumier and the collection of late oil tycoon Armand Hammer, with works by Rembrandt, Monet, and Pissarro. The museum's true gem is Vincent Van Gogh's *Hospital at Saint Rémy*. Hammer purportedly wanted to donate his collection to the L.A. County Museum of Art, but demanded that the works be shown together in a separate wing. The museum refused, telling Hammer to build his own place—which he did. The center hosts traveling exhibitions throughout the year, as well as free summer jazz concerts and seasonal cultural programs. *(10899 Wilshire Blvd., at the corner of Westwood and Wilshire Blvd. ☎310-443-7000; www.hammer.ucla.edu. Open Tu*

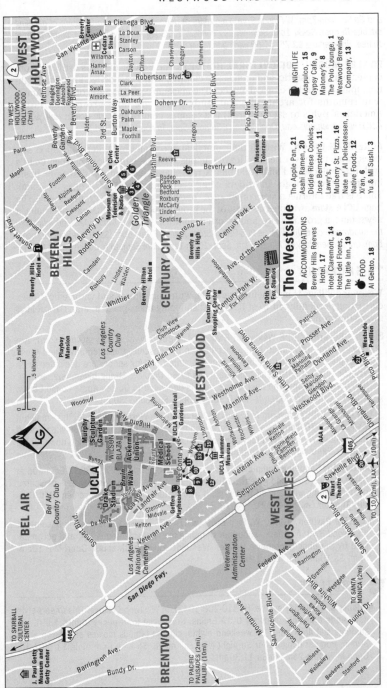

and Sa-Su noon-7pm, W-F noon-9pm. Free tours of permanent collection Su 2pm; of traveling exhibits Th 6pm, Sa-Su 1pm. Summer jazz concerts F 6:30-8pm. $5, seniors $3, under 17 free, Th free. 3hr. parking $2.75, $1.50 each additional 20min.)

FOWLER MUSEUM OF CULTURAL HISTORY. The Fowler displays artifacts from contemporary, historic, and prehistoric cultures with a vast collection of both ethnographic and archaeological objects. The museum's preservation of Native American remains for archaeological study (there are laws protecting Native Americans' rights to sacred burial) is a campus controversy. *(In Haines Hall. ☎825-4361; www.fmch.ucla.edu. Open W and F-Su noon-5pm, Th noon-8pm. Free.)*

ACKERMAN UNION. With all their practical needs met by Ackerman Union services, students never need to leave campus. Visitors can enjoy the **Food Court's** grill, pizza place, and smoothie bar. A ride-share board on the first floor posts information on drivers and riders going everywhere from Las Vegas to Miami. There is free Internet access on Floor A (one floor up from the ground floor). The huge **UCLA Store** swallows up most of the ground floor with UCLA paraphernalia, a newsstand, a grocery store, and assorted sundries. *(308 Westwood Plaza, downhill from the quadrangle on Bruin Walk. ☎206-0833. Store open M-F 9am-6pm, Sa 10am-5pm, Su noon-5pm. Union open daily mid-June to late Sept. 10am-11pm; late Sept. to mid-June 8am-11pm.)*

⌐] SHOPPING

Westwood Village is imminently walkable, with chain stores and vintage boutiques coexisting peacefully. In West L.A., most shopping takes place in malls or tucked-away storefronts.

Rhino Records, 2028 Westwood Blvd. (☎474-8685; www.rhinowestwood.com), two blocks north of Olympic Ave. Specializes in the obscure, the alternative, and those never-played promotional albums. Even the store's parking spaces are dedicated to an eclectic array of musicians from Madonna to Bo Diddley. Strong blues, jazz, exotica, and dance sections. The back of the store is dedicated to Golden Apple Comic Books. 4-for-$1 comic box. Open M-Sa 10:30am-10pm, Su noon-7:30pm.

City Rags, 10967 Weyburn Ave. (☎310-209-0889), in Westwood Village. This small but well-stocked 70s retro-wear shop has a friendly staff and great bargains on vintage stuff that's actually wearable. If they don't have what you need, they can hunt it down. Shirts $12-16. Pants $18-30. Open daily 11:30am-7:30pm.

Century City Shopping Complex, 10250 Santa Monica Blvd. (☎277-3898). Exit I-405 at Santa Monica Blvd. and go east. 140 stores, boutiques, and cafes in a well-manicured outdoor setting with arched walkways. It also features a popular 14-screen **AMC Century Theater** (☎289-4262).

Westside Pavilion, 10800 W. Pico Blvd. (☎474-6255; www.westsidepavilion.com), at Westwood Blvd. A generic, suburban shopping mall transplanted in L.A. and accompanied by the obligatory movie theater—**Westside Pavilion Cinemas.** Open M-F 10am-9pm, Sa 10am-8pm, Su 11am-6pm.

◙ NIGHTLIFE

Maloney's, 1000 Gayley Ave. (☎310-208-1942), in Westwood Village. This *Cheers*-style hangout is a favorite of thirsty UCLA Bruins. No college town prices (drinks $3-9), but students still flock here. On weekend nights, clips of famous movies are shown every 30min. Popular hangout for Su night NFL. Full menu. Su after 9pm pints $1.50-2.50. Open M-W 4pm-2am, Th-Su 11:30am-2am.

Gypsy Cafe, 940 Broxton Ave. (☎310-824-2119), in Westwood Village. Though modeled after a sister spot in Paris, this late-night restaurant has a Turkish feel and Italian food. It's easy to spend a long night lingering on the sidewalk patio smoking flavored tobacco out of ornate hookahs ($12 per hr.). Beer $4.25-5.25. Wine $6.50. Open Su-Th 7am-2am, F-Sa 7am-4am.

Westwood Brewing Company, 1097 Glendon Ave. (☎209-2739) at Kinross Ave. in Westwood Village. Homemade brew and bar food. A UCLA favorite. Opt for the leisure suit sandwich (pita with turkey, roasted red peppers, and guacamole) or the law suit (pita with mozzarella, eggplant, and zucchini), both served with a cup of soup and side salad ($8.45). Westwood brew $2.75, other pints $3.50.Open daily 11:30am-2am.

Acapulco, 1109 Glendon Ave. (☎208-3884). Hacienda-style decor accompanied by hefty drinks. Margarita maxima ($8) lives up to its name. M $2 margaritas, $0.75 tacos. Happy hour daily 4-7pm; drinks half-price. Open M-Th 11am-11pm, F 11am-midnight, Sa noon-11pm, Su noon-10pm.

BEL AIR, BRENTWOOD, AND PACIFIC PALISADES ☎310

Home to many celebrities, these three incredibly wealthy residential communities don't offer much to the economizing traveler in terms of accommodations, but world-class art at the Getty Museum and breathtaking scenery along Sunset Blvd. are both free of charge.

▬ TRANSPORTATION

Sunset Boulevard winds through Bel Air, Brentwood, and Pacific Palisades all the way to the PCH. **Bus #2** follows Sunset Blvd. from Hollywood to Pacific Palisades. **Bus # 761** and **BBBus #14** stop in Brentwood at the Getty Center.

◖ FOOD

▨ **A La Tarte,** 1037 Swarthmore Ave. (☎459-6635), off Sunset Blvd. in **Pacific Palisades.** The rolling green hills through the gabled windows of this country cottage-style bakery/ bistro are part of an impressive *trompe l'eoil* mural. Equally impressive are leisurely breakfasts in the sunny front room or spectacular scones to-go ($2.25). The French chefs who run the place also whip up decadent lunches and aren't afraid to push the boundaries of their craft. Open Th-Sa 7:30am-4pm, Su 8am-4pm. ❷

Gladstones 4 Fish, 17300 PCH (☎454-3474), at Sunset Blvd., in **Pacific Palisades.** Stop in to enjoy seafood, scenery, and weekend song. Sa-Su evenings at sundown, Gladstones's entire staff drops everything and belts out the tune "We Love L.A." while dancing a conga line through the restaurant. While most entrees begin at $20, the portions are huge, and its take out foil-sculptures are nearly as famous as the fish. Cheaper options include the Down Home Lobster Roll, served with chips and coleslaw, for $12. Open M-Th 11am-10pm, Fr 11am-11pm, Sa 8am-11pm, Su 8am-10pm. ❺

◙ SIGHTS

▨ **J. PAUL GETTY CENTER AND MUSEUM.** Above Bel Air and Brentwood in the Santa Monica Mountains shines a modern masterpiece—"The Getty." The 16,000 tons of gleaming travertine marble used to build this museum came from the same quarry as that of the Roman Coliseum. Wedding classical materials to modern shapes, renowned architect Richard Meier designed the stunning $1 billion complex, which opened to the public in 1997. The museum consists of five pavilions overlooking the Robert Irwin-designed **Central Garden,** a living work of art that changes with the seasons. The gardens delight landscape aficionados and young children—grassy hills perfect for somersaults slope down to patios shaded by iron "trees" dripping with bougainvillea. The pavilions contain the permanent Getty collection, including Vincent Van Gogh's *Irises*, located in the West Pavilion, *and* Impressionist paintings, Renaissance drawings, and a fantastic Rembrandt collection in the East Pavilion. The Getty's Special Pavilion displays temporary exhibits. Equally impressive is the sweeping, panoramic view of the Los Angeles Basin from the Getty's numerous balconies and gardens. The museum also hosts gallery talks by local artists, lectures, films, and a concert series. The "Friday Nights at the Getty" program features plays, films, and readings. (*1200 Getty Center Dr. Take I-405 to the Getty Center Dr. exit. Public transportation is strongly recommended: take either Santa Monica BBBus #14 or MTA #761 to the Getty Center. Free off-site parking, also serviced by shuttle. Parking $5. A "panorami-tram" takes visitors up the hill to the museum.* ☎ *440-7300; www.getty.edu. Open Tu-Th and Su 10am-6pm, F-Sa 10am-9pm. Free. Audio guides $3.*)

SKIRBALL CULTURAL CENTER. Dedicated to the preservation of Jewish culture, this dynamic cultural institution explores the connection between 4000 years of Jewish heritage and American democratic ideals. It contains one of the world's largest collections of Judaica, a children's Discovery Center, and interactive exhibits. (*2701 N. Sepulveda Blvd., just a few minutes north of the Getty.* ☎ *440-4500; www.skirball.org. Open Tu-Sa noon-5pm, Su 11am-5pm. 1hr. tours depart from the entrance daily at noon, 1, and 2:45pm. $8, seniors and students $6, under 12 free.*)

▧ CELEBRITY TOUR

Many of today's stars live in Bel Air, Brentwood, and Pacific Palisades. The best way to see their cottages and compounds is to pick up a star map, available at the Santa Monica Pier, local newsstands, or from vendors along Sunset Blvd. Lurking around celebrity neighborhoods might get you a peek at their landscaping or a picture of their mailbox, but it's doubtful you'll ever see them taking out the trash.

North of UCLA is the posh neighborhood of **Bel Air.** From UCLA's northeastern corner, head north on Copa de Oro Rd., where dopey-eyed **Nicholas Cage** lives at 363 Copa de Oro Rd. Return to Sunset Blvd. and head west a few blocks to Bel Air Rd. Turn right and look for the fictional **Beverly Hillbillies** mansion at 750 Bel Air Rd. **Judy Garland** lived at 924 Bel Air Rd., and **Alfred Hitchcock** hatched new plots at 10957 Bel Air Rd. Head back to Sunset and take a left onto St. Cloud Rd. and then a right onto Nimes Rd. to find violet-eyed **Elizabeth Taylor** at 700 Nimes Rd. Head left toward St. Pierre Rd., and then right onto St. Pierre Rd. Make your way to Beverly Glen Blvd. and turn left. **Steve Martin** lives out his L.A. story at 1005 Beverly Glen Blvd. Turn around and head south on Beverly Glen to 111 N. Beverly Glen where you can see **Tom Cruise's** former residence.

East of UCLA, head east on Sunset Blvd. and take a right onto Mapleton Dr., in the tony Holmby Hills area. **Lauren Bacall** and **Humphrey Bogart** resided at 232 Mapleton Dr. Producer **Aaron Spelling's** mansion, 594 N. Mapleton, is larger than the Taj Mahal. Wife Candy Spelling's closets reportedly take up an entire wing. To glimpse the home of infamous, invite-only, racy parties, turn around and head toward Sunset until you hit Charing Cross Rd. and turn right. The estate at 10236 Charing Cross Rd. is the **Playboy Mansion.**

Farther west on Sunset Blvd., on the other side of I-405, is **Brentwood,** preferred address of national scandal-starters. Take a left onto Bundy Dr. and another left onto Darlington Ave. The owner of America's greatest blue dress, former White

House intern **Monica Lewinsky** resides in southern Brentwood at 12224 Darlington Ave. A one-time Oval Office darling herself, **Marilyn Monroe,** was found dead at her home at 12305 5th Helena Dr. in 1962. To get there, return to Sunset Blvd., head west, and take a right onto Helena Dr. Farther west and a right off Sunset Blvd. brings you to **O.J. Simpson's** old estate at 360 Rockingham Ave., which was repossessed and auctioned off for a meager $2.63 million. Celeb-studded Brentwood also includes the homes of **Michelle Pfeiffer, Harrison Ford,** and **Meryl Streep.**

The considerably more secluded and hilly **Pacific Palisades,** above the gorgeous westernmost stretch of Sunset Blvd., brings the stars closer to the ocean and farther from the *paparazzi.* Travel west on Sunset Blvd. to Capri Dr. and turn right for **Kurt Russell** and live-in love **Goldie Hawn's** residence at 1422 Capri Dr. **Whoopi Goldberg** is in town at 1461 Amalfi Dr. (continue west on Sunset Blvd. and take a right onto Amalfi Dr.), just down the road from **Steven Spielberg,** who lives in the house at 1513-1515 Amalfi Dr. that belonged to David O. Selznick while he was producing *Gone with the Wind.* The man with the master plan, bodybuilder, laconic movie star, and governator **Arnold Schwarzenegger,** and his wife, Maria Shriver, loved their lot so much they bought out their neighbor's for $5.4 million. When he's not in Sacramento, Arnold practices family fitness at 14205, 14209, and 14215 Sunset Blvd.

BEVERLY HILLS ☎ 310

Beverly Hills glows in the televised mystique of expensive hotels, ritzy boutiques, and movie stars galore. Its very name evokes images of palm-lined boulevards, tanned and taut skin, and million-dollar homes. Although many silver screen starlets no longer call 90210 their postal code, Beverly Hills is still an opulent spectacle. You can live it up on a budget here simply by throwing on your trendiest jeans, slipping on the shades, and making clerks work for the money they think you have.

▐ TRANSPORTATION

Santa Monica Boulevard cuts diagonally through Beverly Hills, connecting it with Westwood in the southwest and West Hollywood in the northeast. **Rodeo Drive** runs straight through the "golden triangle" formed by Santa Monica Blvd., Wilshire Blvd., and Beverly Dr. **Bus #4** runs along Santa Monica Blvd.

▐ ACCOMMODATIONS

Beverly Hills's central Westside location makes it an attractive place to stay, and though the Beverly Hills Hotel is probably out of the question, there are a few places that cater to travelers on a budget.

> **The Beverly Hills Reeves Hotel,** 120 S. Reeves Dr. (☎271-3006; www.bhreeves.com). This recently renovated mansion near Rodeo Dr. offers both affordability and location. Rooms with A/C and TV. Continental breakfast included. Parking $6. Rooms $50, with bath $69. Weekly rooms $315/$450. ❹

> **Hotel del Flores,** 409 N. Crescent Dr. (☎274-5115). Eclectic, dated decor and a community of long-term guests give this bargain hotel a bohemian feel. TV and fridge in every room. Shared kitchen. Rooms with 1 bed $65, with 2 beds $85. ❹

FOOD

Yes, there is budget dining in Beverly Hills—just avoid Rodeo Dr. and Wilshire Blvd. unless you want designer food to go with your clothes.

Al Gelato, 806 S. Robertson Blvd. (☎659-8069), between Wilshire and Olympic Blvd. Though known for its homemade gelato, Al Gelato also serves large portions of pasta with a delicious basil tomato sauce. Popular with the theater crowd. Giant meatball $5.25. Rigatoni $12. For dessert, stick to the famous gelato ($4-6) and made-to-order cannoli ($4.50). Open Tu-Su 10am-midnight. No credit cards. ❸

Mulberry Street Pizzeria, 240 S. Beverly Dr. (☎247-8100), in Beverly Hills. Additional location at 347 N. Canon Dr. Great pizza by the slice is hard to come by in L.A., which makes this shop all the more exceptional. The wide, flat pizza (slice $2.50-4, whole pie $16) is among the best anywhere. Open Su-W 11am-11pm, Th-Sa 11am-midnight. ❶

Nate 'n Al Delicatessen, 414 N. Beverly Dr. (☎274-0101; www.natenal.com), near Little Santa Monica Blvd. This East Coast-style delicatessen has whipped up hand-pressed *latkes* (potato pancakes; $8.75), blintzes ($9), and Reuben sandwiches ($12) since 1945. The waitresses wear pink pinstripes and there's a bottle of Hebrew National Deli Mustard on every table. Open daily 7am-9pm. ❸

Lawry's, 100 N. La Cienega Blvd. (652-2827). Upscale dining room with tremendous prime rib ($26-40) and seafood. Excellent sides. No t-shirts or torn jeans. Open M-Th 5-10pm, F 5-11pm, Sa 4:30-11pm, Su 4-10pm. ❺

Xi'an, 362 N. Canon Dr. (☎275-3345), north of Wilshire Blvd. Healthy and upscale contemporary Chinese cuisine in the heart of L.A.'s ritziest shopping district. Strut your stuff and pronounce it "shee-ahn." Prices drop significantly for lunch specials such as chicken chow fun ($10) served with salad or soup. Entrees $9-13. Open M-W 11:30am-10pm, Th-F 11:30am-10:30pm, Sa noon-11pm, Su 5-10pm. ❸

Yu & Mi Sushi, 9475 S. Santa Monica Blvd. (☎273-7437). Snag a coveted counter seat and order from the fresh fish display. Lunch specials offer the best value, including fried tofu and California roll served with miso soup, salad, and rice ($7.50). Higher dinner prices, with 6-piece rolls $9-11. Open M-F noon-3pm and 6-10pm, Sa 5:30-10pm. ❹

◉ SIGHTS

MUSEUM OF TELEVISION AND RADIO. A gorgeous Richard Meier building houses the West Coast branch of the original New York museum. Complete with a radio broadcast studio and two theaters, this museum's highlight is its library, which holds 117,000 television, radio, and commercial programs. Request your favorite tube hits and five minutes later the library staff will have full-length episodes ready and waiting at your own private screening station. Hirschfeld caricatures of television stars decorate the walls, and there is always someone watching *I Love Lucy. (465 N. Beverly Dr., at the corner of Santa Monica Blvd. ☎786-1000. Open W-Su noon-5pm. Suggested donation $10, students and seniors $8, under 14 $6. 2hr. free parking in the museum's lot off Little Santa Monica Blvd.)*

BEVERLY HILLS HOTEL. A ludicrously extravagant retreat as famous as the starlets who romanced here, the pink Beverly Hills Hotel sits among 12 acres of tropical gardens and pools. Marilyn Monroe reportedly had trysts with both JFK and RFK in one of the 22 "bungalows." The hotel is home to the **Polo Lounge,** where countless industry deals have been negotiated. International luxury hotel magnate The Dorchester Group owns the complex as well as sister hotels in London, Paris, and Milan. In case you were wondering, rooms run $380-470, bungalows $430-4590, and suites $820-5000. *(9641 Sunset Blvd. ☎276-2251.)*

CIVIC CENTER. Just south of Santa Monica Blvd. is **Beverly Hills City Hall.** This Spanish Renaissance building was erected during the Great Depression and is now engulfed by Beverly Hills's new Civic Center, which took nine years to build at a cost of $120 million. *(455 N. Rexford Dr. ☎285-1000.)* The Civic Center houses what might be the country's most extravagant police and fire headquarters, as well as the **Beverly Hills Public Library,** which has a Thai marble interior but a less impressive collection of books. *(444 N. Rexford Dr. ☎ 288-2222; www.bhpl.org. Free Internet. Open M-Th 10am-9pm, F-Sa 10am-6pm, Su noon-5pm.)*

BEVERLY HILLS HIGH. It may only be a local public high school, but it is still a mild marvel. The indoor swimming pool is open in the summer and has a sliding floor cover that converts the pool into a basketball court, where Jimmy Stewart and Donna Reed danced the Charleston in *It's a Wonderful Life.* The school is still a popular filming location. *(241 Moreno, between Olympic Blvd. and Spalding. ☎ 551-5100. Pool open in summer M-F noon-1:30pm, Sa 12:30-2pm. Adult lap swim 8:15-9pm. $3, seniors and children $2.)*

MUSEUM OF TOLERANCE. This high-tech museum seeks to promote good will with interactive exhibits on the Holocaust, the Croatian genocide, the L.A. riots, the US civil rights movement, and the recent global refugee problem. In front of the entrance, required orientation sessions run every 10-12min. The displays on the main floor of the museum take about 2hr. to get through—patience is encouraged. Visit the **Point of View Diner,** a re-creation of a 50s diner that serves a menu of controversial topics on video jukeboxes, or pick up a "passport" of a child from Nazi-occupied territory and plug it into a computer kiosk to read the victim's biography. The second-floor **Multimedia Learning Center** houses artifacts from concentration camps and original letters by Anne Frank. The museum has hosted many influential world figures, including the Dalai Lama. Holocaust survivors relate their experiences in regularly scheduled speeches. Diagonally across the street is the **Simon Wiesenthal Center** for Holocaust research. *(9786 W. Pico Blvd., at Roxbury St. ☎ 553-8403; www.museumoftolerance.com. Open M-Th 11:30am-6:30pm, F 11:30am-3pm, Su 11am-7:30pm; last entry 1½-2hr. before closing; Apr.-Oct. also open F until 5pm. Holocaust survivor speeches M-W at 1 and 2pm, Su every hr. 1-4pm. $10, seniors $8, students and ages 3-10 $7. Free parking.)*

LOS ANGELES

📷 SHOPPING

The heart of designer shopping beats in the **Golden Triangle** formed by Beverly Dr., Wilshire Blvd., and Santa Monica Blvd. The area is known for its flashy clothing boutiques and jewelry shops, which reach saturation point on **Rodeo Drive.** Built like an old English manor house, **Polo Ralph Lauren** (444 N. Rodeo Dr.) stands out from the white marble of neighboring stores. **Cartier** (401 N. Rodeo Dr.), **Gucci** (347 N. Rodeo Dr.), and **Chanel** (400 N. Rodeo Dr.) occupy some of the area's prime real estate, where rents approach $40,000 per month. At the south end of Rodeo Dr. (the end closest to Wilshire Blvd.) is the pedestrian-only shopping complex of **2 Rodeo Drive,** a.k.a. **Via Rodeo,** which houses **Dior, Tiffany, Versace,** and numerous salons frequented by the stars. Don't be fooled by the cobblestones and lampposts: the ersatz promenade was only constructed in the 1990s. Across the way is the venerable **Regent Beverly Wilshire Hotel,** 9500 Wilshire Blvd., where Julia Roberts went from Hollywood hooker to Richard Gere's beloved in *Pretty Woman.* A peek at the lobby will give you a good idea of just how extravagant the rooms must be. Just north of the Golden Triangle is Santa Monica Blvd., which is lined with a series of small but pleasant parks. One such park, between N. Camden and N. Bedford Dr. on Santa Monica Blvd., contains the most varieties of **cacti** in one place in the world—an interesting, dusty sight amidst the opulence.

The prime example of bigger and better, the **Beverly Center,** 8500 Beverly Blvd., at La Cienega Blvd., is a monstrous neon mega-mall complete with voyeuristic escalators snaking up the building's glass siding. *(☎ 310-854-0070; www.beverlycenter.com. Open M-F 10am-9pm, Sa 10am-8pm, Su 11am-6pm.)* Behind the

Beverly Center, and infinitely more unique, ◪**West Third Street** and **North Robertson Boulevard** are packed with beautiful furniture galleries, young designers' boutiques, and vintage clothing and shoe stores.

⬛ CELEBRITY TOUR

The reason all the maps to stars' homes only seem to show dead stars is that, while the A-list may still shop in Beverly Hills, most no longer live here. Exquisite residences still house plenty of multi-millionaires and live up to visitors' expectations, but the real money has moved away to areas that afford greater privacy (see **Bel Air, Brentwood,** and **Pacific Palisades,** p. 413).

A 1914 trolley car replica is a conspicuous way to tour the town. The 40min. tour of the city and stars' homes leaves from the corner of Rodeo Dr. and Dayton. (☎248-1000. Tours every hr. Sa noon-4pm.) For a more discreet approach, go solo with a star map ($10) sold along Sunset Blvd. (but not within Beverly Hills), or take the following *Let's Go* abbreviated tour.

From Hollywood, drive west on Sunset Blvd. Just after you pass Hillcrest Ave. on your left, keep your eye out for 9401 Sunset Blvd., home to rock star **Phil Collins**. At the next intersection, take a left onto Palm Dr. and look for **Faye Dunaway's** residence on your left at 714 Palm Dr. Return to Sunset Blvd. and continue another four blocks. Turn right onto Lexington Dr. and then a quick right onto Coldwater Canyon Dr. The NRA's renowned **Charlton Heston,** whose residence featured prominently in Michael Moore's *Bowling for Columbine*, polishes his rifles at 2859 Coldwater Canyon Dr. Now backtrack, but before you reach Lexington Dr., turn left onto Rexford Dr. and look for **Meg Ryan's** home at 805 Rexford Dr. Head north on Rexford Dr. back to Sunset Blvd. and turn left. Take your next right on Beverly Dr. and pop in an old **Meat Loaf** CD while coasting by his house at 908 N. Beverly Dr. Continue on Beverly Dr. to the home of laconic action hero **Sylvester Stallone** at 1121 Beverly Dr. Turn around, take Beverly Dr. south across Sunset Blvd. and turn left on Canon Dr., which is one block south of Sunset Blvd. You will find **Kirk Douglas** at 707 Canon Dr. Backtrack to Sunset Blvd. and head west; turn left onto Roxbury Dr. for a glimpse of material girl **Madonna** (1015 Roxbury Dr.). If you're into old-school actors or salad dressing, return to Sunset Blvd. and head west another block. Turn right onto Whittier Blvd. and look for **Paul Newman** at 907 Whittier Blvd. Back on Sunset Blvd., continue west another block and look for Copley Dr., a small street off to the left. Another long-time star, **Gene Hackman,** lives at 9901 Copley Dr. At this point, pop in the "oldies but goodies" tunes and relive the **Elvis** era. The king had two homes in L.A. He purchased the first at 1174 Hillcrest Dr. shortly after his marriage to **Priscilla** in 1967, but quickly relocated to 144 Monovale Dr. because it offered more privacy. (Hillcrest Dr. is farther east on Sunset Blvd., one block east of Palm Dr., where Faye Dunaway lives—see Elvis's first house on the return trip.) A couple blocks west of Gene Hackman's place on Copley Dr., turn right onto Carolwood Dr. and then a quick right onto Monovale Dr. **Priscilla** remains near those memories at 1167 Summit Dr. To get there from Monovale Dr., go straight and take a left onto Lexington Dr., a left onto Benedict Canyon Dr., and then a right onto Summit Dr. **Bruce Springsteen** and **Eddie Murphy** are close by—turn around and take a right onto Benedict Canyon. "The Boss" is at 1224 Benedict Canyon and the famous comedian and actor is at 2727 Benedict Canyon. Return to Summit Dr. and turn right. At the fork, turn onto Ridgedale Dr. Everyone's favorite couple, **Brad Pitt and Jennifer Aniston,** beautify 1026 Ridgedale Dr. For those who love saccharine songs, look for a small road called Hanover Dr. and take it to Carolwood Dr. Hook a left and look for **Barbra Streisand's** old home at 301 Carolwood Dr. and **Walt Disney's** former residence at 355 Carolwood Dr.

WEST HOLLYWOOD ☎ 310 AND 323

Once considered a no-man's-land between Beverly Hills and Hollywood, West Hollywood is now the proud abode of L.A.'s gay community. Though spanning only 2 sq. mi., the area is packed with more restaurants, galleries, boutiques, theaters, and clubs than most cities. The section of Santa Monica Blvd. around San Vicente Blvd. is its oldest gay district. WeHo (as it is trendily abbreviated) is also home of the legendary Sunset Strip, a 1½ mi. stretch of Sunset Blvd. between Doheny Dr. and Crescent Heights Ave. Following its heyday in the 1940s and 50s, the Strip was a den of L.A.'s rock 'n' roll scene in the 60s and a haven for burnouts in the 70s. Today it is the epitome of diversity, as the established stars from the Westside mix with the up-and-comers from the east, creating the ultimate in L.A. nightlife.

▐ TRANSPORTATION

Sunset Boulevard and **Santa Monica Boulevard,** between La Cienega and La Bread Blvd. are WeHo's main drags. **Bus #2** runs on Sunset Blvd., **#4** goes down Santa Monica Blvd. The **CityLine** runs at night along Santa Monica Blvd. (☎800-447-2189. Su-F $0.25, Sa $0.50.)

▐ ACCOMMODATIONS

Orbit Hotel and Hostel, 7950 Melrose Ave. (☎323-655-1510 or 877-672-4887; www.orbithotel.com), a block west of Fairfax Ave. Orbit sets new standards for swank budget living. With a spacious retro kitchen, big-screen TV lounge, small courtyard, and late-night party room. Bright, fashion-conscious furniture. Centrally located. Dorms accept only international students with **passport.** Internet access. Breakfast included. 6-bed dorms $21; private rooms for up to 4 $70-90. ❷

Bevonshire Lodge Motel, 7575 Beverly Blvd. (☎323-936-6154). Seconds from CBS Studios, the staff welcomes *The Price is Right* contestant hopefuls. Rooms come with A/C, mini-fridge, cable TV, daily maid service, and access to outdoor pool, and parking. Singles and doubles $55-65; 5-person suites $70-80. King-size bed with kitchen for 2 $61-71. 10% ISIC discount. ❹

FOOD

The Griddle Café, 7916 Sunset Blvd. (☎323-874-0377). One of the most popular brunch spots on the strip, the Griddle prides itself on hipness and creativity. Especially popular are the "Apple Cobbler French Toast" ($7) and "Black Magic" (Oreo crumb-filled flapjacks; $8). Consider sharing the enormous portions. A 45min. wait is not uncommon on weekends. Open M-F 7am-3pm, Sa-Su 8am-3pm. ❷

Cobras and Matadors, 7615 Beverly Blvd. (☎323-932-6178). Hip and attractive waitstaff serve delicious tapas to a similarly hip crowd. Though the restaurant itself doesn't serve wine, you can buy Spanish wines at the shop next door. They'll even help you pair a wine with your meal. Tapas around $6, but expect to pay at least $20 to fill up. Open Su-Th 6-11pm, F-Sa 6pm-midnight. ❹

Duke's Coffee Shop, 8909 Sunset Blvd. (☎310-652-3100). Legendary Duke's is the best place to see hungry, hungover rockers. The walls are plastered with autographed album covers. Try "Sandy's Favorite" (green peppers, potatoes, and scrambled eggs; $7.25). Entrees $5-11. Open M-F 7:30am-8:30pm, Sa-Su 8am-3:30pm. ❷

Bossa Nova, 685 N. Robertson Blvd. (☎310-657-5070). At lunchtime the patio of this laid-back Brazilian/Italian restaurant fills up with stars in shades, who come for the incredible plantains and inventive pizzas. By the end of the night, everyone's here. Entrees $10-18. Open daily 11am-4am. Reservations recommended. ❹

Tenmasa Sushi Bar, 9016 Sunset Blvd. (☎310-275-7808), serves lunch and dinner to a sedate crowd. Lunch specials (M-F 11:30am-3pm) include a sushi roll with a garden salad ($7). For dinner, *maki* ranges from a $4 shiitake roll to a $19 lobster tempura roll. Open M-F 11am-11pm, Sa 6-11pm. ❸

Chin Chin, 8618 Sunset Blvd. (☎310-652-1818; www.chinchin.com). Other locations in Brentwood, Beverly Hills, Studio City, and Marina del Rey. Trendy youngsters come here in hopes of spotting a celebrity. Lunchtime brings handmade "dim sum and then sum" ($12), an array of dim sum with your choice of soup, salad, mushu, rice, or roasted meat. Signature Chinese chicken salad ($9) is the sort of Chinese-Californian cuisine befitting a restaurant whose name means "to your health." Open daily 11am-11pm. ❷

SHOPPING

Bring your walking shoes and spend a day on the 3 mi. strip of **Melrose Avenue** from Highland Ave. west to the intersection of Doheny Dr. and Santa Monica Blvd. The avenue began to develop its funkiness in the late 1980s, when art galleries, designer stores, lounge-like coffee shops, used clothing and music stores, and restaurants began to take over. The most trafficked stretch lies between La Brea and Fairfax Ave. While much of what is sold here is used, don't expect drastic markdowns. Find outlandish vintage outfits at **Aardvark's** (p. 421), grab an enhanced smoothie at **Hollywood Smoothy's,** 7275 Melrose Blvd. (☎323-933-4803; open daily 11am-7pm), and rest your feet at ⊠**Elixer** (see p. 422), as you rejuvenate in its peaceful Zen gardens with an herbal tonic. North of the Beverly Center is the **Pacific Design Center,** 8687 Melrose Ave. (☎310-657-0800; www.pacificdesigncenter.com), a sea-green glass complex nicknamed the Blue Whale and constructed in the shape of a rippin' wave. In addition to 172 design showrooms, most of which showcase home and furnishing projects, this rich man's Home Depot has a public plaza and a 388-seat amphitheater called the Silver Screen, which stages free summer concerts and art exhibits. (Call for schedules. Open M-F 8:30am-5:30pm.)

Retail Slut, 7308 Melrose Ave. (☎323-934-1339; www.retailslut.com). Draws all manners of punks and goths. The place to find fetish gear and old-school punk-rock basics. Be sure to check out their famous flyer rack, packed with info on clubs and gigs around town. Open daily noon-8pm.

▧ **Book Soup,** 8818/8820 Sunset Blvd. (☎310-659-3110; www.booksoup.com). A maze of new books in every category imaginable, with especially strong film, architecture, poetry, and travel sections. The comprehensive newsstand that wraps around the building includes industry mags and international newspapers. **The Addendum** next door features major discounts (up to 50%) on hardcover art, photo, and design books, as well as fiction and non-fiction books. Main store open daily 9am-11pm. Addendum open daily noon-8pm.

▧ **Necromance,** 7220 Melrose Ave. (☎323-934-8684; www.necromance.com). A window display greets pass-ersby with a child's coffin from the late 1800s, a tame precursor to this shop for the seriously morbid. Genuine human temporal bones $10; real human skulls $125-600. Open M-Sa noon-7pm, Su 2-6pm.

A Different Light, 8853 Santa Monica Blvd. (☎310-854-6601; www.adlbooks.com), at San Vicente Ave. The nation's largest gay and lesbian bookseller has an incredibly diverse selection: gay fiction and classics, biography and autobiography, self-help, travel, law, and queer theory. The shop also has videos, magazines, music, gift items, readings, and book signings. Open daily 10am-11pm.

Mr. Musichead, 709 N. Sierra Bonita (☎323-658-7625), at Melrose St. Although the store has plenty of 60s-70s rock and jazz, it's better known for its posters and collectibles from the same era. Posters $1-1500. Open daily 11am-7pm.

Aardvark's, 7579 Melrose Ave. (☎323-655-6769), at Curson St. Additional location at 85 Market St. (☎310-392-2996), in **Venice.** Used gear galore, from used Levi's ($20-25) to funky wigs ($20). While primarily a clothing store, costume and vintage pieces are always up for grabs. Open M-Th noon-8pm, F-Sa 11am-9pm, Su noon-7pm.

Out of the Closet, 8224 Santa Monica Blvd. (☎323-848-9760). With 17 stores in the L.A. area, this is the granddaddy of resale retail. You can find anything you need in at least one of their stores. Profits are donated to AIDS Healthcare Foundation. Look for OOC's trademark neon storefronts or call for other locations. Open 10am-8pm (HIV testing 4-8pm). Most stores open daily 10am-7pm.

Baby Jane of Hollywood, 7985 Santa Monica Blvd. (☎323-848-7080; www.babyjaneofhollywood.com), at Laurel St. in the French Market restaurant. Gorgeous Provencal building holds an eclectic collection of posters, records, tabloids, and autographed glossies ($25-75). It also has a huge collection of Pez, "Penises on Parade" Mardi Gras videos, and film industry collectibles. Open daily noon-8pm.

THE LOCAL STORY

PRICELESS POOLS

Scattered throughout L.A. are some of the country's most exclusive hotels, catering to pop stars, trust-fund kids, and anyone with a platinum card. For most budget travelers, the $300 per night prices and $20 valet tips make these hotels off-limits, and the hope of hobnobbing with the rich and famous is but a pipe dream.

However, if you dress appropriately, act cool, and buy a couple of expensive drinks at the bar, you may very well be able to claim a chaise lounge by the side of the pool and people-watch without being challenged. If you do get caught, though, you're on your own!

Mondrian, 8440 Sunset Blvd. (☎323-650-8999), in West Hollywood, is an Ian Schrager-owned, Philippe Starck-designed beacon of trendiness. The lounge is perfectly designed for preening and posing. **Hollywood Standard,** 8300 Sunset Blvd. (☎323-650-9090), in Hollywood, has mod styling and an incredible view of the Los Angeles basin. **W Hotel,** 930 Hilgard Ave. (☎310-208-8765), in Westwood, is part of a posh chain, and features two exquisite pools.

A Touch of Romance, 6650 Hollywood Blvd. (☎323-962-4776; www.atouchofromance.com), at Cherokee Ave. Racy adult shop with an extensive collection of lubes, fetish outfits, videos, and toys. Furry handcuffs $20. Helpful and professional staff. Open M-Th 11am-9pm, F 11am-10pm, Sa 10am-10pm, Su noon-7pm.

Hollywood Toys and Costumes, 6600 Hollywood Blvd. (☎323-464-4444 or 800-554-3444; www.hollywoodtoys.com). Enormous warehouse of makeup and accessories. The largest wig store in Hollywood, selling wigs of all colors, styles, and fashions ($25-700). Open M-F 9:30am-7pm, Sa 10am-7pm, Su 10:30am-7pm.

▓ NIGHTLIFE

West Hollywood nightlife is a vast and diverse grab bag of comedy clubs, greasy spoons, trendy clubs, and gay hot spots. The **Sunset Strip** is densely packed with straight clubs, while gay bars and clubs line **Santa Monica Boulevard.**

LATE-NIGHT RESTAURANTS AND COFFEEHOUSES

▨ **Elixer,** 8612 Melrose Ave. (☎657-9300), just east of San Vicente Blvd. Nestled in dense foliage and a bit removed from the street, Elixer provides a calm inspired by celebrities' spiritual trends—look for red Kabbalah bracelets. Outdoor garden imitates a tranquil tropical paradise. An enormous collection of tonics ($4-5) based on Chinese herbal traditions and international teas. Free live music most Tu night; chess, checkers, Chinese checkers, and other board games are always ready for takers. Licensed herbalists are on duty daily 11am-6pm for spontaneous consultations (call ahead for a comprehensive one-on-one session). Open M-Sa 9am-midnight, Su 10am-10pm.

The Rainbow Bar and Grill, 9015 Sunset Blvd. (☎310-278-4232; http://rainbowbarandgrill.com), next to the Roxy. Dark red vinyl booths, dim lighting, loud music, and colorful characters set the scene. Marilyn Monroe met Joe DiMaggio on a blind-date here. Brooklyn-quality pizza $6; calamari $8; grandma's chicken soup $3.50. Open M-F 11am-2am, Sa-Su 5pm-2am.

Mel's Drive In, 8585 Sunset Blvd. (☎310-854-7200; www.melsdrive-in.com), right on the Sunset Strip. Additional locations: 1660 N. Highland Ave. (☎323-456-2111), in **Hollywood,** and 14846 Ventura Blvd. (☎818-940-6357), in **Sherman Oaks,** with more limited hours. This 50s-style diner is a picture-perfect re-creation of the era. The original Mel's (in Modesto) was in the movie *American Graffiti,* although that Mel's didn't have the valet parking option. Play your part by ordering a cheeseburger, fries, and a vanilla milkshake—all for under $12. Free valet parking. Open 24hr.

Jerry's Famous Deli, 8701 Beverly Blvd. (☎310-289-1811), at San Vicente Ave. Additional locations: 10925 Weyburn Ave. (☎310-208-3354), in Westwood, and 12655 Ventura Blvd. (☎818-980-4245), in Studio City in the Valley. An L.A. deli with sleek red leather and sky-high prices. Note the menu's height—Jerry is rumored to have wanted "the longest menu possible while still maintaining structural integrity." Something on it is bound to be perfect for your 4am snack. Known for its jumbo triple-deckers ($13-14) and salads served in a pizza crust ($10-13). Open 24hr.

COMEDY CLUBS

Comedy Store, 8433 Sunset Blvd. (☎323-650-6268). 3 rooms each feature a different type of comedy. The Main Room and Original Room host headliner comics (Cover M-F $15, Sa-Su $20; Main Room only open Sa). Belly Room provides a testing ground for up-and-comers (no cover). 21+. Drinks $5-9; 2-drink min. Showtimes vary; call a week ahead to reserve tickets. Open daily until 2am.

The Laugh Factory, 8001 Sunset Blvd. (☎323-656-1336; www.laughfactory.com). Young talent launches here—you can say you saw them first. Audiences have been graced with the likes of Richard Pryor, Jerry Seinfeld, Damon Wayans, and Arsenio Hall.

L O S   A N G E L E S

see Hollywood map, p. 429

Hollywood Area

▲ ACCOMMODATIONS
Bevonshire Lodge Motel, 41
Orbit Hotel and Hostel, 30

♦ FOOD
Bossa Nova, 23
Canter's, 38
Carlitos Gardel, 31
Chin Chin, 3
Cobras and Matadors, 40
Duke's Coffee Shop, 17
The Griddle Café, 10
Nyala Ethiopian Cuisine, 44

Pink's Hot Dogs, 33
Tenmasa Sushi
  Bar, 16
Versailles, 43
Zankou Chicken, 2

★ ENTERTAINMENT
The Comedy Store, 4
The Laugh Factory, 8

■ NIGHTLIFE
7969 Peanuts, 20
Abbey Cafe, 24
Barney's Beanery, 19

Bourgeois Pig, 1
El Carmen, 42
Elixer, 29
Formosa Café, 22
Grounding Theater, 32
Here, 25
Highland Gounds, 35
Jerry's Famous Deli, 37
Key Club, 11
The Larchmont, 36
Largo, 39
Mel's Drive In, 18
Micky's, 26

Miyagi's, 6
North, 9
The Palms, 28
Rage, 14
Red Grill, 12
Roxy, 13
The Shelter, 7
Standard Lounge, 5
Stir Crazy, 34
Trunks, 27
Whiskey a Go-Go, 15
Ye Coach and
  Horses, 21

With nightly themed showcases: M Latino night; Tu open mic night for the first 15 people in line at 5pm. 18+. Cover M and F-Su $12, Tu-Th $10. 2-drink min. Shows M 8pm; Tu 5pm; W-F 8pm; Sa 8, 10pm, midnight; Su 8 and 10pm.

BARS

■ **Miyagi's**, 8225 Sunset Blvd. (☎323-650-3524), on Sunset Strip. With 3 levels, 7 sushi bars (rolls $5-7), 6 liquor bars, and indoor waterfalls, this Japanese-themed restaurant, bar, lounge, and hip-hop dance club is a Strip hot spot. "*Sake* bomb, *sake* bomb, *sake* bomb" $4.50. Open daily 5:30pm-2am.

El Carmen, 8138 W. 3rd St. (☎323-852-1552), near Crescent Heights Blvd. Border-style bar with velvet seats, Mexican professional wrestling masks on the walls, and 300 varieties of tequila behind the counter. Sidle up to one of the frilly-shirted barmaids and ask for one of the several varieties of *mescal* (a Oaxacan drink similar to tequila). Open M-F 5pm-2am, Sa-Su 7pm-3am.

North, 8029 Sunset Blvd. (☎323-654-1313), between Laurel Ave. and Crescent Heights Ave. A classic L.A. undercover bar where the entrance is hard to find and you need to be "in the know" to go there. Good-looking people buy good-looking drinks and dance until the morning. Drinks $6. DJ spins hip-hop and house Th-Sa nights. Open daily 6pm-2am.

CLUBS

■ **Largo**, 432 N. Fairfax Ave. (☎323-852-1073), between Melrose Ave. and Beverly Blvd. Intimate sit-down (or, if you get there late, lean-back) club. Original rock, pop, folk, and comedy acts. Cover $2-12. Open Su-Th 8pm-2am, F-Sa 8:30pm-2am.

The Shelter, 8117 Sunset Blvd., (☎654-0030), just west of Crescent Heights Ave. The newest and hottest addition to the Sunset Strip club scene, this lounge and dance club spins different beats in each of its 7 rooms. Hip-hop thumps on the main dance floor. Cover $20. Open F-Sa 10pm-2am.

Key Club, 9039 Sunset Blvd. (☎310-274-5800), on the Sunset Strip. A colossal, crowded multimedia experience complete with black lights, neon, and a frenetic dance floor. Live acts and DJ productions, depending on the night. 4 full bars. Cover $10-55. Open on club nights 10pm-2am, on live music nights 7pm-2am.

Roxy, 9009 Sunset Blvd. (☎310-278-9457), on the Sunset Strip. Known as the "Sizzling Showcase," it's one of the best-known Sunset Strip clubs. Bruce Springsteen got his start here. Live rock, blues, alternative, and occasional hip-hop. Many big tour acts. All ages. Cover typically $10-40. Opens at 8pm.

Whisky A Go-Go, 8901 Sunset Blvd. (☎310-652-4205). Historically, this was the great prophet of L.A.'s music scene. It hosted progressive bands in the late 70s and early 80s and was big in the punk explosion. The Doors, Janis Joplin, and Led Zeppelin played here. All ages. Cover M-Th $10, F-Su $13. Shows begin 7pm.

7969 Peanuts, 7969 Santa Monica Blvd. (☎323-654-0280), just west of Fairfax. Sometimes a strip club, sometimes a drag show, sometimes a go-go dance party—not for the faint of heart. Call for the crazy schedule. Most nights feature a mixed gay, straight, and lesbian crowd. Many nights 18+. Cover varies. Open daily 10pm-2am.

GLBT NIGHTLIFE

■ **Abbey Cafe**, 692 N. Robertson Blvd. (☎310-289-8410), at Santa Monica Blvd. 6 candlelit rooms, 2 huge bars, a large outdoor patio, and a hall of private booths make this beautiful lounge and dance club the best gay nightspot in town. The comfy couches cry out for some lovin'. Open daily 8am-2am.

Micky's, 8857 Santa Monica Blvd. (☎310-657-1176). Huge dance floor filled with delectable men. On a weekend night when bars close, head to Micky's for another 2hr. of grooving. Music is mostly electronica and techno, although hip-hop is sometimes sprinkled into the mix. M night drag shows. Happy hour M-F 5-9pm. Cover $3-10. Open Th-F 4pm-2am, Sa 11pm-4am, Su 11pm-2am.

Here, 696 N. Robertson St. (☎310-360-8455), at the corner of Santa Monica Blvd. Known for Su nights when the bartenders dress up in scandalous surfer shorts, this sleek gay bar and dance club caters to the well dressed and trendy. DJ's spin a mix of house and hip-hop. Th lesbian night. Don't miss the frozen cosmopolitans ($8). Happy hour daily 4-8pm; drinks $2-3 off. Open daily 4pm-2am.

Trunks, 8809 Santa Monica Blvd. (☎310-652-1015), a friendly and popular neighborhood gay and lesbian bar. Open daily 1pm-2am.

Arena, 6655 Santa Monica Blvd. (☎323-462-0714). Paired with sister club **Circus,** this club lends itself to frenzied techno and Latin beats. Gay nights W and Sa at Arena, Tu and F at Circus; drag shows start at midnight on those nights. Cover $10-15. Open Su-Th 9pm-2am, F-Sa 9pm-4am.

Rage, 8911 Santa Monica Blvd. (☎310-652-7055). Its glory days have passed, but this institution rages on with nightly DJs that spin house 'til you drop. Mostly gay men; some lesbians during the day. A rowdy scene. Full lunch and dinner menu served daily noon-9pm. W Latin night. Happy hour daily noon-6pm; $2 off drinks, $5 well drinks. 6pm. F-Sa 18+. Open daily noon-2am.

The Palms, 8572 Santa Monica Blvd. (☎310-652-6188). Pool room and full bar with lots of drink specials like W $1 drinks and domestic beers. DJ Th-Sa; music ranges from house to disco to salsa. Men are welcome but may feel very alone. Don't hesitate to hop in the 2-person dance cage. Open M-F 5pm-2am, Sa-Su 4pm-2am.

WILSHIRE DISTRICT AND FAIRFAX ☎323

L.A.'s culture vultures drive south from Hollywood to peruse the Wilshire District's museums, which glorify everything from tar to Model Ts. Developed in the 1920s, the city's first shopping district was designed for those arriving in those newfangled gizmos called automobiles. Fairfax Ave. houses much of L.A.'s Jewish population, and synagogues and kosher delis abound.

▐ TRANSPORTATION

Museum Row is on the **Miracle Mile** (Wilshire Blvd. from Fairfax to La Brea Ave.). **Fairfax Avenue,** which runs north from I-10 up to Santa Monica Blvd., is the main artery of the Fairfax district. **Bus #20** runs on Wilshire Blvd.

▐ FOOD

Inexpensive ethnic (often kosher) restaurants dot **Fairfax Avenue** but health nuts should stay away—there's no keeping cholesterol down in these parts.

▨ **Canter's,** 419 N. Fairfax Ave. (☎651-2030), north of Beverly Blvd. An L.A. institution and the heart and soul of historically Jewish Fairfax since 1931. Grapefruit-sized matzoh ball in chicken broth $4.50. Giant sandwiches $8-9. Visit the Kibbitz Room for nightly free rock, blues, jazz, and cabaret-pop (from 10pm). Lenny Kravitz is known to make appearances in the audience. Cheap beer ($2.50). Open 24hr. ❷

Nyala Ethiopian Cuisine, 1076 S. Fairfax Ave. (☎936-5918), 2 blocks south of Olympic Blvd. The Fairfax area may be known for its kosher delis, but it's also the backbone of L.A.'s Ethiopian community. Nyala's decor combines traditional African influences with Western table settings, but there's no fusion with the food—just large plates of spongy flatbread (*injera*) topped with spicy stews (lunch $8; dinner $11). The vegetarian lunch buffet (M-F 11:30am-3pm) is a steal at $6. Open daily 11:30am-11pm. ❷

Versailles, 1415 S. La Cienega Blvd. (☎289-0392). Additional location at 10319 Venice Blvd., on the corner of an unassuming shopping strip. Cuban food at its best. Family-oriented and always crowded. Appetizers from $3. Entrees $8-15. Lunch specials M-F 11am-3pm ($6-9). Open Su-Th 11am-10pm, F-Sa 11am-11pm. ❸

🔘 SIGHTS

In the crowded Wilshire District a good, green place to start is the well-manicured **Hancock Park,** in the Miracle Mile stretch of Wilshire Blvd. between Fairfax and La Brea Ave. The park contains two famous museums and is near the Petersen Automotive museum. The CBS studios are slightly north of the park. Picnickers should be wary of the odorous tar pits, which may conflict with an otherwise sweet-smelling lunch. (Park open daily 6am-10pm. Free.)

LOS ANGELES COUNTY MUSEUM OF ART (LACMA). Opened in 1965, LACMA is the largest museum on the West Coast, with six main buildings around the **Times-Mirror Central Court.** LACMA's renowned collection of art contains ancient, contemporary, and everything in between. The **Steve Martin Gallery,** in the Anderson Building, holds the famed comedian's collection of Dada and Surrealist works, including R. Magritte's *Treachery of Images.* (This explains how Steve was able to roller skate through LACMA's halls in the film *L.A. Story;* see p. 22.) The latest additions are **LACMA West** and its **Children's Gallery.** The museum sponsors free jazz, chamber music, film classics, and documentaries, and a offers variety of free daily tours. *(5905 Wilshire Blvd., at the southwestern end of Hancock Park. General info ☎ 857-6000, Docent Council 857-6108; www.lacma.org. Open M-Tu and Th noon-8pm, F noon-9pm, Sa-Su 11am-8pm. $9, students and seniors $5, under 18 free. Free 2nd Tu of each month and daily after 5pm. Free jazz F 5:30-8:30pm; chamber music Su 6-7pm. Films $8, seniors and students $6. Parking $5, after 7pm free.)* LACMA's **Bing Theater** shows classic films on the big screen, sometimes for less than a video rental. *(☎857-6010. Shows Tu 1pm, F-Sa 7:30pm. Tu $2, seniors $1. F-Sa $9; students and seniors $6.)*

PETERSEN AUTOMOTIVE MUSEUM (PAM). This slice of Americana showcases one of L.A.'s most recognizable symbols—the automobile. At 300,000 sq. ft., PAM is the world's largest car museum, containing over 150 race cars, classic cars, hot rods, motorcycles, and movie and celebrity cars. The museum also features a 1920s service station, a 1950s body shop, and a 1960s suburban garage. Call to set up a guided tour. *(6060 Wilshire Blvd., at Fairfax. ☎ 930-2277; www.petersen.org. Open Tu-Su 10am-6pm; Discovery Center closes 4pm. $10, students and seniors $5, ages 5-12 $3, under 5 free. Parking $6.)*

GEORGE C. PAGE MUSEUM OF LA BREA DISCOVERIES. The smelly **La Brea Tar Pits** fills the area with an acrid petroleum stench and provides bones for this natural history museum. Thirsty mammals of bygone ages drank from these pools of water, only to find themselves stuck in the tar that oozed below. Most of the 3 million specimens pulled from the pits are on display here, along with reconstructed Ice Agers and murals of prehistoric L.A. The only human unearthed in the pits stands out in holographic horror; discovered in 1914, the 4ft. 8 in. tall La Brea woman was presumably thrown into the tar 9000 years ago after having holes drilled into her skull (not on display). A viewing station exists at Pit 91, where archaeologists continue to dig from July to September. *(5801 Wilshire Blvd., at Curson Ave. Buses stop in front of the museum. ☎934-7243. Open M-F 9:30am-5pm, Sa-Su 10am-5pm. Tours of grounds Tu-Su 1pm; museum tours Tu-Su 2:15pm. $7, students and seniors $4.50, ages 5-12 $2. 1st Tu of each month free. Parking $6 with validation.)*

CRAFT AND FOLK ART MUSEUM (CAFAM). Originally a small gallery in a local restaurant whose art began to win Angeleno hearts, the CAFAM now has its own space and features traveling exhibits from around the world. The museum's permanent collection consists of international folk art. Call ahead to ask about the frequent lectures and seminars. In the summer the museum offers demonstrations and workshops for individuals and families. *(5814 Wilshire Blvd., 3 blocks west of La Brea Ave. ☎937-4230; www.cafam.org. Open W-Su 11am-5pm. $3.50, seniors and students $2.50, under 12 free. Street parking.)*

HOLLYWOOD ☎ 323

Hollywood's mythical glamour has long been the dream of aspiring starlets, but in truth, Hollywood ceased to be the home of the American movie industry decades ago. In the 1930s, all the major studios (except Paramount; see p. 390) moved over the Hollywood Hills to the roomier locale and lower taxes of the San Fernando Valley. Visitors to Tinseltown may be shocked by the unromantic squalor of the place. What remains are a few fragments of the silver screen industry: the Academy Awards, the star-studded Walk of Fame, a handful of historic theaters that host premieres, and an aura of nostalgia that brings in visitors by the busload despite the relatively high proportion of pimps, panhandlers, and porn shops.

☎ ♂ TRANSPORTATION AND PRACTICAL INFORMATION

Public Transit: Buses **#2** and **3** run along Sunset Blvd., **#4** along Santa Monica Blvd., **#10** and **11** along Melrose Ave. $1.35; transfers $0.25. Weekly pass $11.

Parking: Ample metered parking on the street. $0.25 per 30min. Many public lots, rates from $1.50 per hr. to $10 per night. Public lot north of Hollywood Blvd. at Cherokee St. offers first 2hr. free, $1 additional hr. for up to 3 more hours.

Visitor Information: (☎960-2331), on the 2nd fl. of the Hollywood and Highland Mall. Helpful staff with info on accommodations, reservations, sightseeing, and directions. Open M-Sa 10am-10pm, Su 10am-7pm.

Currency Exchange: Cash It Here, 6565 Hollywood Blvd. (☎464-2718), at Whitley St. 2.25-5% commission. Open M-F 24hr., Su 8am-5pm; Sa hours vary.

Police: 1358 N. Wilcox Ave. (☎213-485-4302).

Hospital: Queen of Angels Hollywood Presbyterian Medical Center, 1300 N. Vermont Ave. (☎213-413-3000). 24hr. emergency room.

Internet Access: Cyber Java, 7080 Hollywood Blvd. (☎466-5600). $1.75 per 15min., $6 per hr., $30 for a 10hr. card. Open daily 7am-11:30pm. **@coffee,** 7200 Melrose Ave. (☎938-9985). $1 per 10min., $2 per 30min., $6 per hr. Open M-Sa 8am-9pm, Su 10am-8pm. **C&C Internet Cafe,** 7070 W. Sunset Blvd. (☎462-8100). $2 per 23min., $4 per hr., $10 per 3hr. Open 24hr.

Post Office: 1615 Wilcox Ave. (☎464-2355). Open M-F 8:30am-5:30pm, Sa 8:30am-3:30pm. **Postal Code:** 90028.

♠ ACCOMMODATIONS

Staying in Hollywood puts you smack in the middle of it all, which is a blessing for some and a curse for others. Though the area crawls with people by day, avoid the streets late at night. Always exercise caution while scouting out the budget hostels on or around Hollywood Blvd., especially east of the main strip. Overall, the accommodations here are a much better value than most others in L.A.

▓ **Hollywood Bungalows International Youth Hostel,** 2775 W. Cahuenga Blvd. (☎888-259-9990; www.hollywoodbungalows.com), just north of the Hollywood Bowl in the Hollywood Hills. Free parking. This newly renovated hostel cultivates a wacky summer-camp atmosphere. Spacious rooms and nightly jam sessions. Outdoor pool, billiards, weight room, big-screen TV, and mini-diner. On-site Universal Rent-a-Car (see p. 384). Internet $2 per 10min. Breakfast $3.50. Dinner $10. Lockers $0.25. Check-in 24hr. 6- to 10-bed dorms with bath $15-19; private rooms for up to 4 $59. ●

▓ **USA Hostels Hollywood,** 1624 Schrader Blvd. (☎462-3777 or 800-524-6783; www.usahostels.com), south of Hollywood Blvd., west of Cahuenga Blvd. Buzzing with young travelers, this lime-green edifice is filled with energy and organized fun. Special events nightly, including free comedy W and Su. **Passport or proof of travel required.** Stay for 4 days and get free pickup from airport. Free beach shuttles run Tu, Th, Sa. All-you-can-eat pancakes included. To use lockers, bring your own lock or buy one for $0.50. Free street parking; parking lot $4.50 per day. 6- to 8- bed dorms with private bath $17-25; private rooms for 2-4 people $55-65. Prices $1-2 less in winter. ❷

Hollywood Hotel and Hostel, 1921 N. Highland Ave. (☎876-6544), just north of Hollywood Blvd. An 8-story maze of rooms offering peace, quiet, and quick access to sights. Private rooms are well furnished and large. Lounge with free billiards, TV, and video games. Internet $1 per 10min. Laundry (wash $1, dry $0.75). 4-bed dorms $15-19; private rooms $40-80. ❶

Orange Drive Manor, 1764 N. Orange Dr. (☎850-0350). A pleasant, converted mini-mansion in a residential neighborhood. Grandeur (and lack of sign) disguises this hostel. Spacious rooms with antique furniture. Cable TV lounge, limited kitchen. Internet $1 per 10min. Lockers $0.75. Parking $5. Reservations recommended. 4- to 6-bed dorms (some with private baths) $19-24; private rooms $40-52. $2 discount with ISIC. Cash or traveler's checks only. ❷

Liberty Hotel, 1770 Orchid Ave. (☎962-1788), south of Franklin Ave., 1 block north of Hollywood Blvd. This small hotel, located on a quiet residential street has large, clean rooms that more than compensate for the bare walls. Free coffee and parking. Internet $1 per 10min. Laundry (wash $1, dry $0.50). Reception 8am-1am. Check-out 11am. Singles $65; doubles $73. ❹

Student Inn International Hostel, 7038½ Hollywood Blvd. (☎469-6781 or 323-462-9269 or 800-557-7038; www.studentinn.com), on the Walk of Fame. Right in the thick of it all. Free pickup from airport, bus, and train stations with 4-night stay. Small kitchen, and cable TV lounge. Internet access ($2 per 30min.) and free use of scanner, printer, and xerox machine. Continental breakfast, linen, and lockers included. Only 13 rooms, so call far in advance for reservations. Dorms $18-20; rooms with 2 double beds and private bath $50-54. Work at reception in exchange for a night's stay. ❷

Hollywood International Hostel, 6820 Hollywood Blvd. (☎463-0797 or 800-750-6561; www.hollywoodhostels.com), overlooking the Walk of Fame and the new Kodak Theatre. This hostel hops with aspiring actors and screenwriters of all ages. 44 rooms. Discounted tours and car rentals. Lounge with TV, billiards, and old arcade games. Internet $1 per 10min. Toast and tea breakfast. Lockers $0.25. Laundry (wash $1, dry $0.25). Reception 24hr. Reserve ahead. Single-sex and coed 4- to 6-bed dorms $19; private rooms $40. Weekly dorms $119. ❷

◖ FOOD

There is no need to play the "starving actor" when dining in Hollywood—it has some of L.A.'s best budget dining. Despite the inexpensive eats, you may find celebrities in the next booth over. **Hollywood** and **Sunset Boulevards** have excellent international cuisine. **Melrose Avenue's** chic cafes feature outdoor people-watching patios. Since Hollywood is near the heart of L.A.'s pounding nightlife, many of its best restaurants are open around the clock.

▨ **The Bungalow Club,** 7174 Melrose Ave. (☎964-9494; www.thebungalowclubla.com), 1 block west of La Brea Ave. A romantic oasis with waterfalls, candlelight, and private bungalows. Eclectic world fusion dishes. Free, live comedy shows featuring comedians from Letterman, Leno, BET, and Comedy Central. On weekends without acts, groove upstairs to the DJ dance party (F-Sa). Free live jazz M 8pm in summer. Appetizers $6-10. Entrees $16-22. Open Su-Th 11am-11pm, F-Sa 11am-1am. Dinner reservations recommended. ❹

Roscoe's House of Chicken and Waffles, 1514 Gower St. (☎466-7453), at the corner of Sunset Blvd. Additional location at 5006 W. Pico Blvd, in **West L.A.** The down-home feel and menu make this a popular spot for regular folk and celebs. Try "1 succulent chicken breast and 1 delicious waffle" ($7.40). Expect a 30min.-1hr. wait on weekends. Open Su-Th 8:30am-midnight, F-Sa 8:30am-4am. ❷

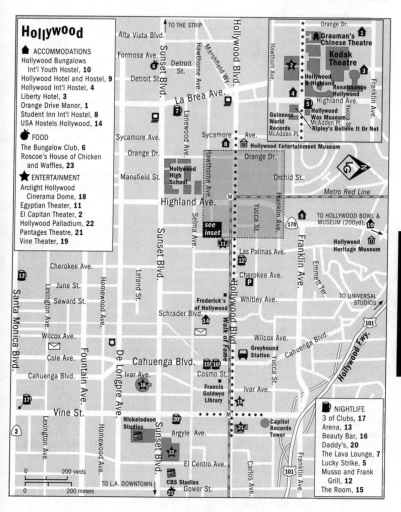

Hollywood

▲ ACCOMMODATIONS
Hollywood Bungalows
  Int'l Youth Hostel, **10**
Hollywood Hotel and Hostel, **9**
Hollywood Int'l Hostel, **4**
Liberty Hotel, **3**
Orange Drive Manor, **1**
Student Inn Int'l Hostel, **8**
USA Hostels Hollywood, **14**

🍴 FOOD
The Bungalow Club, **6**
Roscoe's House of Chicken
  and Waffles, **23**

★ ENTERTAINMENT
Arclight Hollywood
  Cinerama Dome, **18**
Egyptian Theater, **11**
El Capitan Theater, **2**
Hollywood Palladium, **22**
Pantages Theatre, **21**
Vine Theater, **19**

🍸 NIGHTLIFE
3 of Clubs, **17**
Arena, **13**
Beauty Bar, **16**
Daddy's, **20**
The Lava Lounge, **7**
Lucky Strike, **5**
Musso and Frank
  Grill, **12**
The Room, **15**

L O S   A N G E L E S

Pink's Hot Dog Stand, 709 N. La Brea Ave. (☎931-4223; www.pinkshollywood.com), at Melrose Ave. An institution since 1939, Pink's serves up chili-slathered goodness in a bun. The aroma of meaty chili and freshly cooked dogs has lines of tourists and Angelenos wrapped around the block. Rumor has it that Sean Penn proposed to Madonna here. Try the special "Ozzy Osbourne Spicy Dog" for $5. Chili dogs $2.40. Chili fries $2.20. Open Su-Th 9:30am-2am, F-Sa 9:30am-3am. Cash only. ❶

Carlitos Gardel, 7963 Melrose Ave. (☎655-0891; www.carlitosgardel.com), 1½ blocks west of Fairfax Ave. Argentine restaurant with Italian influences. Bread comes accompanied by chimichurri sauce so addictive, you'll want to hunt down a bottle to bring home. Try the signature "Papas Fritas Provenzal" ($6) or "Ojo de Costilla a la Criolla," a rib-eye steak marinated in chimichurri ($34). Entrees $12-38. Open M-F 11:30am-2:30pm and 6-11pm, Sa 6-11pm, Su 5-10pm. Reservations recommended. ❹

Zankou Chicken, 5065 W. Sunset Blvd. (☎665-7842). Unassuming Lebanese chicken joint tucked into a strip mall. Juicy chicken ($8.50) and excellent hummus ($3.50), not to mention rock-bottom prices, draw hipsters in by the trucker-hat load. Open daily 10am-midnight. Cash only. ❷

⦿ SIGHTS

Exploring the Hollywood area takes a pair of sunglasses, a camera, some cash, and a whole lot of fortitude. It is best to drive through the famous Hollywood Hills for beautiful views and incredible houses, and then park and explore **Hollywood Boulevard** on foot. Running east-west at the foot of the Hollywood Hills, this strip is the center of L.A.'s tourist madness. The boulevard itself, home to the Walk of Fame, famous movie theaters, souvenir shops, and museums, is busy day and night, especially around the intersection of Highland St. and Hollywood Blvd. and then west down Hollywood Blvd. Recent efforts to revitalize the storied area and attract tourists have so far been fairly successful.

HOLLYWOOD SIGN. Those 50 ft. high, 30 ft. wide, slightly crooked letters perched on Mt. Lee in Griffith Park are a universally recognized symbol of the city. The original 1923 sign read HOLLYWOODLAND and was an advertisement for a new subdivision in the Hollywood Hills. The sign was taken over by the Chamber of Commerce in 1949 and three decades later was replaced by a steel replica unveiled for Hollywood's 75th anniversary. It has since been a target of many college pranks, which have made the letters read everything from "Hollyweird" to "Ollywood" (after the infamous Lt. Col. Oliver North). A fence keeps you at a distance of 40 ft. (*Getting as close to the sign as possible requires a strenuous 2½ mi. hike. Take the Bronson Canyon entrance to Griffith Park and follow Canyon Dr. to its end, where parking is free. The Brush Canyon Trail starts where Canyon Dr. becomes unpaved. At the top of the hill, follow the road to your left; the sign looms just below. For those satisfied with driving, go north on Vine St., take a right on Franklin Ave. and a left on Beachwood, and drive up until you are forced to drive down.*)

GRAUMAN'S CHINESE THEATRE. Loosely modeled on a Chinese temple, this monumental theater is a Hollywood icon and still rolls out the red carpet for movie premieres. The exterior columns, known as "Heaven Dogs," were imported from China, where they once supported a Ming Dynasty temple. Inside is a collection of over 200 celebrity footprints as well as other star trademarks—Whoopi Goldberg's dreadlocks, R2D2's wheels, and George Burns's cigar. (*6925 Hollywood Blvd., between Highland and Orange St. ☎323-461-3331. 4-5 tours per day; call ahead. $7.50, under 6 free.*)

KODAK THEATRE AND HOLLYWOOD AND HIGHLAND MALL. Four levels of over 70 specialty stores, mall retail regulars, fancy restaurants, and a nightclub surround the Babylon Court, a 64,000 sq. ft. complex that serves as an outdoor gathering place and event venue. Stand in the center of the court and see the Hollywood sign perfectly framed by the large arch. (*Mall info ☎323-960-2331.*) The centerpiece of the complex is the **Kodak Theatre,** a huge $94 million theater built specifically to be the new home of the Academy Awards. The monolithic arena has a seating capacity that ranges from 2200 for live theater to 3500 for concerts and award shows. (*6801 Hollywood Blvd. Box office ☎323-308-6363. Open daily 10am-6pm; on performance days until 9pm. Tours in summer every 30min. 10:30am-4pm; in winter 10:30am-2:30pm. $15, seniors and children under 12 $10.*)

WALK OF FAME. Pedestrian traffic along Hollywood Blvd. mimics L.A.'s congested freeways as tourists stop mid-stride to gawk at the sidewalk's over 2000 bronze-inlaid stars, which are inscribed with the names of the famous, the infamous, and the downright obscure. Stars are awarded for achievements in one of five categories—movies, radio, TV, recording, and live performance; only Gene Autry has all five stars. The stars have no particular order, so don't try to find a method to the madness. Recent inductees include Mary Kate and Ashley Olsen (one star, two girls, half the calories) in front of Hollywood and Highland Mall. To catch today's (or yesterday's) stars in person, call the Chamber of Commerce for info on star-unveiling ceremonies. (☎ 323-469-8311; www.hollywoodchamber.net. Free.)

HOLLYWOOD BOWL AND MUSEUM. The hillside Hollywood Bowl is synonymous with picnic dining and classy summer entertainment. All are welcome to listen to the L.A. Philharmonic at rehearsals on Mondays, Tuesdays, Thursdays, and Fridays. The Bowl also hosts a summer jazz concert series. A small but cozy museum tells the history of the Hollywood Bowl through a collection of photographs, recordings, archival films, programs, and artifacts, including several listening stations where you can groove to recordings of Jimi, the Beatles, Dylan, and BB King. (2301 N. Highland Ave. ☎ 323-850-2058, concert line 850-2000; www.hollywoodbowl.org. Open July-Sept. Tu-Sa 10am-8pm; Oct.-June Tu-Sa 10am-4:30pm. Free.)

HOLLYWOOD HERITAGE MUSEUM. This museum provides a glimpse into early Hollywood filmmaking history. In 1913, famed director Cecil B. DeMille rented this former barn as studio space for Hollywood's first feature film, *The Squaw Man*. Today, antique cameras, costumes worn by Douglas Fairbanks and Rudolph Valentino, props, vintage film clips, and other memorabilia fill the museum. The surrounding hills provide an ideal picnic area. (2100 N. Highland Ave, across from the Hollywood Bowl. ☎ 323-874-2276; www.hollywoodheritage.org. Open Sa-Su 11am-3:45pm; call ahead. $5, ages 3-12 $1, under 3 free. Ample free parking, except during Bowl events.)

HOLLYWOOD ENTERTAINMENT MUSEUM. This landmark offers a behind-the-scenes look at the four arts of entertainment—radio, television, film, and recording—with set design, costume, and props displays. The original sets from *Star Trek* and *Cheers* deserve ooh- and aah-ing. The *Cheers* bar serves up drinks for Monday Night Football and Super Bowl Sunday. See where the stars carved their initials in the bar during the final episode. (7021 Hollywood Blvd., 1 block east of La Brea at Sycamore Ave. ☎ 323-465-7900. Open June-Aug. daily 10am-6pm; Sept.-May Th-Su 11am-6pm. Tours every 30min.; last tour at 5:25pm. $10, students $5, under 5 free. Parking off Sycamore Ave.; $2.)

WEIRD MUSEUMS. The hit-and-miss accuracy of the **Hollywood Wax Museum's** over 200 life-sized pop icon figures has visitors droning, "That looks nothing/just like...." Choose your own object of distraction, from Legends to Super Heroes and Blockbusters to Chart Toppers. Don't miss the Hall of Presidents and the Horror Chamber. (6767 Hollywood Blvd. ☎ 323-462-5991. Open daily 10am-midnight. $11, ages 6-12 $7, seniors $8.50, under 6 free.) The **Guinness World of Records Museum** showcases the tallest, shortest, heaviest, most tattooed, and other curious superlatives. (6764 Hollywood Blvd. ☎ 323-463-6433. Open daily 10am-midnight. $11, seniors $8.50, ages 6-12 $7, under 6 free. Combined admission with wax museum: $16, children $9.) **Ripley's Believe It or Not!** "odditorium" aims to prove that Ripley was not "the world's biggest liar." Displays include a section of the Berlin Wall and the world's largest tire. (6780 Hollywood Blvd. ☎ 323-466-6335. Open Su-W 10am-11pm, Th-Sa 10am-midnight. $11; ages 6-12 $8; military, seniors, and students $9; under 6 free.) **Frederick's of Hollywood,** a lingerie store and mini-museum, gives a free peek at celebrity-worn corsets and bras, including those that gave Madonna, Marilyn Monroe, and Pamela Anderson their crucial push-up to pinup stardom. Less sexy are Forrest Gump's boxers. (6608 Hollywood Blvd. ☎ 323-957-5953. Open M-Sa 10am-9pm, Su 11am-6:30pm.)

LOS ANGELES

CAPITOL RECORDS TOWER. This tower is the preeminent monument of the modern recording industry and has appeared in many L.A. films. The cylindrical building, constructed in 1954, was designed to look like a stack of records, with fins sticking out at each floor (the "records") and a needle on top that blinks H-O-L-L-Y-W-O-O-D in Morse code. *(1750 Vine St., ¾ block north of Hollywood Blvd.)*

EL CAPITÁN THEATRE. "Hollywood's First Home of Spoken Drama," this cinema house hosted the 1941 world premiere of *Citizen Kane*. Restored by Walt Disney Co. in 1991, it is now a first-run theater for Walt Disney Pictures. Movies are not shown every day; call in advance for showtimes, and be sure to ask whether the movie opens with a live stage show. *(6838 Hollywood Blvd., just west of Highland Ave. ☎323-467-9545 or 800-347-6396; www.elcapitantickets.com. Tickets $11, seniors and ages 3-11 $8; with live stage show $13-24/$11-20. Box office open daily 11am-7pm.)*

▣ SHOPPING

▨ **Amoeba Music,** 6400 Sunset Blvd. (☎245-6400; www.amoebamusic.com). Parking garage under the store. Quite simply the largest and best indie record store in the country. A huge building holds all the quirky offerings you could possibly desire, with plenty of listening stations. Extensive collection of underground music. Huge daily $1 clearance sales in each musical category. Live music 2-3 times per week; call ahead for times. Open M-Sa 10:30am-11pm, Su 11am-9pm.

▨ **Samuel French Bookshop,** 7623 Sunset Blvd. (☎876-0570), 5 blocks east of Fairfax Ave. Additional location at 11963 Ventura Blvd. (☎818-762-0535), in Studio City, in the **Valley.** Get prepped for your audition at this haven for entertainment industry wisdom, with acting directories, TV and film reference books, trade papers, and a vast selection of plays and screenplays. Lists local theaters that are currently casting. Occasional script signings by local playwrights. Hollywood location open M-F 10am-6pm, Sa 10am-5pm. Studio City location open M-F 10am-9pm, Sa 10am-6pm, Su noon-5pm.

The Studio Wardrobe Department, 1357 N. Highland Ave. (☎467-9455). Everything (including the register) is vintage in this brick warehouse of denims, furs, graphic tees, and polyesters. Known for its unscheduled but regular 50-items-for-$1 and 25-pairs-of-jeans-for-$5 sales. Open M-Sa 10am-10pm, Su 10am-8pm.

Larry Edmunds Bookshop, Inc., 6644 Hollywood Blvd. (☎463-3273). One of the world's largest collections of books and memorabilia on cinema and theater. With 6000 movie posters that date back to 1932 and hundreds of biographies on big names and no-names in the entertainment world, this is the place to search for a book on, or full-length poster of, your favorite obscure actor. Open M-Sa 10am-6pm.

Counterpoint Records and Books, 5911 Franklin Ave. (☎957-7965; www.counterpointrecordsandbooks.com), at Bronson Ave. One of L.A.'s best vinyl collections (from $0.50). A smaller collection of used CDs (from $1), videos, and tapes. Everything from blues to punk. Doubles as a used bookstore crammed with both popular and obscure titles. Open M-Th 11am-11pm, F-Sa 11am-midnight, Su 1-8pm.

Aron's, 1150 N. Highland Ave. (☎469-4700), between Santa Monica and Sunset Blvd. Loved for its massive new and used CD collection, which ranges from ska to showtunes, and its large LP collection, which features an extensive classical music section. Buys, sells, and trades. Open Su-Th 10am-10pm, F-Sa 10am-midnight.

◧ NIGHTLIFE

A wildly popular nightlife destination in L.A., Hollywood provides a grab bag of options. Clubs here are not for the faint of heart—get your glow stick and game face ready because the hot and the hip are around every corner. For a more relaxed night, head for a bar or lounge. 24hr. restaurants and coffeehouses ensure breakfast is served at any hour.

LATE-NIGHT RESTAURANTS AND COFFEEHOUSES

Highland Grounds, 742 N. Highland Ave. (466-1507; www.highlandgrounds.com). Intimate, laid-back coffeehouse and restaurant. Excellent breakfasts (served until 4pm; $5-9) and an outdoor patio with a fire pit. Live music every night (check the website). Lunch and late-night entrees $7-9. Beer and wine $0.50-6.50. Open M 9am-5pm, Tu-Th 9am-midnight, F-Sa 9am-1am, Su 9am-4pm.

Bourgeois Pig, 5931 Franklin Ave. (☎464-6008; www.bourgeoispig.com). Screenwriters tap away at their laptops and confer with their agents as they sip coffee ($1.75-4.25) and scarf down turkey sandwiches ($5). At night, locals head to "The Pig" to play pool or to indulge in a pot of Moroccan mint tea (serves 2; $6) in the intimate, dimly lit Moroccan back room. Open 8am-2am. No credit cards.

Barney's Beanery, 8447 Santa Monica Blvd. (☎654-2287). Since 1920, Barney's has been serving over 600 items from their newsprint menus, including 125 bottled beers and 28 draft beers. Not a place for the indecisive. Janis Joplin and Jim Morrison were regulars. Pool, ping-pong, air hockey, and video games. Karaoke Su-M and W 10pm-2am. Happy hour M-F 4-7pm; drafts $2, well drinks and house wines $2.50; appetizers $3. Valet parking $4. Open daily 11am-2am.

Stir Crazy, 6917 Melrose Ave. (☎934-4656), between Highland and La Brea Ave. By day, students read quietly; by night, a loud social scene takes over. Coffee drinks $2.50. Original sandwiches $5.50. Open daily 9am-9pm. No credit cards.

G.A.L.A.X.Y. Gallery, 7224 Melrose Ave. (☎936-2074), 3 blocks west of La Brea Ave. Much more than just a coffee shop, this spacious tobacco store has art on display, a collection of African djembe drums, and an enormous bong and hookah selection for your (ahem) tobacco needs. Acid jazz jams on some weekend nights. Hemp coffee $1.75. 18+. Cover varies. Open M-Sa 11am-10pm, Su noon-9pm.

COMEDY CLUBS

Groundling Theater, 7307 Melrose Ave. (☎934-4747; www.groundlings.com). One of the most popular improv and comedy clubs in town. The Groundling's alums include Pee Wee Herman and many current and former *Saturday Night Live* regulars like Will Ferrell, Julia Sweeney, and Chris Kattan. Don't be surprised to see *SNL* producer Lorne Michaels sitting in the back. Lisa Kudrow of *Friends* also got her start here. Polished skits. Tickets $13-20. Shows W-Th 8pm, F-Sa 8 and 10pm, Su 7:30pm.

BARS

Standard Lounge, 8300 Sunset Blvd. (☎822-3111), in the Standard Hotel. No dress code, no cover, no guest list, but you'd never know it. Insanely chic—Carrie Bradshaw drank here in the "Sex and Another City" episode of *Sex and the City.* Nightly DJ. Drinks $9. Open daily 10pm-2am.

3 of Clubs, 1123 N. Vine St. (☎323-462-6441), at the corner of Santa Monica Blvd., hidden in a strip mall. Simple, classy, and spacious hardwood bar famous for appearing in *Swingers.* Live bands Th. DJ F-Sa. Open daily 6pm-2am.

Beauty Bar, 1638 Cahuenga Blvd. (☎464-7676). Where else can you get a manicure while sipping a cocktail? Martinis are *so* much headier when sitting under an old-school hair dryer. Beautify while boozing on drinks like the "perm" or the "platinum blonde" ($8, with manicure $10). DJ nightly 10pm. Open Su-W 9pm-2am, Th-Sa 6pm-2am.

The Room, 1626 N. Cahuenga Blvd. (☎462-7196). Mood lighting and heavy beats turn the bar area into a dance floor as the night progresses. M reggae. Tu-Su hip-hop. No advertising, no sign on the door. Additional location in Santa Monica at 14th St. and Santa Monica Blvd. Open daily 9pm-2am.

Daddy's, 1610 N. Vine St. (☎463-7777), between Hollywood and Sunset Blvd. Low-to-the-ground booths, candle lighting, and the cheapest jukebox in town. $6 drinks and $5 beers. Open M-F 7pm-2am, Sa 8pm-2am, Su 9pm-2am.

Ye Coach and Horses, 7617 Sunset Blvd. (☎876-6900). Former speakeasy-turned-pub. The bartenders know all the local legends. Expect a blended crowd of neighborhood locals and PBR swilling hipsters. Alfred Hitchcock was a regular. Beer $4-5. Happy hour M-F 4-8pm; $2-3 beer. Open M-Sa 11am-2pm, Su 5pm-2am.

Lucky Strike, 6801 Hollywood Blvd. (☎323-467-7776). Entrance is on Highland Ave., ½ block north of the Highland and Hollywood Blvd. intersection. Reminiscent of 1940s bowling clubs, 12 bowling lanes blend with an upscale bar and lounge with pool table. Drinks $6. 21+ after 7pm. $5-8 per person per game; shoe rental $4. Prices increase gradually as the night wears on. Open daily 11am-2am.

The Lava Lounge, 1533 N. La Brea Ave. (☎876-6612; www.lavala.com). Fun young bar with a tropical theme—surf rock and Pacific Island sounds. Sip a "Blue Hawaiian" ($12) under an impressive twinkling star ceiling. Live entertainment from 10pm. Cover $1-5. Open daily 8:30pm-2am.

CLUBS

The Larchmont, 5657 Melrose Ave. (☎323-467-4068). Each night is a different theme. DJ promos bring a good mix of trance, house, and hip-hop. Nonstop dancing on both floors and the outdoor patio. Cover $5-20. Open M-Tu 7:30pm-1am, W 10pm-4am, Th 9pm-2:30am, F-Sa 9pm-4am.

LOS FELIZ, SILVER LAKE, AND GRIFFITH PARK ☎323

The hilly east Hollywood communities of Los Feliz and Silver Lake are home to kitschy knick-knack shops, retro greasy spoons, and L.A.'s verdant public playground, Griffith Park. Though gentrification has begun to sneak in, the area maintains a bohemian-hipster neighborhood vibe. Come here to write the next great screenplay at the House of Pies, grab incredibly cheap, fresh Mexican food, or throw back a few beers at one of the area's laid-back watering holes.

▐ TRANSPORTATION

Los Feliz, Silver Lake, and Griffith Park sit in the hills east of Hollywood. In Los Feliz the action is below Griffith Park on **Vermont Avenue**; in Silver Lake, **Sunset Boulevard** is the main drag. **Bus #2** runs on Sunset Blvd.

◖ FOOD

Silver Lake and Los Feliz host a healthy mix of inexpensive ethnic restaurants and retro diners catering to hungover rockers and freelance screenwriters.

▩ **Malo,** 4326 Sunset Blvd. (☎664-1011), in **Silver Lake.** Hip decor, customers, and jukebox can't outshine the Chicano food. 4 incredible salsas ($4 each), including a unique Spanish chocolate and arbol sauce, complement "fried to order" chips. Entrees $6-15. Open Su-Th 6pm-midnight, F-Sa 6pm-2am. ❸

Fred 62, 1850 N. Vermont Ave. (☎323-667-0062), in **Los Feliz.** "Eat now, dine later." An edgy crowd dines on breakfasts fit for the King, such as Hunka Hunka Burning Love Pancakes with peanut butter, chocolate chips, caramel sauce, and powdered sugar ($7.20). The apple waffles ($4.70) are divine. Open 24hr. ❷

Millie's, 3524 W. Sunset Blvd. (☎661-6163), in **Silver Lake.** Millie's cooks up breakfast delights the old-fashioned way, with fresh eggs, real butter, and dye-free cheese. Weekend mornings, diners crave this chemical-free food to counteract the effects of the night before. House specialties include chicken fried steak ($9) and *huevos rancheros* ($7). Open daily 7:30am-4pm. ❷

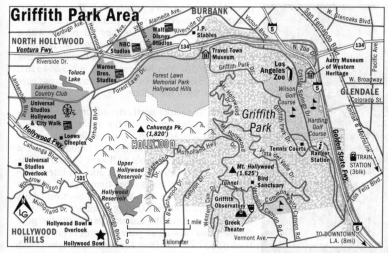

Griffith Park Area

Casbah Cafe, 3900 W. Sunset Blvd, (☎664-7000), in **Silver Lake.** A unique cafe/dress shop combo. Eclectic world menu includes pita sandwiches ($6), empanadas ($4.50), and *mate* tea served in a gourd ($5). Laptop-friendly. Open daily 7:30am-10pm. ❶

◎ SIGHTS

GRIFFITH PARK AND GLENDALE

Nestled in the hills between U.S. 101, I-5, and Rte. 134. Traveling by bus is not recommended, as it affords little flexibility within the park; that said, if coming from downtown, take bus #96, which goes north through the park along Crystal Springs Dr. From Hollywood, take bus #180 or 181 to the intersection the of Los Feliz Blvd. and Riverside and transfer to #96 north.

For a breath of fresh air and a respite from city life, take to the rugged, dry slopes of Griffith Park, the nation's largest municipal park. A stark contrast to the concrete heights of downtown and the star-studded streets of Hollywood, the park is the site of many outdoor diversions. Fifty-two miles of hiking and horseback trails, three golf courses, tennis courts, a planetarium, an enormous zoo, several museums, a 6000-person amphitheater, and dozens of restaurants are all contained within its rolling 4107 acres. Several mountain roads through the park (especially Vista Del Valle Dr.) afford panoramic views of the L.A. basin from downtown to Century City. The 5 mi. hike to the top of Mt. Hollywood, the highest peak in the park, is quite popular. Keep a lookout for deer, opossum, and the solitary cougar.

For info on trails, golf, tennis, biking, and horse rides, stop by the **visitors center and Ranger Headquarters,** 4730 Crystal Spring Dr. (☎323-913-4688, emergency 323-913-7390. Park open daily 5am-10pm.) The park has numerous equestrian trails and places to saddle up, such as **J.P. Stables,** 914 S. Mariposa St., in Burbank. No experience is necessary, and guides are provided. (☎818-843-9890. Open daily 7:30-6pm. 1st hr. $20, $12 each additional hr. Cash only.)

PLANETARIUM AND OBSERVATORY. The world-famous white stucco and copper domes of the castle-like mountaintop observatory would be visible from nearly any point in the L.A. basin were it not for the smog. The observatory parking lot affords a terrific view of the Hollywood sign and the flat wastes of L.A. You may remember the planetarium from the James Dean film *Rebel Without A Cause*, or more

THE LOCAL STORY

STARRY-EYED BARS

Bogart. Sinatra. Hepburn. Gable. Monroe. The greatest actors of a generation slowly destroyed their livers here. Those who say L.A. has no history need look no further than the bottom of their martini glass at these venerable old Hollywood bars. Here's looking at you, kid!

Barney's Beanery, 8447 Santa Monica Blvd. (☎323-654-2287), in West Hollywood. Some like it hot—especially Marilyn Monroe. While filming the picture of the same name, she'd drop in for chili. Odd, because this rough-and-tumble Rte. 66 roadhouse is more suited to Janis Joplin, who partied here the night she died. Open daily 11am-2am.

Chez Jay, 1657 Ocean Ave. ☎310-395-1741), in Santa Monica. A tiny, crusty beachside dive festooned with Christmas lights, red checkered tablecloths, and pictures of Sinatra. Ol' Blue Eyes dented the red vinyl bar here regularly in his day. Open M-Sa 5pm-2am, Su 5:30pm-1:30am.

Ye Coach and Horses, 7617 W. Sunset Blvd. (☎323-876-5900), in Hollywood. A dark, tiny hole-in-the-wall. Richard Burton started his benders here. Open M-Sa 11am-2am, Su 5pm-2am.

The Gallery Bar at the Biltmore Hotel, 506 S. Grand Ave. ☎213-624-1011), in downtown L.A. This was the last place aspiring starlet Beth Short (nicknamed "the Black Dahlia" for her sexy black dresses) was seen alive,

recently from *Charlie's Angels: Full Throttle*. Unfortunately, the observatory and planetarium are closed until early to mid-2006, when they will reopen with a 35,000 sq. ft. extension. *(Drive to the top of Mt. Hollywood on Vermont Ave. or Hillhurst St. from Los Feliz Blvd., or take MTA #180 or 181 from Hollywood Blvd. ☎323-664-1181, recording 323-664-1191; www.griffithobs.org. Grounds open Tu-F 1-10pm, Sa-Su 10am-10pm.)*

L.A. ZOO. The park's northern end furnishes habitats for rare animals from around the world. The Komodo dragon and Red Ape Rain Forest exhibits, along with the elephants and the chimps, are among the most popular spots in the zoo's well-kept 113 acres. The Children's Zoo offers a petting zoo, an interactive adventure theater, and a story-time area. Watch the sea lion training in the Aquatics Section (daily 11:30am and 2:30pm.) During summer, the heat is often too much for the animals, especially the poor penguins, so viewing all your favorites is not guaranteed. *(5333 Zoo Dr. From Los Feliz Blvd., take Crystal Springs Dr. into the park; the zoo will be on your left. ☎644-4200; www.lazoo.org. Open daily Sept.-June 10am-5pm; July-Aug. 10am-6pm. Animals are put away for the night starting 1hr. before closing. $10, ages 2-12 $5, seniors $7.)*

AUTRY MUSEUM OF WESTERN HERITAGE. The Autry Museum draws the line between Old West fact and fiction in its exhibits on pioneer life, outlaws, and movies. City slickers and lone rangers may discover that the American West is not what they thought—the museum insists that the real should not be confused with the reel. Still, costumes worn by Robert Redford and Clint Eastwood are as much artifacts as the authentic saddles and spurs of California's first cowboys, the *vaqueros*. Check out "The Shoot-Out at OK Corral," a simulation of the legendary 1881 10-person gunfight waged by renowned desert lawman Wyatt Earp (who died in L.A.), his brother Virgil, and their sweet-shooting comrade, Doc Holliday. The Holdout Arm Cheating Device for concealing cards and the extensive Colt firearms collection in the Community Gallery are also worthwhile. During July and August, the museum sponsors live swing music in its outdoor atrium; call for times. *(4700 Western Heritage Way. From Downtown, take MTA bus #96 up Crystal Springs Dr. From Los Feliz Blvd., take Crystal Springs Dr. into the park; the museum will be on your right. ☎667-2000. Open Tu-W and F-Su 10am-5pm, Th 10am-8pm. $7.50, ages 2-12 $3, students and seniors $5. Free Th after 4pm.)*

FOREST LAWN CEMETERY. A final resting ground for the famous, Forest Lawn Cemetery is a quiet alternative to the Walk of Fame. Among the illustrious dead are Clark Gable, George Burns, and Jimmy Stewart. The cemetery has a 30 ft. by 15 ft. reproduction of Leonardo da Vinci's *The Last Supper. (Every 30min. 9:30am-4pm.)* A 20min. narrated show unveils the "largest religious painting on earth," the 195 ft. by 45 ft. *Crucifixion,* which is so large it had to be transported from Europe in sections wrapped around telephone poles. *(Every hr. 10am-4pm.)* If you're still obsessed with oversized art, swing by the Forest Lawn in Hollywood Hills (only a 10min. drive) to see *Birth of Liberty,* America's largest historical mosaic—a 160 ft. by 30 ft. masterpiece composed of 10 million pieces of Venetian glass. *(1712 S. Glendale Ave. From downtown, take MTA #90 or 91 and get off just after the bus leaves San Fernando Rd. to turn onto Glendale Ave. From I-5, take Los Feliz Blvd. east and take a right onto Glendale Ave.; from the Glendale Fwy. (Rte. 134), take San Fernando Rd. north and a right onto Glendale Ave. ☎800-204-3131. Open daily 8am-6pm. Mausoleum open 9am-4:30pm.)*

TRAVEL TOWN MUSEUM. At the very northern tip of the park, this museum is the resting place of several antique train cars, donated by the railroad companies to the children of L.A. Locomotives pulling freight cars, passenger cars, and cabooses are scuffed by kiddie shoes daily as pint-size visitors are invited to climb aboard. Although most of the historic automobiles and fire engines were donated to other museums, a few are still on display. Children will demand to take a ride on top of one of the miniature trains. If you are around on a weekend, be sure to check out the complex miniature model of L.A., replete with dozens of model trains zipping through the city. *(5200 Zoo Dr. ☎662-5874. Open Apr.-Oct. M-F 10am-5pm, Sa-Su 10am-6pm; Nov.-Mar. M-F 10am-4pm, Sa-Su 10am-5pm. Model: ☎662-9678. Open Sa-Su 10am-5pm. Free. Train ride $2, seniors $1.50, children 3 and older $2; free steamer train rides Su 11am-3pm.)*

SHOPPING

Chulerias, 3743 W. Sunset Blvd. (☎665-9772), in **Silver Lake.** Distinctive global gifts such as woven handbags, essential oils, and silk scarves. Inexpensive ethnic gifts. Open daily 10am-6pm.

Soap Plant, 4633 Hollywood Blvd. (☎663-0122) in **Los Feliz.** Kitschy, daring, and naughty gifts surround a local art gallery. Everything from mood rings ($3) to exquisitely detailed porn star action figures ($24; must be 18+ to purchase). Open M-W 11am-7pm, Th-Sa 11am-9pm, Su noon-6pm.

Skylight Books, 1818 N. Vermont Ave. (☎660-1175; www.skylighbooks.com), in **Los Feliz.** Neighborhood bookstore specializing in California favorites—film and politics. Authors and other speakers nearly every night. Open daily 10am-10pm.

back in 1947. Five days later, her severed body was found, making her the most famous victim of an unsolved murder case in the city's history. Open daily 4:30pm-1:30am.

Formosa Cafe, 7156 Santa Monica Blvd. (☎323-850-9050), in Hollywood. Make like Lana Turner and cozy up in a booth to drink all you want, but avoid the "Chinese" food at all costs. Open M-F 5pm-2am, Sa-Su 6pm-2am.

Musso & Frank Grill, 6667 Hollywood Blvd. (☎323-467-7788), in Hollywood. Bogie boozed, Sinatra swilled, and Bukowski blew his cash here. Raymond Chandler immortalized Musso's gin and lime juice concoctions in "The Long Goodbye." Open Tu-Sa 11am-11pm.

The Polo Lounge at the Beverly Hills Hotel, 9641 Sunset Blvd. (☎310-276-2251), in Beverly Hills. The loudest thing here is the pink paint on the walls. Order up a Singapore Sling and dream about the days when Katharine Hepburn and Marlene Dietrich held court here. On F mornings, the terrace tables are a classic place for striking movie deals. Open daily 7am-midnight.

Trader Vic's at the Beverly Hilton Hotel, 9876 Wilshire Blvd. (☎310-274-7777), in Beverly Hills. A great place for celebrity affairs, owing to its two exits. The piña colada is served in a whole pineapple; a floating gardenia graces the gin-laced scorpion bowl. Open Su-Th 5pm-1am, F-Sa 5pm-2am.

NIGHTLIFE

The Derby, 4500 Los Feliz Blvd. (☎663-8979; www.the-derby.com), at the corner of Hillhurst Ave. in **Los Feliz.** Still jumpin' and jivin' with the kings of swing. Ladies, grab your snoods; many dress the 40s part. Choice Italian fare from Louise's Trattoria next door. Full bar. Free swing lessons Su 6:30pm. Cover F-Sa $5-12. Open daily 7:30pm-2am. Back bar open daily 5pm-2am (no cover).

Zen Sushi, 2609 Hyperion Ave. (☎665-2929), in **Silver Lake.** Excellent traditional (sushi, *sashimi,* etc.) and experimental (wasabi mashed-potatoes) Japanese food served in 3 luxurious dining rooms. Upstairs *Kabuki* stage and smaller downstairs stage host live performances, from indie rock to drag shows. $1 *sake* shots and a smoking patio seal the deal. Entrees $10-15. Open daily 5pm-2am. Kitchen closes at 11pm.

The Roost, 3100 Los Feliz Blvd. (☎664-7272), in **Los Feliz.** This neighborhood bar by day is invaded by Hollywood hipsters at night. Laid-back and friendly. Bottled beer $2.50-6. Open daily 10am-2am. Cash only.

DOWNTOWN L.A. ☎213

Say "downtown" to Angelenos and they'll wince—either because they don't know what you're referring to, they know but don't go there, or they work there and are none too happy about it. It is L.A.'s netherland—the place over there. Mayor James Hahn and City Hall strive valiantly to project downtown as a paradigm of L.A.'s culture and diversity, but the Westside powers have a solid grip on the culture, and the neighborhoods in L.A. County are sharply defined by homogeneity of race and class. In downtown, an uneasy truce prevails between the bustling financiers and the street population, but visitors should be cautious—**the area is unsafe after business hours and on weekends.**

TRANSPORTATION AND PRACTICAL INFORMATION

The **DASH Shuttle** runs six lines downtown that cover most of the major tourist destinations. ($0.25; see p. 382. References to DASH shuttles in the listings below are for M-F travel.) If driving, park in a secure lot, rather than on the street. Due to expensive short-term lot parking ($3 per 20min.) and exorbitant meter prices ($0.25 per 10min.), it's best to park in a public lot ($5-10 per day) and hit the pavement on foot. The **L.A. Visitors Center,** 685 S. Figueroa St., between Wilshire and 7th St. should have pamphlets and answers to your travel queries. (☎689-8822. Open M-F 8am-4pm, Sa 8:30am-5pm.)

ACCOMMODATIONS

Downtown L.A. is probably not the best place to look for accommodations. Although busy and fairly safe by day, the area empties and becomes less safe at night. If you have an overwhelming desire to stay downtown, some relatively affordable lodgings can be found. If possible, travel in groups.

Days Inn Metro Plaza Hotel, 711 N. Main St. (☎213-680-0200 or 800-223-2223), at Cesar Chavez Ave. near Union Station. Well-managed chain hotel with big, spotless rooms, TVs, fridges, and safes. Free parking. Singles $75; doubles $85. $10 per additional person. ❹

Hotel Stillwell, 838 S. Grand Ave. (☎627-1151 or 800-553-4774). Bustling and informal with a hostel feel, the Stillwell accommodates many budget travelers. Low rates, in-house Indian and Mexican restaurants, and Hank's Bar. A/C. Parking $4.50 per day. Reservations recommended. Singles $56; doubles $67. Weekly singles $285; doubles $370. Prices include tax. $5 discount with ISIC. ❹

Milner Hotel, 813 S. Flower St. (☎627-6981 or 800-827-0411). Take the Prime Shuttle ($14) from the airport, bus, or train station, and get reimbursed when you stay at this downtown spot near the Pantry restaurant (see p. 439). Small, well-furnished rooms with A/C, cable TV, and continental breakfast. Parking next door in the garage; $10 per night. Singles $70; doubles $80. ❹

🍴 FOOD

Financial District eateries vie for the businessperson's coveted lunchtime dollar. Their secret weapon is the lunch special, but finding a reasonably priced dinner can be a challenge.

Philippe, The Original, 1001 N. Alameda St. (☎213-628-3781; www.philippes.com), 2 blocks north of Union Station. A longtime fixture, Philippe is one of downtown's most popular lunch eateries. The invention of the French Dip sandwich occurred here in 1918 when Philippe allegedly dropped a sliced French roll into a roasting pan filled with juice still hot from the oven. The policeman Philippe served loved the dipped sandwich so much, he showed up the next day with a dozen cop buddies requesting the same. Choose from pork, beef, ham, turkey ($4.40), or lamb ($4.70). Top it off with apple pie ($2.75) and $0.09 coffee. Free parking. Open daily 6am-10pm. ❶

The Pantry, 877 S. Figueroa St. (☎213-972-9279). Since 1924, it hasn't closed once—not for the earthquakes, not for the 1992 riots (when it served as a National Guard outpost), and not even when a taxicab drove through the front wall. There aren't even locks on the doors. Owned by former L.A. mayor Richard Riordan, this diner is known for its large portions, free coleslaw, and fresh sourdough bread. Giant breakfast specials $6. Lunch sandwiches $8. Open 24hr. No credit cards. ❷

La Luz del Día, 1 W. Olvera St. (☎628-7495), tucked inside El Pueblo Historic Park along the circular walking path. Family-run and completely authentic Mexican restaurant. The park's trees and performance artists are a nice complement to the great food. Specialties are the homemade tortillas ($0.20), tacos, and rice and beans ($5-6). Open Tu-Th 11am-9pm, F 11am-10pm, Sa 10am-10pm, Su 8:30am-10pm. ❷

Zucca Ristorante, 801 S. Figueroa St. (☎213-614-7800), in the Financial District. This classy and upscale Italian restaurant is popular with downtown businessmen. Antipasti $9-13. Pasta $15-18. Fish $18-20. Children under 12 eat free. Open M-Th 11:30am-2:30pm and 5-9pm, F 11:30am-2:30pm and 5-10pm, Sa 5-10pm, Su 5-9pm. ❹

Cafe Dolcini, 865 S. Figueroa (☎622-0140), A friendly sandwich joint with a selection of dirt-cheap lunch eats (turkey, ham and cheese, veggie, or roast beef $4). Wash it all down with a smoothie ($3). Open daily 7am-5:30pm. ❶

👁 SIGHTS

Though people do work downtown, it lacks any overpowering energy. Pick up the detailed **Angels Walk** brochure (available at the visitors center, central library, and museums), which plots out a worthwhile 15-point walking tour around El Pueblo, the Civic Center, the Financial District, and Little Tokyo. Each guide has a map and helpful MTA information. The **Los Angeles Conservancy** also offers free, printable self-guided walking tours geared toward architectural landmarks on its website as well as a variety of docent-led Saturday tours featuring downtown's historic buildings. (☎623-2489; www.laconservancy.org. Make reservations at least 1 week in advance. No strollers or young children. Tours $10.)

EL PUEBLO HISTORIC PARK. The historic birthplace of L.A. is now known as **El Pueblo de Los Angeles Historical Monument.** In 1781, 44 settlers established a pueblo and farming community here; today, 27 buildings from the eras of Spanish and Mexican rule are preserved. (*Bordered by Cesar Chavez Ave., Alameda St., Hollywood Fwy.,* *and Spring St. DASH B.)* Established in 1825, the **Plaza,** with its Moreton Bay fig trees and huge kiosk, is the center of El Pueblo. It is the site of several festivals including the Mexican Independence celebration (Sept. 16), *Día de los Muertos* celebrations (Nov. 1-2), and *Cinco de Mayo* (May 5); see **Seasonal Events,** p. 390. Dates of festivals are subject to change, so call ahead to confirm. Walk down **Olvera Street,** which resembles a colorful Mexican marketplace, and bargain at *puestos* (vendor stalls) selling everything from Mexican handicrafts and food to personalized t-shirts. The **Avila Adobe** (c. 1818), is the "oldest" house in the city. Following the earthquake of 1971, which damaged the house severely, it was restored as an example of L.A. life in the 1810s. *(10 E. Olvera St. Open daily 9am-3pm.)* On the first floor of the **Sepulveda House** (1887) is the **visitors center,** where you can request to view *Pueblo of Promise,* an 18min. history of L.A. *(622 N. Main Street. ☎ 628-1274. Open M-Sa 10am-3pm. Walking tour maps $0.50. Free walking tours Tu-Sa 10am, 11am, and noon beginning at the Hellman-Quon Bldg., off Los Angeles St. near the Firehouse Museum. Reservations required for groups of 10 or more.)*

CHINATOWN. Today's **Chinatown** is home to less than five percent of the city's Chinese population. With its pagoda-like gates, pedestrian lanes, restaurants, *dim sum,* and kitsch vendors, the neighborhood is lively and vibrant. For a very different experience of Chinese-American culture, visit Monterey Park, 6 mi. to the east. *(Roughly bordered by Yale, Spring, Ord, and Bernard St. DASH B.)*

CIVIC CENTER. The **Civic Center** is a solid wall of bureaucratic edifices south of El Pueblo Park. Unless you have a hearing for that parking ticket you got by Staples Center, there isn't much reason to go inside. *(Bound by U.S. 101, Grand Ave., 1st St., and San Pedro St. DASH B and D.)* One of the best-known buildings in SoCal, **City Hall,** "has starred in more movies than most actors." *(200 N. Spring St.)*

MUSIC CENTER. Reminiscent of Lincoln Center in New York, the Music Center is an enormous, beautiful complex that includes **The Dorothy Chandler Pavilion,** home of the L.A. Opera, former site of the Academy Awards, and until very recently, home of the world-renowned L.A. Philharmonic and the L.A. Master Chorale. *(☎ 972-8001; www.laopera.com.)* Across the street rise the radical silver slices of the Frank Gehry-designed ◪**Walt Disney Concert Hall,** the Music Center's fourth and newest performance venue. This gleaming 2265-seat structure is the home of the L.A. Phil and the L.A. Master Chorale, and also hosts theatrical productions, touring shows, and other popular cultural performances. *(151 S. Grand Ave. ☎ 972-7211; www.disneyhall.org.)* Also part of the Music Center are the **Mark Taper Forum,** honored for its development of new plays (many award-winning Broadway plays had their start here), and the **Ahmanson Theatre,** best known for its world-class dramas, musicals, comedies, and classical revivals. *(☎ 628-2772; www.taperahmanson.com. Tours M-F 11:30am, 12:30, and 1:30pm as performance schedules permit. Go to the outdoor information booth in the large outdoor courtyard between the theaters.)*

LITTLE TOKYO AND THE ARTS DISTRICT. Founded with the opening of a Japanese restaurant in 1886, Little Tokyo served as the spiritual, cultural, and commercial center for Japanese immigrants and their descendants until deportation during WWII. After returning from internment camps, many Japanese-Americans moved to the suburbs, but successful efforts to rejuvenate the area have helped Little Tokyo return to its status as a community center. *(Southeast of the Civic Center, east of 2nd and San Pedro St. DASH A.)* **The Japanese American Cultural and Community Center** is the largest Asian-American cultural center in the country. It is home to a plaza designed by the internationally renowned Japa-

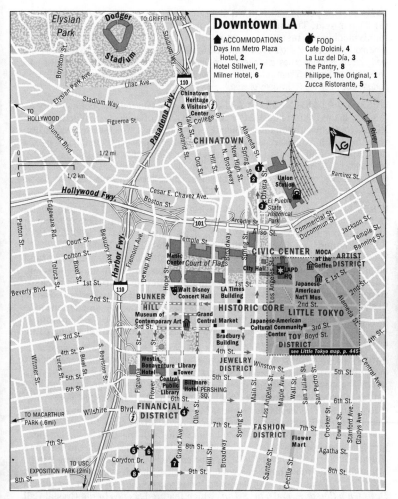

Downtown LA

⌂ ACCOMMODATIONS
Days Inn Metro Plaza
Hotel, **2**
Hotel Stillwell, **7**
Milner Hotel, **6**

🍎 FOOD
Cafe Dolcini, **4**
La Luz del Día, **3**
The Pantry, **8**
Philippe, The Original, **1**
Zucca Ristorante, **5**

nese-American artist Isamu Noguchi; a Japanese-American Veterans Memorial that honors Japanese-American soldiers who died in America's wars; and the Doizaki Gallery, an art gallery that presents work from local and international artists as well as special exhibits on calligraphy, *ikebana* (flowers), and other traditional art forms. Make sure to visit the serene **James Irvine Garden,** better known as *Seiryu-en*, or "Garden of the Pure Stream." *(244 S. San Pedro St. ☎628-2725; www.jaccc.org. Gallery open Tu-F noon-5pm, Sa-Su 11am-4pm. Small donation may be requested.)* The **Japanese-American National Museum** has a Resource Center with interactive computers and access to WWII relocation camp records. *(369 E. 1st St. ☎625-0414; www.janm.org. Open Tu-W and F-Su 10am-5pm, Th 10am-8pm. Resource Center closes 5pm. $8, seniors $5, students and ages 6-17 $4, under 5 free. Th after 5pm and third Th of each month free.)* The Frank Gehry-renovated **MOCA at The Geffen Contemporary** was once the garage for the LAPD fleet. The "Temporary Contemporary" eventually became permanent to the delight of its adoring public, and is now leased for $1 per year. The museum closely resembles a warehouse and presents highly acclaimed installation art exhibitions. *(152 N. Central Ave. ☎626-6222; www.moca.org. Open M and F 11am-5pm, Th 11am-8pm, Sa-Su 11am-6pm. Occasional art talks led by artists, authors, critics, and curators; call ahead for schedule. $8, students and seniors $5, under 12 free. Free Th 5-8pm. Admission good for both downtown MOCA locations. Shuttle transportation between the 2 locations offered.)*

MUSEUM OF CONTEMPORARY ART (MOCA). The Museum of Contemporary Art (MOCA) in the California Plaza is a celebrated piece of modern architecture. Arata Isozaki found inspiration for the facade's curve in L.A.'s sweetheart, Marilyn Monroe. Along with temporary installments, the museum houses a compelling permanent collection of Western modern visual art. *(250 S. Grand Ave. ☎213-626-6222; www.moca.org. Open M and F 11am-5pm, Th 11am-8pm, Sa-Su 11am-6pm. Occasional art talks led by artists, authors, critics, and curators; call ahead for schedule. Free with admission. $8, students and seniors $5, under 12 free. Free Th 11am-8pm.)*

OTHER SIGHTS. L.A.'s history is etched in stone on the sides of the respected **LA Times** building. The public relations department offers tours, call to set up an appointment. *(Between 1st and 2nd St. at the corner of Spring St. ☎800-528-4637.)* Bargain hounds can haggle to their hearts' delight in the **Fashion District.** On Saturdays, these small, open-front wholesale stores sell their flimsy brandname knockoffs individually. Spend mere pennies on classy finds like sequin tube tops, push-up bras, colored contacts (nonprescription), or packs of socks. *(Along Los Angeles St. between 6th and 9th St.)* The equally well-stocked **Grand Central Public Market** (see **Food,** p. 388) has its own stars embedded in the sidewalk out front, each bearing the name of a Chicano celebrity—a *rambla de fama* to complement Hollywood's. An L.A. fixture, the market is one of the best spots to taste some local flavor.

SOUTHERN DISTRICTS. The **Financial District** is a fusion of glass and steel, where gigantic high-rises soar above the flat L.A. basin. *(Bound roughly by 3rd, 9th, Figueroa, and Olive St. DASH B and C)* The tallest building between Chicago and Hong Kong at 1017 ft., **Library Tower,** punctuates the L.A. skyline with its distinctive glass crown. *(633 W. 5th St.)* The **Westin Bonaventure Hotel** is composed of five sleek cylinders sheathed in black glass, and has appeared in *Rain Man, In the Line of Fire,* and *Heat.* The easily amused can spend hours in the high-speed, glass-walled elevators. The view from the 32nd floor is better than that from most helicopters. *(404 S. Figueroa St.)* Slightly southeast of the Bonaventure is the historic **Biltmore Hotel,** a $10 million, 683-room hotel designed by Schultze and Weaver (best known for New York's Waldorf-Astoria). It was a filming location for *Dave, Independence Day, Ghostbusters,* and *The Sting,* which featured scenes in the Crystal Ballroom. *(506 S. Grand Ave.)* Before **Bunker Hill** sprouted skyscrapers, it was a residential area with expensive Victorian homes. The one remaining relic from this era is **Angels Flight,** "the shortest railway in the world." Unfortunately, the railway closed indefinitely after an accident in February 2001. The **Bunker Hill Steps** are a fantastic, florid maze of escalators, stairs, and landings modeled after the Spanish Steps in Rome. *(On the southwest side of the hill along 5th St.)*

EXPOSITION PARK

Southwest of downtown, off the I-110 Exposition Blvd. exit, bounded by Exposition Blvd., Vermont Ave., Figueroa St., and Martin Luther King, Jr. Blvd. From Downtown, take DASH F or MTA #81 or 442. From Hollywood, take MTA #204 or 754 down Vermont Ave. From Santa Monica, take MTA #20, 22, or 720 on Wilshire Blvd., and transfer to #204 at Vermont Ave. Parking at Figueroa St. and Exposition Blvd.; $6.

Once an open-air agricultural market and upscale suburb, Exposition Park began to decline in the early 1890s as wealthier citizens moved west. This population vacuum was filled by immigrants, who were barred from the Westside by home-owners' associations. The resulting low-cost, high-density housing further depressed the neighborhood. This deterioration was counteracted when the Olympic Games came to town in 1932, and the neighborhood was revitalized again for the second Olympic Games at the park in 1984. Today, the area is much better off, and its museums are generally safe and well visited, but **visitors should exercise caution outside the park, especially at night.**

CALIFORNIA SCIENCE CENTER (CSC). Dedicated to the sciences of California, the interactive exhibits in this modern building educate kids and adults about West Coast issues—earthquakes, smog, traffic, and studio production. Eleven human embryos and fetuses are preserved in the World of Life gallery, and the display on California's fault line jarringly recreates an earthquake. You can even design your own earthquake-proof buildings. *(700 State Dr. ☎ 323-724-3623; www.casciencectr.org or www.california-sciencecenter.org. Open daily 10am-5pm. Free.)* The seven-story, 91 ft. wide **IMAX Theater** shows critically acclaimed, often stunning 45min. films on nature, space, and special effects. *(☎ 213-744-7400. Shows every hr. M-F 10am-5pm, Sa-Su 10am-6pm. Evening shows often sell out; call ☎ 213-365-3500 to reserve tickets; $2 surcharge. $7.50, students and seniors $5.50, ages 4-12 $4.50. Discounts for purchasing more than 1 ticket.)* The CSC's formal **rose garden** is the last remnant of the blessed days when the park was a horticultural exposition. The beautiful garden has over 19,000 specimens of 165 varieties of roses that wind through seven acres of lawn surrounding gazebos and a large fountain. When the roses bloom (usually in late spring or early summer), the brilliant fragrance and colors are incredible. *(Open daily 8:30am-sunset. Free.)*

OTHER MUSEUMS. The **California African-American Museum** showcases the history of African Americans and their experience in California via rotating exhibits. *(600 State Dr. ☎ 213-744-7432; www.caam.ca.gov. Open W-Sa 10am-4pm. Free.)* The **Natural History Museum** is best known for its "habitat halls," where North American and African mammal specimens appear in lifelike poses. The museum also features some of the nation's best collections of Native American and Latin American artifacts. The hands-on **Discovery Center** is a must for children, who get to dig for dinosaur fossils and meet Jay and Cecil, the 12 ft. Burmese python and the 6 ft. iguana. *(900 Exposition Blvd. ☎ 213-743-3466. Open M-F 9:30am-5pm, Sa-Su 10am-5pm. Discovery Center animal presentations M-F 3pm, Sa-Su 11am and 3pm. $9, seniors and ages 13-18 $6.50, ages 5-12 $2, under 5 free. Free 1st Tu of each month.)* The cavernous, Frank Gehry-designed **Aerospace Museum** has a blue and white F-104 Starfighter bolted to its south face and a host of intriguing exhibits and displays inside. Design and launch your own model planes, pretend to pilot an L.A.P.D chopper, or strap on a pair of wings and feel the wrath of a wind tunnel. *(700 State Dr. Open M-F 10am-1pm, Sa-Su 11am-4pm.)*

UNIVERSITY OF SOUTHERN CALIFORNIA (USC). North of Exposition Park, USC's 30,000 students bring a youthful character to the streets of downtown. The alma mater of world-famous celebrities including Neil Armstrong, the school has had a gold medal-winning athlete in every summer Olympics since 1912. While it has kept busy churning out incredible athletes, USC's band has become the only US marching band to sell two platinum records. L.A. college sports fans salivate when the burnished USC Trojans clash with the blue-and-gold UCLA Bruins in annual football and basketball classics. *(University Park Campus. From downtown, take Figueroa St. south and turn right into campus on 35th St., or Exposition Blvd. exit from I-110. ☎ 213-740-2311; www.usc.edu. Campus tours offered M-F every hr. 10am-3pm.)*

LOS ANGELES

PASADENA

☎ 626

Every New Year's Day snowbound TV audiences jealously tune-in to sunny Pasadena, home of the Tournament of Roses Parade and Rose Bowl football game. For the nation, Pasadena is the home of the Rose Bowl; for Californians, it is a serene, ritzy suburb. With world-class-museums, graceful architecture, a lively shopping district, and idyllic weather, Pasadena lacks only a coastline. Old Town combines intriguing historic sights with a lively entertainment scene.

◨◪ TRANSPORTATION AND PRACTICAL INFORMATION

Pasadena lies northeast of downtown L.A. at the base of the San Gabriel Mountains. From Downtown, take I-110 north (Pasadena Fwy.). In Pasadena, I-110 turns into the Arroyo Pkwy. Continue north and take a right onto Colorado Blvd. to reach Old Town Pasadena. The splendid **Convention and Visitors Bureau,** 171 S. Los Robles Ave., is a useful first stop in Pasadena, with numerous promotional materials and guides to regional events. (☎795-9311; www.pasadenacal.com. Open M-F 8am-5pm, Sa 10am-4pm.) **Art Buses** shuttle the loop between Old Town and the downtown area around Lake Ave. approximately every 15min. Each of the twelve buses has a theme (e.g., performing arts, Arroyo Seco desert, multiculturalism) reflected in its decor. (☎744-4055. Shuttles run downtown M-Th 11am-7pm, F 11am-10pm, Sa-Su noon-8pm; uptown M-F 7am-6pm, Sa-Su noon-5pm. $0.50.)

◖ FOOD

Eateries line **Colorado Boulevard** from Los Robles Ave. to Orange Grove Blvd. in Old Town. The concentration of restaurants and sights around the boulevard make it pleasant and walkable.

▨ **Fair Oaks Pharmacy and Soda Fountain,** 1516 Mission St. (☎799-1414), at Fair Oaks Ave. in South Pasadena. From Colorado Blvd., go south 1 mi. on Fair Oaks Ave. to Mission St. This old-fashioned drug store with soda fountain and lunch counter has been serving travelers on Rte. 66 since 1915; now, a bit of Pasadena's upscale boutique flavor has crept in. An infamous phosphate drink made of flavored syrup splashed with water and secret "potion" is a fountain favorite ($2). Hand-dipped shakes and malts $4.25. Deli sandwiches $5.50. Soda fountain open M-F 11am-9pm, Sa 11am-10pm, Su 11am-8pm. Lunch counter open Su-F until 5pm, Sa until 8pm. ❷

Pita! Pita!, 927 E. Colorado Blvd. (☎356-0106), 1 block east of Lake Ave. Never has a flatbread deserved so many exclamation points. Free appetizers of green olives, yellow pepper, and tasty toasted pita. Spicy chicken pita $6. Lamb kebab served with salad, rice, and beans $8. Open Su-Th 11am-9pm, F-Sa 10am-10pm. ❷

Pie 'n Burger, 913 E. California Blvd. (☎795-1123), just east of S. Lake Ave., near Caltech. A classic 1963 diner, complete with Formica counters and friendly waitresses. Though it does serve other dishes, burgers ($5.50) and pies (19 varieties; $3.15-3.65) are the things to order. Open M-F 6am-10pm, Sa 7am-10pm, Su 7am-9pm. ❷

Holly Street Bar & Grill, 175 E. Holly St. (☎440-1421), between Marengo St. and Arroyo Pkwy. From Colorado Blvd., go 2 blocks north on Marengo. Contemporary eatery featuring California cuisine, such as southwest fettuccini served with a cilantro cream sauce, and the obligatory "oriental" chicken salad. Dine in the peaceful garden or among leopard-print decor. Live jazz complements the elegant dining experience F-Sa (7pm). Live classical guitar at Su brunch. Salads $9. Entrees $8-22. Full bar. Beer $3.50-4, cocktails $6. Open M 11am-2pm, Tu-Th 11am-2pm and 4:30-9:30pm, F-Sa 11am-2pm and 4:30pm-12:30am, Su 10am-2:30pm and 4:30-9pm. Bar open later. ❹

👁 SIGHTS

Besides spectator sports, Pasadena's main draw is **Old Town Pasadena**, bound approximately by Walnut St. and Del Mar Ave., between Pasadena Ave. and Arroyo Pkwy. This vibrant and trendy, shopping and dining arena has reinvigorated buildings dating back to the 1880s and 1890s. The **Plaza Pasadena** contains a 14-screen movie cineplex, shopping mall, and gourmet supermarket just east on Colorado Blvd. On the north side of Plaza Pasadena is the beautiful **City Hall,** 101 N. Garfield Ave. with an open courtyard, lush gardens, and a fountain (☎ 744-4228).

▓ NORTON SIMON MUSEUM OF ART. Rivaling the much larger Getty Museum in quality, this world-class private collection chronicles Western art from Italian Gothic to 20th-century abstract. The museum features paintings by Botticelli, Raphael, Van Gogh, Monet, and Picasso, as well as rare print etchings by Rembrandt and Goya. The Impressionist and Post-Impressionist hall, the Southeast Asian sculptures, and the 79,000 sq. ft. sculpture garden, by California landscape artist Nancy Goslee Power, are particularly impressive. *(411 W. Colorado Blvd., at Orange Grove Blvd. From I-110 N., exit at Orange Grove Blvd. and take a left onto Orange Grove Blvd. Continue 2 mi. and turn right on Colorado Blvd. Take MTA bus #180 or 181 west on Colorado Blvd. between Lake and N. Orange St. ☎ 449-6840; www.nortonsimon.org. Open M, W-Th, and Sa-Su noon-6pm, F noon-9pm. $6, seniors $3, students with ID and children under 18 free. Free parking.)*

ROSE BOWL. In the gorge that forms the city's western boundary stands Pasadena's most famous landmark. The sand-colored, 90,000-seat stadium is home to "the granddaddy of them all," the annual college football clash on New Year's Day between the champions of the Big Ten and Pac 10 conferences. The Bowl Championship Series comes every four years, and the UCLA Bruins play regular-season home games here as well. *(1001 Rose Bowl Dr. ☎ 577-3100; www.rosebowlstadium.com. Bruins info: ☎ 310-825-29469; www.cto.ucla.edu.)* The Bowl also hosts an enormous monthly flea market that attracts upwards of 2000 vendors, selling nearly one million items. *(☎ 323-560-7469. Held the 2nd Su of each month 9am-4:30pm. Admission 5-7am $20, 7-8am $15, 8-9am $10, 9am-3pm $7.)*

FENYES ESTATE. Built in 1905, the estate sits on the same grounds as the **Pasadena Museum of History** and the Pasadena city archives. It houses an impressive collection of Renaissance furniture, Egyptian sculpture, and local art amassed by Eva Scott Fenyes of the Scott

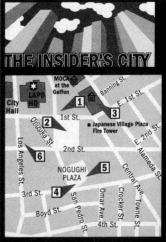

THE INSIDER'S CITY

LITTLE TOKYO

Little Tokyo is an active cultural center in downtown.

1 Little Tokyo Visitor Center, 307 E. 1st St. (☎ 213-613-1911), has maps and info.

2 Japanese Village Plaza, 300 E. 2nd St., is a fusion of US malls and Japanese design.

3 Japanese American National Museum, 369 E. 1st St. (☎ 213-625-0414). Housed in a Buddhist temple and an annex by designer Roy Obata.

4 Japanese American Cultural and Community Center, 244 S. San Pedro St. A showcase of community art.

5 Aratani Japan American Theatre, 244 S. San Pedro St. A handwoven silk *doncho* (curtain) opens on cultural events like Kabuki theater.

6 A Thousand Cranes, 120 S. Los Angeles St. Overlooking Japanese gardens, this restaurant serves pricey but popular shabu-shabu tempura ($48).

GRIDIRON GRIDLOCK

On fall Sundays, while football fans in 32 US cities organize tailgates, spill beer, and run around in the stands, forlorn Angelenos are stuck at home. L.A. has lacked a professional football team since 1994, when the Rams fled for St. Louis, Missouri and the Raiders moved north to Oakland due to poor ticket sales. In pro football, if a team doesn't sell out 48hr. before kickoff, local television networks can't air the game. This practice is called a blackout and aims to get hometown fans out of their recliners and into the stadium. Because its teams share television revenues and ticket sales equally, the National Football League (NFL) needs to ensure that teams are located in cities with sizable, loyal, ticket-buying fan bases.

Now, after almost a decade, negotiations to bring an NFL team back are in the works. Officials from both L.A. and the NFL are hopeful that a team will relocate and be ready to play by the 2008 season. The Indianapolis Colts, New Orleans Saints, and San Diego Chargers are all likely candidates. Proposals to build a new stadium on a 157-acre landfill in Carson or renovate the historic Pasadena Rose Bowl are also being hashed out.

Until the NFL returns to L.A., football fans will have to get their fix rooting for (or against) the UCLA and USC football teams.

Paper Company. Two galleries on the grounds have regularly rotating exhibitions. *(470 W. Walnut St., off Orange Grove Blvd. ☎577-1660. By tour only. W-Su 1:30 and 3pm. $4, seniors and students $3. Gallery admission $5, seniors and students $4, under 12 free. Combined admission $7.)*

PASADENA MUSEUM OF CALIFORNIA ART. The Pasadena Museum of Contemporary Art is the only museum in Southern California devoted solely to Californian Art. Regularly rotating exhibits are dedicated to California art, architecture, and design from 1850 to the present. *(490 E. Union St. ☎568-3665. Open W-Su noon-5pm. $6, seniors and students $4, under 12 free. First F of each month free.)*

PERFORMING ARTS. The **Pasadena Playhouse** cultivated the careers of William Holden, Dustin Hoffman, and Gene Hackman, among others. Founded in 1917 and restored in 1986, it now offers some of L.A.'s finest theater. *(39 S. El Molino Ave., between Colorado Blvd. and Green St. ☎356-7529. For more info, see Theater, p. 392.)* Housed in the concrete labyrinth of the Pasadena Center, the **Pasadena Civic Auditorium** is the centerpiece of the city's Spanish-influenced architecture. The auditorium hosted television's **Emmy Awards** each year until 1998, when the ceremonies moved to L.A. Since it is a rented venue, events are forever changing, but this 3000-seater usually features the Pasadena Symphony and the Distinguished Speaker Series, which hosts guests from Sharon Peres to Bob Woodward to Rudy Giuliani. *(300 E. Green St., at Marengo St. ☎449-7360, Distinguished Speaker Series tickets 800-508-9301. Box office open M-Sa 10am-5pm.)* For a more athletic performance, visit the **Pasadena Ice Skating Center,** which holds public skate sessions Thursday through Sunday. *(310 E. Green St., in the Pasadena Center. ☎578-0801. Open Th 7:30-9:30pm, F-Sa 8-10:30pm, Su 1-3:30pm. $7 admission; $3 skate rental.)*

TECHNOLOGY. Some of the world's greatest scientific minds do their work at the **California Institute of Technology (Caltech).** Founded in 1891, Caltech has amassed a faculty that includes several Nobel laureates and a student body that prides itself both on its staggering collective intellect and its loony practical jokes. These jokes have ranged from simple frathouse pranks, like unscrewing all the chairs in a lecture hall and bolting them in backwards, to nationally televised Rose Bowl scoreboard messages poking fun at competitor prankster school MIT. *(1201 E. California Blvd., about 2½ mi. southeast of Old Town. Tours leave from the admissions office at 355 Holliston Ave. Take I-110 N. until it becomes the Arroyo Pkwy. Turn right on California Blvd. and go 1¼ mi. Turn left on Hill Ave., left on San Pasqual St., and right on Holliston Ave.*

☎ *395-6327. Tours M-F 2pm.)* **NASA's Jet Propulsion Laboratory,** about 5 mi. north of Old Town, executed the journey of the Mars Pathfinder. Ask to see pictures of the face of Mars. *(4800 Oak Grove Dr. ☎ 818-354-9314. Free tours by appointment, call ahead to make reservations. Tours fill as early as 4 months in advance.)*

PASADENA OUTSKIRTS

▓ **HUNTINGTON LIBRARY, ART GALLERY, AND BOTANICAL GARDENS.** This institute commemorates Henry Huntington, a wealthy Californian railroad and real estate developer. Founded in 1919 and opened to the public in 1928, its stunning 150 acres of gardens are broken into thematic areas including the Rose Garden, the Shakespeare and herb gardens, and the Japanese Garden. (Picnicking and sunbathing among the greens is strictly forbidden.) The library holds one of the world's most important collections of rare books and British and American manuscripts, including a Gutenberg Bible, Benjamin Franklin's handwritten autobiography, a 1410 manuscript of Chaucer's *Canterbury Tales*, and a number of Shakespeare's first folios. The art gallery is known for its 18th- and 19th-century British paintings, but also holds Rogier Van Der Weyden's *Madonna and Child* (1460) and a strong collection of American art, including Edward Hopper's *The Long Leg* (1935) as well as works by John Singleton Copely. The Arabella Huntington Memorial Collection displays Renaissance paintings and 18th-century French decorative art. No visit is complete without taking tea in the **Rose Garden Tea Room.** *(1151 Oxford Rd., between Huntington Dr. and California Blvd. in San Marino, south of Pasadena, about 2 mi. south of the I-210 Allen Ave. exit. Take bus #79 and 379 from Union Station to San Marino Ave. and walk 1½ mi. ☎ 405-2100; www.huntington.org. Open Memorial Day-Labor Day Tu-Su 10:30am-4:30pm; Labor Day-Memorial Day Tu-F noon-4:30pm, Sa-Su 10:30am-4:30pm. $12.50, seniors $10, students $8.50, ages 5-11 $5, under 5 free. Free 1st Th of each month. Rose Garden set tea $15; reservations required.)*

DESCANSO GARDENS. The 165-acre garden includes one of the world's largest camellia forests, a historic rose collection, and man-made waterfalls. Events include tutorials on home gardening, bug displays, and cool night walks. Blooming peaks in early spring. *(1418 Descanso Dr., by the intersection of Rte. 2 and Rte. 210. ☎ 818-949-4290. Open daily 9am-5pm. $6, students and seniors $4, ages 5-12 $1.50. Events $7-10.)*

SOUTHWEST MUSEUM OF THE AMERICAN INDIAN. Recent remodeling and innovative exhibits have given this Highland Park museum the attention it deserves. The palatial Spanish-Moorish building has Native American cultural artifacts, including an 18 ft. Cheyenne teepee. *(234 Museum Dr. Take MTA bus #83 to Museum Dr. By car, take I-110 to Ave. 43 and follow the signs. ☎ 323-221-2164; www.southwestmuseum.org. Open Tu-Su 10am-5pm. Call for tours. Library open by appointment. $7.50, students and seniors $5, ages 7-18 $3, under 7 free.)*

RAGING WATERS. California's largest water park overflows with 50 acres of slides, pools, white-water rafts, inner tubes, and fake waves. Hurl yourself over the seven-story waterslide **Drop Out** or rush down **Speed Slide.** *(111 Raging Waters Dr. in San Dimas. Just north of the I-10, I-210, and I-57 interchange. Exit I-210/57 at Raging Waters Dr. ☎ 909-802-2200; www.ragingwaters.com. Hours vary; call ahead or check website. $28, seniors $18, under 48 in. $17, under 2 free; after 4pm $15, under 48 in. $12. Parking $7.)*

▓ NIGHTLIFE

The Ice House, 24 N. Mentor Ave. (☎ 577-1894; www.icehousecomedy.com). The 30-year-old granddaddy of clubs whose celebrity alums pop in occasionally. Read the building's facade for famous past performers. The Annex has stand-up comedy Tu-Th 8:30pm, F 8:30 and 10:30pm, Sa 7, 9, and 11pm, Su times vary. Cover $10-16. 2-drink min. Reservations recommended.

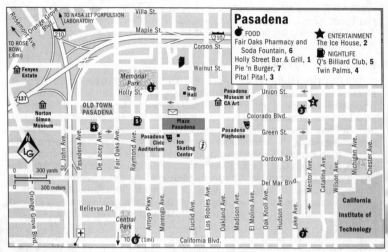

Pasadena

● FOOD
Fair Oaks Pharmacy and Soda Fountain, **6**
Holly Street Bar & Grill, **1**
Pie 'n Burger, **7**
Pita! Pita!, **3**

★ ENTERTAINMENT
The Ice House, **2**

■ NIGHTLIFE
Q's Billiard Club, **5**
Twin Palms, **4**

Twin Palms, 101 W. Green St. (☎577-2567). From Colorado Blvd., take De Lacy Ave. 1 block south. Inside it's hoppin', but outside, beneath the spacious tent and beside the stage, it's even crazier. Formerly owned by Kevin Costner. Regular live music and dancing; call ahead for schedule. Beer $4, martinis $7. Happy hour M-Th 4-7pm, F 4-6pm, Sa-Su 3-5pm. Cover F-Sa after 10pm $10.

Q's Billiard Club, 99 Colorado Blvd. (☎405-9777), just west of Arroyo Pkwy. Play pool, sip cocktails, or dance the night away to a bumping mix of hip-hop, techno, and house. 3 full bars (one on each level). A prime place to watch any sporting event—they've got over 40 televisions. Happy hour M-F 4-7pm. Open daily 11am-2am.

SAN FERNANDO VALLEY   ☎818

The Valley can't seem to shake the infamy it gained for breeding the Valley Girl, who started a worldwide trend in the 1980s with her huge hair, and, ohmigod, like, totally far-out mall adventures. Though it's usually 15°F hotter and always several degrees less posh than the Westside, the Valley deserves some respect; all of the major movie studios (and many pornographers) make their blockbusters here.

▐▌ TRANSPORTATION

The San Fernando Valley can be accessed by **I-405, I-5,** and **U.S. 101.** The movie studios in Burbank and Universal City are off U.S. 101 and Rte. 134. The **Metro Red Line** runs to Universal City.

▐▌ FOOD

Burbank is packed with eateries that are in turn often packed with workers in "the industry." The rules of star-gazing dictate that you can stare and envy them all you want, but don't bother them or ask for autographs.

Sushi Mac, 15030 Ventura Blvd. (☎986-6450), in Sherman Oaks. Adorn your 4-piece California roll or 6-piece salmon roll with the ginger and wasabi that travel past diners on a conveyor belt. All sushi is $2.50 (tax included). Free self-serve Japanese tea. Open daily 11:30am-9pm. ●

Bob's Big Boy, 4211 Riverside Dr. (☎818-843-9334), in Burbank. Don't miss this classic 1940s joint. The oldest remaining establishment of the once-large chain was declared a State Point of Historical Interest in 1993. Daily specials $7-9. Burgers $5-7. Classic Car Night F 6-10pm; Sa-Su 5-10pm offers a carhop service. Open 24hr. ❷

Miceli's, 3655 W. Cahuenga Blvd. (☎323-851-3344), in Universal City. From Hollywood Blvd., go north on Highland Ave., which turns into Cahuenga. Additional location at 1646 N. Las Palmas (☎323-466-3438), in **Hollywood.** Dinner guests feast on hearty Italian fare ($8-15) while the waitstaff serenades them. Open M-Th 11:30am-11pm, F 11:30am-midnight, Sa 4pm-midnight, Su 4-11pm. Lunch served M-F 11:30am-3pm. ❸

◎ SIGHTS

Passing Burbank on Rte. 134, you may catch glimpses of the Valley's most lucrative studios: **Universal, Warner Bros., NBC,** and **Disney.** To best experience the industry, attend a **free TV show taping** (see p. 390) or take a studio tour.

▧ **UNIVERSAL STUDIOS.** A movie and television studio that happens to have the world's first and largest movie-themed amusement park attached, Universal Studios Hollywood is the most popular tourist spot in Tinseltown. Located north of Hollywood in its own municipality of Universal City (complete with police and fire station), the park began as a public tour of the studios in 1964. It has since become a full-fledged amusement park with rides, attractions, and live shows based on some of Universal's classic films. The signature Studio Tour tram brings riders face-to-face with King Kong and Jaws, rattles through a massive earthquake, and wanders past blockbuster sets from America's movie tradition, including *Apollo 13, Jurassic Park,* and *Psycho.* For some, however, the tour plays second fiddle to the park's interactive adventures. While the movie may not have been wildly successful, the live stunts and pyrotechnics at the **Waterworld** spectacular are impressive. Careen through time on Doc Brown's Delorean in **Back to the Future: The Ride,** take a magical bike trip with **E.T.** across the galaxies, or brave the blazing inferno in **Backdraft.** Don't miss **Animal Planet Live!** and the **Special Effects Stages.** *(Take U.S. 101 to the Universal Center Dr. or Landershim Blvd. exits. By MTA rail: exit North Hollywood Red Line at Universal Station. ☎800-UNIVERSAL; www.universalstudios.com. Open July-Aug. M-F 9am-9pm, Sa-Su 9am-10pm; Sept.-June M-F 10am-6pm, Sa-Su 10am-7pm. Shuttles to park leave across the street from the subway and bus stops every 15min. Su-Th 7am-10pm, F-Sa 7am-11pm. $50, under 48 in. $40, under 3 free. Parking $8.)*

UNIVERSAL CITY WALK. This neon-heavy, open-air strip of shopping, dining, movie theaters, and nightlife is the Valley's more colorful but less charming answer to Santa Monica's Third St. Promenade. The mammoth green guitar outside the Hard Rock Cafe, a lurid King Kong sign, and the towering IMAX screen at the Cineplex Odeon cinemas set the tone for the vivid, larger-than-life complex. *(At Universal Studios. ☎818-622-4455; www.citywalkhollywood.com. City Walk parking $8; $2 rebate with purchase of 2 or more movie tickets.)*

MISSION SAN FERNANDO REY DE ESPAÑA. Founded by Father Fermin Lasuen in 1797, the San Fernando Mission is rich with history and is the largest adobe structure in California. The building that stands today is an amazing re-creation of the original destroyed by the 1971 Sylmar earthquake. The grounds, with museum and gift shop, are beautifully kept and definitely worth a visit. *(15101 San Fernando Mission Blvd. ☎361-0186. Open daily 9am-4:30pm. Mass M-Tu and Th-Sa 7:25am, Su 9 and 10:30am. $4, seniors and ages 7-15 $3, under 7 free.)*

MAGIC MOUNTAIN. At the opposite end of the Valley, 40min. north of L.A. in Valencia, is thrill-ride heaven **Magic Mountain.** Not for novices, Six Flags Theme Parks's Magic Mountain contains the most roller coasters in the world.

Its newest addition, **Scream!,** is Southern California's first floorless mega-coaster where your feet dangle in the air as you scream through 4000 ft. of twists, dives, plunges, and loops. **X** flips, spins, and rotates riders 360°, creating a sensation of flying. **Goliath** hits 85 mph and hurtles through an underground tunnel. Other highlights of the park include: **Revolution,** one of the earliest coasters to do a full loop; **Colossus,** California's largest wooden roller coaster; **Viper,** the world's largest looping roller coaster; **Tidal Wave** (stand on the bridge for a soaking); **Deja Vu,** a coaster with a "boomerang" track; the suspended **Batman;** and the 100 mph **Superman** (6½ seconds of weightlessness). Temperatures here frequently soar above 100°F in the summer, so bring a hat, sunblock, and plenty of bottled water. Next door, Six Flags's water park **Hurricane Harbor** features the world's tallest enclosed speed slide. *(Take U.S. 101 N to Rte. 170 N. to I-5 N. to Magic Mountain Pkwy. ☎ 661-255-4100; www.sixflags.com. Open Apr.-Sept. 6 daily; Sept.-Mar. weekends and holidays. Hours vary. $47, seniors and under 48 in. tall $30, under 2 free. Parking $8. Hurricane Harbor: ☎ 661-255-4527. Open May-Sept.; hours vary. $24, seniors and under 48 in. $17, under 2 free. Combined admission to both parks, which can be used on the same day, consecutive days, or for a return visit, $57.)*

AROUND L.A.

Once you leave the city limits of Los Angeles (or, some might argue, even the Westside), the glam factor drops considerably. The cities and neighborhoods that surround L.A. and Orange County are a little hotter and a lot less cool than the urban core, but what these neighboring cities lack in glitz, they more than compensate for with natural beauty. Santa Monica National Recreation Area, just north of Malibu, is a stunning park even by Californian standards, and some of the world's most renowned beaches are an hour's drive south from L.A. in Orange County. Catalina Island, 22 mi. west of Long Beach, offers a peaceful retreat from the manic mainland with beautiful coves perfect for snorkeling. And if all this doesn't cause you to burst out in song, the choreographed merriment of Disneyland just might do the trick.

HIGHLIGHTS OF L.A. AND ORANGE COUNTIES

HUNTINGTON BEACH. Huntington Beach (p. 468) is a classic surfing town, with legendary waves and a lively beach scene.

CATALINA ISLAND. Great hiking, camping, and snorkeling are only 22 mi. offshore on beautiful, rugged Catalina Island (p. 455).

DISNEYLAND. The happiest place on earth. Need we say more? (p. 463).

MISSION SAN JUAN CAPISTRANO. The arched adobe building is among the most beautiful missions in California, as well as a famous roost for swallows (p. 470).

IDYLLWILD. Rock climbers are attracted to Tahquitz and Suicide Rock, while artists head to this beautiful mountain town to gain inspiration and find a kindred community spirit (p. 484).

SOUTH OF L.A.

Catalina Island's sandy campsites and snorkeling spots are the closest SoCal gets to a tropical island paradise. Directly east across the San Pedro Channel, Long Beach's droves of coeds and large GLBT community fuel a growing nightlife and shopping scene.

LONG BEACH ☎ 562

Long Beach (pop. 430,000) is, according to its Chamber of Commerce, "the number one container shipping port in the world," and nothing could be more evident to the first-time visitor. A thriving entertainment district helps make up for the ten-story loading cranes, neon-lighted oil refineries, and container barges that punctuate views of the skyline. Immaculately clean 2nd St. in Belmont Shores offers moderately priced boutique shopping and dining.

The **Parade of a Thousand Lights** features a display of decorated boats along the harbor in mid-December. The **Toyota Grand Prix of Long Beach** (☎436-9953) revs along downtown streets in early April. Summer sounds jazz up downtown during **Jazz Fest** (☎424-0013; www.longbeachjazzfestival.com), in mid-August, and **Long Beach KKJZ Blues Festival** (☎985-1686; www.kkjz.org), in late August or early September. Pro basketball players train during the NBA summer basketball league at the **Long Beach Pyramid** in July (☎985-4949). For more on seasonal events, contact the Convention and Visitors Council (see p. 452).

☐ TRANSPORTATION

Airport: 4100 E. Donald Douglas Dr. (☎570-2619, recorded info 570-2600; www.long-beach.gov/airport.) From I-405 exit Lake Blvd. north; Donald Douglas Dr. is 2 stoplights down on the left. Served by LBT, MTA, OCTA.

Buses: Greyhound, 1498 Long Beach Blvd. (☎218-3011). Open daily 5:30am-9:15pm. Buses run to: **L.A.** ($10); **San Diego** ($15); **San Francisco** ($44).

Public Transportation: Long Beach Transit (LBT), 1963 E. Anaheim St. (☎591-2301), is the nation's safest transit agency. Most buses stop downtown at the newly renovated **Transit Mall,** on 1st St. between Pacific Ave. and Long Beach Blvd. High-tech bus shelters have route maps and video screens with bus info. $0.90, students $0.75, seniors $0.45; transfers $0.10-0.35. **Long Beach Passport,** 1963 E. Anaheim St. (☎591-2301), a separate division of the LBT, offers free service along Ocean Blvd. and Pine Ave. as well as to the Queen Mary (every 15min.). One route runs from downtown to Belmont Shores ($0.90). Most routes operate daily 6am-midnight.

Car Rental: Budget, 249 E. Ocean Blvd. (☎495-0407). Also at Long Beach Airport (☎421-0143). $28 per day, unlimited mileage. 25+ with major credit card. Open M-F 8am-5pm, Sa-Su 8am-4pm.

Bike Rental: Bikestation (☎436-2453), at 1st St. and the Promenade downtown. Bikes $8 per hr., $32 per day. Open M-F 7am-6pm, Sa-Su 10am-5pm.

Auto Repair: AAA Road Service, 4800 Airport Plaza Dr. (☎496-4130, emergency help 800-400-4222). Open M-F 9am-5pm.

✴❷ ORIENTATION AND PRACTICAL INFORMATION

AROUND L.A.

Long Beach is 24 mi. south of downtown L.A. and down the coast from South Bay. By **public transit,** take the Metro Blue Line from LAX, the Green Line from downtown, transferring to the Blue Line at Imperial, or Bus #232 ($1.35). By **car,** take I-405 (San Diego Fwy.) and switch to I-710 S (Long Beach Fwy.), which runs right by the shipping ports into downtown Long Beach.

Long Beach's main tourist attractions lie by the bay. **Pine Avenue,** the backbone of downtown, runs north from the bay, and **Ocean Boulevard** runs west to the boutiques of Belmont Shores. Just south of Ocean Blvd. and east of the Convention and Entertainment Center is an enormous mural of life-sized whales, cited by locals as the largest in the world. **Be cautious** in the inland areas of industrial Long Beach.

Visitor Information: Long Beach Convention and Visitors Bureau, 1 World Trade Ctr., #300 (☎436-3645 or 800-452-7829), at Ocean Blvd. and I-710 (Long Beach Fwy.). Tons of help and free brochures. Open M-F 8am-5pm.

Laundromat: Super Suds, 250 Alamitos Ave. (☎436-1859). Video games and jungle gym. Wash $1.25 per lb., dry $0.75. Open daily 7am-10am.

Police: 100 Long Beach Blvd. (☎435-6711).

Post Office: 300 N. Long Beach Blvd. (☎628-1303). Open M-F 8:30am-5pm, Sa 9am-2pm. **Postal Code:** 90802.

☐ ACCOMMODATIONS

Though good budget accommodations are scarce in Long Beach, the city is close enough to be a reasonable daytrip from L.A. Nevertheless, there are a few reasonably priced surf motels along Ocean Blvd. between Belmont Shores and downtown. The **Beach Plaza Hotel ❹,** 2010 E. Ocean Blvd., at Cherry Ave., has a bright turquoise exterior that matches the ocean. Spacious, clean rooms have cable TV, fridge, and large windows to let in the light. (☎437-0771. Pool and private beach access. Parking included. Reserve ahead. Doubles $70-90, with ocean view and kitchenette $90-170.) A less expensive option, **Beach Inn Motel ❸,** 823 E. 3rd St., has basic rooms with fridge, satellite TV, and A/C. (☎437-3464. $5 deposit for in-room phone. Parking included. Doubles $70, with hot tub $80.)

FOOD AND NIGHTLIFE

The panoply of eateries lining **Pine Avenue** between 1st and 3rd St. aren't all expensive, despite the valets along the sidewalk. There are also budget-smart eateries in **Belmont Shores.** Buy cheap produce at the **open-air market** on Promenade St. (F 10am-4pm.) Long Beach supports a vibrant blues and jazz scene; try the **Blue Cafe,** 210 Promenade St. (☎983-7111), on any night, or **Captain's Quarters,** 5205 E. Pacific Coast Hwy. (☎498-2461), on Friday and Saturday nights. Most **gay and lesbian** nightspots center around **East Broadway** and **Falcon Avenue.** The 16-screen **AMC Theatres,** 245 Pine Sq. (☎435-4262), is centrally located.

The Shorehouse Cafe, 5271 E. 2nd St. (☎433-2266), in Belmont Shores. Wicker beach furniture and wooden ceiling fans add to a comfy diner setting where you can order "anything at any time." The menu is vast and vegetarian-friendly. Great for lunch or late-night meals. Omelettes made with your choice of fillings from $6.45. Stone-hearth pizzas ($13-17) are a house favorite. Pasta $13-15. Open 24hr. ❸

The Omelette Inn, 108 W. 3rd St. (☎437-5625). Choose your own filling at this restaurant devoted to those delightful egg pockets. The health-conscious can choose egg white omelettes, brown rice, and veggie bacon strips. There's real hickory-smoked bacon, too. Create-your-own omelettes $5.50-8. Sandwiches and burgers $5-7. Early-bird specials ($4.50) served until 9am. Open daily 7am-2:30pm. ❷

The Library, 3418 E. Broadway (☎433-2393). This bookstore in the middle of Long Beach's gay neighborhood serves attitude with its coffee. Books line the walls (from Danielle Steel to Bertolt Brecht; $1-10) and studious types settle into plush antique seats. Purchase a magazine or newspaper from their attached newsstand to read while you sip on gourmet coffee ($1.50) or Italian sodas ($2.25). The huge assortment of cakes wins many loyal fans. Live music F-Su 9pm. Sa-Su breakfast omelette bar 7am-1pm. Open M-Th 6am-noon, F 6am-1am, Sa 7am-1am, Su 7am-midnight. ❶

Alegría, 115 Pine Ave. (☎436-3388; www.alegriacocinalatina.com). Latin cooking and dancing in an excruciatingly hip Miró-inspired interior. The menu is a bit pricey, but the musical entertainment attracts friendly and dance-happy crowds. Tapas $2.25-7. Check the website for guest performers and events. Open M-W 11:30am-11pm, Th 11:30-midnight, F 11:30am-2am, Sa noon-2am, Su noon-11pm. ❹

Shannon's Bayshore, 5335 E. 2nd St. (☎433-5901), Belmont Shores. With California State University Long Beach right up the road, this neighborhood bar by day (the longest bar in the US, with long lines at the door to match) becomes one of the liveliest of 2nd St.'s many night-spots. For decades, drunk Long Beach couples have carved their names into the bar. As you carve, swig Shoot-the-Root ($3.50), a shot of root beer schnapps in a cup of beer. Pool table $0.50. Happy hour daily 11am-7pm; drafts and well drinks $2.75. Free food M-F 4-7pm. Open M-F 11am-2am, Sa-Su 9am-2am. ❶

SIGHTS

Shipping is Long Beach's central industry; tourism is clearly an afterthought, and beach life is, well, not a thought at all. Waves and beachgoers here are minimal due to the breakwater of the busy port. The shipping center does have some attractions, though.

QUEEN MARY. The legendary 1934 Cunard luxury liner has been transformed into a swanky hotel with art exhibits, historical displays, and upscale bars. There are still remnants of the days when she was a troop ship called "The Grey Ghost." During WWII, she carried the greatest number of passengers of any floating vessel: 15,740 troops and 943 crew. The Grey Ghost was so crucial to the Allied war effort that Hitler offered the highest honors to anyone who sank her. A tour of the ship is worthwhile; you won't be able to see more than the engine room, deck, and gift shops otherwise. *(At the end of Queen's Way Dr.* ☎ *435-3511; www.queenmary.com. Open daily 10am-6pm. $23, seniors and military $20, children $12. Free self-guided tour maps. Guided tours are an extra $5, ages 5-11 $3.)* A Cold War-era Russian submarine code-named **Scorpion** is moored right next to the Queen Mary. *(From Rte. 710 S, take a right onto Queen's Way and follow the signs. Combined admission $28, seniors and military $25, ages 5-11 $17.)*

LONG BEACH AQUARIUM OF THE PACIFIC. A $117 million, 156,735 sq. ft. celebration of the world's largest and most diverse body of water, the aquarium is situated atop one of the world's busiest and most polluted harbors. Meet the dazzling creatures of the deep that struggle to coexist with Long Beach's flotsam, jetsam, and effluvium. Among the most striking of the 12,000 displaced inhabitants are the unborn sharks floating about in semitransparent embryos. The seals, sea lions, otters, sharks, and jellyfish are also sure to please. There are shark feedings at 11am and 2pm and regular performances by the seals and sea lions. *(100 Aquarium Way.* ☎ *590-3100; www.aquariumofpacific.org. Follow Rte. 710 S into downtown, take a right on Queen's Way, and follow the signs. Open daily 9am-6pm. Animal Vision 3-D Movie every 30min. $19, ages 3-11 $11, seniors $15.)*

MUSEUM OF LATIN AMERICAN ART. The MoLAA specializes in showcasing artists who are well known in their own countries but not in the US. Do not be put off by the drab exterior; superb contemporary art and brilliant colors await inside. Renovations are currently underway. *(628 Alamitos Ave. From downtown, take 3rd St. east and make a left on Alamitos Ave.* ☎ *437-1689; www.molaa.com. Open Tu-Sa 11:30am-7pm, Su 11am-6pm. Free family art workshops Su noon-2pm. $5, seniors and students $3, under 12 free.)*

LONG BEACH MUSEUM OF ART. Initially built at the turn of the 20th century by famed Pasadena architects Greene and Greene, the Long Beach Museum of Art is now augmented by a new building in the style of the original. It hosts a small permanent collection of impressionistic paintings by Jean Mannheim, Maurice Braun, and George Henry Melcher, but most of the museum is devoted to rotating exhibits and videos by its grant recipients. Seaside Jazz concerts are hosted in the summer. *(2300 Ocean Blvd., on the waterfront. From L.A., take Rte. 710 S to Shoreline Dr. and make a right on Ocean Blvd.* ☎ *439-2119. Open Tu-Su 11am-5pm. $5, students $4; 1st F of the month free. Summer garden concerts Th 7-10pm. $27.75.)*

NAPLES ISLAND. Waterside cottages, curvy and narrow streets, peaceful canals, and footbridges. Sound like Venice? Almost. Arthur Parson, an American real estate developer, began creating this picture-perfect Italian community (with the obvious omission of Italians) in the early 20th century. Today it's an ideal place for a dusk stroll or a romantic gondola ride. *(Take 2nd St. east from downtown. For moonlight cruises, call* ☎ *433-9595; www.gondolagetawayinc.com. 1hr. bread-and-cheese cruise for 2 $65.)* It also harbors **Alamitos Bay,** from whence the *S.S. Minnow* set sail on its infamous 3hr. tour, according to the opening sequence of *Gilligan's Island.*

BEACHES. The family-oriented beach of **Belmont Shores,** Long Beach's upscale, uptown neighborhood, is reputed to be the city's best. Park at meters near the intersection of Ocean Blvd. and La Verne St. *($0.25 for 15min.; 10hr. max.)*

CATALINA ISLAND   ☎310

The idyllic island retreat of Catalina sits only 22 mi. off the coast of Southern California. Hills, rugged canyons and gorges, secluded beaches, unbeatable snorkeling and diving, and wild bison combine with crystal-clear air and water to create a splendid escape from the mainland's hustle and bustle. The island finds no need for traffic lights, since cars are rare and most people use golf carts and bikes instead. Avalon, the island's largest town (1 sq. mi.; pop. 3500), is home to a casino without gambling, a memorial without a dead body, and a 3rd St. without a 1st or 2nd, as well as the majority of the island's restaurants and hotels. To truly experience Catalina's beautiful and unspoiled land, head inland with any of the various tour companies or purchase a bike permit and set out on your own (hiking passes are free). The island's natural beauty is preserved mostly by the efforts of the Catalina Island Conservancy, a non-profit group that owns 88% of the island and strives to ensure the survival of the island's rare and endangered species.

▐▀ TRANSPORTATION

Ferries: One way to get to Catalina is via the **Catalina Express** (☎800-618-5533; www.catalinaexpress.com), which runs to either **Avalon** or **Two Harbors.** Shuttles depart to Avalon from **San Pedro** (1hr.), **Long Beach** (1hr.), and **Dana Point** (1½hr.); and to Two Harbors from **San Pedro** (1½hr.). Though there are over 30 departures each day, reservations should be made in advance. Round-trip $48, ages 2-11 $38, seniors $44, under 2 $3. **Catalina Explorer,** 34671 Puerto Pl. (☎877-432-6276; www.catalinaexplorerco.com), goes to Avalon and Two Harbors from **Dana Point** (1½hr.; departs daily 9am, returns 5pm; $41, seniors $37.50, ages 3-11 $31, under 2 $5). **Catalina Passenger Service,** 400 Main St. (☎800-830-7744; www.catalinainfo.com), in Balboa, ferries vacationers on the *Catalina Flyer* catamaran to Avalon from **Newport Beach** (1¼hr.; departs daily 9am, returns 4:30pm; round-trip $44, ages 3-12 $27, seniors $41, under 2 $3).

Public Transportation: Santa Catalina Island Company runs a safari bus between **Avalon** and **Two Harbors,** stopping at a few campgrounds en route (2hr.; departs daily 10:30am, returns 4pm; $20). Call the Visitor Bureau (☎510-1520) for more info. The **Island Hopper,** a tram that leaves from Catalina Ave. between 3rd and Beacon St., will take you to the Botanical Gardens or the Casino ($1.50).

Bike and Golf Cart Rentals: Brown's Bikes, 107 Pebbly Beach Rd. (☎510-0986), 360 ft. from the boat dock. Single-speed bikes $5 per hr., $12 per day; 21-speed mountain bikes $9/$20; 6-speed tandems $12/$30. Open daily summer 9am-6pm; winter 9am-5pm. **Island Rentals,** 125 Pebbly Beach Rd. (☎510-1456). Golf carts $30 per hr. with $30 deposit. 25+. Open daily summer 8am-6pm; winter 8am-5pm.

▟▐ ORIENTATION AND PRACTICAL INFORMATION

Visitor Information: Chamber of Commerce and Visitor Bureau (☎510-1520; www.catalina.com), on the left side of Avalon's Pleasure Pier. Open summer daily 8am-5pm; winter M-Sa 8am-5pm, Su 9am-3pm. **Catalina Island Conservancy** (☎510-2595). This nonprofit group owns 88% of Catalina. Hiking permits (free), maps ($0.25), and trail advice available here. Open daily 8:30am-5pm. **Biking permits** ($60, families $85) are required outside of Avalon. They can be obtained at the Conservancy, as well as the Catalina airport and the Two Harbors Visitors Center (☎510-4205).

Tours: Santa Catalina Island Company (**SCIC;** ☎800-322-3434; www.scico.com) is ubiquitous on the island and runs major sightseeing tours, as well as campgrounds, hotels, and restaurants. Tram tours $10-80. Boat trips $25-100.

AROUND L.A.

AROUND L.A.

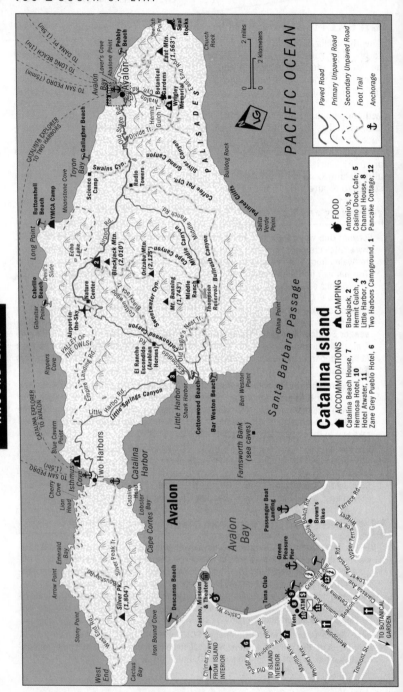

PACIFIC OCEAN

Paved Road
Primary Unpaved Road
Secondary Unpaved Road
Foot Trail
⚓ Anchorage

Santa Barbara Passage

Catalina Island

▲ ACCOMMODATIONS

Catalina Beach House, 7
Hermosa Hotel, 10
Hotel Atwater, 11
Zane Grey Pueblo Hotel, 6

▲ CAMPING

Blackjack, 2
Hermit Gulch, 4
Little Harbor, 3
Two Harbors Campground, 1

🍴 FOOD

Antonio's, 9
Casino Dock Cafe, 5
Channel House, 8
Pancake Cottage, 12

Avalon

Avalon Bay

Passenger Boat Landing
Green Pleasure Pier
Descanso Beach
Casino, Museum & Theater
Tuna Club
Brown's Bikes

2 miles
2 kilometers

TO LONG BEACH (1hr)
TO DANA PT. (1.5hr)
TO SAN PEDRO (15min)
CATALINA EXPLORER TO TWO HARBORS

ATM: US Bank, 303 Crescent Ave. **SCI Information Center** ATM across from Green Pier on Catalina St.

Laundromat: Catalina Coin Wash, in the Metropole Market Place next to Vons. Wash $1.50, dry $0.25 per 15min. Open 7am-10pm.

Showers: Public facilities on Casino Way across from the Tuna Club. $1 per 5min. Towel $1. Assorted preening implements $0.25-3 each. Open daily high season 7am-7pm; low season 7-11am and 3-5pm.

Police: ☎510-0174.

Medical Services: Hospital ☎510-0700.

Post Office: 118 Metropole St. (☎310-510-0084), in the Arcade Bldg., between Metropole and Sumner St. in Avalon. **Postal Code:** 90704.

PHONE CODES. All 7-digit phone numbers on Catalina begin with **510.** Locals may often give phone numbers with only four digits (1234), requiring confused mainlanders to supply the missing ones (☎510-1234).

ACCOMMODATIONS

Hoteliers on the island know they have a captive audience; in summer, accommodation prices skyrocket way out of budget range. Though inexpensive lodgings do exist, securing them requires advance planning. On most summer weekends, and some weekdays, there are no accommodations available on the island at all. **Call as far in advance as possible.**

Catalina Beach House, 200 Marilla Ave. (☎510-1078 or 800-974-6835). One of the island's oldest hotels (est. 1912), tucked into the countryside on a hill a couple blocks above the ocean. Rooms with TV, VCR, kitchenette, and fan. Some have hot tubs. Free video library. Doubles in summer $60-70; in winter $35-45. ❹

Zane Grey Pueblo Hotel, 199 Chimes Tower Rd. (☎510-0966 or 510-1520). A Hopi Indian-style pueblo built by local literary great Zane Grey in 1926. Now a delightful B&B perched on a hillside with spectacular ocean views and grounds (including a pool). Living room with fireplace. 16 rooms have fan, queen-size beds, wicker furniture, and private baths; some have balconies. Rooms Apr.-Oct. $135-179; Nov.-Mar. $59-110. ❹

Hermosa Hotel, 131 Metropole Ave. (☎510-1010). This hotel's motto, "sleep cheap," is a welcome sentiment in pricey Avalon. Clean, inexpensive rooms, some with ocean views, in a relaxed atmosphere maintained by the friendly management. 18+. 2-night min. stay on weekends. Doubles $25-65, with bath $35-85, with kitchen $55-110. ❷

Hotel Atwater, 125 Sumner Ave. (☎800-322-3434), half a block from the ocean. The inexpensive rooms are small but clean, with cable TV and fans. Rooms in summer from $76; in low season from $44. ❹

CAMPING

While no wilderness camping is permitted, the five campgrounds on Catalina each offer distinct camping experiences. You must check in at Two Harbor Visitors Center at the foot of the pier (Two Harbors is 14 mi. west of Avalon). Reservations (required) for any of the five campgrounds should be made at www.catalina.com/camping. A two-night minimum stay applies at Hermit Gulch and Little Harbor from July to August and on holiday weekends. Unless otherwise noted, the camping charge is $12 per adult and $6 per child; discounts may be available from November to March. Hermit Gulch is closest to Avalon, but you can get closer to

AROUND L.A.

THE BIG SPLURGE

DOUBLE THE MINT, DOUBLE THE FUN

In 1921, William Wrigley, Chicago Cubs owner and bubble gum magnate, built a home on Catalina Island, naming the house and the mountain on which it was built after his wife, Ada. The site of the house was carefully chosen to catch the very first morning light and the last rays of the setting sun. In his abode atop Mt. Ada, Mr. Wrigley entertained Presidents Calvin Coolidge and Warren Harding, and the Prince of Wales.

These days, Wrigley's gorgeous white-columned and green-roofed Georgian colonial home has been converted into the luxurious **Inn on Mt. Ada,** where anyone can enjoy delicious views previously reserved for politicians and members of the upper crust. On clear days, the view stretches across the 85 mi. San Pedro Channel to Long Beach.

Most of the spacious rooms have ocean views and fireplaces (one also has a private deck), and run from $300-640. While the price may be steep, it includes breakfast, lunch, fresh fruit, champagne, and freshly baked cookies. Guests are also given golf carts to make the 3min. drive into Avalon, or just to zoom around in.

398 Wrigley Rd. (☎510-2030). No children under 14. 2-night min. stay on weekends.

nature at the other four campgrounds, all run by **Two Harbors Management** (☎510-2800). To get to any of these sites from Avalon, take the shuttle bus; you may have to hike 1½ mi. from the nearest stop.

Little Harbor, southeast of Two Harbors, on the western side of the island. 16 incredible beach sites offer a secluded cove, potable water, cold showers, picnic tables, and chemical toilets. ❶

Hermit Gulch, a 1½ mi. walk inland from the Avalon boat landing. Populated by carousing campers. Hot showers, flush toilets, a coin microwave, barbecues, a vending machine, and a limited number of stoves and lanterns ($5). No gear, no problem—they also rent teepees ($30), tents ($10-16), and sleeping bags ($11). ❶

Blackjack, accessible by Airport Shuttle, Safari bus, or a 9 mi. hike from Avalon. 10 large, secluded pine forest sites near the island's highest point. Cold showers, running water, and fire rings, but prepare for large herds of buffalo ambling by. ❶

Two Harbors Campground, ¼ mi. east of Two Harbors. The most popular beach camping, with 45 campsites, cold showers, chemical toilets, and rental gear. Tents $10-25; sleeping bags $11. 2- and 4-bunk "Catalina Cabins" (Nov.-May) $30. ❶

⬛ FOOD

Avalon, centered on **Crescent Avenue,** is Catalina's largest town and is the island's main restaurant and recreation scene. Crescent Ave. curves along Catalina harbor from the pier, where cross-channel boats arrive at the iconic Avalon Casino. Eateries and bars line the street—a pedestrian-only walkway—affording diners a quiet opportunity to enjoy the sand and bottle-blue water. **Green Pleasure Pier** intersects Crescent Ave. and bustles with fish 'n' chips joints and cotton-candy vendors. Many of the larger restaurants host live music and karaoke nightly, and inexpensive food is easy to find. For groceries, visit **Vons,** 121 Metropole Ave. (☎510-0280. Open daily 7am-10pm.)

🍸 **Antonio's,** 230 Crescent Ave. (☎510-0008). The seaside home of the island's best pizza. Walls are adorned with colorfully defaced one-dollar bills, and floors are strewn with peanut shells. Outside seating on the deck. Huge pizzas $12-17. The Catalina Calzone ($11) is stuffed with spinach, ricotta, and jack cheese. Open Su-Th 8am-11 pm, F-Sa 8am-midnight. ❷

Casino Dock Cafe, 2 Casino Way (☎510-2755), at the end of the Via Casino. In the shadow of the Casino overlooking the placid harbor; one of the best views in

Avalon. Burgers $5-9. Swordfish sandwich $8. Beer $3-4, pitcher $11. Live music in summer Sa-Su 3-6pm. Open M-F 8am-5pm, Sa-Su 8:30am-6:30pm. ❶

Pancake Cottage, 118 Catalina Ave. (☎510-0726). Always packed with hungry islanders, but the Breakfast Special (2 pancakes, 2 eggs, 3 strips of bacon; $6) or stack of buttermilk pancakes (3 for $5) justifies the wait. Sandwiches $6-8. Open M-F 6:30am-1:30pm, Sa-Su 6am-1:30pm. No credit cards. ❷

Channel House, 205 Crescent Ave. (☎510-1617). Continental cuisine in an elegant dining hall or on a secluded patio overlooking the sea. Lunch $8-16. Dinner $15-25. Full bar. Early-bird specials M-Th 4:30-6pm. Open M-Th 11am-3pm and 4:30-9pm, F 11am-3pm and 5-9:30pm, Sa-Su 10am-3pm and 5-9:30pm. ❹

👁 🏔 SIGHTS AND OUTDOOR ACTIVITIES

The **Santa Catalina Island Company** runs a slew of tours. The **Skyline Tour** or the more complete **Inland Motor Tour** are your best bets; go to the Discovery Tours Center at Catalina and Crescent Ave. (Skyline Tour $29, seniors $26, children $14.50; Inland Motor Tour $49.50/$44.50/$24.75.) The best way to see underwater life is to **snorkel.** Before going down below, gather dive gear at **Catalina Diver's Supply,** on the lefthand side of Pleasure Pier. (☎510-0330 or 800-353-0330. Mask, snorkel, and fin package $7 for 2hr., $12 per day; wet suit $11/$15.) Just east of Avalon, **Lover's Cove** is the most convenient snorkeling spot and the best for novices and those who wish to avoid strong sea currents. It is also an excellent place to eavesdrop on the tips shouted out by snorkeling guides. The best place to snorkel among the bright orange garibaldi is in the kelp forests off **Casino Point.** On rare occasions divers may swim among leopard sharks. Rent near the cove from **Catalina Snorkeling Adventures.** (☎510-8558. Open Apr.-Oct. Mask, snorkel, and fins $3 per hr., $6 per day; wet suits $6/$12. Deposit required.) For a slightly less crowded beach and fewer boats, walk past the Casino to **Descanso Beach** (day use $1-2). You can rent equipment just before the beach at **Descanso Beach Ocean Sports.** (☎510-1226. Mask and snorkel $3.50 per hr., $6 per day; fins $3.50/$6; wet suits $6.50/$12; single kayak $15-48.) Alternatives to snorkeling include **Glass Bottom Boat Trips** (30min.; $10.50-13.50, seniors $5.25-6.75, ages 2-11 $5.25-6.75) or the fantastic submarine **Undersea Tour** (45min.; $10.50-13.50, ages 2-11 $5.25-6.75, seniors $9.50-12.25).

The **Casino Building,** at the end of Crescent Ave., was never a gambling den; chewing gum magnate and former owner of the island William Wrigley, Jr. built the $2 million dance hall in 1929 (*casino* means "gathering place" in Italian). The architectural tour of the building is well worth it. (☎510-7400. Tours $13.50, seniors $12.25, children $7.) You can also sneak a peek at the building's elegant Art Deco murals by catching a film in the 1000-seat **Avalon Theater;** F-Sa showings include a free concert on the antique page organ. (☎510-0179. Films M-Th 7pm, F-Su 7 and 9:45pm. $7.50, seniors and ages 3-11 $5.) The casino hosts occasional **jazz concerts** and a **New Year's Eve bash** that recreates the Catalina of the 30s and 40s, when it was a paradise for the sultans of swing. Ask about June's **Silent Film Festival** (for tickets, call ☎510-2414) and the **Halloween Costume Ball** (☎888-330-5252). Beneath the casino is the **Catalina Island Museum,** with exhibits on island history, Native American inhabitants, and author/filmmaker Zane Grey. (☎510-2414. Open daily 10am-5pm. $3, ages 6-15 $1, seniors $2, under 6 free.) Zane Grey's **Avalon pueblo** is now a hotel (p. 457) overlooking the Casino from the high bluffs above.

At the end of Avalon Canyon Rd. (2 mi. outside Avalon), you can pick up the hilly **Hermit Gulch Trail,** a 3½ mi. loop past canyons, secluded coast, and the monolithic **Wrigley Memorial.** The memorial no longer holds the chewing gum magnate's remains, which were removed from the island in the 1940s to L.A.'s Forest Lawn Cemetery. Past the memorial are the **Botanical Gardens.** (☎510-2288. Open daily

8am-5pm. Suggested donation $3.) The gardens, covering 38 acres, contain eight plant species native to Catalina, as well as a vast, needle-filled cactus garden with sweeping Pacific views that extend all the way to the mainland on clear days. The memorial and gardens are accessible by walking straight up Avalon Canyon Rd. or by taking the **Island Hopper** (see p. 455) from Avalon. **Bison and wild boars** inhabit the area along the 4 mi. **Blackjack-Cape Reservoir Loop.** The two or three hundred buffalo here are the descendants of the 25 originally ferried over for the filming of Zane Grey's 1924 *The Vanishing American.* The rigorous 8 mi. **Blackjack Trail** leads to Little Harbor. Pick up either of the last two trails at the Blackjack Junction, accessible by the **airport shuttle** ($14.50 round-trip).

ORANGE COUNTY

Directly south of L.A. County lies Orange County (pop. 2.9 million). Composed of 34 cities, it is a microcosm of Southern California: dazzling sandy shoreline, bronzed beach bums, oversized shopping malls, homogenous suburban neighborhoods, and frustrating traffic snarls. As one of California's staunchest Republican enclaves, Orange County (and no, they don't actually call it "The O.C.") supports big business, and has the economy and the multi-million-dollar hillside mansions oozing luxury cars and disaffected teens to prove it. It is also one of the safest areas in the country.

Disneyland, the stronghold of the Walt Disney Company's ever-expanding empire, is the premier inland attraction, home to dancing cartoon characters in the midst of the suburban sprawl. The self-proclaimed "Happiest Place On Earth" is now even happier as a result of the construction of California Adventure and Downtown Disney. Orange County's aesthetic appeal increases as one moves closer to the shore. A drive down the Pacific Coast Highway (PCH to locals) from Huntington Beach to Laguna Beach is well worth it. The coast runs the gamut from the budget- and party-friendly surf burg of Huntington Beach to the opulent excess of Newport Beach and the artistic vibe of Laguna. A little farther south lies the quiet mission of San Juan Capistrano, set amid rolling hills that spill onto the laid-back beaches of Dana Point and San Clemente.

▐ TRANSPORTATION

Airport: John Wayne Airport, 18601 Airport Way (☎949-252-5200), in Santa Ana. 20min. from Anaheim. Domestic flights only.

Trains: Amtrak (☎800-USA-RAIL/872-7245; www.amtrakcalifornia.com) stations, from north to south: **Fullerton,** 120 E. Santa Fe Ave. (☎714-992-0530); **Santa Ana,** 1000 E. Santa Ana Blvd. (☎714-547-8389); **Irvine,** 15215 Barranca Pkwy. (☎949-753-9713); **San Juan Capistrano,** 26701 Verdugo St. (☎949-240-2972).

Buses: Greyhound (☎800-231-2222) has 3 stations in the area. **Anaheim,** 100 W. Winston Rd. (☎714-999-1256), 3 blocks south of Disneyland. Open daily 6:30am-9:15pm. **Santa Ana,** 1000 E. Santa Ana Blvd. (☎714-542-2215). Open daily 6:15am-8:30pm. **San Clemente,** 2421 S. El Camino Real. (☎949-366-2646). Open daily 7am-9pm.

Public Transit: Orange County Transportation Authority (**OCTA;** ☎714-636-7433; www.octa.net.), 550 S. Main St., in Orange. Thorough service is useful for getting from Santa Ana and Fullerton Amtrak stations to Disneyland and for beach-hopping along the coast. Long Beach, in L.A. County, serves as the terminus for several OCTA lines. Bus #1 travels the coast from Long Beach to San Clemente (every hr. until 8pm); #25, 33, and 35 travel from Fullerton to Huntington Beach; #91 goes from Laguna Hills to San Clemente. $1, day pass $2.50.) **Info center** open M-F 6am-8pm, Sa-Su 8am-5pm. **MTA Info** (☎213-626-4455 or 800-266-6883) available by phone daily 5am-10:45pm. MTA buses run from L.A. to Disneyland and Knott's Berry Farm.

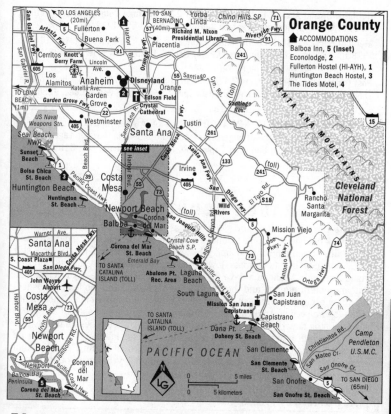

Orange County

▲ ACCOMMODATIONS
Balboa Inn, **5 (Inset)**
Econolodge, **2**
Fullerton Hostel (HI-AYH), **1**
Huntington Beach Hostel, **3**
The Tides Motel, **4**

AROUND L.A.

🛈 PRACTICAL INFORMATION

Visitor Information:

Anaheim Area Visitors and Convention Bureau, 800 W. Katella Ave. (☎714-765-8888; www.ana-heimoc.org), in Anaheim Convention Ctr. Lodging and dining guides. Open M-F 8am-5pm.

Huntington Beach Conference and Visitors Bureau, 301 Main St. (☎714-969-3492 or 800-729-6232; www.hbvisit.com). Good maps and brochures. Open M-F 9am-5pm.

Newport Harbor Area Chamber of Commerce, 1470 Jamboree Rd. (☎949-729-4400), in Newport Beach. Free maps and info. Open M-F 8am-5pm. 24hr. automated answering service.

Newport Visitors Bureau, 110 Newport Center Dr., #120 (☎949-719-6100 or 800-942-6278), in Newport Beach. Eager-to-help staff, maps of area attractions, and events brochures. Open M-F 8am-5pm.

Laguna Beach Visitors Bureau, 252 Broadway (☎949-497-9229). Open M-F 9am-5pm, Sa 10am-4pm, Su noon-4pm.

San Clemente Visitors Center, 1100 N. El Camino Real (☎949-492-1131). Open M-F 8:30am-5pm, Sa 9am-2pm, Su 9am-1pm.

GLBT Resources: Gay-Lesbian Community Center, 12832 Garden Grove Blvd., Ste. A (☎714-534-0862), in Garden Grove. Open M-F 9am-9pm.

Police: Anaheim, 425 S. Harbor Blvd. (☎714-765-1900). **Huntington Beach,** 2000 Main St. (☎714-960-8811).

Hotlines: Sexual Assault Hotline, ☎714-957-2737. **Orange County Referral Hotline,** ☎714-894-4242. **Surf and Weather Conditions,** ☎213-554-1212.

Medical Services: St. Jude Medical Center, 101 E. Valencia Mesa Dr. (☎714-871-3280), in Fullerton. **Lestonnac Free Clinic,** 1215 E. Chapman Ave. (☎714-633-4600), in Orange. Hours vary; call for an appointment.

Post Office: 701 N. Loara St. (☎714-520-2639 or 800-275-8777), 1 block north of Anaheim Plaza, in Anaheim. Open M-F 8:30am-5pm, Sa 9am-3pm. **Postal Code:** 92803.

ORANGE COUNTY AREA CODES. 714 in Anaheim, Fullerton, Fountain Valley, Santa Ana, Orange, and Garden Grove; **949** in Newport, Laguna, Irvine, Mission Viejo, San Juan Capistrano, and surrounding areas; **310** in Seal Beach.

INLAND ORANGE COUNTY   ☎714

In the late 1950s, Anaheim (pop. 300,000) was considered the city of the future. Californians flocked to Orange County's capital city, where booming industry and Uncle Walt's dream machine created jobs and revenue galore. Today, people still pour into the city, but the tourists flowing in far outnumber the residents, and Disneyland has made Anaheim a slave to the tourist dollar. Still, the city is a true hub of fun and entertainment, and though most roads in Anaheim do lead to Disneyland, a few other (mostly Disney-related) venues pull their weight. The Mighty Ducks play hockey at Arrowhead Pond and the Angels play baseball at Edison Field, while the new House of Blues and The Grove attract the best in music. Disney recently built a new theme park adjacent to Disneyland, called "California Adventure," which, combined with the new "Downtown Disney," provides an enclave of restaurants, shops, and shows. Without Mickey, Orange County comes dangerously close to resembling Middle America.

█ ACCOMMODATIONS

Countless budget chain motels and garden-variety "clean, comfortable rooms" flank Disneyland on all sides. Keep watch for family and group rates posted on marquees, and seek out establishments offering the **3-for-2 passport** (3 days of Disney for the price of 2). The good news about the construction of California Adventure is that it inspired hotel owners to revamp their establishments; the bad news is that hotel prices have gone up as a result.

Fullerton Hostel (HI-AYH), 1700 N. Harbor Blvd. (☎738-3721), in Fullerton, 10min. north of Disneyland. Shuttle from L.A. Airport $21. OCTA bus #43 runs along Harbor Blvd. to Disneyland. In the woods and away from the thematic craziness of nearby Anaheim, this hostel has an international feel. The enthusiastic, resourceful staff invites questions but forbids drinking. Kitchen, relaxing living room, communal bathrooms. Linen $2. Laundry (wash $0.75, dry $0.75). 7-night max. stay. Check-in 8am-11pm. Reservations encouraged. Open June-Sept. Single-sex and coed dorms $18.70, nonmembers $21.70. ❷

Econolodge, 1126 W. Katella Ave. (☎533-4505; www.econolodge.com), in Anaheim at the southwest corner of Disneyland. One of what seems like a trillion chain motels, this Econolodge has clean, newly revamped rooms with HBO, phone, and A/C. Balconies offer a good view of Disney's nightly fireworks. Small pool, many kids. Reservations recommended. Rooms $50-150. 10% discount with Internet reservations. ❹

🚶 FOOD

Resist the siren call of the countless fast-food places near Disneyland and try one of the inexpensive ethnic restaurants in strip malls. Many specialize in takeout or will deliver to your motel room.

Rutabegorz, 211 N. Pomona Blvd. (☎738-9339; www.rutabegorz.com), in Fullerton. Also at 264 N. Glassell St. (☎633-3260), in Orange; and 158 W. Main St. (☎731-9807), in Tustin. With a name derived from the often unloved rutabaga, this hippie-*cum*-hipster joint has a 20-page recycled newsprint menu. Crepes, curries, quesadillas, and club sandwiches are all fresh and veggie-heavy. Heaping salads with homemade dressings $4-9. Mexican casserole $7. Smoothies, veggie juices, and coffee drinks $2-4. Open M-Th 11am-10pm, F-Sa 11am-11pm, Su 4-9pm. ❷

Angelo & Vinci's Cafe Ristorante, 550 N. Harbor Blvd. (☎879-4022), in Fullerton. Padded red chairs, iron-rod table lamps, and indoor awnings are all part of the cluttered Sicilian motif. The food is unmistakably the stuff of family recipes (Cannelloni Vinci $11.50), with more than enough to feed the family at the lunch buffet ($6). Su champagne brunch 11am-3pm ($10). Open Su-Th 11am-9pm, F-Sa 11am-10pm. ❸

Inka Anaheim, 400 S. Euclid Blvd. (☎772-2263), in Anaheim. Locals congregate under a backlit mural of Machu Picchu while devouring great Peruvian food. The *arroz con pollo* (rice with chicken; $8) is delicious. *Mazzomorra morada* (purple corn pudding; $3.50) makes an excellent dessert. Occasional live Andean music F-Sa 7:30-10pm. Open M-Th 11:30am-9pm, F 11:30am-11pm, Sa noon-11pm, Su noon-9pm. ❷

Watson Drugs and Soda Fountain, 116 E. Chapman (☎663-1050; www.watson-drug.com), in Orange. Established in 1899, the oldest drugstore in Orange County has been the set for a number of movies, including Tom Hank's *That Thing You Do.* Located in Old Towne Orange, the soda fountain and surrounding streets are a trip back in time. Serves burgers ($5-7) and sweet treats like milkshakes and ice-cream sodas ($3-4). Open M-Sa 6:30am-9pm, Su 8am-6pm. ❷

👁 🎭 SIGHTS AND ENTERTAINMENT

DISNEYLAND

Main entrance on Harbor Blvd., and a smaller one on Katella Ave. By car: take I-5 to Katella Ave. From L.A., MTA bus #460 travels from 4th and Flower St. to the Disneyland Hotel (about 1hr; service to the hotel begins at 4:53am, service back to L.A. runs until 1:20am). Free shuttles link the hotel to Disneyland's portals, as does the Disneyland monorail. The park is also served by Airport Service, OCTA, Long Beach Transit, and the Gray Line (see p. 460). Parking $8. ☎781-4565; www.disneyland.com. Disneyland open Su-Th 8am-11pm, F-Sa 8am-midnight; hours may vary so call ahead. California Adventure open Su-Th 9am-10pm, F-Sa 9am-10:30pm. Disneyland passport $50, ages 3-9 $40, under 3 free; allows repeated single-day entrance. California Adventure passport prices are the same as Disneyland's. Combination ticket $70, ages 3-9 $60. Lockers are located west of the ticket booths and at the lost and found facility on Main Street, USA, in Disneyland.

Disneyland calls itself the "Happiest Place on Earth," and the daily throngs of visitors seem to agree. After a full day there, your wallet, however, may not. In terms of lines, weekday and low-season visitors will undoubtedly be the happiest, but the clever can wait for parades to distract children from the epic lines. Walt's innovative Disney team has finally arrived at a line-busting solution: the **FastPass** program. Available at most major rides, FastPass lets you pick up a reservation ticket when you insert your park ticket into a computer terminal. The ticket specifies a time window during which you can walk right on and ride, cruising past the bulk of the lines. If you are willing to ride without your friends, **Single-Rider** tickets allow you to skip almost the entire line. *The Guide to the Magic Kingdom* has parade and show times, as well as important shopping information.

MAIN STREET, USA. This is Walt's idea of clean, idyllic small-town America. His designers skewed the perspective on Main Street so that the street seemed longer upon entering and shorter upon exiting, thereby creating visitor anticipation and making the walk to the car less daunting after a long day. Main Street's shops stay open an hour after the park itself closes, but don't be fooled into thinking you'll get your souvenirs on the way out—everyone else has the same idea.

FANTASYLAND. The geographical and spiritual center of the park, Fantasyland contains **Sleeping Beauty's castle,** as well as the scintillating **Matterhorn Bobsleds** and numerous kiddie rides like the trippy **It's A Small World,** which will fiendishly engrave its happy, happy song into your brain. This area is best enjoyed when the rides light up at night, the crowds go home, and you have twenty bucks to blow on addictive **churros** (cinnamon-sugary sticks of fried dough; $2.75).

ADVENTURELAND. To the left of Main Street is the home of **Tarzan's Treehouse,** a walk-through attraction that replaced the Swiss Family Robinson Treehouse. The **Indiana Jones Adventure** is just next door. Pass the time in line by decoding the inscriptions inside the Temple of Maya (hint: the ride is sponsored by AT&T). Indiana Jones fans' palms will sweat when an animatronic Harrison Ford suggestively says, "You were good in there…very good." The **Jungle Cruise** next door has a new landing with a swing band to entertain the poor souls languishing in the hot sun. For lunch, the **Bengal Barbecue** offers vegetable, chicken, and beef skewers ($3), and strawberry and banana parfaits ($3).

NEW ORLEANS SQUARE. The best shops and dining in Disneyland are in the west corner of the park. Find New Orleans cuisine at the **French Market** (dinner $10-12) or the much more expensive ◪**Blue Bayou,** which serves the best food in the park. The low-key but entertaining rides are evocative of lazy evenings on the humid Southern bayous. Try the creepy, campy **Haunted Mansion,** or the ever-popular, if now politically correct, **Pirates of the Caribbean.**

FRONTIERLAND. Wild West fetishists will find amusement galore here, especially on the speedy **Big Thunder Mountain Railroad.** Grab a bite at the **River Belle Terrace,** famous for its Mickey Mouse-shaped pancakes. The **Mark Twain riverboat** tours around Tom Sawyer's Island, which looks suspiciously like a clever way to isolate obnoxious children from harried adults.

CRITTER COUNTRY. Most of the park's cuter creatures lurk in this section, where the main attraction is **Splash Mountain,** a soaking log ride past singing rodents and down a thrilling vertical drop. Its host, **Brer Rabbit,** originated in the humorous, if un-p.c. "Uncle Remus" stories of the Reconstruction-era South. You might enjoy the snapshot they take of your horror-frozen face on the way down.

MICKEY'S TOONTOWN. At the rear of the park, this cartoon playland provides the key source of fun for the 10-and-under crowd. Mickey and Co. can often be found strolling about, followed by a stampede of kids in hot pursuit. Disney seems to be phasing out Mickey's old-school compadres like Donald, Goofy, and Chip 'n' Dale, in favor of newer, sexier favorites Ariel, Simba, Aladdin, and Belle. This is the best place to enjoy the park's signature Mickey Mouse ice cream bar ($3.25).

TOMORROWLAND. To the right of Main Street is this futuristic portion of the park, recently remodeled after Disney executives realized that its supposed imagination of the future was gloriously stuck in the 1950s. Though the **Astro-Orbiter**—rockets that circle around moving planets—will thrill young children, the overwhelming favorite of the rush-seeking set is still **Space Mountain**, a darkened roller coaster that banks and swoops beneath a mountain of sheer exhilaration. **Star Tours** promises a routine shuttle to Endor, but delivers an exciting simulation ride.

CALIFORNIA ADVENTURE. Just recently, Disneyland introduced its new kid brother, "California Adventure," to the theme park family. The park features ambitious attractions divided into four districts. **Sunshine Plaza**, the gateway to the park, is anchored by a 50 ft. tall sun enlivened by a flood of red, orange, and yellow lights at night. **Golden State** offers an eight-acre mini-wilderness, a citrus grove, a winery, and even a replica of San Francisco. **Paradise Pier** is dedicated to the so-called "Golden Age" of amusement parks—with rides such as **California Screamin'** and **Mulholland Madness**. Finally, the **Hollywood Pictures Backlot** realizes your aspirations to stardom without those embarrassing before-you-were-famous nude photos hanging over your head. Admission to California Adventure is not included in admission to Disneyland, but combined passes are available (see p. 463).

(K)NOT(T) DISNEYLAND

KNOTT'S BERRY FARM. Back in 1932, Walter Knott combined a red raspberry, a blackberry, and a loganberry to make a flavorful superberry he called the boysenberry. The future site of **Knott's Berry Farm,** his popular roadside stand quickly grew into a restaurant. When he imported the Old Trails Hotel (from Prescott, AZ) and the last narrow gauge railroad in the country to form "Ghost Town," the precursor to the first theme park in America was born. After the opening of Disneyland in Anaheim in 1955, Knott's Farm added more rides and other theme sections such as Fiesta Village. Knott's is a local favorite and aims at being "the friendliest place in the West"—it has long since given up on being the happiest place on Earth. The park's highlights include roller coasters like **Montezooma's Revenge, Boomerang,** and **Ghostrider,** the largest wooden roller coasters in the West. The latest addition is **Xcelerator,** bringing you from 0 to 80 mph in three seconds. If you are brave enough, try **Supreme Scream**, the tallest thrill ride of its kind, where you will fall 30 stories in three seconds. The Doolittle-ish **Birdcage Theater** is where comedian Steve Martin got his start, and now showcases special seasonal entertainment. At Halloween, the park is rechristened and redecorated into **Knott's Scary Farm,** and at Christmas, **Knott's Merry Farm.** While the rides at Knott's might one-up Disney's, the Wild West atmosphere pales in comparison; after all, you're pitting a hybrid fruit against a charismatic mouse. The best deal for food is **Mrs. Knott's Chicken Dinner Restaurant ❸**, located just outside the park. The Mrs. offers soup or salad, corn, biscuits, chicken, and dessert for only $13. Prepare to line up; this is a popular place for a hearty meal or just a tasty piece of pie (slice $2.69, whole pie $8.25). Boysenberry is, of course, the way to go. *(8039 Beach Blvd., at La Palma Ave., 5 mi. northeast of Disneyland. From downtown L.A., take MTA bus #460 from 4th and Flower St.; 1¼hr. If driving from L.A., take I-5 south to Beach Blvd., turn right at the end of the exit ramp, and proceed south 2 mi. Recorded info ☎ 220-5200. Open Su-Th 9am-10pm, F-Sa 9am-midnight; hours may vary, so call ahead. $43, ages 3-11 $13, under 3 free; after 4pm all tickets half-price. Summer discounts available. Parking under 3hr. free, each additional hr. $2; all-day parking $8. Mrs. Knott's Chicken Dinner: ☎ 220-5080. Open Su-Th 7am-9pm, F 7am-9:30pm, Sa 7am-10pm.)*

SOAK CITY USA. This 13-acre water park marks Knott's latest effort to make a splash in the already drenched local theme park scene. Its 21 water rides and attractions are fashioned after the longboards, surf woodies, and waves of the 1950s Southern Californian coast. *(Next to Knott's. ☎ 220-5200. Open Su-Th 10am-6pm, F-Sa 10am-8pm; hours may vary—call ahead. $25, ages 3-11 $13, under 3 free.)*

RICHARD NIXON LIBRARY AND BIRTHPLACE. Farther inland in Yorba Linda is this highly uncritical, privately funded monument to Tricky Dick. The first and only native Californian to become president was born in this house, which has evolved into an extensive museum. Rotating exhibits cover such fashionable topics as "Barbie as First Lady," with the presidents' wives all dolled up, and "Secret Treaties" from Westphalia to Spy Paraphernalia. Skeptics can investigate the Watergate Room and listen to the tapes themselves. Throughout the museum are letters from "small Republicans" to their big GOP idol, who was laid to rest here alongside his wife. Museum curators consistently portray Nixon as a victim of circumstance, plotting enemies, and his own immutable honor—an interpretation of history that admittedly has a certain charm. *(18001 Yorba Linda Blvd. ☎ 993-5075. Open M-Sa 10am-5pm, Su 11am-5pm. $6, students with valid ID and seniors $4, ages 8-11 $2, under 8 free.)*

CRYSTAL CATHEDRAL. Seating 3000 faithful in Garden Grove, the cathedral is where televangelist Dr. Robert H. Schuller's weekly TV show *Hour of Power* is taped. The 40 acres on which it sits is a nondenominational Protestant "campus" with impressive and modern glass towers. The Crystal Cathedral also provides the opportunity for In-Car Worship at a huge outdoor television. *(12141 Lewis St. ☎ 971-4000; www.crystalcathedral.org. 45min.-1hr. tours M-Sa 9am-3:30pm. English services Su 9:30 and 11am; Spanish service 1pm. Free. Broadcast on UPN, channel 13 in Orange County, and on the Discovery Channel.)*

HSI LAI TEMPLE (INTERNATIONAL BUDDHIST PROGRESS SOCIETY). This temple gained notoriety for its involvement in a Clinton-Gore fundraising scandal during the 1996 election; however, Hsi Lai's recent political abstinence has hardly extinguished "Buddha's Light" from its halls. The Bodhisattva Hall up the stairs from the main gate anticipates the main shrine with miniature bodhisattva sculptures lining the walls. For a dollar, you can get your fortune-cookie readings or *dharma* (translated as "religion" or "duty"). In the main shrine are three huge enamel Buddhas, each holding a different symbolic object. Toss pennies at a bell in the Statue Garden; hit it one, two, or three times and receive increasing levels of health, intelligence, and prosperity. Informative signboards along the pathways and in front of shrines make the largest Chinese Buddhist temple outside China as much a museum as a place of worship. Don't forget that it is the latter, though—no shorts or tank tops may be worn in the main shrine. *(3456 S. Glenmark Dr., in Hacienda Heights. From Anaheim, take Rte. 57 N to Rte. 60 W; exit Hacienda Blvd. and go south to Glenmark Dr. ☎ 961-9697. Vegetarian lunch buffet M-F 11:30am-1pm, Sa-Su 11:30am-2pm; $5. Chanting Service Su 10:30am.)*

SOUTH COAST PLAZA. True shopaholics head to this mother of all malls, one of the largest, most profitable, and most popular in the United States. The 300 stores and a 1.6-acre garden path in the mall are impressive, and the novice L.A. shopper will appreciate the free maps. *(3333 Bristol St. in Costa Mesa, off the I-405 Fairview exit. ☎ 714-435-2000. Open M-F 10am-9pm, Sa 10am-8pm, Su 11am-6:30pm.)*

SPORTS. For more evidence of Disney's world domination, catch a game by one of the teams they own. The major league **Anaheim Angels** play baseball from early April to October at **Edison Field.** *(☎ 940-2000 or 800-626-4357. General tickets $9-30.)* To check out some NHL action, catch a **Mighty Ducks** hockey game at **Arrowhead Pond.**

ORANGE COUNTY BEACH COMMUNITIES

Orange County's various beach communities have cleaner sand, better surf, and less madness than their L.A. County counterparts. Other than the ocean view, sights are scarce along the 35 mi. stretch of the Pacific Coast Highway (PCH) between Huntington Beach and San Clemente, with the exception of the graceful Mission San Juan Capistrano. L.A. residents seek refuge among Orange County's natural wonders—its surf, coastal cliffs, and wooded canyons.

◤ ACCOMMODATIONS

Orange County's prime coastline and pricey real estate result in a dearth of bargain rates. Those without multi-million-dollar summer homes in the area can try their luck along PCH or **Newport Boulevard** in Newport Beach.

■ **Huntington Beach Colonial Inn Youth Hostel,** 421 8th St. (☎714-536-3315), 4 blocks inland at Pecan Ave. in **Huntington Beach.** Take OCTA #29 (which also goes to Knott's Berry Farm) or #50. From PCH, turn onto 8th St. This large, early 20th-century yellow and blue house was once a brothel, but things have calmed down since (quiet hours after 10pm). Common bath, large kitchen, reading/TV room, coin-op laundry, Internet access, deck, and shed with surfboards, boogie boards, and bikes. Breakfast and linen included. Key deposit $5. Check-in 8am-11pm. Reserve 2 days in advance for summer weekends. 3- to 4-person dorms $23; doubles $55. ❷

Balboa Inn, 105 Main St. (☎949-675-3412; www.balboainn.com), on the sand in **Newport.** From PCH, follow signs to Balboa Peninsula and turn onto Main St. This recently renovated historical landmark offers rooms with ocean or bay views and is close to area attractions. Relax in the pool or hot tub. Room service available. Continental breakfast, fans, cable TV, and fridge included. Rooms from $139. Overnight parking $8. ❺

The Tides Motel, 460 N. Coast Hwy. (☎949-494-2494; www.tideslaguna.com), in **Laguna Beach.** 1 block from the beach and 4 blocks from downtown. Small collection of relatively inexpensive, basic rooms surrounding a nice pool. A/C, cable TV, and free parking. Singles in summer $110; in winter $99. Senior and AAA discounts. ❺

◤ CAMPING

Orange County's state beaches have campgrounds, but they are somewhat cramped and crowded. Reservations are required for all sites (reservation fee $7.50). Reserve through ReserveAmerica (☎800-444-7275; visit www.parks.ca.gov for current rates) a maximum of seven months in advance and as soon as possible in the summer. Beachside camping outside official campgrounds is both illegal and unsafe. The most popular Orange County campground is **Doheny** ❷, 25300 Dana Point Harbor Dr., along PCH in **Dana Point.** The Doheny Blues Music Festival arrives in mid-May with loud music, big crowds, and late nights. (☎949-496-6172. Fire rings, grills, showers, volleyball nets, and bike and in-line skate rental. Beachfront sites $31; non-beachfront $21.) Ocean bluffs, a nature trail, and coin-operated hot showers draw all kinds of folks to **San Clemente** ❷, 3030 Del Presidente, in **San Clemente.** (From I-5 North, exit at Christianitos and turn right onto Del Presidente and then left onto Calafia after three-quarters of a mile; from I-5 S, exit at Calafia. ☎949-492-3156. Sites $21, with hookup $30.)

◖◗ FOOD AND NIGHTLIFE

Orange County's restaurants tend to serve light California Cuisine and exquisitely fresh seafood.

Laguna Village Market and Cafe, 577 S. Coast Hwy. (☎949-494-6344), 5 blocks south of Broadway in **Laguna Beach.** Located on top of a cliff, the restaurant is housed in an open-air gazebo selling art and jewelry by local artists and designers. Its oceanfront terrace is the main draw. Lap up the view along with some seafood or the house specialty, Village Huevos ($9.50). Calamari plate $9. Open daily 8:30am-dark. ❷

Ruby's (☎714-969-7829), at the end of the **Huntington Beach** Pier. A 5-7min. trek down the pier. With windows on all sides, this flashy white and neon-red 50s-style diner has great burgers ($8) and a fabulous ocean view. ❷

Cafe Zoolu, 860 Glenneyre (☎949-494-6825), in **Laguna Beach.** This small evening restaurant offers an opportunity to dine on the freshest fish in a bustling atmosphere, undoubtedly enhanced by zebra-striped and leopard-print chairs. It's best to pick from the seafood specials like the scallop salad. Nothing prepares you for Alaskan halibut ($28) like ahi tartar ($15). Open Tu-Su 5-9pm. ❺

Joe's Crabshack, 2607 Pacific Coast Hwy. (☎949-650-1818; www.joescrab-shack.com), in **Newport Beach.** Brightly colored chairs, neon beer lights on the walls, and a fantastic view of the harbor create a beach party vibe for the whole family. Locals applaud the Dungeness Crab ($22). Appetizers from $6. Entrees from $10. Open M-F 11am-10pm, Sa-Su 11am-11pm. ❸

The Dutch Bakery, 32341 Camino Capistrano (☎949-489-2180), in **San Juan Capistrano.** In the Vons Center plaza down the street from the Mission. This bakery provides excellent chicken, turkey, ham, salami, and roast beef sandwiches, all on fresh-baked ciabatta bread (all $7). The chicken paisano (with havarti cheese, tomato, lettuce, and paisano mayo) is unbeatable. Wash it down with a strawberry banana smoothie ($3). Open Tu-F 6am-4pm, Sa 7am-3pm. ❷

Taco Laguna, 211 Broadway (☎949-497-4341), at PCH, in **Laguna Beach.** Fill your stomach for just a fistful of dollars at this high-quality Mexican fast-food restaurant. Chicken, fish, calamari, and shrimp tacos $2-3. Open daily 10:30am-8:30pm. ❶

The Cottage, 308 N. Coast Hwy. (☎949-494-3023), at Cliff Dr., across from the Laguna Art Museum, in **Laguna Beach.** In a turn-of-the-century "board and batten" beach home—a Laguna landmark. Overflowing portions of home-style cooking (surfer's breakfast $10) and omelettes galore ensure that guests are fed like family. Prices go up for dinner. Breakfast served daily until 3pm. Open daily 7am-3pm and 5-9 pm. ❸

Streetlight Espresso Café, 201D Main St. (☎714-969-7336), 2 blocks inland from the Pier, in **Huntington Beach.** Entrance is on Walnut St. off Main St. As bohemian as staid Huntington Beach gets. This nondenominational cafe hosts Christian rock bands F-Sa nights. Its board games get regular play. The supersweet white chocolate mocha ($3-3.50) is a godsend. Delectable desserts $1-3. Open M-Th 10am-midnight, F 10am-1am, Sa 7am-midnight, Su 10am-midnight. ❶

The Boom-Boom Room, 1401 S. Coast Hwy. (☎949-494-7588; www.boomboom-room.com), at Mountain St. in **Laguna Beach.** Lively gay hangout has an international reputation, pool tables, live DJs spinning everything from house to hip-hop, and a "surfing, muscle-bound, cruising, tanned" clientele. Boom-Boom specials include "Beer Busts" Tu-Th and Sa-Su 4-8pm; $1.25 draught beer and free sunset buffet. "Go-go Boys" Su night. Dinner entrees $10-15 in Boom Cafe. Cover begins at 9pm. Open Tu-F 11:30am-2am, Sa-Su 9am-2am. ❸

◨ ⬤ BEACHES AND SIGHTS

Apart from prefabricated amusement park joy, fun in the sun Orange County-style lies along the Pacific Coast Highway (PCH). On average, the beaches are cleaner and less crowded than those in L.A. County; the beachgoers are younger and more toned. Nevertheless, visitors should not be lulled off-guard by the crashing waves. As in any city, pedestrians should take care after dusk.

HUNTINGTON BEACH

From L.A., take the I-405 S to Hwy. 39 (Beach Blvd.). Follow Hwy. 39 S to PCH, then turn right (north). The pier is on the left at the intersection of PCH and Main St.

The prototypical Surf City, Huntington Beach is a perfect beach bum playground. This town has surf lore galore, and the proof is on the **Surfing Walk of Fame** and in the **International Surfing Museum.** *(Walk of Fame: the sidewalk along PCH at Main St. Museum: 411 Olive St.* ☎ *714-960-3483. Open daily noon-5pm. $2, students $1.)* You can join the wave-riding for about $40 per hr. for an instructor, board, and wet suit. Inquire at any of the local surf shops or make an appointment with the lifeguard-staffed **Huntington Beach Surfing Instruction.** *(*☎ *714-962-3515.)* The pier is the best place to watch the cavalcade of official surfing contests. By night, H.B.'s bars become a beach party brouhaha. Sink your toes in the sand at **Duke's** barefoot bar. *(*☎ *714-374-6446.)* **Perq's** is Orange County's oldest rock and blues house. *(117 Main St.* ☎ *714-960-9996.)* **Main Street,** Huntington Beach's central lane, is still surf shop central, but malls and shiny new bars have recently replaced the rustic charm of Huntington's classic surfing subculture.

NEWPORT BEACH AND BALBOA PENINSULA
From L.A., take I-405 or I-5 (San Diego Fwy.) S to Hwy. 55 (Costa Mesa Fwy.) and head west. Hwy. 55 turns into Newport Blvd., the main drag leading to the peninsula.

Multi-million-dollar summer homes, the world's largest leisure-craft harbor, and Balboa Peninsula are all packed closely enough on the Newport Beach oceanfront to make even New Yorkers feel claustrophobic. The young, scantily clad hedonists partying on the sand are a solid mix of locals and out-of-towners. Surfing and beach volleyball are popular, as is strolling on the residential streets of Balboa Peninsula. The Newport Pier is an extension of 22nd St. at West Balboa Blvd.

BALBOA PENINSULA. The sands of Newport Beach run south onto the two- to-four-block wide Balboa Peninsula, separated from the mainland by Newport Bay. **Ocean Front Walk,** which extends the length of the peninsula and is lined with neat rows of expensive cottages, is the best place to stroll. The Balboa Pier, flanked by beautiful sands, is at Main St. and East Balboa Blvd. Basketball games can be found at the ocean-side courts at 13th St. At the farthest tip of the peninsula, **The Wedge** encourages bodysurfing where the ocean depth changes suddenly and waves that appear safe suddenly rise to over 20 ft. near the shore.

On the opposite side of the peninsula, at the end of Main St., is the ornate **Balboa Pavilion.** Once a stomping ground of big band great Benny Goodman, it is now a hub for harbor tours and whale watching. The double-deck *Pavilion Paddy* offers cruises. *(*☎ *949-673-5245. 45min. $7, under 5 $3; 1½hr. $10, under 5 $3.)* The *Catalina Flyer* leaves for Catalina Island (see p. 455). A harborside mêlée, **Funzone** stretches its Ferris wheel and bumper cars west of the pavilion. *(*☎ *949-673-0408. Open daily 11am-10pm)*

Most of the crowds navigate Newport Beach and the Balboa Peninsula by bicycle, five-person bicycle surrey, or in-line skates. Stands everywhere rent all necessary gear. *(Bikes $5-7 per hr., $15 per day; skates $3-6 per hr., $15 per day; boogie boards $5-6 per day.)* Bikers should pick up *Bikeways,* a map of trails in Newport Beach, at the visitors center (see p. 461).

BALBOA ISLAND. Across the harbor from the pavilion where Errol Flynn, Shirley Temple, Humphrey Bogart, and other celebrities once docked their yachts is Balboa Island, a haven for ice cream shops (locally famous for Balboa bars and frozen bananas), artsy gift boutiques, and bikini stores. It was once just a sandpit, but the area was dredged and filled right before WWI. A vintage **ferryboat** travels there from the peninsula. *(*☎ *673-1070. Runs daily every 5min., but expect a delay at rush hour. Car and driver $1.50, each additional passenger $0.60, children $0.30; bikes $0.50-0.80.)* The island's outermost sidewalk, which traces the shore, is a popular place for morning walks and runs; no biking or skating permitted. *(Balboa Island is also accessible from PCH via the Jamboree Rd. bridge.)*

OTHER SIGHTS. Newport's **Harbor Nautical Museum,** aboard the 190 ft. *Pride of Newport,* displays Newport maritime history and extraordinary model ships. *(151 E. Pacific Coast Hwy. ☎ 949-675-8915: www.nhnm.org. Open Su and Tu-Sa 10am-5pm. Free.)* In what was formerly Corona del Mar, the **Sherman Library and Gardens** is a museum of living plants where pristine botanical collections range from desert cacti and succulents to tropical blooms. *(2647 E. Pacific Coast Hwy., a few miles east of the harbor. From I-405, take MacArthur turn-off south to PCH. Turn left on PCH and then right onto Dahlia. ☎ 949-673-2261; www.slgardens.org. Gardens open daily 10:30am-4pm. Library open Tu-Th 9am-4:30pm. $3, ages 12-16 $1, under 12 free.)* Get a dose of O.C. style at **Fashion Island.** Divided into seven courts, this outdoor mall has all the amenities of a regular mall and allows you to get a tan while shopping. *(Just inland from the PCH, between MacArthur Blvd. and Jamboree Rd.)* If you haven't had enough amusement park action, make a splash on one of the over 40 waterslide rides at **Wild Rivers Waterpark.** *(8770 Irvine Center Dr., in Irvine, off I-405. From I-405, take the Irvine Ctr. Dr. exit, turn south one block to Lion Country Rd., and turn left into the park. ☎ 949-788-0808; www.wildrivers.com. Open daily 10am-8pm. $28, under 48 in. $18, seniors free. Parking $8.)*

LAGUNA BEACH

From L.A., take I-405 S to Hwy. 133 (Laguna Canyon Rd.); follow it to Laguna Beach.

Punctuated by rocky cliffs, shady coves, and lush hillside vegetation, this lovely, artsy beach town's character is decidedly Mediterranean. **Ocean Avenue,** at the Pacific Coast Hwy., and **Main Beach** are the prime parading areas. **Westry Beach,** which spreads south of Laguna just below Aliso Beach Park, and **Camel Point,** between Westry and Aliso, are welcoming and liberal beaches. For beach access, park on residential streets to the east and look for "Public Access" signs between private properties, or shell out $7-10 for the convenience of a beach parking lot.

From the turn of the century, Laguna has been an artists' colony. The latest incarnation of the original 1914 Laguna Beach art association is the **Laguna Art Museum.** The collection showcases local and state art, including some excellent early 20th-century Impressionist works. Pick up the museum's guide to local art, which lists information on over 100 **art galleries** in the immediate Laguna Beach area. *(307 Cliff Dr. ☎ 494-8971; www.lagunaartmuseum.com. Open daily 11am-5pm. Tours daily 2pm. $9, students and seniors $7, under 12 free. Free 1st Th of each month 5-9pm.)* Art festivals abound in the summertime; ask for the *What's On Laguna Beach Arts* brochure at the Visitors Center.

SAN JUAN CAPISTRANO

30min. south of Anaheim on I-5. From L.A., take I-5 S to the Ortega Hwy., make a right, and follow it downtown. ☎ 949-234 1300; www.missionsjc.com. Open daily 8:30am-5pm. Self-guided tours available in English, Italian, Spanish, and German; call ahead. $6, seniors $5, ages 3-12 $4.

The **Mission San Juan Capistrano** was founded in the same year as the United States of America, 1776, and is the birthplace of Orange County. Full of romance and beauty, the mission stands as a monument to Native American, Mexican, and European cultures. Established by Father Junípero Serra, it is considered the "jewel of the missions." Although most of the original structure collapsed in an 1812 earthquake, this is the only standing site where Serra himself is known to have given mass, and the oldest building still in use in California. The crumbling walls of the beautiful **Serra Chapel** are warmed by a 17th-century Spanish altar and Native American designs. Gregorian chants evoke the spiritualism that Serra once envisioned. On March 19th each year, the city of San Juan Capistrano gathers here for the famous "Return of the Swallows," a celebration of the migrating birds that always return to the Mission.

The Swallows Inn has been a local favorite in San Juan for over 50 years. It is home to one of the largest chili cook-offs in the country and is the best place to catch the **Swallows Day Parade** in March. *(31786 Camino Capistrano. ☎ 949-493-3188.)* San Juan Capistrano's **village** offers abundant evidence that the West lives on. John Wayne lovers must take an afternoon to stroll the few square blocks and absorb the feel of a small Old West town.

DANA POINT AND SAN CLEMENTE

To get to Dana Point from L.A., take I-5 (San Diego Fwy.) S to PCH. Follow PCH toward Dana Point Harbor. To get to San Clemente from L.A., take I-5 south to El Camino. Exit in San Clemente. Don't miss your exit; there are no exits for 30min. through Camp Pendleton.

Dana Point's spectacular bluffs were popularized in namesake Richard Henry Dana's 1841 account of Southern California's sailing culture, *Two Years Before the Mast.* The harbor holds 2500 yachts and also serves as a point of departure for Catalina Island. Dana Point's **swimming beach** lies at Salt Creek and the Strands.

Neighboring **San Clemente,** a "small Spanish village by the sea," provides the powerful waves of Huntington and Newport minus the beach party noise and antics. Its downtown is now known as "Antique Mecca," where unrivaled antique stores and historic buildings are reminiscent of the Revolutionary days. In stark contrast, the US Marine Corps flexes its modern military might at **Camp Pendleton,** located along the coast. Farther south is **San Onofre State Beach** and its "Trestles" area, a breakpoint and thus a prime surfing zone for experienced thrill-seekers.

FESTIVALS

Strawberry Festival (☎ 714-638-0981; www.strawberryfestival.org), on the village green in downtown **Garden Grove.** Late May. Garden Grove is the US's leading producer of strawberries, and the festival includes some arduous strawberry pie-eating contests.

Festival of Arts and **The Pageant of the Masters,** 650 Laguna Canyon Rd. (info ☎ 949-494-1145, tickets 800-487-3378; www.foapom.com), in **Laguna Beach,** take place together in the Irvine Bowl July-Aug. Life literally imitates art in the Pageant as actors re-create famous paintings. Festival grounds open daily 10am-11:30pm; $5, seniors $3. Pageant shows nightly 8:30pm; tickets $15-80. Box office opens Dec. 1 for the following summer, and tickets sell out quickly. For reservations, contact the Festival of Arts, P.O. Box 1659, Laguna Beach 92652. See **No Work, All Play,** p.472.

Sawdust Festival, 935 Laguna Canyon Rd. (☎ 949-494-3030; www.sawdustfestival.org), across the street from The Pageant of the Masters in **Laguna Beach.** July-Aug. Lots of local art. Grounds open daily 10am-10pm. $6.50, ages 6-12 $2, under 6 free.

Christmas Boat Parade of Lights (☎ 949-729-4400), in **Newport Harbor.** The week before Christmas, over 200 boats and innumerable lights create a dazzling display.

NORTH OF L.A.

Government protection ensures prime hiking and camping in the vast expanse of park land north of Los Angeles. Unspoiled coastline, chaparral, and rolling hills stretch from Ventura to the Santa Monica Mountains.

VENTURA   ☎ 805

Ventura (pop. 102,000), is blessed with great weather and easygoing charm. Visitors to the "California Coast's Rising Star" flock to the recently revitalized downtown, now home to numerous restaurants, museums, thrift stores, and an

PAGEANT OF THE MASTERS

For years, artists around the world have sought to imitate life by immortalizing it upon canvas. The **Pageant of the Masters** in Laguna Beach does the opposite: it uses life to immortalize some of the finest and most famous works of art. During the 2hr. extravaganza, volunteers from around the world create living replicas of famous works, from Norman Rockwell prints to Da Vinci's *Last Supper* (the perennial finale). The actors, heavily made-up and costumed, step into a painted background as the piece is framed in front of the audience. The lights dim, and when the picture is revealed, the actors seemingly disappear into a two-dimensional canvas. In addition to paintings, the Pageant also replicates statues and sculptures, brilliantly imitating marble, stone, gold, and countless other mediums. In all, more than 30 works are re-created each year, encompassing everything from Renaissance to contemporary art.

Developed over 70 years ago and enhanced by lighting techniques, the pageant's ability to eliminate a dimension from the human perspective is truly awesome. With musical accompaniment and the anticipation of the crowd, the extravaganza is extremely unique.

In the Irvine Bowl, July-Aug. ☎949-494-1145; www.foapom.com. $15-80.

emerging cultural district for performers of all genres. Ventura Harbor, a bustling center of activity with over 30 cafes and shops, lies 10min. from downtown by car.

■ ▮ ORIENTATION AND PRACTICAL INFORMATION.
Ventura lies 30 mi. south of Santa Barbara and 70 mi. north of L.A. off U.S. 101. **Main Street** runs east-west in the historic downtown area on the east side of town, intersecting with **California Street,** which leads down to the pier. **Ventura Harbor** lies south along the coast; from downtown, take Harbor Blvd. to **Spinnaker Drive.**

Pick up maps and tourist info at the **Ventura Visitors Bureau,** 89 S. California St. From U.S. 101 N, exit at California St. (☎648-2075 or 800-333-2989; www.ventura-usa.com. Open M-F 8:30am-5pm, Sa 9am-5pm, Su 10am-4pm.) Those interested in visiting the **Channel Islands National Park** (see p. 475) should seek out the **National Park Visitors Center,** 1901 Spinnaker Dr. (☎658-5730. Open daily 8:30am-5pm. Tidepool talks Sa-Su at 11am and 3pm. A movie on the islands is shown every 30min.) **Ventura Bike Depot,** 239 W. Main St., rents bikes. (☎652-1114. $21 per half-day, $30 per day. Open Sa-Su 9am-5pm, M-F by appointment only.) Other services include: the **police,** 1425 Dowell Dr. (☎339-4400); **County Hospital,** 3291 Loma Vista Rd. (☎800-746-8885); and the **post office,** 675 E. Santa Clara St. **Postal Code:** 93001.

▮ ▮ ACCOMMODATIONS AND CAMPING.
Prior to its rejuvenation, Ventura was treated exclusively as a stopover point along coastal routes. As a result, the city has a number of budget motels, particularly along **East Thompson Avenue,** though many are decades old and in desperate need of renovation. A good bet is the **Mission Bell Motel ❹,** 3237 E. Main St., near Pacific View Mall. Most rooms have a kitchenette. (☎805-642-6831. Rooms with queen-size bed or double beds $55; 2 beds $60; king-size bed $60.) For something fancier, try the **Clocktower Inn ❺,** 181 E. Santa Clara St. Once a firehouse, the inn is located minutes away from the heart of the city and has an outdoor hot tub. (From Main St., go south 1 block on California St. and turn right on Santa Clara. ☎805-652-0141. Some rooms have balconies and fireplaces. Singles and doubles in high season $73-160; in low season $69-120.)

Beach camping is abundant around Ventura, but conditions tend to be primitive. Reservations through ReserveAmerica (☎800-444-7275) should be made months in advance. **McGrath State Beach Campground ❷**, 5mi. south of town off U.S. 101 in Oxnard via Harbor Blvd., is a popular spot with 174 campsites. (☎968-1033. Sites $21, low season $16.)

[❑❑] **FOOD AND ENTERTAINMENT.** A **Farmers Market** descends on the corner of Palm St. and Santa Clara St. on Saturdays (8:30am-noon). Cheap food in Ventura clusters along **Main Street,** in the heart of historic downtown. **Franky's ❷**, 456 E. Main St., between California and Oak St., is a Ventura institution, showcasing local art on the walls and offering healthy, delectable pita pockets ($7-8) and turkey burgers ($6.75). Wash down your meal with a jam jar of soda. (☎648-6282; www.frankysplace.com. Open daily 7am-3pm.) **Top Hat ❶**, 299 E. Main St., at Palm St., is a roadside burger shack serving chili cheeseburgers ($2.25), hot dogs ($1.50), and fries ($1) to a largely local crowd. (☎643-9696. Open Tu-Th 10am-5pm, F-Sa 10am-7pm.) **Jonathan's at Peirano's ❹**, 204 E. Main St., is a popular spot for Mediterranean food. Its beautiful patio, adjacent to a well-manicured park and large fountain, makes for a pleasant dining experience. (☎648-4853; www.jonathansatpeiranos.com. Lunch $5-15. Dinner $8.50-27. Open M-Th 11:30am-2:30pm and 5:30-10pm; F-Sa 11:30am-2:30pm and 5-11pm.) If the desire for pasta strikes, try **Capriccio Restaurant ❷**, 298 Main St., at Palm St. This quiet, warm Italian restaurant is popular among both the lunch and dinner crowd. Some patio seating is available. (☎643-7115. Lunch entrees $7-10. Dinner entrees $8-15. Open M-Th 11:30am-9pm, F-Sa 11:30am-10pm, Su noon-9pm.) One of the few late-night establishments, **Nicholby's Night Club ❷**, 404 E. Main St., offers two bars and dancing. The first 50 ladies get in free. (☎653-2320. Cover after 9:30pm $6-10. Open Th-Sa 8:30pm-1:45am.) In Ventura Harbor many of the restaurants overlook the harbor. Head to **Hornblowers Restaurant and Comedy Club ❸**, 1559 Spinnaker Dr., for seafood ($10.50-18.50) and comedy on Friday and Saturday nights. (☎805-658-2202. 21+. Cover F-Sa $12. Shows F 8pm, Sa 8 and 10pm. Open Su-Th 11am-9pm, F 11am-10pm, Sa 11am-11pm.) **The Greek at the Harbor ❹**, 1583 Spinnaker Dr., serves Greek cuisine ($15-20) amidst gyrating belly dancers. (☎805-650-5350; www.greekventura-harbor.com. Shows Tu-Th and Su 7:30pm, F-Sa 7:15 and 9pm. Open daily 8-10:30am, 11am-10pm; F-Sa until 11pm.)

[❑❑] **SIGHTS AND BEACHES.** Billed as California's "Gold Coast," the clean beaches near Ventura roar with fantastic surf. **Oxnard State Beach Park,** about 5 mi. south of Ventura, is quiet and peaceful except on weekends. **San Buenaventura State Beach,** at San Pedro St. and Harbor Blvd., entertains families and casual beachgoers with its bike path, volleyball courts, and nearby restaurants. **Surfer's Point,** at the end of Figueroa St., has the best waves around, but be forewarned that the surfers tend to be territorial. Pick up insider surfing tips and Patagonia gear at **Real Cheap Sports,** 36 W. Santa Clara St. The store has little in the way of surfing gear, but the employees are friendly, knowledgeable local surfers. From Main St., go 1 block south on Ventura Ave. and turn right onto Santa Clara St. (☎650-1213. Open M-Sa 10am-6pm, Su 10am-5pm.) For info on surf sessions, call ☎648-2662 or check out www.surfclass.com.

Inland from Ventura Harbor, on Olivas Park Dr., the **Olivas Adobe** sits on almost 5000 acres of land that the Mexican army gave to Raymundo Olivas for services rendered. The restored 1847 home is decorated in period furnishings and is a tribute to the early *rancho* period of Ventura's history. Olivas was not only one of the richest ranchers in California, but also an early benefactor of budget travelers. Next to the visitors' beds, Raymundo placed bowls of coins from which guests could draw some pocket change. From U.S. 101, take the Telephone Ave. exit south to Olivas Park Ave. and turn right, look for signs. (☎644-4346. House open Sa-Su 10am-4pm. Grounds open daily 10am-4pm. Free.)

Mission San Buenaventura, 211 E. Main St., still functions as a parish church, although it also houses a tiny museum of treasures from the 18th century. Enter through the museum gift shop next door. (☎643-4318. Open M-F 10am-5pm, Sa 9am-5pm, Su 10am-4pm. Suggested donation $1.) Across the street is the **Museum of History and Art,** 100 E. Main St., which displays one permanent and two rotating exhibits. Among the works are over 200 George Stuart Historical Figures shown in rotating groups of about 25. The figures comprise an internationally acclaimed collection of intricate small-scale sculptures of people from world history that George Stuart, a historian, created to accompany his lectures. He occasionally gives presentations at the museum. (☎653-0323; www.vcmha.org. Open Tu-Su 10am-5pm. $4, seniors and AAA members $3, ages 6-17 $1, under 6 free.)

SANTA MONICA MOUNTAINS
NATIONAL RECREATION AREA   ☎805

Extending 46 mi. west from the Hollywood Bowl to Point Mugu in Ventura County, 150,050 acres of oaks, dry brush, low mountains, and arroyos comprise the world's largest urban national park. Two indigenous groups, the Chumash and the Gabrielleno-Tongva, made their home here. The highest peaks in Santa Monica Mountains National Recreation Area border the ocean, creating spectacular ocean-side landscapes along the Pacific Coast Highway.

The hills are braided with more than 570 mi. of hiking trails of varying difficulty; ask a ranger for advice before heading out. *Hike Los Angeles, Vol. 1 and Vol. 2* ($10 each; sold at the visitors center), feature popular hikes, with relevant info about the area's ecology and history. *M*A*S*H* was shot at **Malibu Creek.** Much of the set was dismantled after the television show's shooting ended in 1982, and more of it was destroyed in subsequent fires, but an easy 1½ mi. hike from the Crags Rd. trailhead leads to the remaining jeep and ambulance. The flat area above the bank was the helipad. Die-hard hikers might want to try **Backbone Trail,** a 70 mi., three- to five-day journey from Point Mugu to Sunset Blvd. Consult a ranger before making the trek.

The National Park Service administers the **Paramount Ranch Site,** which was used as a location for several Paramount films between 1927 and 1953. Director Cecil B. DeMille and actors Gary Cooper and Mae West all worked here. The versatile ranch served as colonial Massachusetts in *The Maid of Salem* (1937), ancient China in *The Adventures of Marco Polo* (1938), and early San Francisco in *Wells Fargo* (1937). After purchasing the property in 1980, the US Park Service revitalized the old movie set, which is now open to visitors. Rangers conduct regular tours. In summer, Paramount Ranch screens silent movies from the 1920s with live musical accompaniment; call for dates. To reach the ranch, take U.S. 101 to Kanan Rd. exit (in Agoura Hills). Continue for half a mile and turn left onto Cornell Way, veer right onto Cornell Rd., and continue 2½ mi. to the entrance on the right.

On the western edge of the recreation area lies Rancho Sierra Vista/Satwiwa. At one time, a nearby Chumash village had the name Satwiwa, which means "the bluffs." Park rangers or special Native American guests host fire circles as part of the fascinating twilight program at the **Native American Indian Culture Center.** (Center ☎375-1930; www.satwiwa.org. Open Sa-Su 9am-5pm. Fire circles Sept.-May Su 6:30-8pm; June-Aug. Sa 6:30-8pm.) The 8 mi. hike from this site down through Big Sycamore Canyon to the sea is one of the park's most rewarding.

The best place for info is the **National Park Service Visitors Center,** 401 W. Hillcrest Dr., in Thousand Oaks, off U.S. 101 at the Lynn Rd. exit. (☎370-2301. Open daily 9am-5pm.) Call to request *Outdoors,* the recreation area's quarterly calendar of events and programs. Reserve state-run campsites through ReserveAmerica (☎800-444-7275). **Leo Carrillo State Park ❶** (☎818-880-0350; sites $20; low season $15), **Point Mugu State Park ❶** (☎818-880-0350, sites $15-20/$11-15), and **Malibu Creek State Park ❶** (☎818-880-0367; $20/$15) are all good options. **Topanga State Park** (☎310-455-2465) allows backcountry camping.

CHANNEL ISLANDS NATIONAL PARK   ☎805

Ventura and Santa Barbara are the only two points of departure to the windswept, desolate Channel Islands, home to ancient Chumash sites, historic ranches, underwater kelp forests, seals, and wildflowers. The **Channel Islands National Park Visitors Center,** 1901 Spinnaker Dr., distributes info and has an observation tower that looks out on the islands, an indoor tide pool, a native plant garden, and other exhibits. (☎658-5730. Open daily 8:30am-5pm.)

The park consists of five islands. **Anacapa** (time to the island by ferry 1-1½hr.) is composed of three islets and is home to the largest brown pelican rookery on the Pacific Coast. The largest island, **Santa Cruz** (1-1½hr.), is said to be a miniature of what Southern California looked like more than 100 years ago. It is renowned for pristine beaches, lonely canyons, and one of the world's largest sea caves, Painted Cave. The Chumash called **Santa Rosa** (3-3½hr.) *Wima* (driftwood) because currents washed ashore logs from which they built canoes. It features deep canyons, a coastal lagoon, and sand dunes that house large deer mice and island fox. **San Miguel** (4-5hr.), the westernmost island, has severe weather that makes landings difficult. If you are able to land through the surf, however, you will be greeted by no fewer than 30,000 seals and sea lions. Though tiny **Santa Barbara** (4-5hr.) is only 1 sq. mi. and farthest from the mainland, it boasts magnificent views of steep volcanic rock cliffs rising above rocky shores. It is also home to the giant Northern elephant seal and a rare plant called live-forever, which is only found on this island. Due to island geography, it is usually faster to sail out of Santa Barbara when visiting Santa Rosa or San Miguel. Ventura is the preferable point of departure for Anacapa or Santa Barbara. Santa Cruz is equally far from both cities.

The best part of a Channel Islands trip can be the **boat ride,** on which you may spot flying fish, sea lions, whales, and pods of common dolphins playing in the boat wake. Those averse to long hours on a swaying, rolling boat can consider flying to Santa Rosa Island in just 25 min. Contact **Channel Islands Aviation,** 305 Durley Ave., in Camarillo. (☎805-987-1301; www.flycia.com. Half-day excursions or surf fishing safaris $130, ages 2-12 $105. Camping $200.) Unless you happen to have brought your own boat with you, you'll have to ride with one of the park's "official concessionaires" to the islands. The concessionaires offer various diversions on each island, such as camping, hiking, kayaking, and tours. **Island Packers,** 1691 Spinnaker Dr., in Ventura Harbor, has a virtual monopoly on island transport from Ventura. (☎642-7688, reservations 642-1393. Daytrips and overnight camping excursions depart around 8am. Anacapa daytrip $37, overnight $48; Santa Cruz $42-48/$54-60; Santa Rosa $62/$80; Santa Barbara $49/$75; San Miguel overnight only, $90. Island Cruise with no landing $25. Gray whale-watching tours Dec. 26-early Apr.; 3-3½hr.; $25. Blue whale-watching tours Jul.-Aug.; 9am-4 or 5pm; $60.) **Truth Aquatics** also runs occasional boats to the islands from Santa Barbara. (☎805-962-1127 or 805-963-3564; www.truthaquatics.com. Call or check website for schedule.)

All recreational gear must be rented in advance. Full-day guided kayaking tours, a safe and enjoyable way to see wildlife and island formations, are run by **Channel Islands Kayak Center,** 1691 Spinnaker Dr. (☎644-9699), in Ventura, and 3600 S. Harbor Blvd. in Oxnard. (☎805-984-5995; www.cikayak.com. Transportation to Santa Cruz, Santa Rosa, or Anacapa, kayaking gear, a kayaking lesson, and a guided tour through the sea caves, reefs, and beaches included. Tours $170.) For snorkel and dive gear, try **Pacific Scuba Center,** 480 S. Victoria Ave., in Oxnard. (☎805-984-2566; www.pacificscuba.com. Scuba package $40 first day, $20 each additional day. Snorkel package $40/$15.) **Camping ❶** at the islands requires your own gear, food, and in most cases water since all sites are primitive. (Reservations ☎800-365-2267; http://reservations.nps.gov. Sites $10.)

EAST OF L.A.

L.A.'s huddled masses who yearn to breathe free often pack up their kids, cell phones, and cares and head for the hills. Granite mountains, scenic hiking trails, campgrounds, and scented pine forests are a mere 45min. drive above and beyond the inversion layer (the altitude at which the smog ends). In the mountains, outdoor activities abound at all times of the year, but winter is undeniably the high season. While the Sierra Nevada resorts around Lake Tahoe (see p. 237) and Mammoth Lakes (see p. 286) are the destinations of choice for serious California skiers, daytrips to the smaller resorts of the San Bernardino mountains have become increasingly popular. Temperatures typically allow ski resorts to operate from November through April, but always call ahead to check conditions. Even when the snow melts, the coastal mountains are an ideal getaway. The Angeles and San Bernardino National Forests sprawl across majestic mountains and have many campgrounds, hiking trails, and mountain villages.

ANGELES NATIONAL FOREST   ☎626

National forests cover about one quarter of L.A. County north of Pasadena and east of Valencia. Cradling the northern edge of the L.A. Basin and the San Gabriel Valley are the San Gabriel Mountains, whose highest peak, Mt. San Antonio ("Mt. Baldy"), tops out at 10,064 ft. This area attracts mountain bikers, anglers, birdwatchers, and hikers year-round. Harsh weather and frequent brush fires often rearrange the place, but rangers give helpful directions. Skiers will probably find Big Bear more worthwhile than the closer resorts at Mt. Baldy (☎909-982-0800) and Mt. High East and West (☎760-249-5808).

▐ PRACTICAL INFORMATION

The national forest is divided into three ranger districts: Los Angeles River, San Gabriel River, and Santa Clara/Mojave Rivers. Each houses a district office, a visitors center, and an information station, with info specific to the district. For general forest information, call ☎626-574-5200 or visit the Forest Headquarters (see below). In an **emergency,** contact the Angeles National Forest Dispatcher (☎818-447-8999 in the Arcadia area, 661-723-7619 in the Lancaster area). All ranger stations listed below are open Monday through Friday 8am to 4:30pm.

Angeles National Forest Headquarters, Supervisor's Office, 701 N. Santa Anita Ave. (☎626-574-1613), in Arcadia. Comprehensive forest maps $6-8.

Los Angeles River Ranger District, 12371 N. Little Tujunga Canyon Rd. (☎818-899-1900), in San Fernando. **Chilao Visitors Center** lies on Rte. 2 (Angeles Crest Hwy.), 26 mi. from La Cañada (☎626-796-5541). Open M and F-Su 8am-4:30pm. Rte. 2 leads into the south-central area of the forest, north of Pasadena. 27 campgrounds in this district; many are high-country camps.

San Gabriel River Ranger District, 110 N. Wabash Ave. (☎626-335-1251), in Glendora. **Mount Baldy Visitors Center,** on Mt. Baldy Rd. north of Ontario. Open daily 8am-4:30pm. The southeastern district of the forest has 8000 ft. peaks, hiking trails, the San Antonio Falls, and scenic Glendora Ridge Rd. 4 developed campgrounds.

Santa Clara/Mojave Rivers Ranger District, 30800 Bouquet Canyon Rd. (☎661-296-9710), in Saugus, northwest of the main forest. Two visitors centers: **Big Pines,** on the east end of Rte. 2 (Angeles Crest Hwy.) near the turn-off for Valyermo (☎760-249-3504; open M and F-Su 8am-3:30pm), and **Grassy Hollow,** also on Rte. 2, 6 mi. west of Wrightwood (☎626-821-6737; open Sa-Su 10am-4pm). Pyramid, Elizabeth, and Castaic Lakes have boating and fishing.

⚑ CAMPING

The US Forest Service maintains 557 mi. of well-groomed hiking trails and camping facilities. Many of the trails cross, so maps are vital. Most campsites run by the Forestry Service are free, though parked vehicles must display a **Golden Passport** or an **Adventure Pass** ($5, available at ranger stations, visitor centers, and various local retailers; see p. 479). Campsites run by concessionaires are $10-15 per night. Sites do not accept reservations (14-night max. stay), and many are closed in the winter. There are many campgrounds along Big Pines Hwy. that are convenient and free, but they offer little seclusion. Backcountry sites afford more privacy and security, though probably no drinking water or bathrooms.

Chilao Recreation Area (☎818-790-1151), 5300 ft., off Rte. 2, 26 mi. northeast of La Cañada Visitors Center, 1 mi. north of the campground and south of Three Points and Devil's Canyon trailheads. Offers walks, talks, and children's activities. The 111 sites have fire rings, tables, water, and toilets. No hookups. Sites $12. ●

Buckhorn, 6300 ft., on Rte. 2, 26 mi. southwest of Wrightwood and 36 mi. northeast of La Cañada, has 38 sites surrounded by lush ferns and redwoods. Near Burkhart Trailhead. Fire rings, tables, water, and toilets. No hookups. Open June-Nov. Sites $12. ●

Table Mountain, 6500 ft., off Rt. 2, 1 mi. north of the Big Pines Visitors Center, has secluded individual and group sites near a number of trailheads. Easy access to Devil's Punchbowl. Fire rings, tables, flush toilets, and drinking water. No hookups. Sites $13.

Glenn Trail Camp, 2000 ft., off Rte. 39 North. The end of the West Fork National Bike Trail (16 mi. round-trip). Walk or bike in from a gate. The physically challenged can get a driving permit; contact the San Gabriel Ranger Station (☎626-335-1251). 10 free sites with vault toilets. Stream water only; treat before drinking. Free. ●

👁 ⚑ SIGHTS AND OUTDOOR ACTIVITIES

HIKING

Just outside the national forest in a county park, the **Devil's Punchbowl** entices hikers and climbers with its spooky sandstone formations. (Take Longview Rd. from Hwy. 138 to Devil's Punchbowl Rd., where a right turn will take you into the park.) For a moderately easy and scenic morning or afternoon hike, try **Charlton Flat to Vetter Mountain** (3 mi.). The trail climbs past pine, oak, and a wide variety of birds and flowers from near the Charlton Flat picnic area (off

Rte. 2) to an old fire lookout point on Vetter Mountain, providing mountain views. A different trailhead from Charlton Flat leads to **Devil Peak,** another short and enjoyable hike. A popular, moderate full-day hike leads from **Vincent Gap to Mt. Baden-Powell** (8 mi.), climbing 2800 ft. through ancient pines and peaking at 9400 ft. with spectacular views of the San Gabriel range, including Old Baldy and, on clear days, the looming desert. The trailhead is located in the Vincent Gap parking lot, off Rte. 2, 52 mi. from La Cañada. The **Blue Ridge Trail** to **Mt. Baldy** (12 mi.), the highest peak in the San Gabriel range at 10,064 ft., is a challenging, high-elevation hike that should only be attempted by the fit. Those who summit, however, will be rewarded with unsurpassed views of the alpine country. To reach the trailhead, drive 1½ mi. west of Big Pines on Rte. 2 to Blue Ridge Rd. From there, it is three miles to the Blue Ridge campground and the trailhead.

The three- to seven-day **Gabrielino Trail** (53 mi. round-trip) connects Oak Grove Park and the north end of Windsor Ave., in La Cañada Flintridge. The five-day **Silver Moccasin Trail** (53 mi. one way), once a rite of passage for adventurous Boy Scouts, is now a popular backcountry route. The trail connects Chantry Flats with Vincent Gap, crossing forest, stream, mountain, and canyon. Long hikes such as these necessitate **trail camping**. Fortunately, it is free and legal, but fire permits (available at ranger stations) are strictly required for anything with a flame, including cigarettes, and camping is not allowed within 200 ft. of any stream. There are also numerous opportunities to hike a portion of the renowned **Pacific Crest Trail** (see **From Crest to Crest: The Trail of the West,** p. 237). Trailheads are scattered along the length of the **Highway 2** (Angeles Crest Hwy.).

ST. ANDREWS ABBEY

Visitors in search of a more contemplative experience may care to stop at the Benedictine **St. Andrews Abbey** in the village of **Valyermo.** Three-day weekend retreats, including room and board, begin at $125, and focus on diverse theological themes like spirituality in modern cinema and the writings of C.S. Lewis. Visitors are welcome at mass. **Rooms ❹** with A/C are also available on a regular basis for $60 per person per night. (Retreat office ☎661-944-2178; www.valyermo.com. Take Valyermo Rd. from Hwy. 138. Open daily 9am-5pm; mass daily noon-1:30pm.)

SAN BERNARDINO NATIONAL FOREST

The San Bernardino National Forest makes up over 700,000 acres of pristine, mountainous public land on the northeastern edge of Southern California's urban expanse. Five federally designated wilderness areas—Cucamonga, San Gorgonio, Bighorn Mountain, San Jacinto, and Santa Rosa—feature largely undisturbed snow-capped peaks, desert transition zones, deep canyons, green meadows, and dark blue lakes. Outside the wilderness areas are more developed attractions like Big Bear and Arrowhead Lakes.

BIG BEAR   ☎909

Big Bear is easily Southern California's most popular mountain and lake resort. In the summer, the central lake provides ample opportunities for fishing, sailing, and watersports, while the nearby mountains and forest offer enjoyable hikes and well-preserved campgrounds. The village surrounding the lake is a quiet slice of civilization in the woods, with snow chalets and mountain cabins mainly geared toward the skiing set, which arrives en masse from L.A. and elsewhere around December.

TRANSPORTATION

To reach Big Bear, take **I-10** to **Route 30** in San Bernardino and follow Rte. 30 north to **Route 330** (Mountain Rd.), which turns into **Route 18,** a winding 30-45min. ascent. Rte. 18 hits the west end of Big Bear Lake and splits into a continuing Rte. 18 branch along the south shore, where it is called Big Bear Blvd., and **Route 38** along the north shore. A less congested, longer route approaches from the east via **I-10** to Redlands and then Rte. 38 to Big Bear Lake. Driving time from L.A. is about 2½hr., barring serious weekend traffic or road closures. The loneliest route to Big Bear Lake curls in from the north, across the high desert along Rte. 18 through the Lucerne Valley, from **I-15** in Victorville. Weekend day skiers should wait until after 6pm to head home in order to avoid the 4pm rush. Driving to Big Bear should not be attempted during the winter without checking road conditions with **CalTrans** (☎427-7623; www.dot.ca.gov). **Mountain Area Regional Transit Authority (MARTA)** runs two **buses** per day from the Greyhound station in San Bernardino to Big Bear. (☎584-1111. $5, seniors and disabled $3.75.) Buses also run the length of Big Bear Blvd. (1hr.; $1, students $0.75, seniors, and disabled $0.50.) MARTA also operates **Dial-A-Ride.** ($2; students $1.50, seniors and disabled $1.)

ORIENTATION AND PRACTICAL INFORMATION

The **Big Bear Chamber of Commerce,** 630 Bartlett Rd., in Big Bear Village, dispenses glossy brochures and info on lodging, local events, and skiing and road conditions. (☎866-4608; www.bigbearchamber.com. Open M-F 8am-5pm, Sa-Su 9am-5pm.) Located directly above the Chamber of Commerce, the **Big Bear Lake Resort Association** arranges lodging and ski packages. (☎866-7000 or 800-424-4232; www.bigbearinfo.com. Open M-F 8am-6pm, Sa-Su 9am-5pm.) **Big Bear Discovery Center (BBDC),** on Rte. 38 4mi. east of Fawnskin and 1¼ mi. west of the Stanfield Cutoff, is a ranger station that sells the **National Forest Adventure Pass** (day $5, year $30), which is required for vehicles at

IN RECENT NEWS

LIVING AND DYING IN NATURE

Southern Californians love the area's unique landscape, which combines coastal regions, deserts, mountains, and forests. Everyone, it seems, wants their own house in the hills in order to get close to nature. Recently, however, the San Bernardino County Planning Commissioners have considered trying to protect the forests and the county's inhabitants by banning construction in the mountains.

The county is home to some severely dry forests due to record low precipitation in the area for the past several years. While this is a natural occurrence and fires are part of an ordinary forest cycle, development in the mountains and forests can contribute to erosion and make it easier for fires to spread.

Scientists fear that there is significant risk of a fire and flood in the area, which could put tens of thousands of residents at risk. A 2003 autumn fire and Christmas Day flood led to 23 casualties.

Critics of a ban on building argue that there's no point in preserving nature if Californians can't enjoy it. The argument may seem strange, but then again, this is a place where some people admire the influence of smog on beautifully colored sunsets, and others devote their entire lives to saving individual trees.

campsites that charge no additional fee. (☎866-3437. Open daily Apr.-Sept. 8am-6pm; Oct.-Mar. 9am-5pm.) The pass can also be purchased at ranger and information stations throughout the state, through a number of private vendors, or at www.fsadventurepass.org. In **emergencies,** call ☎383-5651 to reach a ranger station. Free **Internet access** is available at **Big Bear Public Library,** 41930 Garstin Dr. (☎866-5571. Open M-Tu noon-8pm, W-F 10am-6pm, Sa 9am-5pm.) The **post office,** 472 Pine Knot Blvd., is off Big Bear Blvd. (☎866-7481. Open M-F 8:30am-5pm, Sa 10am-noon.) **Postal Code:** 92315.

ACCOMMODATIONS

As Big Bear is a year-round destination, rooms below $50 a night are often only found down the mountain in San Bernardino (see p. 483). **Big Bear Boulevard** is lined with lodging possibilities, and groups can find the best deals by sharing a cabin. Solo travelers and couples may have better luck at chain motels. **Mountain Lodging Unlimited** arranges lodging and lift packages. (☎866-5500. Packages from $100 per couple. Open in ski season 7am-midnight; low season 9am-midnight.)

Robinhood Inn, 47097 Lakeview Dr. (☎866-4643 or 800-990-9956). Unlike its namesake, this chalet-style motel won't rob from the rich or poor. Courtyard complete with spa and barbecue. Fireplaces, kitchenettes, and coffeemakers in many rooms. John Wayne once stayed here. Singles and doubles from $59; suites for up to 6 people under $100. ❹

Big Bear Frontier, 40472 Big Bear Blvd. (☎800-798-3960). This lakeside property features spacious log cabin-style motel rooms. The lodge house offers free Internet access, free videos to borrow, and breakfast in the mornings. Singles and doubles $59-129. ❹

Hillcrest Lodge, 40241 Big Bear Blvd. (☎866-7330, reservations 800-843-4449; www.hillcrestlodge.com). Pine paneling and skylights give these cozy rooms a stylish feel. Hot tub, cable TV, and free local calls. In winter small rooms $48-119; 4-person units and suites $79-159. In summer small rooms $48-70; 4-person units with kitchen $90-140; 2-bedroom suites with hearth and kitchen $100-150. ❸

Vintage Resort, 41078 Big Bear Blvd. (☎866-4978). Friendly hosts, an unbeatable location on Big Bear Lake, and a surf and turf restaurant are great perks. Kitchenettes in some units. Singles and doubles Su-Th $70-80, F-Sa $90-100; 2-room units with kitchenette $100-150. ❹

CAMPING

Camping is permitted at many surrounding US Forest Service sites. Several of these sites accept reservations through the National Recreation Reservation Service (☎877-444-6777; www.reserveusa.com) or the US Forest Service (☎800-280-2267). Most are open from May to November. Campers can pitch a tent on US Forest Service land if they stay 200 ft. from water and roads and a quarter mile from developed areas. The entire north shore of Big Bear Lake is national forest and contains many campsites. The Big Bear Discovery Center (see p. 479) offers free visitors permits and info about Remote Camping Areas and Yellow Post Sites.

Serrano, 40650 N. Shore Ln. (☎866-8021, reservations 877-444-6777), 6500 ft., right off Hwy. 38 in Fawnskin. The most popular campground in Big Bear, with the highest occupancy of any national forest campground. Only a few hundred feet from the lake. All 132 sites (including 28 RV) have showers and flush toilets. Many sites are reserved up to 8 months in advance, so make reservations early. Sites $23. ❷

Pineknot, 7000 ft., on Summit Blvd., south of Big Bear. Amid thick woods, these 48 sites are secluded and cool, with access to a number of trails. At the base of steep Snow Summit, mountain bikers rule the single-track. Flush toilets and water. Wheelchair accessible. Sites $18. ❷

Hanna Flats, 7000 ft., on Forest Rd. 3N14, 2½ mi. northwest of Fawnskin. Lush vegetation surrounds 88 roomy sites. Hiking, water, pit and flush toilets. Sites $17. ❷

Holcomb Valley, 7400 ft., 4 mi. north on Polique Canyon Rd. 2N09, then east for ¾ mi. on Forest Rd. 3N16. 19 sites. Pit toilets; no water. Near the PCT. Sites $10. ❶

◘ FOOD

Those with kitchens can forage at **Stater Bros.,** 42171 Big Bear Blvd. (☎866-5211. Open daily 7am-11pm.) Many cutesy eateries offer all-you-can-eat specials.

Peppercorn Grille, 553 Pine Knot Ave. (☎866-5405). Lunch specials, including pasta, salads, and other American and California cuisine, for $7. Gourmet pizza ($8-10) is perfect to share. Open daily 11am-3pm and 5-9pm. ❷

Grizzly Manor, 41268 Big Bear Blvd. (☎866-6226). A local favorite for breakfast. Get some combination of the breakfast staples of eggs, bacon, and potatoes for $4-8, or just go with "The Mess" ($7.50). Open W-F 7am-2pm, Sa-Su 6am-2pm,. ❷

Virginia Lee's, 41003 Big Bear Blvd. (☎866-3151). A motley collection of hot dogs, tamales, ice cream, fancy hot chocolate, and potato and pasta salads make the menu at this little roadside shack. Everything $2-4. Open W-Su 10am-4pm. ❶

La Paws, 1128 W. Big Bear Blvd. (☎585-9115), in Big Bear City. A fun little family-run spot serving authentic and inexpensive Mexican specialties (burritos $4-6) and American favorites. Open daily 7am-8pm. ❶

Boo Bear's Den, 572 Pine Knot Ave. (☎866-2162). With a relaxing outdoor patio in the heart of downtown Big Bear, this local den is your best bet for casual dining near the lake and village shops. The "Boo Burgers" ($5-7) are a good choice. Sandwiches $6-9. Entrees $11-16. Open M-F 8am-9pm, Sa-Su 8am-10pm. ❸

◪ OUTDOOR ACTIVITIES

HIKING

Although hiking often takes a backseat to higher-velocity recreation in Big Bear, the trails in the surrounding mountains are a superb way to explore the San Bernardino wilderness. Maps, trail descriptions, and the *Visitor's Guide to the San Bernardino National Forest* are available at the Big Bear Discovery Center. Perfect for an afternoon stroll, the 3½ mi. **Alpine Pedal Path** runs its gentle, paved course from the Stanfield Cutoff on the lake's north shore to the Big Bear Discovery Center. The moderately difficult 2½ mi. **Castle Rock Trail,** starting 1 mi. east of the dam on Hwy. 18, is a short but steep haul, finishing atop a colossal granite boulder (the final rock scramble can be a tad risky). The views of Big Bear Lake and the surrounding area are stupendous. A more challenging day hike, **Cougar Crest Trail** (5 mi.) starts a half-mile west of the Discovery Center on Rte. 38 and ascends to meet the Pacific Coast Trail. Continuing east to the summit of **Bertha Peak** (8502 ft.), it affords unobstructed views of desert. Serious hikers may want to catch a longer piece of the **Pacific Crest Trail (PCT),** which extends 2638 mi. from Mexico to Canada, and is moderately difficult in this area. (For more info, see **From Crest to Crest: The Trail of the**

AROUND L.A.

West, p. 237.) The trail runs parallel to the lake on the north shore and then continues to the east of the lake; the Big Bear Discovery Center can direct hikers to any of the multiple entry points in the area.

BIKING

When the snow melts, **mountain biking** takes over the Big Bear slopes. In the San Bernardino National Forest, mountain biking is allowed on all public trails except the PCT and within designated wilderness areas. Grab a *Ride and Trail Guide* at the Discovery Center or at **Snow Summit,** 1 mi. west of Big Bear Lake, which runs lifts in summer so armored adrenaline monsters can grind serious downhill terrain. (☎866-4621. $10 , ages 7-12 $5; day pass $20/$10. Helmet required. Open Su-F 9am-4pm, Sa 8am-5pm.) **Team Big Bear,** 476 Concklin Rd., operating out of the **Mountain Bike Shop** at the base of Snow Summit, rents bikes and sponsors organized bike races each summer. (☎866-4565. Bikes $9 per hr., $27 per 4hr., $50 per day; helmet included. For more race info, call daily Apr.-Oct. 9am-5pm, or write Team Big Bear, Box 2932, Big Bear Lake, CA 92315.) **Big Bear Bikes,** 41810 Big Bear Blvd., rents and sells the best bikes on the mountain. (☎866-2224. Front suspension $7 per hr., $35 per day; full suspension $10/$50. Open daily 10am-5pm, extended F-Sa hours if it's busy.)

FISHING

Stocked during fishing season with a mighty supply of rainbow trout and catfish, Big Bear Lake is a major angling attraction in the summer. State **fishing** licenses are available at area sporting goods stores (1 day $10, season $28). Any part of the lake will afford good fishing, but only the north shore is accessible to all; the south shore is mostly private property. The dam at the west end of the lake has the deepest water, making it the best fishing area on the lake. For weekly updates on stocking info, call ☎562-590-5020. **Boats** can be rented at any one of Big Bear's marinas, including **Holloway's Marina and RV Park,** 398 Edgemor Rd., on the south shore. (☎866-5706 or 800-448-5335; www.bigbearboating.com. $50-175 per day.)

WINTER RECREATION

When snow conditions are favorable, ski areas run out of lift tickets quickly. **Tickets** for the resorts listed below may be purchased through Ticketmaster (☎714-740-2000). The crowded mountain roads can challenge both vehicle and driver. Gas stations are scarce on the way up the mountain, and signs notify drivers of tire chain requirements. Call CalTrans (☎800-427-7623) for info on road conditions.

Cross-country skiing is a popular way to enjoy the mountain's wintertime scenery. The **Rim Nordic Ski Area,** across the highway from Snow Valley, is an undulating network of cross-country ski trails. An Adventure Pass ($5) is required (see p. 479).

For those renting ski and snowboard equipment, hitting the ski stores along Big Bear Blvd. can save you up to half the price of renting at the mountains. The following resorts cater to **downhill skiing and snowboarding:**

Big Bear Mountain Resorts (www.bigbearmountainresorts.com) runs 2 separate mountain resorts, **Bear Mountain,** 43101 Goldmine Dr. (☎585-2519, activities report 800-BEAR-MTN/232-7686; www.bearmtn.com), 1½ mi. southeast of downtown Big Bear Lake, and **Snow Summit,** 880 Summit Blvd. (☎866-5766, activities report 888-786-6481; www.snowsummit.com), 1 mi. east of Big Bear Lake. With 195 acres of terrain, including huge vertical drops, expert runs, and undeveloped land for adventure skiing, Bear Mountain is geared toward freestyle skiing and snowboarding. Snow Summit is a more family-oriented resort with snowmaking, night skiing, and a well-rounded assortment of beginner runs. Between the two resorts, there are 23 lifts and over 55 runs; lift tickets are interchangeable, and a shuttle runs between the two parks. Lift tickets $43, ages 13-19 $35, ages 7-12 $14; holidays $50/$50/$21. Skis $25 per day; snowboards $30 per day. Deposit required. Beginner packages available.

Snow Valley (☎867-2751, snow report 867-5151), near Running Springs. 12 lifts, 800-5000 ft. runs, snowmaking, night skiing, and a skate park in the summer. The most family-oriented resort in Big Bear, with a children's obstacle course and beginner trails. Lift ticket $37, ages 6-13 $23. Skis $17 per day; snowboard $30 per day.

SAN GORGONIO WILDERNESS AREA ☎909

The rugged 60,000-acre San Gorgonio Wilderness Area is set aside from the rest of the San Bernardino National Forest and protected from development. Wheeled vehicles, anything mechanized, and fires of any sort are prohibited. Almost 100 mi. of trails converge on remarkable summits, the highest of which is **Mount San Gorgonio** (dubbed "Old Grayback" for its barren summit), at 11,500 ft. the tallest in California outside the Sierras. On a clear day, the panoramic summit view includes the southern Sierras, Mexico, the Pacific Ocean, and the Mojave Desert. There are no campgrounds within the Wilderness Area, but backcountry camping is allowed.

To forge into the backcountry, you must have a **wilderness permit**. Obtain these for free up to three months in advance from the **Mill Creek Ranger Station**, near Mentone, 40 mi. from Big Bear on Rte. 38 (☎909-794-1123; open M-F 8am-4:30pm, Sa-Su and holidays 7am-3:30pm; in winter daily 8am-4:30pm), or at the **Barton Flats Visitor Information Center**, on Rte. 38 about 25 mi. from Big Bear (☎909-794-4861; open June-Oct. W-Su 8am-4:30pm). An easier way to access the wilderness from L.A. is to take I-10 to Redlands, take any exit to Rte. 38, and head east.

All but the toughest trekkers will need two days to traverse Mt. San Gorgonio (typical routes are 15-22 mi. round-trip). Consult rangers at Barton Flats or Mill Creek for indispensable local info and excellent topographical maps ($6). The **South Fork Trail**, a challenging 22 mi. haul, is one way to reach the summit, though the **Fish Creek Trail** will start you off higher and get you to the top faster. The **Vivian Creek Trail** is the shortest and steepest path to the top, and is used as a training spot for those preparing to climb Mt. Whitney. While backcountry camping is free, parking isn't. Anyone who uses a trail needs an **Adventure Pass** for each day of parking (see p. 479). The thin, dry air quickly dehydrates hikers, so bring ample water.

If you prefer seeing San Gorgonio from the road, there are a handful of campgrounds along a 5 mi. stretch of Rte. 38 near Barton Flats Visitor Center. **San Gorgonio** and **Barton Flats Campgrounds ❶**, near the visitor center, are the most expensive ($20) and have showers; **Heart Bar ❶**, toward Big Bear, is the cheapest ($15). Sites fill up quickly on summer weekends, and reservations (☎800-280-2267) are recommended for the more developed campgrounds.

SAN BERNARDINO ☎909

San Bernardino (pop. 181,718), the seat of America's largest county, is a generic southern Californian smog-bowl. Despite its self-billing as the hub of the Inland Empire, the only real empires in this sulfurous city are the rampant corporate franchises—the side benefit being the inexpensive food and lodging available for those en route to Big Bear or another more palatable destination.

Rosa Maria's ❶, 4202 N. Sierra Way, serves up quick and delicious Mexican food. Dispose of the house favorite "Garbage Burrito" for $4.25. (☎881-1731. Open daily 10am-5pm.) The **original McDonald's** once stood at 1398 N. E St., but don't expect fifteen-cent burgers anymore. The only thing offered at this half-hearted historic site is a growing display of Golden Arches memorabilia and Happy Meal toys. While San Bernardino lacks a critical mass of local eateries, nearby Redlands and its up-and-coming downtown district offer a number of cafes and restaurants. A favorite is **The Royal Falconer ❷**, 106 Orange St., a British pub with pool tables and heaping burgers. Try the Irish Nachos ($6), a french fry plate with everything on top. (☎307-8913. Open daily 11:30am-2am. Kitchen open until 10pm.)

The area along Mt. Vernon Ave. (old Rte. 66) is not so safe, especially at night, so out-of-towners should stick to either the north end of town or **Hospitality Lane**, which crosses Waterman Ave. just north of I-10. Lodging prices **do not include the 10% accommodations tax.** At the **Guesthouse Inn ❸**, 1280 S. E St., the rooms have fridges, and continental breakfast is included. (☎888-0271. Rooms with 1 bed $50; 2 beds $60.) **Motel 6 ❸**, 1960 Ostrems Way, at the University Pkwy. exit off Rte. 215, is near Cal State University, San Bernardino. (☎887-8191; www.motel6.com. Singles M-F $38, Sa-Su $47; doubles M-F $44, Sa-Su $53. Lower prices online.) The three-star **Hilton San Bernardino ❺**, 285 E. Hospitality Ln., is reasonably priced (for a Hilton) and offers all the amenities of an upscale hotel. (☎889-0133. Singles and doubles $100-$130.)

The **Metrolink trains**, 1204 W. 3rd St., connect L.A. and San Bernardino with 15 trains running daily on weekdays and eight on weekends. (☎800-371-5465. $6-8 one-way, $11-15 round-trip.) **MARTA buses** (☎338-1113) run to Big Bear via Arrowhead (3hr., 2 per day, $5). For a **taxi**, call YellowCab (☎884-1111). The **San Bernardino Convention and Visitors Bureau**, 201 N. E St. #103, at the 2nd St. exit off Rte. 215 N or the 3rd St. exit off Rte. 215 S., distributes a thin selection of visitor guides and maps. (☎889-3980. Open M-Th 7:30am-5:30pm, F 7:30am-4:30pm.) Other services include: the **police** (☎384-5742); **San Bernardino Community Hospital**, 1805 Medical Ctr. Dr. (☎887-6333), with 24hr. emergency care; **Internet access** at **San Bernardino Public Library**, 555 W. 6th St. (☎381-8201; open M-W 10am-8pm, Th-Sa 10am-6pm); and the **post office** downtown at 390 W. 5th St. (☎800-275-8777; open M-F 8am-5pm). **Postal Code:** 92401.

IDYLLWILD AND SAN JACINTO MOUNTAINS ☎909

Unlike the teeming resort hubs of Palm Springs and Big Bear, Idyllwild refuses to become overrun by tourists, despite its many attractions and natural beauty. Amid the scrub and stocky pines of the San Jacinto mountains, Idyllwild offers outdoor enthusiasts many steep and dusty challenges. Hundreds of miles of well-maintained hiking trails, including routes to the nearly 11,000 ft. summit of Mt. San Jacinto, surround the town. Full-service and wild backcountry campgrounds abound, as do chalet-style accommodations for the less rugged. The monstrous granite of Tahquitz Rock and Suicide Rock tests rock climbers of all abilities. To top it off, Idyllwild is regularly named one of the 100 best small art towns in the country. Nestled in the mountains more than 6000 ft. above the desert, this Californian version of an alpine village not only escapes the incinerating heat that besieges the desert, but also enjoys snowy, blustery winters.

■ ▶ ORIENTATION AND PRACTICAL INFORMATION

From L.A. to the west or Palm Springs to the east, the swiftest approach to Idyllwild is via **I-10** and **Highway 243** south from Banning. The scenic **Palms-to-Pines Highway** (Hwy. 243) climbs 6000 ft. from the desert to a temperate alpine climate. The

The Inland Empire

MOJAVE DESERT

AROUND L.A.

Palm Springs Aerial Tramway (see p. 541) offers the only **public transportation** to Mt. San Jacinto. There is a network of trails leading from the tram into Idyllwild—buy a map to the San Jacinto National Forest while in Palm Springs.

Visitor Information:

Idyllwild Chamber of Commerce, 54295 Village Center Dr. (☎659-3259; www.idyllwildchamber.com), downstairs in the *Town Crier* (the local paper) building across from the Idyllwild Inn. Info and restaurant coupons. Open M-F 9am-1pm.

San Jacinto Ranger Station (US Forest Service), 54720 Pine Crest Ave. (☎659-2117). Maps of hiking trails and campgrounds $1-6. Free mandatory wilderness permits for day hiking and overnight backpacking in the San Jacinto National Forest. Buy an Adventure Pass ($5) if you plan to park your car on US Forest Service property, which includes all picnic sites and trailheads. Open daily 8am-4:30pm.

Mt. San Jacinto State Park and Wilderness Headquarters, 25905 Hwy. 243 (☎659-2607). Free mandatory wilderness permits. Maps $1-8. Open daily 8am-4:30pm.

Aerial Tram Info (☎888-515-8726/TRAM), on Tramway Rd. off N. Palm Canyon Dr. in Palm Springs. Tram from Palm Springs to Mt. San Jacinto runs every 30min. Round-trip $19, seniors $17, children 5-12 $12.50. Open M-F 10am-8pm, Sa-Su 8am-8pm.

Equipment Rental: Nomad Ventures, 54414 N. Circle Dr. (☎659-4853), sells a vast array of hiking, camping, and climbing gear. Rock climbing shoe rentals $7.50 per day. Open M-F 9am-5pm, Sa 8am-6pm, Su 9am-5pm; in winter closed Tu-W.

Emergency: Riverside Mountain Rescue Unit (☎659-2900). Search-and-rescue missions for injured or lost hikers in the San Jacinto mountains.

Police: Riverside County Sheriff Department (☎800-950-2444). Open 24hr.

Library and Internet Access: Idyllwild Public Library, 54185 Lower Pinecrest (☎659-2300). Open M and F 10am-6pm, W 11am-7pm, Sa 10am-4pm.

Laundry: Idyllwild Laundry Service, on Marantha Rd., across from the Fire Station near the junction of Rte. 243. Wash $1.75, dry $1 per 30 min. Open daily 7am-8pm.

Post Office: 54391 Village Center Dr. (☎659-1969), in the Strawberry Creek shopping center. Open M-F 9am-5pm. **Postal Code: 92549.**

🏠🏕 ACCOMMODATIONS AND CAMPING

Hiking and camping enthusiasts could stay here for weeks on a pittance. **Idyllwild Lodging Information** (☎659-5520) provides a rundown of options. For Forest Service campsite reservations, call ☎800-280-CAMP/2267. For State Park campsites at Idyllwild or Stone Creek, call ☎800-444-7275, or go to www.reserveamerica.com. Sites fill up quickly in summer; make reservations or plan on arriving early. Check with the rangers for other camping options.

▨ Atipahato Lodge, 25525 Scenic Highway 243 (☎888-400-0071; www.atipahato.com). Cozy and romantic, each room at this immaculate alpine chalet has antique and outdoors-themed furniture, a kitchenette, and a private balcony. Rooms look out on the lodge's 5 acres of wooded land, which connects to local hiking trails. Rooms with one queen-size bed M-F $59, Sa-Su $69; beautiful cabins with hot tubs, fireplaces, and full kitchens $135-159. ❹

Idyllwild Inn, 54300 Village Center Rd. (☎659-2552), across from the Strawberry Creek Shopping Center. The wooded acres and idyllic rooms and cabins will make you forget you're right in town. Cabins include well-stocked kitchens, and there's a supermarket just a stone's throw away. Rooms Su-Th from $70, F-Sa from $83; Cabins sleeping up to 6 from $152. ❹

Dark Canyon Campground, 5800 ft., located 6 mi. north of Idyllwild on Hwy. 243. This Forest Service Campsite is tucked away amid tall pines and large rocks. RVs up to 22 ft. in length are welcome. All 22 sites have water, fire pits, vault toilets, and access to hiking trails. Nearby sites at **Fern Basin** (6300 ft., 22 sites) and **Marion Mountain** (6400 ft.; 22 sites) are just as lovely. Both are accessible to RVs up to 15 ft. All sites $12. ❶

Idyllwild Campground, 5400 ft., located off Hwy. 234, just south of Idyllwild. This County Park campsite offers a few more amenities, but less seclusion than Dark Canyon. Nonetheless, most of the 90 sites are quiet and pretty. Water, restrooms, coin-operated showers, grills, and fire rings. Sites $15. ❶

🍴 FOOD

Restaurant bills rise with the altitude, making the supermarket an attractive option. **Fairway Supermarket,** 5411 Village Center Dr., in the Strawberry Creek Shopping Center, has reasonable prices. (☎659-2737. Open spring-fall M-Sa 9am-9pm, Su 9am-7pm; in winter M-Sa 9am-8pm, Su 9am-7pm.)

The Bread Basket, 54710 N. Circle Dr. (☎877-659-3506; www.thebreadbasket.net). This European-style bakery is one of Idyllwild's most beloved eateries. Hearty breakfast omelettes ($8-10), specialty sandwiches ($9-10), and a wide variety of dinner entrees ($12-15). The apple loaf is popular with locals. Plenty of vegetarian options. Open Su-Tu 8am-8pm, W-Th 8am-3pm, F-Sa 8am-9pm. ❸

Cafe Aroma, 54750 N. Circle Dr. (☎659-5212; www.cafearoma.org). A funky combination bistro, gallery, and "social club." In this casual but classy restaurant, art is on the walls, and artists are on the waitstaff. Live music acts include jazz bands, pianists, and even an opera-belting waiter. Fine Italian fare (entrees $10-20) with full wine list. Open M 7am-4pm, Tu-Th and Su 7am-9pm, F-Sa 7am-10pm. Reservations recommended. ❸

Restaurant Gastrognome, 54381 Ridgeview Dr. (☎659-5055). "The Gnome," as locals fondly refer to it, serves up steaks, seafood (lobster tacos $25), and pasta under dimmed lights. For decades Idyllwild's top eatery. Dinner entrees $12-25. Open Su-Th 11:30am-2:30pm and 5-9:30pm, F-Sa 5-9:30pm. ❹

Idyllwild Pizza Company, 54391 Village Center Dr. (☎659-5900), in the Strawberry Creek Shopping Center. Relaxed atmosphere. Often packed with Lakers fans. Pizzas $8-13. All-you-can-eat pizza and pasta M-F $7. Open Su-Th 11:30am-8:30pm, F-Sa 11:30am-9pm; in winter daily 11:30am-8pm. ❸

Squirrel's Nest, 25980 Hwy. 243 (☎659-5274). Fresh Californian and Mexican grill specialties at reasonable prices. Popular for takeout. Open daily 11am-7pm. ❶

OUTDOOR ACTIVITIES AND FESTIVALS

Visitors come to this largely undiscovered, uncommercialized town to explore the rough alpine terrain of the San Jacinto range. Hundreds of miles of established trails snake through the boulder-strewn slopes, and the glacier-polished granite of Tahquitz and Suicide Rock teem with wiry rock climbers. The comparatively high altitude keeps the temperature reasonable even when Palm Springs swelters in hellish torment a vertical mile below. Winters often dump glorious powder on the San Jacinto range, blessing cross-country skiers with ample cause to frolic.

The **Palms-to-Pines Highway,** the section of Hwy. 243 that connects Rte. 74 with I-10, rises from the low Colorado Desert into the sky. The highway offers spectacular views and a fascinating opportunity to study the ecological transition from the desert's tumbleweeds to a temperate, lush alpine forest. Though Idyllwild is only 26 mi. from I-10, plan to spend some time navigating the steep and curvy road and stopping for pictures and views from the many scenic turn-offs.

The **Ernie Maxwell Scenic Trail** (2½ mi.), great for day hikes, is a scenic, downhill path through the forest. This is one of the few trails that do not require a wilderness permit. The trail starts from Humber Park near the town center. More serious backpackers can travel a section of the 2600 mi. **Pacific Crest Trail** (55 mi. lie in the San Jacinto District; for more info, see **From Crest to Crest: The Trail of the West,** p. 237). The trail picks up at Hwy. 74, 1 mi. east of Hwy. 371, or at Black Mountain's scenic **Fuller Ridge Trail,** which is a strenuous hike (14½ mi. round-trip) to the 10,834 ft. summit of **Mount San Jacinto.** Alternately, reach the top of Mt. San Jacinto from **Devil's Slide Trail** (16 mi. round-trip); its lower portion provides dramatic views out to Tahquitz Peak and the desert below. Those who want great views with only a moderately strenuous hike should try the **Deer Spring Trail** (3¼ mi.) to Suicide Rock, which continues out to Strawberry Junction Campground. On summer weekends, the limited number of permits for this area run out very quickly, so get to the ranger station early (see **Practical Information,** p. 485).

Idyllwild ARTS, 52500 Temecula Dr. (☎ 659-2171), at the end of Toll Gate Rd. off Hwy. 243, gives free dance, drama, and music performances, as well as exhibitions and workshops. The **Jazz in the Pines** festival is held every August. (☎ 659-4885. Tickets $40-45.) Sophisticates can imbibe culture and bubbly during the fall's **Art Walk and Wine Tasting,** a walking tour of Idyllwild's art galleries. Contact the **Idyllwild Gallery of Fine Art** for details. (☎ 659-1948 or 888-882-5264.) The **Incredible Edible Art Tour** in June is a chance to sample house specialties from over a dozen popular Idyllwild restaurants. (☎ 866-439-5278. Tickets $20.)

SAN DIEGO

The locals call it "America's Finest City," and visitors pulling into this picturesque port will soon understand why. In a state where every other town has staked a claim as paradise, San Diego may be Southern California's best return on the promises of a golden state. Never too hot or too cold, the weather is sunny and beautiful year-round. The city's gardens are lush and verdant, its beaches are inviting, and the demeanor of its inhabitants is happy and friendly. Although downtown San Diego is pleasant, to truly enjoy the majesty of San Diego, escape the hustle and bustle of the city in favor of the more natural settings of Balboa Park, Old Town, and, of course, the world-class beaches.

The city was founded by the Spanish in 1769 and was the first permanent European settlement on the western coast of what would become the United States. San Diego remained a nondescript town until 1941 when, after the bombing of Pearl Harbor, the US Pacific Fleet established its headquarters here. Today, over a dozen naval and marine installations exist in and around San Diego, and the military presence shapes both the economy and the local culture. San Diego is undoubtedly quieter, more reserved, and more conservative than L.A. Its vibrancy lies with its phenomenal natural beauty and climate, making it a top family travel destination any day of the year.

HIGHLIGHTS OF SAN DIEGO

San Diego Zoo. One of the best places in the world to view animals in captivity, the San Diego Zoo (p. 499), located on over 100 acres in beautiful Balboa Park, is famous for its panda bears.

LA JOLLA. Home to UC San Diego, great beaches, and fun cafes, this neighborhood is one of the liveliest and most attractive in the city (p. 506).

PETCO Park. San Diego's perfect weather adds to the appeal of watching sports in this brand new stadium, which features themed seating areas (p. 502).

 AREA CODE. For most of San Diego, including downtown, Coronado, and Ocean Beach: **619.** Northern San Diego area codes (including Del Mar, La Jolla, parts of North County, and Pacific Beach): **858** and **760. Unless otherwise specified, the area code for the San Diego area is 619.**

✈ INTERCITY TRANSPORTATION

San Diego is in the extreme southwest corner of California, 127 mi. south of L.A. and 15 mi. north of the Mexican border. Three freeways link the city to its regional neighbors: **I-5** runs south from L.A. through the North County cities of Oceanside and Carlsbad and skirts the eastern edge of downtown on its way to the Mexican border; **I-15** runs northeast through the desert to Las Vegas; and **I-8** runs east-west along downtown's northern boundary, connecting the desert with Ocean Beach. The downtown core is laid out in a grid, making it easy to navigate. In **North County,** the **Pacific Coast Highway** runs parallel to I-5 and is known as Old Hwy. 101, 1st St., or Carlsbad Blvd., depending on location.

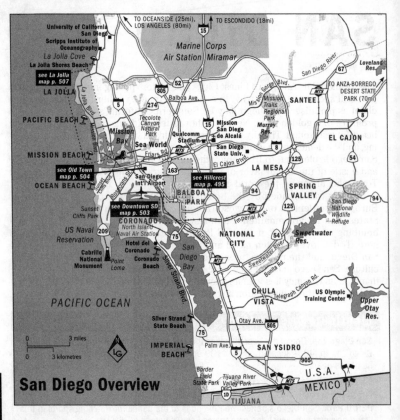

San Diego Overview

Airport: San Diego International (Lindbergh Field), at the northwest edge of downtown. Call the Travelers Aid Society (☎231-7361) for info. Society open daily 8am-
11pm. Bus #992 goes downtown ($2.25), as do cabs ($8-10). **Cloud 9 Shuttle**
(☎800-974-8853) offers affordable shared van transportation throughout the region.

Trains: Amtrak, 1050 Kettner Blvd. (☎800-872-7245), just north of Broadway in the
Santa Fe Depot. Station has info on bus, trolley, car, and boat transportation. Ticket
office open daily 5:15am-10pm. To **L.A.** (11 trains per day 6am-8:30pm; $25-28).

Buses: Greyhound, 120 W. Broadway (☎239-8082 or 800-231-2222), at 1st St. Ticket
office open 24hr. To **L.A.** (30 per day 5am-11:35pm; $15) and **Tijuana** (16 per day
5am-11:35pm; $5).

■ ORIENTATION

The epicenter of **inland** San Diego tourism is historic **Balboa Park,** home to the
world-famous **San Diego Zoo** and a cluster of diverse museums and cultural
attractions. Northwest of the park is the stylish **Hillcrest** neighborhood, the city's
gay enclave, which has great shopping and restaurants. San Diego's **downtown**
attractions are concentrated in the corridor that includes its business and **waterfront** districts—all testaments to San Diego's continuing renaissance. Within this

center of commerce and entertainment are the city's skyscrapers and its modern **Convention Center. Seaport Village** sits on W. Harbor Dr. in olde-time tourist splendor. The **Gaslamp Quarter,** the nexus of San Diego nightlife, sits in the southern section of downtown between 4th and 6th St. and contains many of San Diego's signature theaters, nightclubs, and restaurants. Farther to the north and near the water, **Little Italy** is its own tiny international epicenter of food and entertainment. Just north of downtown in the southeast corner of the I-5 and I-8 junction lies a little slice of old Mexico known as **Old Town.** Discriminating travelers may find Old Town's touristy kitsch a bit contrived, but the fantastic Mexican food and lively scene make this place worth a visit. San Diego is surprisingly safe, but nevertheless, always exercise reasonable caution and avoid the somewhat rundown, eastern section of downtown that abuts I-5.

Along the **coast,** San Diego Bay opens up south of downtown, bounded by classy **Coronado Island.** Coronado offers sunny outdoor fun in the form of surfing and cycling; it may, however, be too pricey for most budget travelers. Northwest of town sits the collection of shiny beaches and man-made inlets known as **Mission Bay.** The beaches north, south, and west of the bay are some of the finest urban beaches in America. Don't forget to get splashed by the flopping, spurting water creatures at the original **Sea World.** A jaunt up the coast leads to the swanky tourist haven of **La Jolla** (see p. 506), where a profusion of upscale shops and Euro-designer brand names often distracts tourists from the area's real riches: the excellent snorkeling at La Jolla Cove, the sparkling beaches at La Jolla Shores, and the relaxing grounds of the surrounding parkland. Up the coast beyond La Jolla are the laid-back, sun-soaked beach communities of the **North County** (see p. 511).

LOCAL TRANSPORTATION

PUBLIC TRANSPORTATION. The city of San Diego provides fairly extensive public transportation through the **San Diego Metropolitan Transit System (MTS).** MTS's automated 24hr. information line, **Info Express** (☎685-4900), has info on San Diego's buses, trains, and trolleys. For live assistance, visit the **Transit Store** at 1st Ave. and Broadway, which has timetables, a free pamphlet with tips for riding, and bus, trolley, and ferry tickets. Be sure to pick up a one- to four-day **Day Tripper Pass** if you plan to use public transit of any kind more than once. (Open M-F 8:30am-5:30pm, Sa-Su noon-4pm. Day pass $5, 2 days $9, 3 days $12, 4 days $15.) The **Regional Transit Information Center** is also a good source for information. (☎233-3004. Open M-F 5:30am-8:30pm, Sa-Su 8am-5pm.) **Bus** fares range from $1 to $3.50 depending on the route. Transfers are good for 1½hr. after they are issued. They require exact fare but accept dollar bills. All buses are wheelchair accessible. If getting to a bus stop is a problem, call the door-to-bus-stop service **DART.** (☎887-841-DART/3278. Operates M-F 5:30am-8pm. $2.25.) The **COASTER** sends trains daily between San Diego (downtown and Old Town) and the coastal communities of Solana Beach, Encinitas, Carlsbad, and Oceanside. (☎800-COASTER/262-7837; www.sdcommute.com. $3.75-5.25 one-way; 10-trip pass $29-43.)

The bright red **San Diego Trolley** consists of two lines leaving from downtown for El Cajon, San Ysidro, and points in between. The El Cajon line leaves from 12th Ave. and Imperial St.; the San Ysidro line leaves from the Old Town Transit Center (at Taylor St. and San Diego Ave.) and continues to the Mexican border. Don't be fooled by the lack of turnstiles: inspectors do check for tickets, and the fine for riding without one is considerable. (☎231-8549; www.sdcommute.com. Runs daily 5am-1am. $1.25-3.) The downtown trolley fare allows unlimited travel to and from downtown stations for 2hr.

BY CAR. Southern California is the land of the automobile: renting a car will make your life easier and your trip more enjoyable. Most rental agencies do not rent to drivers under 21. However, if you have a letter from your insurer stating that you are covered for rental-car collisions you might have better luck.

> **@West Rent a Car,** 3045 Rosecrans St., #215, (☎619-223-2343; www.atwestren-tacar.com), just north of downtown San Diego. From $20 per day. Under-25 surcharge $5-25 per day. Insurance $17 per day if driving to Mexico. Open daily 8am-8pm.

> **Bargain Auto,** 3860 Rosecrans St. (☎299-0009). Used cars available to renters 18+. Cars from $19 per day with 150 mi. free, $105 per week with 500 mi. free. Under-25 surcharge $6 per day, $35 per week. Insurance $39 per day if driving to Mexico. Credit card required. Open M-F 8am-6pm, Sa-Su 8am-4pm.

> **Dollar,** 2499 Pacific Hwy. (☎234-3388; www.dollar.com), at the airport. Cars $28-54 per day with unlimited mileage. Must be 21+ with credit card. Under-25 surcharge $20 per day. Insurance $25 per day if driving to Mexico. Open daily 5:30am-midnight.

BY BIKE. San Diego has an extensive system of **bike routes.** Some are separate from the road and some are specially marked outer lanes. The flat, paved route along Mission and Pacific Beaches toward La Jolla affords ocean views and soothing sea breezes. Bikers beware: pedestrian traffic along the beaches rivals car traffic on the boulevards. Riding downtown and through Balboa Park is also popular. Buses with bike racks make it possible to cart bikes almost anywhere in the city (call ☎233-3004). For more bike info, contact the **City Bicycle Coordinator** (☎533-3110) or **CalTrans** (☎231-2453).

RENTALS: BIKES, BOARDS, AND BLADES. Gear is available throughout San Diego and the surrounding communities. Most rental stores are cheap enough for the budget traveler and bolster San Diego's reputation as an outdoor-sports haven.

> **Action Sports,** 4000 Coronado Bay Rd. (☎424-4466), at the Marina Dock of the Loews Coronado Bay Resort on **Coronado Island.** Beach cruisers and mountain bikes $10 per hr., $30 per 4hr. Open M-F 9am-6pm, Sa-Su 8:30am-6:30pm.

> **Bikes and Beyond** (☎435-7180), at the ferry landing on 1st St., on **Coronado Island.** Mountain bikes $6 per hr., $18 per 4hr. In-line skates $5/$15. Pedal surrey $15 per 30min., $25 per hr. Locks, protective gear, and maps included. Open 8:30am-dusk.

> **Bike Tours,** 509 5th Ave. (☎238-2444), in the **Gaslamp Quarter.** Well-maintained mountain bikes $18 per day, $50 per week. Lock, protective gear, maps, and roadside assistance are included. Open daily 8am-7pm.

> **Cheap Rentals,** 3221 Mission Blvd. (☎858-486-5533 or 800-941-7761; www.cheap-rentals.com), in **Mission Beach.** Beach cruisers $6 per hr., $15 per day. Skateboards $6/$15. Open daily 8am-6pm.

> **Dana Landing Boat Rentals,** 1710 W. Mission Bay Dr. (☎226-2929), on **Mission Bay.** 14 ft. Capri sailboats $20 per hr. Other watersports equipment, including jet skis and power boat, are also available. Open daily 6am-10pm.

> **Little Sam's,** 1343 Orange Ave. (☎435-4058), near the Hotel Del Coronado on **Coronado Island.** Beach cruisers $6 per hr., $14 per half-day, $20 per day. In-line skates $5/$14/$20. Surfboards $15 per hr., $25 per day. All gear comes with safety equipment, locks, maps, and advice. Open daily 8am-6pm.

> **South Coast Longboards,** 5037 Newport Ave. (☎223-8808), in **Ocean Beach.** Soft surfboards $5 per hr., $25 per day; glass boards for the more experienced $10/$50. Credit card or cash deposit of $250 for soft boards, $350 for glass boards. Open June-Aug. M-Sa 9am-7:30pm, Su 10am-6:30pm; Sept.-May daily 9am-6pm.

Star Surfing Co., 4652 Mission Blvd. (☎858-273-7827), in **Pacific Beach.** Surfboards $5 per hr., $20 per day. Bodyboards $3/$12. Driver's license or credit card required for deposit. Open daily 10am-6pm.

Windsport, 844 W. Mission Bay Dr. (☎858-488-4642; www.windsport.net), in **Mission Beach.** Kayaks $15 per hr., $75 per day . 2½hr. kayak tours including equipment rental $60 per person. Includes equipment rental. Open M-F 10am-6pm, Sa-Su 9am-6pm.

WALKING. Downtown, Balboa Park, and Old Town can easily be covered on foot, but beaches are less accessible because of the wide distances between them. **Walkabout International**, 4639 30th St., Ste. C, sponsors about 100 free walks each month, from downtown architectural strolls to 20 mi. La Jolla treks. (☎231-7463. Open M-F 10am-2pm.) Because jaywalking is actively prosecuted in San Diego, pedestrians almost always heed the walk signals.

🖪 PRACTICAL INFORMATION

TOURIST AND FINANCIAL SERVICES

Visitor Information:

International Visitor Information Center, 11 Horton Plaza (☎236-1212), downtown at 1st Ave. and F St. Helpful, multilingual staff dispenses publications, brochures, and discount coupons. 3hr. parking validation for lots with entrances on G St. and 4th Ave. Open daily 9am-5pm.

Just Call (☎615-6111) is an information line operated by the city of San Diego. For free 24hr. assistance with accommodations in San Diego county call ☎1-800-SANDIEGO.

Old Town and State Park Info, 4002 Wallace Ave. (☎220-5422), in Old Town Sq. Take the Taylor St. exit off I-8 or bus #5. Free walking tours daily 11am and 2pm. Open daily 10am-5pm.

San Diego Convention and Visitors Bureau, 401 B St., #1400, Dept. 700, San Diego 92101 (☎236-1212; www.sandiego.org), also provides info.

Budget Travel: San Diego Council of American Youth Hostels, 521 Market St. (☎525-1531; www.sandiegohostels.org), in the Metropolitan Hostel at 5th St. Offers budget guides and info. Open daily 6:30am-midnight.

American Express, 7610 Hazard Center Dr. (☎297-8101). Open M-F 9:30am-6pm, Sa 10am-3pm. Call for other locations throughout the area.

LOCAL SERVICES

Library: San Diego Public Library, 820 E St. (☎236-5800), offers foreign newspapers, borrowing privileges for visitors, a California information room, and an ongoing concert, film, and lecture series. 1hr. free Internet. Branches throughout city, call for more info. Open M-Th 10am-9pm, F-Sa 9:30am-5:30pm, Su 1-5pm.

Community Services: Senior Citizens Services, 202 C St. (☎236-6905), in the City Hall Bldg. Provides senior ID cards (W 9am-12:30pm) and plans daytrips. Open M-F 8am-5pm. **The Access Center,** 1295 University Ave., #10 (☎293-3500, TDD 293-7757), in Hillcrest. Attendant referral, wheelchair repair and sales, emergency housing, motel/hotel accessibility referral. Open M-F 9am-5pm. **Accessible San Diego,** 1010 2nd Ave. (☎858-279-0704), also has info. Open M-F 9am-5pm. **The Center for Community Solutions,** 4508 Mission Bay Dr. (☎233-8984, 24hr. hotline 272-1767), at Bunker Hill St. in Pacific Beach. Offers rape and domestic violence counseling, as well as legal services. Open M-F 8am-4:30pm.

GLBT Organizations: Lesbian and Gay Men's Center, 3909 Centre St. (☎692-2077), provides counseling and info. Open M-Sa 9am-10pm. The **Gay Youth Alliance** (☎233-9309) is a support and social group for people under 24. For a listing of queer events and establishments, check *Update* (☎299-0500), available at virtually all queer businesses, bookstores, and bars. The *Gay and Lesbian Times*, published every Thursday, provides event, bar, and club listings.

Ticket Agencies: Ticketmaster (☎220-TIXS/8497, concert info 581-1000). High service charge. Get half-price tickets from **Times Arts Tix** (☎497-5000), at the corner of 3rd and Broadway. Open Su 10am-5pm, Tu-Th 11am-6pm, F-Sa 10am-6pm.

Laundromat: Metro Wash and Dry, 724 4th Ave. (☎544-1284), between F and G St. Wash $2, dry $0.25 per 8min. Open daily 6am-7:30pm.

Weather Conditions: Weather Report (☎221-8824). Updated daily—as if the weather ever changes. The average daily temperature is 70°F, with nighttime lows around 60°F.

EMERGENCY AND COMMUNICATIONS

Police: ☎531-2000. 1401 Broadway.

Auto Repairs: AAA Emergency Road Service, ☎800-400-4222.

Medical Services: Kaiser Foundation, 4647 Zion Ave. (☎528-5000). **Columbia Mission Bay,** 3030 Bunker Hill St. (☎858-274-7721), in Mission Bay.

Hotlines: Lesbian and Gay Men's Center Crisis Line, ☎800-479-3339. **Women's Center Rape Hotline,** ☎233-3088.

24hr. Pharmacy: Rite Aid, 535 Robinson Ave. (☎291-3705), in Hillcrest.

Radio: News/talk on KSDO (1130 AM), National Public Radio on KPBS (89.5 FM), popular Top 40 on 90.3 FM.

Post Offices: Hillcrest Station, 3911 Cleveland Ave. (☎295-5091). Open M 7:30am-5pm, Tu-F 8:30am-5pm, Sa 8:30am-2pm. **Postal Code:** 92103. **Linda Vista Station,** 2150 Comstock St. Open M 7:30am-5pm, Tu-F 8:30am-5pm, Sa 8:30am-noon. **Postal Code:** 92111.

⌐ ACCOMMODATIONS

Rates rise on weekends and during the summer season. Reservations are recommended for all of the below listings, particularly in summer. San Diego is littered with generic chain motels, which are generally safe and clean but are a little more expensive than hostels or residential hotels. There is a popular cluster known as **Hotel Circle** (2-3 mi. east of I-5 along I-8), where summer prices begin at $60 for a single and $70 for a double during the week ($70 and $80, respectively, on weekends). If you choose to stay in a motel, be sure to pick up one of the traveler discount coupon books at a visitors center. There are also several state beaches in North County and one on Coronado that allow camping.

INLAND SAN DIEGO

▨ **USA Hostels San Diego,** 726 5th Ave. (☎232-3100 or 800-438-8622; www.usahostels.com), between F and G St. in the **Gaslamp Quarter.** This colorful Euro-style fun house is right in the middle of a popular clubbing street. Festive common areas. Hosts frequent parties and organizes Tijuana tours ($10.50) and Gaslamp pub crawls ($4). International passport or out-of-state student ID required. Pancake breakfast included. Free linen and lockers. Coin-op laundry with free detergent. Reserve private rooms in advance. Dorms $21; private rooms $46-50. $1 off for ISIC, VIP, and BUNAC cardholders. $3 off with brochures available at other USA hostels. ❷

▨ **San Diego Downtown Hostel (HI-AYH),** 521 Market St. (☎525-1531 or 800-909-4776, ext. 156; www.sandiegohostels.org), at 5th Ave., in the heart of the **Gaslamp Quarter.** Clean and quiet almost to the point of sterility, this hostel caters to the calm traveler.

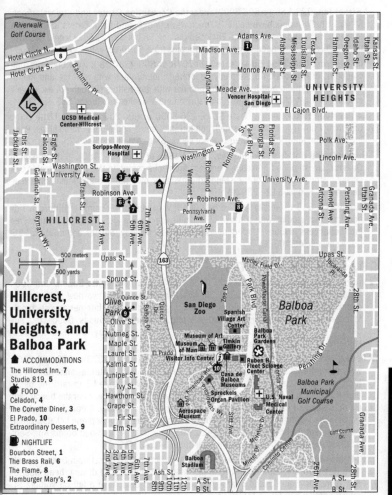

Hillcrest, University Heights, and Balboa Park

ACCOMMODATIONS
The Hillcrest Inn, 7
Studio 819, 5

FOOD
Celadon, 4
The Corvette Diner, 3
El Prado, 10
Extraordinary Desserts, 9

NIGHTLIFE
Bourbon Street, 1
The Brass Rail, 6
The Flame, 8
Hamburger Mary's, 2

Airy common room. No alcohol. Breakfast included. Lockers (bring a lock) and laundry available. Reception 6:30am-12:30am. IBN reservations available. Groups welcome. 4- to 6-bed dorms $18-25, nonmembers $21-28; doubles $45-56. ❷

Old Town Inn, 4444 Pacific Hwy. (☎ 800-643-3025), near I-5 and I-8, a 10min. walk from **Old Town.** Clean rooms with standard amenities. Across the street from the trolley station; perfect for those without cars. Some rooms have kitchenettes. Pool access. Large continental breakfast included. Standard rooms $56-80. ❹

Heritage Park Bed and Breakfast Inn, 2470 Heritage Park Row (☎ 299-6832 or 800-995-2470; www.heritageparkinn.com), near **Old Town.** This Victorian mansion in the quiet enclave of Heritage Park now functions as a cozy B&B, and hosts afternoon teas and nightly screenings of vintage films. Each of the 12 guest rooms is unique. Reserve at least 1 month in advance. Rooms from $160. ❺

J Street Inn, 222 J St. (☎696-6922), near the **Convention Center** and ritzy waterfront. All 221 studio rooms have cable TV, microwave, fridge, and bath. Caters to long-term travelers. Gym and reading room. Enclosed parking $8 per day, $26 per week. Reservations highly recommended. Singles and doubles from $199 per week. ❹

The Hillcrest Inn, 3754 5th Ave. (☎293-7078 or 800-258-2280; www.bryx.com/hillcrestinn), in **Hillcrest.** 45 tastefully decorated rooms, each with a fridge and microwave. Sunning patio and hot tub. Very popular with gay visitors (though not exclusively catering to a gay clientele). 2-day min. stay on most weekends. Rooms $65-85. ❹

La Pensione Hotel, 606 W. Date St. (☎236-8000 or 800-232-4683), in **Little Italy.** Charming Euro-style hotel with small, comfortable rooms and modern furnishings. Parking available. Many rooms feature harbor views. Singles and doubles $75. ❹

Horton Grand Hotel, 311 Island Ave. (☎544-1886 or 800-542-1886), in the **Gaslamp Quarter.** Lavish period furnishings and gas fireplaces complete the Victorian feel in this classy historic hotel. All of the standard amenities, plus many extras including a resident ghost. Rooms $129-289. ❺

Studio 819, 819 University Ave. (☎542-0819; www.studio819.com), in **Hillcrest.** Tidy and compact studios with a range of amenities, including kitchenettes. Laundry. Free Internet access in lobby. Underground parking $10 per day. Singles and doubles $55-63; weekly $345-400. ❹

COASTAL SAN DIEGO

▓ **International House,** 4502 Cass St. (☎858-274-4325), in **Pacific Beach,** and 3204 Mission Bay Dr. (☎858-539-0043), in **Mission Beach.** These two new sister hostels offer excellent service, clean and airy rooms, comfortable beds, Internet access, breakfast, free surfboard and boogie board use, and great beach locations. Out-of-state student ID or international passport required. 28-day max. stay. Dorm rooms $20, students $18. Weekly dorms $110. ❷

▓ **Ocean Beach International (OBI),** 4961 Newport Ave. (☎223-7873 or 800-339-7263; www.oceanbeach.com/hostel), in **Ocean Beach.** Look for international flags. Free transport from airport, train, and bus terminals. If driving, take I-8 toward the beach until it becomes Sunset Cliffs Blvd. and turn right on Newport Ave. Near the beach, with clean rooms and cable TV. Cheap beach gear rental and laundry. Proof of international travel in the last or next 6 months required (stamped passports or plane tickets). Breakfast included. Barbecue Tu and F night. 29-day max. stay. 4- to 6-bed dorms Apr.-Sept. $19; Oct.-Mar. $16. Doubles (some with bath) $40-43. ❷

HI-Point Loma, 3790 Udall St. (☎223-4778), 1½ mi. inland (east) from **Ocean Beach.** Take bus #35 from downtown to the first stop on Voltaire St. If driving, head west on Sea World Dr. from I-5 and bear right on Sunset Cliff Blvd. Take a left on Voltaire St., then a right on Worden St.; Udall St. is 1 block away. Large kitchen, courtyard with ping-pong, and common room with cable TV. Laundry. Pancake breakfast included. Reception 8am-10pm. 14-night max. stay. Reserve at least 2 days in advance. Dorms $15-18; private rooms $38; triples $54. $3 more for nonmembers. ❷

Shell Beach, 981 Coast Blvd. (☎858-459-4306 or 888-525-6552; www.lajollacove.com), in **La Jolla.** Considering its beachfront location, this is one of the most reasonably priced accommodations in the area. The otherwise expensive oceanfront property has a few cheap and tiny studios. Comfy, older rooms are mere steps from the beach. Non-oceanfront studio with queen-size bed $65. Lower rates Sept.-May. ❹

Inn at Mission Bay, 4545 Mission Bay Dr. (☎858-483-4222; www.innatmissionbay.com), near **Mission Bay.** Standard rooms and amenities including kitchenettes. Singles and doubles in summer $79-99; in winter from $54. 10% AAA discount. Frequent online specials. ❹

Silver Strand State Beach Campground (☎ 435-5184), along the 7 mi. strip connecting Coronado Island to the mainland. An endless ribbon of sand and waves. Excellent surfing. No reservations for the small and undeveloped RV sites. Sites $13. ❶

🗂 FOOD

With its large Hispanic population and proximity to Mexico, San Diego is renowned for exemplary Mexican cuisine. Old Town serves up some of the best authentic Mexican food in the state. San Diego also offers a spectacular assortment of ethnic and more traditional eateries, concentrated in both the Hillcrest neighborhood and the trendy Gaslamp Quarter.

INLAND SAN DIEGO

Frequented by both locals and visitors, **Old Town** has the best Mexican food in San Diego, which is saying a lot. Don't be intimidated by the gigantic lines: Old Town's colorful and authentic restaurants have perfected the art of "move 'em in, move 'em out" without compromising quality. Many Old Town eateries are in the **Bazaar del Mundo,** a cluster of restaurants and stores near Calhoun St. accessible only by foot. For a few extra dollars, excellent cuisine abounds in the **Gaslamp Quarter.** The food court at the **Horton Plaza,** a large shopping center between 1st and 4th Ave., and E and G St. sells super-quick bargain-basement chow—it's cheap, but it aspires to be more than just fast food. The best food near Balboa Park is in nearby **Hillcrest** and **University Heights.** These trendy, youth-oriented, gay-friendly neighborhoods are home to an array of inexpensive restaurants offering many low-fat and vegetarian options. Shop for organic groceries in Hillcrest at **Whole Foods Market,** 711 University Ave. (☎ 294-2800. Open daily 8am-10pm.) Grab groceries downtown at **Ralph's,** 101 G St. (☎ 595-1581. Open 24hr.)

🍽 **Casa de Bandini,** 2754 Calhoun St. (☎ 297-8211), in the Bazaar del Mundo in **Old Town.** Repeatedly voted best Mexican restaurant in San Diego. Set in a Spanish-style architectural landmark (built in 1829), Bandini dishes out superb food and boisterous *mariachi* music. The combo plates ($5-9) are fantastic, but the heavyweight margarita ($4-7) is what's truly responsible for Bandini's iconic status. Many outdoor tables on a beautiful tiled patio with fountain. Open Su-Th 11am-9:30pm, F-Sa 11am-10pm. ❷

🍽 **The Corvette Diner,** 3946 5th Ave. (☎ 542-1001), in **Hillcrest.** The ultimate flashback to the days of nickel milkshakes, this 50s-style diner has more chrome than Detroit and more neon than Las Vegas. Extraordinary greasy-spoon classics and a number of unique creations like the Rory Burger (peanut butter and bacon burger; $7). Costumed waitresses give as much lip as service. Open Su-Th 11am-10pm, F-Sa 11am-midnight. ❷

Kansas City Barbecue, 610 W. Market St. (☎ 231-9680), near **Seaport Village.** The setting for *Top Gun*'s Great Balls of Fire bar scene. While the wooden piano remains, all that's left of Goose, Maverick, and Charlie is an abundance of autographed posters and neon signs. Vegetarians will find themselves in the Danger Zone in this barbecue-slathered meatfest. Entrees $9-16. Open daily 11am-1am. ❷

Zócalo Grill, 2444 San Diego Ave. (☎ 298-9840), in **Old Town.** This contemporary bistro grills fabulous fish and other seafood. Happy hour 4-6:30pm; famous Brigantine Fish Taco $2.50. Tapas ($10) are perfect to share. Open daily 11:30am-10:30pm.

The Fish Market, 750 N. Harbor Dr. (☎ 232-3474), within walking distance of **Seaport Village.** This local landmark serves up an amazing array of the freshest seafood; the menu is updated twice a day based on the catch. Ask for a patio table and enjoy your meal with an incomparable view of the bay. Entrees $12-35. Open daily 11am-10pm. The swankier **Top of the Market** is located directly upstairs. While the catch is the same, the added linens, view, ambience, and gourmet names will cost an extra $10 per plate. Su brunch 10am-2pm. Open M-Sa 11am-10pm, Su 10am-10pm. ❹

Celadon, 540 University Ave. (☎297-8424), in **Hillcrest.** This candlelit Thai joint seems out of place among the people-watching restaurants in Hillcrest. Beautifully presented Thai favorites, including pad thai and curries. Despite its award-winning chef and long weekend lines, lunch combos are a bargain at $6, and dinner starts at $8. Open M-Sa 11am-11pm, Su 4-10pm. ❷

El Prado, 1549 El Prado (☎557-9441; www.pradobalboa.com), in the heart of **Balboa Park.** This Latin-Italian fusion restaurant gets rave reviews. The patio seating is beautiful any time of the year, and the calamari appetizer is big enough to be a meal ($10). Paella takes a while to prepare, but is worth the wait. Dinner entrees from $18. Open M-Sa 11:30am-9:30pm, Su 11am-8pm. ❺

Trattoria Fantastica, 1735 India St. (☎234-1735; http://trattoriafantas.signonsandiego.com), in the heart of **Little Italy.** This family-owned restaurant serves heaping portions of scrumptious Italian food. Try the popular *calamari parmigiana* ($15.75) or the *gnocchi alla Romana* ($16). Outdoor seating available. Wood-fired pizzas $10. Entrees $10-25. Open daily 11:30am-3pm and 5-10pm. ❸

Berta's, 3928 Twiggs St. (☎295-2343), off San Diego Ave., in **Old Town.** Dozens of authentic Guatemalan, Honduran, Venezuelan, Peruvian, and Costa Rican specialties ($9-14). Tapas $2-5. Open Tu-Su 11am-10pm. ❸

Extraordinary Desserts, 2929 5th Ave. (☎294-7001; www.extraordinarydesserts.com), next to **Balboa Park.** Additional location: 1430 Union St. in **Little Italy.** Decadent mounds of chocolate, cake, fruits, and other delectables at this desserts-only restaurant. The Asian-influenced decor and rich chocolate may lull you into a state of bliss. Whole cakes available for carry-out ($35-42). Open Su-Th 8:30am-11pm, F 8:30am-midnight, Sa 11am-midnight. ❸

Gaslamp Strip Club, 340 5th Ave. (☎231-3140), in the **Gaslamp Quarter.** Don't be fooled by the name, the 21+ age requirement, the occasional bachelor party, or the red lights and red leather: the only meat on display here are the fine 8-20 oz. steaks and kabobs ($10-20). This retro lounge allows you to order a raw steak, throw it on a grill, and cook and season it to your own taste. Open Tu-Su 5pm-late. ❸

Old Town Mexican Cafe, 2489 San Diego Ave. (☎297-4330 or 888-234-9836; www.oldtownmexcafe.com), in **Old Town.** Serves 115 varieties of tequila, and makes tortillas in the front window. Huge combo plates from $8. Open daily 7am-2am. ❷

COASTAL SAN DIEGO

Mission Beach and **Pacific Beach** are crowded with youth-oriented bars and surfer dives. To bag your own meal, head to the supermarket **Ralph's,** 4315 Mission Blvd. (☎273-0778. Open 24hr.) Most of **Ocean Beach's** inexpensive restaurants and bars are along the westernmost stretch of **Newport Avenue,** one of San Diego's trendiest drags where shots for the movie *Almost Famous* were filmed. **Prospect Street,** the main drag in **La Jolla,** is crammed with upscale shops and galleries, but tucked among these are a number of excellent eateries. **Girard Avenue** and its side streets also hold their own.

▓ Kono's Surf Club, 704 Garnet Ave. (☎483-1669), across from the Crystal Pier in **Pacific Beach.** Identifiable by the line stretching down the block, Kono's is a surfer's shrine. Breakfast served all day ($3-5). Try the huge Egg Burrito #3, which includes bacon, cheese, potatoes, and sauce ($4). Open M-F 7am-3pm, Sa-Su 7am-4pm. ❶

World Curry, 1433 Garnet Ave. (☎689-2222; www.worldcurry.com), in **Pacific Beach,** farther east along the main drag. The amazingly quick service delivers delicious curries from all over the world for $6. Mango, green tea, and Thai tea frappes ($3) provide relief from the heat. Open M-Sa 11am-10pm, Su 4-9pm. ❷

The Spot, 1005 Prospect St. (☎858-459-0800), in **La Jolla.** Popular with local yuppies and college students, this neighborhood bar has a long menu of delicious pastas, pizzas, and steaks. Try the Garbage Burger ($12), with any topping imaginable, along with some La Jolla Gold beer. Open daily 11am-2am. ❷

Jay's Gourmet, 8008 Girard Ave., #220 (☎858-454-2222), in **La Jolla.** With a breath-taking ocean view, Jay's serves some of the best Italian food in the area. Seafood specialties are favorites at this casual seaside eatery. 3-course meal specials offered year-round. Entrees from $10. Open M-Th 11am-9pm, F-Su 11am-10pm. ❸

Zanzibar, 976 Garnet Ave. (☎272-4762), in **Pacific Beach.** Local artwork indoors, people-watching outdoors. Enjoy gourmet pizza ($7-9) and big all-day breakfasts ($4-8). Full-service cafe has coffees and espressos from around the world. Open M-Th 6:30am-11pm, F-Sa 6:30am-midnight. ❷

The Living Room, 1010 Prospect St. (☎858-489-1187), in **La Jolla.** Home to mis-matched sets of comfy chairs and amazingly large sandwiches ($6.50), this coffee-house in the village is a local fave. The cauldron-sized hot chocolate ($4) is good for at least two. Open daily 6:30am-midnight. ❷

Eatopia, 5001 Newport Ave. (☎224-3237; www.eatopiaexpress.com), in **Ocean Beach.** Earthy vegan fast food with refreshing smoothies and excellent wraps. The popular Cosmic California wrap is especially delicious ($4.75). Open daily 10am-8pm. ❶

Rhinoceros Cafe and Grill, 1166 Orange Ave. (☎435-2121), on **Coronado Island.** Fresh pasta, salads, and seafood with plenty of outdoor seating and affordable drink prices. Try their specialty, penne a la vodka (lunch $9, dinner $14). Open daily 11am-2:30pm and 5-9pm. ❸

◎ SIGHTS

San Diego's world-famous attractions are extremely varied, offering more than enough to keep any traveler engaged. Community events take place regularly, especially during the summer. Pick up a free copy of the weekly *Reader*, available at most stores, for local event listings. The **San Diego 3-for-1 Pass** ($92, ages 3-9 $67) offers unlimited admission for five consecutive days at a discounted price to three of the city's premier sights—Sea World, the San Diego Zoo, and the San Diego Wild Animal Park. Visit www.sandiegozoo.org or the websites of the other two parks for information and online ticketing

BALBOA PARK

Balboa Park was created from the baked dirt of an abandoned pueblo tract when pioneering horticulturists planted its first redwood seedlings in 1889. Today, the park nurtures these spectacular trees and a veritable profusion of plants. The centerpiece of the park is the world-famous San Diego Zoo, which houses a diverse array of animals in authentic and humane habitats. South of the zoo is a Spanish-style promenade lined with museums and other cultural attractions. You can reach the park by bus #7, and parking is free. Most museums offer free admission at least one Tuesday a month.

▨ SAN DIEGO ZOO

2920 Zoo Dr. From the north or south, take I-5 or I-15 to Rte. 163, get off at the Zoo/Muse-ums exit (Richmond St.), and follow the signs. From the east, take I-8 to Rte. 163 S, exit at Park Blvd. and turn left; the zoo entrance is off Park Blvd. at Zoo Pl. ☎234-3153, Giant Panda viewing info 888-MY-PANDA/697-2632; www.sandiegozoo.org. Open daily late June-early Sept. 9am-10pm; early Sept.-late June 9am-dusk. Most of zoo is wheelchair accessible and wheelchairs can be rented, but assistance may be necessary on the zoo's steep hills. $21, $32 with 35min. bus tour and 2 tickets for the aerial tramway; ages 3-11 $14/$19.75; military in uniform free. Free on Founder's Day, the 1st M in Oct.

With over 100 acres of exquisite habitats, this zoo deserves its reputation as one of the finest in the world. Its unique "bioclimatic" exhibits group animals and plants together by habitat. The **Polar Bear Plunge** is one of the most elaborate habitats, housing Siberian reindeer, arctic foxes, fish, and of course, the polar bears themselves. Visitors observe the bears underwater through a gigantic glass-walled pool. The legendary **panda** exhibit is the most timeless feature of the park, and the zoo invests over $1,000,000 a year on panda habitat preservation in China. Zoo-goers have a chance to see gorillas and bonobos up close, who act remarkably like those watching them. The koala exhibit show these furry marsupials (not bears) playing on trees while posing for photographs.

The most thorough way to tour the zoo is on foot. During the summer, while sweaty tourists wander about in the sun, the wily animals often snooze in shade hidden from the guests; the best time to visit is early morning or late afternoon, when the sun isn't at its peak. Visitors can also board the educational 40min. **double-decker bus tour** that covers about 75% of the zoo. The non-narrated express bus will take you to any of five stops throughout the park anytime during the day. The **Skyfari Aerial Tramway** rises 170 ft. above the park and lasts about two minutes but can save on walking time. Don't expect to see anything but a pleasant view of the tops of trees and the skyline. *(One-way $2. Coupons for the total experience admission ticket are in almost every tourist publication.)*

BALBOA PARK AND EL PRADO MUSEUMS

Most of the museums reside within the resplendent Spanish colonial-style buildings that line **El Prado Street,** which runs east-west through the Park's central **Plaza de Panama.** These ornate structures—designed for the Panama California Exposition of 1915-16 and for the International Expositions of 1935-36—were originally intended to last two years. As many of the buildings are now nearly 80 years old, they are now being renovated with more permanence in mind. The Passport to Balboa Park ($30) provides admission to (and is available for purchase) at all park museums. The Best of Balboa Park passport ($55) also includes admission to all ticketed options at the Zoo. The **Balboa Visitors Center,** 1549 El Prado, is in the House of Hospitality at the Plaza de Panama. It sells park maps ($0.50) and the Passport to Balboa Park. (☎ 239-0512. www.balboapark.org. Open daily in summer 9am-4:30pm; in winter 9am-4pm.)

MUSEUM OF MAN. Creationists beware: this museum dedicates an entire floor to the 98.4% of DNA we share with chimpanzees. Exhibits trace human evolution from primates to man, with life-sized mannequins and staged civilizations. The real treat, however, is on the outside and doesn't require admission; formerly a state building, the museum's oft-photographed tower and dome gleam with beautiful Spanish mosaic tiles. *(On the west end of the park. ☎ 239-2001; www.museumofman.org. Open daily 10am-4:30pm. $6, seniors $5, ages 6-17 $3; free 3rd Tu of each month. Special exhibits usually $8.)*

NATURAL HISTORY MUSEUM. At the east end of Balboa Park, this museum was entirely redone in 2002. Though rotating exhibits are hit or miss, the new IMAX theater is a consistent winner. All shows are free with admission. *(Near the intersection of Park Blvd. and Village Pl. at the east end of Balboa Park. ☎ 232-3821; www.sdnhm.org. Open daily Memorial Day-Labor Day 9:30am-5:30pm; Labor Day-Memorial Day 9:30am-4:30pm. $9, seniors, military, and students $6, ages 3-17 $5; free 1st Tu of each month.)*

AEROSPACE MUSEUM. One of 62 Star Station One sites nationwide that provide information on the International Space Station project, this museum displays 24 full-scale replicas and 44 original planes. Aviation exhibits in the drum-shaped Ford Pavilion chronicle the history of man's quest to soar, including the Apollo 9 command module. *(2001 Pan American Plaza. ☎ 234-8291; www.aerospacemuseum.org. Open daily 10am-4:30pm; extended summer hours. $9, seniors $7, ages 6-17 $4; under 6 and military free; free 4th Tu of each month.)*

REUBEN H. FLEET SPACE THEATER AND SCIENCE CENTER. The Fleet houses the world's very first Omnimax theater, complete with 153 speakers and a hemispheric planetarium. The science center features interactive exhibits that change several times per year. *(1875 El Prado Way. ☎ 238-1233; www.rhfleet.org. Open daily 9:30am-8pm. $6.75, with Omnimax show $11.75; seniors $6/$9.75; ages 3-12 $5.50/ $8.75. Free 1st Tu of each month.)*

CASA DE BALBOA MUSEUMS. The small, ultra-modern **Museum of Photographic Arts (MOPA)** showcases contemporary photography in eight to ten exhibits per year. Its film program ranges from cult film festivals to technical and thematic examinations of classic cinematic works. *(☎ 238-7559; www.mopa.org. Open M-W and F-Su 10am-5pm, Th 10am-9pm. $6, students, seniors, and military $4; free 2nd Tu of each month. Films $10.)* The **San Diego Hall of Champions,** a slick sports museum complete with Astroturf carpeting, chronicles the San Diego sports scene and immortalizes local heroes like Carlsbad native and skater legend Tony Hawk. Only an odor-proof glass pane separates you from jerseys and shoes worn by Ted Williams and Bill Walton. *(☎ 234-2544. Open daily 10am-4:30pm. $6, seniors and military $4, ages 6-17 $3; free last Tu of each month.)* The recently renovated 1915 Electricity Building houses the **Museum of San Diego History.** *(☎ 232-6203. Open M-W and F-Su 10am-5pm, Th 10am-8pm. $6, seniors and military $5, ages 5-12 $2; free 2nd Tu of each month.)* Also in the building are the **Research Archives.** *(Open W-Sa 10am-5pm. $6.)* Downstairs, hobbyists can drool in the **San Diego Model Railroad Museum.** *(☎ 696-0199. Open Tu-F 11am-4pm, Sa-Su 11am-5pm. $5, seniors and students $4, military $2.50; free 1st Tu of each month.)*

ART IN THE PLAZA DE PANAMA. The **San Diego Museum of Art** has a collection ranging from ancient Asian to contemporary Californian works. At the adjoining outdoor **Sculpture Garden Court,** a sensuous Henry Moore piece presides over other large abstract blocks. *(☎ 232-7931; www.sdmart.org. Open Tu-W and F-Su 10am-6pm, Th 10am-9pm. $9; seniors, students, and ages 18-24 $7; ages 6-17 $4. Special exhibits $2-20.)* **Mingei International Museum,** one of the more interesting museums in Balboa Park, emphasizes unusual media and art from outside the US and Europe. *(Across from the visitors center. ☎ 239-0003; www.mingei.org. Open Tu-Su 10am-4pm. $5, students and ages 6-17 $2; free 3rd Tu of each month.)* Across the plaza, the **Timken Art Gallery** houses a newly restored portrait by Rembrandt and a collection of Russian church icons. *(1500 El Prado Way. ☎ 239-5548; www.timken-museum.org. Open Oct.-Aug. Tu-Sa 10am-4:30pm, Su 1:30-6pm. Free.)* **Spanish Village** is a colony of 300 artists at work in 36 studios. *(At the end of El Prado; if driving, take a left onto Village Pl. ☎ 233-9050. Open daily 11am-4pm. Free.)*

BALBOA PARK GARDENS. The fragrant **Botanical Building** may like a giant wooden cage, but it's filled with plants, not birds. The **orchid collection** is particularly striking, set among murmuring fountains. The **Desert Garden** and **Rose Garden** prove a salient floral contrast. The Desert Garden is in full bloom from January to March, while the roses are best admired between April and December. Free ranger-led tours leave Tuesday and Sunday at 1pm. Free volunteer-led tours meet on Saturdays at 10am; each Saturday tour covers a different set of sights within the park. *(2200 Park Blvd. ☎ 235-1100, tour info 235-1121. Botanical Building open M-W and F-Su 10am-4pm. Free.)*

PERFORMANCE SPACES. Performances at the **Spreckels Organ Pavilion,** which houses the world's largest outdoor musical instrument, can be heard for miles around. Local and visiting organists perform here throughout the week; call for times. *(☎ 226-0819. Free performance Su 2pm.)*

SAN DIEGO

SEA WORLD

On SeaWorld Dr., 10min. north of downtown San Diego. From I-5 take the SeaWorld Dr. exit. ☎ 800-380-3203, TDD 226-3907; www.seaworld.com. Open daily in summer 9am-11pm. The park opens at 10am in winter, but closing hours vary. $49.75, ages 3-9 $37.75; 2 consecutive days $53.75, ages 3-9 $43.75. Parking $7, RVs $9. Rental wheelchairs $8, electric wheelchairs $30.

Take Disneyland, subtract most of the rides, add a whole lot of fish and marine life, and you've got Sea World. Though critics have long condemned the practice of training highly intelligent marine mammals to perform unnatural circus acts, the goofy shows are surprisingly charming. The A-list star and poster-whale is the killer whale **Shamu,** whose signature move is a cannonball splash that soaks anyone in the first 20 rows. The original Shamu died long ago, but each of his successors has proudly borne the same name. The best show in the park, however, is **Fools with Tools,** a delightful takeoff on Tool Time from *Home Improvement.* Tim Allen gets pushed aside as precocious sea lions and otters take the stage. The nearby dolphin show is also a favorite. In addition to the performances, there are habitats for sharks, penguins, and other water-dwellers including the endangered manatee, and also shows featuring watersports and daredevil jet-ski riders. Visitors receive a map and schedule at the parking lot entrance; even the most popular events occur only a few times each day, so take a quick look at the schedule. One of the newest attractions is the **4-D movie theater** in the back of the park. If Shamu's splash wasn't wet enough, head toward **Shipwreck Rapids,** Sea World's first adventure ride. While a dousing is almost guaranteed, the gurgling voyage is less than thrilling. Those looking to cool down who don't want a face full of salt water should head to the free **Budweiser's Beer School** and brewery. The 30min. class, ■**free beer,** and general merriment come courtesy of Anheuser-Busch, the proud owners of Sea World.

DOWNTOWN

■ **PETCO PARK.** The new home of the San Diego Padres offers fans a close-up view of the action, with excellent views from almost every seat. The stadium is just like San Diego itself: beatiful and relaxed. Sections are named after neighborhoods, and the garden by the outfield is one of only a few of its kind in the Major League. Many attendees report buying great seats near trolley stations at terrific prices from scalpers. *(Games Mar.-Oct. Check www.padres.com for schedule and tickets.)*

GASLAMP QUARTER. Antique shops, Victorian buildings, trendy restaurants, and busy nightclubs make the Gaslamp quarter a hot, hot place to be at night. Formerly the city's Red Light District and now home to Hustler, a three-story adult store, new upscale bars and bistros continue to invade the area (see **Nightlife,** p. 508). By day, the area's charm lies in its fading history. The **Gaslamp Quarter Foundation** offers guided walking tours as well as a small museum. *(William Heath Davis House, 410 Island Ave. ☎ 233-4692; www.gaslampquarter.org. Museum open Su and Tu-Sa 11am-3pm. $3 donation suggested. 2hr. guided walking tours Sa at 11am. $8; students, seniors, and military $6; under 12 free. Self-guided tour maps $2.)* The **Horton Grand Hotel,** like most old buildings in San Diego, is supposedly haunted. Believers may catch a glimpse of Wild West lawman Wyatt Earp or baseball legend Babe Ruth. *(311 Island Ave. ☎ 544-1886. Tours W at 3pm. Free.)*

SAN DIEGO MUSEUM OF CONTEMPORARY ART. This steel-and-glass structure encases 20th-century works of art from the museum's permanent collection and loaned works on a rotating basis. It's a smaller branch of the main museum (see p.

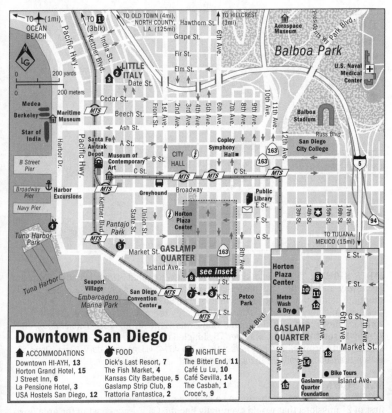

Downtown San Diego

🔺 ACCOMMODATIONS

Downtown HI-AYH, **13**
Horton Grand Hotel, **15**
J Street Inn, **6**
La Pensione Hotel, **3**
USA Hostels San Diego, **12**

● FOOD

Dick's Last Resort, **7**
The Fish Market, **4**
Kansas City Barbeque, **5**
Gaslamp Strip Club, **8**
Trattoria Fantastica, **2**

■ NIGHTLIFE

The Bitter End, **11**
Café Lu Lu, **10**
Café Sevilla, **14**
The Casbah, **1**
Croce's, **9**

507) in La Jolla. Artists represented in the permanent collection include Andy Warhol, John Baldessari, and Philip Guston; works include a wall that looks as though it breathes. *(1001 Kettner Blvd. ☎234-1001. Open Su-Tu and Th-Sa 11am-5pm. Free.)*

SAN DIEGO MARITIME MUSEUM. Housed within some of San Diego's oldest ships, this museum showcases San Diego's rich maritime history and maintains three ships, including the magnificently restored 1863 sailing vessel *Star of India* (the world's oldest merchant ship), the ferryboat *Berkeley*, and the steam yacht *Medea*. During the summer, there are weekend movie screenings on the *Star of India* and sleepovers aboard the ships. *(1492 N. Harbor Dr. ☎234-9153; www.sdmaritime.org. Open daily 9am-8pm. $8; seniors, military, and ages 13-17 $6; ages 6-12 $5. Movies $12, under 13 $7. Sleepovers $65.)*

EMBARCADERO. Spanish for "dock," the Embarcadero, San Diego's waterfront, has boardwalk shops and museums that face moored windjammers, cruise ships, and the occasional naval destroyer. Military and merchant marine vessels are anchored here, and the distantly visible North Island Naval Air Station, Point Loma Submarine Base, and South Bay's mothballed fleet all serve as reminders of the US Navy's prominent presence in San Diego. *(Sites begin on the south end of Broadway. Most afternoon tours of naval craft free.)*

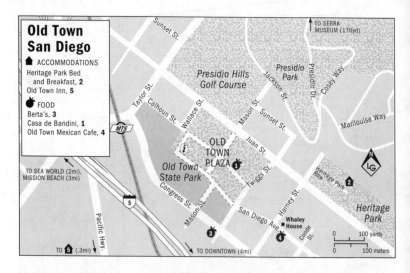

**Old Town
San Diego**

▲ ACCOMMODATIONS
Heritage Park Bed
and Breakfast, **2**
Old Town Inn, **5**

🍎 FOOD
Berta's, **3**
Casa de Bandini, **1**
Old Town Mexican Cafe, **4**

Sunset St.

↑ TO SERRA
MUSEUM (170yd)

*Presidio Hills
Golf Course*

*Presidio
Park*

Presidio Dr.

Cosey Way

Taylor St.

Calhoun St.

Wallace St.

Jackson St.

Mason St.

Sunset St.

Marilouise Way

MTS

i

OLD
TOWN
PLAZA ❶

Juan St.

TO SEA WORLD (2mi),
MISSION BEACH (3mi)

*Old Town
State Park*

Twiggs St.

Heritage
Row

Heritage Park

❷

Congress St.

Mason St.

Harney St.

San Diego Ave.

■ Whaley
House

*Heritage
Park*

5

Pacific Hwy.

❸

❹

Conde St.

0   100 yards
0   100 meters

TO ❺ (.3mi)

TO DOWNTOWN (4mi)

OTHER SIGHTS. The jewel of San Diego's redevelopment efforts is **Horton Plaza,** at Broadway and 4th St. This pastel-hued urban creation is an open-air, multilevel shopping center that covers seven blocks. The **Santa Fe Amtrak Depot,** three blocks west, is a masterpiece of Mission Revival architecture. Its gorgeous arches welcomed visitors to the 1915 Panama California Exposition. *(1050 Kettner Blvd.)* The kitschy **Seaport Village** houses over 75 shingled boutiques, ice cream shops, and a century-old carousel. *(649 W. Harbor Dr. ☎235-4014. Village open daily 10am-10pm; off-season 10am-9pm. Carousel $1. 2hr. parking free; $1 per additional 30min.)*

OLD TOWN

In 1769, Father Serra, supported by a brigade of Spanish infantry, established the first of 21 missions that would eventually line the California coast in the area now known as Old Town. The remnants of this early settlement have become one of San Diego's tourist mainstays. At the center of Old Town is the State Park, where nine original buildings house a number of museums. The rest of Old Town fans out from this center in a somewhat contrived arrangement of shops in reconstructed adobe huts. Although Old Town is certainly a tourist trap, it does offer visitors a genuine glimpse into California history while stuffing them silly with the best Mexican food around (see **Food,** p. 497).

OLD TOWN STATE PARK. The most popular of the area's attractions, the park's early 19th-century buildings houses museums, shops, and restaurants. **Seely Stable** houses a huge museum devoted to the 19th century's primary mode of transportation: the horse and carriage. *(☎220-5427. Open daily 10am-5pm. Tours every hr. 11am-2pm.)* Take a tour of the **Whaley House,** which stands on the site of San Diego's first gallows. It is one of two **official haunted houses** recognized by the State of California (the other is Winchester Mystery House in San Jose; see p. 181). The house also displays a piano from the *Gone With the Wind.* *(2482 San Diego Ave. ☎298-2482, tours 293-0117. Open daily 10am-4:30pm; last entry 4pm. $5, seniors $4, ages 3-12 $2.)* Across the street is **Heritage Park,** a group of seven 150-year-old Victorian buildings (six houses and a temple) collected from around the city. Four are open to the public, one of which you can stay in (see p. 495).

SERRA MUSEUM. The Serra Museum's stout adobe walls were raised at the site of the first fort and mission in 1929. Beautiful Presidio Park surrounds what remains of the original building. While the small exhibits documenting the settlement leave something to be desired, the grounds are spectacular. A truly huge flagpole at the top of the hill marks the former location of **Fort Stockton.** *(2727 Presidio Dr., in Presidio Park. ☎ 297-3258. Open F-Su 10am-4:30pm. $5; seniors, students, and military $4; ages 6-17 $2.)*

COASTAL SAN DIEGO

CORONADO ISLAND

Lovely Coronado Island is now actually a peninsula: a slender 7 mi. strip of hauled sand known as the "Silver Strand" tethers it to the mainland down near Imperial Beach. Famous for its elegant colonial Hotel Del Coronado (see below), the island is perfect for a number of outdoor activities. Water babies love the frothy waves that break along the southern shore, and outdoor enthusiasts jog, in-line skate, and bike along over 7 mi. of paved trails. Coronado also has a huge military presence, and its entire northern chunk comprises the **North Island Naval Air Station,** the birthplace of American naval aviation. In fact, it was a group of diligent navy men who carted wheelbarrows full of sand to connect the island to the rest of Coronado in 1947. Among the island's many naval enterprises is the training area of the elite Navy SEAL (sea, air, and land) special forces teams.

Coronado's most famed sight is its Victorian-style **Hotel Del Coronado,** 1500 Orange Ave. (☎ 435-6611), one of America's largest wooden buildings. The long white verandas and the vermilion spires of the "Del" were built in 1888. It has since become one of the world's great hotels (rooms start at $270 per night), hosting 10 presidents and one blonde bombshell—Marilyn Monroe's 1959 classic *Some Like it Hot* was filmed here. *Wizard of Oz* author L. Frank Baum wrote a number of his books from the porch. The hotel is right on the beach, with boat and bike rental agencies within walking distance. **Coronado Touring** offers easy 1½hr. walking tours of the area around the hotel departing from the lobby of the Glorietta Bay Inn, 1630 Glorietta Bay Blvd. (☎ 435-5993. Tours Tu, Th, Sa 11am. $8 per person.)

Built in 1969, the graceful **Coronado Bridge** guides cars to Coronado from downtown San Diego along I-5. Bus #901 follows the same route, carrying passengers from the Hotel Del Coronado to San Diego and back ($2.25). Those who would rather skim the ocean can take the **Bay Ferry** (leaves for Coronado every hr. 9am-9pm; returns every hr. 9:30am-9:30pm; $2; bikes $0.50). Tickets are available at San Diego Harbor Excursion, 1050 N. Harbor Dr. (☎ 234-4111), and at the Ferry Landing Marketplace on the Coronado side. Once across, the **#904 Shuttle** carries passengers from the landing to the Hotel Del Coronado and back (every hr. 10:30am-6:30pm, $1). Another scenic route is I-5 S to the Palm Ave. exit. Follow the signs to Silver Strand Blvd., which goes north into Coronado.

POINT LOMA

Although the US government owns the outer two-thirds of this peninsula, most of it remains open to citizens and visitors. The **Cabrillo National Monument,** at the tip of Point Loma, is dedicated to the Portuguese explorer Juan Rodríguez Cabrillo, the first European to land in California, but is best known for its views of downtown San Diego and migrating whales. The **visitors center** offers hourly videos or slide presentations as well as information about the monument. (☎ 557-5450; www.nps.gov/cabr/. Visitors center open daily 9am-5:15pm. 7-day pass $5 per vehicle, $3 per person on foot or bike. Golden Eagle Passport accepted.) **Whale-watching** season runs from mid-December to February. The **Bayside Trail** (2 mi.) has stations that explain native vegetation and historic military installations and offer magnificent views of the bay and Coronado Island. Point Loma's oceanfront is rife with tide pools; turn right off Rte. 209 onto Cabrillo Rd. and drive down to the parking lot at the bottom of the hill. At the highest point of the peninsula sits the interesting museum at **Old Point Loma Lighthouse.** (Open daily 9am-5:15pm.)

OCEAN, MISSION, AND PACIFIC BEACHES

Much of San Diego's younger population flocks to these communities for the surf and hopping nightlife; unsurprisingly, noisy bars and grills crowd these shores (see **Food,** p. 498, and **Nightlife,** p. 508). The three beaches line up consecutively, but each has its own flavor. **Ocean Beach (O.B.)** cultivates a homegrown, earthy atmosphere. With local hippies lounging in the gentle surf, O.B. is the most laid-back of the beaches and the best place to learn the art of wave-riding. Anglers can try their luck on the Western Hemisphere's longest fishing pier. On the pier itself, **O.B. Pier Cafe and Baitshop** rents fishing poles and buckets of bait. No license is required as long as you use no more than one pole. (☎226-3474. Open Su-Th 8am-9pm, F-Sa 8am-10pm. $14 per day.) From atop the majestic **Sunset Cliffs Park,** romantics can smooch in the ocean breeze while watching the sun set over the surfers and the area's best waves. (Gates open 4am-11pm; quiet hours after 7pm. No camping.) Ocean Beach also hosts an awesome **Farmers Market.** (Open W 3-9pm.)

Farther north, **Mission Beach,** at the corner of W. Mission Bay Dr. and Mission Blvd., is a people-watching paradise. **Belmont Park,** a combination amusement park and shopping center, draws a youthful crowd. Take advantage of the rare free parking and rattle your brains on the bumpy **Giant Dipper** roller coaster ($4).

Pacific Beach and its boisterous **Garnet Avenue** is the most lively of the three beaches and home to the best nightlife. The **Ocean Front Walk** is always packed with joggers, walkers, cyclists, and the usual beachfront shops. Although all the beaches accommodate those who want to limit their physical activity to rotating on their towels to get an even tan, beachside sports are also very popular. Swimmers and boogie boarders should avoid prime surfing areas.

LA JOLLA

The Spanish named this area *La Jolla* ("The Jewel") for its physical beauty. Later, the hilly promontory developed as an exclusive hideaway for wealthy Easterners, and today it remains true to its tony roots. The gaudy pink hues of opulent **La Valencia Hotel,** 1132 Prospect St., testify to an age of seaside luxury. While La Jolla is still an upscale enclave, it has evolved into a more inclusive area. With brand-name shopping districts and the rugged beauty of La Jolla Cove, this eclectic community is a must-see. Take the Ardath exit west from I-5 or bus #30 or 34 from downtown.

BEACHES. La Jolla features some of the finest beaches in the city. ▦**La Jolla Cove** is popular with scuba divers, snorkelers, and brilliantly colored Garibaldi goldfish. Wander south along the cliffs to a striking semicircular inlet known as **The Children's Pool.** Established in 1931 by local philanthropist Ellen Browning Scripps as a wildlife preserve, the pool's inhabitants are a famously thriving community of sea lions who frolic and cavort in the sun. Don't feed the animals, and confine yourself to the established viewing areas lest you disrupt the fragile ecological enclave. Some of the best breaks in the county can be found in La Jolla at **Tourmaline Beach** and **Wind 'n Sea Beach.** However, these spots are home to notoriously territorial surfers, so outsiders might be advised to catch a wave elsewhere. **La Jolla Shores,** next to Scripps and UCSD, has gentle swells ideal for new surfers, boogie boarders, and swimmers. ▦**Black's Beach** is not officially a nude beach, but that doesn't seem to stop sunbathers from throwing off their swimsuits. The north end generally attracts gay sunbathers. At **Torrey Pines Glider Port** hang gliders leap into the breeze for unadulterated views of the beaches

La Jolla, Pacific Beach, and Mission Beach

▲ ACCOMMODATIONS

Inn at Mission Bay, 11
International House Mission Beach, 12
International House Pacific Beach, 8
Shell Beach, 1

🍴 FOOD

Jay's Gourmet, 2
Kono's Surf Club, 6
The Living Room, 3
The Spot, 4
World Curry, 10
Zanzibar, 9

◼ NIGHTLIFE

Canes Bar and Grill, 13
The Comedy Store, 5
Pacific Beach Bar and Grill and Club Tremors, 7

below. *(To reach the Glider Port, take I-5 to Genesee Ave., go west, and turn left on N. Torrey Pines Rd. Black's beach is accessible by a steep staircase just south of the Glider Port and is very popular with surfers.)*

MUSEUMS. The ◼**Birch Aquarium at the Scripps Institute of Oceanography** has great educational exhibits including a portly octopus, half a dozen different types of oozing jellyfish, a large collection of sea horses, and a 70,000-gallon kelp and shark tank. *(2300 Expedition Way. ☎858-534-3474; http://aquarium.ucsd.edu. Open daily 9am-5pm. $10, students with ID $7, seniors $8.50, ages 3-17 $6.50.)* The **San Diego Museum of Contemporary Art** houses a rotating exhibition of Pop, Minimalist, and Conceptualist art from the 1950s onward. It shares its collection with the downtown branch (see p. 502). The museum is as visually stunning as the art it contains, with gorgeous ocean views, high ceilings, and light-filled spaces. There are daily guided tours at various hours in both English and Spanish. *(700 Prospect St. ☎858-454-3541; www.mcasd.org. Open M-Tu and F-Su 11am-5pm, Th 11am-7pm. $6; students, seniors, military, and ages 12-18 $2. 3rd Tu and 1st Su of every month free.)*

OTHER SIGHTS. The somewhat isolated **University of California at San Diego (UCSD)** sits above La Jolla. Be sure to check out the terraces and buttresses of **Geisel Library,** a space-age structure endowed by La Jolla resident Theodore Geisel, better known as Dr. Seuss, the late and beloved children's books author. Kiosks on Gilman and Northview Dr. dispense maps and give information about campus tours. *(Buses #30 and 34 take you to campus, but cars or bikes are invaluable for getting to the campus's many residential and academic colleges. ☎858-534-2208. Open M-F 7am-9pm, Sa-Su 7am-5:30pm.)* At the foot of Girard Ave. in La Jolla Village is **Scripps Park,** where great waves shake the rocky shore, sending up plumes of silvery sea spray. Ocean lovers—or lovers of any kind—stroll here in the evenings.

ELSEWHERE IN SAN DIEGO

MISSION BASILICA SAN DIEGO DE ALCALÁ. In 1774 Father Serra moved his mission, California's first church, some 6 mi. away from the settlement of rough and unholy soldiers to its current location. The mission is still an active parish church and contains gardens, a small museum, and a reconstruction of Serra's living quarters. *(Take bus #43 or I-8 east to the Mission Gorge Rd. exit. Go north and turn left on Twain Ave; the mission will be 2 blocks ahead on the right. ☎281-8449. Visitors center open daily 9am-4:45pm. Mass held daily at 7am and 5:30pm; visitors welcome. $3, students and seniors $2, under 12 $1. 45min. tote-a-tape guided tours $2.)*

QUALCOMM STADIUM. Home to a number of Super Bowls (including the 2003 drubbing of the Oakland Raiders at the hands of the Tampa Bay Buccaneers) and the **San Diego Chargers** (the city's pro football team), the "Q" is now a football-only venue. *(West of the Mission near the junction of I-8 and I-15 in Mission Valley. Chargers tickets ☎280-2121. Padres tickets ☎877-374-2784.)*

IN THE NAVY NOW. Freedom lovers can take a free tour of the gigantic **USS Constellation** (the vessel with the number "64" on its superstructure, visible from San Diego's downtown waterfront) and other aircraft carriers. *(☎545-2427. Daily tours at 10am, 1, and 3pm. Reserve at least 48hr. in advance for weekend tours.)*

🎭 ENTERTAINMENT

Constructed in 1937, the **Old Globe Theater** in Balboa Park is the oldest professional theater in California. Classical and contemporary plays are performed at the adjoining **Lowell Davies Outdoor Theatre** and the **Cassius Carter Center Stage.** Tickets for all three stages can be purchased at the box office. *(☎239-2255; www.theoldglobe.org. Call for listings, show times, and ticket prices.)* At the **Starlight Musical Theater,** also in Balboa Park at the Pan American Plaza, actors occasionally freeze mid-soliloquy and wait for the roar of passing aircraft to subside before resuming. *(☎544-7827.)* Downtown, the **Balboa Theatre,** 225 Broadway Ave. *(☎544-1000),* and the **Horton Grand Theatre,** 444 4th Ave. *(☎234-9583),* are both excellent theaters. Call for show information; ticket prices vary. The **La Jolla Playhouse,** 2910 La Jolla Village Dr. *(☎858-550-1010; www.lajollaplayhouse.com.),* presents shows at the Mandell Weiss Theatre on the UCSD campus in La Jolla. To get there, turn onto Expedition from N. Torrey Pines Rd. On Coronado Island, sophisticates can take in a performance at the **Lamb's Players Theatre,** 1142 Orange Ave. *(☎437-0600; www.lambsplayer.org.),* San Diego's only year-round professional theater.

🎵 NIGHTLIFE

Nightlife in San Diego is concentrated in several distinct pockets of action. Posh locals and party-seeking tourists flock to the **Gaslamp Quarter,** where numerous restaurants and bars feature live music. The **Hillcrest** area, next to Balboa Park, draws a young, largely gay crowd to its clubs and dining spots. Away from downtown, the **beach areas** (especially Garnet Ave. in Pacific Beach) are loaded with clubs, bars, and cheap eateries that attract college-age revelers. The city's definitive source of entertainment info is the free *Reader,* available in shops, coffeehouses, and visitors centers. Listings can also be found in the *San Diego Union-Tribune*'s Thursday "Night and Day" section.

LATE-NIGHT RESTAURANTS

Although the restaurants below offer complete meals, they are better known as nightspots, be they bars, music clubs, or dance clubs.

Pacific Beach Bar and Grill and **Club Tremors,** 860 Garnet Ave. (☎858-483-9227), one of the only dance clubs in **Pacific Beach.** A DJ packs the 2-level dance floor with a mostly college-aged crowd. The Bar and Grill has respectable food (entrees $7-11) and more than 20 beers on tap. Live music Su. Comedy W. Cover $5 if you enter through Club Tremors, but the same club is accessible through the Grill for free. Club open Tu-Sa 9pm-1:30am. Bar open 11am-1:30am. Kitchen closes at midnight.

Canes Bar and Grill, 3105 Oceanfront Walk (☎858-488-1780 or 858-488-9690), in **Mission Beach.** One of the best live music venues in the city, this beachside bar has unbeatable sunset views from the 2nd-story terrace and dancing every night until 2am. Directly on the water. Canes features standard Mexican fare; the Tacos Supremas ($9-10) are a favorite. Open daily 11am-2am.

Dick's Last Resort, 345 4th Ave. (☎858-231-9100), in the **Gaslamp Quarter.** Buckets of Southern grub attract a wildly hedonistic bunch. Dick's stocks beers from around the globe, from Africa to Trinidad, as well as native brews like the Dixieland Blackened Voodoo Lager. Indulge in greasy french fries and ribs. No cover for the nightly rock or blues, but you'd better be buyin'. The staff's schtick is to give guests a hard time. Lunch burgers $6-7. Dinner entrees $10-18. Open daily 11am-1:30am.

Café Lu Lu, 419 F. St. (☎238-0114), in the **Gaslamp Quarter.** Coffeehouse designed by local artists. See and be seen as you sip a raspberry mocha in this low-key alternative to the aggressive bar scene. Standing room only after midnight on weekends. Open Su-Th 9am-1am, F-Sa 9am-3am.

CLUBS AND BARS

▨ **Croce's Top Hat Bar and Grille** and **Croce's Jazz Bar,** 802 5th Ave. (☎233-4355), at F St. in the **Gaslamp Quarter.** A combo rock/blues bar and jazz bar opened by Ingrid Croce, widow of singer Jim Croce. Live music nightly from 8:30pm. Cover $5-10 (includes 2 live shows). Top Hat open F-Sa 7pm-1:30am. Jazz Bar open daily 5:30pm-12:30am.

The Bitter End, 770 5th Ave. (☎338-9300), in the **Gaslamp Quarter.** This 3-level dance club is always packed with those dressed to impress, so leave the torn Levi's and sandals at home. DJs spin everything from hip-hop to Top 40 to trance on the upper floors, while live music pounds below. Happy hour Th-F 3-7pm; free buffet. 21+. Cover $10 after 9pm. Open daily 5pm-2am.

The Casbah, 2501 Kettner Blvd. (☎232-4355), at Laurel St., near the **airport.** Eddie Vedder of the alternative rock legend Pearl Jam owns this intimate nightspot, one of the best live music venues in the city. Call ahead for a schedule, as tickets sometimes sell out. Cover varies. 21+. Hours vary; usually 5pm-2am.

The Comedy Store, 916 Pearl St. (☎858-454-9176), in **La Jolla.** Sister to the landmark Hollywood club. Go for your big break on open mic Su nights. Drinks $3. 21+. Shows W-Sa 8 and 10:30pm. Cover W-Th $5-10; F $15; Sa $20; Su free but 2-drink min.

Café Sevilla, 555 4th Ave. (☎233-5979; www.cafesevilla.com), in the **Gaslamp.** Live band gets patrons' hips swaying to Latin beats from salsa to flamenco. F night flamenco show includes a 3-course meal, flamenco show, and admission to the club ($50). Dress to impress. 21+ downstairs. Open daily 5pm-late.

GAY AND LESBIAN NIGHTLIFE

Lesbian and gay clubs cluster in **University Heights** and **Hillcrest. The Flame,** 3780 Park Blvd., in Hillcrest, is one of the most popular lesbian dance clubs in the nation. (☎295-4163. 21+. Open daily 5pm-2am.) Find line-dancing drag queens at **Hamburger Mary's,** 308 University Ave., one of Hillcrest's most popular bars.

(☎491-0400. No cover.) **Bourbon Street,** 4612 Park Blvd., in University Heights, is a neighborhood bar with a gay following. (☎291-0173. 21+. Open M-F 2pm-2am, Sa-Su 11am-2pm.) **The Brass Rail,** 3796 5th Ave., in Hillcrest, was the first gay bar in San Diego. It features dancing on weekends. (☎298-2233. 21+. Cover F-Sa $5-10 after 9pm. Open daily noon-2am.)

✿ FESTIVALS

Gorgeous weather and a strong community spirit make the San Diego area an ideal place for local festivals. The following is by no means a comprehensive list, so check the beach community weeklies for additional festival information.

Annual Comic-Con International (☎491-2475), at the Convention Center. Last weekend in July. The city swarms with visitors dressed as Darth Vader and other movie and comic characters during the largest comic convention in the world. Includes a number of sneak previews and a costume ball.

Penguin Day Ski Fest (☎858-270-0840), at De Anza Cove in Mission Bay. Jan. 1, 2005. This festival invites participants to water-ski in the Pacific and lie on ice without a wet suit. Those who do get a "penguin patch"; those who fail get a "chicken patch."

Ocean Beach Kite Festival, 4726 Santa Monica Ave. (☎531-1527), in Ocean Beach. 1st Sa in Mar. Kite-construction and kite-flying competitions.

San Diego Crew Classic (☎858-488-0700), at Crown Pt. Shores in Mission Bay. 1st weekend in Apr. Crews from around the world compete at the only major collegiate rowing regatta on the West Coast. Tickets $5.

San Diego Earthfair (☎858-496-6666; www.earthdayweb.org), in Balboa Park. One day in mid-Apr.; 10am-5pm. World's largest environmental festival. Kids' activities, booths, exhibits, and dancing. Free.

Summer Stargazing (☎594-1415), at San Diego State University's Mt. Laguna Observatory. July-Aug. Free tickets available through the US Forest Service.

Summer Pops 2004 (☎235-0804), on a stage in the harbor. Late June-Sept. 2 Performances by the San Diego Symphony. Tickets begin at $15.

Ocean Beach Street Fair and Chili Cook-Off (☎226-1936). Last weekend in June. Newport St. is lined with arts booths during this 2-day festival.

Taste of Pacific Beach and Restaurant Walk (☎858-273-3303). One in early May and one in mid-Sept. Reduced-fare eats from more than 20 Pacific Beach restaurants.

Beachfest (☎858-273-3303), in Pacific Beach on the Boardwalk. Mid-Oct. Live entertainment, arts and crafts, food, and family fun.

Hillcrest Cityfest Street Fair (☎299-3330), on 5th Ave. between Ivy Ln. and University Ave., in the heart of San Diego's gay community. August 14. Arts, crafts, food, live entertainment, and beer garden.

US Open Sand Castle Competition (☎424-6663), at the Imperial Beach pier. 3rd weekend in July. Sand-sculpting demigods exercise their craft in the largest and oldest American sand-castle event. Parades, fireworks, and a children's castle contest.

SummerFest La Jolla Chamber Music Festival (☎858-459-3724), at the La Jolla Museum of Contemporary Art. 1st 3 weeks of Aug. Be prepared to shell out money for this highbrow event. Concert tickets can exceed $50.

La Jolla Rough Water Swim (☎858-456-2100). Early Sept. Start and finish at the La Jolla Cove. Largest annual rough water competition in the US.

⚡ DAYTRIPS FROM SAN DIEGO

SAN DIEGO WILD ANIMAL PARK. A look at the free-roaming endangered species of the 2100-acre **San Diego Wild Animal Park** is an essential part of any visit to San Diego. While some of the exhibits are similar to those in any other zoo, the highlight of the park is the large enclosures where many species roam freely. African safari creatures like rhinos, giraffes, gazelles, and tigers can be found throughout the park plains. The baby animals warm even the coldest of hearts. The best way to see these enclosures is via the open-air **Wgasa Bush Line Railway,** a 1hr. monorail safari included in park admission that travels through four habitat areas. If possible, sit on the right for a better view. The park has typical shops, restaurants, and animal shows, but for adventure, try the 1 mi. **Heart of Africa** hike, meant to simulate a real African safari. The open-air **Photo Caravan** offers up-close and personal views of the animals. Or snooze to the sounds of elephant snores at the **Roar and Snore** overnight camping safari. (*From I-15, take the Via Rancho Pkwy. exit (County Rte. S78) and follow the signs.* ☎ *747-8702; www.wildanimalpark.org. Park open daily from 9am; closing times vary with the season. Rail tours June-Aug. 9:30am-9pm; Sept.-May 9:30am-4pm. $26.50, ages 3-11 $19.50. Parking $6. Discounts are often available at tourist bureaus and hotels. Most of the park, including the monorail, is wheelchair accessible, but steep hills may require detours. Photo Caravan:* ☎ *619-718-3050. 1¾hr. safari $99, 3½hr. safari $145. Reservations required. Roar and Snore:* ☎ *619-718-3050. Apr.-Oct. F-Su nights $126; includes park admission, all meals, camping equipment, and special tours and programs.*)

MOUNT PALOMAR. Although the Hale telescope at Palomar Mountain's **Palomar Observatory** is over 40 years old, it remains one of the world's largest and greatest astronomical instruments. Diehard science buffs will find the sparse museum fascinating. (*The observatory is accessible via S6.* ☎ *742-2119. Open daily 9am-4pm. Free.*) **Cleveland National Forest** contains the observatory and several excellent campgrounds. S6 passes the wooded **Fry Creek ❶** and more airy and open **Observatory campgrounds ❶,** both of which provide water, toilets, and access to hiking trails. **Palomar Mountain State Park ❶** offers camping, showers, hiking trails, and fishing, but swimming is not allowed. All of these campgrounds are above 5000 ft., so warm clothing is a necessity even in summer. (*Northeast of Escondido. From San Diego, take I-15 N to S6. Palomar Mountain State Park: Turn left onto S7 at the mountaintop store.* ☎ *800-444-PARK/7275; www.parks.ca.gov. Advance reservations necessary on summer weekends. Campsites closed in winter. Sites $12; hiker/biker sites $3; vehicles $2.*)

MISSION SAN ANTONIO DE PALA. The **Mission San Antonio de Pala,** on the Pala Indian Reservation, is one of California's only operational missions. Originally an outpost of Oceanside's Mission San Luis Rey in 1816, it has since converted thousands of Native Americans. The beautiful grounds are worth a visit. (*West of Mt. Palomar on Rte. 76, 6 mi. east of I-15.* ☎ *742-3317. Open W-Su 10am-4pm. $2.*)

SAN DIEGO'S NORTH COUNTY

San Diego's North County is a nearly unbroken expanse of beachfront stretching north from La Jolla toward L.A., an ocean playground that appeals to lovers of sun and surf. North County towns are easily accessible along I-5 and U.S. 101 by car, bike, or bus. Take North County Transit District bus #301 from La Jolla's University Towne Centre as far as Oceanside. (Daily every 30min. 5am-10pm; $1.50; free transfers.) The Coaster, a high-speed commuter train, also provides transportation from North County into downtown and Old Town San Diego. (☎ 800-COASTER/ 262-7837; www.gonctd.com. 11 trains daily. 5am-7pm. Fares $3.75-5.25 depending on distance.) Trains stop in Oceanside, Carlsbad, Encinitas, and Solana Beach. For more North County Transit info, call ☎ 800-266-6883.

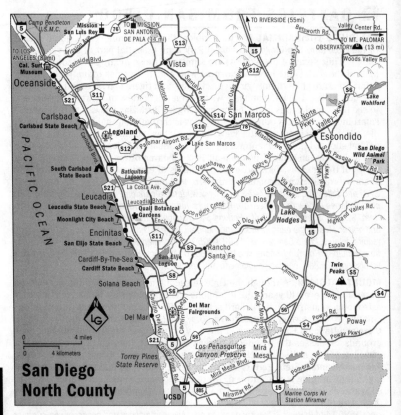

San Diego North County

Opportunities to sportfish off a pier or to book passage on a deep-sea fishing charter abound up and down the coast (see p. 516). The waters off the coast from North County all the way down to Baja California teem with monstrous yellowfin tuna, giant grouper, and the ultimate trophy fish—the marlin.

DEL MAR   ☎858

North of La Jolla, the affluent suburb of Del Mar (pop. 5400) is home to thorough-bred racehorses and famous fairgrounds. Many small boutiques and restaurants line Camino Del Mar. During June and early July, Del Mar hosts the San Diego County Fair, one of the largest fairs in California. Solana Beach to the north boasts the Cedros Design District, full of warehouses converted into artist studios.

⊟☎ TRANSPORTATION AND PRACTICAL INFORMATION. The architectur-ally impressive **Amtrak** station, 105 Cedros Ave. (☎800-USA-RAIL/872-7245), in Solana Beach sends 11 trains per day to L.A. ($22). The **Del Mar Chamber of Com-merce and Visitor Center,** 1104 Camino Del Mar, #214, has brochures and handouts. (☎755-4844; www.delmarchamber.org. Open Tu-Th 10am-4pm.) **Internet access** is available at the **Del Mar Public Library,** 1309 Camino Del Mar. Call ahead to reserve a 1 hr. slot, or drop in to use one of the computers for 15min. (☎755-1666. Open Tu 10am-6pm, W-Th 10am-8pm, F-Sa 10am-5pm, Su 1-5pm.)

◨◪ FOOD AND NIGHTLIFE. Surf-weathered locals favor **Board and Brew ❶**, 1212 Camino Del Mar, for its cheap beer ($2-2.50) and delicious sandwiches such as the California Delight ($4.50), which is stuffed with turkey, cream cheese, and sunflower seeds. (☎481-1021. Open daily 10am-7pm.) Those craving curry head to **Bangkok Bay**, 731 S. Hwy. 101, in Solana Beach, for outstanding noodle and seafood entrees. Their appe-"thai"-zer boat ($13) is as superb as the pun is bad. (☎858-792-2427. Open M-Th 11:30am-9:30pm, F 11:30am-10pm, Sa noon-10pm, Su noon-9:30pm.) For awesome deep-dish pizza and "grog," try **Pizza Port ❷**, 135 N. Hwy 101 in Solana Beach. Expect a wait; the place is usually packed. (☎481-7332; www.pizzaport.com. Pizzas from $6. Pints from $3. Open Su-Th 11am-11pm, F-Sa 11am-midnight.) The **Belly Up Tavern**, 143 S. Cedros Ave., off Lomas Santa Fe Dr. in Solana Beach, was once a warehouse but now hosts blues, rock, reggae, and jazz. Keep your eyes peeled for some well-known acts. Purchase tickets in advance (☎481-8140 or 220-8497; www.bellyup.com) or at the door. (☎481-9022. Live music nightly. 21+. Cover varies with artist; expect $5-40. Open daily noon-2am.)

◧◪ SIGHTS AND BEACHES. The celebrity-studded **Del Mar Thoroughbred Club**, at the corner of Via de la Valle and Jimmy Durante Blvd., draws racing fans from late July until the week after Labor Day. Founded in 1937 by Bing Crosby and Pat O'Brien, the racetrack is one of the most beautiful in the world. (☎755-1141 or 795-5533; www.delmarracing.com. M and W-F 8 races per day, Sa 10 per day, Su 9 per day. First post 2pm. Gates open M and W-F noon, Sa-Su 11:30am. General admission $5, clubhouse $8.) **Torrey Pines State Reserve and Beach**, along the coast just south of Del Mar, is one of only two native torrey pine groves on earth. (The other is on Santa Rosa Island in Channel Islands National Park; see p. 475.) Look for the entrance at 12600 off N. Torrey Pines Rd. about ½ mi. south of Del Mar Village. (☎755-2063; www.torreypine.org. Park open 8am-sunset. $4 per vehicle; pedestrians and bicyclists free.) The **Torrey Pines Lodge**, at the top of the hill on the entrance road, provides info on activities and hiking trails, as well as an exhibit on why the torrey pines are so unique. (Open daily 9am-5:30pm.) The park trails are wonderful for runners, cyclists, hikers, and rule-abiders—there is no camping, no picnicking, no food, no smoking, no dogs (even if kept in cars), and no straying off the established trails. Try the beach trail down for amazing views (1½ mi., round-trip). Hang gliders love the 6 mi. stretch of rocky beach.

CARLSBAD, ENCINITAS, AND LEUCADIA
☎760

Along the Pacific Coast Highway north of Del Mar lie the towns of Encinitas and Leucadia, which show traces of their hippie past in their hallucinogenic beauty and tie-dyed inhabitants. Farther up the coast is the charming lagoon hideaway of Carlsbad, where U.S. 101—known here as Carlsbad Blvd.—winds past silky sands and shingled homes adorned with wild rosebushes.

◪ PRACTICAL INFORMATION. Orient yourself at the **Carlsbad Convention and Visitors Center**, 400 Carlsbad Village Dr. (☎434-6093; www.carlsbadca.org. Open M-F 9am-5pm, Sa 10am-4pm, Su 10am-3pm.) **Internet access** is available at the **Georgina Cole Library**, 1250 Carlsbad Village Dr., near downtown (☎434-2870; open M-Th 9am-9pm, F-Sa 9am-5pm), or the **Carlsbad City Library**, 1775 Dove Ln., off El Camino Real (☎602-2039; open M-Th 9am-9pm, F-Sa 9am-5pm).

◪◪ ACCOMMODATIONS AND CAMPING. Inexpensive rooms are difficult to find in these resort communities. **Surf Motel ❹**, 3136 Carlsbad Blvd., has large, comfy rooms located across the street from the beach and a block from Carlsbad

Village. (☎729-7961. Rooms $109-149; in winter $55-69.) **Motel 6 ❸**, 1006 Carlsbad Village Dr., is just east of Carlsbad Village. (☎434-7135. Singles $50-58; doubles $56-66. If that's full, there's another location on Raintree Dr.; ☎431-0745.) The **Portofino Beach Inn ❺**, 186. N. Hwy. 101, in Encinitas, has nice rooms and a hot tub near the beach. (☎944-0301. Singles $109-169; doubles $139-169.)

Camping near the beach is allowed at **South Carlsbad State Park ❶** or in nearby Cardiff-by-the-Sea at **San Elijo State Park ❶**. Both campgrounds are situated atop cliffs and don't offer much in terms of privacy. However, the beaches below are beautiful. Reservations for both campgrounds can be made up to seven months in advance by calling ☎800-444-7275 or via www.reserveamerica.com. (South Carlsbad ☎438-3143, San Elijo 753-5091. Water, restrooms, showers, general stores, picnic tables, grills, and fire pits available. Reservations essential in summer. Oceanside sites $20, inland $16. Call for availability of RV sites.)

❍ FOOD. There are a number of great beachfront restaurants along S. Coast Hwy. 101. Locals and tourists cram into the intimate dining area at **Trattoria I Trulli ❸**, 830 S. Coast Hwy. 101, for good reason: the food at this Italian bistro is simply delicious. (☎943-6800. Dinner entrees from $10. Open Su-Th 11:30am-2:30pm and 5-10pm, F-Sa 11:30am-2:30pm and 5-10:30pm.) Taste the other side of the Pacific at **Ogata,** 615 S. Coast Hwy. 101, which serves the beach's best sushi and teriyaki dishes ($8-10) and also offers plenty of vegetarian options. (☎753-6451. Open M-F 11:30am-2:30pm and 5-9pm, Sa 5-9pm.) At **Kim's,** 745 S. Coast Hwy. 101, large Vietnamese noodle bowls ($5) and seven-course beef dinners ($20) await hungry beachgoers. (☎942-7816. Open M-Th 11am-9pm, F-Sa 11am-9:30pm, Su noon-9pm.) Life is sweet at **Honey's Bistro and Bakery ❶**, 632 S. Coast Hwy. 101, in Encinitas, where they concoct large, fresh salads ($6), sandwiches ($5), and soups ($4), as well as mouthwatering baked goods. (☎942-5433. Open daily 5:30am-3:30pm.)

◐ ▧ SIGHTS AND FESTIVALS. In Encinitas, truth-seekers can partake in restorative contemplation at the New Age ▧**Self-Realization Fellowship,** 215 K St. The lush and immaculate gardens ensure meditative serenity, especially when lit by a setting sun. (☎753-1811. Retreats available; call for reservations. Gardens open Tu-Sa 9am-5pm, Su 11am-5pm. Free.) The **Quail Botanical Gardens,** 230 Quail Gardens Dr., is home to one of the world's most diverse plant collections. Be sure to check out the lush bamboo groves and the waterfall. (☎436-3036; www.qbgardens.com. Open daily 9am-5pm. Free tours Sa 10am. $8, seniors $5, ages 5-12 $3.) **Legoland,** 1 Legoland Dr., is a fun, goofball tribute to the interlocking blocks that have inspired countless junior architects. Exit I-5 in Carlsbad at Cannon Rd. (☎918-5346. Open in spring Su-M and Th 10am-5pm, F-Sa 10am-6pm; in summer daily 10am-8pm; in fall M and Th-Su 10am-5pm. $44, ages 3-16 $38. Parking $7.) Shake, rattle, and roll at the extensive **Museum of Making Music,** 5790 Armada Dr., in Carlsbad, where over 450 vintage musical instruments chronicle the history of 20th-century American music. (☎438-5996 or 877-551-9976; www.museumofmakingmusic.org. Open Tu-Su 10am-5pm. $5; seniors, students, and ages 4-18 $3.)

On the first Sunday in May and November, the famous biannual ▧**Carlsbad Village Street Faire,** the largest one-day fair in California, attracts over 900 vendors and 80,000 people. From early March to late April, the kaleidoscopic **Flower Fields** bloom with diverse wildflowers on 1 mi. of hillside along I-5 north of Palomar Airport Rd. Take the Palomar Airport exit off I-5, head east along Palomar Airport Rd. to the light at Paseo del Norte, and turn left. (☎431-0352. $4, ages 3-12 $2.) **U-Pick Strawberries,** north of Cannon Rd. at Paseo del Norte in Carlsbad, opens its farms to the public for harvesting. (Open May to mid-July daily 8:30am-6:30pm. Small bucket $4, large $8.) Indulge your materialistic appetites at the weekly **Seaside Bazaar,** which peddles trinkets, jewelry, crafts, food, and other odds and ends, along U.S. 101 at the north end of Encinitas. (☎753-1611. Open Sa-Su 9am-4:30pm.)

◪ **BEACHES.** The California state park system maintains a number of beautiful beaches in the area. **Carlsbad State Beach** is long and attractive, marred slightly by the mammoth power plant that occupies the coast to the south. **Offshore Surf Shop,** 3179 Carlsbad Blvd., rents boogie boards and 6-8 ft. "soft" surfboards. (☎729-4934. Boogie boards $3 per hr., $10 per day. Surfboards $5/$25. Use a credit card for rentals; otherwise, a deposit of $50 for boogie boards and $300 for surfboards is required. Open daily 9am-7:30pm.) The **Encinitas City Beach** has multiple access points. Try the **stone steps** at the end of South El Portal St. to reach over 3 mi. of public sands. Surfing neophytes can score a board at **Leucadia Surfboards,** 1354 N. Hwy. 101. Woody, the chill manager, is always happy to help. (☎632-9700. Open M-F 10am-5pm, Sa-Su 9am-5pm. Boards $5 per hr., $20 per day.) Cardiff-by-the-Sea is near **San Elijo Beach State Park** (☎753-5091) and **Cardiff State Beach.** If you have a car, these beautiful beaches are worth the drive.

OCEANSIDE ☎760

Oceanside (pop. 161,029) is the largest and least glamorous of San Diego's coastal towns, but Harbor Beach, one of the Pacific's best surfing beaches, keeps things buzzing year-round. Buccaneer Beach and Breakwater Way attract crowds from L.A. and San Diego, as well as a variety of bird species. Oceanside may not have the fancy resorts and affluent residents of its neighbors to the south, but serious beachgoers will appreciate the area's warm waters.

◲◪ TRANSPORTATION AND PRACTICAL INFORMATION. The **Oceanside Transit Center,** 195 S. Tremont St., houses the local **Amtrak** (☎800-USA-RAIL/872-7245 or 722-4622) and **Greyhound** (☎722-1587) stations. The newly renovated **California Welcome Center,** 928 N. Coast Hwy., has info about goings-on and a toll-free hotel reservation line. (☎721-1101 or 800-350-7873. Open daily 9am-5pm; closed holidays.) **Internet** access is available at the **Oceanside Public Library,** 330 N. Coast Hwy., in the Civic Center (☎435-5600; open M-W 10am-8pm, Th-Sa 10am-5:30pm), and at the **Oceanside Public Library Community Computer Center,** 321 N. Nevada St. (☎435-5660; open M-Th 10am-9pm, F-Sa 10am-5pm, Su noon-5pm).

◪◪ ACCOMMODATIONS AND FOOD. Unlike its ritzier neighbors, Oceanside offers many inexpensive lodgings. Budget motels line **Highway 101** throughout the town, though not all are reputable. **Oceanside Inn & Suites ❸,** 1820 S. Coast Hwy., offers spacious rooms with a fridge and microwave. (☎433-5751. Rooms $45.) For delicious dockside dining, head to **Harbor Fish & Chips,** 276 S. Harborside Drive. (☎722-4977. Crabcakes $6. Burgers $4-5. Open Su-Th 11am-9pm, F-Sa 11am-10pm.) Power up before hitting the waves at **The Longboarder ❶,** 228 N. Coast Hwy., which serves burgers ($6) and heaping omelettes ($8) to its surfer crowd. (☎721-6776. Open M-F 7am-2pm, Sa-Su 7am-3pm; in summer also Th-Sa 7-10pm.)

◪◪ SIGHTS AND OUTDOOR ACTIVITIES. The pier gets crowded during the **World Body Surfing Championships** in mid-August. Call the Oceanside Special Events Office (☎435-5540) for more info. Oceanside also plays host to the National Scholastic Surfing Association nationals and other major competitions, drawing surfers from across the planet. With its wealth of surfing history, Oceanside is the perfect place for the **California Surf Museum,** 223 N. Coast Hwy. (☎721-6876. Open M and Th-Su 10am-4pm. Free.) You can catch your dinner by renting gear at **Helgren's Sportfishing Trips,** 315 Harbor Dr. South (☎722-2133. Fishing license $7.25 per day. Surface fishing rods $10; deep fishing rods $12. Half-day fishing trips $29; full-day $55. Daily harbor cruise $10, ages 5-12 $5. Times vary with season.) **Mission San Luis Rey,** 4050 Mission Ave., was founded in 1798, but the only original building still standing is the church built in 1807. Follow Mission Ave. east from N. Coast Hwy. for 4 mi. or take NCTD bus #303 at Rte. 21 and Mission Ave. (☎757-3651. Open daily 10am-4:30pm. $5, students and seniors $3, ages 8-14 $1. Cemetery free.)

BAJA CALIFORNIA

Called *"el otro Mexico"* (the other Mexico), Baja ("under" or "lower" in Spanish) California is somehow not at all California, yet nothing like mainland Mexico. Cradled by the warm, tranquil Sea of Cortés on the east and the chilly Pacific Ocean on the west, the peninsula claims one of the most spectacular and diverse landscapes in the world. Sparse deserts surround barren mountains jutting into cloudless sky, high-altitude pine forests fill with winter snow, and unbelievably blue-green water laps at thousands of miles of white sandy beaches. A solid stream of tourists flows from California across the border to surf and drink to their hearts' content. To explore Baja south of Ensenada, pick up a copy of *Let's Go: Mexico.*

HIGHLIGHTS OF BAJA CALIFORNIA

ENSENADA. Warm beaches, clear water, and the West Coast's largest geyser draw visitors south to the Bahía de Todos Santos in Ensenada (p. 526).

REVOLUCIÓN. The wild main drag in Tijuana (p. 520) douses young partiers with drink specials and foam parties—the drinking age in Mexico is only 18.

BAJA ESSENTIALS

EMERGENCY! For emergency help in Baja California, dial ☎060. You can also dial ☎078 for the round-the-clock Tourist Assistance Hotline.

GETTING THERE AND GETTING AROUND

Baja is a popular vacation spot, but be prepared for rugged driving conditions—potholes in the pavement, livestock milling around on the asphalt, and a general lack of guardrails. Driving in Baja can be reasonably secure if you go slowly, never drive at night, and keep your tank full. The **Ángeles Verdes (Green Angels;** ☎800-888-0911) patrol **Mex. 1 (The Transpeninsular Highway)** to provide motorists with roadside assistance. If you are driving in from the US, obtain a **vehicle permit** at the border, which is required south of San Felipe on the Sea of Cortés side and Ensenada on the Pacific side. Those visiting Baja for more than three days should get a tourist card (US$18) and a free permit (show the vehicle's title and proof of registration) at a border station. It is a good idea to pick up additional **car insurance** (about US$9.50 per day) at a drive-through insurance store in **San Ysidro** (the southernmost California town, just before the Mexican border) or through AAA.

MONEY

If your travels in Mexico will be limited to the cities in this book, you will probably not need to exchange your dollars for pesos; the vast majority of shops and restaurants near the US are happy to take greenbacks. Those staying overnight will want

BORDER TRAFFIC. At the world's busiest border crossing, northbound lanes often have backups of more than 150 cars. To minimize the wait, cross during a weekday morning, generally the slowest time. The southbound ride tends to be smoother, but weekends can be rough in both directions. If you're crossing into Tijuana for a day or so, it's easier to leave your car in a lot on the US side and join the crowds walking across the border, though you will still encounter long lines returning to the US. Remember that you need a **tourist card** (US$18) if you plan to travel farther south than Ensenada or San Felipe. Bring proper ID—ideally a driver's license or passport—and leave your fruit, livestock, drugs, and weapons behind.

to convert if the hotel or motel does not accept credit cards—paying in dollars is sometimes more expensive. Any travel farther south will require exchanging currency. As a rough guide, US$1 was equivalent to 11.4 Mexican pesos in Aug. 2004.

FOOD- AND WATER-BORNE DISEASES

Traveler's diarrhea, or *turista*, is one of the less charming experiences encountered by many visitors to Mexico. Symptoms include cramps, nausea, vomiting, chills, and fever, and generally last two to three days. Scientifically speaking, *turista* is a temporary reaction to new bacteria in food ingredients. Impure water and poorly cooked food are the major culprits. Never drink unbottled water (don't even brush your teeth or rinse your toothbrush with tap water) and avoid ice cubes. **Drink only purified, bottled water** (*agua embotellada*). If you must purify your own water, bring it to a rolling boil (simmering isn't enough) for about 30min. or treat it with **iodine drops or tablets.** Many choose to follow the golden rule in Mexico: don't drink the water, drink tequila—did we mention that the drinking age is 18?

If you have the common misfortune of developing *turista*, eat things like tortillas and salted crackers to keep your energy up. The most dangerous side effect of *turista* is dehydration; drink lots of bottled water with ½ tsp. of sugar or honey and a pinch of salt, uncaffeinated soft drinks, and bottled juices. If you develop a high fever or your symptoms don't go away after four days, consult a doctor.

TELEPHONES

To call Mexico from outside the country, dial the international access code of your home country, then 052 (Mexico's country code),

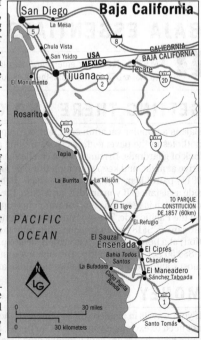

and then the Mexico city code (see the city's **Practical Information** section). The **LADATEL phones** that have popped up all over the country have revolutionized the way Mexico calls. To operate one, obtain a colorful **prepaid phone card,** available at most *papelerías* (stationery stores) or *tiendas de abarrotes* (general stores)—look for the posted "De venta aquí LADATEL" signs. Cards come in 30-, 50-, and 100-peso increments. To call home directly, insert your LADATEL card and dial 00 (to get an international line), the country code of the place you are calling, the area code, and the phone number. Making direct international calls can get very expensive, so you might want to talk quickly. At 5 pesos per min., calling the US is only somewhat pricey. Dial ☎*87 on a LADATEL phone for toll-free assistance or go online at http://www.telmex.com.mx/internos/deviaje/tladatel.htm for calling costs information.

To call from Mexico using a calling card, contact the operator for your service provider by dialing the appropriate toll-free Mexico access number: **AT&T:** ☎01 800 288 2872 (using LADATEL phones) or 001 800 462 4240; **Sprint:** ☎001 800 877 8000; and **MCI WorldPhone Direct:** ☎001 800 674 7000. If your provider does not have a Mexico access code, inquire beforehand as to the correct dialing procedures.

If you speak Spanish and can't reach the international operator, dial 07 to make a collect call through the national operator *(llamada por cobrar)*, who will connect you. Calling from hotels is usually faster, but beware of exorbitant surcharges. There can be a fee of 5 pesos for collect calls that are not accepted.

ALL THE SPANISH YOU WILL EVER NEED.
agua purificada; refrescos: purified water; soft drinks
avenida; calle; centro: avenue; street; city center or downtown
barato/a; caro/a, gratis: cheap; expensive; free (the -a ending is feminine)
borracho/a: drunk
¿Dónde está el baño? (DOHN-day es-tah el BAN-yo): Where is the bathroom?
casa de cambio: currency exchange house
comida; desayuno; almuerzo; cena: food; breakfast; lunch; dinner
dinero: money
extranjero; gringo; turista: foreigner; American (slang); tourist or diarrhea
hotel; motel: hotel; motel

TIJUANA ☎ 664

Just minutes from San Diego lies the most notorious specimen of border subculture: Tijuana (often referred to as "TJ"; pop. 2 million). The city's cheap booze, haggling vendors, and kitschy, unapologetic hedonism attract 30 million US visitors each year. But Tijuana is more than just another Sin City. As one of Mexico's wealthiest cities, it teems with megastores, museums, and monstrous industrial activity. Most travelers stick to *Revolución*, the city's main strip, which reverberates with *mariachi* bands, thumping dance beats from the packed nightclubs, and the sounds of eager tourists unloading wads of cash on everything from *jai alai* gambling to slimy strip shows. In recent years, the city's officials have made an effort to clean the place up, virtually eliminating sex shops and prostitution from the town center. This is not to say Tijuana has lost its sleazy luster; TJ is one of the largest ports of entry for illegal drugs and undocumented migrants into the US. As an introduction to Mexican culture, flashy, shady TJ is about as unrepresentative and unrepentant as they come.

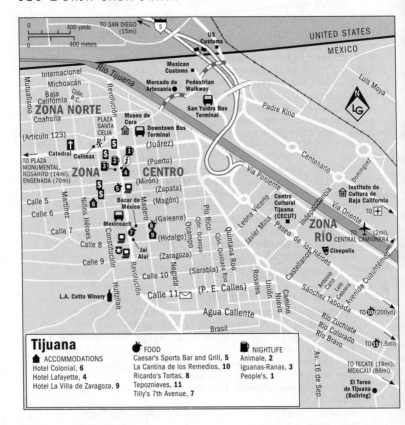

Tijuana

⌂ ACCOMMODATIONS
Hotel Colonial, **6**
Hotel Lafayette, **4**
Hotel La Villa de Zaragoza, **9**

● FOOD
Caesar's Sports Bar and Grill, **5**
La Cantina de los Remedios, **10**
Ricardo's Tortas, **8**
Tepoznieves, **11**
Tilly's 7th Avenue, **7**

■ NIGHTLIFE
Animale, **2**
Iguanas-Ranas, **3**
People's, **1**

▐ TRANSPORTATION

From San Ysidro: Take the red **Mexicoach** bus (☎619-428-9517 in the US) from its terminal at Border Station Parking. It stops right in the middle of all the Revolución madness (every 20-30min. 9am-9pm, US$2). Alternatively, just follow the signs to the *centro* on foot through the pedestrian footbridge; head for the tall, slender arch at the top of Revolución (15min. walk). Either of these methods is preferable to a taxi (US$5).

From San Diego: Grab a trolley on the blue line and take the 25min. ride down to the border (approx. US$3). From there, follow the instructions for San Ysidro above.

From Rosarito: Head north on Mex. 1 until Agua Caliente and turn left to reach the *centro*. From 1D, drive in on Calle 2A, which continues east to Revolución.

Buses: Tijuana has 2 main bus stations. **Downtown Station** is conveniently located just 1 block away from the top of Revolución. **Greyhound** (☎688-1979) runs to **L.A.** (3hr., every hr. 6am-1am, US$20). **Subrubaja** (☎688-0082) sends buses to **Ensenada** (3¾hr., every 3hr.). The **Central Camionera** is right near the airport and accessible only by overpriced taxi (US$12-15) or local bus (30min., 5½ pesos). To get from Central Camionera to Tijuana's city center, leave the main exit, turn left, walk to the end of the building, and take one of the "Centro/Buena Vista" buses. These will let you off on Calle 3 and Constitución, 1 block west of Revolución. At Calle 1 and Constitución, you can catch the bus back to the Central. **Autotransportes de Baja California** (☎621-2424, ext. 1214) runs from the Central to **Ensenada** (1½hr., 32 per day 6am-midnight, 80-89 pesos). There is a separate **Mexicoach station** on Revolución between Calles 6 and 7 that sends buses to the **San Ysidro border crossing** (30min., every 20-30min. 8am-9pm, US$2) and **Rosarito** (1hr., every 2hr. 9am-7pm, US$5; *colectivos*—see below—are much cheaper).

Taxi: Traditional **yellow cabs** prey almost exclusively on tourists and charge absurd rates; set a price before getting in. White and orange **taxis libres** are likely to offer slightly better value. Much cheaper *colectivos* or **taxis de ruta (route taxis)** are a popular option with locals, running designated routes painted above the rear tires and on the windshield for 10-20 pesos. Most originate on or around Madero or Constitución between Calle 1 and Calle 5. These colorful station wagons go to: Parque Morelos (orange and gray; 5 pesos); Rosarito (yellow and white; 10 pesos); and El Toreo bullring (red; 5 pesos), among other destinations. **Tipping** cabdrivers is not a common practice in Mexico, but drivers will often refuse to make change.

🔅🔢 ORIENTATION AND PRACTICAL INFORMATION

For the vast majority of visitors, Tijuana simply *is* **Avenida Revolución**, in the middle of **Zona Centro**, the tourist hot spot. *Calles* run east-west and are named and numbered; *avenidas* run parallel to Revolución and perpendicular to the *calles*. While crowded during the day, the Zona Centro can be unsettling at night; it's advisable to take a cab if you need to cross this area. **Exercise caution when walking at night.** Officials recommend avoiding the notorious **Zona Norte**, downhill from Calle 1, which is filled with prostitution and drugs—**not a safe place for tourists.**

Visitor Information: Tourist Office (☎685-2210), in the small booth on the corner of Revolución and Calle 3. English-speaking staff offer good maps and advice. Open M-Th 10am-4pm, F-Su 10am-7pm. They also have branches inside the Mexicoach station (next to the ticket office) and at the border crossing. **Customs Office** (☎683-1390), at the border on the Mexican side after crossing the San Ysidro bridge. Open 24hr.

Consulates: US, Tapachula Sur 96 (☎622-7400 or 681-8016), in Col. Hipódromo, next to the racetrack southeast of town. **Canada,** Gérman Gedovius 10411-101 (☎684-0461, for after-hours emergency assistance 800-706-2900), in the Zona Río. Open M-F 9am-1pm. **UK,** Salinas 1500 (☎681-8402, after-hours emergency assistance 681-5320), in Col. Aviación, La Mesa. Open M-F 9am-5pm. In an **emergency,** call the San Diego office (☎619-692-2154) and leave a message and phone number; an officer will return your call. Open M-F 8am-4pm.

Currency Exchange: Banks along Constitución exchange money and traveler's checks at the same rates. **Banamex** (☎688-0021; open M-F 8:30am-4:30pm), on Constitución at Calle 4, has shorter lines than more central **HSBC**, Revolución 129 (☎688-1914), at Calle 2. Open M-F 8am-7pm, Sa 8am-3pm. Both have 24hr. **ATMs.** *Casas de cambio* offer better rates but may charge commission and refuse to exchange traveler's checks.

Car Rental: @West Rent a Car, 3045 Rosecrans St., #215, just north of downtown San Diego, rents to drivers ages 18-25 and charges decent rates. (☎619-223-2343; www.atwestrentacar.com.) Open daily 8am-8pm. **Budget,** Paseo de los Héroes 77, next to the Hotel Camino Real (☎634-3303; open M-F 8am-7pm, Sa-8am-4pm), and **Hertz,** Av. Centenario (☎607-3949; open M-Sa 8am-6pm), offer similar rates.

Police: (☎685-6557), on Constitución at Calle 8. English spoken. Specialized tourist assistance (☎688-0555).

Red Cross: (☎621-7787, emergency 066), on Gamboa at Silvestre. English spoken.

Pharmacy: Farmacia Internacional (☎685-2790), at Constitución and Calle 2.

Medical Services: Hospital General, Centenario 10851 (☎684-0237 or 684-0922), in the Zona Río. **IMSS** (☎629-6342), at Agua Caliente and Francisco Zarabia. Both have 24hr. emergency service.

Internet Access: Matrix Internet Place, at Revolución and Calle 5 (☎688-2273; open 8am-1:30am; 10 pesos per 30min., 15 pesos per hr.), and **CNIS,** at Revolución between Calles 8 and 9 (☎688-3840; open 24hr.; 15 pesos per hr.).

Post Office: (☎684-7950), on Negrete at Calle 11 (Elías Calles). Open M-F 8am-5pm, Sa 9am-1pm. **Postal Code:** 22000.

ACCOMMODATIONS

As a general rule, hotels in Tijuana become less reputable the farther north you go. Avoid any in the area downhill from Calle 1 (the Zona Norte). Rooms at some motels may not fit the standards of cleanliness expected by US travelers.

Hotel Colonial, Calle 6 1812 (☎688-1620), between Constitución and Niños Héroes, in a quiet, residential neighborhood away from Revolución. Large, very clean, comfortable rooms have A/C and private baths. Singles and doubles 260 pesos. ❷

Hotel Lafayette, Revolución 325 (☎685-3940 or 685-3339), between Calle 3 and 4. Quiet considering its location in the middle of Revolución's chaos. Large rooms have color TV, phone, fans, and private bath. Singles 245 pesos; doubles 320 pesos. ❷

Hotel La Villa de Zaragoza, Madero 1120 (☎685-1832), between Calle 7 and 8. Semi-affordable luxury for those too squeamish for Tijuana's truly budget offerings. Spacious rooms come with TV, phone, king-size beds, bottled water, and towels. Laundry, room service, and 24hr. security. Singles from 393 pesos; doubles 474 pesos (excluding tax). Credit card reservations accepted. ❸

FOOD

As with most things in Tijuana, loud, in-your-face promoters try to herd tourists into the overpriced restaurants lining **Revolución.** For ultra-cheap food, **taco stands** ❶ all over the *centro* sell several tacos or a *torta* for 10 pesos. The supermarket **Calimax** is at Calle 2 at Constitución. (☎633-7988. Open daily 6am-midnight.)

La Cantina de los Remedios, Diego Rivera 19 (☎634-3065), on Paseo de los Heroes in the Zona Río. Local memorabilia, competing *mariachis,* a huge range of tequila, and a big crowd. Authentic Mexican cuisine (from 80 pesos) extends well beyond the usual options. Open M-Th 1pm-midnight, F-Sa 1pm-12:30am, Su 1-10pm. ❷

Ricardo's Tortas (☎685-4031), at Madero and Calle 7. Popular among both locals and *gringos,* Ricardos serves the best *tortas* in town (25-40 pesos). Try the *super especial,* with ham, *carne asada,* cheese, avocado, and tomato (47.50 pesos). Open 24hr. ❶

Tilly's 7th Avenue, on Revolución and Calle 7, next to the Jai Alai palace. Airy atmosphere and exceptional Mexican dishes (US$7.50). Caters mainly to tourists. Happy hour daily 4-7pm; beer US$1. Open Su-Th 9am-9pm, F-Sa 9am-10:30pm. ❷

Tepoznieves, Blvd. Sánchez Taboada 4002, in the Zona Río. The strangest ice-cream parlor ever, with cheese, tequila, pear, celery, and 100 other flavors. Cups and cones 15-30 pesos. Open daily 11am-9pm. ❶

Caesar's Sports Bar and Grill, on Revolución between Calle 4 and 5. This place claims to be the home of the Caesar salad. Have the genuine article lovingly prepared at your table (US$7)—it might just be the best you ever taste. Open daily 9am-late. ❷

SIGHTS

Many of the most entertaining sights in town are right on Revolución. While the so-called "attractions" of the main tourist drag also suffer from mind-numbing predictability, such as zebra-painted donkeys and gaudy costumes, Tijuana's cultural assets and parks counter its one-dimensional image.

■ **CENTRO CULTURAL TIJUANA (CECUT).** The most visually striking feature of Paseo de los Héroes is probably the huge sphere and plaza of Tijuana's cultural center. The superb **Museo de las Californias** traces the history of the peninsula from its earliest inhabitants through the Spanish conquest and the Mexican-American War to the 20th century. Exhibits are attractively presented and (unlike the city outside) provide the best possible introduction to the peninsula's cultural heritage. CECUT also hosts free science and art exhibitions and showcases Tijuana's cultural vitality with dance performances, concerts, and opera in the **Sala de Espectáculos.** Panoramic films are shown on a vast 180° screen every hour in the afternoon in the spherical building **Cine Omnimax.** There's also the charming **Jardín Caracol,** a garden with reproductions of pre-Columbian sculptures. (☎ 678-9633. Museum open daily 10am-7pm. 20 pesos, students and children 12 pesos. Cine Omnimax films 40 pesos, students and children 21 pesos. For showtimes, call ☎ 687-9700.)

MUSEO DE CERA. Eighty-six life-size figures await visitors in this wax museum, one of three in Mexico. Memorable combinations (and there are several) include President Vicente Fox and Fidel Castro towering over Mother Theresa and Mahatma Gandhi. (Calle 1 and Madero. ☎ 688-2478. Open daily 10am-7pm. 15 pesos.)

PARQUE MORELOS. This sprawling state-run park offers pleasant walks, rides, an open-air theater, and a small zoo. (Blvd. de los Insurgentes 26000. Take an orange and grey communal cab (5 pesos) on Calle 4 and Madero. ☎ 625 2470. Open Tu-Su 9am-5pm. 5 pesos, children 2 pesos. Parking 10 pesos.)

L.A. CETTO WINERY. Established in 1926 by Italian immigrants, this family-run winery maintains its vineyards in the Valle de Guadalupe, northeast of Ensenada. Underwhelming tours are preceded by a video presentation on the vineyards' resources, traditions, and exports; the real draw is the chance to sample and purchase the products. (Cañón Johnson 2108. Follow Constitución away from the party district to Calle 10a and turn right; the winery is on the left. ☎ 685-3031. Tours M-F 10am-6:30pm, Sa 10am-5pm; avoid coming during lunch hour around 1-2pm. US$2; includes tasting.)

🎵 **ENTERTAINMENT**

If you're in town on the right Sunday, you can watch the graceful and savage battle of *toreador* versus bull in one of Tijuana's two bullrings. **El Toreo de Tijuana,** southeast of town just off Agua Caliente, hosts the first round of fights. Catch a bus on Calle 2 west of Revolución. (May-Aug. every other Su at 4pm.) The seaside **Plaza Monumental** hosts the second round (Aug.-Oct.). Mexicoach sends buses (roundtrip US$4) to Plaza Monumental on fight days. Alternatively, take the blue-and-white local buses (5 pesos) on Calle 3 at Constitución all the way down Calle 2. Tickets to both rings go on sale at the gate (☎ 685-1510 or 685-1219) or at the Mexicoach office (☎ 685-1470) on Revolución between Calle 6 and 7 the Wednesday before a fight. (Tickets 95-400 pesos.)

📷 **SHOPPING**

As soon as tourists cross the footbridge from the US, they're bombarded with vendors peddling everything a *gringo* could possibly desire. The gaudy shopping scene continues most of the way up Revolución, as far as the intersection with Calle 7. Other spots for assorted tourist-oriented wares include the **Mercado de Artesanía,** on Calle 1 under the pedestrian footbridge, the vendors on **Plaza Santa Cecilia,** near the arches on Revolución, and the **Bazar de México,** on Revolución at Calle 7. **Bargaining** is a must, as quoted prices can be over twice the bottom line.

BAJA CALIFORNIA

NIGHTLIFE

In the 1920s, Prohibition drove US citizens south of the border to revel in the forbidden nectars of cacti, grapes, and hops. The flow of *gringos* thirsty for booze remains unquenched, with many taking advantage of Mexico's drinking age (18) to circumvent US laws. Stroll down Revolución after dusk and you'll be bombarded with thumping music, neon lights, and abrasive club promoters hawking "two-for-one" margaritas at the not-so-low price of US$5. Those who prefer laid-back nights of good conversation are in the wrong place.

Animale, on Revolución at Calle 3. The biggest, glitziest, and loudest hedonistic haven of them all. 2 drinks for US$5. Open daily 10am-4am.

Iguanas-Ranas (☎685-1422), on Revolución at Calle 3. A sublimely wacky, tacky world of life-sized plaster clowns, balloons, and kitschy US paraphernalia. Pound beers (US$3) in an authentic yellow school bus. Slogans and beer jokes plaster the walls. Packed with teenagers on weekends. Open M-Th 10am-2am, F-Su 10am-5am.

People's (☎688-2706), at Revolución and Calle 2. Fluorescent constellations and crudely painted sportsmen decorate the purple arches of the open-air terrace, where revelers guzzle 10 beers for US$15. Open M-Th 10am-2am, F-Su 10am-4am.

ROSARITO   ☎661

Baja's youngest city, Rosarito (pop. 120,000) has recently transformed from elite hideaway to all-out *gringo*-magnet where the two most widely accepted languages are English and the American dollar. Just 15 mi. from the border, Rosarito remains a popular Hollywood filming site while expanding at breakneck pace. You probably won't find the "real Baja" here, but if weekend hordes of SUV-driving visitors don't bother you, the placid beaches and throbbing clubs are yours to enjoy.

▐ TRANSPORTATION. To get to Rosarito from **Tijuana,** grab a yellow-and-white *taxi de ruta* (30min., 9 pesos) from Madero near Calle 3. In Rosarito, taxis congregate in front of the Rosarito Beach Hotel and can be flagged down anywhere along northbound Juárez. **Mexicoach** runs to Tijuana (US$5) from the Rosarito Beach Hotel and also serves Foxploration (p. 525) on request. Just behind where the taxis wait is the **ABC bus terminal** (☎613-1151). **Buses** run to Ensenada (1¼hr., 4 per day, 53 pesos); you can also ask the station to call the Tijuana station to ask that their next hourly Ensenada bus pick you up. To **drive** from Tijuana to Rosarito take Mex. 1 cuota (toll road) and exit at Rosarito Sur.

▐▌ ORIENTATION AND PRACTICAL INFORMATION. Mex. 1 runs straight through Rosarito, becoming **Juárez,** the city's main drag, before continuing south. Most of the town's businesses are concentrated at the southern end of Juárez, between the PEMEX at the corner of Avenida Cipres and the Rosarito Beach Hotel. Police recommend staying in this area of town and warn that the area around Col. Constitución and Co. Lucio Blanco is particularly unsafe.

The **SECTUR tourist office** is inconveniently located in the very northern end of town. (☎612-0200. Open M-F 8am-8pm, Sa-Su 9am-1pm.) **Banamex,** on Juárez at Ortiz Rubio, has a **24hr. ATM,** but most visitors get by with US dollars. (☎612 1556. Open M-F 9am-4pm, Sa 10am-2pm.) In an **emergency,** call ☎060, or contact the **police** (☎613-0612 or 613-3411), at Juárez and Acacias next to the post office, or the

Red Cross (☎613-1120, emergency 066), on Juárez at Ortiz Rubio, around the corner from the police; some English is spoken at both. Other services include: **laundry** at **Lavamática**, on Juárez near Acacias (40 pesos for wash and dry; open daily 9am-9pm); **Internet** access at **El Tunel.com**, Juárez 208, near Cárdenas in the yellow building with the arcade (☎612-5061; 20 pesos per hr.; open M-F 9am-10pm, Sa-Su 10am-10pm); the pharmacy **Farmacia Roma**, set back from Juárez at Roble (☎612-3500; open 24hr.); and the **post office** on Juárez, near Acacias (☎612-1355; open M-F 8am-3pm, Sa 8am-noon). **Postal Code:** 22710.

ACCOMMODATIONS AND FOOD. Most budget hotels in Rosarito are cramped or situated on the outskirts of town. Prices soar during spring break, holidays, and summer weekends. Close to the bars and clubs in the southern end of town is **Motel Sonia, Juárez and Palma ❸**. These rooms provide the bare necessities on a first come, first served basis. (☎612-1260. Singles and doubles $20-35.) **Hotel Palmas Quintero ❷** is a well kept secret, tucked away on Privada Guadalupe Victoria 26. To find it, head north on Cárdenas from Juárez and follow it until it becomes a dirt road, continue for one block, and turn left; the hotel is ahead and to the right. Large rooms have cable TV and clean baths. (☎612-1359. Singles Su-Th US$25, F-Su US$35; doubles US$40/US$50.)

Although Rosarito's culinary scene caters mostly to tourists who consider US$10 cheap, careful searching yields quality budget eateries. **❏La Flor de Michoacán ❷**, Juárez 291, at the north end of town, is a pork lover's paradise that serves huge *órdenes de carnitas* (65 pesos) with either "solid" or "mixed" pork (mixed includes tongues, stomachs, and all sorts of good stuff). Those with lots of friends or impressive appetites can order by the kilogram. (☎612-1858. 240 pesos per kg. Open Su-Tu and Th-Sa 9am-10pm.) Delight in heaping plates of ordinary and not-so-ordinary Mexican dishes at local favorite **Las Mañanitas,** at Juárez and Cardenas, attached to a nightclub of the same name. (☎100-2156. Entrees $4-9. Open daily 10am-10pm.) Find the best tacos in town at **Macho Taco ❶**, Juárez 60, across from Hotel Festival Plaza. The special combo—two tacos, rice, beans, and a soda for US$3.50—can't be beat. (☎613-0630. Open daily 10am-2am.)

SIGHTS AND ENTERTAINMENT. Rosarito entices visitors with posh resorts, beautiful shores, and wild nightlife. Spanning the coast two blocks west of Juárez, **Rosarito Beach** has soft sand and gentle surf. Rosarito's long connection to Hollywood (many stars vacationed here in years past) continues in the form of the **Foxploration** tourist park, 1 mi. south of Rosarito. Constructed for Fox's blockbuster *Titanic*, the park is next to Fox Baja Studios, a regular filming site. Exhibits include original sets and props, though don't expect to find the ship. (☎614 9444; www.foxploration.com. Open Su-M and Th-Sa 9am-5pm. Tours $12.)

Rosarito's nightlife revolves around the mega-clubs packed with drunken revelers on the streets behind the Hotel Festival Plaza. **Iggy's,** at Nogal and Coronado, is a behemoth of a nightspot with its own pool, foam party, ATVs on the beach, and even bungee jumps from an on-site crane. The three bars offer all-you-can-drink cocktails. (☎612-0537. Cover around US$10. Open 8pm-3am, later on weekends.) Across the street is **Papas and Beer,** a multilevel party palace that can accommodate up to 7000 guests, plus a mechanical bull. (☎612-0444. Drinks US$1.50-7. Open Su-Th 11am-3am, F-Sa 11am-4am.) **Tequila Safari,** on Juárez between Roble and Encino, is a good place for cheap drinks, with happy hour specials (5-7pm; 5-all drinks half-price) and buckets of six different beers available for US$10 all day. (☎612-0202. M-Th noon-10pm, F-Su noon-2am.)

BAJA CALIFORNIA

ENSENADA ☎ 646

Nestled in the beautiful Bahía de Todos Santos (Bay of All Saints), Ensenada (pop. 370,000) still maintains some of the salty atmosphere of a fishing harbor, but the biggest catch these days is likely to be schools of tourists from the cruise ships. An easy daytrip from San Diego, Ensenada will get you slightly closer to the "real Mexico" than will Tijuana.

▊ TRANSPORTATION. Ensenada is 50 mi. south of Tijuana on **Mex. 1D** (a *cuota* or toll road; cars 23 pesos or US$2.10). The last 20min. stretch of the 1½hr. drive is particularly breathtaking. The less scenic, poorly maintained **Mex. 1** parallels the *cuota* inland. As there are no streetlights on Mex. 1, use the *cuota* at night. Follow signs to downtown Ensenada or "Centro"; these lead to **Costero,** which runs by the harbor, one block south of Mateos. Local *urbanos* (☎ 178-2594) leave from Juárez at Calle 6 and from Calle 2 at Macheros (5½ pesos for most destinations in the city). **Buses** from Tijuana arrive at the **Central de Autobuses,** at Calle 11 and Riveroll. To get to the *centro,* turn right as you come out of the station, and walk south 10 blocks to Mateos. **Autotransportes de Baja California** (☎ 178-6680) runs buses to Tijuana (1½hr., every 30min. 5am-11pm, 90 pesos). **Transportes Brisas** (☎ 178-3888), Calle 4 771, near Macheros, runs buses to small towns nearby.

▊▊ ORIENTATION AND PRACTICAL INFORMATION. Mateos, the main tourist drag, is also called **Primera** (Calle 1). *Calles,* including **Juárez** (Calle 5), run east-west, parallel to Mateos. Alphabetized *avenidas* run north-south, starting with Alvarado and moving east. Street signs are nonexistent more than one block from Mateos. After sundown, **exercise caution** near the shore and in the region bounded by Miramar, Macheros, Mateos, and Calle 4.

The English-speaking staff at the **tourist office,** Costero 540, at Azueta Friendly, doles out maps and pamphlets. (☎ 172-3022; fax 172-3081. Open M-F 8am-8pm, Sa-Su 9am-1pm.) The closest bank is **Santander Serfín,** at Ruíz and Calle 3. (☎ 174-0009. Open M-F 9am-5pm, Sa 10am-3pm.) The **police,** (☎ 176-4343), on Calle 9 at Espinoza, speak some English. The **Policía Federal Preventativa,** Mateos 1360 (☎ 176-1311), near the post office, may help with information on roads in the surrounding countryside. Other services include: **Hospital General,** on Mex.-1 km 111 (☎ 176-7800); **San Martín pharmacy** at Ruíz and Calle 8 (☎ 178-3530; open 24hr.); **Internet** access at **Café Internet MaxiComm,** on Mateos between Miramar and Macheros, upstairs from the souvenir stalls (☎ 175-7011; 15 pesos per 30min., 20 pesos per hr.; open M-F 9am-9pm, Sa-Su 9am-8pm); and the **post office,** on Mateos at Espinoza. (☎ 176-1088. Open M-F 8am-6pm, Sa 9am-1pm.) **Postal Code:** 22800.

▊ ACCOMMODATIONS. In Ensenada, budget motels cluster around the eastern end of Mateos. Accommodations in Ensenada frequently sell out in the summer; those arriving at night should call ahead. **Motel América ❷,** on Mateos at Espinoza, has huge rooms with overhead fans, baths, and cable TV; some have kitchens. (☎ 176-1333. Singles US$24-28; doubles US$32-36.) **Motel Caribe ❶,** Mateos 627/8, is in the lively center of town. The main building's rooms are spacious and carpeted, with cable TV, fans, and baths, while those in the building across the street are more modest and cheaper. (☎ 178-3481. Singles US$15-20; doubles US$25. US$5 more on weekends.) One block off Mateos, on Alvarado at Calle 2, **Hotel Hacienda ❶** rents large rooms with phones, cable TV, and tiny showers. (☎ 178-2344. Singles Su-Th 180 pesos, F-Sa 210 pesos; doubles 300/340 pesos; jacuzzi suite 350/430 pesos.) A more comfortable alternative is the **Hotel Villafontana ❸,** Mateos 1050, which offers rooms with queen-size beds and spacious bathrooms. (☎ 178-3434; www.villafontana.com.mx. Rooms Su-Th US$41, F-Sa US$46.)

🄲🄵 FOOD AND NIGHTLIFE. At the waterfront fish market, **loncherías** sell savory fish tacos for under US$1 apiece. **Calimax** sells groceries at Gastelum and Calle 3. (Open daily 7am-11pm.) **Mariscos Playa Azul ❶**, on Rivveroll between Mateos and Calle 2, serves seafood as cheap as water. (☎ 174-0622. Entrees 50-60 pesos. Open daily 10am-10pm.) Tasty breakfasts are cooked up in a homey setting at **La Holandesa ❶**, at Mateos and Rayón. (☎ 177-1965. Shrimp omelettes 50 pesos. Open M-F 7am-10pm, Sa 8am-10pm, Su 8am-5pm.) **Los Farroles Villa Mexicana ❶**, at Riveroll and Calle 2, serves quick, yummy *tortas* (25 pesos) at its outdoor counter. (Open daily 7am-4pm.) No trip to Ensenada would be complete without a pilgrimage to ⬛**Hussong's Cantina,** Ruiz 113, possibly the most famous watering hole in all of Mexico, in business since 1892. This cantina was a salon to a number of expatriate writers who found inspiration in a bottle of tequila. (☎ 178-3210. Beer 20 pesos. Margaritas 30 pesos. Open daily 10am-1am.) Cross the street to the modern, rowdy bar/dance scene at **Papas and Beer.** (☎ 174-0145. 40-peso margaritas. DJ Su-Th. Live music F-Sa, cover US$5-10. Open M-W noon-midnight, Th-Su noon-3am.)

🄶 SIGHTS. A cosmopolitan dream by North Baja standards, Ensenada has enough museums and other cultural attractions to fill a few pleasant days. All of the museums are small by California standards and may be seen in under an hour. The lovely Moorish buildings and perfectly maintained gardens of the huge **Riviera del Pacífico,** on Costero one block from the tourist office, once housed a world-famous casino and still welcomes visitors into its elegant interior. Stop for a drink at the original **Andaluz Bar** or the **coffee shop.** The museum also houses temporary exhibitions in the **Galería de Arte de la Ciudad.** (☎ 176-4310; www.ensenadahoy.com/riviera. Open daily 8am-8pm. Bar open Su-Tu and Th-F 4pm-midnight, W and Sa 9am-midnight. Coffee shop open daily 9am-9pm. Galeria open M-F 8am-7pm, Sa 10am-4pm. Free.) The permanent display at **Museo de Historia,** in the Riviera, charts the history of the region in a cavern-shaped gallery. (☎ 177-0594. Open M-F 9am-5pm, Sa-Su 10am-5pm. 7 pesos, under 12 5 pesos.) Originally built in 1886 as a barracks, the **Museo Histórico Regional,** on Gastelum between Uribe and Mateos, houses an eclectic range of exhibits on the Spanish conquest and the history and lifestyle of indigenous tribes. (☎ 178-3692. Open daily 10am-5pm. 22 pesos.) The highlight of the geology and natural history exhibits at **Museo de Ciéncias,** Obregón 1463, at Calle 14 near Mateos, is the Noah's Ark boat outside displaying photographs and info on Baja's endangered species. (☎ 178-7192. Open M-F 9am-5pm, Sa 10am-3pm. 20 pesos, children 14 pesos.)

The mild, dry climate of Baja's northern coast is perfect for growing grapes, and the **Bodegas de Santo Tomás,** Miramar 666, at Calle 7, has been distilling those grapes into wine since 1888. Tours conclude with a wine tasting with breads and cheeses. (☎ 178-3333. Tours daily 10, 11am, noon, 1, and 3pm. Tours US$5 with tasting of 5 wines, US$10 with a wider selection.) At the top of Calle 2, the **Chapultepec Hills** offer a stunning view of the bay and the city.

🄲🄽 BEACHES AND OUTDOOR ACTIVITIES. A car, ideally with 4WD, is needed to reach many of the sights near Ensenada. Tijuana and San Diego are the best bets for rentals (see **Tijuana: Car Rental,** p. 521). Ensenada's shoreline is devoted to shipping rather than sunbathing, so daytrippers stream southwest along the Punta Banda Peninsula to a series of beautiful beaches and ocean views in **Bahía de Todos Santos.** On the northern side of the bay, **Playa Estero** is packed with volleyball courts, banana boats, and *norteamericanos*. Sea lions come ashore during low tide. Access the bay through the Estero Beach Resort. (Take a right at the "Estero Beach" sign on Mex. 1 heading south. Free parking in the first hotel lot. Or catch a bus marked "Aeropuerto," "Zorrillo," "Maneadero," or

"Chapultepec" from Pl. Cívica.) Five mi. south of Ensenada, **Playa El Faro** is similarly crowded but has slightly better sand and allows **beach camping ❶**. Signs warn swimmers about strong offshore currents. Horse rentals are often available at nearby **Playa Santa María**. (☎177-4620. Sites US$7 per car. Hookups US$12.) Undeterred by the rocky beach, surfers flock to **Playa San Miguel**, to the north. Drive west on Calle 10, which joins Mex 1D, continue to the toll gate, make a U-turn, and then turn right onto the cobbled road. (24hr. parking.) **Camping ❶** (☎174-7948) facilities include hookup and hot baths for US$10. (All-day surfing until 8pm US$6. Prices drop with stays of several days.)

Punta Banda, the peninsula at the southern end of the bay, boasts beautiful solitary trails and more secluded beaches than the north. Heading south on **Mex.1,** take a right on Mex. 23 at "La Bufadora." **Baja Beach's** clean, soft sands are buffeted by small waves that provide some of the best swimming in the area. A number of remote hiking trails start from **Cerro de la Punta,** under the radio tower on the road to La Bufadora near the end of the peninsula. The ascent to the top provides sweeping views of the surrounding area. You can also descend to secluded rocky coves along the shoreline. Most of the trails are unmarked footpaths, but be sure to stick to them; trailblazing damages the flora. ■**La Bufadora,** the Pacific coast's largest geyser, is one of Ensenada's biggest attractions. Once you've reached the end of the curving road and peninsula, there's no missing the trinket stalls and churro stands on the way to the blowhole. (Parking US$1-2.)

Situated 1650m above sea level, the thick mountain pine forest of the **Parque Nacional Constitución de 1857** is unlike the rest of Baja. A long desert drive winds its way high up into an enchanting landscape of deep greens, excellent trails, and isolated ranches. The focal point of the park is **Laguna Hanson,** a small lake with small campsites along its perimeter (US$7). Bring warm clothes and a good sleeping bag—temperatures drop dramatically at night.

THE DESERT

California's desert is one of the most beautiful places in the world; it's also one of the loneliest. Roads cut through endless expanses of barren earth and landscapes that seem untouched by human existence. Only a few hours from the complicated hustle of L.A. lies the wide-open space of the Mojave. Exploration turns up elusive treasures: diverse flora and fauna, staggering topographical variation, and scattered relics of the American frontier. Throughout the year, the desert switches from a pleasantly warm refuge to an unbearable wasteland and back again.

HIGHLIGHTS OF THE DESERT

WONDERLAND OF ROCKS. The split-granite at Wonderland of Rocks in Joshua Tree National Park (p. 531) draws hard-core climbers into the hot desert.

CIRQUE DU SOLEIL. Contortionists, exhibitionists, and impresarios perform three mind-bogglingly inventive shows in three different Las Vegas casinos (p. 559).

MITCHELL CAVERNS. These limestone caves under the lonely Mojave National Preserve (p. 568) offer stunning stalactites and reprieve from the heat.

◆ ORIENTATION

California's desert divides into the Low and High Deserts, names that indicate differences in both altitude and latitude. The **Colorado,** or **Low Desert** (see p. 569), occupies southeastern California from the Mexican border north to Needles and west to Anza-Borrego. The **Mojave,** or **High Desert** (see p. 531), averages elevations of 2000 ft. and spans the southern central part of the state, with Joshua Tree National Park at its southern border, San Bernardino to the west, the Sierra Nevadas to the north, and Death Valley in the northeast. Four major east-west highways cross the desert. **I-8** hugs the California-Mexico border, running straight through the low desert, while **I-10** runs between the Mojave and Colorado Deserts, connecting Joshua Tree and Palm Springs. Cutting through the heart of the Mojave is **I-15.** From Barstow, the Mojave's central pit stop, I-15 continues on to Las Vegas, while **I-40** runs east through Needles to Arizona's deep red desert.

▌ DESERT SURVIVAL

Here, **water** is life. The body loses at least a gallon of liquid per day in the desert (two gallons during strenuous activity), so keep drinking. Consuming huge quantities of water to quench your thirst after physical exertion is not as effective as drinking water before and during activity, even if you're just driving. Whatever you're doing, tote **two gallons of water per person per day.** Designate at least one container as an emergency supply. In the car, keep backup containers in a cooler. Drink the water you have. Avoid alcohol and caffeine, which cause dehydration. Keep your strength up for long stays with a high-quality beverage that contains potassium compounds and glucose, such as **ERG** (an industrial-strength Gatorade). If you are planning to hike, bring at least 1 pint of water per mile with you.

Most people need a few days to adjust to the heat, especially before difficult hikes. Sunglasses with 100% UV protection, sunscreen, and a wide-brim hat are essential **sun protection,** but proper clothing is the most effective shield. Light-colored clothing helps reflect the sun's rays. Although it may be uncomfortable to wear a sweaty shirt, it prevents dehydration more effectively than going shirtless.

The Desert

Heat is not the desert's only climatic extreme. At high elevations, temperatures during winter nights can drop well below freezing (a sweater is often necessary even in summer). Fall and spring **flash floods** can cause water to rush down from rain-drenched higher elevations and wreak biblical devastation upon lands below, turning dry gulches into raging rivers. Don't walk in washes you can't scramble out of, beware of thunderstorms on the horizon, and never camp in washes or gullies. For more advice, consult the excellent *Desert Survival Handbook* (Primer; $8).

DRIVING IN THE DESERT. Conditions in the desert are as grueling on cars as they are on bodies; only recently serviced cars in good condition can take the heat. Bring at least five gallons of radiator water, extra coolant, a spare tire, proper tools for minor repairs, and a few quarts of oil (car manuals recommend appropriate oil weights for varying temperatures). Avoid running out of gas by keeping your tank more than half-full; gas can be hard to find in the desert. Beware of gravel roads that turn to sand. A board and shovel may also be useful for stuck cars.

Although towns are sometimes sparse, major roads usually have enough traffic to ensure that breakdowns are noticed. Still, isolated areas of the parks pose a threat, especially in summer when few tourists visit. **Stay with your vehicle if it breaks down;** it is easier to spot than a person and provides crucial shade. Turn off **air-conditioning** immediately if the car's temperature gauge starts to climb. Air from open windows should be sufficiently comfortable at highway speeds. If your car overheats, pull off the road and turn the heater on full force. If radiator fluid is steaming or bubbling, turn off the car for 30min. If not, run the car in neutral at about 1500 RPM for a few minutes, allowing the coolant to circulate. Never pour water over the engine or try to lift a hot hood. **Desert water bags** ($5-10) are available at hardware or auto stores. When strapped onto the front of the car and filled with water, these prevent overheating by speeding up evaporation. Pick up a manual with more specific desert driving tactics if you plan to be traveling extensively in the Mojave. The above-mentioned *Desert Survival Handbook* is a good choice.

 PHONE HOME. Mobile phones may not get service in remote parts of the desert. Take note of emergency roadside phones and pay phones instead of relying on your cell phone.

THE MOJAVE DESERT

The Mojave Desert is the very picture of desolation. Atop a plateau, the desert unfolds at heights around 5000 ft. The Mojave conceals unlikely treasures for those patient and hardy enough to explore it. Genuine summer attractions are rare, but temperate winters allow travelers to trudge across drifting dunes and creep through ghost towns. Some of the best bouldering and most fascinating plants in the US await climbers and botany enthusiasts at Joshua Tree.

JOSHUA TREE NATIONAL PARK ☎ 760

When devout Mormon pioneers crossed this faith-testing desert in the 19th century, they named the enigmatic tree they encountered after the Biblical prophet Joshua. The tree's crooked limbs resembled the Hebrew general, and, with arms upraised, seemed to beckon these Latter-Day pioneers to the Promised Land. Even today, Joshua Tree National Park inspires reverent awe in those who happen upon it. Towers of wind-sculpted boulders, guarded by the legions of eerie Joshua Trees, continue to evoke the devastation of the walls of Jericho. The park's five oases appear lushly Edenic against the desolate desert backdrop.

THE DESERT

Modern climbers, campers, and daytrippers from Southern California add to the mosaic. "Josh," as outdoor enthusiasts call it, has become a world-renowned mecca for both casual and elite climbers. The boulder formations strewn across the desert badlands have nearly limitless potential. History buffs will appreciate the vestiges of human occupation: ancient rock petroglyphs, 19th-century dams built to catch the meager rainfall for livestock, and ruined gold mines. But the most attractive aspect of Joshua Tree is its remoteness and freedom from the commercial mayhem of many national parks. Its natural beauty is disrupted only by a few paved roads and signs, with vast tracts left almost untouched since the days when miners coaxed precious metals out of the scarred terrain.

At the north entrance to the park lies Twentynine Palms, settled after World War I by veterans looking for a hot, dry climate to soothe their battle-weary bodies. Today the town also houses the world's largest US Marine Corps base, as well as murals depicting people and events from the town's past.

AT A GLANCE: JOSHUA TREE NATIONAL PARK

AREA: 794,000 acres.

FEATURES: Pinto Mountains, Hexie Mountains, Eagle Mountains, Little Bernardino Mountains, High/Low Desert Transition Zone, Lost Palms Oasis.

HIGHLIGHTS: Climbing virtually anyplace in the park, hiking to to the bottom of Lost Palms Oasis, navigating the 4WD-only Geology Tour Rd.

GATEWAY TOWNS: Joshua Tree, Twentynine Palms, Yucca Valley.

CAMPING: Reservations available for groups. Wilderness permit required for backcountry camping.

FEES: Entrance fee $10 per vehicle, $5 per pedestrian or bicyclist. Valid for 7 days.

WHEN TO GO. Due to intense heat and aridity, it's best to avoid visiting June-Sept. The park's most temperate weather is in late fall (Oct.-Dec.) and early spring (Mar.-Apr.); temperatures in other months span extremes (summer highs 95-115°F; winter lows 30-40°). For more advice, see **Desert Survival**, p. 529.

✷ ▮ ORIENTATION AND PRACTICAL INFORMATION

The park is ringed by three highways: **Interstate 10** to the south, **Route 62 (Twentynine Palms Highway)** to the west and north, and **Route 177** to the east. The northern entrances to the park are off Rte. 62 at the towns of **Joshua Tree** and **Twentynine Palms.** The south entrance is at **Cottonwood Spring,** off I-10 at Rte. 195, southeast of Palm Springs. The **park entrance fee,** valid one week, is $5 per person, $10 per car.

Visitor Information: There are 4 useful visitors centers in the park.

    Headquarters and Oasis Visitor Center, 74485 National Park Dr. (☎367-5500; www.nps.gov/jotr), ¼ mi. off Rte. 62 in Twentynine Palms. The best place to familiarize yourself with the park. Friendly rangers, plus displays, guidebooks, maps, restrooms, and water. Open daily 8am-5pm.

    Cottonwood Visitor Center, at the southern gateway of the park, 7 mi. north of I-10 and 25 mi. east of Indio. Information, water, and picnic areas. Open daily 8am-4pm.

    Indian Cove Ranger Station, 7295 Indian Cove Rd. (☎362-4367). Open Oct.-May daily 8am-4pm.

    Twentynine Palms Chamber of Commerce, 6455 Mesquite Ave., Ste. A (☎367-3445). Info on transportation, accommodations, and food. Open M-F 9am-5pm; may close for lunch.

Gear rental and Instruction:

    Nomad Ventures, 61795 Twentynine Palms Hwy. (☎366-4684), in the town of Joshua Tree. Lots of gear for sale or rent. Well-qualified staff; experienced climbers will especially appreciate their help. Open daily 9am-6pm.

THE DESERT

Joshua Tree National Park

0 ___ 5 miles
0 ___ 5 kilometers

TO AMBOY (30mi)
TO AMBOY (48mi)

MOJAVE DESERT

SHEEPHOLE MOUNTAINS

TO MARINE CORPS AIR
GROUND COMBAT CENTER (3mi)

Amboy Rd.

Adobe Rd.

Twentynine Palms

Oasis Visitor Center
Oasis of Mara
North Entrance Station

TO PARKER (55mi)

Aqua Peak
(4,416')

COXCOMB MOUNTAINS

177

TO BLYTHE (30mi)

Kaiser Rd.

COLORADO DESERT

MOJAVE DESERT
Transition Zone
COLORADO DESERT

PINTO BASIN

Black
Eagle
Mines

EAGLE MOUNTAINS

10

Chiriaco Summit

Gold Crown Rd.

Black Eagle Mine Rd.
Old Dale Rd.

PINTO MOUNTAINS

Pinto Mountain
(3,983')

Pinto Basin Rd.

Eagle Mtn.
(5,350')

Lost Palms Oasis

TO MECCA, SALTON SEA (13mi)

195

62

Entrance Station

Indian Cove Rd.

Canyon Rd.
Fortynine Palms Oasis

Queen Mtn.
(5,677')
Barker Dam
Skull Rock
Ryan Mtn.

7
8

Cholla Cactus Garden

HEXIE MOUNTAINS

Monument Mtn.
(4,834')

Pinkham Canyon Rd.
Cottonwood Canyon
Pinkham Canyon

Cottonwood
Visitor Center

9

COTTONWOOD MOUNTAINS

Thermal Cyn.

TO MECCA, SALTON SEA (8mi)

Joshua Tree

West Entrance
Station
Wonderland
of Rocks

Boy Scout Tr.

Wonderland of Rocks

2

3
Hidden Valley

Quail Mtn.
(5,814')

Geology Tour Road

6
5
Lost Horse Mine
Ryan Mtn.

PLEASANT VALLEY

Berdoo Canyon

MOJAVE DESERT
Transition Zone
COLORADO DESERT

Dillon Rd.

SAN ANDREAS FAULT

111

INDIO HILLS

Indio

Coachella

86

111

62

247

Yucca Valley

Morongo Valley

Palmer Ave.
Joshua Tree
Alta Loma

Yucca Trail
Yucca Valley
Joshua Lane
Visitor Center

Twentynine Palms Hwy.

La Contenta Rd.

California Riding and Hiking Trail

Eureka Peak
(5,516')

Inspiration Peak

Keys View

LITTLE SAN BERNARDINO MOUNTAINS

Desert Hot Springs

Indian Ave.

10

Cathedral City

Rancho Mirage

Palm Springs

111

TO LOS ANGELES (98mi)

LG

N

Freeway
Major Paved Road
Minor Paved Road
Unpaved Road
4WD Only
Trail

THE DESERT

Joshua Tree Rock Climbing School (☎800-890-4745; www.rockclimbingschool.com), south on Hillview off Twentynine Palms Hwy. and then right onto Desert Air Rd. Gear, guiding, and instruction, regardless of experience. Inquire about their climber's cabins ($125).

Coyote Corner, 6535 Park Blvd. (☎366-9683). Sells gear that smells of incense. Showers available. Open daily 9am-6pm.

Medical Services: 24hr. dispatch (☎909-383-5651). Call collect. **Hi-Desert Medical Center,** 6601 White Feather Rd. (☎366-3711), in Joshua Tree. 24hr. emergency care.

Library and Internet Access: Twentynine Palms Branch Library, 6078 Adobe Rd. (☎367-9519). Open M-Tu noon-8pm, W-F 10am-6pm, Sa 9am-5pm. **Joshua Tree Branch Library,** 6465 Park Blvd. (☎366-8615), north from the Twentynine Palms Hwy. Open M-F 10am-6pm.

Post Office: 73839 Gorgonio Dr. (☎800-275-8777), in Twentynine Palms. Open M-F 8:30am-5pm. **Postal Code:** 92277.

ACCOMMODATIONS

Those who cannot stomach the thought of desert campgrounds can find inexpensive motels in Twentynine Palms, the self-proclaimed "Oasis of Murals."

29 Palms Inn, 73950 Inn Dr., (☎367-3505; www.29palmsinn.com.), off Twentynine Palms Hwy., is a tourist attraction in its own right. Its 23 distinctly different rooms and bungalows face the Mara Oasis, which has supported life for over 20,000 years. More recently, the life here has been of the celebrity genus, with guests like Charlize Theron, Michelle Pfeiffer, Nicholas Cage, and Robert Plant, who composed his post-Zeppelin hit "29 Palms" here. Check out the garden and enjoy its produce in the restaurant. Reservations required Feb.-Apr. Doubles Oct.-May Su-Th $60-95, F-Sa $85-135; June-Sept. Su-Th $50-75, F-Sa $75-115. Adobe cottages for 4-8 people also available. ❸

Motel 6, 72562 Twentynine Palms Hwy. (☎367-2833; www.motel6.com.). Clean and reliable, with a pool and laundry. Singles $40-44; doubles $46-50. $3 per additional person. Online reservations $3-4 less. ❸

Harmony Motel, 71161 Twentynine Palms Hwy. (☎367-3351; www.harmonymotel.com.) U2 stayed in one of the 10 units here while creating the album *Joshua Tree* in 1987. Rooms were recently refurbished and have A/C and access to a communal kitchen. Singles and doubles $60-70; negotiable rates in the summer. Bartering is also possible. ❹

CAMPING

Camping is an enjoyable and inexpensive way to experience the beauty of the park, except in the scorching heat of summer. Even then, when the sun goes down, the temperatures may drop to comfortable levels. Spring weekends and holidays are the busiest times. Pre-noon arrivals are the best way to guarantee a site, since most campgrounds in the park do not accept reservations (campgrounds that require separate fees do take reservations). Reservations can be made for group sites at Cottonwood, Sheep Pass, Indian Cove, and Black Rock Canyon via the Internet at www.nps.gov/jotr. Well-prepared and experienced campers can register for a backcountry permit at the visitors center or at self-service backcountry boards located throughout the park. Regulations require camping at least 1 mi. from roads and 500 ft. from trails; rangers provide maps of designated wilderness areas. All established campsites have tables, fire pits, and pit toilets, but no hookups. Only campgrounds that take reservations offer water or flush toilets; visitors who plan a longer stay should pack their own supplies. (14-day max. stay Oct.-May; 30-day limit per year.)

Indian Cove, 3200 ft., on the north edge of Wonderland of Rocks. Enter at the north entrance on Indian Cove Rd. off Twentynine Palms Hwy. Popular spot for rock climbers. 101 sites, including 13 for groups. Sites $10; group sites $20-35. ❶

▩ **Jumbo Rocks,** 4400 ft., near Skull Rock Trail on the eastern edge of Queen Valley. Take Quail Springs Rd. 15 mi. south of Oasis Visitors Center. The highest and coolest campground. Front spots have shade. 125 sites. Wheelchair accessible. Sites $5. ❶

White Tank, 3800 ft., on Pinto Basin Rd., south of Belle campground. Few people, but watch for coyotes that may try to keep you company as you gaze at the Pinto Mountains. Cowboys built up White Tank as a reliable watering hole for cattle. 15 sites amid huge boulder towers. Sites $5. ❶

Hidden Valley, 4200 ft., in the center of Queen Valley off Quail Springs Rd. Secluded alcoves are perfect for pitching tents. Enormous shade-providing boulders serve as perches for viewing the sun at dawn and dusk. Hidden Valley's proximity to numerous popular climbing boulders makes it a rock climber's heaven; the 39 sites fill up quickly. Sites $5. ❶

Sheep Pass, 4500 ft., on the trail to Ryan Mountain. Huge boulders and lots of Joshua trees make this site fairly cool and secluded. The 6 group spots can be reserved up to 3 months in advance. Sites $20-35. ❷

Belle, 3800 ft., on Pinto Basin Rd., south of the Oasis Visitor Center. An ideal place to stare at the starry heavens. 18 sites tucked in the crevices of big boulders. Hold out for one of the sites on the road's second loop. Sites $5. ❶

Ryan, 4300 ft., off Park Blvd., on the trail to Ryan Mountain. Fewer rocks, less privacy, and less shade than other campsites. The 3 mi. round-trip trail ascends to Ryan Mountain, which served as headquarters and water storage for the Lost Horse mine. The sunrise is spectacular from Key's View (see p. 536). 31 sites. Sites $5.❶

Black Rock Canyon, 4000 ft., at the end of Joshua Ln. off Rte. 62 near Yucca Valley. Good for those who haven't camped before; close to Yucca Valley, water, and a ranger station. A great place to spot animals, with various hiking trails nearby. Flush toilets. 100 sites. Wheelchair accessible. Reservations accepted. Sites $10. ❶

Cottonwood, 3000 ft., near the Cottonwood Visitor Center. The easiest place to see the Colorado Desert and its famous spring wildflowers. Flush toilets and running water. 62 sites (30 in summer); 3 are for groups. Wheelchair accessible. Sites $10; group sites for 10-70 people $25. ❶

▣ FOOD

Although there are no food facilities within the park, Twentynine Palms Hwy. offers both groceries and grub. If you are willing to cook, the **Stater Brothers** supermarket, 71727 Twentynine Palms Hwy., has a good selection and saves you a bundle. (☎367-6535. Open Su-Th 6am-10pm, F-Sa 6am-11pm.)

Wonder Garden Cafe, 73511 Twentynine Palms Hwy. (☎367-2429). Locals recommend this spot—an organic juice bar, fresh sandwich deli, and smoothie joint. Adjoins a natural foods market. Open M-F 6:30am-6pm, Sa 8am-5pm, Su 8am-4pm. ❷

Edchada's, 73502 Twentynine Palms Hwy. (☎367-2131). Good for margaritas ($4) or meals. The airy layout offers respite from the heat. Lunch specials $5. Dinner $9-11. Open 11am-9pm. ❷

Andrea's Charboiled Burgers, 73780 Twentynine Palms Hwy. (☎367-2008). Wise old men and others in the know dine here for hearty eggs, pancakes, and burgers ($2-7). Open daily Su-F 7am-9pm, Sa 7am-3pm. ❶

Chen's, 73501A Twentynine Palms Hwy. (367-5888). The take-out Chinese spot of choice. Satisfying $5 lunch specials and generous $7 dinner combos at one of the area's only Asian restaurants. Open Tu-F 11am-9pm, Sa noon-9pm. ❷

The Beatnik Cafe, 61597 Twentynine Palms Hwy. (☎366-2090). Soothe your heat-addled brain with beer or ice cream ($3-4). Call or check door for live music schedule. **Internet** $2 per 15min., $3.50 per 30min., $6 per hr. Open Su-Th 7am-midnight, F-Sa 7am-2am. ❶

OUTDOOR ACTIVITIES

Over 80% of Joshua Tree is designated wilderness, safeguarding the park against development (including paved roads, toilets, and campfires) and providing truly remote territory for backcountry desert hiking and camping. Hikers eager to reap the rewards of this primitive terrain should pack plenty of water and keep alert for flash floods and changing weather conditions. Be sensitive to the extreme fragility of the desert and refrain from venturing off established trails.

The tenacious **wildflowers** that struggle into colorful bloom each spring (mid-Mar. to mid-May) attract thousands of visitors. Get updates via the **Wildflower Hotline** (☎367-5500); the menu at this number is also useful for weather and tour information. The trees and reeds of the oases host golden eagles and bighorn sheep. Kangaroo rats, lizards, and stinkbugs scamper about by day, while wily coyotes, bobcats, and the occasional rattlesnake stalk their prey (including your unleashed pet) after dusk.

SCENIC DRIVES

The craggy mountains and boulders of Joshua Tree acquire fresh poignancy at sunrise and sunset. A self-paced driving tour is an easy way to explore the park and linger until sunset. All roads are well marked, and signs labeled "Exhibit Ahead" point the way to unique floral and geological formations. One of these tours, a 34 mi. stretch winding through the park from Twentynine Palms to the town of Joshua Tree on **Park Boulevard**, provides access to the park's most outstanding sights and hikes. An especially spectacular leg of the road is **Keys View** (5185 ft.), 6 mi. off Park Blvd. and just west of Ryan Campground. On a clear day, you can see to Palm Springs and the Salton Sea. The sunrise from here is renowned. The longer drive through the park from Twentynine Palms to I-10 traverses both High and Low Desert landscapes and the Pinto Basin with its impressive views. The **Cholla Cactus Garden**, a grove of spiny succulents, lies just off the road.

Those with **4WD** vehicles have even more options, including the 18 mi. **Geology Tour Road,** west of Jumbo Rocks off Park Blvd., which climbs through striking rock formations and ends in the Little San Bernardino Mountains. Though dry years leave the roads sandy and difficult to navigate for cars without high clearance and 4WD, in the spring and fall of wetter years even **cyclists** can enjoy these roads, especially the unpaved and relatively unpopulated 4WD-only roads through **Pinkham Canyon** and past the **Black Eagle Mines,** both beginning at the Cottonwood Visitor Center. Cyclists should check with rangers for info regarding the opening of bike trails.

> **THE DANGERS OF GOING DOWN.** Do not enter abandoned mine shafts, as they are unstable and often filled with poisonous gases.

HIKING

Hiking is perhaps the best way to experience Joshua Tree. The desert often appears monotonous through a car window, and walking allows appreciation of the park's subtle beauty. On foot, visitors can tread through sand, scramble over boulders, examine the occasional historical artifact, and walk among the park's namesakes. Anticipate slow progress even on short walks; the oppressive heat and the scarcity of shade can strain even the hardiest hikers. Drinking 1 liter of water an hour is not unreasonable on desert hikes.

Although the 1 mi. **Barker Dam Trail,** next to Hidden Valley Campground, is often packed with tourists, its petroglyphs (though sadly vandalized) and eerie tranquility make it a worthwhile stroll, especially at twilight. **Lost Horse Mine** (4-8¼ mi. round-trip), near Keys View, rests at the end of a 2 mi. trail, commemorating the region's gold prospecting days with rusted machinery and abandoned mine shafts. If you

THE DESERT

don't want to return yet, keep following the trail up to the saddle of Lost Horse Mountain and beyond; it eventually loops around back to the trailhead. From the top of **Ryan Mountain** (3 mi. round-trip), off Park Blvd., the boulders in the encircling valley share an uncanny resemblance to enormous beasts of burden slouching toward Bethlehem. Bring lots of water for the strenuous, unshaded climb to the summit. Or head to the northern edge of the park and hike the 1½ mi. moderately strenuous climb to the pristine **Fortynine Palms Oasis** (take Canyon Rd. from Twentynine Palms Hwy). Visitors centers have info on the park's other hikes, which range from a 15min. stroll to the **Oasis of Mara** to a three-day trek along the 35 mi. **California Riding and Hiking Trail.** The ranger-led **Desert Queen Ranch Walking Tour** ($5; call for reservations) covers the restored ranch of resourceful homesteader Bill Keys.

ROCK CLIMBING

The crack-split granite of Joshua provides some of the best rock climbing and bouldering in the world for experts and novices alike. The renowned boulders at **Wonderland of Rocks** and **Hidden Valley** are always swarming with hard-bodied climbers, making Joshua Tree the most climbed area in America. Adventurous novices will find thrills at the **Skull Rock Interpretive Walk,** which runs between Jumbo Rocks and Skull Rock. The walk offers not only info on local plants and animals, but also exciting yet non-technical scrambles to the tops of monstrous boulders. The area's potential for climbing is limitless; for guides and instructors see p. 534.

PALM SPRINGS ☎ 760

From its first known inhabitants, the Cahuilla Indians, to today's geriatric fun-lovers, the restorative oasis of Palm Springs (pop. 43,520) has attracted an odd menagerie of old and young people. The medicinal waters of the city's natural hot springs ensure not only the vitality of its wealthy residents, but also its longevity as a resort town. With warm winter temperatures, celebrity residents, and a casino, this city is a sunny break from everyday life. But beach lovers beware: while the warmth, desert sand, and sparkling blue pools may put you in the mood for the surf and sand, the only waves rolling in are composed of dry summer heat.

▐ TRANSPORTATION

Airport: Palm Springs Regional Airport, 3400 E. Tahquitz-Canyon Rd. (☎318-3800). Small airport with in-state and very limited national service.

Trains: Amtrak (☎800-872-7245), at the corner of N. Indian Canyon Rd. and Train Station Dr., a few blocks south of I-10Service to L.A.

Buses: Greyhound, 311 N. Indian Canyon Dr. (☎325-2053 or 800-231-2222), downtown. Open daily 8am-6pm. At least 1 per day to L.A., San Diego, and Las Vegas, NV. Rates and times vary widely.

Public Transportation: SunBus (☎343-3451) is the local bus connecting all Coachella Valley cities. Info office open daily 8am-5pm. Lines #23, 24, and 111 cover downtown and surrounding locales. $1; transfers $0.25. The *SunBus Book,* available at info centers and in most hotel lobbies, includes schedules and a system map.

Taxi: Yellow Cab (☎345-8398) and **Ace Taxi** (☎321-6008).

Car Rental: Most rental cars about $35 per day (excluding insurance); more in winter. **Rent-A-Wreck,** 67555 Palm Canyon Dr., #A102 (☎324-1766 or 800-535-1391; www.rentawreck.com), in Cathedral City. Usually 21+. Under-25 surcharge $10 per day. **Budget** (☎327-1404 or 800-221-1203), at Palm Springs Regional Airport. 21+ with major credit card. Under-25 surcharge $20 per day.

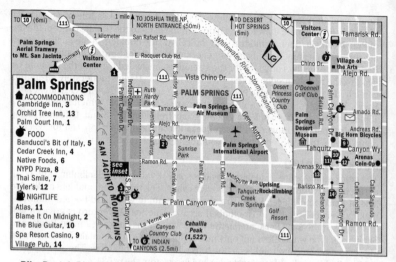

Palm Springs

▲ ACCOMMODATIONS
Cambridge Inn, **3**
Orchid Tree Inn, **13**
Palm Court Inn, **1**

● FOOD
Banducci's Bit of Italy, **5**
Cedar Creek Inn, **4**
Native Foods, **6**
NYPD Pizza, **8**
Thai Smile, **7**
Tyler's, **12**

◗ NIGHTLIFE
Atlas, **11**
Blame It On Midnight, **2**
The Blue Guitar, **10**
Spa Resort Casino, **9**
Village Pub, **14**

Bike Rental: Bighorn Bicycles, 302 N. Palm Canyon Dr. (☎325-3367). Mountain bikes $8 per hr., $22 per 4hr., $29 per day. Bike tours available to Las Palmas and Indian Canyon. Open early Sept.-June Th-Tu 8am-4pm. **Tri-A-Bike,** 44841 San Pablo Ave. (☎340-2840), in Palm Desert. Mountain bikes $7 per hr., $19 per day, $65 per week. Open M-Sa 10am-6pm, Su noon-5pm.

✴ 🄵 ORIENTATION AND PRACTICAL INFORMATION

Palm Springs is a 2hr. drive from L.A. along **I-10.** Exit I-10 at Hwy. 111, which becomes **Palm Canyon Drive,** the major north-south road through the city. The north-south stretch of **Indian Canyon Drive,** the city's other main drag, also connects to I-10. Indian Canyon and Palm Canyon Dr. are one-way streets in the downtown area. East Palm Canyon Dr. (Rte. 111) borders the southern edge of the city, and leads to Palm Desert and other cities in the Valley. The two major east-west boulevards are **Tahquitz-Canyon Road,** which runs east to the airport, while **Ramon Road,** four blocks south, which provides access to I-10.

Visitor Information: Visitors Center, 2781 N. Palm Canyon Dr. (☎778-8415 or 800-347-7746; www.palm-springs.org), 1 block beyond Tramway Rd. Free hotel reservations and friendly advice. Pick up *The Official Visitor's Guide* or *Weekender* for attractions and entertainment. Open daily 9am-5pm. **Chamber of Commerce,** 190 W. Amado Rd. (☎325-1577; www.pschamber.org). Grab the seasonal *Palm Springs Visitors Guide*, buy a map ($1), or make hotel reservations. Open M-F 8:30am-4:30pm.

Laundromat: Arenas Coin-Op, 220 E. Arenas Rd. (☎322-7717), ½ block east of Indian Canyon Dr. Wash $2, dry $0.25 per 10min. Open daily 7am–9pm; last wash 8pm.

Police: 200 S. Civic Dr. (☎323-8116).

Hotlines: Rape Crisis, ☎568-9071. **Road Conditions,** ☎800-427-7623.

Medical Services: Desert Regional Medical Center, 1150 N. Indian Canyon Dr. (☎323-6511).

Library and Internet Access: Palm Springs Public Library, 300 S. Sunrise Way (☎322-7323), at the corner of Baristo Rd. 30min. free Internet. Open M-Tu 9am-8pm, W-Th and Sa 9am-5:30pm, F 10am-5:30pm.

Post Office: 333 E. Amado Rd. (☎800-275-8777). Open M-F 9am-5pm, Sa 9am-1pm. **Postal Code:** 92262; General Delivery 92263.

▛ ACCOMMODATIONS

Despite Palm Springs's reputation as a luxury getaway, affordable lodgings do exist. Motels cut prices 20-40% in the summer. Many offer discounts through the visitors center, and promotional publications often have terrific coupon deals, featuring rooms for as little as $25. Reservations may be necessary in the winter. Prices listed below don't include the county's **11.5% accommodation tax.**

Orchid Tree Inn, 251 S. Belardo Rd. (☎325-2791 or 800-733-3435), behind the main downtown strip and near good shopping. Large rooms with tasteful Spanish decor overlook a courtyard with lush gardens and pool. Singles and doubles in winter from $145; in summer $99-$119. Studios, suites, and bungalows also available. ❺

Miracle Springs Resort and Spa, 10625 Palm Dr. (☎251-6000 or 800-400-4414; www.miraclesprings.com), in Desert Hot Springs. The newer, classier, and more luxurious of 2 hotels atop the famed hot springs. 110 spacious units with bedrooms and living areas, some of which overlook the 8 pools of "miracle" water. Rooms in winter from $119; in low season from $99. ❺

Cambridge Inn, 1277 S. Palm Canyon Dr. (☎325-5574 or 800-829-8099). Large, bland rooms in a prime location. Laundry, pool, and hot tub. Continental breakfast included. Rooms Sept.-June $69-125; July-Aug. $44-60. ❸

Palm Court Inn, 1983 N. Palm Canyon Dr. (☎416-2333 or 800-667-7918), between I-10 and downtown. Behind the melon-colored facade are 107 rooms as well as a pool and hot tub. Oct.-May singles $69; doubles $79. June-Sept. singles $49; doubles $59. All prices slightly higher on weekends. Look for discount coupons in visitor guides. ❸

▛ FOOD

Palm Springs offers an array of culinary treats, from standard burger joints to ultra-trendy fusion cuisine. Prices can get pretty steep, especially in Palm Desert and Desert Hot Springs. To cook for yourself, head to **Ralph's,** 451 S. Sunrise Way, for groceries. (☎323-9799. Open daily 6am-1am.)

▨ Thai Smile, 651 N. Palm Canyon Dr. (☎320-5503). Just as friendly as the name implies, Thai Smile serves satisfying and inexpensive Thai cuisine. Classy wood-heavy decor and a fashionable wine rack. Vegetarian options (tofu *pad thai* $8). Don't miss the $5 lunch specials. Open daily 11:30am-10pm. ❷

THE HIDDEN DEAL

PAR FOR THE COURSE

Golf exemplifies the leisurely life in Palm Springs, where a stress-full day might include 18 holes and a dip in the pool.

Though many of the area's courses charge $150 for a round of golf, two of the most beautiful courses are a steal compared to the others in the area. The Arnold Palmer-managed Tahquitz Creek Golf Resort gets four stars from *Golf Digest* magazine but is publically owned by the city of Palm Springs. The 36-hole regulation course gives out summer tee times for under $30. The Desert Willow Golf Resort, owned by the city of Palm Desert, offers similar off-season deals. Both of the challenging championship courses are beautifully landscaped yet require no membership or special connections. Each resort has affordable rentals for those without the right gear, and the staff is anything but snobbish. The public courses have restaurants, pro shops, and clubhouses, proving that if you want to hit the links, you don't need to bust the bank.

*Contact **Tahquitz Creek**, 1885 Golf Club Dr. (☎328-1005), in Palm Springs, or **Desert Willow**, 38-995 Desert Willow Drive, (☎346-7060), in Palm Desert, to arrange a tee time.*

■ **Cedar Creek Inn,** 1555 S. Palm Canyon Dr. (☎325-7000). Charming eatery with outdoor patio, fresh flowers, and an extensive wine list. Pasta specials $5. Lobster dinners $15. Happy hour 4-9pm. Open daily 11am-10pm. ❷

Banducci's Bit of Italy, 1260 S. Palm Canyon Dr. (☎325-2537). The promise of delicious Italian food draws plenty of locals to this Palm Springs staple every night of the week. The rich fettuccine alfredo ($14) comes with antipasto, minestrone soup, and buttery garlic bread. Entrees $8-20. Open Su-Th 5-9:30pm, Sa-Su 5-11pm. ❸

Native Foods, 1775 S. Palm Canyon Dr. (☎318-1532). Hidden in the back of a strip mall, this vegetarian's haven, ensures that diet-conscious Californians don't go hungry. "Handholds" (wraps) and hot bowls $8-12. Open M-Sa 11:30am-9pm. ❷

Tyler's, 149 S. Indian Canyon Dr. (☎325-2990). A trendy lunch spot with classic American fare—tasty burgers, malts, and root-beer floats. Don't let the low prices fool you; everything is *a la carte*, so it adds up. Burgers $4-6. Soda-fountain drinks $2.50-4. Open M-F 11am-4pm, Sa 11am-5pm; in summer Tu-Sa 11am-4pm. ❷

NYPD—New York Pizza Delivery, 260 N. Palm Canyon Dr. (☎778-6973). An alternative to the high prices and suffocating trendiness of Palm Springs. Pizza ($2) and other filling pizzeria fare. Open M-F 11am-9pm, Sa-Su 11am-10pm. ❶

👁 🎨 SIGHTS AND OUTDOOR ACTIVITIES

Most people seek Palm Springs's balmy winter climate for partying, golfing, lounging poolside, and schmoozing with celebs, but the city also has its share of sights. **Mt. San Jacinto State Park,** Palm Springs's primary landmark, offers a variety of outdoor recreation. Hiking trails in the park are accessible year-round via the aerial tram, and cross-country skiing is available in winter at higher elevations, though access is easier and cheaper from nearby Idyllwild (see p. 484). Despite its benign appearance in the crowded winter season, the desert surrounding Palm Springs is a summertime furnace, with highs consistently over 100°F.

■ **INDIAN CANYONS.** Just minutes from downtown Palm Springs are four canyons that hold the city's only naturally cool water, as well as remnants of the Cahuilla communities. Ranger-led tours demonstrate how the Cahuilla Native Americans once utilized the area's flora and fauna, including the world's densest patch of naturally occurring palm trees. In the cooler months, the canyons provide beautiful places to bike, hike, picnic, or horseback ride. *(3 of the canyons are located 5 mi. south of town at the end of S. Palm Canyon Dr. ☎325-3400 or 800-790-3398; www.indian-canyons.com. Open daily 8am-5pm. Tours M-Th 10am-1pm, F-Su 9am-3pm. $6; students, seniors, and military $4.50; ages 6-12 $2; under 6 free. Tours $6, children $2. Tahquitz Canyon is located at the west end of Mesquite Rd. It has a separate visitors center, as well as a spectacular 60 ft. waterfall during the winter. ☎416-7044. Tours $12.50, children $6.)*

DESERT HOT SPRINGS SPA. A trip to Palm Springs would not be complete without a visit to the town's namesake. This spa features eight naturally heated mineral pools of different temperatures, as well as saunas, massages, and body wraps. *(10805 Palm Dr. in Desert Hot Springs. ☎800-808-7727. Open daily 8am-10pm. $3-7; includes admission to pools, dry sauna, and locker rooms.)*

PALM SPRINGS DESERT MUSEUM. This museum features frequently changing exhibits centered on art, history, and culture, as well as a sculpture garden. The museum sponsors performances in the 438-seat **Annenberg Theatre** (☎325-4490). In the winter, curators lead field trips into the canyons. *(101 Museum Dr. Take SunBus #111. ☎325-7186. Open Tu-Sa 10am-5pm, Su noon-5pm. $7.50; seniors $6.50; students, ages 6-17, and military $3.50. 1st F of each month free.)*

UPRISING ROCKCLIMBING CENTER. Prep for nearby Joshua Tree at this gigantic outdoor climbing structure, the only one of its kind in the US. Whether you're a beginner or expert, you'll find a fun challenge in the shaded plastic rock. The center provides instruction and supervision, and arranges excursions to Joshua Tree, Idyllwild, and Mission Gorge by arrangement. *(1500 Gene Autry Trail. ☎ 888-254-6266; www.uprising.com. Open Sept.-June M-F 10am-8pm, Sa-Su 10am-6pm; July-Aug. Tu-F 4-8pm, Sa-Su 10am-6pm. Day pass $15. Equipment rental $7. Lessons from $45 per day. Parking in the Knotts lot $6.)*

PALM SPRINGS AIR MUSEUM. With its extensive collection of beautifully restored WWII aircraft, the Palm Springs Air museum will impress aviation buffs and novices alike. Aviation shows run from October to March. *(745 N. Gene Autry Trail, near the airport. ☎ 778-6262. Open daily Sept.-May 10am-5pm; June-Aug. 9am-3pm. $8, seniors $6.50, children $3.50.)*

PALM SPRINGS AERIAL TRAMWAY. If Mt. San Jacinto's 10,804 ft. peak is too much for your legs to take, this world-famous tram can whisk you to the top in 10min. At 8516 ft., the observation deck has great views of the Coachella Valley. Travelers planning to take one of the beautiful hikes from the upper tram station should note that temperatures are invariably 20-30°F cooler than on the desert floor. *(On Tramway Rd. off N. Palm Canyon Drive. ☎ 325-1449 or 888-515-8726; www.pstramway.com. Trams run at least every 30min. M-F 10am-8pm, Sa-Su 8am-8pm. Last tram down 9:45pm. Round-trip $21, ages 3-12 $14, over 60 $19, under 3 free.)*

TENNIS AND GOLF. Palm Springs has several public tennis and golf facilities. There are eight courts at **Ruth Hardy Park.** *(700 Tamarisk Dr., at Avenida Caballeros. Open dawn-dusk.)* **Tahquitz Creek Golf Resort,** managed by Arnold Palmer, claims to be one of the nation's top municipal golf courses. *(1885 Golf Club Dr. ☎ 328-1005. 18 holes. Open daily 6am-6pm. $25-75; includes golf cart. Lower prices afternoons, summer, and weekdays.)*

LIVING DESERT WILDLIFE AND BOTANICAL PARK. Arabian oryx, camels, meerkats, and more crazy animals live at this desert zoo. Wear sunscreen and bring water; there isn't much shade, though hand-held misters are available. *(47900 Portola Ave., Palm Desert, 1½ mi. south of Rte. 111. ☎ 346-5694; www.livingdesert.org. Open daily Sept.-June 9am-5pm, last admission 4pm; July-Aug. 8am-1:30pm, last admission 1pm. Sept.-June $8.50, seniors $7.50, ages 3-12 $4.50; July-Aug. $6.50, ages 3-12 $3.50.)*

CELEBRITY TOURS. Find further evidence that celebrities are wealthier and more glamorous than you—just don't expect to see an actual celebrity. Your closest brush with fame might be seeing a gardener weeding the estate of a dead celebrity like Frank Sinatra or Bob Hope. The 1hr. narrated tour drives past 30-40 celebrity homes. *(4751 E. Palm Canyon Dr., Ste. D. ☎ 770-2700. Open in winter daily 8am-5pm; summer Tu-Sa 7:30am-2:30pm. $20, seniors $15, under 17 $8.)*

WIND FARM TOURS. The unusual topography and outrageous temperatures of the Palm Springs region generate some of the world's strongest sustained winds. On the Wind Farm, about 3500 high-tech windmills harness this energy. Even if you forgo the tours by **Windmill Tours, Inc.,** a drive down I-10 will take you past this oddly spectacular forest of whirling blades. Drive with caution, as the high winds may shift your car around on the highway. *(1¼ mi. west of Indian Canyon Dr. on 20th Ave., just across I-10. ☎ 251-1997. Tours M-Sa 9, 11am, 1, 3pm. Reservations required. $23, seniors $20, students $15, ages 6-13 $10, under 6 free.)*

DATES AND OASES. Since the Coachella Valley is the self-proclaimed "Date Capital of the World," slick back your hair, suck down a breath mint, and head to the **Shields Date Gardens** in nearby Indio. This palm grove sets itself apart with its amusing free film *The Romance and Sex Life of the Date*. A date

THE DESERT

crystal milkshake ($3) proves how sweet a good date can be. *(80225 Rte. 111.* ☎ *347-0996 or 800-414-2555. Open daily Sept.-May 8am-6pm; June-Aug. 9am-5pm.)* Zoo-lovers can enjoy the rugged **Big Morongo Canyon Preserve,** a nearby wildlife sanctuary. *(Off Rte. 62 on East Dr.* ☎ *363-7190. Open daily 7:30am-dusk. Free.)* The **Coachella Valley Preserve's Visitors Center** can help you plan a hike through mesas, bluffs, or the **Thousand Palms Oasis,** a grove of palm trees that is home to the protected fringe-toed lizard. *(Northeast of Palm Springs in Thousand Palms.* ☎ *343-2733 or 343-4031. Open Sept.-June sunrise-sunset.)*

☎ NIGHTLIFE

The glitz of Palm Springs doesn't disappear with the setting sun; this city's nightlife is almost as heralded as its golf courses. Although a night of total indulgence here might cost a small fortune, several bars provide drink specials and lively people-watching. Palm Springs is a major destination for GLBT travelers. The gay scene sparkles with bars, spas, and clothing-optional resorts. Gay establishments concentrate along **Warm Sands Drive,** off Ramon Rd. Almost a dozen gay resorts with restaurants, bars, and pools stay busy late into the night. *The Gay Guide to Palm Springs,* available at the visitors center, also provides a wealth of pertinent info.

> **Village Pub,** 266 S. Palm Canyon Dr. (☎323-3265.) Relive your college days with tourists and locals swapping jokes, swilling beer, and grooving to folksy live rock at this popular bar. The crowd is usually 25+, but it gets younger on the weekends. Those under 21 are restricted to the front eating area after 9pm. Open daily 11am-2am.

> **Atlas,** 210 S. Palm Canyon Dr. (☎325-8839). Ultra-modern restaurant and dance club in the heart of downtown; a spectacle of glow sticks, hot bodies, and techno beats. Its fusion specialties are as modern as its music. Entrees $15-25. Local DJs nightly. Club 21+. Open daily 11am-2am.

> **The Blue Guitar,** 125 E. Tahquitz Canyon Way. (☎327-1549.) Live music from local and touring minstrels Th and Su from 8pm, F-Sa from 9pm. Cover varies.

> **Spa Resort Casino,** 100 N. Indian Canyon Drive. (☎800-854-1279; www.sparesortcasino.com.) The Cahuilla Indians have brought a bit of Vegas to Palm Springs with this swanky resort, busy late into the night with table and slot players, as well as lounge entertainment and bars.

> **Blame It On Midnight,** 775 E. Tahquitz Canyon Way (☎323-1200). Close to downtown. A subdued, upscale restaurant and bar popular among gay travelers. Open Su-Th 5-10pm, F-Sa 5-11pm.

❀ FESTIVALS

Downtown, **Village Fest** takes over Palm Canyon Dr. between Amado and Baristo every Thursday night. Vendors hawk food, jewelry, and arts and crafts, while people of all ages enjoy live entertainment and cool evening air. This weekly event is a great time to bring the kids. (☎320-3781. Th 6-10pm; June-Sept. 7-10pm.)

Attempting to fulfill his campaign promise to heighten Palm Springs's glamour quotient, former mayor Sonny Bono instituted the annual **Nortel Networks Palm Springs International Film Festival** (☎778-8979). The annual **National Date Festival,** on Rte. 111 in Indio, is not a hook-up scene but rather a bash for dried fruit lovers. (☎863-8247. Feb. 18-23 in 2005.) Palm Springs is also famous for its tennis tournaments and its professional golf tournaments, like the annual **Bob Hope Chrysler Classic** (☎346-8184; Jan. 24-30 in 2005) and the LPGA's annual **Kraft Nabisco Championship** (☎324-4546; Mar. 21-27 in 2005).

DEATH VALLEY NATIONAL PARK ☎760

The devil owns a lot of real estate in Death Valley: he grows crops at Devil's Corn-field and hits the links at Devil's Golf Course, and the park is home to Hell's Gate itself. The area's extreme heat and surreal landscape explain this identification with the dark side. Stare into the abyss from Dante's View, one of several panoramic points approaching 6000 ft. in elevation, or gaze wistfully into the distant, cool heavens from Badwater, the lowest point (282 ft. below sea level) in the Western Hemisphere. Wildflowers, snow-capped peaks, and some of the hottest, driest land in the world miraculously coexist in this corner of California. It rains very infrequently in the park, but when it does, the hard, compacted ground is prone to flash floods. Winter temperatures dip well below freezing in the mountains, and summer readings in the valley average 115°F. The second-highest temperature ever recorded in the world (134°F in the shade) was measured at the valley's Furnace Creek Ranch on July 10, 1913. Despite these killer temperatures, the region sustains a motley crew of rugged plants and animals. Although much of the land seems desolate and barren, over 500 different species of plants grow and many threatened and endangered species—including the desert tortoise and the desert bighorn sheep—inhabit Death Valley. If you see something unusual, go to a visitors center and fill out a wildlife sighting card.

Human inhabitants have a long history inside the valley as well. The Shoshone Indians lived in the lower elevations during winters and retreated into the cooler peaks during summers. During the Gold Rush, prospectors came here searching for a shortcut across the Sierras. They were unsuccessful and skedaddled as soon as they could find a way out—but not before several lives were lost. Looking back at their scene of misery, someone said, "Goodbye, Death Valley!" and the name stuck. Later, miners looking for gold found borax instead and boom towns grew around the mines. Once the borax supply was depleted, the prospectors took off and left behind a medley of skeletal towns like Skidoo and Rhoylite. These ghost towns now lend Death Valley a deserted, post-apocalyptic atmosphere. The desolate beauty gave rise to the tourism industry; in 1933, the US government set aside over three million acres as a national park. The park entrance fee ($10 per vehicle, $5 for non-vehicles), valid for one week, is collected at Furnace Creek Visitors Center, Grapevine, Stovepipe Wells, and the ranger station in Beatty.

AT A GLANCE: DEATH VALLEY NATIONAL PARK

AREA: 3.3 million acres.

CLIMATE: Very arid.

FEATURES: Badwater, Mosaic Canyons, Telescope Peak, Scotty's Castle.

HIGHLIGHTS: Peering down at the valley floor from Dante's View, driving to the bottom of Ubehebe Crater, photographing the Death Valley Sand Dunes.

GATEWAYS: Beatty, NV (p. 550), Lone Pine (p. 297), Shoshone (p. 551).

CAMPING: 30-day max. stay, 14-day max. stay in Furnace Creek. Free backcountry camping; check in at the visitors center.

FEES AND RESERVATIONS: Entrance fee $10 per car, $5 per pedestrian or cyclist.

⌐ TRANSPORTATION

Cars are virtually the only way to get to and around Death Valley (2½hr. from Las Vegas; 5hr. from L.A.; 7hr. from Tahoe City; 10½hr. from San Francisco). If you are sharing gas costs, renting a car can be cheaper than any bus tour. The nearest rental agencies are in Las Vegas (see p. 567), Pahrump, Barstow, and Bishop.

THE DESERT

WHEN TO GO. Although the average high in July is 115°F and the nighttime low 88°F, summer visits can be enjoyable with wise planning. The Furnace Creek Visitors Center distributes the free pamphlet *Hot Weather Hints.* Some summer days are simply too hot to hike, even with abundant water. Severe heat exhaustion strikes even the fittest; don't overestimate your tolerance. (See **Desert Survival,** p. 529.) You can drive through and admire the beauty of the Valley in July and August, but to enjoy the hiking and camping options, visit between November and April. Winter is the coolest time (temperatures average 39-65°F in the Valley, with freezing temperatures and snow in the mountains) and also the wettest, with infrequent but violent rainstorms that can flood canyons and obliterate roads, trails, and ill-placed tract housing. Call ahead to find out which areas, if any, are washed out before exploring the park. Desert wildflowers bloom everywhere in March and April, but the season is accompanied by tempestuous winds that whip sand and dust into a blinding frenzy for hours or even days. Over holidays and three-day weekends, congested trails and campsites, traffic jams, and long lines for gas plague the area.

Conditions in Death Valley are notoriously hard on cars. **Radiator water** (*not* for drinking) is available at critical points on Rte. 178 and 190 and Nevada Rte. 374. There are only four **gas stations** in the park (see **Gas Stations,** p. 545), and though prices are as much as $0.50 more per gallon than outside the valley, be sure to keep the tank at least half full at all times. Check ahead with park rangers for road closings and do not drive on wet and slippery backcountry roads.

Although **4WD vehicles** and high-clearance trucks can handle the narrow roads that lead to Death Valley's most spectacular scenery, be sure to check with the visitors center about current road conditions if you have limited off-road driving experience. Always travel with 2 gallons of water per person per day. In the case of a breakdown, stay in the shade of your car. (For more **driving tips,** see p. 531.)

Of the seven **park entrances,** most visitors choose Rte. 190 from the east. The road is well maintained and the visitors center is relatively close. However, since most of the major sights adjoin **Badwater Road,** the north-south road, the daytripper can see more of the park by entering from the southeast (Rte. 178 W from Rte. 127 at Shoshone) or the north (direct to Scotty's Castle via Nevada Rte. 267). Unskilled mountain drivers in passenger cars should not attempt to enter on the smaller Titus Canyon or Emigrant Canyon Dr.

■❄️🔆 ORIENTATION AND PRACTICAL INFORMATION

Death Valley is on the eastern edge of the state, next to Nevada and south of Inyo National Forest. Rte. 190 cuts east-west across the valley. Many sites fall along Rte. 178, which runs north-south through the lower part of the park. Most of Death Valley is below sea level.

Visitor Information:

Furnace Creek Visitors Center (☎786-3244; www.nps.gov/deva), on Rte. 190 in the Valley's east section. For info, write: Superintendent, Death Valley National Park, Death Valley, CA 92328. Guides and hiking maps ($4-8), schedules of activities, and weather forecasts. Park entrance fee can be paid here. Open daily 8am-6pm.

Contact Stations: Weather reports, park info, and emergency assistance are available at each station. **Grapevine** (☎786-2313), at Rte. 190 and 267 near Scotty's Castle. **Shoshone** (☎832-4308), at Rte. 127 and 178 outside the Valley's southeast border. **Beatty, NV** (☎702-553-2200), on Nevada Rte. 374. All are technically open daily 8am-5pm but are staffed sporadically.

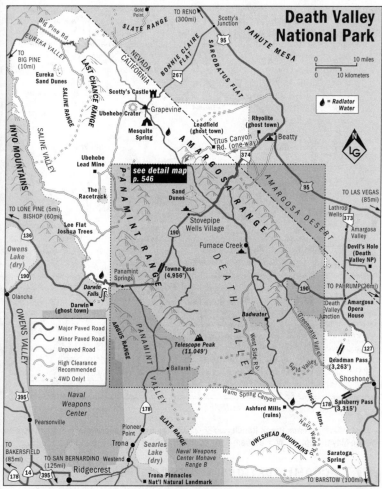

Death Valley National Park

Hiking Information: The private website www.deathvalley.com has general information on Death Valley, as well as message boards and detailed hiking resources.

Gas Stations: Fill up outside Death Valley at Lone Pine, Olancha, Shoshone, or Beatty, NV. Once in Death Valley, gas costs $0.15-0.50 more per gallon. Don't play macho with the fuel gauge; fill up often to maintain a high gas level. For gas in the valley, head to Furnace Creek, Stovepipe Wells Village, Panamint Springs, or Scotty's Castle. Be sure to have a credit card, because the stations are often unstaffed in the evenings, so you won't be able to use cash. **AAA towing service, minor repairs, propane gas,** and **diesel fuel** available at the Furnace Creek Chevron.

Laundromat: At Furnace Creek Ranch (☎786-2345). Wash $1, dry $1. Open 24hr.

Showers: Stovepipe Wells Village (☎786-2387). Non-guests $2. Open daily 8am-midnight. **Furnace Creek Ranch** (☎786-2345). $2. Open daily 7am-11pm.

24hr. Ranger Dispatch and Police: ☎786-2330. **Emergency road service:** ☎760-876-4600.

THE DESERT

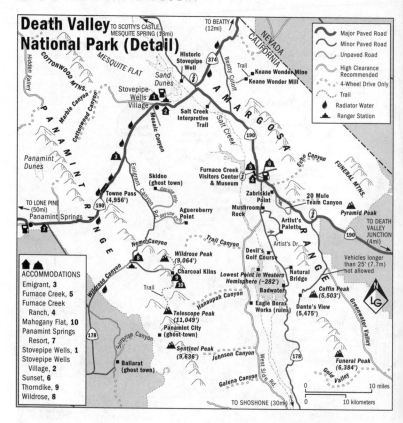

Death Valley National Park (Detail)

ACCOMMODATIONS
Emigrant, **3**
Furnace Creek, **5**
Furnace Creek Ranch, **4**
Mahogany Flat, **10**
Panamint Springs Resort, **7**
Stovepipe Wells, **1**
Stovepipe Wells Village, **2**
Sunset, **6**
Thorndike, **9**
Wildrose, **8**

Post Office: Furnace Creek Ranch (☎ 786-2223). Open Oct. to mid-May M-F 8:30am-5pm; mid-May to Sept. M, W, F 8:30am-3pm, Tu and Th 8:30am-5pm. **Postal Code:** 92328.

ACCOMMODATIONS AND FOOD

In Death Valley, affordable beds and inexpensive meals can be as elusive as the desert bighorn sheep. Motel rooms in surrounding towns are cheaper than those in Death Valley, but can be over an hour away from top sights. Never assume that rooms will be available, but your chances (and the prices) will be better in the summer. (For more affordable accommodations outside the Valley, see **Gateways to Death Valley,** p. 550.) For groceries, **Furnace Creek Ranch Store** is well stocked but pricier than most supermarkets. (Open daily 7am-9pm.) **Stovepipe Wells Village Store** is smaller and also expensive. (**ATM** inside. Open daily 7am-9pm.) Both stores sell charcoal, firewood, and ice.

▨ **Furnace Creek Ranch** (☎ 786-2345; www.furnacecreekresort.com), in Furnace Creek. Supremely convenient location next to the visitors center, with a cafe, bar, restaurant, laundromat, post office, and grocery store in the same complex. Singles and doubles in summer from $85; in winter from $105. ❺

Stovepipe Wells Village (☎ 786-2387), 30 mi. northwest of Furnace Creek Visitors Center on Rte. 190, is at sea level, though nothing seems more remote than the ocean. The village provides comfortable rooms (with A/C) and a mineral water swimming pool—a blessing when it's too hot to camp. RV sites available. The dining room offers plenty of food at stiff prices. Breakfast buffet 7-10am ($8). Dinner buffet 6-9pm ($17). Singles and doubles $60-100. Full hookups $22. ❶

Panamint Springs Resort (☎ 775-482-7680; www.deathvalley.com), 33 mi. west of Furnace Creek. This remote resort sits on a relatively high elevation, offering relief from the heat. The complex, popular with park regulars, includes 14 rooms, RV hookups, campsites, a restaurant and bar (dinner $12-25), and gas. The only tie to civilization here is the overhead roar of naval fighter jets on maneuvers from China Lake Naval Weapons Station. Doubles from $65; sites $12; RVs $10-25. ❶

☂ CAMPING

The National Park Service maintains nine campgrounds in Death Valley, all of which provide an inexpensive way of seeing the park. Some of the hottest sites are closed from May to September (Sunset, Texas Spring, and Stovepipe Wells), while Thorndike and Mahogany Flat are closed due to snow and ice from December to February. Pay attention to elevation; the higher up you are, the more comfortable your visit will be when the temperature climbs into the triple digits. Unfortunately, the higher campsites tend to be farther from the park's main sights. The Furnace Creek Visitors Center keeps records about site availability; be prepared to battle for a space if you come during peak periods (see **When to Visit,** p. 544). All campsites have toilets, but none have showers. All provide water (except Thorndike and Mahogany Flat), and the visitors center has unlimited free water (as warm as bath water), but never depend heavily upon any source of water except that which you carry with you. Collecting wood is forbidden, so pack your own firewood. Since fires are prohibited outside of fire pits, a camping stove may prove useful. Roadside camping is not permitted, but **backcountry camping** is free and legal, provided you check in at the visitors center and pitch tents at least 2 mi. from your car and any road and a quarter mile from any backcountry water source. All sites limit stays to 30 days except Furnace Creek, which has a 14-day limit.

Furnace Creek (☎ 800-365-2267), 196 ft. below sea level, north of the visitors center. Furnace Creek is particularly uncomfortable in summer, even though many of the 136 sites are shaded. Fills up before other campgrounds in winter, especially with RVs. Near Furnace Creek Ranch's facilities ($3 shower; laundry). 14-day max. stay. Reservations (Oct.-Apr.) can be made 5 months in advance. Sites in winter $16; in summer $10. ❶

Sunset, 196 ft. below sea level, and **Texas Springs,** at sea level, in the hills above the Furnace Creek Ranch Complex. These 2 sites are the best places for tents near Furnace Creek activities. Over 1000 sites available, some with shade. For wind protection, stick close to the base of the hills. Generators prohibited. Water, some fire pits, and some tables. Flush toilets and dump station. Open Oct.-Apr. Sites $10-12. ❶

Wildrose, 4100 ft., off Emigrant Canyon Rd. An old summer residence of the Shoshone Indians, this 23-site campground is nestled between 2 hillsides and is a comfortable summer option, well protected from sandstorms. Convenient base for trips to Skidoo, Aguereberry Point, and Telescope Peak. Water, fire pits, and pit toilets. **Free.**

Emigrant, 2100 ft., off Rte. 190, 9 mi. west of Stovepipe Wells Village across from the ranger station, on the way down from Towne Pass through Panamint Range. Gorgeous view of Stovepipe Wells and the valley's sand dunes, though sites are located directly next to Rte. 190. The 10 tent-only sites can be relatively comfortable even in the summer. Flush toilets and water. No fires. **Free.**

Stovepipe Wells, at sea level, near the airstrip, 4WD trails, and sand dunes. Reminiscent of a drive-in movie lot. Tents compete with RVs for 190 gravel sites. Spots near the trees offer better protection from sandstorms. Hotel and general store nearby. A few tables and fire pits. Open Oct.-Apr. Sites $10. ❶

Mesquite Spring, 1800 ft., near Scotty's Castle, 2 mi. south of Grapevine Ranger Station. Located in a small valley among dry brush, some of the 30 gravel sites offer shade and protection from wind. Listen for the howls and hoots of coyote and owls. Picnic tables, fire pits, water, and flush toilets. Sites $10. ❶

👁 🏔 SIGHTS AND OUTDOOR ACTIVITIES

Planning your approach to Death Valley and avoiding backtracking saves precious gas (see **Transportation,** p. 543). If exploring the Valley in one day, adopt a north-south or south-north route. For longer visits, get your bearings first at the Furnace Creek Visitors Center on Rte. 190 (which connects east-west). Camera-toters should keep in mind that the best photo opportunities are at sunrise and sunset. Rangers can provide the distances and times of recommended hikes. Ranger-led programs are generally unavailable in summer, but a number of guided hikes may take place when the rangers feel like arranging them. Astronomy buffs should speak to one of the rangers, since they often set up telescopes at Zabriskie Point and offer freelance stargazing commentary during meteor showers.

DANTE'S VIEW. From this 5475 ft. summit, one can truly appreciate the astonishing and primeval landscape of the valley's floor. A palette of light hues washes over a 100 mi. stretch of land. Temperatures at the summit are around 20°F cooler than in the valley, and the area is perfect for a breakfast picnic when the rising sun fills the valley with golden light. *(From the visitors center, drive 14 mi. east along Rte. 190. Turn right at the Dante's View turn off. The 13 mi. climb is especially steep at the top.)*

ZABRISKIE POINT. Just a stone's throw away from Rt. 190 is one of the most beautiful views of Death Valley's corrugated badlands, especially when the first or last rays of the sun soften the colors. For an intimate view of the valley, take the short detour along **20 Mule Team Canyon Road.** The well-maintained dirt road is named for the gigantic mule trains that used to haul borax 130 mi. south to the rail depot at Mojave. The view of the dry lakebeds and undulating yellow rock formations is particularly stunning late in the day. *(3 mi. south of Furnace Creek by car. Take the turn-off from Rte. 190, 1 mi. east of the museum.)*

BADWATER. A briny pool four times saltier than the ocean, this body of water is huge in the winter but withers into a salt-crusted pond by summer. The surrounding flat is the lowest point (282 ft. below sea level) in the Western Hemisphere. The pools shelter the extremely threatened Badwater snails. The boardwalk provides a closer look at the strange orange floor, but getting in the water is prohibited. *(18 mi. south of the visitors center on Badwater Rd.)*

DEVIL'S GOLF COURSE. Lucifer himself couldn't stay below 100 strokes on this "golf course,"—actually a vast expanse of gnarled salt pillars formed by cyclical flooding and evaporation. This is Death Valley at its most surreal; the jagged crystalline deposits, some quite delicate and beautiful, stretch as far as the eye can see. In the summer you can occasionally hear tinkling sounds as hollow structures expand and shatter. *(15 mi. south of the visitors center. on Badwater Rd.)*

ARTIST'S DRIVE. This one-way loop winds through brightly colored rock formations. The loop's early ochres and burnt siennas give way at **Artist's Palette** to sea green, lemon yellow, periwinkle blue, and salmon pink mineral deposits in the hillside. The scene is most dramatic in the late afternoon, when the setting sun causes rapid color changes in the deposits. The dizzying and intense 9 mi. drive turns back on itself again and again, ending up on the main road only 4 mi. north of the drive's entrance. *(10 mi. south of the visitors center on Badwater Rd.)*

DEATH VALLEY'S SAND DUNES. Two miles from Stovepipe Wells, these large dunes made of extremely fine quartz sand may seem out of place in the Valley, but they make for a great day hike that feels good between the toes. Take note that perceived distances can be misleading; peaks that appear close may really be a 2hr. arduous climb. Ask at the visitors center for the handout on photographing in the setting or rising sun to make like Ansel Adams. *(22 mi. north of the visitors center.)*

MOSAIC CANYON. A half mile corridor of eroded marble walls, this site stands out as a true natural wonder. A simple and relatively flat 2 mi. trail leads from the parking lot around the canyon to some awesome vistas. Occasional bighorn sheep sightings are a bonus. *(Take the turn-off from Rte. 190, 1 mi. west of Stovepipe Wells.)*

EMIGRANT CANYON ROAD. This winding road leads from the Emigrant Campground to Wildrose Canyon Dr. In between, there is a turn-off for the 4WD skedaddle to the ruins of **Skidoo**, a ghost town 5700 ft. up in the Panamint Range. Skidoo was the backdrop for the only full-length movie ever shot in Death Valley, Erich von Stroheim's *Greed* (1923). A few miles down Emigrant Canyon Rd. is the turn-off for the dirt road to **Aguereberry Point** (may require 4WD), which is known for its fine sunset views. A left turn at Wildrose Canyon Dr., followed by a 10 mi. drive (last 2 mi. unpaved gravel), brings you to the 10 beehive-shaped furnaces known as the **Charcoal Kilns**, huge ovens built in 1876 that once fired 45 cords of wood at a time to process silver and lead ore, adding even more heat to the scorching valley.

TELESCOPE PEAK. This trail through the **Panamint Mountains** leads to the summit of the park's highest peak (11,049 ft.). The strenuous hike begins at Mahogany Flat campground and winds 3000 ft. up past charcoal kilns and bristlecone pines, providing unique views of Badwater and Mt. Whitney. Buy topographical maps at a ranger station. The trek becomes a technical mountain climb in winter, requiring axes and crampons, but is snow-free by June. Let a ranger know when you'll be climbing and when you'll return. *(7 mi. one way.)*

TITUS CANYON ROAD. This 27 mi. one-way road off Rte. 374 winds through rugged and colorful mountains and passes Indian petroglyphs and the Leadfield ghost town. A high-clearance vehicle is needed to drive through the canyon. Those without such vehicles can hike in via either end. *(The entrance to the canyon is off Rte. 374, 21 mi. east of the junction with Rte. 190.)*

SCOTTY'S CASTLE. Remarkably out of place in the desert, this castle's imaginative exterior rises from the sands, complete with minaret and Arabian-style colored tile. The saga of the castle's construction began with the friendship between Chicago insurance millionaire Albert Johnson and infamous local con man, Walter Scott (a.k.a. "Death Valley Scotty"). Scott had conned wealthy Easterners (including Johnson) into investing in his nonexistent gold mine. After Scott and Johnson became friends and then partners in crime, Johnson built this ridiculous vacation home and told people it was built on the gold fortune. The museum and "living" tour guides provide more details on the bizarre story. *(From Rte. 190, look for the sign near mile marker 93 and take road junction to Park Rte. 5; follow Rte. 5 33 mi. to the castle. ☎ 786-2392. Open daily 9am-5pm; last admission 4pm. Tours every hr. May-Sept.; more frequently Oct.-Apr. $8, seniors $6, ages 6-15 $4.)*

THE DESERT

UBEHEBE CRATER. This vast volcanic blast site is nearly 1 mi. wide and 600 ft. deep. It can be seen by car, but take the gravel trail leading to the floor of the crater to truly appreciate the hole's dimensions. Be careful—the climb back out is grueling. A unpaved road (4WD required) continues 23 mi. south of the crater to the vast **Racetrack Playa**, a dried-up lake basin with access to Hidden Valley and White Top Mountain. See the trails left by mysterious **moving rocks** on the basin floor. For an outstanding view of the Racetrack, follow **Ubehebe Peak Trail** from the Grandstand parking area along a steep, twisting pathway. *(8 mi. west of Scotty's Castle. Ubhebe Peak Trail 6 mi. round-trip.)*

GATEWAYS TO DEATH VALLEY

BEATTY
☎**775**

The small town of Beatty, Nevada, is a convenient place to stay while visiting Death Valley. Situated 90 mi. northwest of Las Vegas on U.S. 95, Beatty offers weary travelers gaming, great accommodations, and that all-important A/C. All casinos are theoretically open 24hr., but by 2am the dealers start eyeing the clock.

Info can be found at **Beatty Visitor Information Center**, 119 E. Main St. (☎553-2424. Open M-F 10am-3pm.) The **Beatty Ranger Station** is well stocked with books, maps, and safety info for desert-bound drivers. (☎553-2200. Open Tu-Sa 8am-4pm, though the hours aren't strictly observed.) The comfortable **Happy Burro Hostel ❶**, 100 Main St., located in a former brothel, offers international clientele a "John Wayne" breakfast. (☎553-9130. 3-bed dorms $15.) Sleep in peace at the **Stagecoach Hotel ❸**, on U.S 95, half a mile north of town. Amenities include a pool, hot tub, casino, and bar. (☎533-2419. Singles from $35; doubles from $40.) Slightly cheaper rooms can be found at the **El Portal Motel ❷**, on Rte. 374, one block from the junction with U.S. 95. (☎553-2912. Singles $30; doubles $33.) Don't miss the authentic Baja cuisine at **Ensenada Grill**, 600 U.S. 95, which serves heaping plates of fish tacos and seafood enchiladas. (☎553-2600. Entrees $7-10.) For a cold beer, check out the **Sourdough Saloon**, 106 Main St., the favorite bar of auto industry engineers who test top-secret prototype cars in the valley. Every year, each test team leaves a memento. Be sure to check out the brilliantly engineered BMW birdhouse to the left of the door. (☎553-2266. Open daily noon-midnight.) There is public **Internet** access for a nominal fee at the **Beatty Public Library.** (☎553-2257. Open M and W-Th 9am-3pm; Tu noon-7pm; Sa 9am-noon.)

PAHRUMP
☎**774**

Halfway between Las Vegas and Death Valley is the town of Pahrump, just an hour's drive on Rte. 160 from I-15. Pahrump is the only gateway to Death Valley with supermarkets, drug stores, and other essentials. It's still close enough to Las Vegas to have $0.99 breakfast specials and cheap prime rib dinners at its casinos. The **Saddle West ❸** offers a full casino, poolside bar, and showroom populated by local country singers painfully struggling to make it big. The spacious rooms range $45-60. You'll find plenty of Pahrumpans at **Sheri's Ranch**, 10551 Homestead Rd., a sports bar off Rte. 160 (☎751-5111).

OLANCHA
☎**760**

Ghost towns like **Darwin** and a few slightly more populated communities are the only developments that remain on Rte. 190 west of the park. In **Olancha**, the **Ranch Motel ❸**, on U.S. 395, provides clean, homey cottages at great rates for groups. (☎764-2387. Singles $30; doubles $50; cabins for up to 6 $125. Rates may vary with the Lone Pine Film Festival or on other holiday weekends.) Farther north along U.S. 395 at the junction with Rte. 136 is **Lone Pine.** Sitting at the base of Mt. Whitney, the town stays pleasantly cool compared to the desert. (See **Lone Pine,** p. 297.)

DEATH VALLEY JUNCTION ☎ 760

In Death Valley Junction, at Rte. 127 and 190, 29 mi. from Furnace Creek, lives mime and ballet dancer Marta Becket, whose **Amargosa Opera House** is the sole outpost of high culture in the desert. Becket incorporates parts of classical ballet, modern dance, and pantomime into a one-woman show with 47 different characters that draws packed houses. (☎852-4441. Performances Jan.-May and Oct.-Dec. Sa 8:15pm; Nov. and Feb.-Apr. also M. $15.)

SHOSHONE AND TECOPA ☎ 760

The town of **Shoshone,** at Rte. 127 and 178, 56 mi. southeast of Furnace Creek, serves as a gateway to Death Valley and a base for outdoor adventures. The **Charles Brown General Store and Service Station** is a good place to stock up and fill your tank. (☎852-4242. Open daily 7am-8:30pm.) Next door is the brown **Shoshone Inn ❹,** which offers clean (but slightly tacky) rooms, a swimming pool, and cable TV. (☎852-4335. Rooms $63.) The nearby **Shoshone RV Park ❶** has RV hookups, showers, a pool, and even some shade. (☎852-4569. Sites $10; hookups $15.) Stop by **Cafe C'est Si Bon ❷,** a relaxing outpost of French cuisine in the middle of the desert. Crepes, coffee, and **Internet** access come at fair prices. (☎852-4307. Crepes $5-7. Internet $1 per 5min. Open M and W-Su 7am-5pm.)

South of Shoshone is the small town of **Tecopa,** which offers hot springs and a hostel for outdoor adventurers. The hot springs are available in single-sex bathhouses run by Inyo County. The springs are free for bathers. Be sure to follow the two basic rules: no clothing and no photographic equipment allowed. Follow the signs to **Desertaire Hostel HI-AYH ❷,** 2000 Old Spanish Trail Hwy., for cheap sleep. The hostel also has a full kitchen and sells groceries. (☎852-4580. Check-in 5-9pm. Open July-May. Dorms $20.)

LAS VEGAS ☎ 702

Rising out of the Nevada desert, Las Vegas is a shimmering tribute to excess. Those who embrace it find the actualization of a mirage, an oasis of vice and greed, and one very, very good time. This playground town was founded on gambling, whoring, and mob muscle. These days, however, it's rather family-oriented. Lavish hotels on the Strip recreate Paris, New York, Venice, ancient Egypt, and medieval England in attempt to entice visitors to their poker tables and nightclubs. Drawn by the glitz, people flock to this flashing, buzzing corner of the desert to get married, celebrate anniversaries, and then bring their kids. Sleeping (and decision-making) can be nearly impossible with sparkling casinos, cheap gourmet food, free drinks, and spectacular attractions everywhere. Nowhere else do so many shed inhibitions and indulge with such abandon. Know thy tax bracket; walk in knowing what you want to spend and get the hell out when you've spent it. In Las Vegas, there's a busted wallet and a broken heart for every garish neon light.

◢ ORIENTATION

The drive to Las Vegas from L.A. is a straight 300 mi. shot on I-10 E and then I-15 N (4-5hr.). From Arizona, take I-40 to Kingman, then U.S. 93 N.

Las Vegas has two major casino areas. The **downtown** casino district has been converted into a pedestrian promenade. Some of the oldest and most famous casinos cluster close together beneath a shimmering space-frame structure called the

Fremont Street Experience, which spans five city blocks. The other main area is **the Strip,** a collection of mammoth hotel-casinos along **Las Vegas Boulevard.** Parallel to the Strip and in its shadow is **Paradise Road,** which is also dotted with casinos. Both areas are very busy; traffic can be frustrating. For faster travel north or south, use one of the major roads farther east, such as Maryland Pkwy.

As in any large city, some areas of Las Vegas should be avoided, especially downtown areas far from the casino district. Always stay on brightly lit pathways, and do not wander too far from the major casinos and hotels on foot. Despite (or perhaps because of) its debauchery, Las Vegas has a **curfew.** Those under 18 aren't allowed in most public places late at night (Su-Th 10am-5pm, F-Sa midnight-5am), unless accompanied by an adult. Laws are even harsher on the Strip, where no one under 18 is allowed unaccompanied 9pm-5am—ever. **The drinking and gambling age is 21.** People under 21 may walk through the casinos, but loitering on casino floors is prohibited. Some casino employees report more pressure on weekends to ask for identification.

⌐ TRANSPORTATION

Airport: McCarran International (☎261-5743), at the southwestern end of the Strip. Shuttle buses run to the Strip ($4.75) and downtown ($7); taxis $10-15 to the Strip, $16-20 downtown.

Buses: Greyhound, 200 S. Main St. (☎384-9561 or 800-231-2222), downtown at Carson Ave., near the Plaza Hotel/Casino. To **L.A.** (5-7hr., 22 per day, $38) and **San Francisco** (13-16hr., 6 per day, $69).

Public Transportation: Citizens Area Transit (CAT; ☎228-7433). Bus #301 serves downtown and the Strip. Buses #108 and 109 serve the airport. All buses wheelchair accessible. Buses run daily 5:30am-1:30am (24hr. on the Strip). Strip routes $2, residential routes $1.25; seniors and ages 6-17 $1/$0.60. For schedules and maps, try the tourist office or the **Downtown Transportation Center,** 300 N. Casino Center Blvd. (☎228-7433). **Las Vegas Strip Trolleys** (☎382-1404) cruise the Strip every 20min. daily 9:30am-1:30am. Trolley fare $1.75 per trip; day pass $5. The brand new **Monorail** (www.lvmonorail.com) runs along the Strip, connecting the major casinos daily 8am-midnight. $3 per ride; day pass $15.

Taxi: Yellow, Checker, and **Star** (☎873-2000). $3 base, $1.80 per mile. For pickup, call 30min. ahead of time. Wheelchair accessible cabs available. McCarran Airport departures are an additional $1.20. No extra charge for up to 4 passengers.

Car Rental: Sav-Mor Rent-A-Car, 5101 Rent-A-Car Rd. (☎736-1234 or 800-634-6779), at the airport. From $24 per day, $110 per week. 21+. Under-25 surcharge $12 per day. Open daily 5:30am-1am. Airport window opens 7am.

Parking: Free parking abounds. Major casinos offer both valet and self-park areas. Both are free, but tip the valet. Downtown lots generally require validation inside the casino.

⟩ PRACTICAL INFORMATION

Visitor Information: Las Vegas Convention and Visitors Authority, 3150 Paradise Rd. (☎892-0711), 4 blocks from the Strip in the big pink convention center by the Hilton. Up-to-date info on headliners, shows, hotel bargains, and buffets. Open M-F 8am-5pm.

Tours: Coach USA/Gray Line, 795 E. Tropicana Ave. (☎384-1234 or 800-634-6579), at the corner of Swenson St. Evening tours (5hr., 1 per day, $40). Bus tours from Las Vegas to **Hoover Dam/Lake Mead** (7hr., 1 per day, $62) and the **Grand Canyon's South Rim** ($150). Discount coupons in tourist publications. Reserve in advance.

Bank: Bank of America, 1140 E. Desert Inn Rd. (☎654-1000), at the corner of Maryland Pkwy. Open M-Th 9am-5pm, F 9am-6pm. Phone assistance 24hr.

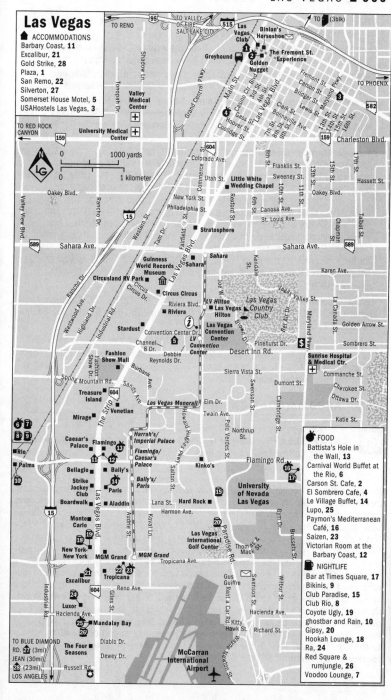

Las Vegas

ACCOMMODATIONS
Barbary Coast, **11**
Excalibur, **21**
Gold Strike, **28**
Plaza, **1**
San Remo, **22**
Silverton, **27**
Somerset House Motel, **5**
USAHostels Las Vegas, **3**

FOOD
Battista's Hole in the Wall, **13**
Carnival World Buffet at the Rio, **6**
Carson St. Cafe, **2**
El Sombrero Cafe, **4**
Le Village Buffet, **14**
Lupo, **25**
Paymon's Mediterranean Café, **16**
Saizen, **23**
Victorian Room at the Barbary Coast, **12**

NIGHTLIFE
Bar at Times Square, **17**
Bikinis, **9**
Club Paradise, **15**
Club Rio, **8**
Coyote Ugly, **19**
ghostbar and Rain, **10**
Gipsy, **20**
Hookah Lounge, **18**
Ra, **24**
Red Square & rumjungle, **26**
Voodoo Lounge, **7**

THE DESERT

ATMs: Plentiful in all major casinos, but there is at least a $2 charge for each use. ATMs at gas stations or banks often charge lower fees.

Laundry: Cora's Coin Laundry, 1099 E. Tropicana Ave. (☎736-6181), at the corner of Maryland Pkwy. Wash $1, dry $0.25 per 10min. Open daily 8am-8pm.

Gaming Lessons: Blackjack, roulette, craps, Caribbean stud poker, three-card poker, and baccarat. Free at major casinos. Call Aladdin (☎785-5555) for session times.

Library and Internet Access: Clark County Library, 1401 E. Flamingo Rd. (☎507-3400). 15min. free Internet. Open M-Th 9am-9pm, F-Su 10am-6pm. **Kinko's,** 395 Hughes Center Dr. (☎951-2400), at the corner of Paradise and Flamingo Rd. $0.20 per min. Open 24hr.

Marriage: Marriage License Bureau, 200 S. 3rd St. (☎455-4415), in the courthouse. 18+ or parental consent. Licenses $55; cash only. No waiting period or blood test required. Witness is required. Open Su-Th 8am-midnight, F-Sa 24hr. **Little White Wedding Chapel,** 1301 Las Vegas Blvd. (☎382-5943; www.alittlewhitechapel.com.). From 3min. drive-through whirlwinds to elaborate fantasy-themed extravaganzas, this Vegas wedding chapel is legendary among the city's matrimonial traditions. Vegas luminaries like Frank Sinatra and Liberace as well as Britney Spears have been hitched here. Basic drive-through packages begin at a friendly $40 and end at the limits of imagination. All wedding necessities are provided, including photographer, tux and gown, flowers, and, for honeymooners on the go, a lollipop-pink Caddy. Be sure to pick up your marriage license first. No reservations required for the drive-through services. Open 24hr.

Weather Conditions: ☎263-9744.

Hotlines: Compulsive Gamblers Hotline, ☎800-LOST-BET/567-8238. **Gamblers Anonymous,** ☎385-7732. **Rape Crisis Center Hotline,** ☎366-1640. **Suicide Prevention,** ☎731-2990 or 800-885-4673.

Police: ☎229-3111. Corner of Russell Rd. and S. Las Vegas Blvd.

Post Offices: 301 E. Stewart Ave. (☎385-8944), downtown. Open M-F 8:30am-5pm. **Postal Code:** 89101. Closer to the Strip: 4975 Swenson St. (☎736-7649). Open M-F 8:30am-5pm. **Postal Code:** 89119.

ACCOMMODATIONS AND CAMPING

> **TIP** **CHEAP SLEEPS.** Many of the larger casinos offer discounted rates for gamblers. Call the hotel and ask for a "casino rate," which is often considerably lower than regular rates.

Room rates in Las Vegas fluctuate greatly, and a room that costs $30 during a slow period can cost hundreds during a convention weekend. **Vegas.com** (www.vegas.com) has some of the best rates. Local, free, readily available publications such as *What's On In Las Vegas, Today in Las Vegas, 24/7, Vegas Visitor, Casino Player, Tour Guide Magazine, Best Read Guide,* and *Insider Viewpoint of Las Vegas* list discounts, coupons, general info, and schedules of events. If you get stuck, call the **Room Reservations Hotline** (☎800-332-5333).

Strip hotels are at the center of the action and within walking distance of each other, but their inexpensive rooms sell out quickly. A number of motels cluster around **Sahara Road** and **South Las Vegas Boulevard.** Motels also line **Fremont Street,** though this area is a bit desolate at night.; if you want to stay downtown, it is best to stay in one of the casinos in the **Fremont Street Experience** (see Casinos, p. 557) itself. Inexpensive motels also stretch along the southern end of the **Strip,** across from ritzy Mandalay Bay. In the room rates listed below, the **hotel taxes of 9%** (11% for downtown Fremont St.) are not included.

▩ **Barbary Coast,** 3595 S. Las Vegas Blvd. (☎737-7111), at Flamingo Rd. With the best location on the Strip, mere minutes from Bally's, Caesar's Palace, and Paris, Barbary Coast is perfect for those looking to be in the middle of everything. Large rooms and low table limits make this popular with a young crowd. Restaurants, bars, and casino floor always buzzing. Rooms Su-Th $49-79, F-Sa $69-129. ❸

▩ **Excalibur,** 3850 S. Las Vegas Blvd. (☎597-7777), at Tropicana Ave. The best value of all of the major resort casinos. This King Arthur-themed castle features a moat and drawbridge, 2 pools, a modern spa and fitness center, a large casino and poker room, and a monorail station to Luxor and Mandalay Bay. Many of the 4000 rooms have been recently renovated. Rooms Su-Th $49-79, F-Sa $79-129. ❸

San Remo, 115 E. Tropicana Ave. (☎800-522-7366). Just off the Strip, this is a smaller, quieter version of the major players. Delicious prime rib draws an older crowd. Live entertainment every night, featuring the "Showgirls of Magic" ($39). Rooms may go as low as $32 during slow periods, but are usually Su-Th $45, F-Sa $70. ❸

Silverton, 3333 Blue Diamond Rd. (☎800-588-7711; www.silvertoncasino.com). This Old West mining town-themed gambling den has new rooms and a bass fishing store. Free Las Vegas Blvd. shuttle until 10pm. Doubles Su-Th $35-45, F-Sa $69; $10 per additional person. RV hookups $23-30. $3 energy charge. ❸

USAHostels Las Vegas, 1322 Fremont St. (☎800-550-8958 or 385-1150; www.usahostels.com). Though it's located far from the action of the Strip in a dreary section of downtown, this hostel's laid-back staff keeps guests comfy and entertained. Sparsely furnished rooms. Free trips including a champagne limo tour of the Strip. Pool, hot tub, laundry, and billiard room. Free pickup from Greyhound station 10am-10pm. International passport, proof of international travel, or out-of-state college ID required. Dorms Su-Th $15-19, F-Sa $17-21; suites Su-Th $40-42, F-Sa $40-49. Prices roughly $3 higher in the summer and peak holidays. ISIC discount. ❷

Gold Strike Hotel & Gambling Hall, 1 Main St. (☎800-634-1359), in Jean, NV, 20min. from the Strip on I-15. Cheap restaurants (prime rib $7; buffet $7.50), loose slots, and low-limit tables. Spacious rooms. Make reservations for lower prices. Rooms Su-Th $15-20, F-Sa $40-50. $3 per additional person. ❷

Somerset House Motel, 294 Convention Center Dr. (☎888-336-4280; www.somersethouse.com). A no-frills establishment within walking distance of the Strip and the Convention Center. Rooms are large and many have kitchens. Dishes and cooking utensils provided upon request. Some of the best weekend rates. Singles Su-Th $35, F-Sa $44; doubles Su-Th $44, F-Sa $55. $5 per additional person. Senior discount. ❸

Plaza, 1 Main St. (☎800-634-6575; www.plazahotelcasino.com), the western anchor of the Fremont Street Experience. Many rooms have great views of the Strip. Casino has low stakes games and is more modern than other downtown casinos. Tennis courts, barbershop, salon, and pool. Singles Su-Th $30-50, F-Sa $79-99. ❸

Circusland RV Park, 500 Circus Circus Dr. (☎734-0410). Pool, hot tub, convenience store, showers, and laundry. RV hookups Su-Th $18-28, F-Sa $20-30. ❷

◗ FOOD

From swanky eateries run by celebrity chefs to gourmet buffets, culinary surprises are everywhere in Las Vegas, and usually at a great price. Inexpensive does not always mean low-quality in this town, since food operations are a major part of casino marketing. Be sure to check the marquees of major hotels for specials. $0.99 shrimp cocktails and $5 prime rib can always be found somewhere. Long lines for a buffet are generally a good sign, since the food tends to be fresher.

THE HIDDEN DEAL

SOMETHING FOR NOTHING

Enjoying penthouse suites with butlers, champagne brunches, boxing tickets, spa treatments, Grand Canyon helicopter tours all or free—high-rollers at Las Vegas casinos are treated like royalty. But even if you don't have enough dough to bet $2500 a hand on blackjack, getting "comped" in this town is easier than ever.

Comps are the rewards casinos give to players to keep them wagering. Both slot and table players are eligible for comps, and sometimes, cash back. Here's how to get in on the deal:

1) Join the players club. Show your ID to a club employee, who will issue you a card. Join the club wherever you play, and be sure to ask if there are any promotions going on. You'll often get something just for joining.

2) Play. Insert your card into the card reader on slot machines, or give your card to the table dealer.

3) Get comped. Go to the players club center, an automated comp machine, or the pit boss to check your balance and get a reward. The easiest comp to get is a buffet voucher.

But be careful; don't play just to get comps, because statistically, you'll lose about twice the value of the comp. You may also get a lot of mail offering free hotel rooms to encourage you to come back, which wouldn't necessarily be so bad...

☒ **Le Village Buffet,** 3655 Las Vegas Blvd. (☎946-7000), in the **Paris,** French cuisine at 5 stations, each representing a different region. Begin with heaps of fresh shellfish and cheeses and then order fresh fruit crepes. Beef and veal sit at carving stations, while a pastry chef prepares more than 40 *gateaux*. Breakfast $14. Lunch $18. Dinner $24. Open daily 7am-10pm. ❺

☒ **Carnival World Buffet,** 3700 W. Flamingo Rd. (☎222-7757), at the **Rio.** The line can be long, but the 12 themed food stations, from sushi to Mexican, are sure to delight those who wait. Breakfast $13. Lunch $16.Dinner $25. Open daily 7am-10pm. ❹

Victorian Room, 3595 S. Las Vegas Blvd. (☎737-7111), in **Barbary Coast.** Home to the best night-owl breakfast special (full breakfast $3; midnight-7am) and excellent Chinese food. Also serves pasta, steak, seafood. Fast, friendly service around the clock. Entrees $7-20. Open 24hr. ❷

Carson Street Cafe, 129 Fremont St. (☎385-7111), in the **Golden Nugget.** Exhaustive menu features large of salads, burgers, pasta, steak, and even Korean kalbi and Japanese udon. Save room for one of the dozens of homemade desserts. Locals love the bread pudding. Entrees $7-24. Open 24hr. ❷

El Sombrero Cafe, 807 S. Main St. (☎382-9234). Where locals go for authentic Mexican food. Small room, huge portions, friendly staff. Their combination plates offer a lot of food for a little money ($9-11). Lunch $7. Open M-Sa 11am-9:30pm. ❷

Paymon's Mediterranean Cafe, 4147 S. Maryland Pkwy. (☎731-6030). Some of the best Mediterranean food in the city. Try the delicious combo plate with hummus, tabouli, and stuffed grape leaves ($10), or a big falafel and hummus pita bread sandwich ($6). Attached to **The Hookah Lounge** (see p. 560). Open M-Th 11am-1am, F-Sa 11am-3am, Su 11am-4pm. ❷

Battista's Hole in the Wall, 4041 Audrie St. (☎732-1424), behind the Flamingo. 33 years' worth of celebrity photos, novelties from area brothels, and the head of "Moosolini" (the fascist moose) adorn the walls. Generous portions; many diners share. An accordion player adds to the charm. Dinner ($18-34) includes all-you-can-drink wine. Open Su-Th 4:30-10:30pm, F-Sa 4:30-11pm. Reservations recommended. ❹

Saizen, 115 E. Tropicana Ave. (☎739-9000), in **San Remo,** behind the slots on the 1st fl. Meticulous owners are known to use only the best ingredients, giving it the reputation as the best sushi bar on the Strip. Entrees $10-24. Open daily 5:30pm-midnight. ❹

Lupo, 3590 S. Las Vegas Blvd. (☎740-5522), in **Mandalay Bay,** beside a number of classy nightspots and dining options. Celebrity chef Wolfgang Puck's first Italian restaurant. Pizzas and salads ($11) are filling and well presented. The perfect prelude to Rumjungle and Red Square (see p. 560). Open M-Th 5-10pm, F 5-11pm, Sa 11:30am-4pm and 5-11pm, Su 11:30am-4pm and 5-10pm. ❸

CASINOS

Casinos spend millions of dollars attracting big spenders, and they do this by fooling guests into thinking they are somewhere else. Efforts to bring families to Sin City are evident everywhere, with arcades and thrill rides at every turn. Still, Vegas is no Disneyland. With the plethora of steamy nightclubs, topless revues, and scantily clad waitresses serving up free liquor, it's clear that casinos' priorities center on the mature, moneyed crowd. Casinos, bars, and some wedding chapels are open 24hr., so whatever your itch, Vegas can usually scratch it. Almost every casino resort has a full casino, several restaurants, a club or two, a buffet, a feature show, and other attractions to lure in gamblers. There is valuable art, thrill rides, and startling architecture at every corner. Look for casino "funbooks" that feature deals on chips and entertainment. **Gambling is illegal for those under 21.**

> **LIMIT YOURSELF.** If you're gambling, be sure to set a daily limit for yourself. Big early losses can ruin a trip.

THE STRIP

The undisputed locus of Vegas's surging regeneration, the Strip is a fantasyland of neon, teeming with people, casinos, and restaurants. The nation's 10 largest hotels line the legendary 3½ mi. stretch of Las Vegas Blvd., named an "All-American Road" and "National Scenic Byway." Don't let the glitter dupe you—this shimmering facade was built on gamblers' losses.

Mandalay Bay, 3950 S. Las Vegas Blvd. (☎632-7777; www.mandalaybay.com). Undoubtedly Vegas's hippest casino, Mandalay Bay tries to convince New York and L.A. fashionistas they haven't left home. With all the swank restaurants and chichi clubs, gambling seems an afterthought. Shark Reef has 100 aquatic beasts from all over the globe, including 15 shark species. House of Blues shelters some of Vegas's best music.

Bellagio, 3600 S. Las Vegas Blvd. (☎693-7444; www.bellagio.com). The world's largest 5-star hotel, made famous in the remake of *Ocean's Eleven*. Houses a gallery of fine art and a beautifully maintained floral conservatory that changes with the seasons. Spend your winnings on Prada, Hermes, Gucci, or other bling in the Via Bellagio Shops. Muscle your way up for a view of the spectacular fountains, where water is propelled several stories into the air during daily free water ballet shows, set to Italian opera songs.

Venetian, 3355 S. Las Vegas Blvd. (☎414-1000; www.venetian.com). Singing gondoliers serenade passengers on the 3 ft. deep chlorinated "canal" that runs through this palatial casino. The Guggenheim Hermitage Museum presents modern artwork from around the world. For those who dig the representational, there's Madame Tussaud's wax museum. Elaborate architectural replicas of Venetian plazas, bridges, and towers adorn the exterior. Fine restaurants and upscale shops line the canals.

Caesar's Palace, 3570 S. Las Vegas Blvd. (☎731-7110; www.caesars.com). At Caesar's, busts abound; some are plaster while others are barely concealed by the low-cut get-ups of cocktail waitresses. Few are real. The pricey Forum Shops led the high-end shopping craze at Strip casinos. With constant construction and ever-changing attractions (including Celine Dion), Caesar's continues to set the standard for excitement.

Luxor, 3900 S. Las Vegas Blvd. (☎262-4000; www.luxor.com). This architectural marvel recreates the majestic pyramids of ancient Egypt in opaque glass and steel. Luxor has all sorts of diversions when gambling loses its appeal; there's an IMAX Theater, a full-scale replica of King Tut's Tomb, Club Ra, and the Blue Man theater.

Paris, 3655 S. Las Vegas Blvd. (☎946-7000; www.parislasvegas.com). From restaurants that look like French outdoor cafes to replicas of the Arc de Triomphe, the French Opera House, and even the Eiffel Tower, this themed resort adds a Parisian *je ne sais quois* to Las Vegas glam.

The Mirage, 3400 S. Las Vegas Blvd. (☎791-7111; www.mirage.com). Arguably the casino that began Vegas's reincarnation in the early 90s. Shelters 8 bottlenose dolphins and a garden of white tigers and lions. A volcano that puts science fair projects to shame erupts every 15min.

MGM Grand, 3799 S. Las Vegas Blvd. (☎891-1111; www.mgmgrand.com). A huge bronze lion guards Las Vegas's largest hotel (5000 rooms), which echoes the green glamour of the Emerald City from *The Wizard of Oz*. Cowardly and brave felines dwell in the Lion Habitat. The MGM often hosts world-class sporting events and concerts.

New York-New York, 3790 S. Las Vegas Blvd. (☎740-6969; www.nynyhotelcasino). Towers mimic the Manhattan skyline and re-create the Big Apple. Walk under a replica of Brooklyn Bridge or visit Coney Island to ride the Manhattan Express open daily 11am-11pm, $12), the wildest ride on the Strip.

Treasure Island (TI), 3300 S. Las Vegas Blvd. (☎894-7111; www.treasureisland.com). Refurbished and fully embracing the wave of pirate chic, this once-tired casino is trying to reinvent itself as an "in" spot for young crowds. See the *Sirens of TI* for a sultry sea battle in one of Vegas's most skin-baring free outdoor shows. Shows daily at 7, 8:30, 10pm and 1:30am.

Circus Circus, 2880 S. Las Vegas Blvd. (☎734-0410; www.circuscircus.com). While parents run to card tables and slot machines downstairs, children watch free circus acts and spend their quarters in the enormous video game arcade upstairs. Adventuredome, inside the hotel complex, is the one of the world's largest indoor theme parks. Rides include a double-loop roller coaster and a towering free-fall machine.

Stratosphere, 2000 S. Las Vegas Blvd. (☎800-998-6937; www.stratospherehotel.com). World-class dining and a theme park sit at the highest point in Vegas and one of the tallest observation decks in the world, on top of this futuristic-looking resort.

 CASINO TIPPING. While gambling, players are served free cocktails, and $1 is the standard tip for servers. Leave at least $1 per person for the drink server and bussers at a buffet. Many players reward a good table-game dealer with a $1 tip next to their main bet for the dealer.

DOWNTOWN AND OFF-STRIP

The tourist frenzy that grips the Strip is less noticeable in "old" Downtown Vegas. **Glitter Gulch** offers smaller hotels, cheaper alcohol and food, and some serious gambling with table game limits as low as $1. The family atmosphere that the Strip tries to cultivate is substantially lacking here; the feel is grittier, and the focus is on gaming. Years of decline were reversed with Las Vegas's city-wide rebound and the 1995 opening of the **Fremont Street Experience.** Now there's a protective canopy of neon, and construction of a pedestrian promenade has furthered the area's renaissance. Despite the renewal, don't stray far from Fremont St. at night.

Golden Nugget, 129 Fremont St. (☎385-7111; www.goldennugget.com). An outpost of Strip-like class downtown, this 4-star hotel charms gamblers with marble floors, elegant chandeliers, and high-end gambling. Without the distractions of roller coasters and replicas, the Golden Nugget stands for what Vegas used to be.

Binion's Horseshoe, 128 Fremont St. (☎382-1600). The Binion family brought their love of high-stakes gaming from Texas. A place to learn the tricks of the trade by observation rather than playing, this casino has been the site of the World Series of Poker—a serious gambler's paradise. Come at night to watch the large poker room in full swing, where tourists take on local hustlers, usually unsuccessfully. High craps odds, single-deck blackjack, and a willingness to honor almost any bet are Horseshoe hallmarks.

Palms, 4321 W. Flamingo Rd. (☎942-7777; www.palms.com). Owned by thirty-something marketing genius George Maloof, who is on his way to becoming the next casino mogul, the Palms is the ultimate venue to spot celebrities and party with the young and beautiful. The Skin Pool Lounge has swings and cabanas to enjoy before you hit the bars and clubs on the property.

♫ ENTERTAINMENT

Vegas entertainment revolves around the casinos. Casino-sponsored productions feature marvels such as waterfalls, explosions, fireworks, and casts of hundreds (including animals). You can also see Broadway plays and musicals, individual entertainers in concert, and critically acclaimed performance art. All hotels have city-wide ticket booths in their lobbies. Check out some of the ubiquitous free show guides—*Showbiz, Today in Las Vegas, What's On*—for summaries of shows, times, and prices. For a more opinionated perspective, try one of the independent weeklies—*Las Vegas Mercury, City Life, Las Vegas Weekly,* or *Neon,* the *Las Vegas Review-Journal's* weekly entertainment supplement. It's worth setting aside some money to see one of Vegas's most elaborate shows. There is also plenty of free entertainment, but lounge singers and dancers are nothing compared to some of these big-ticket performances.

Cirque du Soleil's creative shows—*O, Mystère,* and *Zumanity*—are awe-inspiring but bank-busting ($93.50-150). Performed at the Bellagio, ⬛O is easily the best of the three, with agile performers suspended above a moving pool. **Mystère,** at Treasure Island, is almost as impressive, and often has $60 discount seats. At New York-New York, **Zumanity,** hosted by a drag queen, caters to an adult audience. ⬛**Blue Man Group,** at the Luxor, pushes the limits of stage entertainment with unique percussion and audience participation. Las Vegas' step into more than just the spectacular, the show is postmodern performance art without snobbishness ($75-85). Those looking for an illusionist will be thrilled by **David Copperfield** (appearing often at MGM; $90-100) and **Lance Burton** (at the Monte Carlo; $65-75). For a cheap laugh, **Second City,** at the Flamingo, is an improvisation show featuring some of the country's best up-and-coming comedians ($20). The group inspired the show Saturday Night Live, and many company members went on to write or perform for the show. For a performance by one of the musical stars who haunt the city, such as **Celine Dion** (at Caesar's Palace), **Gladys Knight** (at Flamingo), or **Wayne Newton** (at Stardust), you'll have to fork over at least $50. Incredible impersonator/singer/dancer **Danny Gans** entertains at The Mirage ($100).

▣ NIGHTLIFE

Nightlife in Vegas starts late and powers on until everyone drops, runs out of money, or drunkenly stumbles to the chapel. And just like the themed casinos that house them, Vegas clubs are always one-upping each other with spectacular attractions. Most clubs have dress codes; in general, leave the shorts and sneakers at home and wear something snazzy.

ghostbar and **Rain,** 4231 W. Flamingo Rd. (ghostbar ☎938-2666, Rain 940-7246), in the **Palms.** Indisputably the hottest Vegas nightspot. Rain features over 25,000 sq. ft. of dance floor and intense displays of fire, fog, and rain. You may have to wait in line for

THE BLUE MAN GROUP

Let's Go sat down with the director and cast of the Blue Man Group, a performance art trio costumed like blue aliens that busts out mesmerizing percussion beats while overloading the audience with unusual treats like Twinkies and tissue paper.

Identifying the failures of modern society, director Carrie Hanson said, "Look at us today. I've got my pager, cell phone, three email addresses, 900 cable channels—we're not relating to the people around us, just these gadgets." Hanson views the show as a move away from the days when the elite just stood back and intellectualized art. "Blue Man wants to create life in music, art, and science. And if you can't feel it, we're gonna show it to you so you can see it."

While many performers see New York and Hollywood as gateways to success, the group sees Vegas as a symbol of hope for many performers. "I was determined to make something of myself artistically, instead of just working in a factory, so I came to Las Vegas," said one Blue Man, who got the job through an open casting call.

And living in Las Vegas? Cast member Isaac Eddy captured it perfectly: "I'm from Puritan New England, which means I need to work to get my dessert, and there's just too much desert here to make me feel comfortable."

hours, but once you're in, be ready to groove with the hottest bodies in Vegas while DJs throw down beats. The Skin Lounge Pool offers respite from the 3 levels of sweaty dancers. Cover $10 Th, $20 F-Sa. Open Th 11pm-late, F-Sa 10pm-late. The beautiful and well-dressed relax at ghostbar on the hotel's 55th floor, with a deck and 360° view of Vegas. Open daily 7pm-late.

rumjungle and **Red Square,** 3950 Las Vegas Blvd. (☎632-7407), in **Mandalay Bay.** Fashionable international visitors are welcomed to rumjungle with a wall of fire and volcanic eruptions of rum set to hip-hop and R&B. Cover $10-20 F-Sa. Red Square, a Miami Beach import, pulls off post-Communist chic with ease. Fashionably smug capitalists sip amazing martinis and frozen vodkas ($9-11) surrounded by quaint remnants of Leninism. Open Su-Th 5pm-1am, F-Sa 5pm-5:30am.

The Bar at Times Square and **Coyote Ugly,** 3790 S. Las Vegas Blvd. (The Bar ☎740-6969, Coyote Ugly 740-6330), in **New York-New York.** The Bar features two dueling pianos playing crowd favorites on demand. Patrons cheer on the performers and toast each other with drinks from the full bar. Cover $10 F-Sa. Open Su-Th 8pm-2am, F-Sa 8pm-3am. In Coyote Ugly, inspired by the famed New York bar, gorgeous waitresses dance on a saloon-style bar, embarrassing visitors by bringing them up to dance in front of a loud crowd. Lucky victims are rewarded with a shot poured into their mouths. Cover varies, but often free before 9pm. Open daily from 6pm.

VooDoo Lounge, Club Rio, and **BiKiNiS,** 3700 W. Flamingo Rd. (☎949-1127), in **The Rio.** Start a Rio evening at the VooDoo Lounge (no cover before 8pm). Sunsets look beautiful through a beer at this bar on top of the Rio. Live music. On the casino floor, grab free admission cards to Club Rio, where Th is the most popular Latin night in town. If you can't get in free (cover men $20, women $10), head to BiKiNiS, where hard-bodied lifeguards and swimwear-clad bartenders add to the South Beach motif. Ladies free, $20 cover for men. Open Th-Su from 10pm.

Gipsy, 4605 Paradise Rd. (☎731-1919). The center of the GLBT scene in Las Vegas heats up every night with a different theme, including drag queen nights and lip-sync contests. Gipsy becomes one of the town's most hopping scenes late at night. Happy hour daily 9pm-2am; all drinks $2. Cover $5-10, W free. Open daily 9pm.

Hookah Lounge, 4147 S. Maryland Pkwy. (☎732-3203). Features more than 20 flavored tobaccos (all legal) in a fun and intimate atmosphere. Perfect before a night on the town or as post-poker relaxation. Full bar and flavored teas. Open M-Th 5pm-1am, F-Sa 5pm-3am.

Ra, 3900 S. Las Vegas Blvd. (☎262-4949), in the **Luxor.** Egyptian-themed nightclub where resident and famous guest DJs spin a variety of sounds from old-school 80s to chart-topping hip-hop tracks. Vegas's most popular club, with a strictly enforced dress code (not casual), especially for men. Call about special events or to inquire about what's on the turntables that night. Cover men $20, women $10. Open W-Sa 10pm.

Club Paradise, 4416 Paradise Rd. (☎734-7990), across from Hard Rock Cafe. Repeatedly voted best gentleman's cabaret (read: strip joint) in America. It's safe and the G-strings stay on. About as sophisticated as a topless bar gets. Beer $6. Cocktails $6-10. Cover $20, $10 before 9pm. Open M-F 4pm-6am, Sa-Su 6pm-6am.

DAYTRIPS FROM LAS VEGAS

The mountains and lakes outside Las Vegas offer opportunities for outdoor excitement. Travelers stop to marvel at the monumental engineering of the Hoover Dam, boaters enjoy the waters of Lake Mead, and hikers and climbers test the canyons and crags of Red Rocks. While Las Vegas swelters in heat and sin, the higher elevations around it are cooler and more pristine.

RED ROCKS. Less than 20 mi. west of the bright neon of the Strip lie the bright geological formations of Red Rock Canyon National Conservation Area, an astounding network of crimson sandstone bluffs and washes formed hundreds of millions of years ago from the remains of ancient marine life. You can stick to the 13 mi. scenic auto route, hike into the desert, or climb through the red rocks. The most popular **hikes** are those through the washes of **Calico Hills** and **Calico Tanks,** accessible from the first few turnouts along the scenic road. Take the **Sandstone Quarry Trail** to climb right onto the red rocks. The waterfalls seen from the **Ice Box Canyon** and **Lost Creek Trails** are not mirages; both trails make for short, worthwhile hikes, especially in the early spring or after it's rained. An excellent **visitors center** introduces the flourishing desert ecosystem, and a **campground ❶** sits off Hwy. 159, 2 mi. east of the visitors center, with picnic tables, grills, water, and toilets. *(From Las Vegas, take I-15 or the 215 Beltway to Charleston Blvd./Rte. 159 W. Visitors center: ☎363-1921. Camping: ☎515-5352. Sites $10. Backcountry camping and overnight climbing require free permits; for info, call ☎515-5050.)*

HOOVER DAM. Built to subdue the flood-prone Colorado River and provide vital water and energy to the southwest, this looming ivory monolith, also known (by New-Deal Democrats) as the Boulder Dam, took 5000 men five years of seven-day weeks to construct. By the time the dam was completed in 1935, 96 men had died. Their labor rendered a 726 ft. colossus that now shelters precious agricultural land, pumps more than 4 billion kilowatt-hours of power to Las Vegas and L.A., and furnishes the liquid playground of Lake Mead amid the sagebrush. Though the dam has altered the local environment, it is a spectacular engineering feat, weighing 6,600,000 tons and measuring 660 ft. thick at its base and 1244 ft. across the canyon at its crest. It is a lasting tribute to America's "think-big" era. Tours and an interpretive center explore the dam's history and future. *(From Las Vegas, take U.S. 93/95 26 mi. to Boulder City. From Boulder City, head east 5 mi. on U.S. 93. ☎866-291-8687. Open daily 9am-5pm. Self-guided tours with short presentations $10, seniors $8, ages 7-16 $4. Parking on the Nevada side costs $5; free on the Arizona side.)*

LAKE MEAD. The largest reservoir in the US and the site of the country's first national recreation area, Lake Mead was created by the construction of the Hoover Dam across the Colorado River in the 1930s. Despite diminished water levels due to drought, the lake is a water recreation haven with nearly 500 mi. of shoreline. Park service-approved outfitters rent boats and more along the shores; visit www.funonthelake.com for more info. First-time visitors to the lake will benefit from a trip to the **Alan Bible Visitors Center,** where the helpful staff dispenses informative brochures, maps, and the *Desert Lake View*, the lake's newspaper and guide. Popular **Boulder Beach ❶,** the departure point for many water-based activities and home to one of the area's many campgrounds, is accessible from Lakeshore Dr. at the south end of the lake. *(From Las Vegas, take Lake Mead Blvd./Hwy. 147 off I-15 east 16 mi. to Northshore Rd. Entrance fee $3 per pedestrian, $5 per vehicle. Visitors center: 4 mi. east of Boulder City on U.S. 93. ☎ 293-8990; www.nps.gov/lame. Open daily 8:30am-4:30pm. Boulder Beach Campsite: Restrooms, water, no showers. Sites $10.)*

VALLEY OF FIRE STATE PARK. A fun, solitary drive through desert foothills brings you to Valley of Fire State Park, named for its diabolical rock formations that seem to bleed in the sun. There is a splendid **campground ❶** near the ancient petroglyph site of Atlas Rock. *(50 mi. northeast of Las Vegas. Take I-15 north to Rte. 169. Campground: ☎ 397-2088. No electricity or hookups. Sites $13.)*

GRAND CANYON   ☎ 928

Long before its designation as a national park in 1919, the Grand Canyon captured the imagination of those who strolled up to its edge and beheld its inconceivable magnitude. The biggest attraction in the Southwest, the canyon never fails to elicit individual thought and reflection. Over 227 mi. long and over 1 mi. deep, with shifting hues due to millions of years of geologic history, it overwhelms the human capacity for perception.

The Grand Canyon extends from Lee's Ferry, Arizona all the way to Lake Mead, Nevada. In the north, the Glen Canyon Dam backs up the Colorado River into mammoth Lake Powell. To the west, the Hoover Dam traps the remaining outflow from Glen Canyon to form Lake Mead. Grand Canyon National Park proper divides neatly into three sections: the popular South Rim; the more serene North Rim; and the canyon gorge itself.

AT A GLANCE: GRAND CANYON NATIONAL PARK	
AREA: 1,218,376 acres.	**GATEWAY TOWNS:** Flagstaff, Williams.
FEATURES: The Canyon, Colorado River, North Rim, South Rim, West Rim, Kaibab Plateau, Tonto Platform.	**CAMPING:** Mather Campground on the South Rim and North Rim Campground require reservations. Backcountry camping requires a permit ($10, plus $5 per person per night, $10 per group).
HIGHLIGHTS: Taking a mule ride to Phantom Ranch, rafting in luxury down the canyon, backpacking from Rim to Rim on the South and North Kaibab Trails, standing in awe at the edge of either rim.	**FEES:** $20 entrance fee per car, $10 entrance fee per pedestrian or cyclist. Valid for 7 days.

SOUTH RIM   ☎ 928

During the summer, everything on two legs or four wheels comes to this side of the Grand Canyon. If you plan to visit at this time, make reservations well in advance for lodging, campsites, and/or mules, and prepare to battle the crowds and search for parking spaces. A friendly Park Service staff, well-run facilities, and beautiful scenery help ease crowd anxiety. Fewer tourists brave the canyon's winter weather, and many hotels and facilities close during low season. Leading up to the park entrance, Rte. 64 is winds through Kaibab National Forest and encompasses the North Rim.

▐ TRANSPORTATION

There are two park entrances: the main **south entrance** is about 6 mi. from the Canyon View Information Plaza, while the eastern **Desert View** entrance is 27 mi. away. Both are accessible via Rte. 64. From Las Vegas, the fastest route to the South Rim is U.S. 93 S to I-40 E, and then Rte. 64 N. From Flagstaff, head north on U.S. 180 to Rte. 64. Free shuttle buses to eight rim overlooks run along **Hermit Road** in the west (closed to private vehicles in the summer). Avoid walking on the drive; the rim trails are safer and more scenic.

Public Transportation: Free shuttle buses run along the West Rim to Hermits Rest (1¼hr. round-trip; operates daily May-Sept. 1hr. before sunrise to 1hr. after sunset) and the Village Loop (1hr. round-trip; operates daily 1hr. before sunrise to 10pm) every 10-30min. May-Sept., the Hermits Rest shuttle is the only way to access the West Rim area. A free **hiker's shuttle** runs between the info center and the South Kaibab Trailhead, on the East Rim near Yaki Point. Early buses run June-Aug. at 4, 5, and 6am.

Taxi: ☎638-2822.

ORIENTATION AND PRACTICAL INFORMATION

Posted maps and signs in the park make orientation easy. Lodges and services concentrate in **Grand Canyon Village**, at the west end of Park Entrance Rd. To the east lie the visitors center, campground, and general store, while most of the lodges and the challenging **Bright Angel Trail** are in the west section. The shorter but more difficult **South Kaibab Trail** is off **Desert View Drive** east of the village. The **entrance pass** is $20 per car and $10 for travelers using other modes of transportation, including bus passengers; the pass lasts one week. For most services in the park, call the main switchboard at ☎638-2631.

Visitor Info: The **Canyon View Information Plaza** (☎800-858-2808; www.grandcanyon.com or www.nps.gov/grca), across from Mather Point just after the entrance to the park, is the one-stop center for Grand Canyon info. The visitors center stocks copies of *The Guide* (an essential), assorted pamphlets, and plenty of information on hiking. To get there, park at Mather Pt., then walk ½ mi. to the info plaza. The Park Service, through the Grand Canyon Association, sells a variety of informational books and packets. The **transportation info desks** in the **Bright Angel Lodge** and the **Maswik Lodge** (☎638-2631) handle reservations for mule rides, bus tours, plane tours, Phantom Ranch, taxis, and more. Open daily 6am-8pm.

Equipment Rental: At the gear counter in Canyon Village Marketplace in Market Plaza. Comfy hiking boots with socks ($8), sleeping bags ($9), tents (2-person $15, 4-person $16), day packs (large $6, small $4), and other camping gear (stoves $5). Deposits required. Open daily 7am-8:30pm. Major credit cards accepted.

Weather and Road Conditions: ☎638-7888.

Medical Services: Grand Canyon Clinic (☎638-2551). Turn left at the first stoplight after the South Rim entrance. 24hr. emergency aid. Open M-F 7am-7pm, Sa 10am-4pm.

Post Office: Grand Canyon Market Plaza, next to the Marketplace (☎638-2512.) Open M-F 9am-4:30pm, Sa 11am-3pm. **Postal Code:** 86023.

ACCOMMODATIONS

Summer rooms on the South Rim should be reserved 11 months in advance; call ☎888-297-2757 or write to Xanterra, 14001 E. Iliff, Ste. 600, Aurora, CO 80014. That said, there are frequent cancellations; if you arrive unprepared, check for vacancies or call the operator (☎638-2631) and ask to be connected with the proper lodge.

Bright Angel Lodge (☎638-2631), in Grand Canyon Village. The cheapest indoor lodging in the park, located in a historic building right on the rim. Very convenient to Bright Angel Trail and shuttle buses. Rustic lodge singles and doubles $55, with bath $71; historic cabins (some of which have fireplaces) for 1 or 2 people $84-107. $7 per additional person. ❸

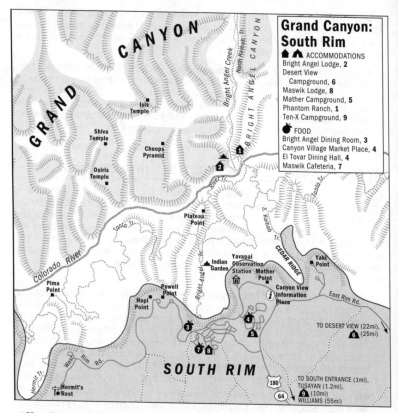

Grand Canyon: South Rim

▲ ♠ ACCOMMODATIONS
Bright Angel Lodge, **2**
Desert View
   Campground, **6**
Maswik Lodge, **8**
Mather Campground, **5**
Phantom Ranch, **1**
Ten-X Campground, **9**

🍴 FOOD
Bright Angel Dining Room, **3**
Canyon Village Market Place, **4**
El Tovar Dining Hall, **4**
Maswik Cafeteria, **7**

Maswik Lodge (☎ 638-2631), at the west end of Grand Canyon Village. Small, clean cabins with showers. Motel rooms with queen-size beds and ceiling fans also available. Singles $79; doubles $121; cabins $77. $7-9 per additional person. ❹

Phantom Ranch (☎ 638-2631), on the canyon floor, a day's hike down the Kaibab Trail or Bright Angel Trail. Breakfast $17; box lunch $8.50; stew dinner $20, steak dinner $28, prepared the same way for over 50 years; vegetarian option $20. Reservations can be made up to 23 months in advance. If you're dying to sleep on the canyon floor but don't have a reservation, show up at the Bright Angel transportation desk at 6am on the day prior to your planned stay and take a shot on the waiting list. Male and female dorms $26; seldom-available cabins for 1 or 2 people $72, $10.50 per additional person. ❷

🏕 CAMPING

While lodgings in the park are usually filled years in advance, camping is a definite possibility. Mather Campground (see below) usually fills by reservation, but there are many other options located just outside the park where you can pitch your tent. Reservations for some campgrounds can be made through **SPHERICS** (☎ 800-365-2267). If you run out of options, and darkness is closing in, you can pull off a dirt road and camp for free in the **Kaibab National Forest,** along the south border of the park. No camping is allowed within a quarter of a mile of U.S. 64. **Dispersed**

camping sits conveniently along the oft-traveled N. Long Jim Loop Rd.—turn right about 1 mi. south of the south entrance station. For quieter and more remote sites, follow signs for the Arizona Trail into the national forest between miles 252 and 253 on U.S. 64. Fires are heavily restricted or even banned in some of these areas; make sure you know the rules. Sleeping in cars is not permitted within the park, but it is allowed in the Kaibab Forest. For more info, contact the **Tusayan Ranger Station,** Kaibab National Forest, P.O. Box 3088, Tusayan, AZ 86023 (☎ 638-2443).

Ten-X Campground (☎ 638-2443), in Kaibab National Forest, 10 mi. south of Grand Canyon Village off Rte. 64. Removed from the highway, Ten-X offers 70 excellent, shady sites surrounded by pine trees. Toilets, water, no hookups, no showers. No reservations. Open May-Sept. Sites $10. ❶

Mather Campground (reservations ☎ 800-365-2267), in Grand Canyon Village, 1 mi. south of the Canyon Village Marketplace; follow signs from Yavapai Lodge. 320 shady, relatively isolated sites with no hookups. Those on foot or bike can snag a spot in one of the communal hiker/biker campsites that are usually available on a walk-up basis. 7-night max. stay. For Apr.-Dec. reserve up to 5 months in advance; Jan.-Mar. first come, first served. Sites $15; hike/bike $4. ❶

Desert View Campground (☎ 638-7888), 25 mi. east of Grand Canyon Village. Short on shade and far from the hub of the South Rim, but a perfect place to avoid the crowds. 50 sites with phone and toilets, but no hookups or campfires. No reservations. Open mid-May to Oct. Sites $10. ❶

■ FOOD

The **Canyon Village Marketplace** ❶, at Market Plaza 1 mi. west of Mather Point on the main road, has a deli counter with the cheapest eats in the park, a wide selection of groceries, camping supplies, and enough Grand Canyon apparel to clothe each member of your extended family. (☎ 638-2262. Sandwiches $2-4. Open daily 7:30am-8:30pm.) **Maswik Cafeteria** ❶, in Maswik Lodge, serves a variety of food from themed food stations focusing on grilled entrees, country favorites, and Mexican specialties. (Sandwiches $3-5. Hot entrees $6-7. Open daily 6am-10pm.) **Bright Angel Dining Room** ❷, in Bright Angel Lodge, is popular with families and serves hot sandwiches ($7-9) and breakfasts ($6-7), while pricey dinner entrees range $10-15. (☎ 638-2631. Open daily 6:30am-10pm.) Just outside the dining room, the **Soda Fountain** ❶ at Bright Angel Lodge chills eight flavors of ice cream (1 scoop $2) and stocks a variety of snack-bar sandwiches. (Open seasonally; hours vary.) The classiest dining in the park can be found at **El Tovar Dining Room** ❹, in the El Tovar Hotel in the Village. The grandly appointed dining room provides a great view of the canyon, and the food lives up to its posh surroundings. (☎ 638-2631, ext. 6432. Open 6:30am-10pm. Dinner reservations recommended.)

■ HIKING

Hikes in and around the Grand Canyon can be broken down into two categories: day hikes and overnight hikes. Confusing an overnight hike for a day hike can lead to disaster and permanent residency in the canyon. Hiking to the Colorado River is reserved for overnight trips. All overnight trips require permits obtained through the Backcountry Office. In determining what is an appropriate day hike, remember that the canyon does not have any loop hikes. Be prepared to retrace every single footstep uphill on the way back. An enjoyable hike usually means beginning before 7am for day hikes and consulting a ranger and the displays at the Canyon View Information Plaza before heading out. Park Service rangers also present a variety of free, informative talks and guided hikes; times and details are listed in *The Guide*.

The **Rim, Bright Angel, South Kaibab,** and **River Trails** are the only South Rim trails regularly maintained and patrolled by the Park Service. While other trails do exist, they are only for the experienced hiker and may contain steep chutes and technical terrain. Consult a ranger and *The Guide* before heading out.

Rim Trail (12 mi. one way, 4-6hr.). With only a mild elevation change (about 200 ft.) and the security of the nearby shuttle, the Rim Trail is excellent for hikers seeking a tame way to see the canyon. The trail is wheelchair accessible to Maricopa Point in the west and has 8 viewpoints along Hermit Rd. and 3 east of it. Near the Grand Canyon Village, the Rim Trail resembles a crowded city street, but toward the eastern and western ends, hikers have a bit more elbow room. Hopi Point is a great place to watch the sun set with its panoramic canyon views—*The Guide* lists times for sunsets and sunrises, and the "Choose your view" kiosk at the visitors center has previews of typical scenery at different locations and times of day.

Bright Angel Trail (up to 18 mi. round-trip, 1-2 days). Bright Angel's frequent switchbacks and refreshing water stations make it the into-the-canyon choice of moderate hikers. Depending on distance, the trail can be either a day or overnight hike. Departing from the Rim Trail near the western edge of the Grand Canyon Village, the first 1-2 mi. generally attract droves of day hikers looking for a taste of canyon descent. Rest houses are strategically stationed 1½ and 3 mi. from the rim, each with water May-Sept. **Indian Gardens,** 4½ mi. down, offers restrooms, picnic tables, 15 year-round backcountry campsites, and blessed shade. From rim to river, the trail drops 4460 ft. The round-trip is too strenuous for a day hike—do not attempt to make it one. With a permit, overnighters can camp at Indian Gardens or on the canyon floor at Bright Angel Campground, while day hikers are advised to go no farther than Plateau Point (12¼ mi. round-trip) or Indian Gardens (9¼ mi. round-trip). The **River Trail** (1¾ mi.) runs along the river, linking the Bright Angel with South Kaibab.

South Kaibab Trail (7 mi. to Phantom Ranch, 4-5hr. descent, 4880 ft.) is for those seeking a more challenging descent. Beginning at Yaki Pt. (7260 ft.), Kaibab is trickier, steeper, and lacks shade or water, but it rewards the intrepid with a better view of the canyon. The South Kaibab avoids the safety and obstructed views of a side-canyon route and instead winds directly down the ridge, offering panoramic views across the expanse of the canyon. Day hikes to Cedar Ridge (3 mi. round-trip) and Skeleton Point (6 mi. round-trip) are reasonable only for experienced, well-conditioned hikers due to the trail's steep grade. Kaibab meets up with Bright Angel at the Colorado River. Fewer switchbacks and a more rapid descent make the South Kaibab Trail 1¾ mi. shorter than the Bright Angel to this point—guests staying at the Phantom Ranch or Bright Angel Campground can use either trail to reach the ranch.

⚠ OUTDOOR ACTIVITIES

Beyond using your feet, there are other ways to conquer the canyon. **Mule trips** from the South Rim are expensive and booked up to one year in advance, although some do cancel. (☎303-297-2757. Daytrip to Plateau Point 6 mi. down the Bright Angel Trail $120; lunch included. Overnight including lodging at Phantom Ranch and all meals $325 per person.) Looking up at the Grand Canyon from a **whitewater raft** is both popular and pricey. Trips into the Grand Canyon proper vary in length from one week to 18 days and are booked far in advance. The *Trip Planner* (available by request at the info center) lists several commercial guides licensed to offer trips in the canyon; check the park website for info well in advance of your visit. **Smooth-water rafting** trips are also available for those not quite ready for a wet, wild, and expensive time in the heart of the canyon. Drifting from Glen Canyon Dam to Lee's Ferry generally takes a half-day. **Wilderness River Adventures** arranges such trips. (☎800-528-6154. $62, children $52.) If the views from the rim fail to dazzle you, try the higher vantages provided by one of the park's many **flightseeing** companies, all located at the Grand Canyon Airport outside of Tuyasan. **Grand Canyon Airlines** flies 45min. canyon tours hourly during the summer. (☎ 866-235-9422. $79, children $49. Reservations recommended, but walk-ins generally available. Discount for lunch-time tours, 11am-2pm.) For a list of flight companies in the park, write the Grand Canyon Chamber of Commerce, P.O. Box 3007, Grand Canyon, AZ 86023.

HAVASUPAI RESERVATION ☎ 928

To the west of the hustle and bustle of the South Rim lies the tranquility of the Hava-supai Reservation. Meaning "people of the blue-green water," the Havasupai live in a protected enclave bordered by the national park. Ringed by dramatic sandstone faces, their village, Supai, rests on the shores of the Havasu River. Just beyond town, rushing crystal-clear water cascades over a series of spectacular falls. Such beauty attracts thousands each year, but a grueling 10 mi. hike separates the falls from any vehicle-accessible surface and prevents over-exposure of the reservation. For most, blistered feet or a saddle-sore rump make bathing in the cool waters even sweeter.

Supai and the campground can be reached only by a trail originating on the rim at the Hualapai Hilltop. To reach the trailhead, take I-40 E until Rte. 66 at Seligman; fol-low Rte. 66 for 30 mi. until it meets with Indian Rd. 18, which ends at the Hilltop after 60 mi. No roads lead to Supai, although mules and helicopters can be hired to carry bags or people. For mule reservations, contact **Havasupai Tourist Enterprise.** (☎ 448-2141. Groups leave at 10am. One-way $70, half of which is required as a deposit; includes 4 pieces of luggage not exceeding 130 lb. total. **Skydance Helicopter** flies between the hilltop and village four days per week. (☎ 800-882-1651. Flights every 15-20min. Su-M and Th-F 9am-3pm. One-way $70. No reservations.) The hike is not to be underestimated. The well-marked trail is a grueling, exposed 8 mi. to Supai and then an additional 2 mi. to the campground. Do not hike down without a reserva-tion—you may have to turn around and walk right back to the trailhead.

Reservations for the campground, lodge, and mules can be made by calling the Havasupai Tourist Enterprise. Visitors must check in at the **Tourist Office** in Supai before heading onto the campground. In the village, there's a Post Office, a general store, and a cafe. Prices are high because everything must be brought in by mule or helicopter. Bringing your own food to the campground is advised, but all trash must be packed out. No **gas** or **water** is available past Rte. 66; stock up beforehand.

The Havasupai tribe operates two accommodations: the ◪**Havasupai Campground** ❶ and the Havasupai Lodge, both on the canyon floor. The friendly campground, 2 mi. beyond Supai, lies between Havasu and Mooney Falls, bordering the blue-green water of the Havasu River and swimmer-friendly lagoons. The tribe charges a one-time entry fee ($20 per person, $10 per night) at the campground. There are no showers, and the non-flush toilets tend to smell up the sites. A spring provides fresh water, and the falls are a quick jaunt away. The **Havasupai Lodge** ❷, in Supai, offers basic accommodations ($75-96 for up to 4 people, plus the entrance fee; low season $45-66). The trail from Supai to the campground extends to **Mooney Falls** (1 mi.), **Beaver Falls** (3 mi.), and the **Colorado** (8 mi.). The steep hike down to Mooney Falls may turn your stomach. Extreme caution should be exercised—shoes with good tread are a must. Swimming and frolicking are both permitted and encour-aged in the lush lagoons at the bottom of the falls.

BARSTOW ☎ 760

Midway between L.A. and Las Vegas at the crossroads of I-15 and I-40, Barstow (pop. 23,056) is a classic rest-stop town with inexpensive motels and fast food chains. However, it is also an ideal gateway to the California desert for those will-ing to explore the hot, desolate area.

THE DESERT

East Main Street offers an endless line of motels. Prices fluctuate depending on the season, day of the week, and whether Vegas accommodations are full. The **Desert Inn ❸**, 1100 E. Main St., near I-15, is a newly renovated motel with HBO and amazing A/C. (☎256-2146. Singles $27; doubles, triples, and quads $30.) Eight miles north of Barstow, the adventurous can pitch tents at the **Owl Canyon Campground ❶** while visiting the arid beauty of the **Rainbow Basin Natural Area**. To get there, head north on N. 1st St. away from Main St. in Barstow. Take a left onto Fort Irwin Rd, continue for 7 mi., then turn left onto Fossil Bed Rd. Follow this dirt/gravel road for 3 mi. until you see signs to the campground and scenic loop. Hikers can investigate the colorful canyon, search for the desert tortoise, and gaze at a night sky unpolluted by city lights. The 31 camping sites are equipped with fire rings, drinking water, and pit toilets. (☎256-8313; www.ca.blm.gov/barstow. Sites $6.) For more information and maps, contact the **California Desert Information Center**, 831 Barstow Rd. (☎255-8760; www.caohwy.com/c/caldesic. Open daily 9am-5pm.)

Every restaurant chain imaginable has a branch on **Main Street**, but Barstow's local food may be more promising. The aroma of savory dishes fills the festive and oddly decorated dining room of **Rosita's Mexican American Food ❷**, 540 W. Main St. (☎256-9218. Lunch specials Tu-F under $5. Dinners $6-15. Open Tu-Sa 11am-9pm, Su 11am-8pm.) For some good, hearty Italian food, head to **DiNapoli's Firehouse Italian Eatery ❸**, 1358 E. Main St. Traditional pizzeria fare is served in a recreated old-fashioned firehouse, complete with the front of a fire engine and a fire pole. (☎256-1094. Dinner entrees $8-15. Open Su-Th 11am-9pm, F-Sa 11am-10pm.)

Amtrak, 685 N. 1st St. (☎800-USA-RAIL/872-7245), lacks a ticket counter, so buy tickets by phone or online. One train per day departs for L.A. (4am, $26). **Greyhound** buses, 681 N. 1st St. (☎256-8757 or 800-231-2222; open M-Sa 9am-2pm and 3:30-6pm), go to L.A. ($24.50) and Las Vegas ($26.50). The **Barstow Chamber of Commerce**, 409 E. Fredricks St., off Barstow Rd., has info on hotels, restaurants, and attractions. (☎256-8617. Open M-F 10am-4pm.) Other services include: the **police**, 220 E. Mountain View Rd. (☎256-2211); **Barstow Community Hospital**, 555 S. 7th St. (☎256-1761); and the **post office**, 425 S. 2nd Ave. (☎256-9304; open M-F 9am-5pm, Sa 9am-noon). **Postal Code:** 92311.

MOJAVE NATIONAL PRESERVE
☎760

WHEN TO GO. While many of the Mojave's mystical features can be enjoyed year-round, the summer months can be particularly brutal, with temperatures regularly reaching above 100°F, making the rocky paths of the Mojave's hiking trails feel like burning lava. The best time to visit is Mar.-Apr., when wildflowers are in full bloom and before the oppressive heat steals the small bodies of water.

The 1.6 million acres of Mojave National Preserve, a federally stewarded desert, encompass dry lake beds, volcanic cinder cones, sweeping sand dunes, and the occasional splash of water. Dramatic geological formations rise from the seemingly infinite landscape and resilient creatures crawl along the scorched terrain. Most drivers press onward, praying that their cars are up to the task (see **Desert Driving**, p. 529), missing the stark beauty of the area.

This area was first encountered by European explorers guided by Native Americans in the 1770s; it soon became a trade route. Along this corridor are the **Kelso Dunes**, which blanket a spectacular, barren landscape within the preserve. Stretching 4 mi. and reaching heights of 700 ft., the dunes offer a 2-3hr. one-way hike from the trailhead, located 4 mi. west of Kelbaker Rd. Keep in mind that the sand acts like a giant oven in the summer—don't get baked. From the top you can hear the dunes sing on a windy day; the shifting sand groans like bending metal. The dunes are 44 mi. southeast of Baker via Kelbaker Rd. from Barstow; either take I-40 to

Kelbaker Rd. exit (80 mi. to the east) or I-15 to Baker. **Kelbaker Road** itself offers phenomenal views of every conceivable desert formation from the Kelso Dunes and crusty lava flows to glacier-hewn granite heaps. **Dune buggies** and **jeeps** are still permitted at **Dumont Dunes**, just off Rte. 127 about 33 mi. north of Baker. Look for the 3½ mi. road turning off Rte. 127 just after Harry Wade Rd. There is no sign; keep your eyes peeled. The dunes are strewn with man-made striations—those from WWII training exercises are still visible in parts of the Mojave. Tracks remain in the sand for decades; don't leave a legacy.

The **Hole-in-the-Wall Rings Trail** allows even the most novice **rock climber** to blaze through rock formations like a pro with the help of rings installed by rangers. The trail is in the center of the park on Black Canyon Rd. Inside the preserve lies a sep-arate state park, the **Providence Mountains State Recreation Area**, a popular, high-altitude (4000-5000 ft.) region with six **primitive campsites** (☎928-2586; sites $10) and a **visitors center**, on Essex Rd., 17 mi. north of I-40. In addition to beautiful desert vistas, you'll be able to view the spectacular **◪Mitchell Caverns** on an infor-mative 1½ mi. tour through the stalactite-cluttered limestone chambers. (Tour res-ervations ☎928-2586; $2 surcharge. 1½hr. tours depart Sept.-May M-F 1:30pm, Sa-Su 10am, 1:30, 3pm. June-Aug. Sa-Su 1:30pm. $4, under 17 free.)

Hunting and **fishing** are allowed in the preserve, but finding water may be an angler's toughest challenge. For those with the required California hunting license, deer and quail are popular targets in season. Watch out for protected desert tortoises sunning themselves on desert roads and avoid disturbing them in the desert, their last natural stronghold.

One of the best ways to explore the Mojave is from **Baker,** one of the few towns along I-15 in the desert. The **Mojave National Preserve Information Center** is open daily throughout the year, where free maps are available round-the-clock just out-side. Baker is home to the **world's tallest thermometer** and not much else. The **Wills Fargo ❸**, 72252 Baker Blvd., just off I-15, has simple rooms at simple prices. (☎760-433-4477. Singles $36; doubles $40.) There are 61 primitive but beautiful sites sur-rounded by piñon and juniper trees at the unseasonably cool **Mid Hill ❶** (5600 ft.) and **Hole-in-the-Wall ❶** (4200 ft.) in the East Mojave National Scenic Area. The road into Mid Hill is unpaved and not recommended for RVs. From Essex Rd., follow Black Canyon Rd. to Mid Hill or Wild Horse Canyon Rd. to Hole-in-Wall. (Limited water, pit toilets, no hookups, no reservations. Sites $12.) The **Mad Greek Cafe ❷**, 72112 Baker Blvd., is a popular stop on the way back from Vegas. A friendly staff serves gigantic gyros and Greek specialties, along with burgers, malts, and other diner fare. (☎760-733-4354. Entrees $5-10. Open daily 6am-midnight.)

THE COLORADO DESERT

The Colorado Desert, home of Anza-Borrego Desert State Park and the Salton Sea, is at first glance flat and barren, with few easily observed signs of life beyond the artifi-cial tourist oasis of Palm Springs and the date groves of Coachella Valley. Only a few resilient species have learned to flourish amid the dust and broken rocks, but there is a striking beauty in the mountain vistas and the toughness and fragility of desert life.

ANZA-BORREGO
DESERT STATE PARK
☎760

The largest state park in the continental US, Anza-Borrego is layered with both nat-ural and human history. A short drive from San Diego or Palm Springs, this harsh desert sprouts over 1000 different plant species, many of which are found nowhere else in California. Barbed cholla cacti, bruise-blossomed indigo bush, and thirsty

THE DESERT

tamarisk flourish in the withering heat. The scrub sprawls over a diverse landscape of dunes, badlands, mountains, oases, and active faults. Hidden among these natural wonders are the abandoned dwellings of Native Americans, Spanish settlers, and oil pioneers. Over 56 species of reptiles or amphibians and 30 species of mammals, including the endangered bighorn sheep, live within the park's borders.

Though Anza-Borrego is just as beautiful as Death Valley or Joshua Tree, it remains less popular than the national parks because the state lacks the funding to adequately maintain and develop roads, campgrounds, and facilities. The park is also far from major highways and therefore relatively difficult to access. The beauty of Anza-Borrego can only be found by a true desert adventurer. Visit in the winter or early spring when temperatures are more manageable; high summer temperatures can make daytime activity in the desert dangerous.

TRANSPORTATION. To reach the park from the west, take **State Route 78** east from I-15 or I-5. From the south, take **State Route 79** northbound from I-8 to Rte. 78. From the east, take **County Route S22** west from Rte. 86, which connects to I-10 in Indio. Once in the park, head to **Borrego Springs**, its only town, via **County Route S3** for info, lodging, and food. No roads approach Anza-Borrego from the north. The **Northeast Rural Bus System** serves the region. (☎767-4287. Info line open daily 7am-noon and 2-5pm.) **AAA Emergency Road Service** (☎800-222-4357) can refer troubled motorists to a towing company.

ORIENTATION AND PRACTICAL INFORMATION. For backcountry and safety info, stop by the **Anza-Borrego Desert State Park Visitors Center**, 200 Palm Canyon Dr., Borrego Springs. They have topographical maps, books, exhibits, and slide shows. (☎767-4205. Open Oct.-May daily 9am-5pm; June-Sept. Sa-Su 9am-5pm.) In summer months, call the **Anza-Borrego State Park Headquarters** (☎767-5311; open M-F 8am-5pm) or stop by the **Borrego Springs Chamber of Commerce and Visitor Center**, 786 Palm Canyon Dr. (☎767-5555, weather conditions 289-121. Open M-F 10am-4pm). The **Borrego Medical Center**, 4343 Yaqui Pass Rd., Borrego Springs, on Rams Hill, provides medical assistance. (☎767-5051. Open June-Sept. M-Tu and Th-F 9am-1pm, W 1-6pm; Oct.-May M-F 9am-5pm, Sa 9am-1pm.)

ACCOMMODATIONS AND CAMPING. The small community of Borrego Springs provides adequate accommodations for park visitors, from basic motels to resorts of the Palm Springs variety. Though bargains are hard to find, the rates at **Stanlunds ❸**, 2771 Borrego Springs Rd., are manageable. Breakfast is included on weekends and Internet access is available for those with laptops. (☎767-5501. Pets welcome. Oct.-Apr. $60-85; May-Sept. $48-68.) **Hacienda del Sol ❹**, 610 Palm Canyon Dr., has comfy, well-worn rooms. (☎767-5442. Singles and doubles $60. $15 per additional person.) The Western-themed **Palm Canyon Resort ❺**, 221 Palm Canyon Dr., offers more niceties, including two pools, a fitness center, restaurant, saloon, and laundry. (☎800-242-0044. Singles and doubles Oct.-Apr. $95-130; May-Sept. $70-85.)

Since lodging prices in Borrego Springs tend towards the high side, the park is a great opportunity to practice your tent-pitching skills. **Backcountry** sites must be 100 ft. away from water and any road, and fires are not permitted unless they're in a metal container. The daily $4 park fee must be paid prior to camping; park entrance is free if you are not camping. Besides backcountry camping, Anza-Borrego hosts four developed campgrounds and ten primitive campgrounds. Make reservations with ReserveAmerica (☎800-444-7275; www.reserveamerica.com). **Borrego Palm Canyon ❶** has 123 developed sites for tents, RVs, and groups. (Flush toilets, water, showers, sunshades, fire rings, and picnic tables. Sites $10-19.) **Tamarisk Grove ❶** has 27 developed sites for tents and RVs. (Flush toilets, water, showers, sunshades, fire rings, and picnic tables. Sites $10.) For those who wander in without the aid of machines, **Horse Camp ❶** has 10 developed sites for horses and people only. (Flush toilets, water, showers, fire rings, and picnic tables. Sites $14-17.) **Bow Willow ❶** has 16 sites for tents or RVs. (Vault toilets, water, picnic tables, sunshades, and fire rings. No showers. Sites $7.) Call ahead to check if all camps are open in the summer, as some may be closed due to inadequate funding. The primitive campgrounds all have vault toilets (except Yaqui Pass, Dos Cabezas, and Sheep Canyon) but no distinct sites or other amenities.

◖ FOOD. Center Market, 590 Palm Canyon, Borrego Springs, sells groceries and supplies. (☎767-3311. Open M-Sa 8:30am-6:30pm, Su 8:30am-5pm.) Across the street is the local favorite, **Kendall's Cafe ❷**, 528 Palm Canyon Dr. Entrees ($6-10) include half-pound buffalo burgers. (☎767-3491. Open daily 6am-8pm.) Those thirsty for a cold one can follow the locals into the one nightspot option in town, **Carlee's Bar and Grill ❷**, 660 Palm Canyon Dr. (☎767-3262. Entrees $7-15. Open daily 11am-2am.) Other restaurants with finer fare can be found in the resorts in Borrego Springs.

◖◣ SIGHTS AND OUTDOOR ACTIVITIES. Hiking and desert exploration opportunities abound in Anza-Borrego. The **Palm Canyon Creek Trail** (3 mi. round-trip) leads up to a huge fan palm oasis, where desert bighorn sheep come for water in the summer months. The trailhead is located in the back of the **Borrego Palm Canyon** campground. Another short but rewarding hike can be found at **Slot Canyon.** Exit Rte. 78 east of Borrego Springs on a small dirt road labeled "Buttes Pass Rd." and bear left at the first fork. About 1 mi. down the road is a small parking area; Slot Canyon is below. The **Southern Emigrant Trail**, a 26 mi. self-guided auto-tour, follows a wagon trail used by Mormon settlers. Along the trail is a sod stage station built in 1852. **Font's Point,** accessible with a 4WD vehicle, looks down on the spectacular Borrego Badlands—bare knuckles of pink-hued rocks and gullies. Those without 4WD can view the badlands from S22 east of Borrego Springs. Continue east on S22 to reach the huge, salty **Salton Sea.** The park's chief attraction is **wildflower** season, which transfigures barren wastelands into blossoming wonderlands in spring after just the right amount of rain has fallen. Some years, no flowers bloom at all due to inadequate rainfall. Call the **Wildflower Hotline** (☎767-4684) to learn if the unpredictable blooming has occurred. Rangers also offer special guided activities; check the schedules at the visitors center.

THE DESERT

INDEX

Numerics

17 Mile Drive 347
848 Community Space 124
90210 415

A

AAA (American Automobile Association) 45
Academy Awards 430
Adams, Ansel 16, 106, 260
  Gallery 265
additional resources
  alternatives to tourism 74
  film 21
  music 23
  travel books 21
Admiration Point 277
adventure trips 59
aerogrammes 49
airplane travel
  fares 40
  standby 41
airports
  Castle, Merced 316
  Fresno-Yosemite International 254
  Inyokern 297
  John Wayne 460
  Los Angeles (LAX) 377
  McCarran International, NV 552
  Monterey 342
  Palm Springs Regional 537
  Reno-Tahoe International 248, 286
  Sacramento International 304
  San Diego International 490
  San Francisco International 77, 184
  San Jose International 178
  Santa Barbara Municipal 367
Alabama Hills 299
Alameda County (AC) Transit 77, 145
Alcatraz 83, 118
alcohol 33
Alonzo King's Lines Contemporary Ballet 122
America's Finest City 489
American Express 30, 50
American Red Cross 37
Amoeba Music 121, 125, 143, 432
Anaheim 462
Anaheim Angels (baseball) 466
Ancient Bristlecone Pine Forest 295
Angel Island State Park 119
Angeles National Forest 476
Aniston, Jennifer 419
Año Nuevo State Reserve 192
Anza-Borrego Desert State Park 569
apple orchards 324
aquariums
  Birch 507
  Cabrillo Marine 407
  Long Beach Aquarium of the Pacific 454
  Monterey Bay 346
  Morro Bay 366
  Roundhouse Marine Studies Lab and Aquarium 407
Arcata 223
Arizona
  Grand Canyon 562
  Grand Canyon South Rim 562
  Havasupai Reservation 567
Armstrong Woods State Park 177
Around L.A. 451–476
Artist's Drive 548
arts
  architecture 15
  fine arts 15
  literature 16
  music 17
Ashland, OR 207–210
aspen 9
ATM cards 30
auto transport companies 46
Avalon 455
Avenue of the Giants 228–230
avocados 14

B

backpacks 58
Badwater 548
Badwater Ultramarathon 302
Baja California, Mexico 517
  Angeles Verdes (Green Angels) 517
  Bahía de Todos Santos 517, 527
  beaches 517, 525, 527
  bullfights 523
  car rentals 521
  Ensenada 526
  Mex. 1 517, 526, 528
  Parque Nacional Consitutición 517, 527
  Rosarito 524
  Tijuana 519
  traveler's diarrhea 518
Bakersfield 317
Balboa Park 499
Balboa Peninsula 469
bargaining 31
Barstow 567
Battery Point Lighthouse 222
Battery Spencer 159
Bay Area Rapid Transit (BART) 77, 80, 83, 136, 145, 180
Bay Area. See San Francisco Bay Area.
beaches
  Avila 364
  Bahía de Todos Santos 517, 527
  Baldwin 244
  Belmont Shores 454
  Black Sands 232
  Black's 506
  Bonny Doon 335
  Cabrillo 407
  Calawee Cove 244
  Camel Point 470
  Cardiff State 515
  Carlsbad State 515
  Carmel River State 351
  Children's Pool 506
  Corral State 402
  Crescent 222
  Dana Point 471
  Del Mar 513
  Dunes 193
  East 371
  Encinitas City 515
  Francis 193
  Gaviota State 373
  Goat Rock 236
  Gold Bluffs 220
  Gold Coast 473
  Gray Whale Cove 193
  Half Moon Bay 193
  Hearst State 358
  Hearts Desire 156
  Hermosa 407
  Hidden 222
  Jones 233
  La Jolla 506
  La Jolla Cove 506
  Laguna 470
  Leadbetter 371
  Lester 244
  Limantour 156
  Main 470
  Manchester State 236
  Manhattan 407

HOSTELLING INTERNATIONAL USA-San Diego

WHERE WORLD TRAVELERS STAY

HI-USA, San Diego Downtown

- Let's Go's Thumbs Up hostel 2002/03/04
- Located in the heart of the Gaslamp Quarter
- Only hostel in San Diego with 24 hrs Front Desk staff
- Dormitory style rooms and private rooms (with or without bath)
- Minutes away from airport, bus and train station
- Free continental breakfast
- Free daily activities and guided walking tours

521 Market St, San Diego, CA
Phones: (619) 525-1531 /
1-888- GO-HIUSA / 1-888-464-4872 # 156
Email: downtown@sandiegohostels.org.

HI-USA, San Diego Point Loma

- "Homestay hostel in a big city"
- Minutes away from the ocean and town of Ocean Beach.
- Relaxed atmosphere; sunny patio; BBQ and fire pit.
- Private rooms and dormitory style rooms
- Free breakfast
- One block from public transportation
- Lockable surfboard storage

3790 Udall Street, San Diego, CA
Phones: (619) 223-4778 /
1-888- GO-HIUSA / 1-888-464-4872 # 157
Email: pointloma@sandiegohostels.org.

REAL TIME ONLINE RESERVATIONS AT

www.sandiegohostels.org

ABOUT LET'S GO

GUIDES FOR THE INDEPENDENT TRAVELER

At Let's Go, we see every trip as the chance of a lifetime. If your dream is to grab a machete and forge through the jungles of Brazil, we can take you there. If you'd rather bask in the Riviera sun at a beachside cafe, we'll set you a table. We write for readers who know that there's more to travel than sharing double deckers with tourists and who believe that travel can change both themselves and the world—whether they plan to spend six days in London or six months in Latin America. We'll show you just how far your money can go, and prove that the greatest limitation on your adventures is not your wallet, but your imagination. After all, traveling close to the ground lets you interact more directly with the places and people you've gone to see, making for the most authentic experience.

BEYOND THE TOURIST EXPERIENCE

To help you gain a deeper connection with the places you travel, our researchers give you the heads-up on both world-renowned and off-the-beaten-track attractions, sights, and destinations. They engage with the local culture, writing features on regional cuisine, local festivals, and hot political issues. We've also opened our pages to respected writers and scholars to hear their takes on the countries and regions we cover, and asked travelers who have worked, studied, or volunteered abroad to contribute first-person accounts of their experiences. We've also increased our coverage of responsible travel and expanded each guide's Alternatives to Tourism chapter to share more ideas about how to give back to local communities and learn about the places you travel.

FORTY-FIVE YEARS OF WISDOM

Let's Go got its start in 1960, when a group of creative and well-traveled students compiled their experience and advice into a 20-page mimeographed pamphlet, which they gave to travelers on charter flights to Europe. Four and a half decades later, we've expanded to cover six continents and all kinds of travel—while retaining our founders' adventurous attitude toward the world. Our guides are still researched and written entirely by students on shoestring budgets, experienced travelers who know that train strikes, stolen luggage, food poisoning, and marriage proposals are all part of a day's work. This year, we're expanding our coverage of South America and Southeast Asia, with brand-new *Let's Go: Ecuador*, *Let's Go: Peru*, and *Let's Go: Vietnam*. Our adventure guide series is growing, too, with the addition of *Let's Go: Pacific Northwest Adventure* and *Let's Go: New Zealand Adventure*. And we're immensely excited about our new *Let's Go: Roadtripping USA*—two years, eight routes, and sixteen researchers and editors have put together a travel guide like none other.

THE LET'S GO COMMUNITY

More than just a travel guide company, Let's Go is a community. Our small staff comes together because of our shared passion for travel and our desire to help other travelers see the world. We love it when our readers become part of the Let's Go community as well—when you travel, drop us a postcard (67 Mt. Auburn St., Cambridge, MA 02138, USA) or send us an e-mail (feedback@letsgo.com) to tell us about your adventures and discoveries.

For more information, visit us online: www.letsgo.com.

MAP INDEX

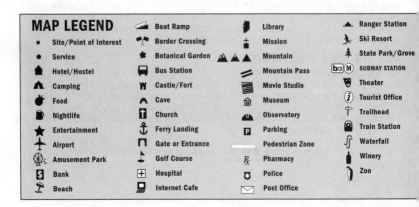

MAP LEGEND						
■	Site/Point of Interest	⚐	Boat Ramp	▮	Library	▲ Ranger Station
●	Service	⚑	Border Crossing	✝	Mission	🎿 Ski Resort
🏠	Hotel/Hostel	🌳	Botanical Garden	▲▲▲	Mountain	🌲 State Park/Grove
⛺	Camping	🚌	Bus Station	⟋	Mountain Pass	bart Ⓜ SUBWAY STATION
🍴	Food	🏰	Castle/Fort	🎬	Movie Studio	🎭 Theater
🍷	Nightlife	⋀	Cave	🏛	Museum	ⓘ Tourist Office
★	Entertainment	⛪	Church	⚲	Observatory	⊤ Trailhead
✈	Airport	⚓	Ferry Landing	P	Parking	🚉 Train Station
🎡	Amusement Park	⊓	Gate or Entrance	- - -	Pedestrian Zone	∫ Waterfall
$	Bank	⛳	Golf Course	℞	Pharmacy	🍇 Winery
🏖	Beach	⊞	Hospital	✚	Police	🦒 Zoo
		💻	Internet Cafe	✉	Post Office	